THE LUTHERAN CHURCH IN
PAPUA NEW GUINEA

The First
Hundred Years
1886-1986

edited by
Herwig Wagner
Hermann Reiner

Lutheran Publishing House, Adelaide

Cover design: Graeme Cogdell; layout: Annette Eckermann

The cover design for this volume incorporates:

1) the baptismal font in the Sattelberg church (the first two
   baptized Christians at Sattelberg depicted in the carving
   typify the story of this volume);

2) the crucifixion carving in the Kalasa church;

3) an illustrative band, adapted from original artwork by
   Margaret Cramer, giving traditional PNG motifs a
   Christian symbolism: the drum (to announce the Good
   News); the battle spear and snake (Christ's victory over
   sin and Satan); the conch shell (the call of the Miti); the
   dove (the Holy Spirit); the fish (the Church). All symbols
   are superimposed on the coconut, the symbol of life in
   many parts of PNG.

National Library of Australia
Cataloguing-in-Publication data

The Lutheran Church in Papua New Guinea.
The first hundred years: 1886-1986.

Bibliography.
Includes index.
ISBN 0 85910 382 X.

1. Evangelical Lutheran Church of Papua New Guinea — History. 2. Lutheran Church — History.
3. Lutherans — Papua New Guinea — History. 4. Missions, German — Papua New Guinea — History.
5. Missions, Australian — Papua New Guinea — History. 6. Missions, American — Papua New Guinea — History.
I. Wagner, Herwig.

284.1'953

First printing July 1986

Printed and published by
Lutheran Publishing House,
205 Halifax Street, Adelaide, South Australia.   LPH 86-191

To the glory of God
and in grateful memory
of all God's people,
both indigenous and expatriate,
who have embraced the *Miti*
and shared it with others
in Papua New Guinea

The Bishop's Preface

The Evangelical Lutheran Church of Papua New Guinea is the largest Protestant church in the country, with a membership of over half-a-million baptized Christians; and it is a rapidly-growing church, too. It is a missionary church also in the sense that it grew out of the missionary activities of several overseas churches. Its beginning is marked by the arrival of the first missionary, Johann Flierl, at Finschhafen, exactly 100 years ago.

The background history shows that this church emerged from three different church/mission organizations: Finschhafen, Madang, and Siassi/Menyamya. Closer fellowship with the Gutnius Lutheran Church in the Enga Province is still ahead of us. Even before those three church/mission bodies united, all their congregations participated in effective missionary activities in their own mission fields in PNG. The expansion of the missionary movement was enormous, especially when large areas were opened up in the Highlands shortly before and after World War II. Overseas missionaries and local evangelists worked together side by side in order to spread the Gospel of salvation to all

people of our country. The congregations felt responsible for their mission fields, and showed this by sending men, money, and other material support for their workers in the mission of the church. It was only in later years, when the regional churches had become united, that this missionary zeal began to decline.

When the former leaders thought about uniting these regional churches, they did not have a proper planning of the new church organization. The indigenes were, to a certain extent, forced to agree that there be one church, although the church itself was not yet prepared to be united. The Evangelical Lutheran Church of New Guinea (ELCONG) was born in 1956 as a result of this.

Ever since ELCONG was formed, a structural dilemma has been felt and encountered. The church structure was drawn up with the hope of better organization and effective communication. But it turned out to be negative in communication between the national church, the Districts, and the village congregations, and this often created misunderstandings and distrust among church leaders of all levels. Sometimes the paternalistic

4

attitudes of expatriate missionaries in decision-making procedures over-ran the opinions of timid indigenous church leaders. This resulted in expatriates making decisions for the church in its initial stage, and implanted the idea that, when the expatriate missionary was there, things would always be to the better.

One can see consequences of this attitude still today, though this church is an autonomous church. Lack of closer cooperation and of a spirit of humble sharing and working together gradually has deepened the gap between young and old, between leaders and people, between the educated and the less educated. Some young elites of this church have been emotionally attracted to and have joined other religious groups and movements. Some of them have been ordained overnight, claiming to be pastors without having received any formal theological education. Sons and daughters of Lutheran pastors and evangelists are even the forerunners in some religious movements in the country. This is one of the greatest concerns of our church. Blindly to ignore these growing movements will result in worse consequences for the future ministry of this church. We have both the manpower and the spiritual resources available; but to mobilize them into concrete and workable programs is still another thing, something yet to be accomplished.

We leaders of this church today have seriously to concern ourselves with the future of this church. Again, the re-organization of the church must be carefully studied as we plan for another 100 years ahead. One thing, I feel, is at the core of all the problems which our church faces today: the need for a renewed sense of belonging to the church of Christ by all those who have been baptized into our church. When that need is met, people will be responsive in all matters pertaining to the upbuilding and spiritual nurturing of the people inside and outside of the Christian congregations.

Despite all our shortcomings, however, there is a host of committed pastors, evangelists, teachers, elders, expatriate missionaries, youth leaders, women's workers, and still more congregational members who are to be commended for having humbly and faithfully served their Master Jesus Christ, who is the Power and the Wisdom of God. This church strongly believes that 'the word of the cross is folly to those who are perishing, but to us who are being saved it is the power of God' (1 Cor. 1:18). May God grant us that Wisdom!

Ash Wednesday, 1986   Getake S. Gam
National Bishop
Evangelical Lutheran Church of
Papua New Guinea

The Editors' Preface

No church has its origin in itself. Apart from the first congregation in Jerusalem, all have received the Word of God from elsewhere (1 Cor. 14:36); and in every case, the Holy Spirit acted through people: apostles, evangelists, teachers, messengers of many kinds. The New Testament clearly shows this evangelistic advance from town to town, from region to region, and from one continent to the next. No church should be ashamed to recall its own missionary beginnings.

The Lutheran Church in Papua New Guinea has its own record of missionary outreach during the past one hundred years. Soon after the first Christian congregations had been founded from elsewhere, their own local missionaries followed suit in an evangelistic movement carrying the Gospel of Peace to ever-new regions of their country. New Guinean missionaries — both ordained and, in far greater numbers, unordained — surely outnumber those who have come from overseas churches in Germany, Australia, America, and Canada.

In the year of the centennial anniversary of the beginning of Lutheranism in Papua New Guinea, the overseas partner churches have pooled their resources so that a comprehensive volume of the historical developments in this church could be presented in word and picture. Almost all chapters have been written by former missionaries in New Guinea. In its own way, this volume exemplifies the cooperation of various Lutheran churches on three continents for and with those in Papua New Guinea.

New Guinean Christians have contributed in many ways to this volume, some in writing, others by interviews, and some by making available their personal experiences in the mission of the church. Indeed, we look forward to the time when this account of the missionary advance in New Guinea will be enhanced by a history written by New Guinean scholars. It is clear that there is scope for further research work into this history. Written accounts by New Guinean missionaries and evangelists are rare. Many of those who carried out the very pioneering work in new mission areas have now joined the church in heaven. It will be up to future local researchers to tap the available oral traditions, and perhaps the memory of sons and daughters who grew up with their parents at the

6

remote evangelists' stations, and heard details of how the *Miti* spread into those areas far away from vehicular roads and modern lines of communication. The present volume could not attempt to accomplish this; it remains a challenge for a forthcoming generation of Christian historians in New Guinea.

A large section of this volume is concerned with the toil and labour of those men and women, both expatriate and New Guinean, who all too often go unmentioned in church and mission histories: teachers, builders, agriculturalists, doctors, nurses, technicians, etc. They should not be called 'laymen', in the hierarchical connotation of the word; quite a number of them were also preachers in the pulpit; many more were active witnesses to the Lord through their dedicated service, reflecting the love of God to man in their loving service to their neighbours. A New Guinea church history would be rather deficient if it did not gratefully remember their share in the common work.

To ask men and women to be contributors to this volume who were co-workers in the mission, or even founded a specific field of church work, has been a risky undertaking. No one would be better acquainted with the historical events, yet one cannot expect a detached, objective view from those who have given their heart and their lifetime to the Lord's service. On the other hand, their contributions to this volume convey some of the original flavour of the respective period of the church's history. The Last Day alone will reveal how much of it was built with gold, silver, precious stones, wood, hay, or stubble (1 Cor. 3:12).

As this volume will be read by many people who are less familiar with the land and the languages of New Guinea, some special maps relevant to the church's history have been inserted. The spelling of vernacular names has also been consistently simplified (for example, omitting diacritical marks like â, ê, ô, and c for the glottal stop). In some cases, the now-common Anglicized form of names and terms is used (Yelso for Je'elso, or Pidgin for Tok Pisin); in other cases, the international linguistic spelling is followed (such as Jabem for Yabim, or Meziab for Mesiab). As far as possible, geographical names are given as in the *Encyclopedia of Papua New Guinea* (Peter Ryan ed.) listed in the Selected Bibliography.

The writing and printing of this volume was made possible by generous grants from the overseas churches, through their Departments of World Mission: the Evangelical Lutheran Church of Bavaria, the Lutheran Church of Australia, the American Lutheran Church, and the North Elbian Evangelical Lutheran Church. And only the unrelenting willingness to cooperate by many staff in the Neuendettelsau, Adelaide, Minneapolis, and Barmen offices and archives enabled so much verification and documentation to be presented; to them too we want to express our heart-felt thanks. Special acknowledgment is due to the respective Boards who accepted the responsibility of supplying complete lists of their commissioned personnel to New Guinea, and to the secretaries who had the unenviable work of compiling these names for the appendix at the rear of the book. Credit for selecting and providing captions for the numerous historical illustrations goes to one of the authors, Mr Wilhelm Fugmann; only one who was so closely acquainted with many New Guinean and expatriate staff of the past was in the position to identify people on historic photographs. Translations of German contributions have been made by Mrs E. Franz of Weissenbronn, the Revd and Mrs H. Bamler of Kleinhaslach, and Mrs S. Dellbruegge of Neuendettelsau. And finally: no book such as this is finally ready for the printer until the manuscripts have been typed and re-typed — up to five times! — by many willing helpers, too many to be named individually. All involved in this publication have made their contribution because they are dedicated to the work of the Lutheran Church in Papua New Guinea; and they pray that the Lord may bless it on into its second century, indeed, until he will come at the end of time.

Neuendettelsau   Herwig Wagner
March 21, 1986   Hermann Reiner

AELC	Association of Evangelical Lutheran Churches
ALC	American Lutheran Church
ALM	Australian Lutheran Mission
AMAF	Australian Missionary Aviation Fellowship
ANGAU	Australian New Guinea Administrative Unit
APO	Aid-Post Orderly
BFM	Board of Foreign Mission (of Iowa Synod)
CBS	Christian Broadcasting Service
CCC	Christian Communication Commission
CCMC	Churches' Council for Media Coordination
CEC	Christian Education Council
CMC	Churches' Media Council
C-MC	Church-Mission Council
CoEv	Committee of Evangelism
CTICR	Committee on Theology and Inter-Church Relations
CYCOM	Commission on Younger Churches and Orphaned Missions
ELCA	Evangelical Lutheran Church of Australia
ELCONG	Evangelical Lutheran Church of New Guinea
ELC-PNG	Evangelical Lutheran Church of Papua New Guinea
GLC	Gutnius Lutheran Church
LCC-W	Lutheran Church Council - Wabag
LC-MS	Lutheran Church - Missouri Synod
LES	Lutheran Economic Service
LMF	Lutheran Mission Finschhafen

LMM	Lutheran Mission Madang
LMNG	Lutheran Mission New Guinea
LMS	London Mission Society
LSN	Lutheran School of Nursing
LWF	Lutheran World Federation
MAF	Missionary Aviation Fellowship
MATS	Melanesian Association of Theological Schools
MCC	Melanesian Council of Churches
MCH	Maternal Child Health program
MEO	Mission Education Officer
NGC	New Guinea Company
NGCC	New Guinea Coordinating Committee
NGLM	New Guinea Lutheran Mission
PCC	Pacific Council of Churches
PNG	Papua New Guinea
RMS	Rhenish Mission Society
SDA	Seventh Day Adventist
SVD	Society of the Divine Word
UELCA	United Evangelical Lutheran Church in Australia
UPNG	University of Papua New Guinea
WCC	World Council of Churches

Contents

LIST OF MAPS

Part I

The Growing
Church

The Traditional Context

Cultural and Religious

by Carl E. Loeliger

History, Culture, and Religion

The history of the Lutheran Church in Papua New Guinea cannot be considered apart from the history, culture, and religion of its Papua New Guinean context. Any review of the history and life of the church anywhere is unable to avoid consideration of the history, culture and pre- or non-Christian religion of the area in question. Mission and church history cannot and should not appear to be divorced from its wider historical context. This calls for a sensitive awareness of the people whose history, culture, and religion are the focus of attention. These remarks may seem superfluous, for early Lutheran missionaries were among the first Europeans to appreciate and to study Papua New Guinean history, culture, and religion. But people not directly involved, in particular, need to be reminded of this necessary sensitivity.

Like Christinas anywhere in the world, Papua New Guinean Christians have acquired their identity from their place in the universal Christian Church and from their own historical, cultural, and religious roots. Any Christian account of these more specific roots will want to recognize also the universality of the Christian Church and the Lordship of Christ over all. This recognition does not mean the abandonment of a critical approach or the adoption of either negative or romantic views; it rather allows for the development of a positive but critical approach, or, stated in another way, it permits the growth of both deep respect and healthy suspicion. The history, culture and religion of Papua New Guinea or of Melanesia are to be viewed with the same deep respect and healthy suspicion as those of any other nation or culture area.

The extent to which Papua New Guinea peoples were interested in their history and historical reflection prior to 1884 is a matter of debate. Although Papua New Guinean people were non-literate prior to the advent of European colonization and the arrival of Christian missionaries, it seems they had their history and interest in history. The evidence for this interest and reflection is to be found in their attitudes to, and stories about, the ancestors, migration stories, myths of origin, legends and stories of many kinds, and this is still largely uninvestigated.

Careful study of their oral literature is only one of a variety of means by which it is now possible to discover something of the history of non-literate peoples. The impressive feature of human history in Papua New Guinea is its considerable time-depth. Recent archaeological discoveries suggest that this history goes back as far as about fifty thousand years ago. There is also archaeological evidence to argue that agriculture was practised in the New Guinea Highlands as early as anywhere in the world. Against this kind of time-depth, the periods of mission and colonial history seem very insignificant. Papua New Guineans may well point to the length of human habitation in their land with pride. The scholarly study and interpretation of this long period of human history has barely begun. Even the study of the more-recent past in Papua New Guinea is still in its infancy, as also, it may be argued, is the study of mission and church history, particularly from Papua New Guinean perspectives.

Perhaps the changes which have come to Papua New Guinea in the period of European colonial and Christian missionary activity have been unprecedented in their scope and rapidity; but these cannot be used to support the view that before this era there were no major changes among Papua New Guinean peoples. Migration, contact with other peoples, major changes in economy (e.g., from hunting and gathering to agriculture), introduction of new domestic animals (e.g., pigs) and crops (e.g., sweet potato), major natural disasters (e.g., earthquakes and volcanic eruptions), all brought major changes. Even apart from such major factors, it cannot be assumed that Papua New Guinean societies were static and unchanging before 1884, the beginning of the colonial period.

The term 'culture' is used here in the anthropological sense of the whole way of life of people in society and everything that results from that way of life, the implication being that there is no people without culture. Religion is always closely integrated with culture, and particularly so in 'primal' or 'traditional' cultures. The term 'religion' is employed broadly in this chapter to refer to the beliefs, values, and rituals of all peoples, the implication being that no people, ancient or modern, has been without a religion of some kind.

It is important to recognize 'ideals' and 'realities' in any survey of religion and culture. In

Ancestral house (Madang District about 1880).

every society there are ideals which are set before people but which are not always upheld or suitably fulfilled, just as there are the harsh realities of human life; any balanced account will take note of both the ideals and realities. Papua New Guinean communities before 1884 had their ideals, high and not so high, and their realities, harsh and not so harsh, just as they do today.

As far as is known, pre-Christian Papua New Guinean peoples made little or no distinction between 'culture' and 'religion'. This is borne out by the confusion some people have experienced even in recent times on hearing the calls of government ministers and others to preserve — even to rediscover — traditional culture. For some people the question has immediately arisen whether these calls involve a return also to traditional religion. At least until the arrival of Christian missions and European cultures, Papua New Guinean peoples seem not to have viewed culture and religion separately, and certainly not separately as many present-day European people do. The arrival of Christian missions did open up the possibility of a different religious base for, and new attitudes to, culture. In particular, belief in Christ made possible a positive but critical attitude to culture; it brought a freedom from, and for, culture.

An Appropriate Christian Attitude

Discussions of traditional culture and religion raise the question of appropriate attitudes to culture and pre-Christian religions. An appropriate Christian attitude to culture is positive but critical: positive because of God's relationship with and attitude toward human beings; and critical because of human beings' failure to be or to become what they are, and all the problems which result from that failure. The question of appropriate attitudes to other religions seems a more difficult question; but, as has been mentioned, the questions of relationship to other cultures and to other religions are closely related.

Submission to the Lordship of Christ does not mean Christians are not free to recognize that which is good in other religions. A point which Roland Allen has made may be helpful here: 'Missionary zeal is wholly independent of our ideas as to the value or character of heathen religions . . . Christians who recognize much truth in heathen religions are not less zealous in preaching Christ than those who recognize little.' [1] Whether one can speak of any positive attitude to non-Christian or pre-Christian religion depends at least partly on one's view of the activity of the Holy Spirit. Do missionaries bring God to non-Christian people, or do they bring the Good News of a God who has already been speaking to these people (see Romans 1:18 ff)?

Whilst the unique nature of the relationship of Jesus Christ and the early Church to the Old Testament tradition and Judaism cannot be overlooked, there is much in that relationship which is instructive for working out Christian relationships to culture and religion in any place. By way of hindsight, it has been possible to state that the whole of Old Testament history was the prelude to Jesus the Messiah and his Church. The attitudes of Jesus and the early Church to the Old Testament were certainly positive, but were also critical. These attitudes were critical because there now was a new and final authority: a Son (Hebrews 1:1 ff) whose words and works provided the norms for Christian

belief and life. Nevertheless, the early Church cannot be understood apart from the Old Testament and Jewish religion and culture. So also Papua New Guinean Christianity must be seen in its context: traditional Papua New Guinean religion and culture. As in the case of Jewish religion and culutre in the time of the early Church, however, the words and works of Jesus have provided a new basis for the evaluation of religion and culture. Early Christian attitudes to Old Testament religion and culture provide ideas for appropriate attitudes to traditional religion and culture in Papua New Guinea.

Within the Old Testament literature itself, there is evidence of the peoples' struggle to work out attitudes and relationships to the religion of the patriarchs or ancestors, to various features of their own culture, and to foreign religions and cultures in the light of their commitment to Yahweh, the God who revealed himself particularly in the liberation from Egypt. It is appropriate to speak of a struggle because the attitudes could not simply be totally negative or totally positive, and particularly in respect of the religion of the ancestors. Christians may at times disagree with some of the Old Testament attitudes to religion and religions, and to culture, but there is much to be gained from the study of the Old Testament for the understanding of Papua New Guinean religion and culture, and the struggle of Papua New Guinean Christians to relate to their heritage. [2]

The Importance of Primal (Traditional) Religion

It is essential to realize the importance of primal (often in the past called 'primitive' and still called 'traditional') religion among the world's religions. In the study of religion and religions, primal religions have only in more recent times received due recognition. One scholar has suggested a six-feature analysis for primal religion: 1) Kinship with nature, 2) Human weakness, 3) Man is not alone, 4) Relations with transcendent powers, 5) Man's after-life, 6) The physical as sacramental of the spiritual. [3] This analysis will not be strictly followed here, but it shows at a glance the impressive breadth and depth of primal religions. There is no reason why primal religions should not receive the same attention

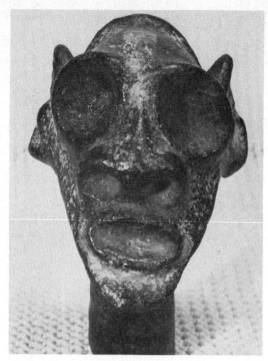

Ancestral sculpture used as magic (Finschhafen).

to grow. Papua New Guinean Christians have been reflecting on their primal religious background for nearly one hundred years, and it is still important that they do so. They must continue to reflect also, it is understood, on the universal Christian heritage. Unless Papua New Guinean Christians continue to come to grips with their own religion and culture, they will not be mature Christians, nor will there be mature national churches. [4] This does not mean that one generation's reflections will take the same course as that of the previous generation, but the activity of reflection must continue.

Great Cultural Complexity

The cultural and geographical area known as Melanesia, and the modern state of Papua New Guinea (which is a substantial part of Melanesia) are areas famed for their cultural complexity. This complexity is well illustrated by the existence of some 1200 languages in Melanesia, and some 700 languages within Papua New Guinea. Lutheran missionaries also encountered these cultural and linguistic complexities within the areas in which they worked. While they encouraged the continuing use of local vernacular languages, Lutheran missionaries also promoted the use of some as church languages, such as the Kate, Jabem, and Graged languages. Of these, Kate in particular came to be used as a church language far outside its original confines. This cultural and linguistic complexity has caused many scholars — missionaries included — to be very wary of making generalizations about the indigenous culture and religion of smaller regions, let alone an area the size of modern Papua New Guinea.

There are as yet no satisfactory explanations for this great cultural and religious complexity. It is possible to cite the geographical features of Papua New Guinea as one substantial reason for the isolation of peoples, but one is also able to point to the evidence of trading links, words common to a number of languages, and commonly-held stories, to show that the isolation of peoples was not nearly as complete as some have suggested. The little historical research which has already been done suggests that there will be no simple explanation for the great cultural complexity of Papua New Guinea.

as, say, Islam or Buddhism. No primal religion has ever been a missionary religion in the way these two religions have been; but primal religions have been the basic, fundamental religion of all Papua New Guineans. Now that situation has changed, and change continues apace, but the importance of primal religions has not altogether diminished. Certainly the impact of Christian missions has changed the commitment to primal religions, but their legacy cannot be easily ignored or forgotten. Here the Old Testament provides interesting material for consideration and comparison in the way that the religion of the ancestors or patriarchs has been accounted for in Israel's trans-tribal religion born in the context of the deliverance from Egypt.

European primal religions have clearly left their mark on European Christianity, so it should be no surprise if Papua New Guinean Christianity clearly reveals its contact with indigenous primal religion. In any event, it is appropriate that Papua New Guineans retain some interest in, and knowledge of, their primal religion, the context in which Papua New Guinean Christianity has grown and continues

18

Papua New Guineans themselves (eg Narakobi[5]) have tried to point out features common to all or most peoples in Papua New Guinea, and to emphasize a 'unity in diversity'. Christians considering this problem of complexity have good reasons for trying to identify cultural features and historical experiences which are shared, and those which are not. Since the Lutheran and other major denominational churches in Papua New Guinea cross very many of the linguistic and cultural boundaries, it is important for their wider communal harmony for their members to know what can be considered as their common heritage. As long as wider and universal connections are not forgotten, there is also no reason why people should not remember and cherish their specific cultural heritage and historical experiences, for these are an important part of any people's identity. To repeat an earlier assertion, it is the people's specific religious and cultural heritage and their historical experiences which have given, and will continue to give, Christianity in this region its particular identity. There is no such culture as a Christian culture; one more descriptive term has always to be added (for example, African, Chinese, German); and so, Papua New Guinean Christian culture is to be expected and welcomed.

In view of the great variety and complexities of Melanesian religion and culture, and the consequent reluctance of many scholars to generalize, any attempt to delineate the central and most important features of Melanesian or Papua New Guinean religion and culture has to be treated as tentative. Comment has already been made on how Papua New Guineans have traditionally seen the world as a whole; if life and experience were divided at all, they certainly were not divided into religion and culture, or into the religious and the secular, as people of many modern societies do. The western divisions of life into economic, political, social, psychological, and religious aspects also had no parallels in this total view. This total view involved an intense relationship with the whole environment, an I-Thou rather than I-It relationship — as our modern western societies have come to see relationships with the environment. This did not mean a naive

Mogus, *an image of the village spirit (Markham Valley).*

appreciation of the environment; Papua New Guinean peoples have had their own impressive ways of categorizing plants, animals, birds, and marine life, but these have not been seen just as things to be exploited. The spiritual and physical natural worlds were inseparable; so, in addition to the main (ancestral) spirits and deities, there were in most places a multitude of lesser localized spirits with which to contend in everyday life.

The Community of People and Ancestors and 'Gutpela Sindaun'

If there is one central, constant and almost universal feature in Melanesian and Papua New Guinean primal religion, it must be the ancestors and the respect in which they are held. Details vary from place to place, but everywhere, it seems, the ancestors are extremely important. To understand religion and culture, including social structure, the central place of the ancestors must be appreciated. Roderic Lacey's comments on the Enga (Highlands) world-view seem generally pertinent:

Three ideas are at the heart of life:

1. A person does not live in isolation as a single individual. His life, identity, and way of acting flow from the heritage which has come to him through many generations of ancestors. He and his ancestors are sharers in this common life.

Mask (Finschhafen).

Asa festival (near Bogadjim about 1890).

2. Man lives in a community made up not only of men and women who are alive now and present to him, but in a community of men and spirits all of whom are alive. Some of these persons, because they are spirits and hence their power is not so restricted as when they were men, are more powerful than others. One needs to relate to these persons in a balanced way.

3. Life is a continual, changing, and dynamic pattern of relationships between persons, some men, some spirits, all living. The good life is maintained by maintaining appropriate relationships with the proper people. [6]

While the details may vary from locality to locality, these three essentials of the Enga world-view seem to reflect ideals about community and the community of people and (ancestral) spirits held almost everywhere in Melanesia. A sense of community and appropriate relationships were (and are) everywhere important. Without these, there could be no good life. To state that Melanesian religion is concerned with only socio-economic welfare does not do justice to the central concern of

20

'continuation, protection, sustenance and celebration of life'. [7] These ideals bring to mind the Old Testament literature where blessing, peace, and happiness and the state of salvation can be experienced only in community. They are far removed from the modern western emphasis on the individual. Loneliness is seen as abnormal and inhuman. The wisdom of the strategy of the conversion of communities rather than of individuals, as was promoted early in Lutheran missionary activity by Christian Keysser, is obvious.

It is in this setting of community and appropriate relationships that the search for salvation in Melanesian or Papua New Guinean religion is to be seen. [8] For a full appreciation of salvation or the search for salvation, a broad view of Old Testament ideas is particularly useful background. [9] In the Old Testament literature, the liberation from oppression in Egypt, seen as God's greatest act of salvation, is used as the model or pattern for reflection on God's other saving acts. This however, is only one aspect of salvation; the people were also brought to a productive land which made the 'good life' possible (Deuteronomy 26:9). The

Old Testament portrayals of the condition or state of salvation present visions of the 'good life' which seem to be similar to those expressed in the *Tok Pisin* term *gutpela sindaun*. [10] The blessing activity of God in the Old Testament, of which the so-called 'Aaronic blessing' (Numbers 6:22-27) gives a concentrated account, also has to be taken into consideration. The key aspect of God's blessing activity is *shalom* (inadequately translated as 'peace'), and the context of *shalom* is community with others and properly-maintained relationships which are the foundations of complete life.

There are great differences between the Old Testament and Melanesian views of salvation, but, in respect of the condition or state of salvation, the holistic view of life, and the place given to community and right relationships, there is much that is comparable. Throughout the colonial and mission period of Papua New Guinea's history, there have been numerous new religious movements that are frequently referred to as 'cargo cults'. These complex and controversial movements have often revealed that Papua New Guineans traditionally have recognized that human conditions mostly are far from the ideal, and that the problems are largely due to ruptured relationships. The people involved in these many-sided movements do not seek 'cargo' in any narrow sense, but a whole new life with proper relationships — or, as has eloquently been argued, salvation. [11] While there are recently-introduced elements in these movements, they also reflect traditional beliefs and concerns. These movements always, it seems, assume the community of people and ancestral spirits as the basic community in which salvation is to appear. Whether pre-Christian Papua New Guinean peoples had any expectations of a Messiah or eschatological figure is uncertain; Messiah figures have been expected or have appeared in comparatively few of the new religious movements in Melanesia.

Lo, Ritual and Magic

How to describe Papua New Guinean attitudes and feelings toward the ancestors has been a controversial issue. It is likely that attitudes and feelings varied. Perhaps some went as far as worship and great fear; veneration or deep respect may be more appropriate terms

in other instances. In the Old Testament literature, the basic relationship between God and his people is expressed in terms of the covenant, a covenant the demands of which God fulfils, but which his people fail to meet. The *Tok Pisin* word *lo* has among other things a meaning similar to that of covenant or contract. This concept of *lo* also has to do with all the relationships in which people find themselves; it provides the framework for that fulfilment of relationships in which the ancestors and gods are obliged to guarantee success and fertility. [12] *Lo*, then, is about appropriate relationships, and is central to Melanesian views of salvation. An example of festivals which could be compared with Old Testament covenant renewal ceremonies are the pig festivals which are still held in some areas, particularly in the New Guinea Highlands. These elaborate festivals have among their aims the restoration and renewal of relationships, both people with the ancestors, and people with people. There is also a clear connection with the maintenance of fertility generally.

Festivals in traditional Papua New Guinea life deserve more than a brief note, but only that is possible here. The phrase 'celebration of life' quoted above is fitting for the attitude toward life which was evident in the numerous festivals, in their component rituals, dances, songs, and drama. Even in modern *singsings* in which traditional dances, songs, and drama are performed out of their original context, something of this 'celebration of life' and the accompanying excitement can still be felt.

The extent to which Melanesian or Papua New Guinean peoples have believed that ancestors, spirits, and gods could be manipulated by the performance of the right rituals remains controversial. The argument that there were major differences between Coastal peoples and Highlands peoples on this issue of manipulation cannot be maintained, because — as in other matters — the complex situation cannot be so easily described. Ideas about manipulation of spiritual powers are not confined to Melanesia; they were also found among the ancient Israelites, as can be seen from the powerful blasts of the prophets like Hosea and Jeremiah against such ideas in respect of the relationship with God.

The traditional Melanesian world-view can

Celebration of life which was evident in numerous festivals (Mt Hagen).

be described as magical, but it is not only that. [13] Magic and religion have always been mixed up, but neither religion in general nor primal religion in particular can be dismissed as simply magical practice. Magic can be seen to have a positive sense; it can reflect the freedom of human beings to attempt to control and to change their environment by manipulating the world's mysterious powers. Magic can have a positive purpose. For example, garden magic was (and is) performed to ensure a bountiful crop; it does not have a destructive aim. Sorcery seems to present the other side of the coin. Sorcerers also tried to manipulate the world's mysterious powers, but for destructive purposes: to bring about ruin, injury, or death. Sorcery was also used to explain deaths, and particularly untimely or accidental ones. The practice of magic and sorcery has been widespread in Melanesia, but the interest in sorcery has not been the same in all regions. As with other aspects of Melanesian culture, the details of the activities of magicians and sorcerers varied considerably from place to place. The fear of sorcery and sorcerers is still great in some areas.

22

Given-ness of Life

Melanesians, like the people of the Old Testament, have not had any concept of luck or fate, but have believed that events in the material and human realm are caused by someone rather than something. [14] Whether events be of the kind that bring happiness or that bring anguish, they are often attributed to spirit forces or to human beings who have successfully used magic or sorcery. As has been stated, properly-maintained relationships in the community of people and spirits is absolutely essential; disaster and suffering are inevitable if relationships are allowed to deteriorate.

One feature of God's activity toward people in the Old Testament is its 'given-ness'. Given-ness can also be seen as a feature of Melanesian belief and thought. Almost everywhere there is the recognition that many things in the environment and all aspects of culture have been given to people by someone — by gods, ancestors, other spirits, culture heroes, or other beings. This recognition, it seems, is related to the general recognition of the 'creaturehood' of human beings. A distorted awareness of the given-ness of things is evident in some of the 'cargo cults', where people seem to have waited for the products of modern technology to be given to them rather than working for them. The people involved in these movements have well known that garden produce, for example, does not come without work. The expectations found in these movements that the ancestors will appear bringing wealth with them can be regarded as extensions of the traditional idea of the given-ness of things.

As the leading part the ancestors played in belief, thought, and life clearly illustrates, Melanesians have had a universal belief in the after-life. Existence changes after death, but death is not the end. At death, a person leaves the 'living living' and joins the 'living dead', but remains within the community of people and spirits. Details of belief in the after-life varied enormously, as did burial practices. Belief in the resurrection of the dead was found in a number of places; and so the Motu in Papua, for example, were not surprised by Christian belief about the resurrection of the dead. The evidence from the cargo cults also suggests that there were widespread expectations of the return of the ancestors from the place of the dead. There are instances where this expectation is different; among the Enga people in the Highlands of Papua New Guinea, for example, it is hoped rathat that the living will join the sky people. There is still much research to be done on these expectations among Melanesian people.

Supreme Being

It may seem inappropriate that mention of a Supreme Being or God should be made only after referring to the ancestors. While it may be assumed that the ancestors are almost everywhere important, the same assumption cannot be made about belief in, or knowledge of, a 'Supreme Being' in pre-Christian Melanesian religion, as a recent article has shown. [15] In some areas, missionaries and the local people have been able to use the local name of the Supreme Being for the God of the Christian proclamation, the famous example for Lutheran mission experience being Anutu. In the case of Anutu, the name and variations of it are widespread. Its designations also are divergent — from a remote creator-god to that of a culture hero like the well-known Kilibob and

Manup of the Madang region. The use of the name Anutu for God has become widespread among Papua New Guinean Lutherans, but it must be noted that the name has achieved a new significance for those who knew it from local tradition, while others have accepted it as a new, but nevertheless Papua New Guinean name, for the Christian God. As Fr Theo Aerts has shown in his comprehensive article, it is extremely difficult to make generalizations about traditional Melanesian gods, beliefs in and about them, and how these might or might not be employed in the expression of Melanesian Christianity. Here, as in other areas, Papua New Guinean beliefs and traditions must be treated with respect and sensitivity and, at the same time, critically. It is at this point again that outsiders must tread very carefully and leave the final judgment to Papua New Guinean Christians.

Diversity is found also in the case of totems and totemism. Some Melanesian societies had and have their totems, usually birds, animals, fish, plants, or special objects; others have not. For some societies, totems are important for their relationship to ancestral origins; for others, totems are more like emblems of special significance, but not in connection with human origins.

A number of scholars have attempted to identify key concepts generally found in Melanesian religion. Earlier in the study of primal religions, the term 'animism' was used, but it is no longer used by scholars in respect of Melanesian religion; whichever way it is defined, it does not refer to a general key concept in Melanesian religion. Codrington's thesis that *mana* (power, powers) is a basic concept in Melanesian religion is widely accepted. Theo Ahrens has argued that the *Tok Pisin* word *pawa* (might, strength) and its vernacular equivalents represent key concepts in Melanesian religion. [16] In this case also there is comparable Old Testament material. *Pawa* does seem to designate a basic concept, but whether it does so everywhere in Melanesia is a matter for debate.

From the evidence of the cargo cults it would seem that Melanesian religion is concerned also with the search for the 'secret'. These movements have among their features the finding of the 'secret' which Europeans

Men's house with totem emblems (Taemi 1895).

have, but which has been thus far denied to Melanesians. [17] The search for the 'secret' is also found in Old Testament literature, particularly in the wisdom and apocalyptic literature. A case has been made that religion, for Melanesians, is more a secret than a mystery; [18] but whether this holds generally is open to question. It cannot be said that in Melanesian primal religion there is no sense of mystery.

It is legitimate and necessary to search for key concepts in Melanesian primal religion, but it cannot be expected that such a search will lead to a simple explanation of a very complex religious situation. It can be argued that fear is the dominant emotion and attitude in this religion, [19] but it seems that this must be seen over against the more important concern of maintaining right relationships within the community of people and spirits. As some have argued, the concern for the community and right relationships must further be seen over against the concern for life in the broadest sense and for the celebration of that life. [20]

Kinship Societies

An appreciation of the role of the ancestors is also extremely important for understanding

the basic social units, and how Melanesians or Papua New Guineans felt and still feel about them. Melanesian societies are kinship societies. [21] The basic social units are those considered to have descended from a single ancestor. The clan, a smaller social unit than the tribe or phratry, remains a strong social unit, and its strength is felt even in modern politics. The important role of the extended family in Melanesian societies is consistent with the importance of the clan. The details of social structure differ greatly from society to society, but everywhere ancestors, clan, and extended family have been, and mostly still are, central. For Papua New Guineans, as for southern Africans, human beings have always been a family. A Papua New Guinean can say as easily as can an African: 'I am because I participate'. [22] The institution of marriage also reflected the importance given to family and clan. Marriage not only brought two individuals together; it involved their families in a new and important relationship. Early in their association with Papua New Guinea societies, Lutheran missionaries recognized the social structure as providing a strong foundation for the establishment of Christian societies.

The term 'village' appropriately refers to social units in some areas, but is not suitable to refer to basic social units everywhere. While Charles Rowley, for example, has used the title *The New Guinea Villager* for his classic work, he has in the same work pointed out that the term 'village' by no means covers all the situations in which people have lived. [23]

Related to the importance of ancestors, clan, and extended family are Melanesian peoples' anthropocentricism and earth-centredness. There is anthropocentricism also in the Old Testament literature, but there it is overshadowed by theocentricism. The earth-centredness of Melanesian views of the world is in some cases referred to as ethnocentricism. [24] Clans or villages tend to regard themselves as better than any other group of people, [25] a tendency which, of course, is not confined to groups of people in Melanesia. In view of these points it is not surprising that there were, and are, deep attachments to the land, and particularly the land of one's ancestors, clan, and family. Land boundaries were something to be argued and fought about, but land itself was not something to be bought and sold. In respect of this relationship to the land, there is comparable material in the Old Testament literature (see especially 1 Kings 21).

It may be safely contended that all Melanesian societies have had their traditional moral codes, but in respect of the relationships between these codes and religious beliefs there has not been uniformity. These codes can be set out in a way similar to the statement of the Ten Commandments of the Old Testament. [26] In some societies, it was believed the spirits, or a god or gods, took an interest in people's observation of the moral code; in others, no connection seems to have been made between moral behaviour and the spirits or gods. There was one aspect of the basis of traditional moral codes and ethical concerns which seems to have been universal: The well-being of the community took precedence over that of the individual. [27]

Inter-Clan Relationships, Payback, and the Principle of Give and Receive

Hostility and warfare were regular features of relationships between societies and clans, and in some areas still occasionally mark inter-clan relationships. The peace which colonial rule and mission influence brought was widely welcomed. Hostility, however, was not the only possible kind of relationship, as the evidence of extensive trading circles and peace-making efforts shows. Nevertheless, seen against the difficulties of inter-society and inter-clan relationships, the bravery and courage of the early New Guinean Lutheran evangelists who dared to travel, live, and work among peoples little known to them, are remarkable indeed.

Particularly because of the publicity given to 'payback killings' in more recent times, a comment should be made on retribution and reciprocity in Melanesian societies. [28] Retribution or 'payback' for injuries or wrongs done is not, of course, found only in Melanesian societies, but it does seem that in pre-colonial times there was little delay in carrying out retributive action. The aim of such action was usually the well-being and protection of the community and its life. [29] If the member of a clan had been killed, then one of the offending clan had to be killed. Action against another clan was generally indiscriminate; any life would be taken, unless a known sorcerer or magician was involved. It has been argued that the peace between clans brought about by the colonial governments and missions increased the tension within some communities in one respect, because sorcery suspicions were moved from outsiders to people within the community. [30] Although compensation in goods or money is replacing payback killings, people still fear the possibility of swift payback for death or injuries sustained in road and other accidents.

Reciprocity or the principle of give-and-receive and a sense of balance in exchanges have been as important in Melanesian societies as in any other. Exchanges of wealth, reciprocal giving and receiving were a very important feature of the life of communities, and essential for the maintenance of good relationships; they continue to be important. [31] Some traditional exchanges have become distorted, and seem to be considered more as payments; a conspicuous example of this is the exchange of wealth associated with marriages, which is now often referred to as bride-price payment. The concern for balance in all dealings was, in some

Chief Matagong (Bukawa).

societies at least (such as the Tanga in the Madang province), developed in a systematic way with special terms to describe situations of balance and imbalance. The relationship between Papua New Guineans and Europeans in colonial times was seen as one of imbalance, not only in respect of authority, but in material possessions and technology. It is possible to see one of the aims of cargo cults as an attempt to redress, or even reverse, this imbalance.

The traditional political units in Melanesia, the clans (or even sub-clans), were small, particularly in contrast with those of Polynesia. In traditional political leadership there also was a contrast between Polynesia and Melanesia; Polynesian communities were more highly stratified than Melanesian societies, and leadership was hereditary. Traditional Melanesian societies are usually described as egalitarian, although there are areas where there is clear stratification (such as Manam Island, parts of the North Solomons). It is very difficult to generalize about traditional political leadership in Melanesia, for there is a diversity extending from hereditary chieftainship to the situation where the position of 'big man' was

open, at least theoretically, to anyone willing to work at acquiring the necessary prestige and influence.

Leadership

Melanesian societies are generally regarded as having been male-dominated, but there are areas (such as Mekeo and Roro in Papua) where women have been very influential. In most societies, if not all, the older men, because of their greater knowledge and experience, were highly respected and had considerable authority. The elders as custodians of the clan's traditions also had the duty to teach the young men. Initiation was an important event in every young man's life. For a period of months the young men were taken from the village to an isolated place to be taught, trained, and tested for adult life. Periods of initiation and initiation rites and methods varied considerably, but the aim was always similar: to begin to teach young men the range of traditional knowledge, and to prepare them for adult life in the community.

In many societies, initiated men lived in the large men's house, and spent a minimum of time with their wives and children. The men's house was a place for ritual, continuing education, story-telling, discussion, and planning. Young women were also prepared for adult life, but generally not the same attention seems to have been given to their preparation. Yet women have played a very important part in the overall life of societies, a part which has not always received due recognition. In addition to other areas of competence, women usually were the experts in gardening and pig husbandry.

Economy and Technology

The traditional pre-colonial economy of Papua New Guinea is generally described as 'subsistence'. Even now the subsistence sector has subsidized the so-called modern sector. Subsistence agriculture has a long history in Papua New Guinea (up to 8000 years?); although Papua New Guineans did not have access to iron and steel before the colonial period, they did have impressive and appropriate gardening techniques, and could produce a wide range of crops. In the case of crop failure, people used their knowledge of uncultivated plants to obtain food. Drainage of

Markham pottery.

swamps and irrigation schemes were known and carried out long before the colonial period. In most areas people were able to produce a surplus of food from time to time for trading and festive purposes.

A further comment is warranted concerning traditional Melanesian technology. Seen against the seemingly-spectacular achievements of modern technology, it is all too easy to underestimate the technological achievements of Papua New Guineans prior to the coming of Europeans. The more obvious manifestations of these achievements could be seen in such things as buildings, bridges, canoes — large and small, pottery manufacture, weapons, tools and utensils made of stone and wood, ceremonial and ritual objects, animal and fish traps, and irrigation and drainage schemes. In this material culture there was much which Europeans could describe as works of art, as works of highly-skilled people. Papua New Guineans, however, seem not to have been interested in art for art's sake, at least in the past.

In this article, very little attention has been given to specialists in Melanesian societies. Although in very small societies there may have been little specialization, in many societies there were degrees of specialization. There were priests and prophets (also prophetesses), [32] people skilled in traditional medicine, and craftsmen and women of different kinds. As has been noted, women were often the experts in agriculture; they also were the experts in pottery-making where that was practised.

Baptismal font (Finschhafen).

While this chapter is concerned mainly with the more traditional culture and religious context of the growing Lutheran church, at least brief reference must be made to the impact on this context of the colonial powers, with their policies and administration, and of the presence of a range of foreigners with their interests. The impact of these outside influences was not felt to the same extent everywhere, but particularly in the New Guinea segment (former German New Guinea) the impact in a number of regions was severe. The changes in colonial powers from German to Australian (under the League of Nations), to Japanese, back to Australian (under the United Nations), and particularly the Pacific War of 1942 to 1945, greatly affected traditional society, religion and culture, and the missionary effort. As well, introduced economic activities such as copra production and gold mining brought major changes to all aspects of life. All these influences complicated an already-complex cultural and religious situation. An account of these additional complexities cannot be given here, but they must be kept in mind as part of the context of the growing Lutheran Church in Papua New Guinea.

27

Worthy of Respect and Continuing Reflection

As ways of life which have supported people for thousands of years, Papua New Guinean primal religion and culture are worthy of respect. At the same time their deficiencies and problems cannot be overlooked. Whether this primal religion and culture are considered to have provided bridges or obstacles — or both — for the proclamation of the Gospel and the development of a Melanesian Christian culture, they must be treated absolutely seriously as the context in which Christian missionaries have worked, and in which indigenous Melanesian Christianity has grown.

An article such as this cannot do justice to the complexity and richness of Papua New Guinean religion and culture, nor to the great amount of research and writing which has been done on Papua New Guinean peoples, religion, and culture. Lutheran missionaries have made significant contributions to the generally-available knowledge of Papua New Guinea and its peoples. With their specialized training and their long-term commitments to particular peoples and communities, Lutheran missionaries have had opportunities to get to know Papua New Guinean peoples and their ways of life as few outsiders, other than missionaries, have had. Apart from the extent of the contribution to the recorded knowledge of peoples and cultures, there is the question, perhaps more important, of whether the knowledge gained by missionaries is reflected in the life and worship of the Lutheran Church in Papua New Guinea. It is appropriate to ask to what extent the understanding of Papua New Guinean religion and culture gained by missionaries has contributed to the development of a truly mature national or local church. Implicit in this question is the equally-difficult question of the extent to which Lutheran missionaries were able to disentangle the Christian Gospel from their own European cultural background, and to relate it to the Melanesian context in which they lived and worked. It was observed earlier that the 'celebration of life' was a central feature of Melanesian religion. The question arises as to whether not more of this sense of celebration, which was manifested in festivals, song, and dance, could not have found its way into the liturgy of the church. This sense of celebration has found its way into special festive occasions (for example, the dedication of new church buildings), but is not really in evidence in the regular worship liturgy.

The interpretation of Papua New Guinean primal religion and culture, and their past and present relationship with Christianity, will continue to be controversial. The most important interpretations will continue to be those of Papua New Guineans themselves, and will deserve respect from outsiders. Papua New Guineans have reacted in a diversity of ways to their own cultures in the light of their experience of Christianity and foreign cultures. Whichever way people have accommodated the new to the old, Christian belief and foreign cultures to traditional religion and culture, they have not been able to avoid the impact of the new, nor to reject the old as though it was no longer important or had gone away. There has been dramatic change, but there also is continuity with the past. We may speak and write of Papua New Guinean Christianity and Papua New Guinean Christian culture.

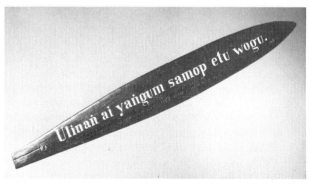

Jabem: 'Behold I make all things new' (Rev. 21:5).

Endnotes

[1] Roland Allen, *Missionary Principles*, (London: Lutterworth Press, 1968), 60,61.

[2] See my paper, 'Melanesian and Old Testament Cosmologies', in *Melanesian Institute Orientation Course Notes*, Goroka, 1979.

[3] Harold Turner, 'The Primal Religions of the World and Their Study' in Victor C. Hayes ed., *Australian Essays in World Religions* (Adelaide: Lutheran Publishing House, 1977), 30 ff.

[4] See Darrell Whiteman, 'From Foreign Missions to Independent Church', *Catalyst* IX (2, 1981), 73-91.

[5] See the collection of Bernard Narakobi's articles, *The Melanesian Way: Total Cosmic Vision of Life* (Port Moresby: Institute of Papua New Guinea Studies, 1980).

[6] Roderic Lacey, 'A Glimpse of the Enga World View', (unpublished paper) 5-6. A shorter version of this paper appeared in *Catalyst* III (2, 1972). 37-47, under the title: 'Enga World View'.

[7] See Philip Gibbs, 'Blood and Life in a Melanesian Context', *Point* 1977, 167.

[8] See Gernot Fugmann, 'Salvation in Melanesian Religions' in Ennio Mantovani ed., *An Introduction to Melanesian Religions* (Goroka: Melanesian Institute, 1984), 279 ff.

[9] See my paper, 'Melanesian and Old Testament Cosmologies', 13 ff.

[10] See Fugmann, 282.

[11] See John Strelan, *Search for Salvation* (Adelaide: Lutheran Publishing House, 1977), 62 ff.

[12] See Fugmann, 284-287.

[13] See Fugmann, 'Magic: A Pastoral Response', in Mantovani ed., 214.

[14] See Donald McGregor, 'Basic Papua New Guinea Assumptions', *Catalyst* VI (3, 1976), 181 ff.

[15] Theo Aerts, 'Melanesian Gods', *Bikmaus* IV (2, 1983), 1-54.

[16] Theo Ahrens, 'Concepts of power in a Melanesian and biblical perspective', *Point* 1977, 61 ff.

[17] See Joe Knoebel, 'A Pattern in Dreaming and Hoping', *Point* 1, 1974, 89-91.

[18] See Hermann Janssen, 'Traditional Religion in Melanesia', *Melanesian Institute Orientation Course Notes*, Goroka, 1972, 1.

[19] See, for example, Merlyn Wagner, 'The Enga Concept of Fear' in Paul Brennan ed., *Exploring Enga Culture* (Wapenamanda: Kristen Pres, 1970).

[20] See Ennio Mantovani, 'Traditional Values and Ethics', in Darrell Whiteman ed., *An Introduction to Melanesian Cultures* (Goroka: Melanesian Institute, 1984), 284 ff, and Whiteman, 'Melanesian Religions: An Overview', in Mantovani ed., 106 ff.

[21] See Kenneth McElhanon and Whiteman, 'Kinship: Who is Related to Whom', in Whiteman ed., 106 ff.

[22] John V. Taylor, *The Primal Vision* (London: SCM Press, 1972), 85.

[23] Charles Rowley, *The New Guinea Villager* (Melbourne: Cheshire, 1972), 32 ff.

[24] Theo Aerts, *The Old Testament Through Melanesian Eyes* (Bomana, 1978), 4.

[25] McGregor, 1977.

[26] See, for example, Albert Maori Kiki, *Ten Thousand Years in a Lifetime* (Melbourne: Cheshire, 1968), 44-45.

[27] See Mantovani ed., 206 ff.

[28] On these difficult topics see Garry Trompf, 'Retributive Logic in Melanesian Belief', in *Religion in Melanesia* part C, option I, compiled by G.W. Trompf and C.E. Loeliger (Port Moresby: University of Papua New Guinea, 1980), 97 ff.

[29] Mantovani ed., 206.

[30] Trompf, 100-101.

[31] Mantovani ed., 204-205.

[32] See Garry Trompf ed., *Prophets of Melanesia* (Port Moresby: Institute of Papua New Guinea Studies, 1981).

The following books and articles have not been specifically cited in the notes:

Aerts, Theo, 'Christian Art From Melanesia', *Bikmaus* V (1, 1984), 27-83.

Evan-Pritchard, E.E., *Theories of Primitive Religion* (Oxford: Oxford University Press, 1965).

Fugmann, Gernot, 'An Interview with Waga Miridji', *Catalyst* XIV (3, 1984), 207-219.

Koschade, Alfred, *New Branches on the Vine* (Minneapolis: Augsburg Publishing House, 1967).

Lawrence, Peter, 'Religion and Magic', *Encyclopedia of Papua New Guinea* (Melbourne: Melbourne University Press, 1972), vol. 2.

Lawrence, Peter, *Road Belong Cargo* (Melbourne: Melbourne University Press, 1964).

McGregor, Donald E., *The Fish and the Cross* (Goroka: Melanesian Institute, 1982).

Narakobi, Bernard, 'What is religious experience for a Melanesian?', *Point* 1977, 7-12.

Runne, Maria, 'Religion of My People', *Catalyst* XIV (3, 1984), 220-228.

Somare, Michael Thomas, *Sana: An Autobiography*, (Port Moresby: Niugini Press, 1975).

Whiteman, Darrell, *Melanesians and Missionaries* (Pasadena: William Carey Library, 1983).

Chapter 2

Beginnings at Finschhafen

The Neuendettelsau Mission jointly with the Australian Lutheran Church

by Herwig Wagner

The wondrous story of the future Lutheran Church of Papua New Guinea began to unfold when the Neuendettelsau missionary Johann Flierl landed on the shores of New Guinea on July 12, 1886.

On the Verge of Colonial Rule

Finschhafen,[1] a small but well-protected harbour on the eastern point of the Huon Peninsula, marked the first beginning. From November 5, 1885, it had sheltered the first tiny settlement of the New Guinea Company, a company endowed with sovereign power in the colony by the new German Empire. In November 1884, through a symbolic flag-hoisting at three locations on the mainland (one of which was Finschhafen) plus four island sites, Germany had claimed as its colony the northern part of Eastern New Guinea under the name 'Kaiser-Wilhelmsland', as well as the protruding Bismarck Archipelago. Holland had already acted in similar fashion in 1824 by annexing the western half of the island to its Indonesian colony. In 1888, England finalized its hold on 'British New Guinea',[2] comprising the southern part of the eastern half of the island (adjacent to Australia) and the near-by islands not claimed by Holland.

The economic expectations of Germany in New Guinea and the Bismarck Archipelago were quite unrealistic. It was only after the 1870s that two German trading firms, Hernsheim and Co., and the German Plantation and Trading Company, both located in Hamburg, established small business settlements on New Britain (then Neu-Pommern) and on New Ireland (then Neu-Mecklenburg).[3] In Germany, however, high economic expectations were placed in the mainland;[4] by establishing plantations and good trading connections with Europe, lucrative profits were hoped for. At the same time, the migration of enterprising Germans or of German people in Australia was seen as a possibility. With such bright hopes in view, Adolf von Hansemann founded a plantation and trading organization which called itself the New Guinea Company, and established the first settlement of the Company in Finschhafen. It soon became evident, however, that both Finschhafen and the Madang area were unsuitable for this purpose. In fact, their hopes for New Guinea and the

Finschhafen, harbour entrance.

Bismarck Archipelago to become a profitable dependency were never fulfilled.

Missionary Pioneers in New Guinea

The first missionary to come to Kaiser Wilhelmsland was Johann Flierl. Previously there had been a short and unsuccessful mission attempt on Umboi Island[5] by the French Roman Catholic Order of the Marists in 1848.[6] The Catholics had planned their settlement on Umboi to be a second mission station of the Vicariate Apostolic of Melanesia and Micronesia, branching out from their mission centre on Woodlark Island (Papuan Islands). However, the appointed Bishop for Melanesia and Micronesia, Jean-Georges Collomb, died of malaria in the same year, shortly after he had arrived at his mission station on Umboi. The following year, this very first missionary outreach to New Guinea collapsed altogether. A second attempt on Umboi (1852-55) by missionaries from the Milan Institute for Foreign Missions was just as short-lived.[7] When Woodlark was also abandoned as a mission centre in 1855, the Vicariate Apostolic of Melanesia for almost 30 years remained only a

Johann Flierl.

strategic plan for Roman Catholic missions in that area. In 1882, missionaries from the Order of the Most Sacred Heart of Jesus, acting on the advice of Pope Leo XII, resumed work in the orphaned Vicariate Apostolic of Melanesia. They established their first mission station on the Gazelle Peninsula of New Britain, next to the

32

German trading companies. Their station Kiniguna was soon dubbed Vunapope (that is, the seat of the 'Popies' or Catholics). Later, Vunapope became the seat of the new Vicar Apostolic for New Britain, Bishop Coupé.

The resumption of Roman Catholic work in Melanesia was, in fact, preceded by the Australian Methodist Mission, also on the Gazelle Peninsula. Their pioneer missionary, Wesley Brown, had begun work there in 1875. Brown had previously been in Samoa, and had heard reports there from German traders about New Britain. In his heart, he longed for an entirely new mission opportunity which, in fact, he found in New Britain. His connections with European traders enabled him to establish an amazingly-quick contact with the local people. Within two years he had a foothold in no fewer than 23 villages on New Britain, New Ireland, and the smaller Duke of York Island in between.[8] He most certainly must have viewed the appearance of the Catholic missionaries in his immediate neighbourhood as menacing competition. On the suggestion of the German administration, the Gazelle Peninsula was divided in 1890 into two mission areas for the Methodists and the Catholics.[9] Unfortunately, this well-meant government action produced no results whatsoever. The regrettable competitive situation between two Christian mission bodies continued, even though there was at that time no other Christian mission activity in the vast area.

In British New Guinea, two missions were already at work in those early years. Their activities began with missionaries from the London Mission Society, Samuel McFarlane and A.W. Murray (1871), William Lawes (1873), and James Chalmers (1877). Three of them came as experienced missionaries from the Pacific mission field, and brought indigenous co-workers with them to New Guinea. The large but hardly-known island of New Guinea constituted a special missionary challenge to them. Each of these men could be classified as a pioneer in his own right in British New Guinea: McFarlane made the first contacts on some islands in the Torres Strait and in Milne Bay; Lawes was the first European missionary to Hanuabada (near the later Port Moresby); James Chalmers became the pioneer of the Gulf region and the Fly River, where he died as a martyr on Easter Sunday 1901, together with a group of co-workers, when they were unexpectedly attacked on Goaribari Island by a group of suspicious villagers.

The second mission in British New Guinea was begun in 1885 on Yule Island by the French missionaries of the Roman Catholic Order of the Most Sacred Heart of Jesus. The initiator of this new work was Louis-Andre Navarre, who later became Archbishop and Vicar Apostolic of British New Guinea. The actual pioneer in the work, however, was the energetic Italian, Henry Verjus. After 1908, Alain de Boismenu, successor to Archbishop Navarre, took over the work of both these men.

The Australian Anglicans were the third Christian mission to begin work in British New Guinea. After the State of Queensland had annexed that part of the island in 1883, the Anglican General Synod regarded it as its task to care spiritually for the Australians who migrated there, as well as to bring the Gospel to the indigenes. In 1891, the work of the Anglican Mission was started by C. King and A. Maclaren on the Dogura Plateau on the north-east coast.

The first British Governor of the colony, Sir William McGregor, was very sympathetic toward Christian mission work; in 1891, he also invited the Methodists to take part in evangelizing the land. Reaching out from Dobu Island, William Bromilow, with a group of co-workers from Fiji and Tonga, began working in what came to be called the Papuan Islands, where 40 years earlier the French Marist missionaries had broken off their unsuccessful mission attempt.

In order to keep denominational peace among the four missions working in his territory, McGregor advocated a regional working agreement between them, similar to that of the German administration in New Britain. The Anglicans were to consider the north-east coast of British New Guinea up to the boundary of the German colony as their mission field; the Methodists the coast-line islands; the London Mission Society was to concentrate its efforts on the south coast and down to the Gulf region. It was the Roman Catholic Mission which again opposed the suggested gentlemen's agreement; they were unwilling to have their work restricted to certain areas by the claims of other missions. The Catholic mission claimed the right of religious liberty; no government

33

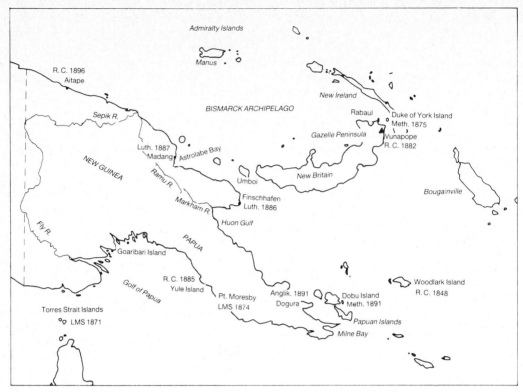

Early Christian Missions PNG

1848	Rom. Cath.	Woodlark Island	1885	Rom. Cath.	Yule Island
1871	LMA	Torres Strait Islands	1886	Luth. (ND)	Finschhafen
1874	LMS	Hanuabada/	1887	Luth (Rh)	Astrolabe Bay/
		Pt Moresby			Madang
1875	Methodist	Duke of York Islands	1891	Methodist	Dobu Island
1882	Rom. Cath.	Gazelle Peninsula/	1891	Anglican	Dogura Plateau
		Vunapope	1896	Rom. Cath.	Aitape

should have the right to interfere with the work of individual religious groups.

Except for the conflicts with the Catholic missionaries, denominational differences between the Christian churches presented no big problem in those initial years of mission work in New Guinea. On the whole, the working areas of the individual missions were far apart, except in New Britain. A converging of the different denominations in urban or other built-up areas was not yet foreseen. Both the British and the German colonial administrations tried hard to create an atmosphere of orderly conduct between the various missions. the Neuendettelsau missionaries in Finschhafen suffered the least from denominational

competition. Johann Flierl was at that time the first and the only Christian missionary in what was then called Kaiser Wilhelmsland. A year later, the Rhenish Mission, with whom the Neuendettelsau Mission was on friendly terms, began its work in Astrolabe Bay (see ch 3). For decades, the Finschhafen Mission was fortunate to be spared denominational upheavals.

Beginning of Lutheran Work by Johann Flierl

To begin mission work in New Guinea had not been on the agenda of the Neuendettelsau Mission Society at all. This small Franconian village had become a spiritual centre of the Bavarian Lutheran Church through the activities of its pastor, Wilhelm Loehe († 1872). Through his powerful preaching, a genuine awakening began in that area. Young women were prepared to serve as deaconesses, and young men were trained and sent out as preachers to the German immigrants in North America. Similar services soon followed for the migrants to Australia and Brazil. Up to that time, Loehe's Bavarian church was not in the position either spiritually or administratively to undertake any work which would extend beyond the boundaries of its homeland, nor to take over the responsibility for it. Following trends of that time, Loehe in 1849 established the *Gesellschaft fuer Innere Mission im Sinne der Lutherischen Kirche*,[10] which aimed to support, both spiritually and financially, the rapidly-growing work at home and abroad. Even before that, Loehe had considered it necessary already in 1846 to train young men for an overseas ministry. From a very modest beginning, this activity grew into a full-fledged training institution for missionary service, later called *Missions- und Diaspora- Seminar*.[11] It remained in operation until 1985.

Johann Flierl (born April 16, 1858, in Buchhof, Bavaria) received his training at that seminary. On Easter Sunday 1878, he was commissioned to go to Australia to work among the Aborigines in the interior of that large continent. His fervent wish always had been to become a missionary in a foreign land. When the Lutheran Immanuel Synod in South Australia requested such a co-worker from Neuendettelsau Mission, Flierl felt the call and spontaneously volunteered for Australia.[12] His intentions, however, were in fact aimed at something still greater:

> I would rather go to a totally untouched heathen people, not yet trampled on, oppressed and pushed aside by white settlers, as is the case on the mainland of Australia. There, behind Australia, that large island of New Guinea, that would be my idea.[13]

However, those were his private thoughts. His assignment from the Australian Immanuel Synod first of all led him (for some seven years, 1878-1885) to Bethesda Mission Station in the interior of South Australia. There he was to work among the Aboriginal tribe of the Dieri.

His idea of going to New Guinea, however, had not been forgotten. When he received news about the German colonial beginnings in New Guinea, he recorded in a rather-lengthy letter his vision of expanding mission work to that near, yet so far-away, unknown island:

> As for myself I am ready to move on to an outpost. I am prepared to live there with only the most necessary equipment as soon as I receive the call and assignment from the committee to do so . . . I will forgo every comfort which I have grown used to and put up with any kind of inconvenience. My dear wife would also comply, even though it means a separation, until such time when most of the initial difficulties are overcome.[14]

Flierl sent this letter to his Mission Society in Neuendettelsau, as well as to the Mission Committee of the Immanuel Synod in South Australia, since he was firmly bound to the latter through his work at the Bethesda Mission.

A positive answer came surprisingly fast from Neuendettelsau. The most important sentence of the letter by Mission Inspector J. Deinzer read: 'My advice is: In God's name, forward to New Guinea, but quickly and quietly!' The Mission Committee in South Australia reacted just as positively.[15]

Thus, from the very beginning, mission work in New Guinea became a joint effort of the Mission Society in Neuendettelsau and the Lutheran Immanuel Synod in South Australia. The Australian Mission Committee released Flierl from his work at Bethesda so that he was free to go to New Guinea. On November 8, 1885, he was commissioned for that task during a worship service of the Tanunda congregation in South Australia. His wife, Louise, née Auricht, a member of that congregation, had to wait until 1888 to join him.

However, in spite of its willingness to participate, the Immanuel Synod had to stress that its own strained financial position demanded that the responsibility for the start of this big undertaking had to rest with Neuendettelsau. 'We are happy to help with advice, but the responsibility for the actual work has to be in Germany.'[16] Even with this limitation in mind, it must be stated that from the outset the Lutheran congregations in South Australia felt spiritually responsible for the new mission work in New Guinea and gave some financial assistance. Thirty years later, this co-operation was urgently needed for the Mission's survival during and after World War I.

Flierl's expedition to the new German colony proved to be even more difficult and time-consuming than either he himself or the mission boards in Germany and Australia had imagined. At first, it was the New Guinea Company which had second thoughts. Then, after its Board of Directors in Berlin had agreed, the Company's local agent in Cooktown delayed Flierl's passage an additional five months. Flierl simply had to wait, for no other ships went to Kaiser Wilhelmsland except those of the Company. Yet he did not remain idle during this delay. Supported by the Queensland Government, he started to work as missionary among the Aborigines in Northern Queensland. There and then he established the new station Elim. [17]

However, his destination was New Guinea. Finally, on July 8, 1886, he started out, and on July 12, he landed in Finschhafen as the first Christian missionary in Kaiser Wilhelmsland.

The First Mission Station: Simbang

Flierl's arrival in Finschhafen was more pleasant than he had expected after his initial experiences with the New Guinea Company. The newly-appointed Governor of the Colony, Admiral Georg von Schleinitz, had arrived there shortly before Flierl, and showed himself quite co-operative toward Flierl's mission venture. Apparently a change of attitude had also taken place among the Board of Directors in Berlin; they gave instructions 'to support the missionary as much as possible under the prevailing circumstances'. [18] Flierl was asked to conduct Sunday worship services for the people of the Company, and, at the start, he even gave religious instruction to the children of the Governor.

However, this was not the purpose for which Flierl had come to New Guinea; his main concern was mission work. He gave himself three months to find a suitable site for a mission settlement somewhat away from the Company. Finally, he chose Simbang, a village at the mouth of the Bubui (Mape) River in Langemak Bay, about one hour's walk from Finschhafen. One week after his first co-worker, Karl Tremel, had arrived from Germany, Flierl hired a Company boat to take them with all their personal belongings to Simbang. The date: October 8, 1886.

36

Simbang, birthplace of the Church.

Looking back, Simbang was an ideal place for the first settlement. From there, the coastal as well as inland mountain tribes could be reached comparatively easily. On the other hand, being away from Finschhafen also meant a certain measure of independence from the Company and its administration. However, through ignorance of local customs, Flierl made the mistake of settling directly next to a village; and he also did not seek the explicit permission of the village leaders to settle on their land. Flierl himself remembered:

> I tried to explain the reason of our coming to the local people of Simbang and thought I had their permission. We also had obtained the permission from the Land Office [of the Company] and were granted a small piece of land ... But the reception by the Simbang people was anything but friendly. It seemed that they had understood my repeated announcements of our coming only to the point that we merely wanted to visit them for a short while with welcome presents. When they saw that we already had come with building materials, such as corrugated iron for a permanent building, their faces grew dark, and the old chief Duke shouted abuse. [19]

The appearance of two white men with their belongings must have raised uncertainty, even spontaneous rejection, on the part of the Simbang people. Flierl and Tremel were immediately made aware that they were not welcome. Even to this day, stories are told in Simbang village of how they at first wanted to drive the two strangers away through trickery, thievery, and actual assault. Not knowing the language of the people, the two missionaries could hardly make themselves understood in regard to the simplest daily needs, to say nothing of explaining to the villagers the reasons for their coming. Furthermore, besides the annoyance they caused by their illegal claim of village land, they were also seen as a religious threat. Did these two men perhaps ascend from the region of the dead and spirits? It was their white skin which might have suggested that, because only the spirits of the deceased were believed to be colourless. Could one, then, have contact with them without running into danger?

In spite of these partly self-inflicted initial difficulties, Flierl and Tremel managed to get a foothold in Simbang. They built a house with a corrugated iron roof, planted gardens, and started a small chickenyard for their own subsistence. Initially, the Simbang people were in no way inclined to assist the missionaries in their daily work. However, Flierl was fortunate enough to obtain six young men from the Methodist Mission on New Britain as workers for some time. [20] Without this help, the beginning in Simbang would have been even harder.

Besides doing necessary construction work, the two pioneer missionaries were handicapped in their missionary activities by malaria. Even though the Neuendettelsau missionaries were spared fatalities in the first eight years, the almost-regular malaria attacks every two or three weeks, which in serious cases culminated in the so-called black-water fever, posed a serious threat to their health. The question arose whether Europeans would ever be able to live in a tropical climate for a longer period of time. Only at the turn of the century was tropical medicine in a position to identify the actual cause of malaria (a certain kind of mosquito), and to use quinine in the right dosage as a preventative. In the first months of 1891, a particularly malicious form of tropical malaria swept over the Company settlement in Finschhafen, causing the death of nearly one-third of its members — and finally, the physician himself. This terrifying experience caused the Company to give up its headquarters in Finschhafen and to move to Stephansort (Bogadjim) on Astrolabe Bay, almost 200 km further up the coast.

Should the missionaries and their families join them? If not, would not isolation caused by irregular shipping and postal services and lack of proper medical care make their living conditions difficult and endanger their life? Most importantly, they would have to depend upon themselves, without the protection of the German colonial authorities. Flierl was aware of the urgency of the situation. How could he make such a far-reaching decision with the same haste as the departure of the Company people? He wrote to the Mission Board in Neuendettelsau:

> On the surface it looks as if we, with our whole mission here, are standing at a turning point, but our parole can only be: Remain and hold on! For us, leaving this area would mean unfaithfulness and foolishness, after having done so much preliminary work, and having settled down and familiarized ourselves to such a degree. [21]

It was a courageous decision of the missionaries to stay on at Finschhafen, trusting solely in God's protection. In the long run, it was the wisest decision they could have made. By their action, the missionaries affirmed more effectively than by words that in their commitment and their work they were independent of the colonial administration and the trading interests of the Company. As a result, in later years they had the advantage of not being categorized with the rest of the Europeans in the country. In addition, they were able to extricate themselves from the trading habits of the Company, which were rather ruthless when annexing native land. The neighbouring missions in Madang and on the Gazelle Peninsula had to suffer a lot because they were not free of these complexities. Even today, there are noticeable characteristics in the Finschhafen (Kate) District of the Church which are due, among other things, to this decision of 1891. For more than a generation, the growing church in the Finschhafen area had the chance to develop according to its own spiritual foundations.

How to Approach People?

Through his activities among the Aborigines in Australia, Flierl had been rather well prepared for his missionary service in New Guinea. However, the mistake of establishing the first station on village ground at Simbang certainly did not help. Flierl and Tremel — in addition to all their other initial difficulties — faced the handicap of rejection by the village

37

The first school building at Simbang. Schoolboys with (from left) Held, Mrs Vetter, Vetter, Mrs Hansche, Hansche, and Bamler.

leaders. How would they be able successfully to carry on mission work under such circumstances?

The only model for propagating the Gospel familiar to them was that of holding worship services similar to those at home. This, however, proved to be totally inadequate in New Guinea. Their invitations to services on Sundays at the mission station were neither appreciated nor heeded. In the everyday life of a New Guinea villager, there was no actual link to the worship habits of the missionaries whatsoever. 'We are tired of your words. Our ears hurt. Your axes are good, but your talk you can keep for yourselves!' [22] Strangeness to, and misunderstanding of, the missionaries' aims could hardly have been expressed more bluntly.

From the beginning, it was Flierl's idea to achieve a breakthrough with the people by approaching the youth. With this in view, he built his first station house in Simbang large enough for half of it to be used as a classroom. Yet even here he failed completely in the beginning, for in traditional New Guinea life, formal schooling was unknown. How could missionaries expect boys (or even girls!) to attend school regularly?

38

After all, going to school would not be of any advantage anyway. Within three months after their arrival, the missionaries tried to conduct classes; but the result was exactly nil. [23] If there was anything at all which was interesting to the people, it was the white men's iron tools, tobacco, and glass beads. Tremel wrote:

> They want to be paid for attending school. We went into the near-by village to call the children together and bring them to school, but often, when we stooped and entered the huts at the front door, the pupils slipped away at the back, clearing through under the grass roof. [24]

Yet, the idea to use the school — that is, the younger generation — as a basis for the missionary approach proved successful, though in a different way. In 1889, Labita, a close relative of a chieftain from nearby, and 14 young men appeared at the missionaries' place, declaring themselves ready to learn and to work with the missionaries for five months. [25] All came from neighbouring villages, some so far away that it was necessary to house them on the station. Thus began what the German missionaries afterwards used to call *Kostschule* (boarding school). It was community life, shared by missionaries and pupils alike. Normal morning school routine in the classroom was only a part of it. The pupils regarded that as a necessary evil, through which they would obtain what they were really looking for: the use of iron tools in the afternoon work program. Quite accidentally, the missionaries had found an approach to the New Guinean people. Working under the guidance of the missionaries, the pupils learnt the techniques of handling iron tools, and became familiar with hitherto-unknown tropical fruits like corn, pawpaw, and pineapple. All this was part of their schooling as they were being introduced to a Christian-oriented community life, consisting of daily devotions, Christian songs, and prayers. Actually, it was quite simple: the young men did not come to hear the Gospel, nor did they want to learn how to read, write, and count; most of all, they were interested in being paid. On the other hand, they were fascinated by the cultural innovations of the newcomers to their land. In this way they became connecting links between the missionaries and the local people. Since the Finschhafen area had hardly any contact with the outside world, an almost ideal condition developed for a peaceful acquaintance with a 'new era'. Later, the new era would reach the people without fail. The more the missionaries became familiar with the rights and customs of the local people, the less they caused friction by interfering with the complicated land and property codes. The relatively quiet and undisturbed phase of pioneer work around Finschhafen is due largely to these favourable circumstances when mutual trust and confidence was established.

Swift Expansion: Tami Islands

While Flierl and Tremel were still suffering under the frustrating initial difficulties in Simbang, the Mission Board in Neuendettelsau was already in the position to send out additional missionaries: Georg Bamler (1887), Georg Pfalzer and Konrad Vetter (both 1889). The additional personnel put the now five-man Mission team in a position to enlarge the working area. Their attention was drawn to the Tami Islands, approximately 12 km out to sea from Simbang. In November 1889, a second mission station was started there, and Tremel and Bamler were assigned there. The selection

of Tami was made primarily from a strategical viewpoint. Being islanders, the Tami people were seafaring. With their imposing sailing canoes, they had established trading links with the neighbouring mainland villages as well as with those around the Huon Gulf. They were also sailing north as far as Siassi Islands and the east point of New Britain. The hopes and expectations of the missionaries to use the trading routes of the Tami islanders later for the spreading of the Gospel were fulfilled.

Sattelberg

Health problems at Simbang right on the coast forced Flierl to look for a station site at a somewhat higher altitude, where it was hoped that malaria would be less prevalent. In 1890 he moved the mission station from Simbang to a nearby hill, Gaigeresa (Simbang II). However, Flierl's ideas went far beyond that: he had longer-range plans for establishing a mountain station which could serve as a recreation centre for the missionaries and their families, as well as being the first step in reaching the population of the Finschhafen hinterland. [26] In planning such a station, he had Sattelberg in mind, a mountain which overlooks the whole Finschhafen area. [27] During a first exploration trip there in 1892, Zake of Bare, [28] the local chieftain who was Flierl's guide at that time, urged the missionary to return soon — with iron tools; if so, his people would build a house for him on the mountain ridge. This time Flierl was careful not to repeat his early mistake made in Simbang. At Sattelberg he was by no means an intruder. Even though the land rights were much too complicated for Flierl to understand, this mission station was started on the basis of the invitation and expressed consent of the landowners. Payment for the land was made with iron tools and mediums of exchange of that time. Toward the end of 1892, Flierl and his family moved to the new station on the mountain.

Up to this time, not a single baptism had taken place. When the Board at home wanted to have more visible results, the missionaries called for 'great patience and faith' in view of a comparatively-successful start. Unperturbed, they continued building up their small chain of mission stations under the leadership of the senior missionary, Johann Flierl. To expand

39

Sattelberg, first station building.

Pola mission station.

their work further, the missionaries were depending on their church for additional personnel; [29] at the same time, they skilfully used the existing traditional routes of communication. It soon became evident that the message of the new way of life was spreading to the villages faster than the missionaries were able to make visits there. It was chiefly the young men who had lived with the missionaries on their stations who took back to the villages what they had learnt. In fact, they were the most effective communicators of the Gospel.

Finschhafen Area

For the first two decades, the missionaries were busy with expanding and intensifying their evangelistic efforts in the Finschhafen area. In 1902, Vetter built the station Obasega (also called Jabem), near Ngasegalatu village in the Jabem-language area. Finschhafen itself regained some of its former importance when the New Guinea Company established a coconut plantation there at the turn of the century. The missionaries followed suit in 1903 by establishing a mission station at Finschhafen, which was given its local name: Pola. The station was started by the missionaries Georg Pfalzer and Johann Ruppert. Pfalzer also took care of the business matters of the Mission. [30]

Because of these new stations, Simbang lost its importance, and the missionary, Ernst Schnabel, changed his working area to the Kate-speaking inland region. In 1906, the mission station itself was relocated at Masang. In order to intensify the work among the mountain tribes, missionary Andreas Zwanzger started a new station called Wareo, north of Sattelberg on the thickly-populated Wamora Mountain Ridge (1903). Later, under Leonhard Wagner, Wareo was to become an important starting-point for the mission to the mountain tribes north of Finschhafen.

The growth and importance of the Kate mountain stations of Sattelberg and Wareo made it necessary to establish a coastal base station that was nearer than Finschhafen. Accordingly, Flierl handed over the Sattelberg station to Christian Keysser in 1904, and moved to the coast near Busum Bay, where the Administration had given the Mission a large piece of land for a coconut plantation. The new station was named Heldsbach in memory of the missionary Friedrich Held who had died three years before. Heldsbach later became an important school station and plantation site, but the small Heldsbach congregation for a long time remained in the shadow of the two larger stations.

The setting up of a rather tight net of stations, however, was in no way the goal of the missionaries — least of all, of Senior Flierl. To the south, the trading connections of the Tami people with the village people around the Huon Gulf were favourable to the spreading of the Gospel. The swift advance of the mission movement was marked by the founding of three additional mission stations: Deinzerhill [31] by the initiative of Georg Bamler in 1899; Bukawa [32] under the direction of Stephan Lehner in 1906, and Malalo on the opposite side of the Huon Gulf by missionaries Karl Mailaender and Hermann Boettger in 1907.

To the north, the situation was more difficult because there were less trading and tribal connections; the message of the Gospel did not spread so easily from one village to the other. In 1905, Flierl went with the newly-arrived missionaries, E. Schnabel, L. Wagner, and K. Wacke, to explore the coastal region to the north; however, after one-and-a-half day's travel, they were turned back at the village of Kanome. The people were anything but happy about their arrival, and forcibly blocked their way. Maybe the frightening earthquake of 1906, which terrified the whole Finschhafen populace, had a good effect; on the next exploration trip, the approach was much easier. In fact, the Sialum and Qambu people gave the missionaries a friendly reception, and even invited them to settle in their midst. In 1907, Karl Wacke and Michael Stolz, later joined by Karl Saueracker, founded Sialum, the first mission station north of Finschhafen.

First Baptism

The first baptism took place in 1899. After 13 long years of missionary toil, two station workers in Simbang: Kaboing with the baptismal name Tobias, and Kamunsanga with the baptismal name Silas, became the first-fruits of the future New Guinea church by receiving Holy Baptism administered by Pfalzer at the

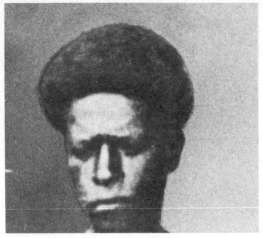

Tobias Kaboing, the first Christian.

First Tami Christians.

Simbang Station. During the next five years, 36 more people from Tami Island and from the coastal villages near Simbang were added to their number. For the missionaries, these baptisms were the first visible fruit of their hard labour; [33] yet, they still had made no real inroads into the realm of the people's traditional religion with its strong binding powers. The first people baptized were, in fact, members of the missionaries' households, and as such had little impact on the local communities. That the locals still held a wait-and-see attitude was clearly shown by the small number of village people attending the first baptismal celebrations — a vivid contrast to the large crowds of later years, when even those not yet baptized were most anxious to come and see. The missionaries had not yet recognized the

Starting at Malalo (1907). From left: missionaries Mailaender, Flierl, Boettger.

vigour and depth of the religious life of the New Guinean people.

Twenty years had passed since Flierl's landing at Simbang, but the Mission was still a small cause. It had established itself in Finschhafen proper and along the coast to the north and to the south. Since the beginning at Simbang, a further ten mission stations had been founded. The number of baptized people was still small; but a modest beginning with indigenous Christian congregations had been made in all the mentioned places.

The Great Breakthrough

The mission in Finschhafen was pioneering work in every respect. Missionaries sent out by Neuendettelsau were not able to fall back on any great missionary experience within their own society, for New Guinea was Neuendettelsau's first mission field. [34] At that time, no students on New Guinea anthropology or on mission methods were available. The missionaries followed the customary approaches of their time; in their preaching, they followed the pattern of their homeland, the only method familiar to them. In a long process of learning, they finally began to question their own evangelistic approach.

One of the first to do so was Konrad Vetter. [35] He soon started to detach himself from the ways of preaching at home:

> We don't deliver lengthy sermons to the people ... We simply sit down among them, whether they are many or few, and try through conversation to direct their attention toward that which contributes to their peace. [36]

At the first large baptism on the newly-founded station of Obasega in 1906, the *Miti* [37] was presented impressively to the public. There were more people than ever before present, yet the majority in no way considered themselves as future candidates for baptismal instruction. Prior to the actual baptism, the new Christians revealed to the women and children the carefully-guarded secret of *balum*, the ancestor festival. In front of all the people, the baptismal candidates handed the ceremonial wooden whirlers over to be burned. [38] The fact that Vetter could dare to have these symbols shown in public and to have them burned, indicated how significant a change had taken place: The *Miti* had left the close borders of the mission stations and had taken root in the villages.

The same year, Flierl reported on a visit to the Bukawas, undertaken to negotiate for land for a new mission station:

> How friendly the group were who received us on the beach, and led us to the village where the old, friendly chieftain sat on the porch of his house. First, he desired a devotion (!) for himself and his people. Afterwards, we all went to look for a suitable station site ... What a difference between the beginning here and that of our first start at Simbang! [39]

Steadily over a long period, the good tidings of the *Miti* as the message of peace had spread from village to village, and had prepared

Konrad Vetter.

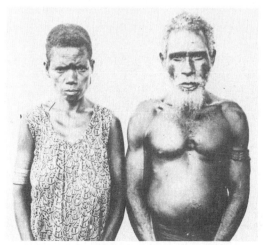

Bockulung and wife (Bukawa), early Christians.

43

Bukawa mission station with baptismal candidates.

the way for the arrival of the missionaries. When Lehner was given the task of establishing the Cape Arkona (Bukawa) Station, he was received upon arrival as a long-awaited friend. After his long years of service in Bukawa, in which he came to know well the religion and culture of that tribe, a somewhat strange honour was accorded him. He became the main character of a local myth, in which he was truly not a foreigner, but rather the son of a Bukawa woman who chanced to have given birth to him in Germany. [40] Peculiar and doubtful though this myth might be, it never would have been told if the *Miti* had reached the Bukawa people as a foreign religion, or even as one forced on them. It reveals a first glimpse of the later development in the history of the expanding church: the unfolding of the congregations' own missionary zeal and accomplishment.

Around this time, developments inland from Finschhafen brought the decisive breakthrough for the Gospel among the mountain people. This work had its centre at the mission station of Sattelberg, where, as at Simbang, Flierl had started a boarding school. From that school the two first-fruits of the Kate

congregation: Aijang and Kupa, came forward to be baptized in 1904.

However, the decisive breakthrough for the whole area was initiated by Christian Keysser. He originally was assigned to be an assistant teacher for the missionaries' children at Sattelberg. Those duties, however, in no way

Evangelist Kupa and wife Fondeng.

Christian Keysser.

Chief Zake, Keysser's friend.

satisfied the talented and energetic young missionary. His free time after lessons was spent in the surrounding villages learning about the life and habits, customs and traditional legal systems, of the people. He soon enjoyed a great respect among the villagers. His keen eye could not miss the sorcery and fear which controlled the lives of the people. He saw that this was the root from which in endless succession came enmity and murder, revenge and reprisal. Keysser noticed that this applied not only to individuals, but even more so to the larger units of clans and tribes. Yet how could a missionary coming from outside intervene in this web of sanctioned confrontation and fighting?

Keysser, after consulting with the chieftain Zake of Bare (who had already been co-operative with Flierl, and whom Keysser had befriended in even greater measure) decided on an unusual step. Together with Zake, he sent out invitations to a traditional dance festival. [41] According to custom, the host could impose certain regulations for his festival. Keysser's and Zake's ruling was that no guest be permitted on the festival grounds with weapons. Despite a marked hesitance on the part of the guests, they eventually complied and laid down their spears in front of the festival grounds in a forest clearing. Nearly 200 people had appeared, among whom were the leading men of the nearby villages. The festival was celebrated according to tradition: dancing continued until daybreak, and the host treated his guests to sufficient food. Then, after daylight, that part of

the festival which was essential to Keysser was initiated. During the ensuing debate, Keysser broke the taboos by openly stating that through sorcery, which was practised everywhere, murder and manslaughter held the villages in anxiety and fear. However, that was only the beginning! Keysser reports:

> He [Zake] made a big impression by confessing that he was guilty of Moga's murder (February 1902). Chieftain Sane delivered a vehement speech in self-defence and denied any sorcery. But finally he had to admit that he had ordered sorcery to be carried out. He even mentioned the neighbouring chieftain Gambangge as one whom just recently he had wanted to get rid of through this dark power; but his sorcery did not work. Gambangge responded disclosing that he likewise had wanted to kill Sane through sorcery, but also without success. Bai, perhaps the most evil sorcerer of all, defended himself without much chance and finally was silenced ... After several hours, the debate was closed with the admonition to all those assembled that the now-recognized evil should be avoided and God's reality be heeded. [42]

Keysser had already become almost a New Guinean himself. He knew that his admonition, to avoid the evil and to heed the *Miti,* God's Word, would not at this moment lead to a decision. Basically, however, the decisive thing had already happened: the much-dreaded sorcery and the sorcerers themselves had been called by name; leading men had publicly admitted practising death sorcery, and having others committed to murder. These public

45

Chief Gera, from Masanko.

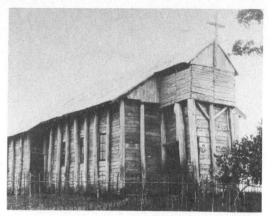

First Sattelberg church (1903).

confessions did not let the matter rest. Finally, even Chieftain Gera from Masangko village acted on Keysser's invitation and came to the mission station in order to bury the old war threats and make peace, and the breakthrough of the *Miti* became evident. Almost as a matter of course, the mission station at Sattelberg became the centre for the surrounding villages, where people regularly came to hear more about the 'peace talk of the *Miti'*. A year after the dance festival, Keysser started the first baptismal class. On May 7, 1905, the first large baptism took place at Sattelberg.[43] It was regarded as an affair that concerned all the surrounding villages. Even though only ten people actually received Holy Baptism, the spell was broken; the path of the *Miti* to the Kate people was opened.

The Congregations' Share in the Spreading of the Gospel

It has been pointed out that the pupils at the so-called boarding schools took the tidings of the *Miti* home with them when returning to their villages. *Miti* was the New Way of Life, as experienced at the mission station. Very deliberately the missionaries emphasized in their baptismal instruction that in Baptism only a beginning of the new life is made; by no means is it completion already reached. For the newly-baptized this meant they had to develop for themselves a form of Christian living in the villages, including the responsibility for church services and daily devotions. Soon an additional

task fell to them: With the rapidly-increasing number of baptismal candidates, the missionaries could not possibly conduct all the classes themselves. The newly-baptized Christians had to take over at least part of the baptismal instruction for their fellow-villagers. Thus, from the very beginning, the fledgling congregations were drawn into a kind of mission work.

It was, however, a different story with regard to the expansion of the *Miti* beyond the local village boundaries. Traditionally, there was hardly any starting-point; except for occasional trading contacts, each village and/or tribe was independent — and usually hostile to the neighbouring clans as well. For activities and communication with unrelated tribes, a strong feeling of reluctance had first to be overcome.

The credit for making the very first missionary attempts among people other than their own is to be given to Christians from Deinzerhill.[44] In July 1907, a few young men went to the traditional Taemi trading partners — the Kela people on the other side of the Huon Gulf — to teach them Bible stories and some Christian hymns. Joel Lokumu, the first baptized Christian from the Taemi congregation, was even ready to stay for five months with the Kela people. Later, this evangelistic activity of Taemi Christians (together with their families) was extended to up to two years.

In the same year, 1907, the small Heldsbach congregation made a modest

46

beginning of their own on the north coast. Senior Flierl had acquired a piece of land for a new mission station at Duburi. [45] He later gave up the plan for a close network of mission stations, but wanted to keep Duburi as a rest station on the way to Sialum. The Heldsbach congregation sent one of their baptized members, Anu, and his family there to look after the rest house for travelling missionaries. However, Duburi grew into a real evangelistic station for the population along the Qorafung coast. Hongkenare from Heldsbach, one of the first group of trained teacher-evangelists, became an effective missionary for the part of the coast north of Heldsbach.

New Guinean 'Foreign' Mission

The great challenge, however, for New Guineans to be missionaries to far-away tribes was still to come. In 1907, four young men from the Sattelberg congregation — Kupa, Haringke, Mainao, and Fungmo — presented themselves to their missionary, and told him that they would be prepared to serve as evangelists. Keysser reports about that meeting:

I let them explain their decision, and then I asked them the critical question: 'How long are you prepared to work among a strange new tribe?' They seemed surprised, and then one of them answered for them all: 'We do not think of returning!' They were prepared to serve without a time limit. Had these young men really considered such a grave decision? [46]

This was the turning-point for a further basic decision: Keysser was not prepared to accept the sole responsibility for such a far-reaching undertaking. During the church service on the following Sunday, he announced the names of the four candidates for mission service, and asked the congregation for their consent. This was risky, indeed — and even more so since three of the four men came from the same village: Ziwewaneng. One of the four was the last son of the still-unbaptized chieftain Sane. Sane, who was present, replied: 'I am an old man, and giving up my only son is like sacrificing my right hand; but since *Anutu* [God] calls him to go, I will not hold him back.' These were the decisive words, and the congregation agreed. Furthermore, the congregation assumed the spiritual and financial responsibility for those who were

Group of Kate chiefs (Sane second from left).

47

departing as their missionaries. This indeed was the birth of the specific type of mission carried out by congregations rather than individuals.

For the Sattelberg congregation, the Hube tribes were a God-given missionary opportunity. An exploratory trip into this unknown area had already been carried out two years earlier by the Sattelberg Christians together with Keysser. Now, as a first step they needed the Hube people's consent for the evangelists to settle among them. In the meantime, Keysser trained the men for their future task, and furnished them with the most necessary equipment for survival in a foreign area. He also assumed the spiritual guidance and over-all responsibility for the congregation's mission work — without, of course, freeing the Sattelberg congregation of the missionary obligation which they had accepted.

On September 6, 1908, the congregation commissioned their missionaries with prayer and accompanied them on the first leg of their trip to their new mission field among the Hube people. Kuluntufu, a village above the Mongi River, was the first mission station — one which

Evangelist Haringke.

was never directed nor occupied by an European. Two-and-a-half years later (1911), when the first four Sattelberg missionaries received reinforcement from their home congregation, Kuluntufu became the parent of two further mission stations: Haringke went to the Kuat people in Tobou, and Mainao to the

Group of evangelists at Kulungtufu.

48

Burum people in Ogeramnang. The Hube Mission as carried out by the Sattelberg congregation [47] became a model for further New Guinean mission activities in heathen areas.

Keysser had pointed out to the four Sattelberg missionaries that first they should simply settle down, build houses, and plant gardens where they were given land to do so, and that they should by no means begin to preach too early. Following his advice, the men and their families learnt the local vernacular and lived as New Guineans among the Hube people, whom they had not known before at all. In these first years, it was the evangelist's lack of fear, their impartiality, and their mediating role in feuds which raised their esteem in the eyes of the Hube. Only later did they begin to preach, that is, to tell Bible stories about *Anutu*, the creator of all things, and about His love to mankind in Jesus. And it took a long time before the spell of sorcery, revenge, and the ancestors-cult was broken in Hube-land, and the victory of the Gospel became evident. The first baptism took place in 1917. Not without pride did

Greeting ceremony (Burung Valley).

First church at Kulungtufu.

49

Tinonga, a famous Hube chief.

Keysser report: 'This result was achieved without formal schooling!' [48] Even though the mission schools were valuable in the beginning, and later attained new significance as congregational schools, congregational mission in New Guinea had proved that formal Western education was not an indispensable prerequisite for evangelistic work.

Keysser was consistent in taking the congregation's responsibility for their Hube mission seriously. When the time of the first baptism drew near, Keysser found that he was unable to get there; but that was no cause for the initial baptism to be postponed. He sought and obtained the Sattelberg congregation's consent that Kupa, the responsible leader of the mission work in Kuluntufu, be authorized to baptize. By doing so, Keysser certainly departed from the usual missionary practice. However, such an unprecedented situation — as congregational mission continually presented — demanded extraordinary decisions.

Even in a wider sense, this beginning of congregational mission was epoch-making. Without doubt, the European missionary stood behind the Sattelberg evangelists, helping and

50

advising them. And they certainly also profited from the great respect in which Keysser was generally held among the people. Yet in the very persons who went as emissaries of the Sattelberg Christians to the Hubes, the *Miti* had detached itself from the white missionary and from the characteristics of his European culture, as well as from direct contact with the then German colonial power. In those New Guinean missionaries, the Gospel found its own indigenous way into the interior of the country.

The 'Miti' moves on

The first mission stations had been well planned; the missionaries always had a strategic goal in mind. Tami and Deinzerhill had been started in the hope that they would prove to be a door to the remaining coastal villages around the Huon Gulf; Sattelberg was to be an outpost to the mountain population. These hopes were not in vain. With the emergence of the first New Guinean Christian congregations around these stations, and, above all, with the exemplary beginning of the congregational mission, the small Finschhafen mission venture saw an almost breathtaking advance.

The message of the *Miti* spread faster than the missionaries could envisage. The establishment of the stations of Bukawa (1906), Malalo (1907), and Sialum (1907), was but the beginning of expansion both to the north and south of Finschhafen. In 1910-11, no less than six further stations were founded. At the same time, the concept of congregational mission took hold, partly by supplementing the European mission stations, partly by establishing independent indigenous mission settlements (evangelists' stations). Especially in the difficult, rugged mountain regions, the indigenous evangelists were the ones who introduced the *Miti* to one tribe after another.

It took them years of patient work to penetrate the land and establish a close web of new Christian congregations. This impressive advance of the *Miti* cannot be described as the history of the white missionaries alone. It rather was a close cooperation between European missionaries and New Guinean co-workers; both have to be mentioned in one breath. It is a default of earlier mission chronicles that, for the most part, only the names of the white missionaries are recorded; the names of the many New Guinean evangelists, teachers, and other co-workers deserved mention at least as much. Here lies a wide field for local historical research work which has hardly been touched.

Without question, those early years from 1910 on were an especially-rich and blessed period in the history of the New Guinean Lutheran Church. The story can be told here only in outline form, highlighted by a few outstanding events.

Mission Work in the Markham Valley

The ongoing evangelization of the people living around the Huon Gulf had its origins in the Bukawa and Malalo congregations. Between the two localities lies the wide basin around the mouth of the Markham River. The region is rather thinly populated: south of the river is the home of the Labo tribe, and to the north the Lae people have settled. The whole area, however, lived in fear and terror of the warlike Lae-Wampar (old spelling: Lae-Womba). They lived about a day's journey upstream, and frequently attacked their neighbours downstream; the Lae as well as the Labo people faced the continual threat of annihilation. In 1907, the Lae-Wampar even succeeded in putting to flight an armed government expedition. Indeed, this tribe was a constant threat to the population of the Lower Markham Valley.

Through their traditional connections with the Bukawa people, the Lae and Labo tribes had contact with the Mission rather early. Initially,

they looked for protection to the missionaries, whom they thought powerful enough to fend off the Lae-Wampar. That idea might easily have come from a misconception of both mission and government, since both were represented by Europeans. Naturally, the missionaries were unable to give them the protection they sought, for such power rested with the government.

In 1909, the missionaries Lehner, Keysser, and Mailaender, and the anthropologist Dr Neuhauss, decided to take a new initiative. They were rowed about 20 km up the Markham in river canoes by the Labo people who were acquainted with the locality. The desired contact with the Lae-Wampar people, however, did not eventuate. Evidently, the tribe became aware of the expedition well in advance, and the entire population hid in the bush. However, before turning their canoes downstream again, Lehner decided to indicate their willingness to communicate with the people by leaving a few New Guinea valuables and some European barter articles openly hanging on a tree. After his companions lit a fire nearby in order to call attention to the place, they began their return trip. Naturally, the people had been watching everything, and came out of their hiding places after the group had left. They well understood the sign, and accepted the offer. Fourteen days after that canoe trip, a Labo man presented Missionary Lehner with a Lae-Wampar sword; he had received it from the dreaded enemies as a sign that they had accepted the gifts and were

Magi, chief of the Kela people who went to Bukawa to 'fetch' a missionary.

Early Bukawa Christians with chief Obogo in the centre.

51

Gowi, a typical coastal gulf village.

Three men from Lae-Wampar.

willing to make peace. Their message was: 'In five days a peace meeting shall take place. The people from Lae, Labo, Apo, and Bukawa [all their traditional enemies] are supposed to take part.' 49

The meeting took place, and a truce was actually achieved; ultimately peace was celebrated between tribes hostile to each other

52

from times immemorial. No missionary was present at those functions; the Lae-Wampar people had not thought of inviting them. But at the peace celebrations, an invitation was extended to Lehner to come and visit them. A month later (June 1909), Lehner (together with six Christians of the Bukawa congregation, and accompanied again by Dr Neuhauss) travelled overland to the Lae-Wampar, and they received him with all honours as a friend.

Thus, the missionaries succeeded in making a peace which the government expedition had not been able to achieve two years earlier. What a missionary challenge! It meant that the Gospel, the great message of peace, could be brought in its fullness to the entire population of the lower Markham Valley: to the Lae, Labo, Musong, and Apo people, and to their pursuers, the Lae-Wampar. To achieve this, the mission conference decided to build two new mission stations, one at Ampo (Lae) on the coast, and a second one at Gabmazung, a day's journey up-river, in the area of the Lae-Wampar tribe. By this time it had become an established pattern in the Finschhafen Mission that the new Christian congregations accept

Teachers and preachers from Gabmazung/Lae-Wampar.

their active share in missionary outreach. Gottfried Schmutterer at Ampo, as well as Friedrich Oertel and Karl Panzer at Gabmazung, could never have accomplished the evangelistic work among the Lae and the Lae-Wampar people without indigenous co-workers. The Bukawa congregation sent Jakotung, and the Sattelberg congregation sent Gapenuo as evangelists into the work, not to mention dozens of Bukawa Christians who helped with building the two stations and who volunteered as carriers to Gabmazung.

Among the Lae-Wampar, ten full years passed before the first baptism took place in 1921. Panzer reported about the marked change in the whole tribe, quoting them as saying: 'Our whole life has been changed through Baptism.' [50] The practical verification soon followed: the most-feared warriors became co-workers in further propagation of the Gospel. Together with Labo and Lae Christians, they participated in the ongoing mission work among the Musom and Waing peoples in the foothills north of the Markham Plains.

Mission Work in the Morobe and Waria Area

After the New Guinea Company had transferred its location from Finschhafen to Bogadjim (Stephansort) in 1891, the Finschhafen Mission was left almost entirely on its own. Rarely had the German administration interfered — and, when it did so, it had not always been in the most peaceful manner. The missionaries, however, were not dependent on the firearms of the government. The German administration did not think it necessary to establish a government post at Morobe on the southern coastline of the Huon Gulf until 1909. What motivated them to do so may have been the near boundary with Papua (former British New Guinea), and, perhaps even more so, the assumption that gold was to be found in the river area of the Waria. At that time, Morobe was the only permanent government station in the area of the Finschhafen Mission.

The mission conference followed suit by founding the mission station of Ongga (1910 by Georg Stuerzenhofecker) next to the Morobe government station. However, it was given up ten years later in favour of Zaka station, established in 1911 by Mailaender at the mouth

53

Zaka mission station.

of the Waria River. Mailaender had come from Malalo, and the congregation there had placed Jabem-speaking Christians at his disposal for the new beginning in the Waria area. To their surprise, however, they found that the Zia vernacular spoken at Zaka belonged to the non-Melanesian language group, and therefore one which the Malalo people found difficult to learn. Thanks to the good relations which the Malalo congregations maintained with the Kate congregations in Finschhafen, Sattelberg came to their rescue. They sent a number of evangelists whose mother tongue was closer to the language of the Morobe and Waria people. Zafinu and Bapiangnu were Mailaender's co-workers in Zaka and the Waria Valley; Enareka and Farenu were stationed as evangelists in Morobe (Ongga). Mailaender himself had no other choice than to switch from Jabem to the non-Melanesian Zia vernacular and to Kate, the language of his co-workers. The work in the Waria area spread amazingly fast after the administration built a road across the mountains from Morobe directly into the middle and upper Waria area. With this a better approach to the huge population in the

54

mountains was accomplished. The story of this work will be taken up later in this chapter.

Expansion to the North

Heldsbach and Sialum had been the first stations along the path which the *Miti* took to the north of Finschhafen. In 1911, the same year that mission work began in the Markham Valley and in the Waria area, M. Stolz founded a coastal station further north: Sio. [51] It soon became apparent that the Sio people spoke a Melanesian rather than a Papuan language, as did the neighbouring villages. To avoid the difficulties experienced at Zaka, Stolz right away requested the Bukawa congregations to send a Jabem-speaking co-worker. For many years Samuel served as his faithful and conscientious partner. Because of Samuel, a delegation of unbaptized people took part in a celebration of the Bukawa congregation in October 1919. The Sio people were so moved by their experiences in Bukawa that, on their return, a genuine evangelistic movement began in their village. Yet, even in Sio it took ten years before the community would make the decisive step toward the *Miti*. In March 1922, the first large

Missionary G. Bamler with a group of Christians from Siassi.

baptism took place, and in 1927 the whole community finally joined the Christian congregation.

During those years of open doors (1910-11), the old trade connections of the Tami people with the Siassi islanders also began to bear fruit. Already in 1892, G. Bamler had joined a canoe trip from Tami to Umboi (Rooke Island), the main island of the Siassi group. The gradual turning of the Tami people toward Christianity did not remain unnoticed by their trading partners on Siassi. Soon after a small congregation was established on Tami Island, individual Tami Christians started to proclaim the *Miti* at least for a short time on Siassi Island, and not without evident results. During their occasional visits to Tami, the Siassi people repeatedly asked for a missionary. Finally, in 1911 the mission conference decided to follow up their request. The obvious choice was G. Bamler; now, for the fourth (!) time, he had the task of building up a new station. Five co-workers from the Tami and Deinzerhill congregations supported him in his new assignment.

In spite of the local request for a missionary, the work on Siassi was hard in every respect. The population certainly did not turn out to be as open as expected; indeed, sometimes they were even hostile. The connection with the Mission on the mainland was maintained under great difficulties. Even Bamler's visits to the evangelists on the smaller islands of Tuam and Malai were risky and time-consuming. The first baptism took place in 1914 on the small island of Tuam. Others followed, yet the great breakthrough that had happened in other places did not eventuate on Siassi. Perhaps this was partly due to the fact that the missionary had to be recalled to the mainland from 1920-23 because of the staff shortage of the post-war years. In 1928, after having served on the Siassi Islands for another five years, G. Bamler was accidentally killed by a falling tree at his station of Karapo. Again, Siassi was without a European missionary for one-and-a-half years. In 1936, when the Finschhafen Mission needed all available workers for the newly-begun Highlands mission, the Siassi work was handed over to the Evangelical Lutheran Church of Australia (ELCA).

The First World War

The turmoils of World War I left New Guinea almost unscathed. News of the outbreak of war in Europe on August 4, 1914 reached the faraway colony within eight days. But it still took a full six weeks before Herbertshoehe, the seat of the German Colonial Governor, near Rabaul, was taken by Australian Marines after an insignificant exchange of fire; with that, the era of German colonial rule in New Guinea came to an end. For the missionaries at Finschhafen and in the Huon Gulf region, the political change became evident only on January 8, 1915, when the Morobe government station was taken over by Australian forces.

On the whole, the conditions of surrender were rather moderate. The life and property of Germans in the colony were to be safeguarded; the German government officials were allowed repatriation to their home country; the German missionaries were assured they could continue their work unhampered, with the sole restriction of absolute political neutrality. All German mission members swore the demanded oath of neutrality.

This peaceful arrangement was upset by only one unfortunate incident. At the takeover of the Morobe government station, the four German officials briefly managed to get away. Two missionaries, Hans Raum of Malalo and Willy Flierl of Zaka (the oldest son of the senior missionary), were blamed for having given assistance to the four German fugitives, [52] and were taken into custody and later interned in Australia. Mission Inspector Steck, who happened to be on a visitation to New Guinea at the beginning of the war, and who was a German reserve officer, refused to swear the demanded oath of neutrality. As a result he was treated as a prisoner of war, and also interned in Australia.

Unfortunately, one of the Morobe officials, the land surveyor Captain H. Detzner, successfully avoided capture by the Australians. He hid for four years in the villages of the Huon Peninsula, predominantly in places around Sattelberg, and surrendered to the Australian authorities only at the end of the war. [53] Though Keysser had explicitly barred Detzner from the mission station, he supplied him through a third party with medicines and the most necessary

things for survival. This was, in a very strict interpretation of the law, a breach of oath. Subsequently, Keysser was refused a re-entry permit when he wanted to return to New Guinea after a well-deserved furlough in Germany in 1920. [54]

Who Will Come to the Rescue?

The prospects for the German mission in New Guinea at the beginning of the war did not look too hopeful. The Mission's economic situation was rather dismal; the field was cut off from Germany, and thus economically isolated. The Mission supply house was relatively well stocked at the beginning of the war; yet, even with the most frugal use of supplies, such a situation could not be expected to last long. In addition to that, war conditions meant that the Missionaries and their families could not take their furlough in a better climate — not to speak of necessary replacements of staff.

Under these critical conditions, Senior Flierl contacted the Lutheran congregations in Australia which had always served as his second home-base. [55] These friends knew that the moment had come to take an active role in the rescue of the New Guinea Mission. In Pastor F.O. Theile of Bethania, Queensland, the Mission had a warm supporter and an active advocate. The first thing he organized was a shipment of urgently-needed goods to Finschhafen. He also organized relief supplies for the families of the Rhenish Mission in

Pastor F.O. Theile.

56

Madang. Both Theile and Flierl turned to Lutheran congregations in U.S.A. for help, especially to the Iowa Synod and its president, Dr F. Richter; they asked for mission offerings to be sent to Australia to provide for the orphaned mission field (for more details, see ch 4). Theile continued to throw himself whole-heartedly into organizing relief consignments, acting as a 'Business Manager for the New Guinea Mission' throughout the war years, in addition to his duties as a parish pastor near Brisbane. Thus, from a first call for help and its spontaneous reply, a continuing Australian-American relief program developed for both the orphaned German missions in New Guinea.

The hour of an even greater testing came at the war's end with the signing of the Versailles Peace Treaty. Had the treaty been fully applied, it would have meant the termination of Lutheran mission work in New Guinea. In contrast to the mild conditions of surrender in 1914, it called for the expulsion of all Germans from the former German colonies, including missionaries. The expropriation of all German holdings in the colonies was alleviated for mission societies only insofar as mission property would continue to be used for missionary activities — but not by Germans. [56] From then on, the German missionaries lived as if 'the sword of Damocles hung over them', [57] that is, under the threat of being expelled from the country. The Australian government, which had been entrusted with the mandate of the League of Nations for the former German colony of New Guinea, first set a deadline that all German missionaries had to leave by 1922. Thanks to the persistent and skilful negotiations of F.O. Theile, the harsh deportation clause was eased bit by bit, until it was dropped altogether in 1925.

Nevertheless, the situation regarding personnel of the two German missions in New Guinea right after the war looked desolate. During these years of great need, the Lutheran congregations in U.S.A. and Canada — who so far had willingly given offerings to the New Guinea work — now stepped in by also sending personnel. In the same way, the Australian partner in the work (who since 1902 had sent a number of missionaries to New Guinea) now intensified its involvement, and also sent additional staff. [58]

A Time of Suspense

The great concern after World War I was: Will it be possible to save the great work in New Guinea for the Lutheran Church? If it was to be saved at all as a Lutheran mission, a reorganization of the two German mission bodies at Finschhafen and Madang was a matter of urgency; the leadership could not remain in German hands. The Australian government actually wanted the work of both Neuendettelsau and the Rhenish Mission Society to be entrusted to an English Protestant church or mission, regardless of denomination. [59] However, this purely politically-motivated intervention into church affairs floundered, among other things, because of the firm standing of the respective Australian churches. They claimed they were not in the position to take over the huge Lutheran mission work in New Guinea. Here not only mere practical reasons played a part, but also their ecumenical commitment; they preferred not to be a party to such a political act of expropriation of the German missions. After long negotiations with the Australian government, Director Theile and Dr Richter, president of the Iowa Synod, finally achieved their goal: In May 1921, the two mission fields of Madang and Finschhafen were united under the name of Lutheran Mission New Guinea, and jointly administered by the United Evangelical Lutheran Church in Australia [60] and the Iowa Synod. From 1923 on, Pastor Theile was relieved of congregational duties so that he could dedicate his energies full-time to the New Guinea work as its Mission Director. With these organizational steps, [61] the continuation of Lutheran Mission New Guinea was safeguarded, even though Barmen as well as Neuendettelsau had 'lost their New Guinea mission field', as it was commonly described in Germany at that time.

In 1926, when Germany entered the League of Nations, the political situation eased. According to the League's rules, all member nations had access to its mandate territories. That also applied to German missionaries in the Australian-ruled Territory of New Guinea. [62] Now the road was open for both Barmen and Neuendettelsau to resume their activities in New Guinea — but with some limitations. For one thing, all the mission property was still held by an Australian Board of Trustees, and no government provisions were made to change that status. Another question was how the four partners in New Guinea mission work — the Australians, the Americans, Neuendettelsau, and Barmen — could agree on terms with regard to administrative functions and co-operation. Each had invested so much in the work that it would have been unfair to exclude any one of them from directive and administrative responsibility in the future. The problem was that, according to the definition of the other partners, the Rhenish Mission Society was not considered to be strictly Lutheran. Moreover, there were some doubts that the missionary principles of Keysser and his staunch supporter, Inspector Steck, were genuinely Lutheran. All this caused unrest among the overseas partner churches. Should not the Madang and Finschhafen fields better be separated again?

Two Attempts to Settle the Issue

Representatives of all the four Boards involved met in Brisbane in May 1929. It was agreed that the Rhenish Mission should be given back its former Madang field. Neuendettelsau was invited by the American and Australian Mission Boards to participate in the joint direction and administration of the Finschhafen field. In order to leave each party some room for self-determination, the former Finschhafen field was to be divided into two 'spheres of interest' with a field inspector at the head of both. The two new districts — Finschhafen and Finisterre — were each to have its own President. [63]

This solution of 1929 seemed to be a fair compromise in view of the conflicting interests of all partners concerned — yet the plan could not be realized. Any division based on geographical lines which would separate the Finschhafen and the Finisterre districts proved to be impracticable in view of the evangelistic outreach of the older congregations into the interior of the Huon Peninsula. The same was true of the Upper Ramu Valley, where evangelists of the Madang and Finschhafen congregations had met on their way into the foothills of the Central Highlands. Reorganization of the mission field along the national lines of the home Boards no longer was
58

adequate for a situation that required far wider strategies. While the home representatives were negotiating a partitioning of the New Guinean mission into the above three separate fields of interest, quite a different development was beginning to take shape which would later lead to the establishment of a united Lutheran Church of New Guinea, comprising the mission areas of both Madang and Finschhafen and even the evolving church of the Highlands. This greater vision, however, was not in the minds of the men assembled in Brisbane.

By 1932 the situation had changed again. When the Rhenish Mission Society no longer saw any possibility of keeping its New Guinea mission field, the American Lutheran Church [64] agreed to take over the work, the property, and the personnel. At a consultation of Board representatives in Columbus, Ohio in May 1932, the transfer of responsibilities was settled. As a result, the situation in New Guinea improved considerably. Instead of three working fields and mission bodies; there were now only two: Finschhafen Lutheran Mission (Neuendettelsau) and Madang Lutheran Mission (ALC). That also put an end to the joint American/Australian administration of both former German missions.

Fortunately, the organizational changes in the aftermath of World War I did not have any immediate effects on the growing church in New Guinea. Its evangelistic outreach and its congregational work continued to thrive in spite of what foreign mission Boards thought best for the growing church. On the other hand, the chance for an organizational solution beyond the narrow issues of the day had been lost. Instead of looking ahead and aiming at one indigenous Lutheran church in New Guinea served by an international mission body, the Boards fell back on the old pattern of national working fields. Seemingly, the time was not yet ripe for such a change. Today we cannot but have mixed feelings as we read how enthusiastically the *Neuendettelsauer Missionsblatt* carried the news that 'we have got our mission field back'. [65] Friends of the Mission in the Bavarian church, however, responded very positively; since 1927 they have in increasing amounts provided men and means for the work in New Guinea. Both were, in fact, urgently needed for meeting the new missionary challenge in the Central Highlands in the 1930s (see ch 5).

The Great Period of Congregational Mission

Events during World War I and subsequent organizational problems have brought us far ahead into the 1930s. Now it is time to return to the very history of the growing church. Despite political and economic difficulties in those years, the missionary advance continued — at even greater pace than before.

During the years of extreme shortage of both money and supplies, the missionaries from overseas could not possibly think of starting new stations. Instead, the New Guinean congregations took up the Great Commission as their task. They sent their own missionaries to new fields of missionary opportunities. [66] These Christians, trained teachers and evangelists, and their untrained helpers, sometimes illiterate people, began the painstaking pioneer work of evangelizing the heathen regions further out, and of establishing new congregations. By so doing they, without doubt, followed the missionary example of apostolic times. For this reason, the term 'congregational mission' (*Gemeinde-Mission*) was coined, and will be used here, too. The fact that Baptism was administered regularly by the European missionaries in no way belittles the accomplishments of the New Guinean congregational missionaries. The two teacher-training institutions at Hopoi and Heldsbach placed well-trained evangelists at the disposal of the congregations. In those years the ministry of teacher-preacher-evangelists proved itself as the great missionary asset of the growing church. Faithfully and with untiring vigour, the New Guinean evangelists and teachers carried the Gospel further out, from village to village, and from tribe to tribe. This advance of the mission is a glorious page in the annals of the early New Guinean Lutheran Church. [67]

Malalo Congregation

The Malalo Congregation, in the southern region of the Finschhafen Mission, after initial hesitation finally accepted the idea of congregational mission. For them it was not exactly difficult to find a missionary outlet; their missionary Friedrich Bayer wrote in 1920: 'We are surrounded on all sides by heathen tribes. Even a day's walk from the station brings us right into the heathen area.' [68] It was mainly the work among the mountain tribes of the Hote, Kaiwa, and Kaidemui (today known as Buangs), which challenged the missionary capacity of the Malalo congregation. Small as it was still at that time, the congregation vigorously took it up, and — to say the least — they thereby gained spiritually.

Zaka Congregation

Zaka at the mouth of the Waria River was the southernmost station of the Finschhafen Mission. Compared with other areas, here was an exception: The coastal region and the Middle and Upper Waria Valley had already been

Evangelist (later pastor) Elia from Taemi.

Evangelist Mainao from Sattelberg. Among others he started work in the middle Waria.

opened by the government, so it was not advisable to delay mission work further inland until a congregation had been established on the coast. As mentioned before, a plea by Zaka missionary Mailaender to the Kate congregations for evangelists was soon answered by sending eight evangelists. Among them were Noreewe, Zafinu, Enareka, Haegao, and Mainao (one of the very first evangelists in the Hube area). At the end of 1916, they began their work in the Middle Waria Valley, starting out from the newly-established evangelist station at Kipu. Immediately after the first baptism in Zaka (Advent 1922), the new congregation sent five of their newly-baptized men there as reinforcement. During the previous year, the evangelists had moved on to the heavily-populated Upper Waria area. There they started a new evangelist station at Erep (Sim), which is two days' walk from Kipu.

From there, together with Mailaender, they crossed the watershed of the Owen Stanley Range on an exploratory trip, and pushed forward as far as the valley of the Biaru River. This trip could have ended fatally. When they reached the first Biaru village one afternoon, their initial contacts with the people were friendly; they were even offered a house for resting. At dawn, however, a group of young men from a neighbouring village arrived, and openly showed the guests that they were not welcome at all. Heavily armed, they encircled the guests' resthouse, and openly and menacingly displayed their bows and arrows. Although this was highly alarming, Mailaender and his group remained calm. No arrows had been shot, but there was no way of escape as long as the warriors watched the house. Mailaender himself reports: 'We were reminded of the men of God in the Old and New Testament who had faced similar threats of life. Was God going to spare our lives? We all gathered in prayer: "O God, make them blind or put them to sleep!" After midnight, indeed, in spite of rain and cold, we found them all fast asleep.' Calmly, one by one they left the house and sneaked through the close circle of warriors, leaving behind almost all their belongings. In the cold rain and without the help of a lantern, they crossed the high mountain range again to get back to the safety of the Erep village from where they had started to bring the

message of peace to the Biaru people. 'God has saved us from their hands', Mailaender concludes his account. [69]

Two years later, in 1924 friendly contact was made with the Biaru people, and in 1925 the evangelists could establish there a further station, Ilup. Meanwhile, in the Middle and Upper Waria Valley, the first group of people was ready to accept Christianity, and the first baptism took place at Kipu in 1926, ten years after the station was founded. The leading evangelists were: Pinao at Kipu, Haegao in the Upper Waria, and Totonu in the Biaru area. Mailaender describes the years 1926-27 as the 'years of harvest'. 'The storm wind of the *Miti* has finally uprooted the strong cedars of heathendom', it says in the *Kate Church History* (143), when reporting about the work in the Waria region.

Congregational mission had shown its strength and vitality. Mailaender and the Kate evangelists were the motivating force behind it. The Zaka congregation, however, also responded to the missionary call immediately after the first baptism in 1922. It should be noted that their 'mission area' involved a 7-8-day walk from the coast and even crossing over a ridge of the mountains. The main load of the work was done by the New Guinean evangelists from Finschhafen jointly with the local people from Zaka and Morobe. Carrying the Gospel further was no longer solely the white missionary's task.

Azera Mission in the Upper Markham

After work had begun among the Lae-Wampar, the missionaries made their first excursions further afield. The thickly-populated grassland area of the Upper Markham was visited by Keysser, Pilhofer, L. Flierl, and Oertel for the first time in 1912. From 1914 on, Oertel made regular trips from Gabmazung to the Azera people further up the river. In early times the Lae-Wampar and Azera people had once formed a larger unit; when the missionaries came on to the scene, this relationship had been severed. The Azeras in the Upper Markham were just as exposed to continuous attacks from the Lae-Wampar as were their neighbours to the south. The actual Azera Mission began in 1917, starting out from the evangelists' station at Zifasin, located half-way between the Lae-Wampar and Azera. Oertel in 1917 reported: 'An area of over 100 villages with one and the

Evangelist Jaengwoga and family at Sangang (Markham).

same language, all rather peaceful and friendly, is open to us here.' Thus, even before the first baptism had taken place at Gabmazung, the missionaries had gone further afield. Important help came from Bukawa, and later also from Deinzerhill/Taemi. Both congregations readily sent evangelists into the work among the Azera people. They regarded Azera as 'their mission field'. As early as 1919, the missionary could list some ten (!) evangelists' stations spread out over the whole tribal area. In 1918, the mission station of Kaiapit was founded as the centre for the Azera work, with Fritz Oertel as the logical missionary in charge. The people were ready to accept the *Miti.* As soon as the evangelists had familiarized themselves with the language, baptismal classes began at the various stations. The Kaiapit missionary was full of praise for his evangelistic co-workers from the coastal stations: 'They are all highly respected ... They successfully strive to make peace everywhere through their goodwill, and their zeal, and courage.' [70] The first large Azera baptism took place in 1924. Following the example of the older coastal congregations of Bukawa and Taemi, the young Azera congregation took on

its missionary task among its neighbours, the people on the Ramu Plains (evangelists' station Garamari) and on the upper course of the Leron River.

At the Doorsteps to the Central Highlands

Kaiapit and the evangelists' station at Garamari on the Ramu Plains also served the Kate Congregations in Finschhafen as gateway stations for their drive onward to the Gazub foothills of the Highlands, west of the Markham Valley (1922), and the Ramu Valley (1926).

After the missionary breakthrough was attained in the Hube area in 1917, the Sattelberg congregation considered their immediate missionary obligations there as completed; however, they were in no way inclined to sit back. On the contrary, they wanted to share with the newly-won Hube Christians the spiritual blessings which they themselves had received through their engagement in mission work, and to begin a joint new mission venture. As incredible as it sounds, within their immediate vicinity no such opportunity existed any more. On the other hand, they did not want to interfere with the work of neighbouring congregations,

61

Evangelists and their families (Markham Valley), (Missionaries Oertel, left, and Pietz, right).

so they started to search for a new mission further afield. They found it at the open end to the west of the Azera mission area. With the consent of the Kaiapit missionary, the Sattelberg congregation stationed the first four evangelists in the Gazub foothills west of the Markham in 1922. The leader among them was Gapenuo Ngizaki, who was fluent in the Lae-Wampar as well as in the Azera language. [71]

Leonhard Flierl, the successor of Keysser as missionary at Sattelberg, undertook to expand the new mission field of his congregations even further into the Central Highlands. From the evangelist station Garamari as the base, he established a further station at Rihona on the fringe of the Highlands. It was from there that he made the first trip into the Central Highlands in 1927. Starting these new stations was in line with the concept of the on-going mission work carried out by the Sattelberg/Hube congregations. The long distance from the home base was beyond what a traditional New Guinean villager could conceive; here the original concept of the congregations' neighbourhood mission met its logistic limits.

62

The evangelization of the Highlands is a new chapter in the joint work of the overseas and indigenous missionaries.

The 'Miti' Reaches the Interior of the Huon Peninsula

Congregational mission had been initiated by the Sattelberg congregation among the Hube tribes, but other congregations soon followed. One after the other felt called to do 'Miti work', to evangelize the neighbouring tribes. They even competed with one another, and got into fights about which congregation should be allowed to evangelize the next region. For the 'mother' congregations it was a matter of course: As soon as the first baptism had taken place, the 'daughter' congregations were given their share in the missionary task; they too were motivated to appoint workers from their own ranks for the next step ahead. Only thus was it possible between 1908 and 1950 to evangelize the mountainous interior of the Huon Peninsula, a region which at the time was regarded as almost impenetrable to outsiders.

Huon Peninsula

First contacts in the Rawlinson Mountains.

Evangelist Ronggao and family at Samanzing (Rawlinson).

Rawlinson Mountains

The Kate congregations of Heldsbach and Wareo soon followed the Sattelberg line of congregational mission. Later, Qembung, perhaps the oldest of all, did not want to be left behind. [72] They felt called for missionary work among their neighbouring tribes, the Zuqong and Kosorong people. In 1916, evangelist Bazakie founded the new station of Ebabaang in that area. When the Kosorong work proved to be comparatively limited, the Qembung congregation began work in the Rawlinson Mountains. [73] The first evangelists' station was Mumelili (1917), on the upper course of the Buso River.

Since the Rawlinson mountain region is almost three times the size of the Hube region, the further the evangelists advanced within this rugged mountain area, the further they became removed from their base at Qembung. Gradually it became easier for them to contact the Gabmazung mission station rather than their own mother congregation in faraway Qembung/Finschhafen. Teacher Zurenare (the head of the evangelists' team) and his co-workers suffered greatly from this isolation. Altogether, the Qembung congregation provided 32 teachers and evangelists for that work, yet the task proved almost too large and too difficult for them. Under those circumstances, fast and spectacular results were denied to them. Evangelists' and school stations like Samanzing, Kasanombe, Gaeng give evidence of the steady work of men like Ronggao, Bafinu, Ronu, Sesinu — to mention just a few. At great personal sacrifice, they carried the Gospel to the people of the Rawlinson mountains and beyond. Finally, after twelve years of tedious work, the Finschhafen Mission came to their support. In 1932 a new mission station was built at Boana. Gustav Bergmann was stationed there, and remained the 'father' of the congregation for over 40 years. His friend Basawepe, one of the early Qembung evangelists, finally became the first circuit pastor of Boana after World War II.

The Boana congregation followed in the footsteps of its 'mother' by faithfully spreading the Gospel in the remaining heathen areas on the southern slopes of the Saruwaged mountain range. From the experience of the Qembung evangelists and teachers, however, an

Pastor Basawepe, a church leader in the Boana circuit.

important lesson in mission strategies had been learnt, viz. how vital it is for the growth of any mission that the sending congregation keep in close contact with its emissaries into a new area.

First Step to the North-west

Soon after their first trained teachers became available, the Wareo congregation began mission work among its neighbours. In 1913 they established an evangelists' station at Hompua, with Baafecke as teacher-evangelist in charge. After his early death, Elisa, also a trained teacher, took his place. Two years later, they expanded their work with a new station, Zageheme, a day's trip away from Hompua. There Babarigao and Goreepe, and later Bamiringnu and Wahao, became 'fathers in the faith' to the Dedua people. Relatively soon — four years after the evangelistic work had begun — the Dedua tribes at a large public gathering decided to accept the *Miti* and to make peace with each other. It took two more years before they disclosed the secret of the ancestors to their women folk. With that, the biggest hindrance had crumbled, and the path for Baptism was open (1919 in Hompua, 1922 in Zageheme).

Gawamba and family from Kalasa.

Missionary Karl Wacke and young Christians.

The Wareo congregation had fulfilled its missionary call among its nearest neighbours, the Dedua tribes, surprisingly fast. Their mission zeal, however, was by no means exhausted. From then on they supported the Sialum missionary Wacke in his difficult work among the Ono tribe, living on the eastern slopes of the Cromwell mountain range. The Ono people put up considerable resistance to the Gospel. The evangelists Nikodemo, Jona, Tamae, and Bajape from Wareo made a start in evangelizing, and were later supported by local Christians from Sialum. To intensify the combined efforts to win the Onos for Christ, Wacke in 1919 moved his station from Sialum to Kalasa, right within the Ono tribal area. It was then that the *Miti* began to take a first hold among the Ono tribe. The hostilities gradually ceased, and the people made peace with each other. Finally, they also disclosed the ancestors' secret. As in other instances, this was the decisive turning-point. Wacke in his 1921 report wrote:

> The difficulty is now that 5000 Ono people are hungry for the Gospel; everyone wants to have instruction … What God has done to the population of this circuit, can hardly be described in words. I thank God every day that He found me worthy to be a witness to all this.

A Second Step — At the Same Time

At almost the same time, other missionaries from the Wareo congregation began to work in the Komba region (on the northern slope of the Cromwell Range), thereby reaching the very interior of the Huon Peninsula. In 1911, the missionaries L. Flierl and G. Pilhofer had set out on an exploratory trip inland from the Hube area. They then realized how thickly populated this area was, compared with coastal regions, but evangelistic work was not feasible for another seven years. In October 1918, L. Wagner from Wareo and Wacke from Sialum/Kalasa made the next trip with the definite intention of opening up the Komba area as a new mission field for their congregations. Finally, in August 1919, everything was set for the start: three main villages, Indagen, Ununu, and Darasimbit, were chosen to be evangelists' stations, with several evangelists and teacher-preachers stationed at each place. Among them were Norerawe, Honenu, Muka, Jowanu, Rapenao, to mention at least a few of the pioneers in the Komba region. Two more deserve a special mention: Akikepe and Firiepa, evangelists who later were ordained. [74] Under their leadership, Ununu soon developed into a spiritual centre for the whole area. Since the new mission field of the Wareo congregation was five days' march away from home base, and separated from the coast by the high Cromwell mountain range, the evangelists and teachers had to be rather self-reliant in their work. However, their home congregations did not neglect them, even though supporting them meant long trips overland. This was done fairly regularly several times a year.

Evangelization was not easy among the Komba people, for they were used to living in a

Akikepe, early Komba evangelist, later Ulap pastor.

state of constant warfare with each other. The evangelists and teachers — foreigners to the local people — were more than once in danger of being killed. Living in a remote mountain region, they could hardly rely on direct protection from the Administration, or on the moral authority of the missionary. The evangelist Firiepa once said to the warring Kombas: 'We didn't come to you on our own behest, but God has sent us here. It is also He who protects us through His angels.' The turning to the new way of the *Miti* began surprisingly soon. Perhaps this was due to Christian trading partners from the coast and in the Hube mountains; most likely they told the Komba people what had happened to them since the arrival of the *Miti*. Again there was the fear that the Gospel was running quicker than the pace at which evangelists and the missionaries were able to carry it. In May 1926 the first baptism took place at Ununu.

Firiepa at the end of his life wrote in retrospect about his Komba mission work:

The menacing threats [of paganism] we have experienced as evangelists among the heathen. Since they did not want to give up their old ways,

Village with church in the Komba area.

they dangerously came near us. In their fury they wanted to destroy our houses and even kill us. Yet we have not let ourselves be intimidated, nor did we flee. When their women and girls came to embrace us, we did not falter. When they met us on bush tracks and took off their grass skirts, we did not become weak. When they threatened us with bows and arrows, or with axes and knives, we did not forsake our mission task. As our fathers taught us courage and steadfastness in the pagan times, so has Jesus granted us power and strength, and above all His peace. Thus, when Satan in his might approached us, he could not withstand us and was overcome. The light of the Gospel finally found its way to the heathen. And now while I sit here, ELCONG is born. For that all praise belongs to our heavenly Father. Amen.

Pressing On and On

The mission to the Kombas was but the beginning of a huge movement in which all coastal Kate-speaking congregations took part. Included were the newly-established ones among the Deduas and those on the Qorafung coast, the Sialum, and, finally, the Ono congregations. Fanning out from Heldsbach-Qorafung, more evangelists' stations (Iloko, Selepet, Kabwum, Ulap) in the Selepet area bordering on the Komba land were established in 1919-1922. [75] Ranangme at Selepet and teacher Tinkewe at Ulap were considered the leading evangelists in that work. As the older congregations grew in numbers, their mission areas spread into the mountain region of the Huon Peninsula, and required every available hand for the great harvest. It was as if there was nothing which could stop the missionary advance.

Starting out from the Selepet area, the next river region of the Timbe could be reached only by mountain trails under greatest difficulties. The Ono congregation stationed their evangelists in the villages of Hengune, Etaitno, and elsewhere. The Dedua congregation occupied Sambanga, Heman, and Leweman. Among the many workers which the congregations sent into the work, the Dedua evangelist Manasingnu in Sambanga and the Ono teacher (later, pastor) Batamae were outstanding leaders. It was one of the most exciting times in the onward rush of the *Miti*, and many more evangelists, teachers, and their helpers ought to be mentioned. The untiring

work of Ulap missionary Saueracker should also be remembered. Likewise, the readiness of the home congregations to support their workers; they were the ones who spiritually carried the mission outreach and provided personnel and finances according to their capacities. The links through regular visitations were important for their commissioned workers, and also for the newly-begun congregations. These were the times when the overseas churches were almost unable to support the mission work in New Guinea financially, or to send additional staff. Yet, in those same years, thanks to the fervent mission zeal of the congregations, the Kate District of the church grew and spread out over the entire Huon Peninsula, up to the Finisterre Mountains in the north, and south as far as Zaka and the Waria Valley.

In 1925, the Kalasa congregation founded a new mission field on the upper course of the Orowa River. Boksawin village became its spiritual centre through the almost 50 years' work of Niniju, the Kalasa evangelist, and Isai, the teacher. Niniju was the recognized spiritual authority for the whole area, and also for the evangelistic co-workers which the Kalasa congregation stationed there. That did not even change in the next generation when young Orowa Christians took over the work load in schools and congregations.

Irresistibly the evangelists pressed on. Beyond the Som River, Kalasa evangelists reached the densely-populated Jupna Valley. In

Evangelist Niniju (left) and teacher Isai (right), Boksawin.

1929 the first evangelists were placed in Keiweng and Isan. In the Jupna area, the chieftain Japit himself proved to be helpful to the evangelists right from the beginning. Isan became the centre of the area, particularly through the work of the evangelist Ragewe. Retrospectively, one may say it was divine providence that the Mission at that time did not have enough people to station white personnel in the large mountain area of the Huon Peninsula, and that it was left to the New Guinean congregations to find ways and means for mission outreach into new areas, as well as for spiritual leadership in the new congregations. Being challenged in that way, and also having to care for their own emissaries, meant spiritual blessing as well as growth in the task to win their own people for Christ.

Evangelist Ragewe, Jupna.

There was no let-up in the missionary penetration of the very rugged mountains of the Huon Peninsula and the bordering Finisterre mountains. Following the successful beginning of the work in the Komba, Timbe, and Selepet areas, a mission station was established at Ulap in 1928. For years the indigenous missionaries had been working far from their home congregations; now, with the establishment of Ulap as a base station, they felt somewhat relieved. Missionary Saueracker, an untiring traveller and friend to his indigenous brethren, was now somewhat nearer. He never failed to keep close contact with his co-workers, and that included even the remotest outstations.

Missionary Karl Saueracker.

Chief Japit (middle), father of the evangelists in Jupna.

Men from Wantoat, shortly after having been contacted.

Crossing the Mountains

Soon after the first people were baptized and formed Christian congregations in the Komba, Timbe, and the other areas mentioned, they could not be denied the privilege of participating in the great mission movement. However, their neighbours of the Orowa and Jupna river basins had meanwhile received evangelists and teachers from Kalasa. Since they would have understood a reinforcement of workers from the new Ulap congregations as an intrusion rather than a help, the Ulap congregation had to look for a new mission field. This they found on the southern slopes of the high Saruwaged mountain ridge. A first survey trip to the Wantoat Valley in 1927 had shown a population of approximately 5000 people not yet reached by any Christian mission. And so, in 1929, the first Ulap evangelists were stationed among the Wantoat people. Teacher Bafinu from Komba (later ordained) made Mupiapun the new spiritual centre for the Wantoat; he himself became something like a spiritual father to the people. Other evangelists from Ulap/Komba followed him.

A painful lesson — which others had learnt before — the Ulap congregation had to learn in a particular way: Mission work also claims human lives. Whatever the circumstances, an unusually high number of Ulap workers died in Wantoat. Nevertheless, the home congregation did not become disheartened; replacements were sent for those who were buried on the mission field.

There was one factor which Saueracker had not taken into consideration when looking for a new mission field for the Ulap congregation. Wantoat is much nearer to the Kaiapit Circuit than Ulap, and therefore Kaiapit claimed the right to evangelize in Wantoat. An unpleasant clash between the evangelists from Ulap and Kaiapit resulted from the claims in the Wantoat area. In their fury over the alleged interference, the old Komba warring mood flared up, and, as in former tribal feuds, they set fire to the houses of their Azera/Kaiapit co-workers. [76] This was the other side to the coastal congregations' rush for new mission areas. Perhaps a traditional concept of owner-relationship played a role in this unforeseen incident: Whoever discovers has certain rights

70

of ownership. Should such claims of 'mother congregations' be established also toward their 'daughter congregations' within the Christian church? No doubt, the mother/daughter relationship was a universally-accepted pattern in the early New Guinea church. The course of history showed, however, that this inevitably would lead to conflicts, though not necessarily as violent as the one mentioned above. Despite such all-too-human shortcomings, however, in those years before and after World War II, the *Miti* ran like wildfire throughout the Huon Peninsula.

From the Wantoat Valley, mission work was carried further into the regions of the Leron and the Rumu rivers up to the borders of the Boana mission area at Erap. Thus, the course of the Gospel had completely encircled the central Saruwaged Mountain Range of the Huon Peninsula.

Only in 1960 did it become possible to build a mission station at Wantoat as a centre for the very isolated Ulap evangelists. Guenther Herrlinger was put in charge of the new work. After some uncertainty, the Wantoat Circuit, which originated from the mission work of both Ulap and Azera evangelists, finally became a part of the Lae District.

Pastor and congregational leader Kitangnuwe from Tapen.

Still Unevangelized Fields

The work of the Ulap congregations was by no means completed with Wantoat. There were further regions untouched by the *Miti*. In 1930, the Ulap missionary Saueracker, together with Hans Neumeyer and the American missionary Paul Fliehler, for the first time travelled through the hinterland of Saidor/Biliau in the Finisterre Mountains. The area is called Nankina after the main river. Quite rightly it has been called 'the last mission field' of the Ulap congregation. Here the area of the Finschhafen Mission already touches the Madang District; the boundaries were never exactly defined. In 1936, the first evangelists from the Timbe area began their work in the village of Gumbaion. Later, however, Bambu would become the centre in the Nankina area, chiefly through the work of the evangelist Nowatuo.

In 1951, a mission centre was built for the widespread evangelistic work of the Kalasa and Ulap congregations at Tapen, high up the coastal slopes of the Finisterre Mountains. The station was built by Konrad Munsel, who for many years was in charge of that rugged country, 'father' to the Orowa, Jupna, and Nankina people.

The coastal people from Sio to Saidor are both linguistically and ethnically widely different from the mountain population. While the evangelistic approach to the relatively thickly-populated mountain region was made overland by crossing from one river basin to the next, the coast remained the mission field of the Sio congregation. Only in the years shortly before and after World War II were the coastal congregations united with the Ulap and Tapen centres.

Advance to the South

While the Kate-speaking congregations were busy within their vast mission field in the interior of the Huon Peninsula, the Jabem-speaking congregations advanced up the Markham Valley and to the south of it: the Malalo hinterland, Bulolo Valley, Buang Mountains, Watut River area, as well as Mumeng. For the Musom and Waing area north of the Markham, a working agreement was reached between the

Kate and Jabem districts; the Lae evangelists were not to go any further up into the very mountain area which later was to become the Boana Circuit. To compensate for the loss in the Waing area, G. Schmutterer directed the attention of the Lae and Labo congregations to the area along the Wamped River. Thus, in 1925 Gurakor was established as an evangelist station — the station where (the later Lae District President) Gedisa Moale had his first assignment as a teacher-preacher. Some years later, the Wamped area and parts of the Buang Mountains were united, and a new station established at Mumeng with Georg Vicedom in charge. Mission work in that region was anything but easy, for the gold rush at Wau and in the Bulolo Valley was at its height.

Nevertheless, evangelists and teachers pressed into an unknown area toward the Kukukuku country. [77] The government had declared it an 'uncontrolled area', and no permanent government patrol post had yet been established there. The tribal people to the south had hardly ever been contacted. (In 1936 the missionaries Lechner from Malalo, Reiner from Mumeng, and Maurer from Lae, made an extensive exploratory trip through this unknown country and had proceeded as far as the watershed of the mountain range close to the Papuan border.)

The Lae and Waing people, jointly with the Mumeng congregation, accepted this new area as their mission field and willingly provided evangelists and teachers. However, the fact that it was an 'uncontrolled area' meant that not even New Guinean teachers and evangelists were free to settle wherever they were welcomed by the people. Nevertheless, they could not be prevented from bringing the message of peace to a tribe as warlike as the Kukukuku. The advance, however, was brought to a temporary standstill during the war years. The harvest time was to come only after World War II.

Meanwhile, the second great mission period of the Lutheran Church was in its initial stage in the Central Highlands. The older Jabem- and Kate-speaking congregations — which in their missionary zeal and fervour are almost unparalleled in history — had taken on another, still-greater mandate. In the Highlands, the continuation of the congregational mission of the 1920s and 1930s proved itself on an even

Round hut in the Kukukuku country.

Missionary Lechner and Evangelist Hiob, Malalo area.

larger scale. The missionary penetration of the mountainous country around the Huon Gulf and up to the threshold of the Highlands had been first and foremost the achievement of the New Guinea congregational mission, with the actual mission activity being carried out from dozens of evangelists' stations. Few of those stations need be mentioned here; today, most of them have been given up. More important than names of places are the names of evangelists, teachers, pastors, and their co-workers who, for the sake of the Gospel, had left their villages and homes to become strangers in unknown country. By their steady and dedicated work, under incredible hardships and temptations, they carried the *Miti* onward, from village to village, from valley to valley, and from tribe to tribe. Future research must uncover their names, and save them from oblivion. They were the saints of their time, who became apostles in their own right and for their own country. They were builders of today's Lutheran Church in Papua New Guinea.

Baptism — and Then What?

The missionaries' toil for the first 15 years showed hardly any visible results, and this was hard to bear. Thirteen years passed before the first baptism in Simbang had taken place. The years from 1903 to 1906 brought the first awakening for the Gospel at Finschhafen. After that, the numbers of candidates for baptismal classes steadily increased. In spite of the ever-increasing pressure of work in the newly-established congregations, the early missionaries never lost sight of the fact that the missionary zeal of the congregations should not be hindered.

In those early years, a large number of additional missionaries arrived from overseas. Their arrival meant that the opening doors all around the Huon Gulf and in the interior of the Peninsula could be entered and made the most of. However, the task of strengthening the new Christian congregations, and of giving them a firm structure, could never have been accomplished by the missionaries alone. They realized that the newly-baptized had a genuine Christian responsibility in their own right. Both the missionaries and the new Christians took this seriously. Mission outreach, as outlined in this chapter, was the one (and most characteristic) side; the way of Christian living in the community the other. It was a basic decision in those early years that the missionaries keep the traditional social structure intact also within the Christian congregation. The decisive step of turning from the old ways to the Gospel was not normally made by individuals, as it would be in a European context; it was always a matter of the entire community. As long as the social group with their chieftains and leading men opposed the new way of the *Miti*, an individual's decision for baptism was rendered relatively insignificant; it may even have had a negative effect if the group viewed it as an offence against the community, for that would mean stronger resistance to the Gospel. In an increasing measure, the missionaries realized that the decision for the *Miti*, if it was to have a lasting effect, had to be made by the group as such, or at least that the rest of the clan should give its consent to those ready to be baptized. [78]

The beginnings of such mission methods specifically aimed at the New Guinean situation are already visible in Vetter's and Lehner's work, referred to earlier in this chapter. However, it is particularly apparent in Keysser's approach; unlike any before him, he strove to understand fully the way the people lived, and studied their customs, traditions, and legal system. His missionary pioneering was marked by this kind of extraordinary sensitivity toward Melanesian culture; and so was his concept of building up a living Christian congregation in a genuine New Guinean setting. [79]

His philosophy of Christianizing peoples, rather than individuals, did not remain undisputed among his fellow-missionaries. A long and heated discussion on missionary methods was launched in 1914-15 when the Neuendettelsau Mission Inspector Karl Steck visited the Finschhafen field. At the missionaries' Field Conference in Heldsbach in January 1915, Steck summarized in four sentences the insights he had gained on his extensive information trip through the mission field:

1. This is New Guinea, and not Europe.
2. You are not a pastor, but a missionary and a teacher.

3. Contents rank before form.
4. Any egotism is out of place here. [80]

With these points, Steck wanted to stress a genuinely New Guinean pattern of church and Christianity as the goal of the missionaries' work.

This statement, however, was understood — at least by some of the missionaries — as supporting Keysser's ideas and his ways of working in the Sattelberg congregation. At this point Steck met with opposition from a majority of the group, who were not prepared to follow what they considered to be Keysser's extravagances. Today it is hard to understand the battle-lines in this argument — and even less the pungency with which even Senior Flierl thought he had to defend himself against Steck and Keysser. [81] The outcome of the long-drawn-out and often exaggerated discussion, however, is amazing: Since 1928, whenever new Neuendettelsau staff have come to New Guinea, the above-sketched guidelines for mission work and congregational organization have been accepted as the 'Neuendettelsau Approach', for all missionaries sent out from Neuendettelsau since World War I were students of Keysser at the Mission Seminary. In this way, Keysser's experiences and insights continued to bear manifold fruit in the New Guinea Mission, even though the Australian administration had refused to let him return to his former field of work.

Congregational Elders

Together with the decision on missionary principles, the methods of how to build up the life of a congregation after baptism also changed. No longer could the mission station be the sole centre of the growing congregation; the new life after baptism should also engender new life in the villages based on the *Miti*. This should apply not only to Sundays, when people willingly used to come to the worship service on the mission station; more important was the actual form of congregational life at home. According to the New Guinean pattern of village life, this all hinged on reliable elders. [82] At first, they were considered as 'eyes and ears of the missionary', and their appointment was seen by the missionaries from a rather pedagogical angle. [83] However, much more was at stake: This was the very first step of the New Guinea

74

Congregational leaders and elders from Sattelberg.

congregations toward becoming an indigenous church. With the elders, the first local office of the growing church was created, even though it did not at first seem so. Maybe the missionaries regarded the elders as more or less dependent on their own leadership and shepherd position. Such an assumption, however, had no consequences, owing to the grace of outward conditions. The village elders never received any payment out of mission funds. Their office was an honorary one. And, above all, it was (and still is) an office of the Christian congregation, and not an institution of the mission organization. [84] Indeed, the elders did inform the missionaries of all important happenings in their villages; but they were independent in their essential activities. They saw to it that daily devotions were held, and reprimanded those who did not attend. Soon they were given the ministerial task of visiting the sick and old people and of praying with them. Later, they were commissioned for the hearing of confessions and for performing other pastoral acts, such as conducting weddings and funerals. The so-called village devotions also included the repetition of Bible stories: a simple form of preaching. It is quite justified to view the New Guinean elders' office as a pacemaker of the Office of the Word in the church. [85]

Congregational Authority

An important adjunct to the office of the elder was the congregational meeting. In a traditional Melanesian society, the chieftain was bound to obtain the consent of his followers. His claim to leadership was not simply based on authority; he continuously had to gain and to sustain the loyalty of his people. Even this traditional pattern of leadership was now carried over to the Christian congregation. It should not be overlooked, however, that the congregational meetings in many respects resembled traditional village meetings, where each and every concern of the community used to be discussed. Christians came to see that, if the Gospel were become the guiding force in daily village life, first and foremost it had to be shaped by the community as a whole. Since the Gospel was understood as the great message of peace, it was obvious that from now on every village or clan make peace with its enemies. In fact, new ways of communication had to be

75

established between neighbouring villages. So, for instance, road-building between the villages could be carried out as *Miti*-work. The decision on such matters was solely in the hands of the congregational meeting.

Since *Anutu* (God) had created all things — above all, man and woman — a neat village site and even personal cleanliness now belonged to the way of the *Miti*. Thus, in congregational meetings mothers were admonished to keep their children clean; at other times it was decided to bury all the dead in a common cemetery outside the village. All such duties of the community as well as of individuals were regarded to be a result of the *Miti*. It is important to see that the vernacular term *Miti*, as it was taken up by Christians, comprises God's Word as well as the New Life of the Gospel. This shows the oneness of Gospel and life, which is characteristic for most primal cultures. The theological differentiation between the indicative and imperative of the Gospel (that is, between justification and sanctification) cannot be ascertained by this New Guinean Christian key word *Miti*. The congregational meetings defined the *Miti* in its second sense, and unfolded it in the form of correct instructions and assignments of duties.

On the other hand, it cannot be denied that such a change could result in a new kind of legalism. This happened more than once, the most consistent case being that of the Sattelberg congregation. In 1910 they worked out their own Order of Life and Work.[86] It is a matter of speculation how far Keysser's own ideas on a genuinely-tribal structure of the Christian congregation or his personal influence were responsible in swaying the energetic Sattelberg leaders to set up such a kind of communal order; Keysser himself disclaimed any responsibility for it. Yet, whatever the case may have been, he was all for it. He praised it as 'a Christian tribal order', and as 'a means to educate the tribes'.[87]

In this order, new Christian regulations of social life were to replace the old pagan standards of social behaviour. For instance, to achieve greater tribal unity, it forbade any living in individual hamlets. For the sake of all, community working hours were introduced. Binding rules for village life were laid down (for instance, which animals could be kept in the

76

village and which had to stay outside). Men were strictly forbidden to beat their wives (there were apparently reasons for such a rule!). For policing such rules, *Songangs* (work elders) and Head-*Songangs* were installed. The order even went so far as to empower the Christian congregation to take over civil jurisdiction in the absence of a governmental authority (the government and its officials were far away!). Punishment by hard labour, beatings, even imprisonment,[88] and expulsion from community life as the highest form of punishment, could be imposed by the elders as the representatives of the village community, which was considered identical with the Christian congregation.

Keysser allowed all this to happen, and even supported the Sattelberg Order by occasionally trying to argue its Christian validity. He thus earned a great deal of criticism — ironically, more from his missionary colleagues than from the German colonial administration.[89] The latter viewed the matter as a welcome help for their own task of keeping order, since they at best could only partly enforce it. The Sattelberg Order, however, did not gain general consent, even in the Finschhafen area. In the period of the Australian administration which followed, it would only have increased the issues of conflict with government officials.

Church discipline was regularly practised in all Christian congregations.[90] This was not only because the missionaries had taught them so; the congregations themselves enforced it. Later, they even established a system of appeal first to the local congregation, then to the Circuit, and finally to the District Conference, according to the seriousness of the respective case. Most commonly, cases of adultery and polygamy by individual Christians were settled by disciplinary means. As well, there were cases when, according to the pattern of community living, whole villages were excluded for a certain length of time from receiving the Sacraments. Such community measures were well understood and accepted at that time by the Christian congregations concerned.

In such matters they felt themselves called upon to act as a community rather than as individuals.[91] It was the congregational meeting, and not the missionary or an individual leader, that took measures against open wrong-doers in their midst. It cannot be denied, however, that, in dealing with matters of church discipline, traditional patterns of punishment and retaliation sometimes tended to over-ride the call to repentance and the proclamation of the Gospel.

Congregational Schools

In the context of the set-up of the Christian villages, the congregational schools must be mentioned briefly. (For a more detailed presentation, see ch 13.)

Right from the very beginning at Simbang, Flierl had thought of schools, though it was much too early. To him, the opening of schools was a kind of missionary approach. This was the general practice at that time, but it was an entirely European concept. It was generally considered that through an educational routine the younger generation could gradually be led to a Christian way of life. However, this did not work. Regular school attendance and an orderly work schedule for the day was not at all to the liking of the village boys and girls. These methods seemed to be rather unsuitable for New Guinea — at least in the pioneer years.

Christian village schools, planned after the great missionary breakthrough, must be seen in a different context. The missionaries as well as the people now considered schools to be a necessary consequence of Baptism. [92] Neither education as such, nor the passing on of (Western) knowledge was the goal, but first and foremost the teaching of basic biblical values; the children needed to be strengthened in faith and introduced to a Christian way of life. 'They shall not grow up in ignorance as we did', said the older people.

While the ultimate goal of the mission schools was to provide the New Guineans with an access to the written Word of God, the schools also taught general subjects, such as reading, writing, numbers, and social subjects.

The setting up of a Christian education system linked to Baptism demanded determined planning. The rapid expansion after 1906 made it impossible for the missionaries also to be schoolteachers, and this led to the early establishment of teachers' seminaries. The importance of such indigenous teachers for the growth of the fledgling congregations

can hardly be overestimated. The major emphasis in such schools was put on religious instruction, a subject for which the teachers were specially trained. This enabled them also to be preachers in the villages. Teaching children in the classroom was only one part of their assignment at that time; preaching the Word of God to the adult congregation was the other. Thus, the office of the elder was supplemented by an office of public preaching. While elders and teachers alike shared the commission, neither of them were ordained ministers. And yet both of them were regarded as duly recognized preachers of the Lutheran Church. [93]

Trials and Temptations

During the first 30 years, the Christian congregations in the Finschhafen area, living in an insignificant corner of the great island, were spared harmful interference by inimical forces. When the German New Guinea Company abandoned Finschhafen as its headquarters in 1891, the area was more or less left to itself. The colonial government opened its only outpost in the Morobe District as late as 1909 at the southernmost tip of the country, at the small place called Morobe. Since initial hopes for profitable plantations at Finschhafen and other places in the Huon Gulf area were not realized, the recruiting of workers during the first decades of colonial rule was also negligible. This fact also facilitated the missionaries' efforts to win the people by building up living Christian congregations. Outside interference was practically unknown in the Finschhafen district for more than two decades.

This, however, changed after World War I. The Australian administration was suspicious of the church work of the Finschhafen Mission, and regarded it as a German 'state within the state'. Senior Flierl was soon able to establish a good relationship with the top administration people, but there were plenty of opportunities for lower-ranked *Kiaps* (government patrol officers) to challenge the established order of Christian conduct in the villages. Some of them regarded it as their national duty to take a stand against the 'usurped' government-like authority of the 'German Mission' (as they expressed it). Keysser's ideas of local Christian congregations somewhat resembling a tribal community faded

Senior Flierl shortly before retirement.

away — after proving itself for many years in the Kate congregations and beyond. But how, for instance, could church discipline be practised if young *Kiaps* encouraged sexual permissiveness? Divorces (which in earlier times were difficult to secure) could now be obtained by order of the *Kiap* — or, even more easily by the consent of the government-installed local *Luluai*.[94] Congregational meetings could no longer limit the number and length of traditional dances; *Kiaps* would order the people to have traditional *singsings* (festive dances) with their usual pagan backgrounds.

Missionaries had over many years obtained a deep insight into, and respect for, the indigenous culture. They certainly were not prepared to uproot this valuable heritage as long as it did not clash with Christian ethics; on the contrary, it was accepted policy to integrate Christianity into the existing cultural background. This was no longer possible under the new conditions. Unexpectedly, the young Christian congregations faced a new and bewildering situation. Mistrusted by government officials, the missionaries could no longer speak up for them. Even indigenous

78

Christian leaders dared not invoke the missionaries' authority in situations where their Christian way of living clashed with the *Kiap's* ambitions. Unfortunately, the New Guinea congregations were not yet equipped for this new development. After 10 or 15 years of Christianity, they certainly were on their way to taking up public responsibility, but the process of learning was hampered by an abrupt change in government authority, an authority which showed little or no interest in the claim of the oneness of Gospel and life also in public life.

A second challenge was the encounter with a modern, and yet pre-Christian, world. Even during the German colonial period, some young men used to work on plantations or in other services for white settlers and traders, usually on the basis of a three-year contract. Every year at Christmas, many of these workers returned to their home villages.[95] In order to define their status anew in the tightly-knit home community, these returnees tended to show off on the basis of their newly-won experiences in the outside world. This was most easily done by opposing Christian moral standards, as represented by the elders and congregational authorities. Often they also displayed magic utensils and practices which their own communities had given up long ago.

Gold Rush

Right up to the early 1920s, the congregations were still able to meet the partly-secular, partly-old-religious challenge. The situation, however, became more critical in 1925, when rich gold deposits were discovered in the area of the Bulolo River, far in the mountains east of Malalo mission station. A hectic gold fever brought many adventurous characters to New Guinea.[96] Directly affected was the Malalo congregation and its mission field in the Buang Mountains. Since the goldfields could be reached only by a four-day walk across a rugged mountain range, the gold prospectors required carriers for their gear. Often recruiting was done even with the support of *Kiaps*; whoever looked physically fit was forced to work. The carrying job itself was next to murderous. F. Bayer's reports on Malalo Station covering those years are full of complaints about injustices done to the people:

Toward the end of 1926, nearly 70 people were

taken by the administration from the Piololo villages; all at one time. Since I knew most of the people, I could keep track of them ... From their number, 13 died, some in Salamaua, some on the way. 16 had to be sent home early due to sickness. From these another two died. A small village, named Bugweb, was especially hard hit. Six men were taken, and only one returned. [97]

In 1926, Senior Flierl submitted a memorandum to the government administration specifying the degrading and even scandalous conditions under which local people were pressed into service. However, even the government had lost control. Mission Director Theile then turned to the Colonial Minister. He also spoke to the Administrator whom Flierl already had addressed, pointing out the embarrassing, even inhuman, conditions of the people. In spite of government investigations, hardly anything was changed. 'One cannot doubt the good will of the Administration', wrote Theile in his report for 1926, 'but when the greediness for gold seizes a person, then there is no more thought of one's fellow man. What difference does a black man make to them ...', he complained, 'what difference does Administration and its laws make to them?' [98]

The consequences of the discovery of gold were felt throughout the country. Recruiting became a regular occupation for a certain type of European. The practices of such men were ruthless; they had no consideration whatever for the social situation when combing through villages for able-bodied men of working age.

Decker wrote in 1938:

> It is really a pity that the young men go to the gold fields and stay five, even ten, years there ... And so marriages are ruined, and the population diminishes. Even the younger lads don't come home. The young women of marriageable age sit and wait for years.

'About 600 girls and young women have no husband, and many children have no father', Wacke of Kalasa complained. [99]

Such rude methods of recruiting were a great concern to the people. No wonder the Mission felt called upon to act as advocate for the exploited population. G. Pilhofer quotes Proverbs 31:8 as a word which he had often heard from the mouth of Senior Flierl [100]: 'Open your mouth for the dumb and for the rights of all who are left desolate'. Flierl wrote a detailed report to the Administration in Rabaul, based on the testimonies from people who had turned to him for help. Finally, he was at least successful in that a Royal Commission investigated the cases recorded, and ordered compensation to be paid for damages done. [101]

Decline and Revival at Sattelberg

The Kate congregations of Sattelberg, Wareo, Heldsbach, and Qembung had experienced a great spiritual awakening after the missionary breakthrough in 1904-06. In their mission activities among the Hube and Dedua tribes, they saw the Gospel spreading far and wide. The congregations were blessed with outstanding elders and teachers, of whom at least their spiritual leaders Zurenuo (later ordained), Songangnu, and Rowosae should be mentioned. Keysser possessed the great gift to recognize leaders awakened by God, and to entrust them with various spiritual tasks. Throughout the whole area, it seemed, the days of paganism with its fears of sorcerers and resorting to old magic had vanished. Such practices would never be rekindled on a large scale — so the missionaries thought.

Pastor Zurenuo from Sattelberg.

Meanwhile, the problems of any second generation of Christians caught up with the mountain congregations around Sattelberg. Whatever the depth of their own turning to Christ may have been, they were unable to hand it on to the following generation. To no small degree this was due to the fact that their beloved spiritual father Keysser had to leave New Guinea, never to return. [102] For more than 20 years he had been with them, and now they felt like orphans. But that was not all. When Keysser left, two of the most outstanding congregational leaders, Songangnu and Aijang, accompanied him to Madang, and there both of them were taken ill and died, away from home. All of a sudden, the congregation was robbed of three of its spiritual leaders, and the result was a decline in congregational life. How difficult it must have been for Leonhard Flierl, Keysser's successor, to step in.

In the years after 1922, the Sattelberg congregation was exposed to a first wave of the cargo cult. Two young men — Mutari and Tutumang — brought some new-fangled ideas with them when returning home after a long period of work at Rabaul. In the seclusion of remote mountain villages, they developed strange ideas and practices with the intent of making money — and they found willing listeners. For a long time they were able to hide their activities from the missionary. As fraudulent as such 'magic money-making' may appear to the outsider, many village people were led astray by this alleged way of finding access to a new quality of life.

At about the same time, an authority crisis also developed — thanks to another returnee from Rabaul: Serembe, a man with exceptional leadership qualities. The Australian administration made him Paramount *Luluai*, which gave him great authority. Serembe cleverly used the existing leadership vacuum at Sattelberg to become the local leader. To make matters worse, Serembe tried to pit his political office against the Christian congregation, thus counteracting Keysser's aim and efforts to form a Christian unit of both tribal community and Christian congregation. As time went on, the tensions between political authority and congregational leadership became so strong that even the respected spiritual leader, Zurenuo, had to leave Sattelberg for some time.

During those years, the spiritual life of the congregations almost came to a standstill. The fear of the old sorcery customs and the new magic practices, believed to have been overcome, again flared up. Church discipline became ineffective. Congregational elders were at a loss as regards their authority in the village community. Serembe was certainly not interested in strengthening the role of the congregational authorities. His relationship to the missionary, L. Flierl, was likewise strained.

Then something happened in June 1927 which changed the whole picture. In his Sunday sermon, L. Flierl again reproached the congregation, as he had done many times before. In vivid picturesque language, he scolded his listeners: 'You are not good bananas. You are wild ones, which are thrown away.' With such words, he hoped that some of the people would repent. But the result of his sermon was astounding: Serembe himself, his strong opponent, withdrew to his field hut —and repented. There, in his solitude, he experienced a spiritual conversion. After some days, he contacted the pious teacher Desiang (who sometimes in the past had tried to reprimand him), seeking his counsel. At Desiang's suggestion, Serembe called a meeting of 25 leading men from the surrounding villages. What followed, however, was Serembe's own idea: The food he offered his guests was nothing but wild bananas. 'Yes, eat them. This is what we have become, and so I prescribe for you wild food.' It was a strange mixture of obstinacy over against the missionary, an admission of his own indolence and sin, and at the same time a new start with earnest confession and new listening to the Gospel. *Eemasang*, a revival movement of the Sattelberg congregation, was born. [103]

Only gradually did the movement spread from the small group of the 25 to the rest of the congregation. Later, they began to make regular evangelizing visits, village by village. Their main concern was to lead the ordinary village Christians to a 'spiritual house cleaning': listening anew to the Word of God, confessing sins and accepting Christ's forgiveness, and, most of all, starting a new life in strict obedience to the *Miti*. Within three years, the *Eemasang* movement spread to all Sattelberg villages and even beyond. As a genuine revival movement it was carried on by special prayer meetings, sometimes with great emotional outbursts. Neither old nor young, neither respected nor ordinary church members were left out; the cleaning up was thoroughly done. The actual leaders were Desiang, Manasupe, and Serembe; later also, L. Flierl joined them. Though he had started off the movement with his preaching, he was not even informed at first. The *Eemasang* movement was and basically remained a genuine New Guinean movement; overseas missionaries were allowed to participate only marginally.

It is not clear to this day when and how the revival leaders became involved in Mutari's magic money-making. The fact remains, however, that this is what happened at some later date. Obviously, the *Eemasang* leaders did not have the spiritual insight to recognize Mutari's cargo cult involvement, nor did they have the spiritual strength to overcome it with the *Miti*. Desiang, one of the leaders, saw the revival potential fade away during the years following 1931. [104] Later attempts to revive it were unsuccessful.

Looking back today, it must be said that the *Eemasang* movement remains a shadowy one, at least as long as no additional historic facts can be uncovered. Yet it definitely had genuine spiritual roots which should not be obliterated by later events.

The Second World War

Unlike World War I, World War II brought the fighting to the very shores of New Guinea. As far as the Mission was concerned, the war began in 1939 when the Australian government started to intern the German missionaries. The Finschhafen region was hit the hardest, for all the ordained missionaries living there were Germans apart from Martin Helbig. Only three in the Jabem District and three in the Kate District were permitted to stay on, at least for some time; later, they also were interned. Five lay missionaries, most of them Australian citizens, were allowed to stay until 1942. [105] So that the Kate and Jabem stations as well as the inland stations were not left vacant, [106] American personnel from Madang helped out with as many as could be spared. After Japan entered the war, everybody had to leave, apart from Lehner and Decker; for some unknown reason, they were allowed to stay on their stations. Adolf

Missionary Adolf Wagner †.

Wagner avoided internment by escaping and hiding in the mountains.

The Japanese occupation of New Guinea at first was limited to Rabaul (January 1942) and Salamaua/Lae (March 1942). The main thrust was southward toward Port Moresby. No Australian troops worth mentioning were stationed in the Huon Gulf area. Finschhafen was taken by Japanese troops in late 1942, without a shot being fired. Except for devastating Allied air raids, the area was so far battle-free. In September 1943, the Allied forces began to re-occupy New Guinea by landing troops at Lae (Sept. 9) and at Finschhafen (Sept. 24), forcing the Japanese troops back into the interior of the Huon Peninsula. This meant a time of great suffering for the people living in that region.

The removal of the overseas missionaries from their stations disrupted the work in the congregations as well as in schools. At Malalo, M. Lechner had started a first pastor's training course for candidates from the Jabem-speaking congregations; this came to a premature end when the missionary was interned in July 1940. The Jabem Teacher Training School at Hopoi was able to continue for a while since Lehner was not interned. However, after a severe Japanese air raid, the school community withdrew to a temporary settlement near Apo in the Bukawa hinterland; regular instruction continued there until the Japanese army arrived on the spot in September 1943. The Jabem Secondary School at Logaweng continued to function a few weeks after that. After the approach of the Japanese army, the head teacher Gedisa also relocated this school to Bukawa at a place called Abongapu, and instruction continued until finally the Japanese army forced all students to serve as carriers.

At the Kate Education Centre at Heldsbach, regular work was disrupted as early as 1939 when G. Pilhofer was interned. Earlier, he had begun a first course to train Kate pastors; with his departure the course came to an abrupt end. The Teachers Training School at Heldsbach, where Wagner was in charge, continued to function much longer, even after the Japanese forces had already occupied Finschhafen.

Finally, in February 1943, Wagner and some of his students retreated to the village of Zageheme in the Dedua mountains on account of heavy bombing attacks. Later, they had to withdraw even further into the bush country to Jamino. While trying to keep the school going, Wagner sandwiched in many trips, visiting orphaned congregations, preaching, giving Holy Communion, and comforting the suffering people in their plight. However, all this came to an end toward the middle of 1943, when the Japanese army fled in the face of the Allied onslaught.

Adolf Wagner's Death

Adolf Wagner, having been born in New Guinea as the son of a missionary, felt more bound to his fellow New Guineans and to the spiritual ministry than to any ordinances, whether they came from the administration or from his mission authorities. After being trained in Germany, both as a qualified teacher and an ordained missionary, [108] he had returned to New Guinea in December 1937, and was stationed at the Heldsbach school centre. At the outbreak of war, he was spared the first wave of internment in 1939 which brought most German missionaries to Australia, and he was able
82

legally to continue his work at the Heldsbach school until February 1942.

After the Japanese had landed at Rabaul, it became obvious that the Australian administration would have to bring the remaining overseas personnel out of the country, and Wagner as well as the congregational leaders felt great concern about the future. And then, very suddenly, a ship arrived at Finschhafen to evacuate the last foreigners. Adolf Wagner, however, made up his mind to flee. During the night, before he had received orders to board the ship, he mounted his horse and fled to the Dedua mountains. Nobody knew his hiding place, and so the search was given up. Five weeks later, in March 1942, when the Australian administration had practically ceased to function, he reappeared in Heldsbach and continued his class work at the Teachers Training School.

Meanwhile, Finschhafen was actually in no-man's-land; the Australians had retreated, but the Japanese had not yet arrived. Finally, in December 1942, the Japanese occupied Finschhafen/Heldsbach, and soon after Finschhafen became the object of Allied bombing. The school was destroyed. The students could no longer be kept on the station; indeed, some had already left. With the remaining students, Adolf set out again for the Dedua mountains. (The evangelist Bamiringnu had previously invited him.) Zageheme was like a second home for Adolf. With about thirty students he resumed his usual class work.

The situation came to a dramatic head in September 1943 when the Allies began to retake the mainland of New Guinea. The Japanese force, a defeated, suffering army, streamed through the New Guinea mountains like a plundering mob. Adolf repeatedly had to flee to even-more-impenetrable bush places. However, in the end there was no more escape; in October 1943 he must have been captured by the Japanese military police. The fact that he was a German, and as such actually an 'ally', didn't help him much. The Japanese army conscripted him as an interpreter, mainly in order to enlist carriers for their forces. For another two months Adolf suffered under an enormous physical and emotional strain. Whenever Japanese soldiers committed acts of violence, Adolf stood up for his fellow New

Guineans. It is reported that occasionally he found the ears of officers, but that only made him even more hated by the military police. With the help of his New Guinean friends, he could perhaps have fled and fought his way through to the Allied troops, but he regarded this as breaking his word of honour given to the Japanese. Thus, he remained a captive in the hands of the Japanese armed forces until he was murdered by his captors.

Adolf Wagner died on December 9, 1943, near the village of Hudewa in the Dedua mountains. It seems, according to what has become known, that he was murdered by soldiers on a bush track. His faithful companion, Gahazia, escaped by seconds from suffering the same fate; he heard a shot, which may have been meant for him or for Adolf. Months later, after the war had ended, Adolf's bones were discovered in a shallow pit in the bush, not far from the place where Gahazia had heard the shot. The Dedua people have kept the memory of Adolf alive by erecting a stone cross at the place where he was shot dead. The Christians of the Finschhafen area consider him as their true brother; 'Adoli' they used to call him, and still lovingly call him when talking about war time.

We do not know how many New Guinean men and women were killed during the war, how many were executed by the Japanese forces for alleged assistance to the enemy, or how many perished while fleeing or starved to death in the bush. Dozens? Hundreds? Two Finschhafen missionaries paid with their lives: Adolf Obst who was killed in New Britain while on military duty, and Adolf Wagner, who because of his missionary calling went into utmost peril and then was murdered.

But the Church Lives

When the overseas missionaries were taken away in 1939-42, nobody knew how the congregations would react when left on their own. There was no strong regional church structure. The local congregations even lacked an ordained indigenous ministry. The first two courses of regular pastors' training at Malalo and Heldsbach had ended prematurely. [109] In some instances, missionaries before leaving hastily commissioned reliable men to administer the Sacrament of Baptism in their congregations, but these were but emergency measures. Structurally, the Finschhafen/ Morobe congregations were not sufficiently prepared for what lay ahead of them.

Yet, in spite of all shortcomings, the Christian congregations stood the test. Their leaders, ordained or not, kept steadfast in faith. Elders and teachers, as well as evangelists who returned home from their stations, became ministers and servants to the mother congregations. At that time, a complete translation of the New Testament was already available in both church languages, Jabem and Kate, and their own Christian songs had been recorded in printed hymn books (see appendix to ch 13). When some of the hard-pressed coastal congregations had to hide in the jungle —some villages lived there for months! — they were not without the Word of God. Faithfully they would conduct their daily devotions and Sunday services. Under the leadership of their elders and teacher-preachers, the congregations proved able to stand on their own feet much more than anyone would have dared to predict. Thus, the war years became a forced time of independence for the church in New Guinea. The church had to rely on the Lord — and it was not forsaken. When the first American missionaries returned after the war, they saw the devastation done to mission stations, church buildings, schools, and institutions; the scaffold was in ruins. But they also saw the church — alive! Thanks be to God who kept His Church, even without the scaffolding.

Some Specific Observations on Partnership Involving the Australian Church

By Gordon Gerhardy

Beginnings in Partnership

After many years of missionary work, Johann Flierl still looked back to a few congregations in Australia as his 'Antioch'. Referring to St Paul having been commissioned in Antioch and then going to preach and suffer in Asia Minor while these believers 'lifted praying hands to the Lord to grant the Good News victory in the neighbouring country', Flierl acknowledged that the same had happened for him in the small Immanuel Synod in South Australia. This was where, seven years earlier, he had been ordained into the ministry of the Lutheran Church in Australia, and where, on November 8, 1885, at Langmeil, Tanunda, he was now being commissioned for the first major heathen mission outreach for the Neuendettelsau Mission Society. Flierl continued:

> The brothers in the faith in South Australia were already heavily burdened with their own total church program and their mission to the heathen in the interior on their own land. Now, besides this, they energetically directed their concern to our work in German New Guinea which was at first so difficult, but has now been blessed by the grace of God. [110]

From the very outset, the Lutheran Church in Australia had a share in supporting this mission work in New Guinea. It began with no claims to leadership nor to giving direction nor to a particular mission policy. Its role, in very humble circumstances, was merely a support role for Flierl's and Neuendettelsau's program

to bring the Gospel of Christ to this neighbouring island. When Flierl was sent, the Australian church promptly commissioned a layman, Johann Biar, to accompany him and support him, and that with offerings to help. [111] Over the years this support and partnership grew and developed side by side with the Lutheran church in PNG, and needs to be considered for an understanding of the international partnership which now exists within the Lutheran church of PNG today.

In 1885, when Flierl made his first approach to his leaders with the request to be sent to New Guinea, Lutheranism in Australia was far from unified, being widely dispersed and divided in several synods. The Immanuel Synod was one of the smaller ones, having only about 2000 confirmed members, served by nine pastors. [112] By 1898 it had 18 pastors, 16 of whom had come from Neuendettelsau. [113] This group, enthused for mission work, had virtually become an overseas arm or base for Neuendettelsau. [114] At the same time, for Flierl and the missionaries who followed, it became a stepping stone or launching platform for entrance into New Guinea. The strategic position of the Australian church was obvious from the beginning, but became much clearer only 30 years later with the outbreak of World War I.

Johann Flierl's seven years' mission orientation in Australia, as it has been called, [115] was not only with the Australian Aborigines, but was an experience in partnership with another supporting church, a partnership which developed with him in New Guinea itself. This cooperation took an unexpected course in the early years; the first support personnel sent from Australia were the wives of six of the early German missionaries: Louise Auricht (Johann Flierl), Christine Geyer (K. Tremel), Clementine Doehler (S. Lehner), Margarete Koschade (A. Zwanzger), Magdalene Doehler (K. Wacke), and Agnes Rechner (K. Saueracker). The contribution of these and other courageous wives of missionaries in these early times deserves to be recognized. It was these German missionaries, in their reports, letters, and visits to Australian congregations, who stimulated interest and understanding there, and it is from these missionaries that come some of the most beautiful expressions of international partnership in mission work in New Guinea. Outstanding in this respect is the contribution of Stephan Lehner who, in later years, became Field Inspector for Lutheran Mission New Guinea. [116]

With the increase in the number of mission stations in the 1890s, the need for lay missionaries became very clear. They were needed for building and maintaining mission stations, for transport, and also for generating income on the plantations. In the early decades, most of the lay workers came from Australia. The first was Gottlieb Keppler, who arrived in 1902 and worked at Sattelberg and Heldsbach. [117] In 1904, his sister, Rosette Keppler, began her long period of medical service. Others who followed were Paul Helbig (in later years ordained), Samuel Jericho, captain of the *Bavaria*, Gottlieb Schultz, and Wilhelm Schulz. The number of lay missionaries from Australia gradually increased so that, of the number of lay workers in the service areas, the Australian church provided over half during the 100 years. [118]

The *Deutsche Kirchen- und Missions-zeitung* (German Church and Mission News), of which Flierl's father-in-law, Pastor J.C. Auricht, was the founder and editor, became the main channel in Australia for promoting support for mission, even beyond the Immanuel Synod. The synod felt a commitment now to contribute financially both to the Elim mission station in Northern Queensland and to New Guinea. Regular mission letters and reports were printed, and gifts acknowledged in this weekly newspaper. No doubt the extent of the support fluctuated, but the gifts show a degree of self-sacrifice and unmistakable love for mission work. [119]

World War I and the Beginning of the Theile Era

By 1914, young New Guinean congregations, both Jabem and Kate, were well established in their own 'foreign' mission to other tribes. This brought a political transformation as fighting died down and the Gospel of peace emerged as victor. The evangelist-missionary became a glowing example of a Christian whose tribal allegiance or 'nationality' became merely incidental over against his commission to proclaim Christ. A deep awareness of the rule of God transformed the society. Some of the great questions about the *Miti* in its political context these congregations had come to master in just a few years — only to find their expatriate missionaries now struggling and even floundering with the same questions.

While the main concern for the young New Guinean church was the spiritual battle against demonic powers resisting the coming of Christ's kingdom, the concern elsewhere was the devastating war in Europe of 1914-1919. Combining both of these, however, there was another conflict building up and seriously threatening the Lutheran Church in New Guinea. And it was at the centre of this that the Lutheran Church in Australia found itself under suspicion from its own national government.

The difficult situation for the missionaries during and after the war, together with all the problems relating to the Australian government, are described earlier in this chapter and in chapter 4. However, the position of the Australian church in this crisis needs further mention.

Quite suddenly the Australian Lutheran church now found itself called on to increase drastically its support for what its government suspected to be an enemy-based mission in New Guinea. Feelings of hostility in Australia against Lutherans were directed in particular against their congregations. [120] How support for New Guinea could increase under these conditions was a valid question. Ultimately, it could only be by the grace of God which had

85

already brought two major influences to bear in the Australian church in the previous century.

Firstly, mission had always been a major concern of all the Lutheran synods in Australia from their beginnings, 80 years earlier in 1838. By far the majority of pastors who came to Australia in these years were trained in mission seminaries in Europe. [121] To think of the church was to think of mission. The second factor was that most of the Lutherans who had migrated to Australia in the early years had left their homeland in order to be free to confess their faith according to the Confessions of the Lutheran Church. [122] This determination was strengthened by the missionaries and pastors who came from Neuendettelsau Mission Seminary in Germany from 1875 onwards. [123] A love for the Gospel, and a concern for others also to have it, had to be the prime motivation. Apart from this, there was a very human factor. The church had strong German roots, and these were not easily given up.

The nearest effect when the war broke out in 1914 was felt by the Queensland Synod which had worked closely with the Hope Valley (Elim) mission since 1902. [124] Neuendettelsau contact and support were cut off; but of far greater significance was the resulting isolation of the mission in North East New Guinea now under Australian military rule. Responsibility for the welfare of the missionaries passed automatically to the Australian church, both as partner and as the only channel open for organizing emergency supplies for entry into the territory.

For a number of years, Pastor Otto Theile, as secretary, had represented his Queensland Synod in work with the Hope Valley Mission, and had also been acting for the Finschhafen Mission in the ordering of supplies. From this point on, he became a key figure in the total mission program, and continued to be so for a further 30 years. He had been born in Australia, and so could claim government recognition. During these critical years when New Guinea came under the government of an opposing power, Theile's position as representative and subsequently Director of the Mission required very sensitive, but far-sighted and firm political negotiation. [125]

At the same time, a deep pastoral compassion was needed for the missionaries

isolated in New Guinea and for the New Guinean congregations, to say nothing of an endless capacity for all the hard work required to rally and coordinate the support now needed from Australia and America to keep the missions going. In this respect, it was of great advantage that Neuendettelsau had been the seminary for Theile's theological training. Contacts were made in Germany and America on which relationships of trust could subsequently be built.

During the war years, it was a matter of great urgency for the Iowa Synod in America and the Lutheran Church in Australia to raise money for supplies. Theile was often under great financial pressure, but then each gift was recognized as evidence of the help of God. [126] However, he wrote of a further burden resulting from the Lutheran Church already being suspected of disloyalty by its own Australian government. He was personally under surveillance by military intelligence, and had to submit to all his correspondence being censored. [127] He wrote:

> To live through those long years of continuous insecurity and fear — both with regard to personal freedom and to the future of the missionary undertakings themselves — constituted a strain that was almost too great. It was of the Lord's mercies that we were not consumed. [128]

In 1915, Flierl had also brought to Theile's attention the desperate plight of the Rhenish missionaries in the Madang area. Since they had no support from outside, and their credit in Sydney was gone, [129] necessary help was sent as soon as possible. Theile also commented at this time that he was receiving many letters from the staff in the two New Guinea mission fields. [130] Those who were interned he visited where possible; he also arranged for extra supplies and books to be provided for them regularly. [131]

The Lutheran Church in Australia will always affirm its deep respect and love for the senior missionary, Johann Flierl, for the support and encouragement he gave through his attitude to mission work, even in these difficult years. His was an attitude which rose above all bias of nationality or culture or language. For him 'every true missionary will in the first instance be a missionary and a servant of Jesus Christ our Lord'. [132] Through this stance he earned and built up respect with the government while still in Australia, and later with officers of the Australian administration in New Guinea. From this vantage-point he could openly appeal 'for the freedom of Christian mission' in 1919, after the war had ended; [133] in the same Open Letter, he reminded English people of the debt they owed to the German missionaries of the nineteenth century. He elaborated further on this in 1920 in another public appeal entitled: 'Memorial to Friends of Foreign Mission and True Christians in English-speaking Countries'. [134] His later warning against the evil influences of Western culture showed this international understanding of mission to be based on a deep concern for the Gospel and for the welfare of the New Guinean people. [135]

In addition to the help of the Immanuel Synod and his own Queensland Synod, Theile managed to get some support from other synods in Australia. This cooperation, added to the hardships of the war, became a God-given preparation for the union of five synods into the United Evangelical Lutheran Church in Australia (UELCA) in 1921. Only then was there a Lutheran synod in Australia large enough and ready for the time when the most critical negotiations with the new colonial government were necessary. It was as though the Australian church was developing side by side with the church in New Guinea for responsibility together. In Australia, the church was also learning that the mission of Christ operates by sheer grace, even in spite of government and nationality. Through its part in the spread of the church in New Guinea, the Australian church was learning the power of the *Miti* in its own political context.

The Crisis after World War I

After the Treaty of Versailles in 1919, the Australian government was clearly rigid in its intention to enforce the removal of all German missionaries from the Territory of New Guinea. The threat this posed for the Finschhafen and Madang missions has already been mentioned, and is shown in further detail in chapter 4. The intention of the Australian Prime Minister, Mr W.M. Hughes, and of his government, to turn the two German missions over to other Protestant churches that were English, came as a serious shock to Australian Lutherans; it meant the loss

of what they had regarded, in part, as their own Australian mission, and which they and their own missionaries had supported for almost 35 years. Parts of the church had also formed close attachments to the Rhenish Mission. [136] Most of the burden of this crisis now fell on Pastor Theile in negotiations with the Australian government. In his report to the Second Synod of the UELCA in 1922, he wrote:

> We learnt to pray: 'Who are we, Lord, that we should build up your kingdom in New Guinea?' There we felt the Lord's word: 'Without me you can do nothing!' [137]

The help and support of the Iowa Synod, through the visit of its President, Dr Richter, in 1921, was of great significance. It not only encouraged the uniting of the synods to form the UELCA: Dr Richter also played a valuable role in interviews with the Prime Minister and some members of his Cabinet. Only with the help of this American Synod could the venture into the management of Lutheran Mission New Guinea be considered. And the Australian government had to be convinced that there was a Lutheran Church which was Australian, and which was of some significance in the Australian community and beyond, before it reluctantly agreed.

Of considerable importance also was the support of the Anglican Church — without doubt the main influence in the Australian Missionary Council — for asking that German missionaries be allowed to remain in their New Guinea fields. [138]

When news was received by the members of the UELCA that the Australian government had agreed to the control of Lutheran Mission being transferred to them, there was much relief, joy, and heartfelt thanks to God. Theile had been greatly encouraged in his negotiations by many telegrams and letters from pastors and laymen of the church urging him to accept the control of the Mission. [139]

Similarly, in the *Neuendettelsauer Missionsblatt* the following remarks appeared:

> What matters is not so much that the New Guinea Mission should remain ours by law, but that God is still charging us with this mission, even though we may at present remain its friend only without being able to do anything for it. What our American and Australian friends have been to us for the last thirty-five years: unassuming helpers, that we shall

be able to be for them too, as long as it is required. And God knows and gives counsel and right. [140]

At first the priority was to provide supplies and replacement personnel for the Neuendettelsau field. [141] However, this distinction was soon removed, and the Rhenish field was given equal status and support. Residences purchased in Toowoomba, Queensland, and in Light Pass, South Australia, were set up for missionaries coming to Australia for long-overdue furlough. Arrangements were made for the education of missionaries' children in Australia, and for the fiancées of German missionaries to be admitted to New Guinea.

Slowly the grace of God unfolded. First, the missions were given over to the Lutheran Church in 1921; then, German missionaries were allowed to remain at first for two years, then for four, and finally altogether. By 1925 it had become increasingly clear that Australian and American missionaries could not make up for the experience of the resident German missionaries, [142] so a further three-year deferment of their departure was applied for. And this would have been granted, had the way not been opened for German missionaries to remain permanently (when Germany joined the League of Nations in 1926). But even then it all depended on the grace of God, for human weakness was all too evident in some congregations; furloughing missionaries complained that all too many members lacked interest, and that mission work was seen as a burden rather than as a blessing for the home church. [143]

In the period between the two wars, the four visits which Theile made to the Finschhafen and Madang fields of Lutheran Mission New Guinea as Director were very important. [144] These totalled a period of almost two-and-a-half years. He tried to visit every station and to discuss the work with every staff member in order to become fully informed, and to gain a sympathetic understanding of the difficulties of each missionary. He also needed to keep the supporting churches and their Boards in touch with the total picture as it affected the supporting partners, the government in Australia and its administration in New Guinea, the supplying companies, and new developments such as radio and land

88

settlement questions. As far as individual missionaries and their families were concerned, this meant Theile getting an understanding of their health needs and travel requirements, for all missionaries needed to be met and helped in Australia, whether staying or only passing through. Because of strong pressure, also from Neuendettelsau, all missionaries had to learn English, and this need was most conveniently met in Australia and arranged through Theile's office.

In the period when it was thought that all German staff would have to be replaced, the church in Australia appealed strongly for new personnel. [145] By 1922 a further seven laymen had been placed in the two fields, and that number increased to 30 by 1939. The first Australian-ordained missionary entered the field only in 1933. He was Martin Helbig, who had been born in New Guinea, the son of Paul Helbig.

Re-organization on the Field

As some of Theile's concerns with the government eased, strain appeared from another direction: The Rhenish Mission made very strong moves to recover its former Madang field. Neuendettelsau also indicated its desire for some control. For the Finschhafen field this raised the difficult and involved question of how ownership and control could be exercised by the American, Neuendettelsau, and Australian partners in the work.

These very significant negotiations are adequately described elsewhere; so also is the eventual outcome in 1932, with Neuendettelsau having its own Finschhafen Mission and America the Madang Mission. The 1931 convention of the UELCA had resolved to withdraw from active control of the Mission in New Guinea; [146] however, it also resolved to give support in personnel and funds to help both fields. In a letter to President Stolz in 1933, Theile summed up the situation as follows:

> The UELCA today has the same relationship with New Guinea as it [Immanuel Synod] had before the war. Possibly it is more ... intimately connected, even though it has no legal right to property nor in administration. [147]

Clearly, Theile now found himself in an awkward position. He was still the New Guinea Mission Director for Neuendettelsau and for the

ALC, though now handling their finances in separate accounts. [148] Much of the business and land settlement was still in his hands, for, even though the Australian church had declined to accept control, Theile was registered as managing director of the two missions as companies. [149] It seems that the Australian Board also made the situation more difficult for him by not appreciating the degree of independence from the Board which he had in this position. [150]

Theile was obviously distressed that the field had been divided into a German and an American field. In his opinion, too many decisions were being made by the Boards at home without consulting the field. [151] This affected not only mission staff, but also the New Guinean church. Writing about this 'unfortunate division of the mission field', Theile stated:

> It is touching to see what the New Guineans say to it all, and they are absolutely correct, as little as one may like to admit it. It was human and not divine reason which caused the division. The human reasons may seem clear and important, but the whole development is shameful proof how little we like to carry out God's thoughts. [152]

The reference to 'New Guineans' arose, at least in part, from a lengthy letter in the Jabem language which Theile had received from Michael of Malalo, with translation by Stephan Lehner (November 5, 1932). To what extent Michael regarded Theile as responsible for this division is not clear, but what he wanted was that Pietz, the American missionary, be left at Kaiapit in the German field. The letter was written as an 'appeal to our people who care for us':

> O people ... we cannot imagine what suddenly has happened with you, that mission work does not go on as before; we cannot imagine it. And on the other hand, you cannot imagine what the situation is like out here with us.
>
> Now, please listen to us. You sent us the missionaries, and they always told us: 'People, stay together, work together, do as we whites do. We are the people from USA, some from Australia, and some others from Germany. We all came here to your land to proclaim the Word of God.' This talk made us feel ashamed and troubled us until we could become one and work together ... This kind of talk [of the fields dividing by nationalities] really disturbs us. So now, how does this fit together? On the one hand, they encourage us to work together; on the other, they separate ... We black people want to overthrow the decision

> you have made ... so that the *Miti* can spread and grow ...
>
> Or do you think we, the black people, look at our missionaries as strangers? No, never. We consider ourselves brothers from one clan; therefore, if you are thinking about the stationing of one of the missionaries ... we ask you please to tell us about it, ask us about it for once. If you continue to act as you did this time, how can we still believe the *Miti?* ...
>
> We people [congregation] of Kela have written this to you people who care for us in the wide world (in different villages). The grace of our Lord Jesus Christ be with you when you read this paper, and with us too.
>
> Mikaele, Malalo. [153]

In the previous 20 years, which had often rendered overseas mission programs humanly helpless, with missionaries hurled together in crisis and great hardship, the New Guinean church had grown to a maturity and a deep understanding of the Gospel and the church universal, from which their Western brothers and sisters in the faith could learn a lesson.

Over those years, much of Theile's efforts had been taken up in establishing a relationship of trust between the international partner missions for the New Guinean church and the Australian government. With the outbreak of World War II, it was as though this work had to begin all over again, and his correspondence at this time reflects the full burden of this situation. In all this, the Australian church, often falteringly, tried to stand behind him. It had learnt how the church is strengthened in times of hardship, and had come to realize that the grace of God could spare missionaries (even by internment) for further service in the New Guinean church after the disaster of war had passed.

Pastor Otto Theile's service spanned a period of 30 very difficult years of service for the Lutheran Church in New Guinea, and in many respects during this time he stands out as a central figure. [154] He died in office on August 17, 1945, two days after the war in the Pacific ended.

Developing from Neighbour to Partner Churches in the South Pacific

The war in the South Pacific had one far-reaching political effect on the nations, colonies, and territories of the area: A common enemy to their freedom had drawn them together and made them more aware that they were neighbours, compared with the great distance from the older nations on the other side of the world on which they had formerly been so dependent. For Lutherans in Australia, the church in New Guinea had also, in a sense, come closer. Where troops had fought in the war, there the church could also fight for the Gospel. In the emergency situation at the end of the war, the ALC had willingly assumed control of both the Finschhafen and Madang fields. [155] Pastor Theile's death left the UELCA with a serious gap in understanding of the Mission's affairs, and it took a number of years to recover. However, by 1947, the church had sent fourteen (either former or new) missionaries to the field.

A further stage in maturity of the Australian church's role in mission became evident by 1950. Out of its graduating class of eight pastors from the UELCA seminary, four were sent to New Guinea as missionaries. Gradually, the number of ordained missionaries has grown, most of them serving in the educational program of the church in the vernacular, Pidgin, and English. The Australian church had no desire to detract from the importance of the vernacular languages; however, because of its own past experiences and difficulties in the transition to the English language, it foresaw similar problems for the church in New Guinea (at least to some extent) if the church did not improve its facility in English, the language of the government's education policy.

The percentage of lay missionaries in all fields of service also rose rapidly after the war. [156] So many lay missionaries were needed that the American and German partners asked the UELCA to provide staff, while they would support financially. This was done because of the nearness of Australia, and also because the political situation was more readily understood by Australians. In this way, even to the present time, the Australian Lutheran Church has been able to provide a level of staff personnel which was beyond its financial capacity to support.

The same trend to increased staff showed itself in the mission of the Evangelical Lutheran Church of Australia (ELCA). This synod, comprising approximately the other half of the Lutheran membership of Australia, had been working on the Rooke-Siassi Islands since 1936 (see ch 7).

90

In 1959, the UELCA made its first official contacts with the HKBP, one of the Batak churches of Indonesia. [157] As the Australian Lutheran church has developed its scholarship program for Papua New Guinean and Indonesian students, the opportunity for more contact and closer understanding between members of the ELC-PNG and of the Batak churches has opened up.

Mergers of Lutheran synods in Australia could not take place without their effect also being felt by the New Guinean Lutheran Church. This has happened on two occasions in particular. The first was the formation of the UELCA in 1921, when, as already shown, the critical years of mission and church in New Guinea under a different government began. The second occurred in 1966, when the two synods, ELCA and UELCA, united to become the Lutheran Church of Australia (LCA).

The fact that these two synods had previously been engaged in two different mission programs had led to New Guinean people being divided in their church allegiance in their own country, some for a period of over forty years. [158] In this situation of support and division, the Lutheran Church in Papua New Guinea provided for its partner in Australia, the LCA, a valuable exercise in church co-operation. And this was done in a way which upheld and treated in all seriousness the confessional tradition of the original overseas supporting churches and the confessing faith which had brought about such tremendous expansion in the history of the Lutheran Church in New Guinea.

Discussions in New Guinea from 1963 onwards between members of the Lutheran churches and missionaries of the overseas supporting partners resulted in *A Statement of Faith* being presented to the church in 1972. Whether this document can validly be called a New Guinean statement can be left as a debatable question. What did occur was a significant exercise in confession of the faith together, as a beginning to a broader witnessing together of the faith and of the universal church in this part of the globe, and as an exercise for the New Guinean church's mission in the future. The LCA's centenary project of presenting ELC-PNG with Luther's *Large Catechism* in Pidgin is another token of thankfulness for this partnership in the faith.

Since 1981, the Lutheran Church of Finland has also contributed missionaries for the work in association with ELC-PNG. These personnel have been supplied by the Lutheran Evangelical Association of Finland through the Board for Overseas Mission and Church Co-operation of the LCA. Originally, the Australian Finnish congregations in the LCA acted as the stimulus for this venture. Four Finnish missionaries have so far shared the love of Christ with ELC-PNG in this way. In this program, the Lutheran Church of Australia has welcomed the opportunity to provide some orientation and language study in English, as it also does for missionaries from Neuendettelsau and the North Elbian Mission Centre before they enter Papua New Guinea.

Finally, perhaps the most significant development in church co-operation in recent years began in 1979, when ELC-PNG made its decision to engage in an overseas mission program of its own in Australia. Pastor Nawon Mellombo of Biliau Circuit in the Madang District was commissioned on March 11, 1979 for a ministry among the Wujal Wujal Aboriginal community near Cooktown in northern Queensland. He was succeeded in this work by Pastor Aldal Wagim in 1984. In a remarkable way, the Papua New Guinean church has traced the path of Johann Flierl in reverse, helping the Australian church with a task which he left unfinished in 1885, and using mission insights with Aboriginal people which the Australian church as a Western church needs.

However, there is a consideration which goes beyond this being simply a partnership in the faith with Aborigines. The presence of ELC-PNG in Australia becomes an invitation — and, indeed, a test — to leaders and members of the LCA to examine their own Western church in the light of the spiritual and theological insights which a century of the church in Papua New Guinea offers. Whether the Lutheran Church of Australia has the maturity — and, indeed, the humility — to do this, is a question which the future will answer.

Endnotes

[1] The first overseas traveller, Dr Otto Finsch, named the inlet Deutschlandhafen; later, it was renamed Finschhafen in honour of the famous South Sea explorer.

[2] Alerted by reported German colonial interests in New Guinea, Queensland had already annexed that territory in 1883. Encouraged by Australian gold miners and traders, supported also by missionaries of the London Mission Society, England on November 4, 1884 declared this territory its Protectorate; this was less than a month before the Germans raised their flag at Finschhafen on November 27, 1884. In 1888 the southern part became an English Crown Colony.

[3] The best organized trading venture in this region was that of Emma Forsayth ('Queen Emma') and her trading partner Thomas Farrell; both, however, were not linked to Germany.

[4] New Guinea, geographically, is the largest island in the world apart from Greenland. That is why it is often referred to as mainland, in contrast to the islands of Melanesia.

[5] Known today as Rooke Island, the main isle of the Siassi Islands group, between the mainland and New Britain.

[6] Ralf M. Wiltgen, *The Foundation of the Roman Catholic Church in Oceania, 1825 to 1850* (Canberra: Australian National University Press, 1979), 474-487.

[7] Reiner Jaspers, *Die Missionarische Erschliessung Ozeaniens* (Muenster: Aschendorff, 1972), 255, 279.

[8] John Garrett, *To Live among the Stars.* Christian origins in Oceania (Geneva/Suva: World Council of Churches, 1982), 233-236.

[9] Details by Reiner Jaspers, 'Kolonialismus und Missions-taetigkeit' in H. Waldenfels, ed., ... *denn ich bin bei euch* (Glazik-Willeke-Festschrift), Zurich/Cologne: Benziger, 1978), 169-182.

[10] In 1888 its name was amended to: 'Society for Home and Foreign Mission'.

[11] Georg Pilhofer, *Geschichte des Neuendettelsauer Missionshauses* (Neuendettelsau: Freimund Verlag, 1967), 14.

[12] Johann Flierl, *Fuehrungen Gottes* (Neuendettelsau: Verlag des Missionshauses 1899), 17.

[13] Johann Flierl, *Gedenkblatt der Neuendettelsauer Heidenmission in Queensland und New Guinea* (Tanunda: Auricht's Printing Office, 1909. Neuendettelsau: Verlag des Missionshauses, 1910), 6.

[14] Letter (undated) sent from Bethesda sometime in May 1885 (Neuendettelsau Archives). Reprinted with some omissions in *Kirchliche Mitteilungen*, 10/1885.

[15] Both replies are likewise printed in *Kirchliche Mitteilungen*, 10/1885.

[16] *Ibid*.

[17] This beginning proved very promising. Work among the Aborigines is still carried on today as the Hope Vale Mission of the Lutheran Church of Australia. See also ch 9.

[18] Letter of July 26, 1886 in *Kirchliche Mitteilungen*, 7/1886. Preceding difficulties were explained away by delays in mail and misunderstandings in the correspondence between Australia and Berlin.

[19] J. Flierl, *Gedenkblatt*, 23.

[20] W. Flierl lists the helpers by name in the way they were remembered by the older people of Simbang, in the Kate Church History *Miti Fua Ngeing Ewec* (Madang: Lutheran Mission Press, 1962), 7 (hereafter cited as: Kate Church History).

[21] Letter of April 4, 1891 in *Kirchliche Mitteilungen*, 7/1891.

[22] Quoted by Georg Pilhofer, *Geschichte der Neuendettelsauer Mission in Neuguinea*, 3 vols. (Neuendettelsau: Freimund Verlag, 1961-63), vol. I, 108 (hereafter cited as: G. Pilhofer, volume and page number).

[23] The station school in Simbang remained unused for three years. Kate Church History, 14.

[24] Quoted by G. Pilhofer I, 104.

[25] J. Flierl, *Gedenkblatt*, 29. The report makes it clear that these were not schoolchildren, but rather young men who dared to undergo the experiment of the new.

[26] In the beginning these mountain people were called Kai; later, Kate = forest-people.

[27] The highest peak being a little over 900 metres above sea level. The mountain was named by the Germans for its appearance from the north-east coast.

[28] Today the Pidgin term *Bikman* is preferred to 'chieftain'. In many local languages, the corresponding words tend to speak simply of an important (big) man. In this chapter, however, the traditional title 'chieftain' is retained.

[29] For the names of German and Australian mission staff in Finschhafen, see the appendix. The Kate Church History, and E.A. Jericho, *Seedtime and Harvest in New Guinea* (Adelaide: UELCA New Guinea Mission Board, n.d.), 79-157, have almost identical name-lists.

[30] For details see ch 18. It is still confusing that, in addition to the official name Finschhafen, every single small settlement has its own local name. See map on p 584. Today Finschhafen covers an area of about 40 km along the coast and about 10 km inland, with a total of not more than approximately 5000 people.

[31] A village named Taemi (Taminugidu), a settlement of Tami people on the mainland. The name Deinzerhoeh (Deinzerhill) was given *in memoriam* of the late Mission Inspector Johannes Deinzer of Neuendettelsau.

[32] Then known as Cape Arkona, sited on a cliff above the sea, about half-way between Finschhafen and Lae.

[33] It is striking how restrained are the reports of Pfalzer and Hoh in their letters about the first baptisms. The news in *Kirchliche Mitteilungen* for the friends of the Mission Society was made up in a similar way. Only K. Vetter has reported in more detail, *Kirchliche Mitteilungen*, 11-12/1899.

[34] Basically, this was also true for the co-workers of the Australian Immanuel Synod, if one does not take into account the experiences gained in the mission to the Australian Aborigines (which, however, was quite different in approach).

[35] Unfortunately, he had to leave New Guinea in 1906 because of illness. He died in Australia on his way home to Germany.

[36] K. Vetter, *Die Predigt des Evangeliums in Neuguinea* (Neuendettelsau: Freimund Verlag, 4th edn, 1917), 12.

[37] This word, taken from the Jabem language, stands for Word of God, Gospel, New Life. It was quickly accepted in the Finschhafen area, and later became a kind of trademark of Christianity even in other New Guinea languages. The original meaning of the adjective *miti* is: skilled (in an art), clever, qualified for something, well-done, peaceable.

[38] K. Vetter, letter of Dec. 18, 1905, *Kirchliche Mitteilungen*, 6-7/1906.

[39] J. Flierl, *Gedenkblatt*, 67.

92

[40] Reported by Wesley W. Kigasung, *Change and Development in a Local Church. A History of the Bukawa Church since 1906* (MA Thesis, University of PNG, 1978, unpublished), 75.

[41] The dance festival at Bare (or Dobeo — it is the same locality) was described several times by Keysser, most explicity in *Zake, der Papuahaeuptling* (Neuendettelsau: Freimund Verlag, 3rd edn, 1957), 48-51. More readily available in *Anutu im Papualande* (Neuendettelsau: Freimund Verlag, 1958), 25-27.

[42] Ch. Keysser, *Anutu*, 27.

[43] Detailed report by E. Schnabel in *Kirchliche Mitteilungen*, 10/1905.

[44] G. Pilhofer I, 184.

[45] Geographically today Bluecher Point, about half-way between Heldsbach and Sialum.

[46] Ch. Keysser, *Anutu*, 73.

[47] The beginnings of the congregation's mission (in German: *Gemeindemission*) among the Hube was described by Keysser several times. In addition to the already-quoted book, *Anutu im Papualande*, mention must be made of *Der Prophet von Tobou* (Haringke), (Berlin: Heimatdienstverlag, 1940), and *Gottes Weg ins Hubeland* (about the conversion of the Burum tribes) (Neuendettelsau: Freimund Verlag, 2nd edn, 1949).

[48] Annual Station Report for 1918 (Neuendettelsau Archives).

[49] S. Lehner in *Kirchliche Mitteilungen*, 12/1909.

[50] K. Panzer, Report dated 6.3.1921 (Neuendettelsau Archives).

[51] Sio is about a day's journey north-west of Sialum; formerly also called Dorfinsel (Village Island) because the original settlement of the Sio people was on a small island off the coast.

[52] *Neuendettelsauer Missionsblatt*, 8/1920.

[53] Hermann Detzner, *Vier Jahre unter Kannibalen* (Berlin: A. Scherl, 1920).

[54] Details in the autobiography by Ch. Keysser, *Das bin bloss ich* (Neuendettelsau: Freimund Verlag, 1966), 120.

[55] Missionary Mailaender got a letter of Flierl's through from Zaka across the border to Papua (British New Guinea) to his nearest Australian missionary colleague, Rev. C. King in Ambasi, hoping that it would find its way to Pastor F.O. Theile in Bethania near Brisbane. This letter never arrived at Theile's; however, a request from King to help the isolated Lutheran missionaries with food and medicines was received (Circular O. Theile, dated Sept. 12, 1929, Neuendettelsau Archives).

[56] E.A. Jericho quotes the pertinent paragraphs of the Versailles Peace Treaty in *Seedtime*, 25-26.

[57] G. Pilhofer II, 27.

[58] Up to 1930, the American Lutheran Church (then still the Iowa Synod) sent a total of 21 missionary personnel to New Guinea, among them seven women and seven ordained missionaries. The much smaller Australian Lutheran church body (UELCA) committed itself even more vigorously: by 1921 there were 17 missionary personnel in service in New Guinea; in the years 1921-1930 eleven more were added.

[59] Apparently Protestant churches of British origin in Australia were meant. See letter of Dr F. Richter to Neuendettelsau, dated April 23, 1921 (Neuendettelsau Archives).

[60] This merger of two groups of Lutheran synods, under the leadership of the Immanuel Synod, into the United Evangelical Lutheran Church in Australia (UELCA) was accomplished in the spring of 1921, just in time to take responsibility for the orphaned missions in New Guinea.

[61] For details of the financial side of this reorganization, see ch 18.

[62] The Australian government confirmed this new legal situation in a letter to Director F.O. Theile. G. Pilhofer II, 104, quotes a circular of Theile dated February 25,1927.

[63] Minutes of the Conference of Representatives, held in Brisbane, May 15, 1929 (Neuendettelsau Archives). According to the decisions of that conference, the Aboriginal Mission at Hope Vale (North Queensland) also was part of the Lutheran Mission of New Guinea, being an 'Australian sphere of interest'. The exact division of working areas in New Guinea could not be resolved at the Brisbane Conference. It was worked out later on recommendations of the Field Conference at a smaller Board Representatives' meeting in January 1930, also held in Brisbane. This question of working areas, however, was never resolved satisfactorily (for details see ch 4). The Field Inspector (for both areas) was to be S. Lehner; the President of the Finschhafen District was W. Flierl, the President of the Finisterre District G. Hueter.

[64] In this merger of three American Lutheran Synods in 1930, the partner in New Guinea, the Iowa Synod, was also absorbed.

[65] Mission Director Eppelein commented on the results of the Columbus Conference in the *Neuendettelsauer Missionsblatt* 9/1932, p 66, under the heading 'Nun danket alle Gott'. Much less enthusiastic is the official note of the American Lutheran Church, sent to Neuendettelsau, dated August 30, 1932 (*ibid*, 74-75).

[66] In earlier literature those New Guinean missionaries are often referred to as 'assistants' (German: *Gehilfen*), in contrast to the ordained European missionaries.

[67] The simultaneous development of mission work in all coastal congregations, both in the Jabem- and Kate- speaking areas, from Zaka to Sialum, makes it necessary to ignore the exact chronological order of progress in favour of a smooth presentation.

[68] F. Bayer, Annual Report 1920, *Neuendettelsauer Missionsblatt*, 9/1921.

[69] F. Mailaender, Annual Report 1922 (Neuendettelsau Archives).

[70] F. Oertel, Annual Report 1921 (Neuendettelsau Archives).

[71] Gapenuo Ngizaki had his reminiscences written down and later translated into German by Johannes Flierl, *Braune Fackeltraeger: Erfahrungen und Bewahrungen, 1923-1963* (Neuendettelsau: mimeographed, n.d.), a very worthwhile source for New Guinean church history of the early years.

[72] Qembung was started as a mission station by E. Schnabel only in 1920; however, it carries the tradition of the historic first mission station of Simbang. It was abandoned as a mission station after World War II. Its congregational area is the lower Mape Valley, its congregational centre today is Suqang, about one hour's walk from Simbang, Flierl's historic landing site.

[73] Actually, it was thought that the Bukawa congregation had made these mountains their mission field. First attempts had indeed been made when the call came in 1917 to begin the Azera work. The Qembung congregation, though much farther away, finally accepted the work in the Rawlinson Mountains, and pressed on past the Adler (Busa) River region as far as the Erap River, with great sacrifices by teachers and evangelists.

[74] Firiepa and Akikepe are two of the very few New Guinean pioneers who in handwritten memoirs reflected on the experiences of their mission work: *Geschichte und Gemeindeerfahrungen des Pastors und Lehrers Filiepac* (tr. from Kate by Hans Wagner), and *Bericht von Pastor Edo Akikepe* (tr. from Kate by Hans Wagner). Both manuscripts are in the Neuendettelsau Archives.

[75] Later Ulap became a mission station.

[76] A. Metzner, Report about the Ulap mission work in Wantoat (Mimeographed, 1937. Neuendettelsau Archives). G. Pilhofer, II, 148 quotes an un-named missionary who is said to have sarcastically remarked: 'I wish we had (more) such congregations who find it necessary to fight over mission areas'!

[77] In early German literature, the people of the area are referred to as *Rock* Papuas — skirt people — because of the grass skirts men and women alike used to wear. 'Kukukuku' is a rather derogatory name given to them by outsiders. Experts advise against its use; however, a better alternative to cover the whole populace of the area has not yet been found.

[78] An example is the touching story of Jakabonga of Kuluntufu. Keysser was advised by the Sattelberg congregation to delay his baptism until Jakabonga had the consent of his Hube community. Ch. Keysser, *Anutu*, 133-135.

[79] On Keysser's missionary approach, see above pp 45,46. His work and experiences in the Sattelberg and Hube area have been described in many smaller pamphlets and in two larger books: *Eine Papua-Gemeinde* (Neuendettelsau: Freimund Verlag 2nd edn, 1950); in English: *A People Reborn* (Pasadena: Wm Carey Library, 1980), and *Anutu im Papualande* (see note 41). A bibliography of Keysser is found in *Bayerisches Missions-Jahrbuch* 1952, 111-121. For an interpretation of his theological position, see Herwig Wagner, 'Die geistliche Heimat von Christian Keysser', in the Gensichen Festschrift, *Fides pro Mundi Vita* (Guetersloh: Verlagshaus G. Mohn, 1980), 119-132.

[80] K. Steck's addresses to the Field Conference were printed in a summarized form in *Neuendettelsauer Missionsblatt*, 2-8/1922. See also Hanfried Fontius, *Mission — Gemeinde — Kirche* (Erlangen: Verlag Evang. Luth. Mission, 1975), 72-75, and G. Pilhofer, II, 30-42.

[81] J. Flierl, *Die volkstuemliche Missionsarbeit im Sinn und Geist unserer lutherischen Kirche* (Typescript, Neuendettelsau Archives). A surprisingly-short summary of this long essay is given by the author in *Wunder der goettlichen Gnade* (Tanunda: Auricht's Printing Office, 1931), 272-277. A somewhat different emphasis is given in the English edition, *Christ in New Guinea* (Tanunda: Auricht's Printing Office, 1932), 135, and in Ch. Keysser, *Einheit und Gemeinsamkeit unseres Missionswerkes* (Typescript, Neuendettelsau Archives).

[82] In Kate: *Songang*; in Jabem: *Gejobwaga* ; originally: the shepherd, the one who cares and supervises and bears responsibility.

[83] G. Bamler, *Gedanken und Vorschlaege zu einer Gemeindeordnung, zur Hauptkonferenz*, 1906; H. Zahn, Annual Report 1910; Ch. Keysser, Annual Report Sattelberg, 1911; J. Ruppert, Annual Report Pola, 1914; H. Boettger, Annual Report Logaweng, 1915 (Neuendettelsau Archives).

[84] In German mission reports, and then also in literature, the expression *Gehilfen* (helpers) is frequently used for 'elders'. This term lends itself to a subordinate interpretation, though the missionaries knew very well how much they actually relied on the village elders. It seems that the early terminology differs significantly from the importance the elders were given by both villagers and European missionaries. Today the term *Gehilfen* has become obsolete.

[85] See also H. Fontius, *Mission*, 50.

[86] There is no exact written form available of the 'Sattelberg Works-and-Self-Improvement Order'. Ch. Keysser in various publications described and commented on it: *Eine Papuagemeinde*, 206-211 (*Reborn*, 185-189). Also in *Allgemeine*

Missionszeitschrift 1913, Supplement 2. The most detailed account is given in his unpublished essays *Die Seele der Papua-Christen* (Neuendettelsau: typescript, n.d.), vol. II/1, 90-92 (Neuendettelsau Archives).

[87] *Ibid*, 88.

[88] We must, however, realize that the *kalabus* (prison) was only a simple bamboo structure in the village, from which any youngster could have escaped. It is said that the door of the *kalabus* was not even locked. The pronounced punishment as such was shameful enough.

[89] Ch. Keysser, *ibid:* 'The Order was approved by the German Governor in a letter dater March 16,1911'. However, it was declared void with little formality in a speech by the Australian Capt. Ogilvy, addressed to the Kate Sonangs summoned to Finschhafen in October 1915. Ch. Keysser, *Songangnu* (Neuendettelsau: Freimund Verlag, 1923), 24.

[90] On matters of church discipline, see: L. Flierl, 'Gemeindezucht in Neuguinea' in *Jahrbuch fuer Mission*, 1931, pt. 2, 60-67; Hans Neumeyer, 'Gemeindedienst und Lebensordnung', in *Hilfsbuch der Bayerischen Missionskonferenz 1942*, 53-59; and J. Herrlinger, 'Gemeindedienst an der Gemeinde durch die Gemeinde', op. cit., 77-96. Reports on actions of discipline are found quite frequently in the missionaries' correspondence.

[91] The impact of this type of congregational church discipline was felt for many years afterwards. A spectacular case in more recent times happened at the Kate District Meeting at Tapen in 1961, when the whole Kalasa Circuit was placed under church discipline for a year because of its involvement in a cargo cult. The station missionary at that time declared himself in solidarity with the Kalasa congregation, and allowed his own child to be baptized only after the disciplinary ban for the whole area was lifted. Twice during that year, the neighbouring Sattelberg Circuit sent a delegation to the Kalasa congregations to call them to repentance and to renewal of faith. Here church discipline was practised in a truly evangelical manner.

[92] See expecially ch 13. For the early philosophy of Christian education, see G. Vicedom, 'Struckturwandlungen und Schulfragen in Neuguinea', in *Evangelische Missionszeitschrift* VII (1955), 104-113.

[93] The dispensing of the Sacraments was normally the privilege of the ordained missionaries. In expectional cases, especially-capable elders and teachers were also commissioned for this.

[94] Village chiefs with the authority to settle lesser disputes.

[95] The contract year was identical with the calendar year — hence the old Pidgin expression *Krismas* (Christmas) for 'year'.

[96] The story of goldmining in New Guinea was written from a rather romantic perspective by Ion L. Idriess, *Gold-Dust and Ashes* (Sydney: Angus and Robertson, 1933, and many reprints). With an historian's accuracy, Hank Nelson, *Black, White and Gold. Goldmining in Papua New Guinea 1878-1930* (Canberra: ANU Press, 1976).

[97] F. Bayer, 'Wirkungen des Goldes', *Neuendettelsauer Missionsblatt, 10/1928.*

[98] Quoted by G. Pilhofer, II, 119. Such barbaric carrier service ended with the second phase of the gold-mining operation by the New Guinea Gold Co, when primitive gold washing was replaced by organized, machine-operated mining. This was possible only after planes had been put into service. After 1929, all necessary supplies and heavy machinery (which otherwise could not have been brought into the mountains) were flown in.

[99] J. Decker, Deinzerhoeh-Bukawa Report 1938; K. Wacke, Kalasa Report 1935. Both quotations from G. Pilhofer, II, 123-124.

[100] *Ibid.*

[101] J. Flierl, *Report for Government and Missions about the maltreatment of a peaceful population and the illegal recruiting, in company with recruiters in the Hinterland of Finschhafen, by Mr S. Hawkes, W.O., in June and July of this year. Heldsbach, August 4, 1927* (Neuendettelsau Archives). In an especially grave case, the recruiter concerned was sentenced to a term of 18 months in jail.

[102] The reason for this was the adverse case of the German Captain Detzner as described earlier in this chapter. Keysser was accused of having violated his oath of neutrality. Besides, the expulsion of all German missionaries from the former colony was pending at that time.

[103] Literally: The Great Clean-up. For this, see the monograph of L. Flierl, *Eemasang. Die Erneuerungsbewegung in der Gemeinde Sattelberg* (Guetersloh: C. Bertelsmann, 1931).

[104] Private correspondence and interview, September 1971.

[105] S. Lehner (Bukawa), J. Decker (Deinzerhill), H. Boettger (Logaweng), W. Hertle (Sattelberg), W. Zischler (Kalasa), and A. Wagner (Heldsbach). The Finschhafen lay missionaries were A. Obst, L. Behrendorff, K. Kirsch, D. Rohrlach, and E. Wagner.

[106] E. Pietz to Lae, M. Ackermann to Malalo, Dr A. Hoeger to the Finschhafen hospital, and R. Boettcher to the Maneba Supply House. In the Highlands, J. Kuder took over Ogelbeng Station, H. Hannemann Ega, A. Frerichs Raipinka. Only Helbig, as an Australian, was allowed to remain at Asaroka.

[107] Only in 1950 was it possible for the course to be resumed by A. Metzner at Sattelberg with the same people; many had survived the war. For more details, see ch 12.

[108] Adolf Wagner kept a private diary even during the last months of his service in New Guinea. Excerpts have been published by his widow, Thilde Wagner, *Es kommt die Nacht ... Aus dem Tagebuch meines Mannes Missionar Adolf Wagner* (Neuendettelsau: Freimund Verlag, 1964). This source and additional material form the basis of a short biography by Wilhelm Fugmann, *Und ob ich schon wanderte im finstern Tal ... Vom Leben und Sterben zweier Zeugen Jesu Christi [Adolf Wagner and Yot Begbeg]* (Neuendettelsau: Freimund Verlag, 1982). For a critical historian's view, see Hank N. Nelson, 'Loyalties at Sword Point: The Lutheran Missionaries in Wartime New Guinea, 1939-45', *The Australian Journal of Politics and History*, XXIV (August 1978), 199-217. His remarkable last sentence reads: 'And there can only be anguish for Adolph Wagner. Amid conflicting loyalties and reviled by men of two armies he saw a clear track; and he kept on it even when he knew that it would lead to his death.'

[109] After M. Lechner (who had begun the first Jabem pastors' course at Malalo) was interned in 1940, S. Lehner brought the course to an early conclusion. Lehner then prepared three more capable and proven men for ordination in Hopoi/Apo. For details, see ch 12.

[110] J. Flierl, *1885-1910 Gedenkblatt der Neuendettelsauer Mission in Australien und Neuguinea* (Neuendettelsau: Verlag des Missionshauses, 1910), 5. This support in the faith was often referred to by Flierl. See also: *Von einem alten Australier* (J. Flierl), *Ein Ehrendenkmal fuer die Ehrwuerdigen Heimgegangenen Vaeter der Lutherischen Kirche in Australien* (Tanunda: Auricht's Druckerei, 1929), 15.

[111] Biar subsequently remained in North Queensland to help care for the Aboriginal work at Elim which Flierl needed to leave behind when proceeding to New Guinea.

[112] Th. Hebart, *The United Evangelical Lutheran Church in Australia (UELCA)*, English version, edited by J.J. Stolz (North Adelaide: Lutheran Book Depot, 1938), 104.

[113] *Deutsche Kirchen- und Missionszeitung fuer die evangelische-lutherische Kirche Australiens*, (Tanunda, May 31, 1898), 77.

[114] Flierl provided a description of the Neuendettelsau influence, enthusiasm for mission, and family atmosphere at synodical conferences. J. Flierl, *Missions-Vortragsreise durch drei Erdteile* (Selbstverlag des Verfassers, 1911), 5ff. By 1894, the Immanuel Synod had accumulated another mission station. This was the Hermannsburg Aboriginal Station in Central Australia, which it had to support fully.

[115] Correspondence of J. Deinzer to J. Flierl, 1885, in J. Flierl, *Dreissig Jahre Missionsarbeit in Wuesten und Wildnissen* (Neuendettelsau: Verlag des Missionshauses, 1910), 52.

[116] S. Lehner's correspondence reflects a deep pastoral concern to promote love and respect among all the nationalities involved. See, for example, correspondence of S. Lehner to F. Eppelein, August 17, 1932.

[117] Obviously, lay witness was appreciated. Flierl commended Keppler's service, and considered him 'exemplary in his working together with New Guinean people'; see J. Flierl, *Forty Five Years in New Guinea*, transl. W. Wiederaenders (Columbus, Ohio: Lutheran Book Concern), 96. Lehner and others made similar comments in reference to the early lay-workers; see correspondence of S. Lehner to Mission Inspector, February 10, 1905.

[118] See Appendix of Mission personnel.

[119] A sample of such an acknowledgement of donations illustrates how mission interest permeated the everyday life of the church: 'Heathen mission receipts no. 1, 1898. ... from 4 tea meetings, 5 persons at 4s (shillings) each, £1 (pound); from 3 shows, 4 persons at 1s each, 12s; at the cricket club, 3 persons at 5s each 15s; for tobacco not smoked £1-12s; 10 loads of firewood carted without having a drink at 6d (pence) each, 5s; in addition 1s. ... family mission box 3s 4½d' (*Deutsche Kirchen- und Missionszeitung*, May 31, 1898), 78.

[120] This hostility in the Australian community showed itself, among other ways, in the extent to which Lutheran churches were burned down — even as late as 1925, six years after the Peace of Versailles; see Th. Hebart, *UELCA*, 133.

[121] The majority came from Neuendettelsau and Hermannsburg, but Basle, Leipzig, Gossner, Breklum, and other mission societies were also represented. See Th. Hebart, *UELCA*, and A. Brauer, *Under the Southern Cross*, History of Evangelical Lutheran Church of Australia (Adelaide: Lutheran Publishing House, 1956).

[122] See W. Iwan, *Um des Glaubenswillen nach Australien. Eine Episode Deutscher Auswanderung* (Breslau: Verlag des Lutherischen Buchvereins, 1931).

[123] In 1884, while still at the Bethesda field, Johann Flierl and his cousin resigned from the Immanuel Synod for a brief period in protest against what he regarded as a weak stand by the church in its Lutheran confessional witness. See correspondence of J. Flierl to the Mission Board, April 16, 1884.

[124] This was the United German and Scandinavian Lutheran Synod of Queensland.

[125] In a tribute to Theile's work, J. Stolz, President of the UELCA, wrote in 1921: 'What we are especially thankful for is that he has the confidence of the government, who have learned that he is a man to be trusted during a time when mistrust against all of German descent was common.' *Lutheran Herald*, October 26, 1921, 117.

[126] Numerous examples, such as in correspondence of F.O. Theile to L. Kaibel, February 7, 1915; F.O. Theile to Mission Committee Immanuel Synod, August 7, 1915.

[127] Correspondence of F.O. Theile to L. Kaibel, February 4, 1915. A similar situation prevailed again in World War II, when Theile had his house searched for latest correspondence. Correspondence of F.O. Theile to J. Stolz, October 11, 1940.

[128] F.O. Theile, *One Hundred Years of the Lutheran Church in Queensland* (Brisbane: UELCA, 1938), 109.

[129] *Deutsche Kirchen-und Missionszeitung*, December 21, 1915.

[130] Correspondence of F.O. Theile to L. Kaibel, December 23, 1915.

[131] *Ibid.*, December 10, 1915; August 7, 1916. Theile was able to visit W. Flierl and H. Raum. However, permission to see Steck was not granted.

[132] Numerous instances of this attitude appear in correspondence; for example, see J. Flierl to Mission Committee South Australia, April 16,1884.

[133] J. Flierl — Open Letter to Children of God of Different Nationalities and Different Confessions, November 10, 1919.

[134] This lengthy appeal to the public was printed in *Church and Mission News*, February 10, 1920.

[135] One of the writings which expressed Flierl's cultural concern was written in his retirement in Germany in 1937, and printed in South Australia under the title: *Observations and Experiences — Is the New Guinea Primitive Race Destined to Perish at the Hands of European Civilization?* (Tanunda: Auricht's Printing Office, 1937). It was significant that Flierl could write of his early years in Australia when he was no longer a German citizen nor a naturalized Australian. He assumed his German citizenship again only in the 1890s. J. Flierl, *Zum Jubilaeum der Lutherischen Mission in New Guinea 1886–1936 III* (Tanunda: Auricht's Printing Office, 1936), 20. And yet, in 1929 he published a booklet under the anonym 'By an old Australian': (*Ein Ehrendenkmal*); the witness is that of St Paul, being all things to all men for the sake of the Gospel.

[136] E.A. Jericho, *Seedtime and Harvest* (Adelaide: UELCA Mission Board, n.d.), 35.

[137] *UELCA General Synod Report* 1922, 35.

[138] Correspondence of F.O. Theile to R. Taeuber, December 10, 1924, tells of the Anglican Bishop of New Guinea collecting materials (to be passed on to Canon Hughes in Australia) which aimed to soften the government's attitude to the removal of the missionaries. Also, in the *Lutheran Herald*, November 17, 1924, there is mention of the Anglican Province of Queensland at its regular meeting voting unanimously in favour of this appeal for German missionaries to be readmitted.

[139] *Church and Mission News*, May 31, 1921, 163.

[140] *Lutheran Herald*, October 10, 1921, 95-96.

[141] Correspondence of F.O. Theile to J. Stolz, June 21, 1921. There was evidently doubt in both America and Australia that enough replacement staff could be provided for both missions. Theile reacted to a hesitancy on Dr Richter's part, saying that pastors with Basle Missionary Society background in Australia were strongly in support of the former Rhenish Mission.

[142] *Lutheran Herald*, August 17, 1925, 260.

[143] *Supplement to the Lutheran Herald*, April 7, 1924: Letters from K. Wacke and K. Mailaender, 2-4.

[144] Theile's visits were: September 1921 to July 1922; August 1927 to March 1928; September to December 1930; and July to December 1933.

[145] *Church and Mission News*, May 31, 1921, 163.

[146] Correspondence of S. Lehner to F. Eppelein, November 7, 1931. Lehner, as field director, expressed his sadness that the UELCA had withdrawn from leadership.

[147] Correspondence of F.O. Theile to J. Stolz, February 13, 1933.

[148] *Ibid.*, January 13 and 14, 1933. Theile, in a quandary about his own position, felt reassured when he received payment for part of his salary from the ALC. Similarly, in correspondence with Eppelein, November 21, 1932, he found it helpful to know that he was given authority to send Australian personnel directly to the field.

[149] F.O. Theile, *Lutheran Mission Madang, a Supplementary Report on My Visit to the Mission Field in the Year 1934*, 1-2. It was also a legal requirement for two-thirds of all shareholders to be British subjects, a condition which avoided land problems in World War II. See also correspondence of F.O. Theile to J. Stolz, September 11, 1939.

[150] Correspondence of F.O. Theile to J. Stolz, January 14, 1933.

[151] *Ibid.*, August 3, 1932.

[152] *Ibid.*, January 3, 1933.

[153] *Ibid.*, an accompanying letter.

[154] In 1934 the Neuendettelsau Society for Home and Foreign Mission (*Gesellschaft fuer Innere und Aeussere Mission Neuendettelsau*) declared Theile an honorary member, and in 1939 Wartburg Seminary of the ALC conferred on him the degree of Doctor of Divinity In recognition of his services.

[155] *Report of Ninth General Synod UELCA, 1947*, 111. In 1945, the UELCA had again promised support 'to the best of our abilities without a share in the control' (*General Synod Report*, 1945, 29).

[156] By 1972 there were 79 lay missionaries and 24 ordained from the merged church, approximately one-third of the total staff (*LCA General Synod Report, 1972*, 250).

[157] The Revd T. Sihombing, General Secretary of the Huria Kristen Batak Protestan, accepted an invitation as an official visitor to the 1959 General Synod of the UELCA.

[158] Even though merger in Australia had taken place in 1966, Siassi became a district of ELC-PNG only on May 6, 1977; the Menyamya congregation joined the Jabem District on October 27, 1974.

Chapter 3

Beginnings at Madang

The Rhenish Mission

by Hermann Reiner

Preparations

In 1884, the Imperial German Government laid claim to the northern part of Papua New Guinea by raising her flag in various harbours of the country. Australia also claimed this territory, and it was not until April 6, 1886 that an agreement was signed in London. Germany was allocated the territory north of the line of demarcation which divided the areas which later came to be called Papua and the Territory of New Guinea prior to independence in 1975. The newly-established German colony included the north-eastern third of the island, then known as Kaiser-Wilhelmsland, and the islands of the Bismarck Archipelago.

The Imperial German Government conferred territorial rights on the New Guinea Company (NGC), which had been founded in 1880. It was entitled 'to exert governmental authority within the territories designated by the German Empire', and 'to practise the exclusive right of appropriating unclaimed land and to make contracts with the natives concerning land and ground entitlements'.[1] This arrangement continued until April 1899, when the German Empire assumed direct authority by installing a government official in the town of Rabaul.

In Germany, the foundation of the new colony prompted both the Neuendettelsau Mission and the Rhenish Mission in Barmen to extend their mission work to that territory. The differing positions of the two institutions at that time vitally influenced the course of their work. The Neuendettelsau Mission, then a newly-founded organization, had not yet been engaged in any mission field of its own. Thus, it was much freer and more flexible in its decisions, and able to concentrate all its efforts on Papua New Guinea right away.

The Rhenish Mission, meanwhile, needed much more time for careful deliberation and cautious planning before it could venture into an additional field of mission. That may explain why the first missionary from Neuendettelsau began his work in Papua New Guinea one year ahead of the first Rhenish representative. Johann Flierl, the pioneer from Neuendettelsau, was at that time a missionary among the Aborigines in Australia. As soon as he heard of the new German acquisition, he sent an overture to Neuendettelsau with his proposals

99

for spreading the Christian faith in Papua New Guinea and promptly received permission to start his work in Finschhafen. The early history of the Rhenish Mission on the northern coast of the island, on the other hand, was much more involved and complex.

In 1885, from October 27 to 29, a special conference was held in Bremen, at which nine leaders of German mission societies participated. (Neuendettelsau was not represented at this conference.) The main issue of their debate, under the chairmanship of former Rhenish Mission Inspector Dr Fabri, was the new situation created by the rising colonial ambitions of the Imperial Government. The delegates considered the introduction of Christianity to the new colonial territories as a vital challenge. A small group of German nationalists, who wanted to restrict the mission work in German colonies to German missionaries only, and to subject its aims to German national interests, was overruled by the moderate majority of the assembly. The final resolution stated that mission work was not a national task, but a universal one transcending national interests. This fundamental position was also endorsed by the representative of the Empire at the conference, Consul Raschdau.

When the Rhenish Mission delegate, Dr Schreiber, reported the results of the conference to headquarters in Barmen, the Board decided 'to introduce a mission program in Papua New Guinea, but to start out in a very cautious manner'. They did not want the new project to affect their mission fields in China, Africa, and — the most promising of all — among the Bataks in Sumatra. After the Board's recommendation was accepted by the Main Assembly on May 12, 1886, numerous contributions for the work in New Guinea began pouring in, although no missionary had yet been sent out. This enthusiastic and generous financial support by friends and congregations was a signal for the Society to go ahead.

Difficult negotiations with the New Guinea Company now began. These were more complex than expected, and it was not until November 25, 1886 — Johann Flierl had already settled in New Guinea — that the Rhenish Mission received the 'General Conditions for the Admission of Evangelical Missionaries in New Guinea'.

According to these conditions, the NGC claimed the right to determine the location of the mission stations and the boundaries of the mission territories. The Rhenish Mission was to take responsibility for its missionaries and assistants, for they would be subject to the laws and regulations of the official authorities. Beyond that, the Rhenish missionaries were expected to 'instruct the natives in every kind of useful knowledge and skill, familiarize them with regular work, and teach them how to farm.' Furthermore, the missionaries were to serve the administration as interpreters in negotiations etc., without receiving any pay for this work. The cost of maintenance of the missionaries and the mission stations was to be met by the Mission Society. The NGC, for its part, instructed its employees to support the missionaries in the pursuit of their task. They committed themselves, as much as was in their power, to offer the missionaries all available facilities regarding transportation, enlistment of labour, purchase of land, and medical care.

While the Neuendettelsau Mission was making good progress in Finschhafen, the Rhenish Mission struggled with difficulties from the very start. The problems and obstacles they encountered were largely due to the political developments in the Madang region, which were taking a course exactly opposite to that in Finschhafen. When the Neuendettelsau missionaries first settled in Finschhafen, they had the advantage of being situated in close proximity to the current German official, von Schleinitz. Under the protection of the colonial administration, they enjoyed access to the administration's transport and communication facilities, as well as personal contact with the authorities. All of that enabled them to secure a firm position for themselves. And just when the people were beginning to become aware of the drawbacks of colonial rule, tropical diseases killed more than half of the Europeans in Finschhafen in 1891, inducing the colonial administration to transfer its main office from malaria-ridden Finschhafen to Stephansort on Astrolabe Bay. This move obviated any development of unrest and tension in the Finschhafen region. The Neuendettelsau missionaries were able to continue their work without being disturbed by the tensions and

100

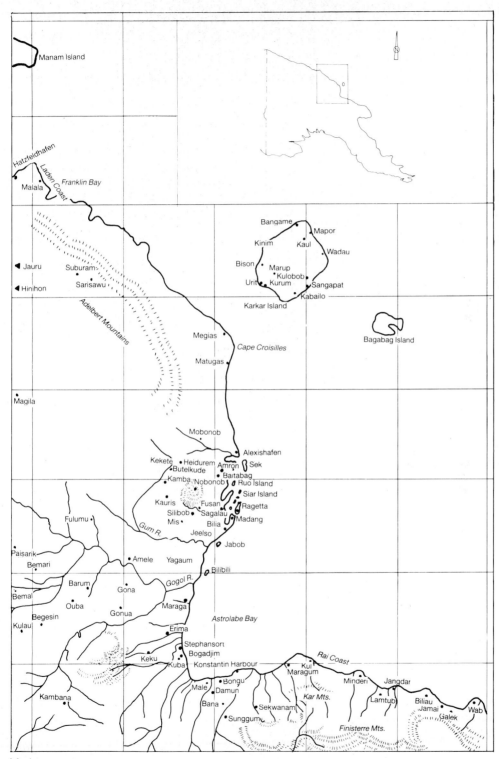

Madang area

problems related to the centres of political and economic power.

The Rhenish Mission, on the other hand, was established at Astrolabe Bay in the Madang region at a time when the area was far from the political centre of the colony. They had a difficult start because of their isolation and the necessity of dealing with inefficient subordinate authorities. Then, with the transfer of the government and business administration of the NGC to Astrolabe Bay, the territory of the Rhenish Mission suddenly became the administrative and commercial centre. That circumstance changed the attitude of the local population. All their resentment against the colonial administration — for abolishing their traditional laws and creating new ones, for depriving them of their land and treating them as inferiors — was now directed also against the missionaries. Because of the similar colour of their skin, they were associated with the unwelcome white intruders — although there are also instances illustrating that the local inhabitants could well distinguish between missionaries and white government officials.

A letter dated May 24, 1909 from the Mission Board in Barmen to its missionaries in New Guinea points to another possible cause of the many setbacks:

> We would like to add another reason ... why your work has not made such good progress as that of our Neuendettelsau brothers ... Unlike them, you were not content to concentrate your work on the established mission stations; again and again attempts were made to venture out into other, more densely populated areas that appeared more promising. The Neuendettelsau missionaries began their work in Simbang under extremely difficult conditions. It was their strategy to wait until they had gained sufficient strength, and the necessary resources, before they dared to advance into other regions to set up new mission stations. They always took care not to jeopardize the position of the already-existing stations by the establishment of new ones. We recommend that in the future ... we follow their example. [3]

It is hard to tell whether this reproof is justified or not. Actually, the Rhenish missionaries always tried to assign two missionaries to each station. But often these plans were upset by the high toll demanded by diseases. Many missionaries died or had to

return to Germany prematurely (more of that later).

It may well be true, though, that the Rhenish missionaries were working under the pressure of producing spectacular results similar to those achieved among the Bataks on Sumatra. Because of that, they were continually on the lookout for more promising areas; yet, all their hopeful endeavours turned out to be of no avail. Interestingly enough, the home Board often had encouraged that strategy, rather than opposing it.

The Beginnings

Unlike Neuendettelsau, the Rhenish Mission had a number of experienced missionaries at its disposal. So, Barmen decided to send out two proficient missionaries to New Guinea: Wilhelm Thomas and Friedrich Eich. They had both been born in 1843, and had done their studies together at Barmen, but they had not seen each other since their time together at the seminary. After years of mission work in Nias (Indonesia), and German South-West Africa (Namibia) respectively, they were now in their mid-forties. Thomas was not actually called to be a missionary in New Guinea. But since he was due for furlough from his field in Indonesia, the Board asked him to detour to New Guinea on his way home to Germany, and to assist Eich in setting up the first Rhenish Mission station. (Eich was to remain on in New Guinea, undertaking the actual work with younger graduates from the seminary who were soon to follow.) Due to better travel connections, Thomas was the first Rhenish missionary to set foot on New Guinea, arriving on February 17, 1887. Eich was somewhat delayed, leaving London only in mid-February, and arriving in Finschhafen on April 16, 1887.

Thomas became weary of the long wait, and before Eich's arrival went on to Astrolabe Bay. As Johann Flierl had already established the mission station of Simbang in Finschhafen, Thomas wanted to look for another field of work for the Rhenish Mission. He turned his attention to the region of Astrolabe Bay, 200 km to the north. Sixteen years before, this region had been explored by the brillant Russian scientist, N. Mikloucho-Maclay. The harbour where he disembarked from the ship he named Port Constantine after a Russian prince; from there

Missionary Wilhelm Thomas.

Missionary Friedrich Eich.

he pushed inland until he reached the Finisterre Range. Maclay stayed in the region for about 15 months, and in 1876 he returned for another year. The Rai Coast, where he stayed the second time, is a constant reminder of the explorer, for 'Rai' is the local version of his name. The first missionaries attributed their initial success in establishing good relationships with the local people to the 'excellent impression' which the first white visitor, Maclay, had made. [4]

By this time the NGC had set up two trading posts on the north coast of New Guinea: the one at Hatzfeldhafen, [5] the other on Astrolabe Bay, at Port Constantine (renamed Konstantinhafen by

Bogadjim beach, first settlement of Rhenish Mission.

the Germans). Here Thomas arrived on March 16, 1887. As a temporary housing arrangement, the local jail was made available, a small desolate room without partitions. He wrote about it:

> The small house, truly jail-like, had two small windows with grille bars. A piece of an old coffee sack served not only as a curtain against the sun, but also as protection against the rain, alternating from one window to the other. Otherwise, the wind would have driven the rain through the whole jail. Normally, jails do not grant their inmates a free view of the outside. In my jail, however, through the cracks of the shrunken boards, I was able to look in all directions. The rain poured inside to such an extent that I had to take my clothes off the nail quickly. But apart from that, I felt quite at home in my peculiar dwelling place. [6]

Thomas did not remain idle while waiting for Eich's arrival. He wandered through the coastal region of Astrolabe Bay, and visited the villages of Bongu and Bogadjim (Bogatim). He also went to the small island of Bilibili, located at the outlet of the Gogol River, and to Friedrich-Wilhelmshafen (later named Madang). His aim and hope: a suitable location for the first mission station.

On May 13, 1887, Thomas could finally welcome Friedrich Eich. Together, they immediately travelled on the same boat to Hatzfeldhafen to investigate the possibility of locating a second mission station there. From his excursions, Thomas had gained the impression that the hinterland of Astrolabe Bay was very sparsely populated, and he wanted to start the mission in a more densely settled area.

In Hatzfeldhafen the two missionaries had the good fortune to be invited to join a scholarly expedition led by C. Schrader up the Sepik River (then still known as Kaiserin-Auguste River). Two observations made on that expedition from June 22 to July 14 confirmed the two missionaries in their decision to favour a site near Hatzfeldhafen as the location of their first mission station. First, they had noticed that there were many people living along the river; and secondly, they saw that the river would serve as a convenient waterway to carry them further inland. However, the uncooperative attitude of the local official of the NGC (at that time still wielding governmental authority) ultimately forced them to give up their plan for Hatzfeldhafen.

The said local officer of the NGC, Mr Kubary, a former ornithologist, was a Pole of Hungarian origin; as a refugee, he had entered the services of the NGC, and was now a faithful administrator of his employer's interests. And the NGC was viewing the activities of the Mission with great suspicion. Undoubtedly, they were afraid that the presence of the missionaries might hinder them in the exploitation of the local population. A company representative is reported to have stated: 'We do not want to have the missions and the missionaries around here, because they act as our conscience, and are therefore entirely unwelcome and a great nuisance.' [7]

Kubary, under the threat of a fine of up to 1000 Marks, forbade the missionaries to settle at any site that he had not first brought under his control. Possibly Kubary had already thought of giving the territory around Hatzfeldhafen to the Catholic Mission (who later on were able to establish themselves there). In any case, his decision meant that the Rhenish Mission had to be satisfied with Astrolabe Bay. The Annual Field Conference reported to Barmen in 1889:

> The results of the negotiations with the NGC and the local representative have proven ... that the Rhenish Mission in New Guinea must be content, for the time being, with the Astrolabe Bay region. As for the establishment of mission stations in Hatzfeldhafen territory, the Rhenish Mission could not see any prospect at the moment of receiving any concession there. [8]

Thus, the founding of the first mission station was delayed, and Thomas had no chance to witness the first modest success. After a trip to the Bismarck Archipelago, where he and Eich managed to purchase the first small boat for the Rhenish Mission, Thomas suddenly went down with a severe fever. He was rushed to Cooktown, Australia for medical treatment, and eventually was well enough to continue his trip back to Germany. After his well-deserved furlough, he returned to his field in Nyasaland, where he worked until his death in 1900.

For the time being, Eich was alone. After difficult negotiations with Kubary, he finally succeeded in securing a piece of land for the first mission station near the village of Bogadjim. Colonial law did not permit him to purchase the site himself, as only the NGC was

Bogadjim village.

authorized to buy land from the New Guineans. The NGC, therefore, acquired a four-hectare piece of land in exchange for three hatchets, three knives, and a packet of tobacco, and in turn sold it to Eich for a commission of 120 Marks. The first station of the Rhenish Mission in New Guinea was thus founded when Eich moved to Bogajim on November 8, 1887. [9]

As time went on, relations with Kubary improved; he became friendly and more positive in his attitude when he realized that his interests were not being infringed. For the setting up of the mission station, he put the transportation facilities of the NGC at Eich's disposal, and later assisted the Rhenish missionaries in recruiting workers.

The first mission house was very simple: level with the ground, constructed of bush material and timber planks. But at least Eich was in the position to welcome the newly-arriving Rhenish missionaries in his own house and on his proper grounds. The two new missionaries, Gustav Bergmann and Wilhelm Scheidt, arrived on January 8, 1888. Eich was again suffering from a serious attack of malaria at the time, and was barely able to make it down to the shore to meet the newcomers.

The Bogadjim people, after whom the station was named, lived close together in four villages. According to the first statistics, there were altogether about 175 houses. In spite of the fact that the area was obviously well populated, the three missionaries aimed to establish a second mission station as soon as possible.

One of their plans — to expand in the direction of the Solomon Islands — had to be abandoned because of insufficient transport facilities. However, in 1889 and 1890, two island stations were founded: one on Siar, an island in the harbour of Madang, the other on Dampier Island (today known as Karkar). As soon as sufficient number of missionaries was available, two smaller stations could be added: Ragetta, which was affiliated with Siar, and could be reached by rowboat in about 30 minutes; and Bongu, which was associated with Bogadjim village, located 10 km away on the other side of Konstantin Harbour.

Until 1904, these five stations were the bases from which the Rhenish Mission pursued its work — even though it was very hard at times to keep all of them going. From the beginning, the work had suffered from the frequent turnover of personnel, caused by serious illnesses and death. Even the arrival of a mission doctor from Germany, Dr Wilhelm Frobenius, who was stationed on Siar and provided medical care from 1890 to 1900, could not reverse this development.

105

A conference report of 1904, sent to the home Board, itemizes a list of events to explain why so little progress could be made:

1894 Helmich comes; Kunze leaves.
1895 the Bergmanns and Hanke come; Barkemeyer is killed in an accident.
1896 Holzapfel comes; Dr Frobenius leaves.
1898 the Kunzes and Frobenius come; the Bergmanns and Hoffmann travel home.
1900 the Bergmanns and Hoffmann come back; the Kunzes have left, and Frobenius is about to leave.
1901 Nebe and Koolen take up their work; after 6 weeks Nebe dies of malaria; Koolen becomes seriously ill and has to leave the country after 5 months.
1903 Brother Weber comes; Brother Ostermann goes home.
1904 the Helmichs come; the Bergmanns retire. [10]

A number of casualties are not even mentioned in this list: The death of Herman Wackernagel by drowning in the Bubui River at Finschhafen on December 17, 1888; the death of Mrs Eich on October 4, 1889; the death of Missionary Klaus on November 27, 1890; and the murders of Scheidt and Boesch near Malala in 1891. Mrs Boesch died in October 1891, Mrs Kunze on April 24, 1892, Missionary Arff on July 4, 1893, and Mrs Hanke in 1900. The phrase 'going home' used in connection with Heinrich Ostermann refers to his eternal home; he died of black-water fever on January 21, 1904. In the same way, the 'retirement' of Brother Bergmann refers to his death (April 26, 1904 in Sydney).

The Murder Incident of Malala

As the chronicle in the previous paragraph indicates, hardly any other mission society had to pay such a high blood tribute in Papua New Guinea as did the Rhenish Mission. In a church history such as this one, the most painful incidents call for a more detailed description.

The extension in the direction of the Sepik River (Hatzfeldhafen), which the Mission had planned several times, was held up by the negative attitude of the NGC. When the difficulties were cleared away at last, an attempt was made in 1891 to set up a new mission station. This was not in Hatzfeldhafen, however, where the NGC had an official agency, but in Malala (Franklin Bay), which was somewhat

closer to Astrolabe Bay. On his visit there a year earlier, Scheidt had discovered a suitable site — and what he believed to be friendly inhabitants.

Together with the young missionary Friedrich Boesch, Scheidt boarded a NGC steamer heading north, and arrived at the proposed location in Malala near Hatzfeldhafen on May 18, 1891.

The people appeared to be friendly when they met the two missionaries, and Scheidt had no misgivings when he went back to Hatzfeldhafen to pick up some construction material (mainly corrugated iron sheets). He returned to Malala on May 27. An official of the NGC, von Moisy, and 11 New Guinean oarsmen and workers were with him. [11] As the boat was

Martyr-Missionary Wilhelm Scheidt.

Martyr-Missionary Friedrich Boesch.

about to beach, a group of men jumped toward the boat as if to help pull it ashore. All of a sudden, spears were flying through the air. Scheidt and von Moisy were hit, and then the entire boat-crew was massacred. A mere two of the hired workers, although injured, managed to escape to Hatzfeldhafen to spread the news of what had happened. However, no one has ever found out what fate befell Boesch and his five workers. Most likely they were murdered soon after Scheidt had gone to Hatzfeldhafen, sometime between May 22 and 26. [12] Perhaps the second massacre was planned and executed to cover up the first one, because the people obviously had not expected Scheidt to return so soon and with so many men.

The question that has puzzled many people is: What instigated the people to commit these murders? Kriele's theory, [13] suggesting that the people merely wanted to have the iron tools and the other belongings of the two white men, is not convincing. Kunze may be closer to the truth when he assumes that the people of Malala believed that Scheidt and Boesch were planters who were going to set up a plantation. [14] The local people may well have been afraid that this would lead to the same kind of restrictions and deprivations at their settlement as the establishment of the plantations in Hatzfeldhafen had brought to the residents there. Hostile encounters between settlers and locals in the Hatzfeldhafen area three years earlier had caused the colonial authorities to inflict severe punishment on the population. [15]

The bitterness and tensions created in connection with the expropriation of land also help to justify Kunze's theory. Right from the beginning, the NGC's strategy of land appropriation failed to recognize the people's customary understanding with regard to property. The privilege conferred upon the NGC by the German government 'to appropriate unclaimed land' was obviously based on the assumption that in New Guinea there was such a thing as 'unclaimed' or unused land — a grave misconception! The uncultivated land (grassland as well as forests) formed the hunting and grazing regions of the respective tribes, and was an integral part of the local economy. When the colonial authorities took over this seemingly-unclaimed land, they actually were expropriating. 'Every inch of soil,

each useful tree in the forest, each fish in the streams has its proprietor.' [16]

Kunze on Karkar was the first missionary to receive news of the tragic event at Malala. Some men reported to him: 'The missionaries Scheidt and Boesch are dead! The villagers of Laden killed them with spears.' When Kunze learnt that this news came from the village of Kurum, which had trade connections with Malala, he sent them a message asking them to come to see him at the mission station. After about six days, several people from Kurum arrived, but Kunze still did not get any further details of the affair beyond the information that 15 workers had also been killed. Kunze later reported:

> Anyway, the Kurum villagers appeared less anxious to share information with me than to find out what would happen to the murderers ... I told them: 'I am a friend of Jesus ... We will not beat the inhabitants of Laden'. ... I noticed that at this remark some men of the group were given signals with a wink of the eye. [17]

Obviously, these were men from Malala who wanted to find out what punishment awaited them.

However, the offenders did not go unpunished, as Kunze had wished. A steamer of the NGC shortly thereafter brought in a unit of German colonial troops, and they burnt the village of the culprits to the ground. Later, Kunze established contact with the Malalas through the Kurum people in order to show them that they did not have to fear any blood revenge from the missionaries. He used the occasion to refer them to Jesus, the peacemaker. The people from Laden must have felt greatly relieved at that:

> As I finished speaking, the Malalas fetched coloured bushes which grew there and planted them in the ground before my eyes. We sat around in a circle holding each other by the wrists. Then I broke off some twigs from the bushes according to the number of Malala villages that were represented. I handed the twigs to the villagers so that, upon their return home, they could plant them in the ground as a confirmation of our peace treaty ...

It was not possible for Kunze, however, to pursue his plan to bring the Gospel to the Malalas; in 1894 he had to leave Karkar. In the following years, the Malalas as well as the entire region of Hatzfeldhafen became associated with the Catholic Mission. Relations with the Rhenish

Men from Malala.

First settlement at Nobonob.

108

Mission were obviously so impaired through the events that, in spite of Kunze's endeavours, feelings of mistrust and shame among the local population were never completely overcome.

Four Graves on Karkar Island

Karkar Island is another place where Rhenish missionaries in New Guinea displayed exceptionally strong faith and endurance in the face of great suffering and hardship. Here there was a string of tragedies. Eventually the missionaries felt so worn out and disheartened that they had to give up.

The pioneer of the Karkar mission was Georg Kunze. He arrived in New Guinea in December 1888. After language study, he was given the task, together with Klaus and Boesch, to build up a new mission station on Karkar Island. Thanks to the friendliness and cooperation of the village chief, Madom, Kunze acquired a suitable piece of land, located on a hill above the village of Kulobob. But even before the missionaries had finished building the mission stations, the first grave had to be dug. Missionary Klaus died on November 27, 1890, presumably of pneumonia; he had been in New Guinea for just ten months. Then Boesch left Karkar in May 1891 for Malala, and met a violent death there, as described above. Kunze was now alone.

At that time, Karkar was quite isolated, and reefs made the access for shipping very difficult. Kunze lived in this solitude until March 1, 1891, when he was able to celebrate his wedding with his fiancée who had arrived from Germany. Mrs Kunze discovered already on her wedding day what it means to be a pioneer missionary. The mission station in Bogadjim, where the ceremony was held, was like an emergency hospital. Kunze describes the situation as follows:

> On one side lay the Bogadjim Missionary Arff and his young wife, both seriously ill. On the other side, the mission doctor Frobenius, who lived with them. Dr Frobenius was ill with dysentery ... Under these circumstances, we could hardly think of a joyful wedding celebration. Nor was there any such thing as a wedding meal with wedding guests. Who would want to think of such things in the midst of disease and misery! Even the wedding cake, which is part of the simplest wedding, could not be baked; for the care of the sick claimed all our time. [18]

Missionary Georg Kunze.

The happiness of the Kunzes on the solitary island did not last long. After a year, Mrs Kunze caught a fever, became seriously ill, and died on April 24, 1892. Her husband writes about her last hours:

> I saw how the high fever was burning up her body and how she became weaker and frailer, tormented by terrible restlessness. I called to God. However, the longer I struggled, the more certain I became that the Lord had something else in mind for us, different from what we had thought ... I wanted to pray once more for her recovery. She heard me and said: 'Don't hold me back any longer — I am going to the Lord Jesus, I'm going ...' On Saturday evening she said: 'Please write on a piece of paper: "We are afraid, but not in despair!" (2 Cor. 4:8), and hang this verse at the foot of my bed ...' Finally, she bade farewell to me and asked me to give her last greetings to all those in her German motherland that she loved. When she saw that grief was overwhelming me, she said: 'Give me your word that you will reconcile yourself to my death. Will you thank the Lord for it? Please promise that; otherwise I can't be happy.' With the word: 'So, now I will lie down in peace', she prepared herself for her last hour. [19]

Next to the grave of Missionary Klaus, the lonely widower laid his wife to her last rest.

Only nine months later, Kunze raised the third mound there. August Pilkuhn, who had shared the solitude of Karkar for a few months as boatman and lay missionary, died from his first attack of malaria. He had been in the country less than six months.

Kunze was able to train the young missionary Dassel (who arrived in December 1892) for two years before his own health was ruined. In December 1894 he had to leave New Guinea. He returned in December 1898, but after a year his poor health forced him to return to his homeland permanently.

Dassel continued the work on Karkar. However, on June 16, 1895, an unexpected eruption of the volcano on Karkar occurred. The missionaries (Heinrich Helmich was now working with Dassel) ran out of provisions. On top of that, a pox epidemic broke out on the island and drastically reduced the population. For weeks it was not possible for ships to get to Karkar because of the heavy sea. On July 2, Missionary Johann Barkemeyer and his faithful boat-crew finally managed to reach the island. They brought the order to abandon the mission station because the local population also planned to abandon the island. With the smoking volcano in the background and ash-filled air around them, both missionaries preached in the village of Kulobob for a final time. There had never been so many attentive listeners.

Before the departure, yet another terrible misfortune occurred. Barkemeyer went to shoot a pigeon for their meal, but finally had to return to the house without a bird. Tired from the heat, he was dragging the gun behind him, but had forgotten to engage the safety catch. Suddenly a shot went off, and the buckshot pierced the ill-fated man at point-blank range. He died a few hours later in great pain.

Thus, the row of graves on the island was extended by a fourth one. That marked the end of the Karkar mission for the time being.

Mission Approaches

For 16 years up to 1903, the statistics of the Rhenish Mission show no measurable success; that is, there were no baptisms. Nevertheless, these years were certainly not wasted years. Although the efforts of that long period to gain the confidence of the people seemed of no avail, the struggle eventually bore rich fruit. Sadly, only a few of the mission pioneers lived to see those results.

From the very beginning, the Rhenish missionaries set to work with a clear concept. With the help of local teachers and assistants, they wanted to develop their own school system as soon as possible, and train people to help them in their educative program. Moreover, through the children they hoped to improve the contacts with the older generation.

With this concept in mind, Eich tried to recruit New Guinean teaching assistants from the London Mission Society in British New Guinea. He believed the preaching provided by New Guineans to be much more effective than that of European missionaries. Unfortunately, his plan failed. The idea of recruiting some evangelists from the Rhenish Batak Mission had to be discarded, too. [20]

At last, the missionaries realized that they would get nowhere unless they first learnt the local language themselves. Only that would enable them to start their own program of training the kind of helpers they needed. But there, too, they were faced with endless problems. Even in the small Astrolabe Bay area, the language fragmentation was so diverse that practically each missionary had to pursue his own language studies. This was complicated especially in Bongu and Bogadjim, where the inland Papuan languages were spoken — and that in an area where normally the different coastal Melanesian languages were used. As the goal of the mission work was to advance further inland eventually, it would have been opportune to adopt one of the inland languages as the official church language and to spread it through mission schools. However, the proud Melanesian coastal inhabitants would never have condescended to use the language of inland mountain people, whom they despised. Hence, the efforts to set up a standard church language in the Madang region at the outset of the mission work were frustrated. In the following years, only limited results were achieved in adopting the Graged or Bel language. Later on, with the development of Pidgin as the *lingua franca*, these endeavours became unnecessary.

The other major problem was that again and again colleagues who had become proficient in the language would become unavailable because of death or disease. Difficulties arising due to the limited knowledge of the language were still complained of in the Conference Reports of 1899. Native listeners would say after a sermon: 'We have heard all

A school class at Bongu.

that before.' Just how hard these beginnings were can be seen from the resolution of the Mission Conference of 1890:

> Therefore it appears advisable to hold short meetings with the natives only once a week, preferably on Sundays. That will provide an opportunity to discuss some of the questions with them that may have come up in conversation with individual people during the week. At the same time, people can be pointed to the significance of reading and writing. If then one or the other feels the urge to learn how to read and write, it will be an opportune moment for the schools to set in. [21]

The first references in the annual reports to numbers of students appear after 1898. Four schools with 80 to 100 children are mentioned. But these impressive figures by no means imply that the students attended school regularly. Often the children had to be enticed to come to school by promises and gifts — if not to the children themselves, then to their parents. One gets the impression that the people thought that by school attendance they were doing the missionary a favour. They simply could not yet see what benefit it would bring to their own lives. [22]

In order to improve the discipline and the level of teaching, Kunze strongly pleaded for the establishment of so-called *Kostschulen* (boarding-schools). What he had in mind were schools where the children would spend not only part of the day, but where they would live for weeks on end under the influence of the missionary; at the same time, they would be removed from the customary pagan environment of village and home. In fact, a good deal of the success of the Neuendettelsau Mission was attributed to local helpers who themselves had been trained at such schools. That was the model Kunze had in mind when he repeatedly advocated the establishment of boarding-schools. Eventually, boarding facilities for up to 20 students were added to the normal mission schools. The boarding students grew their own food in fields that they took care of themselves. Beyond that, they earned something toward their keep by working on the plantations of the Mission. All that helped to keep the expenses down.

Such boarding-schools proved effective also in the Madang territory. A large proportion of the first Christians had been students at such

111

schools. Even from remoter areas, boys applied for admission to the boarding-schools. Afterwards, when they returned to their villages, they became the missionaries — or they served as contacts when the Rhenish Mission later extended its work to those areas. The relations with villages on the Rai Coast, for instance, developed with the help of such former students (see also ch 13).

Along with the school teaching and the language studies, another major concern of the missionaries was translation work. It was essential to produce lesson material, especially biblical stories, prayers, and songs in the vernacular. This required a better knowledge of and discrimination between the respective local school languages. Accurate translation is of vital importance in mission work. In the early stages, the news of the Gospel is in constant danger of being misunderstood. This may happen when a translator uses an incorrect term, or does not realize the ambiguity of a term, or is unaware of fine shades of meaning associated with a given word.

Meticulous care was essential, and delayed the progress of the translation program. [23] Moreover, the thorough language studies needed to be accompanied by endeavours to find out more about the local pre-Christian religion; Christian truth could be expressed clearly only with reference to and in distinction from these heathen concepts and ideas. At the conference in 1898, Missionary Hanke advocated the coordination of these efforts. He proposed that a chronicle be kept at each station, in which the missionaries would conscientiously record all remarkable events and their observations with regard to local customs and religious usage. [24]

At last, in 1899 Hoffmann reported at the Annual Conference that he had translated several texts into the Bogadjim language: some Bible stories of the New Testament, a summary of the Passion story, the first two articles of the Creed, the Ten Commandments, and a number of prayers.

To be sure, although the beginning work showed so few visible results, there were subtle aspects that played a vital role in eventually attracting the attention of the population to Christ. The Christian way of life of the first mission families, their deep Christian faith, their love of God and of their fellowmen, all left their mark on the environment and impressed the heathen population.

In the midst of the customary monotonous village life, the mission station with its strangeness became a popular centre, possessing a certain fascination for the New Guinean population. It was inevitable that the daily life of the mission family would also be noticed and remarked upon. The people noticed how the Christian Sunday was observed, and took note of the daily morning and evening devotions: 'Be quiet! Kunze is reading the Jesus book.' [25] They contemplated the Christian pictures and verses on the walls, and asked for their meaning. They experienced joy and sorrow, baptism and death with the missionary's family.

A young warrior once said to Kunze:

When you first arrived here on our island, I would have thrown my spear at you if the men of the village had said: 'Let us kill Kunze'. But today I couldn't do it. There [pointing to the mission graveyard] you buried Missionary Klaus, Pilkuhn, and your wife. When I think of that, I turn weak inside; and as I see you, I feel compassion, and the spear in my hand sinks to the ground. [26]

Of course, the missionary helped out with his first-aid resources and his medical knowledge when injured people were brought to him or he was called to a sick-bed. The people did not take it for granted that the missionary would help them medically, and were immensely grateful when he did. Kunze records the incident of how he was pursuing some thieves to a village on Karkar Island. There one of the warriors attacked him, pierced his hat with a spear, and was raising the second spear. Now we let Kunze speak:

There — what do I see? — suddenly a woman flung herself against the man who had pointed his spear at me. She grabbed the spear and forcibly pressed it to the ground. The man, now even more enraged, tried to wrench the spear from her hands. But she held on tight, and they struggled with one another. [27]

That woman probably saved Kunze's life. He learnt later that, several weeks before, Scheidt had bandaged a wound for her.

Any record of methods in mission work is incomplete without the mention of the quiet influence exerted by the missionaries' wives on the female population, especially of the younger

112

generation. Already at the Second Mission Conference in 1890, it was considered 'very meaningful to have lessons in needlework for the girls, which should be provided by the missionaries' wives'. On the veranda of every mission house, women and girls met for the 'women's hours' and learnt how to sew (later also how to knit).

> Of course, during this sewing hour there was not only sewing, but lively gossip as well. The ... women and girls had usually saved all kinds of thoughts and thousands of questions for this occasion. In her replies, my wife always tried to touch the students' souls, too, and told them something of the Saviour. She also always had a notebook within reach to record every strange phrase or idiom for the enrichment of our vocabulary. [28]

The First Baptism

By the turn of the century, the missionaries believed they had won the trust and affection of the inhabitants, and that the turning to Christ would now be only a question of time. On December 28, 1903, the milestone was reached: The first convert was baptized by a Rhenish missionary.

The first convert of the Rhenish Mission was Gumbo of Bogadjim village. As a child, he had broken a valuable piece of his father's ornaments. Being afraid of his father's wrath, he had run away to the house of Missionary Hoffmann in Bogadjim, and had hidden there for several days. A deep friendship developed

Gumbo, first Christian at Bogadjim.

between Gumbo and the missionary family because of the kindness he had experienced through them.

Later on, Gumbo became the house boy for the Hoffmanns, and stayed with them for some years. When he returned to live with his family, he had difficulties in readjusting to the pagan environment. Missionary Hoffmann writes about Gumbo's spiritual growth up to the time of his baptism:

> In the month of August last year, our former house boy Gumbo came and asked us to take him into our home again. He said he did not want any payment, just work 'lana' (for nothing). We soon realized that the young man was moved by something deeper than external circumstances. He appeared completely changed. Soon he approached me with the wish to be baptized. I began to observe him closely for some time; and what I saw was positive. One day his relatives organized a pagan celebration. The entire family was expected to participate, lest they provoke the ill-will of their ancestors and spirits. We were anxious to see how Gumbo would handle the situation. We could observe a touching scene. All the relatives came, one after another, and tried to persuade him to take part in the ceremony. Finally, his elderly parents came and pleaded with him. They told him just to put a feather in his hair and watch from afar. But the young man stood his ground and kept giving one-and-the-same answer: 'I want to become a Tamo (man) of Christ; Jesus does not want the celebration'. Thereupon I started with lessons for baptism, and I remember many wonderful hours when we felt the presence of God ...
>
> After Gumbo had received baptismal lessons for three months, I decided not to put off the baptism any longer. Brothers Bergmann and Hanke, whom the young man went to see, shared my opinion. We chose Christmas as the date for the baptism because the Child of Bethlehem is proclaimed to be the comfort and light for all the heathen ...
>
> There were about 250 people altogether. The ceremony started at 8 o'clock in the morning. The glory of God was sung in three different languages. A short sermon based on John 3:16 made reference to the meaning of Christmas and the significance of baptism. Then the candidate was examined to show his knowledge of Bible stories, the Ten Commandments, the Apostles' Creed, the Lord's Prayer, and the Order of Baptism. The answers to my questions were given calmly and clearly. Every pastor at home would be

happy if their candidates were as firm in their examination... In reply to my question whether he believed whole-heartedly what he had confessed with his lips, he answered joyfully Yes. He then stated before his fellow countrymen and family that he was determined to be a Christian and made the following baptismal pledge: 'I renounce the customs of my ancestors. The Asa [celebration of the ancestral spirits] has been instituted by my forefathers through deception. I know that they have invented the pagan deities. I believe in the Rote [God] Jehovah. He is the only God; he created the heavens and the earth and all things. I believe in Jesus Christ. He is God's only Son. Jesus has forgiven me my sins. He delivers me from the devil. He frees me from hell. I used to walk the ways of my fathers, but now I will go the way of Jesus. O Rote Jehovah, I have spoken to you and you have heard me. O Jehovah, help me. Amen!' After this confession, Gumbo knelt down, and I baptized him in the name of the Father, the Son, and the Holy Ghost. I laid my hands on his head and blessed him.

Dear Inspector, you will understand that at this solemn moment my knees were shaking and tears came to my eyes. I could hardly control my voice to speak the Order of Baptism and the blessing. I got stuck more than once. Many a thought came to my mind at that sacred moment. I was thinking of the faithful perseverance of so many children of God who have been praying for New Guinea; of my own doubts and lamentations; of the brothers who have sacrificed their lives and had been longing for this day, which the Lord has now granted to us. Surely, they were looking down upon us from the 'cloud of witnesses' together with our dear departed Inspector Dr Schreiber. Gumbo has chosen the name Paul as his Christian name, which I then bestowed upon him. [29]

That report was received by the Mission in Barmen with great joy and excitement. The Board wrote a jubilant letter to the missionaries. These are the most moving lines:

That should and must be the first, that we and the congregations at home gratefully join with you in the thankful hallelujah. Finally, the long anxious wait has been answered, and the first heathen has been baptized. For 16 years we have been yearning for this event, and have repeatedly asked ourselves: 'Guardian, is the night soon over; guardian, has the night soon passed?' And 12 brothers and sisters have sunk to their graves without the opportunity of seeing even a trace of what they so much had hoped for. And now it has happened: 'The first-born fruit of the seed that was laid with sacrifices and tears is there'.. [30]

The jubilation and optimism of all the people who witnessed this event is understandable. However, reality was soon to bring them back to earth. For one thing, Gumbo could not really live up to the high hopes placed in him. The separation from his past and from his relatives and from everything else that he had once cherished must have consumed much of the strength of his personality and character. He eventually became a rather half-hearted and faltering Christian. Beyond that, other incidents during the following year proved that it was false to believe that the confidence of the native population had been gained.

The very next Conference in 1904 put the question to the home Board 'whether the time has not come to turn our stations — as far as they are to be kept up — over to the Neuendettelsau Mission'. [31] What had happened to cause such a drastic change?

The First Madang Rebellion

In 18 years of administration, the German colonial government in New Guinea had established new laws in place of the traditional concepts that existed in the country. Outwardly the local population did not seem to object to such measures. The Melanesians of Astrolabe Bay had not shown that their national feelings were continually hurt — until events came to a climax in 1904. Only then did the German officials and the missionaries realize how precarious was their situation. The missionaries reported to Barmen as follows:

To give a full picture, we must refer to incidents that occurred back in January and February 1904 in Bongu and Bogadjim. In January 1904, a young Bongu boy came to Brother Hanke one day. He reported that the people of Bongu and Bogadjim, as well as the tribes that lived in the mountains nearby, had united and decided to kill all the Europeans, including the missionaries, in Stephansort and Konstantin Harbour. (Meanwhile we have learnt that the murder plan at that time originated from Siar and Bilibili. But Siar and Bilibili were only supposed to get the uprising started, and then Bongu and Bogadjim wanted to continue with the massacre.) In any case, Brother Hanke did not pay any attention to this rumour. Late in the evening of February 4, the same boy came to Brother Hanke a second time with the same story. But now he added some details of the people's plan: They wanted to ask the Europeans for firearms, pretending that they intended to shoot birds for them. They were going to massacre the whites with their own weapons. Although Brother Hanke could not really believe this, he felt obliged to pass the information on to the administration in Stephansort. Luckily, it remained only rumour, and nothing happened at that time.

Nevertheless, the latest tragic incidents in the Siar region clearly prove that the boy's reports to Brother Hanke had not been just empty rumour after all. On the morning of July 26, at about 9.30, shots were heard in Friedrich-Wilhelmshafen. Brother Helmich at Ragetta, who was just returning home from school as on any other morning, did not pay any attention to the shots. The sound of shooting was often heard in Friedrich-Wilhelmshafen from the regiment stationed there. He was soon roused from his apathy, however, when shouts and screams reached his ears from the village of Ragetta. He hurried into the village, where he learnt that the shots had been aimed at the people of Siar and Ragetta. While he was still conversing with the people, the local official arrived with policemen to check whether the missionaries and their families were still alive. Other boats with police-soldiers were heading for Siar. The local official told Helmich that the natives of Siar, Ragetta, and Bilibili had come to attack Friedrich-Wilhelmshafen; at the last moment, a young man from Bilia had disclosed the plan, and the revolt could be suppressed. One young man from Ragetta was killed, another one was taken into custody. The rest of the people had dispersed in all directions. The young man from Bilia had testified as follows:

Some people of Siar and Bilibili had called on the inhabitants to fight against all Europeans. But the people of Bilia did not want to take part in the attack because they were afraid of the consequences, should they be defeated. The Siar people had told them that they first wanted to kill the officials of the government and the Company in order to get their guns. From there they wanted to go up to the European hospital and the doctors' residence in Bilia, and massacre the whites there. Then they wanted to murder Missionary Weber at Siar, and finally Helmich at Ragetta. As for the two women, Sister Bergmann and Sister Helmich, they did not want to kill them, but to take them as wives. Likewise, the little Theo Bergmann was to be spared. Should the scheme in Friedrich-Wilhelmshafen fail, they wanted to pretend that they had gone to Friedrich-Wilhelmshafen to do road work, and then they could have counted on the support of the missionaries.

Man from Siar Island.

The mission people of Siar and Ragetta refused to believe the statements of the Bilia man ... Also, the people of Siar kept protesting their innocence. The government, fortunately, stood firm and believed what the man had reported. The local official, Assessor Studehardt, acted calmly and moderately. First of all, he put six Siar men in jail on July 29 and August 4, and interrogated them. People from Bilibili were supposed to be arrested, too, but the rough sea made it impossible to reach the island. When the sea became calmer, the men had quietly escaped to the Rai area...

We considered it necessary to close the Siar mission station for the time being. Brother Weber moved to Ragetta, and Sister Bergmann went to visit Bongu and Bogadjim. Most of the people of Siar had left their village, and were hiding in their fields near the coast.

On August 9, the six prisoners were transferred from Siar to Herbertshoehe [seat of the Governor, near Rabaul]. The next day, four more men were taken into custody on Siar, and on August 12 the local official claimed pigs, weapons, and fruit as reparation payment. On Ragetta, five men were arrested on August 15 and 16. Here, too, the people had to make reparation payments. It was hoped that gradually peace and harmony would return to the district, although the prisoners' fate had not been decided on yet. The exile of the ringleaders was considered as a possible punishment.

August 17 brought an unexpected change of events. The administration staff of the New Guinea Company in Friedrich-Wilhelmshafen had in the meantime drafted a petition to be presented to the Governor. It urged the Governor, in view of the serious incidents in the Siar territory, to inflict severe punishment on the delinquents. An official of the NGC also approached Brothers Weber and Helmich with this petition for their signature. Since the petition did not request anything but the severe punishment of the key figures, there was no reason for us to refuse our signature. If we did not sign, we would give the impression of siding with the culprits. The Brothers in the Siar region had made this impression anyway, because at first they had been convinced of the innocence of the people. Yet Missionary Helmich did not sign directly, but first checked whether the petition would be handed to the local authority as well. This being affirmed, the Siar missionaries sent the petition to President Hoffmann. When he had signed, Weber and Helmich signed too. Afterwards it turned out that we and the local authority had been deceived. The petition was handed to the Governor without the knowledge of the local government official. As a result, Vice-Governor Knake, acting for the Governor, Dr Hahl, who was away, came with police-soldiers to take the necessary action. But soon Mr Knake became convinced that his presence was unnecessary, that the situation was being handled correctly by the local government official, and that peace could be restored. As the ship was ready for sailing, the Vice-Governor decided to depart, taking the prisoners with him.

Suddenly everything changed for the worse. An official of the administration in Friedrich-Wilhelmshafen brought new reports that the Namalas [people from Finschhafen][32] who were working for the Company were also supposed to have participated in the general conspiracy. One Namala, already a Christian, who worked for Brother Weber, was immediately summoned from Ragetta. He was said to have acted as a mediator between the Siar and the Namalas. Fortunately, the innocence of this young man could be proved. The situation regarding the other Namalas, though, has not yet been clearly established. In any case, the rumours were obviously sufficient to cause the departing Vice-Governor to impose the state of martial law on the entire territory.

At around noon, Missionary Helmich received his appointment as a member of the court-martial

jury. The court martial was convened at two o'clock that very afternoon. The natives Mas Maian and Aman Kinau from Siar, and Ijai, Matan, Mirop, Dum, and Karik from Ragetta, were sentenced to death. Three of these men were recommended to the mercy of the Governor, but the other four were shot at Siar at about 4 o'clock. To this day nobody knows what will happen to the rest of the prisoners. Most likely there will be another execution. It is also still uncertain what will happen to the rest of the people here. There is a rumour that all the people of Siar and Ragetta may be banished to the Bismarck Archipelago. The island of Bilibili has already been confiscated by the German Empire. The Siar peope have left their island by now. Only a few adults have remained in Ragetta. [33]

Causes of the Uprising

The missionaries' report to Barmen on the Madang events also reflects on the possible causes of the uprising:

When the question arises regarding the motives for the revolt, the only spontaneous answer can be that the people want to be free again from outside influence — although they must admit that they have been profiting considerably in a cultural sense. The people themselves have said: 'We want to be free for ourselves again; then we can do what we like.' And that's the way it is. They do not want their traditional customs to be destroyed. The government recently mobilized the people for road construction. Although they were paid for their work, it created a considerable commotion. For the most part, the people had to be coerced to go to work. Several times the Siar had to pay with pigs for their insubordination. When an old stone landmark was destroyed, during road construction, the people were quite upset. They were convinced that the swine fever that killed all their pigs was a result of that sacrilegious act.

Recently a rumour was spread that chiefs would be appointed here, just as had been done on the Bismarck Archipelago. Such things breed great anxiety among the people — even if without cause. Although from the viewpoint of the natives, these issues may be the reasons for discontent, it must be emphasized that the government cannot be blamed for the uprising...

In any case, it is hard to understand how the people could rush so blindly into disaster. After all, they had witnessed several shocking instances of the power of the authorities and the effect of their guns. We are, therefore, inclined to assume that the belief in the power of magic must have played a significant part. The Bilibili have the reputation of being great sorcerers. Presumably they made the people believe that the magic made them immune to bullets and shots. [34]

Consequences of the Uprising

The report also comments on the situation now facing the Mission:

Up to now, we were certain that we had acquired the confidence of the people, and so in turn we had trusted them. But this conspiracy proves with appalling clarity that we were mistaken. And we do not see any chance of overcoming or eliminating this mistrust in the near future. On occasions such as these, the natives can observe that the missionary has verbal and written contact with the government authorities. That this is necessary is more than they can understand. Perhaps they are willing to accept that kind of collaboration if decisions are made to their advantage. But even if they are rightly to be punished for an offence, they expect the missionary to intervene on their behalf and to help them out of the dilemma. If he fails to do so, he is rejected as well. We are certain that under these circumstaces, mission work — as we have done it in spite of all the hardships —is no longer possible. Also, even if Siar really continues to exist, the whole territory will become unsafe for some years, for blood revenge is still common practice here. [35]

The report speaks for itself. Disappointment and genuine indignation provoked the missionaries to use some unfair and harsh formulations regarding the New Guineans. The report also reveals hardly any sympathy for the legitimate desire of the Melanesians to be free to do what they wanted, as their fathers had been able. The missionaries evidently did not realize what it meant for the New Guineans to be dependent on well-meaning intruders who tried to patronize them in every way.

Even more clearly, these lines manifest the missionaries' loss of self-confidence. One of their own ranks, Missionary Helmich, had been a member of the court-martial jury that pronounced the death sentence. The missionaries felt, with good reason, that this would be a fatal impediment in any future endeavours. In addition, they experienced great disappointment with regard to the attitude of the local inhabitants. They had assumed that they had won the trust and affection of the population, but now they saw that the people had not shown their true feelings. The feeling

that they had been deceived made the missionaries react in a resentful and offended way. Was this the reward for all their sacrifices? Moreover, even their willingness to understand and to forgive, and their warm sympathy for the New Guineans, had been taken advantage of by the rebellion leaders in a cold and calculated way. All that made the missionaries doubt the sense of their work.

The home Board reacted calmly. For the time being, everyone was encouraged to stay at his place and to continue as if nothing had happened. This directive was read at the Field Conference on January 22, 1906. This did not evoke objection — as one might expect — but agreement, for in the interim a new situation had evolved. The most-dreaded consequences of the rebellion had not come to pass. The entire population of the guilty villages had not been deported, nor had relations with them deteriorated as much as had been expected. As a result, the resolution of the home Board could be accepted. The Conference asserted 'that our general situation is better than we dared hope when we drew up the report to the Board'. [36]

A Religious Awakening

During the period that followed, a strange unexpected phenomenon could be observed: Paganism began to disintegrate and lose its strength. It was not the number of applications for baptism that pointed to this development, for there were still very few. [37] Rather, syncretistic elements began to make themselves felt, which indicated that the intellectual and spiritual interaction between paganism and Christianity had set in. When the first occurrence of this kind became known to the missionaries, they did not yet recognize its actual significance, but dismissed it rather off-handedly. A man from the Siar-Ragetta area declared that he had seen the god of the whites on an island. He described him as a huge man, black but with a white face. He had admitted, among other things, to having given guns to the whites, but he had not meant them to be used for shooting blacks. Also he had said that the great ancestor-spirit celebration and the secret cult associated with it were part of the New Guinean tradition and therefore good, whatever the missionaries might have said to the contrary. He had also suggested that the natives should discuss among themselves whether they wanted to have the whites in their land any longer. He did not understand their language, but that should not be a problem. They should use certain signs, such as nodding, to tell him the result of their consultation. He had said that, if they desired the departure of the whites, he would 'write a paper' and then all the whites would have to leave. [38]

This story spread along the coast and induced great expectations among the local people. President Hanke commented on this unusual story with indignation: Obviously the people want to revive the belief in spirits and even claim the God of the whites as an advocate of their cause. [39]

Such a reaction is understandable, of course. In the historical context, however, the event will be evaluated differently. The failure of the rebellion, together with experiences before that event, had evoked a deep crisis with regard to meaning of life and values for the New Guineans. The white conquerors had proved their superiority in every way; opposition had become useless. The only thing for the people to do was to adapt to the new situation, and to try to save as much as possible of their own identity. If this was true of all the other areas of life, why not of religion as well?

The fact that the God of the whites in the story is black with only his head being white shows that he is accepted as a person of vital significance for the black population too. Even more: He is really a black; only his face is white, that is, only what is 'visible' of him at the first moment: his preference of whites and the preaching of the missionaries presenting him as a white. And he is much more tolerant and merciful than the rigoristic preaching of the missionaries implies; he does not object to the inclusion of traditional forms of devotion, cult objects, and other notions into the new religion. Above all, he is not partial to white people, but is, in fact, willing to send them back to their homeland as soon as the New Guineans want that. On the other hand, he acts like a white government official at his desk: he does not know the local language, and merely needs to write a paper or a decree. With his signature, the matter is settled. Thus, even the authoritative German administration had contributed to the development of this native image of God.

To the sensitive observer, this story reveals the beginning of trust in the God proclaimed by the Mission, although disguised to such an extent that one cannot blame the missionaries for their lack of understanding at that time.

They had a more positive approach to another movement which originated on the mainland shortly thereafter. Hanke of Bongu reports:

On November 13 some people came to the Bongu mission station in great excitement and reported some very peculiar happenings. Finally they asked me to come with them to their village with the 'Book of God's Teachings' [Bible]. I myself became infected by their excitement and went with them immediately. In the village I met the men from Bongu and about 30 other people from Kul and Maragum. Everyone was sitting there silently, completely against the normal Papuan behaviour, occupied with the question: 'What shall we do?' I sat down among the people and quietly waited to be addressed. As no one spoke, I asked them why they had called me. Thereupon an elder from Kul began to speak and related the following: In the deep of the hinterland, a *lan-tamo* [man from heaven] had descended to earth with his child. This *lan-tamo* broke all the spears, arrows, bowstrings, and magical implements. They [the people to whom the *lan-tamo* first had come] were then directed to pack the broken things into baskets, to take them to the next village, and to tell the inhabitants to do the same thing there. Furthermore, the *lan-tamo* had packed the peelings and pits of all fruits into another basket to show that everything belonged to him. He, the *lan-tamo*, had created all things, so they were his property, and not that of men. Into another basket he placed his child. Finally, he declared that the *Ai* [spirit ceremony] was a lie, and that the implements used in the celebration should be shown to the women and children and then be burnt. Then he said that everything the missionaries had told the people of Bongu and others about the Word of God was correct and true. Therefore they should take to the missionary the baskets of broken spears, arrows, bowstrings, and magical implements, the basket with the fruit peelings, and the basket with the child, and hand them to him and to no one else. They should handle the basket with the child very cautiously. If their path should go through forest, they should first clear the way so that no branches would brush against the basket. Likewise, they should first make a smooth path through tall grass. The baskets containing the arrows —there were nine of them — should be burnt; but the basket with the child should stay closed until the father himself came. These were the words that were brought to them together with the baskets. The baskets were in the house. Hanke should convince himself of the truth and examine them. [40]

Then they showed him ten baskets, each covered with a sacred plant. When they asked Hanke if anything was written in his Bible about this, he told them the story of the Creator who had sent his Son. He clearly realized that all of a sudden a door had been burst open where before he had met only solid walls. The people then followed the missionary to the mission station, where they carefully set down the baskets. Only a young man was allowed to carry the basket with the child.

Moved by the experience, 23 men applied for baptism lessons the following day, and nine girls the day after that. In his report, Hanke added a few more details:

The site where the *lan-tamo* was supposed to have appeared with his instruction to break the weapons and to take them to the missionary keeps changing. The tall man is described as follows: His body had radiated like the sun, but only the elders had been able to perceive him. The young men were dazzled by the bright gleam. They made him offerings. They slaughtered a pig and a dog, cooked them and placed them before him. The *lan-tamo* actually consumed the food, but not as people would; rather, the food disappeared from the dishes at his glance. He then complained that the souls of the dead arrived in the other-world all covered with wounds. He was tired of healing these souls and gave orders to keep peace. He told them to break their arrows and spears which they had fought with and to destroy their magical implements. If any more souls should come covered with wounds, from now on he would throw them into the fire. [41]

On December 18, the ceremonial implements of the spirit cult were actually burnt, and this was done in the presence of the women. 'Those 15 minutes were a memorable event for the people of Bongu. The men arrived with their ceremonial musical instruments and played on them once more before breaking them to pieces and throwing them into the fire. The women, who had been summoned by the men, were trembling all over with fear.'

On the day after Christmas, the unusual procession reached the mission station in Bogadjim. Missionary Schuetz writes about it:

Not a woman or child was to be seen. All homes were closed. On one side of the village square, the men of Bogadjim were sitting in deep silence, awe and fear on their faces, while the procession of people formed a circle. Gumbo (so far the only Christian in Bogadjim village) came to me and asked what they should do now. I told him they should patiently wait and see what else would happen. But soon I saw Gumbo entering the circle with a coconut, dividing it, and handing a piece to each individual person. Thereupon the men set down the baskets with the greatest care. I asked Gumbo, who had come back to me, why he had divided the coconut. He said he did not know himself what it meant, but that the leader of the procession had told him to do so. A downpour of rain ended the gathering just as the mountain people wanted to speak. The next morning I was called for once more. I went to the village again. This time, I found all the women assembled as well, and the men of Bogadjim were standing and sitting in groups. Everybody was extremely excited, and I was told that now the *Asa* instruments were to be burnt, according to the directive that had been brought with the baskets. A large pyre was set up in the large square; the men gathered wood and other fuel; and then the pile was set on fire. The men were given a sign to bring

Asa *masks.*

119

forward the *Asa* instruments: pipes, rattles, long bamboos, and so forth. But as soon as the women saw the instruments that had always been anxiously hidden from female eyes, and when they heard the men blow into them, they behaved as if they were struck by lightning. They were scared, and tried to run away in all directions. But in no time the men had formed a circle around them and did not let anyone escape. It was a touching scene that then took place. The women looked absolutely terrified. They frantically clung to one another as if they wanted to seek refuge behind each other, or as if they all were to die together. They acted as if they were out of their minds, and it took them a long time to calm down.

During this panic I did not notice what else happened. I just saw how a man, one of the main sorcerers, produced a series of mysterious sounds with the long bamboo; then he broke it and threw it into the blazing fire. I had never realized that the *Asa* exercised such frightening power on the women. When they finally relaxed, I addressed the assembly with a 'Jehovah speech', and implored the people to open their hearts to these words. After singing and praying, I dismissed them. The main sorcerer applied for baptism lessons the next day. [42]

Thus suddenly began a period of growing success for the Rhenish Mission. Reports of baptism ceremonies kept coming from all the mission stations, though the total number of baptisms was still modest when one considered the size of the population. In 1911, the Rhenish Mission could still count only 83 baptized Christians.

A certain tradition grew up around the ceremony of baptism, with the following elements:

> An examination of what had been studied in the pre-baptismal lessons;
> the candidate's confession concerning his former pagan way of life;
> the public incineration of the magic and cult implements.

These elements eventually became a part of an official ritual through which the conversion was openly demonstrated to society. [43]

More striking than the number of baptisms was the increase in worship attendance. In 1911, Diehl reported from Bogadjim that the average attendance had climbed to 140 or 150. People from the nearby mountains arrived already on Saturday to celebrate Sunday at the mission station. [44]

120

Even in the Siar-Ragetta region, where the tale of the *lan-tamo* had hardly any influence, and where, because of the penalties after the revolt, the reserve of the people against the missionaries was the strongest, paganism began to lose strength. The first large baptism was celebrated on Trinity Sunday 1906, when 14 adults and four children were baptized by Helmich.

There were people from Seg Island and — what is even more significant — from the Rai Coast among the candidates at this baptism, people who had attended Helmich's boarding-school. That was all the more remarkable, for through these people the missionaries were soon able to establish contacts which opened up the possibility for evangelist-teachers to be stationed in that region. President Hanke, therefore, had good reason to report to Barmen in 1906 that the Rhenish Mission 'was now well on her way toward the real goal of mission work'. [45]

Six Samoan Pastors at Work

In 1912, there was a second attempt by the Siar-Ragetta people to rebel against the white authorities; apart from that, there followed a tranquil time of consolidation and steady development for the Rhenish Mission. Six Polynesian pastors, who came to New Guinea around this time to support the German missionaries, did much to contribute to the success of the Rhenish Mission.

As was mentioned above, the Rhenish missionaries had from the very beginning considered employing local co-workers from young neighbouring churches. All such plans had failed, however. Now, all of a sudden, another possibility presented itself. The German Pastor Heider, who was working for the London Mission Society on German Samoa, wrote several letters to the Rhenish Mission offering to the Mission for its work Samoan pastors who had graduated from the Theological Seminary in Malua (Upolu). His reason for doing so was the circumstance that not all of these pastors could be employed by their own church. The London Mission Society in British New Guinea, who previously had absorbed the surplus, was now planning to give its own graduates the chance of joining the mission staff.

These Samoan pastors had completed a four-year theological training course after six years of village school and four to six years of district school education. They were ordained, and were entitled to a yearly salary of 400 Marks, as well as a certain quantity of clothing and household items for themselves and their families. Every six years they could take a one-year furlough to go home.

At the conference at Siar in July 1909, Mission Inspector Kriele informed the missionaries of the details of the plan that had been worked out with the London Mission Society. In spite of some scepticism, the conference decided to accept the Samoans. The first two to arrive in New Guinea in July 1912 were Jerome and Kurene. In September 1913, four more came: Siliva, Faiupu, Taeao, and Asafo. The outbreak of World War I stopped this influx of personnel; after the war there simply was no money for this.

The six pastors made a significant contribution to the Christianization of what later became the Madang District of the Lutheran Church. And their sacrifices in terms of human life were equal to those of the missionaries. In a letter asking for additional personnel, Jerome records:

> On October 2, 1917, Pastor Siliva died of black-water fever. Other people who died:
> Mele, daughter of Pastor Taeao (January 28 to February 26,1915); Aisoo, wife of Pastor Kurene, died on April 5, 1915 of malaria and tuberculosis; Leman, wife of Pastor Siliva, died on October 6, 1916, of black-water fever; Milivi, son of Pastor Asafo (November 14 to November 17, 1917). [46]

The newcomers set to work with great enthusiasm. At the same time, they had to face many problems. For one thing, they were not accepted as whites by the natives because of the colour of their skin and their poverty; on the other hand, they were not considered as natives, either. But eventually they earned respect and approval through their cheerful energy and their skills, especially in fishing.

Jerome was assigned to lay missionary Schamann, and was stationed on the island Ruo, where the Ragetta language was spoken. He had very little trouble with learning the language because his native Samoan and the Melanesian languages both belong to the same Austronesian language-group. For Kurene, who

Jerome, one of the Samoan pastors (with Missionary Krueger).

worked in Bongu, it was much more difficult, for he had to cope with the non-Melanesian language of that inland area.

In the beginning they were quite willing to accept the Rhenish missionaries as their seniors. Later, it must have been extremely frustrating for them; despite their many years of experience, they were again and again assigned to positions that were subordinate to those of even German newcomers. Many tensions developed because of this — above all, for Jerome who, as the elected speaker of the Samoans, repeatedly had to voice their grievances very distinctly. From the start, the six men took on an enormous work-load. After nine months of language studies with Helmich, Jerome came to Ruo on February 18, 1913. He built a school first, and started lessons as early as February 21; only after that did he begin to build his own living quarters. Saturday mornings from 7 to 9 and Sunday afternoons from 3 to 5, he gave lessons to the seven catechumens in the baptism class; on each weekday apart from Wednesday he taught arithmetic, writing, and religion to 18 students. In addition, he held the morning and evening devotions and Sunday worship service for the people. And yet, his modest income forced him to support himself mainly by the work of his hands, through farming and fishing.

Already only the third Sunday after his arrival, five more men applied for baptism lessons. In 1914, 50 to 120 villagers (of a total population of 193) attended the Sunday worship services. In later years, however, Jerome had to struggle with great problems. One of the events that contributed to the stagnation of mission work in the area was the baptism ceremony in Ragetta in 1919. The fact that at this celebration the cult implements of the *Meziab* (spirit cult) had been publicly burnt in the presence of the female population deeply offended the remaining pagan Ruo men. According to traditional heathen practice, villages where the women had been admitted to the secrets of the cult used to be ruthlessly eradicated.

From 1923 to 1930, Jerome worked on the Rai Coast. There were eight assistant teachers assigned to him, who were stationed in the villages of Galek, Wab, Jamai, Bilia, Wassi, and Langtub. Here, at last, Jerome had the opportunity to work with a more open-minded and receptive population. His reports do not sound depressed any longer, but proud and happy. On September 5, 1926, the first baptism took place; 95 people were baptized, all of them adults. And in 1929, one year before his transfer to Karkar, Jerome was able to celebrate a remarkable baptism in Galek with 166 male and 182 female candidates.

From 1912 to 1930, Jerome had done his work as a missionary in New Guinea without any home leave. After his leave, when he was transferred to Karkar, the collaboration with the Rhenish Mission ended on a discordant note. For one thing, it had already exasperated him that his resolute wife, who had an excellent command of the language, had not been permitted to preach. But what irritated him even more now was that the Rhenish Mission refused to engage any new Samoans on the grounds that 'the salary demands were too high'! In October 1932 he wrote a last letter in his own style of English: 'If you say: Samoans, go home, thank you, we go home; if you say stay, we stay here until death — thanks. We stay for the work.' [47] Yet, despite many disappointments, he remained loyal to the Rhenish Mission until Barmen withdrew from its New Guinea field in 1932.

The working career of Kurene was much shorter. He was stationed in Bongu with Hanke. He held school lessons and Sunday school for the children, and taught the candidates for baptism in the villages of Male, Sungumana,

Damun, and Bau. After the death of his wife, he stayed for another two years, and then returned to Samoa.

Siliva, the third Samoan pastor, was in service for only three years. He died of black-water fever in 1917. He was assigned to Schuetz at Mabonob. Later, the village people built a house for him in Kekete, from where he looked after the regions of Kekete and Mabonob. In one of his reports, he mentions that he taught 23 students. Regarding his contacts with the inhabitants, he writes briefly but significantly:

> All the people of Mabonob and Kekete like me and provide me with everything, like taro and jam, so that I don't have to buy them ... Formerly, when we first came, only a few people attended baptism classes. Today [December 1914] there are many more men, from Mabonob and Kamba, Butellekude and Kamis, and all the chiefs, five altogether. [48]

Faiupu has recorded very little information of his experiences. He had first been sent to Mabonob to learn the local language. Then Schuetz stationed him in Heidurem, close to the border of the Catholic territory. He mentions a church and school dedication in Kamba, at which pagan cult implements were burnt. He reports virtually nothing about his own activities. On December 31, 1921, he returned to Samoa.

Asafo was much more communicative. In fact, thanks to him, we have some vivid descriptions of the pagan time on Karkar. Together with Taeao, he was first assigned to Jerome in Ruo to get used to the new environment and to learn the Ragetta language. On March 28, 1916, both of them were sent to Karkar, where they worked faithfully and with great success.

By December 1919, when Asafo wrote his first semi-annual report from Bangame (north coast of Karkar), he was already accepted and respected by the population, even though he had difficulties with the non-Melanesian language of his region. Apart from his main work, the school in Bangame, he soon opened another school in the neighbouring village of Kinim. He was asked by the villagers to do so because their children did not yet dare to go to Bangame. Thus he had quite a teaching load for five days a week: He taught 64 boys and 30 girls in Bangame in the mornings, and then hurried to Kinim to teach 20 boys and 12 girls there in the afternoon. One of his casual remarks shows how restless the region still was at his time: He wrote that on his way to the villages he had to beware of the spear-heads that were stuck into the ground around the villages to injure prowling enemies at night.

As often as possible, Asafo also visited other villages, both in the neighbourhood or farther away. [49] In 1921, the church building in Bangame had to be enlarged to accommodate the people of the neighbouring villages who were taking part in the worship services. The same development is reported from Kinim.

Asafo must have been a very courageous and self-assured man. Listen to what he has to say in June 1920 about the early days:

> On my property there are two pagan deity stones. One of them was lying on the spot where my house stands now. When I wanted to clear the site, I called to some men standing there: 'Come on, let's roll away this stone.' Thereupon they ran away screaming. I then turned to my boys: 'Come on, let's roll away the stone, it is no god.' The boys came and rolled the stone away. When I was visiting the village, I noticed a pig with a lame leg and asked the people about it. 'All our pigs are like that; the bad stone has done it', they said. The next day I went to the stone, where I met the man who was guarding it. He showed me where the stone was. As I wanted to go near the stone, he got frightened and exclaimed: 'This night your leg will get bad!' Nevertheless, I climbed onto the stone. The next morning the man came to my house. I went down to him and said: 'Look at me and you can believe that this stone is no god.' He agreed with me. [50]

Another similar proof of courage is reported of Asafo's resolute wife, who supported him actively in his work, especially at school:

> Recently I was absent. My wife spoke with the people about their death magic, and said to them that it was all lies. To that, a tall man said: 'My magic is no lie, indeed. When I cast a spell, the man dies. I can also do the fish magic.' My wife said to Masar, as the sorcerer was called: 'Good, make your spell, and give me the fish to eat.' Masar said to her: 'Cut some of your hair off and give it me; I will cast a spell, and you will die.' My wife got a pair of scissors, cut off some hair, and gave it to Masar. He took the hair and wrapped it in a banana leaf, tied everything together, and cast his spell over it. His hands trembling, he said: '*Mana marek ararara palta*: Stones of god, come here, come here! Today I say to you people: You should know

that today I cast my spell publicly so that you know what I am saying, today she will die.' The people dispersed to go to sleep. Early in the morning the people came to see my wife. My wife said to Masar: 'Come here, I am still alive. What do you say about your magic now?' Masar said: 'Yes, today I know that my magic is a lie, today I will stop it.' Then he said to the people: 'Today I stop practising magic because it is a lie ...' Since that day, Masar treats me like a friend. [51]

On Sunday, May 4, 1924, the great day had come for the first baptism in Bangame. On the day before, the old magic implements were burnt. In a solemn Sunday worship service, 97 men, 80 women, and 59 children were baptized. The church was overcrowded. More than 1000 people attended the ceremony. Among them were the missionaries Eckershoff, Hannemann, Jerome, and Holtkamp. Many guests had come from Karkar, Bagabag, Ruo, Siar, Ragetta, Bilia, Jabob, Bilibili, Amele, and the Rai Coast.

By this time, Asafo was already in charge of nine schools, with a total number of 723 school children. Moreover, some newly-baptized men applied to become evangelists in the still-pagan regions of the island. Small wonder that Asafo concluded his report of November 10, 1924 with the following words: 'This year, our work was full of joy. The customs have changed, the old has passed away; all has become bright. The people are now taking care of their bodies and of their spiritual life as well.'

Asafo was able to continue his work for only two more years. During his home leave in Samoa in 1926, he caught the black-water fever and died.

Taeao came to New Guinea together with Asafo. He and Jerome were the only Samoan pastors who held their positions until the Rhenish Mission gave up the mission field. In March 1916, he was stationed at Mapor in northern Karkar, and was responsible for the Waskia region. In January 1920, he reported his first success: Two villagers had been baptized, and 38 were attending catechetical instruction; 64 children were at the school that he had opened. His achievements made him more communicative than he had been before, and one could see that he enjoyed the success of his work. He sent another report in June of the same year:

> I work with great joy, for the work is beginning to thrive. At present there are 99 catechumens, adult

men and women and their children, all of whom have chosen to follow Jesus ... Many who have learnt the Word at school tell it to people who live farther away and don't understand the Ragetta language but have their own language. [52]

Shortly before his home leave, which Taeao began in December 1921, he celebrated his first large baptism, when 58 adults and 52 children stood before the baptismal font. At the same time, 246 catechumens were still being taught. After that event, there is hardly any news; there is merely one last letter written in 1932. By this time, the excitement and enthusiasm of the early years had largely subsided, and the change can be felt in Taeao's report. He compares the Waskia community to a sick man. Two elders have had to be excluded because of bigamy, the offerings have been decreasing, and fewer and fewer people have attended Communion. Actually, such a development should not have come as a complete surprise; the people converting to Christianity usually had unrealistically high hopes with regard to the new faith, hopes that could not be fulfilled. But Taeao was completely puzzled by the development.

The fact that Taeao and Jerome, despite so many disappointments, remained dedicated to their work gives the Samoans a rank that is equal with that of the Rhenish missionaries in New Guinea. The words of St Paul to the Corinthians (1 Cor. 4:2) apply especially to them: 'It is required that those who have been given a trust must prove faithful'. And faithful they were!

During and After World War I

The preceding account of the work of the Samoan pastors has taken us far into the 1920s; but it does not include any details with regard to World War I or the transfer of the mission field to Lutheran Mission New Guinea.

The time before and during World War I is marked by four features: missionary outreach into the hinterland of Astrolabe Bay; secondly, establishment of mission work on the Rai Coast; thirdly, resumption of work on Karkar Island; and fourthly, resistance against the increasing pressure from the Roman Catholic Mission.

A new phase of the Rhenish Mission work began with the second attempted revolt in 1912. In contrast to 1904, the incident of 1912 did not catch the missionaries unawares. Helmich had

observed for some time a stagnation in his work and a revival of the *Meziab* cult. It had certainly been no coincidence that Christmas Day 1911 had been chosen for a big spirit celebration; Christianity was to be openly resisted. At the closed ceremonial houses in Ragetta and Siar, high poles could be seen towering defiantly above the buildings. They were decorated with feathers, which were continually vibrating while inside the voice of the ancestral spirit *Meziab* resounded in the roar of the buzzing timber blades. In addition, the ceremonial pipes were blown and the drums beaten. The missionaries felt that a storm was brewing. And yet, for six months everything remained calm. But on August 23, the same man who had exposed the murder plot of 1904 disclosed the plans for a new revolt. All the whites were to be murdered, including the missionaries. The intended date of the uprising had been August 7; however, as the conspirators did not manage to gather punctually, the revolt was postponed to August 24. On the evening before that day, the colonial administration intervened, and 16 ringleaders were taken into custody. In addition, all the people who had been involved in the conspiracy were banished from their native villages and islands, although they were allowed to decide for themselves where they would be deported to. Some of them went to Karkar and Megias, north of Madang, but the majority went to the Rai Coast. Helmich and Blum were authorized to accompany the deportees to the Rai Coast. The exiles were also given tools so that they would be able to survive in an unaccustomed environment. Luckily, the exile was of short duration. At the outbreak of the war in 1914, the Australians took over the administration of German New Guinea, and a return home was granted to the exiles immediately.

Of course, nobody could foresee this development in 1912, and the mission people felt quite dejected at the turn of events. Once more they would have to make a new start. This is the response from Barmen to the reports from New Guinea:

> The conspiracy of the natives against the lives of the whites and the removal of all the villagers to other regions are disastrous for our work in Siar-Ragetta. All at once, Siar-Ragetta has been deprived of its mission objects. That is an extremely bitter fact. [53]

First church at Nobonob.

But once again, later events showed the great distress caused by the setback to be unfounded. In the period following the revolt, the same phenomena evolved as after the first rebellion in 1904. The work did not stagnate; on the contrary, it gained new impetus. The inhabitants of Bongu and Bogadjim regarded the punishment of the Siars as a divine judgment, and were more open to the Gospel than before. The number of applicants for baptism in Bongu and Bogadjim rose to over 250 in 1913. Indeed, even the Nobonobs on and around Mt Hansemann, who had previously been strongly influenced by the Siars, now burnt their pagan magic and cult implements and turned to the message of the missionaries. They did it even though Schuetz, missionary at Nobonob since 1906, had advised them to make a decision of such importance only when they were definitely determined to accept the Gospel.

On the threshold of World War I, President Hanke was able to write in a letter of January 11, 1914, of 'a period of calm development and good progress', and mentions a list of evangelists' mission stations which had been established in the hinterland of Astrolabe Bay, in the area of Bogadjim. These were Erima, Bana, and Maraga, and Mabonob-Heidurem, north of Nobonob. Hanke emphasized 'that the people in charge of these branch mission stations are, without exception, assistants from their own people'. [54] Some of them hadn't even been baptized yet.

By the end of November 1915, the number of mission schools in the Bogadjim region, which Eiffert was in charge of, had risen to 12. Schuetz, from Nobonob, had opened five schools. Seven years earlier, not a single one had existed there.

The hinterland of Astrolabe Bay was also more and more open to the Gospel. The proportion of mountain people attending the worship services in Bongu and Bogadjim grew steadily. On October 8, 1917, Hanke baptized the first 154 people of the inland villages in Bongu. [55] That was a decisive breakthrough. The mission work was focused more and more on inland areas, and in October 1916 Wullenkord founded the first real inland mission station at Amele. In June 1918, the station in

125

Teachers Training School at Amele with Missionary Wullenkord.

Bongu was abandoned and transferred to the inland village of Keku.

In the meantime, there was also a surprising development on Siar and Ragetta, due to the unexpected behaviour of the deportees themselves. Immediately following the German capitulation in New Guinea in 1914, the deportation order covering the insurgents was annulled. [56] Missionary Blum expected that the exiles would return with an attitude of defiance and even greater opposition, but he was mistaken. In 1915, Blum observed that every Sunday 10 to 12 canoes filled with people from Siar came to Ragetta for the worship service without any inducement from him to do so. [57] At Ragetta, even the chief Sabu himself

Baptism at Ragetta 1923.

began to come to the worship services regularly. Some 40 people were participating in baptismal lessons; among them was Guleng, who had publicly admitted to have slandered Missionary Weber. [58]

The rebellion and exile had yet another unexpected effect. The connections that the deportees had established with their places of exile on the Rai and Megias coasts proved to be extremely helpful later when these regions were reached by the missionaries from Siar and Ragetta. After the great baptism on Ragetta on March 4, 1923, five of the newly-baptized volunteered to work as evangelists on the Rai Coast. But that takes us too far ahead of events.

Baptism at Ragetta

The next important event on Ragetta was the first baptism of 70 men and 60 women on November 30, 1919. Before that could take place, there were long deliberations and discussions about what should happen with the magic packages and the *Meziab* cult implements. Blum wrote about this as follows:

> Finally the debate about this issue was concluded by Dulau (the warden of the Spirit House): 'Who is authorized to decide about the *Meziab*: all of you or me alone? I alone can do so, not Blum. And I say, it is going to be burnt; but first, we will play on the instruments once more, as Blum has said, and that's all' ... Much was being said by the missionaries and also by the Samoan preacher. I want to quote only what two natives said. Dulau, a grey-haired man from Ragetta, stood up and said: 'Listen to me! Look at me! Is there anyone who does not know me? You all know me! You know who I am. You, people from Mis, from Fusan, from Silibob, from Kamba, from Guntabak. You, people from the mountains and from the islands! When you landed here with your canoes, ready to celebrate the *Meziab*, I was here to welcome you. Decked with a feather head-dress, with shell ornaments, and with my comb. I was decorated with ornaments on my arms and on my legs, the wild boar tusks on my chest, a shell-arrow through my pierced nose. My body was covered with magic. That is how I stood before you, me, the great man. Look at me, it is still me! But my head is shaven now, my head-dress is burnt. You all have seen it this morning in church. There are no more ornaments on my body; no more magic covers my body, nor do I wear a magic loincloth. Everything has gone. That is how I stand before you. Something new has begun, the old ways have

passed. I have become a Christian. I have given up my sins and will now live in God.'
> That is approximately what the old man said, but his speech was far more vivid and embellished than I can recount here. It is really impossible to reproduce his manner of speaking. The orator himself, his whole mannerism, his movements and gestures, his facial expressions etc., all these were vital parts of the speech.

Turning of the Tide at Karkar

Not only the mainland mission experienced an unexpected turn; the same thing happened on Karkar (the former Dampier Island), where Kunze had sown the first seeds.

With the acquisition of the steamboat *Rheno-Westfalia* by the Rhenish Mission, a dependable connection to the mainland was established, and in 1912 missionaries took up their work on the island again. Eckershoff was assigned to the eastern part, and George to the western part of the island. Two years earlier, the faithful teacher Madoi, a student of Helmich, had already opened a school at Kulobob; he continued his work there for many more years with great success. The new mission station was set up at Kurum, because it was much easier for ships to reach the island from that side, through the coral reefs.

The turn toward Christianity began in the north-western part of the island, simultaneously along the coast and in the mountain villages of the Waskia region. In many villages, the cult implements of the *Barak* (as the secret cult was called there) and all the magic objects were burnt without the missionaries exerting any pressure. Already in September 1915, Eckershoff could hold his first baptism; in August 1918, a second one followed. Even so, the total number of Christians was small: only 11 men, four women, and 10 children. But the attendance of more than 1000 guests from all parts of the island at the baptism celebration in 1918 indicated that these few candidates were the beginning of a movement. On July 31, 1921, the first large baptism, with over 100 candidates, took place.

When George returned to Karkar in July 1921, after a furlough of one-and-a-half years, he was overwhelmed by the change in such a short time. He wrote:

> Several hundred people came to the station. And this happened every Sunday when there was a

School class at Karkar with teacher Madoi.

Missionary Heinrich George.

worship service. When I think of earlier times ... In many villages there are only a few people left who are neither baptized nor in baptism instruction. And even they will not be able to hold out much longer. [59]

The mission on Karkar suffered a setback through a serious influenza epidemic which killed many people. Immediately some local

inhabitants tried to blame Christianity for the deaths. For instance, the people from the village of Bison asked George to withdraw the evangelists; they did not want to hear the Word of Jesus any more for they feared for their lives. George promptly went to Bison together with a number of Christians and baptism candidates — including the former sorcerer Labong, who gave an eloquent address, and succeeded in changing the people's minds.

The following account gives interesting detail about the confrontation between Labong and Igom, the spokesman of the pagan group:

Igom, go on and call your parents, I see that they aren't here. I would be happy to see them. What, you don't call them? Why don't you get up and get them? Why don't you go? Please, do me the favour, you have done so many others for me. Why don't you want to do it? Listen, Igom, don't you have any ears? You are supposed to call your father and your mother, I want to greet them. How stubborn you are today with your mouth tightly shut! You don't even answer, nor do you call. What are you ashamed of? What makes you turn your back on me? Don't be afraid, we are not going to hurt you. We just want to talk to you. So, go and get your parents. Call out loud, so that they can hear you. Didn't you say that no one dies here, and only the Christians in Kurum, Biu, Marup, Kabailo have to die, because they have God's Word? But you don't have God's Word here — and your parents had not previously heard anything of it. So, they certainly cannot have died here and are still here. Aren't they, Igom? You want the evangelists to leave your village because God's Word kills, and if you don't hear it any more you will stay alive. According to your arguments, your parents must still be alive. So, call them, do you hear me? Oh, Igom, poor soul. Why don't you admit — I know it anyway — you can't call them. They lie buried under your house, isn't that right? Why don't you admit it? I know it quite well. Open your mouth and speak. Didn't Uruwut die? Isn't my great father dead, who did not know God's Word? Didn't the great Begloi die, who was twice as tall as we? Aren't all the other tall strong men of Kurum and Bison dead? All of them are dead, dead despite the powerful magic of their old evil customs. Isn't that true? You see, a person also died without God's Word. All of you will die, too, without God's Word. Even you will die, Igom, do you hear me? Why do you say that only the Christians must die? Look at me, Igom, I am Labong, the great man and powerful sorcerer. Look at me, look at how old I am already! Do you know how great my fame was? Everyone was afraid of me and my skill. My magic used to be strong and sure. My word was full of power and awe. All the villages feared me. All the villages knew my name. Who could do what I did? Is there a dance that I couldn't dance before you? Didn't I serve the *Barak* [the secret cult] first? Do you know any spirits that I don't know? I drummed, not you, and everyone came! I was the first to offer great feasts to visitors of the dance, not you. You see, that's what I used to be, but now no longer am. Today I am different, completely different. I buried all my skills and evil implements under my house. [The Papuans used to bury their dead under their houses.] There all of it can rot, I don't want it anymore. My children are Christians, two of them teachers. They followed the call of Jesus before I did. I don't want to be left behind. Formerly I spoke and they obeyed, and you all obeyed. Today I want to be silent and listen to them. What the elders say, that is right for me now. What the congregation decides, I accept. That is what I do now, although there's hardly any hair left on my head and I am very old. I know now that my word was evil and theirs is good and true. That makes me happy. Therefore I have given up my former fame, and follow Jesus. If I have done so, you should follow and do the same. Didn't you follow me in everything before? You know, you won't be able to keep up your resistance against Jesus. Whoever

follows him will be saved and come into his glory. Do you know where the others will end up? They will end up at a place that is awfully hot, where the big fire is burning. There you will become so thirsty, that your tongue, stiff like a piece of wood, will hang down to your waist. You will try to scream for water, but you won't be able to make a sound. Anyway, there won't be any water there. That's where you will end up if you refuse the Word of Jesus and send away the evangelists. There are only these two paths, and we have to choose one of them. Choose the good one, as I have done, Igom, do you hear? Take my advice. It's the great Labong advising you.'

Thus spoke Labong. During that entire speech, he fixed his eyes upon the ground. After some silence, Igom began to grumble and said: 'I didn't mean it like that. But when my relative in Kurum died, I became angry and said that the Christians cast an evil spell on the others so that they die; we don't want any Christians here, nor do we want to become Christians ourselves. That's what I said when I was angry. But now they can stay. You are right, we all have to die, too. Keep on sending teachers, elders and Christians to us, and light the fire so that it will become bigger and bigger. I myself am rooted in the old tradition with all its evil, and can never get away from it on my own. Therefore, you must light the fire, so that eventually everything will be burnt, just as you have done in your villages.' [60]

An Ecstatic Movement on Karkar

From this period, a report also exists about an ecstatic movement, which began in Wadau, in the eastern part of Karkar. Presumably it was an early form of the cargo cult, similar to the *Eemasang* movement of Sattelberg; unfortunately, the details are not precise enough to verify this assumption.

In June 1920, a young female candidate for baptism had a vision. She said that she saw Jesus himself, and that he announced to her his imminent return, and that she should, therefore, spread his teachings and propagate the public confession of sins and genuine repentance among her people.

A case of clairvoyance added to the fame of the movement. A man suddenly said during a journey: 'Dalit is dying'. (Dalit was the father of the prophetess who had founded the new movement.) Even though his travel companions laughed at him, he persisted with his statement. And, indeed, Dalit had been speared at that time by a renegade Christian.

Great excitement and commotion seized the whole village. People sang, prayed, fasted, and kept each other awake. The over-tired people then had visions and heard voices, which increased the expectations even more. A woman fainted on her way to the fields. People carried her into the house, thinking she was dead. When she regained consciousness, they believed that she had risen from the dead. It is not suprising that, with the accumulation of such incidents, the movement continued to grow.

After the highly-respected teacher Madoi invited his friends to a banquet, the Wadau people spread strange stories about it. In reality, Madoi had given a speech at the banquet. He had taken two stones and asked his listeners to throw them away. The first one burst into many pieces; the second one was solid and did not break. By this symbolic action, Madoi wanted to illustrate the steadfastness of the Gospel in contrast to the brittleness of the old heathen tradition. The leaders of the new sect, however, interpreted the celebration in their own fanciful way: They proclaimed that Madoi had gathered his people, and they had eaten all the pigs because the return of Jesus was immediately at hand; a spring had opened up under Madoi's house; all the pigs and dogs had suddenly dropped dead, etc.

The Wadau people took steps to spread their movement. In processions they passed from village to village, demanding confessions of sins and true repentance. Whoever refused to confess his sins was beaten severely with a rope that they carried with them. Often people were pressed to confess sins that they knew nothing of. In the village of Wadau, 'a temple with an outer court' was built. Opponents were attacked with a knife that Jesus was said to have handed over to them. When Eckershoff was bandaging a man who was badly injured with that knife, he was called names such as 'doubting Thomas' and 'Satan'. The movement survived for only a few years. It vanished as quickly as it had appeared. [61]

In spite of its presumably-syncretistic character, this movement indicates that Christian ideas were making their way into the religious thinking and feeling of the inhabitants of Karkar Island. The prominent role of women in this movement is another interesting aspect,

130

possibly pointing to their changing social status. In traditional religion, women were not permitted to take part in cult ceremonies. The change with regard to the status of women in traditional society can only be ascribed to the influence of Christian teaching.

Developments on Karkar during the following years have already been described. An important part was played by the two Samoan pastors, Taeao and Asafo. The only item that remains to be added is that the Karkar mission extended its work to Bagabag Island in 1919. Evangelists from the village of Kabailo did most of the mission work there.

In the late 1920s, the Karkar evangelists also took charge of the Laden region and Matugas, located on the mainland opposite the island.

Advance on the Rai Coast

The Rai Coast has already been mentioned earlier in this chapter, when the Samoan pastor Jerome and his evangelists from Siar-Ragetta extended their activities to that area. Some incidents of the early history of the area must be added here.

Already in 1907, Helmich had made an exploratory journey to this region. [62] In Medise (Minderi) he found a ceremonial house of more than local importance. Helmich himself decided to enter the building; however, he let his companions decide for themselves whether or not they wanted to go with him, and none of them refused. A man from Bogadjim was the first to jump over the threshold. The inside of the ceremonial house proved rather disappointing; there was nothing in it but an old pot with a few broken teeth, a lower human jaw, a small ancestral figure, and a jar with lime. Helmich told his men to leave everything as it was. But the rumour of their venture spread like the wind as far as Ragetta and Bilibili, and there was a great amazement when Helmich and his companions returned safe and sound. Some people asserted that there had been an earthquake at the time the group had entered the house. Others said that they had seen the sun grow dim.

An advance in May 1913 into the hinterland of the Rai Coast must also be recorded. In the Finisterre Range lived the dreaded Raua people. The wife of a plantation worker in the Raua area had been murdered. Fearing blood revenge, the manager sent a delegation with gifts of atonement (12 bush knives and 4 axes) to the home village of the murdered victim. Missionary Hanke, who joined the delegation which turned out to be successful, summarized afterwards:

> I regard it as a success that the first encounter between Europeans and the Raua people … was so peaceful. It helped to lift the secrecy which had surrounded the Rauas. As a result, the strained relationships between the Rauas and the inhabitants of the coast, both native and white, have improved. Moreover, four villages — Bongu, Maragam, Sekwanam, and Jenglam — have established direct contact with the Rauas after this journey. The Raua people who accompanied our delegation back home stayed at the mission station and in Bongu for three days, and came into contact with the greatest and most glorious gift that exists for sinful human beings: the Gospel. [63]

The 1914 Field Conference decided that the missionaries Welsch and Blum should establish the long-planned mission station on the Rai Coast. However, the outbreak of World War I and the ensuing restrictions prevented the realization of the plan. That project had to wait until Jerome was sent to the Rai Coast in 1923.

Competing Roman Catholic Mission

An east-west line approximately 15 km north of Madang (touching the northern tip of Seg Island) gives the general borderline between the Rhenish Mission and the territory of the Roman Catholic Mission. This border was for a long time respected by both, but, beginning in 1914, repeated complaints of Catholic trespassing into the Rhenish region are recorded. Of course, mutual accusations with regard to proselytism in such border areas are common, and in most cases each side gives the other reasons for complaint. In this case, however, the initiative for expansion was obviously on the Catholic side, for the Rhenish missionaries had absolutely no interest in a northern expansion because of lack of funds and personnel. It sounds almost naive when the 1914 Conference Report declares:

> We could do nothing but accept the fact that the Catholic Mission had established themselves in Alexishafen, where they now control over 2,000 hectares of land, with primary and secondary schools as well as a training seminary for native assistants, and where they have a constant staff of 40 whites. But we had hoped that at least we would remain unmolested in our comparatively small territory for a number of years. [64]

It is not recorded when exactly a letter from the Catholic Mission at Alexishafen to the President of the Rhenish Mission officially revoked the boundary agreement. [65] But the Field Conference of 1914 was already pre-occupied with the Catholic intrusion and how to counteract it. The complaints were coming from all sides. The trespassing of the Catholics on the islands of Ruo, Seg, and Bilibili was reported by Eiffert. Schuetz complained that they had come to Madang (Friedrich-Wilhelmshafen) and even wanted to purchase the entire harbour. Blum was afraid that the Rhenish Mission could be cut off from their entire inland territory.

Having no real strategy, the Rhenish Mission first did nothing but react to this kind of intrusion. They felt compelled, for instance, to set up plantations to provide their own young people with an opportunity to earn money. Otherwise, they said, 'the Catholic Mission would be sure to entice all the able-bodied people from Dampier, Rich Island, and from the hinterland of Mt Hansemann to come to them'. [66] When the Rhenish missionaries were asked by the adminsitration to teach German to native soldiers and policemen, they agreed to do so simply because 'if the soldiers were taught by the Catholic Mission, they might believe that the Catholics must be right for them since the *Kiap* (government official) uses them as teachers for his men'. [67] They were particularly afraid of the Catholic influence in the hinterland, from where so many colonial troops were recruited.

Eventually the Catholics tried to gain influence even in the Huon Gulf area, in the midst of the Neuendettelsau Mission field. That finally prompted the Rhenish and the Neuendettelsau Missions to cooperate in developing a real strategy against Catholic expansion. The two Protestant missions met in Madang for mutural consultation and cooperation in April 1919. The outcome of this was an agreed resolution: 'Because the main pressure [from the Catholics] is directed toward the region of the Rhenish Mission, which is too weak to withstand this pressure, the Neuendettelsau Mission comes to its assistance'. [68]

To help their distressed brothers in Christ, the Neuendettelsau Mission offered them some New Guinean evangelists from the Sattelberg congregation. They would be assigned to the Rhenish district missionary, but at the same time remain under the supervision and maintenance of their home congregation. The evangelists were, in this case, baptized laymen who would move to pagan villages together with their families, and there testify to their Christian faith with the Word and their way of life. Instead of working at different locations, far apart from each other, groups consisting of six or more families were to get together and form 'mission colonies' in the Amele region. Later on, trained evangelists would join them, to do the school teaching and hold worship services. Already in 1920, the first nine men from Sattelberg arrived in Amele with their families and were stationed at Fulumu. Their names were: Herupe, Ekizia, Ereepa, Rengqai, Tio, Makung, Zangekio, Kanggu, and Futu.

Welsch, together with Keysser and Oertel, made an exploratory trip from Madang through the Ramu and Markham Valleys into the Neuendettelsau mission field, and used the occasion to pay a visit to the congregational mission in the Azera area. He compares the work of the New Guinean evangelists with that of the Samoan pastors and comes to the following conclusion:

The Samoan preachers are strangers who are not familiar with the needs of the Papuans. Besides, they will probably never be able to understand fully how the Papuans think and feel. The evangelists from Finschhafen, however, are New Guineans just like the people among whom they work, and therefore they are acquainted with all the deceptions of the Papuan religion. They know all the tricks and habits of their people. They make a deep impression on their fellow New Guineans because they themselves have fought their way out of the darkness of paganism to Christ and his light ... These evangelists are sent by their congregations and are also supported by them. I did not see any long faces when some evangelists were told that their home congregation couldn't give them any financial support this year. They see themselves as members of their congregations and don't want to be exceptions. They are thankful for whatever they receive. [69]

The Rhenish Mission, too, now began to rely on *Totols* (as their congregational emissaries came to be called), who were often poorly-trained, but nevertheless efficient, evangelists. Thereby their work gained an unforeseen consolidation. Such evangelists, who are typical of the Lutheran Mission in New Guinea, finally became a characteristic element of the Rhenish Mission as well. Thanks to their achievements, the pressure from the Catholic Mission was eventually released. Already in 1926, Kraushaar stated:

The great advantage we have over against the Catholics is the work of our evangelists. The few catechists of the Catholic Mission have, so to speak, the position of contract boys; they are not allowed to preach nor to conduct worship services. [70]

Baptism at Amele with Missionary J. Welsch.

132

One year later, Wullenkord reported that 'in our boundary region up to the Gogol River, evangelists have been placed in almost every village'. [71] There was a total of seven evangelist stations in this area; and Wullenkord announced that the Sattelberg evangelists might now be withdrawn gradually and be replaced by Madang evangelists.

The evangelists' efforts also greatly contributed to the accomplishments of the Karkar mission. George reported in 1924 that the people of the inland villages came to see him with the desire to hear the Word of Jesus. At once he held a conference with his congregations, and the results of the discussion surpassed all expectations. They divided the inland villages up among the Christian congregations and, two by two, young baptized volunteers went to these villages as evangelists. [72] In this way, 28 villages received evangelists, and virtually the entire island was covered, enabling the whole population to hear the message of the Gospel.

Epilogue: Working as Part of Lutheran Mission New Guinea

As mentioned above, the war years had hardly any harmful effect on the process of Christianization in New Guinea. However, we should not forget that the missionaries themselves had to put up with great hardships and restrictions. Contact with Barmen was almost completely cut off, and so were the finances and material supplies. The missionaries were virtually dependent on the little support that the Mission's own plantations yielded.

Of the first-generation missionaries, Hanke died in 1918. In 1921, the European personnel of the Rhenish Mission consisted of 15 adults. All had been in New Guinea for more than eight years, some of them for 14 or 15 years without any leave. Their salaries had not been paid punctually by the Rhenish Mission for years. It would have been impossible for them to make ends meet without the support of the Australian Lutherans and the American Lutherans (Iowa Synod) who regularly granted them loans free of interest. At the time when the two German mission bodies in New Guinea merged to form the Lutheran Mission New Guinea, the Rhenish Mission was in debt to the amount of £5,386. [73]

After the war, the Board in Barmen intended to resume its financial support, and also promised to send new personnel. [74]

However, the Treaty of Versailles and its consequences also affected the German missions in New Guinea. The Australian government, whom the League of Nations had put in charge of Kaiser-Wilhelmsland as a Mandated Territory, decided to expropriate all German property, including that of the German missions. In addition, all Germans were supposed to leave New Guinea, and no new missionaries were to be allowed to enter the country. It was this situation which compelled the Australian and American Lutherans to intervene (see ch 4).

Their initial aim, 'to help the old German mission societies to regain their property', could not be achieved; but, in May 1921 the Australian government transferred the mission fields of the Neuendettelsau and Rhenish missions to the United Evangelical Lutheran Church of Australia (UELCA) and the American Lutheran Iowa Synod. The properties of both missions in New Guinea were transferred to a Board of Trustees in 1926, and administered by the Mission Board of the UELCA. The protest of the Rhenish Mission against this decision was in vain; there was no other choice for the Board in Barmen — as for the Neuendettelsau Mission — but to agree to a merger with the Australians and Americans to form the Lutheran Mission New Guinea.

During the last regular Field Conference of the Rhenish Mission in Ragetta in June 1921, news was received from Australia that the UELCA jointly with the Iowa Synod had taken over the Rhenish Mission in New Guinea. Pastor F.O. Theile, newly-appointed Chairman of the Board of Foreign Mission in Australia, invited the Rhenish missionaries to continue their work and join the new Lutheran Mission New Guinea. All the missionaries who were present at the conference agreed. [75] The new Board took over the overdue salary debts, and employed the missionaries under the same conditions, rights, and duties as their own personnel. That is how the Madang field became a part of the Lutheran Mission New Guinea.

The Mission Board in Barmen wrote in its farewell letter, dated January 16, 1922:

Before the war, 96 Christians; at the end of 1920,

133

Missionary Wilhelm Blum.

church leaders had a special relationship to Neuendettelsau. Many of them had, in fact, studied at the Mission Seminary in Neuendettelsau at some time or other; an equally-cordial relationship to Barmen did not exist. So, the Neuendettelsau influence was much greater, and soon became a decisive factor in personnel decisions. Initially, missionaries were to be called again from Germany as soon as this was feasible, but from Barmen only confessional Lutherans would be eligible. However, as that time drew near, positions hardened, and the relationships grew increasingly tense.

On October 2, 1926, Senior J. Flierl from the Neuendettelsau Mission wrote very harshly:

A truly Lutheran mission would not be able to employ new young missionaries from Barmen in the same way as the old meritorious missionaries, who were here in the hour of need, and had done this kind of work for a long time and grown fond of it. These people should certainly have the possibility of staying here. A young candidate, on the other hand, could only be accepted in exceptional cases: He must be genuinely determined — not just ad hoc — to join the Lutheran Church; at his ordination he ought to be willing and able to pledge absolute loyalty to the Lutheran Confession. The Lutheran Church, according to its principles, can call only Lutheran ministers into the offices of church and mission. Its pastors and missionaries cannot be interdenominational in normal times. [76]

In view of this uncompromising confessional stance, it is not surprising that the Rhenish Mission did not feel comfortable in Lutheran Mission New Guinea, and sought to regain its former independence as soon as possible. However, the old Rhenish missionaries actually experienced very little change under the new administration, apart from the circumstance that now they were working side by side with American (Hannemann, Hueter) and Australian (Holtkamp) missionaries.

School Work

At that time, the school and mission station of Amele began to thrive, and ultimately became the centre of inland mission work. The first baptism took place in 1922. Among those baptized was Gugulu, who later became a strong church leader, and Ud, who is famous for his church hymns. In 1924, two years after the

1264. Zero outposts before the war; now 41, with 1500 people participating in baptism instruction as well! The fields that used to be thorny and full of rocks are now yielding rich harvests. That makes the parting even more painful. The time has come to say farewell to a place that has become dear to so many faithful Christians here at home; to a place where, after a long period of darkness, after many sacrifices, tears, and loss of human lives, the sun is rising brightly.

Of course, the 'farewell' referred to in the above letter was not as dramatic as it may sound. The reports of the missionaries in New Guinea continued to appear in the publications of the Rhenish Mission. Besides, the Rhenish Mission was still a partner in the Lutheran Mission New Guinea — although, due to financial difficulties in Barmen, the contributions in terms of money and personnel were very small.

However, being an interdenominational mission, the Rhenish Mission had the role of an outsider within Lutheran Mission New Guinea; all the other partners were strict members of the Lutheran denomination. Besides, the principal people among the Australian and American first baptism, Wullenkord opened a training centre for evangelists and teachers there.

Language was a problem. Although Schuetz advocated the adoption of the Nobonob language, Wullenkord decided to intoduce the Amele language as the official school language. His next project was to translate and design teaching material. In 1921, a handbook of Bible stories appeared, in the Amele language, and in 1928 a catechism with Bible verses appended.

The recruitment of students was not easy, either. Job opportunities in the expanding city of Madang and on the nearby plantations were much more attractive for the local young people than life as a poor mission student and church school teacher. Wullenkord refers to that problem in his report of December 2, 1925: 'The natives are paid 20 shillings for every boy they bring [to the white employers]. That is tempting … Often 9- or 10-year-old boys are employed.' Small wonder, therefore, that the number of boarding-students dropped from 50 to 30 in the course of two years. Moreover, Nobonob refused to send any students at all because of the language rivalry. Nor did they want to employ any of the Amele graduates. [71]

In spite of all these difficulties, the school station at Amele developed excellently. In the area surrounding Amele, one school after the other was opened. In 1928, Wullenkord already began to lament that the supervision of the numerous evangelists — graduates of Amele — was taking too much of his time. [78] When Mission Director Theile was visiting New Guinea in 1927, he was amazed at the change that had taken place, thanks to the 'systematic training of teachers and assistants':

> While the Mission was in touch with 15,000 to 20,000 natives in 1921, it reaches 35,000 to 40,000 today. In 1921, there were about 1,000 baptized, whereas now there are about 6,000, and many more thousands are preparing for the sacrament of baptism. [79]

The visitor was also struck by the fact that, on his tour through the villages, he did not encounter as many sick people or natives covered with wounds as he had five years earlier. He attributed this to the medical care provided by the missionaries throughout the area.

While Amele was the prominent centre of the inland area, Kurum on Karkar became significant for the region of the Siar-Ragetta language on the mainland coast (later called Graged). George opened a teachers' training school at Urit on Karkar Island in 1925. Unlike Wullenkord, George had the possibility of using the relatively-rich teaching material which the many coastal missionaries before him had produced, particularly Helmich.

The annual report of 1926 gives an impression of what was required and taught at both of these training centres. Wullenkord provided some details of the final examination: The students were required to know the five main sections of the Catechism, a number of Bible stories from the Old and New Testaments, church history up to the Reformation, and the characteristic differences between Protestantism and Catholicism. The skills in writing and arithmetic were also tested. He mentions the following essay-themes:

1. Why do the heathen react negatively when first confronted with the Gospel?
2. What moves the heathen to accept the Gospel?
3. How can the mission worker make sure that the newly-established congregation remains true and faithful to the Gospel?
4. Jesus' attitude toward sin and the sinner.
5. What does Jesus expect of his disciples?
6. How did the Gospel happen to pass from the Jews to the Christians?

While the work on the outskirts of the Madang field made good progress, the central part (that is, the area around Madang, Bongu, and Bogadjim) experienced a decline in activities. A development of this kind is common at the time of transition from the first to the second generation, and even more so when the third generation takes over. In the Madang region, the disintegration of the old village structure caused by urbanization and itinerant work aggravated the situation. Moreover, the Australian administration continued to watch the activities of the German missionaries with suspicion, and often supported elements that were antagonistic toward the Mission.

That is what Director Theile refers to when he writes:

> [The officials] even support the bad elements of the people. Thanks to the influence of Christianity, the majority of the people in Madang district has stopped practising polygamy. But now the D.O. [District Officer] seems to consider it his special

duty to appoint only those men as *Luluais* [village chiefs] and *Tultuls* [village elders] who have two wives. The government officials openly display their preference for those people who still practise their heathen dances. Often these people speak about the Mission in the meanest fashion, and seek to bring it into discredit. The result is that the good-for-nothings show off insolently and rudely in the villages, and pose as *Kiap* people, in contrast to the Mission people ... Even the jurisdiction is affected by this opposition against the Mission, and our Christians obviously suffer because of it. [80]

According to Theile's judgment, it was therefore not surprising that the young congregations were infected by half-heartedness, and that the fresh enthusiasm of the first love had worn off.

The Rhenish Mission Gives Up Its New Guinea Work

The 1926 protest of the Rhenish Mission against the transfer of their property to the Lutheran Board of Trustees came as a surprise to the partners of Lutheran Mission New Guinea, who had considered the joint administration of both mission fields as a permanent arrangement. They now realized that the Rhenish Mission regarded it as a temporary solution. Theile, therefore, urged the Barmen mission administration to explain clearly what they intended to do regarding Madang.

Senior Flierl of Finschhafen, with his rigid Lutheran position, took the following stand: 'Should Barmen insist on sending new people to New Guinea again, this is conceivable only if they resume full responsibility for their former mission field.' [81]

At a conference in Brisbane in May 1929, the churches and mission societies concerned resolved to give the Rhenish Mission its independence once more; its field, however, was drastically reduced. As a sign of gratitude for the emergency help during and after the war, Barmen gave up all claims to certain areas, and ceded them to Lutheran Mission New Guinea (in particular, to the American Iowa Synod); these areas included the Rai Coast with its hinterland and the Mission properties there and the store in Madang.

The outcome of the negotiations with the Rhenish delegation at Brisbane elicited great joy in Barmen. New plans were made. The field

136

administration asked for three new missionaries and four lay missionaries. The work among the lepers on Pig Island was to be reinforced, too.

However, it became apparent very soon that, with its limited field and no possibilities of expanding it, the Rhenish Mission could not survive. Moreover, the financial situation of the Mission Society was badly affected by the world economic crisis. Thus, after only two years of independence, the Rhenish Mission decided — regretfully — to offer their entire New Guinea work to the Americans. That decision was made at a conference in Columbus, Ohio, in 1932. The American Lutheran Church, the church body that was established in 1930 when the synods of Iowa, Ohio, and Buffalo had merged, took over the remaining Rhenish mission field on January 1, 1933.

This abrupt resolution struck the Rhenish workers in New Guinea like a thunderbolt. Of the ordained missionaries, Krueger as a member of the Reformed Church was not able to join the new mission body for confessional reasons. The other ordained Rhenish missionaries were accepted by the Americans. The lay missionaries Dahlhaeuser and Hermann were rejected without any reason given. It was surely not very tactful to inform the two men of this decision in the presence of all the other missionaries; humiliated and embittered, tortured by self-doubts, they walked out of the gathering. After all, Dahlhaeuser had achieved remarkable results in his work. With great vigour and determination, he had succeeded in winning back the Ruo congregation after the Catholics had got hold of it. [82] In like manner, he had revived the Ragetta congregation, which had become increasingly indifferent. Even those missionaries who were accepted, had a hard time adjusting to the changed situation. [83]

Eiffert expressed everyone's feelings in his farewell report of October 24, 1932:

In 1921 there were 1463 baptized, and today there are close to 11,000 who have joined the Christian community ... In baptism classes, according to the statistics, there are 3836 people ... With long patient work, we sowed again and again. And now that the seed is finally sprouting, and the harvest can begin, we must relinquish the field ... So, then we part from you, cherished Rhenish mission field, land of so many tears and prayers —both here and at home. We mourn for you, dear Rhenish mission

Missionary Georg Eiffert.

field, as for the loss of a dear friend and brother. May God bless the work of the new administration and help it to grow. [84]

For many years thereafter, Rhenish missionaries worked loyally within Lutheran Mission New Guinea — for instance, the widowed Mrs Welsch until 1963, and Missionary Schoettler until the 1970s.

The former field of the Rhenish Mission is now one of the districts of the ELC-PNG. It contributes to the life of the Lutheran Church with its special character, impressed on it by the work of the Rhenish Mission.

Endnotes

[1] Kaiserlicher Schutzbrief vom 17. Mai 1885, as quoted in Dr A. Schreiber, Bericht an die Deputation der Rheinischen Mission (Barmen Archives).

[2] Allgemeine Bedingungen fuer die Zulassung evangelischer Missionare in Neuguinea, quoted by E. Kriele, *Das Kreuz unter den Palmen* (Barmen: Verlag des Missionshauses, 1927), 18.

[3] Letter of the Board to its missionaries in New Guinea, dated May 24, 1909 (Barmen Archives).

[4] N. Mikloucho-Maclay, *New Guinea Diaries 1871-1883*, translated by C.L. Sentinella (Madang: Kristen Pres, 1975), 324.

[5] Situated at Dalua Bay, between Madang and the Ramu outlet.

[6] E. Kriele, 26.

[7] N. Mikloucho-Maclay, 325.

[8] Conference Report 1889 (Letters, Barmen Archives). It is understandable that the Rhenish Mission did not spell out in detail these problems in its publications. Kubary is referred to only as 'K'.

[9] The purchase itself became legal with the transfer of the purchase deed on February 25, 1888.

[10] Conference Report 1904 (Barmen Archives).

[11] Most of them were from the island of Mioko in the Bismarck Archipelago, who were enlisted for labour by the German colonial administration. The Rhenish Mission hired some of these men from the New Guinea Company. They were steadfast oarsmen, first-rate swimmers, and good workers.

[12] E. Kriele, 72-76. G. Kunze, *Im Dienst des Kreuzes auf ungebahnten Pfaden* (Barmen: Verlag des Missionshauses, 3rd edn, 1925), 105-110.

[13] E. Kriele, 73.

[14] G. Kunze, 109.

[15] Conference Report 1890,6. The most drastic incident of this kind occurred on July 23, 1887, when a white plantation settler and his 20 Javanese workmen were attacked. One of the Javanese was killed; six were wounded, four of them seriously. The delinquents in this case came off rather lightly, thanks to the attitude of the Commander of the German warship *Sophie*, who 'did not feel like taking any drastic measures just for the sake of one single Malayan who had been speared by a native'.

[16] N. Mikloucho-Maclay, 324.

[17] G. Kunze, in the work cited above.

[18] *Ibid*, 83.

[19] *Ibid*, 162.

[20] Conference Reports 1889 and 1890.

[21] Conference Report 1890.

[22] The Conference Report of 1903 records that Ostermann hit a boy at school. The result was that the father wanted to take the boy out of school, and another man even threatened to kill Ostermann with a spear.

[23] G. Bergmann describes very vividly how he scrutinized each word of the Lord's Prayer before he decided upon a certain term. Not only central words such as 'Father', 'God', 'Creator', 'Holy Spirit' had to be chosen with utmost care to prevent misunderstanding; the same deliberation was required for seemingly-simple words like 'our', 'holy', 'prayer', 'will', 'kingdom'. See also Reports of the Language Conference 1898 (Barmen Archives).

[24] Conference Report 1898.

[25] G. Kunze, 190.

[26] *Ibid*, 202.

[27] *Ibid*, 205.

[28] *Ibid*, 156.

[29] *Berichte der Rheinischen Mission* 1904, 227-229.

[30] Letter of the Board to its missionaries, dated May 9, 1904 (Barmen Archives).

[31] Conference Report 1904.

[32] In the Jabem language, *ngamala* = human being; here, people of the Neuendettelsau mission area.

[33] Report to Barmen, August 27,1904 (Barmen Archives).

[34] *Ibid.*

[35] *Ibid.*

[36] Minutes of 1906 Field Conference at Bongu, 14.

[37] Conference Report 1906. 'For the first time since the existence of the New Guinea Mission we could enter in our annual report the column 'Candidates for Baptism' with figures — though low ones ... It appears significant to us that there aren't just individual applicants who are coming ... but several ... and at several stations.'

[38] *Berichte der Rheinischen Mission* 1906, 86.

[39] Hanke, *ibid.*

[40] *Berichte der Rheinischen Mission* 1907, 29-30.

[41] *Ibid*, 54-55.

[42] Schuetz, *ibid.*

[43] Schuetz, *Berichte der Reinischen Mission* 1906, 217.

[44] Diehl, *Berichte der Rheinischen Mission* 1912, 11.

[45] Hanke, *Berichte der Rheinischen Mission* 1906, 93.

[46] Letter to the President of the Rhenish Mission, dated December 30, 1918 (Barmen Archives).

[47] Letter to the President of the Rhenish Mission, dated October 1932 (Barmen Archives).

[48] Siliva, Report to the Annual Field Conference 1914 (Barmen Archives).

[49] Asafo, Report for the first six months of 1921: 'The mountain villages I visited are Mangangkarab, Pangsick, Ola, Narer, Sikentika, Komangkuting, Tulakotam, Kial, Ukamtika, Orara, Afare, Sangana, Tikosori, Keng, and Mom' (Barmen Archives).

[50] Asafo, Report to the Annual Field Conference 1920 (Barmen Archives).

[51] *Ibid.*

[52] Taeao, Report, June 1920 (Barmen Archives).

[53] As quoted by Hanke in his Report to the Field Conference 1906 (Barmen Archives).

[54] Letter to the Board, dated January 11, 1914 (Barmen Archives).

[55] *Berichte der Rheinischen Mission* 1917, 83 et seq.

[56] On September 10, 1914, the Australian forces occupied Rabaul, the seat of the German colonial government. On September 25, 400 to 500 Australians under Major Martin occupied Freidrich-Wilhelmshafen. Germans were allowed to stay on and to pursue their former occupations as long as they took the oath of neutrality. This also applied to the missionaries.

[57] Letter to the Board, dated October 28, 1915 (Barmen Archives).

[58] This slander resulted in the tensions between Weber and the government. Weber had to leave New Guinea in 1908 and to resign from the mission. Later, he returned as a private farmer to Umboi (Siassi). He was murdered there in 1912.

[59] *Berichte der Rheinischen Mission* 1922, 170-171.

[60] *Berichte der Rheinischen Mission* 1921/22.

[61] *Berichte der Rheinischen Mission* 1921, 168 et seq.

[62] *Berichte der Rheinischen Mission* 1907, 163-164.

[63] Minutes of Field Conference 1914 (Barmen Archives).

[64] Conference Report 1914, 19.

[65] von Kraushaar's report of May 15, 1926 simply says 'a few years ago'.

[66] Conference Report 1914, 67. The areas named were the main fields of work of the Rhenish Mission; they are now known as Karkar Island, Bagabag Island, and among the Nobonob people.

[67] *Ibid*, 50.

[68] Minutes of a Consultation between Keysser and Oertel of the Neuendettelsau Mission and Blum, Wullenkord, and Welsch of the Rhenish Mission at Ragetta, April 12, 1919 (Barmen Archives).

[69] *Berichte der Rheinischen Mission* 1920, 101.

[70] von Kraushaar, Travel Journal, March 15, 1926 (Barmen Archives).

[71] Wullenkord, Report of 1927.

[72] *Berichte der Rheinischen Mission* 1924, 161.

[73] O. Theile, First Report 1921/22, 4.

[74] Letter of the Board to its missionaries in New Guinea, dated January 11, 1920 (Barmen Archives).

[75] Present were: Blum, Eiffert, Wullenkord, Welsch. Absentees George, Eckershoff, and Schuetz agreed later. Graeb was ill and had to return to Germany.

[76] Letter to the supporting Mission Boards, dated October 2, 1926 (Barmen Archives).

[77] After the departure of Schuetz in 1926, 21 students from Nobonob immediately joined the school at Amele. This fact clearly shows that the white missionaries themselves must be held responsible for much of the unfortunate disagreement.

[78] Conference Report 1928.

[79] O. Theile, Report 1927, 2.

[80] O. Theile, Report 1926, 4.

[81] Letter to the supporting Mission Boards; see note 76.

[82] Dahlhaeuser was taken over by Lutheran Mission Finschhafen. He served at Sattelberg until 1939. After his internment in Australia, he returned to Germany.

[83] For the names of the Rhenish Missionaries who were taken over by Lutheran Mission Madang (ALC), see the following chapter, note 55.

[84] Eiffert, Farewell Report to the Rhenish Mission Board, dated October 24, 1932.

Chapter 4

Partnership across Oceans

The American Lutheran Church

by Gerhard O. Reitz

What part did American Lutherans play in bringing the Gospel to Papua New Guinea? Why should Americans be interested in a far-off island in the western Pacific, when America itself was still very much a mission area in 1886?

An Early Relationship

The Lutheran churches in middle America were so busy in the first 50 years of their existence with the need to minister to the tens of thousands of immigrants by training pastors, building schools, and gathering congregations, that they did not begin overseas mission work of their own. But, since many midwest pastors had been classmates in Neuendettelsau and other Lutheran training schools in Europe of men who became missionaries in Australia, South America, Asia, and Africa, they were very interested in their work and supported these overseas missions by sending regular contributions to the mission societies in Europe. [1]

Therefore, from the very beginning of the Neuendettelsau Mission Society's work in New Guinea, congregations and pastors of the Iowa Synod in America became partners of the work.

The great majority of gifts still went from Neuendettelsau to America for support of missionaries, circuit riders, teachers, and schools. And it also went the other way: Pastors of the Iowa Synod supported Neuendettelsau's New Guinea mission work through their gifts, right from the beginning.

Already in 1886, in November, Pastor Michelson sent 625 Marks as a gift to Neuendettelsau from the Iowa Synod for the mission work in New Guinea. In April of 1887, he sent M 490, and in August of 1887 another M 412. [2] Mission Inspector J. Deinzer of Neuendettelsau exclaimed: 'We didn't expect that almost 45 years after we had scattered bread upon the waters we would now find it again after such a long time'. [3] When in 1899 the students and friends of Inspector Deinzer, who were serving in America, heard that funds were required for the fourth mission station to be established in the Finschhafen area, they decided to gather the funds as a memorial to Inspector Deinzer who had died in 1897. [4]

So, from the very beginning the Iowa Synod had contributed to the mission work in New Guinea. These gifts grew, until at the beginning

141

of the First World War they amounted to about one-third of all receipts for the mission.[5] Many pastors of Iowa Synod, together with their congregations, considered the Neuendettelsau Mission in New Guinea 'their' mission. Neuendettelsau had sown the seed of the Gospel in America, and reaped a harvest for mission work in New Guinea.

American Lutherans Identify with the New Guinea Mission

The coming of World War I suddenly brought many difficulties for the mission work in New Guinea. Both the Neuendettelsau and the Rhenish Mission Society were German societies. Germany declared war on France on August 3, 1914, and next day England, an ally of France, declared war against Germany. Soon most major nations in Europe, Australia, and later also the USA, were involved in a terrible war.

On September 11, 1914, an Australian military force landed at Rabaul, the administrative centre of the German colony. The German administration surrendered after a short fight on September 17. On September 21, Madang was occupied by British and Australian forces, but it was not till January 8, 1915, that the Patrol Post of Morobe was taken.[6] When the German administrators at Morobe fled into the bush, together with Captain Detzner who was to survey the border, the young missionaries W. Flierl and H. Raum were blamed for aiding their escape, and were later interned in Australia. Also detained and later interned was the visiting Neuendettelsau Inspector Steck, who had refused to take an oath of neutrality as was required of all German nationals.[7] Because of these events, the German missions were regarded by suspicion throughout the war and also later by some Australian administrators.

Because of a sudden lack of communication, and also of shipping and of regular mail service, all kinds of rumours spread about the missionaries in New Guinea. First, it was reported in the United States that all German missionaries were prisoners of war, cut off from families and congregations. Later, the rumour was spread that all German missionaries were taken as prisoners to England, and their wives and children left in New Guinea.[8] Because of these rumours, Prof.

142

G. Fritschel of Wartburg Seminary and other pastors contacted the British Embassy and the United States State Department to find relief for the wives and children of the missionaries. All the rumours were officially denied.

Lutherans in America, however, soon realized that the war in Europe would not be over very quickly, and that German missions in Africa, Asia, and the Pacific would require special help. Dr M. Reu of Wartburg Seminary said in his *Kirchliche Zeitschrift:* 'We must help, we can help, we will help'.[9] When approached, the US State Department contacted the Australian government, and was assured that all German missionaries in New Guinea were still at work and that the Iowa Synod could send funds according to arrangements made by the State Department.[10]

Specific news about need was slow in coming from New Guinea to Australia and to the United States. One letter was evidently sent by W. Flierl, dated December 24, 1914, from Ongga via Anglican missionaries in Papua to Pastor Art. Reuther in Australia. Pastor Reuther passed on the news to his brother-in-law, Pastor H. Senft, in Georgia, Iowa. W. Flierl reported that the missionaries were getting on well, but that supplies were short.[11] Much earlier, on October 23, 1914, Senior Flierl had written to the Revd F. Otto Theile in Bethania, Queensland, saying that the missionaries were in need of food supplies. The letter of Flierl did not reach Theile. Instead, a letter from the Revd Copeland King, a neighbouring Anglican missionary in Papua, who sent Flierl's letter on, did arrive, giving the message intended by Senior Flierl. The letter of King must have arrived in the first week of January 1915.[12]

The Revd Theile immediately took action. First of all, permission was obtained from military authorities to send food supplies to New Guinea via the Anglican missionary, the Revd King.[13] Next, the Australian Board of Missions (Anglican), on Theile's request, sent instructions to their missionaries in Papua to help Lutheran missionaries wherever possible. Theile promised funds, even though he had none available. He possessed only £20 destined for the Hope Vale mission in North Queensland. But he went ahead and ordered the most needed supplies, and sent them off to

Finschhafen. The news of the first shipment caused great joy among missionaries in Finschhafen. Many sent letters of thanks to Theile. [14]

In the meantime, Senior Flierl, and also Pastor Theile, had written to the mission friends in America to help pay for necessary supplies. Before these appeals were generally known, people like Dr Reu spoke out for massive aid. He pointed out that in 1914 the Neuendettelsau Mission had spent M 321,000, but had received only M 210,000. He continued: 'So now we must help much more energetically'. [15] Dr F. Richter, responding to a letter from Senior Flierl, wrote that the Lutherans of the Iowa Synod would stand together with the Lutherans of Australia in giving necessary and regular mission support. [16] The first gift of £700 from the Iowa Synod arrived in Brisbane at the beginning of July.

But now other needs pressed themselves upon Senior Flierl. Missionaries Zwanzger, Hoh, and Pfalzer were absent from the field, and H. Raum and W. Flierl were interned. G. Keppler, an Australian layman, was on medical leave in Australia when war came. Flierl repeatedly asked Theile if Australian missionaries could be sent to help out, but that was not possible; neither was it for Americans. [17]

Another need became urgent. The Hope Vale Mission in Queensland had been receiving £500 annual support from Neuendettelsau, and this was now no longer available. Dr Richter assured Theile of support, promising that Hope Vale should not suffer. The Rhenish mission in Madang was likewise in serious need, and the Iowa Synod agreed that relief aid should be shared also with the Madang missionaries. [18]

The war in Europe dragged on, demanding ever greater sacrifices of blood and agony. The pastors in the Iowa Synod recognized that aid for the New Guinea mission would have to be gathered in a better way than previously. By January 1916, the mission magazine *Die Missions-Stunde*, started in 1913, had a list of 2,300 subscribers. That number was insufficient. So, a drive was begun to increase subscriptions to 5,000 by October 31, 1917 [19]

The Fourth Missions Conference of the Dakota District was held from May 29 to 31, 1916, at Wishek, N.D., and made plans for a mission aid society (later called The Mission Auxiliary) to support further appeals for help. The aid society was to cover all districts of the Synod. [20] The inaugural meeting of this aid society for New Guinea was established on May 30, the last day of the missions conference, with 80 friends present. The Revd W. Kraushaar was elected chairman, the Revd R. Taeuber secretary, and Pastor A. Hoeger treasurer. The meeting said:

> Since we are bound together with Neuedettelsau through the bonds of love and common work, so shall the society first of all be an aid society for New Guinea. As such, the society will take over special projects of the work over there ... It will also be a goal of the society to win missionaries out of our circles, so that the Lord cannot make the justified accusation, you indeed gave of money but you were unwilling to bring an offering of flesh and blood. [21]

By January of 1917, the New Guinea Aid Society had 1,019 members, by the end of 1919 it had over 3,000. [22]

From September 1914 to July 1919, funds of the Iowa Synod for 'our mission' rose from $1,308 to $13,000. The total for that period was $86,438. [23]

Dr F. Richter, President of Iowa Synod.

So, in a marvellous way, God took care of the missions in Finschhafen and in Madang during the emergency of World War I. Despite the scarcity of supplies and funds, and despite the fact that the missions were understaffed, and missionaries sick and in need of furlough, God blessed the Gospel and the work of the congregations, so that the Word of the Lord grew and bore much fruit.

American and Australian Lutherans Save the Former German Missions in New Guinea

The official situation for the German missions in New Guinea did not change immediately at the end of the war which came on November 11, 1918, when Germany asked for a truce. Only two years later did the Australian government take action concerning the German mission in New Guinea.

In the meantime, the Lutherans in America and Australia continued their support of the mission work. The period of emergency help stretched out for almost seven years. Relief given by Australian and American Lutherans was primarily given for the Finschhafen Mission. What was given for the Rhenish Mission in Madang was given as a loan.

In August 1917, the General Synod of Iowa, meeting in Dubuque, had authorized the Synod itself to take over all responsibility for the mission in New Guinea if necessary. To make such a move possible, a Heathen-Missions Committee of the Evangelical Lutheran Synod of Iowa and Other States was chosen. Members of this committee were Prof. George Fritschel (secretary), Pastors G. Gundel (chairman), A. Hoeger, R. Taeuber, and F. Braun (treasurer). The first meeting was held on July 16, 1919, in Sioux City, Iowa. Present also was Dr F. Richter. He reported that Synod gave complete support to the Rhenish Mission in New Guinea and to the Leipzig Mission in East Africa. Dr Richter also reported that the Iowa Synod had made a claim on the New Guinea mission through the National Lutheran Council and the International Missionary Council. [24]

The World Alliance of Churches, meeting in the Netherlands in October 1919, stated that German missions should be allowed to continue. The Revd Shaw of the Anglican Mission in Papua attended the Lambeth Conference of the Anglican Church in London

144

in 1919, and spoke in support of the Lutheran mission in New Guinea. [25] Why the concern? In paragraph 119 of the Versailles Peace Treaty, Germany had to renounce her right and title to all overseas possessions. Paragraph 122 gave the legal right to all governments in charge of former German colonies to expel all German missionaries and to transfer the missions and all their belongings to other churches. On the other hand, paragraph 438 of the Treaty gave some hope that the mission work should have a future. It reads as follows (the emphasis is mine):

> The Allied and Associated Powers agree that where Christian religious missions were being maintained by German societies or persons in territory belonging to them, or of which the government is entrusted to them in accordance with the present Treaty, the *property which these missions or mission societies possessed, including that of trading societies whose profits were devoted to the support of missions, shall continue to be devoted to missionary purposes.* In order to ensure the due execution of this undertaking, the Allied and Associated Governments *will hand over such property to boards of trustees, appointed by or approved by the Governments and composed of persons holding the faith of the Mission whose property is involved.* [26]

The concern over the future of the New Guinean mission was very real. Lutherans of German background in America, and especially in Australia, were regarded with suspicion of disloyalty during the First World War. In fact, in many places in Australia, German-language Lutherans were regarded as enemies of Australia. Articles written for local newspapers continually attacked Australians of German origin, and also their churches, schools, and missions. Many people had forgotten the pioneering work of German Lutheran settlers.

An article published already in March 1919 in the Iowa Synod, in view of the situation, expressed real concern for the missions in New Guinea:

> The German societies will possibly have to give up the fruit of much work of love, the result of much faithful giving and sacrificial care, to others who will reap where they have not sown. Where the carcass is, there gather the vultures ... We lay claim to the New Guinea mission. For tens of years we have prayed, wrestled, preached, worked, offered, and given a portion, and in part of it the inner life of our

Iowa Synod lies over there on the green island in the peaceful ocean. And thousands of strengths, of faith, of love, and of hope bind us with her. If it no longer dares be a Neuendettelsau mission, then it must be an American. Then it shall be ours. Can we carry the burden? [27]

At the second meeting of the Board of Foreign Missions (BFM) of Iowa Synod, held on September 9, 1919 in Minneapolis, calculations were made as to additional funds necessary each year from America to carry on the Neuendettelsau work in New Guinea on the level of the work before the war in 1913. What was not considered was that in both Finschhafen and Madang there had been tremendous growth in the work. In addition, considerable debts had accumulated, with unpaid bills for supplies and unpaid salaries. Nevertheless, the Board proposed to Synod to raise $75,000 for 1920, $80,000 for 1921, and $85,000 for 1922. [28]

The first priority of the Iowa Synod, in the case of possible loss of the German missions of the Lutheran Church, was to completely take over the Neuendettelsau mission, since Iowa had always regarded that mission as its own. The second priority was to hold and possibly take over the Rhenish mission in Madang, if the Rhenish missionaries there would be willing to work under a Lutheran administration. [29]

Compared to other German missions, the New Guinea missions of German churches suffered least during the war period. The most important task after the war was the replacement of missionaries and the addition of new workers, because of the growth of the work. There was also a need that someone should study the situation at first hand. The Iowa Board thought that possibly Senior Flierl could come to America, or that someone from America or Australia could go to New Guinea. Both were impossible.

Some months later, the Revd Theile impressed upon the Iowa Board that furloughs for missionaries were immediately required. The Board agreed, and sent $2,500 to Australia to make furloughs possible. But then came the report from Theile that missionaries would not be allowed to go on furlough. In negotiations with the Australian government, Theile had received the impression that Neuendettelsau would not be allowed to continue mission work,

and that the Lutherans in Australia and the United States would have to take over. The Iowa Board accepted in principle a proposal by Senior Flierl that Australian Lutherans, Neuendettelsau, and the Iowa Synod should carry on the work together, and that legal ownership be in the hands of Australia and the Australian Board executive. [30]

The Mission Auxiliary (or the New Guinea Aid Society), which had published *Die Missions-Stunde* (The Mission Hour) since 1913, and the BFM of Iowa decided that it was necessary to publish an English-language monthly magazine, called *The Lutheran Missionary*, in order to contact a much larger membership in the Synod. *The Lutheran Missionary* began publication in January 1921, and did an excellent job of publicity for mission work in New Guinea by publishing regularly articles, reports, and statistics of missionaries. Already in February 1921 a complete list of all missionaries and their families in the Finschhafen field was given.

To meet the needs of the developing situation, Dr Richter, president of the Iowa Synod, left for Australia and arrived there safely on February 4, 1921. He began immediate intensive negotiations with the Revd F. Otto Theile concerning the union of Lutherans in Australia and the propositions to be placed before Australian authorities. God blessed the consultations, and on March 21 the United Evangelical Lutheran Church in Australia was formed and the decision made to take over the German missions in New Guinea and to carry out the mission work in partnership with the Iowa Synod. [31] This was the first time that union of Lutherans in Australia became important for the history of the Lutheran Church in New Guinea. [32] And the decision was made just in time.

The Australian government was not in the mood to permit the German missions in New Guinea to continue under any Lutheran supervision or control, whether Australian or American. It was necessary to contact other Protestant churches in Australia for support. The government wanted to have assurances that other Protestant mission boards could not, or were unwilling to, take over the New Guinea work. So, on February 17, Theile and Richter met with the United Missionary Council of

145

Australia in Sydney. The Council represented Anglicans, Presbyterians, and Methodists. The Council affirmed:

That this Council representing all the Protestant missionary societies in Australia is of the opinion that in view of the great and important work carried on by the Lutheran Mission in late German New Guinea the matter of the repatriation of German missionaries should not be unduly hurried. We endorse the proposal of the Australian Lutheran Church that it take control of this mission supported by the Lutheran body in America, that new members appointed to the mission should be Australian or American citizens and that gradually so far as possible, an Australian staff should be created.

The above resolution was part of a submission made by the Revd Theile, who was now chairman of the Board of Foreign Mission of the UELCA, and by Dr Richter, President of the Iowa Synod, to the Australian Prime Minister Hughes on March 24, 1921. They had already met with the Prime Minister on March 15.[33] In the same submission, the Lutheran representatives also asserted that they had met with the Revd J.G. Wheen, Secretary of the Methodist Foreign Mission Board, and with the Revd Jones, Chairman of the Anglican ABM in Sydney, on February 17, and with Archbishop Donaldson of Brisbane on February 22.

These three gentlemen emphatically declared that their boards were not in a position to take care of the Lutheran Mission in New Guinea. This mission is a field of such magnitude and requires so many workers and such large annual expenses that they are unable to think of accepting the responsibility for same.

In the second part of the submission, Theile and Richter go on to say:

The Foreign Mission Board of the United Evangelical Lutheran Church of Australia in taking control of the Lutheran Mission in New Guinea is determined to send only Australian-born and American-born workers; ordained missionaries, lay helpers, nurses, teachers, physicians, etc., to New Guinea. Since it is far beyond the means of the Australian Lutheran Church to carry on the work in New Guinea on its own accord, the United Evangelical Lutheran Church in Australia needs the assistance of the American Lutherans, which is freely offered by the Evangelical Lutheran Synod of Iowa a.o.S. As soon as the chairman of the board of Foreign Missions of the said church, has had an

opportunity to inspect the field personally and his report can be acted upon, an Australian will be sent to New Guinea to take the office of superintendent of the mission and he would be the person with whom the civil administration at Rabaul would have to deal in all matters pertaining to this mission.

Other important needs of the New Guinea mission mentioned in the submission included: (1) the need for experienced missionaries who spoke the language to continue the work, (2) the need of furloughs for the missionaries, and (3) the importance of uniting German brides with their missionary husbands in New Guinea. Although the Prime Minister had requested early replacement of German nationals in New Guinea, the two Lutheran representatives assured him that by the end of the present decade they would 'see that the present missionary staff is replaced by Australian and American staff'.

Another interview with the Prime Minister was scheduled for April 18. For that occasion, Dr Richter prepared a submission in which he stated the following: (1) 'We are ready to take control of the mission in New Guinea — with the understanding that the missionaries be permitted to stay until 1925 and that the Foreign Mission Board of the UELCA then be permitted to request an extension if necessary.' (2) 'We take it for granted that children of the missionaries will be able to go to proper schools in Australia and missionaries needing furloughs will also be able to come to Australia.' (3) He mentioned the importance of a decision concerning fiancées of missionaries being allowed to come to New Guinea.

Thereupon the Prime Minister let Dr Richter know that no further interview was necessary, and that there was acceptance of the need for missionaries to take furloughs, and for children to go to proper schools in Australia. The question of missionary brides would still have to be considered by Cabinet. But on the question of the missionaries themselves, Dr Richter reports:

I left Mr Dean (Secretary to the Prime Minister) assured that we would be given control of the mission and that the missionaries would be permitted to stay eight years — four of which would be given to us now, the other four later.

The Revd Theile also contacted Mr A. Wienholt, a member of the Lutheran Church and also a member of Parliament, who now personally contacted the Acting Prime Minister, Mr Joseph Cook. The personal representations of Mr Wienholt resulted in a statement from the Prime Minister's Office. Mr Joseph Cook wrote on June 22, 1921, as follows:

(a) That the Australian Lutheran Church, supported by the Lutheran organization in America, shall be permitted to take control of the Lutheran missions in the Territory of New Guinea on lines discussed between Dr Richter, Rev. Theile and the Prime Minister recently;

(b) That such of the German missionaries at present attached to the mission as are prepared to take an oath of loyalty shall be permitted to remain in the Territory for a period of four years, as from June 1, 1921, and then to be replaced by Australian-born and American-born missionaries;

(c) That during this period of four years children of German missionaries may be sent to proper schools in Australia and the missionaries allowed to enter Australia for purposes of furlough;

(d) That fiancées of the limited number of missionaries referred to by Dr Richter should be permitted to come from Germany to New Guinea;

(e) The foregoing concessions to be conditional on adequate guarantees being furnished of loyalty to the Administration and abstention from any act or word which might prejudice the Administration. [34]

On June 28, the Revd Theile responded to the Acting Prime Minister concerning the conditions mentioned in Mr Cook's letter to Mr Wienholt. Attached to the letter was a list of 28 ordained missionaries and four laymen of German extraction, and two laymen of Australian extraction, at work in Finschhafen. At the moment, the Revd Theile forgot to include the names of the Madang missionaries.

In a short note of July 15, the Acting Prime Minister, Joseph Cook, stated in reference to his letter of June 22, that, after reconsideration, the government still thought that every effort should be made to replace the German missionaries in four years; in view, however, of representations as to the difficulty which will be experienced in providing trained substitutes it (the government) has now decided that a further period of three years will be granted' (which would bring the period of grace to 1928).

However, all problems were still not solved. Dr Richter returned to America and reported orally to the Iowa Synod Board of Foreign Mission concerning all that had happened in his negotiations with the Australian government. On the basis of Dr Richter's report, the Board resolved to send out all missionary candidates to New Guinea who passed the necessary qualifications. [35]

In order to take legal responsibility for the German mission property in New Guinea, the nine members of the UELCA Board of Foreign Missions were also nominated, to the government of Australia, as trustees. [36] This made possible the official legal takeover of the properties and the administration, beginning on September 30, 1921. Both Madang and Finschhafen were treated as one mission, with the Superintendent of Finschhafen serving as chief executive for the whole. The Revd F. Otto Theile became the official director of the mission field in 1923, appointed by the Iowa Synod and UELCA Boards of Foreign Mission. The Iowa Synod Board insisted that he resign as both chairman and member of the UELCA Board. Theile remained as chairman of the Board of Trustees. [37]

First American Missionaries Sent to New Guinea

The time had come for the Iowa Synod to send missionary personnel to New Guinea. To find volunteers for overseas assignment after World War I was not an easy task. From 1921 to the end of 1925 only two ordained missionaries were sent. The first Americans actually to arrive in New Guinea were Mr and Mrs Fred Knautz, and Misses Ida and Ludhilde Voss. [38] Mr Fred Knautz had planned to go to Finschhafen with the others, but on arrival at Madang on October 24, 1921, he met the Revd Theile who told him he was to be stationed at Ragetta (Graged) Island. Mr Knautz was to be the first of many American laymen to serve in New Guinea with distinction. At Ragetta, the Knautzes took over the work of supply for missionaries and the care of the mission station at Maulon, previously served by pioneer missionary Blum. Mr Knautz was a very shrewd businessman, as well as an all-round handy man. His skills saved the

Mission much money. Mr Knautz did not return to New Guinea after his term of service because doctors said he would lose his sight if he continued to take quinine for malaria.

The Voss sisters arrived in Finschhafen on October 28, 1921. Ludhilde, a trained teacher, was stationed at Sattelberg. In 1926 she was married to the Revd E. Hannemann, but she died in 1929 on Karkar. Her sister Ida was a trained deaconess. Her medical service started in a very simple way, helping village people at Pola and Maneba stations (Finschhafen). A provisional hospital was built in 1924, halfway between Pola and Salankaua. In between work at the hospital, trips were made to villages or to Sattelberg to give medical service when needed. Later married to the Australian lay missionary V. Koschade at Sattelberg, she continued her medical work wherever the two were stationed. From June 1923, Ida Voss was very thankful for the presence of Dr A.B. Estock, the first medical doctor from the United States, who worked at Finschhafen until 1926.

The fifth and sixth Iowa Synod missionaries to arrive in New Guinea in July 1922 were laymen. Mr William H. Siemers, an experienced carpenter and an outstanding example of a Christian builder, was to give 22 years of dedicated service in New Guinea under very difficult conditions. In 1924, Siemers began an Industrial School with eight young men as students. The students contracted to stay three years, during which time they were taught elementary carpentry. At the end of the training period they were to return to their home congregations with a set of tools to build schools, desks, benches, and churches, as well as better homes. Through the years, Siemers emphasized Christian behaviour and Bible study among the young men he trained. His regular reports on special festival days held on the occasions of baptisms, confirmations, church dedications, and so on, provided inspiring reading for mission friends in America.

The other layman who travelled with Siemers was Mr Andrew Freese. When Freese heard of the lay people who left for New Guinea in 1921, he determined to offer his gifts as a farmer to God in the mission field. When Freese arrived in New Guinea, he was assigned to Malahang Plantation at Lae, where he relieved Missionary Georg Stuerzenhofecker, who then took charge of Gabmazung mission station. Stuerzenhofecker had been planting coconuts at Malahang since 1916, as an emergency measure to find funds for the Mission during the war-time period.

Although the Revd and Mrs E. Pietz were among the first group of missionaries to leave America, they did not arrive in New Guinea until September 22, 1922, since the Revd Pietz was required to take care of the three congregations served by the Revd O. Theile in Brisbane, who from October 1921 to August 1922 made a thorough inspection trip of the missions in New Guinea.

The Pietzes were assigned permanently to Kaiapit among the Azera people, 60 miles inland up the Markham valley. At Kaiapit in 1924, Pietz found conditions rather primitive. He reports: 'Here in New Guinea in such primitive conditions, spade, hoe, and hammer often become the tools used by the missionary'. Not much time was left for school work and language study. In Kaiapit the missionary had to master the local Azera language, and at the same time be proficient in Jabem for work in schools and with the evangelists.

Revd E. Pietz. The first ordained American missionary in New Guinea.

148

During the pioneer years in Kaiapit, a faithful evangelist from Bukawa, named Geyammalo Apo, who was working among the Amari people across the Markham River, made some of the first contacts with the Gazub people of the Eastern Highlands, thus opening the way for an historic evangelistic thrust by Kate evangelists in the Eastern Highlands, beginning in 1922. Pietz very early recognized the remarkable work of the local evangelists, who often were exposed to great danger.[39] He promoted some of the best traditions of evangelistic work that had been found to be successful by the early Neuendettelsau missionaries.[40]

Arriving at Madang on December 30, 1923, E. Hannemann was assigned to Ragetta (Graged) station to study the Graged (Bel) language and culture, under the Rhenish pioneer missionary W. Blum. The assignment of E. Hannemann to Graged proved significant later in the 1930s, since the Graged (Bel) language was selected by the new Madang mission of the American Lutheran Church as the church and school language of the whole Madang mission. On April 12, 1928, the

Revd E. Hannemann.

Hannemann family moved to Kurum on the island of Karkar to take care of the missionary work among the numerous Takian and Waskian villages. The Karkar people at that time, and also through the years, required much medical attention. Hannemann was saddened by the high infant mortality rate. Little did he realize that less than two years later, on November 11, 1929, his young and talented wife Ludhilde was to die from blackwater fever at Kurum.

In the years 1923 and 1924, the Iowa Synod sent out five single women to serve in a variety of ways. The first one to arrive in May 1923 was Sophie Deguisne (later Mrs Lehner), with the purpose of helping wherever possible. Four others came to New Guinea in December of 1924: Tennie Kalkwarf and Louise Reck (both stationed at Sattelberg, at the school for missionaries' children), and Emma and Hattie Engeling. Emma was a trained teacher; she served first on Sattelberg. After having been married to the Mission ship's captain, T. Radke, they moved to Madang, where she taught in the Chinese School. After her husband's death in February 1944, in Japanese imprisonment, she returned after the war to New Guinea to teach Chinese and mixed-race children until 1963.

Emma's sister Hattie, a nurse by profession, took over the small clinic at Amele in Madang. Her first five years at Amele were to be an excellent introduction for Hattie, who later married Dr Braun. She continued to give a total of 48 years of dedicated care to the sick and the training of indigenous nurses in New Guinea.

Finally, in 1926, the Iowa Synod was able to send an additional three ordained missionaries to New Guinea to help fulfil a burning need. George Hueter took over Nobonob station from the Revd Schuetz, who was the founder of the mission station and now badly required furlough. Nobonob territory bordered Roman Catholic mission work spreading west and south from Alexishafen, and therefore suffered much from religious competition.

Two other single ordained men arrived in November 1926. R. Hanselmann was assigned work at Keku station, south of Madang. Hanselmann developed a system of instructing young men as evangelists, who participated in telling the Gospel in an ever-increasing number of villages under the supervision of the elders.

149

Paul Fliehler, who arrived with Hanselmann, was stationed on the Markham river at Gabmazung, replacing G. Stuerzenhofecker, who had gone without furlough from 1904 to 1927. Eight months after his arrival in August, Fliehler began to preach regularly in the local language. He worked hard to become acquainted with the evangelists and the people.

In 1927, two additional ordained men arrived in Madang: J. Mager and Fred Henkelmann. Mager was sent to Kurum on Karkar, and Henkelmann was stationed at Ragetta to do his study of the Graged language under E. Hannemann. Henkelmann was a gifted linguist, and when the E. Hannemann family left after half a year, in April 1928, Henkelmann was able to continue the work on his own. Already during his first years of activity, Henkelmann observed an over-emphasis on law in indigenous preaching, poorly attended village-wide morning and evening devotions, the practice of sorcery and magic, village quarrels, a lack of community cooperation in keeping village schools in order, the evil influence of nearby secularized Europeans in Madang, and the proselytizing of Lutherans by Roman Catholics. Henkelmann started English services for the European population of Madang, and encouraged Pidgin services for plantation workers.

A lay worker named William Pfeiffer travelled with Mager and Henkelmann to New Guinea. Pfeiffer, a German living in the USA, never forgot his promise to his father to remain true to his faith confessed in confirmation. When he heard of the need for workers in New Guinea, he volunteered. He was assigned to care for Malahang Plantation, where A. Freese had served. After six years of service, he died from malaria at Bunabun on the north coast, where he had gone to prepare the new mission station.

Another lay-worker, Carl Bertram, left San Francisco with two Neuendettelsau men, M. Lechner and H. Streicher, in 1928. He arrived in New Guinea in May, and was assigned to take the place of Joh. Ruppert at Pola/Finschhafen. Bertram was relocated to Madang in 1932, when the mission fields were divided. After a seven-year term of service, he left New Guinea in 1935 in ill health.

150

Together with C. Bertram, H. Streicher, and M. Lechner, came Miss Gretchen Taminga. At first she served in the hospital at Finschhafen. In 1932 she was transferred to Madang, where she served until 1937. She, too, left because of illness.

Thus, in the years 1921 to 1929, the Iowa Synod sent a total of 21 missionaries to New Guinea: 3 teachers, 1 doctor, 3 nurses, 2 plantation men, 2 businessmen, 2 domestic workers, 1 builder, and 7 ordained personnel. During that same period the UELCA sent 11 laymen and 2 laywomen to New Guinea (plus several brides of missionaries). Although this section speaks of the American and Australian Lutherans 'taking over' the German Mission fields in New Guinea, this really applies only to the legal responsibility to the Australian government, and to the financial support that continued to make possible Lutheran misison work in New Guinea during the 1920s. The majority of personnel at work were still from Neuendettelsau and Barmen, although many had to leave temporarily or permanently during this period. The 34 Americans and Australians were new strengths that made continuity in the congregations' ever-expanding evangelism program possible.

A Temporary Solution: The New Finisterre District (1929)

Although the question of ownership of the two Lutheran Missions in New Guinea assigned to Australian and Iowa Synod Lutherans seemed to have been solved by the decision of the Australian Government in 1921, there remained many unsolved questions and problems. [41]

The German mission property in New Guinea had not been expropriated, as other German private property was. It was left as mission property, though under different stewardship. When it was clear that the Australian government would accept as trustees for such property only people living in the Commonwealth, the UELCA proposed, already in 1922, the names of nine Lutherans. Yet it took until March 1926 for them to be acknowledged and named to the Board of Trustees of Lutheran Mission New Guinea. This Board was given wide-reaching rights in respect to the management and use of the property of

Neuendettelsau and the Rhenish Mission. At the same time, it was made clear that, although there were only Australians on the Board, the Government fully acknowledged that the ownership and the control of the mission property involved both the Iowa Synod and the UELCA, and that nothing should be decided without agreement of these two churches.

Meanwhile, the Rhenish Mission Society protested to the Australian Government against this transfer of property rights. In their view, the American and Australian churches were only 'place-holders'. Neuendettelsau's position, however, was different. After it was decided that their missionaries could stay on the field, they desired a partnership in work with UELCA and Iowa Synod, and wanted the question of ownership and control to be left open to the future.

During this period of thinking and acting about the question of legal ownership of the former German mission in New Guinea, the Iowa Board of Foreign Missions sent its secretary, the Revd W.F. Kraushaar, on an inspection trip to New Guinea (August 1925 – February 1926). His report was quite positive. In the case of the Madang field, Kraushaar was still under the illusion that Barmen had already formally given up any property or mission claims. In the case of Neuendettelsau, he thought that there might be a problem when Neuendettelsau desired to take over a share in the administration. 'A discussion with the brethren', said Kraushaar of the Neuendettelsau missionaries, 'had this result, that not a single one of them refused to work on under the new leadership if the situation would make it impossible for Neuendettelsau to step into the work again. The welfare of the work is for them the highest law.' [42]

Since Barmen had protested to the Australian government against the transfer of the Madang Mission to the Australian trustees, Theile asked for a decision from the Government about turning over the Madang field to Barmen again, and about Neuendettelsau taking part in a tripartite leadership of the Finschhafen field. To this inquiry, Theile received no answer.

Thereupon, because of the uncertainty that prevailed, the Revd F. Braun, the treasurer of the Iowa Synod BFM, was sent to Germany in February of 1929 to clarify matters with the societies concerned, so that, at a later conference planned for the same year, all parties would have a clear view of the issues involved. It appears that the Revd Braun hoped to obtain the final consent of Barmen to relinquish the Madang field to the Iowa Synod and the UELCA Boards of Foreign Mission. However, this hoped-for goal was not accomplished.

Barmen insisted that they had never given up the Madang field, even though past correspondence from Director Kriele seemed to indicate that to be the case. In view of their decision, the Rhenish Mission Society agreed to repay all debts taken over by the Iowa Synod, and all funds used for purchase of missionaries' personal property in ten installments. As a friendly gesture, Barmen proposed to turn over a part of its Madang field to the Iowa Synod. [43]

The long-awaited conference took place in South Brisbane, Queensland, from May 6 to 15, 1929. It was called a Representative Conference of those concerned with the German Lutheran missions in New Guinea.

After days of serious discussion, involving the deepest emotions of all present, Neuendettelsau declared that it was willing to work together with Lutheran Mission, that is, with the Iowa Synod and the UELCA, in a unity with whatever administrative arrangements were possible. Both the Iowa and the UELCA mission boards considered a tripartite leadership impossible.

Concerning Barmen, the situation proved to be more complicated. Barmen made it clear that they had never agreed to giving up their Madang field. Under the circumstances in which the UELCA trustees exercised ownership rights over the mission properties, Barmen desired to fully take over their Madang field. Barmen was also willing to keep some Australian and American missionaries in the Madang area, who would be supported by their home churches. Director Theile expressed the position of both the UELCA and the Iowa Synod when he stated that it was not possible on the basis of their confessions to work with Barmen, which represented union churches, but he said it was possible to work with Neuendettelsau, which represented only Lutheran churches. Mission Director Schmidt from Barmen could not

151

understand why it was not possible to work together from an ecumenical standpoint.

Eventually, the decision was made that Barmen should take over the Madang field if the Government permitted such an action, and that Neuendettelsau, the Iowa Synod, and the UELCA should work together as a unity. Barmen would turn over the Rai Coast area to the American missionaries, to which Neuendettelsau would add Siassi and the Long Island groups, Ulap and Sio, and the Amari-Garamari areas of Kiapit in the upper Markham valley, including the new Kate work in the Eastern Highlands. In Finschhafen there were to be two spheres of interest, but one mission. The two spheres of interest were called Finisterre District (to be manned mostly by Americans) and Finschhafen District (to be manned mostly by Neuendettelsau missionaries). UELCA missionaries were to serve in both areas. [44]

The decisions of the Brisbane Conference were seconded by meetings held in New Guinea and later also in Australia. The main conference of Australian, American, and Neuendettelsau missionaries met at Sattelberg on December 1-15, 1929, and accepted the Brisbane proposals. The Revd Lehner was elected superintendent of the whole mission. The Revd G. Hueter was chosen as president of the Finisterre District, and the Revd Wm. Flierl as president of the Finschhafen District. [45]

A final meeting of Neuendettelsau, Iowa, and the UELCA representatives, together with Director F.O. Theile, took place in Sydney from January 29-31, 1930. From now on, it was clear that UELCA missionaries would work under American and Neuendettelsau leadership, with all matters relating to recruitment, training, furloughs, and retirement to be the responsibility of the Australian Church. [46] Thus ended the partnership between the UELCA and the Iowa Synod, created in an emergency during the years from 1915 to 1921 and continued in an official way from 1921 to 1929, for a total of 15 years.

Consequences for the American Staff

What were some of the immediate effects of the Brisbane decisions as far as American personnel in New Guinea were concerned? For

Senior Flierl with (right) Pastor Dr Eppelein from Neuendettelsau and Pastor Dr Taeuber (left) from USA. After Field Conference 1929.

After the Brisbane Conference 1929, at Bogadjim: Revd Hanselmann, Pastor Taeuber (both Iowa Synod) Elder Anang from Bogadjim, Revd Hoffmann, Revd Wullenkord (both Rhenish Mission).

the pioneer F.E. Pietz, who was on furlough in 1930, no immediate change was required, since Kaiapit — or at least Amari and Garamari — were located in the Finisterre District. The Pietz family returned to Kaiapit after furlough. Also for E. Hannemann, who went on furlough in late 1930, there was no immediate change. In 1932 he returned to Tagub, the evangelist school on Karkar at Kurum. Mager was required to serve as business manager and storeman of the Finisterre District while located at Madang, until a permanent decision could be made concerning a supply centre for the new district. From January to November 1932, Mager also served as the President of the Finisterre District, after the G. Hueter family went on furlough. Neither was change necessary for F. Henkelmann, who was located at Galek on the Rai Coast. In 1932 the station was moved some miles to the west to Biliau.

For others, the new arrangements meant radical change. Missionary Hueter and his wife had worked themselves well into the Nobonob circuit. Now they were suddenly required to pull up roots and move to Heldsbach/Finschhafen, where Hueter was expected to organize and make functional the new Finisterre District, which was far removed from Heldsbach.

The Paul Fliehler family, which had put down firm roots in Gabmazung, where the Jabem church language was used, was now required to move to Ulap, where Kate was the

Revd P. Fliehler.

153

school and church language. In a similar way, the R. Hanselmann family, which had been at Keku where the Amele language was used, were moved to Awelkon on Siassi Island, where Jabem was the church language.

Miss Hattie Engeling, already on her sixth year of service as a single woman in medical work in the Madang area, was transferred to Finschhafen in 1930 to help the newly arrived Dr T. Braun establish his hospital work.

During the short life of the Finisterre District (till 1932), only a few new missionaries from America arrived in New Guinea. The sending body now was the American Lutheran Church (ALC), which resulted from a union of the Buffalo, Ohio, and Iowa Synods, all from a German background. The first of these missionaries was Dr Theodore G. Braun, son of Pastor F. Braun, a long-time supporter of the mission work in New Guinea.

A nurse, Lydia Seidler, arrived in July 1930 together with the Revd and Mrs Henry J. Foege. From mid-1931 to mid-1932, she was stationed in the Finschhafen area, and then married Missionary P. Fliehler at Ulap. Henry J. Foege was the only ordained missionary sent from America during this period. He was assigned to the new station of the Finisterre District inland from Kaiapit, called Amari. After studying the Kate language, he proceeded to Kaiapit to assist Missionary Oertel and to plan the building of Amari station. But there was still great indecision as to the wisdom of all aspects of the Brisbane decisions concerning the two spheres of interest within the Finschhafen mission area. American and Neuendettelsau missionaries began to regard the building of a station among the Gazub people of the Eastern Highlands as having a higher priority than the building of Amari.

One more worker from America arrived during this period: Hans Schwarz. He was assigned to be the bookkeeper and then the business manager of the Madang Supply House.

What was the result of the decisions of the Brisbane Conference of 1929? The American representative at this conference, the Revd Taeuber, had said that Iowa 'never thought to take the heart of Neuendettelsau. Finschhafen belongs to the mother society and we will seek something which appends itself to

154

Finschhafen.' [47] Since the Rhenish Mission Society took over the Madang area, and Finschhafen was to be Neuendettelsau area, the Americans could have a few stations in between. The eventual result, called the Finisterre District, however, had little chance of survival at that time.

The serious problems — shortage of missionaries and of finance — caused by the first World War, were unavoidable as far as the missionaries and Christians in New Guinea were concerned. With few exceptions, the mission work grew remarkably during the war and post-war period (see chapter 2). The Brisbane decisions, however, caused problems on all sides. American missionaries who had long since established themselves in the Madang area were to be uprooted and sent elsewhere. Congregations and mission areas which formerly belonged together were to be separated. Evangelists from the Ragetta congregation (Madang) at the Rai Coast now found themselves in a completely new district, the Finisterre District. The Ulap congregation, and all the evangelist positions in the mountains behind Ulap, had intimate connections with Kalasa and Wareo, but now Ulap was to belong to a different 'sphere of interest'. Mission executives and missionaries had made decisions without consulting New Guinea congregations, thereby creating confusion and distrust.

The overseas supporting societies and churches each wanted to have their own mission field. [48] But the Christian congregations in Madang and Finschhafen were not consulted. It is surprising that missionaries in New Guinea agreed to the proposals of their Boards so quickly. They had a missionary representative from Madang and one from Finschhafen at Brisbane, but neither was an American.

It did not take long before dissatisfaction with the arrangements began to appear. In order to assist with establishing the new mission and administrative arrangments, Theile made a third trip to New Guinea from August to December 1930. The Annual Conference, and also the two district conferences, were held at Sattelberg from November 26 to December 5, 1930. The Conference as a whole came to the conclusion that the Middle Watut (Mumeng), Gazub (Kambaidam), and Rawlinson (Boana) areas should be the locations of new mission stations immediately, since gold prospectors were causing many problems for the evangelists. Because of this need, the building of the proposed Amari station in the Finisterre District was to be delayed. At the same time, the Conference said that the best location of the main hospital, planned for Dr Baun, was Finschhafen. [49]

However, the Americans in their Finisterre District were far from the proposed hospital site, far from the supply bases, ships, central schools, rest homes, and any decent harbours. Therefore the Conference unanimously proposed that Kalasa and Wareo be included in the Finisterre District. Such an arrangement would bring the area of the Finisterre District much closer to the centre of things in Finschhafen.

The proposals of the December 1930 Conference concerning Kalasa and Wareo must have caused considerable excitement in Neuendettelsau. The Direktorium met, together with missionaries on furlough, and stated that the proposals were unacceptable. On the other side, the ALC's position was influenced by the attitude of its missionaries on the field. In a letter to his Home Board, G. Hueter pointed out that at the December 1930 Conference the ALC men had consented to many things because of the united support for the new proposals. Hueter considered the Neuendettelsau rejection as seriously 'jeopardizing cooperation here on the field'. He continued: 'If the home societies will force measures upon the missionaries on the field against their will, the whole work here will suffer immensely'. [50] No one was more disturbed by the dissensions on the field and the growing management problems than was Theile in Brisbane. He lost much of his previous joy because of the situation. [51]

A Final Solution (1932)

During this period, other events were happening which eventually led to a solution for that time. The Rhenish Mission Society was finding it difficult to keep up debt payments on the ALC and to find adquate new staff for the Madang field. On the urging of Neuendettelsau, the executive of the Rhenish Mission, meeting in Barmen on January 4, 1932, decided to use the good offices of Neuendettelsau to see whether the ALC would be willing to take over the Madang mission field. Subsequently, a preliminary telegram was also sent to the ALC. [52]

In New Guinea, quite ignorant of events in Europe, the missionaries gathered for Annual Conference from January 8 to 22, 1932, at Sattelberg. The Finisterre District held an extraordinary meeting at the same time as the Finschhafen District was holding its separate meeting. The emotions were intense. G. Hueter resigned as president of the Finisterre District; J. Mager was elected in his place. The Brisbane arrangments were at the point of a complete collapse. But suddenly God provided a solution which restored joy and mutual relationship between the Neuendettelsau and ALC missionaries. The minutes read:

On the fourth session on January 20 in the afternoon it was announced that a telegram was received on the previous evening from Brisbane which has overwhelmed and completely overthrown all of our plans till now. The telegram reads, 'BARMEN WISHES NEGOTIATIONS IN VIEW OF TRANSFER MADANG DISTRICT TO US'. Hueter proposes that we should let the BFM know that we are prepared to take over the field of the Rhenish Mission in New Guinea but we request earnestly that Welsch and Wullenkord or one of the two come back. [53]

The Finisterre District meeting immediately made plans for stationing all missionaries in the Madang area when and if that field became the field of the ALC. At the same time, they also felt more gracious in financial questions toward their Neuendettelsau brethren.

Months of anxious waiting were still ahead, since official proposals by Barmen to the ALC were not possible before a full meeting of the Rhenish Mission Society was held. Only then could a joint meeting with the ALC take place. The proposals from such a meeting would also require approval of the supporting church and society.

In the anxiety of their last Finisterre District meeting, the ALC missionaries emphasized that, in a situation where several mission societies and boards overseas exercised executive decisions concerning the field, unity on the field could be maintained only if leadership decisions were made on the field. This suggestion was prophetic. The great missionary expansion and growth in the New Guinea mission field of the Lutheran Church was yet to come, and it would happen in a radical situation where leadership was largely exercised on the field, and where local congregations, circuits, and districts would play an increasingly important part in decision-making.

The American Lutheran Church Takes Over the Madang Field

The official negotiations between the Rhenish Mission Society and the American Lutheran Church concerning transfer of the Madang field to the American Lutheran Church took place at Columbus, Ohio, May 10-12, 1932. Present were Inspector Friessler of the Rhenish Mission Society and also Director Eppelein of the Neuendettelsau Society. The American Lutheran Church representatives were President Dr C.C. Hein, Stewardship Director Revd H.F. Schuh, and the members of the Board of Missions. The decisions reached included the following:

1) The ALC was to take over the Rhenish mission field in the Madang area, including the Rai Coast;
2) Neuendettelsau was to take over its complete former mission field, including the stations that had been handed over to the ALC, such as Ulap, Siassi, Kaiapit, and Amari-Garamari. [54]

Other arrangements included legal interests, financial obligations, and matters concerning personnel. The Australian trustees were requested to resign, and to turn over their rights to two new sets of trustees, one for Lutheran Mission Finschhafen (LMF) and the other for Lutheran Mission Madang (LMM). Each group of trustees was to have a number of Australian citizens as members. Under the new agreement, the Australian Church no longer participated in management, but continued to support both LMB and LMM with personnel and by other means.

Meanwhile, in Finschhafen, the American members of LMF met, and asked all ordained Rhenish missionaries in the Madang field to stay on if they were willing to serve under the confessional basis of the ALC. Most of them welcomed the opportunity to continue their life's work. [55] The Americans also elected to

156

support only the Bel (also called Ragetta or Graged) language, for future school and church use. Bel was strictly a Melanesian language. This decision caused misgivings among some missionaries, and especially among the people who were effected, that is, the Nobonob and Amele-Begesin congregations, with their school systems. The English language was adopted as the official language for use among the missionaries, although some American missionaries continued to display their skill in German by continuing to write their reports in that language.

The actual transfer of the field took place on January 1, 1933. The First Field Conference of the new Lutheran Mission Madang (LMM) took place from February 25 to March 9, 1933, at Ragetta Island next to Madang. Many changes in personnel were necessary, which caused difficulties for both missionaries and people. E. Pietz now ended his long service among the Azera people at Kaiapit, and became the new Superintendent of the LMM, with the Nobonob circuit as his congregational assignment. This meant a fourth (!) New Guinea language for him. P. Fliehler, who had served at Gabmazung (Jabem language) and Ulap (Kate language), was now assigned to Biliau on the Rai Coast, where he was required to learn the Bel language. R. Hanselmann, who had started his missionary career at Keku, and was then assigned to Siassi, now was to return to Keku again after two years. F. Henkelmann, who had made a great effort to build up the mission work on the Rai Coast, was shifted to the Amele Teachers Seminary to teach the Bel language to the Amele Seminary students, whose school books, Bible stories, readers, and so on, were all in the Amele language. Every station or area of work was affected by the change.

Supplementary Services

What support facilities had been established in the past in the Madang area, and how did these serve the Madang mission? (See also chapter 18, on the Socio-economic Concern of the Mission and Church.) First of all, the Americans inherited a reasonably good supply centre (called Lutmis), established by F. Knautz. H. Schwarz continued to serve as bookkeeper, business manager, and storekeeper until he left in 1938, when R. Boettcher took his place.

A very important facility in New Guinea missions is boat **transport**. From the Rhenish Mission, LMM had inherited the *Rheno-Westphalia*, a motor vessel already 26 years old, allowed to carry 27 passengers (but often overloaded with passengers and tons of freight). In addition, there were a number of smaller boats and pinnaces available. A replacement of the *Rheno-Westphalia* was now necessary. The Sunday-school children of the American Lutheran Church provided the means with their pennies, nickels, and dimes, and also voted for the name *Totol* (meaning angel or messenger). T. Radke left for Hong Kong in March 1937, and negotiated for the building of a solid boat built by Chinese craftsmen for a very modest $9,400 HK. On December 4, 1937, the *Totol* left on a maiden voyage to Finschhafen. During the next four years, the sight of the *Totol* on its regular runs always gladdened the hearts of New Guineans and missionaries. But its life was to be cut short in 1942. After participating heroically in the rescue of defenders and other Europeans fleeing from Rabaul after the invasion of the Japanese, the *Totol* was sunk in the inner muddy swamp-area of Nagada harbour to prevent her capture. Later, an Allied plane spotted her, and the bombing and subsequent fire made her useless.

Due to the scarcity of mission funds from 1914 to 1932 because of the World War I emergency and the post-war difficulties, existing buildings everywhere were in need of complete **rebuilding**. In addition, for proper schooling, medical work, printing, and adequate living, an enormous amount of building had to be undertaken in LMM after January 1, 1933. But the 1930s were also a time of serious world-wide depression, low commodity prices, and scarce funds. The laymen who served in building and in the industrial area of the Mission gave of themselves unselfishly in service. The veteran builder and trainer of indigenous craftsmen, W. Siemers, served as a shipwright, and was also in charge of building the Amele Hospital, the Madang chapel, and residences at many locations. Thereby he kept on with his training of indigenous craftsmen in sawing and planing of timber and in building. Mr Victor Koschade, an Australian layman, first worked in the store at Madang but then spent eight months in 1933 building the road to Amele from the Gum river near Madang. For the next three years Koschade cleared the site and supervised the building of the new central school, located on a beautiful ridge overlooking the whole Madang area, called Amron-Gonob. His last major task was to erect a new printery at Gonob and, although not a printer by trade, to put it into operation with old and new presses and type.

Another area of lay activity was **plantation** development and supervision. (For details on Kurum, and Nagada Plantation, see chapter 18 and the List of Workers appended.) The plantations were considered a support for the Mission, as well as a training school and work opportunity for local Christian young men. The lay missionaries saw it as their specific calling regularly to conduct Bible studies and daily devotions with the workers, in addition to giving them training for various jobs.

Besides the various Australian laymen serving for LMM in pre-war years (B. Jaeschke, J. Lindner, A. Bertelsmeier, R. Barber) and the veteran Rhenish lay-missionary H. Schamann, two ALC members are to be mentioned: Andrew Mild and H. Thogerson. Mild came from Ohio, and arrived in New Guinea in December 1938. For most of his years of service he worked on Karkar Island. In 1942 he fell into the hands of the Japanese, but survived imprisonment. After the war, he returned to New Guinea as an ordained missionary. The other ALC man, Thogersen, was a native of Denmark and not yet a fully naturalized citizen of the US. He served from 1935 to 1940 in various building assignments and on plantations.

Another important department supportive of Lutheran Mission in Madang was **Medical Mission**. This department was to be led in a most remarkable and dedicated way during the next 40 years (that is, from 1932 to 1972) by a medical mission couple, namely Dr and Mrs T.G. Braun. They were married on July 5, 1932, at Finschhafen. When the Americans were to take over the Madang mission, the Brauns moved there in October 1932, and Amele mission station was selected as the hospital site. Mrs Braun already knew the Amele language well. Although it was impossible to go to Amele for the time being, Dr Braun was not idle. He was interested in the complete missionary activity of the church, where the various tribes lived, how they could be contacted, and what was necessary in personnel, equipment, programs, and finance to spread the Gospel in an effective way. He made long trips with various missionaries, including the first major exploration trip into the highlands, in order to have a personal understanding of what was needed by the mission.

Part of Dr Braun's objective was to make modern medical care available for both the people and the missionaries. His next concern was to teach especially the missionaries how to take care of themselves in a malarial country. Very early, the Madang area repeatedly demonstrated the vicious types of malaria and other tropical diseases endemic there. W. Pfeiffer fell victim to malaria at Bunabun in 1933. C.A. Lewald, an Australian layman from Queensland, who arrived in Madang in 1935, also died from malaria 16 months later, in 1936.

If a hospital at Amele was to be a reality — and the Women's Missionary Federation of the ALC had provided the funds — a road would have to be built from Madang to Amele, a total distance of 28 kilometers. From 1933 on, a succession of missionary laymen worked on the building, the rebuilding, and the maintaining of the road, assisted by hundreds of local people. Hospital construction was carried out by W. Siemers, assisted by two Chinese carpenters and other Europeans, and many trainees of Siemers. By the end of 1934, all medicines, instruments, and dispensary equipment could be moved into completed rooms of the hospital. During 1935, construction continued. The hospital was finally dedicated on May 17, 1937.

On November 11, 1935, Dr Agnes Hoeger from North Dakota arrived in Madang to begin a 30-year career in medical mission work. She was thankful for the introduction given by Dr and Mrs Braun before they left on furlough in May of 1936. She soon noticed the poor health of the mission staff, and hoped that a planned health station would bring some relief. She called immediately for more nursing staff, both for the hospital and for the outstation patrols. She took over the training program of indigenous medical staff which had been begun by Dr and Mrs Braun. The most elementary facts of anatomy, of physiology, and of the most common diseases had to be taught, together

158

with practical work with patients. As with Dr Braun, there was no rest for Dr Hoeger. During 1937, she reported, she was seldom at the hospital for two consecutive weeks before being called on an emergency trip. In ten months she made 15 such trips.

After Dr and Mr Braun returned from furlough, LMM enjoyed the blessing of two medical doctors, until Dr Hoeger was sent to Kakoko Hospital in Finschhafen in September 1940 to take over there, after Dr Stuerzenhofecker was interned in Australia. More staff meant better training of workers. In 1939 Dr Braun reported nine men in the Amele school as medical helpers. Two of the most distinguished of these trainees were Fulalek from Amele and Siming from Bel. (For details of Medical Mission and names of overseas and New Guinean personnel, see chapter 17.)

Through the years, almost every mission station also had a local dispensary, where sick people were cared for. The small hospital at Tagub on Karkar continued to minister to thousands of ill patients year after year. Dr Braun had promoted the idea of a special hospital for lepers through the years, but without success. The Government denied permission in 1937. At first, all lepers were sent hundreds of miles by sea to isolated Kavieng on the Island of New Ireland. Actually, some lepers were isolated on Pig Island near Madang.

Apart from the congregational village schools, which will be dealt with in connection with the various circuits or congregations, a very important area of mission work was represented by the **teacher-evangelist seminaries**, at first called 'helper' schools.

The Amele Teachers Seminary was begun in February 1923, by the Revd A. Wullenkord. The first class graduated in November 1926. Some of the first graduates were Aik, Ud, Gulal, and Digon, who gave notable service in mission. In the first class were 31 Amele and nine Keku students. At that time the Nobonob missionary and people refused to send students to be trained in the Amele language. The third class of the Seminary began in September 1930, with over 150 students. But in 1933 the school was to change over from Amele into the new church language, Bel, which caused many problems. Due to the change, the class was kept on for two more years until early January 1935, when there were only 31 students left. Despite the problems of the last class at Amele Seminary, the graduates of the school successfully brought the Gospel to the whole Amele area and became pioneers of the advance into Begesin, the Ramu, and trans-Ramu. Some graduates also served in the inland at Kerowagi.

The Karkar 'Helpers' School, at the station called Urit, was begun in 1925 by the Rhenish missionary H. George. Altogether, three classes with a total of 158 students were graduated from the Urit school under the missionaries George, Lindner, Hannemann, and W. Stahl, and the local teachers Mileng, Jas, and Sapush. The school was brought to completion in September 1936.

Meanwhile, E. Hannemann was assigned to start a central school at Amron. Instructions began on November 17, 1934, with 76 students, who came from Nobonob (13), Ragetta (10), Karkar (22), Rai Coast (18), Keku (10), and Amele (3). The Waskians sent Lapan, and the Grageds sent Los to assist in teaching. Both Nobonob and Ragetta congregations gave generous help in getting the school gardens planted, and the station buildings erected.

E. Hannemann spent much time trying to establish a new tradition in school work. He disavowed strong disciplinary methods executed by the European missionary, and instead established a system of discipline supervised and enforced by the student body and their local teachers, a system similar to that exercised in the villages. Hannemann also expected Christian villages and congregations to discipline students who ran away from school or who misbehaved.

Hannemann spent an enormous amount of effort preparing school materials for students and teachers. Continuing to encourage native arts and crafts, he revised and increased the hymns in the hymn book (Kanam Buk). With the participation of both students and teachers from all areas of Madang, the Bel language hymn book eventually had a content of 75 per cent indigenous melodies and hymns. Melodies from the various areas were taught by the students to each other by use of rhythm techniques peculiar to Melanesia. In a short while, hundreds of Christian songs were being sung with local melodies all over the Madang district. The spread of the Gospel received a tremendous boost.

At Amron, a largely successful attempt was made to produce a larger number of local assistant teachers. By 1938, six local teachers were at work: Lapan (Waskia), Tanggoi (Takia), Pah (Nobonob), Gulal (Amele), Jabon (Siar), and Los (Graged). Each year, missionaries and local teachers at Amron participated in holding refresher courses for village teachers and evangelists.

In September 1940, the first of 42 evangelists and teachers from Amron's six-year course were graduated. However, a total of 86 failed to complete the course.

The Amron school program eventually required a second European teacher. In 1937, J. Mager joined the teaching staff. Mager was a gifted student of New Guinean languages and culture. He prepared two dictionaries, one for the Waskia language and another for the Bel language. He also participated in a number of exploratory mission trips among hostile tribes in the Adelbert mountains north and west of Madang. In 1940, when Hannemann left on furlough, Mager took charge of the Amron school. He continued his service after the war until 1950.

For years, the school program suffered because of misconceptions of village people and students. Magical views looked upon the skills of writing, and especially arithmetic, as providing the key to the secret of earthly goods. When students returned home year after year without the secret magic formula for miraculously producing steel axes, knives, and a whole host of desired articles, they were at times kept back by parents or relatives, since there was no evident benefit of schooling. In 1937, two students admitted to Hannemann that the study of geography had freed them from 'As Bilong Kago' ideas (ideas related to magical production of earthly goods).

For school and congregational purpose, a **printing program** was urgently required. Missionary H. George had begun a printery in 1924 at Urit on Karkar. In 1935, V. Koschade built a new printery building at Gonob, Amron, and in 1936 relocated the old press to Amron. Although not a printer by trade, he was able to get the printery operational. J. Mager, who had operated the press previously at Urit for several years, arrived in late 1937 at Gonob, and took over until 1940, when Mr Walter Krebs, an American layman, arrived, and was given the job of operating the new printery, which he faithfully carried out until imprisonment by the Japanese.

Two other small enterprises were begun by LMM. One was a school for the Chinese children in Madang, begun by Mrs Emma Radke in 1935 at the request of the Chinese.

A school for missionaries' children was started in 1936 at Amele by Miss Irma Taeuber. Mrs H. Hannemann, who, because of government restrictions, could not proceed with her husband to Kerowagi in the inland, provided a home for the children.

A Survey of the Madang District Congregations

What was the missionary and congregational picture of the new American field in Madang, and how did that picture change until World War II? At the end of 1932, the retiring president of the Rhenish Mission in Madang, the Revd Eiffert, gave a short description of each congregation or circuit (as they were later called). [56] His description will be incorporated in this survey of the Madang circuits, beginning with the oldest and ending with the newest mission areas.

The original mission station was located at **Bogadjim** in Astrolabe Bay. Later moved to Bongu, the station was relocated at **Keku** in June, 1918. The American missionary R. Hanselmann was stationed there from late 1926 until the end of 1929. Then W. Doege, a Rhenish missionary, took over for two years until March 1933. Later that year, R. Hanselmann returned to Keku from Siassi.

Eiffert said that in the whole circuit the older generation which had been influenced by the Gospel was dying out, and the younger generation grew up without having experienced the Gospel, but instead they were greatly influenced by plantation workers who practised sorcery and witchcraft. Doege, in his short time, had worked intensively among the evangelists and teachers, also in the Raua area, but with mixed results. Many workers became tired, and returned to their home villages. This meant that no firm base existed in the home villages which would support an evangelist at work far away

160

from home. Eiffert said that if Keku was to be rebuilt, two missionaries should be stationed there.

When Hanselmann arrived back in Keku on July 5, 1933, he was quite enthusiastic, because new mission areas in the Ramu river area and the trans-Ramu area on the slopes of the Bismarck mountains were wide open, due to the spread of governmental authority. But the old leadership of the congregations, like that of the elders Muls and Maraisi, had died out, and the new leadership was ineffectual. 'The present Christianity', said Hanselmann, 'has no outward recognizable shape or form for its members, and this became also well known so that people from other areas said, "Our roads, our houses, churches and hospitality are better than what the Christian congregations have to offer".' The life of the congregation was further described as 'weak', 'indifferent', and 'lacking self-assurance'. In part, the many changes of missionaries, their methods, and lack of a consistent language policy had contributed to the present situation, according the Hanselmann. To expect Keku congregations to actually carry out mission work across the Ramu was 'idle talk', and therefore Hanselmann proposed to open an evangelists' course for 20 men.

Later in December 1933, Hanselmann reported that all teachers stopped teaching after the July native conference, when they heard the new district language was to be the Bel language. The teachers had been trained in Amele. In many villages where catechumen instruction had been given for five to ten years, the catechumens were growing tired because they could see no hope of being baptized. Villages closest to Keku seemed to give a poor impression, and those further away a much brighter picture. Despite the dark picture painted by Hanselmann, five successful helpers' stations were located across the Ramu river: Koroba, Danaru, Gajebara, Waimiriba, and Goni. Seven of the twelve men occupying these stations were Amele trained. The population (in 1933) of the circuit was estimated at 6,469, with 27 helpers at work. There were 1,238 children of school age, but only 177 were registered pupils. On the other hand, 287 young men were absent on contract labour with Europeans.

In his 1934 report, Hanselmann said that all village schools had closed, that the long-term catechumens, who were finally baptized, did not really understand Christianity, and that those young people baptized as infants had grown up as heathen.

In 1934, R. Hanselmann gave the missionaries a special report, written in both German and English, called *Ass Bilong Cargo.*[57] In it, he explained some fundamental beliefs of the Melanesians and their complaints against the Europeans. Because the title was given in Pidgin, the language hated by many missionaries, and a language very likely effectively used by Hanselmann, the report did not win admiration from many missionaries. But Hanselmann must be given credit for revealing a very basic problem which grew to monumental proportions, not only in the Madang area after World War II, but far beyond. Hanselmann explained in the report that in the past nothing bore fruit for Melanesians unless there was some mystical or magical power at work. 'Why is it', they say, 'that today the fundamental power which will make all things possible for us is not revealed to us? Why is it that we are permitted by the Europeans to advance only so far but then cut off so that we will not discover for ourselves the secret of wealth?' This particular problem lay heavily on the hearts of the people, especially after the 1933 native conference. They claimed that each time they gathered in elders' conferences with others, this problem was never really dealt with, always only circumvented or pushed aside. Hanselmann said that under the basic viewpoints of the people, all kinds of variations, of hopes, dreams, and expectations are possible, and that one simple picture will not describe the full thought-world of the Melanesian.

In 1935, Hanselmann went on furlough and never returned. Some important missionaries were very critical of what he had written and said. But later generations of missionaries have reason to be thankful to him for exposing a fundamental problem of communications that existed and still exists in Melanesia today.

The next Keku missionary was P. Fliehler, who came after considerable experience at Gabmazung and Ulap. After arriving in Madang on August 11, 1935, he immediately set out on a trip over the Raua mountains with E. Hannemann and J. Kuder. Kuder became seriously ill on the trip, and had to be carried out via Keku to Madang. So Fliehler's first experience was to arrive at Keku by the back door as an unknown. The impression on him was devastating. He wondered how a missionary could continue to administer the sacraments to such lukewarm people. He quoted L. Flierl as saying that there are two ways of evaluating catechumens to be baptized. The one way is to teach and influence them slowly, and the other way is to face the people squarely with an ultimatum. Fliehler chose the way of ultimatum.

Fliehler said that Keku was a beautiful location, but there were no people living in the vicinity, and the two closest villages were apparently heathen. He maintained that the following factors seemed to be inter-related: 1) the location of the station; 2) the frequent change of missionaries; 3) the use of Pidgin as a means of communication; and 4) the spiritual state of affairs. He saw no hope for a resolution of the language problem in the next five years. Where Hanselmann reported 27 helpers at work, Fliehler reported only 17.

During 1936, 1937, and 1938, Fliehler tried to rebuild and reactivate the Keku station. He mentioned poor statistics and poor congregational records. But what is quite evident, and was also mentioned by Fliehler, is that the influence of European cuture, especially through large numbers of returning labourers, was breaking down the natural controls of the clan in the Melanesian society. Government, business, and mission all had a part in this deteriorating situation, said Fliehler, and the people did not know how to deal with their problems. By 1938, eight village schools with 212 pupils were again in operation, and 20 evangelists were still at work. Ten new evangelists had volunteered, and Fliehler hoped to instruct them in 1939.

A new missionary, the Revd Harry Dott, from Pittsburg, Pennsylvania, had arrived in November 1937, and was gradually being introduced into the mission work. In late 1938, Fliehler and Dott began to move the station to a place close to its original location at Bogadjim, to a place named Kubal. Dott continued the program begun by Fliehler, made many mission trips, and participated in the stationing of seven new helpers. Unfortunately, Dott's ministry was cut short by the invasion of the Japanese and his early martyrdom.

The **Ragetta** congregation or circuit was begun in 1889 by G. Bergmann on Siar island. The mission station was later removed to Ragetta (Graged) island, and served the villages Bilibil, Jabob, Bilia, Graged, Siar, and Ruo scattered to the north and south of Madang. By 1933, most of the people were Christian, and they now faced all the problems usually associated with second-generation Christians. The natural trading connections had made the Rai Coastal area the mission area of the circuit already before any missionary help was located there. From 1930 to 1932, the Rai Coast area belonged to the Finisterre District, and so was formally cut off from Madang. Fortunately, in practice not all contact was cut off. But Dahlhaeuser, the Rhenish missionary in charge in 1932, complained that Siar village had many young men, but few volunteered for mission work, and if they did volunteer they were not very faithful. It seems that the system of worshipping only at the central church had broken down, and permanent school churches were being built at each village.

The Samoan Pastor Jerome, who had arrived in New Guinea in 1912, spent the last months of his ministry on Ragetta in 1933 before retiring from mission work on November 20, 1933. He had given faithful service at Madang, Karkar, and the Rai Coast.

From 1934 through to the end of this period, the Ragetta circuit had no true resident missionary. Missionaries involved with administration, shipping, and building lived on the two mission properties on Graged Island, that is, at Maulon and Nashadamon, and thus, because of their location and work, had almost daily contact with the people of nearby coastal and island villages.

Since E. Hannemann had been their missionary in the past and knew their culture and language intimately, he was assigned the mission oversight of this circuit while serving as headmaster of the large central school at Amron. The arrangement had benefits both ways. The congregations became supportive of the central school, and the villages received many benefits from the school in return.

To solve the problems of lethargy, lack of interest, weak leadership, suspicion and fear of sorcery, and the like, Hannemann encouraged local Melanesian responsibility and leadership, as he did at the central school. Living in such close proximity to Madang, the people were constantly enticed by the flow of wealth and goods which they helped to unload from incoming ships and to distribute. As a result of the enticement of material goods, a serious problem arose. Some parents were led to sell their daughters or to rent them to the police and other workers, Chinese as well as Europeans. And this practice greatly discouraged the young men of the village, and destroyed communal solidarity.

Hannemann mentioned in detail the ban on the Sacraments put in force by the missionaries and the Native Conference in 1936 (see below), but in 1937 he reported that nothing had been accomplished, but that rather a retrogression had taken place. Although the congregation was 35 years old, Hannemann said the people had the peculiar temperament of coastal or island people, they had problems thinking through the economics of Europeans, and they suffered because of their close proximity of Madang.

We shall next take a look at the **Karkar** congregation or circuit, which was begun in July 1890 at Kulobob by G. Kunze, given up in 1895 because of the volcanic eruption, and re-established in July 1911 at **Kurum** by H. Eckershoff, who was joined by H. George in 1912.

In 1932, G. Lindner was in charge of the schools at Urit, and W. Stahl was in charge of congregational work among the 8,000 inhabitants who were almost all under the influence of the Gospel. By the end of 1932 there were over 2,000 baptized Christians in Takia alone, of whom 1,645 took Communion. Both Stahl and his wife had contracted frambesia (yaws) and severe cases of malaria. This situation required a medical furlough to Australia, beginning in March 1933. His replacement was J. Mager, who arrived on March 28.

Mager, Lindner, and the Samoan Pastor Taeao, selected a new station site on the north end of the island at **Narer**, among the Waskia people. (Kurum was located among the Takian tribe.) On November 28, 1933, Mager could move into a new house at Narer built by a Chinese carpenter under the direction of the Kurum plantation manager, Schamann. [58]

For the next several years, Mager was kept busy supervising the helpers and their catechumen classes, giving instruction to the weekly elders' meetings, inspecting the village schools, and strengthening the Christians in the villages by his visits and preaching. Mager was often absent on long mission trips, exploring the mission areas of the Adelbert mountains south of Bunabun, and also participating in the trips to the Central Highlands in 1934. He was fluent in the Bel language, and also mastered Waskia while at Narer. He left on October 18, 1935 from Narer for a much-needed first furlough.

The Revd D.E. Spier from North Dakota arrived at Narer on September 5 in 1935. Spier was first introduced into the Karkar mission field on the north coast at Bunabun and in the Adelbert mountains on the trip he took with Mager, Doege, and Stahl shortly after he arrived in September, and thus attended the first baptism in Bunabun at Sarisawu on September 15, 1935. In his 1936 report, Spier mentioned that Karkar had sent out 23 young men to Bunabun (Laden), nine more to Karkar proper, two to Bagabag island, and one to the Amron school. He mentioned great plans for the Karkar congregation, and hoped to win the Waskian people for the schools at Urit and Amron. Unfortunately, his plans for ministry were cut short by his untimely death on March 26, 1937.

The Revd A. Frerichs arrived in New Guinea on August 29, 1937. During 1937 and 1938 he was assigned to the Karkar congregation, where he worked under the supervision of F. Henkelmann, who was at Bunabun, the Karkar mission field. He reported poor church attendance, much fear of sorcery, much dancing, especially on the many plantations on all sides of Karkar, and few new volunteers for mission work. Otherwise, he had a favourable impression of the work of the helpers and teachers. Henkelmann, in his 1938 report, questioned whether the ban on the Sacraments had done any good for Karkar. He suggested that the ban had been a burden on the faithful Christians, and did not concern the weak Christians.

Revd A. Frerichs.

The Rhenish missionary, W. Stahl, returned to Karkar from furlough on January 17, 1939. He gave a devastating commentary on the effect of the ban on the Sacraments (see below), and remarked that 80 per cent of the Waskian congregation was now asleep (although the picture of the Takian congregation was much better). He cited a number of reasons: 1) too many changes of missionaries; 2) the many commercial plantations on Karkar, and their negative influence, especially the influence of the anti-church attitude of the European managers; and 3) inadequate preparation of elders, teachers, and helpers to meet the pastoral needs of the changing situation.

Stahl was forcibly removed in September 1939, since he was not yet a naturalized Australian citizen, and put under house arrest at Nobonob and eventually interned. His place at Narer was taken, for short while, by the Revd H. Enser, and then in 1940 and 1941 by A. Mild, a layman. Mild was assisted by the arrival of the Revd J. Hafermann, who had previously spent some months of internship with missionary Welsch at Begesin.

The Karkar and Bagabag people were involved in a very powerful repentance movement called *Kukuaik* in 1941 and 1942. The movement began on the island of Bagabag, where the leading elder Jas encouraged the Christians to stop personal animosities and subsequent fear of sorcery by confessing to each other regularly and publicly events or words which caused them concern. Encouraged by a decision of an elders' conference in March 1941 at Did to become involved in *Kukuaik* (which means 'to shrink back from evil or danger'), the movement spread throughout Takia in the second half of 1941, and by November also in Waskia. Because of the rumours of war and natural phenomena produced in the sky and bush by a prolonged drought of over ten months, the climate was right for all kinds of misinterpretations and abuses to be added to the original repentance movement. These later additions included prayers to ancestors, special revelations and unusual dreams, special and prolonged forms of prayer, new pentecostal joys, and end-of-the-world fears and hopes. When on New Year's Day thousands of plantation workers on Karkar left their jobs to await the second coming of Christ, the European plantation managers panicked and called the police by radio to stop what they considered was an insurrection against authority.

Mileng, the chief congregational leader, who had consistently counselled moderation, became the scapegoat for false accusations, and was banished for life to a prison far away. Fortunately, the Japanese bombs that fell on Madang soon after, opened the doors of the prison, and he, like Peter and John of old, returned to his congregation to continue a fruitful ministry during the war and afterwards. The Government after the war did not think it wise to carry out the pre-war judgment. [59]

Nobonob congregation or circuit also experienced many missionary changes from the late 1920s to the early 1930s. The pioneer Nobonob missionary who developed the Nobonob language and promoted it throughout the area was F. Schuetz, from the Rhenish Mission. He was followed by G. Hueter from the US from 1926 to 1929, and then by a Rhenish missionary, E. Krueger, who left in 164

1933 after baptizing a large class of catechumens. According to Krueger, the congregation indicated a willingness to adopt the Amele dialect for church and school use which had been resisted previously, but then came the American decision to promote Bel, which was probably more acceptable to the Nobonobs. The use of Nobonob continued in the worship and mission of the congregation.

The Revd F. Pietz was assigned as the new missionary for Nobonob, and he was expected to serve as the president of LMM as well. Through the next years until the Pietz family left on furlough, Pietz did not think that he could do justice to the congregational work as well. But the shortage of missionaries left him no choice. He participated in a mission trip overland to Bunabun, and also in the great trek over the Bismarcks to establish Kerowagi in the inland. He hoped that the participation of the workers on the inland trip would lead to increased mission zeal in Nobonob itself.

Although the transition from the use of Nobonob as a school language to the use of Bel went reasonably smoothly in Nobonob, which pleased Pietz, the village schools still did not make much progress because of inadequate school literature and programs. Another problem concerned Confirmation instruction. People were eager for Baptism, but only half-hearted about Confirmation. Again, problems of communication, lack of materials, and inadequate instructors hindered solutions to the problem. [191]

The last Nobonob missionary before the war was the Revd R. Inselmann, who was originally from Germany but migrated to Iowa in 1921, and after graduation from Wartburg Seminary arrived in New Guinea in February 1936. He lived and worked in Nobonob until 1942. Then he moved inland to the mission area of Nobonob, and lived at Magila from April 1942 until February 20, 1943.

Inselmann was a gifted and hard-working missionary. He prepared a Nobonob-English dictionary, revised a short Nobonob grammar, edited a Nobonob Hymnal, and translated parts of the New Testament into Nobonob.

Inselmann's first observations at Nobonob were not positive. He noticed the absence of schools in many places, and even where there were schools, half of the children were unable to read. In religious matters he suspected they were ignorant. On the other hand, Inselmann was pleased with Confirmation and catechumen instruction. In the years that followed, Inselmann maintained a close contact with the people and workers near the station, as well as in the mission areas trans-Gogol and on the south slopes of the Adelbert Mountains. Those people affected by Roman Catholic competition seemed to Inselmann never to have understood the meaning of Christianity.

In the last report for 1940, Inselmann mentioned a dance called *Letub*, which he said originated in neighbouring Catholic villages. The people met for the dance at the cemetery, and swayed their bodies back and forth, calling on their ancestors. The ancestors were to send material gifts to their descendants. Some *Letub* practitioners became healers. In the eight Nobonob villages, where *Letub* was practised, all congregational work ceased. Inselmann said that the *Letub* dance revealed a great distrust of the Europeans, so he suspended the Lord's Supper and Baptism. As in the Keku area with *Ass Bilong Cargo*, the *Letub* movement was another manifestation of what was later called the 'cargo-cult' movement. It was an indication of the missionary task still remaining. [60]

The Revd H. Ander from Texas joined the mission staff in November 1940. After orientation and language study, he was stationed at Nobonob in 1941. When the Japanese came, he was taken captive and became a martyr. However, Inselmann, inland at Magila, had a chance to escape the Japanese in 1944.

The next major centre or circuit to be established was **Amele**. For a number of years, Amele was the centre for a large evangelistic outreach, reaching to the Ramu and including the area of the circuit later known as Begesin. In his 1929 report, missionary J. Welsch from the Rhenish Mission, who later joined the American staff, outlined three areas belonging to Amele's supervision: 1) from the sea-coast to the Gogol river; 2) from the Gogol to the watershed of the Ramu; and 3) the watershed of the Ramu. In the first area, where many baptisms had taken place, there was a reaction against the Gospel. In the second area, which included Begesin, Bemari, Gonua, and Barum, the people were prepared for their first baptism and were eagerly

doing away with their magical 'leaves, creepers, herbs, climbers, stones, pieces of iron and marbles'. A newcomer would be tempted to laugh at seeing all the rubbish which kept the ignorant people captive in fear. Welsch, however, said: 'Each time, when in a few hours all this rubbish passes before me and I get a glimpse of the depths of depravity, I am deeply and strongly moved'.

Much of the evangelistic outreach of the Amele congregation was due to the excellent training school for evangelists conducted by Wullenkord. J. Welsch served as evangelistic missionary, and Wullenkord as trainer of evangelists. This system of stationing two capable men together at one station proved very successful, especially since these two knew how to divide the duties and how to work together. But then came the news of the decision of the Americans to develop only the Bel language as the language for schools and evangelists. Eiffert in 1932 reported: 'This (decision) is for the time being the best as we start work on the north coast. Otherwise the Ragetta (Bel) language is much easier to learn than any other mainland language ... The older Amele brethren will be sorry if the Seminary here would cease to function.'

What happened to the evangelists' school has already been reported. Fr. Schoettler, a young Rhenish missionary who joined the ALC staff, reported in 1932 that his many trips from Amele to the Begesin area were always a great joy for him. He wrote of baptisms in Begesin village, in Kulau, and in Ouba. The schools in the mission area, however, were bad, he said, since the teachers represented the Law and used whips, thereby destroying any interest in God's Word.

In 1933 some Amele Christians voiced their objection to the introduction of the Bel language in the schools, and Schoettler made it his goal to make the transition acceptable. The old congregations at Amele seem tired, he remarked, but evangelism was going ahead in Begesin. On five evangelist stations, 400 baptisms took place, and one also occurred at Paisarik, a village on the edge of a large area of bush country.

In 1934, the main objective of both missionaries and people in Amele was to establish Kerowagi station in the inland. Foege,

Braun, and Schoettler made a tremendous trek inland from May 4 to June 22 to survey the unknown territory and people. A later trip, requiring hundreds of carriers, was required to establish the station. One old elder, Ogam of Fulumu, died near the head of the Chimbu river on the return journey.

But in Amele itself, work among confirmands and young people was proving difficult. A new rage for dancing developed, and the chief of Amele seemed to turn more and more to the old ways. In 1935, many of the elders agreed to no longer contribute to heathen festivals which included dancing, and to accept nothing from the host of such festivals. Those who still participated were excluded from the congregation, and their children denied Baptism.

In Amele there were a number of high points during 1936. The first event was the ban on both Sacraments, decided by the Executive Committee of LMM in order to win back the backsliding brethren. Schoettler said the decision was taken due to the dance and to the hold of sorcery. Secondly, rumours from the Rai Coast spoke of the appearance of two angels and Elias, and of their prediction of the end of the world. Because of these rumours many polygamists and sorcerers cleaned house, the churches were filled, and a total darkness was awaited. Then came the elders' conference, when polygamy and the dance were discussed. Some congregations rejected the elders' decisions to ban the dance. Concerning the Lord's Supper, the Amele elders maintained that they would be prepared for the sacramental meal after Christmas.

Immediately after the elders' conference, there was great disenchantment. The rumours from the Rai Coast were considered a lie. There was no star from heaven. So, more and more people gave up baptismal instruction. The young people seemed to respond better, but by and large the life of the congregation was filled with ups and downs. Only nine new students from Bilibil and Jecelso left for Amron. The other villages refused to send students to a Bel language school.

From April 1937 to August 1938 the F. Schoettlers were on furlough, and Welsch exercised oversight over both Begesin and Amele from Begesin. Ud, the leading Amele

elder, was stationed at Amele, and was chosen and ordained by the congregation to give Communion to the sick. When Schoettler returned in 1938, Ud was appointed to be in charge of the Amele circuit, while Schoettler was to give Baptism and Confirmation instruction.

Welsch was deeply concerned with the problem of cargo beliefs ever since the elders' conference in Bogadjim in 1933. He said: 'Why can't the people distinguish between truth and lies?' During 1938 and 1939, most congregations again celebrated the Sacraments, but Welsch questioned the ban itself. He asked: 'Were really all the people in the areas not worthy to receive them?'

When the war began in Europe, Schoettler was not allowed to leave Amele station. Later, when invasion by the Japanese threatened, Welsch was recalled to Amele to be on hand for Executive Committee meetings, and Schoettler went to Begesin. It was from there that he was escorted to the Central Highlands by Australian soldiers and thus escaped Japanese captivity.

At this point we shall continue with the account of **Begesin**, since it was a mission field closely connected with Amele, and often under common oversight by Welsch together with Amele. Amele evangelists had advanced to the Ramu river before Begesin was assigned a European missionary. H. Foege, who arrived in New Guinea in mid 1930, was assigned to various duties and mission stations due to the constant change of personnel during the years of transition, 1930-32. In 1932, with W. Bergmann, he took part in the first exploration flight through the Central Highlands to plan for a missionary advance there. Finally, Foege returned to the Madang area, and began in a small bush house as first resident missionary at Begesin in October 1933. Half a year later, in March 1934, he was assigned to the new station to be started at Kerowagi in the Central Highlands. After Welsch returned from furlough, he replaced Foege by moving into Begesin at the end of 1934.

Welsch, as usual, entered into his daily duties with devotion and much energy. He thought that the Begesin people should have an identifiable centre. The various helpers' stations had the effect of decentralizing the congregational work. 'Unless centralization is

166

achieved', declared Welsch, 'there will be no strong development, neither inwardly nor outwardly.' In 1935, Welsch enlarged the station. In 1937 a girls' training course, established by Mrs Welsch, was added. By 1939, 15 girls were under training.

Shortly before leaving Begesin, Welsch moved the station further inland to Kasual, so that he could be closer to the larger population groups of the Galia and Sop people. On Christmas Day 1939 the message arrived at Kasual which ordered all wives of missionary personnel to evacuate. With sorrow, Welsch accompanied his wife out from their beloved Begesin to Madang. He never saw her again on this side of heaven.

A mission area of Lutheran Mission Madang was the **Rai Coast**, which had been incorporated into the Finisterre District in 1930, but became part of the ALC Mission in Madang at the beginning of 1933.

Pastor Jerome, one of the six pastors who had been requested by the Rhenish Mission from the Samoan church (see chapter 3), was to make the first start of organized missionary efforts at the southern-most part of the Rhenish mission field. Pastor Jerome said that the people on the Rai Coast had been contacted from 1912 on. Actually, there were business contacts between the Rai Coast people which predated the coming of the whites. The 1912 date marks the official banishment of some Madang villagers to the Rai Coast. Some of these Ragetta people were Christians.

Jerome left for the Rai Coast on January 9, and settled at Galek. Four Siar and three Graged teachers were sent to assist him.[61] F. Henkelmann took over from Jerome during the period 1930 to 1932. During 1932, the station was moved to Biliau. In 1933, Henkelmann left Bilaiau to take over the Amele Evangelists School. This assignment was made because Henkelmann knew and used the Bel (Graged) language.

The new missionary for Biliau was P. Fliehler, coming from Ulap. For someone acquainted with the mission work of Kalasa and Ulap evangelists, the Rai Coast situation presented serious problems. Evidently, Jerome and the teachers under his supervision evangelized, for the most part, only the coastal villages. In the foot-hills inland from the coast,

only two hours' walking distance, there were still many unevangelized people who practised murder, sorcery, and other evils, and the coastal people were very afraid of them. Only 12 teachers and helpers were still at work, two from Karkar, four from Ragetta, and the rest from the Rai Coast or the Kar mountains. Fliehler remarked: 'The very life of the Rai Coast congregation is at stake ... They are well on the way to spiritual death.'

Polygamy seemed to be a big problem. The Christians desired Communion, so Fliehler suggested three possibilities: 1) all should come except the backsliders; 2) villages which have Christians living in open sin should not commune; or 3) the entire Rai Coast congregation should accept the burden as belonging to all, and therefore not commune until action was taken to correct the evils. The elders accepted the third proposal, and planned to admonish the polygamists. If this step was unsuccessful, the polygamists were to be excommunicated, and then the people would receive Communion the following Easter.

The next misionary for Biliau was to be the Revd J. Kuder from Niagara Falls, NY, who was to spend six years on the Rai Coast. The Kuder family arrived in New Guinea in May 1934, and had little opportunity for orientation. In July, Kuder joined E. Hannemann on the Rai Coast, who was to introduce Kuder to the work there. Kuder reported both positive and negative impressions in his first report. Negatively, he said that the Roman Catholics would station a priest at Bang, and from then on there would be opposition to Lutheran workers. He lamented the lack of teachers and helpers necessary to properly evangelize the people. On the coast, he reported that Christian villages and heathen villages were living side by side, and only two-and-a-half hours' walk inland the villages were all heathen. He had questions relating to the celebration of Communion, church discipline, and missionary method.

During 1935, Kuder made a number of important mission trips. Together with E. Hannemann, a trip was made southeast of Kar, where 2,000 people were found in the Jambarra region. From Jambarra, the journey led to the Jangdar valley, where there were 1,500 people never before contacted by whites, and in the Mot river valley another 2,000 people were discovered. In August, a party consisting of Kuder, Fliehler, E. Hannemann, and helpers crossed the tremendously lofty Finisterre range and entered the Nahu valley on the south slopes, and were greeted by a population of two to three thousand. After a conversation with A. Metzner, the LMF missionary at Ulap, it seemed likely that Ulap evangelists would cross over into the Rai Coast mountain areas to evangelize uncontacted people there, especially in the area between the Mot and Jupna river valleys.

A serious illness kept Kuder absent from Biliau during the latter part of 1935 and early 1936. When he returned to the station in late February 1936, he was shocked at the condition of the congregation. He said that the work seemed to go ahead when the missionary was present, but fell down when he was absent. Together with the elders, a visitation program covering all villages under contract was begun. In the visitation, it was agreed to emphasize community responsibility for the Christian faith, life, and outreach to the unevangelized. The visitation was carried out, but with only partial success. Before definite progress could be expected, Kuder suggested that more instruction for elders and leaders would be necessary, and an understanding of what Christianity truly means would have to be more thoroughly rooted among the people.

Kuder reported the 1936 prophet movement, which caused such a stir in the Madang area. Under influence of the heathen prophets from the Jangdar valley, people rid themselves of sorcery articles, went through a form of baptism, and expected the second coming of Christ to be accompanied by earthquakes and the levelling of mountains.

Gradually, in the next three years, congregational renewal and participation in evangelistic outreach improved. Additional helpers were sent from Madang, and others from the Rai Coast volunteered. By 1938, the Kate congregations at Ulap and Kalasa had sent 51 helpers, who were at work in ten stations in the mountains, and in 1939 an additional five stations were being planned by them.

The Rai Coast Finisterre mountain chain taxed the physical resources of any missionary, especially if the range had to be crossed to make visits to evangelists possible in the valleys on the south side. Kuder hoped for extra

missionary help in 1939, which finally materialized when the Revd Paul Freyberg from Bradner, Ohio, arrived in Madang in September 1939, and was later sent to Biliau.

When Kuder was asked to go to the inland station Ogelbeng during the wartime emergency, Freyberg was required to take over the vast Rai Coast field. He did so while mastering both the Kate and Bel church languages in a few years. When the Japanese occupation of Madang was accomplished, P. Freyberg and J. Lindner were ordered out over the mountains by government officers. Their escape involved an exhausting trek through Japanese lines in the Markham Valley to safety. [62]

Another true mission area of the Americans was on the Laden Coast, northwest of Madang, where a station called **Bunabun** was eventually established. This was the coast near Malala village, where the Revd F. Boesch and the Revd W. Scheidt were murdered on May 27, 1891, before there were any Catholics there (see chapter 3). In general, the coastal villages were later occupied by Roman Catholic priests or catechists, but through the years there were consistent contacts between the people on the Laden Coast and the Karkar people.

In 1932, J. Mager and G. Lindner made a trip to the villages of the Laden people, both coastal and mountain villagers, who had sent an invitation. Two teachers, Kautil and Jeros, were placed at Malala, and another teacher at Rurunot. The visit extended to a number of villages in the mountains, such as Sarisawu, Aben Latnen and Tanlak, Tinami, and Jauru.

Mager knew the area reasonably well, having made a first exploratory trip with George in February 1929, and later going to Suburam in May of that year by himself. In September 1930, Mager, Stahl, and E. Hannemann went as far as Jauru in the mountains. [63]

The station at Bunabun was established because of the good work on the coast and in the mountains by the evangelists, who totalled 11 or 12. Pfeiffer began building a temporary house in April 1933. Shortly after Doege arrived, Pfeiffer became very ill, and died on May 21 from malaria.

It became evident that a mosquito-proof house was necessary. Therefore, Siemers was sent to Bunabun to erect a permanent residence. During his first year at Bunabun, Doege made four exploratory trips into the mountains, once with Mager, and several trips to coastal villages. He became convinced that in the long run a station in the mountains would be necessary.

The number of helpers and teachers from Karkar and Bagabag increased, and this made a good beginning possible in the work of bringing the Gospel to both coastal and mountain villages. In 1934, evangelists from Bagabag were present, who made a fine contribution in the years ahead, strong-willed and independent as they were. They were Balun, Jaun, Jong, Kisou, Malis, Umat, and Wasek. From Karkar the following were at work: Giok, Jeros, Kautil, Kumarar, Kuriring, Lom, Live, Longsei, Mateki, Nagu, Talmel, and Udil. In the years that followed, Karkar supplied an additional 17 evangelists, but some ran away when they realized what real heathen in the mountains actually looked like. After the first baptisms, the mountain villages in Bunabun, especially, participated in sending evangelists to the unevangelized heathen. In one way, their service was an act of self-preservation, for to have untouched cannibals as neighbours was dangerous at all times. More than 32 local men volunteered during the next few years, and often became excellent evangelists in difficult situations. [64]

The first two baptisms at Bunabun took place at the coast on June 2, 1935, and at Sarisawu in the mountains on September 15, 1935. On the coast, 64 men, women, and children from Tawulte, Bunabun, and Garum were baptized, and there were 147 people at Sarisawu. The great leader of the mountain people, Kamong, knew that his life was in danger because he had given up heathen customs and practices. So he continued to admonish his people to be faithful. Scarcely five weeks after the baptism he was treacherously murdered by heathen neighbours. To become a Christian in the Bunabun mountains was extremely dangerous in those days.

On May 2-15, 1934, a long dangerous exploratory trip was made across the Adelbert mountains from Bunabun to Nobonob by Pietz, Mager, Welsch, and Doege. Since the ridges of the Adelberts lie from east to west, travelling in those rugged mountains proved very difficult,

especially since there were no paths and the fearful heathen were ready to fight at the slightest impulse. The women in the mountains wore no clothes whatsoever, and the men a very brief bark loin-cloth. [65]

In 1936, from May 16 to 31, another special trip was made by Schoettler, Spier, and Doege to clarify the location of a mountain station, since Bunabun was considered only a coastal support station. In the central range of the Adelberts, the men estimated that five to eight thousand people lived, who were totally uncontacted until that time. About 15 helpers' stations would be required to bring the Gospel to them. The men proposed that if a station at Sarisawu could not be built, then a station much further inland would be necessary. Consequently, in July, a missionary conference resolved to establish a station at Sarisawu. 1936 marked the time of the first Communion celebrations in Bunabun, when 90 per cent or more of the Christians participated. Unfortunately, 1936 was also the year when a ban on the Sacraments was imposed by the Mission Executive and later the native conference.

In 1937, Doege made valiant efforts to strengthen the entire mission effort, spending over 215 days away from home. In July, together with Pietz, he visited four or five proposed new evangelist stations near Hinihon on the very top of the range, and received requests from large population groups on the Ramu side of the mountains. Both missionaries rejoiced over the progress made. But a deep shadow was cast over the whole work by the ban on the Sacraments. Due to land slides at Sarisawu, which partly destroyed the planned station site, Doege now proposed a new site near Hinihon, which would definitely involve plane transport. The elevation of the site was 1,415 metres. 1937 was the last year of Doege's service in New Guinea. He went on leave on January 16, 1938, and through the misfortune of war was caught in the Philippines by the Japanese invasion, where he and his family spent many difficult years in imprisonment.

F. Henkelmann arrived at Bunabun on December 18, 1937, and took over the work from Doege in 1938. Two extensive trips were made in 1938, one in April with Mager and Thogersen, and one in August with the same men, accompanied by about 17 carriers, several evangelists, and one elder. The purpose was to solve the problem of locating the proposed station site. Starting on August 4, the party had crossed the main range three times by August 15. On August 18, the party was attacked by hostile suspicious people from the village of Kridematau. In defending themselves, the party killed a fight leader from Kridematau, but Mager received an arrow in the back. It took eight days of day and night travel under the most adverse conditions to carry Mager out to the coast and to medical help. [66]

In the years 1939 to 1942, Henkelmann continued to commit himself heart and soul to the great evangelistic task. During 1939, steps were taken to establish a station at Hinihon. But most of his time — over 200 days each year — was spent visiting the evangelists' stations, encouraging, advising, and helping in whatever way possible. The battle for the hearts and minds of the heathen was a monumental struggle. Where the Gospel was accepted, there peace ruled, but there was still the ever-present danger of attacks from those still uncovered. Even the wives of the evangelists were fair game if a hungry man caught them unprotected in a bush garden.

On the coast, Protestant villagers experienced considerable opposition from their Roman Catholic neighbours, who threatened to close trade stores to them and who refused to buy their village produce.

Henkelmann continued to work faithfully throughout 1942, even after the Japanese landed in Madang. Finally, he too was brought into captivity, and he lost his life as a martyr in an unknown location, possibly near Bunabun, in March of 1943. In his last years at Bunabun, Henkelmann had the assistance of Ray Barber, who built up and maintained the station property, planted trees, and took care of the domestic animals. In addition, he ministered to the many sick.

In the early enthusiasm of the missionaries of the American Lutheran Church in 1932, when they realized the Madang area would be their mission, they planned a mission advance across the Ramu river to the north slopes of Mount Wilhelm to an area called Iwam. G. Eiffert and W. Foege were to establish a station at a site called **Faita** (Ene). Thus, on April 4, 1933, Eiffert

170

and Foege left Amele with 35 carriers, but found Ene occupied by Roman Catholic catechists. So they went west to Faita, where a Lutheran evangelist station was already established. There E. Hannemann joined them for a trip to the Iwam country. In the Iwam they constantly heard the words Popi (for Roman Catholic) and Taltal (for Lutheran) used as descriptions of opposing forces. Instead of continuing on further, they returned to Faita and built a small house, where Eiffert settled in.

Later, from June 5 to 26, Foege made a trip over the Bismarcks to the Upper Purari or Hofa region with Hanselmann, returned, and visited Faita and the Iwam again with Eiffert. He came to the conclusion that Faita would not amount to anything, that the station had little or only partial support for missionaries and local people, and therefore asked the Executive for another assignment. He was subsequently assigned to Begesin.

Eiffert tried valiantly to put life into the advance at Faita. He himself was inclined to use a very personal individualistic approach to evangelism, and in this way differed with Foege. In 1933 there were precious few evangelists available in the Madang area, and in 1934 all strengths were focused to an advance to the inland on the south side of Mount Wilhelm to Kerowagi.

Faita never had much hope of success. Few people lived in the vicinity, and the Iwam area could be reached only by a strenuous day of climbing over foot-hills to the valley of the Imburum river. The Roman Catholics eventually established an aerodrome at Bundi on a mountain ridge on the edge of the Iwam country. However, Bundi village, and others first contacted by the Amele evangelists, continued to be loyal to their first commitment.

Specific Missionary Problems

Before concluding this section by considering the mission advance into the Central Highlands, some consideration should be given to some special problems facing the missionaries in their attempt to bring the Gospel to the people in the Madang area.

Polygamy, the practice of having more than one wife, was a common custom of important men in the pre-Christian society. Very early, the Christians made a decision that before

Baptism could be received a polygamist must keep only one wife. The other wife or wives should be given in marriage to men without wives, since about one-third of men in the heathen society could not be married due to the shortage of women.

Polygamy and Christianity do not mix: that was the united Lutheran Mission practice, and a principle of the indigenous church. Polygamy remained a problem for many years in the Madang district, especially in the mission area of the Rai Coast. On many occasions, the evangelists dealt with the problem of polygamy in a very legalistic manner. Sometimes divorced women committed suicide, rather than take another husband.

F. Henkelmann mentioned polygamy on the Rai Coast as a problem in several reports. He noted that the congregational practice of dealing with polygamists in a legalistic way caused problems: 1) for the conscience of the missionary; 2) for the wives of the polygamists; 3) for the children of polygamists; and 4) for the divorced wives and children of polygamists. Fliehler, who followed Henkelmann on the Rai Coast, recommended to the congregation that those who became polygamists after baptism, or those who took back wives previously dismissed, should be denied Communion. His recommendation was accepted.

Traditional dancing was also considered a serious problem by both missionaries and early Christians. All activities in the pre-Christian society were connected with belief in magic, fear of sorcery, worship and fear of ancestors, adultery, murderous thoughts, and the like. Since dancing was usually a joyful community occasion, often associated also with exchange of pigs and other valuables in the economy, it stood at the centre of the pre-Christian life. But the Madang District prohibited it. The decision was taken at an elders' conference at Sagalau in 1936, though it was not unanimous. It was a very important decision for Ud, the leader from Amele, and for his missionary, Welsch, but the Ragetta congregation did not support it. Elders from other congregations supported Ud, but their decision was not accepted unanimously by people back home.

In 1934, at the Annual Field Conference in January, and in the Ministerial Conference in July, E. Hannemann, in a three-part paper,

discussed the native dance and its implications, but specific resolutions were not passed. Stahl reported previously that the dance had largely ceased in Takia in 1932. Mager said of the Waskians in 1933, that the Christians gave up the dance. They said: 'The dance is evil. It is the chief source of sins that prevail among us. It is devilish.' In 1934, Kuder at the Rai Coast wondered whether Christians who danced could be admitted to Communion. Inselmann reported in 1937 of the Nobonob people that they said that the mission had forbidden the dance but the government had allowed it. In respect to the dance, he said that there had been no improvement since the Sagalau Conference in 1936. [67]

In connection with many baptismal festivals, dances of the past were performed by the people, and the meanings of the various dances were recalled. Some dances were quite vicious, even involving attempted murder, incitement to murder, temptation to adultery, and so on. But not all dances were equally evil. Some told stories and myths of the past. Wherever evangelists became excessively legalistic about dancing, there the dance was occasionally used as a weapon against the congregation. Sometimes the law made the dance more sinful than it had been.

Another serious missionary problem was the decision to make the Bel language the **school language** for the whole district. It was unfortunate that a decision for a unifying language had not been made in the previous 45 years. When the decision was finally made by the American missionaries, the Amele language school system covered a large area from within a few miles of Madang to the Ramu river. The Nobonob congregation was also used to its own printed literature. No one proposed using Pidgin, which was well known in the entire Madang area wherever labourers had entered the contract-labour system.

In 1933, Schoettler reported that the congregation had arguments about the introduction of the Bel language. In the same year, Pietz reported that the Nobonob people were willing to switch from the Amele language in schools to the Bel language. Even though the Nobonobs were willing to change, reports in the following two years indicate that many years

171

would pass before a satisfactory Bel language school system was possible.

After the central school at Amron had been operational for one-and-a-half years, E. Hannemann said that although many students knew the Bel language, too few used it, since Pidgin was so handy. In 1936, Schoettler noted that most people in the Amele congregation were still opposed to the introduction of the Bel language, and in a combined report covering both Amele-Begesin in 1938, Welsch explained that since the Bel language had made little progress, it was necessary to continue with the Amele language and Amele teachers in schools.[68]

The time was far too short. The Urit schools did not attract students from either Amele or Nobonob in the past. And the Amron school, with its six-year course, could not possibly effect a change in such a short time. A wiser decision might have been to continue all schools, the schools at Urit and Amele, for a few additional years, and only later discontinue them. With inadequate missionary and indigenous teaching staff, the decision made was not practical. Hannemann, Mager, and the six local teachers at Amron made a tremendous contribution, but the fruits of their labour were cut short by the war.

The most debatable mission method of this period was the use of the **ban on the Sacraments** in order to discipline and to awaken Christian congregational members, who, according to the missionaries, displayed inadequate zeal in putting away old customs and in encouraging Christian customs in the villages, or who were lax in selecting and sending out missionaries to the unevangelized. This practice was not new to Madang. It was commonly also practised in Finschhafen by elders and missionaries. In a 1933 report of Keku, R. Hanselmann stated that the use of the Sacraments was forbidden except for a few individual Christians, but that this ban was accepted with indifference by the people. Pietz reported from Nobonob in the following year that the people thought that if they were denied Communion once or twice, that would be sufficient to repay any guilt. In 1935, Hannemann wrote that the Ragetta congregation did not celebrate Communion. The reason given was that the congregation

172

should become more congregation-conscious and attain greater solidarity before commemorating the sacramental meal.

Also in 1935, Fliehler at Keku cited the use by Jabem and Hube congregations of LMF of the ban on the Sacraments, and mentioned the condition of the Keku congregation as a reason for instituting a ban at Keku. He decided that it was better to use ultimatums with the Keku people rather than the slower method of teaching and influencing the people. In support of this decision, he quoted L. Flierl on a number of possible ways of dealing with a baptismal class that has problems.[69]

The ban became obligatory for all missionaries in 1936, when the 16th Executive of Lutheran Mission Madang decided the following:

> We are of the opinion that all congregations are suffering a retrogression, that the majority of the natives with whom we are in contact are indifferent and do not realize a common aim, nor the principles of basic Christianity. It will be well if the natives themselves then bring forth the obstacles which have hindered them from taking steps toward this aim. God has given us the 'tools' with which we are to work and has promised us the strength necessary. If we fail to give in return or make proper use of them, we forfeit our right to receive them ... From now on no missionary will baptize or give communion until such a time as the congregation has given proof it has realized and taken steps to carry out their Christian duty ... Each member of the staff will include himself under these restrictions. This means members of the white staff will not baptize their own children nor celebrate communion. (Faithful members of the mission may have communion or baptism in emergency.)[70]

In the 17th Executive meeting in 1936, the minutes record the following:

> They say that potentially the Papuan Church has the right and the duty to administer the means of grace, Word and Sacrament. It is an erroneous idea that we whites are the proprietors of the means of grace. It is evident that the people do not understand these things and have not done their Christian duty. In order to make this known to the congregations we propose dispensing for the time being with the administration of the sacraments.[71]

Subsequently, the decision of the Executive was brought before the Sagalau Elders' Conference of 1936, and endorsed by the congregational leaders. The leaders hardly had any other choice, since permission to administer the Sacraments had not yet been given.

What was the result of the decision? The missionaries were faced with a great missionary task, both in the Madang area and in the newly-opened area in the inland. There were an inadequate number of evangelists available, and the congregations did not display the enthusiasm felt by the missionaries.

Some cautious support for the ban was expressed. Fortunately, the Bunabun congregation had celebrated Communion successfully early in the year, with 90 per cent attendance after the first baptisms of 1935. At Nobonob, the congregation took steps for self-examination, and all expressed their desire to have Baptism and Communion again, since the congregation had rejected sorcery, immorality, and so on. Kuder on the Rai Coast hoped that the decisions of the Sagalau conference would bear fruit. At Keku, Fliehler said that the Sagalau decisions were a step in the right direction. [72]

However, soon former Rhenish missionaries — including Welsch who was on the Executive — expressed other observations and opinions. Schoettler said that the ban on Communion made no impression on indifferent Christians at Amele. In Begesin, Welsch reported that the Sagalau decisions made no impression on the Begesin people, except the people in Bemal. The most critical observation, however, soon came from an experienced former Rhenish layman, H. Schamann, the plantation supervisor. He complained about the ban on the Sacraments, and said that it is right to forbid the Sacraments to evident and open sinners, 'but because of them one does not have the right to forbid the sacrament on the whole mission field'. According to his opinion, the Executive had overstepped its right. 'The ban', he said 'has absolutely no effect on Karkar. Yes, in some villages some old and new magical things were burned, but what does that mean? They can easily provide substitutes again.' [73]

In 1937, the Sangapat Elders' Conference gave the right to use the Sacraments again to Amele congregations, but the rest remained under the ban. The Ameles had stood solidly together, and impressed the meeting. Fliehler at Keku was disturbed about that decision, since

he was having difficulties with disobedient Amele helpers on Keku circuit outposts. Doege at Bunabun, who participated in the Executive meeting, now questioned whether it was right to deny Communion to the many catechumens in Bunabun. Inselmann at Nobonob advised that the resumption of the use of the Sacraments should not be delayed too long, lest a hopeless attitude develop among the people.

In 1938, Kuder said that in considering the effect of the ban, an unqualified 'Yes' could not be given, but he thought the ban helped to bring home to the people the responsibility of the Christian life. [74]

E. Hannemann defended the ban on the Sacraments until he went on furlough, but others became very critical, and many pointed out that on weak Christians it had no effect at all. Stahl gave a devastating report of the effect on the Karkar congregation. Before the ban, Kaul village had 200 catechumens ready for Baptism. In 1939, all had given up. The Bangame church was usually well attended, now only a few children gathered. At other villages, worship services also lost their attraction, and people no longer came to devotions. He said that the ban had a negative effect. The people said: 'Now there will be no more nourishment, therefore we can also not work, we have no more strength'. And the lukewarm people said: 'There is no passover, no Lord's Supper any more, so we can go ahead and sin and we will not have to confess our sins any more'. [75]

Due to the growing dissatisfaction, the Annual Elders' Conference at Bangame on Karkar, on July 22-25, 1939, decided after lengthy discussion that the ban should be lifted for all other congregations still under the ban. Later, the Karkar congregation, under the leadership of Mileng, proposed a number of specific situations in which people were to be denied the Sacraments. These proposals were presented to the 1940 Elders' Conference at Bongu, and approved. [76]

The people were now free to receive the Sacraments again, but in 1941, shortly before the war, due to two discipline cases involving two missionaries, the Executive Committee meeting at Maulon on July 11-14, 1941, decided not to celebrate Communion. [77] The missionaries were also sinners.

Advance into the Central Highlands

The opening of Kerowagi mission station in the Wagi river valley of the Central Highlands represented participation by the Americans in the great mission outreach into the highlands in the 1930s. The Eastern Highlands had been occupied by evangelists from LMF from 1922, and by a permanent missionary, W. Bergmann, in 1931.

Following a government exploration mission into the Wagi valley and Western Highlands in early 1933, it was decided by the Executive of both LMF and LMM to make a survey flight westward from Kainantu in October 1933. The Executive of LMM chose Foege and Fliehler to represent LMM on the survey flight. However, Pietz later replaced Fliehler. On October 24, in a very small plane that could take only two passengers (W. Bergmann and W. Foege) in addition to the pilot, they made the exploration flight. Each man with compass, paper, and watch made a map of the terrain, gardens, and villages seen on his side of the plane. At the end of the flight, both men acknowledged that the Wagi valley to Hagen held an enormous population. Both LMF and LMM agreed that only a united effort would make possible a mission outreach into the new areas. [78] Since the administration had asked for Lutheran cooperation in opening up the new fields, the Lutherans considered the discoveries as a Macedonian call to help. (See also chapter 5.)

In January 1934, the Annual Conference of LMM agreed to cooperate wholeheartedly with LMF in the inland work. Urgent requests were sent to the home board for advice and for additional men and funds. At a Special LMM Conference in March, 1934, a cable message was received from the ALC which said: 'ALC will not neglect work in the new inland districts. Make a start. We hope to be able to send additional missionaries.' The same special conference assigned Foege to the new inland work, and authorized an overland exploratory expedition to be made with Braun, Schoettler, and congregational representatives, plus carriers. Pietz and Braun were to go to Finschhafen to arrange for a joint expedition with LMF. [79]

The third Executive meeting of 1934 took place at Finschhafen on April 13. Pietz and

174

Braun met with Lehner, W. Flierl, and Herrlinger from LMF. It was decided to make a joint overland expedition, with both parties meeting in the Eastern Highlands on May 13, at Rabana. The Madang group, made up of Foege, Braun, and Schoettler, plus carriers and congregational representatives totalling 143, left Madang on May 4, and arrived on schedule at Rabana. After a rest day, the joint party, including Bergmann, Herrlinger, and Lechner from LMF, went west through Benabena, Gafuka, and Marifuteikar valleys to the Wagi valley, running from east to west. After the joint party had been together two weeks, they arrived at a point one day's walk from Mount Hagen. There the two groups parted. Both parties agreed that ways and means must be found to bring the Gospel to so many unevangelized people. They also agreed that both LMF and LMM must work together because of the heavy population.

After parting, the Madang group went northeast, crossing the Jimi river valley and the Schrader range before arriving at the Ramu. This very difficult trip took two weeks. They noticed that the whole area west of Faita had a very sparce population. Since not all objectives of the trip had been fulfilled, Schoettler was sent to Begesin and Amele with the bulk of the carriers, and Foege and Braun proceeded to explore a direct way to the inland via the Iwam country. On Sunday morning of June 17 they stood on the Chimbu river valley watershed at 9,100 feet, and saw the heavily populated valley before them. They had found a very old and much-used trade route over the Chimbu pass. The men were very grateful to God. On the long trip, lasting seven weeks, their whole group had remained fit, they had had no accidents, and neither were they ever attacked by any of the thousands of people they met. [80]

In the meantime, several further exploratory trips were made, and Eiffert improved a trail from Faita to the Iwam country. In July, LMF and LMM representatives meeting at Nobonob decided that LMF was to establish Ega and Hagen, and LMM Kerowagi, with the hope that LMM would start another station in 1935 between Kerowagi and Hagen. September 1 was set as the start of the expedition to begin Kerowagi station. [81]

Revd H. Hannemann.

Foege had been selected as the lead missionary in establishing the Kerowagi station, and H. Hannemann, a new arrival from the US and a brother of E. Hannemann, was to serve as the second missionary. H. Hannemann was to serve for the next 34 years among the Kuman people of the Wagi valley. On September 1, a missionary party including Pietz, Welsch, Foege, Mager, H. Hannemann, and Radke left Amele with 140 carriers, including some evangelists and elders, each carrier loaded with a 25 lb. pack of supplies. On the way, Eiffert joined the party. In the Iwam, instead of following the way discovered by Braun and Foege, the local people led the expedition on a by-path wasting precious miles and taxing the strength of the whole party, until the divide was reached at a considerably higher elevation at 10,500 feet. But the view of the treeless valley ahead, with gardens up to 9,000 feet, inspired everyone. Instead of going down the Chimbu to the Wagi valley, the party crossed over to the Koro river valley, and on a Saturday, two weeks after leaving Madang, reached the Wagi valley. One carrier died a couple of days after arrival, and one Fulumu elder died in the Chimbu valley

on the return journey. These were the sacrifices the congregations made in the founding of Kerowagi. Others were soon to follow.

A station site was purchased from local people, and immediately work was begun on an airstrip of 800 by 60 yards. For the time being, everyone lived in small grass huts. Two weeks after arrival, 120 carriers left with four missionaries for Madang, and only Foege, Hannemann, and Radke remained. A test plane was to arrive on October 15, but finally came two weeks later. Bad weather had interfered. The pilot declared the strip to be the fourth best he had used in New Guinea.

Strenuous efforts were made day by day, with saw crews preparing timber for a permanent house. The planes brought in roofing and flat iron. On December 1 the house had a roof and one room ready, and the missionaries were happy to escape the fleas so prevalent in the local grass huts. Before departing after a three months' stay at Kerowagi, Radke remarked that in the Wagi there was sufficient work for 30 white missionaries and 1,000 local evangelists. [82] This prediction eventually proved to be more than correct. But fulfillment awaited the much greater resources of post-war years.

In the months and years that followed, strenuous efforts were made by both missionaries and evangelists to learn and record the local language, and to make contact with an ever-widening circle of the local population. To establish contact with people further removed was not easy, because of the enmity of clan with clan and the many local disputes. A number of missionaries from Madang spent shorter or longer periods at Kerowagi, either to assist the work or to relieve the men assigned to Kerowagi, so they could come out to the coast and see their families from whom they had been separated. A young Canadian missionary, F. Doering, originally from Latvia, arrived in October 1935. It was not till 1937 that Doering was given permission to stay permanently in the inland. He and Bertelsmeier were assigned to begin a new Wagi station, which was never begun before the war. Later, during the war-time emergency, Doering took charge of the work at Kerowagi until he was evacuated.

175

In early January 1936 an unfortunate event occurred at Kerowagi, which was reported personally by Foege to the patrol officer at Kundiawa. Foege then left by plane for Lae and Madang. On February 12 he was informed that his permit would not be renewed for inland work. On April 30 he was called to Salamaua for a preliminary court hearing, and on July 16 sentenced to two years' hard labour in prison at Rabaul. Foege was soon pardoned by the Australian Prime Minister on October 1 that year, because of representations by mission and church authorities. He had become a victim of administrators who were not friendly to the Gospel. In this way, the American pioneer missionary to the inland was lost to the work. The loss of Foege was a great blow to LMM. [83]

The famous Administrator McNicoll order of mid-1936, forbidding all New Guinean evangelist stations apart from the main European stations, caused hundreds of Lutheran evangelists to be withdrawn from the Central Highlands, and severely hindered the work before the war. The order especially affected the Lutheran work. (For details, see chapter 5 and appended Document 2.)

War Time Again: Australian and American Missionaries Take Charge

As the year 1939 dawned, the missionaries in LMF and LMM were very much aware of the world political situation. Pilhofer and Lehner, with five other LMF guests, attended the seventh Field Conference of LMM on January 7-13, 1939. Pilhofer spoke to the assembled missionaries of the critical situation facing the two missions, which he felt could jeopardize the whole future of the Lutheran Church.

In a covering letter to the minutes, President Fliehler mentioned the severe financial situation facing LMF. Debts, mortgages, and a lack of new men for the field were all part of the picture. Pilhofer considered that LMF might have to give up mission stations — and also the inland work — and then call on LMM to take over the inland stations and also the operation of the plane. Fliehler underlined the statement: 'Lutheran Mission Finschhafen is facing ruin'. [84]

Fliehler reported that the plane *Papua* had suffered an accident, and was not covered by insurance. 'At any moment during this year', he
176

said 'Lutheran Mission Finschhafen may turn to the ALC to take over their entire field.' Fliehler went on to explain that the Finschhafen missionaries had been unofficially informed that if New Guinea became definitely Australian, that is, British, and if Germany received some of her other colonies back, then even the small funds now received for mission work would be cut off and LMF would be forced to turn over their mission field to some other church. According to the letter, September 1, 1939, was the date set by Hitler for the return of all former German colonies. If the situation feared by LMF came to pass, Fliehler said that LMM was 'ready to do anything possible to help save the situation for the Lutheran Church'. [85] As a result of the situation in LMF, the Madang missionaries resolved to economize as much as possible, since 'the work of the two Lutheran Missions in New Guinea is not the work of individuals nor of societies but the work of our Lord and Saviour'. [86]

What had been feared, happened, when news arrived that war had been declared in Europe in September. On September 26, 1939, the first German missionaries were interned in Australia. Others soon followed. At Finschhafen only a few of the older German missionaries, like Decker and Lehner, and the young A. Wagner, were allowed to stay. LMF was not taken over by legal action of the Australian government, as was the case after World War I, but the missionary emergency was much more devastating with the loss of the majority of the missionary staff.

In Madang, Welsch and Schoettler were not touched. The women were evacuated later, in December 1941, with the exception of the medical personnel of LMM, who elected to stay on. [87]

In order to take care of the most urgent needs of missionary supervision, representatives of LMF and LMM met together four times from October 1939 to June 1940 to plan for strategy and missionary replacements. H. Hannemann took over supervision at Ega in September of 1939, while Doering remained at Kerowagi. At first, it was planned to put Frerichs at Ogelbeng, but eventually Kuder received permission from the administration to go to that isolated inland station. Frerichs took over Raipinka, and Pietz became the Superintendent of LMF to be stationed at Lae, where he could exercise supervision over the Markham Valley congregations. The Australian layman, P. Helbig, was taken over by LMM and served at the inland station of Asaroka until evacuated. [88] On August 18, 1940, the Revd Martin Ackermann arrived from Minnesota to help out in the emergency. He was assigned to Malalo circuit of LMF, south of Lae, where he worked until 1942, when he was evacuated.

The districts of Madang and Finschhafen had cooperated closely during the emergency of the First World War until 1930, when LMF and LMM were separated once more. Then followed increasing cooperation because of the requirements of evangelization and the great mission thrust into the Central Highlands. Finally, because of the new emergency of World War II, thoughts of boundaries, mission ownership, and rights, vanished in the need to stand by the congregations in their life of faith and witness. All American missionaries who served in LMF or were located there or in the Highlands were safely evacuated by order of the authorities. All except one in the Madang area suffered a different fate. [89]

Imprisonment, Suffering, and Martyrdom under the Japanese

After December 7, 1941, when the Japanese attacked Pearl Harbour in Hawaii, the missionaries realized that New Guinea might also become an active war zone. The Australian government ordered the evacuation of all European women and children, but permitted doctors and nurses to continue their service. Mrs T. Braun, Miss Frieda Klotzbuecher, Miss Marie Kroeger — all Registered Nurses — and Dr Hoeger, who had gone to Finschhafen, chose to stay. The men decided to stay unless they were ordered to leave by the government. All considered that it was their duty to continue to minister as true shepherds (John 10:12).

New Guinea became a war zone much sooner than anyone expected. Already on December 8, Japanese troops were landed on the coast of Malaya. On December 10 they began a full invasion of the Philippines. The Japanese thrust was so rapid that on January 21 both Madang and Rabaul were heavily bombed. Rabaul was invaded on the 23rd by the Japanese 4th fleet, and was soon under

Japanese control. The islands of Ambon and Timor off the western tip of New Guinea were invaded on January 31 and February 20 respectively. [90]

When Madang was bombed heavily on January 21, most of the civilian population fled by foot to Kainantu and eventually to Mount Hagen, from where they were flown out by air. Several other air raids were suffered in the following weeks. The plantations were deserted by their labourers, and fleeing labourers from other centres told wild stories of events. [91]

Although bomb shelters and trenches were dug in Madang town by order of the District Officer, the first serious bombing raid happened so suddenly that Wilbur Wenz, the business manager of Lutheran Mission Madang, had no time to reach shelter. Because of his narrow escape, he suffered such shock that he was sent to Kubal (Bogadjim) to the Revd Dott to recuperate.

By that time, the news came that Europeans, soldiers and civilians, fleeing from Rabaul required help to evacuate. A Captain G.C. Harris commandeered the mission ship *Totol* from Madang and the *Umboi* from Siassi to go to the rescue which took place on the north coast of West New Britain between March 8 and March 21, when a larger vessel, the *Lakatoi*, evacuated several hundred to Australia and the *Totol* and *Umboi* were allowed to return. Captain Ted Radke played an important part in this rescue. [92] After returning to Madang, Captain Radke hid the *Totol* in a slough deep in the inner harbour of Nagada, where he let the boat sink in the mud. A bomb from an Allied plane caused a fire to burn the superstructure, and the hull could no longer be made useful after the war.

The Japanese invasion bypassed Madang at first. Rabaul, the Solomon Islands, Lae, Salamaua, and Port Moresby were more important strategically. The Revd Pietz, the Revd Ackermann, and Dr Hoeger, together with others in the Finschhafen and Lae areas, were ordered evacuated after the fall of Rabaul and travelled overland to Wau and then to the Papuan coast via the 'Bulldog' Trail. Dr Hoeger was flown to Port Moresby from Wau.

On March 8, a force of 3,000 Japanese landed at Lae and Salamaua. After some months of careful preparation, the Japanese planned a double strike at Port Moresby and northern Australia, with the intent to invade Port Moresby. The famous Coral Sea battle, in which each side, the Americans and the Japanese, lost an aircraft carrier, fought between May 5 and 8 effectively halted the rapid Japanese advance for the time being.

Then followed the invasion of Gona and Buna, Anglican mission stations on the north coast of Papua on July 21. Milne Bay was occupied on August 25-26. Instead of attacking Port Moresby by the sea, the Japanese decided to go overland, crossing via the Kokoda trail to within a few kilometres of Port Moresby, where they were halted at Imita Ridge on September 17.[93] There followed months of unbelievably difficult fighting on the Kokoda trail before Kokoda was recaptured on November 2, Gona on December 9, and Buna first on January in 1943.

In the meantime, the missionaries in Madang had hopes that the invasion forces would bypass Madang. But increasing attacks by Allied planes caused such losses among Japanese ship convoys that attempts were made to keep the supply lines open with the use of barges travelling along the coast at night and hiding along the shore by day. On December 18, 1942, a large Japanese convoy was spotted off the north coast of Madang already in the forenoon. Before dark, many Japanese ships could be seen off Karkar Island. During the night, the Japanese landed in strength at Madang, although the ships suffered many losses at sea.

Now began the internment of the Madang missionaries. Superintendent Paul Fliehler, who lived on Graged Island at the mouth of the harbour, was taken during the night to Madang to the headquarters of the general and was never seen again. Mr Ted Radke, who also lived on Graged Island, was taken the next day. When it was discovered he was a ship's captain, he was put to work repairing ships, especially their engines, since many had been damaged. Mr A. Bertelsmeier, the Australian plantation manager at Nagada, and the Revd Hans Ander were also interned on December 19. Since they did not give much information, they were tied to trees for two weeks, and almost starved to death. The Revd Welsch, stationed 16 miles inland at Amele, heard of the suffering of Bertelsmeier

and Ander and thought he might be able to help, since he was a German national. But when he arrived at the Japanese headquarters, he too was tied to a tree for three days without food or water in the sun before he was given a hearing. After having complained to the general, Welsch was asked to lead a party of soldiers to Amele, where Dr and Mrs Braun, Miss Frieda Klotzbuecher, Miss Marie Kroeger, and Mr Alvin Kuehn were working. Dr Braun and Kuehn were made to sit on a bench for five days and nights, while the women were allowed to continue working under guard.

On December 26 the Japanese occupied Amron and interned the Revd J. Mager and Mr Walter Krebs, at first leaving Mr Siemers behind. They returned on January 2, 1943. On each occasion the captain ordered the ordinary soldiers to cook him a big meal from the chickens and garden supplies available. The captain who interned Siemers discovered he was a Lutheran, and told Siemers that he too was a Lutheran and had gone to a Lutheran school. Fortunately, Siemers was allowed to take along a knapsack which he had carefully prepared with essential tools and supplies.

On February 5, the Revd Henkelmann and Mr R. Barber were brought in from the north coast from Bunabun, and the Revd J. Hafermann and Mr A. Mild also arrived that same evening. The seven Amron, Bunabun, and Karkar men were kept at Sek, the Catholic Mission headquarters, where they were held captive together with 20 priests, 40 lay brothers, and 25 nuns.

The Revd R. Inselmann and the Revd H. Ander had been at Nobonob, a high hill overlooking Madang. An Australian lookout post was also located there. When the invasion came, the officer fled inland, taking Ander and Inselmann with him. He soon sent Ander back, who was immediately interned. Inselmann was stationed at Magila, some miles inland. The local people hid and protected him, and he eventually made a notable overland trip, crossing mountains and swamps and rivers to reach Port Moresby and the USA.

On February 23, the seven Lutherans at Sek were taken by barge to Graged Island, so that all the Lutherans could be united. The missionaries at Amele had been brought down, and now only Missionaries Dott and Wenz were unaccounted for. Rumours that the Japanese had killed them later turned out to be true. They had been forced to accompany a Japanese party over the mountains to the Ramu Valley. There the Revd Dott was shot, and his body was found lying on the ground near Dumpu. Mr Wenz's body was found in a grave near a village called Orgaruna. He had been beheaded.

At Graged, crowded into one house, were 14 Lutheran missionaries, a young lad named Nagi who had been adopted by the Revd Welsch, and a plantation manager, Mr Johnson. Alvin Kuehn and Marie Kroeger who had been engaged for some time, got married because of the danger evident in the situation for a single woman. The group soon busied themselves converting the copra shed into a bomb shelter, since the Graged Island location was essentially part of the Madang town complex, and thus a daily target for Allied planes. On the other hand, the Japanese warned that if anyone tried to escape, all would be shot.

Due to the war emergency, Mr Radke had planted a large garden on neighbouring Pig Island. When the Japanese were told about the garden, they and the missionaries made good use of the garden's fruits, and daily some missionaries were escorted to the island to enlarge the planted area. Regularly, the soldiers took the best garden products and allowed the missionaries to eat the leftovers.

Gradually, the Japanese officers removed liberties and increased the restrictions. New officers on March 22 refused to allow further trips to the large garden. The soldiers had eaten all chickens except three wild ones, and so no more eggs were available. One after the other of the cattle, milk cows, and calves were taken away. By necessity, the missionaries began to clear and plant gardens among the coconuts on the stony, coral ground of Graged Island. They distilled salt from ocean water. Additional food became available when the Japanese soldiers and officers discovered that the missionary women could mend torn clothes, and that Mrs Braun was an excellent nurse, able to cure malarial fevers with quinine. Once, a group of Japanese ships were bombed to the north, and later, dozens of pounds of dead fish washed up on shore near the new bomb shelter built by the missionaries. The crop of fruit from the mango trees was especially good during May. From time to time the Japanese issued a ration of rice. Thus God preserved the missionaries from starvation, and no one was injured despite the almost daily bombing and strafing.

Gradually, the meagre diet began to affect some. Mrs Braun was ill, and Mrs Siemers suffered from a severe diarrhoea. As the pressure of war increased, more and more soldiers moved on to the island with the missionaries, and set up machine-gun and anti-aircraft-gun positions, which increased the problems for the prisoners.

On Sunday evening, August 1, a Japanese major took the Revd Henkelmann along with him on a trip up the north coast to Bunabun, so that he could serve as an interpreter. Henkelmann was never seen again.

On August 10, 1943, the missionaries were all moved over to Siar Island, one mile away. Native canoes, by order of the Japanese, provided transport. The Japanese said that it was not fitting that the missionaries lived in a house, while they, the 'noble Japanese soldiers', had to live in tents. The missionaries suspected that the real reason for the move was the carefully cultivated garden, with its sweet potatoes, beans, pumpkins, and other vegetables, which was almost ready for harvest.

At Siar Island, bush houses had to be built, and gardens planted even in the local cemetery. An early missionary had lived on the island and built an underground cistern. This was turned into a bomb shelter, and a well was dug for a water supply. The missionaries helped the local Siar people with small jobs, repairing tools, and taking care of their sick, and in return were helped by the people with what meagre supplies of food they had. During September, after Lae was retaken by the Allies on September 11, bombing became very intense. That was because airstrips were being built in large numbers in the Markham and later in the Ramu valleys, reducing drastically the flight time of bombers and fighters.

Practically all of the missionaries were now sick from flu, dysentery, or malaria. The local people were also very sick, many children dying of dysentery. Dr Braun was no longer allowed to treat them.

Hardly were the gardens on Siar ready to bear some fruit, when the missionaries were brought to Madang on the evening of October

21, and together with some Catholic missionaries loaded on a boat and shipped north to the island of Manam. There the missionaries were off-loaded and told to walk 18 kilometers to the west side of the island, where the new camp was to be set up on a Catholic Mission station. Fortunately, the local people helped the weak missionaries carry their few belongings. Since a large number of Catholic missionaries were to be housed at the station as well, the Lutherans built their own small village with bush materials under several large bread-fruit trees, where the huts were completely hidden from any planes. The station at Manam was never bombed.

The local Japanese captain on Manam had not permitted the soldiers to loot the peoples' gardens, but encouraged the people to plant large gardens. The people were required to feed the missionaries, but the food was first brought to the Japanese officers, who selected their requirements and gave what was left to the missionaries. The local herd of 30 cattle was gradually reduced for the needs of Japanese on the mainland. If the missionaries helped with butchering, they got heads, livers, and stomachs of the butchered cattle. One old horse was finally left, and the superstitious Japanese did not want any of it, but allowed the missionaries — 157 Roman Catholics and the Lutherans — to share it. Once in a while the men caught a rat, but at that time Mrs Braun, who was very ill, received most of the meat. Fruit-bats, snakes, insects, and lizards all furnished part of the daily diet. Daily the missionaries prayed, sang hymns, and meditated on God's Word. The time spent on Manam, a beautiful tropical island, was peaceful, and the active war seemed far away.

Actually, the terrible war had passed through one Lutheran congregational area after another, bringing destruction, disease, hunger, and death to many. After nine months of struggle from Papua over the mountain ridges and along the coast, the Allied forces finally recaptured Salamaua on September 11. On September 16, Lae was taken. On September 19 and 20, Kaiapit, near the headwaters of the Markham, was entered by Allied troops. Scarlet Beach near Heldsbach, Finschhafen, was the scene of a troop landing on September 22, but Sattelberg, the missionary health station only a

few miles away, first fell to Australian troops on November 25. Now the Japanese at Madang were being pressed on two fronts: on one by an advance up the coast from Finschhafen to the east, and on the other by an advance via Shaggy Ridge from the Ramu valley to the south. [94]

In the new year, 1944, toward the end of January, many planes were about, and there was a lot of bombing on the mainland. On the morning of Wednesday January 26, Dr Braun was called to headquarters, and told that the missionaries would be moved in two or three days. On Friday, the missionaries celebrated Holy Communion, and on Saturday morning, January 29, they were ordered to walk eight miles to a landing and at night cross over to Hansa Bay on the mainland, where many bombs had fallen. The Lutheran groups, together with others, making a total of 75, were to go ahead. Day after day the guards and missionaries waited in vain for a ship. Finally, on the afternoon of February 5, an armoured troop transport arrived, about 60 feet long, with mounted anti-aircraft guns. All prisoners were ordered on deck, and were told to lie flat on the deck, face down, if planes were heard. One hundred Japanese soldiers were also to be transported north on the same ship.

The ship left harbour near midnight, but soon an American plane came over. The guns fired, but there was no hit. Twice reconnaissance planes appeared over the ship, which meant that the ship's position was known. On Sunday, February 6, 1944, the prisoners were greeted with a beautiful tropical sunrise, but soon the quiet splendour was disturbed by the sound of Allied planes. All prisoners tried to lie face down on the deck, but there was hardly room. Soon bombs dropped, but there were no hits. Then the steel bullets came like hail from all sides, tearing through the armoured plating as if through rotten wood. The anti-aircraft guns fired, but to no effect.

One report tells that after the first round of strafing, the human damage was so awesome that Dr Braun and a few others stood up and tried to wave the planes off.

Suddenly, everything was quiet. The ship was only six miles off the coast from Wewak. The deck of the ship was covered with dead and dying missionaries. Captain Radke, lying in front of Siemers, jumped up and asked: 'How many are hurt?' and then dropped over dead. The Revd Welsch said a few words of farewell for his wife's sake, and died. Sister Klotzbuecher, Ander, and Krebs were dead. Severely wounded were Mr and Mrs Kuehn, Bertelsmeier, with a broken leg, and Mr Johnson, with a dreadful back wound. Mr Siemers also had serious wounds, but the Revd Mager, Mr Barber, the boy Nagi, and Dr Braun had only slight wounds, and Mrs Braun was not hit at all.

The ship immediately headed for shore. Of the Catholic group of 138, seven priests, 14 lay brothers, 28 nuns, and seven others were dead. All the rest but six were wounded. Few soldiers in the hold were hurt. At Wewak all were taken off the ship, and the dead were lined up on a hillside. Mr Kuehn died while being taken off ship. Japanese army doctors gave some first aid to the wounded.

Toward evening, all the living had to reboard the ship. Most had to be carried on. Then the ship voyage began again. Many were fearful of another attack, but none came. On Tuesday, February 8, the ship arrived at Humbold Bay, then Hollandia, Dutch New Guinea. There was no place for the prisoners, so they suffered under the hot sun on deck all afternoon. But finally the prisoners were off-loaded and put in a large barrack made of bush material near the beach. Of the 92 prisoners left, 60 were unable to help themselves. All were put in the open-sided building, 20 feet wide and 100 feet long. Those able to walk gathered swamp grass as bedding for the wounded. Meanwhile, Dr and Mrs Braun and a Catholic lay brother tended the sick and wounded.

The missionaries helped one another physically and spiritually as best they could. Siemers, though terribly weak himself, made splints for those with broken bones. Dr and Mrs Braun used the few medications available to help in emergencies, which were many. Father Mai had to have a leg amputation to save his life. The operation was completed successfully by Dr Braun with the aid of a carpenter's saw. Soon, even the least wounded missionaries became ill, because there was so little food, and the condition of the barracks encouraged dysentery.

The camp had to be moved. One bombing raid had missed the barracks, but others were surely coming. A suitable place about ten and a half kilometres inland was found and prepared by those able to walk. On March 15, the first patients, including Mrs Kuehn, were carried in over the muddy swampy road. By the 17th all patients had been successfully transported. In the meantime, seven additional Roman Catholic missionaries had died, including the bishop. Another group of Roman Catholic missionaries were sent from Wewak to join the camp, which now numbered 120 prisoners.

A big building project had to be carried out to adequately house everyone. All able to help, offered their skills. By April, the building program was finished.

Mrs Kuehn (Marie Kroeger) had been suffering a great deal from a large open wound just above her left thigh. On the evening of her death, she said: 'I am glad that I will soon be taken to my heavenly home. I'll meet Al again, that I know for sure.' (Her husband, Al Kuehn, had died at Wewak.) She died on the morning of March 30. Now the martyrs of the Madang missionaries numbered eleven: four in the Madang area and seven since the ship's voyage began.

In the meantime, God provided that the suffering was to be shortened. The Americans had landed at Saidor in the Madang area on January 2. Then they made a giant leap forward, and chose Hollandia as the next amphibious landing. On the morning of April 22 there was much bombing and shelling of the harbour area ten kilometres away. The guards heard of an American landing, and immediately ordered all the prisoners to get ready to march inland. All pleading by Dr Braun and others fell on deaf ears. Only those too weak to move were allowed to stay; all others had to struggle toward the interior. By night, not a great distance had been covered through the mud and water. There was no adequate shelter. Other Japanese soldiers came to the camp, and forced the prisoners to sleep out in the rain. During the night additional Japanese continued to arrive in great excitement. Before dawn, the Japanese prepared to march on. Before leaving, the guards called Dr Braun to step forward, and told him that they could no longer take care of the prisoners, and so the prisoners were free.

It was Sunday morning, April 23, and there sat the pitiful, emaciated group of wounded and sick missionaries. A miracle from God had

Memorial Lutheran Church Madang. Erected in memory of those members of Lutheran Mission Madang who died or were killed during World War II.

saved them. They could so easily have been shot by the guards, as happened many times during the cruel war in the Pacific and Asia. But now the ragged bunch was free to go back to their camp. In the confusion, it seems that the young lad Nagi Welsch was taken along by the Japanese. He was never seen again.

On Monday April 24, all missionaries had made it back to their previous camp, and on the next day contact was made by three from the camp with the troops at the beach. At 4 pm on that day, 200 American soldiers suddenly surrounded the camp. The joy and thanksgiving of the missionaries at their release cannot be described. Soon, a defence perimeter had to be prepared and fox-holes dug for the night, for no one knew whether Japanese soldiers were near. One old nun died that night, very likely from a blow given her with the butt of a gun by one of the departing Japanese guards. Early the next morning, after the funeral, those who could walk did so. The rest were carried high over the swamp waters by the six-foot-tall soldiers, to the beach. Two days later, the missionaries were moved to a place selected for a hospital site.

182

On Sunday April 30, the missionaries were evacuated, sailing down the coast to the east in the late afternoon on a large landing barge. On Wednesday May 3, the barge reached Finschhafen, and all missionaries were taken by ambulance to the military hospital. Soon, most were sent on to a hospital in Brisbane for futher medical attention. Only Mr Siemers and Mrs Braun were too weak, and Dr Braun stayed behind to be with his wife.

Recovery for Mrs Braun, W. Siemers, and some of the others took many months. All except Siemers eventually returned to serve their Lord once more in New Guinea. William Siemers never fully recovered, and spent his last years praying for the Lord's work in New Guinea, while staying at the Deaconess motherhouse in Milwaukee, Wisconsin.

Meanwhile, the congregations throughout the coastal region of New Guinea in both Finschhafen and Madang slowly tried to resurrect a normal existence again. The terrible war and bloodshed in the Pacific continued for another 15 months. In Europe, Asia, and the Pacific, 45 million human beings lost their lives during the conflict. The people in New Guinea also asked the question: 'Does Christianity make any sense at all?'

This draws to a close this account of the American contribution to the mission work in New Guinea, which began in 1886 through the regular offerings of American Lutherans of Iowa Synod and continued with even greater participation through the emergency of the First World War and the 1920s. The account also covers full participation during the 1930s, and the emergency of the Second World War, which was climaxed by unbelievable suffering and martyrdom. A brighter future of a new day lay ahead in the combined Lutheran Mission New Guinea and the independent Evangelical Lutheran Church of Papua New Guinea.

Endnotes

[1] E. Clifford Nelson, ed., *The Lutherans in North America* (Philadelphia: Fortress Press, 1975), 279; Abdel Ross Wenz, *A Basic History of Lutheranism in America* (Philadelphia: Fortress Press, 1964), 185.

[2] *Kirchliche Mitteilungen* (Neuendettelsau), 11/1886; 4 and 8/1887.

[3] *Ibid*, 1/1887.

[4] *Ibid*, 10/1889. The station was then named Deinzerhill.

[5] *The Lutheran Missionary* (Jan. 1921), 5. In 1913 the Iowa Synod had 113,000 members, 526 pastors, and 75 mission locations in the United States. In May of that year it was proposed to raise $133,000 for mission (*Die Missions-Stunde*, May 1913).

[6] F. Braun and C.V. Sheatsley, *On Both Sides of the Equator* (Columbus, Oh.: The Lutheran Book Concern, 1937), 90; G. Pilhofer, *Die Geschichte der Neuendettelsauer Mission in Neuguinea*, vol. II (Neuendettelsau: Freimund Verlag, 1963), 18, 19.

[7] *Ibid*, 19. *Correspondence* of Henry Lambert, W.M. Conference, London, to Prof. G. Fritschel on remarks by the Governor General of Australia, June 25, 1915. According to the Governor General, Inspector K. Steck was detained at Ongga because: 1) he stated he was a German soldier, 2) he refused to take the oath of neutrality, 3) he assisted a German officer to evade capture. The third reason given was denied by W. Flierl and H. Raum. But all three, W. Flierl, H. Raum, and K. Steck were interned because of it. The men were first placed under house arrest, and in July 1915 taken to internment camp at Liverpool, NSW.

[8] *Die Missions-Stunde*, February 1915; April 1915.

[9] *Ibid*, October 1914.

[10] *Ibid*, March 1915.

[11] *Ibid*.

[12] *Correspondence*: F.O. Theile to L. Kaibel, January 8, 1915.

[13] *Ibid*, January 16, 1915.

[14] *Kirchen-und Missions-Zeitung*, No. 23, June 8, 1915.

[15] *Die Missions-Stunde*, April 1915.

[16] *Ibid*, November 1915.

[17] *Correspondence*: F.O. Theile to L. Kaibel, November 25, 1915; October 13, 1916.

[18] *Ibid*, December 23, 1915.

[19] *Die Missions-Stunde*, January 1916.

[20] *Ibid*, April 1916.

[21] *Ibid*, June 1916.

[22] *Ibid*, January 1917; January 1920.

[23] *The Lutheran Missionary*, January 1921.

[24] Minutes: Iowa Synod BFM, July 16, 1919; *The Lutheran Missionary*, January 1921.

[25] F. Braun and C.V. Sheatsley, 103.

[26] *Ibid*, 101-102.

[27] *Die Missions-Stunde*, March 1919.

[28] Minutes: Iowa Synod BFM, September 9, 1919.

[29] *Ibid*, July 16 and September 9, 1919.

[30] Minutes: Iowa Synod BFM, July 14, 15, 1920.

[31] For details see: Th. Hebart, *The United Evangelical Lutheran Church in Australia,* English version by J.J. Stolz (Adelaide: Lutheran Book Depot, 1938; facsimile ed., Lutheran Publishing House, 1985), 135-137.

[32] The second occasion was the union of the UELCA and the ELCA in 1966, which aided the union of Siassi and Menyamya Lutheran congregations with the ELC-PNG and the cooperation with the Gutnius Lutheran Church of Papua New Guinea.

[33] *Correspondence*: F.O. Theile to Prime Minister, March 26, 1921.

[34] *Correspondence:* F.O. Theile to Dr Richter, May 19 and May 27, 1921; Minutes: Iowa Synod BFM, May 27, 1921.

[35] Minutes: Iowa Synod BFM, June 9, 1921.

[36] These were: The Revd J.J. Stolz, the Revd J. Zwar, Mr H. Mickan, Mr G. Kruger, the Revd J. Simpfendorfer, the Revd A. Hiller, the Revd L. Doehler, Mr M.T. Schneider, and the Revd F. Otto Theile.

[37] E.A. Jericho, *Seedtime and Harvest in New Guinea* (Adelaide: UELCA New Guinea Mission Board, 1961), 27 and 35; Minutes: Iowa Synod BFM, September 15, 16, 1924.

[38] All biographical and other data of the American missionaries in New Guinea have been taken from their Annual Reports and Personal Files, as kept in the ELC-PNG Archives, Lae. For a list of all missionary personnel 1886-1986, see appendix.

[39] Geyammalo Apo, *Recollections and Experiences of a New Guinea Evangelist*, tr. F.E. Pietz (Dubuque, Ia.: 1971).

[40] One can recognize the influence of S. Lehner, F. Oertel, G. Pilhofer, and C. Keysser in Pietz's work. Pietz did not accept the past traditions blindly, but was able to adapt and change wherever necessary. Cf F.E. Pietz, *Christianizing New Guinea* (ALC-BFM, NG section).

[41] The period from 1921 to 1929 was that of the Revd F.O. Theile's greatest activity on behalf of Lutheran Mission Finschhafen and Lutheran Mission Madang. It is best documented in his detailed Annual Reports and his supplementing Circular Letters, which were circulated among the missionaries and the Boards of Foreign Missions in the United States, Australia, and Germany. They are to be found in the respective Archives.

[42] W. Kraushaar, *Report*, March 15, 1926 (duplicated by the Australian BFM). See also F. Braun and C.V. Sheatsley, 115.

[43] *Ibid*, 119-121.

[44] Minutes: Representative Conference, Brisbane, Queensland, May 6-15, 1929. The takeover was to occur on January 1, 1930. Lutheran Mission agreed that its Mission Director Theile would also represent the Rhenish Mission before the Australian Government.

[45] Minutes: LMF Main Conference, Sattelberg, December 1-15, 1929.

[46] Minutes: Representative Conference, Sydney, January 29-31, 1930. The UELCA took over complete responsibility for the Aborigines' Mission Hope Vale in Northern Queensland as its 'Sphere of Interest'.

[47] Minutes: Representative Conference, Brisbane, Qld., May 6-15, 1929.

[48] F. Braun and C.V. Sheatsley, 124.

[49] Minutes: LMF Main Conference, Sattelberg, November 26- December 5, 1930.

[50] *Correspondence*: G. Hueter to R. Taeuber, June 2, 1931. Cf *Gutachtung* (opinion) appended to Minutes of LMF Conference, Sattelberg, January 8-22, 1932.

[51] F.O. Theile, *Annual Report*, 1931.

[52] *Ibid; Correspondence*: F. Keppler to F. Eppelein, January 5, 1932; Minutes: ALC-BFM, February 2, 1932; *Correspondence*: F. Keppler to R. Taeuber, February 6, 1932.

[53] Minutes: LMF Main Conference, Sattelberg, January 8-22, 1932.

[54] F. Braun and C.V. Sheatsley, 130,131. The agreement was ratified by the Executive of the Rhenish Mission Society on June 27, by the General Convention of the Rhenish Mission Society on July 21, and by the ALC General Convention on October 14-20, 1932. Cf Certificate of Transfer, ELC-PNG Archives, Lae.

[55] Minutes: American members of LMF Meeting, Finschhafen, October 10, 1932. ALC took over from the older Rhenish missionaries, the Revds G. Eiffert, F. Schuetz, and J. Welsch, and veteran lay worker H. Schamann; and of those who arrived after 1929, the Revds W. Doege, F. Schoettler, and W. Stahl, plus ship's captain H. Alt (see also chapter 3).

[56] G. Eiffert, *Comprehensive Conference Report*, October 24, 1932.

[57] R. Hanselmann, *Annual Reports*, 1933 and 1934; special report: *Ass Bilong Cargo*, 1934.

[58] J. Mager, *Chronology of the Karkar Congregation*, ELC Archives, Lae.

[59] A pastoral account of the whole movement was written by F. Henkelmann, called *Kukuaik*. Fortunately, the manuscript was preserved, and from it we gain an insight into the heart and life of a great missionary who became a martyr shortly afterwards. F. Henkelmann, *Kukuaik*, ELC Archives, Lae.

[60] R. Inselmann, *Annual Reports*, 1936-1940; R. Inselmann, *Letub, the Cult of the Secrets of Wealth*; M.A. Thesis, Kennedy School of Missions, Hartford Seminary Foundation, 1944.

[61] Jerome Ilaoa, *Galek Report*, June 30, 1923.

[62] Personal Conversation, P. Freyberg.

[63] J. Mager, *Airdromes and Arrows* (unpublished manuscript), ELC Archives, Lae.

[64] Official lists of Evangelists prepared for Government report — Bunabun Station, 1934-35. Also Minutes; Bunabun Elders' Conference, 1935-1940, ELC Archives, Lae.

[65] W. Doege, *Trip Report*, May 2-15, 1934.

[66] J. Mager, *Seeking an Airdrome in New Guinea* (unpublished manuscript), ELC Archives, Lae. J. Mager, *The Arrow That Flieth by Day* (unpublished manuscript), ALC-BFM, St Paul, Minn.

[67] Cf *Annual Reports*, W. Stahl (1932), J. Mager (1933), J. Kuder (1934); Minutes: Annual Conference, LMM, 1933, 1934; *Annual Reports*, R. Inselmann (1937), W. Doege (1935), F. Henkelmann (1941); W. Foege, *Trip Report — Iwam* (1934); Annual Missionary Reports re Amele, late 1930s.

[68] *Annual Reports*, F. Schoettler (1933, 1936), F.E. Pietz (1933, 1935), R. Inselmann (1936), E. Hannemann (1935), J. Welsch (1938).

[69] *Annual Reports*, R. Hanselmann (1933), F.E. Pietz (1934), E. Hannemann (1935), P. Fliehler (1935).

[70] Minutes: 16th Executive Meeting, LMM, April 17, 1936.

[71] Minutes: 17th Executive Meeting, LMM, May 18, 1936.

[72] *Annual Reports* for 1936 of: W. Doege, R. Inselmann, J. Kuder, P. Fliehler.

[73] *Annual Reports* for 1936 of: F. Schoettler, J. Welsch, H. Schamann.

[74] Minutes: Sangapat Elders' Conference, June 26-28, 1937. *Annual Reports*, P. Fliehler (1937), W. Doege (1937), R. Inselmann (1937), J. Kuder (1938).

[75] W. Stahl, *Annual Report*, 1939.

[76] Minutes: Elders' Conference, 1939, 1940.

[77] Minutes: 23rd Executive Meeting, LMM, July 11-14, 1941.

[78] Minutes: 5th Executive Meeting, LMM, September 8-12, 1933; W. Foege, *Annual Report*, 1933.

[79] Minutes: 2nd Field Conference, LMM, January 21, 1934; Special Conference, LMM, March 12-14, 1934; 6th Executive Meeting, LMM, April 4, 1934.

[80] Minutes: 3rd Executive Meeting, LMM, April 13, 1934 ; W. Foege, *Annual Report*, 1934.

[81] Minutes: 8th Executive Meeting, LMM, July 22, 1934; Meeting of Representatives LMM and LMF, Nobonob, July 21, 1934.

[82] T. Radke, *A Brief Report on the Establishment of the New Station Kerowagi*, 1934.

[83] Cf Frieda Foege, *Our Days in New Guinea* (unpublished personal manuscript, 1978); see also chapter 5, note 36.

[84] Minutes: 7th Field Conference, LMM, January 7-13, 1939; P. Fliehler, *Covering Letter*, January 20, 1939.

[85] *Ibid.*

[86] Minutes: 26th Executive Meeting, LMM, January 14, 1939.

[87] A. Frerichs, *Anutu Conquers in New Guinea*, first edn. (Columbus, Oh.: The Wartburg Press, 1957), 66-70.

[88] Minutes: LMF and LMM Representatives, October 5, 1939; January 12, January 22, June 1, 1940.

[89] Much of the following section was written on the basis of William H. Siemers, *The Story of the Japanese Invasion of New Guinea: The Imprisonment of Our Missionaries of the Madang District, and How Some Live to Tell the Story* (mimeographed), ELC Archives, Lae.

[90] Lionel Wigmore, *The Japanese Thrust* (Sydney: Halstead Press, 1957).

[91] Dudley McCarthy, *South-West Pacific Area — First Year* (Sydney: Halstead Press 1959), 49-50.

[92] L. Wigmor, 660-661. Cf. also *The Lutheran Missionary*, 4/1951, 22.

[93] For details, see D. McCarthy, 80-81.

[94] David Dexter, *The New Guinea Offensives* (Adelaide: The Griffen Press, 1961), XIX and XX.

Chapter 5

Missionary Advance to the Highlands

by Kurt-Dietrich Mrossko

A Difficult Beginning

Anyone travelling for the first time to the Highlands by road from Lae will be impressed by the mighty mountain walls which tower up from north and south along the Markham Valley and which envelop it more and more. For instance, the Kraetke Range, the outermost mountains of the southern range, which merge into the Bismarck Range in the west, rise from 1,000 to over 3,000 metres.

It was chiefly due to this powerful defiance of nature that the Highlands, hidden behind these slopes, were hardly known to the outside world until well into the 20th century. Contact between the people of the Highlands and those of the Lowlands was sporadic. Inquiring minds could not gain access to the area. Hence, there could be no thought under these circumstances of opening up the region economically and politically. The only question was how long an area of this size could escape the notice and the interest of the outside world.

The beginning of the century had already seen the first steps in the direction of the Highlands. This was in no way systematic, however, nor was it urged on by man's desire to explore the unknown or to develop the region. Scarcely heeded by the public, hardly promoted by the then German colonial government, and not supported by any business enterprise, it was the Neuendettelsau Mission in New Guinea which created the real basis for opening up the Highlands by starting work in the Markham Valley. In retrospect, the founding of the mission stations at Lae (1910), Gabmazung (1911), and Kaiapit (1918), proved important steps on the way.

At the time when the foot of the Highlands was reached, the outward situation of the Mission was as black as night. The old familiar colonial government of the Germans had had to make way after defeat in World War I to another foreign administration, namely, that of the Australians. Its mistrust of everything German was understandable, and its measures reflected this. At a time when staff were already desperately short, all efforts to send out missionaries from Germany were stopped. All Germans, even the missionaries, were threatened with deportation. Furthermore, material help of any significance could not be expected from a fleeced Germany (however, it

187

Mission station Gabmazung.

was just at this time that the ecumenical involvement of Australian and USA Lutherans was proving significant).

The slopes of the Kraetke Range thus seemed to become an important mark of fate for the Lutheran Mission. It was as if a sign had been set up there for the tidings of peace of Jesus of Nazareth, received with so much openness and good faith by the Azera and Amari peoples in the Markham and Central Ramu Valley: 'Thus far and no farther!' (Initially, this was not regarded as a great cause for sadness. For one thing, the tasks in the area opened up so far were still considerable. And for another, nobody really suspected that a new field of work existed beyond the mountains.)

Two factors now became crucial, and no one can say that human foresight alone made them such. One was that the work of Lutheran Mission had long ceased to be borne by white missionaries only. They had long been joined by New Guinean missionaries from the 'old' congregations of the coastal region who regarded it as their Christian duty to take over the major part of the task of preaching the Gospel in areas that had just been opened up.

(For the detailed account, see ch 2.)

The second was that the slopes at the edge of the Highlands were not so high as to prevent regular meetings of those above and below. The term 'meetings' is certainly a euphemism for what took place between the two regions: robbery, assassination, and war.

The evangelist Geyammalo Apo from the village of Ee near Taemi (Finschhafen area) comments about this in his memoirs:

> The Amaris inhabit the Markham Valley in a long row of villages, from Ragiampoan to Marawasa. The Amaris, however, are not the only ones who live in this region. Parallel to their villages, farther up on the mountain slopes, live three groups of people, the Asasobs, the Orapanas, and the Oraunas; they are known by the name of Gazub and were once highly feared as warring tribes ... As a rule, they came down from the mountains before the break of dawn, between four and five, to lie in ambush in a field. When the owners, suspecting nothing, arrived for work, the Gazubs attacked and killed them. Such was the situation when I started work amongst the Amaris. [1]

On the whole, the Mission's work in and around Kaiapit from the outset proved an event whose effect spread right to the fringes of the

Geyammalo Apo and family.

'They are known by the name of Gazubs and were highly feared.'

189

Highlands. In particular, the striving for peace and reconciliation, despite all the devastating setbacks, became the dominant feature of the Christian preaching.

The curiosity and interest of the Lutheran Mission was aroused. In January 1920, an exploratory party of three European and several New Guinean missionaries started out from Kaiapit with the aim of exploring the Highlands, at least in part. The whole expedition ended in disaster after only a few days. After the group had been hospitably received by the Binumarian people, they were drawn into a deadly battle by the Pundewatenos (or Pundeos, Pundebazas) as they continued their journey. The outcome: the death of the head of the tribe, and two injured on the Pundewateno side; several wounded among the travellers.

'It can only be deeply regretted that that journey of exploration, whose purpose was after all to establish friendly relations with the people in the mountains, ended so tragically', wrote the first chronicler of these events, Leonhard Flierl.[2]

Nevertheless, the Lutheran Mission did not give up trying to make contact with the inhabitants of the Highlands. In 1921, a group of evangelists, accompanied by Leonhard Flierl, embarked on a journey through the region in which the station of Wampur was later established. It passed off without any unpleasant incidents, but also without tangible success.

In 1922, when it seemed that the Binumarians were ready to have evangelists, the Sattelberg congregation despatched some.

One of those sent, Ngizaki Gapenuo, depicts the laborious process of building the foundations in the following words:

Finally, four evangelists travelled with me on 5 May 1922 from Finschhafen over the sea to Lae. From there we walked to Gabmazung and Azera. Four members of the congregation accompanied us on this first trip out. They were to help us carry our most necessary personal belongings through the hot Markham Valley, and see us through the initial difficulties. So, we nine men packed our bags and started out on this long walk of over 100 kilometres along the Markham plains. After walking for some days, we reached — with God's help — the mission station of Kaiapit. Jakabonga and I went into the Gazub mountains at the beginning of 1923 on a first exploratory trip. We climbed right up to the Binumarian people, who had received us hospitably in February 1920 on our first visit with the missionaries Pilhofer, Oertel, and Stoessel.

This time, too, the chief Bano gave us a friendly welcome in his house and looked after us. When this became known in the village, however, the men gathered in front of the chief's house, armed to fight, and struck up a threatening pose. Whereupon the chief, likewise armed, stepped out of the house in front of the warriors and declared: 'I have received these men as guests. Anyone who lays a hand on them will be killed!' On the next day the men of the village again gathered, armed. They surrounded the house threateningly. The chief said to them: 'These people come neither as beggars nor are they poor people, but they are prosperous, and it can only be to our advantage to win them as friends!'

Evangelists accompanied by Missionary L. Flierl.

Gapenuo Ngizaki, the apostle of the Gazubs.

My companion Jakabonga was full of fear. So I said to him: 'Have no fear! Jesus will protect us, he will look after us!' We stayed there another two days to get to know the people better and to become more friendly with them. We also had a small garden in which we planted sweet potatoes and taro. The Azera boys who had accompanied us up the mountains, being fearful, had returned secretly to their village. On the third day we returned to Kaiapit, and took two more evangelists with us to the Binumarians to help us build the first dwelling and extend the garden.[3]

The work rested entirely on the shoulders of the New Guinean missionaries. They knew how to establish a certain trust with the host villages and tribes. However, their attempts to make peace were frustrated often enough. It is hard to imagine that, with all the setbacks they had to endure, including constant exposure to the moods and threats of their hosts and their isolation in strange surroundings, they did not give up.

Letters and visits from their home congregations helped to mitigate this unhappy situation. In particular, Leonhard Flierl, the missionary in the Sattelberg and Hube area, visited the evangelists (most of whom came from his circuit) every year until his health failed in 1929.[4] From 1925 onwards, government officials appeared more frequently in the eastern Highlands, but they scarcely brought relief to the indigenous missionaries in their outposts; sometimes, in fact, the very opposite. The appearance of other white people (gold prospectors, for instance, or goldfield recruiters

Evangelists: the main work rested on their shoulders.

191

with their often rough ways) only deepened the local people's mistrust of anything foreign. Yet, despite all the difficulties, by the end of the 1920s it was feasible to retain and develop the following stations: Wampur, Arau (or Ambesia), Barora (or Asinu), Apimuri in the Gazub region, Rihona (or Lihona) in the Hazung region. [5]

From the Edge to the Centre of the Eastern Highlands

From the beginning, the Highlands Mission was carried alone by the faith, enthusiasm, and the readiness to make sacrifices, of some Christian congregations. In particular, the Sattelberg, Hube, and Bukawa congregations were notable in this respect, supported by their European missionaries.

But was this basis sufficient in the long run? Was not the Highlands Mission a challenge which all, expatriates and locals alike, had to accept equally? It was noticeable that the New Guinean missionaries were more anxious to push ahead than the expatriate Mission.

At the Missionary Conference held at Sattelberg in December 1930, the arguments for and against were aired once more. How could an extension of the field of work be envisaged when everywhere there was already a lack of staff, particularly of European missionaries? How were the transport problems to be overcome in this country without roads, when the distances from the coast to stations in the Highlands were becoming longer and longer?

Added to this were the troublesome money worries. One source of income was drying up that very year: The coconut harvest was hardly worthwhile in the Mission's own plantations near the coast because of low copra prices, and G. Vicedom suspected that the Mission was fully occupied with preserving its 'achievements from a [financial] catastrophe'. [6] And thanks to the catastrophic world economic crisis in 1929, no great support could be expected from the home churches in Australia, the USA, and Germany.

Yet a positive decision was taken. The Highlands Mission was recognized as part of the Mission as a whole, and a large station was to be set up. Wilhelm Bergmann was entrusted with the task. [7] His departure took place quietly and quickly in January 1931. Wilhelm Bergmann,

192

Missionary W. Bergmann and his wife moved into a new house at Kambaidam.

his young wife, and some helpers travelled westwards along the Markham Valley from Malahang (Lae), taking the two cows and one horse which were provided on that first journey. The group naturally made use of the missionary infrastructure which had been created in the meantime: travelling via Gabmazung and Kaiapit, [8] they headed for the evangelist station of Wampur on the north-east edge of the Highlands.

Two hours walk from Wampur in the direction of Arau, Wilhelm Bergmann found a suitable place for a new station, approximately 30 hectares in size. There was no trouble at all in acquiring the land; the owners, with *Luluai* Andalau at the head, were kindly disposed toward the Mission. The site was called Kambaidam. By March 18, 1931, Wilhelm Bergmann and his young wife were able to move into a new house, built largely of local materials.

Now an overseas missionary experienced at first hand what the New Guinean evangelists had experienced for roughly a decade. The neighbouring villages waged almost constant war with each other. The missionaries were drawn into these hostilities — sometimes more, sometimes less — in spite of their continual striving for peace and trust. The stations of Menefinka in the Hanzung region and Arau and Apimuri in the Gazub region were destroyed that same year, usually not by the host villages, but by the attacking enemy; Kambaidam itself

Another visitation together with missionary Johannes Flierl.

was besieged at times. But none of the stations was given up. Those which were destroyed were built up again and occupied anew when the situation had become more settled. Wilhelm Bergmann saw no enmity toward Christianity in these excesses, but quite different reasons; to be precise, 'very material reasons were decisive'. [9] Such pillage often provided attackers with valuable goods — even if just the harvest from the evangelists' gardens. The evangelists themselves and their families were often brutally blackmailed and threatened, but nobody was seriously harmed.

How difficult it was to win the trust of the local people was experienced also by the government in its growing number of expeditions to this area. In contrast to the missionaries, however, they won respect for themselves by the use of their firearms, when necessary.

But the periods of peace were long enough for the evangelists in the Hazung and Gazub areas to be able to meet several times in Kambaidam in 1931. Some of them, along with Wilhelm Bergmann, managed to visit all the stations in the area on a trip to the Hazung

district from Rihona. The next year, too, a visitation was made, in which the missionary Johannes Flierl took part.

At the beginning of December 1932, emissaries from the Finschhafen and Madang Lutheran Missions, continuing as two separate organizations, met in Rihona to delineate the fields of work in the Highlands. [10] The agreement reached never became effective; the times called for new perspectives.

So far, the work of the Lutheran Mission in the eastern Highlands had proceeded from the periphery. From there, the evangelists tried cautiously to infiltrate the interior. In establishing the station of Kambaidam, the mission organization followed this pattern. But soon Kambaidam came to be regarded as provisional; the goal became a central point from which the whole area could be reached equally well in all directions, and the search began in September 1932. In March 1933, some land at Onerunka was acquired by Wilhelm Bergmann as an appropriate place for a new central inland station. [11]

To illustrate what material facilities were available (or, more precisely, were not available)

193

in setting up a new station at that time, note the following eye-witness description written roughly a year after the establishment of Onerunka:

> We had no reason to suppose we were near a mission station. Bergmann had set up his new centre in the middle of the bush . . . The tree trunks in the forests still lie criss-cross everywhere you turn; the saws move only slowly in their task of making shelves out of trunks. A two-room hut of corrugated iron is the centre of the station, and in these two rooms is housed everything that one would like to keep safe. There is a living room, bedroom and nursery, dining room and workroom, study and washroom, pharmacy and shop — in short, everything has to be squeezed into these two rooms. It is really crowded here! . . . For him [Bergmann] it has all become a matter of course, and not worth talking about. That's why someone else has to say it for him, so that people know what it means to set up inland stations. He was there with his wife and two children — and that for the second time. [12]

Within this modest framework, the whole of the missionary work in the eastern Highlands developed steadily. But it became increasingly plain that the Lutheran Mission was only one of many outside elements influencing life in this area. An element of unrest and often brute force continued to characterize the presence of the gold prospectors and, to a lesser extent, the recruiters. Relations with government officials fluctuated between generous support and open hindrance, and it often depended on individual officers. And, for the first time, the Mission had to recognize that another mission was taking up work in its area: In July 1934, the Seventh Day Adventists settled in Kainantu.

A vital factor in the work of the Lutheran Mission continued to be the relationship of the evangelists with the local people. Wilhelm Bergmann describes the relationship between the two groups as follows:

> Usually the evangelists are given a friendly reception at first. But then some sort of disappointment sets in. Perhaps the local people do not receive as many material goods as they had expected, perhaps some notice that their heathen thought and actions are somehow endangered, either because their magic no longer works, or because the evangelists are always exhorting to peace, etc. Briefly, after a little while, a contrary reaction begins. When this time is over and the

Onerunka mission station.

locals have learnt to trust the evangelists, a better time begins for them. [13]

Wilhelm Bergmann sees the latter phase as having been reached in the area of Onerunka at the end of 1934. By this time, there were 15 evangelist stations, the western-most of which was situated in Sigoija on the Bena-Bena river. At ten of them it had been possible to start intensive schooling with some 150 young people. Katé was generally accepted as the language of tuition. Baptismal classes were being held at two of the stations. And most important of all: on September 15, 1934, following thorough preparation by the capable evangelist Gapenuo, the first group of Highlanders was baptized at Wampur.

By this time it was already clear that the missionary activity in the Highlands was assuming new proportions. Johannes Flierl and Georg Hofmann were chosen as European missionaries to continue the work in Onerunka, for a new task was awaiting Wilhelm Bergmann.

On the Advance

What had happened? Missionary Georg Vicedom expressed it realistically and vividly in the following words:

> 1932! Deep in the heart of New Guinea, extensive high valleys with some hundred thousand people had been discovered ... We missionaries had heard about them and had often discussed whether we would have enough funds and energy to bring the Gospel to these people also. Sadly, we always came to the same conclusion: It is not possible, not for the time being.

'On the advance' missionaries (from left) Vicedom, Helbig, Bergmann, Horrolt, and Zimmermann.

1934! The order to begin work was suddenly there. It came from the people, but was manifestly from God. So there was no hesitating. [14]

The situation of the Mission in regard to staff and finance was just as bleak in 1934 as before. What, then, had changed?

Gold prospectors and government officials, sometimes working in close collaboration, had been penetrating deeper and deeper into the unknown Highlands. To the forefront in this activity in the early 1930s were the Leahy brothers. In March 1933, a government expedition explored the area between Bena Bena and Mt Hagen. The Acting Administrator, T. Griffiths, who had taken part personally, encouraged — yes, almost ordered — the Lutheran Mission to move into this area to take up its work of peace and preaching. [15] The government's readiness to cooperate certainly did not derive from pure friendship with the missionaries; primarily, it may be assumed, the administration wanted to be relieved. As far as the outcome was concerned, however, that was of no consequence; the leaders of the Missions in Madang and in Finschhafen accepted the challenge. [16]

The first step was taken when Wilhelm Bergmann received orders from Stephan Lehner [17] on October 12, 1933 to carry out a reconnaissance flight with two missionaries from Madang over the unexplored interior as far as Mount Hagen. [18] By October 24, 1933, all the preparations had been completed, and the missionaries Henry Foege from Madang [19] and Wilhelm Bergmann set out from Kainantu in a hired aeroplane. [20] The result of the three-hour flight was basically: 'More information is certainly needed'. [21]

Since that information had to be obtained by a land expedition, preparations were immediately set in train: The expedition that followed constituted the second energetic step into the interior of the Highlands.

On May 14, 1934, a group of 106 men including six European and American missionaries started from the evangelist station of Rabana, high up over the Bena Bena valley, where the two groups from Finschhafen and Madang, roughly equal in size, had met. [22]

For people some 50 years later, it is extraordinarily difficult to appreciate properly even the physical achievements of such early

People from Rabana with evangelist Agajo.

missionary workers. Nowadays, thanks to modern means of transport and a well-developed infrastructure, distances have shrunk to a comfortable journey of hours or even minutes; those same distances at that time called for a maximum of physical strength consistently maintained over several days. In addition, there were the difficulties which the organizational preparation involved, particularly when so many people were concerned.

That is why this trip must go down in history as one of the successful large-scale enterprises of Lutheran missionaries in this part of the world. It went from the eastern Highlands through the geographically-difficult Chimbu area to Mt Hagen, then south to the foot of Mt Jalibu, and back. There were no serious incidents; however, the sick had to be carried, bad weather in impassable terrain had to be overcome, and the utmost care had to be taken when contact with new groups of people was made, so that no dangerous misunderstandings occurred despite all the language-barriers.

On this expedition, Lutheran and Catholic missionaries met for the first time in the Chimbu

region near Kurukuru (Mingende); near Mt Hagen, they came across the first airfield built by the Leahy brothers.

The joint exploration completed, the group from Madang headed north from Mt Hagen, travelling over the Bismarck Range through the Jimi Valley to the Ramu Valley in a trek in which they endured great privation. From there they proceeded to the coast at Madang. The group from Finschhafen basically followed their outward route. Forty-three days after leaving Onerunka, they arrived back there on June 23, 1934.

'We, who made the journey together, became one on the way: Kate, Jabem, Leawomba, Kela, Azera, Hube, etc ... Yes, even black and white became completely irrelevant when we carried and bore one and the same lot day after day.' [23]

In addition to all the findings of the trip in terms of geography, population statistics, and anthropology, Missionary J. Herrlinger regarded that as an important result — by no means the least in a period torn by nationalism and racism.

The Lutheran Mission's third step into the interior of the Highlands followed surprisingly

196

The Beginnings in Chimbu (Ega).

quickly. An extraordinary missionary conference, held on July 10-11, 1934 in Lae, adopted the suggestion of the fact-finding missionaries that the Finschhafen section should set up a station in the Chimbu area and one at Mount Hagen, and the Madang section one in the western Chimbu area. Bergmann was chosen to begin in Chimbu, and Georg Vicedom in Hagen. Two other important decisions were taken at this conference: Work in the Chimbu region should be carried out primarily by the Kate congregations, and work in the Hagen area by the Jabem congregations. So that the Mission might be able to cope somewhat with transport problems, the Mission Board in Germany was asked to provide an aeroplane.

On the morning of September 5, 1934, a party of 45 New Guineans, mostly evangelists, and four missionaries set out from Onerunka.[24] On September 12, they reached the place which the exploratory expedition had regarded three months earlier as favourable for a new station. That day may be considered the day on which the station of Ega was founded. Work began immediately on building houses and making preparations for an airfield.

Almost at the same time, on September 15, 1934, the Lutheran missionaries from Madang arrived in the valley of the Koro river, approximately a day's walk west of Ega, and began to set up the station of Kerowagi.[25]

The missionaries, G. Vicedom and G. Horrolt, and all the evangelists helped in the task of beginning the station of Ega. In the same way, Bergmann and some evangelists proceeded to set up the station at Hagen. When this group reached the spot that had been picked out on the exploratory trip, they found it now occupied by the Roman Catholic mission. It took till the end of November before they found another place considered suitable:

> The people called it Ogelbeng. At 8 o'clock we began to clean the place. This day (November 21, 1934) may therefore be recorded in the history of the inland station as the day on which this station was founded.[26]

With these three new stations, the Lutheran Mission had reached the limits of its capacity; over the next few years only one more station was set up, that of Asaroka (July 13, 1937 by Georg Hofmann) to cover the large gap

197

between Onerunka/Raipinka and Ega. The five mother stations determined the picture of the Lutheran Highlands Mission in New Guinea for over 10 years; the question of how far World War II prevented the establishment of more stations must remain unanswered.

The establishment of such stations, run by expatriate missionaries, did not constitute the essence of the Lutheran Mission. The strain of beginning the Highland Mission rested almost entirely on the shoulders of the New Guinean missionaries from the coastal regions, and this did not alter fundamentally even after the establishment of Onerunka, Asaroka, Ega, Kerowagi, and Ogelbeng.

Let Ega serve as an example. On September 12, 1934, the group of missionaries

First building at Ogelbeng.

arrived there. By September 21, 1934, the first evangelist station had been set up a few hours' walk away from Ega:

> It is to be called Pare. That is what the people there call it. We built the first hut together, still on the same day, then we left the evangelists there, namely: Tiemengte, Kapingnuwe, and Laenuwe. The people were very friendly and helpful. [27]

And that work continued at a steady rate. Just under a month later, 10 evangelist stations had been established, and 30 New Guinean missionaries had found their sphere of activity, reaching out to some 10,000 people in their vicinity.

George Vicedom wrote from Ogelbeng at the beginning of 1935 that he was even further advanced with the establishment of the work than at Ega. [28] And in the Asaroka and Onerunka/Raipinka circuits, the evangelists had long been working at their stations before the main station was set up. Only Kerowagi suffered greatly at the beginning from the lack of preachers; they were only gradually won in the Madang region for the work in the Highlands. [29]

All the main stations had one feature in common: the airfield. This was an indication of a basic problem not just for the Mission, but for New Guinea as a whole: transport. How bad the situation was is revealed in Vicedom's deep sigh: 'Not money, but transport was the main problem' [30] — almost a perverse remark in view of the Mission's consistently-weak financial situation!

Ogelbeng evangelists with Vicedom, Bergmann, and Horrolt.

198

Even the beginning of the Highlands work was overshadowed by doubts as to how essential goods could be transported from the coast; but now the distance to Ogelbeng of more than 400 kilometres, sometimes over the most impassable terrain, seemed a sheer impossibility. Aircraft and freight space could be hired, it is true; but the long-term cost of doing that far exceeded the funds which the Mission had available. [31]

On September 12, 1934 — the very day on which Ega was founded, of which the outside world knew nothing yet — the Board of Neuendettelsau Mission thousands of miles away in Germany decided to buy an aeroplane. [32] How it was to be paid for, nobody knew at the time. However, many donations (including those from the Sattelberg-Hube evangelists, who in 1934 decided to go without their pay —little enough anyway) meant that it was possible to raise the money after all.

On March 5, 1935, the aircraft, which had been called *Papua*, [33] made its first inland flight to Ega. Of course, the Mission was not suddenly free of all its transport problems through the purchase of the plane. But the plane had become a symbol of hope. The Chimbu people elevated this plane by calling it 'Mother of the Whites', whom it provided for. [34] Both New Guinean and expatriate missionaries knew that help was closer at hand in the event of sickness or trouble.

That was, however, the last positive report from the Mission in the interior of New Guinea for a long time.

Evangelist (later pastor) Tirie with his wife (Raipinka).

Setbacks

Two major catastrophes now befell the work in the Highlands that had begun with such high hopes.

The first began when two Catholic missionaries were killed by some villagers north of Ega: Father Morschhaeuser on December 19, 1934, and Brother Eugen on January 8, 1935. The government responded sharply to these incidents. Admittedly, the foreigners already in the Highlands were allowed to continue to live and work there; but no new people were allowed in — not even members of the family of missionaries. As well, the expatriate missionaries were under police supervision to the extent that they had to notify the local officer in advance of any overland journeys, and, on their return, to report their observations to him. Drastic as these measures were, they were understandable in the circumstances.

But far worse was to come. On August 1, 1936, the laws were tightened. All the evangelists had to leave their outstations, and were allowed to stay only at those stations where an expatriate missionary was in residence. [35]

There has been much speculation over the real reasons for this measure. Officials, for instance, declared that the peace of the inland tribes was seriously threatened by people from other tribes. If that were so, why did the restrictions apply solely to the evangelists? Were not the policemen and government clerks also from outside the area, some even from the same regions as the evangelists? Another reason given was that the parity of the missions had to be preserved — a point which could refer only to the Lutheran and Catholic missions. The restriction had the greatest effect on the Lutheran Mission, for its program in particular was based on the work of evangelists. [36]

Whatever the reasons, this ruling was a catastrophe for the Lutheran Mission. Some 70 evangelists were affected in the Ega district, 40 in Ogelbeng, 20 in Kerowagi, and 100 in the Onerunka region. As none of the evangelists was threatened by his hosts, or involved in any violent incident at the time, this break in the Mission's work was hard to explain to the people. That was the effect of the measure in practical terms.

Even more catastrophic, though, was the human side of the affair. People who had lived

199

Highlanders listening to the Gospel (Onerunka).

together for years — some for far more than a decade in the Eastern Highlands — were torn apart. Bonds of trust, friendships, even the situation of people having grown accustomed to each other — all that was suddenly wiped out. Bergmann himself went out to bring in his evangelists from their stations. He summarizes the impressions in the villages, the weeping and grieving, the self-mutilation resulting from despair, the hopelessness, the disbelief of the inevitable, his own shock and bitterness, in the following words:

> So much grieving I had never seen before. Poor people! ... If we could only help them! If the men who had made these laws could only see! But they would probably only mock and laugh. [37]

From that time on, the evangelists could visit their former villages only in the company of the missionary, and that, of course, was possible only rarely. How the evangelists and the inhabitants of the villages themselves felt is reflected in a letter from the evangelist Sekung:

> We Kate evangelists established two stations in the Chimbu area. In September 1936, however, on the government's orders, we all had to give up our places and go to the mission station at Ega. The

government has also forbidden us to go around and visit the people in their villages. We are very sorry about that. It really isn't true that the heathen are tired of us and have become hostile toward us. Only with the missionary are we allowed to pay visits. So, on December 10 we went with the missionary to several deserted places and visited the people again. Everywhere they asked Missionary Bergmann: 'Are you bringing us our evangelists again?' He answered: 'No, I am not allowed to do that.' When the men grew angry on hearing that, he said to them: 'I am not the one who took your evangelists away. It was done on the *kiap's* orders. You must turn to him.'

> Everywhere we went, the people mourned our departure. They covered themselves with dirt and ashes as if bewailing the dead, and wept dreadfully. As far as the order of the government is concerned, namely, that we had to leave our stations, we are of the same opinion as the people: It is a matter here of our, the brown Papuans', country, and not that of the whites. If the brown heathen want us brown Christians, how then can the whites, strangers to the country, put up a barrier between us and forbid us to settle with our friends? Furthermore, they are preventing the spread of the Word of God, which brings us brown people so much good. That we do not understand. [38]

The solutions which tried to make the best out of the situation naturally were not wholly satisfactory. In general, all the evangelists were moved to the main stations. Some of the boys who had previously attended the schools at the evangelist stations were sent by some village communities to continue their schooling at the main stations. Altogether, some 400 gathered at Ega, some 300 at Raipinka — numbers of people for which these stations originally were certainly not intended. At Ogelbeng the number of pupils alone was 150.

In the Onerunka/Raipinka area, a remarkable peace movement developed in response to the government regulation. The evangelist Gapenuo Ngizaki portrays it thus:

> The second chief Arowe of Waianofira set out in 'icy' silence with his two evangelists on the six-hour walk back to the evangelists' station. There he sat down on a block of stone, surveyed the fine, semi-circular building, and suddenly began to weep lamentably. A large crowd gathered. 'You proud warrior, weeping like a woman?', cried out some of the men to him. Whereupon he jumped up and cried: 'All you Waianofira people come to this place tomorrow morning! Then I shall tell you why I am weeping!' And with that he disappeared into the bush.
>
> The next morning, the whole group of villagers, whose number ran into the hundreds, appeared at the evangelists' station. Suddenly Arowe comes out of the bush, steps in front of the assembled crowd, and announces the shattering message from the Administrator, declaring: 'Now all our evangelists whom we have come to love must leave us! We ourselves are to blame with our wretched magic, blood vengeance, and feuds. How often have I warned you, but you didn't listen to me! This is our undoing! Our downfall!' Breathless silence. Then up jump a few men and cry: 'Down with magic and blood revenge! Down with murder and war!' Finally, everyone jumps up, and from all sides comes a hubbub of cries: 'Down with magic!' 'Down with murder!' 'Down with war!' 'Our messengers of peace shall stay!'
>
> Then finally Arowe declares: 'Only when peace has returned to all the area, to the whole of the Kafe-Gazub area, will our messengers of peace be able to stay! So, let's go — from village to village — let us make peace!'
>
> So the cry for peace travelled, slow-moving but steady, from place to place, from valley to valley, from mountain to mountain — until, a few months later, the whole of the Kafe-Gazub area was

'We want peace!'

201

covered, with weapons collected region by region and taken to the government official in Kainantu, where all solemnly declared: 'We want peace; we want to build paths, to clean the villages; the evangelists shall come back to us; we want to "put into our nose" [hear and accept] the message of peace.'

On the suggestion and orders of the Mission and the government, the villages in the whole area were cleaned after three to four months, and tidy walking and riding paths laid out, so that a senior officer from the government headquarters at Rabaul could make a journey of inspection on a horse belonging to the Onerunka station through the previously wild and impenetrable region of the Kafe-Gazub tribes, and recognize that peace reigned in the country. Thereupon the central government lifted the ban completely, and allowed all the evangelists to work without restriction in the whole of the region. That was at the beginning of 1937.[39]

Pleasing as this was for the people of the Onerunka area, the harsh ruling remained basically in force for other areas until 1947.

The second major catastrophe was the outbreak of World War II. Certainly its early effects were not as severe as those of World War I, particularly in the Highlands. Since Germany was now at war with England, and therefore also with the Commonwealth of which Australia was a member, most of the German missionaries were interned immediately. As early as the end of September, the Highlands missionaries with their families were taken from Ogelbeng, Ega, Asaroka, and Raipinka. Fortunately, there were American missionaries to replace them.[40]

The 1930s were undoubtedly the most eventful, dramatic years for the Lutheran Mission in the Highlands. Although it sometimes looked as if incomparably-fruitful times were just around the corner, there were also moments in which the situation looked utterly bleak. And hardly a ray of hope shone on the horizon at the end of the decade, as far as external influences were concerned. Would the Gospel be able to take root under these circumstances?

When the historic exploratory expedition had arrived back in Onerunka on June 23, 1934, Bergmann chose Luke 12:49 as the text for the devotion: 'I have come to set fire to the earth, and how I wish it were already kindled!' He was able to interpret that text as words with

202

which Jesus wanted to encourage the missionaries for the great task ahead of them. But now another fire had broken over the world whose devastating power threatened to wipe out everything that had been built up so diligently over the past years. Was there still room for hope?

Ruins, Sorrow, and New Impulses

The blaze which had been set alight in Europe in 1939, and which swept the world, was felt only faintly in New Guinea at first. Apart from the restrictions the government had imposed previously, the Lutheran Mission had to manage with even fewer white members of staff than before. 'A change of [government] officers often took place, and not all of them were kindly disposed to the missionary activities. Yet the work was not entirely forbidden'[41] was how Bergmann described the situation at Ega.

From Chimbu come reports of a kind of conversion movement at that time. People came to the station at Ega, surrendered their magic devices to Herbert Hannemann, and asked for guidance at their time of prayer. The places of worship they subsequently established were a thorn in the government officer's side. Without informing the missionary, he sent out his policemen to pull them down. As strange as this was, it would certainly have been tolerated more patiently, had not the situation grown worse.

New Guinea was really drawn into the war on January 22, 1942 when Rabaul was occupied by the Japanese, closely followed by Lae and Madang. The Ramu and Markham Valleys and the coastal region became the scene of devastating battles; the Highlands, by contrast, remained almost completely untouched. Admittedly, they were struck by air raids, of which more will have to be said later; but by and large, the Highlands were only indirectly affected by a war which the population did not understand, which did not concern them, and which was a matter between white and yellow people.

But the consequences soon made themselves felt. Early in 1943, the American and Australian missionaries had to leave the Highlands, too. Some of them fled in a dramatic way by foot to the coast of Papua. The deserted stations soon housed all manner of 'guests'; it is said of Ega that at times there were up to 30 Australian and Chinese people lodged there.

Particularly severe was the fate of the evangelists. They were given no special status because of their coastal origin, and certainly not because of their work. They were sometimes called upon, like every other Highlander, for menial tasks, and were often the target of suspicion and hostility.

> When Japanese aircraft flew over the station of Ega, the evangelists were forbidden to stay at or near the station. They had to move to the villages, live among the people, and dress exactly as they did (that is, they were not allowed to wear loin cloths or jackets any more). Is it surprising that they became tired of this life and wanted to return to their home places? Many requested permission to return, and were granted this. Those in charge let them go — even went with them part of the way, and then left them to look after themselves. On the way they met with sickness and death. [42]

This is how it was later reported to Wilhelm Bergmann. The villagers also told him that the police had gone around to destroy most of the evangelists' houses which were still standing, and to set up government rest houses — often on the same site. Leading members of the village communities who protested against this were said to have been whipped until they bled.

Fortunately, however, there were also more cheerful reports. When Ogelbeng was destroyed by Japanese bombs, the head of the tribe, Gope, broke out in tears at the sight of the ruins, and promised the evangelists in future every help. And he kept his word as well as circumstances permitted. [43] Even after the bombardment of Ogelbeng station, regular Sunday services were held at the station school by former pupils such as Filip, Pagum, Jung, Ik, Gure, Pok, and others. [44] These pupils often took over functions in other places, too, although hardly anyone had expected this of them, and for which they were in no way specially prepared. From Kerowagi, John Kuder reported of these pupils:

> All on their own, and with the help of the local population, the older school pupils had gone out, gathered the children together, and held classes. Without textbooks (except for the books held by the teachers themselves), without paper, pencils, ink, blackboard, or chalk, they had made a beginning in instructing their people. [45]

At Raipinka, A. Frerichs, the departing missionary, had entrusted the evangelists to the special protection of the government official. He had them assemble at Raipinka from the various places in the circuit and gave them food.

Bombs also fell on the Eastern Highlands area. Since there could be no thought of regular mission work because of this, the Sattelberg missionaries were recalled by their home congregations in 1944, and they accepted this call.

The report from this area would be incomplete, however, without taking note of a signal event in the year 1942. Shortly before all expatriate missionaries had to leave the Highlands, 30 adults were baptized at Rihona after eight years' preparation — the second baptism in the Highlands, after Wampur in 1934. [46]

A Long Way Back to Normality

No war leaves people and circumstances unchanged; it is impossible to pick up things exactly from where they were before. The first Lutheran missionaries who returned to the Highlands after the war were acutely aware of this. Their reports reveal their apprehension: What would remain of the work that had been begun? What would the external conditions be? And how would the inner state of the people manifest itself?

Felix Doering's report on Ogelbeng makes this clear almost allegorically. [47] He describes only a minute parte of the world as it was then, full of ruins, degradation, sadness, and tears. The situation is nonetheless indicative of the contrast in the Highlands between external destruction and spiritual growth:

> Ogelbeng was a place of material desolation when we arrived. The station had borne the brunt of the Japanese attack and therefore had been bombed extensively. Anything that had not been destroyed by the bombs and was lying around loose had been pillaged — mostly by whites ... What was left of it was almost a complete wreck.

This was offset, however, by the happy astonishment at the Gospel's power of survival:

> Over this scene of material desolation, which at times had a tendency to bring on a feeling of depression rather than cheers, there shone a brighter light, which helped one to forget the ruins around ... For the seeds of the Gospel which had been sown in pre-war years had taken root and were now showing evidence of new life, which

Missionaries F. Doering (left) and H. Strauss (centre) with Christians from Mt Hagen.

even the strong weeds of war had not been able to choke out.

Much of this strength of the Gospel, and also the desire for new intensive missionary activity, is reported by John Kuder after his first round-trip in the Highlands.[48] On his visit, the people of Ogelbeng presented him with a rope with 19 knots, symbolizing 19 places where churches and houses of prayer had already been set up, and were being run by former pupils of the station school at Ogelbeng. But on the rope were another 22 knots, symbolizing places possessing churches, but no one to preach the Gospel. Over and above this, Kuder was told, there were numerous villages waiting for missionaries to come, but which had not yet set up any houses of prayer.

The demand for teachers and staff at Kerowagi and Ega was similarly large. The figures are impressive: At Ega, 2,000 children were waiting for lessons from the Mission, but there were only two teachers from the coast available, and one missionary. In Asaroka, 5,000 to 6,000 people gathered to listen to the Sunday service, and the village and tribal leaders asked Kuder for new missionaries.

204

Of course, there were also obstacles in the way of these challenging positive perspectives. The former German missionaries who had worked in this area were no longer in Australian internment camps by 1947, but they were only gradually allowed to leave for New Guinea. New missionaries did come from America and Australia (but not from Germany), but in inadequate numbers.

The harsh pre-war restrictions on the evangelists' work were completely lifted on July 1, 1947.[49] That does not mean, however, that there were immediately enough church workers from the coast. Nor could the former pupils of the station schools who had plugged many a gap eagerly and painstakingly — and without pay — be expected to continue to work like that under normal circumstances.[50] Elements of the traditional religion also surfaced again.[51] Yet the first steps toward a steady resumption of the work could be taken. When, for instance, Bergmann could return to Ega at the end of 1947 (after working for 10 months at Sattelberg), 23 preachers' families, 90 people in all, went with him to the Highlands to continue the Mission's work.[52]

'All our work is directed toward the goal of Baptism.'

Hope and Encouragement

The end of this decade, which had begun in such a sombre and bloody way, brought the Highlands Mission new signs of hope and encouragement. External pressure was less than ever; the missionaries' efforts could be concentrated entirely on the task of the Mission derived from the Gospel.

> All our work is directed at the goal of baptism. All our preaching and the years of instruction are but preparation for baptism. [53]

Large-scale baptismal ceremonies now shaped the picture of the work in the Highlands for over two decades. Gapenuo Ngizaki reports on what is widely held to be the first of these great ceremonies in the Highlands, when 323 people were baptized in Raipinka on March 9, 1949:

> Missionary Frerichs told the story of Zacchaeus. The effect was astonishing. The people returned all the stolen goods they had taken possession of from the deserted Mission and European stations during the turmoil of the war, or they paid for them. Also what they had stolen from among themselves was given back. The preachers put the money they received for the stolen goods not in

their own pockets but in the Mission's collection box. [54]

In the interior of the Highlands, the first baptismal ceremony was held in Ogelbeng on Sunday, June 8, 1949. A single date is misleading, however; the ceremonies in those years were events which lasted several days. When the guests from Kerowagi and Ega, themselves numbering over 200, arrived on foot on the Thursday before, they were received by some 6,000 people from Hagen. The next day, the crowd swelled to an estimated 10,000 to 12,000 people at a dance on the airfield. By Sunday, the actual day of the baptisms, the crowd had increased to roughly 15,000.

Government officers and their families were present; clergy from the Roman Catholic mission were also there. Members of the Lutheran Mission who could disengage themselves from their own duties also came. The evangelists from the various stations supplemented the program with symbolic performances. President John Kuder gave the bapismal sermon in Medlpa. [55] Then:

> Those who were to be baptized [went] in groups of 12 to 15 up to the platform, knelt down there, and

Gathering at Ogelbeng.

were baptized by missionaries Doering and Kuder. In all, there were 120 adults and 40 children. The large assembly of heathen was generally calm and quiet during the ceremony. They watched what was happening here. It was, after all, the first time that people had been baptized there. What might they have been feeling in their hearts?[56]

Bergmann's rhetorical question must remain unanswered. At any rate, the reponse to this event was that the wish to be baptized spread and spread.

The first baptisms were performed at Ega on October 31 of that same year. Those baptized were the former pupils of the station school, of whom mention has already been made, along with their families. All in all, there were 87 young men, 47 women, and 17 children.

> Now we had the first 'congregation' in Ega. But also a special sort of congregation, for it was already one hundred per cent involved in the missionary work.[57]

Before the end of the 1940s, steps had been taken to extend the Mission's activities in the Highlands. In 1948 the station of Omkolai was set up, and in 1949 those of Tarabo and Monono were in preparation.[58]

During a baptismal service at Ogelbeng.

206

Chief Bongelo from Ega, 'a true friend'.

From Pioneer Mission to Church

Each decade in the Highlands Mission since 1920 may have had its own focal point, but they all had one thing in common: They were part of a real pioneer mission. This situation changed, however, the moment new congregations began in the Highlands as the result of baptisms — a stage reached about 1950.

This was when mission lost its exclusive character, and became part of church work, as had happened in the older areas of the Lutheran Mission on the coast. Mission and congregational activities now became linked and intertwined, requiring the vigilance of the clergy in equal measure. Would they be up to this dual task — yes, would they recognize the task in time? Undoubtedly, it was a challenge to prepare people for the missionary goal of baptism to fire their enthusiasm, to motivate them. But what then? The clergy in the Highlands, the missionaries from New Guinea, America, Germany, and Australia, were what one might loosely call specialists in baptism. They performed this task brilliantly in all humility. (We will have more to say about that later.) But would they now know how to motivate the new Christians to keep their faith, so that it was not relegated to a position of secondary importance, or became something they turned their backs on in disappointment? Would they be able to stimulate the new congregations to keep, and even increase, their enthusiasm?

This was an enormous problem, but not one that concerned the Highlands alone; regularly it also had to be resolved anew in the core areas of the Lutheran Mission in New Guinea. From now on, development in those areas and the Highlands ran more or less parallel; more and more details, tasks, and problems occurred in all areas at the same time. This trend began in the 1950s, and increased with each new decade. The way to the one Lutheran Church of Papua New Guinea — in which all parts would have the same status, the same duties, and fundamentally the same cares — had thus begun. [59]

The Government and Other Missions

The Australian mandate government in the 1950s certainly had no completely-formulated policy toward the indigenous population, but at least it aimed at more autonomy, more schooling facilities, and greater economic development. Toward the Lutheran Mission in the Highlands, too, a relationship of tolerance and correctness was pursued. [60] The following declaration from an official to a gathering of indigenous and expatriate church workers in 1957 has been handed down: 'Each institution has its own task: the government and the Mission. Both must work together.' [61] Practice right up to the time of the country's independence in 1975 largely confirmed this simple motto.

Not entirely without its problems, however, was coexistence between the various denominational missions. Particularly in the Chimbu area, in the Wagi Valley, and later in the new territories of the Southern Highlands, there was considerable confrontation between the different denominations. In the beginning, the Roman Catholics and Seventh Day Adventists chiefly opposed the Lutherans; but later, many other missions were also involved.

Before the war, some personal agreements had been forged between Catholics and Lutherans to define each one's areas of work; [62] after the war, however, there were no records of any such agreements, and the principle of 'First come, first served' was followed — sometimes aggressively. Manipulation was an extremely common practice, and claims sometimes even had to be settled by the police or the courts. This inter-denominational rivalry caused tremendous confusion among the people. One of the Lutheran teachers concerned, who had not experienced this disunity among Christians at his home on the coast, described the situation thus:

> This is the sixth year of our work. But we are not the only ones here. The Adventists, the Baptists, and the Catholics are working alongside us. Because four different missions are here, the people are becoming confused and don't know what to do. When the nemuja trees blossom, the butterflies and other insects fly from one tree to another. The people here are doing just that, too. They are constantly flitting back and forth. [63]

The administration had promised freedom of religion, and more and more missionary groups felt encouraged to go to New Guinea. At the beginning, some of them turned to the experienced Lutheran Mission for advice:

> All these people have consulted with us before going in … We cannot refuse to let these people go in. We have not the men, and they have. So far they have not entered into active competition with us; they have gone into areas where we had not begun. [64]

And, indeed, the misfortune of Christian disunity was first felt on the fringes of the respective mission areas. It often manifested itself in mutual suspicion, direct enticement, the spreading of hostile rumours, and large-scale distribution of gifts.

This rivalry soon penetrated areas which had hitherto been uniform in confession. [65] With the best will in the world, one could no longer say that this served the good of the people or furthered preaching of the Word of God; it was clearly aimed at weakening or even ousting other religious communities. Only much later did the trend toward uniform action become stronger, particularly when confrontation with secular demands and traditional forms of belief proved in the long run to be too great a challenge for one group to overcome alone. [66] Alcoholism, gambling, polygamy, offences against property, the revival of traditional fighting, and every form of violence were major catalysts in this development.

The Emerging Church in the Highlands

The 1950s and 1960s were marked in the Highlands by more tremendous expansion for the Lutheran Mission. This entailed a two-fold thrust: the expansion and consolidation of the

208

structures in areas which already had missionaries, and the opening up of new regions. Never were so many mission stations set up, never were so many staff employed by the Lutheran Mission, as in those two decades.

The most decisive step in this expansion was certainly the opening up of the Southern Highlands from the latter half of the 1950s on into the 1960s. Work began in the Jalibu area in 1955. Both pastoral aspects and strategic considerations determined the choice of such a place:

> There is no doubt that to the South lie our greatest possibilities; and, if we intend to begin there, our present location is ideally suited for paving the way. [67]

That follow-up stage was reached a few years later. In 1958, an area still further south, situated in the former Australian colony of Papua, was visited to evaluate its suitability for missionary activity. Bergmann describes the procedure as follows, drawing attention at the same time to significant changes since the pre-war period:

> Starting in a new area is quite different today from 20 or 30 years ago. [68] Then we could go where we wanted without asking a lot of questions or requesting permission. The work developed gradually. The neighbouring tribes got to know us and our preachers, and it usually didn't take long for them to ask for evangelists, too. Today, the government … does not allow the Mission to enter areas in which it has not already 'made the peace'. Hence, the government has usually been in the new territories for a number of years before it gives us permission to begin our missionary activities there. It has to declare the area 'open' for other whites. [69]

Bergmann was asked to help select the location for a new station; the outcome of this was the mission area of Wabi. [70] In the Southern Highlands, Tiripini was added in 1961. Other new stations can also be seen as part of the trend to push the Lutheran Mission's activity south, even if the border with Papua was not crossed. In this connection we can list Alkena and Rongo (both 1958), Agotu, Ponampa and Karepa (all 1960/61), and finally the last linked Highlands area where real pioneer missionary work was begun: the area of Wonenare and Marawaka (1964 and 1967).

A number of stations developed when it was realized that the original circuits were too

Church at Tiripini (Southern Highland).

large to be looked after intensively enough from one place. The following stations owe their existence to this: Finintugu as an offshoot from Raipinka (1963/64),[71] Bena-Bena from Asaroka(1964), Banz from Kerowagi (1950), and Kotna (1958) and Tiria (1961) from Ogelbeng. Expansion on a smaller scale took place in the mountainous, impassable north; Kogl (1956) and Sumburu (1958) should therefore be mentioned here.

Lutheran Mission had limited its work to the west, for it had surrendered the region west of Ogelbeng Circuit to American Lutherans of the Missouri Synod as a mission field. Finally, the urban circuits of Goroka (1963), Mt Hagen (1964), and Kainantu (1970) must be added.

From the few pre-war bases of Lutheran Mission which were scattered over the extensive Highlands, a fine-meshed network had now developed to provide an organizational framework for the immense task of winning the people over to the Gospel. The setting up of a central station did. not just mean that a missionary started there; at the same time, a number of evangelists and teachers came too, to be stationed in the surrounding villages which

wished to have them.[72] Thus the work grew, and churches, schools, and medical stations were set up.

The structure became more refined with the years. Meetings of the church staff were held; and once or twice a year all the evangelist stations were visited by a missionary and as many other church representatives in the circuit as possible.[73] After baptism (sometimes even before), elected members of the newly-developing congregations took part in these events. With the indigenous church testing its wings of independence after 1956, attention was also given in the Highlands to having New Guinean leaders take their place alongside expatriate missionaries. These were known as Circuit Presidents, at first equal in rank, and later superior to the missionaries. Often, these men had had no theological education; they were reliable, experienced evangelists and teachers who were given pastoral tasks with all the rights and duties associated with that office. As time passed, pastors and teachers with more thorough education from the old training centres on the coast or from the new ones in the Highlands joined their ranks. The mission

The urban circuit church at Mt Hagen.

stations (which gave their name to a whole circuit) became the focal point for all the activities of a carefully-organized church life. Small business enterprises, shops, trading in coffee, and special projects (less often) like cattle breeding or vegetable gardening, all represented on the one hand attempts to serve the needs of the people, and on the other to strengthen the usually-weak financial basis of the circuit.

The circuits then began looking for greater organizational union at a higher level:

> Now there were Christian congregations at almost all the old inland stations. They hardly had any links with each other, however, except through the white missionaries. That is why it was time to bring the representatives of these congregations together ... To make a start, we invited representatives of the other congregations to come to Ega in the middle of the year. [74]

Following this step in 1952, the Highlands Conference became established as a regular institution. In 1961, the Conference recommended that the Highlands be divided into three more clearly-defined areas: the Goroka District (or the District of the Eastern Highlands), the Chimbu District (or the Central

210

District), the Hagen District (or the District of the Western Highlands). [75] The borders of these districts largely corresponded to those of the government districts at that time (the later Provinces). The Highlands church had now received its outward form, which it retained for decades to come.

At the head of these districts from the outset were New Guinean District Presidents. [76] A district missionary was assigned to each as adviser. In other respects, the Highlands regions and districts increasingly resembled the structure of the church as a whole. They were equal to the coastal districts of the Evangelical Lutheran Church of New Guinea (ELCONG).

Each district had its own district school. [77] The Pastors Seminary established in 1960 at Ogelbeng was primarily intended to serve students from the Highlands, but it also accepted students from the coastal region. A training centre for teachers, with Neo-melanesian Pidgin as the language of tuition, has operated at Rintebe since 1964. [78] At Kotna a hospital run by the church was set up, and in Awande a special clinic for sufferers from the Kuru disease (1962-1968). An agricultural

First group of Highland Leaders.

Enareki † (Goroka)

Baina (Goroka).

Baniepe † (Chimbu).

Mambu (Hagen).

211

school opened its doors in Banz in 1955. In Asaroka an English High School was established in 1956. The above list offers only a selection from a tremendous range of activities.

How would the young church manage them, especially when the number of expatriate missionary workers would decrease — as was the aim? Would the indigenous church be able to afford this wealth of institutions when they had to be funded from its own resources? Would they even want to take over the structures which had evolved in the early days of the church in the Highlands, structures which largely bore the stamp of expatriate missionaries?

Such questions still await a final answer. But a word from the former bishop of the Hagen District, Mabu Jeremiah, is indicative: 'The old structure will probably disappear, if only because our native pastors can work more easily with smaller and more distinct congregations.' [79] Is that a friendly, yet clear, indication that an intricate entity will emerge from the phase of expansion whose external form was not appropriate for the country, its believers, and its spiritual workers? Time alone will tell.

Harvest Time

It cannot be emphasized often enough how much the Lutheran Highlands Mission has been the work of the New Guinean missionaries right from the beginning. The few expatriate clergy who were part of that work would never have been able, by themselves, to initiate such a mass movement as that which brought Christianity to the inland of New Guinea. They provided the organizational and logistic framework, the skeleton, so to speak; they were able to help in many questions concerning the Mission and the Gospel. Through their presence, they encouraged, helped, supported, provided authority and backing — aspects that should not be underestimated.

But the instruments of the Gospel on the spot were unquestionably the New Guinean missionaries, originally from the coastal region only, later from the Christian congregations of the Highlands themselves. [80] Their work cannot be praised adequately enough within the scope of this account. The names of most of them are no longer known; even their exact number

212

Pastor Kewengu and wife (Raipinka).

cannot be determined. [81] Each one of them could feel supported by the home congregation, from where they originally received their pay; [82] that support was so valuable as they adapted to the requirements of a new environment: new climate, strange food, other languages, unusual customs. There was one other thing they could also be sure of: They were warmly welcomed. No evangelist was posted to a station against the will of the host villages. In fact, reports from those decades are full of complaints that the requests for evangelists could not be fully met. The motives of those issuing the invitations may initially have been superficial, for they could not know what to expect. They may have been looking for a share of the (relative) wealth of the Mission; their motive may have been pure curiosity, or a desire for change. However, there is no known instance of an evangelist having been driven out after the local people grasped what their guest's real concern was. On the contrary, the scenes of mourning after the government restrictions of 1936, and the dramatic demands for missionary helpers at the end of World War II, speak for themselves.

Many of the evangelists were highly-educated, impressive personalities. Others had not been to school, [83] and knew only a few Bible stories and the catechism by heart; several had not even been baptized. Indeed, almost annually a number had to be sent back home again on account of misdemeanours and irregularities (mostly adultery — particularly when married men were not joined promptly by their wives and children); some did not have the strength to see their task through. The majority, however, performed their mission task with astonishing devotion and perseverance. The fruit of this tough, patient labour was a tremendous desire on the part of the Highlands people to become Christians. The development of Asaroka may illustrate this:

1934	Beginning of the evangelists' work in the Asaroka area
1937	Setting up of the central station
1950	Still no baptisms
1951	151 baptisms (native pupils at the station)
1952	106 baptisms (villagers)
1953	497 baptisms
1954	223 baptisms
1955	75 baptisms
1956	185 baptisms
1957	1,237 baptisms
1948	1,667 baptisms
1949	1,694 baptisms
1960	2,447 baptisms
1961	4,806 baptisms

Even with such astonishing figures, Asaroka was not an exception.[84] Already in 1953, W. Bergmann wrote the following, in view of the tremendous developments in his area:

We had begun our work here ... What tremendous changes there have been here in these more than 20 years! What I said then —that we would probably only be able to do a sower's work — has not proved true, for we have also been able in the last few years to reap the harvest.[85]

There is no reason to mix the wine with water. This powerful development of the Gospel could in no way have been anticipated. And the discerning among the active workers realized in their humility that this triumphant advance of Jesus' message was not their doing, but that the Lord was at work. Nevertheless, voices were raised quite early in warning:

Can we with a good conscience form Christian congregations by baptizing people, knowing that there are no others than some appointed illiterate (though often faithful) elders who know only a few Bible stories by heart which they recite every Sunday as a substitute for a sermon, and who are not able to lead a congregation into a deeper relationship with their Saviour? The result: People get tired ... What is the aim of our missionary work? Leading people to baptism and then leaving them on their own?[86]

Reports of diminishing interest among the members of the congregation after baptism are numerous. Had, then, the newly-baptized had wrong expectations, and were they now disappointed?

However that may be, the church and the Mission were now faced with the tremendous spiritual challenge of ministering to those who had been baptized by encouraging them to remain active and devout Christians, as far as this can be asked of people at all. The temptation, however, to regard baptismal 'fruits' as a final, irrevocable success was and is enormous. To keep the metaphor: How the ground must be treated to remain fruitful, to make it produce new harvests, is the question that the spiritual leaders will continue to ask themselves. But that is a problem not only for the Highlands, and not even only for Papua New Guinea.

Public square in Goroka today.

Endnotes

This account is based on facts and conclusions drawn from Wilhelm Bergmann's 10-volume report entitled *Forty Years in New Guinea*; the wealth of this monograph is by no means exhausted by the present writer. Also important were the relevant parts of the Mission Histories of W. Flierl, A. Frerichs, G. Renck, H. Hage, and, of course, the almost-unequalled standard work of G. Pilhofer (in which, however, large parts of W. Bergmann's biography have already been evaluated).

Important for me was to give room to as many Neu Guineans as possible, for example, to the biographies of Geyammalo Apo and Gapenuo Ngizaki. An unexpected treasure proved to be letters from Kate Christians to Christian Keysser, their former missionary, in Germany, which he had translated into German. Another source of high atmospheric and historic value, hitherto hardly used, I found in the reports in the Kate church magazine *Aakesing*, whose most important contributions the same untiring Christian Keysser translated into German until shortly before his death in 1961.

This material and many other sources were made available to me by the Neuendettelsau Archives. An inexhaustible wealth of information is contained in the annual reports of the station missionaries. A very under-rated source seemed to me to be the small booklets by former missionary staff in New Guinea, whose statements have always stood up to critical analysis. However, this contribution is based only on the sources of the Archives of Neuendettelsau, and I was able to write on the American and Australian involvement in the Highland Mission only as far as material was available there.

[1] Geyammalo Apo, *Erinnerungen und Erfahrungen eines Evangelisten in Neu Guinea* (Recollections and Experiences of a New Guinea Evangelist), as told by Geyammalo Apo to his son Janadabing in 1964. Original in Jabem, tr. into German by J.F. Streicher (mimeographed, n.d.), 8-9. Unfortunately, it is not clear from Geyammalo's account exactly when he began his work, and when he first established contact with the Gazub people. In all probability, it was at the end of 1918.

[2] Leonhard Flierl, *Unter Wilden* (Neuendettelsau: Buchhandlung der Diakonissenanstalt, n.d.), 10.
This bloody beginning is like the warning sign: 'mene, mene, tekel, upharsin' over the work in the Highlands, for the credibility of the Mission's peace work depended entirely on how the missionaries approached the new groups of people and how they shaped their relations with them. How seriously the evangelists regarded this incident is seen from the fact that two of them wanted to offer themselves to the Pundawateno tribe to atone for the death of their leader. They had to be forcibly restrained by their native communities.
There were, however, many excuses and explanations for using weapons. The white missionaries, who ultimately had to answer for the shots, even if they were fired without their express command, were responsible for a large number of natives accompanying them, and were clearly in a situation which called for self-defence. Moreover, they were encountering a people accustomed to battle, who did not see in them preachers of the Gospel — there was neither the time nor the opportunity to make that clear — but absolute enemies. The names of the German missionaries involved were: Georg Pilhofer, Friedrich Oertel, and Johann Stoessel.
However, that was the only man killed in the history the Lutheran Highlands mission. In sharp contrast was the quick and often unscrupulous use of firearms by government officials and especially by commercial agents. Indeed, to New Guineans in most areas the feature which differentiated the Mission from other white groups was initially that the ones did not shoot and kill, whereas the others did. The government allowed new areas to be entered only if a suitable number of firearms was carried; that also held good for the missionaries. It was most fortunate that the Lutheran missionaries had to use these weapons so rarely; Christians will acknowledge this as God's mercy, for which they have to be grateful.
The Pundawateno tribe retained their warlike attitude toward their neighbours, the government, and the Miission for many years. Their first baptism took place in 1951, to which they invited Wilhelm Bergmann, the first white missionary to gain their trust.
The portrayal of a still-earlier attempt to establish contact with the people in the mountains is found in Stephan Lehner's booklet, *Siehe, ich mache alles neu!* (Neuendettelsau: Freimund-Verlag, 1937), 11 ff. Regrettably, it is not entirely clear when Lehner, his evangelists Kemadi, Buase, Dema, and Gamung from Bukaua and the eight other helpers paid their two-day visit to the Gazub people. Presumably it was already in June 1917. On the subject of firstcomers, see too: Ian Willis, 'Who was first?', *Journal of the Papua New Guinea Society*, 3, 1 (1969), 32-45.

[3] Gapenuo Ngizaki, *Braune Fackeltraeger: Erfahrungen und Bewahrungen eines braunen Evangelisten im Hochland Neuguineas 1923-1963* translated from Kate into German by Johannes Flierl, (Neuendettelsau, n.d., mimeographed), 8-9. Gapenuo Ngizaki was one of the most prominent New Guinean missionaries of the pioneering epoch in the Eastern Highlands; L. Flierl calls him 'the most efficient of the evangelists', and Jakob Herrlinger a 'fine man'. Gapenuo worked mainly in Wampur, where he prepared the first baptismal class of the Highlands. Moreover, Gapenuo was a regular contributor to the Kate churchpaper *Aakesing* where his contributions are found right on into the 1950s.

[4] Particularly remarkable is L. Flierl's journey from the end of July to the beginning of August 1927. Besides the New Guinean helpers, the missionary Karl Saueracker was also a member of this group. Whereas most of the previous expeditions to the Highlands from Kaiapit had taken the shortest route through the Onga region to Wampur, these men followed the Markham Valley westwards up to the place where it merged into the Ramu Valley. On a level with the evangelist station of Garamari, they ascended the slopes of the Bismarck Range where the evangelist station of Rihona was set up in 1926, travelled in a wide arc south-west, and touched the Upper Ramu plateau before returning to the Markham Valley. This expedition passed off without casualties; on the contrary, contacts were made which were later fruitfully strengthened.

[5] The designations Gazub and Hazung, which have now lost their importance politically and geographically, are names for the lowlands east of present-day Kainantu (Gazub), and the mountainous region west of it (Hazung).

[6] Letter from G. Vicedom to Hans Bock, March 29, 1930.

[7] Bergmann was the European missionary who knew the Highlands best at this early date. He had already made two explorations into the Highlands, the first from August 26 to October 5, 1929 with Georg Pilhofer, and the second with Willy Flierl from July 27 to September 1, 1930. For Pilhofer this was also the second trip to the Highlands (he had taken part in one in 1920); meanwhile, however, as the leading man in the schoolwork at Finschhafen, he could not be spared. W. Bergmann (born 1899) was one of the first German missionaries after World War I to be given permission by the Australian mandated government (in 1928) to travel to New Guinea. Before he received orders to go to the Highlands, he worked in Heldsbach and Qembung. In 1929 he married Louise Gutebier. Bergmann now lives in retirement in Queensland, Australia with one of his daughters. His 10-volume work, *Vierzig Jahre in Neuguinea* (Mutdapilly, Qld., n.d., mimeographed) is the main source for this account (hereafter cited as: W. Bergmann, volume and page number).

[8] Kaiapit was given a key function in the opening up of the Highlands because of its favourable close location. The irony was that the Kaiapit missionary, Friedrich Oertel, was against the establishment of a new Highland station at that time. That did not prevent him, however, from supporting the undertaking fairly and loyally.

[9] W. Bergmann, II, 236.

[10] As early as Pentecost 1931, 14 evangelists from the Amele circuit came to visit Rihona. They were looking for a new mission field in the Highlands. An expatriate missionary did not accompany them. The visit was initially without consequences (W. Bergmann, II, 136).

[11] An important factor in the choice of Onerunka was its proximity to Kainantu, which was developing into the government centre for the Highlands (including the airfield). A basic reason for the station being moved to Raipinka in November 1936 was the latter's even greater proximity to Kainantu. The old site at Onerunka became important particularly after World War II as a district evangelists' school, later on a 'District *Tok Ples* School'.

[12] Report by J. Herrlinger of August 18, 1934; this description refers to the beginning of Onerunka in May 1934. This was the second station Bergmann started; the first one was Kambaidam. Because of illness, Mrs Bergmann and the children were at the coast at the time referred to.

[13] W. Bergmann, IV, 182.

[14] Georg Vicedom, *Ein neuentdecktes Papuavolk* (Neuendettelsau: Freimund-Verlag, 2nd ed., 1940), 30.

[15] Bearer of this message was the Lutheran Mission's contact with the Australian government, the untiring and meritorious Australian Mission Director Otto Theile. (See his letter of August 3, 1933, the first document appended to this chapter.)

[16] Significant was the attitude of the German Mission Board in Neuendettelsau. They fully supported the step to penetrate further into the Highlands, but dared give their approval only in a coded telegram. The Mission in Germany was becoming increasingly isolated. Since January 30, 1933, the National Socialists under Adolf Hitler had been in power, with an ideology diametrically opposed to the aims of the Mission. Already in 1933 it had been declared: 'Every penny for the heathen mission is a crime against the German people'. A ban on private collections, issued in 1934, also affected offerings for the Mission. Gottfried Schmutterer, the earlier missionary from Lae, and his wife were fined severely for an alleged infringement of this prohibition. Strict foreign exchange regulations hindered, and at times prevented, the transfer of funds from Germany to New Guinea even before the outbreak of war. Funds, nevertheless, were raised by loyal donors. The paradox was that, despite all this, a number of German missionaries in New Guinea were considered supporters of Hitler.

[17] Stephan Lehner was Field Inspector at this time, that is, head of the Finschhafen Lutheran Mission, of which Bergmann was a member.

[18] What accelerated the pace at that time, a period that had no ecumenical ideas of any kind, was the rumour that the Catholics were already becoming established there. This rumour proved to be true. The 'race' to the Highlands by various denominations was not viewed positively everywhere. The *Pacific Island Monthly* of June 22, 1934 described it as 'ridiculous'.

[19] The aircraft proved too small for the second missionary from Madang, Edward Pietz.

[20] It was a 'Foxmouth' aeroplane, piloted by Mr Goerner.

[21] W. Bergmann, Report of November 1, 1933.

[22] The missionaries concerned were: Wilhelm Bergmann, Matthias Lechner, and Jakob Herrlinger from the Finschhafen group, and Friedrich Schoettler, Henry Foege, and Dr Theodore Braun from the Madang group. Ironically, it is the names of those who fell ill on that arduous journey, or who otherwise had trouble, which have been preserved through the reports of the New Guinean participants. Mention should be made here of Christian and Jaselung from Malalo, Davidi Anam (a Jabem teacher who later became famous as a woodcarver and painter, see ch 15), and Gesengsu and Zangezia (Kate evangelists).

[23] J. Herrlinger, Report of August 18, 1934.

[24] Besides Bergmann and Vicedom, Martin Helbig went for Chimbu, and Georg Horrolt for Hagen.

[25] There were six missionaries who had come from the coast: Edward Pietz, Herbert Hannemann, Henry Foege, John Mager, Jakob Welsch, and Theodore Radke; only three of them were to remain in Kerowagi on a long-term basis. There were also some church leaders from the Madang district: Sapuz (Bel), Mileng (Karkar), Nai (Nobonob), Ud and Samiaip (Amele), and Jagenip and Simgaip from Begesin (who returned after a while). The number of evangelists, however, was very small; Bergmann speaks of five.

[26] W. Bergmann, V, 3.

[27] *Ibid.,* IV, 200.

[28] G. Vicedom, letter to Christian Keysser of February 28, 1935.

[29] Kerowagi therefore asked for evangelists from other circuits. There was a complete lack of teachers, for instance. One who was 'borrowed' from neighbouring Ega was the teacher Sorenuka from the Sattelberg area. He was one of the members of the first expedition to the Highlands in 1934. Sorenuka subsequently worked in the Chimbu area for 37 years, and became the first President of the Kerowagi Circuit. In 1956 he was ordained a pastor (according to the *New Guinea Lutheran* of April 1972).

[30] Georg Vicedom, *Purimetl* (Neuendettelsau: Freimund-Verlag 1937), 10.

[31] The Mission is greatly indebted to Martin Boerner for his services in overcoming the transport problems before the arrival of the aeroplane. For instance, he organized caravans through the Markham Valley; with six mules and a few horses he transported approx. one ton of goods each trip. After all, every nail and every medicament, to say nothing of all the other utility goods, had to be transported to the Highlands in this way.

[32] This purchase was immediately severely criticized by a senior representative of the National Socialist Party in power in Germany.

[33] It was a Junker F-13 aeroplane with the registration VH-UTS. The first pilot was Fritz Loose, who describes his experiences in New Guinea in his book *Zu Wasser, zu Land und in der Luft* (Steinebach-Woerthsee: Luftfahrt-Verlag Walter Zuerl, n.d.).

[34] G. Vicedom, *Purimetl*, 15. One problem could not be solved by the purchase of the aircraft: all the passenger traffic into the interior. When the government's strict regulations of 1936 were eventually eased enough for the families of the Highlands evangelists and teachers to be able to join them, troops of women and children with some men to accompany them were regularly assembled in Lae to travel to the Highlands on foot right up to Ogelbeng. That was a trek of some 20 days. It is probably one of the most moving sights in the history of the Highlands Mission '... when they trail along with their children for weeks on end through hot plateaus, torrential rivers, and wild rugged mountains, in order to be reunited at last with fathers and husbands, to help in their work and to share their troubles' (H. Strauss, '19 Tage Marsch', *Missionsblatt* 7, 1935).

[35] Administrative Regulation of May 20, 1936 (see Document No. 2 appended).

[36] Certainly a contributory factor was that the government saw its own position challenged by the powerful development of the Mission; with the restriction it wanted to make clear who was really in charge. But probably national pride also played a part. The Lutheran Mission in the Highlands, for example, was dominated by Germans and Americans; why should the Australian administration support their activities? The draconian sentence imposed on the American missionary Henry Foege thus becomes understandable. Foege had a lad bound, who was strongly suspected of theft, to prevent him from escaping. When Foege himself reported it to the local officer, he was charged (only officers were authorized to bind people), sentenced to imprisonment, and expelled from the country. This measure altogether conforms to our present-day sense of justice. However, as things were then, when even the use of firearms against New Guineans was still the custom, and corporal punishment was no criminal offence, it had to be seen as a pure demonstration of power by the government, and illustrated the prevailing atmosphere (see also ch 4, note 83).

[37] W. Bergmann, V, 216.

[38] Sekung, in a letter to Christian Keysser from Ega on January 1, 1937, translated into German by Keysser. The indication 'two stations' refers to those which had been equipped directly by his home congregation. Altogether, there were far more stations in the Ega district.

[39] Gapenuo Ngizaki, *Braune Fackeltraeger . . .,* 21 ff; 'Kafe' is a group of languages around Henganofi (Eastern Highlands). The corresponding report by the missionary in charge, Johannes Flierl, is (partly) printed in: G. Pilhofer, *Die Geschichte der Neuendettelsauer Mission in Neuguinea* (Neuendettelsau: Freimund-Verlag, 1963) II, 245. On this, see also Robin Redford, 'Burning the Spears', *Journal of Pacific History,* 12 (1977), 40-54.

[40] In Ogelbeng, John Kuder replaced Hermann Strauss; in Ega, Herbert Hannemann replaced Wilhelm Bergmann; in Raipinka, Albert Frerichs replaced Martin Zimmermann. G. Hofmann from Asaroka was also interned, but his father-in-law, Paul Helbig, an Australian, was allowed to stay.

[41] W. Bergmann, VII, 165.

[42] *Ibid.,* VII, 168.

[43] Letter from H. Strauss to G. Vicedom of November 28, 1949.

[44] Undated report by F. Doering. Unfortunately, it has not been possible to establish the exact date of this report. What is known, however, is that Doering returned to Ogelbeng in 1946.

[45] Report by John Kuder, *Lutheran Standard,* April 26, 1947.

[46] Gapenuo Ngizaki, *Braune Fackeltraeger . . .,* 22.

[47] See note 44.

[48] J. Kuder had meanwhile become President of the whole of the Lutheran Mission in New Guinea, even though the (American) Madang branch and the (German/Australian) Finschhafen branch of the Mission were formally united in the 'Lutheran Mission New Guinea' only in 1953. The reference here is to the report of April 26, 1947, mentioned in note 45.

[49] Until then, even evangelists who had stayed in the Raipinka area during the war, or returned evangelists who had been able to move about relatively freely before the war, had had to stay in Raipinka and have their baptismal class come there for instruction (Report by Kuder, see note 45).

[50] The first baptisms in Ega (October 31, 1948) were for these young pupil-evangelists (see later in this chapter).

[51] At Rugli, for instance, 25 kilometres from Ogelbeng, because non-christian customs had been revived, the inhabitants no longer went to church for the Sunday service. But they gathered outside and listened to the Gospel from there — which was no handicap, in view of the flimsy structure of the church (Report by F. Doering of 1946).

[52] The return of the former (German) missionaries meant a gain not only for the spiritual work. W. Bergmann (Ega) and H. Strauss (Ogelbeng) could now continue their scientific research. Both involved themselves deeply in the language and the culture of their areas. The outstanding fruits of these labours are: H. Strauss, H. Tischner, *Die Mi-Kultur der Hagenberg-Staemme* (Hamburg: Commissions-Verlag Cram, de Gruyter & Co. 1962), and W. Bergmann, *Die Kamanuku. Die Kultur der Chimbu Staemme,* (Mutdapilly, Qld, 1970, mimeographed) 4 vols.

This is perhaps also the place to mention other outstanding works by German Lutheran missionaries on the culture of the Highlands: G. Vicedom, H. Tischner, *Die Mbowamb — Die Kultur der Hagenbergstaemme* (Hamburg: Friederichsen, de Gruyter & Co. 1943/48), 3 vols. Guenter L. Renck: *A Grammar of Yagaria* (Canberra: Australian National University, 1975). Another volume, in part about the Highlands, is Friedrich Steinbauer, *Melanesische Cargo-Kulte* (Munich: Delp'sche Verlagsbuchhandlung, 1971). It must be added that the permission given to German missionaries at this time to continue their work was a sign of generosity on the part of the Australian administration. Germany and the Germans were still greatly restricted as to their rights everywhere else in the world at that time after the defeat in war and the crimes committed by the National Socialists.

[53] W. Bergmann VIII, 36.

[54] In *Aakesing,* September 1949, translated into German by Chr. Keysser.

[55] He had been a missionary in Ogelbeng for several years (1939-1942).

[56] W. Bergmann, VIII, 15. The film taken at this ceremony by Rev. Maahs must sadly be presumed to be lost.

[57] *Ibid.,* VIII, 45. The first baptismal ceremony for non-pupils took place in Ega shortly afterwards on January 8, 1950. Part of the Lutheran ceremonies was the disclosure of magic charms, previously held secret. This took place only with the agreement of all the tribal leaders, not just of those to be baptized. However, these disclosures sometimes caused heated protest in villages which still stuck to the traditional religion. Bergmann (IX, 19 ff) reports that some groups lodged complaints in 1951 with the Australian officials in Goroka and Kundiawa. An official investigation confirmed that the Christians had voluntarily given up their magic, and so the government saw no reason to intervene.

[58] For the history and later development of Tarabo Circuit, see F. Steinbauer, *So war's in Tarabo* (Neuendettelsau: Freimund-Verlag, 1969).

[59] This chapter, which is limited in scope, can only deal with publications concerning the Highlands and must set wider-ranging subjects aside. The time limit for this is 1962 when the Highlands districts were created. Details, statistics, notes, etc. from the following years will be used whenever they illustrate general tendencies or when earlier indications are lacking.

[60] The missionaries' reports include hardly any more complaints about the officials' behaviour; this had not been always the case. One of the last major basic conflicts was in 1947 when the Mission reproached an official for reviving girls' dances in Chimbu in places where the population expressly did not want them (W. Bergmann, VII, 169 ff).

[61] Hans Wagner, *Die Ernte ist gross* (Neuendettelsau: Freimund-Verlag, 1958), 32.

[62] W. Bergmann, IV, 193 ff, 227.

[63] Report by Tuao (Joanggeng) in *Aakesing*, September 1954; from Jaibosi, Jaramanda (Ogelbeng Circuit).

[64] Letter from Dr J. Kuder to G. Vicedom, May 13, 1949.

[65] One example is Tarabo, originally a purely Lutheran area; in 1968 there were 14 other missions besides the Lutheran (Hartmut Gericke, Tarabo Report of 1968).

[66] 'Whether [in the early years of mission work] a dialogue took place on a broad basis between the heathen and the Christians, no one can remember. Tackling the problems of modern times was not done within the framework of the Church' writes a missionary from personal experience (Juergen Trantow, Report from Tiria of 1975). Attempts to make up for this are made, for instance, by the (inter-denominational) Melanesian Institute for Pastoral and Socio-Economic Service. It is part of the history of the Mission and the Church in the Highlands, for the Institute is located in Goroka.

[67] Len A. Tscharke, Report from Jalibu of 1956.

[68] 'Today' refers to 1958; '20 or 30 years earlier' refers to the mid-1920s and the 1930s.

[69] W. Bergmann, X, 13.

[70] On his flight to Wabi in 1948, Bergmann had the satisfaction of seeing areas which he had already got to know on foot on the great expedition in 1934. So he returned to where he had started.

[71] Finintugu is a particularly clear example to show that the establishment of a central station could not automatically be equated with a pioneer mission. The area of Finintugu was one of the Highlands areas that came into early contact with Christianity; the evangelist station at Rihona is part of this area. The establishment of Finintugu can perhaps be interpreted as an attempt to find forms of intensive congregational life in cooperation between expatriate and New Guinean church workers both from coastal and local circuits, over and beyond the phase of baptismal preparation.

[72] 'Various other villages also asked for evangelists,but we had to tell them that we didn't have any at the moment. One of these villages was called Osena. When we arrived at this village, the village elders insisted that we leave an evangelist behind. When we refused their request, one of the chiefs pressed 8 shillings and 6 pence into my hand, saying: "We would like to buy an evangelist"' (A. Frerichs, Account of a Journey of 23 November 1950 from the Raipinka circuit). Such, admittedly, was not an everyday occurrence, but it makes plain how much in demand evangelists generally were.

[73] Among the special events of church life in the Highlands were annual visits by delegations from the coastal circuits. Their primary aim was to maintain contact with their evangelists and teachers in the Highlands.

[74] W. Bergmann, IX, 51.

[75] Resolution of the Highlands Conference of August 19, 1961 in Monono, and adopted at the General Synod of October 11-14, 1962, in Boana (see Document 3 appended to this chapter).

[76] According to the files of the Mission Archives in Neuendettelsau, Pastor Rungwo (Hagen District), Pastor Kaman Fungkepa (Chimbu), Pastor Enareki Kopai (Goroka) were the first New Guinean district presidents.

[77] Onerunka for the Goroka District, Kewamugl for the Chimbu District, and Kentagl for the Hagen District.

[78] These had been preceded by English schools since 1952.

[79] Wilhelm Fugmann, *Mambu Jeremiah* (Neuendettelsau: Freimund-Verlag, 1977), 55.

[80] A list may make clear the origin of the church coworkers. It comes from the Wabi Circuit one of the last pioneer areas, and dates from 1964. From the coastal regions: Biliau, 2 evangelists: Bukawa, 6 evangelists; Kalasa, 8 evangelists; Lae, 5 evangelists; Malalo, 1 evangelist; making 22 in all. From the Highlands Circuit, Alkena, Asaroka, Monono, 1 evangelist each; Ega, 8 evangelists; Kerowagi, 8 evangelists; Ogelbeng, 4 evangelists; making a total of 23. The number from the Highlands and from the coast is roughly the same.

[81] The highest number of evangelists in my research was 800 for the year 1935, that is, for the pre-war period (see E. Schnabel, *Der Missionar und seine Gehilfen* (Neuendettelsau: Freimund-Verlag, 1936), 3. And for the post-war period, 1,400 in 1962 (see G. Vicedom, *Junge Kirche in Neuguinea* [Stuttgart: Evang. Missionsverlag, 1962], 50). The latter's English original is *Church and People in New Guinea*. World Christian Books (London: Lutterworth Press, 1961).

[82] Sadly there are only very few records of the financial side of the evangelists' work. At any rate, payment by the home congregation worked only in a limited fashion; on the other hand, the host areas hardly had any funds to speak of. Of the year 1957, Hans Wagner reports as follows: 'The evangelists let it be known that they could no longer manage on their annual salary received from general church funds (equals approximately DM 100 a year) because of steadily rising prices

and costly living conditions. Whereas they used to be able through bargaining to get a small pig in return for a bush knife or some valuable shells, they would have to pay DM 50 to 100 for it today. A tin of fish costs DM 1.80, which isn't even enough for a family' (H. Wagner, *Die Ernte ist gross*, 15). It is difficult to figure out the exact value of DM 100 in current currency, but that is not so important. What H. Wagner's report points out very clearly is the relation between salaries and some essential goods. W. Bergmann (VII, 15) also mentions unpleasant disagreements over pay. Another statistic which speaks for itself: the salary for pastors in 1967 was $20 Australian, and for the evangelists $5 (H. Gericke, Report from Tarabo, 1967); and it may safely be assumed that even these amounts were not paid everywhere.

[83] Samples of the proportion of illiterate evangelists: Banz 1958, 60%; Asaroka 1961, 120 out of 158; Agotu 1966, 22 out of 37. Nevertheless, these men must have worked satisfactorily, for the 1963 District Conference of Mount Hagen expressly recommended: 'However, new circuits can still use "uneducated" evangelists'.

[84] However, this dramatic upward curve flattened out considerably in the 1960s. The figures are taken from the reports on Asaroka from the listed years, mainly written by R. Goldhardt.

[85] W. Bergmann, IX, 66.

[86] Werner Jacobsen, Report from Asaroka, 1963.

Documentation

Document 1

The Superintendents
Lutheran Missions
Finschhafen & Madang

Rabaul, 3/8/33

Dear Brothers,
The Administrator was at Mt Hagen roughly two weeks ago. The number of natives he saw there made a great impression on him, and their friendliness and openness quite surprised him. He asked me to see to it that one of our missionaries be stationed there as soon as possible. The Administration will be going away again from there for the time being, for there is no gold there, and so they have no reason to stay, but the natives there have shown themselves to be so open, and will sorely miss the whites when they go, so that he would be very pleased if we could relieve his officials there with one missionary.

The area I am talking about is in the Madang administrative district. That is definite.

The area on the Upper Purari and on the upper course of the Ramu is also part, geographically speaking, of the Madang district, but it has been made part of the Morobe district for administrative purposes on account of the gold deposits there.

I shall, I hope, have the opportunity to discuss this question with you. The Administrator is really very keen to have the Lutheran Mission there, although he personally is a Catholic.

Yours sincerely,
O(tto) T(heile)

(Translated from German)

Document 2

TERRITORY OF NEW GUINEA

The Superintendent
Lutheran Mission
FINSCHHAFEN

C.A. 1601/6
Central Administration
RABAUL, May 20, 1936

Reverend Sir,

As a result of the recent disorders in the uncontrolled areas of the Territory, it has been decided, after serious consideration, that the peace of such areas is seriously endangered by the presence of natives from other districts who are living in places where no Europeans reside, and who visit villages unaccompanied by Europeans.

In the interest of the native inhabitants of such areas, the requirements of the Administration in bringing them under control, and the administration of justice generally, the Regulations under the Native Administration Ordinance have been amended to make it illegal for natives, not being natives of such areas, to visit villages in uncontrolled areas unless accompanied by a European, or to reside in any place within an uncontrolled area, excepting where the European in charge of them resides. The amendment will be published in the next issue of the New Guinea Gazette and will come into effect on August 1, 1936. As this measure will affect natives engaged in mission work in an uncontrolled area in places where no European missionary resides, it is desired that you will cause to be withdrawn from such places, within the period of two months allowed by the new Regulation, any members of your native staff affected by the amendment, and further that you will instruct your members that henceforth no native, who is not a native of the area, is to be permitted to visit villages in an uncontrolled area, unaccompanied by the European in charge of him.

I deeply regret that the necessity has arisen for this provision, but I feel confident that, after due consideration, the members of your Mission will appreciate the position, and will facilitate the withdrawals required. Your attention is drawn to Section 9 of the Uncontrolled Areas Ordinance 1925-1935.

Yours faithfully,
(signed) W. Ramsay McNicoll
ADMINISTRATOR

(Original in English)

Document 3

HIGHLANDS DISTRICT REORGANIZATION PROPOSAL

Our church order par. III, 13 says:

'As soon as there is an adequate number of Christians in a group of organized circuits, a separate district may be established according to the principles of this action.'

WHEREAS in our Highlands District the population has reached the following figures (1960 statistics):

the present	Eastern Highlands District	307,323
	Western Highlands District	160,500
	Southern Highlands District	37,000
	Total population	504,823

and
WHEREAS the Highlands District has more than double the population of the three coastal districts together:

Kate District	99,895
Jabem District	78,873
Madang District	60,934
Total population	239,702

and
WHEREAS now the total number of Christians living in the Highlands is 68,742 and the number of Catechumens in 1960 was 12,516 and a steady increase of Christians can be expected, and

WHEREAS the Highlands District is scattered over a very large area over 250 miles in length, which makes the administration, travelling, visiting, and supervision very difficult and expensive, and

WHEREAS it would be a big help for the Missionaries of a District, if they could meet from time to time to discuss their work and their problems, and

WHEREAS the Annual Highlands Conference is steadily growing and extending, and causes a lot of transportation troubles and increasing expenses, and

WHEREAS during the Highlands Conference the Native Delegates often do not come to the point where they are able to discuss their special and local problems, and

WHEREAS our New Guineans are supposed to grow into an indigenous church — which is very hard for them — as long as the Highlands District is so large, and

WHEREAS our New Guinean Elders, Pastors, Teachers and Evangelists themselves want to grow together on a higher than circuit level, and

WHEREAS all the New Guinean Churchworkers need better supervision on a higher than circuit level, and

WHEREAS the church order II, 4 says:
'The District exercises control over all congregational circuits and is responsible for the functioning of the church order
a) It supervises the training and stationing of the teachers
b) It supervises the training and stationing of the pastors
c) The District is supervisory authority over the schools
d) It seeks to eliminate community evils (home mission)
e) It assists needy circuits and congregations
f) It assists a mission district with men and means
g) It has the right of discipline over the pastors in connection with the respective circuits and congregations,'

and
WHEREAS these supervisory duties cannot be fulfilled by such a loosely organized big church body, as our present Highlands district represents, and

WHEREAS the fifteenth Annual Field Conference transferred the matter of dividing the Highlands District to this conference for further discussions and recommendations

BE IT RESOLVED that we recommend to our next Field Conference the following:

The 1961 Highlands Conference at Monono recommends that the Highlands District should be divided into
three Districts:

A. EASTERN HIGHLANDS DISTRICT: consisting of the following circuits: Asaroka, Agotu, Ponampa, Raipinka, Rongo, Tarabo and Wonenara. The population of this District would be 169,000 (1960 statistics).

B. CENTRAL HIGHLANDS DISTRICT: consisting of the following circuits: Ega, Karepa, Kerowagi, Monono, Nomane, Omkolai and Sumburu. The population of this District would be 168,000.

C. WESTERN HIGHLANDS DISTRICT: consisting of the following circuits: Alkena, Banz, Kogl, Kotna, Ogelbeng, Tiria. The population of this District would be 130,000. And as long as a separate Southern Highlands District is not established, the three circuits Jalibu, Tiripini and Wabi with a population of at least 37,000 should be connected to the Western Highlands District. The population of this District would then be 167,000 ...

This is part I of the draft, written by E. Jaeschke. It was adopted by the Highlands Conference in Monono on August 19, 1961. It was finally resolved by the Fourth Synod of the Evangelical Lutheran Church of New Guinea, at Boana, October 11-14, 1962:

62-41 *Resolved*: The Highlands District be divided into three districts as approved by the 1962 Highlands Elders Conference. These districts are to be known as:
    Hagen District
    Chimbu District
    Goroka District.

Chapter 6

Reconstruction and Consolidation

Lutheran Mission New Guinea After World War II

by John F. Kuder

War Had Ended

It was a different world that greeted new and returning missionaries after World War II. It was not only that they were greeted, not with handshakes, but with military-type salutes, especially by the younger generation. Nor was it only that accommodation was provided not by the mission guesthouse or other missionary residence; there was a 'transit camp' for civilians in Lae provided by the military. Rather, it was because there was a new spirit in the air. Contact with the tens of thousands from Japan, Australia, and the United States had opened the eyes of the people to new dimensions of living, and the people were desirous of having a share of the 'good things' which the ships had brought to their shores.

What did 'mission' mean in such a context? To determine this was to be the task of missionaries for the next decades. For Lutheran Mission the beginning was made when a group of newly-arrived missionaries met for their first interim missionary conference in Lae February 28 to March 5, 1946. The task awaiting them, and those who would join them in the following months, was thought of in terms of healing the wounds of war; re-establishing congregational worship; restoring necessary mission centres or stations; rebuilding the ruined schools, hospitals and churches; making provision for the supply service to outstations (which meant ships and boats, vehicles and a plane); and, above all, meeting the challenge of the evangelization of the large Highlands tribes, of which a promising beginning had been made prior to the outbreak of the war. How could all this be done?

Preliminary thinking and planning had been going on in the United States. The Board of Foreign Missions of the American Lutheran Church had called together a meeting of furloughing missionaries in Columbus, Ohio, to deal with matters related to a restoration of the work in New Guinea. Members of the Board, and also officers of the Church, lent their counsel to the solving of problems which arose during the discussions. When it was determined that about 100 persons, both ordained and lay, would be required to undertake the restoration of the program in New Guinea, Dr Henry Schuh, President of the ALC, advised that the Church would balk at such a request, but, if a schedule

223

Dr John Kuder, first Bishop of ELCONG 1956-1973.

Dr Theodore Fricke, former Executive Secretary of ALC.

were drawn up requesting a certain number for each of several years, the request would receive favourable consideration. This advice was followed, and proved to be good.

Dr Schuh had another suggestion. The war had caused great property destruction, but an appeal could be made to the Church for young people to volunteer for two years' service as 'mission builders'. Again this advice was followed, and in due course a group of young men together with four older and experienced men were ready to begin the task of reconstruction. At the same time, the American Lutheran Church initiated a reconstruction appeal to cover the costs of restoring the properties destroyed during the war.

The Board of Foreign Mission also chose Dr Theodore Fricke as executive secretary to succeed Dr Richard Taeuber, who was retiring after years of service as secretary, first for the Iowa Synod and then for the American Lutheran Church's Board. The Board also determined to send Dr Fricke as a special commissioner to establish contact with the leaders and congregations of the United Evangelical Lutheran Church in Australia, and, together with

224

representatives of that Church, to negotiate with Australian government authorities the return of missionaries to New Guinea. Dr Fricke was also to proceed to New Guinea with the Revd John Kuder[1] to make an overall survey and to appraise the needs of the field.

In Australia, interest in the restoration of the work was high. Australian Lutherans had been involved in the New Guinea mission from its beginning, both with financial contributions and numbers of workers, especially for the lay tasks of the Mission. And at the time when German missionaries were interned and their families evacuated to Australia, Lutheran families generously opened their homes to receive the families until such time as the families could be reunited. Between the wars, the Australian Church had selected a Board of Missions to direct its participation in the New Guinea work, with Dr Otto F. Theile of Brisbane as its executive secretary. Dr Theile also represented the German mission society and the American Lutheran Church Board in handling financial matters and in negotiating with the Australian administrative departments. As a result, when World War II broke out, the missions were not treated as 'enemy' institutions, and so were not subject to the 'Trading with the Enemy Act'. Dr Theile did not live to see the actual resumption of the work. He died a few days before Fricke and Kuder left Brisbane for New Guinea on September 7, 1945.

The situation in Germany was uncertain. Most of the German missionaries who were not on extended furloughs in Germany were in internment in Australia. The return of German missionaries to their work in New Guinea depended on what the policy of the Australian government would be. The missionaries had used the time of their internment to review and revaluate their work in New Guinea, and to consider what the future might hold for them if they were permitted to return.

Neuendettelsau *Missionsseminar* had continued to function, and was ready to train additional personnel as needed. Although the Neuendettelsau Mission was not an official organ of the Evangelical Lutheran Church in Bavaria, it enjoyed entree to many of its congregations, and had developed a loyal and interested constituency supporting the work. Because of the post-war economic situation, support for the work could not be great; but, as the country recovered from the effects of the war, both additional missionaries and material support could be expected. Through the mediation of the UELCA leaders, interviews were arranged with Australian government

officials for the re-entry of missionaries. The Australian government was favourable to the request, and Dr Fricke was able to telegraph the ALC mission office in Columbus: DOORS OPEN SEND MEN. In the meantime, Kuder had been able to proceed to Australia, and then joined Dr Fricke in Brisbane to help prepare for the return to New Guinea. They left Brisbane on September 7, and, after a stopover in Townsville, arrived in Lae the following day.

A New Beginning

Among those who welcomed the two mission representatives was Major Horace Niall, administrative officer for the Morobe District. He was very interested in the restoration of the Mission in his district, and in the months that followed was helpful in facilitating the work of restoration. At his suggestion, Fricke and Kuder decided to attend the Sunday service of the war-time village of Labu, some miles inland from Lae, for which Major Niall arranged transport. What a service it was! Instead of a disorganized, confused people, it was a congregation of some 200 people who had brought their children for baptism. The service was led by Pastor

Pre-war aerial view of Lae.

Pastor Philemon (Lae).

Philemon according to the Jabem liturgy, and he also preached the sermon and administered the Sacrament of Baptism.

In the weeks that followed, Fricke was able to see many evidences of a functioning church. Although not every place had overcome the effects of the war to the same degree as the congregations in and around Lae had done, everywhere there was a welcome and a desire expressed for resumption of the Mission's work.

Shortly after the arrival of Fricke and Kuder in Lae, they were informed that a representative of the United States Army Surplus would be in Finschhafen. So they proceeded to Finschhafen, where they were able to negotiate the purchase of a large amount of building materials and supplies. Among the purchases were the fully-operative 119th Station hospital with 250 beds, plus supplies and equipment for another 250-bed hospital; two fully-equipped mobile workshops and radio communication equipment; and a number of large warehouses built of Australian hardwoods. These and many more were available to the reconstruction crew when they arrived to begin the rebuilding of schools, churches, and homes. The 119th

Station hospital at Buangi/Finschhafen was ready for Dr Theodore Braun when he and his nursing staff arrived to resume the Mission's medical service.

Finschhafen had been the pre-war headquarters of the German Neuendettelsau Mission and was much larger than the American Madang Mission. It was felt, therefore, that people of this part of the Lutheran work should be consulted as to their willingness to receive the new Australian and American missionaries needed to replace the German missionaries whose return was at this time still uncertain. Dr Fricke had been authorized by the Commission on Younger Churches and Orphaned Missions (CYCOM) of the Lutheran World Federation (LWF) to represent it in negotiations with the people. Dr Fricke, at a large meeting of church leaders at nearby Heldsbach, presented the plans which had been formulated for the restoration of the work. Would this be acceptable to the people? The response was an immediate acceptance of the proposals. But this was an elite group. What would be the response of the people as a whole?

A good indication of their response would be their willingness to resume their evangelistic responsibility, especially for the Central Highlands which had begun in 1934. With the repeal of the Uncontrolled Area Regulations, the work could proceed. There were many 'open doors' through contacts which had been made with the 'people beyond' before the war. However, during the war most of the coastal evangelists had returned to their home villages, either on their own volition or because of government orders. There they had become reestablished, having built houses, having opportunity to send their children to better schools than those in the newer areas, and having tasted something of the new era ushered in by the tens of thousands of foreign troops with their equipment and mountains of supplies. Would they now be willing to face again the hardships of the newer areas among heathen tribes?

The first response came from Sio. Sio had been evangelized by workers from Finschhafen together with Michael Stolz, the Sio missionary. Besides accepting the Gospel and the Christian way, they had also carried the Gospel to their long-time trading partners on the Rai Coast. The war had interrupted the work, but now the congregation wished to send workers to continue what had been begun in previous years. Soon others were ready to follow the example; many of the former mission areas were again occupied, and new contacts made.

Dr Fricke was able to visit the major centres of the work, both in the coastal areas and also in the Central Highlands. After completing his survey, he left for a short visit to acquaint the Australian church leaders with his findings. From there he went to Manila to complete the negotiations with the American Army Surplus for the purchase of the supplies and equipment at Finschhafen.[2]

Missionaries Arrive

Soon missionaries began to come back. First to arrive were Australians of the pre-war staff. Americans followed soon after. By the end of February 1946, it was possible to hold the first (interim) post-war missionary conference. The meetings were held at the Civilian Transit Camp at Lae. Present were: Leonard Behrendorff, August Bertelsmeier, Roland Brandt (new), Herbert Enser, Albert Frerichs, Paul Freyberg, Emil Hannemann, Martin Heist (new), Martin Helbig, Fred Scherle (new), Carl Schneuker (new), and John Kuder.[3] On this small band rested the responsibility, as representatives of their home churches, for setting in motion the restoration of the two missions: Lutheran Mission Madang, and Lutheran Mission Finschhafen. Later the two Missions were to become Lutheran Mission New Guinea (LMNG), destined to grow into one of the largest Protestant missions in the world.

One of the first steps was to arrange the stationing of staff, both of those already arrived and of those expected in the near future. For 32 positions, 30 missionaries, both lay and ordained, were designated. This may seem a good coverage, but it was actually a very thin line. Edward Pietz, for example, was given responsibility for three mission stations more than 40 miles apart, plus temporary responsibility for two more! Martin Helbig was assigned to the Heldsbach school and also to oversight of the Kate congregations. But it was a beginning; and, as additional people arrived, it was possible to occupy more and more stations.

While the interim conference was in

Missionary Martin Helbig.

session, a communication was received from the Secretary of the Department of External Territories, Mr J.R. Halligan, Canberra, Australia, regarding the return of German missionaries who had been in the work prior to the outbreak of the war in 1941 (see Documentation). We were thankful that the former German missionaries might return. It was hoped that this would be the case after the peace treaty was signed, but Australia had acted on its own even before that. This action was seen as an indication of a favourable attitude toward mission work in New Guinea, as well as a recognition of what had been done by mission workers in the past. As far as this writer is aware, Australia was the first of all the colonial powers to permit workers from former enemy countries to return to their colonies or trusteeships. This decision meant that many more stations could be occupied and other positions filled by persons experienced in the work, persons who had a knowledge of the people, knew their languages, and were aware of the past history of the work.

True to its promise, the Australian government permitted the majority of the

227

former German missionaries to return. The 1947 Field Conference, the first regular field conference, was able to record the names of nine members of the German pre-war staff. Each year the number increased, so that by the 1952 Field Conference nearly all the pre-war German staff members had returned to the work. That year's minutes also contain the names of the first members of the new generation of Neuendettelsau graduates, and eight new Australian names, four of them from the latest seminary graduating class. The total attendance of regular staff had by this time increased to 68. Because of the increased staff, the minutes could also include the names of four new post-war Highlands stations: Omkolai (1948), Monono (1949), Banz (1950), and Tarabo (1950).

New Mission Headquarters

Since the first Neuendettelsau missionary, Johann Flierl, had landed there in 1886, Finschhafen had been a natural location for mission headquarters. It was a good centre from which to reach out both along the coast and into the hinterland. The properties formerly owned by the government and by private owners were sold to the Mission, and these enabled the Neuendettelsau Mission to establish Finschhafen as its centre of operations.

The Rhenish Mission established its work farther west at the district centre of Madang. Madang, likewise, proved to be a good place for developing the work along the coast, on adjacent islands, and inland.

The pre-war Lae had become important because it was the centre for supplying the goldfields from its good airstrip. With the retreat of the Japanese forces from the area and its reoccupation by Australian and American troops, Lae had become an important military supply centre for the Allied advance toward the Philippines and then Japan. With the resumption of civilian activity, Lae now became an important business centre. At the time of this writing, the population is said to be 60,000, making it the largest urban centre in PNG apart from the capital, Port Moresby. Though Lae's later expansion into a most vital administrative and educational centre was not yet foreseen at the time of the First Field Conference in 1947, nevertheless the Conference decided to

establish its new headquarters there.[4] In the light of later events, it appears to have been the right move. However, the move away from Finschhafen and Madang to a degree reduced the importance these centres had enjoyed as the starting-places of the Christian advance. There, to a large extent, the patterns for evangelism methods, educational policies, and church and congregation building had been established. Finschhafen and Madang continued to exert influence on the church (they have not been abandoned), while Lae has served to draw the various sections together — not only Finschhafen and Madang, but also the newer centres in the Highlands and in the outlying coastal islands. For many years, Lae also has continued to be the port of entry for Lutheran and other missionaries, as well as for the general European population living in the northern part of the country.

Mission in Commercial Activities?

It all began very simply: Missionaries bartered with the local people for food. With the passing of time, the local people's wants increased, and the only way to satisfy those wants was to obtain supplies through the missionaries; 'other' trade stores were few and far between, while the mission stations were situated among the people, and received regular shipments of supplies with the *M.V. Rheno-Westphalia*, or the *M.V. Bavaria*, or the launch *Iowa*. Could they not also bring supplies for the local people? They could; and, over the years, the trading increased so that missionaries spent many hours in their trade stores buying and selling. This was not an entirely ill-spent time; when people came from many villages, some from quite a distance, to barter for supplies, quite often they were willing to sit and talk and listen. So the missionary was able to see more people more often than would have been the case with his visits to the villages in the area of his work. But some missionaries were troubled: Was it really a legitimate activity to be engaged in 'business'?

This doubt was expressed again after the war, and, because of opposition of some, no trade stores were opened for some time. However, this decision was opposed by the New Guinea people themselves. They saw in this action a lack of willingness on the missionaries' part to render what the people considered a vital service to them. Meanwhile, traders arrived, some of them with the aim of making a quick profit, and their selling prices were adjusted accordingly. The Mission made some profit as well, but such profits did not benefit any missionary, but were made to aid the Mission's medical and educational programs. In view of these circumstances, it was decided to reopen trade stores, especially at the outstations where such stores were the only source of supplies for the people. [5] One of the results or outgrowths of the post-war trading was the founding of a trading company — sponsored by the Mission, but independent from it — in which New Guineans invested capital and shared in the operation. It bore the name *Native Marketing and Supply Service* (NAMASU) (see ch 18).

Missionary Willy Flierl, pre-war Superintendent Lutheran Mission Finschhafen.

Toward a Unified Mission

Prior to the outbreak of the war, cooperation between the two mission bodies, Lutheran Mission Finschhafen and Lutheran Mission Madang, consisted mostly in sharing of information, sending of representatives to each other's field conference, consultation regarding policies and joint enterprises in the advance into the Central Highlands. Finschhafen also accepted Madang missionary children into its school at Sattelberg (for children of German-speaking missionaries); Sattelberg health station was also available for Madang missionaries convalescing after illness. Through these contacts, the staff of the two missions learnt to know each other and to appreciate each other's work.

For a time after World War I, the two missions had been combined in one operation as a joint Australian/American enterprise. [6] Though this did not last, experience had shown that joint operation was possible, and when the situation after World War II called for a joint operation, it was the right thing to treat the two mission fields as one unit. Cooperative mission efforts are no novelty today, but they were rarer in former years. In New Guinea, the Lutherans were pioneering in this area. Not least of the factors making for joint action was the fact that Lutherans have a common confessional basis.

To begin with, the pre-war German missionaries were still in Australia, and the date of their release and arrival in New Guinea was still uncertain, yet the staffing of the field and the occupation of vacant posts was an urgent matter. The only missionaries available were Australians and Americans. Later, when German missionaries arrived on the field, every attempt was made to restation them at their old posts or, at least, where they were familiar with the languages. It was at this point that Wm Flierl, leader of the German group and former superintendent of the Finschhafen field, proposed that American missionaries who had occupied Finschhafen stations should not be removed to make way for returning German missionaries. This was a generous gesture and evidence of the understanding for a joint operation.

There were other practical advantages to such an operation. Pre-war, each of the two missions had maintained separate staffs, separate supply houses, separate shipping, separate schools for missionaries' children, separate budgets, and separate conferences. With a joint operation, many of these activities could be combined. For example, although there were still two legal corporations, 'Finschhafen' and 'Madang' with two separate budgets, with two separate origins (American Lutheran Church and Lutheran World Federation), they could be administered by a single staff. Thus, the superintendent, treasurer, secretary, and business manager of Lutheran Mission Finschhafen were also officers of Lutheran Mission Madang.

There were additional considerations favouring a joint operation. As Lutherans, the missionaries shared a common Confession and tradition. There was also an historical tie in that some of the Australian and American missionaries came from church organizations which had been supplied with pastors from the same training institution from which the first German New Guinea missionaries had come. An additional factor was the ability of most of the German missionaries to speak and write a good English. All this made communication possible, and enabled common decisions to be reached.

Though these considerations may have seemed supportive to the idea of a joint operation to the workers on the field, this may not have been the case with the supporting churches and their mission boards. Neuendettelsau may well have claimed founders' rights for having begun the Finschhafen work, developed its policies, and engaged a large supporting constituency in congregations throughout Bavaria and in other parts of Germany. The American Lutheran Church might have advanced the consideration that it had acquired the rights of the Rhenish Mission in Madang, and had also won an interested and supportive constituency, particularly in the Women's Missionary Federation. Would there then not be a resulting sense of loss if it were no longer possible to speak of 'our' Mission in the same sense as had been the case previously?

If such sentiments arose, no hint of them reached the field staff in a formal way. The joint operation began through a provisional organization, with the structures of Finschhafen and Madang remaining more or less intact, with finance for Madang coming from America, and for Finschhafen from the Lutheran World Federation as trustee for Neuendettelsau's interests. The UELCA in Australia supported both divisions.

But there were several differences, chief among them being the stationing of personnel. New people, whether they came from Germany, Australia, or America, were stationed where they were needed, and as the individual's qualifications fitted him/her for a particular position; it was not necessary to consider a German, Australian, or American/Canadian sphere of influence. So, a *de facto* situation
230

developed into a good working arrangement with the various elements having a conviction of being part and parcel of a common enterprise.

However, in one area there were some lingering doubts. The Commission on Younger Churches and Orphaned Missions (CYCOM), the Lutheran World Federation's agency dealing with mission relationships, became aware of criticism of its dealings regarding the German New Guinea mission. Suggestions of 'Lutheran imperialism' were voiced by people from other churches: that Americans were taking the opportunity resulting from the impoverished state of Germany to 'take over' a German mission. To clarify this matter was an important item on the agenda for Dr Frederik Schiotz, President of the ALC and Secretary of CYCOM, when he attended the Fourth Annual Field Conference in Madang in February 1950. Dr Schiotz sought assurance that what was envisaged was, in fact, a joint operation, and not, as had been rumoured, an American takeover of the Neuendettelsau Finschhafen Mission. After a lengthy discussion, in which many members participated, Dr Schiotz was convinced that the intention was indeed a joint operation. When the discussion showed this clearly, Dr Schiotz asked that a statement be drawn up expressing the Conference's position. The statement, drawn up by representatives of the different churches, reads as follows:

> Since the war, we on the field as well as the home churches have seen the necessity of continuing this mission as one unified organization. In spite of the fact that the home bodies have in principle agreed to maintain this as a unified field, we are faced with the prospect of a renewed division because the orphaned missions are held in trusteeship until such time as the original societies will be able to resume responsibility and ownership. If this occurs after the lapse of some time, the original owners will, in consideration of their constituencies, be under strong pressure to take them over again as separate units, or at least as separate spheres of influence, which in our case will inevitably lead to the separation of the unified field.
>
> We would remind the home churches of the fact that a similar situation obtained after World War I. At that time the home churches also had agreed to one organization, but they insisted upon separate spheres of interest and dual control. In spite of efforts on the part of the field to maintain unity, the situation led to a division of the field

which was decided upon by the home bodies. Grave consequences resulted in the native church. Missionaries who had gained the confidence of their congregations were uprooted for reasons the natives could not understand, and with which they could not concur. Those missionaries were placed into areas where they did not know the language and had to win anew the confidence of a native people.

Today such a separation would be made more detrimental than it was then. The staff is intermingled to a much greater extent. Furthermore, the native church has assumed a greater voice in the stationing of missionaries, and there is a closer relationship between the native church and the mission personnel. Therefore, a separation of the mission would be almost tantamount to a separation of the church. The critical judgement of the natives having much increased, they would regard such a course as the opposite of what we for years have tried to impress upon them in regard to inter-tribal cooperation and unity. It would amount to a scandal and be injurious to the developing Church.

Because of the foregoing reasons, we, the united staff of Lutheran Mission New Guinea, appeal to the representatives of our home churches to forestall any such development. We would request the home Churches to find ways and means of determining now our future status so that we can continue organizing our work on the basis we have started.

The Conference then went on to suggest how such a joint operation might be structured and financed:

The entire area formerly considered to be the sphere of work of Lutheran Mission Madang and Lutheran Mission Finschhafen, and any additional areas where work may be undertaken in New Guinea and adjacent islands, be considered the unified field of Lutheran Mission New Guinea.

The administration of this field, within the limits set by the constitution, to be vested in the field conference and its officers, and later to be transferred to the indigenous Lutheran Church in ever greater measure.

In all matters of mission policy and method, the conference to look for advice and suggestions to the home Boards.

The several home Churches to be responsible for the private cash salaries of such members of the white staff as have been sent by them to the field, and to be entirely responsible for them as soon as they leave the field for furlough or retirement. This also to include the care for children when they leave the field.

All other costs of maintaining the mission on the field with all its enterprises be met out of a common treasury into which all contributions of the home Churches are paid. The field authorities to render regular account to the home Board on the status of the work and on monetary disbursements and to submit to them their future budgets.

The sending of new personnel to the field to be a matter of negotiation between the field conference and the respective home Board. If, however, a home Board feels that its monetary contribution is not large enough to warrant increase of its personnel on the field, such personnel may be adopted by one of the other home Boards.

We feel that some such arrangements would help us maintain a unified field and Church, and at the same time assure us the continued support of all home Churches.[7]

The statement was adopted by the unanimous vote of all voting members present. Dr Schiotz did not comment on the individual paragraphs of the statement, but declared himself satisfied that the desire for a unified mission was the wish of all sections of the staff. To formalize the organization of the unified field and to govern its operation, a Mission Constitution was proposed at the Second Field Conference in 1948. The original proposal was further discussed at the two succeeding conferences, and adopted in its final form at the 1953 Field Conference.[8]

It might be supposed that this decision would not be entirely welcome to the home constituencies, especially to the congregations in Germany which had supported the work from the beginning. In spite of such possible considerations, the field staff's decision was accepted, and arrangements were worked out for the ongoing work in personnel and funds. As Germany recovered after the war, the congregations increased their support of the work. In the meantime, the Lutheran World Federation continued its support, but, as the German contributions increased, LWF funds were designated for other areas of work.

The decision to function as one mission rather than as two cooperating missions had another favourable aspect. It might be anticipated that the staff, coming from different churches with differing traditions and experiences, would have difficulty in

Dr G. Vicedom, pre-war missionary, greeted by friends (1950).

communicating with one another, and individuals with the group as a whole. Of course, there were differences. Many of the German missionaries had been trained by Christian Keysser in the Neuendettelsau *Missions-seminar*, and were aware of Keysser's missionary approach in dealing with the native communities. Americans, on the other hand, came from training institutions which emphasized individual pastoral methods based on the concept of individual responsibility, individual freedom, individual decision, individual conversion. Their approach to the New Guinea situation would be influenced by this type of training.

In this situation, the annual field conferences, as well as the district conferences, proved to be invaluable in developing common understanding and actions. For the field conferences, each missionary prepared a report of his work, outlining accomplishments as well as the difficulties and problems which he had encountered. When these reports were tabled, the discussions afforded an opportunity for exchange of ideas and led to the formulation of policies and harmonious actions. In addition,

papers were read at each field conference on subjects pertinent to the work. A quick glance at some of the titles reveals a wide scope of subjects reviewed: Development of a Native Clergy; Polygamy and Divorce; Problems of the Second Generation of Christians; Church Discipline; True Understanding of the Sacraments; Church and State; Law and Gospel; More Edifying Preaching; Stewardship; Youth Work; and many more. The preparation of these papers and their subsequent presentation and discussion were a kind of in-service training from which the whole staff derived much profit. [9]

A word should be said here about the support given to the field programs by the Boards of the supporting churches. Early in the post-war era, Board secretaries or other Board representatives were sent out to visit the field. They came from Australia, Germany, Canada, and the United States. Although the supporting churches and Boards did not attempt to dictate policies or make decisions, they did make many constructive suggestions which proved profitable for the work. The fact that these counsellors — for such they were — spoke not

232

to one group, but to the multi-national assembly of missionaries, was a positive contribution toward common understanding and action.

Then, too, many of the missionaries in the now-united Mission had known each other before the war. They formed the nucleus of the fellowship, sharing their knowledge and experience with those who came after them. Some of the American missionaries, for example, had served in the Finschhafen field in the interim following World War I; then, when the American Lutheran Church assumed support of the Madang area, Americans and some Australians transferred to Madang. Since many of them were bilingual, they formed a bridge between the two former separate groups. [10]

Partners in Mission
1. *The Australian Lutheran Mission*

Perhaps this is the place to refer to a sister Lutheran mission established already prior to World War II. Australia had two general Lutheran church bodies prior to 1966: The Evangelical Lutheran Church of Australia (ELCA), and the United Evangelical Lutheran Church in Australia (UELCA). Although the two churches were not in official fellowship, they were, in part, descendants of the same original migrations from Germany. There was communication between the two churches, and negotiations leading to a possible reunion. Each was aware of the other's interests and activities. The members of the UELCA were involved in the New Guinea mission from its very beginning in 1886, providing financial aid and sending personnel for the work. When the UELCA was formed after World War I, this support continued on a much larger scale. These events and subsequent developments were followed with interest by the leaders and congregations of the ELCA, and this led to a desire to have a part in the evangelization of New Guinea. In 1936, the ELCA was offered Finschhafen's mission station in the Siassi group of islands off the north-east coast. With Siassi as a base, the Australians would have an opportunity to become familiar with New Guinea conditions and also to prepare local evangelists for their future new work. The offer was accepted, and work was taken up at Siassi the same year under the name 'Australian Lutheran Mission' (ALM). After the war, a new pioneer work was started among the people in the previously-unreached Menyamya area, west of the Wau/Bulolo goldfields. This was planned to be a joint operation of ALM and LMNG. An additional station was planned for this area, but, since the population was sparse, the LMNG missionaries withdrew. ALM established other stations later on: Kwaplalim, Kapo, Concordia and Kwaikuma (see ch 7).

With the union of the two Lutheran Churches in Australia in 1966, forming the Lutheran Church of Australia, a new relationship came into being for the missions in New Guinea. To begin with, the new church in Australia found itself supporting two missions in New Guinea. It therefore resolved to recommend the merging of the two missions. As a result, all members of the staff of ALM were received as full voting members of the staff of LMNG at its 22nd Annual Field Conference in 1968. For the Siassi islands, this meant a reunion with the parent congregations along the mainland coast, for it was from these congregations that the first evangelists had gone out to the Siassi island group. The Siassi Church resolved in 1976 to merge with the Evangelical Lutheran Church of Papua New Guinea, becoming a district of that Church. The Menyamya congregations had taken this step three years earlier in 1973, becoming part of the Lae District of (then) ELCONG.

The integration of the two staffs thus took place without difficulty. Other actions were also taken to actualize its implications, such as exchange of staff between LMNG and ALM, participation in decision-making for the whole group, operation under a common budget, and additional shipping service. The addition of the ALM staff meant an increase in the Australian membership of LMNG in relationship to American and German personnel. This situation was reflected in the response of the Lutheran Church of Australia to the work at its Second General Synod in 1968. Of a total budget of $551,399, the sum of $160,000 (29%) was designated for work in New Guinea. In the years following, support for the work, both in personnel and finances, continued at an increasing level.

2. New Guinea Lutheran Mission

A reinforcement of a somewhat different character was the coming of missionaries of the Lutheran Church-Missouri Synod from the United States. Shortly after the restoration of mission work in New Guinea, the Revd Harold Freund of the Australian Lutheran Mission approached officials of LMNG inquiring about the possibility of ALM beginning a mission outreach in partnership with the Lutheran Church-Missouri Synod. After some discussion, the area west of the Mt Hagen massif was agreed upon as a possible place for a new mission to be established. The inhabitants of this area were known as Enga. They had contacts with the tribes east of Mt Hagen, and had visited Ogelbeng station. A fomer Ogelbeng schoolboy, Aije, who later became a member of the native constabulary, had some influence with the Enga people and had a verbal agreement with them about 'his' mission beginning work among them. So the preliminary contacts had already been made, and proved to be the entree into the Enga area and the beginning of mission work among them.

In 1948, Dr O.H. Schmidt, Mission Director of the Lutheran Church-Missouri Synod (LC-MS) arrived in Lae to arrange for the beginning of their Mission in partnership with ALM, and was welcomed by the members of LMNG. Dr Schmidt was desirous of securing New Guinea evangelists to assist in their new work, and arrangements were made for him to visit the LMNG schools at Hopoi and Heldsbach where Dr Schmidt appealed to the graduating students for some to volunteer for the new enterprise.

While Dr Schmidt was still in Lae, the first two of his missionaries arrived: Willard Burce and Otto Hintze. Preparations were then made for flights to the Central Highlands where the LMNG stations Ega and Ogelbeng were visited. At Ega, Dr Schmidt could witness the first baptism in the Chimbu area. The date was October 31, 1948, Reformation Sunday. Others with Dr Schmidt were the Revd O.E. Thiele, Executive Secretary of the Board of Foreign Missions of the Evangelical Lutheran Church of Australia, and missionaries Burce and Hintze. [11]

From Ega, Dr Schmidt and his party proceeded to Ogelbeng, the jumping-off place

234

for advancing into the new area, and from there they flew to Wabag, the government post for the Western Highlands. From Wabag it was a long day's march to Yaramanda, the site chosen for a new station. The date was November 3, 1948. Two Australian missionaries and Felix Doering from LMNG mission station Ogelbeng, together with some evangelists and local assistants, had preceded Dr Schmidt, and had erected a temporary bush house to accommodate the newcomers.

The work of what was later called the New Guinea Lutheran Mission (NGLM) developed, and more stations were opened as new personnel arrived to join the work (see ch 8). As it grew, the mission also opened schools and a hospital. In order to share its experience in the various branches of mission work, LMNG invited NGLM to send representatives to its annual field conferences where the preceding year's work was reviewed. The invitation was accepted, and NGLM representatives were present at most of the following annual conferences. From the contacts made through the conferences, there developed a desire for cooperation in various areas of work, and this resulted in NGLM's sharing in the operation and support of the Balob Teachers College at Lae, and later in the planning, building, and support of Martin Luther Seminary at Malahang, Lae. Other cooperative enterprises are the Nurses Training School at Madang, and the major printing and publishing establishment, Kristen Pres, at Nagada, Madang.

3. The Leipzig Mission

The Leipzig Mission has a long history of participation in mission in several places of the world. In 1841 it assumed support of the Danish-Halle mission on the East Coast of India. In 1893, it began work in what was then called German East Africa, now know as Tanzania. When World War II broke out, German missionaries were compelled to leave. After the cessation of hostilities, there were difficulties in the way of resumption of operations to the same degree as previously. Not least of these was the division of Germany into East and West. East Germany, as a Communist country, was not favourable to the support of Christian missions. However, there was a Leipzig-supporting constituency in West Germany, and this group became interested in supporting the work in New Guinea. The first Leipzig missionaries to arrive (in 1955) were Ernst Jaeschke, Friedrich Hoehne, and Hans Dieter Klemm. Jaeschke had served in the Leipzig Mission in Tanzania prior to World War II, and his experience there under the tutelage of the renowned missionary and student of African life, Bruno Gutmann, as well as his own observations of Christian congregational life, were a good preparation for his work in New Guinea. Hoehne served only a short time; on one of his trips through his circuit, he became ill and died before he could return to his station. Leipzig continued its support of LMNG in following years with up to 15 staff members, of whom 13 were ordained missionaries.

4. *North Elbian Evangelical Lutheran Church — Centre for World Mission and Church World Service (NMZ)*

The Leipzig Mission (West) ceased its overseas missionary operations in the early 1970s after the Protestant Churches in the Federal Republic of Germany agreed on a new structural framework for their overseas missionary and ecumenical operations. Following the 1961 integration of the International Missionary Council into the World Council of Churches, the basic idea was that each territorial church in Western Germany would establish its own Board for overseas mission integrating the historical mission societies and concentrating on particular areas of concern. Competition was to be avoided. While the Department of World Mission of the Lutheran Church in Bavaria inherited the Leipzig Mission's East Africa commitments, the North Elbian Lutheran Church took on former Leipzig Mission responsibilities in Papua New Guinea through its Centre for World Mission and Church World Service in Hamburg (in brief, NMZ).

In 1973, Hartmut Gericke and Theodor Ahrens were among the remnant of the Leipzig missionaries who transferred to NMZ, and Gisela Hamann was the first woman to be commissioned by NMZ to serve in PNG. Since then, the North Elbian congregational support of and support to the mission of the Church in PNG has been growing and deepening.

5. *Liebenzell — Evangelical Mission Manus*

Perhaps it is in place here to refer to another mission, which, although not officially connected with the Lutheran Church, has Lutheran missionaries from Germany and the United States on its staff. The Liebenzell Mission was founded in 1899, and has its headquarters in Bad Liebenzell in the state of Wuerttemberg, Germany, and also has offices in the United States and Canada. The mission is working in Liberia, Bangladesh, Taiwan, Japan, Micronesia, and Papua New Guinea. Its work in Papua New Guinea is located in the Admiralty Islands, the main island of which is Manus, where there was an American naval base during World War II.

Missionaries from Manus frequently attended the field conferences of LMNG, and a number of their children also attended the school for missionaries' children at Wau. In addition, indigenous students have attended the Balob Teachers College at Lae. Bishop Kuder also visited the work at Manus, and participated in the dedication of the Mission's town church at Lorengau. Over many years, Lutheran people from the mainland have been offered a spiritual home in the Liebenzell Mission congregations at Manus.

Outreach and Advance

When Kuder accompanied the two New Guinean representatives, Christian Gwang and Mufuanu Butik, to the Minneapolis Assembly of

Bishop Kuder with Christian Gwang (middle) and Mufuanu Butik (left), at Minneapolis 1957.

the Lutheran World Federation in 1957, at their stopover in San Francisco they visited an old Neuendettelsau graduate, Pastor Eberhard Hafermann, in hospital. [12] When he saw the two New Guineans at his bedside, he exclaimed in a voice full of emotion: 'And you had a part in the victorious march of the Gospel in New Guinea!'

Perhaps 'victorious march' is too strong a term for the remarkable advance that took place in New Guinea after the war, particularly in the Highlands. Having discussed at some length the 'apparatus' of mission, it is necessary to recall the purpose of it all. The governing Constitution states as follows: 'The object of Lutheran Mission New Guinea shall be to evangelize the inhabitants of New Guinea, gather them into congregations, and ultimately to establish an indigenous church.' The key words are 'evangelize', 'gather into congregations', and 'to establish an indigenous church'.

Evangelization of the new areas had a high priority in the Mission's post-war activity, especially in the relatively-untouched areas of the Central Highlands. Prior to World War II, a good beginning had been made in 1934: with the establishing of four stations: Raipinka in the

Eastern Highlands, Ega and Kerowagi in the Chimbu District, and Ogelbeng in the Hagen District. A fifth station was established at Asaroka near Goroka in the Eastern Highlands in 1937 (see ch 5).

These five pre-war stations were the centre from which impulses radiated, leading to the founding of new stations around the original five 'mother' stations. Mention must be made especially of Wilhelm Bergmann's part in this outreach. He was one of the founders in 1931 of the very first mission station in the Highlands, Kambaidam, and assisted in the founding of many others right through the Highlands to Wabi, the westernmost station of LMNG. Others, too, were active in the outreach: Albert Frerichs from Raipinka, Hermann Strauss from Ogelbeng, and Robert Hueter, Bergmann's successor at Ega. At Kerowagi, Herbert Hannemann was a dedicated student of the Kuman language spoken in the Chimbu area. Through the activities of these pioneers, and others from Germany, Australia, Canada, and the United States, the number of stations increased to 32, and formed a network covering the three Highlands provinces (see 1973 map).

Lutheran church at Yagusa village, Eastern Highlands.
236

In addition there were also the stations which provided auxiliary services: two secondary hospitals, one secondary school, three sub-vocational schools, four vocational schools, three automobile workshops, and an aviation hangar and workshop. As well, each mission station had a primary school staffed with indigenous teachers (some had European teachers, too).

It was not a 'victorious march', but it was a remarkable achievement, fraught with many difficulties, frustrations, disappointments — and hard work! There were also many accomplishments, and, above all, many evidences of God's Spirit at work through his Papua New Guinean workers and their European fellow-workers.

A Different Mission Approach

The Highlands necessitated, at least in part, some changes in the Mission's method of work. In the coastal areas (especially in the Kate sections, and to some degree in the Jabem area and Madang district), the mission approach to the people was based on the findings of Christian Keysser. As the first of the New Guinea missionaries to realize the communal nature of the indigenous society, Keysser determined that the Gospel approach had to be not to individuals, but to the community itself, of which the individuals were organic members. This approach was successful in the many cases where communities as a whole came under the influence of the Gospel and made a communal decision to accept it. The community decided to accept the Word of God as the basis of their communal and individual living, replacing their old pagan beliefs. As their understanding of the Word of God grew, the community agreed to the baptism of those whose understanding of the Gospel and corresponding conduct warranted it. Those first baptized would, in turn, become guides to others until, in most cases, the whole community was baptized. [13]

This could be done in the coastal areas because the communities made decisions affecting all matters of village life — including, to a large extent, matters affecting individuals within the community. When such a community became Christian, it functioned as a Christian congregation with no devastating effect on the social order. Then, too, the community was challenged by a single religious influence from without. It was a confrontation, so to speak, between *Anutu* (God) and the old pagan order, after the biblical pattern of Elijah versus the priests of Baal (1 Kings 18:21), or of Joshua appealing to the Israelite tribes: 'Choose this day whom you will serve, whether the gods your fathers served ... or the gods of the Amorites ... but as for me and my house we will serve the Lord' (Joshua 24:15).

In the Highlands, however, the situation was different; here there were influential chieftains, 'big men', with their clan retainers. Such chiefs made the decisions and exercised control; the ordinary men had little to say, and could only support their chiefs in their enterprises as ordered.

Because of this situation, the evangelists had to have the goodwill of the chiefs in order to get a hearing for the proclamation of the Gospel. If they were successful in obtaining the goodwill of the chiefs, the preaching and teaching could go on with their support, even if the chiefs themselves held back their decision for Christ and the Christian way, possibly because they were polygamists.

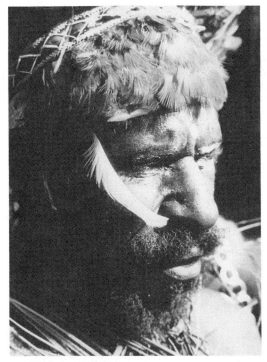

A Highlands chief.

It was not an easy situation for the evangelists, especially for those who came from the Morobe district, where Christianity was represented by a single Mission. Here in the Highlands, they were one of several approaches seeking the people's response. Perhaps it is an exaggeration, but it has been said that in one area there were twelve different mission groups at work. In another case, the Lutheran missionary reported that, after years of instruction and guidance, a community was to be baptized in a few weeks' time. Before that day of baptism arrived, an individual came to the village from a nearby town and baptized the group after telling them that the Lord was soon coming and that, if they were not baptized, they would be lost.

Papua New Guinea is in the process of becoming a pluralist society as these different approaches are made to the people — not only to pagan, unevangelized people, but also to people already baptized and members of congregations, Roman Catholic or Lutheran. The latter naturally consider themselves as the pioneers, as having 'borne the heat of the day', as having assisted in the difficult task of exploring an unknown country and of promoting reconciliation between mutually-hostile tribes, and that the later arrivals have profited from their work.

Be that as it may, the Highland chiefs faced a multiple-choice situation. They could choose whatever group seemed best to them, depending on the advantages being offered and promised. And they brought with them their followers in a kind of *cuius regio, eius religio* situation.

In spite of such difficulties experienced by the evangelists and missionaries, the Highland congregations grew. The first baptisms took place in 1948, and were followed in the succeeding decades by increasing numbers receiving the sacrament — even as many as 700 at one time.

Consolidation

The advances in the Highlands were paralleled by developments in the coastal areas. Some of the stations along the coast and in the foothills and in the Markham Valley were rather far apart. For the missionary, maintaining contact with his indigenous fellow-workers and

Church dedication at Aseki.

with the congregations required weeks of travel, often over very difficult country. For pastors, teachers, and evangelists, as well as for congregation members, visiting their missionary for consultation involved the same time and effort. The Hube tribe in the Huon Peninsula, for example, had been evangelized by indigenous workers without a resident missionary; the Sattelberg missionary could make only infrequent visits to the area. In order to support the pastors, teachers, and elders in their work of deepening the spiritual life of the congregations, as well as to render some economic help, the station of Mindik was established in the Hube area (1965). Tapen was set up for the same reason (1951). Later, Ulap Centre was split into two Circuits, and a station was established at Kabwum (1967). Between Tapen and Kaiapit, the new station of Wantoat was founded (1960), with both Kate and Jabem evangelists and pastors as well as the expatriate missionary. Ranara was a new station (1964) in the Ramu Valley near Dumpu. Mumeng station was relocated at Gurakor (1953) on the Lae-Wau road. Garaina, once an outpost of Zaka on the coast, became a full-fledged station (1961) with a resident missionary in the Upper Waria area. Bogadjim on Astrolabe Bay was relocated at Bongu (1946). Aseki (1958) and Kaintiba (1963) were new stations in the Kukukuku ranges supporting the flank of the ALM stations at Menyamya mentioned above.

To follow the Lutheran diaspora, New Guinea pastors and evangelists were stationed in distant parts of the country and in the neighbouring islands. New centres were opened in the towns and rural areas where mainland New Guinea workers were employed: in Port Moresby, Rabaul (with responsibility for New Britain and New Ireland), Wau (in connection with Katherine Lehmann school), and Bougainville. As well, a considerable number of auxiliary stations which, while not actually mission outreach, provided care for physical needs and nurture for spiritual life. From the materials purchased from the US Army Surplus, it was possible to build and equip two major hospitals: Yagaum near Madang, and Finschhafen; others were the leprosy colony and clinic at Etep near Ulap; the leprosy centre and rehabilitation centre at Asuar near the Gogol River, Madang; a secondary hospital at Wagezaring, Hube; another at Menyamya. A rather distinctive institution is Gaubin Hospital on Karkar Island off the north coast of mainland New Guinea, which is under the direction of Mr Edwin Tscharke, MBE, and Mrs Tscharke. What is especially noteworthy is the cooperation of the local people in the building of the hospital and in its maintenance. The work of the Tscharkes has caught the attention of the international medical community, and studies of the operation of the Gaubin medical program are under way to determine if some of the methods in use there can have a wider application (see ch 17).

In addition to the 'professional' medical work, mention should be made of the fact that medical help has been available to the surrounding people at nearly all the rural mission stations, as well as at some of the urban places. Some missionaries' wives, who were trained as nurses, have carried on this work as their contribution; where this was not the case, missionaries and their wives have done what they could to alleviate fevers, treat ulcers, and help care for infants. Thanks to radio, outstations were able to consult with the doctors

at the main hospital, and so provide additional help. In cases of severe emergency, a plane could be requested wherever there was a landing field in the vicinity.

The establishing of schools and the production of literature and school texts were important contributions to the people's understanding of the world and to their understanding of the Word of God. These are discussed in chapter 13.

Important roles in the work of the mission were played by the many lay persons who came either as career workers or as short-termers. This was true already in the early history of the mission, but the participation was much greater in the post-war era. In addition to the medical staff, many secular callings were represented: for example, specialists in agriculture, building, business, aviation, seamanship, accounting, and, of course, education. The post-war outreach would have been unthinkable without the help of such people, who came from Germany, Canada, the Netherlands, Australia, New Zealand, Finland, Guatemala, and the United States. Some were sent out by the sponsoring churches; others were sent by secular organizations. Some even came for one specific project; for example, a Rotary Club from Australia for one of the units of the Etep leprosy hospital.

Support from Overseas

Such development would have been impossible without the generous support of the sending churches. In order to arrange for this, the Mission budget was submitted to the sponsoring churches in two forms: a maintenance budget for current operations, and a capital budget for buildings nd equipment. The sponsoring churches then analysed the requests, and stated how much they could contribute to each. For some years this was done by each sponsoring church acting separately, but, at the suggestion of the (then) Secretary of ELCONG, Zurewe Zurenuo, representatives of the sending Boards now meet in New Guinea, where the coordinating of the contributions takes place in the context of the ongoing work.

In the early post-war years, it was the policy to isolate the Lutheran World Federation contribution from other income. This was because the LWF contribution was an emergency measure intended to support the Neuendettelsau missionaries until that society could resume its support. Initially, LWF did not support the outreach into new areas, but this was changed when it was pointed out that the term 'mission' implied both inner growth and outreach. When the sponsoring churches agreed to the field unification, they also agreed to a unified budget, for which the amounts given were in proportion to the number of personnel from each supporting church. As the economic situation improved and Neuendettelsau's contribution increased, the LWF participation tapered off. At first, Neuendettelsau's contributions were for the operations budget only, but on an increasing scale. When the sponsoring churches agreed to a unified budget in proportion to the number of missionaries from the separate churches, provision was also made for a church with more money than personnel to help support personnel from another church. Although Neuendettelsau found it difficult to make funds available for the capital budget, it was able to enlist the help of donor agencies for specific projects, such as the Balob Teachers College at Lae. [14] The German organization *Bread For The World* also provided funds for projects of an agricultural nature, such as the Gabmazung rice experimental project in the Markham Valley under Martin Boerner, the Kalasa cattle project at Asak, Kalasa, under Hans-Jakob Wiederhold, and an experimental agricultural project in the Highlands carried on by Guenter Oelschlegel (see also ch 18).

Other donor agencies which have made substantial contributions include the Lutheran World Federation's Community Development and Validation Service. Assistance with personnel, in addition to the worker volunteers who came from the United States, Canada, and Australia, was given by *Dienste in Uebersee*, a German agency providing trained workmen and women for specific assignments. Australian Volunteers Abroad also sent out qualified personnel for various duties. A British organization, *Service Overseas*, participated in the short-term workers' program. Usually the sending agencies assumed a part of or the whole costs of the sending, including salaries, furloughs, medical care, and repatriation.

A word of appreciation is also due to those professors from Neuendettelsau, Dubuque, St Louis, River Forest, St Paul, and Adelaide who used their well-earned sabbatical leave to come to New Guinea to teach in the seminaries.

From Mission to Church

The foregoing pages have served to give a few glimpses into the size and extent of Lutheran Mission New Guinea, and of the varied functions carried out by its expatriate staff after World War II. It is now important to ask how this large organization thought of itself, of its reasons for being, of its role in the Christianization of Papua New Guinea.

When one analyses the decisions, plans, and strategies made at the annual field conferences, it could easily be supposed that the Mission considered itself as an autonomous entity with its own reasons for existence, a foreign enterprise pursuing its own aims and purposes. Some resolutions, for example, have a long-term effect on the church for years to come. Decisions regarding the building and siting of institutions and mission stations are instances of this. True, the siting of mission stations was often the result of the people's own expressed desire, and stations could not be located on particular sites unless the people concerned were willing to sell the land to the Administration for lease to the Mission for a prescribed number of years. It is also true in later years that the indigenous leadership participated in the discussions regarding the location of these institutions. In establishing Balob Teachers College, the voice of the people was heard, even to the extent of using the name Balob proposed by the people themselves. And, after a long search and careful consideration of the alternatives, the indigenous leadership as well as the staffs of LMNG and NGLM agreed on a site on Malahang plantation near the city of Lae for Martin Luther Seminary.

However, it must also be said that many other conference decisions over the years were made by the missionaries acting on their own judgment and perceptions of what was necessary. (This was referred to as 'supervising', 'giving guidance'.) Dr Georg Pilhofer, a leading Neuendettelsau missionary and teacher of teachers, on one occasion said in the presence of the writer: 'But we must set the goals'; yet he was a firm believer in the New Guineans' ability to make decisions regulating their village and church life.

Missionaries' influence was strong in determining policies regarding baptism, confirmation, language, schools, and pastors' training. Missionaries were, of course, the chief negotiators with the sponsoring churches, making the requests for personnel, for the means to support them, and for the planned expansion of the work. Missionaries were concerned about the developments within the villages, especially with the changes being brought about through influences from without, as well as changes that were a part of the old pagan culture. Some of the problems that arose within the indigenous communities were: revivals of the old polygamous practices in some congregations; divorce; the practice of sorcery and the fear of sorcery, especially of the variety known as *sanguma* (which in at least one area was connected with ritual murder); some features of Communion practices, and the neglect of the Sacrament; problems of the second generation; problems of the youth, especially of those living in towns; and many others.

In a class by itself was the movement commonly called the 'cargo cult'. The missionaries who first encountered this movement saw it as an opposition to the Christian way of life, a kind of reversion to old pagan ideas and practices, or even a syncretism of pagan and Christian ideas and practices. Since it is dealt with in chapter 15, it is not necessary to discuss it further here. A number of essays, conference papers, private studies, articles in periodicals, and books written by missionaries testify to the importance of this movement in the thinking of the people, and of the difficulties the missionaries experienced in coping with it. [15]

Later missionaries who also became acquainted with this movement are sometimes very critical of the earlier missionaries' attempts at dealing with it, as if the latter were way off the mark in understanding it, and far too legalistic in their attempts to suppress it. In their view, the cargo cult is not primarily a search for the goods of the white man — as the earlier generation of missionaries supposed — but should be understood as a manifestation of the people's aspirations for a 'better way of life'.

But for those who experienced some of those 'aspirations', or were even victims of them, this was not always apparent. Some of the incidents connected with the movement included the theft of a camera, bed sheet, copy of a mission periodical from the home of a missionary, and the theft of an altar parament from the church. These items were then shown to the initiated as the first-fruits of the movement; they were declared to have dropped from heaven (Kalasa). Another incident had to do with the theft of a Communion chalice from a Roman Catholic church, but which was declared to have mysteriously appeared on a special table in the forest (Karkar). Perhaps it is true that these movements began as genuine revivals, as strivings for a better life, but then degenerated when the reform movements failed to achieve their purpose.

Although they themselves may not appear in the best light as a result of the later investigations and studies, senior missionaries will rejoice at the later findings about the 'cults', and will hope that the present counsellors of the Papua New Guinea Christians and their congregations will be able to direct the people to the 'better way' in union with Jesus Christ.

Impending Changes

A 'legacy' of successes and failures, of hopes realized and hopes dashed, of the passing (in many respects) of the old community in favour of the Spirit's creation of the new community of the people of God through the proclaimed Gospel, and of the passing away of 'Mission' in favour of the establishment of the church: that is the legacy handed on to the villages and congregations of Papua New Guinea.

As the years passed, the Mission continued to carry out its programs and to make decisions and plans, but there was a change in the procedures. An instance of this is the attendance of New Guineans at the annual field conferences as delegates of their various circuits. The first listing of indigenous delegates appears in the 1951 minutes: from Madang 16, from Jabem 17, and from Kate 18. From this date on, New Guineans were regular attendants at the conferences. At first, as may be expected,

Gedisa Moale, former president of the Lae District.

they functioned generally as observers; but there were exceptions. Through their experience in the congregational, circuit, and district meetings, some delegates had overcome all shyness in the presence of their expatriate co-workers, and were able to express their opinions and advocate their positions without hesitation.

Gedisa, the President of the Lae Circuit, put it this way:

> There was a man who had a dog. Now this man, who was a hunter, taught his dog also to hunt. The dog learnt so well that, during a time when his master was absent, the dog continued to hunt successfully on his own. But, when the master returned, the dog was no longer permitted to hunt on his own; he had to hunt only under the supervision of his master.

The meaning of the 'parable' was clear. Fortunately for the Church, Gedisa continued to be a faithful leader of the indigenous Church later as District President; even in retirement he continued his activity in the social service of the Church.

In order to facilitate understanding of the sessions of Conference, which were usually conducted in English, various missionaries acted as interpreters to groups of New Guinean delegates who were sitting together according to their language understanding. Later, through the efforts of Paul Freyberg, a translating system was obtained so that each delegate had an earphone through which he could hear the discussion in the language with which he was familiar.

It was not long, however, before more and more New Guinean voices were heard in the discussions. Missionaries, too, often spoke in the Pidgin *lingua franca*, and this language was also used by the New Guineans when they addressed the assembly. The 1967 minutes show, for example, that the Wednesday evening worship service was conducted by the Lae town pastor Gedisa. Secretary Zurewe Zurenuo preached the sermon, based on Ephesians 2:19-23, in which the 'chief cornerstone' became, in the New Guinea setting, the main 'house post', as it is in the bush churches. Among other things, Zurewe expressed thanks for the coming of the missionaries, but stated that their work is not finished, there is much more to be done to build with the New Guineans the church of Jesus Christ.

At the 1967 Field Conference, a resolution was passed inviting indigenous persons to become full-fledged members of the Mission's standing committees, preferably such persons as could serve over a longer period of time. [16] By this and similar actions, it was hoped that New Guineans would get a better insight into the workings of the Mission, learning from it what might be adaptable to their own operations in the church.

As the New Guineans' understanding of the scope of the Mission's activities grew, it seemed appropriate to think that the time was ripe for the formal organization of the work into a truly indigenous church. Much more was involved in the working of an organization on a national basis, than in the various districts — which were to a certain extent homogeneous — and so help would be avisable, at least for a time, but the experience gained in the smaller groupings would be a good basis for understanding what was involved in the workings of the larger unity.

At the Constituting Synod, Simbang 1956.

The Constituting Synod of 1956

A first formal step toward an organization was the preparation of a constitution — or, as it was called, a church order (the idea being that a church order might seem less formidable than a constitution, although the purpose to be achieved was the same). Such a church order was looked upon as provisional, in that its use in the church could be a testing leading to a more formal and permanent document, namely, a constitution. When the order, drawn up with the assistance of the missionaries, was referred to the Districts for consideration, an objection was lodged to the confessional article subscribing to all the various Christian and Lutheran creeds and confessions. Since the people were not familiar with most of these, how could they subscribe to them? Of course, they were familiar with the Apostles' Creed and Luther's Small Catechism, but none of the others had been translated at that time and made available in any New Guinean church language. [17]

Interest in the proposed organization grew, and it was planned to have the constituting synod at Simbang, Finschhafen, the site of Flierl's first mission station. The first synod, held

in 1956, was also to be a celebration of the 70th anniversary of the landing of Johann Flierl at Finschhafen on July 12, 1886 — in other words, the founding of the Lutheran Mission and Church in New Guinea. The Jabem and the Kate people were the hosts for the synod, and many visitors came from all sections of the Lutheran work. Overseas visitors also attended and participated in the historic occasion, including Director Hans Neumeyer from Neuendettelsau, Dr (later Bishop) F. Birkeli from Norway representing the Lutheran World Federation, Dr M. Lohe, President of the United Evangelical Lutheran Church in Australia, Dr Henry F. Schuh, President, and Dr George Schultz, Secretary, from the American Lutheran Church.

The host congregations had made elaborate preparation to welcome and provide for the many guests, and also prepared a number of dramatizations retelling the history of earlier days in New Guinea. One of these acted out Flierl's landing at Simbang and his reception (not exactly a friendly one).

Another dramatization illustrated the progress of the Gospel from the coast into the

243

The Gospel-fire's progress to the Highlands, Simbang Synod 1956.

Central Highlands. A long wire was stretched with one end representing the coast and the other the Highlands. Cotton had been arranged along the wire and saturated with kerosene. At the appropriate moment in the dramatization the coastal end of the wire was lit and the fire travelled along the wire until it reached the Highlands destination. Perhaps it sounds very simple as written here, but to the people assembled there it was a true representation of the Gospel fire's progress across the country. The hearers listened attentively to the explanation that followed.

In the synodical discussions, the Church Order was the chief topic. At the close of the discussions, the whole assembly arose to vote its adoption, thus approving the establishment of the Evangelical Lutheran Church of New Guinea (ELCONG).[18] The date was February 13, 1956. The synod chose John Kuder as the Church's first bishop.

No doubt, in the minds of the people there were expectations of some immediate benefits, even of a material nature, arising from the formation of the Church. Among some of the church workers, voices were heard against the use of the word 'evangelical' in the Church's title. This term seemed to be related to the term 'evangelist', which represented a lower status as compared with 'pastor' or 'teacher'. Evangelists now wanted to enjoy a higher status, but the word 'evangelical' in the Church's name seemed to preclude that for them. The acronym ELCONG also had a mysterious sound, and was not understood by some.[19]

Now that there was an entity called 'church', it became necessary to activate it meaningfully. It was a gradual process as the Districts chose their leaders to represent them in the councils of the Church. For the missionaries it was a rewarding experience to observe New Guineans, whose sphere of influence had been delimited by the boundaries of sometimes hostile clans and tribes, grow into an understanding of the meaning of church as the *ecclesia* of the whole people of God. A parallel phenomenon was observed in the secular sphere as more and more New Guineans accepted responsibilities in many occupations previously occupied by Europeans.

244

A New Role for Missionaries

Whereas previously there had been a missionary field conference to which the Districts of the Church sent observers/ delegates, there was now a church assembly of representatives of the Districts, called the Synod, which missionaries, also chosen by the Districts, attended. The beginnings of the Church's function in such assemblies were simple as the New Guineans began to grapple with problems previously dealt with in the field conference. In this situation there was further development in indigenous leadership ability and growth in understanding. Men like Liwa and Stahl Mileng of Madang, Zurewe Zurenuo and Mufuanu Butik of Finschhafen, Gedisa Tingasa and Janadabing Apo of Lae, Mambu of Hagen, Boniepe of Chimbu, Enareki and Baina of Goroka, to name just a few, began to see themselves as leaders in a much greater enterprise than they had experienced previously. Helpers in this growth and development of the leadership were the missionaries, now functioning not so much as independent members of a 'foreign' organization, but as members and servers of the Church.

The status of the missionaries became a question for the Church and its indigenous leaders. An explanation which was helpful went as follows: As a Church, it was now possible to have the service of qualified people from many sources. Leadership and responsibility should be in the hands of the indigenous people, but there were many functions in the Church, and the Church was free to call upon qualified people from within its own ranks or from overseas to carry out these functions. This was particularly true in the field of finance; so, for quite a few years, the Church enjoyed the services of qualified overseas personnel to manage the Church's funds.

On one occasion, Dr T. Fricke of the American Lutheran Church interviewed the then Church Secretary Zurewe Zurenuo regarding the type and qualifications of overseas workers desired by the Church. In his reply, Secretary Zurewe explained that the Church was not so much in need of the 'pioneer type' of missionary, such as the original missionaries had been; what was needed now were persons qualified to deal with, and to give

guidance to the Church leadership in dealing with, the present-day situation of the Church. Help was especially needed as regards the new movements developing within the Church itself as well as those coming from without: secularism; the competition from other missions seeking to 'reconvert' Lutheran Christians; the problems of the 'second generation' and of youth; urbanization; etc.

But it was not a one-way street. One of the happy memories of this writer refers to a happening at the last Hagen District meeting which he attended. At the morning service, Hagen District President (later, Bishop) Mambu called a meeting of the missionaries for the Sunday afternoon. When the group gathered, Mambu was not sitting at the feet of the missionaries to learn from their wisdom. Instead, he was counselling them about their work; the missionaries were learning from him.

It goes without saying that the change from Mission organization to the Church situation was not an easy one for some missionaries to make. Would they still be able to apply the fruits of years of study and preparation without the status and without the authority which the position of 'missionary' had previously implied?

The Vision of One Lutheran Church

In the course of time, New Guinean church leaders were prepared to take on a greater share of responsibilities in all areas of work. As communication within the New Guinean community grew, the existence of two and even three separate Lutheran church and mission bodies in the country was no longer seen as an acceptable situation. Church leaders, together with many of their expatriate co-workers in all the church bodies, had a vision of one Lutheran Church in New Guinea. They felt that the time had come to unite.

Through representation at each other's field conferences, as well as through other contacts, missionaries of NGLM, ALM, and LMNG had learnt to know one another as workers engaged in a common task. This was also true of the indigenous members of the several churches. But no formal steps had been taken to explore this situation in depth.

A significant change was indicated in a resolution adopted at the 1962 Field Conference of LMNG, on recommendation of the Committee on Inter-Church and Mission Relations:

> WHEREAS our President has received an informal letter from the New Guinea Lutheran Mission-Missouri Synod approaching us with the view in mind of having informal discussion meetings with our mission on the following matters:
> 1. Our common missionary task and goal
> 2. Our missionary methods
> 3. The progress of our mission work, on the coast and in the Highlands
> 4. Biblical exegesis, therefore be it
> RESOLVED that we invite them to such a meeting, and be it further
> RESOLVED that our President enter into correspondence with [NGLM] concerning this matter. [20]

The response to this resolution of 1962 was brought to LMNG's 1963 Field Conference by Dr H.P. Hamann, Principal of Concordia Seminary, Adelaide, South Australia, and Morris Jordan of ALM, who had just come from the Field Conference of NGLM. After expressing an apology on behalf of the NGLM for their non-representation at LMNG's Field Conference, they presented a resolution passed at NGLM's Conference (it was understood to be a joint NGLM and ALM resolution):

> WHEREAS we are very concerned about the future of the indigenous Church in New Guinea, and
> WHEREAS we must always keep in mind that the European missionary's activity in New Guinea might be curtailed or even terminated, and
> WHEREAS we believe that a united indigenous Lutheran Church is vital for the future of Lutheranism in New Guinea, be it
> RESOLVED that we inaugurate and vigorously pursue regular discussions with LMNG and ELCONG on the basis of the Scriptures and Lutheran Confessions, as has already been suggested, with the view toward the establishment of such a united Lutheran Church in New Guinea.
> WHEREAS we understand that LMNG is going to set a date for the first meeting, be it
> RESOLVED that we ask them to do so without delay. [21]

In reply to this communication, the LMNG Field Conference suggested that a committee of four persons in addition to the President be appointed to enter into discussions with a similar committee of NGLM and ALM. It also recommended that the ELCONG Church Council appoint four indigenous members to

represent it in these meetings. Upon NGLM's suggestion, LMNG's Executive Committee was to set the date for the first meeting. [22]

Two consequences resulted from these resolutions: (1) the appointment of a committee, later known as the One-Church Committee, to make the study suggested in the 1962 resolution; (2) the appointment of a Committee on Theology and Inter-Church Relations (CTICR). Membership on the committees was drawn from ALM, NGLM, LMNG, the Siassi Church, the (then) Wabag Lutheran Church, and ELCONG. The work of the One-Church Committee resulted in the preparation of a tentative constitution for the proposed united Lutheran Church. The CTICR had the task of preparing a statement of the faith as a guide to the Churches, and as a testimony and witness to the Lutheran understanding of the Christian faith expressed in a New Guinea context. The CTICR completed its work on the Statement in 1972.

In the meantime, there were other indicators of a willingness for a united operation. Dr T. Nickel, Second Vice-President of the Lutheran Church-Missouri Synod, was present at the 1965 Field Conference of LMNG. In reply to a welcome extended to him by the President, he brought the greetings of his President, referring in part to 'changes which had taken place ... in New Guinea'.

Further, at the same Conference the CTICR recommendation was adopted:

> That with respect to Resolution 65:1 of the CTICR and the **action taken on it by the Conference of NGLM** (emphasis mine)
> WE AGREE to the setting up of a committee to look into the possibility and practicability of a Joint Board of Publications, and we ask the Executive Committee to appoint two members to act as the representatives of LMNG on this committee. [23]

Dr Willard Burce, Professor at Martin Luther Seminary, Lae, then

> outlined an action taken by the Conference of NGLM ... requesting the Churches and Missions to initiate in 1966 a theological course in English ... namely, to invite other Missions and Churches to set up an ad hoc committee ... to outline objectives, policies and projections involved in the eventual establishment of a combined theological seminary. [24]

Revd Erwin Spruth was the NGLM representative at the 1966 Field Conference. In his remarks at the close of the Conference, Spruth

> expressed his thanks for the opportunity to be present at our Conference, and assured us of their Mission's looking forward to the day when the two Lutheran groups will be one. [25]

In the light of later events, it is significant that the initiative and hopes for the future came from NGLM/Missouri Synod personnel. But in spite of these hopeful resolutions and indications, they could not be realized. At the dedication of the first units of Martin Luther Seminary on January 31, 1971, attended by representatives of the various Lutheran Missions and Churches, the Revd Alwyn Ewald, President of NGLM, informed Bishop Kuder that it would not be possible to continue with talks regarding union because of developments within the Lutheran Church-Missouri Synod in the United States. So, while cooperation has continued at Balob Teachers College, at Ogelbeng and Martin Luther Seminaries, at the Nurses Training School, and in the publishing enterprise, all this is still only a prelude to the hoped- and planned-for union of the Lutheran Churches in Papua New Guinea. The tentative constitution developed for the united church became, with the consent of NGLM, the basis for the new constitution for ELCONG adopted at the 1973 Synod at Balob Teachers College.

One cannot but deeply regret that developments which took place in a foreign country could bring to a sudden halt a step which seemed so right for Papua New Guinea.

The End of Lutheran Mission New Guinea

The 1969 Field Conference accepted the resignation of Dr Kuder as president of Lutheran Mission New Guinea, and chose Rufus Pech from the Lutheran Church of Australia to succeed him. This action was felt to be a necessary step in the developing autonomy of ELCONG. Bishop Kuder was thus freed from the many executive duties associated with the Mission president's office, and could devote his remaining time of service to the affairs of the Church and to helping the indigenous leaders of the Districts in their understanding of responsibility for the life and work of the Church. In the time following his return from furlough in 1971, much of his activity was directed to

Bishop Kuder hands over his office as President of Lutheran Mission New Guinea to Rufus Pech.

helping prepare for the election of his successor as bishop of the Church.

More yet was implied. The more the indigenous church grew in importance, the less the Mission organization would make its decisive influence felt. In 1970, the LMNG Field Conference adopted a revised constitution for its operations, in which it was simply stated: 'The object of Lutheran Mission New Guinea shall be to serve the Evangelical Lutheran Church of New Guinea'. In accordance with this purpose of serving the Church, the size and importance of the Field Conference were greatly reduced, as the By-Laws state:

> II. 1. The Conference shall be constituted by a minimum of 20% of the membership of the field.
>
> 2. The Conference shall concern itself strictly with missionaries' affairs such as salaries, housing, children's education, medical care and benefits, refresher courses, and retreats. [26]

In other words, missionaries would still continue to meet to discuss matters which concerned them personally and their relation with their home churches, but in much smaller, representative conferences. Matters which concerned the Church in New Guinea belonged to the jurisdiction of the Synod or of the District Conferences. Of course, missionaries would also be present at these conferences, exercising their influence and bringing to bear their knowledge and experience on matters of concern to the Church.

The same 1970 Field Conference foresaw the eventual end to its existence as a separate body. In the Constitution adopted at that Conference, Article XI refers to the procedure for the termination of the Conference (implying the end of the Mission as a separate organized entity). After such disenfranchisement of the Mission, missionaries could still meet for discussion of their personal concerns, as mentioned above, and for further study on how to improve the quality of their contribution to the work of the Church.

The missionaries also continued another feature of the Field Conference program: written annual reports on their work, with observations and suggestions concerning the Church's work, which were now sent to the Bishop. The 1975 Book of Reports contains a preface by Bishop Zurewe in which he thanks the writers of the reports, appreciating their comments. He requests that the practice continue as a service to him, as a mutual service to fellow-missionaries, and also as a service to the sending Churches.

Under the capable leadership of Rufus Pech, LMNG continued as a separate body for five more years in its service to the Church. Considerable attention was given to the process of reducing the Mission's authority, and to the steps to be taken to terminate the existence of the Mission as a separate entity.

Several matters needed special attention in this process. Particularly, the auxiliary services conducted by the Mission had to be put on a different basis. For many years such concerns had been matters for the Field Conference to regulate, but it did not seem advisable to load this responsibility on the Church's synod. The auxiliaries in question were: the Lutheran Mission Supply House, Lutheran Shipping, Lutheran Aviation, Kristen Pres, and the plantations (for details see ch 18). These activities were separated into self-managing units, so that they were no longer a part of the Mission's budget. After some time of operating on this basis, Lutheran Aviation was consolidated with Missionary Aviation Fellowship (MAF) as part of their overall service to the various missions. The Madang Supply House was sold to a private entrepreneur. The plantations became the responsibility of Kambang Holdings Limited. Lutheran Shipping continues its separate existence, and has been making regular contributions to the Church's budget. Kristen Pres has been incorporated as a separate entity.

As the Mission clarified and refined its self-understanding, it often recalled the image of the construction of a building. Surrounding a construction is a scaffold, giving the workers a place from which to work and access to the rising walls; but the time inevitably comes when the scaffolding must be removed. That time had come for Lutheran Mission New Guinea, and so it was officially terminated in 1975.

The Church remains. Its true builder is the Holy Spirit. Missionaries still serve — and their services are still asked for in a role alongside the Papua New Guinean workers. Their contributions of service are still a function of the Church. Many of the problems that faced the Mission still remain, and new ones have joined them. But the Holy Spirit does not abandon the Church, nor does his guidance become outmoded. That his guidance will be an ever-present reality in the life and work of the Evangelical Lutheran Church of Papua New Guinea is our hope and confidence.

Endnotes

[1] Missionary John Kuder was nominated by the group and appointed by the Board as Interim Field Superintendent of the Mission.

[2] For a detailed account of Dr Fricke's survey, see: Theodore P. Fricke, *We Found Them Waiting* (Columbus, Ohio: Wartburg Press, 1947).

[3] Gerhard Reitz and Alfred Walck (both new) were delayed in Australia because of bad weather, and did not arrive until the session was over.

[4] It was, in fact, by common agreement rather than by formal resolution that Lae-Ampo became the permanent Head Office first of the Lutheran Mission, then of the Lutheran Church.

[5] Second Field Conference, 1948, Minutes, res. no. 48-8. Also the 1949 Field Conference resolved that 'the missionaries be strongly urged to train natives to operate the stores, whenever possible with native ownership and management as the ultimate goal' (Minutes, p 31).

[6] For a detailed presentation, see chapter 4 of this volume.

[7] Fourth Field Conference, 1950, Minutes, pp 21-23. Already in 1948 at the Second Field Conference, a series of resolutions had been passed regarding unification of the work. One of them reads:
WHEREAS the *development of one united Papuan Lutheran Church* is our aim, and
WHEREAS this development would be greatly hindered by dividing the now unified field into two or more missions or separated spheres of interest, and
WHEREAS the perpetuation of a unified mission necessitates the free interspersion of personnel coming from different home churches, throughout the entire field, therefore be it
RESOLVED that we recommend that the Lutheran Mission be and remain *one homogeneous mission* (Minutes 1948, p 25).

[8] Seventh Field Conference, 1953, Minutes, res. 53-13.

[9] An American missiologist viewing a copy of the annual reports and papers suggested that this material was a veritable fund of missionary understanding that could be made available to others. However, to this date no sympathetic and understanding person has undertaken the task of assembling and evaluating this material.

[10] For a listing of the Lutheran missionary personnel serving in New Guinea 1886-1986, see appendix to the volume.

[11] Wilhelm Bergmann, *Vierzig Jahre in Neuguinea* (mimeographed, Mutdapilly, Qld, n.d.) vol. VIII. O.H. Schmidt, *Globe-Trotting for the Gospel* (New York: Vantage Press, 1962).

[12] Pastor Hafermann's Siegried ('Hy') and Mrs Hafermann were the Board's representatives in San Francisco, assisting missionary families departing for overseas or returning to the United States.

[13] Some later missionaries have been critical of the so-called 'Keysser Method' (a term, by the way, which Keysser himself objected to). See, for example, Peter Koehne, 'Justification, The Ministry and the Keysser Method' in *Lutheran Theological Journal* (17), December 1983, 103-114. Keysser believed that the 'method' of approach — not the content of the message — should be determined by the situation, in the sense of 1 Cor. 9:22: 'I have become all things to all men'.

[14] Additional funds for the Balob Teachers College came from the Swedish Lutherhjaelpen as well as from the Lutheran Church-Missouri Synod.

[15] Among the studies presented to Field Conference meetings are the following:
1948: A. Walck, 'Cargo' (already at the Second Field Conference!)
1950: A. Maahs, 'The Development of the Jali Movement'
1959: Zurewe Zurenuo, 'New Guinea Christian — *Ai bilong em olsem wanem long samting bilong graun*' (We New Guinea Christians in Our Relationship to the Secular World)
1960: T. Gedisa, '*Kristen man i lukim samting bilong graun olsem wanem?*' (Same subject as the one immediately above)
1964: H. Wagner, 'An In-Depth Study of the Buged Circuit'; F. Wagner, 'The Outgrowth and Development of the Cargo Cult'; J. Kuder, 'The Cargo Cult and Its Relationship to the Work of the Church'
1971: R. Hueter, 'The Battle for the Abundant Life'.
In addition to the formal papers on the subject, there were many conference discussions on the subject arising from the annual station reports. See the publications by missionaries Ahrens, Steinbauer, Strelan, Strauss, H. Wagner, as listed in the selected bibliography.

[16] 21st Field Conference, 1967, Minutes, p 30.

[17] Over the years, the original Church Order/Constitution was revised several times. In the 1978 version it reads *(my translation of the Pidgin original)*:

Article II Faith

We join with all Christians of the past in accepting the *Apostles' Creed*, the *Nicene Creed*, the *Athanasian Creed*. We join with other Lutheran Churches in accepting the *Augsburg Confession* and the *Small Catechism of Martin Luther*. By that time, these confessional writings had been translated into Pidgin and some of the church languages. It was perhaps well that the Church Order's character was provisional, for, when it was later submitted to the Lutheran World Federation in an application for membership in that body, the document was faulted because it contained a provision that missionaries (expatriates!) were to carry out certain continuing functions in the Church.

[18] In 1975, because the work had extended into Papua, the southern part of the large island, and also because the name of the independent country was 'Papua New Guinea', the name 'Papua' was also added to the Church's title (ELC-PNG).

[19] On one occasion, a European of the New Guinea secular community remarked: 'ELCONG, what's that? Is it something like Viet Cong?'

[20] 16th Field Conference, 1962, Minutes, p 67.

[21] 17th Field Conference, 1963, Minutes, p 16.

[22] *Ibid*, p 69.

[23] 19th Field Conference, 1965, Minutes, p 19.

[24] *Ibid*.

[25] 20th Field Conference, 1966, Minutes, p 47.

[26] 24th Field Conference, 1970, Minutes, p 26.

Documentation

Luth. Mis. N.G.
Minutes — Int. Conf.

page 11
Feb. 28-March 5, 1946

TERRITORIES OF PAPUA AND NEW GUINEA
RETURN OF MISSIONARIES

The following conditions are those that have been approved by the Commonwealth Government in regard to the return of missionaries to the Territory of New Guinea:

1. Missions to be allowed to resume operations in New Guinea as the areas in which they formerly operated become available and the necessary authority is given for the re-entry of missionaries to those areas.
2. Subject to specific approval in each case, missionaries of German nationality who were resident in the Territory prior to the outbreak of war in 1941 may be permitted to return to the Territory.
3. Until the signing of the Peace Treaty when the matter could be reconsidered, any person who was not resident in the Territory at the outbreak of war in 1941 and who is of German nationality or of German birth or who has received his or her education in Germany shall not be permitted to return to New Guinea as a missionary, lay-worker or employee of any mission operating in the Territory.
4. The Mission concerned to accept responsibility for the activities in the Territory of personnel selected for work with the Mission and agree to withdraw without question any of such personnel

when officially requested to do so. If such a situation arises the matter to be taken up with the Head of the Mission, who is to be advised by the superior authority in the Territory of all the circumstances of the case and the reason why the withdrawal of the missionary is desired.

5. All missionaries to be required to have a reasonable knowledge of the English language before entry to the Territory is approved but, in the case of missionaries who were resident in the Territory prior to the outbreak of the war in 1941, they be required to acquire a reasonable knowledge of English within a reasonable period. Evidence of progress to be to the satisfaction of the Administrator at the end of twelve months and thereafter at the end of each six months and if satisfactory progress is not made the missionary to be removed from the Territory.

Department of External Territories
CANBERRA, ACT
12th February, 1946

(signed) J.R. Halligan
Secretary
Department of External Territories

Chapter 7

Siassi and Menyamya:

The Work of Australian Lutheran Mission

by J.G. Strelan*

In 1836, Pope Gregory XVI approved the formation of the 'Society of Mary', and entrusted to it the Western Pacific as its special mission field. In one corner of the Western Pacific lies the Siassi archipelago, a cluster of 25 islands situated midway between the West New Britain coast and the north-eastern coast of the Huon Peninsula. The largest island in the group is Rooke (or Umboi) Island; the smallest inhabited island is Aromot, less than half an acre in size. The Siassi Islands were the centre of an intricate trading system between New Britain and mainland New Guinea; hence they were well-placed to serve as a springboard for mission work on the New Guinea mainland.

It was, therefore, with high hopes and great expectations that Marist Bishop Jean-George Collomb, accompanied by three colleagues, landed on Rooke Island in 1848. Alas, the missionaries soon discovered that the place was as unhealthy as the people were indifferent. Within six months, Collomb and a colleague had died of malaria. The two remaining Marists withdrew. In 1852, one Marist and four priests from the Milan Foreign Mission Society came again to Rooke Island. Three years later they left, permanently; Siassi was a hostile and fruitless field.[1]

So matters stood for almost 50 years. In 1892 Pastor Georg Bamler of the Neuendettelsau Mission Society had visited Siassi for six weeks. Only in 1911, however, was Bamler able to return to Siassi and take up permanent residence. He arrived at Aromot Island on April 28, 1911; but he settled, after trying several sites, at Gerem, inland from Yangla village on the eastern side of Rooke Island. From Gerem, Bamler and his Taemi and Tami Island co-workers set about the task of bringing the Gospel to the people whose grandparents had rejected it 50 years before. In 1923 Bamler moved from Gerem to Karapo, very close to Yangla village. There, on April 12, 1928, Bamler was killed by a falling tree. He had spent 41 years in New Guinea.[2]

Bamler's successor, the North American missionary Pastor Roland Hanselmann, moved Karapo station to Awelkon, on the western side of the island (not far from where Bishop Collomb's party had landed years earlier). Hanselmann was succeeded by a former banker, Lorenz Methsieder. His ministry,

253

Map of Siassi.

however, was only a short one. His wife became seriously ill; in April 1936 he and his Australian-born wife had to retire to Australia. At this time, Siassi had a population of ca. 5,500. There were approximately 1,500 baptized members of the Lutheran church; 20 teachers and evangelists; and 350 school pupils, including 45 boys at the station school at Awelkon.

Ever since Bamler's death, Lutheran Mission Finschhafen (as the New Guinea mission of the Neuendettelsau Mission Society was known) had been hard pressed to find a resident missionary for Siassi. Hanselmann and Methsieder were stopgaps. The problem was that in the central highlands of New Guinea the Lutherans had entered into a race with the Roman Catholics to claim large portions of the highlands as their 'own'.[3] The human and financial resources of Lutheran Mission Finschhafen were stretched to the limit. No man could be spared for Siassi.

A solution to the Siassi problem came from an unexpected quarter: a Lutheran church in Australia. From the very beginning of Lutheran work in New Guinea, the United Evangelical Lutheran Church in Australia had supported the work in New Guinea with money, personnel, and prayers.[4] But the other major Lutheran body in Australia — the Evangelical Lutheran Church of Australia — had, on confessional grounds, no ties with the United Evangelical Lutheran Church of Australia nor with the Lutheran mission societies which were working in New Guinea. The Evangelical Lutheran Church of
254

Australia, however, had been looking for a mission field of its own since 1926, when it had appointed a committee, under the chairmanship of Professor H. Hamann, to investigate mission prospects in land north of Australia.

Eventually, in 1935, the church formally resolved to 'launch a mission in the northern region of the Mandated Territory of New Guinea'.[5] Specifically, the church intended to commence a mission in the Sepik region, at the junction of the Sepik and Doerfer rivers. The church appointed a 'New Guinea Mission Board', with Pastor F.W. Noack as Chairman.[6] A successful fund-raising campaign was conducted, and two pastors (A.P.H. Freund, and F.W. Noack, a young graduate of Concordia Seminary, Adelaide) and two laymen (V. Neumann and G.J. Noack) were called to form the first missionary team to the new field.[7]

The Evangelical Lutheran Church of Australia never did get to establish a new field in the Sepik. Lutheran Mission Finschhafen, searching desperately for ways to minister adequately to the people of Siassi, saw in the new arrivals from Australia a God-sent solution to the Siassi problem. So in January 1936 Superintendent Willy Flierl proposed to the Evangelical Lutheran Church of Australia that it take over Siassi as its own mission field.[8] Awelkon station and its appurtenances were offered to the Australian church for the sum of £580; an additional £400 was asked for stores and equipment. The Australians saw only advantages in accepting the offer.[9]

'For us', wrote Freund later, 'the benefits were obvious.' He continued:

> By taking over an established mission field, we would have the opportunity to gain the necessary experience, and then in due time be able to train native workers to go out with us into the originally planned Sepik area. Siassi was from the beginning looked upon as a springboard for pioneering mission-work on the mainland.[10]

One question, however, did cause the Evangelical Lutheran Church of Australia, and also the Neuendettelsau Mission Society, some concern, namely: What were the implications for the situation in New Guinea of the Australian church's position on church fellowship? Since the Evangelical Lutheran Church of Australia was in altar and pulpit fellowship with none of

First Missionaries, L to R: Neumann, Freund, F. Noack, G. Noack.

the Lutheran churches or mission societies which were at work in New Guinea, it experienced some pangs of conscience about allowing evangelists and teachers from Lutheran Mission Finschhafen to continue to preach and teach and partake of the Lord's Supper with Siassi Christians.

Lutheran Mission Finschhafen, for its part, apparently had no theological qualms about handing over the Siassi field to the Evangelical Lutheran Church of Australia. Superintendent W. Flierl wrote:

> We recognize that the ELCA is a truly Lutheran church; we can, therefore, with a good conscience entrust the Awelkon congregation, with its teachers and helpers, to the care of the ELCA. We can tell the Christians at Awelkon that even though the new missionaries come from a different school from ours, they nevertheless preach the same Gospel which has until now been preached to them. [11]

Nevertheless, Flierl attached several conditions to the transfer of the Siassi field to the Australians: the teachers and evangelists who were working at Awelkon must be permitted to continue to work there for several more years; they must be permitted to take the Lord's Supper with their fellow-Lutherans at Awelkon; and the Australian mission must make no changes in church customs and practices at Awelkon until the missionaries had won the confidence of the people. [12]

The Australian church accepted Flierl's conditions. But Noack, the Chairman of the Mission Board, had earlier assured President Darsow of the Evangelical Lutheran Church of Australia that the missionaries intended to regularize the 'irregular' situation within two or three years:

> When we have worked our way in, and the time comes to finalize the question of the status of the workers [from Lutheran Mission Finschhafen], we shall give them a choice: those who want to cast their lot with the Siassis may do so, and be absorbed into the island population; those who do not want to make that commitment, shall return to their homeland [and church]. [13]

Thus, in the transfer of the Siassi field from the care of one Mission to another, [14] the seeds were sown for the creation of a rift between the Siassi Lutherans and their fellow-Lutherans on the New Guinea mainland, a rift which was formally healed only forty years after.

255

I. 1936-1945: CONSOLIDATION AND PROGRESS

The missionaries of Australian Lutheran Mission (as the New Guinea Mission of the Evangelical Lutheran Church of Australia came to be known) devoted their attention, in the years between 1936 and 1941, to visiting the villages and gaining the confidence of the people, instructing and examining baptismal classes, inspecting schools, and upgrading the teaching program. [15]

It soon became evident that local teachers (men such as Bingmalo, Yakobus, Labuni, and Yasaking) had been and still were the human keys to opening the villages to the Gospel. These men and their families lived in the villages and exerted an influence for good on the lives of the villagers. Hence, special attention was placed on strengthening and equipping teachers for their work. The first of many teachers' conferences was held at Awelkon in March 1937; its goal was to improve the skills of those who had had little formal teacher-training. The conference — which was really an in-service course — focused on the teaching of Jabem and of Bible stories; reading, spelling, writing, and arithmetic.

The decision to pay special attention to building up a cadre of competent teachers proved in later years to be a vital one for the continuing life of the church on Siassi: these teachers gradually assumed the role of 'pastor' in the villages. During the years of the war with Japan they provided almost all of the pastoral care, and after the war it was from the ranks of the teachers that the church drew many of its evangelists to mainland New Guinea, and its first ordained pastors.

In keeping with long-established Lutheran mission practice, the Australian Lutheran Mission endeavoured to expand its activities in order to meet the legitimate needs of the whole person and the whole society. Thus, in the years prior to the Japanese invasion of New Guinea, the mission laid the foundations for medical work, economic development, and improvement in transport facilities.

Mrs Dorothea Freund, the wife of A.P.H. Freund, had received some basic medical training at Finschhafen, and had begun medical work on Rooke Island shortly after her arrival in October 1936. [16] She was relieved of the major burden of this work only in 1946, when Sister L. Hamdorf, and Mrs Jean Nagel, a trained nurse, arrived on Siassi. The women's guilds of the Evangelical Lutheran Church in Australia and New Zealand assumed reponsibility for supporting the healing ministry in New Guinea. During the 1950s and 1960s, two hospitals and a number of clinics were established on Rooke Island and other islands of the Siassi archipelago. Funds for the building of the two hospitals came from a 'Stamps for Missions' project in Australia. This project, which involved the collecting, cleaning, sorting, packing, and selling of millions of used stamps, was, and still is, directed by stamp expert Ern Unger of Alectown, New South Wales. [17]

Nursing sisters went on long patrols, by canoe, boat, and on foot, offering village women pre- and post-natal care; they conducted clinics in child-health care and hygiene; and they offered general medical care. [18] With the nearest doctor and major hospital 8 to 10 hours away on the mainland of New Guinea, the Siassi people were totally dependent upon the medical services provided by Australian Lutheran Mission.

Another facet of the medical program was the training of New Guinean nurses and medical orderlies. These men and women, trained by a combination of formal lectures and on-the-job experience, not only established clinics in villages throughout the Siassi islands, but also formed an integral part of the mission outreach to Menyamya during the period 1955-1975.

A program of economic development got under way in 1937 when Messrs Money and Reynolds offered to sell their Gizarum plantation to the Mission. The offer was an attractive one, especially since Gizarum possessed the only good all-year anchorage (now known as Luther Anchorage) on Rooke Island, and, furthermore, Gizarum had one of the few sawmills in New Guinea. The missionaries hoped that proceeds from the sale of timber would enable the debt on Gizarum to be paid off within three years. [19]

In 1938 the Evangelical Lutheran Church of Australia approved the purchase of Gizarum. The 'New Guinea Mission Society' was formed to purchase and operate the plantation. In October 1938 the plantation began operations as a plantation of Australian Lutheran Mission; Mr V. Neumann was the first manager.

256

Gizarum functioned not only as a plantation for the production of coconuts and copra; it served also as a centre for training local men in various agricultural skills and in animal husbandry. It conducted management courses in which men were taught how to organize routine plantation work, including the planting of coconut and coffee groves, the care of plantations, and the general principles of plantation economics. Already in these early years, the missionaries saw the necessity of providing young people with the requisite knowledge and skills to enable them to participate in the development of a cash economy on Siassi.

Gizarum Plantation provided opportunities for villagers to add to their cash income by selling timber to the plantation. It also offered advice to villagers on matters connected with copra production, and it acted as agent for the sale of their copra. Furthermore, Gizarum gave on-the-job training to many young men, and gradually gave them positions of responsibility on the plantation. Gilambing Baitol, for example, was first employed at Gizarum as a medical orderly; he later worked as store manager, and finally as head foreman. [20] Other Siassi men were placed in charge of livestock, tractor work, vehicle workshops, and general supervision.

In 1968, Gizarum, by this time controlled by a Board of Management made up of representatives of the church and the government, was offered to the Siassi Local Government Council for $60,000. The offer was rejected. Finally, the church formed the Siassi Cooperative Ltd to take over the Gizarum lease. The transfer was not without its problems. Local villagers laid claim to the plantation, on the basis of traditional land ownership. The government settled the claims, and awarded the lease to the Siassi church. Eventually, Gizarum Plantation was sold to Simon Senat, a member of the group which, in 1975, had claimed to be the traditional owner of the land on which Gizarum stood. [21]

The subject of Gizarum cannot be closed without making reference to the problems of transportation. Obviously, without some form of transport to the New Guinea mainland, Gizarum could not be a viable proposition. Furthermore, the missionaries and the people living on the 25

islands of the Siassi archipelago needed reliable transport in order to maintain communication with each other and with the people of both New Britain and the New Guinea mainland. Traditionally, the canoe was the only form of sea transport. But often this mode of travel was neither possible nor expedient, especially in rough weather.

Until 1937, missionaries travelled by canoe, or they depended on whatever arrangements they could make with the owner of Gizarum, who operated a small schooner, the *Siassi*. In 1937, the situation improved somewhat with the purchase of the *MV Awelkon*; but it was a tiny boat, not really suitable for travel on the open sea or even for inter-island travel. [22] Only in 1940 was a truly-adequate boat obtained; the *MV Umboi*. But even the *Umboi* had no real passenger cabin; the only protection passengers had from the wind and rain was a galvanized-iron shelter.

In 1942 the *MV Umboi* was commandeered by the Australian Army, and used to help in the evacuation of troops from New Britain. It was sunk in 1943, and became a casualty of the war. After the war, a new boat, *Umboi II*, built in Hong Kong, was dedicated in October 1946. The first Mastor of *Umboi II* was Vic. Neumann. He was succeeded, in turn, by L. Noller, R. Uebergang, E. Beck, and E. Carlsen. Pastor Keith Nagel also skippered the *Umboi* on many trips. Toward the end of its life in the service of Australian Lutheran Mission, the

Ships — 'Umboi II'.

257

Captain Sidi.

Umboi was captained by Sidi of Barim; he had obtained his Native Master's Licence in 1964. [23]

The *Umboi* and other boats, such as the little *Karapo*, were essentials in the lives of missionaries and people alike. But perhaps the single biggest factor in changing the relationship of Siassi with the mainland of New Guinea was the airstrip at Lablab on the eastern side of Rooke Island. This light-plane 'strip was constructed by local people, using mainly pick and shovel. The work was supervised by the resident missionary, Keith Nagel. When the 'strip was completed in 1964, Rooke Island was only 40 minutes away from Lae, the administrative, business, and church centre of the Morobe Province.

After this brief excursus on the work of Australian Lutheran Mission in the areas of medical services, economic development, and transport, it is time to double back in history and pick up the threads of the story.

Soon after Pearl Harbour, it became evident that New Guinea would not escape the ravages of a foreign war. In December 1941 the wives and families of missionaries on Rooke Island were evacuated to Australia. Three

258

months later, the three Australian men on Rooke Island (Freund, Zacher, and Neumann) joined the New Guinea Volunteer Rifles. [24] The work on Siassi was committed entirely into the hands of local teachers and elders, under the leadership of Gerson, Yakobus, Yanadabing, and others.

During the war years, the Siassi church leaders continued to preach, teach, administer the Sacraments, and even to build new churches — this despite the fact that the Japanese occupied Awelkon and Gizarum, and many people were compelled, for safety's sake, to move into the bush. Some teachers tried to keep their schools going, but most returned to their homes; there, together with their people, they waited for the war to end.

II. 1946-1965: EDUCATION AND OUTREACH

The war of 1941-45 touched and changed, directly or indirectly, the lives of all Papua New Guineans. Many people had new experiences, both good and bad; they met many different kinds of people from many different countries; they gained new ideas and insights, and they saw new possibilities for the future. Their horizons were extended. The winds of war generated winds of change. Cargo cults and other movements of a religious and socio-political nature, swept the country. [25] Education, which prior to the war had been almost entirely in the hands of the Missions, began to claim a significant and increasing share of the government's interest and budget. The first small moves began toward political independence and church autonomy, imitating faintly the events taking place in nearby Indonesia and distant Africa and India. In short, the two decades after the war promised to be times of rapid social, political, and religious change. Siassi would not be in the mainstream of events; nor, however, would it be entirely excluded or unaffected.

When, in 1946 and 1947 the first post-war groups of Australian missionaries returned to Siassi, [26] they found that they had to work at reconstruction and consolidation, as well as to make plans for future developments. A large number of baptisms took place, including the baptisms of 6-to-8-year-old children who had not been baptized during the war. [27] By 1950 there were only 800 adults on Siassi who had not been confirmed.

In the period immediately after the war, an extensive building and rebuilding program was undertaken. For example: a store was built at Gizarum, and a clinic and hospital at Awelkon. In 1951 a second main mission station was established at Lablab, not far from where Bamler had lived and worked. Pastor Keith Nagel supervised the building of houses, a school, a hospital, a church, and finally in 1964, an airstrip.

It is not possible, within the confines of this brief chapter, to chart all the changes and developments which took place on Siassi during the first two postwar decades. But more than passing notice must be taken of developments in three related areas: education, pastor-training, and mission outreach.

Education

Education on Siassi took a giant step into the future with the opening of Gelem Training Centre in 1948. The expressed aim of this school, which later became one of the first co-ed schools in Papua New Guinea, was to provide future pastors and teachers for the church on Siassi. The planned enrolment was 60; the very first intake was 118, most of them married men with families. The two teachers, Pastor Conrad Eckermann and Teacher Yanadabing, were hard pressed to cope with the numbers. During the early years, and for many years after, Mrs Joan Eckermann devoted herself, her time, energy, and talents to the school, at first to the care and training of the students' wives, and later of the girls who came to study at Gelem. [28]

The first class of teachers was graduated from Gelem Training Centre in 1954; they helped to ease the acute shortage of teachers in the village schools. As Gelem grew, more and better buildings were needed; these were added in 1955. By this time, Standards 1-6 were being taught according to a government-approved syllabus. In 1956 the first graduation took place of teachers whose qualifications were recognized by the government.

As part of the teacher-training program, a practice school was established at Gelem. By 1959 a number of students had completed Standard 6 at Gelem, and 25 of them enrolled at Dregerhafen High School on the mainland

coast. In 1963, enrolments at Gelem climbed to 318, including 91 girls. In the early 1960s a handful of Gelem graduates attended church colleges in Melbourne and Adelaide, Australia.

Teacher-training at Gelem came to an end in 1964. Thereafter, prospective teachers from Siassi received their training at Balob Teachers College in Lae. Balob, a joint institution of the three Lutheran Churches and Missions in New Guinea, opened its doors in February 1965. [29] Gelem Training Centre became Gelem Junior High School (later the 'Junior' was dropped); it continued to function as a preparatory school for those who wished to serve the church as pastors, teachers, or medical workers. Pastor and Mrs Eckermann, who for 20 years had done so much to mould Gelem's unique character, and to foster the Christian *esprit de corps* which was noticed by even the most cynical observer, left Gelem in 1970. One of their legacies to the Siassi church was a sound and effective system of Christian education. [30]

Gelem High School was transferred to Lablab in 1977: there was more land available, and nearby was the airstrip and a good anchorage for boats. This relocation marked the end of the history of *Gelem* Training Centre and High School.

Pastor-Training

In 1955, after less than 50 years of mission work on Siassi, there were 5,000 baptized Lutherans (of a total population of c. 6,000) grouped into 36 congregations, each with its own school, each supporting its own teacher. There were 40 teachers and just over 1,000 students. In addition, 16 evangelists were being supported in mainland areas, chiefly in the Enga Province.

There is no mention, in the previous paragraph, of pastors. So, who did the preaching, counselling, visiting, burying, marrying, and administering of the Sacraments? There were, in fact, three ordained pastors on Siassi at this time (Nagel, Eckermann, and Noller), but these three could not possibly attend to all the pastoral duties, especially since Eckermann was fully occupied at Gelem Training Centre, and Nagel was burdened with many administrative duties. The bulk of the pastoral work in the congregations was done by the teachers, elders, medical

259

Pastor and Mrs Eckermann.

orderlies, church councillors, and evangelists. Of these, the teachers had had some theological training — the older men at Hopoi, the younger men at Gelem. Most of the others were theologically untutored men who were respected and accepted by their people. Most congregations received the benefits of a team ministry: as each man had a gift, so he ministered — in preaching, teaching, singing, counselling, and so forth. The Australian pastor fitted into this team as advisor, occasional preacher, and dispenser of the Sacraments, in particular, the Eucharist.

This system of team ministry worked well for many years. But the key figure was the teacher, and when 'education' became popular as the open sesame to a golden future, the team-ministry system began to disintegrate. All the teachers were expected to devote all their time and energy to students in the classroom — in classrooms which were full to overflowing. The Siassi Christians began to speak about the need for literate, theologically-trained pastors. Members of the Church Council had been authorized to distribute the Lord's Supper in the villages, but this did not solve the basic problem.

Nagel with pastors retrained. Back Row, L. to R.: David, Geyamokwi, Nagel, Bingmalo, Peter. Front L. to R.: Kekongandang, Yasaking, Teopil.

The need for a trained, full-time, pastoral ministry was met by initiating a two-stream program of pastor training: the one stream prepared older, experienced, men for ordination; the other stream provided a longer, more academic, course of studies for younger men. Planning for the implementation of these programs began in the early 1960s. In 1963, Pastor Keith Nagel gathered about him seven Church Councillors, all men with long experience as teachers and evangelists, some with as much as 30 years' experience. In many areas there was not much that one could teach these battle-scarred veterans; more often, the pupil taught the teacher. In due course, the seven completed their studies and their supervised practical work.[31] They were ordained by Pastors Nagel, Freund, and Klein, on November 29, 1964. The new pastors — Bingmalo, David, Geyamokwi, Kekongandang, Peter, Teopil, and Yasaking — were assigned to their parishes by the Siassi Church Board which for some years had had the task of assigning teachers to their posts. Nagel left Lablab and New Guinea in 1965; later training courses for older men were conducted by Pastor Rhyall Klein at Awelkon.

Meanwhile, planning had begun for the establishment of a joint seminary with New Guinea Lutheran Mission (Lutheran Church-Missouri Synod) and the Wabag Lutheran Church (now Gutnius Lutheran Church), to be located either in the Enga Province or at Gelem. This seminary would offer a lengthy course of theological studies, in English, to young men who wanted to prepare for the ordained ministry. It so happened, however, that at the same time as these plans were being made, Lutheran Mission New Guinea and the Evangelical Lutheran Church of New Guinea were exploring the feasibility of establishing an English-language seminary for the training of pastors. Fortunately, common sense and wisdom prevailed, and all the Lutheran missions and churches agreed to establish a joint seminary in Lae, located temporarily on the campus of Balob Teachers College (a pan-Lutheran institution). Australian Lutheran Mission and the Siassi Lutheran Church participated fully in the planning and development of the English Lutheran Seminary (the name was soon changed to Martin Luther

Dick Ngalu and students.

Seminary). They had two representatives on the first Council of the Seminary (Conrad Eckermann and Dick Ngalau), and they assigned a lecturer (Pastor John Strelan) to the three-man Faculty. In the first class, which began work in February 1966, there were three graduates of Gelem High School. A more detailed account of the beginnings and development of Martin Luther Seminary is given in another chapter of the present volume.[32]

Mission Outreach

It is not without significance that, at the first *Sam* (church Convention)[33] to be held on Siassi after the war, a decision was made to send five evangelists to work in what is now the Enga Province. The challenge to begin mission work among the Engas had been taken up by the Lutheran Church-Missouri Synod, but that body had requested help from Siassi and from Lutheran Mission Madang. In July 1948, Harold Freund, Armin Kleinig, and four Siassi men travelled to Ogelbeng in the Western Highlands, and then walked for four days to Yaramanda (Enga Province), where land was purchased and a mission-station established.[34] Here, for many years, more than 20 Siassi teachers and evangelists and their families made an important contribution to the growth of what is now Gutnius Lutheran Church. Their story is told in more detail elsewhere in this History.[35]

The Christians on Siassi supported fully the work of their evangelists in the Enga Province. Thus, for example, when the Awelkon church

261

was dedicated in 1954, the offering of £39 was used to provide blankets for Siassi workers in the cold Enga climate. The Siassi church regularly sent delegations to visit the Enga area for the purpose of encouraging the evangelists, strengthening the neophyte Christians, and keeping the home church informed of the problems and prospects of the highlands mission.

Australian Lutheran Mission and the Siassi Church, however, were still looking for a missionfield of their own on the New Guinea mainland. Their opportunity came when Australian Lutheran Mission staff attended the 1950 *Sam* (Convention) of Lutheran Mission New Guinea, held at Busamang. The *Sam* suggested that the Mission and Church on Siassi should take up mission work among the so-called Kukukuku people of the Menyamya area in the Morobe highlands. The area, with a population of c. 25,000, was at that time untouched by the Gospel and unaffected by Western culture. [36]

The Evangelical Lutheran Church of Australia was ready and waiting for such an opportunity: it had £4,000 set aside, and had already designated Harold Freund as the man to head the move into a new area. The Siassi Church, too, agreed to support the venture by supplying the needed workers: evangelists, teachers, medical orderlies, and carpenters. Lutheran Mission New Guinea had also consented to support the move into Menyamya by providing evangelists for the initial contact period. Thus, the outreach into Menyamya was a joint undertaking — and rightly so, especially in view of the fact that Lutheran Mission New Guinea was already at work in areas on three sides of Menyamya.

Menyamya was, at that time, a restricted area, which meant that no one could enter the area without the permission of the government. In November 1950, an experienced government officer, Lloyd Hurrell, had trekked overland from Wau to Menyamya. He and his party cleared a temporary airstrip for a light aircraft so that a government party could move in and authorize the opening of the area. The mission party which had assembled at Lae consisted of the missionaries Horrolt and Scherle from Lutheran Mission New Guinea, together with twenty Jabem evangelists and

Menyamya Station.

262

their families; from Australian Lutheran Mission came Freund, Kleinig, and newly-recruited teacher Owen Altus. The first group of this party arrived in Menyamya on March 13, 1951, the last on March 29. In April, the site for a mission station and the first bush buildings were dedicated to the service of God.[37]

Owen Altus set up a small school on Menyamya station; this school existed mainly for the purpose of training lads and young men who could assist the evangelists as language informants and as interpreters. The number of young men attending the school gradually increased, even though the routine and discipline of school work was alien to the Menya culture. By the time ten years had passed, the demand for schooling had increased so much that the Mission was hard-pressed to provide enough schools and teachers to meet the demands of the people. It took, however, more than ten years before people felt comfortable about sending their girls to school.

The work of the Jabem evangelists was, at first, severely restricted by the government's requirement that an evangelist could live only where a European was living; in practice, this meant that the evangelists were confined to the Menyamya station. In 1955 the restrictions were eased somewhat: evangelists were permitted to live in villages which were no more than one day's walk from the Menyamya station. The teaching and the influence of the evangelists immediately became more effective.

Many people were still very wary of the missionaries and evangelists; however, on their own initiative the fight-leaders at Kwaikuma, east of Menyamya, set aside a piece of land for a mission station. When Pastor Ted Lutze and two evangelists began to establish a mission station

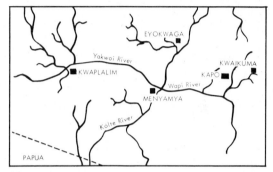

Menyamya area.

Owen Altus.

at Kwaikuma in 1955, the local people cleared the site, made paths to the water supply, dug drains, and built houses — all without pay in cash or kind. Soon a school was started, with an enrolment of 63 boys. All instruction was in the local language except for 30 minutes of Pidgin each day. The curriculum consisted almost entirely of Bible stories.

At Manyamya and Kwaikuma, and environs, the missionaries and evangelists quietly persisted in talking to the people about Jesus Christ. They told his story with the aid of pictures and, often, of a gramophone. This machine was an effective and fascinating resource, especially useful in overcoming the language barrier which existed between the Menyas and the missionaries. Bible stories, Gospel messages, and elementary catechetical lessons were taped by local speakers, and then transferred to records. These were then played on simple gramophones which schoolboys and evangelists took into the villages, and played whenever there was somebody who was willing to listen. Gospel Recordings Incorporated contributed much to this particular ministry. [38]

By 1958, the government had lifted many of the restrictions which it had placed on the evangelists; but by this time, most of the original 20 Jabem evangelists had returned to the coast, frustrated and discouraged by the delays and by the restrictions which had been placed on their movements. These original evangelists were replaced, in a few cases, by fellow-Jabems; but in the main, evangelists from Siassi took up the major part of the load.

The year 1957 was the first year of a decade of growth on many fronts. A new mission station was established at Kwaplalim, west of Menyamya, on land which was formerly a battleground. Pastor Russell Weier, who was to spend the next 20 years at Kwaplalim, was the missionary in charge. [39] Such was the early response to his ministry that ten extra men could have been placed in villages which were requesting the services of an evangelist. Meanwhile, at Kwaikuma, Deaconess Merna Thamm had opened a school for girls, and Pastor Morris Jordan was making good progress in the study of the Menya language — recognized as one of the most difficult languages in New Guinea. [40] Jordan was reducing it to writing, and preparing to translate

264

Gospel portions and other materials for an adult literacy program. At the dedication of the church in Menye village, the people for the first time sang a hymn in their own language.

The first large group baptisms in Menyamya were conducted in 1961 at Kwaikuma station and in the villages of Yinimba and Menye. The baptisms at Yinimba and Menye were notable on two grounds: The candidates had completed a course of instruction given entirely by New Guinean evangelists (Kekongandang and Taekeka), and the baptisms took place in village churches, not on a mission station. These baptismal services were followed by the formation of congregations, with elders being appointed in the various villages.

The Word of the Lord continued to grow, and the demand for education and for baptismal instruction grew apace. New school buildings were constructed and new churches were built in the villages in which evangelists were working. Much of this construction work was done by the versatile evangelists themselves. Buildings of a more permanent nature were erected by John Lewis and his team of Siassi and local carpenters. The timber for these projects was supplied by layworker Ray Ramm (and later, John Blyth), working with a team of Menyas to fell and cut logs in difficult and often dangerous terrain. [41]

The growth of the work in the 1960s presented the church on Siassi with a huge challenge to provide more evangelists and teachers to meet the demands from the Menya villages. The shortage of teachers was a major problem. The clamour for schooling was so great that a number of evangelists had to serve as teachers. The Siassi Christians responded magnificently to the Menyamya challenge: in the mid-1960s the 5,000 baptized Lutherans on Siassi were supporting over 40 evangelists and teachers and their families. In addition, other men from Siassi were working in Menyamya as medical orderlies and carpenters.

Medical orderlies from Siassi made major contributions to the medical program in Menyamya, especially in the village setting. At first, medical work was concentrated at Kwaikuma, where Som Lukas from Siassi [42] and Ken Cramer from Australia worked together to win the confidence of the people, break down

Ray Ramm cutting timber.

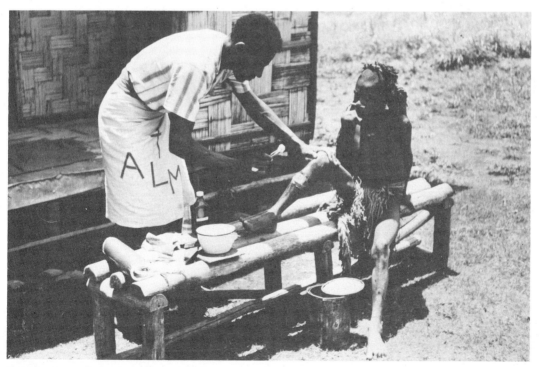

Som Lucas, orderly at work.

Evangelists training 67/68 with Logan.

Freund and Mrs Freund.

John Hartwig.

their distrust of Western medicines, and persuade them to follow basic principles of hygiene and child care. At Kwaplalim, Sister Dulcie Seiffert and her Siassi co-workers were faced with similar challenges. [43] The influence of the Siassi medical orderlies was such that a number of young Menya men determined to train as medical workers. They went for training to Lae, or to the hospitals at Awelkon and Lablab on Rooke Island. Upon the completion of their training, they returned to Menyamya to work side by side with their Siassi elder brothers.

After 1965, when local evangelists and medical orderlies began to work in the villages, the Siassi workers gradually withdrew from the field. In 1980 the last two Siassi evangelists — Seth Yalambing and Stephen Aun — left Menyamya and returned to Kampalap, their home village.

In 1963, the Menyamya Lutheran Church was formed, and thereafter annual *Sams* (church Conferences) were held. At the very first *Sam*, a decision was made to introduce a training course for local evangelists. This training program was begun by Morris Jordan at a new station north of Menyamya station, Eyokwaka. The program was continued, in 1964-65, by Harold Freund and John Strelan, and later by Pastor Cecil Logan. The graduates of this program filled the need for local workers in the congregation until they were replaced in many congregations by fully-trained local pastors.

Eyokwaka was to be the 'education' station of the Menyamya church. The girls' school was shifted from Kwaikuma to Eyokwaka; in addition, a new school (named 'Concordia') was built to provide more advanced training for boys and girls in the Menyamya area. The first Headmaster was Trevor Winderlich.

In 1965, when veteran missionaries Harold and Dorothea Freund left New Guinea after 30 years of service, the Menyamya church counted 1,160 baptized members, with another 1,000 people being prepared for baptism. Freund's successor at Menyamya was Pastor John Hartwig. God required of him only a short ministry in Menyamya: as he was returning from a patrol of his circuit, he was accidentally drowned in the Kotai river which forms one of the boundaries of Menyamya station. Pastor Hartwig died on August 13, 1967. He was the only member of the staff of Australian Lutheran Mission to lose his life in New Guinea.

III. 1966-1985: DISSOLUTION, UNION, AND REUNION

For many years prior to the 1960s, the members of Australian Lutheran Mission, and of the churches on Siassi and in Menyamya, had only spasmodic contact, and no formal ties, with their fellow-Lutherans in other parts of New Guinea. This was due, in part to geographical isolation, in part to the influence of the confessional stance of the 'mother' church, the Evangelical Lutheran Church of Australia.

It is true, the isolation was not total. Missionaries from Australian Lutheran Mission attended annual conferences and other meetings of Lutheran Mission New Guinea and of New Guinea Lutheran Mission, and these visits were reciprocated. Evangelists and teachers from the Evangelical Lutheran Church of New Guinea worked in Menyamya alongside of men and women from Australian Lutheran Mission and Siassi. For many years, evangelists and teachers from Siassi worked with the missionaries of New Guinea Lutheran Mission in the Enga Province. And Lutherans from Siassi and Menyamya who were working away from home joined congregations and gladly accepted the services of pastors of the Evangelical Lutheran Church of New Guinea. Nevertheless, as a group, Lutherans on Siassi and in Menyamya maintained their identities while enjoying generally cordial relations with other Lutherans, on an *ad hoc* basis and in a casual way.

Although this situation began to alter in the early 1960s, dramatic and far-reaching changes in the relationships between all Lutherans in Papua New Guinea took place only in the decade after 1966. During this period, Australian Lutheran Mission was dissolved, and its personnel became members of Lutheran Mission New Guinea; and the Lutheran churches on Siassi and in Menyamya became part of the Evangelical Lutheran Church of Papua New Guinea. The purpose of this final section of the present chapter is to give a brief account of the 'why' and 'how' of these developments.

In May 1963, representatives of New Guinea Lutheran Mission, Wabang Lutheran Church, Lutheran Mission New Guinea, Australian Lutheran Mission, and Siassi Lutheran Church,[44] met in Lae to discuss a proposal put forward by New Guinea Lutheran Mission and Australian Lutheran Mission that serious efforts be made toward bringing about the formation of one Lutheran church in Papua New Guinea.[45] One outcome of the meeting was the formation of a Committee on Theology and Inter-Church Relations, consisting of two representatives of the six Lutheran missions and churches in Papua New Guinea (the churches on Siassi and Manyamya were regarded as one).[46]

The Committee on Theology and Inter-Church Relations held its first meeting at Irelya, Enga Province, in October 1963. At this meeting the Committee announced that its primary aim was 'to draw up a confessional statement which will enable all Lutheran congregations in New Guinea to unite in a common faith in full accord with the Word of God, and in common work to the greater glory of God in New Guinea'.[47] After 13 meetings spread over ten years, the Committee was able to instruct its Executive Secretary to 'inform the heads of the three churches and missions that the CTICR has completed the Statement of Faith, and that if the churches and missions have no more work for the CTICR, the committee be discharged'.[48]

In the meantime, while the Committee in New Guinea was carefully going about its work, important developments had been taking place in the relationship between the two Lutheran churches in Australia, developments which were to affect the future of Australian Lutheran Mission and of inter-Lutheran relationships in New Guinea. The Committee on Theology and Inter-Church Relations in New Guinea had always been aware of the fact that 'one of the major barriers to a United Lutheran Church in New Guinea [might] lie in the relationship of the supporting bodies to one another'.[49] Indeed, the Committee addressed a direct question to the overseas supporting churches: 'Will the lack of fellowship among the supporting bodies hinder full fellowship or union among the Lutherans in New Guinea?'[50] The question was a pointed one especially for Lutherans in Australia, where the United Evangelical Lutheran Church in Australia and the Evangelical Lutheran Church of Australia were, on confessional grounds, not in fellowship with each other — but each contributed funds and personnel to one or more of the Lutheran churches and missions in New Guinea.

For a time it seemed that the apprehensions implicit in the Committee's question were well founded. A joint meeting of the Board of Foreign Missions and the Inter-synodical sub-committee of the Evangelical Lutheran Church of Australia (in March 1964) resolved:

> We agree that the ALM representatives cannot commit the ALM and the native churches to union with ELCONG or other Lutheran groups without the consent of the ELCA, which must be granted the right and opportunity to assure itself that any affiliations entered into by our representatives and native churches is in keeping with Scripture and the Confessions. If this is the case, the ELCA should not withhold approval and consent to our people in New Guinea becoming part of a U-ELCONG. [51]

In a covering letter, the President of the Evangelical Lutheran Church of Australia wrote:

> Our Lord has given us the great command to observe all things He has commanded us. If the confessional principles contained in this command are upheld, the ELCA would have no right to withhold approval and consent to our people in New Guinea becoming part of one Lutheran Church in New Guinea. If these principles are not upheld, however, which God may forbid, we could not with a good conscience give our consent to such a union. [52]

Within two years of the passing of the above-mentioned resolution, the Evangelical Lutheran Church of Australia had agreed to unite with the United Evangelical Lutheran Church in Australia to form one church, the Lutheran Church of Australia. The Document of Union included the following statement:

> We, the uniting churches ... pledge our common support to the Evangelical Lutheran Church of New Guinea, the Wabag Lutheran Church, and the Rooke-Siassi-Menyamya congregations of the Australian Lutheran Mission, because we recognize these three native Lutheran bodies to be confessionally Lutheran in their constitutions, doctrine and practice. [53]

Since the one Lutheran church in Australia was now supporting the work of Lutheran Mission New Guinea and of Australian Lutheran Mission, and since both mission organizations

were fully committed to Lutheran union in New Guinea, the next step was inevitable: the amalgamation of Lutheran Mission New Guinea and Australian Lutheran Mission. In 1966 both parties agreed upon this move; [54] it was implemented in an orderly way over a period of two or three years. By the end of the 1960s the amalgamation had been brought to a *de facto* completion. The final legal dissolution of Australian Lutheran Mission came only on April 5, 1975, the year of Papua New Guinea's political independence.

Thus, almost 40 years to the day from when the Evangelical Lutheran Church of Australia decided to establish a mission in Papua New Guinea, Australian Lutheran Mission came to an end. But its work did not. Many of its personnel, including the veteran missionary Freund, [55] continued to work in New Guinea. And the churches on Siassi and in Menyamya — the fruits of the Mission's work — were, of course, still there, faced now with the question of determining their relationships with the other Lutheran churches in Papua New Guinea.

The Menyamya Lutheran Church had experienced rapid growth in the 1960s. By 1969 it had grown to 7,000 members. Men from Menyamya were attending pastor training at Awelkon; one young man was studying at Martin Luther Seminary; and two-year training programs for evangelists were being conducted in Menyamya. But still local pastors and teachers were in short supply.

With the amalgamation of Australian Lutheran Mission and Lutheran Mission New Guinea, the number of expatriate personnel in Menyamya was gradually reduced. The last, and longest-serving Australian pastor in Menyamya, Russel Weier, left in 1978. By this time, Papua New Guineans were assuming greater responsibilities for the work in Menyamya. Three graduates of Logaweng Seminary were assigned parishes in the Menyamya Church. Three of the station schools had New Guinean headteachers. The Church Council visited every parish every three months, and tried to keep in touch with Menyas working in the towns by visiting them periodically.

In the early 1970s, the Menyamya Church began to look for ways of merging with the Evangelical Lutheran Church of New Guinea. In

1972, the Menyamya District Council called a meeting with the three neighbouring circuits (Aseki, Kaintiba, and Marawaka), with a view of forming a separate District within the Evangelical Lutheran Church of New Guinea. Marawaka withdrew from subsequent discussions, but Menyamya, Aseki, and Kaintiba decided to form the Maka Council, which would become part of the Lae District of the Evangelical Lutheran Church of New Guinea.

On August 15, 1974, at its convention at Akwangi village, Menyamya Lutheran Church formally adopted the *Statement of Faith* which had been published in 1973 and studied by the Menyamya congregations. Finally, on October 24, 1974, special services were held in Menyamya to celebrate the union of the Menyamya Lutheran Church with the Evangelical Lutheran Church of New Guinea. The Bishop of the latter church formally received Menyamya Lutheran Church into membership of the Jabem district, and also acknowledged the Maka Council as an organization within the Evangelical Lutheran Church of New Guinea.

By joining the Evangelical Lutheran Church of New Guinea in 1974, the Menyamya Lutherans were actually several years ahead of their 'fathers' on Siassi. The Siassi Lutheran Church had been formally constituted in 1964. In 1969 the church decided to regard itself as a District (with a view to future union), which was divided into two circuits with twelve parishes. Pastor David Isom was elected President of the Kaimanga Circuit, with headquarters at Lablab; Pastor Rhyal Klein was President of Kowai Circuit, with headquarters at Awelkon; and Pastor Yasaking Yawal, President of the District, had his office at Gelem.

Already in 1971 the Secretary of the Evangelical Lutheran Church of New Guinea (Zurewe Zurenuo) had extended an invitation to the Siassi Church to join with his church on the basis of the *Statement of Faith* prepared by the Committee on Theology and Inter-Church Relations. In 1975 the Siassi Church indicated its willingness to become a part of the larger church, on the condition that Siassi would not be joined with another District, but that it be admitted as a separate District.

At its tenth Synod, in 1976, the Evangelical Lutheran Church of New Guinea voted to receive the Siassi Lutheran Church as a seventh District. The declaration of union took place on May 10, 1977, when delegates of the Siassi Lutheran Church voted 157 to 0 to join with the Evangelical Lutheran Church of New Guinea as its seventh District. [56]

The first President of the Siassi District was Mr Martin Ningau; he was succeeded in turn by Pastor Stephen Sidi and then by Pastor Ben Aiwal. District headquarters were shifted from Gelem: first to Lablab, then, in 1982, to Karapo, the place where Georg Bamler first began Lutheran work on Siassi. So, in more ways than one, the wheel had turned full circle — symbolized, as it were, by the relocation of church headquarters. In Bamler's day, the Lutherans on Siassi had been part of the larger Lutheran fellowship in New Guinea. Then they were separated from it for 40 years. Now they were reunited.

Perhaps some of the sentiments expressed in the 'Declaration' at the time of union between Siassi Lutheran Church and the Evangelical Lutheran Church of New Guinea summed up what the Siassi people themselves thought of much of the history which has been so sketchily recorded in the previous pages:

The Saissi Lutheran Church remembers the overseas missionaries who came to work on Siassi.

From 1911 to 1936, the Neuendettelsau Mission Society and Lutheran Mission Finschhafen, as well as some friends from Buakawa, Taemi, Tami Island, and Jabem, came to work among the Siassi people. From the period 1936 to 1964 the Siassis were the responsibility of the Evangelical Lutheran Church of Australia and the Australian Lutheran Mission.

In 1964 Siassi Lutheran Church was formed, but the Australian Lutheran Mission continued to assist the church. Today we thank God for sending people from other areas who came and worked diligently to establish His Church on Siassi.

The Siassi Lutheran Church also thanks God our Father today because He, by His own mercy, has opened the door for the Siassi Lutheran Church to join the Evangelical Lutheran Church of Papua New Guinea. [57]

Endnotes

* *This chapter, written by Dr J. Strelan, acknowledges the research and an initial draft written by the Revd G.D. Noller.*

[1] A brief account of the Marists' work on Rooke Island is given by Hugh Laracy, *Marists and Melanesians: A History of Catholic Missions in the Solomon Islands* (Canberra: Australian National University Press, 1976), 24,25 and 30.

[2] An account of Bamler's life and work is given by A.P.H. Freund, 'Mission Pioneering', *Challenge*, 1972, 5-12.

[3] See Chapter 5.

[4] See Chapter 2.

[5] Minutes of the Synodical Convention of the Evangelical Lutheran Synod of Australia, Adelaide, March 7-13, 1935.

[6] Board members were: Pastors F.W. Noack, H.E. Temme, T. Reimers; Messrs M. Baltzer, A. Paech, C.M. Nothling. Members-at-large were Pastors R.H. Altus, O. Noske; Messrs B. Koch, E.L. Huf, E. Fisher, H.F. Altmann.

[7] The four men, accompanied by Board Chairman F.W. Noack, left Brisbane on December 20, 1935, and disembarked at Port Moresby on December 27, 1935.

[8] Pilhofer [*Die Geschichte der Neuendettelsauer Mission in Neuguinea*, Volume 2 (Neuendettelsau: Freimund Verlag, 1963), 233] is in error when he writes that the Siassi field was ceded to 'die Missouri Synode in Australien'. The Evangelical Lutheran Church of Australia enjoyed cordial and close relations with the Lutheran Church-Missouri Synod, but the relationship between the two churches was informal, and the Australian church was never an organic part of the Missouri Synod.

[9] The offer, made in January 1936, was accepted by the Executive Council of the Evangelical Lutheran Church of Australia on April 3, 1936. The Neuendettelsau Mission Society gave its formal consent only in September 1936.

[10] A.P.H. Freund, 'A Beginning is Made', *Challenge*, 1963, 6,7.

[11] 'Angebot der LUTHERAN MISSION FINSCHHAFEN an die Ev. Luth. Synode in Australien', January 20, 1936, page 2, section B.1.

[12] *Ibid*, pages 2,3, section B 1,2.

[13] Noack to Darsow, 20/1/36.

[14] The formal handing-over of the Siassi field to the missionaries from the Evangelical Lutheran Church of Australia was carried out by Pastor Stephen Lehner of Lutheran Mission Finschhafen on December 7, 1936.

[15] For accounts of the early years of Australian work on Siassi, see: A.P.H. Freund, 'A Beginning is Made', *Challenge*, 1963, 6,7; A.P.H. Freund, 'The Australian Lutheran Mission', *Challenge*, 1973, 11-15; Dorothea M. Freund, *I Will Uphold You* (Adelaide: A.P.H. Freund, 1985), 46-115.

[16] *Op. cit.* Dorothea M. Fruend, 55 (hereafter cited as Dorothea M. Freund).

[17] 'Stamps for Missions' also provided funds in the 1960s for the erection of two hospitals in the Menyamya area. See T. Wuttke, 'The "Stamps for Missions" Hospital', *Challenge*, 1966, 10-13.

[18] For an account of a typical medical patrol, see L. Menzel, 'Medical Patrol', *Challenge*, 1965, 34-38.

[19] In fact, the first payment to Money and Reynolds was made only in 1940; it was many years before the debt on Gizarum was finally paid off.

[20] A brief biography of Baitol is given in 'People you must Meet: Gilambing Baitol', *Challenge*, 1966, 8,9.

[21] For more information on Gizarum, and its place in the larger context of the plantations of Lutheran Mission New Guinea, see Chapter 18.

[22] Dorothea M. Freund, 63-65.

[23] A brief account of Sidi's life and work is given by E. Thamm, 'Sidi and the Mission Lifeline', *Challenge*, 1967, 26-28.

[24] Zacher and Neumann were conscripted; as an ordained clergyman, Freund was not obliged to join up; nevertheless he did so. He served with the Coast Watchers, and later with the Allied Intelligence Bureau. Cf Dorothea M. Freund, 85-93; also Eric Feldt, *The Coast Watchers* (Sydney: Pacific Books, 1967 [1946]) 45,151-154,166,167.

[25] For a general survey of cargo cults after the war, see John G. Strelan, *Search for Salvation* (Adelaide: Lutheran Publishing House, 1977), 26-50. For a cargo movement on Siassi, see Rhyall Klein, 'Deluded People Without Hope', *Challenge*, 1967, 29-32.

26 Neumann, Freund, and Mrs Freund returned to Siassi in 1946; they were accompanied by new recruits, Sister L. Hamdorf, Pastor Keith and Mrs Jean Nagel, and Mr Armin Kleinig. In 1947 came Pastor Conrad and Mrs Joan Eckermann, together with the laymen F.G. Koop, L. Heppner, M. Sawade, and L. Geue. For an account of conditions at Awelkon in the immediate post-war period, see Dorothea M. Freund, 100-104.

27 Between 1946 and 1963, 2,624 people were baptized on Siassi.

28 See Vida Mibus, 'In His Service', *Challenge*, 1964, 42-44.

29 A brief account of the work of Balob Teachers College is given by the first Principal, Mr Fred Stolz, 'Balob Teachers College', *Challenge*, 1969, 41-48.

30 Eckermann went first to Martin Luther Seminary, Lae, then to parish work in Australia. Ill-health forced an early retirement. Pastor Eckermann died on February 14, 1983.

31 See Keith Nagel, 'Native Pastors ... Really?', *Challenge*, 1964, 4-7; David Isom, 'Brethren, Pray for Us', *Challenge, 1967, 33,34.*

32 See Chapter 12.

33 For a description of a typical *Sam*, see Dorothea M. Freund, 58-61.

34 Dorothea M. Freund, 115-129, gives an account of the early days at Yaramanda.

35 See Chapter 8.

36 On Kukukuku culture, see Beatrice Blackwood, *The Kukukukus of the Upper Watut,* ed. C.R. Halpike (Oxford: Pitt Rivers Museum, 1978). For an account of early European exploration of the Menyamya area, see J.K. McCarthy, *Patrol into Yesterday* (Melbourne: F.W. Cheshire, 1963), 90-126.

37 A first-hand account of the development of the work in Menyamya during the first 14 years is given by Dorothea M. Freund, 133-182. Many details of mission tours (including places visited, linguistic notes, classes conducted, Gospel Recordings used, etc) are contained in the unpublished diaries of Pastor A.P.H. Freund.

38 See Dorothea M. Freund, 146-149.

39 In 1958 Weier was joined at Kwaplalim by Pastor Melvin and Mrs Vivienne Grieger. The Griegers returned to Australia in 1962.

40 See Morris Jordan, 'Learning the Language', *Challenge*, 1963, 18-20.

41 See R. Ramm, 'Timber from the Mountains', *Challenge*, 1963, 21-23; J. Lewis, 'Building for Christ', *Challenge*, 1964, 36-38.

42 See 'People You Must Meet: Som Lucas', *Challenge*, 1966, 8.

43 For brief reports on medical work in Menyamya, see K. Cramer, 'Menyas, Mud, and Medicine', *Challenge*, 1964, 16-18; D. Ramm, 'Report for the Third Quarter', *Challenge*, 1964, 33-35; B. Heinrich, 'Health, Hope, and Happiness for the Children', *Challenge*, 1967, 40-43.

44 The congregations on Siassi actually founded the Siassi Lutheran Church only in 1964.

45 The proposal of Australian Lutheran Mission and New Guinea Lutheran Mission is recorded in the minutes of the 'Inter-Mission Conference, 9th and 10th May, 1963', page 1.

46 Siassi Lutheran Church was represented at all thirteen meetings of the Committee by Pastor Yasaking Yawal and Pastor David Isom. Australian Lutheran Mission was represented by Pastor John Strelan (all meetings), and Pastor Keith Nagel (later by Pastor Conrad Eckermann).

47 'Minutes of the First Meeting of the Committee on Theology and Inter-Church Relations', Irelya, via Wabag, 22-24 October, 1963, Statement 3 (page 2).

48 'Committee on Theology and Inter-Church Relations: Minutes of the Thirteenth Meeting', Lae, November 30-December 2, 1972, Resolution 72:2.

49 'Minutes', October 22-24, 1963, Statement 10 (page 4).

50 *Ibid.*

51 'Minutes of Joint Meeting of BFM and Intersynodical Sub-committee at 261 Stanley St. North Adelaide on February 13, 1964', Point 3.

52 Clemens Hoopmann to John Kuder, 24/3/64.

53 'Document of Union', Paragraph 14.

54 'Minutes of the Meeting of the Combined Executive Committees of ALM and LMNG, held at ELCONG headquarters, Ampo, Lae, Friday 17/6/66', Resolutions 2-4, page 3.

55 Freund and his wife had returned to Papua New Guinea in 1968. They left the country in 1976 for active retirement in Australia.

[56] This decision was subsequently confirmed at the regular *Sam* (Convention) of the Siassi District on May 24-26, 1977. The 'Declaration' of union was signed by Martin Ningau and Dick Ngalau (for the Saissi Lutheran Church), and Zurewe K. Zurenuo, Janadabing Apo, Bapiangnu Buma, and Gedisa Tingasa (for the Evangelical Lutheran Church of New Guinea).

[57] 'Strongpela Tok i Kamap Ples Klia bilong ol Manmeri i ken Harim na Tingim: Siassi Luteran Sios na Evanselikal Luteran Sios bilong Papua Niugini i Bung Wantaim', II,6 (page 3).

Chapter 8

Lutheran Church among the Enga

New Guinea Lutheran Mission/ Missouri Synod

by Erwin L. Spruth

Introduction

The development of the Lutheran Church among the peoples of what is now known as the Enga Province of Papua New Guinea is related to, but significantly different from, the growth of the Lutheran Church in other areas of Papua New Guinea. The community of believers known as the *Gutnius Lutheran Church* (GLC) grew out of the work of Lutheran Mission New Guinea (LMNG), but developed alongside of, rather than being fully a part of, its mission movement. [1] Through the accidents of history, the Enga area opened up to mission development in 1948, soon after the end of World War II, at a time when the resources of LMNG and its supporting bodies were stretched to the limit as they tried to put together the work interrupted by the war. Thus, a new group was invited into the New Guinea work in order to assure a strong Lutheran presence in the Highlands. This in turn introduced a different supporting body with some differing methods and policies. [2] Consequently, an independent Lutheran Church developed in the Enga area alongside of the Evangelical Lutheran Church-Papua New Guinea (ELC-PNG).

The events covered in this brief history took place mainly in the Enga Province of Papua New Guinea, with some overlap into the Western Highlands Province (WHP) and the Southern Highlands Province (SHP). The Enga Province is rugged mountain country cut by many fast-flowing rivers and streams. The people live in areas which lend themselves to the production of sweet potato at altitudes of approximately 4000 to 8500 feet above sea level. There is little flat land even in the larger river valleys. Much of the gardening is done on the slopes of the mountains, and has led to the development of some unique agricultural techniques. The people were and still are primarily subsistence gardeners. Sweet potato is the major food crop, although the people now grow many different types of vegetables as well as some coffee and pyrethrum as cash crops. The rugged terrain seems to have led not only to the isolation of the area, but also to the development of the independent and aggressive character of the people.

In general, the Enga, Ipili, and Duna peoples, as well as the Nete and Hewa fringe-groups, had a similar world-view and cultural

273

outlook. They could be classified as animistic, pre-literate, new stone age, subsistence gardeners who were socially organized into named patri-clans which ideally practised exogamous marriage. While there are distinct cultural features which identify the various groups, all of them would fit into this broad framework, and all view the universe as being three-layered: the sky, people, and spirits above; living human beings and the earthly realm in the centre; and the land of the ancestral ghosts and malevolent spirits below. Each group has developed different rituals for satisfying the ancestral ghosts, but all aim at the same ideal: to live a peaceful and prosperous life in harmony with other people and with both the spiritual and material world.[3]

The Enga people make up the major portion of the GLC. They comprise the largest single language-group in Papua New Guinea (over 200,000), and are continually making their influence felt in the church and throughout the young nation that is Papua New Guinea.

The growth of the Gutnius Lutheran Church took place in that period of history right after World War II when Papua New Guinea was going through many rapid changes. The Australian administration in PNG was working to introduce education in English, economic development, political unity, and independence. For the people of the Enga Province, movement from a non-technological, stone-age-type culture to the highly-developed technology of today's world proceeded at an unprecedented pace: approximately 100 years of development and change for each year for the last 30 to 35 years. Children born at the beginning of this period are today serving as airline pilots, government leaders, teachers, nurses, skilled technicians, artists, and fully qualified medical doctors. The growth of the Church with its problems and successes must always be seen against this background of very rapid change. For this writer, it is only the grace of God and the independent character of these Highland peoples that kept them from being destroyed by all the forces of change and the technological development poured down on them by people and institutions beyond their control.

It is also important to remember that the GLC was not the only Church to develop in this area during this period of history. Gone were the

days of comity which gave different church groups different areas of the country to evangelize. The Roman Catholic, Seventh Day Adventist, Apostolic Church Mission, as well as several neo-Pentecostal sects that arrived after independence, were all trying to win these people to their interpretation of the Word and of the Gospel.

This, then, is the setting in which the history of the Gutnius Lutheran Church was made. Changes of all kinds have flowed rapidly one after another into the lives of these people. Social structures have been disrupted. Law and order has passed out of the control of the clan. Even institutions viewed as being good and helpful, such as schools, have taken their toll. Children who have been introduced to so much new information which their parents neither know nor understand, tend to disregard everything their parents say. The family and the clan are in a state of flux. Young people, particularly those who have not been able to go to school, are floundering between two worlds. But there is also a new stability; a new structure which makes brothers and sisters of people from different clans and language-groups; a new hope and a new peace.

In all of this varied milieu, the Lord of history has been active to bring into being a people called by his name, a new people free to be fully human and to fulfil the purpose for which they were created. What follows will show how God was at work in the growth and development of the Gutnius Lutheran Church-Papua New Guinea.[4]

God Prepares His People

The question is often asked as to when the Church really began in the Enga Province. When did God put in his appearance among the ancestors of the people who today form the GLC? If we speak of the formal organization of the church, we can cite the day and name the people who were present. When we speak of God's involvement with the people in prior times, we cannot put down dates or name names. We can only say that, when the forefathers came to this part of Papua New Guinea, God not only came with them, he was already here.

The ancestors did not know God as creator, nor did they know Jesus Christ as Lord.

Some time in the distant past, they had lost the knowledge of the God who made them and constantly cared for them. There was, however, a longing, a knowledge, a story that life was not always this way, and that there had been a better time. This belief was expressed in the story of the *Water of Life* and how it was lost to the people of earth. [5] Now they could only hope that someday somehow they would find the *tae toko*, the ladder to the sky, the way back to the good life.

We must be clear that this was not always the centre of the life of the people. Often they pushed it aside, did not want to think about it; but the story, the idea, was there. God did not leave his people without a witness.

Long before the missionaries were aware of the people of this part of PNG or came to them with the Gospel, God was feeding, sustaining, protecting, directing, and preparing his people. No matter what the people may have thought or believed concerning their world and the source of all good and happiness, it was God who was demonstrating his love and concern to them (Acts 14:17; 17:24-28). God was involved in the history of these peoples. He was part of their migration and their establishment in the Highlands. He provided them with the sweet potato and their excellent way of gardening. He enabled them to establish the norms of their culture which reflect the partial knowledge of his will in their hearts. Their hopes and their dreams, their ideals of peace and brotherhood, their holding of relationships between people as being of higher value than things, all point to the fact that God was among them, preparing a people to be his own. Their laws reflect 'the law of God written in their hearts' and show a relationship to the second table of the Decalogue: Obey your elders; do not kill; do not steal; do not take another's wife; help your brothers; do not speak evil of another. Often these 'laws' were broken, and harmony did not exist, but the ideal was there, and people were often called to follow it.

We do not want the reader to feel that there was only good in the religious beliefs of these Highland peoples; that would be far from true. But there were those better elements which show God at work among them, and which gave each man or woman the opportunity to seek the truth and to live according to what they had already found.

Most of Enga and Ipili religious practice involved the ghosts of the recent dead and the ancestral spirits. These ghosts were viewed as the ones who caused all the problems of human beings, who brought sickness and death. Thus, the ghosts were feared, and various offerings and sacrifices were made to them to ensure their non-interference in human affairs. At the same time, however, the people did know of a supreme being who was over all, called *Aitawe* or *Gotte*.

Aitawe/Gotte did not play an active role in the lives of the people, but he was there as a court of last resort. He was seen as the ultimate guardian of morality, one who could be called on when a ghost was acting capriciously and would not leave a man alone. It was only after they came to faith in the Lord Jesus and came to know God as their own God and Father that Enga and Ipili people recognized that in some way God had been trying to reach them all along.

Rare of Wangam is a special case. Sometime in his youth (1915?), he had a vision of the 'land of plenty and peace', a place where everything was good. He was told by the 'great one' that he would be able to go to this blessed land, but he would have to leave many of the ways of his people and follow the 'great one' alone. One almost hears an echo of the biblical word: 'Do this and you shall live'. Rare was true to his vision and tried to share it, but people thought he was a fool or even insane. In 1955, shortly after Lutheran mission work began in the Lakaip area of the Enga Province, Rare was brought to the attention of the missionary. After only one meeting, Rare made the connection between his vision and the Lord Jesus. That night Rare died, one who had been waiting for the Lord. Not many people paid attention to Rare during his lifetime, but, as the Gospel spread among them, they remembered and were able to thank God for the witness he had given them (Spruth 1981:41-43).

Wambalipi of Lyaimi is another example of God preparing a people to hear his Word. The scope of this brief history does not allow us to detail his story, but what he did had a profound effect on the spread of the Gospel in the western portion of the Enga Province. Wambalipi and his brothers began a religious movement sometime during 1940 or 1941 which moved from the Lyaimi area eastward to the Lakaip and Sirunki areas and northwest to the Porgera. The movement continued until it was stopped in 1945 by the Australian authorities, who viewed it as some sort of 'cargo cult'. When Wambalipi and other leaders were jailed, the movement petered out (Schaan 1968, Spruth 1981:43-48).

This movement introduced the idea of brotherhood among all people, service to a higher power, organized worship, and a turning away from the fear of the ancestral ghosts and the spirits. It incorporated a ritual cleansing as well as a communal sacramental meal. Parts of the ritual were totally unacceptable to the Christian faith, yet it did prepare people for something that was to come. Wambalipi, now a member of the Lutheran congregation at Unjaka in the Lyaimi area, views his cultic activity as something that basically failed. At the same time, he is convinced that the ideas he had came from God, and that he was fulfilling part of God's plan for his people. Christians in the Porgera go so far as to identify this movement with that of John the Baptist in Jesus' day. They see it as God's way of preparing them to receive the Gospel (Mandita 1978).

What then of Rare and Wambalipi and other prophetic voices? What of this movement that excited the people? Were those men moved by God, or was it just another attempt to deceive the people? The fact remains that the messages and actions of these men did prepare the way for the Gospel. People were living in expectation, and were open to hear the Word of the Lord. [6]

Come Over and Help Us

It was the policy and practice of the Lutheran missionaries who brought the Gospel to the people of the Enga Province to wait for an invitation from the people before beginning work in a given area. There were times when people were encouraged to issue such an invitation, but the missionaries never forced themselves on the people. In the early years of the work, the major problem the Mission had was keeping up with all the invitations to 'come over and help us'.

Lutheran Mission New Guinea had plans to enter the Enga country as soon as the Australian administration opened the area.

One of the first churches at Yaramanda.

Their interest was heightened by the Enga people who came to Mount Hagen, particularly to the Lutheran Mission centre at Ogelbeng, and invited the Lutheran Mission to come and establish work in their area.

LMNG wanted to be sure that there would be a strong Lutheran presence in the Enga area, for that was the next logical step for the development of the Church in the Highlands. Yet, when the time came to enter Enga-land, it became apparent that, with the redevelopment work needed right after the war, LMNG did not have the resources nor the missionary personnel to cope with this new field. They then issued an invitation to the Evangelical Lutheran Church of Australia (ELCA), which was already at work in PNG in the Siassi islands group. Since the ELCA felt that the Enga field was a larger project than they could handle by themselves, they in turn issued an invitation to the Lutheran Church-Missouri Synod (LC-MS) to 'come over and help us'. The invitation was accepted by a unanimous vote of the LC-MS in its 100th anniversary convention in 1947. At a later date, the LC-MS and the ELCA agreed that the LC-MS alone should be responsible for this mission project, although they would be free to call workers from the ELCA. [7] The stage was now set to answer the many calls for the Lutheran Mission to bring the Gospel to the Enga people.

The most persistent calls for the Lutheran Mission came from the people on the eastern border of the Enga. Minjuku Yasima, of the

276

Worshipping at Irelya.

Wawini clan at Yaramanda, was a government-appointed *bosboi* for his group. [8] Early in 1947, he went to Mt Hagen and saw all the development at the Lutheran centre at Ogelbeng. He noted how the Mission helped the people and was a source of material goods. He also saw that the Mission treated the people much better than the government, at least from his point of view: work was paid for, produce was purchased, and people were respected. These were the people he wanted in his area. Again and again he asked the missionary and the church leaders to 'come over and help us' (Waimane and others, 1978).

Kooa Waimane was another young man of the Wawini clan who was instrumental in bringing the *Miti* to his people. [9] Since Waimane had trade relations with some of the Hagen people, he had learnt their language and was able to communicate with them. Sometime in 1947 or early 1948, Waimane heard the Gospel for the first time while visiting Ogelbeng. He was attracted to this message and wanted to learn more, so he enrolled as a catechumen for several months. This new message of a God who loves people, of one who can free people

from the fear of the spirits, gripped his heart. He added his voice to that of Minjuku in pressing the Lutheran Mission to 'come over and help us'.

Through the efforts of Minjuku, Waimane, and others, and in accord with God's will for his people, the invitation to come to Yaramanda was heard. The first Lutheran advocates of the Gospel were: the Revd A.P.H. Freund, senior missionary of the ELCA's Siassi field; Mr A. Kleinig, a builder from Rooke Island; Teacher/Evangelists Teoc, Yasaptung, and three other workers from the Siassi congregations; the Revd F. Doering, LMNG missionary at Ogelbeng; Evangelist Pokon of the Ogelbeng congregation; and Kundi, a catechumen from Ogelbeng who spoke both Enga and New Guinea Pidgin. They arrived at Yaramanda in early August 1948 (NGLM 1948).

Yangomane Yakopya, a *kamongo* of the Talyuru clan at Irelya, [10] was another leader who issued a strong invitation to the Lutheran Mission. Yangomane was a leader in the Enga pig exchange. As such, he had travelled down the Lai River Valley and was aware of the missions beginning to enter the Enga area. He

277

was opposed to the fighting that seemed endemic among the Enga, and hoped the missions would help to keep the people from warring with one another.

The Irelya people had been recruited by the Australian administration to help carry goods and supplies from Mt Hagen to the new patrol post at Wabag. In order to assure a continued supply of carriers, a New Guinea police constable by the name of Apakasa was stationed at Irelya, some three miles from Wabag. He became friends with Yangomane, and urged him to work for peace. He told him that the best way was to invite the Mission to bring them the message of God. Apakasa's witness to his faith was used by God to encourage Yangomane to call for the mission (Yangomane 1978; Kuniame 1978).

Yangomane recalled one of the dreams and prophecies of his father Taingane: 'When someone comes with "white skin", the people will live in peace and have plenty. They will find the way to the skyland, and fulfil all of their longings.'[11] Spurred on by these ideas, Yangomane looked for a missionary to come to his place (ibid).

Yangomane had married a woman from Rakamanda where the Seventh Day Adventist Mission had just begun to set up a mission centre, so he decided to go to Rakamanda to invite the missionary there to also set up at Irelya. When he did this in early 1948, but was refused, he began to look for someone else to help him and his people. About that time, the Lutheran missionaries arrived at Yaramanda some 25 miles down the Lai Valley. When Missionary Freund made his first trip to Wabag in mid-August 1948, Yangomane invited him to send a missionary to Irelya. This he promised to do (Yangomane 1978; NGLM 1948).

Yangomane was pleased that the mission would be coming, but that feeling was not shared by all the leaders at Irelya. The idea of a mission at Irelya was particularly opposed by Imbuni, a leader of one of the other Talyuru sub-clans. But Yangomane did not give up easily; he recruited other leaders. Lyiu Lyilyo of Irelya and Tini of Aeposa saw the advantages, and joined Yangomane in wanting the mission to come. Then Punanji and Neape of Irelya also agreed, and the matter was settled. Yangomane went to Yaramanda and pressed his case. Early in 1949,

278

Missionary Willard Burce and Teacher/ Evangelist Yasaptung arrived at Irelya to begin the work there. Irelya became a centre for the spreading of the Gospel, and is today the headquarters of the GLC (Kuniame 1978; Yangomane 1978; NGLM 1948/49).

Viewing his homeland and his people, Yangomane now tells them that everything he said in the past, the prophecy of his father, has come true. They are living in peace and plenty, and, what is more, they know the way to the true Life (Yangomane 1978).

The scope of this short historical introduction does not allow us the space to tell of the many leaders and others who were used by God to invite the bearers of the Good News into their midst; they are known by God and by the people in their local areas. It is as the writer of Hebrews said as he shared the stories of the great heroes of the faith: 'And what more shall I say? I do not have time to tell about ...' (Hebrews 11:32). The invitations came from pragmatists who wanted more and better things for their people, as well as from religious innovators who saw in the Miti a way to a new life. All, however, saw the coming of the mission as a way of peace. All were used by God for the building of his Church.

The Spread of the Church

Let us now take a broad look at the flow of the Gospel as it passed from one community to another, bringing about a turning to the Lord and the establishment of the congregations and circuits of the Gutnius Lutheran Church. In the early years, the evening prayers of the worshipping groups often included a recital of the way the Word of God had passed from one main area to another, and included a petition that each should be strengthened in their faith, and that the Word of God would continue to be spread. Today, with the large number of communities and major areas that have been reached, such a recital becomes too long and is not used. Occasionally, an older leader will follow at least some of the pattern, ending with: 'and all those farther on who have joined us in following Jesus Christ'.

The pattern of growth generally proceeded from east to west, and from the main valleys to spurs and feeder valleys. It is interesting to note that this is also the way in which it is believed the

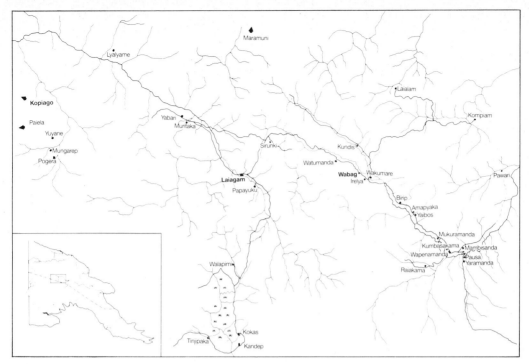

Enga area

Enga people originally migrated into their mountain homeland (Lacey 1975:261): first, up the Lai Valley; then, over the range into the Lakaip; and finally, into the fringe areas and on to other language-groups. The Gospel travelled along many of the normal and usual routes of trade and communication. One sometimes gets the feeling that even the missionaries, be they black or white, were shared by the Enga along these pathways. God used the long-established system of the Enga people to share his love among them.

The Gospel first came overland from the Mt Hagen area, carried by New Guinea evangelist/teachers as well as by missionaries from other lands; together they were used by God to make known the Good News about his Son. In 1947, the administration of Papua New Guinea de-restricted a large portion of the Enga area, [12] opening it up for missions to work among the Enga. The Lutheran Christians of Mt Hagen had been waiting for this time, and they began to share the Good News with their Simbai neighbors. God's full time had come for his Enga people.

Missionaries Freund, Doering, and A. Kleinig, together with teacher/evangelists from the Lutheran congregations in the Siassi islands and workers from the Mt Hagen congregations, travelled overland from Ogelbeng with about 240 carriers. They arrived at Yaramanda in August 1948, and accepted the offer of land from Minjuku and the people of his clan. The first centre from which the Lutheran Church would share the Gospel with the Enga people was established. The task had begun.

The people used by God to carry out his mission task among the people of the Enga area came from coastal villages, small tropical islands, mountain hamlets, great metropolitan areas across the seas, rolling farmlands, and small towns. They spoke different languages and had varied cultural backgrounds — but they all came on the same basis: sent by the same God, empowered by the same Spirit, and carrying the same message of salvation through the Lord Jesus Christ. They were the men and women called by God through their congregations and churches to be missionaries among the peoples in the newly-opened area of the Highlands of Papua New Guinea. These men and women, whether or not they were sent specifically to be evangelistic workers, were advocates of the new life in Christ, pleading on Christ's behalf: 'Let God change you from enemies into friends!' (2 Cor. 5:20).

These 'fathers in the faith' have had tremendous influence on the development of the GLC. For good or bad, the patterns that were set by the pioneer missionaries became the policies of the Church and set the directions of the Mission for many years. While all preached the Good News of Jesus as Saviour and Lord, the different emphasis flowing from differing backgrounds has made for variety within the Church. A total of 42 evangelists and teachers from PNG Lutheran congregations and 254 expatriates served with the GLC in the first 35 years of its history. [13]

All the workers sent by the Kate, Siassi, and Hagen congregations of the Lutheran Church in PNG were engaged in some form of direct evangelism, either as teachers or evangelists or some combination of the two. With the overseas workers, the picture is much different. In addition to the pastors, teachers, and evangelists, there were also doctors, nurses, and other medical staff; builders, mechanics, and other tradesmen; administrators, business staff, and secretaries; teachers, and house-parents for the missionaries' children. Over the years, some 100 of these expatriate missionaries served the GLC in tasks directly linked to the growth of the Church. They, together with the 42 evangelists and teachers from PNG Lutheran congregations, had a special role in the proclamation for the Gospel.

The fact that evangelists and teachers were sent by PNG Lutheran congregations into the wilds of the western portion of the New Guinea Highlands in the 1940s from Siassi, an island off the northern coast of New Guinea, from the Kate congregations, particularly those of the mountain area behind Finschhafen, and from the newer congregations around Mt Hagen was very significant. Their work as witnesses to the Lord Jesus showed the Enga people that the Gospel was not a message restricted to those from outside PNG. The evangelists from Mt Hagen were especially equipped for the task of witnessing to the Enga; they had only recently come out of heathenism, and knew at least
280

some of the problems faced by Enga people as they listened to the Good News.

The service of such PNG missionaries was concentrated in the years between 1948 and 1961. After GLC began sending out their own evangelists and teachers, the need for these men diminished, and many returned home to other tasks within the Church. A difference in church policy between their home congregations and the emerging Enga congregations hastened the departure of some of them. As evangelists and teachers, in their home congregations they were not authorized to baptize, to officiate at the Lord's Supper, or to officially hear confessions; these tasks were reserved for the missionaries and the ordained pastors. In the Enga church, however, each congregation was encouraged to appoint elders who would be responsible for the preaching of the Word and the administration of the Sacraments. The majority of Enga congregations appointed such elders, particularly in the western portion of the Church. 'How can we as fathers feel comfortable receiving the Lord's Supper from those who are our children?' was the way some of them expressed their concern. They returned home with the knowledge that they had done their job well.

Before we continue with the growth and movement of the Good News across the mountains and valleys of the Enga Province, let us get to know at least a few of the early pioneers, those who came first with the story of God's love in Christ Jesus.

Pokon

Pokon was an evangelist of the Ogelbeng Congregation near Mt Hagen. Because he was able to speak Enga, he was given leave of absence from his task, and sent with the team that began the mission among the Enga in August 1948. He was a man with a deep love for his Lord and a desire to share the joy he had found in Jesus Christ. He was forceful in his approach to the Enga people, demonstrating his lack of fear of their spirit powers or their *poisen*. [14] While he did not remain in the Enga area long enough to see the fruit of his labours, he did stir up the hearts of many, causing them to become seekers after God's truth. Pokon was used by God to bring the Gospel to many Enga people. He was the first evangelist to proclaim clearly the Gospel of Christ Jesus in the Enga language. He produced the first Enga language hymns, and helped to establish the principle of using the local language for worship and instruction (NGLM 1948-50).

Teoc

Teoc was a trained teacher, who came from Siassi with A.P.H. Freund and A. Kleinig. By early 1949, he was instructing a group of boys and young men in reading, writing, and numbers, as well as introducing them to the Lord Jesus Christ. Out of these classes at Yaramanda came some of the young men who would become the Church born among the Enga people. Teoc was a good disciplinarian, and established a pattern of education which was carried on in many other schools of the GLC. Teoc served in many teaching duties, including the establishing of the first middle school among the Enga at Ampayaka. In November 1961, he returned to Siassi after 13 years of missionary service (NGLM 1948-61).

Kate Workers

The Kate evangelists and teachers were some of the most enthusiastic of all the New Guinean missionaries. They saw the evangelization of PNG as one of their primary goals in life, and worked hard to make it come about. Occasionally their enthusiasm got them into difficulty — as when Temaonec cut down a tree in a sacred grove near Raiakama — but their work was invaluable in bringing the Enga Church into being. Fusepe, Otasinke, Yasaking, Temaonec, and others left their homeland to spend many years of their life among the Enga, teaching them to know the Lord Jesus and to follow his ways.

One of the disappointments for the Kate workers was the decision by the Mission to use Enga as their language of communication and education rather than Kate, which had been the practice in other Highland areas. Because of their zeal to share the Good News, most of them learnt Enga very quickly, and soon they were witnessing without the need of interpreters. The Kate workers were the first to leave the Enga Church; by 1961, all had either returned to their home congregations or gone on to other mission tasks.

Expatriate Missionaries

The expatriate missionaries from Australia, Canada, and the USA were the people who generally set the tone and the pace of the mission program. From 1948 to 1960, they determined which place would get workers, where missionaries would be stationed, and how the funds would be used; they even made the decision as to which of the catechumens would be baptized, and which were not yet ready. Naturally, they consulted with their PNG co-workers, and later with the catechumens and the baptized Christians, but the decisions were theirs to make in these early years of the development of the GLC. The policies set by the early expatriate missionaries, and the patterns of mission work developed and followed by them, have become the standards by which all other work has been judged by the Church in these first thirty-odd years. Again and again, one will hear older men quote Burce or Hintze or Kleinig or Stotik or Spruth as their authority for certain ideas and/or methods of work. In a sense, these first proclaimers of the Good News in each area have become the apostles to the GLC in the minds and the hearts of the people. Their work is valued highly, and their message seen as the standard by which all others must be evaluated.

None of the expatriate missionaries aspired to the role of setting the patterns and standards of the local church, but the very nature of the situation placed them in that position. Their actions and judgments have been both a help and a burden to the GLC. This is particularly true of those men who were the first into an area, before there was a group of local Christians to help with the mission expansion. When the GLC's own evangelists and leaders became a part of a team going into a new area, the expatriate missionary was viewed as an important part of the group, but no longer the focal figure as before. As we would expect, the influence and directions set by these first advocates is both good and bad. Their dedication to the Lord Jesus and their willingness to work long and hard, to visit the most remote group in order to share the Gospel, has set a pattern of mission interest and dedication which continues in the GLC. Their emphasis on the needs of the whole person has also encouraged the Church to carry on programs and service which link the Gospel with many other needs of the people of this area. On the other hand, their centralized administration, Western patterns of organization, and willingness to be part of the condemnation of certain Enga cultural practices before the full ramifications of such a condemnation were known, have given the GLC problems with which it is still wrestling. [15]

The length and scope of this brief chapter in the story of the Lutheran Church in PNG do not allow us to introduce all of the people used by God to bring about the establishment and growth of his church in the Enga Province. We will, however, mention some of those who were the pioneers in bringing the Good News to these people.

A.P.H. Freund

Missionary Freund was the senior missionary of the Australian Lutheran Mission. He had been in New Guinea prior to World War II, and had served as a Coast Watcher for the Australian forces during the Japanese occupation. [16] Because of his long experience in PNG, he was loaned to the new work in the Highlands for two years. He led the first Lutheran party into the Enga area and established the first centre at Yaramanda in 1948.

Freund helped to set the patterns which the work would follow in this early period: frequent itinerations, exploration, language study, the establishing of many additional satellite centres, and cooperation between expatriate and PNG missionaries. By the time he returned to his work on Siassi in 1950, the new field had established centres at Yaramanda, Irelya, and Yaibos, and many smaller centres throughout the area (Burce 1955:1-5; NGLM 1948,1949).

Willard Burce

Missionary Burce is recognized as senior among the 'fathers' of the GLC. Arriving on the field from the USA in 1948, he has continued his service with the Church through to the present. Dr & Mrs Burce were assigned to the second mission centre to be opened by the Mission, and began their work at Irelya, near Wabag, in February 1949. Burce was a good linguist, and a keen student of the ways and customs of the people. Through his Gospel proclamation and the work he did together with Yasaking and other PNG evangelists, a large number of

Dr Willard Burce.

people around Irelya began to accept the Gospel. It was here that the first baptism of a group of Enga people took place on January 6, 1957.

Burce and his Enga co-workers at Irelya produced the first book of Enga Bible stories in 1955. Later, in 1965, he translated the first portion of Enga Scripture to be printed: the Gospel of Mark. Burce was assigned to establish the Birip School for Church Workers in 1960, and was posted to the joint ELC/GLC Martin Luther Seminary at Lae in 1966. His early work at Irelya has continued to bear fruit as the men he trained became some of the leaders of the GLC. The Revd Dr Waima Waesa, first Bishop of the GLC, was instructed and baptized by Dr Burce.

Otto C. Hintze

Otto Hintze is recognized as the second of the 'pioneer' missionaries from the USA. He arrived in PNG in November 1948 together with Burce, was assigned to the station at Yaramanda, and worked together with Freund until 1950. Hintze did a lot of patrolling throughout the Lower Lai Valley, and was

282

instrumental in establishing the majority of the congregational centres in the area. He put in much effort in reducing the Enga language to writing and establishing it in its present form. In 1963 he was appointed as the first Director of the Enga Language Training Centre for missionaries, and began full-time work in language teaching and missionary orientation. In 1965 when the Hintzes returned to the USA for furlough, he resigned from the field to accept a teaching position at the Springfield Seminary of the LC-MS.

Ian Kleinig

The Kleinigs were seconded to NGLM by the ELCA. They arrived on the field in May 1949. After spending their first few months in PNG at Irelya, Kleinig was given the task of developing the work between Irelya and Yaramanda. He first worked closely with the centre being established at Birip, and then in October 1949 established the centre at Yaibos. Kleinig developed the outreach into the Ninim Valley to the north of Yaibos and in the Aiyale Valley south of Yaibos. He gave a lot of time to the establishing of the school at Yaibos, and was also instrumental in developing the first agricultural program of the Mission.

Together with a team of GLC evangelists and leaders, Kleinig was given the responsibility of opening up the Tarua area when it was de-restricted in 1961. He continued his work at Yaibos until 1963 when he was appointed as the second teacher at the Birip Lutheran School for Church Workers. In late 1965, the Kleinigs were given a peaceable release from their call to PNG in order to accept a call to work in mission in Orissa, India.

Karl Stotik

Stotik arrived on the field from the USA in 1951. After a period of orientation at Irelya, he began the work at Sirunki in April 1952, soon after the area was de-restricted. As a single man, Stotik was able to patrol extensively and to enter into some areas of Enga culture restricted to others. He was the first expatriate to witness the *sangai* (bachelor cult) of the Enga. [17] One of his major contributions in the early years was an emphasis on adult literacy and the development of materials to teach adults to read. For many

years, literacy was a full part of the instruction of candidates for baptism in the Sirunki area.

In 1961, Stotik was assigned to the task of beginning the outreach in the Kandep area. Together with Enga evangelists and leaders and Missionary Vic Heinicke, he entered the Kandep in July 1961, and helped to establish the main centre as well as additional areas for the sharing of the Gospel. In 1962, he was transferred from Sirunki to Irelya and given the position of Adult Literacy Director. In 1963, he was elected President of the NGLM. In subsequent years, Stotik has been a teacher at Timothy Lutheran Seminary, Birip; Circuit Advisor to the Yaibos Circuit of the GLC; and has developed a program of extension education for church workers. He and his family returned to the USA in 1983.

Erwin L. Spruth

The Spruths arrived in New Guinea in January 1953. After an orientation period at Yaramanda, and several months working at Sirunki while Stotik was away, the Spruths were assigned to Papayuku. Special permits to enter the Lakaip area were obtained from the government in July 1954. Soon afterwards, the mission centre at Papayuku was established, and the work in the Lakaip Valley began. Following the patterns established by those before him, Spruth itinerated throughout the Lakaip area establishing preaching places wherever people were willing to hear the Good News. Medical work carried out by Mrs Spruth, a registered nurse, was instrumental in paving the way for the message of the Gospel among many of the Lakaip Enga. Spruth was given the responsibility, along with leaders and evangelists of the GLC, to begin the work at Muritaka in the lower Lakaip when it was de-restricted in 1961. In following years, he was also assigned the task of beginning the work among the Ipili in the Porgera and Paiela areas, as well as starting the work in the Lyaimi Circuit.

In 1964 the Spruths were assigned to Irelya, where Spruth was to serve as Irelya Circuit Missionary and as Counsellor for Evangelism and Stewardship. The Evangelism and Stewardship job was made full-time in 1966. Spruth served the GLC in various tasks related to the evangelistic programs of the Church and its administration. From 1973 until 1978 he served as Administrative Officer of the GLC. When this position was localized in 1978, he was reassigned to the Evangelism Department of the GLC. The Spruths returned to the USA in 1981.

Other Staff

While these men mentioned above have been most influential in the establishment and development of the GLC, they were not the only expatriate advocates of the Gospel. A history of the New Guinea Lutheran Mission-Missouri Synod must be written to tell the full story of all of these men and women of God, used by him for his mission in the GLC. Special mention should be made of William P. Wagner who opened the Kopiago Mission in 1964; Edward Dicke, the first full-time Treasurer/Business Manager who led the Mission into economic development on behalf of the local people; George Hinlicky, the first teacher on the field; Audrey Lafrenz Biberdorf and Wanda Fricke who served as the first nursing staff; and the many wives who worked together with their husbands, carried on programs in education, women's work, medicine, and literacy, and showed the people much love.

The missionary advocates, black and white, were used by God to bring the message of salvation into the lives and hearts of the people in such a way that they turned to Jesus, accepted him as their own, and were incorporated into his Church.

Let us get back to our story of how the Gospel spread among the peoples of the Enga Province. As we have noted above, the Good News spread from the main valleys to the feeder valleys, and generally from the east to the west. Soon after the establishment of the main centre at Yaramanda, the Mission was given an opportunity to begin a second centre at Irelya in 1949. Patrols were carried out to most of the surrounding communities. Wherever people were willing to accept a proclaimer of the Good News, sub-centres were established at which missionaries sent by the Lutheran congregations of PNG shared the Gospel with their Highland brothers and sisters. Work at places where GLC congregations now exist (such as Makaramanda, Injinji, and Birip) was begun, and the strange names of men like Kitingnu, Temaone, Ichatong, Yasaking, 284

Tiopoli, and Moramundi became familiar to the Enga people. Men and women were given the opportunity to hear the Word of the Lord, to come to know Jesus as Saviour, and to find new life in him (NGLM 1948-50).

The physical expansion into new communities continued at a rapid pace. Everywhere people were asking for men to bring them the Gospel. Black or white missionaries were usually sent out to a new area as soon as possible. In 1950 and 1951, eight centres were opened, including a new circuit at Yaibos between Yaramanda and Irelya. In addition, there were many smaller places being reached on an irregular basis through visitations and through people sharing what they had already heard of the Gospel. The labourers were unable to keep up with the demands of the harvest. A certain amount of competition was evident as Lutheran advocates attempted to outpace the Roman Catholic workers, and Catholics tried to outmanoeuvre the Lutherans.

By the end of 1954, two more circuit centres had been established further west: Sirunki in 1952, and Papayuku in 1954. Five circuit centres and 48 preaching-places were regularly bringing the Gospel to over 12,000, and contacting at least twice that number. At this time, the workers who had been sent to make the Good News known and to lead people to discipleship numbered five expatriate pastors and 27 evangelist/teachers from Lutheran congregations in PNG. In addition there were three expatriate builders, two nurses, a teacher, and a business manager. These Christian witnesses, together with their wives and families, were the ones used by God to touch the Enga people with his love.

There continued to be more calls from people who wanted to hear the Gospel than there were workers. There were as yet no baptized Enga Christians; but there were some 540 adults enrolled in membership classes, and it was from this group that much of the manpower came to meet the requests of people for the Good News. Catechumens were instructed each day from Monday to Friday. Those who were able to communicate what they had been taught were sent out on Saturday and Sunday to share the message of the Word they had learnt that week. Thus, from the very

First baptism at Irelya in 1957.

earliest years of the life of the Enga Church, local people were engaged in the task of sharing the Gospel with their own people (NGLM 1948-55). Control was still being exercised by missionaries from outside of Enga-land, but the work was already in the hands of God's people in this place. Without the work of faithful witnesses like Kooa and Powai at Yaramanda, Ete and Natan at Irelya, Apakasa at Yaibos, and others throughout the Church, the sharing of the message of Jesus Christ would have proceeded at a much slower pace.

The emphasis of the work in these years centred around preaching and teaching, establishing simple schools, helping the people with their sickness, beginning some economic development, and learning to know more of the people and their language. The presence of proclaimers of the Good News was not only accepted by most communities, but was desired as a good thing. Some of this desire to have a mission centre in their midst grew out of the hope of finding the way to the 'good life', but the Holy Spirit was opening doors and preparing the way.

Growth Begins

The westward penetration of the Gospel into other Enga lands was halted for six years when the government seemed reluctant to district any additional areas. This led to more concentration and consolidation in the areas already being served. Additional circuit centres were begun at Raiakama in the Saka Valley, at Kundis in the Ambum, at Pawali in the Lower Lai, and at Mambisanda where a hospital was under construction. Many additional preaching areas were opened, the majority initially served by catechumens and later by Enga evangelists.

The year 1957 marks the beginning of the harvest of the Gutnius Lutheran Church which is still going on. First at Irelya in January 1957, then at Yaramanda and Yaibos, groups of Enga people were baptized into the Lord Jesus Christ. At the end of the year, the church had a membership of 658 baptized, 403 of whom were communicants. Thousands were enrolled in membership classes as the Spirit of the Lord moved people throughout the area. Congregations were organized; cooperation was begun between groups that had once been at war with one another; and the local Christians

285

Natan of Irelya, one of the first baptized Christians.

began to take on some of the responsibility for Christ's mission in this place (Burce 1957, NGLM 1957, Spruth 1957 & 1970).

Already in 1956, there had been meetings between the leaders of the various catechumen classes to discuss common matters of practice and commitment. The men who would later be the leaders of the young church came together from all the centres from Yaramanda to Papayuku. In these meetings they came to know and respect one another. They agreed that certain practices of the Enga people such as the *tee* (pig exchange), *laita* (death payments for children), *kumanda* (funeral customs), *sangai/sandalu* (bachelor cult) would have to be abandoned by the Christians. Some of these decisions were later modified by the Church, but a pattern for joint action and mutual decision-making was being established.

Each year saw additional groups being baptized and congregations organized. In 1958, Raiakama, Makaramanda, Sakalimi, Birip, Makapumanda, Watumanda, and Sirunki were added to the number of Christian congregations. The year 1959 saw even greater numbers added as groups were baptized and

congregations organized at Konjamanda, Saka, Potea, Injinji, Konale, Kinapaluma, Tukisanda, Kupalisa, and Papayuku. There were now 27 congregations with a total membership of 4,649 baptized members (3,052 confirmed), and a further 3,200 enrolled in membership classes.

Evangelists were now being sent out by the Enga congregations. In addition, elders were appointed in the various congregations so that the ministry of Word and Sacrament would continue. Each day seemed to bring new opportunities as God opened many doors and hearts to the Gospel. Throughout these years of congregational growth, other aspects of the work and life of the Church were also growing: A hospital had been built at Mambisanda in 1954/55, and was in operation; schools were established in over 70 communities, and a central higher school was also set up at Pausa (NGLM 1948-1960). The whole life of the people was being changed through the total influence of the Gospel and God's love breaking into all areas of life.

At this point, the Christians began to realize that there was much they would not be able to do alone. In order to meet the needs of each congregation, it would be necessary for the congregations to band together and help one another. Training for their leaders and workers and the opportunities for further sharing the Gospel were their major reasons for coming together. First they met to discuss and to plan. A group was appointed in 1959 (Powai of Yaramanda, Elisa of Irelya, and Eriko of Raiakama, along with Otasinke and Teoc as representatives of the coastal evangelists and teachers, and Burce and Hintze from the missionaries) to establish the rules and points of agreement for a continuing conference of Enga congregations. More important than this constitutional committee, however, was the establishment of the Lutheran School for Church Workers at Birip to train leaders and pastors for the congregations (GLC 1959). The Christian people were looking to the future needs of the Church.

A general meeting was held in 1960 at Birip at the time the new school for church workers was dedicated. The proposed constitution was presented and discussed, and then submitted to the congregations for further study. Most of the work of organization was still being done by the

Waema Waesa, first President of Gutnius Lutheran Church.

missionaries, but the Enga people were beginning to find their way.

The meeting at Irelya in 1961 formally organized the Wabag Lutheran Church,[1] and elected Waima Waesa as its first President. This constituting convention also approved a plan for reaching out to other areas of the Enga Province. Four groups were appointed consisting of missionaries and Enga leaders to establish teams for each of the areas which were yet to be opened for mission work. The young Church had dedicated itself to the mission task (GLC 1961).

The Second Geographical Expansion

For several years there had been persistent rumours that the government was about to de-restrict some of the populous areas surrounding the Enga heartland: Tarua to the north, Maramuni to the north-west, Muritaka, Lyaimi, Porgera, and Paiela to the west, and the Kandep and Wake to the south. The newly-organized Church wanted to be ready to meet the needs and opportunities of these areas, and selected teams to be responsible for the evangelistic outreach to each one.

Lanyeta, Kleinig, and a group of elders and evangelists from each area of the Church, were to meet the needs of the Tarua. Morosa and Larson, together with another group of elders and evangelists, were to be responsible for the Maramuni. Niketemos and Kisa, Stotik and Heinicke, together with elders and evangelists from throughout the Church, were to work in the Kandep. Reo and Spruth, along with elders and evangelists from Sirunki and Papayuku and the rest of the Church, were to serve the Muritaka area (GLC 1961). This was a great undertaking for the young Church, involving some of its most able people, and setting a pattern for its thinking and development for years to come. Over 70 evangelists were appointed to this preparation for mission outreach. Never again would this Church deploy so many of its people at one time.

One can see the Lord's hand in all the preparations. The organizational meeting at which these plans were confirmed was held in May 1961. The Committee on Evangelism of NGLM, together with a group of Enga Christian leaders, developed the strategy for outreach into new areas (CoEv 1960/61). In July 1961, the government de-restricted not one or two areas, but all of them at the same time. The area of the Enga province now considered 'open' was more than doubled with one stroke of the pen of the Administrator of the Territory of Papua and New Guinea. By the end of the year, a main centre had been set up in each new area, expatriate missionaries assigned to the Kandep and Muritaka areas, and 63 new preaching-places opened. The local Church took on the support of the evangelists and teachers in these mission areas, making this the largest item in their budget. Mission outreach was viewed as the most important task of the GLC.

The following year, in June 1962, the administration de-restricted additional areas: Lyaimi, Porgera, Paiela, and Wake. The resources of the Church were further strained to meet these new opportunities. Much of the burden fell on the Papayuku and Sirunki circuits to provide additional manpower. At the same time, other new work was also expanding and requesting more staff. All this while the Church was still trying to reach additional people in the older circuits. The leaders and missionary at Papayuku were particularly pressed; they were

Early leaders of Gutnius Lutheran Church: Kasen, Reo, and Kewa.

Evangelists and elders of Papayuku circuit.

288

expected to cover all the new work west of their circuit, which included Muritaka, Lyaimi, Porgera, and Paiela. By the end of 1962, the GLC had sent out 141 evangelistic workers and established 121 centres for sharing the Gospel in the new areas. Sixteen of these were among a people who spoke a different language: the Ipili of the Porgera and Paiela. The resources of both Church and Mission were strained to their limits. Leadership training did not keep up with the demand for workers, leaving some congregations with poor leadership. The GLC had met the opportunities for mission. It remained to be seen how this would affect the over-all growth and strength of the Church.

Growth of Other Programs

Up to this point, we have spoken only of the evangelistic growth and expansion of the GLC. There was, however, also growth and development in programs of education, medical services, and economic development. All these were part of the 'whole man' ministry of the Church, and aided in the spread of the Gospel. School programs went hand in hand with the establishing of centres for sharing the Gospel. Each major centre of the Church had its school program which tried to reach out beyond the main station. Vernacular and Pidgin-language schools were established in many congregations and preaching places, in addition to the English schools at the main centres. A special program of teacher training was set up to provide teachers for the vernacular schools throughout the Church. Many of the workers from coastal New Guinea were teacher/evangelists, and established schools as well as proclaiming the Good News. Teachers and evangelists were sent by the GLC to the new areas to serve the whole community. By the end of 1962, the GLC had a total of 152 schools served by 162 teachers with an enrolment of 3,997. Thirty-five of these schools were in the mission areas which the GLC had begun to reach in 1961 (NGLM 1962). The people were very interested in having schools, for they were viewed as one of the ways in which the group would be assured of having the necessary skills to meet the rapid changes being brought about by the introduction of many new ideas and different material goods.

Medical work, while not as extensive as the educational program, also played an important role in the work of the Church and Mission. All the missionaries offered a certain amount of medical aid in connection with their work. Some, as at Papayuku, established full-time clinics to serve the needs of the local people. Training for local medical orderlies was made an important part of the Mambisanda hospital program. Wanda Fricke (who arrived in 1952) and Audrey Lafrenz Biberdorf (who arrived in 1953) were the nurses responsible for the development of this medical outreach.

Medical staff often accompanied patrols into new areas. The local people wanted and needed medical aid. The Church, however, could meet this need only in a limited way due to lack of trained staff and finance. By the end of 1962, there were nine clinics in addition to the hospital. The medical work was served by a total staff of 25 national and six expatriate workers. The national staff had received much of their training at the Lutheran Hospital at Yagaum near Madang, a further indication of the cooperation between all the Lutheran bodies working in PNG.

At the end of this period (1962), the newly-organized Church found itself supporting a tremendous program of mission outreach. The GLC with a total baptized membership of 15,740 (10,171 communicants) in 86 congregations had sent out 176 workers to eight new areas and established 121 centres for sharing the Gospel with those who still did not know Jesus. This Church in PNG would never again mount such a large program relative to the size of its membership.

The Third Geographic Expansion

There remained one more large area to the west where access was still restricted by the government: that of the Duna people of Lake Kopiago. After contact was made by the Australian administration in the late 1950s, a patrol post was opened, and construction began on an airstrip. Christian Enga government medical workers, police, and general labourers were assigned to the Kopiago Patrol Post. Thanks to them sharing their faith in the Lord Jesus, the Kopiago people asked the GLC to come to this area with the Good News. The Church was quite willing to meet the request, and a team was chosen to begin the

Duna *celebration at Kopiago.*

Kopiago work. In this case, all the evangelists and teachers had to speak New Guinea Pidgin, for the Duna language was unknown to the Enga people. Plans and preparations were focused on entry to the field in either late 1962 or early 1963, but the government did not de-restrict the area until 1964. By that time, some of the original team had gone on to other work; but Evangelist Morosa from Irelya, Elder Eriko from Saka Raiakama, the Revd William Wagner and Teacher G. Cooke were able to begin Lutheran work among the Duna in August 1964.

In the period between the people's invitation and the administration's de-restriction of the area, other mission organizations had also decided to enter this field. An agreement was reached between the Apostolic Church Mission, Christian Missions in Many Lands, and the GLC as to areas of influence; in addition, the Roman Catholic and Seventh Day Adventist groups also entered the area. Many missions/churches were 'competing' for a smallish population. The new areas of PNG were beginning to come to an end.

The work in Kopiago was established rather quickly. Cooke did not remain with the 290

team, but Morosa, Eriko, and Wagner patrolled the so-called Lutheran area, and set up nine centres by the end of the year. This was a new kind of work for the GLC, for it involved the extensive use of interpreters among the Duna (and then later among the Hewa people).

After the establishment of the work in the Kopiago, the GLC entered no other major new areas. Yet there has been a continual reaching out to new people and places through the congregations and circuits of the Church. In 1964, Reo, Pia, D. Schaus, and Spruth made an exploratory patrol from the Maramuni to the Penale people, and then down the Sepik River. On this trip, contact was made with a leader of the people at Yalipa, who also speak Enga. As a result of this contact, the people requested help from the GLC. In September 1964, a team consisting of a medical worker, an evangelist, and a teacher were sent to the Yalipa people.

Additional patrols in 1965 and 1966 were made to the Hewa area from both Kopiago and Porgera, and in 1967, evangelists from the Porgera were placed at three centres. However, because of the nomadic nature of the Hewa, the work developed slowly; at times, the evangelists would be left without their congregations for weeks. Still, the Lord has also called his own people from among the Hewa, people who have been baptized and incorporated into his Church.

Further outreach to fringe-area people was undertaken from the Maramuni and Lyaimi circuits. The local congregations, with support from the GLC, have sent evangelists and established congregations among the Nete people. [18]

As the era of the 1960s drew to a close, the GLC saw itself carrying on God's mission throughout the Enga area, among the Ipili and Duna peoples, and among smaller groups such as the Hewa, the Nete, and the Wapi. Major geographic expansion had come to a close, and the Church had to focus on the needs of the people within its own area. There were great changes taking place in the country and in the everyday life of the people. Both economic and political development were taking up more of the people's time. The evangelists, elders, and pastors had to work much harder not only to reach additional people, but to keep the 'flock of God' faithful. By the end of 1968, the total baptized membership had grown to some 37,000, but there were indications of a slow-down in the life and activities of some of the older congregations and circuits. The rapid growth-patterns would continue for a few more years because of the newer areas, but important changes had to be made in the established congregations lest the people wander away from the Faith.

Expansion in the 1970s

In the changing situation of PNG, the GLC began to see the need for some work in the towns and resettlement areas. Enga people began migrating in search of jobs, a different lifestyle, and adventure. The Church felt a responsibility to go along with its people in order to continue to meet their spiritual needs.

The government established a large resettlement area at Kinding, some 30 kilometres east of Mt Hagen. Land pressures at home influenced many Enga people to apply for resettlement blocks, and their applications were successful. Others went to the same area to work for the commercial tea plantation that was being established at Kinding. In 1968, the GLC called Pastor Waesa Watakau from the graduating class of Timothy Seminary to serve these Enga people in dispersion (as well as people from other parts of PNG). Kinding, of course, was in an area served by ELCONG, and the cause was begun only after consultation and agreement between the Hagen District of ELCONG and the GLC.

Ministries to other towns and resettlement areas were established as the need for them arose, and as the GLC had men who could be entrusted with the task. All such work was carried out in cooperation and partnership with ELCONG. In 1972, Pastor Kewa Kopen was called to serve in the town of Mt Hagen in partnership with ELCONG. The year 1974 saw Pastor Punai begin work at the Avi resettlement block, also in the Hagen area. In 1975, Pastor Pia Tondau became the first GLC pastor to serve the capital city of Port Moresby. Then in 1977, he was sent to begin the work of the GLC among the men in the copper-mining camps of Bougainville. The GLC had become a church with worshipping congregations all over PNG.

During the same period, the Gospel was being carried across another boundary. Bilingual Enga-Huli speakers from the Mariant Valley south of the Kandep had begun to hear of the Lord Jesus from their Enga-speaking neighbours. When they invited the Kandep congregations to send them workers, another mission area was opened in 1975. That work continues; the people are sharing the Good News, and the message is spreading among the still-unreached Huli people toward Mendi.

The work in the Tambul area has a much longer history. In 1949, the area had been visited by Hintze, and land had been purchased (Hintze 1949). When it was later agreed that this area would be served by the ELCONG, nothing more was done from the GLC side. Every few years, however, people from the area who spoke Enga repeated their request for the workers they still wanted. After ELCONG leaders agreed to action by the GLC, a pastor and two evangelists were sent in 1965. This first effort did not work out very well; however, in 1976 the work took hold, and a large number of people accepted Christ. After almost 27 years, people became part of the Church they had invited to bring them the Gospel so many years before.

291

A Growing Church

All during its brief history, the GLC has remained a growing church. In the period of rapid geographical expansion, the Church continued to grow within the established circuits. Some years produced better growth than others, but always one or the other area seemed to be adding more people than were turning away in another place. In later years, the growth-pattern has slowed down, partly because there are not as many people without the Gospel, but partly also because there has been a change in attitude among those who still have not accepted the Gospel.

At the same time, the Church has continued to grow in other areas of its life and work. As will be seen in other sections of this story, the church has been growing in its ability to carry out the mission of Christ, in its organization, and in its service to the wider community. The problems brought on by the government's unilateral action in introducing alcohol to the people of New Guinea, the political independence, [19] and the upsurge in clan fighting have all hurt the Church, but have also strengthened it. There are many new movements of the Spirit of God among the members, particularly the youth. Lay people are often moving ahead of their pastors and elders in non-formalized programs of Christian nuture and spiritual growth, but are working within the framework of their congregations.

In June 1978, the GLC Convention, meeting at Kokas in the Kandep, finalized the adoption of a new constitution, accepted A Statement of Faith, [20] and changed its name. The Church had been looking for a way to express its new situation. No longer is it strictly an Enga church or a regional body. The people see themselves as having a national responsibility and outreach that goes far beyond the confines of Wabag. Thus, the name was changed from the Wabag Lutheran Church to the Gutnuis Lutheran Church-Papua New Guinea.

Not quite two months after that convention, the GLC in August 1978 celebrated the 30th anniversary of the coming of the Good News to this part of PNG. It was a coming prepared for and predicted by God's working among their own prophets and religious innovators. It was a coming sustained by God's Spirit and power in

292

the face of many problems and difficulties, a coming which has changed for all eternity the destiny of many thousands of people, and which has also raised up as God's servant the Gutnius Lutheran Church-Papua New Guinea.

Whole-person Ministry

From the beginning of the mission task in the Enga Province, ministry to the whole person has been part of the task of sharing the Gospel. Neither the Mission nor the Church has seen the task simply in terms of 'winning souls for Jesus', but rather of bringing the love of God and the fullness of salvation to every situation of life. The GLC indicated its concern in the following statement:

> We of the Lutheran Church know that God has given this great work of mission to the church, to work to suppress each sign and problem of sin in the lives of people and to bring them back to God. For this reason, we must work to help people in all of their life with the Gospel. If we talk about the Good News to a person who is sick or hungry, and we do not do anything to live the Good News and help him, then our proclamation will be as a lie and we will not be able to help anyone ... We cannot divide God's mission. We have to follow the example of our Lord Jesus and always have compassion on people and help them in all of their life ... Our work and our mouth must always be in partnership. The Good News is not merely talk (WLC 1975).

Schools and Teachers

Schools were a part of the program of the mission task in the Enga Province from the very beginning of the work. Education went hand in hand with the proclamation of the Gospel and the advocacy for the new life in Jesus Christ. The missionaries viewed education as necessary and part of their task of planting and nurturing the church in the Highlands of PNG. Schools were to be instruments for bringing the Word of God to bear on the life of the community, as well as for preparing future leaders for the church and the Christian community. The people quickly accepted the idea of schools, and saw them as a means for growing in knowledge and in the ability to meet the changing needs of the community (GLC 1978).

The majority of the missionaries sent to the Enga area by Lutheran congregations of coastal New Guinea were teacher/evangelists. They viewed their task as one of proclamation and education. In October 1948, the first school was established at Yaramanda with 40 pupils (all male) enrolled; teaching duties were shared by O. Hintze and the teacher Teoc (NGLM 1948). A similar pattern was followed at Irelya where a school was established soon after the arrival of W. Burce and the teacher Jasaptong in 1949. Burce and Jasaptong shared the teaching task at first, but soon Jasaptong was replaced by Bingmalao. Other schools were set up by the workers at Arumanda, Makaremanda, and Birip. By the end of 1949, there were five schools in operation (NGLM 1949). By as early as 1952, that number had grown to 28 (NGLM 1952). Many of the young men who attended those early classes are in leadership positions in the GLC today.

George Hinlicky, the first fully-qualified teacher to serve with the GLC, came to the Enga area with his family in January 1953. Because of the demand for schools, his primary task was the training of young men who could serve as teachers in literacy-type schools. A training centre for this purpose was established at Amapyaka in 1954. Mr Hinlicky enrolled 20 students who had already had several years of instruction at one of the other station schools. After three additional years at the Amapyaka school, these young men were assigned as teachers to vernacular schools. In 1958, this school was moved to Pausa; there it eventually became St Paul's Lutheran High School (NGLM 1953-60).

The Australian government set the future pattern of formal education in PNG in 1956 by making English the official language of education. English was not to be taught merely as a foreign language; it was to be the medium of education in all recognized and/or registered schools. At the same time, it was made illegal to conduct a school which was not recognized or registered. The Government did, however, allow for a category of 'exempt schools' — schools where the vernacular language was taught, and the major emphasis was on literacy and on religious instruction. The majority of the schools of the GLC were included in this category.

Schools at the major centres, where there was an expatriate missionary who could become registered as a teacher, became registered schools and taught the required government syllabus. The demand for schools and teachers was much greater than the number of available teachers. As a result, a group of 60 young men was enrolled in a special 10-week course in 1957, after which they were assigned to the circuits as teachers under the oversight of the missionaries. A full program of materials was prepared by the mission staff so that these teachers would be able to share with their pupils. Thousands of children were enrolled in these schools and learnt to read and write in their own language as well as to know the Lord Jesus (NGLM 1957/58).

The exempt schools were usually the responsibility of the local community and/or congregation. Some assistance was received from the Church in the form of materials and a small subsidy for teacher's wages. The people believed that education was the way to the future and to all the good things that were being introduced into their area. At a later date (after 1967), they began to reject the exempt school when they came to see that it was not the open door to a paid job and economic advancement (NGLM 1967).

Additional teachers were sent from overseas with an aim to have a teacher at each main centre. In 1957, Kenneth Bauer and Dale Busse were sent from the USA and assigned to the task of building up the new High School at Pausa. Thomas Ango of Irelya became the first Enga to graduate as a certificated teacher. He joined the staff of the Irelya school, having received a call from his home congregation. Thomas set in motion a pattern of localization in the school system of the GLC which came to completion in 1978 when all the teaching positions in both the primary and secondary schools of the Church were held by Papua New Guineans.

The demand for schools grew faster than the supply of teachers. In 1964, the GLC decided not to open any new schools until all the present schools were fully staffed and local teachers were available for new schools. This need for fully-qualified local teachers led the GLC to cooperate with ELCONG in the establishment of Balob Teachers College at Lae. This joint institution has trained the majority of the teachers of the GLC.

Meanwhile, the costs of education were rising more rapidly than the ability of the Church and community to meet them. So, when the government proposed to establish a national teaching service, this was viewed with approval, and finally agreed to in 1970. All certified teachers of the GLC school system are now paid by the national government, and are part of the national teaching service. While this helped the GLC by giving them teachers whom they did not have to salary, it also began to change the character of the schools which were now much more under government control (GLC 1970-78). With the school system growing, and becoming more and more localized, Mr Dale Kambu in 1973 became the first Enga to serve as Education Secretary of the GLC.

Community Education Centres

During the expansion of the English-language school system by the missions, churches, and government, the exempt school program all but died. A survey in 1968 showed that these schools were not meeting the expectations of the parents or the children, who saw education in terms of future employment (Ewald 1968:5). An attempt was made to change these schools so that they would actually help the people in their economic development. At the same time, the people were informed that the main purpose of the schools was to help the students become better people where they were. James Akipane, Itaki Kakapao, and Richard Hilgendorf worked together to develop a program which would continue to offer formal education and literacy to children in the vernacular and in New Guinea Pidgin without promising employment. The *Komuniti Edukesen Senta* program was established for older students with a more practical application to their life at home.

Medical Services

Traditional Enga and Ipili belief attributed all sickness and death to the malevolent influence of spirits (particularly the ghosts of the dead of one's own family), to the *temango*, and to magic. People tended to die at an early age with an infant mortality rate that approached 75% in the first year of life. In this context, the Gospel of salvation included salvation from sickness and the powers of the spirit world.

From the beginning, the missionaries practised 'backdoor' medicine, treating those illnesses for which they had medicines and
294

skills, and praying for all. Through their ministry, many were healed physically, and many more were willing to listen to the message of true healing. Many instances of dramatic healing are remembered where prayer and an injection of penicillin brought back to life those given up for dead.

The needs of the people in terms of medical care, however, were beyond the scope of the 'backdoor' programs, even when administered by a missionary wife who was a trained nurse, such as Lorraine Spruth at Papayuku or Audrey Biberdorf at Pawali. There was a need for a formal program of medicine which also offered training to the people so that they might better care for their own community. Although the Mission had requested professional medical staff already in 1949, the first nurse (Wanda Fricke) did not arrive until 1953, and the first doctor (Eric Hoopmann) until 1955.

Immanuel Lutheran Hospital was built at Mambisanda during 1955-57. Over the years it has developed into one of the better hospitals in PNG, with an excellent program for training community health workers, nursing aids, hospital orderlies, and aid post orderlies. In 1976, it became the Provincial Hospital for the Enga Province, the only church hospital in PNG to serve in such a capacity.

The first Engas to be trained for the medical ministry of the Church began their instruction at Mambisanda in 1955, and received further training at Yagaum Lutheran Hospital near Madang. Some of these young men later transferred to the government medical services, and are still working in the healing ministry.

Until 1971, the Church and Mission operated a medical program parallel to that of the government. Because of the Christian orientation of the staff, their services were often preferred. Small clinics were established in those mission areas where the GLC had sent out evangelists and teachers. Medical services, however, are very costly, and soon the GLC recognized the fact that this was not something that it could do alone; cooperation and integration with the government's medical services became essential. From the point of view of many people in the remote areas, this has resulted in a reduction of services rather than an increase. The combining of church and government medical programs, however, has raised the educational level of the medical staff and provided for adequate salaries for the medical worker.

The medical program continues to be reevaluated by the Church as more and more of the responsibility for these services is taken by the community and the various governmental agencies. The size and scope of that program has been reduced since the government moved the Provincial Hospital closer to Wabag. The Church continues to make its most important contribution to the medical field through the training of medical workers and the supplying of Christian medical staff for various programs throughout Papua New Guinea.

Economic Development

From the time when the task was almost entirely in the hands of the missionaries, the GLC has been engaged in the task of serving the physical and material welfare of the people as well as preaching the Gospel of salvation through Christ. With the understanding that 'God himself always works to care for people, both for their bodies and their souls', and that the Lord Jesus 'also worked to help people in all of their needs', the GLC initiated programs of agricultural and business development to aid the people with their material needs (GLC 1975:9).

At first, the help offered in terms of economic development was more casual and incidental to the task of making disciples. Missionaries purchased produce and services from the local people; they introduced new types of vegetables and improved varieties of sweet-potato; they helped people to obtain chickens and better pigs; they set up small stores where people could purchase some of the new goods they desired at a reasonable cost; they nursed sick pigs as well as sick people, and tried to show concern for the whole life of the people.

The NGLM and the GLC became the major agencies for economic change in the Enga area. Not only were market-garden vegetables introduced; a program of purchasing these vegetables and exporting them to other areas of PNG was established. Mr Ed Dicke, Business Manager of NGLM, arranged to purchase vegetables and potatoes through the various mission centres and to market them in other areas. In 1959, Mr Roland Freund was called as the first agricultural missionary of the GLC. His task was to find ways in which the people could help themselves both by improving their own nutrition and by developing market crops. The Church worked together with the government in introducing coffee, cattle, and improved pigs.

As these various developmental programs grew, it became necessary to formalize the work and put it into proper perspective, lest it become the whole task. In an attempt to continue to help the people in their economic development, but to divorce the actual business involvement from the day-to-day work of the Church, WASO Ltd was founded as a shareholding company in 1964. It was to be the marketing agent for the vegetables and coffee, as well as taking over the supply of goods from the outside to the community. In the beginning, the controlling share of stock was held by the Mission (later turned over to the Church), but provision was soon made for local groups and individuals to buy shares and thus to profit from the development of their own area. Thereafter the GLC held over 30% of the shares of the company, and continued to be very active in its operation. As the country changed, however, Waso Ltd was unable to keep up with the high costs of doing business in the Enga Province. Another factor was that the culture of the local people had not adapted to the capitalistic system of economics; too many goods and services were given away. By 1983, the company was in bankruptcy, even though some of its service to the people continued.

Other economic development programs were started in order to help the people. Tora Motors was set up as a separate business in 1974, a continuation of the automotive workshop that had been run by the Mission. In 1978, it expanded its activities to include all the construction and electrical work of the Church; it also ventured into marketing. But it, too, has had its problems because of the nature of the Enga area. At the present time, it is back to serving only as an automotive enterprise.

Lakaip Entaprais was established in 1975 as a business group serving the circuits in the western portion of the Church. The Papayuku, Muritaka, Sirunki, and Lyaimi circuits worked together to help develop the economy of their own area. Much of their work was involved with marketing potatoes. Mr Ed Bloos was assigned to that area to help with this program.

As with so much that is introduced from one culture to another, the economic program had both good and bad effects. On the one hand, it did introduce other crops and give people access to more 'things'. On the other hand, it did tend to divert people's attention from the main need of both the Church and the community: its continuing connection to Jesus Christ as both Lord and Saviour.

The Indigenous Church

The development of the GLC as a church-body making its own decisions was a long process. Previous pages of this chapter may have often given the impression that the structure was quickly in place, and that the Church then went along doing the work and growing. But there was a long period of time during which the Mission made all the major decisions even after the establishment of the Church. One of the factors that has continued to be a problem for the Church is the difference between traditional leadership and the way leadership is now practised in both church and government. [21] Traditional leadership has always been achieved after many years of work and service to the clan community; it has never been elected or paid for its services, and the clan leader has always operated for the good of the clan first.

The Church was formally organized at Irelya on May 16, 1961. The representatives of the 48 Enga congregations met, adopted the constitution that had been presented to them the year before, and elected officers. The officers chosen were all able leaders, and were drawn from the various areas of the Church. They had the responsibility of leading the Wabag Lutheran Church in its first steps as a group of believers banded together to further the Lord's work. These men were:

> President: W. Waesa of Kundis
> 1st Vice-President: R. Reo of Papayuku
> 2nd Vice-President: K. Niketemos of Sirunki
> Secretary: K. Kewa of Irelya
> Treasurer: K. Tumu of Papayuku
> Council Member: P. Powai of Yaramanda
> Council Member: A. Aloo of Yaibos
> Council Member: E. Eriko of Raiakama

This leadership formed the Church Council, and was responsible for the programs of the GLC. The Mission, however, continued to care for the direction of the finance, evangelistic, educational, and medical programs. GLC men were 'elected' to serve on these Mission committees, but for the time being the real authority rested with the Mission. However, the Mission Executive Committee invited the GLC Church Council to work together with it in the placing of expatriate missionaries and other staff funded by the Mission, and the first joint meeting took place on July 28, 1961. After working together in that way for several years, the Church and Mission agreed to establish a Church-Mission Council (C-MC) in 1964 to oversee the work of both Church and Mission. The missionaries still played the major role in this council, but the Church leadership was learning.

As the Church grew, it expanded its Church Council in order to give full representation to all the circuits of the Church. As a result, the Church-Mission Council began to become unwieldy. There were 21 members of the GLC Council and 11 members on the NGLM Executive Committee, making the meeting almost a mini-conference.

In addition, there was the need to begin to give over more responsibility to the Church, for the leadership of the Church was beginning to feel uncomfortable under the shadow of the Mission. The view was voiced that too much power resided with the missionaries and the Mission Staff Conference. A question they raised was why there was a need for a Mission organization at all. Why should there be two organizations when we are all working in the same task and for the same Lord? The missionaries also began to feel uncomfortable with the relationship of the Church to the Mission as an organization. The time had come for change.

The C-MC took note of the unrest, and appointed a group to try to produce a constitution which would integrate the Church and the Mission and satisfy both the local people and the missionaries (C-MC 1968). The proposed constitution was never fully developed, but the idea did lead to a change in organization.

The Mission was the first to act officially. At their Conference in January 1970, the missionaries suspended part of their Constitution for two years, and gave full authority to their Executive Committee to find the best way to continue God's work in partnership with the local Church. The Executive Committee was authorized to work for full integration if that seemed best for the mission task (NGLM 1970).

Out of the discussions held between the leaders of the Church and the Mission, a proposal for closer integration was presented to the Convention of the Church: Both the Executive Committee of the Mission and the Church Council of the GLC would cease to function for one year; in their place the Lutheran Church Council-Wabag (LCC-W) would be formed (C-MC 1970). The Church agreed to this proposal, and the new council was established. It consisted of one elected member from each circuit of the Church, the officers of the Church, and the Mission Executive Committee. The Revd Reo Raku, President of the Church, and the Revd Victor Heinicke, President of the Mission, were co-chairmen of the Council. At times it was frustrating, for both Church and Mission leaders came to the Council with a different set of priorities, but it was a learning situation through which Church leaders began to see the broader picture, and missionaries began to understand the fears and concerns of the Church leaders. Out of this struggle a common purpose and unity emerged, which led to further development of the Church.

Shortly after the establishment of the LCC-W, an unfortunate problem within the LC-MS in the USA led to a determination by the Church leaders to control their own program as soon as possible. Because the LC-MS was in financial straits, its Board for Missions informed the NGLM of a drastic budget cut for that year, and foreshadowed similar cuts for following years. The missionaries saw that the only way to meet the budget cut was to retrench expatriate staff. This idea was strongly opposed by the Church leaders; but, because finances were involved, and money was controlled by the Mission, they reluctantly agreed to retrench twelve expatriate missionaries (LCC-W 1970). That was a traumatic experience which affected the relationship between the New Guinea Church and the USA, breaking down a certain feeling of trust and shattering the idea that the USA Church would always be there to help. It became obvious to the leaders of the GLC that they would have to control the finances if they were to direct the work and program of their Church.

The initial one-year term of the LCC-W was extended, and the number of missionaries on the Council was reduced. It was agreed between the leadership of the GLC and a representative of the LC-MS that the Mission organization would be discontinued, and that all missionaries would become part of the Wabag Lutheran Church. The missionary staff would continue to be concerned about the support of expatriate workers; all other matters would devolve upon the Church. Provision was made within the Church for a missionary adviser to the President of the GLC.

At a special conference of the Church in September 1971, Waima Waesa was elected as president, providing leadership for the GLC after a period of crisis. [22] President Waesa and his adviser, E. Ewald, began a process which resulted in changes in the organization of the Church. The office of adviser to the President was no longer given ex officio to the Mission president; it was replaced by the elective office of Administrative Officer within the Church. At the same time, the Church made provision for a Secretary for Overseas Personnel who would have special responsibility for expatriate missionaries. Spruth was elected to the position of Administrative Officer, and Stotik to the position of Secretary for Overseas Personnel. Both men were voting members of the GLC Council (GLC 1973).

As the organization of the Church developed, there was a period of time when the leadership became more and more involved in programs involving subsidy to congregations, in determining salary for workers, and in keeping the money coming from the USA. The Church was well on its way to becoming a satellite of the LC-MS, primarily interested in maintaining the status quo and their own subsidy.

At this time, however, a crisis arose in the relationship between the Church in PNG and the LC-MS, brought on by the internal struggle in the American church. Because of the effect this had on its expatriate staff, and on those in the

USA who had worked with the GLC, the Church reacted strongly against what it perceived to be an effort to control them from the USA. They banded together with other Lutheran churches in Asia, and determined to be the church in their area, accepting the final responsibility for the life of the church and its mission task under God. While still concerned about funding from the USA, the leadership became more concerned with the integrity of the Church in PNG. The problems of the Church in the USA made the local Church realize that they could not continue for ever to rely on people from outside their own land. They also saw that it would be advantageous to form relationships with more than one group (GLC 1974).

The Bishops

The on-going development of the GLC led to constitutional changes that were proposed in 1974 and adopted for a trial period in 1976. The GLC divided itself into five regions, and decided to designate its leaders as bishops. Dr Waima Waesa was elected as the first Bishop of the GLC, with Nekotemos Hayene, Philip Kiso, and Reo Raku elected as the first Assistant Bishops.

It is significant to note that Nekotemos Hayene was from the Kopiago area, a non-Enga-speaking part of the Church. In 1978, this new system was confirmed; one change was the election of five Assistant (Regional) Bishops, one for each region of the Church. This was the convention that made the name-change from Wabag Lutheran Church to Gutnius Lutheran Church-Papua New Guinea.

With the new constitution, representation on the Church Council was also changed. Previous representation of one from each circuit had made the Council very clergy-dominated; only one or two members were not directly employed by the Church. The new constitution provided for ten members (two elected from each region) who were lay people not in the employ of the Church. In addition, provision was made for two pastors and two teachers on the Council, as well as the Bishop, Regional Bishops, the Secretary, and the Treasurer. With the 1978 Conference, the expatriate membership of the Council ceased; both the General Secretary (the former Administrative Officer) and the Secretary for Overseas Personnel were now only advisory members.

Consecration of Bishop Waesa (K. Stotik and E. Spruth assisting).

298

The cycle had been completed: The direction of the Church was entirely in New Guinea hands (GLC 1978).

Relationship to Other Churches

The GLC has generally been open to relationships with other churches in PNG. In 1963, it began a series of exchange visits with the Siassi Lutheran Church. It appointed members to a 'One Church Committee', and to the group which drew up a common statement of faith for the Lutheran Churches in PNG. After the two Lutheran Churches in Australia joined together, the Siassi Church became part of ELCONG. With the adoption of *A Statement of Faith* in 1976, the GLC was in full fellowship with the ELCONG. Together they operate Balob Teachers Training College, Martin Luther Seminary, and the Lutheran School of Nursing. Nothing is hindering full unity other than some lingering reluctance to be part of a larger group rather than on your own, and the current political climate in PNG. In the not-too-distant future, there should be only one Lutheran Church in PNG.

In 1972, the GLC became a full member of the Melanesian Council of Churches, and in 1978 joined the Lutheran World Federation. In

Church leaders (Bishops), Gutnius Lutheran Church; from left: Reo, Michael, Pilipo, Niketemos, Waesa, and Philip.

Bishop Waesa ordains Assistant Bishop Niketemos.

Mark Yapao, General Secretary of the Gutnius Lutheran Church, addresses the Church Convention.

299

the continuing crisis with the LC-MS, the GLC was instrumental in forming a relationship with Asian Lutheran Churches in the Philippines, Japan, Korea, Hong Kong, and India. It also has formal ties with the Lutheran Church of Australia and with the Association of Evangelical Lutheran Churches in USA. The GLC has established a policy of relating to those church-groups who agree with it in the understanding of the Gospel. No longer does the Church rely on only one partner for the aid it feels it still needs in finance and manpower.

In the immediate area of its own congregations, the GLC has developed a good relationship with the Catholic Church. The two groups are cooperating in the translation of the Scriptures into Enga. It has also maintained friendly relations with the Western Highlands Baptist Union, with whom it shares a common boundary. On the other hand, relationships with the Apostolic Church and with the Seventh Day Adventists are poor because both these groups seem to feel it is their right to proselytize among members of other churches.

In the last few years an influx of neo-pentecostal churches has encouraged the development of so-called spirit-filled people and congregations. The question, of course, always is: With whose spirit are they filled? There has been tension in the GLC over these charismatic manifestations, especially over the inroads made by the sect which calls itself the 'One Way Church'. There is much in their practice which leads the people back to their animistic roots, and leads to the development of spiritualist-type churches which use a combination of Christian teaching and animistic practice to gather members from all the churches. What will happen in the future cannot be answered in a book that is devoted to history. The GLC will need to review its practice and teaching in order to bring the Gospel to bear on this new situation in ways which will once more enable it to enter into the full life of the people.

A Time of Testing

On September 16, 1975, Papua New Guinea became an independent nation, taking its place among the new nations of the world. The people of the Enga Province were opposed to independence, saying: 'We are not ready yet; we need someone who is strong to help us with

300

our development.' The problems of the last ten years in the Enga Province attest to the insight of those who said: 'We are not ready'. With the strong presence of the Australian administration gone, inter-clan fighting began again. Soon there were more conflicts than there had ever been in the time before the government and missions came to Enga-land. The progress of some 30 years seemed to slip away overnight as every aspect of life in the Enga Province became disrupted. The people of the churches were not immune to the false idea of freedom and independence; they too became involved in clan fighting and other evils, and this began to divide the congregations. The local government was corrupt, with leaders using their position to gain material things for themselves. And the gross abuse of alcohol put the finishing touches to the destruction of the people and the way of peace in which they had lived for over thirty years. [23] It is indeed a time of testing.

The Highlands people in particular became extremely political in everything they did. The idea of getting yourself elected to a high post from which you could then reap personal gain also infected the Church. Soon the choosing of bishops and other leaders became a political game rather than a time for asking God for directions and then finding 'men who were filled with the Holy Spirit'. During this time also, many expatriate missionaries who had served with the Church for many years returned to their homelands. For a while, the GLC was able to keep the political tensions between regional Enga groups in balance; but the call to national political office was strong, and some of the leaders of the Church tried their hand at getting elected to these positions. That seemed to open the floodgate of political action within the Church itself. People began to campaign for office and to make political alliances.

At the Convention of the GLC in 1982, the Revd Dr Waima Waesa was not re-elected as Bishop; he was succeeded in that position by the Revd David Piso of Raiakama, a graduate of Martin Luther Seminary and a former PNG Defence Force Chaplain.

Ever since that election, there has been tension between the new Bishop and those who still support Dr Waesa. Some of the tension is the natural human problem of people from different areas wanting their leader in the top post, but some also stems from the differing approach of the two leaders. It is still too early to describe these differences and what they mean for the Church.

We are not, however, looking at a problem that is unique to the GLC in our time. Even with the strong pull for unity among churches throughout the world, there have been a number of 'splits', including some in Lutheranism. There has been a strong movement within the GLC for at least two of the regions to withdraw to form a separate body, which would then try to join the ELCPNG. Through the efforts of the supporting partners of the GLC (the AELC and the LC-MS), the split has been avoided thus far. [24] As things stand, the Church is the only institution in the Enga Province which still has a hope of bringing some sense of unity and oneness to the people. If it also were to break apart, that would be a disaster

not only for the work of the Gospel, but also for the entire society (Ewald 1985).

One does not want to end the story of a Church with an unresolved problem and a picture of weakness, so let this also be said. Through all this, there continue to be many who hold fast to the Lord Jesus as the one who can help in every situation. There are areas where the Church is still growing, and there are Christians who are more interested in the Gospel than in their own position. The date set for forming a breakaway church has passed, and the GLC is still together. There is evidence that the two sides are now talking to each other, and that cooperation is still possible.

And so, we can close our story with hope — hope that is born of the power of God and of the conviction that these are his people, this is his Church, and 'the gates of hell shall not prevail against it'.

God, save your people! To you alone be the glory now and for ever!

Endnotes

[1] The Church in the Enga area first called itself *Wabag Lutheran Church*, using the name of the main centre to identify itself. As the Church grew and included others who could not be identified with Wabag or the Enga language, the name was changed to *Gutnius Lutheran Church* (GLC). *Gutnius* is the New Guinea Pidgin word for Good News. The new name was adopted in 1978. To avoid confusion, we will use GLC to indicate this Church throughout this outline of its history.

[2] The Lutheran Church-Missouri Synod was not in fellowship with either the American Lutheran Church or the United Evangelical Lutheran Church of Australia. At first, this put some strain on the cooperation needed to carry on the work in the Enga area. It also led to the development of two separate Lutheran Churches in Papua New Guinea.

[3] We do not want the reader to think that these people lived up to their ideals any more than people in the Western world. It is important to note, however, that they had these ideals, and so were open to the Word. When they heard the Gospel and the promise of peace it offers, the message struck a responsive chord in the hearts of many hearers.

[4] We will concentrate on those events and actions which seem to tell most of the story. As much as possible we will concentrate on the local Church rather than on the Mission.

[5] The story of how the people lost the Water of Life and all the good things which went with it is a myth that reminds us of the story of human failure and rebellion in the Scriptures:

In the land of the *yalyakali* (sky people), so the story goes, there is no hunger or pain, no tension among the people, no sickness or death, no fighting or destruction. All is in perfect harmony and peace. In times past, the *yalyakali* set about the task of peopling the earth. The first man found a wife, and they lived together in a land of plenty without the cares, problems, and pain that mar life today. At the birth of their first son, the father knew that he would have to go and draw

301

water from the source of the *Water of Life* to give to the baby. Before he left, he warned his wife not to give the baby any breast milk, even if the baby cried, but to wait until he returned with the water which would ensure the continued prosperity and happiness of all. The trip was rather long, however, and the young mother could not deny the hungry wail of her son, so she fed him from her breast. With this action, humankind was now bound to the earth with all its troubles, anxiety, and death. The *Water of Life* was lost; the way to paradise barred. People were left with only a longing to return and be made whole once more. They had a hope that one day someone would find the way back, would discover the *yalya toko* (ladder to paradise).

[6] Johannes Warneck (1954:156-187) has pointed out the fact that God is often at work among a heathen people, using their prophets and life-situations to prepare a people who are ready to hear the Gospel. Without such preparation, the work in heathen areas would be very difficult. Among other things, he notes how the longing for peace plays an important role in predisposing people to listen to the Gospel.

[7] The New Guinea field had been presented to the LC-MS at its 100th Anniversary Convention held in Fort Wayne, Indiana in June 1947. The Convention unanimously accepted the 'gift', and directed its Board for World Missions to establish this work as soon as men could be found to enter the work.

[8] *Bosboi* is term from New Guinea Pidgin meaning a clan or local leader appointed by the colonial government in the first stages of contact.

[9] *Miti* is the term used by Lutheran coastal evangelists for the Word of God and the whole complex of Christian life and practice. Taken from the Jabem and Kate languages and adopted by Enga, it means the whole of God's message to people.

[10] *Kamongo* is the Enga term for a rich and powerful man; one who has been able to acquire wealth, power, and knowledge, and so brings honour and prestige to his clan as well as to himself; a leader in the *tee* (pig exchange), able to control many pigs and shells.

[11] The Enga possessed a strong desire for peace, and the dream of a land in which people could dwell at peace and would have all that they need. See note 5 above.

[12] After World War II, the Australian government did not allow Christian missions or other expatriates to enter any area of the country that was not under direct governmental control. These 'uncontrolled' areas had restricted access; non-local people were not allowed in. When an area was opened for free access to all people, it was 'de-restricted' by the government.

[13] Both these figures represent the called or appointed workers and do not include spouses and families. The entire Christian community involved from within PNG would total over 160, while the total for the expatriate community would be almost 600.

[14] *Poisen* is a substance or spell with magical properties used to kill or in some way harm an enemy. It is/was much feared by New Guinea people.

[15] An example of this is the position the missionaries took in regard to polygamous marriages, without considering how this would effect the women and children involved. People were told that, to be baptized and become part of the people of God, they would have to be monogamous. The good news about Jesus Christ was changed into the bad news about polygamy. Later, the Church changed this policy.

[16] Coast Watchers lived in the hills with the local people and reported on Japanese ship and troop movements to the Australian and American forces trying to recapture New Guinea.

[17] *Sangai/sandalu* is the name given to a complex of ceremonies used by the Enga as a purification rite for young bachelors, giving them strength and vision, and making them good warriors for the clan. It was a strong moral force among Enga young men.

[18] The Nete are nomadic hunters and gatherers. It has been hard for the Enga to stay among them, for they are not used to the continual migration. In recent years, however, the Nete and Hewa peoples have been changing their patterns, and congregations have been established among them.

[19] The Enga people were opposed to independence from Australia in 1975; they did not think the country was ready to have the strong influence of the *pax Australiana* removed. But they were helpless in resisting this movement of history. In addition to any other factor, the Australian government wanted to be out of PNG. Independence was declared on September 16, 1975.

[20] *A Statement of Faith* was prepared for the Lutheran Churches of PNG by the Committee on Theology and Inter-Church Relations set up by the Church and Missions working together. The work was completed in 1972 and presented to the Churches. The GLC was unable to accept it as its own until it was translated into Enga.

[21] The patterns of leadership which have developed in the GLC over the years have not followed the usual patterns of leadership in the local society. They have, however, certainly been influenced by traditional values. The fragmented nature of social organization among Enga peoples did not allow for formal chiefs at a clan level, much less political leaders of large groups. But this does not mean that there were no leaders, or that Enga people were super-individualists. Individual freedom could be practised within the bounds set by clan practice, but the solidarity and the good of the clan was seen as

the greatest good to be supported by all. Within clan structure, leadership was an achieved status exercised on an informal basis. The *kamongo* exercised his role of authority and power through the relationships he maintained, and by the way he was able to manipulate these relationships for the good of the entire group. Leadership was never absolute, nor was it practised under the threat of punishment. To become a man of influence, a leader, required a great deal of hard work on the part of the individual. His success was measured in terms of prestige and fame, rather than of wealth. A *kamongo* had to use his wealth for the good of the people, and be skilled in manipulating individuals for the good of the group. The coming of Western-type government, and missions imbued with Western organizational patterns and ideas, brought about changes in the leadership role, and a conflict between introduced and traditional leaders. This struggle has not yet been resolved, and is part of the difficulty facing the GLC in 1985. The coming of political independence and the acceptance of Western forms of government seem to give an edge to the new type of leader. Yet the concept of the *kamongo* has not died; today's leaders in government and church are often expected to follow the traditional role — at least, to some extent. Leaders are more often still seen as men who have the knowledge and skills to help the group than as people who make the major decisions for everyone to follow. Furthermore, traditional leaders were always men of wealth, and were not paid to be leaders — as are the men in both political and religious leadership today. This naturally leads to misunderstanding among taxpayers and church members. True leadership remains an achieved status in this part of Papua New Guinea.

22 At the time of the GLC Conference in June 1971, Papua New Guinea was in a state of high excitement. A national parliament was to be elected. Leaders from all over the country and from every clan-group believed they would be able to get elected. The GLC had decided that its top leadership had to remain committed to the tasks of the Church, and should not be involved in running for national office. The Conference made this a requirement for all of its officers. It then proceeded with the scheduled election, and elected Reo Raku as President, and Imbu Imbuni as Vice-President. After their election, both men challenged the Conference's right to limit their political future, and informed it that they had every intention of running for the national parliament. The delegates were divided on the issue, many along clan lines. The expatriate missionaries were also upset, and let it be known that they would be unable to recognize men as their leaders who went against the will of the GLC. Missionary Elwyn Ewald offered his resignation from the Church, and returned to his station. Finally, under pressure from the Conference, the two men resigned from office, and the meeting was adjourned until September. The group had been very close to breaking up, but calmer heads had prevailed.

23 One of the Enga ideals is that people should live together in peace and harmony. At the same time, the Enga have always fought with one another over land and pigs and women. During the years from 1947 to 1977, the power of the Australian government and the influence of the missions was able to stop the clan fighting. It was a time of peace which people enjoyed; they were able to move about freely and to trust one another. As the pain of their warfare faded, older men began to speak of the glory of war and the insults that had never been repaid. Then alcohol was allowed when the Australian administration in PNG changed its laws. This has lead to much pain, death, and a breakdown of law and order. The coming of independence, which was misunderstood by many, led to further fighting. Soon there were more fights than could be controlled, and the new government had no way to really control the situation. Only the church and the Christian community stood between absolute chaos and the way of peace. It may well take another four or five years before peace really comes to the Enga Province.

24 As the society became more and more politicized, and people began to view their leaders as those who were supposed to give them more things, the church also began to suffer. Leaders used the position they had been given to give special help to their own people, and tended to ignore others. Younger men, such as Absalom, began to tell everyone how they would be able to make it better for all. In this setting, David Piso, a former chaplain of the PNG Defence Force and a graduate of Martin Luther Seminary, was elected by the GLC in its 1982 Convention in opposition to Dr Waima Waesa, who had been the leader of the GLC since 1971 and its Bishop since 1976. Because of the political nature of the change, there has been constant tension in the GLC and the threat of a divided church. It is ironic that the AELC and the LC-MS, who went through a split not too many years ago, have been the instruments used by God to keep the GLC together — at least for now. Both groups informed the factions within the GLC in no uncertain terms that there would be no support from the USA for either group, should there be a split. God does work in mysterious ways.

Listed below you will find the sources used for the materials in this chapter whether they are quoted directly or not.

BOARD FOR WORLD MISSIONS, The Lutheran Church-Missouri Synod. *1948-1963 The First Fifteen Years: An Account of the New Guinea Lutheran Mission-Missouri Synod and the Wabag Lutheran Church* (St Louis: LC-MS, 1963).

BRENNAN, Paul W. ed., *Exploring Enga Culture: Studies in Missionary Anthropology.* Second NGLM Anthropological Conference (Irelya, PNG: NGLM, 1970).

BRENNAN, Paul W. 'The Indigenous World View' (NGLM, Mimeo, 1971).

'Communicating a guilt-oriented message in a shame-oriented society' (NGLM, Mimeo, 1973).

Let Sleeping Snakes Lie: Central Enga Traditional Belief and Ritual (Adelaide: Australian Society for the Study of Religion, 1977).

BURCE, Willard. Patrol and Station Reports 1948-52. (GLC Archives, Irelya, PNG)
'Our New Guinea Mission During its First Seven Years' (NGLM Mimeo, 1955)
Newsletter dated October 1, 1956, Irelya, PNG
Newsletter dated January 11, 1957, Irelya, PNG
Annual report, 1960 (GLC Archives, Irelya, PNG)

CHURCH-MISSION COUNCIL, GLC/NGLM
1964 Minutes (GLC Archives, Irelya, PNG)
1965-70 Minutes (GLC Archives, Irelya, PNG)

COMMITTEE ON THEOLOGY AND INTER-CHURCH RELATIONS
1964 Minutes (GLC Archives, Irelya, PNG)

EVANGELISM COMMITTEE, NGLM
1957-59 Minutes (GLC Archives, Irelya, PNG)

EXECUTIVE COMMITTEE, NGLM
1950-70 Minutes (GLC Archives, Irelya, PNG)

EWALD, Elwyn. 'Exempt School Survey', NGLM Study Paper, 1968 (GLC Archives, Irelya, PNG)
Telephone conversation, July 16, 1985

FREUND, A.P.H. 1949 Patrol Reports (GLC Archives, Irelya, PNG)

GUTNIUS LUTHERAN CHURCH-PAPUA NEW GUINEA (GLC) (Formerly the Wabag Lutheran Church)
General Conference Agenda, Reports, and Minutes 1959-80 (GLC Archives, Irelya, PNG)
Constitution, Wabag Lutheran Church, 1961
Revised Constitution, Wabag Lutheran Church, 1967
Constitution, Gutnius Lutheran Church — Papua New Guinea, 1978
Church Council Agenda, Reports, and Minutes 1961-64 and 1974-80.
Executive Committee Agenda, Reports, and Minutes 1961-64 and 1974-80
Official Correspondence 1962-80
Rules of Association of the Wabag Lutheran Church, Incorporated, 1969 (amended 1974 & 1976)
Rules of Association of the Gutnius Lutheran Church-Papua New Guinea, Incorporated, 1978
The Mission of the Church of Jesus Christ, GLC, Irelya, 1975
Gutnius Lutheran Church Plan: 1981-1990

HINTZE, Otto C. Patrol and Station Reports 1948-52
Newsletters 1952-60 (GLC Archives, Irelya)

KUNIAME Sakatao. Interview at Irelya, Novemeber 13, 1978.

LACEY, Roderic John
'Oral Tradition as History: An Exploration of Oral Sources Among the Enga of the New Guinea Highlands' (unpublished PhD Thesis, University of Wisconsin, 1975)

LUTHERAN CHURCH COUNCIL-WABAG. 1970 Minutes (GLC Archives, Irelya)

MANDITA of Porgera. Interview, October 5, 1978.

NEW GUINEA LUTHERAN MISSION-MISSOURI SYNOD
Official Minutes, Reports, Correspondence 1948-70 (GLC Archives Irelya)

RAIAKAMA CONGREGATION
Interview with the Lutheran Congregation at Raiakama April 15, 1976

SCHAAN, Herbert. Tapes and transcript of interview with Wambalipi, including reports of evaluations of Wambalipi by the people of the Lyaimi area, 1968-69

SPRUTH, Erwin L. Various field notes and journals 1954-80
Newsletters, 1955-80, Irelya
'Mission Work in New Guinea', NGLM Report, 1957, Irelya
'Mission Work in New Guinea — Up-date', NGLM, 1959, Irelya
'The Mission of God in the Wabag Area of New Guinea' (unpublished ThM Thesis, School of World Mission, Fuller Theological Seminary, Pasadena, California, 1970).
Tok Bilong God Ran I Go: Stori Bilong Gutnius Luteren Sios, 1980.
'And the Word of God Spread: A brief history of the Gutnius Lutheran Church-Papua New Guinea' (unpublished Doctor of Missiology Thesis, School of World Mission, Fuller Theological Seminary, Pasadena, California, 1981)

STOTIK, Karl. Station Reports 1950 (GLC Archives, Irelya)
Annual Report 1958 (GLC, Irelya)

STRACKBEIN, Lee. Newsletter, November 1955 (GLC Archives, Irelya)

WAIMANE, Kooa and others. Interview at Yaramanda, September 14, 1978

WAGNER, William P. Kopiago. Station Reports 1964 (GLC Archives, Irelya)

WARNECK, Johannes. *The Living Christ and Dying Heathenism* translated by Neil Buchanan (Grand Rapids: Baker Book House, 1954)

YANGOMANE, Yakopya. Interview at Irelya, November 14, 1978

YAPALINI of Kaipale. Interview at Kaipale, November 13, 1978

Chapter 9:

Autonomous Church in Independent Papua New Guinea

by John May

'The autonomy of the church has now begun!' With this 'Declaration of Autonomy', issued on the initiative of Bishop Zurewe on July 2, 1976 to celebrate the 90th anniversary of the arrival of the first Lutheran missionaries, the Evangelical Lutheran Church of Papua and New Guinea (ELC-PNG) quite deliberately echoed the proud proclamation of national independence of the previous year.[1] On reflection, of course, such a declaration of autonomy was of necessity more symbolic than real. It is as difficult to say precisely *when* the ELC-PNG became autonomous as it is to say *whether* Papua New Guinea is even now truly independent in every respect. Both the autonomy of the church and the independence of the nation are more truly seen as a long and painful process of coming of age or of struggling toward maturity at a quite new level of existence and in an unfamiliar network of wider relationships. In this chapter I shall thus try to present the struggle for autonomy as a process that is still going on. Where possible, I shall do so in the words and through the eyes of Papua New Guinean members of ELC-PNG.

My aim is to examine this process in four steps. The first two are more descriptive in character; they concern, first, the transition from mission to church, and second, the resulting structure of ELC-PNG. These will make rather dry reading for those already familiar with the church, but they are indispensable for the more evaluative sections which follow. Thirdly, the question must be put — as it has been to ELC members — whether a certain dependency still detracts from the undoubted growth of the church toward autonomy. Then in conclusion, I should like to raise the issue of the church's sense of its own identity, surely an integral part of autonomy: is it recognizably Lutheran *and* Melanesian, or — and this is no doubt the key question — is a synthesis of both possible, desirable, and in the process of coming about?

It is obvious that no definitive answers to such far-reaching questions can be expected in this chapter, given the paucity of documentary material and the limited opportunities available to me for conducting formal interviews. However, as a Roman Catholic guest of ELC-PNG, I have received every encouragement, especially from its present Head Bishop, the Rt

'Jesus Christ is the living stone' (1 Peter 2:4). Stone-monument in front of church headquarters, Lae.

The Rt Revd Getake Gam, Head Bishop of the ELC-PNG.

Revd Getake S. Gam, to become as familiar with it as possible; and, as a relative newcomer to Papua New Guinea, perhaps I can look at the issues and difficulties facing it with a certain detachment. My admiration for this church has grown as I have watched it trying to find its own way in a situation which is becoming increasingly difficult.

From Mission to Church

Lutheran ecclesiology — which adheres closely to the New Testament, and thus to the example of Paul, the prototype missionary — takes for granted that each local church (the *Landeskirche* of German tradition) should become autonomous as soon as possible. Even so, it is very much to the credit of Lutheran Mission New Guinea (LMNG) that it envisaged from the very beginning of its work the establishment of an indigenous and autonomous Lutheran church in New Guinea; indeed, this intention is implicit in the whole approach of a pioneer missionary like Keysser. After the disruptions of two world wars and the eventual integration of the German, American, and Australian missionary efforts, the

Simbang 1956 — the ELCONG is founded.

Evangelical Lutheran Church of New Guinea (ELCONG) was formally established as early as 1956 with the explicit purpose of taking over by degrees the responsibilities then still incumbent upon LMNG. This historic event took place at Simbang, near Finschhafen, 70 years after the founding of the Mission, and on the very spot where Johannes Flierl landed. Dr John Kuder (ELCONG's inaugural bishop) reports that it was the indigenous leaders who pressed for this step and for the church order which officially inaugurated ELCONG as an organized entity. [2] An event of equal significance, as we shall see, was the election of Zurewe Zurenuo (until then church secretary of the Sattelberg circuit) as the Secretary of ELCONG. [3] It was his vision and energy which helped to fill the bare framework that was ELCONG with the spiritual vigour and administrative self-confidence that were to make ELC-PNG possible.

Dr Kuder, the first bishop of ELCONG, was originally also president of LMNG. At the 23rd Annual Conference of the Mission in Wau in January 1969, he was suceeded as President by Rufus Pech. The intention was that Kuder devote his energies to the development of indigenous leadership of the fledgling church. On the same occasion, the Church Council of ELCONG and the Executive Committee of LMNG were merged to form a joint council. [4]

The following years were devoted to an intensive discussion of the shape and substance of the coming independent church toward which all, indigenous and expatriate, were working. [5] As power gradually devolved from LMNG to ELCONG, [6] a consultation held at Lae from February 25 to March 6, 1970 envisaged departments of Evangelization, Finance, and Education as forming the nucleus of the church's structure. [7] A memorandum from about this period, presumably Zurewe's but unfortunately unsigned and undated, suggests that there were some who felt that Melanesians should be appointed secretaries of these departments, as had already happened in the United Church. However, others were of the opinion that 'we are not ready for this yet', and that the infrastructure of shipping, aviation, education, and medical care should remain the concern of the Mission until the Church felt able to take them over. There were even those who wanted to retain the title 'mission'. [8] There was

309

much talk of 'first things first' and of 'learning to drive' by stages. [9] For all his impatience at the slow progress of localization, Zurewe clearly foresaw the need for continuing support from expatriate missionaries for a considerable time to come. [10]

Despite these understandable hesitations and trepidations, it is important to remember that the progress of ELCONG toward full autonomy was much more orderly and collaborative than the parallel process of wresting the independence of the country as a whole from a mistrustful, not to say sceptical, Australian administration; indeed, the 'when', if not the 'whether', of independence was uncertain until almost the last moment. Yet there can be no doubt that, during these eventful years, independence was in the air, and that the development of what Zurewe called 'a walking Church ... a growing Church ... a changing Church'[11] must be seen in this context. [12]

The Eighth General Synod of ELCONG at Ogelbeng, from August 31 to September 7, 1970, in the presence of the Catholic Bishop Bernarding and the Anglican Bishop Ambo, formally dissolved the joint council of ELCONG and LMNG and established a Church Council, with Dr Kuder as a member, and Rufus Pech and the laymen Arthur Fenske and Don Ruthenberg as advisers; Zurewe was reelected Secretary for a further four years. [13] The overriding question now became: Who would succeed Dr Kuder as Head Bishop: a New Guinean or an expatriate? Meeting at Madang on June 26-30, 1972, the Church Council set up a nominations committee, [14] and Zurewe was well aware that his name was increasingly being mentioned. He revealed both his nervousness (which was even then affecting his health) and his clear ideas about the future structure of the church in a letter to two members of the committee who were also his close confidants: Mambu Jeremia and Mafuanu Butik. Instead of the compromises which are so often the response to 'localization' in Papua New Guinea — a national in the official position with an expatriate in the background — he suggested that the Head Bishop and Assistant Bishop should be either both expatriates or both New Guineans, though an expatriate layman would be acceptable as treasurer. From 1973 on, the

310

bishop's secretary should be concerned with running the office, keeping minutes, and other strictly secretarial tasks. The Circuit Presidents should all be New Guineans, though Circuit Missionaries might still act as their advisers. Above all, at the coming synod the church should aim at consensus; it should not be like the House of Assembly, where competitive elections are the order of the day. [15]

Presenting a draft of the ELCONG constitution to LMNG for study and comment, Bishop Kuder indicated that there was some discussion as to whether the future leader of the church should be called 'bishop' or 'president', but another issue he raised was to be more significant: 'We should stress the fact that the districts are really the working arms of the church, while ELCONG headquarters continues to be a kind of agency to bind them all together and not a ruling organization'. [16] The sentiment is unimpeachably Lutheran; but whether Melanesians would feel at home in the type of organization envisaged is another matter, and this apparently was not given much consideration.

The decisive Ninth General Synod of ELCONG was held at Balob Teachers College, Lae, on January 22-29, 1973. After the expatriate candidate withdrew, Zurewe was elected the first indigenous bishop of the Church, and was installed by Bishops Kuder and Dietzfelbinger (Germany), assisted by District Presidents Boniepe and Mambu, President Grope (Australia) and the Revd Gudmestad (USA). The new constitution was approved and entrusted to a revision committee for further work. [17] The Committee on Theology and Inter-Church-Relations had been working since 1964 on a Statement of Faith, which was provisionally accepted by the Synod. On April 2-5 of the same year, the conference of LMNG at Nobonob near Madang, at which only two representatives of ELCONG were present, formally transferred to ELCONG the responsibility for the operations of the Mission in the fields of aviation, radio, shipping, maintenance, building, plantations and lands; a conference of all missionaries at Wau in 1974 was to complete this transfer. [18] As had been mooted at the Madang Church Council meeting of June 26-30, 1972,[19] a New Guinea Coordinating Committee (NGCC) then

Zurewe Zurenuo, elected first indigenous Bishop of the Church.

replaced LMNG as ELCONG's partner in all matters concerning overseas finance and personnel,[20] and the business and development activities of the church were entrusted to Kambang Holdings and Lutheran Economic Service.[21]

There is no doubt that this complicated process of what today would be called the 'transfer of power' from LMNG to ELCONG was carried out with an admirable sense of responsibility and a prudent concern for administrative detail on both sides. Yet, even though the theological legitimacy of the operation was taken for granted by all concerned, there is little evidence that they realized its full significance in the wider context of decolonization. Throughout the 1950s and 1960s, Asian and then African countries in increasing numbers had achieved their independence, often accompanied by bloody revolutionary and civil wars and followed by acrimonious reprisals against missionaries, whom nationalist leaders tended to identify with the colonial masters from whom they now imagined they had liberated themselves. Under such circumstances, the indigenization of local

churches was a condition of survival. The authenticity of the process was closely scrutinized, and all links to outside supporting agencies were viewed with the greatest suspicion by governments intent on self-reliance.

In a series of lectures delivered late in 1965, Georg Vicedom, who had been a pioneer missionary to the Highlands of New Guinea, confronted both Church and Mission with the full implications of this wider context for their project of achieving autonomy for ELCONG. If some of his warnings had been heeded, ELC-PNG would be in a better position to face many of the problems which plague it today. Vicedom made it quite clear that the mere intention to found a 'self-supporting, self-governing, and self-propagating church' does not necessarily guarantee true independence in reality.[22] Because the missionaries usually placed an indelible Western stamp on the churches they founded, these remained the captives of the 'mission stations' on which they had always depended.[23]

Churches to which autonomy has been granted commonly use most of the fraternal workers and funds from abroad to serve themselves. The fraternal workers seem content to be used. Thus mission seems to have disappeared ...[24]

The problem is not solved by just transferring power to a younger church ... [for the crux of the matter is the acknowledgment] that the younger church is a part of the one church and therefore will be used by God as a base for its mission in that country ... this means that integration can not be realized by new organizational ways, it is always an outcome of the spiritual life of mission and church. There was too much emphasis on the organizational side and not enough on the radical change of attitude and relationship which is demanded.[25]

The question must be put whether the integration of LMNG and ELCONG, which was formally concluded not ten years after these words were written, escapes this judgment. Vicedom had warned: 'Integration as an organizational solution will have disastrous effects where the spiritual presupposition is not given',[26] but here it must be said that ELC-PNG was able to build on an indigenous missionary tradition and was blessed with spiritual leadership of a high order. All in all, we may thank God that, in the course of Papua New

311

Guinea's relatively-harmonious transition to independence, ELC-PNG was spared the traumas that many other churches of the so-called Third World had to endure. When we go on to examine the church structure that emerged, however, we do so against the background of Vicedom's challenging remarks.

The Structure of ELC-PNG

One's first impression of the structure of ELC-PNG is that it is highly centralized, bureaucratic, and hierarchical (though not of course with the theological connotation this word carries for Roman Catholics, and always remembering that any large organization needs a bureaucracy).

The Head Bishop, with the assistance of a *Helpim Bishop*, to whom he may delegate representative and pastoral functions, bears ultimate responsibility for the day-to-day running of the church. The Church Council, to which each District sends three delegates, meets with the Head Bishop and the Assistant Bishop twice a year. Synod meets every two years, and includes delegates from circuits,

parishes, and congregations, as well as District Presidents and departmental heads. The seminaries, high schools, and chaplaincies of the church are also represented. The department of the Head Bishop oversees the general administration of the church and consists of the office of the Assistant Bishop, administrative secretaries for national and overseas staff, and sections for office management, statistics, and archives. A number of committees, either special or standing, report to the Church Council on publishing, social justice, theology, constitutional matters, and scholarships, while the Bishop's Council has committees on pastoral problems and the pastors' work. The remaining departments of the church cover finance, medical services, evangelism, education, and ministerial training, with the recent addition of Lutheran Economic Service as a fully-fledged department by the 1984 Mt Hagen Synod. [27]

An analogous structure is reproduced at district and circuit levels. Annual District Conferences make decisions on policy and

Church headquarters, Lae.

312

administration and receive reports from the various departments, while the everyday running of the district is in the hands of the District President and his staff at the District Office. It would be wearisome to continue describing the further ramifications of these structures; an impression of the whole may be gained from a diagram appended to this chapter.

On closer inspection, we realize that this structure, complex and bureaucratic as it may be in the abstract, includes what we might call a strong participatory or democratic element. All major decision-making, from the congregations upwards, is where possible by consensus; and there is a sense in which the Head Bishop is indeed more truly described as a President, one who presides over this process of communal decision-making (as does the District President at his level). In the congregations, lay elders stand beside the ordained pastors, and the laity are strongly represented in all the administrative and consultative bodies described above. [28] Though the church does not yet ordain women, the presence of women, including those with some theological education, is being felt increasingly at district and national levels. [29]

A certain ambiguity remains after our brief examination of the structure of ELC-PNG. The *way* or 'style' in which the Lutherans of Papua New Guinea go about conducting the affairs of their church is as characteristically Melanesian as the *structures* within which they are constrained to do so are unmistakeably Western. The church is indeed tightly organized — as any national body of over a half-a-million people must be — yet one cannot escape an impression of conflict or even confusion when Melanesians (coming from a culture which stresses communal values and organic structures, and shuns specialization and individualism) are expected to function within a tightly-structured and rationally-organized bureaucratic hierarchy. Is this simply a consequence of over-hasty localization, or do the roots lie deeper, in the failure of the church to maintain and develop the indigenous forms of theological, liturgical, and congregational life which were apparent at the beginning? These are the far-reaching questions to which we must now turn.

Autonomy or Dependency?

In 1977, only a year after Bishop Zurewe's 'Declaration of Autonomy' and the renaming of ELCONG as ELC-PNG, the church was presented with two thorough evaluations: the one of its progress toward true independence, and the other of its general condition. The first was by an international team of experienced Lutheran administrators expecially commissioned for the purpose; [30] but it depended to a considerable extent on an empirical survey carried out locally by the staff of the Melanesian Institute in Goroka, which with the 'objective' techniques of social science reflects the opinions of Papua New Guinean Lutherans about their church. [31] My own observations have led me to believe that, despite improvement in some areas and deterioration in others, the essential problems faced by ELC-PNG have not changed since then. I shall thus draw on these reports in what follows, though I shall supplement them wherever possible with the views of present-day members of the church (who, as they occupy positions of responsibility, shall remain anonymous). [32]

One problem that emerges from this process of self-evaluation is the need for ELC-PNG, in its operations and its outlook, to become a *national* church. [33] The missions from which it originated were established among peoples who traditionally had been sufficient unto themselves. The panoply of organizational structures erected by the architects of ELCONG was to have fused these into a higher unity, following not only the dictates of Christian doctrine but the exigencies of approaching independence. Added to this was the difficulty of ministering to Lutherans, who were used to the vigorous and homogeneous congregational life of rural areas, in the alien environment of the country's rapidly-growing towns. [34] It would seem, however, that circuit, district, and national headquarters have still not entirely succeeded in impressing a sense of belonging to a national unity on the members of village congregations. [35] Though these do expect a certain amount of help and support (both material and spiritual) from the national church, they do not seem to identify with the national church, and they feel little responsibility toward it.

313

Its authority is confined basically to very limited areas, namely: talking with the overseas churches, finance, missionaries, money, looking after church properties, running the educational work. These are the common interests of the districts with regard to the national church and the very narrow common denominator for what might be called 'National Lutheran Church' ... The general feeling on the side of the congregations and circuits seems to be that they do not receive much relevant help from the national church ... [yet] they much overestimate the contribution which they make to the national church. [36]

There is thus 'a great gap in how things are viewed', [37] which echoes Zurewe's judgment of some five years earlier: 'There is a big gulf between the people and the church administration'. [38]

What would seem to be lacking, then, is the conviction of belonging, as Lutherans, to the wider family of Melanesian Christians in an independent nation. This is not without repercussions in the relations of ELC-PNG to other churches and to national and provincial governments. Bishop Zurewe had foreseen this difficulty, and from the beginning had been tireless in urging his fellow-Lutherans to take their share of responsibility in the life of the nation as a whole. In a submission to the Constitutional Planning Committee, [39] he proposed that Christianity should be explicitly recognized and mentioned in the new constitution, stressing particularly 'unity within the church and nation' and 'spiritual development among the people of the nation', as well as the church's traditional role in ministering to social problems. Reminiscing, he told how he had encouraged government ministers to eat at his house, even going to the extent of praying with the Prime Minister in his office: 'I wanted cooperation of State and Church, but on this level: ministers of the government and leaders of the church should come to know and appreciate one another'. [40]

From 1970 on, Bishop Zurewe was Chairman of the Melanesian Council of Churches, and he saw ecumenical work as the responsibility, not just of the national headquarters, but of each district office of the church. [41] He encouraged dialogue with the Roman Catholic Church on Baptism, [42] and with the United Church on Baptism and Holy Communion. [43] Today, the encroachments of

314

fundamentalist sects on traditionally-Lutheran areas pose a new and difficult problem, which can best be met in cooperation with the other major churches. There seems no reason why common ground cannot be found with evangelicals and charismatics, though Lutherans in village congregations, ill-prepared to understand this new breed of Christians, tend to feel threatened by them. There would seem, however, to be a largely untapped ecumenical potential in these congregations, for I was told again and again by pastors and elders that they valued belief in God and Jesus Christ above all denominational affiliations, including their own:

This is what I believe. I don't take notice of what others think. One goes to the Lutheran church — that's good; or to the Methodist — that's good; Catholic — that's good. But I weigh all this and come to the conclusion: ah, Catholic and Lutheran and whatever kind of mission, SDA mission — they're just missions, that's all. But God is one ... there's this and that way of thinking and this and that kind of law — it's nothing; forget it. It was Jesus himself who came to us on the cross; it was he who helped us and bore our sins and died, who came back from the dead to help us. [44]

Some considerable time before ELC-PNG became formally autonomous, its members were warned that they would be expected to 'pull' (support) it, and not the other way around. [45] There was much talk of 'stewardship' based on voluntary offerings by the people for their church. [46] But even today there is still a lingering doubt whether they do, in fact, see the church needing large financial outlays for its complicated operations as *their* church; whether ELC-PNG is in any deeply-felt sense the *people's* church. This lack of conviction has very practical consequences when it comes to deciding how much and from whose resources church workers should be paid. Zurewe, with his usual foresight, vigorously combated the idea of pooling the resources of LMNG and ELCONG as 'cargo cult thinking'. [47] The 1977 self-study revealed that, apart from paying their own pastor — and even here opinion was divided between those who approved of a regular salary and those who wanted payment only for services rendered [48] — that 'close to 74% of respondents are unhappy with the collection', which may suggest 'a crisis of faith and belief in what the Church is'. [49] The people have nothing against the educational, medical, and

The National Parliament, Port Moresby.

developmental services provided by the institutions of the church, but they take for granted that these are supported by business interests and overseas funding; in no way do they regard them as *their* responsibility.[50] The vexed question of the large overseas subsidy rankled with Zurewe, for whom financial autonomy was crucial to true independence: 'Is this church still a child, or does it want to stand on its own like a true church?'[51]

Zurewe's perceptiveness is evident from his disclosure that it was this unhappy situation which provided a large part of his motive in encouraging ELC-PNG pastors to undertake missionary work among the Australian Aborigines:

I wanted to give our church a missionary goal for which it would be worthwhile to make sacrifices. In this way I wanted to strengthen our congregations.

With characteristic frankness he goes straight to the heart of the matter:

All the institutions we have in this country were founded by the mother churches. Nothing comes from our own initiative. Hence we do not regard it as our own. But mission work of our own in another country, that would be an independent initiative, something that belonged to us alone. That was my intention.[52]

But this work has not developed sufficiently to capture the imagination of the congregations.[53] The challenge still remains to find ways of progressively reducing the church's dependence on the overseas subsidy, e.g., by strictly limiting the number of expatriate personnel, and restricting them to positions where they are still indispensable, and by requiring ELC-PNG to find the first K2,000 of their salaries so that this amount would already be covered by the budget in the event of localization.[54]

Although the question of financial dependency is important and unavoidable in discussing the autonomy of a church in what was formerly a mission country, a Christian assessment of autonomy must go deeper. In the end, all such matters of organization and

315

finance are merely symptomatic of the maturity or otherwise of the church's life of faith.

Has ELC-PNG remained — for it undoubtedly was so at the beginning — a truly *spiritual* church? This is what really interested those older and experienced members of the church with whom it was my privilege to speak.[55] 'The Gospel comes first — we don't pay reverence to the powers of the earth!'[56] Another summed up the history of the church thus: 'The light came to drive out darkness', adding that 'the light worked together with problems' which came upon the young church from outside.[57] When asked how they felt about their church at present, both President Gedisa and Bishop Mambu expressed their joy at belonging to it: 'It looks to the Bible and does God's work',[58] and 'the work of evangelization is going ahead'.[59]

Yet the International Evaluation Team discerned the church's three most pressing needs in order of priority as: 'Spiritual renewal, deeper devotion to Christ; Prophetic vision from the leadership, a clear sense of direction; More joyful and authentic worship, especially for the young people'.[60] Bishop Zurewe had insisted on these things in season and out of season:

> [Unlike the Evangelical Alliance and the Melanesian Council of Churches] we of ELCONG have not had one seminar to discuss New Guineans being responsible for the spiritual work. We have only been engaged in writing minutes and attending all kinds of meetings … True spiritual work is when the people join with the pastor in studying the Word of God … [yet our work has been] only organizational.

Properly regarded, the Bishop's Council is to 'discuss the work dealing with the Word of God, Communion, Baptism, prayer, worship and preaching during these changing times'.[61] Discussing development with a representative of the German Lutheran aid agency *Bread for the World*, he said:

> We cannot support the spiritual work in this country without development, because it is a young country and a newly-developing nation. This is the real reason, but the people have lost their spiritual thinking, the way of bringing Jesus Christ to the people. They have forgotten this, and they think only about the development of the nation … The word 'development', I would say, has two branches. One is the 'development of the spiritual life', and the other is the 'development of the nation'.[62]

The immediate practical problem, as Zurewe notes in the same context, would seem to be one of inadequate communication. This affects not so much the church's central task of communicating the unfalsified Word of God through its preaching and the sacramental life of its congregations — which, of course, presents its own difficulties;[63] rather, it involves the flow of information and the understanding of one another's roles between the different levels and branches of the church.

After analysing the quite serious failure of communication between congregations and circuits, circuits and districts, and each of these levels with the national church, the 1977 self-study concludes by asking: 'But what is the real task of the church? Why is it so much concerned with itself?', observing that 'each unit in the church organization seems to rotate around itself', yet 'our vision cannot be to keep the organization going'.[64] Though the catechetical and educational work of the church is the envy of others in Papua New Guinea, a Lutheran working in the media field complained that church members returning from conferences overseas or attending church and government meetings never think of contacting him to report on their experiences.[65] If it is true in general that Christian spirituality is rooted in the life of the community, how much more true must this be of Melanesian Christians! Yet if, as the views quoted above suggest, this dimension of the spiritual life of ELC-PNG is being smothered by organizational forms which absorb much of the church's energy, then the church is seriously handicapped in performing its essential task.

We have looked at ELC-PNG as a national church, a people's church, and a spiritual church as three possible approaches to the autonomy it has achieved. We have seen evidence of missionary outreach and spiritual growth, yet the almost insuperable difficulties of the church in supporting and administering its own operation leave us with the impression of a lingering ambiguity. 'We want to be free', said Zurewe to a German visitor in 1972, 'We want to make our own decisions, but we need advice from the missionaries';[66] and the whole ambivalence of his position and that of ELC-PNG is reflected in his words. Looking back on his years as bishop, he who was the

316

instigator of the 'Declaration of Autonomy' (which he went to the length of declaring was 'even more important than the church's constitution, the confession of faith, so to speak, which the constitution presupposes' [67]) feels compelled to admit: 'Much has still not been accomplished ... I did not achieve my goal ... The independence and autonomy of the church has even now not really arrived, in all areas.' As a seminary student put it even more bluntly: 'They always tell me that ELC-PNG got her independence, but it is skin only'. [68]

Though Zurewe spared no effort 'to develop the villages and make village life attractive again, so that the urban drift can be reversed', he was dissatisfied with the progress made by the church in meeting the challenge of foreign missions and urban ministry; if it fails to understand the urgency of this challenge 'and restricts itself to its traditional village communities, it will have no future'.

Another unsolved problem that 'depresses' him, as he freely admits, is the continuing financial dependence of the church on an overseas subsidy. It is not so much the size of this subsidy that worries him as the fact that the people have still not learnt to give generously. 'All the things I tried, to get them to give more willingly!' The other side of this coin was his impatience at not being 'taken seriously as a partner' by the overseas churches. [69] And yet he has high praise for the dedication of the white missionaries: 'Without their contribution I would not have been able to build up the church', for the simple reason that 'the church as a whole was foreign to our people'. Not a single one of his compatriots was able to help him in this respect. [70]

That these are not just the ramblings of an embittered old man is shown by frequent references to his deteriorating health, almost certainly as a result of the strain he was under in trying to convince both uncomprehending New Guineans and the overseas churches of the rightness and urgency of his vision. Even in a pastoral letter, he admits that the worries of his office have made him too sick to attend district conferences. [71] And yet he was always learning, even from such apparently insignificant experiences as the active participation of the wives of Indonesian Lutherans in a meeting he attended at Medan in Sumatra, which fired him

to write to Mufuanu Butik about arranging refresher courses to inform the wives of ELC-PNG officials about the work of the church. [72] He was always open to new ideas, even such controversial ones as the 'moratorium' on overseas missionaries, in which he saw a possible help toward self-reliance and self-identity; [73] and, after talks with Dr Won Yong Ji, Asian representative of the Lutheran World Federation, his immediate reaction was: Why shouldn't ELCONG join, when its constitution and its Statement of Faith are in preparation? [74] He was quite evidently both a bold thinker and a spiritual leader, though it was his tragedy to be far ahead of his time. The ups and downs of his years as the first indigenous bishop of the church were part and parcel of its struggle to become truly autonomous.

The closing words of his reminiscences make a fitting conclusion to this section:

> The church — that's not Lae with its many offices. When visitors come from Germany or America, they shouldn't think they've met the church when they've seen its leadership in Ampo. That's not the church. The true church — that is the many simple people scattered here and there in the jungle all over the country. How are they to be helped and served? Not with money. Your money doesn't reach the grass roots anyway. But when you visit us, you must go to them if you're looking for the church. Sit down with them, talk to them, eat with them, sleep in their houses. Share their devotions, attend their worship, join them in prayer. Then you'll meet up with the true church. And the blessing will be mutual. They will see something of the great, world-wide church, and you will encounter the hospitality of true Christians. The ordinary people — that is the church. Lae is just an organizational centre. [75]

Lutheran or Melanesian Identity?

Though informed Papua New Guinean Lutherans are generally well aware of the problems involved in their church's achieving autonomy, I have found it hard to interest them in the question of 'identity'. Yet, as Zurewe noted when asking his people to weigh the pros and cons of a missionary moratorium, 'self-identity' is an integral part of 'self-reliance' and thus of autonomy. [76] Though he occasionally used the bureaucratic jargon of 'localization, [77] he seems to have preferred the more theological term

The church is not Lae. It is the people all over the country.

'indigenization' with its connotations of forging a new Melanesian Lutheran identity. Thus, in the memorandum of uncertain date already quoted, he calls for a 'Committee of Inquiry into Indigenization of the Church' and a 'Seminar for District Bishops in Practical Indigenous Theology'.

A passage from a student's essay (whose grammatical imperfections are a poignant testimony to the confusion against which the author is struggling) strikes to the heart of the matter with a telling and very Melanesian metaphor:

> This present church structure that our church is following nowadays have been planned to follow it and use it in proclaiming good news in our country to convert us. And also it has been planned by different people of different countries which have different cultural background of their own which it did not use our cultural background or environment. It has been planned by using the cultural background of different society altogether and, so the church structure we are following have been originated from somewhere and it's brace is also in somewhere. It's roots are also in somewhere but the trunk and it's branches are in our country PNG. Therefore the food and the

water is collected from it's roots which is in somewhere else far away from PNG to it's trunk and branches which is in PNG and it produces fruit here. Therefore I am saying that the Church would change it's structure, since we are converted already and plant the structure in PNG with it's own cultural background and let it grow in the land of PNG, not in somewhere far from PNG. In this way I think it would enforce the work of stewardship (*sic*). [78]

In the second of his 1965 lectures, Georg Vicedom left Church and Mission in no doubt about the anti-Western feelings of the emerging nations — and churches — of Asia and Africa and the legitimate reasons for them:

> One of the most depressing observations is, that nations which received the most of the Western money and technical help, or where Western industrial concerns rule the situation, — these nations became the places of the greatest social unrest and upheavals.

He goes on to point out how alien Western secularism and individualism are to these cultures:

> To have dealings with a man is to deal with a man who has a specific mother tongue, has certain patterns of thoughts given through the cultural

318

setting in which he has been brought up, is affected by specific social customs. These are the depths into which the Gospel wants to put its roots and we have to dig the ground for it.

We too easily assume, however, that the people 'are accepting just what we are teaching', and that 'Christianization ... [is] something substantially continuous with the general progress of human development.' [79]

Yet, when I visited Lutheran seminaries in 1983 on behalf of the Melanesian Association of Theological Schools, the students seemed almost entirely unaware of two of the central ideas of contemporary ecumenical theology: that it is necessary, and indeed inevitable, that they should begin working toward a theology of their own, using Melanesian concepts to address Melanesian problems, while remaining in communion with their Lutheran sister-churches and the world-wide Christian family ('indigenous theology'); and that this theology should be developed in the course of a critical dialogue with the cultural and socio-economic development — or maldevelopment — of their country ('contextual theology'). [80] A Lutheran university student, on the other hand, wrote: 'Theology in Papua New Guinea by and large remains in a State of Teutonic Captivity. The Aryan bias of christian doctrine is perhaps the most serious intellectual obstacle to full ecumenical fellowship with the young church, to our own theological creativity, and christian evangelism.' [81]

In a theological evaluation of the 1977 self-study, Gernot Fugmann pointed out that 'we quite often hear the phrase "misin i pinis" ("the phase of evangelization is over")'. [82] He continued:

> There seems to be no real motivation to go out expanding the church in areas still untouched by the presence of churches. Instead we see the church fully occupied with its organizational problems, constitutions, guidelines, finances, and the issues of localization. They are the concerns on the agendas of the meetings. [83]

And it is precisely this, with the concomitant 'large number of nominal, uncommitted, baptized members, who have not yet identified with the message of the church', which makes ELC-PNG an easy prey of fundamentalist and pentecostalist sects who deny the premise on which its whole work was originally based: That it preaches and lives the Gospel, and nothing but the Gospel, as 'the message of peace and power'. [84] Today, however, in an increasingly-westernized, urbanized, and secularized society, people's needs are more complex. 'What are the theological answers?' [85]

Fugmann's diagnosis is that 'a large percentage of the church members lack a feeling of identity with the church', for the reasons given in Section 3 above, and he calls for 'a theological process in the church, of which he [the pastor] must be a part', noting that 'there are also many specific theological contributions which can be made on the basis of Lutheran doctrines'. [86] In 1982, he organized and led a Study Seminar for pastors from Tanzania and Papua New Guinea at Martin Luther Seminary, Lae (October 25 - November 28), in which these suggestions were taken up in earnest. [87] After a study tour of the church, the Tanzanians quickly came to some of the same conclusions as the 1977 self-study; [88] even more interesting were the cultural affinities and differences they were able to share with their Melanesian colleagues. [89] For the first time, as far as I know, the seminar tried to relate the central confessional documents of Lutheranism to the basic concepts of African and Melanesian cultures, which led to some highly-suggestive results (for example, 'The concept and necessity of suffering in the "theologia crucis" is very strange and in opposition to the traditional views regarding well-being as expression of a faithful relationship to God', [90] even though 'the concept of well-being in the Afro-Melanesian traditional societies has as its equivalent the Christian concept of salvation'. [91]

All in all, it would seem that Papua New Guineans are not overly concerned about their Lutheranness; it is the Gospel itself, with its liberating 'message of peace and power', for which they are profoundly grateful; and this surely is an unmistakably-Lutheran attitude of mind! But they also seem little concerned about the implications of their Melanesianness for their Christian faith. While intent on the 'localization' of what remains essentially an alien and energy-consuming church structure, they have not adverted sufficiently to the more far-reaching process of 'indigenization', fraught as it is with theological challenges. Far from being a medium of communication between their church and the wider society of independent Papua New Guinea, their church organization has tended to become a world in itself, one whose complicated operations preoccupy them fully, whereas they often appear to be ill at ease with the rapidly growing 'modern' sector of their society with its attendant rapid change, cultural dislocation, differentiation of functions, and secular mentality. Though it has participated in, and sometimes pioneered, ecumenical dialogue, and has been an active member of the country's ecumenical bodies, ELC-PNG has perhaps not yet opened itself up sufficiently to the surrounding social context or to the 'Pacific mind' which is slowly but surely emerging — not without significant Christian influence — in the region as a whole. Zurewe's vision embraced all these things, but it has remained unfulfilled. [92] His successsor, Bishop Gam, however, has personally assured me of his commitment to ecumenism.

This might be a fair summary of perceptive Papua New Guinean Lutherans' views of their church. Yet the outsider feels constrained to redress the balance a little. The Lutheran mission to New Guinea broke new ground in evangelizing by community consensus and in entrusting the continuance of this work to indigenous evangelists. The high standard of pastoral care, and the seriousness with which community and individual participation in Baptism and Holy Communion were taken, put down deep roots, which even the ravages of two world wars and the onslaughts of various cargo cults could not tear up. Vernacular hymns with indigenous melodies and respect for Melanesian forms of authority and decision-making led to a thorough-going 'indigenization' and the establishment of 'base communities' decades before these terms became fashionable missiological jargon. It was the transition from LMNG to ELCONG which, in subtle ways which are not easy to pin down, seems to have resulted in the uneasy compromise between 'Melanesianness' and 'Lutheranness' in which the church now lives.

This uncertainty makes it ill-prepared to meet the new challenges which are exerting ever more pressure upon it: the increasingly-questionable politics of a newly-independent country caught in the throes of too-rapid and too-disjointed development; the aggressive evangelism of selfrighteous sects which offer a false security to people insufficiently rooted in their own church; the solidarity of Melanesians in the face of residual colonialism, whether French or Indonesian; and the appearance on the religious horizon of Islam as a possible alternative to Christianity.

Yet I for one am confident that the Lutherans of Papua New Guinea will meet these challenges, as they have those of the past. ELC-PNG will fare well if it finds its own Melanesian way while cleaving to the Gospel faith in its Lord and Saviour.

Endnotes

[1] The document was signed by Zurewe Kamon Zurenuo, Janadabing Apo, Bapiangnu Buma, and Sesengo Narangeng; the signing was certified by Zurewe, Jakotong Saki David, and Angacnukac Peso.

[2] See John Kuder, 'Die Evangelisch-Lutherische Kirche in Neuguinea', in W. von Krause, ed., *Junges Neuguinea: Ein Informationsbuch* (Neuendettelsau: Freimund-Verlag, n.d.), 52.

[3] *Ibid*, 53.

[4] *New Guinea Lutheran* (hereafter cited as *NGL*), VII (March 1969), 3,4.

[5] Thus, we read that ELCONG should not be looked on as a structure peopled by officials, but consists of all Lutheran men and women, both black and white, on the sole basis of their baptism, *NGL*, VII (July 1969), 2,3. It was also pointed out that the 'congregation' is something quite distinct from the mere organizational structure of the church *NGL*, IX (June 1970), 4,5.

[6] *NGL*, IX (March 1970), 2,3.

[7] *NGL*, IX (April 1970), 2,3.

[8] *NGL*, IX (May 1970), 2,3.

[9] That is, L-plates first for learners, then P-plates for probationers, and only after these periods of instruction and practice the unrestricted licence to drive, *NGL*, IX (Sept. 1970) 4,5; (June 1970) 4,5.

[10] Zurewe to Dr Agnes Hoeger on her return to America, May 5, 1966.

[11] Zurewe to Lutheran students, undated, possibly 1968. Clearsighted as always, he stressed to them the church's urgent need for trained personnel: '*Mi laik bikpela moa training i mas kamap kamap*' (emphasis in orig.); see also the undated memorandum mentioned in the text.

[12] *NGL*,X (1971) saw fit to run a series entitled: 'What Is Independence?' One article, 'Ready for Independence?', after pointing out that humankind had sinfully sought independence from God, was content to opt for *inter*dependence! *NGL*, XI (Sept.-Oct. 1972), 4,5. By this time, elections to the House of Assembly had introduced political parties to Papua and New Guinea for the first time, *NGL*, XI (Jan. 1972), 4-6.

[13] *NGL*, IX (Oct. 1970), 4-7.

[14] *NGL*, XI (Oct. 1972), 3.

[15] 'Long wok bilong sios i no wanbel na mekim eleksin, bihain wok bilong lida wantaim wok bilong kongrigesen na ol pasto na deleget baimbai i no ken wanbel na wok i bagarap kwik', Zurewe to Mambu and Mufuanu, September 13, 1972.

[16] Kuder to LMNG, June 21, 1972.

[17] *NGL*, XII (March 1973), 4-7. The missionary advisers, two from each circuit, had a voice but no vote in these proceedings.

[18] *NGL*, XII (June 1973), 3.

[19] *NGL*, XI (October 1972),3.

[20] *NGL*, XIII (July 1974), 2,3.

[21] *NGL*, XIII (March 1974), 4,5.

[22] Georg Vicedom, 'Thoughts on Integration of Mission and Church', mimeographed, 1965, 1. These principles, with the addition of 'self-determination' and 'inter-dependence', were also familiar to Zurewe; see Z. Zurenuo, 'Die Unabhaengigkeit der Kirche in einem selbstaendigen Neuguinea', in Rolf Italiaander, ed., *Heisses Land Niugini: Beitraege zu den Wandlungen in Papua Neuguinea* (Erlangen: Verlag der Ev.-luth. Mission, 1974), 286; he reiterates the first four principles in his 1983 interview (Source 4 as listed in Appendix A below).

[23] '"Mission" means sending; "station" means standing still', Vicedom, 'Integration', cited above, 8.

[24] *Ibid*, 2.

[25] *Ibid*, 3.

[26] *Ibid*, 10.

[27] ELC-PNG, *Namba 14 Sinod: Minis bilong bung i kamap long Kitip, Hagen Distrik*, 16-23 Janueri, 1984, Resolution 84:63. The significance of this step lies in the recognition that 'Sios i lukim wok developmen em i bilong en yet', 36.

At the same Mt Hagen Synod (Resolution 84:61), three new districts were created: Southern Highlands, Wagi, and New Guinea Islands, bringing the total number to 10. There was some controversy about the advisability of this further proliferation of bureaucratic structure; a District President [10] was quite adamant about not setting up the usual District Office in his district, regarding it as a distraction from real pastoral work.

[28] There is often friction, however, between ordained pastors and lay elders, for each tends to strive for 'big man' status in the village, whereas the functions of each in the congregation have never been clearly defined, see Theodor Ahrens, ed., *The Evangelical Lutheran Church of Papua New Guinea: Report on a Fact Finding Survey* (Goroka: The Melanesian Institute, 1977) (hereafter cited as *FFS*), 26. This was confirmed by (8), who made the very revealing remark that, in practice, it is sometimes the family rather than the congregation that 'ordains'!

[29] I was privileged to attend the Madang District Conference at Wanuma, August 25-29, 1983, and in my diary I recorded the deep impression it made on me: 'Somewhat to my surprise, I saw a healthy indigenous church in action, its leaders smoothly orchestrating the complexities of democratic procedure, its representatives participating vigorously in debate, worshipping with feeling and enthusiasm, and over everything that unobtrusive New Guinea hospitality that can be so touching by making a gesture of helpfulness out of the means available'. My only reservation was that there was practically no discussion of properly theological issues in the press of administrative business.

[30] Jonathan Preus, ed., *Report and Recommendations of the International Evaluation Team to the Evangelical Lutheran Church of Papua New Guinea* (Lae 1977), mimeographed (hereafter cited as *IET*).

[31] As cited above in note 28 (*FSS*).

[32] For the same reasons I have refrained from interviewing the present Head Bishop, the Rt Revd Getake S. Gam; I made exceptions for the retired Bishops Zurewe and Mambu and former District President Gedisa. For the mode of referring to this supplementary material, see Apendix A below.

[33] 'It is clear that the real problem is not one of structure, of decentralization, or of finance. Basically the problem is that some leaders, particularly some of the expatriates, lack a commitment to national unity. Indeed, some are openly hostile to anything done at Lae, which is reflected in the attitudes of some Papua New Guineans', *IET*,50.

[34] *FFS*, 22,23, concludes that 'church work in town and church programs are *not really directed at the way of life that is found in town*', and my informants (7) and (10) felt quite strongly about this inadequacy.

[35] The unity of the church was one of Zurewe's greatest worries: 'Tasol planti seket na districk lida, yumi lusim tingting long *BUNG WANTAIM*' (emphasis in the original), Sept. 23, 1975; even in retirement, he insisted that the barrier between Kate and Jabem should be done away with, (4). Details can sometimes be revealing: While waiting for a plane with participants of a Lutheran meeting, I noticed that their luggage was labelled, not with a postal address or with the Province and District of the secular government, but with the District-Circuit-Congregation of the ELC-PNG administrative structure; this seemed to be more real to them than their own nation.

[36] *FFS*, 176.

[37] *FFS*, 175. Some doubt is expressed about the continuing need for circuits, whose purpose was essentially missionary, see 132-3; this concurs with the opinion of (10).

[38] Undated memorandum, presumably Zurewe's, probably 1972; similarly, Zurewe in a letter of February 6, 1972.

[39] Zurewe, January 30, 1974.

[40] Zurewe, (4).

[41] Zurewe, letter of June 6, 1969. An ELCONG planning document of October 10, 1972, under the name of G. Messner, calls on the church to participate in inter-church activities through the Melanesian Institute, the Melanesian Council of Churches, the Churches Medical Council, the Christian Education Commission, and the Churches Council on Media Coordination, as well as local Christian Councils and the Lutheran World Federation. The World Council of Churches is conspicuous by its absence!

[42] *NGL*,XI (Oct. 1972),3.

[43] The minutes of these two consultations, at which the respective delegations were led by Moderator To Burua and Bishop Zurewe, were kindly made available to me by Dr Gerhard Reitz, who was present.

[44] 'Em i olsem bilip bilong me. Mi no tingim arapela man. Arapela man i go long Luteran Sios, em i gutpela; it go long Metodis — em i gutpela; Katolik — em i gutpela. Tasol me yet mi skelim, na mi ting, ah, Katolik na Luteran na wanem kain misin, SDA misin — em i misin tasol. Tasol God em i wanpela ... Narapela tingting, narapela lo — em i nating —maski. Jisas yet i kamap long mipela long kros diwai; em yet i helpim mipela na karim sin bilong mipela na em i dai, na kam bek gen long matmat bilong helpim yumi', (5). Similarly, (1) and (2), who, however, were more concerned about their Lutheran identity: For the sake of family harmony, (1) persuaded his younger brother to renounce the Catholicism he had embraced for rather ulterior motives; and (2), although a pastor, was still troubled by his father's being a Catholic.

[45] *NGL*,IX (July 1970),3.

[46] *NGL*,VII (July 1969),6,7; *NGL*,X (June 1971) 4,5.
There was even a series on 'A Christian and His Money'!

[47] Zurewe to Bishop Kuder, February 25, 1967, expressing his disapproval of the proposal which was apparently current: 'Bungim tresa bilong ELCONG na LMNG i mas wanpela', especially the implication that New Guinean church workers would be paid with overseas money: 'Mi no laikim dispela tok tru ...' ELCONG must be independent '*long moni na long leader* ... TOK BILONG BUNGIM TRESA em i tok bilong Cargo Cult' (emphasis in the original). See also the undated memorandum already quoted.

[48] *FFS*,108,109.

[49] *FFS*,110.

[50] *FFS*,111; and the warning of *IET*,59: 'But there is danger in the success of enterprises and investments; like overseas subsidy, this income can support programs, personnel and services which the people themselves may not want very badly. The church structure could become a hollow shell, supported independently of the real foundation of church finance, the people.' I heard many rumblings of complaint along these lines when talking to members of the church, mainly directed at the German partner churches.

322

[51] Letter of September 23, 1975, in which Zurewe rails against a subsidy of K500,000; because of it, instead of the K16,000 budgeted for local contributions, only K1,500 was actually raised. For the comparative figures over several years, see *IET*,38 (the figures for 1975 do not tally exactly with Zurewe's, but the proportion is roughly the same). See also Zurewe, letter of June 12, 1975. In his 1974 article, 'Unabhaengigkeit der Kirche', 287, he proudly states: 'We don't get a penny from overseas for the workers in the congregations and circuits', adding significantly: 'We object to being told what we are supposed to want' (288).

[52] Zurewe, (4). He adds: 'Unfortunately this wasn't understood', and he goes on: 'All the organizations and works of the church are the legacy of the mission, nothing of our own … the initiative always started with the white missionaries, not with us' (referring to the work of Melanesian evangelists in the Islands and Highlands).

[53] This missionary work in North Queensland was carried out by Pastor Nawon Mellombo, who has since been replaced by another Papua New Guinean missionary.

[54] These and other suggestions were made by Dr John Strelan in a letter to the editor of *Lutheran Theological Journal*, 1/16 (May 1982), 50-53; they would, of course, remove the temptations to call for expatriate missionaries in the knowledge that they, unlike their national counterparts, do not have to be paid for!

[55] Thus (2),(3),(5),(6),(8), and (9).

[56] 'Gutnius em i namba wan — no ken litimapim paua bilong graun'; Gedisa also stressed that 'stewardship' goes beyond money to include social service and pastoral care, (8).

[57] 'Lait i kam long rausim tudak … lait i wok wantaim hevi',(9).

[58] 'Em i lukim baibel na wok bilong God', (8).

[59] 'Wok misin i go het', (9).

[60] *IET*,11.

[61] Memorandum, presumably Zurewe's, probably 1972.

[62] Record of Zurewe's interview with Mr Nickoleit, October 26, 1972.

[63] Thus, (8) observed that the process of evangelization often proceeded too quickly, and that missionaries left people on their own prematurely, so that the Gospel became 'mixed up with local ideas', while (3) gave a graphic description of the havoc wreaked by the cargo cult associated with Yali on the Rai Coast, although he concluded with confidence: 'kago kult i no gat kaikai — i wok nating'.

[64] *FFS*, 178. Earlier (165), it had been noted that in the view of district leaders 'the national office is in danger of becoming a purpose in itself', whereas a national officer is quoted as saying: 'We are not informed about the problems which confront the people in the congregations', 171 — a damaging admission, to say the least. The impression given by the respondents to *FFS* is that the incessant meetings became an empty ritual of resolution-passing without practical consequences, with the danger of the national *church* being equated with the national *office* in Lae. Bishop Mambu insisted that the equation of Ampo with the church must not be allowed to obscure the conviction of the people in the village congregations that '*we* are the church', (9).

[65] (7) extended this criticism to the lack of communication between the church leadership and their own 'grass roots'.

[66] Interview with Mr Nickoleit, October 26, 1972.

[67] Zurewe, (4); he hastens to add that he does not mean the expression 'confession of faith' to be taken literally!

[68] Letter to Mr Onnie Hinkle of the American Lutheran Church, who was recently commissioned by ELC-PNG to report on its progress toward autonomy. Another of his correspondents wrote: 'It is a sad thing that Papua New Guinea has become a "parasite" country in spite of all its natural resources and manpower. Right from the National level down to the community level, from political, social, economical and religious organization, people are crying for money-money-more money! … We need to ask ourselves seriously: Are we Independent? Or are we lazy bones? … Even sad thing is that our National Church ELC-PNG is among the groups who use the above resources for her income' (*sic*).

[69] Zurewe, (4), referring to a recent exchange of students between Martin Luther Seminary and Germany. President Gedisa, (8), echoed these sentiments: The 'mama sios' must become a 'brata sios', but people tend to confuse 'partnership' with 'planti moni'.

[70] Zurewe, (4).

[71] Pastoral letter, March 1976. Earlier in the same year, he had declined an invitation to attend a meeting on village development — a subject close to his heart — saying: 'The doctor has forbidden me to work in my office for at least two months' (Jan. 29, 1976). And toward its close, he was unable to attend the graduation ceremony at the Agricultural Training College, Banz: 'I cannot travel too far by car or by air because I have a heart problem' (Nov. 11, 1976).

[72] Letter of August 4, 1972. Thanking those who had helped him on his visit to Europe and North America for the 450th anniversary of the Augsburg Confession, he remarked that the trip had taught him that all Europeans are by no means rich, yet they still want to give to the church (July 30, 1980).

[73] Pastoral letter, October 28, 1975; his recommendation: *'Skelim!'* (Weigh it!).

[74] Letter of August 7, 1972.

[75] Zurewe, (4). I strongly recommend that ELC-PNG commission a biography of this remarkable man before the inimitable style of his personal reminiscences is lost to it.

[76] Pastoral letter, October 28, 1975.

[77] Transcript of meeting with LMNG representatives and the Revd W. Jacobsen of Neuendettelsau, May 16, 1974, in which the complaint was raised that New Guinean churchmen are too concerned with power and status, though Zurewe hoped that the power of the Holy Spirit was also involved.

[78] Deposition to Mr Onnie Hinkle, April 5, 1984.

[79] Georg Vicedom, 'Culture Contact and Religion', mimeographed, 1965, 4,5.

[80] Significantly, (7) heartily concurred in criticizing these shortcomings, as did several Lutheran university students with whom I spoke.

[81] John Muingnepe, 'Proclamation and Theology in Melanesia', in *The Christian* (UPNG Chaplains' newsletter), 2 (Sept. 1984),3.

[82] Gernot Fugmann, 'The Mission of the Lutheran Churches in PNG', mimeographed, n.d., 1. This offers a poignant contrast to the call so vividly remembered by President Gedisa, looking back to 1931: 'Haiden i redi!' (8).

[83] Fugmann, 'Mission', 1.

[84] *Ibid*, 4. Noting that 'now it is rarely possible to reach a group consensus in religious matters', he goes on to sketch the adverse conditions now obtaining in villages and towns, where 'many church leaders are utterly helpless, when confronted with situations which require new ethical decisions' (3).

[85] *Ibid*, 4.

[86] *Ibid*, 2,5.

[87] Gernot Fugmann, ed., *Struggling for Lutheran Identity: The Relevance of Lutheran Theology in an Afro-Melanesian Context* (Neuendettelsau: Institute for the Study of World Mission of the Department of World Mission, Evangelical Lutheran Church in Bavaria, 1983).

[88] *Ibid*, 7,8.

[89] *Ibid*, 9-11.

[90] *Ibid*, 15.

[91] *Ibid*, 24.

[92] Bishop Mambu, (9), an old-time confidant of Zurewe, mentioned this explicitly: ' *Ol i lusim tingting bilong Zurewe na Kuder*' (They've lost sight of Zurewe's and Kuder's thinking).

Appendix A:

Sources

A selection from the correspondence and papers of Bishop Zurewe, by far the greater part of which is still unsorted and inaccessible, was kindly made available to me by Dr and Mrs G. Reitz, archivists at Ampo.

A selection from material gathered by Mr Onnie Hinkle of the American Lutheran Church in the course of a survey of ELC-PNG was kindly made available to me by the Revd Jim Baital, Gerehu.

The following interviews are referred to in the notes by number:

(1) Highlands student, Martin Luther Seminary, 3/6/1983 (diary entry).
(2) Pastor coastal village, 28/9/1983 (diary entry).
(3) Elder, coastal village, 15/11/1983 (tape).
(4) Bishop Zurewe, 18/11/1983 (German transcript kindly made available by Dr Hermann Reiner, Neuendettelsau; the translation is my own).
(5) Elder, coastal village, 22/11/1983.
(6) Elder, coastal village, 17/6/1984 (Pidgin transcript kindly made available by the Revd Gernot Fugmann, Goroka).
(7) Martin Luther Seminary graduate, urban media, 3/10/1984 (notes).
(8) Retired President Gedisa, 10/10/1984 (notes).
(9) Bishop Mambu, 10/10/1984 (notes).
(10) District President, urban ministry, 21/11/1984 (diary entry).

Fugmann, Gernot. 'The Mission of the Lutheran Churches in PNG', n.d., mimeographed.

Fugmann, Gernot, ed. *Struggling for Lutheran Identity: The Relevance of Lutheran Theology in an Afro-Melanesian Context*. Neuendettelsau: Institute for the Study of World Mission of the Department of World Mission, Evangelical Lutheran Church in Bavaria, 1983.

Kuder, John. 'Die Evangelische-Lutherische Kirche in Neuguinea', in W. von Krause, ed. *Junges Neuguinea: Ein Informationsbuch*. Neuendettelsau: Freimund-Verlag, n.d. 49-57.

Muingnepe, John. 'Proclamation and Theology in Melanesia', *The Christian*, 2 (Sept. 1984), 3,4; *The Christian*, 3 (Nov. 1984), 4.

Strelan, John. Letter to the Editor of *Lutheran Theological Journal*, 1/16 (May 1982), 50-53.

Vicedom, Georg. 'Thoughts on Integration of Mission and Church', 1965, mimeographed.

Vicedom, Georg. 'Culture Contact and Religion', 1965, mimeographed.

Zurenuo, Zurewe, 'Die Unabhaengigkeit der Kirche in einem selbstaendigen Neuguinea', in Rolf Italiaander, ed. *Heisses Land Niugini: Beitraege zu den Wandlungen in Papua Neuguinea*. Erlangen: Verlag der Ev.-luth. Mission, 1974, 284-389.

Abbreviations

FFS = Theodore Ahrens, ed. *The Evangelical Lutheran Church of Papua New Guinea: Report on a Fact Finding Survey*. Goroka: The Melanesian Institute, 1977.
IET = Jonathan Preus, ed. *Report and Recommendations of the International Evaluation Team to the Evangelical Lutheran Church of Papua New Guinea*. Lae 1977, mimeographed.
NGL = *New Guinea Lutheran*.
ELC-PNG, *Namba 14 Sinod: Minis bilong bung i kamap long Kitip, Hagen Distrik*. Janueri 16-23, 1984, mimeographed.

Organization of ELC-PNG

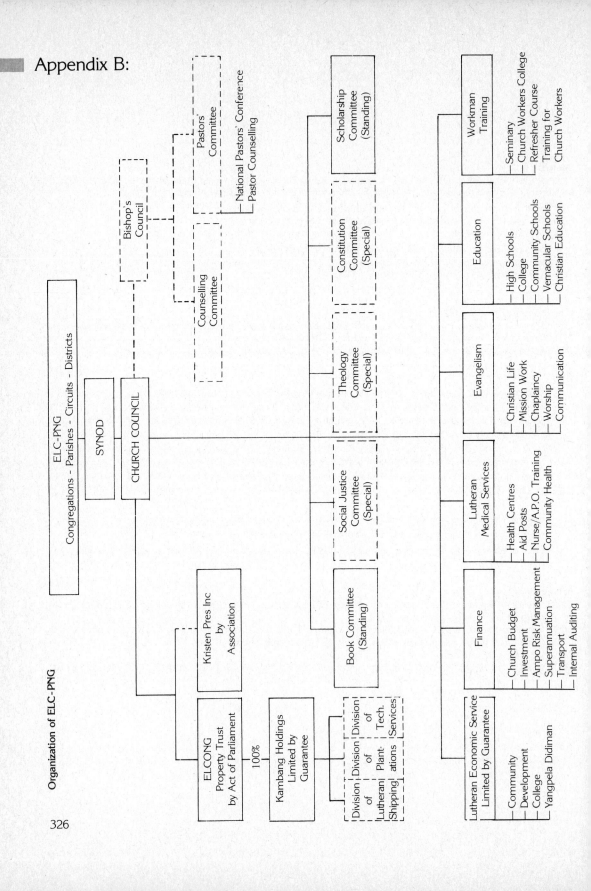

Part II

Portrait of the Church

Chapter 10

The Ecumenical Setting

by Brian Schwarz

The Lutheran Church in New Guinea has not grown in isolation. As it has grown, the church has come into contact with an increasing number of missions, churches, and church agencies within the country and overseas. These various bodies constitute the ecumenical setting of the church's growth.

In this chapter we shall focus on the growing church's ecumenical relations. We shall note that these relations have been of various kinds, ranging from confrontation and opposition to cooperation and fellowship. We shall then review the major ecumenical ventures in which the church participates, and finally consider some factors which influence the church's ecumenical stance and the challenges it faces in this area.

Spheres of Influence

Before the beginning of missionary activity in New Guinea, strife had often occurred between competing missions in various parts of the South Pacific. The London Missionary Society (LMS) and the Methodists were rivals on Samoa; the French Catholics and the LMS on Tahiti. Nineteenth-century Europe was afflicted by interdenominational hostility and strife, and European missionaries who came to the South Pacific brought with them the inter-denominational attitudes that were current in Europe. Missionary documents from the time reveal that the deepest division lay between Catholics and Protestants. [1] Protestants commonly referred to Catholicism as 'popery'. Roman Catholics, in turn, regarded Protestantism in its various forms as 'heresy', and its missionary agents as 'ministers of error'. Roman Catholic missionaries saw the need to combat heresy as being of equal importance with the need to win the heathen to Christ. Sadly, such attitudes were usually passed on to the converts by both groups.

Both the British and German colonial authorities tried to eliminate missionary competition by designating certain areas for the activities of each mission. In 1880, William MacGregor, the Governor of Papua, persuaded the Protestant missions to make an agreement to work in different areas. [2] The Catholics, however, took no part in this agreement and refused to recognize the so-called 'spheres of influence'.

329

Likewise, the German administration sought to keep apart the Catholic and Protestant missions in New Guinea. In 1890, the administration passed a law defining the areas of the Catholic and Methodist missions' activities on the Gazelle Peninsula. Despite this zoning arrangement, the work of the two denominations became intermingled and a feeling of rivalry developed. In 1897, Catholic pressure forced abandonment of the policy.

On the mainland, the German administration did not attempt to legislate the areas of each mission's activity. Nevertheless, when the first Rhenish Missionaries landed at Finschhafen in 1887, the German administration told them to seek another mission field, because Finschhafen belonged to Neuendetelsau Mission, which had come the previous year. Likewise, when the first Roman Catholic missionaries of the Society of the Divine Word (SVD), who arrived in 1896, contemplated working in Astrolabe Bay, where the Rhenish Mission was already active, the authorities encouraged them to move up the coast to the north-west. This policy not only served to minimize the chances of conflict between missions, but also distributed more widely agents of development.

Unity — a First Fruit of the Gospel

When the first Christian missionaries came to New guinea, they were entering the most socially fragmented region in the world. The Melanesian inhabitants were divided into many groups, each one usually having several hundred members, though some highland groups had several thousands. Most groups were without any system of hereditary leadership. People aligned themselves to self-made *bigmen*. When the strength of influence of these men waned, people would transfer their allegiance to another rising leader. Competition between *bigmen* and aspiring *bigmen* made for internal instability. A tendency to divide was checked by fear of hostile neighbours. In some parts of the highlands, people lived in a state of near-constant warfare. Being self-sufficient and fearful of enemies, many people would pass their whole lifetime without venturing beyond their clan boundaries.

The social divisions were accompanied by linguistic divisions. In the eastern part of the

330

Christian Keysser at the time when he left New Guinea (1921).

island of New Guinea, there were over 700 distinct languages. Some languages were spoken by only a few hundred persons. It is understandable that one of the early missionaries is reported to have sighed despairingly: 'Why was Babel transferred to New Guinea?' Mirroring the social and linguistic divisions, and contributing to them, was the physical nature of the land. High mountain ridges, deep valleys, rushing rivers, dense jungles, and vast swamps formed natural boundaries between neighbouring groups.

Unity between the diverse groups of the region seemed unattainable to the first Lutheran missionaries at Finschhafen. Pioneer missionary Christian Keysser recalled the situation:

> The inhabitants of this area were previously anything but a unit. Hardly any of us missionaries would have thought it possible that they could ever be unified into one congregation since there was no coherence between them. On the contrary, every little group of from 200 to 400 souls was a deadly enemy of its neighbours. They fought each other incessantly. They hated, murdered, and then ate those whom they had killed. Once while standing on a mountain I asked my guide about

the people on the opposite range. He replied disdainfully, 'Over there is my hunting group; the people are bad but their flesh is full of fat and tastes very good. I will soon go hunting again, for I am hungry for human flesh.' Another guide had hesitantly brought me into a small village where he behaved in a manner such as I have never seen a New Guinean do. He did not extend his hand in greeting and not a friendly word came over his lips. The look on his face expressed the deepest disdain. When I entreated the man to behave in a more friendly way, he retorted, 'I have never yet been here except with weapons in my hand and every time the cowardly wizard mob ran away. There can be no peace with them, they must be exterminated.' [3]

The barriers to unity seemed insurmountable, but they were overcome, and surprisingly quickly. 'In the course of a comparatively few years, an inner and outer unity and a real Christian congregation has resulted.' [4]

This radical revolution came about by the preaching of the Gospel. The main message as proclaimed by the noted pioneer missionary, Christian Keysser, concerned *Anutu. Anutu* was a local creative deity, whose name the missionaries adopted for the Christian God. Keysser spoke of *Anutu* as having created the whole world and all tribes. In concrete and dramatic ways, he forcefully presented the reality and quality of God. Eventually, the resistance of the people broke down. Convinced of the truth of the message about *Anutu*, they began to prepare for Baptism. As various groups were drawn to *Anutu*, they also found themselves drawn to one another.

> The common experience of God created for the New Guineans a strong feeling of belonging to each other. They all belonged to the new God. If he was their father then they were sisters and brothers. The same word was valid for all and this constituted a mighty incentive toward unification. Old opponents were reconciled, tribes that formerly were completely separated, united ... Now 'the great peace' entered. [5]

Besides the missionaries, the German colonial government also sought to bring peace. One of its first acts was to declare to the local inhabitants of the region that fighting was forbidden, and people must now *sindaun isi*, dwell in peace. Stern penalties were threatened and imposed upon those who did not obey. Such measures were largely effective in bringing about overt peace. Beneath the surface, however, age-old fears, suspicions, and hatred remained. But the inner and outer unity achieved by the preaching of the missionaries far surpassed the expectations of government officials, and even caused some critics of the mission to change their minds. No doubt they would have agreed with Keysser when he wrote: 'Even the most skilful, blameless, strongest government would never be able to accomplish this.' [6]

In time, the common experience of God led to the development of a new social order. [7] The first step in this process was resettlement in new villages. Scattered houses and hamlets were abandoned, and people congregated together into the principal villages of the district. This move enabled all the children to be educated by one teacher and the people to be organized for communal tasks.

A second step was the making of roads. Linking villages to one another and to the mission station, such roads concretely expressed the new ties of a common faith, and enabled people to experience God's wider world.

A further step, taken by thousands, was the adoption of a new language. [8] Such a radical move was not forced upon converts. It was rather, as Keysser explained, the result of the impression made by the new way of life of Christians. So strong was this impression that 'entire tribes have voluntarily renounced their own language and by popular resolution taken the foreign language of the Christians in order to join the Christian congregation and form a true unity together with them.' [9]

While unity in faith was expressed among the Kate-speaking people by adoption of a common social order, there was also a growing understanding that unity in faith transcended cultural and geographical differences.

In 1914, the Christians of the Kate-speaking mountain congregations invited the Jabem-speaking Christians of the coastal region to a joint assembly. The purpose of the meeting was to bring about some kind of union between the two groups. The planned meeting never took place, mainly because of missionary opposition, but the invitation is nevertheless interesting, because it reveals an already-developing awareness of ecumenism, in the

Sattelberg Station (1910).

Chiefs Sane (right) and Tube (left).
332

sense of Christians of the same origin, yet of diverse language and location, as belonging together.

> We elders of the Kate congregation say as follows: ... We, the Kate, are of the opinion, that all of us, coastal inhabitants as well as forest people, have one and the same Word of God. We also have the same God whose word we all hear. But you coastal people always say: 'We dwellers along the seashore are a group by ourselves, and you forest people are a group by yourselves'. Because of this now we would like to meet with you so that we may mutually express our opinions and establish friendship between us ... Please be informed that we Kate people have already met together. At that time we said, 'Unitl now our congregations act independently of each other. It is as if each has his own God. That is not right, because we all have the same *Anutu* and the same Word of God. Why should we therefore then behave as though there were many Anutus and each congregation had its special God? This is indeed pride. At the same time we stagger unsteadily to and fro and do not show any firmness. For this reason we invite you. Please come; then we shall negotiate mutually, do away with all that divides us and join our hand in unity ...[10]

Friedrich Schuetz with evangelists (1919).

Though the planned meeting did not take place, the invitation did achieve an important result.

Like the Kate congregations, the coastal congregations now united and celebrated a so-called Melanesian Day on November 22, 1914. The two groups of congregations thus marched separately, each by itself, and yet this group formation was, after all, an indication of progress.[11]

We now turn to look at the relations between Lutheran and other mission bodies in New Guinea.

Conflict with Catholics on the North Coast

On the north coast, the Rhenish Mission first occupied the Astrolabe Bay area, while the Catholic missionaries of the Society of the Divine Word established stations in the Aitape and Sepik districts. Before long, the two mission groups came into contact. Working from the west, with Tumleo as their first station, the Catholic mission slowly advanced toward the Rhenish field. In 1905, when the society experienced difficulty in getting supplies to their stations along the coast, they sought to establish a supply base near Madang. With Governor Hahl's permission, they settled in Alexishafen. This move brought them into close proximity with the Lutherans. Here, as on the Gazelle Peninsula, the line of demarcation between the fields of the two missions happened to divide tribal entities contacted by both churches. And here, too, rivalry developed and friction followed.

The border between the Lutheran and Catholic territories lay in a line running inland from Sek (Alexishafen) on the coast. Friedrich Schuetz, missionary in the Nobonob circuit, struggled to maintain the allegiance of people in the border area in the face of aggressive Catholic tactics to win them over. In his 1923 report, Schuetz complained that:

Despite written and oral negotiation with the authorities of the Catholic mission Father Nowak has continued his insidious agitation in the border area ... When Father Nowak came to Omondovo and Assikan at the beginning of August the people declared that they belonged to us. Schuetz had come there first ... Now the Father comes and wants to take over these villages. It is understandable that nobody wants to know

333

anything about him apart from the *luluai*, who has his position by the grace of the Father. At his last visit they didn't even want to let him stay overnight and told him to go back to Omondoro and stay overnight in his house. But Nowak insisted on staying. Next morning he required all to appear in order to write their names. Most, however, distanced themselves. It was told that he then spread the knives he had brought along on the ground probably in order to awaken their desire. By and by, ten ventured to accept a knife each ...[12]

Later, after they had been addressed by the Lutheran evangelist, Katmunage, the people gave the knives to the *luluai* with instructions to return them to the priest. They also asked Katmunge to give them an evangelist 'in order to protect them against the priest'.

As the tempo of this battle for souls rose, previous arrangements about spheres of influence were ignored. In 1926, the Catholic Mission established a station at Tabel on the hitherto exclusively 'Lutheran' island of Karkar. In 1933, the Lutherans set up a station at Bunabun on the Catholic-dominated mainland opposite Karkar. Having agreed to allow freedom of religion under the terms of the United Nations mandate, the Australian administration could not restrict mission groups to certain areas.

The intense competition for souls led to a scandalous division on the tiny island of Rivo, situated on the Madang cost between Nagada and Alexishafen. A fence, separating the Lutheran and Catholic converts, was built down the middle of the island. Though it was the local adherents rather than the missionaries who caused this cleavage, critics of missionary activity used this incident to attack the work of Christian missions.

In this struggle to gain people's allegiance, it should not be imagined that the population were simply passive participants, pulled this way or that by the opposing missions. Frequently, they contributed to or influenced the rivalry in subtle ways. Sometimes an individual would try to advance his standing by inviting in a rival mission. Shrewd village politicians became adept at playing off one mission against the other in order to gain the maximum advantage. In their zeal to win converts, missionaries were sometimes blind to these skilful manipulations.

334

Samoan Pastor Taeao.

Samoan Missionaries in Madang

Sickness and death took a heavy toll on the staff of the Rhenish Mission. In the first 25 years, 33 men and 21 women entered the service of the Mission. In that same period, 11 men and 5 women died, and 12 men and 9 women were compelled to leave on account of sickness or the climate. It seemed that Europeans had trouble withstanding the rigours of New Guinea.

It is not surprising, then, that the suggestion of employing South Pacific Islanders as missionaries was raised. This had been done successfully by the London Missionary Society in Papua and the Methodists on the Gazelle Pensinsula. Before starting their work in the Madang area, pioneer missionaries Thomas and Eich had visited the Gazelle Peninsula at the invitation of the German Governor. There they conferred with the Methodist missionaries, and studied their methods. Assuming that South Pacific Islanders would better cope with the harsh tropical environment, the Rhenish Board decided to try to recruit Samoans as an auxiliary force for their New Guinea field.

The London Missionary Society had a seminary at Malua in Samoa (then a German colony), under the direction of a German, Pastor Heider. Missionary Hanke, who was travelling back to the field after furlough in Germany, was asked to visit Samoa and investigate the possibility of recruiting some of the graduates of the seminary. His visit led to the recruitment of six Samoan pastors and their wives. The first of these arrived in 1912. After a preparatory course by the European missionaries, they were assigned to outstations. One pastor and two of the wives died in New Guinea and were buried there. Two pastors, Jerome Ilaoa and Taeao Salua, remained in the service of the mission until 1933.[13] (For more details, see ch 3.)

The Neuendettelsau Mission and the Anglicans

The Neuendettelsau Mission at Finschhafen was able to work in relative isolation for many years. Flierl had received the help of six young Methodists from Kokopo on the Gazelle Peninsula in establishing his first mission station at Simbang. They were employed privately by Flierl, not sent by their church, but they made a good impression and helped to form friendly ties and close cooperation between Lutherans and Methodists.

The few contacts the Neuendettelsau missionaries had with the neighbouring Anglican mission at Ambasi (Papuan North Coast) were also friendly. In January 1912, the Anglican missionary at Ambasi, the Revd Copeland King, invited Missionary Mailaender, who was stationed at Zaka, to visit him on his station. Accompanied by Schultz, an Australian, Mailaender made the visit in July. King received them hospitably, and, with Schultz acting as translator, the two missionaries exchanged views on mission methods, tribal relations along the boundary, language problems, and other matters of mutual interest.[14] Later, King returned the Zaka visit.

This friendly relationship with an Anglican proved to be an important link for the mission when the war broke out several years later. In the first months of the war, German missionaries were cut off from all support and communication. Letters that Flierl wrote to Pastor Theile in Brisbane, urgently asking for assistance, did not arrive. Concerned about the plight of his fellow missionaries, King himself wrote to Theile about the missionaries' needs. He also informed his own church headquarters in Brisbane. The Anglican authorities in Brisbane mediated with the Australian War Ministry and colonial authorities in Rabaul on behalf of the German missionaries. As a result, the goods Pastor Theile had purchased for the needy mission were soon sent to Finschhafen

Missionary Karl Mailaender with Evangelist Benauna.

and quickly cleared for distribution by the Australian authorities.[15]

After the war, when the German mission societies were faced with the forfeiture of their mission fields and property under the conditions of the Treaty of Versailles, the Anglicans again moved to assist. The Revd Shaw of the Anglican Mission in Papua interceded for the New Guinea Mission at the Lambeth Conference, London, in 1919. In 1924, the Anglican Province of Queensland voted unanimously to urge the Commonwealth authorities to rescind the order that all German-born missionaries in the Mandated Territory be deported by July 1, 1928, and sent a message to this effect to the Australian Prime Minister.[16]

The strong support given to Lutherans by Anglicans, undoubtedly influenced the Neuendettelsau Mission to respond favourably to an Anglican request to assist the Anglican Mission to begin mission work near Gasmata on New Britain. In 1925, Missionary Bamler sent three Siassi evangelists to prepare the ground for the Anglican Mission. The Lutheran evangelists established a station at Aisaga and began evangelistic work among the local

335

populace, with whom they had traditional trading ties, continuing on for a year after the arrival of the Anglican Mission in the area. [17]

Expansion in the Highlands

Lutherans began mission work in the Highlands well before other Christian bodies. In 1919, Kemadi, a Jabem evangelist stationed in the Kaiapit circuit, and Bukaua missionary Stephan Lehner, visited the Gazub area on the edge of the Eastern Highlands. The next year, Georg Pilhofer took a well-equipped party through the same region. In following years, Leonhard Flierl made regular patrols into the area, stationing evangelists and making contacts with new groups of people. By 1928, 28 evangelists were stationed in the Eastern Highlands. In 1929, W. Bergmann and Pilhofer became the first Europeans to look into the Goroka valley and see the vast potential for mission in the area. [18]

The Lutherans maintained discreet silence about their explorations and work in the Highlands. They were not ready to move in among the people, and until they had sufficient evangelists for the great field they preferred that others should remain in ignorance. Experience had taught them to be wary of gold prospectors and labour recruiters. But they also wanted to keep out their old rivals, the Roman Catholics. By keeping their knowledge of the people a closely guarded secret, they were able to work alone for years, free from unpleasant competition. Thus, it was not till 1931 that the Lutherans established their first station in the Highlands at Kambaidam.

The Lutheran monopoly on mission in the Highlands was to change soon after the discovery of a large population in the Wagi Valley, about 300 kilometres to the west of Onerunka. The gold prospecting Leahy brothers, Mick and Dan, with government officer Jim Taylor, made an exploratory trip as far as Mt Hagen. They reported the existence of a wide and flat valley that held a teeming population. News of this discovery caused interest and excitement all around the world. It also precipitated a mission rush akin to a gold rush.

One of the first to react to the news was Bishop Wolf of the Catholic Archdiocese of Madang. He decided to send an expedition into

Beginnings at Kambaidam.

the valley under Fr Willie Ross. But before Fr Ross could proceed, Fr Francis Schaefer, the priest stationed at Bundi on the edge of the Highlands, decided to make his own expedition. In 1933, led by a Chimbu *bigman*, Kavagl, Fr Schaefer took an expedition into the Chimbu and up to Mt Hagen, selecting suitable station sites along the route. After meeting the Leahy brothers in Mt Hagen, they returned to establish a station at Mingende in the Chimbu. [19]

The Lutherans also responded quickly to the exciting news. A short time after Fr Schaefer's historic expedition in November 1933, the Reverends Bergmann and Foege made a survey flight over the Wagi Valley, choosing likely sites for stations. In May of 1934, this flight was followed up by a joint expedition of representatives from the Madang and Finschhafen missions. Meeting at Rabana on a ridge above the Bena Valley, the Lutherans moved west, through the Asaro Valley, and into the Chimbu. After selecting a station site at Ega, where the Kundiawa airstrip is now located, they continued deeper into the Highlands.

At Mingende they unexpectedly came across Fr Ross and his companions, who were beginning to establish their station there. It was a cool meeting. Declining Fr Ross's invitation to a cup of tea, the Lutherans proceeded west, first to Kerowagi, and then to Ogelbeng near Mt Hagen.

Following the unexpected arrival of the Lutherans on the scene, Fr Ross and his companions were faced with a dilemma. On the one hand, their bishop had instructed them to start a station close to Bundi. On the other hand, they feared Lutherans might take over the site they had already chosen at Mt Hagen. After a long discussion, they decided to hurry back to Mt Hagen to secure their site. The following account reveals their sense of urgency:

> They packed in a flurry and closed the mission temporarily. As they wanted to get to Hagen in the shortest possible time, they decided to travel light with only six or seven mission workers. A few days later they passed the Lutheran party just outside Ogelbeng where they were resting beside a river. Fr. Tropper could no longer stand the suspense. He took off and ran from Ogelbeng to Kuta many miles away, arriving at the camp quite out of breath and red in the face. [20]

Fr Tropper's run to secure chosen territory before a rival mission could claim it, presaged the intense competition that marked Lutheran and Catholic relations in the years that followed. Both missions disliked the competition, but both also wanted to capture the whole population of an area for their own denomination. Other missions in the area were regarded as a stumbling block in the way of this goal. Since there was no agreement between them to work in defined areas, and as yet no restrictions placed on them by the government, friction was inevitable.

The Catholic missionaries were particularly concerned about the Lutheran practice of placing evangelists in villages. By 1936, there were 300 evangelists in the Highlands; 11 of these were at Kerowagi, and 37 at Mt Hagen. The Catholic policy was to train local boys at school, and then send them back to the villages. It was a much slower method. On his trips into villages, Fr Ross, the Catholic priest at Mt Hagen, would often be told that the Lutheran evangelists were there already. Worried by the success of this Lutheran strategy, he wrote to the government officer at Salamaua in 1934, questioning its legality. A government report noted that 'it would appear that the intention of the Lutheran Society is to flood the area with native helpers and so gain possession of practically the whole district between the Kratkes and Mt Hagen'. [21] Such a prospect was as unwelcome to the administration as to the Catholic Mission.

In late 1935, the intense rivalry between Lutherans and Catholics led to a serious incident at Bundi on the edge of the Highlands. Fr Cranssen, a Catholic priest stationed near Bundi, told his workers to burn the houses of some Lutheran evangelists. As a result of this incident Fr Cranssen was brought to court and sentenced to jail. [22] This incident and its aftermath embittered relations between Lutherans and Catholics. It also prompted the government to impose on coastal church workers the same restrictions as it had shortly before placed on European missionaries, following the killing of two Catholic missionaries in the Chimbu area. [23] Coastal church workers were now confined to main mission stations, where they were required to be under European supervision. By this restriction, the Administration effectively hobbled the activities of all missions in the Highlands for the next decade; but especially the Lutherans, who relied heavily on the evangelistic activities of New Guinean evangelists.

In the Eastern Highlands Province, a similar situation was developing, but here the rivals to the Lutherans were the Seventh Day Adventists (SDAs). In 1934, the Lutheran monopoly on mission work in this part of the country ended when the Adventists established a station at Kaiantu, close to the government station. Soon strife was occurring between them and the well-established Lutherans, and government officers frequently had to deal with disputes between the two missions.

Wearisome as this competitive situation was to government officers, it was mainly of the government's own making. The SDAs had entered the area at the invitation of the government. Behind the government's unusual action lay deep concern about the German nationality of most of the Lutheran missionaries.

During the First World War, anti-German feeling ran high in Australia. Some of the German missionaries working in New Guinea were interned in Australia during the war. After the war, Australia administered the former German colony under a mandate from the League of Nations. As noted above, it initially determined that German missionaries must leave the colony within two years. Though this harsh decision was eventually rescinded, anti-German feeling in the administration remained high. In 1928, a judge openly expressed this feeling when, in his summary of a trial, he wrote with reference to the Neuendettelsau Mission: 'In my opinion this Mission is at heart distinctly disloyal and in spite of their protestations I am convinced that their influence on the natives is not favourable to the Administration'. [24]

With the entry of the missions into the well-populated Highlands region, the Australian administration's concern about the extent of the influence of German missionaries increased. While it strongly suspected the missionaries of disloyalty, it lacked sufficient evidence to take direct action against them. But in the light of actions of officers of the administration in the years preceding World War II, it seems that there was an official, though unwritten, policy to restrict the influence of German missions in general and the Neuendettelsau Lutherans in particular.

338

In 1934, the Rabaul Administration encouraged the Anglican Mission to begin work in the Western Highlands. The previous year, the government anthropologist, Ernest Chinnery, took the unusual step of visiting representatives of the Seventh Day Adventist Mission to invite them to begin work in the Eastern Highlands. He described to them the 'newly discovered Highlands', with '100,000 natives of rather a fine type who were entirely untouched', and showed them aerial photographs of possible station sites near present-day Kainantu. They were quickly convinced that the 'Government Anthropologist would like us to work there, and the sooner the better'. [25] Undoubtedly, the government's motive in making these approaches was to encourage loyal Australian or British missionaries to set up rival missions in areas where German missionaries were at work. [26]

In the following years, the government's lack of even-handedness in dealing with the two missions in the Eastern Highlands became apparent. In 1937, a remarkable peace movement in the Eastern Highlands influenced the government to partially lift the restrictions on missionary activity in that area, and the Lutherans sought to reoccupy their former station at Bena Bena. Before they were allowed to return, however, the SDAs received permission to establish a station there, and immediately occupied the former Lutheran site. The Lutherans protested, and the Adventists were ordered to move. With the outbreak of war in 1939, the German missionaries at Asaroka an Raipinka were interned in Australia. After their departure, and before the arrival of American Albert Frerichs at Raipinka, the SDAs made big advances at the expense of the Lutheran Mission. These advances were due to the favourable treatment given to the Adventists by the government officer at Kainantu. Vigorous protests by Frerichs brought some readjustments in favour of the Lutherans, but by the time the missionaries were evacuated, the SDAs were well established in the Upper Ramu area. [27] By aiding and abetting the SDA Mission, the Administration succeeded in breaking the Lutheran monopoly on mission in the Eastern Highlands. Unfortunately, they also contributed to the intense rivalry between Lutherans and SDAs that has continued up to the present.

Relations in the War

With the arrival of war in New Guinea, the rivalry between Lutheran and Catholic missions temporarily ceased. Catholics and Lutherans were thrown together in evacuation, suffering, and death. In 1942, Lutheran missionaries Kuder and Doering were evacuated from their highland stations with Catholic missionaries Ross and Bernarding. Together they flew to Port Moresby, where they shared a small room. In the close confines of their quarters, they got to know and respect one another. On the ship that took them to Australia, they were allocated the same cabin. Later, Kuder and Bernarding became bishops of their churches. Their time together as evacuees prepared the way for a better relationship between the two churches in the Western Highlands in later years. [28] At Manam Island, 15 Lutherans were interned by the Japanese with 139 Catholic prisoners. On February 6, 1944, while the group was being evacuated by ship to Wewak, the ship was strafed by American planes. Seven Lutheran were among those who died in the attack. Dr Braun was one of the survivors, and throughout the duration of the group's activity and immediately after the attack, he provided basic medical care for his fellow prisoners. [29]

In the calamity of the war, not only missionaries, but also New Guinea Christians, were drawn together by their common faith. Bishop Gaius of the United Church recalled his contact with Lutherans on the Gazelle Peninsula of New Britain during the time of the Japanese occupation there:

> I clearly remember the funeral I conducted for a Finschhafen (Lutheran) woman. This was the first time I heard Christian words singing to native tunes and chants. It had a great impact on me: one of the most moving occasions of my ministry. I suppose being a minority group, those Finschhafen people felt God very near to them. [30]

The Bishop remembered the example of the Finschhafen Lutherans on this occasion as being one of the factors that strengthened his faith during the dark days of the war.

Relations in the Post-War Period

In 1946, Lutheran missionaries began to return to New Guinea. In addition to rebuilding their shattered stations, they faced the challenge of renewing and extending their mission work, particularly throughout the Highlands, whose clans were eager for development and their own missionaries. Despite recruitment of new personnel, it was clear that the task was beyond the capacity and resources of Lutheran Mission New Guinea. President John Kuder therefore invited compatible Protestant churches to come and begin mission work in certain areas of the Highlands. Some who responded were: the Missouri Synod (Lutherans of the USA, who, as New Guinea Lutheran Mission, first established themselves at Yaramanda in the Enga region in August 1948); the Australian Baptists (who began a mission at Baiyer River in 1949, and at Telefomin in 1951); the Australian Methodists (who began work at Mendi in 1950 and at Tari in 1953, in the Southern Highlands), and the Evangelical Lutheran Church of Australia (which began at Menyamya in 1951).

Following the war, rivalry between the established missions to win the favour of the Highland clans was revived. In 1947, the administration lifted the pre-war restrictions on missionary movement, and missionaries were now free to travel where they pleased within controlled areas. Not long after, the Lutheran Mission found other missions beginning to operate in areas which they considered to be solidly Lutheran. In the early 1950s, the Anglican Mission was given a plantation on the range behind the Asaroka station, which the Lutherans had established in 1936. Believing the area over the range to be as yet unevangelized, the Anglicans began to build churches and engage in mission work among the local populace. The Lutherans protested vigorously. The area occupied by the Anglicans lay partly in the Asaroka circuit and partly in the Monono circuit. Forty per cent of the population there were either baptized or under instruction. Several approaches by the Lutheran authorities to the Anglican bishop failed to resolve the situation, and relations between the two missions were strained for a while. [31]

In some of the established Lutheran areas, other missions began to set up English schools. At that time, many people had unrealistic expectations about the benefits of education in English, and these schools proved very attractive to the local people. In the Mission Conference Reports of 1959, it was noted that in the Kaiapit circuit the SDAs were offering teachers, and two villages had shown unwillingness to wait any longer for Lutheran teachers. Two years later, in 1961, it was reported that the newly installed Roman Catholic bishop of Goroka had established six schools run by missionary sisters within the Asaroka circuit. The Lutherans regarded the establishment of these schools as a ploy to gain a foothold in the Lutheran areas. In a letter accompanying the 1961 conference minutes, Dr Kuder wrote to the mission boards of the supporting churches:

> We are now seeing the development of a movement which was pointed out already quite a few years ago, namely, that other missions are attempting to infiltrate our congregations (not just unevangelized areas) and are seeking to gain as converts our baptized people. The inducement is the English School.

In addition to facing increased competition from established churches, the Lutherans found themselves having to cope with an influx of new mission groups. During the war in the Pacific, the attention of the world had been drawn to the hitherto little-known island of New Guinea. Following the war, conservative evangelical groups and small faith missions, originating mainly in the USA, began to arrive in increasing numbers. The Australian administration allowed them entry to the country in accordance with its policy of 'freedom of religion'. Another policy of the administration was to prevent missions from entering uncontrolled areas until government patrols had first contacted and 'pacified' the populace. The effect of these two policies was to intensify mission rivalry, since both the older and newer missions would enter at the same time.

As new areas were opened up to mission activity, each of the mission groups would strive to be the first to enter the new fields. In a description of the beginning of the work in Wiru in the Southern Highlands, Missionary Willi Hertle tells how shrewd observation and initiative enabled the Lutherans to overcome an initial handicap in the race into the new area.

> It was of great importance in the beginning as to which mission entered the Wiru field first ... The government would perhaps have been glad, if the two large denominations, the Lutherans and the Roman Catholic, would have been about equally

represented in Wiru. Now it was no secret for the government officials in Jalibu that the Lutheran Church had by far the most contacts with the Wiru people. Perhaps it is for this reason that the government — for 'purely technical reasons' as they tried to explain to me later — gave the weaker missions, that is, the Catholic and Bible mission, written permission to enter the Wiru area one or two days before we received it. So our mission was almost the last to enter the Wiru district. That we nevertheless entered the field before the Catholic mission got there, was due to the fact that the mission evangelist noticed how the Catholic priest with a large following entered Wiru. When I appeared before the government officials, the written permission, which had already been prepared, was given to me. By a forced march I then reached Wiru before the priest did. So we avoided losing the fruits of our work done in Jalibu and did not have to enter the field as a rear guard. [32]

One of the destinations most favoured by the newly-arriving missions was the Eastern Highlands. In this area, the Tarabo Circuit of the Lutheran Church proved to be particularly attractive to the newcomers. In 1965, the (then) Church Secretary Zurewe reported to the Mission Conference that 11 mission stations of the faith-mission type were operating within the boundaries of that circuit. Since these missions were operated mainly by individuals and lacked a larger body to coordinate their activities, dealing with them was difficult. Their attitude to the Lutheran Mission and Lutheran Christians is well illustrated in the following letter, written to the Revd Mansur in 1957 by a leader of a faith mission:

> Generally we have found that the Lutheran mission in New Guinea with which we were confronted is influenced by a spirit of compromise and apostasy, which for instance becomes evident in the connection to such bodies as the WCC etc. This fact and our experience of an unsatisfactory proclamation of an emasculated Gospel through unholy messengers has led us to view a large area of the so-called 'Lutheran area' to be totally unevangelized. [33]

New Guinea Lutherans deeply resented being regarded as unconverted. They pointed out to the newly arrived missions that they were already instructed and baptized, and told them to go and work elsewhere among the heathen.

Invariably, their protestations fell upon deaf ears. Missionaries in the newer bodies had definite ideas regarding mission, conversion, and church. Measured by their standards, the Lutherans fell short in some way. They lacked the expected institutional structures, or sufficiently well-educated personnel, or the correct forms of conversion or baptism, or the required degrees of holiness. In the Lutheran Church — where the church workers were mainly New Guineans, where the churches and schools were frequently constructed of bush materials, where indigenous languages were employed and people converted in their natural social units — there the newer missions failed to find sufficient evidence of 'real' Christianity. Since in their view the Lutheran Mission had made only a superficial impact, they felt quite justified in bringing to a proper completion what the Lutherans had merely begun.

The Lutherans regarded this influx of other missions into formerly solid Lutheran areas as an invasion. The terminology used in the Mission Conference Reports to describe relations with other missions is often the language of warfare. In the Asaroka circuit, Catholics are described as 'beginning a formidable campaign'; in Raipinka, 'the SDA advance is reverting to a consolidation of their forces'; in Rongo, the New Tribes Mission is working 'in force'; in many areas, missions are 'attempting to infiltrate our congregations'. Behind such language lay a deep concern over the erosion of Lutheran influence and the fragmentation of communities along denominational lines.

In the face of opposition, the Lutherans prepared to defend themselves. A thorough knowledge of the antagonists was considered important. In 1955, the Conference resolved that a paper be presented at the next conference on the teachings and practices of the Seventh Day Adventists. In 1962, it was resolved that pamphlets be printed on the Jehovah's Witnesses, Mormons, and Bahais, and that a booklet on the various missions working in New Guinea be prepared.

Lutheran Mission, which provided physical support for many new missions in the Highlands, also responded with economic sanctions. It drew up a list of missions, designating them either as 'cooperating' or 'non-cooperating'. 'Cooperating' meant that a mutual aggreement had been reached concerning areas of work. 'Non-cooperating'

missions and churches were not allowed Lutheran supply and transport services at discount rates.

In the last 20 years, various Pentecostal organizations have been especially active and aggressive in their efforts to win over Lutherans, particularly the youth. Their activities and the influence of charismatic individuals from the major churches have spawned numerous revival movements. A few of these movements, including one among Lutherans in the Garaina region of the Morobe Province, have broken away to form independent churches. [34]

In the face of aggressive proselytizing, Lutheran indigenous pastors often have a difficult time in holding on to their people. This is partly because they are usually matched against younger, better-educated, and better-supported church workers. Another factor is that the advances of aggressive new mission organizations have largely coincided with a decline in the institutional structure of the mission and a reduction in overseas mission personnel on outstations. Thus, the loyalty of Lutherans has been severely tested at a time when the morale of pastors has been at a low point. In a few cases, bewildered and angered church leaders have resorted to violence to discourage the proselytizing activities of other groups.

After the war, the rapid expansion of mission activity by the older, larger missions in the highlands, and the arrival there of numerous new, smaller missions, resulted in intense competition. [35] Lutherans raced to win people in new territories, and strove to hold on to adherents in areas previously gained. Unfortunately, this scramble for souls compromised the method of group conversion the Lutherans practised, and resulted in an overall weaker Christian commitment. Besides, the rivalry and bitterness that accompanied it, ill-suited those who came as Christ's messengers of peace. At the Lutheran Mission Conference in 1963, Mr Zurewe sadly compared the present divisions caused by competing missions to the past, when people were drawn together by Jesus Christ. It is a matter for profound thankfulness that a new era had already begun, and the next few years would see a revolution in ecumenical relations in Papua New Guinea.

A New Era in Ecumenical Cooperation

While the post-war period brought about an increase in competition between the churches and missions in New Guinea, it also saw the beginning of a movement toward increased dialogue, which eventually resulted in a level of ecumenical cooperation attained in few other countries in the world.

Two important factors in promoting this movement were the wider ecumenical movement and the approach of national independence. As one historian has put it, expatriate leaders of emerging churches 'were becoming conscious that it would be morally indefensible simply to pass on to their indigenous heirs the divisions which Western Christianity had undeniably introduced into the total fabric of Melanesian society'. [36] Similarly, the challenge of nation-building prompted church leaders to work together for a united and Christian independent country. In this movement toward closer cooperation, the Lutheran Church was to play a leading role.

Relations with Methodists

While rivalry and competition have often marked relations between Lutherans and some other mission agencies in New Guinea, Lutherans and Methodists enjoyed friendly ties from the very start. The pioneer missionaries in both the Finschhafen and Madang fields received assistance from the Methodists on New Britain. Immediately following the First World War, the Revd Cox, superintendent of the Methodist Rabaul circuit, conducted services for town-based workers from the mainland, many of whom were Lutherans. [37] When the Lutheran Church stationed Evangelist Wangum from Madang in the New Guinea islands in the mid-1950s, the Methodists housed him in their compound at Malaguna. Later, as more Lutherans were contacted, they moved him to the Rabaul town area and built a house for him on their own property. Since the Lutherans had no place in which to worship, the Methodists allowed them to worship in one of their school buildings. This arrangement lasted for 15 years. The Methodists also ran a primary school, at which all the students were Lutheran. [38]

In Madang, the Lutherans provided pastoral care to Methodists, many of whom were Chinese. It was at the invitation of the

342

Methodist Mission that the Lutheran Mission began working in the Jalibu area of the Southern Highlands.

It was against this background of friendly ties and close cooperation that an invitation was issued to the Lutheran Church to participate in negotiations for a United Church. In 1963, the Methodist United Synod resolved to work for union with the Papua Ekalesia and other churches. Lutherans attended the early meetings as observers, and served on a committee to formulate an acceptable statement of faith. Later, after the committee's proposals on the Lord's Supper were rejected, the Lutheran representatives withdrew. Agreement did not seem possible. At the same time as these negotiations were taking place, relationships between the three Lutheran bodies in New Guinea (the Evangelical Lutheran Church of New Guinea, the Wabag Luheran Church, and the Lutheran congregations of Siassi and Menyamya) were developing through discussions. Agreement between the Lutheran bodies was not only desirable, but also seemed to be possible (see also ch 6). Greater concern was attached to achieving Lutheran unity than to pursuing the faint hope of union with the Methodists and Papua Ekalesia.

Though the Lutherans did not participate in the formation of the United Church in 1968, neverthless relations between the two churches were warm and were strengthened in the following years.

Administration-Mission Conferences

Ironically, an initial stimulus for closer inter-church cooperation after the war came from the Administration, which had previously fostered inter-mission rivalry in the Eastern Highlands. In 1949, the Administrator of the Territories of Papua New Guinea organized a conference of representatives from the Administration and from church and mission organizations. The conference aimed to establish a better working relationship between the Administration and the Christian bodies, and also between the Christian bodies themselves. The Administration also desired to relate to the missions and churches as one body, rather than to many separate organizations. Subsequently, these meetings were held every two years. John Kuder, then president of the Lutheran Mission, frequently chaired these gatherings.

By the mid-fifties, several mission bodies began to feel a need for and express an interest in a forum to discuss common concerns and problems. Foremost among these was the provision of pastoral care for migrants to the growing urban centres. In 1955, the Executive Committee of the Lutheran Mission resolved to contact other missions with the goal of establishing a Missionary Council of Eastern New Guinea. Eventually, in 1959, the Christian Council for Papua and New Guinea was formed. It met at the same time as the Administration-Mission Conference. The Council never became a really effective ecumenical body, but it did represent the first hesitant step toward closer cooperation.

The real impetus for closer church cooperation in Melanesia came from the International Missionary Council. In 1960, this body organized a meeting of Pacific church leaders to plan for a Conference of Churches and Missions in the Pacific. The Conference was held the following year in Samoa, under the sponsorship of the World Council of Churches (WCC). Stahl Mileng and Albert Frerichs attended as representatives of the Lutheran Church. The Conference explored ways in which the churches of the Pacific region could cooperate more closely in theological training and the production of Christian literature via a Pacific Council of Churches (PCC).

In order that the ecumenical impetus generated at the Samoa Conference should be transferred to the various parts of the Pacific, delegates to the Conference organized regional Continuation Committees of the Samoa Conference. In January 1963, the Papua and New Guinea Continuation Committee convened an inter-church study meeting at Bumayong Lutheran Boys High School near Lae. Representatives from the Anglican, Lutheran, Methodist, Baptist, and Papua Ekalesia Churches met to consider together St Paul's letter to the Ephesians. Subsequently, the Continuation Committee promoted increased cooperation in areas where there was a pressing need for common action: in urban centres, youth camps, making submissions to the government regarding the proposed university, and in literacy and Christian broadcasting.

By this time, doubts were arising among church leaders about the benefit of belonging to a Pacific conference. It was generally felt that the Pacific was too remote for effective cooperation. Furthermore, the close association of the PCC with the WCC could hinder some Christian organizations from joining the regional body. In view of the fact that the Territory was large and complex enough to warrant its own council, and had already taken some steps toward that end, it was decided to form a Melanesian Council of Churches.

Melanesian Council of Churches

On June 23, 1965, the inaugural meeting of the Melanesian Council of Churches (MCC) was held at the Boroko Baptist Church, Port Moresby. Founding churches of the Council were the Anglican, Baptist, Evangelical Lutheran, Methodist, and Papua Ekalesia Churches. Later in the same meeting, the Salvation Army also joined the Council.

Non-participation of the Catholic Church in the MCC meant that the Council lacked the voice of the largest church in Melanesia. But the impact of the Second Vatican Council was already beginning to have its effects on Catholic attitudes toward those whom the Council called 'our separated brothers'. The feeling of being competitors with other Christians was changing to that of being co-workers for Christ. By 1969, the Council recognized that the time was ripe to make good the deficiency in its ranks, and at its Annual General Meeting it invited the Roman Catholic Church to join the Council. Approval for this step was given in 1970, and in February 1971 Catholic membership of the Council was formalized. The move was an important event internationally, as well as nationally. Papua New Guinea was one of the first places in the world where the Roman Catholic Church joined a national Church Council.

In 1971, the Wabag Lutheran Church (now Gutnius Lutheran Church) also became a member, making the MCC a council of seven major churches in Papua New Guinea, representing over 80 per cent of the country's population.

In 1964, another grouping of churches was formed under the name of the Evangelical Alliance of the South Pacific Islands. Only one of the 20 full-member churches was active in the

343

Territory prior to World War II. With two exceptions, the churches who are members of the Evangelical Alliance are not members of the Melanesian Council of Churches. Nevertheless, the two bodies maintain cordial relations and cooperate with each other on several inter-church councils and committees.

The Evangelical Lutheran Church's first two bishops both played a prominent role in the MCC. Dr John Kuder, who had been at the forefront in the movement toward ecumenical cooperation from its beginning, gave the council strong support in its period of formation and later as chairperson. His successor in the chair, Mr Zurewe (later Bishop Zurewe), was the council's first Melanesian chairperson and the first widely recognized Melanesian ecumenical leader. During his term of office, Zurewe strove to extend ecumenical involvement beyond cooperation at the national organizational level by proposing that 'ecumenical centres' should be established in the main towns of Papua New Guinea. He envisioned that such centres could lead to combined action on social problems and encourage discussion of 'simple theology' among pastoral workers. [39] Though no such centres have been established, the formation of urban ministers' fraternals and regional inter-church councils has facilitated the kinds of cooperation and discussion Zurewe proposed.

In addition to cooperating in a general way with other churches via the MCC, the Lutheran Church also cooperates with other churches in specific areas of ministry. We shall now briefly consider some of the major ecumenical ventures in which the church is involved.

Kristen Redio

An important area of ecumenical cooperation in PNG is Christian broadcasting. The ecumenical organization which coordinates the efforts of 17 churches in broadcasting is Kristen Redio. The Lutheran Church has played a key role in the establishment and growth of this ministry. [40]

In the early 1960s, the churches and missionary organizations in Papua New Guinea came to realize the opportunity afforded by radio to communicate the Gospel through Melanesia. At the Lutheran Mission Field Conference in 1965, a resolution was passed that the LMNG/ELCONG broadcasting

Kristen Redio, situated at Martin Luther Seminary, Lae.

committee approach other Territory churches with a view to setting up a Board of Christian Churches for Radio Broadcasting.

In June 1965, the Revd John Sievert met with the representatives of Protestant Churches in Papua New Guinea to discuss the possibility of the churches working together to use radio for Christian broadcasting. As a result of this meeting, in November 1965 the committee decided to from the Christian Broadcasting Service (CBS). Mr Geoff Basket, who was working for the Department of Information as Assistant Manager of Radio Wewak, resigned from the government service to take up the position of Manager of CBS.

The Lutheran Mission supported this decision by submitting an appeal to an overseas donor agency for funds to cover the cost of setting up recording studios and staff housing at Rugli in the Western Highlands District.

In 1966, CBS was established not as planned at Rugli, but at the Christian Leaders Training College at Banz. It commenced with regular five-minute programs of devotionals in Pidgin over one station: Radio Wewak. Soon, other stations began to accept its programs. In 1971, the name of the service was changed to Kristen Redio, in line with Kristen Pres.

In 1974, following the changeover from the Australian Broadcasting Commission to the National Broadcasting Commission, it was decided to move the production centre of Kristen Redio from Banz to the campus of Martin Luther Seminary in Lae. The main reason for this move was to enable Kristen Redio to have a closer liaison with the National Broadcasting Commission through their station, Radio Morobe, in Lae. Initially, Martin Luther Seminary made available a small studio, a tape-duplicating room, an office, and staff accommodation. In 1976, grants from overseas enabled Kristen Redio to erect a proper broadcasting complex on the campus of the seminary.

With expanded staff and facilities, Kristen Redio increased both the number and type of programs it broadcast, and it ventured into new fields of service. In 1979, the station was putting to air 121 programs each week. At the same time, a year-long training course, covering all aspects of radio broadcasting, script-writing, and practical production, was offered to

representatives of member churches. In 1984, Kristen Redio further expanded its ministry by setting up a Puppet Training Centre. Here, representatives of the churches are trained to make puppets and present the Gospel through puppet plays.

Kristen Redio is financed by grants from overseas and by a levy on member churches. Kristen Redio has received substantial grants from Lutheran churches in Germany and America. With the largest number of baptized adherents, the Evangelical Lutheran Church of Papua New Guinea is the major local contributor.

The Churches' Council for Media Coordination
The growth of modern mass media in Melanesia has brought the churches new avenues for communication. By cooperating with other churches and agencies in the field of media, the Lutheran Church has tried to make the best use of new methods in making widely known God's message.

Wantok, *a newspaper sponsored by the various churches through the Churches' Council for Media Cooperation.*

Cooperation between Christian bodies in electronic and print media is coordinated by an ecumenical agency known as the Churches Council for Media Coordination (CCMC)[41]. Virtually every Christian denomination in Papua New Guinea holds membership in the Council, either directly or through the Evangelical Alliance.

The main functions of the CCMC are:
— to negotiate with the National Broadcasting Commission over the allocation of time for religious broadcasting;
— to coordinate training in various forms of media, radio, photography, slide or tape presentation, writing, puppet making, and, recently, television;
— to coordinate the communication resources of the churches, and arrange the sharing of personnel, equipment, and facilities;
— to serve as a voice to overseas churches and funding agencies concerning communication in Papua New Guinea.

In recent years, the CCMC has given increased attention to the government's proposal to introduce television broadcasting within Papua New Guinea. Recognizing that television is a powerful medium, which will have a major impact on society in Papua New Guinea, the CCMC has presented to the government the views of the churches on the introduction of television and on its use by the churches.

The Melanesian Institute

Another expression of the ELC's ecumenical commitment is its membership in the Melanesian Institute. Situated at Goroka in the Eastern Highland Province, the Institute is a joint venture of the Catholic, Lutheran, United, and Anglican Churches in Melanesia. Its primary goal is to help Melanesian and expatriate church workers in the process of incarnating the Gospel in the cultures of Melanesia. This goal is expressed in the symbol of the Institute: a snake depicted climbing a cross. In many Melanesian cultures, the snake represents everlasting life. The cross stands for God's gift of new life in Christ. By combining these two symbols, the Institute attempts to portray its primary aim: that the peoples of Melanesia may have abundant life in Christ, and

346

give witness to that life within their own cultural contexts.

The specific areas of interest of the Institute are expressed in its full name: the Melanesian Institute for Pastoral and Socio-Economic Service. The Institute aims to help church workers in their pastoral and socio-economic service by conducting research into specific areas of concern. While most research is for the benefit of all member churches, some projects are undertaken for the benefit of one church. One such project was the Planning Survey of the Evangelical Lutheran Church conducted in 1976. The survey assessed and critically evaluated the situation of the church by investigating major areas of church activity. Research findings are shared with church workers by way of the Institute's publications and courses.

The Institute was originally a Catholic organization. Founded in 1968 by the Association of Clerical Religious Superiors of the Catholic Church in Papua New Guinea and the Solomon Islands, its purpose was to provide new Catholic missionaries with an introduction to cross-cultural ministry. The Institute conducted the first Orientation Course for missionaries at the end of 1969.

Meanwhile, Lutheran missionaries also began to express the need for a better grasp of the cultures of Melanesia. When, therefore, the assistant director of the Institute met with the MCC in 1971 to discuss the involvement of its member churches in the Institute, the Lutheran Church in particular showed keen interest in this opening. Further discussions resulted in members of other churches attending the 1972 Orientation Course at Alexishafen, and the Lutheran Church appointing Dr Theo Ahrens to the Institute staff in 1973. In 1976, the United Church assigned the Revd Brian Turner as its first representative on the staff.

The present staff of the Institute come from three member churches, and seven countries. Most staff members have training or interest in a specific field. Nevertheless, much of the work is done as a team. For example, in the Marriage and Family Life Project currently being undertaken, the staff work together to look at marriage from anthropological, theological, and pastoral perspectives. The strength of the research undertaken by the Institute is largely due to this interdisciplinary cooperation and team approach. And its ecumenical and international composition makes for a stimulating and creative working environment.

Support for the Institute comes from a variety of sources. The stipends of staff members are provided by their sponsoring churches. Approximately 35 per cent of the Institute's operating budget is generated by the Institute itself and contributions from the supporting churches. The remainder comes from overseas funding agencies. [42]

Melanesian Association of Theological Schools

The Evangelical Lutheran Church has also worked closely with other churches in Melanesia through the Melanesian Association of Theological Schools (MATS). Founded in 1969, MATS incorporates 13 seminaries and theological colleges in Papua New Guinea and the Solomon Islands.

Theological education was the main concern that initially led churches to closer cooperation in the South Pacific. The leaders of churches and missionary agencies who met at the Samoa Conference in 1961 recognized that an important common need was to upgrade theological training for ministers and church workers. At that time, most of those who continued their theological education beyond local theological colleges went to Australia, New Zealand, England, USA, and India. Conference participants were convinced that a regional ecumenical college would better serve the majority. The conference resolutions came to fruition in 1966, with the opening of the Pacific Theological College at Suva, Fiji.

In PNG, there was a strong move to establish a similar theological college or faculty in connection with the proposed university. One of the first decisions of the newly-formed MCC was to form an inter-church committee to liaise with the university on this and other proposals. The move, however, fell through when it failed to gain the support of all the churches and ran into opposition within the university. With the support of the churches and the Theological Education Fund of the WCC, a small religious studies department was eventually set up within the university of PNG Faculty of Arts. In 1972, Dr Carl Loeliger, an Australian Lutheran, was appointed to the department as lecturer in Religious Studies.

Failure to establish a common theological college did not inhibit moves to bring about closer cooperation between various denominational colleges. In April 1968, the Theological Education Fund sponsored a Theological Education Consultation in Melanesia. Faculty members from thirteen theological institutes and pastor-training schools assembled at Lutheran Mission, Lae, under the chairmanship of Bishop Kuder. The conference favoured the establishment of an Association of Institutions engaged in theological education, and recommended that a committee be formed to draw up a constitution. The following April, the inaugural meeting of the Melanesian Association of Theological Schools was held at the Catholic Holy Spirit Seminary, Bomana. Four Lutheran seminaries were among the ten founding-member colleges.

MATS has fostered various kinds of cooperation and interaction between various institutions. Exchanges of lectures and students' conferences have brought about encounters between teachers and students of different theological traditions. Study Institutes have promoted reflection on such topics as ordination, worship, and Melanesian theologians at work.

MATS also functions as an academic accrediting agency. A special committee makes regular visits to the various institutions to monitor entrance levels. It also assesses and approves qualifications awarded by member bodies, ranging from lower-level catechetical certificates, through middle-level diplomas, to degrees in theology. The MATS-approved Theology degree has been recognized by the University of Papua New Guinea as a fully accredited first degree, entitling the holder to proceed to the UPNG Master's Program. At its General Meeting in March 1984, the Executive of MATS resolved to work toward the setting up of a full Department of Religious Studies, offering degrees up to a Master's level. The committee also makes recommendations to the various institutions regarding the development of national staff and library resources.

Martin Luther Seminary has played a prominent part in the history of MATS. Because of its central location in the country, it has been the venue for many of the MATS meetings. The MATS textbook library is also housed at the seminary. Three of the seminary's lecturers, Dr W. Burce, the Revd R. Pech, and the Revd K. Kautil have served consecutively as secretary/treasurer of the ecumenical organization.

Churches Education Council

In the last 15 years, the Lutheran Church has also worked with other churches in the field of education. Ecumenical cooperation in education at a national level is coordinated through the Churches Education Council (CEC).

The CEC was formed in early 1969 by the national education secretaries of the Evangelical Alliance and of the United, Lutheran, and Catholic Churches. These churches had opted to become education agencies in the proposed National Education System. Motivation for the council's formation lay partly with the government, which preferred to deal with the churches as a group. But the churches, which at that time controlled two-thirds of the primary schools in the country, also realized it was in their interest to work together and present a united front to the government. The main purposes of the CEC were to protect the rights of the church agencies, to nominate representatives to national committees, and to formulate common policy, such as the development of an agreed syllabus for religious instruction in primary schools.

CEC has played an important role in helping church-agency schools maintain their Christian identities within the National Education System. In 1983, the Council was instrumental in getting the National Education Act rewritten, so that it reinforces the rights of individual agencies. In 1984, the CEC also persuaded the Minister for Education to allow 150 minutes of Christian Education a week (30 minutes each day) within normal school hours.

Balob Teachers College

Again in the educational field, Lutherans are involved in impressive ecumenical cooperation in teacher training at Balob Teachers College, in Lae. The college is a joint

348

A student of Balob Teachers College.

venture of the Evangelical Lutheran Church of Papua New Guinea, the Gutnius Lutheran Church, and the Anglican Province in Papua New Guinea.

Balob grew out of the need for better training for teachers for the growing number of English schools run by the various Lutheran organizations. During the discussions of the Commission on Theology and Inter-Church Relations (CTICR) in the 1960s, the idea evolved of having one institution for the training of teachers for all the Lutheran Churches. A strong factor in bringing this idea to implementation was the encouragement of the Department of Education to consolidate the small teacher-training institutions of the churches, such as Rintebe, Amron, Heldsbach, and Hopoi.

Construction of the college began in 1964, and classes in 1965, although the official opening was not held until November 27 of that year.

The Anglican Church's involvement at Balob stems from that church's decision to move its teacher-training institution from Dogura in Milne Bay to the Northern Province. The Anglicans requested that their students attend Balob temporarily, until they re-established their college at another location. The Lutherans agreed, and in 1969 three staff members and 26 Anglican students resided at the college. Since the Department of Education wanted to reduce the number of small teacher-training institutions, it encouraged the Anglicans not to open another college but to ask to stay on at Balob. This proposal suited the Anglicans, and in 1970 the college's governing council approved a resolution to make the Anglican Church an associate partner with the Lutheran churches at the college.

Over the years, the number of students at Balob has increased greatly, rising from 99 in 1965 to 349 in 1985. In its 20 years' history, well over two thousand graduates have gone out to all parts of Papua New Guinea to serve as Christian teachers.

Churches Medical Council

Ecumenical cooperation in health care is coordinated through the Churches Medical Council (MCC). This body is an expression of the conviction that 'the best use of resources for health action to benefit the most people ... is enhanced by a close communicating partnership between Church and Government health services'. [43]

Organized ecumenical cooperation in health care began with an Anglican initiative by the staff at Dogura hospital. In 1965, the Anglicans, who had long held their own medical conferences, invited other missions to participate. Sisters Merla Garrett and Christa Lindner represented the Lutheran Church. The main thrust of the conference was in the area of nurse training. Qualified nurse teachers realized the need to cooperate with the newly-established National Nursing Council if they wanted recognition of their training and financial assistance. Medical staff also saw the value of other forms of cooperation. Thus, a Combined Mission Medical Council was formed, and continued to meet annually in different places.

Since its formation, the CMC has facilitated various kinds of cooperation between church and mission health agencies. Two areas particularly stand out. One is cooperation in health education, mainly through exchange of ideas and teaching staff. The other is in meeting the health-care needs of people in rural areas by the provision of staff and services.

Another major function of the CMC is to promote better communication and cooperation between the churches' health services and the government Health Department. Rather than dealing with a large number of church health agencies, the government can negotiate with the single representative body. Close cooperation with the government has resulted in a rationalization of health services involving the closing of some hospitals where health services were being duplicated, the changing of function of some health institutions (e.g., Yagaum), and the actual integration of church/government institutions in several areas (e.g., health education, Braun Health Centre, Butaweng). In 1978-79, Sister Merla Garrett served as Church/Government Health liaison officer.

While the CMC has promoted close cooperation with the government, it has also worked to help the churches' medical services retain their Christian identities. At CMC medical conferences, attention is given to the theological basis of the church's healing ministry and its understanding of health in the full biblical sense. Opportunities are also provided for spiritual fellowship between health workers from various churches.

The present Lutheran Medical Secretary, Mr Wilson Waesa, has been involved with the CMC for eight years. From 1978-79, he was Chairman of the ecumenical body, and in 1984 its deputy chairman.

Publishing

The Evangelical Lutheran Church of PNG and the Gutnius Lutheran Church cooperate together in publishing via Kristen Pres Inc. In October 1969, the newly-established organization took over the facilities of the former Luther Press at Nagada. Kristen Pres publishes material in Pidgin, English, and indigenous languages. It operates a retail bookshop in Madang and one in Lae, and also has extensive wholesale distribution through independent Christian and secular bookshops.

In July 1976, an important step took place in ecumenical publishing when the Catholic-owned Wantok Publications became a joint venture of the Catholic, Lutheran, United, and

Anglican Churches. Initially, representatives of the other churches were given positions on the committee of control of Wantok Publications. Later, the other churches became shareholders in a new company called Media Holdings. The Lutheran Church has a 20 per cent equity in this company. Word Publishing, which publishes the Pidgin weekly *Wantok* and the bi-weekly *Times for Papua New Guinea*, is a wholly owned subsidiary of Media Holdings.

Ecumenical Challenges

While cooperation between the Lutheran Church and other churches continues through the MCC and the various ecumenical organizations mentioned above, there is something of a lull in the present ecumenical movement in Papua New Guinea. The enthusiasm generated in the late 1960s and early 1970s by the common task of nation-building has waned. The accidental death of Fr Patrick Murphy in 1978 deprived the movement of an articulate and tireless worker. Most of the Lutheran missionaries who gave leadership to the movement have left the country. The slowing-down of the ecumenical movement in Europe has also influenced the local movement. The rush to cooperate is over. The present mood is one of stocktaking, of assessing what the present situation is, and of pondering the next steps.

While the Lutheran Church has contributed significantly to the high level of ecumenical cooperation in Papua New Guinea, important challenges in this field lie ahead. These are mainly in the development of relations with the region's established churches and emerging religious movements, and with overseas churches and ecumenical organizations.

While the church has cooperated extensively with other churches in the past 20 years, most of this cooperation has been on the practical and organizational level. Little has been done in the sensitive theological level, except with the United Church.

In 1974, the Lutheran Church began a series of discussions with the United Church. The first meeting was concerned with closer pastoral cooperation. Three years later, a second meeting was held to discuss urban work and the Sacraments. In 1980, the two churches brought
350

out an agreed statement on Holy Baptism. In 1981, discussions were held on Holy Communion. Recommendations from these discussions were considered by Synod the following year. The Synod decided to ask the Bishops Council to study the recommendations on joint Communion, and advise the church as to what direction it should take. [44] There the matter rests. Further dialogue between the two churches is planned.

From 1970 to 1973, Papua New Guinea's Anglican and Catholic Churches held theological discussions. Considering the common liturgical heritage the Lutheran Church shares with these two churches, and the friendly relations and close ties it enjoys with both bodies, the basis exists for extensive theological dialogue with these churches too.

In 1985, the Lutheran Church took a significant step toward closer cooperation with the Manus Evangelical Church, with the stationing of a Lutheran pastor on Manus under the supervision of the Manus Church and the declaration that Manus should be regarded as a mission area of the Madang District of the Lutheran Church.

The Manus Evangelical Church is a fruit of the Liebenzell Mission, which originated in Germany (see also ch 6). Many of its mission personnel have been Lutherans, and Manus Evangelical Church members frequently identify themselves as Lutherans and join Lutheran congregations on the mainland. The first two pastor-teachers of the Manus Mission were trained at the Rhenish Mission school at Amele, completing their course in 1932. In the 1950s and 1960s, representatives from the Manus mission frequently attended the annual Lutheran Mission conferences at Wau as observers. In addition to this common ground, the people of Manus and Madang have traditional trading and cultural ties. There is therefore a broad basis for building a closer relationship with this island-based church.

On the regional level, Melanesia's new and ongoing religious movements also present the Lutheran church with a significant ecumenical challenge. In the past, the majority of these movements were cargo cults, syncretistic movements exhibiting a mixture of Christian and pagan elements. In recent years, most of the movements have become more distinctly

Christian in character. In particular, many revival or 'Holy Spirit' movements, stimulated by the activities of fundamentalist and charismatic missions, have sprung up and rapidly spread (see also ch 15).

An established church that seeks to enter into a relationship with such movements faces a difficult task. Members of such movements regard themselves as true Christians. A heavy-handed approach is usually counterproductive. Humility, understanding, and patience are essential in building up goodwill and trust. Most Lutheran leaders have much to learn in how to relate evangelically to these movements. The danger of schism is high, and a program of educating the churches' pastors about the movements is urgently required.

On the international level, the Lutheran Church in Papua New Guinea is challenged to strengthen its ties with other younger Lutheran Churches of the so-called Third World. In November 1982 and in August 1985, pastors from ELC-PNG met with pastors of the Evangelical Lutheran Church in Tanzania to study and reflect upon basic Lutheran theological convictions. While the prime purpose of the meeting was to help the two churches move toward a deeper understanding of their respective Lutheran identities and roles within the African and Melanesian contexts, an important by-product was the establishment of fraternal ties between pastors of the two churches.

ELC-PNG's relations with Lutheran churches in the Asian region, and in particular with the neighbouring Batak Church of the Indonesian Republic and Lutheran Aboriginal communities in Australia, await further development. Since 1977, the ELC-PNG has been a member of the Lutheran World Federation. In 1984, the question of membership in the World Council of Churches was raised. Before long, the relationship of the church in Papua New Guinea to the world body will be an important topic of discussion and debate.

Factors Favouring Ecumenism

Despite the recent levelling off in ecumenical activity in Papua New Guinea, a climate favourable for the further development of ecumenism still exists. Deeply embedded in

many Melanesian cultures is a longing for reconciliation between estranged brothers. In the early years of the Lutheran Church, the Gospel fulfilled this traditional longing to a remarkable degree. Later, interdenominational rivalry introduced new divisions in the name of Christ and cheated more recent converts of the same experience of unity. Today, denominational divisions are generally accepted as part of the Christian reality. But there is still a widespread feeling that brotherhood in Christ transcends these divisions. As the chairman of the MCC, Bishop Zurewe expressed this feeling when he wrote:

> We work together as brothers in Jesus Christ. We should not think and fight about Biblical teachings and doctrinal differences, but we must think of Jesus Christ, the Son of God, and our Saviour and Redeemer. We all believe in him and share in unity. [45]

This recognition of Christian brotherhood in Christ and the longing to realize it more fully makes for openness to the further development of ecumenical relations.

Another factor favouring closer ecumenical ties is the widespread respect for Scripture. Almost all Melanesian Christians regard the Bible as the written Word of God, and as such accept its authority. This widespread respect for the Scriptures and general willingness to place oneself under them gives grounds for optimism in ecumenical dialogue.

Restraining Factors

While the leaders and people of the Lutheran Church in general share the widespread longing for greater Christian unity, certain factors act as restraints upon the church's ecumenical activities. One of the major factors is the present preoccupation of Lutheran leaders with internal Lutheran affairs. In recent years, much time and effort has been devoted to church planning. The Lutheran Church inherited from Lutheran Mission a large and fairly complex organization. Its administration has proved a difficult task for national church leaders. Attempts have been made to simplify the church structure and decentralize certain functions. But despite the changes, management remains a problem. In this situation, where much effort is devoted to the internal organizational aspects of the

351

Lutheran Church, the development of ecumenical relations tends to be given low priority.

Another restraint lies in the concern of ELC-PNG's church leaders about how the development of ecumenical ties with other churches or church bodies would affect existing relations. Of particular concern are the church's relations with its sister church, the Gutnius Lutheran Church, and one of its overseas partner churches, the Lutheran Church of Australia. The Gutnius Lutheran Church is a product of the missionary activity of the Lutheran Church-Missouri Synod. It retains close ties with its parent body, and has a similar ecumenical stance. The ELC-PNG and the Gutnius Lutheran Church accept a common Statement of Faith, have declared themselves to be in fellowship, and cooperate in several ventures, including the training of pastors. Before embarking on new ecumenical initiatives, the ELC-PNG would carefully consider the implications of such moves for its relationship with its sister church.

The Australian Church is a strongly confessional Lutheran body. Its roots lie in the migration of confessing Lutherans to Australia. They chose to leave their home country rather than compromise their confessional principles. In the past, Australian Lutherans have shown their sensitivity to ecumenical developments in New Guinea. [46] Recently, representatives of the Australian Lutheran Church expressed concern about recommendations arising out of the consultation on Holy Communion with the United Church.

The Lutheran Church of Australia has a special relationship with the ELC-PNG. In addition to its long historical ties with Lutheran mission work in New Guinea and its continuing commitment of a high proportion of its resources to ELC-PNG, the Lutheran Church of Australia has declared itself to be in church fellowship with the ELC-PNG and the Gutnius Lutheran Church. For the sake of a united Lutheran Church in Australia, the two former Australian Lutheran synods severed all other church ties, including membership in the Lutheran World Federation. At the Constituting Convention of the Church in 1966, the uniting churches promised to do all in their power to

maintain the confessional Lutheran character of the native Lutheran Churches of New Guinea. [47]

Thus far, the leadership of ELC-PNG has shown respect for the confessional concerns of the Lutheran Church of Australia. Prior to ELC-PNG joining the Lutheran World Federation, Bishop Zurewe expressed concern that such a move would put the church in New Guinea out of step with its Australian partner. Sensitivity to expressions of Australian concern over the consultation on Holy Communion with the United Church has resulted in recommendations of the consultation being put on ice. The risk of disrupting the close relationship with its Australian partner has made for caution and restraint in the further development of ELC-PNG's ecumenical ties.

The Way Ahead

In the ELC-PNG's Statement of Faith, Christian unity is presented as a goal that Christians should pray for and actively seek. The Statement speaks against a mere show of unity which hides fundamental disagreements. It rather urges an honest expression of faith, made in love, as a way toward genuine unity. Furthermore, it states that unity does not depend upon church rules and customs, but rather 'that we are agreed concerning the Gospel of Christ, that we preach the Gospel purely, as Christ gave it to us; and that we administer and receive the Holy Sacraments according to Christ's Word'. [48]

The Statement of Faith clearly and simply sets forth the motive, means, and goal of more intensive ecumenical interaction. The motive for pushing ahead is obedience to Christ. Continued involvement in ecumenical activity cannot be regarded as an option, but rather as a Christian obligation. The means by which the church should continue to seek unity is by inter-church dialogue, characterized by openness and honesty. The goal of the dialogue should be agreement on essentials.

While the church has a clear mandate and guidelines for continued ecumenical activity, at this stage the interests of the local church would be served best by proceeding slowly. ELC-PNG's leaders need time to develop theological maturity and ecumenical confidence. In particular, they need a stronger Lutheran doctrinal identity. While the church

352

leaders can generally sense that which is at variance with Lutheran convictions, few are yet able to articulate what is distinctive in the Lutheran understanding of Gospel and Sacraments. Before Papua New Guinea's Lutheran leaders can be expected to enter confidently into inter-confessional dialogue, they first need more experience in inter-Lutheran dialogue. By continuing to support dialogue, such as that which was held with Tanzanian Lutheran pastors, the overseas partner churches can make a significant contribution to ELC-PNG's continuing ecumenical growth.

Endnotes

[1] N.G. Gash, J.F. Hookey, R.J. Lacey, J.L. Whittaker, eds., *Documents and Readings in New Guinea History, Prehistory to 1889* (Melbourne: Jacaranda Press, 1975), 384-386.

[2] See British New Guinea, Annual Report, 1889-90, 19.

[3] Chr. Keysser, *A People Reborn* (Original: *Eine Papuagemeinde*, tr. A. Allin & J. Kuder) (Pasadena: William Carey Library, 1980), 2.

[4] *Ibid*, 3.

[5] *Ibid*, 17,18.

[6] *Ibid*, 3.

[7] *Ibid*, 56-58.

[8] One of the great difficulties in spreading the Gospel in New Guinea was the great diversity of languages. In Lutheran Mission Finschhafen, the area served by the Neuendettelsau Mission Society, two languages were chosen as vehicles for the Good News. One, called Jabem, was to serve the largely coastal Melanesian language tribes; the other, Kate, the non-Melanesian mountain people. Both of these languages became *lingua francas* in their respective areas of use (and, in the case of Kate, well beyond), and cemented a wider sense of unity and common identity. An attempt to do the same in Lutheran Mission Madang, an area served historically by the Rhenish Mission Society and later the American Lutheran Church, was only partly successful.

Both the German and Australian administrations, and many in the churches too, were opposed to the use of another *lingua franca* that had been developing in the islands for many years. This was New Guinea Pidgin or *Tok Pisin*. Despite attempts to suppress it, Pidgin continued to spread and develop. Today it is the one universal language of Papua New Guinea.

Tok Pisin has been one of the most significant factors in the development of ecumenical relations, both within the Lutheran Church and between the churches. It has enabled people from widely diverse social groupings to come together for worship. The *Nupela Testamen*, the Pidgin New Testament first published in 1969, has also given Christians from various denominations a common basis from which to discuss their faith.

[9] Chr. Keysser, *op. cit.*, 20.

[10] *Ibid*, 191,192.

[11] *Ibid*, 192.

[12] Friedrich Schuetz, Nobonob Station Report, 1923 (Lae Archives).

[13] F. Braun and C.V. Sheatsley, *On Both Sides of the Equator* (Columbus, Ohio: The Lutheran Book Concern, 1937), 81,82.

[14] Mailaender tells of King's visit in a report he wrote on September 9, 1912 (Neuendettelsau Archives).

[15] Flierl spoke gratefully of the assistance given by the Anglicans in a report he wrote about the experience of the mission between August 1914 and March 1915. It was reprinted in the *Neuendettelsauer Missionsblatt*, 1916.

[16] Reported in *The Lutheran Herald*, 4, (Nov. 17, 1924).

[17] James Ayong, a graduate of the Anglican Seminary, Newton College, wrote of the assistance the Neuendettelsau Mission gave to the Anglican Mission in his home area in a paper he wrote while doing post-graduate studies at Martin Luther Seminary, Lae, in 1984.

[18] The pioneering and early evangelistic work of the Lutheran Mission in the Eastern Highlands is sympathetically presented by Robin Radford in *Highlanders and Foreigners in the Upper Ramu: The Kainantu Area 1919-1942*, MA Thesis, UPNG, 1979. See also ch 5 of this volume.

[19] M. Mennis, *Hagen Saga* (Port Moresby: Institute of Papua New Guinea Studies, 1982), 43-52.

[20] *Ibid*, 55.

[21] *Ibid*, 72.

[22] *Ibid*, 72,75.

[23] *New Guinea Annual Reports* 1934/35, pars 33,34.

[24] Quoted by R. Radford, 1979, 169.

[25] *Ibid*, 256.

[26] Historian Peter Munster made this point in a lecture given at the Melanesian Institute in June 1984.

[27] R. Radford, 1979, 264-268.

[28] An account of the evacuation of the Catholic and Lutheran missionaries is given by M. Mennis, *Hagen Saga*, 104-106.

[29] *Ibid*, 112-115.

[30] A. Leadley, 'The Japanese on the Gazelle', *Oral History*, Vol. 3 (March 1975), 69.

[31] The strain in relations between the two missions is reflected in correspondence about the matter. Copies of relevant correspondence were shown to the author by the Revd R.F. Hueter.

[32] W. Hertle, 'The Beginnings of Mission Work in Wiru', translated from the German by the Revd Volkmann (Lae Archives), 5.

[33] This section is quoted from a letter by A.J. Spence to the Revd Mansur, dated Sept. 19, 1957, in W. von Krause, ed., *Junges Neuguinea* (Neuendettelsau: Freimund Verlag, n.d.), 89.

[34] An account of the Garaina *Bilip Grup* is given by Sr Wendy Flannery in *Religious Movements in Melanesia Today (2)*, Point Series No. 3 (Goroka: Melanesian Institute, 1983), 155-193. Since the article was written, the group has become an independent church, known as 'The New Life Church'. See also ch 15 of this volume.

[35] Dr G. Trompf of the University of Papua New Guinea claims that in the Eastern Highlands Province there are 80 distinct missionary groups at work. See *Religion in Melanesia, Part B* (Port Moresby: UPNG, 1980), 64.

[36] R. Pech, 'The Acts of the Apostles in Papua New Guinea and Solomon Islands', in *An Introduction to Ministry in Melanesia*, Point Series No. 7 (Goroka: Melanesian Institute, 1985), 65.

[37] N. Threlfall, *One Hundred Years in the Islands* (Rabaul: Toksave na Buk Dipatmen, 1975), 99.

[38] Information regarding cooperation between Lutherans and Methodists in the New Guinea Islands region in the post-war period was provided to the author by the Revd M. Diemer, resident Lutheran missionary at Rabaul, in 1984.

[39] Zurewe presented his ideas to the Executive of the MCC in 1971, under the title: 'Thoughts on the Ecumenical Council of Churches'.

[40] Information in this section is derived mainly from reports sent to the author by former Kristen Redio manager, Mr Geoff Basket.

[41] In presenting a brief historical background of the CCMC, its first coordinator, the Revd Gaylen Gilbertson, noted:
'In 1966, three significant events took place which were instrumental in shaping the Churches' Council for Media Coordination, although the Council was not actually brought into being for another eight years. These were
1) the action of the Pacific Conference of Churches, taken at its inaugural meeting, calling for a survey of the literature needs of the churches in the South Pacific;
2) the formation of the Christian Broadcasting Service (Kristen Redio) by 28 Protestant churches and missions in Papua New Guina (PNG);
3) the initiation of plans by the Lutheran Church in PNG for a creative literature training centre in Madang.'
(Report of Media Coordinator, Dec. 1975, p 3).
In 1970, the training officer of the Creative Literature Training Centre, the Revd Glen Bays, was instrumental in forming a national Christian Communication Commission (CCC). Several years later, a WCC-sponsored conference on Christian communication recommended that the MCC incorporate the CCC into its scope of operations. This proposal caused difficulties for non-MCC churches which wished to participate fully in the communication body. Therefore, in order to give a broader ecumenical base to communication work, it was decided to form a new organization separate from the MCC, but nevertheless in close working relationship with it. This new organization was known as the Churches' Council for Media Coordination.

[42] This section is based on 'The Melanesian Institute, A Venture in Interdisciplinary and Ecumenical Cooperation', by former Institute staff member, Dr Darrell Whiteman. The article is published in Afeaki, Crocombe, and McClaren, eds., *Religious Cooperation in the Pacific Islands*, (Suva: University of the South Pacific, 1983), 133-143.

[43] Churches Medical Council, PNG, Resolution 73/24, 1973 (Lae Archives).

[44] Report of the 13th Synod of the Evangelical Lutheran Church of Papua New Guinea, 1982, resolution 82/68 (Lae Archives).

[45] Quoted from a letter from Zurewe to MCC secretary, the Revd John Key, March 26, 1971 (Lae Archives).

[46] In 1920, while Ch. Keysser was attending a Lutheran pastors' conference in Adelaide, South Australia, he was criticized for 'entering into a working partnership with a unionist mission'. Earlier that year, in response to repeated pleas from the Rhenish Mission, and acting on the instructions of the mission conference, Keysser had taken nine evangelists to Madang to assist the struggling mission (see ch 3). This action was condemned as being contrary to the Lutheran Confessions. See Friedrich Eppelein, 'Christian Keysser, ein Gefolgsmann Martin Luthers und Wilhelm Loehes?' in *Jahrbuch fuer Mission* 1949/50 (Festschrift zum 70. Geburtstag von Dr Ch. Keysser), 9-24.

In 1936, the great need for mission workers in the Central Highlands, where the Lutherans faced a strong challenge from the Catholic Mission, prompted the Finschhafen Mission to negotiate a transfer of its Siassi field to the Evangelical Lutheran Church of Australia (ELCA). At that time, the ELCA was considering starting a mission in the Sepik area of New Guinea, and was glad to gain the Siassi Islands as a training ground for their missionaries and New Guinea mission workers and as a springboard for their planned new venture (see ch 7).
The decision to transfer the field to the ELCA was made by the missionaries on the field. The Home Board in Germany did not support the decision, though it did not prevent the transfer. The Board feared that the ELCA missionaries would promote division in Lutheran congregations on the mainland.
One of the conditions of the transfer was that for an interim period, while the transfer was being effected, the ELCA missionaries would not emphasize the differences between the two missions. After the transitional period was over, Lutheran workers from the mainland who were transferred to the care of the ELCA were instructed not to commune with their friends from the Finschhafen Lutheran Mission. Thus, a division among Melanesian Lutheran Christians, similar to that which existed between the two Lutheran synods in Australia, was created in New Guinea. The evangelists, however, in 'faithful disobedience' often partook of Holy Communion when back in their home congregations.

[47] 'Document of Union', Sec. 14, in *Doctrinal Statements and Theological Opinions of the Lutheran Church of Australia* (Adelaide: Lutheran Publishing House, 1980), 29.

[48] *A Statement of Faith* prepared and published by the Committee on Theology and Inter-Church Relations (Madang, 1972), 197.

Chapter 11

Viewing Their Own Church

Interviews with Church Leaders

by Hannes Gaenssbauer

When I was asked to provide the material for this chapter, I decided that it would not be appropriate for me at this time to offer my own insights, experiences, and observations based on 20 years' work either in or with the Evangelical Lutheran Church of PNG. The written history of Lutheran work in Papua New Guinea is incomplete if it tells only of the work of missionaries from overseas churches, and if it tells the story only through their eyes. The real history is one of partnership between overseas and local workers, with the latter group supplying the majority of workers and being, in effect, the senior partner. The fact is that very soon after the first acceptance of the Gospel, the people themselves accepted also the Great Commission; they acknowledged their responsibility for bringing the Gospel to their own people in their own land.

So, out of a deep sense of respect for the Christians and their leaders in the ELC-PNG, I attempted to get their own story of how they understand their own church in all the changes which have taken place in their own country. I turned to the members and leaders of ELC-PNG, who carry the brunt and burden of

the daily work in their church. I listened carefully to them, and took notes in a series of interviews conducted in February and March of 1984, in order to be in a position to relate *their story*, not the insights of an outsider.

The Interview Partners

The method I used was the method of representative interviews. I assumed that what interviewees told me is also to a certain extent representative of the basic assumptions, views, and insights of people I had no chance to interview.

Of course, I am aware of the dangers of this particular approach. The selection of certain people may predetermine what one gets to hear. In this situation I relied on my 20 years' direct and indirect involvement with ELC-PNG, and chose the persons I interviewed on the grounds of my close familiarity with members and leaders of the ELC-PNG.

I interviewed the following persons:
1) **Sir Zurewe Zurenuo**, first local Bishop of the ELC-PNG, now retired.
2) **Jeremiah Mambu**, first local Bishop of the Mount Hagen District, Western Highlands

Province. According to his own statement, he is only 'ready to retire when he dies'. He is now living and working in his home District, the Jabem District, and is still active as counsellor and father-figure in the Social Concerns Office of ELC-PNG in Lae.

3) **Gedisa Tingasa**, first local President of the Jabem District, co-founder and experienced counsellor in the 'Social Concerns Office' in Lae. He now lives in his home village.

4) **Honeo Gubung**, teacher, leader, and President of the Sattelberg Circuit, Morobe Province. In his capaity as Circuit President, despite his age, he still patrols the Sattelberg mountains to visit the congregations.

5) **Sanangke Dole**, teacher, first 'local' (as Highlander) Bishop of the Mount Hagen Church District, Western Highlands Province.

6) **Bapiangnu Sike**, President of the Kate District, Morobe Province, interviewed together with

7) **Sam Sorenu**, teacher and Stewardship Director of the Kate District, Morobe Province.

8) **Sila Esori**, voluntary women's worker of the Goroka District, Eastern Highlands Province.

9) **Uram Panok**, Pastor, President of the Wanuma Circuit, Madang District, Madang Province.

10) **Bamokenare Ateike**, teacher, President of the Ulap Circuit, Kate District, Morobe Province.

11) **Zabut Nail**, Pastor in Begesin and Wewak, former youth coordinator of the Madang District, Madang Province.

12) **Yara Muramel**, former gang leader, now Youth Coordinator of the Mount Hagen District, Western Highlands Province.

The 12 people whose names are listed above are able representatives of their fellow-Lutherans in PNG. That is my considered opinion, based on my familarity with the PNG situation and the church people in PNG. Of course, in seven of the cases I was trusting not only my own judgment but also the judgment of the members of the ELC-PNG, who had elected these seven men to be their representatives, to lead them and to speak for them. Thus, I

358

interviewed the first local Bishop of the Lutheran Church, four District leaders (two active, two retired), and three Circuit Presidents who have been in office for many years, and who are trusted and respected by their people. [1]

As I talked with the *older men* — Honeo, Gedisa, and Mambu[2] — I tried to trace the history of Lutheran work as far back as possible, almost to the beginning. Both Mambu and Gedisa had worked in first-contact situations. Both had instructed heathen in baptismal classes. The same is true of Uram. Honeo was part of, and for many people he represents, the centre of missionary activities of the Sattelberg congregation, beginning in the surrounding area and climaxing in the big missionary endeavour in the 1930s: the evangelization of the Highlands of PNG.

Since this chapter also deals with *changes* which took place in Papua New Guinea, it was particularly valuable for me to get the insights and reflections of these old people on the many changes which they experienced during their lifetime of service in their church.

The *younger generation* are represented by Yara (both with regard to his age and his responsibility for youth work), and by younger leaders and workers such as Sanangke, Bapiangnu, Sila, and Zabut.

The customary distinction between the older *coastal church Districts* and the younger (at least in time) *Highlands Districts* is well represented by former Bishop Mambu, who belongs equally to both areas. He was sent by his native Jabem District to work as missionary in Mount Hagen, and in his many years of service there he gained the trust of the Hagen people to such an extent that they elected him as their first local Bishop. Today, he works again in the Jabem District.

Bishop Mambu identifies so much with the Highlanders that he told me: 'For us, missionary work did not start in 1886 with the arrival of a first missionary from Germany, but in 1943 with the beginning of *our* missionary work in the Highlands'. [3]

The majority of the people whom I interviewed had spent most of their life in the *rural areas*, which accurately reflects the distribution of the population in Papua New Guinea, with about 85 per cent living in rural areas.

Although they spent most of their lives in rural areas, both Bomokenare and, in particular, Honeo represent the development of the church in areas with nearly a century of contact with Europeans and, especially, Lutheran missionaries. The statements of Bapiangnu and Sorenu also have to be understood against this background.

As far as the experience in *towns* is concerned, the situation of the church there is portrayed above all by Gedisa through his experience in the Social Concerns Office, by Mambu (Mount Hagen), by Sila (Goroka), by Yara (Mount Hagen), and by Zabut (Wewak and Madang).

The reader will notice that I have included only *one interview with a woman*. This suggests a certain imbalance, and even a sexist bias. In fact, however, it reflects a situation which may not be unique, but which is, at least, easier to explain or understand in Papua New Guinea than in other parts of the world.

Furthermore, intimate conversation in Papua New Guinea presupposes friendship and trust between those conversing. In my case, with direct contacts limited to two months per year, I naturally turned to those whom I once knew well or still have a lot to do with. The situation in PNG is such that my dealings, especially as a Mission executive officer, have been with men, not women.

I know, however, that all of the men to whom I spoke regard their wives as belonging inseparably to their ministry. And most share the insight once relayed to me by the late Bishop Stahl Mileng (Madang): 'Eighty per cent of the faithful congregation consists of women who most probably will no longer put up with all the males in the pulpit and on the District and Church Council'.

Retired Bishop Mambu referred to the baptismal name of his wife, a name which puts her under the same obligation as him in his service for the church. [4] And President Gedisa makes the point that he was able to enrol women in his baptism class only after his wife joined him as a living example of a Christian woman. [5]

In summary: I tried to select a group of people who are working in, and who are familiar with, a variety of situations and contexts. Thus, I tried to ensure that the 'representative interviews' do indeed reflect and represent the 'understanding of the church' in a changing time and in changing situations, which the interviewees not only observed, but in which they fully participated. Sometimes they were agents of change; sometimes they themselves were subjected to the changes which took place in their country and their church.

How They Look at Their Church

The reader will notice the complete lack of abstract statements with regard to the role of the church in major social issues. It is not absolutely clear to me whether this is the result of the way in which I put the questions to the interviewees, or whether it has to do with their lack of readiness to answer this type of question.

Changes brought about by a more prominent role played by the Government or the effects of business development agencies were clearly reflected. Problems of young people, the generation gap, and the effects of ubanization were considered and reflected on by the interviewees. But all these questions were looked at from the point of view of their effects on the church and on the congregations, that is to say, from an *inner-church perspective*. Leaders and members of the church whom I interviewed never took a position of 'objectively' looking at changes, and causes for changes; instead, they always dealt with them in the concrete scope of their task and their responsibility.

The same applies to the questions of *church structure*. With the exception of the first local head bishop, Sir Zurewe Zurenuo, and, to a certain extent, President Gedisa, none of the interviewees dwells on structural issues. Again, their main concern was only to illustrate to what extent their work is hindered or furthered by certain structures. But I was not able to provoke any strong statement with regard to certain principles of church structure, such as congregationalism or a more centralized understanding of the church, although nearly every one of them made a point of stressing the fact that strong and responsible congregations are the basis for a strong and responsible church.

It should also be noted that, contrary to a common interpretation of *conversion* and becoming a member of the congregation, a number of people whom I interviewed pointed out quite clearly that the 'crisis' in the process of making the basic decision to leave the old patterns of their previous life and to become Christians did not take place before baptism, but rather after they were baptized. This is highlighted particularly by Honeo[6] and Bomokenare,[7] but also by Uram[8]. It was the basic question of results, fruits, and even rewards — although not always in the sense of material rewards — which kept occupying and troubling the minds of the already converted and baptized Christians.

A decision against the old 'powers' was made. The liberating experience of peace and harmony with former enemies was thankfully appreciated. But still the basic question: What are the benefits and advantages of being a Christian? was very much on their minds and, obviously, has to be answered again by each generation of Christians. That was exactly the reason I included in all of the interviews a last question as to the *personal motivation* for being a Christian and working in and for the church.

A further observation, which has to do with what I say in the above paragraph, concerns the frequent use of the term *power* in many interviews. It is used quite frequently when referring to the 'old time', the pre-Christian time. It is also used for describing the 'crisis' after baptism, and it is, again, used when referring to their lives as Christians and their work which is supported and carried by the power of God, Jesus, and the Holy Spirit. In other words, Christian life is not seen solely in the context of an independent decision, but in the context of a clear submission either to evil power or to the power of the triune God. This is a concept which is clearly evident in the New Testament, but obviously not very prominent in Western churches.

A final point will probably not be necessary for the attentive reader. I found it, however, so clearly emphasized in nearly all of the interviews that I thought I should briefly mention it, in view of the background of the particular history of Lutheran mission work in Papua New Guinea. What comes so clearly through in Yara's very personal statement[9] and is, again, stressed by Gedisa[10], Sanangke[11], Mambu[12], Sila[13], and others, is the fact that the time of working

360

through the old male leaders of clans in order to bring about *group* conversion is definitely over. The Lutheran Church in the 1980s is clearly working with *individuals*, men and women of any age-group. The only bigger unit they refer to is the nuclear family. This, clearly, is the basis of work with Christians which extends in circles: to clans, villages, circuits, districts, and the national church. From the statements of Papua New Guineans themselves, it becomes crystal-clear that they believe that the only direction in which dynamic church work is done is from the bottom to the top, not the other way round.

Interview 1: with Sir Zurewe Zurenuo
(First local Bishop of the ELC-PNG, now retired)

Sir Zurewe Zurenuo.

On national church and congregations:

The national church is like an 'island in the sea', and there is a lot of water between this island and the congregations. By directly subsidizing districts and circuits, the central church has destroyed the authority of districts and circuits.

In the past, during the 'time of mission', the church was growing from the grass-roots level to the top. This growth was interrupted by introducing a circuit constitution, which gave too much power to the circuit and took away authority from the congregations. This move led to a withdrawal of congregations and members of congregations in terms of involvement and responsibility. New emphasis should be placed on the strengthening of the congregations by returning to them their original responsibility and authority, not only in organizational matters, but also in spiritual matters.

Special programs for women and youth, which were introduced by church and government, destroy the strength of the Christian family, and encourage the establishment of special groups (like youth and women), which do not include the backbone of the old missionary approach, namely the men.

At the same time, I am aware that, with the arrival of political independence, individuality became a strong factor in PNG society. This has not, however, led to a different approach by the church.

The church's leadership is too old. The old structures no longer reach people. People like to make independent decisions, and are no longer ready to blindly follow the government and the church, but rather base their decisions on their own independent judgment.

The decision to join with the mission and church, which was made some time ago by the male leaders, has to be re-evaluated in the light of emerging individualism in PNG, also in view of the fact that the decision was made by leaders for other people some time ago.

So, with regard to the church, a central approach from the top deprives local leaders of their authority and responsibility. [14]

The partner churches of the ELC-PNG are too closely tied to the central church. They should be supporting special projects or programs, such as seminaries.

On church and government:
The two decisive factors for changing society in PNG are the church and the government. Today, the government is closer to the people than the church. The people really like the church, but they are also glad about the support which comes from the government.

On stewardship:
I can illustrate the problem by giving two figures: A certain area makes Kina 30,000 in selling coffee, and gives Kina 12 for the central church.

On incentives for stewardship by creating obligations through subsidies:
This does not work, because the sums given by the government are so large that the church is not seen as a real partner in the reciprocating system. The church cannot match the sums given by government.

On church structure (Districts):
The Districts have no real task. I have made a big mistake. The District missionaries, who were members of the executive committee of Lutheran Mission, worked in a central way which made it hard for local District leaders — and therefore for the Church Council — to take over their responsibility.

Interview 2: with Jeremiah Mambu
(Former Bishop of the Hagen District; at the beginning of his work in the same District, evangelist, teacher, and pastor; sent there as missionary from the Jabem District)

Jeremiah Mambu, former District Bishop.

On changes:
When we think of the beginning of missionary work by the Lutheran Church in Papua New Guinea, you overseas people think of 1886. We PNG people think of the year 1934, when we started mission work in the Highlands.

The heading of what I have to say is: **Light and Darkness**.

The light started to shine; it shone brightly, and we were attracted by this light. We baptized people so they could do their own missionary work. This was our aim.

With the foundation of ELCONG in 1956, the light became truly ours and the church came into existence. Expatriates are no longer the fathers; we ourselves have taken over this responsibility. And we joyfully work. I firmly believe that the light will conquer darkness.

In 1973 [15] I observed a change: The source of light came to us ourselves. Bishop Zurewe in Lae and I in Mount Hagen were entrusted with this light. Now we have been working for 20 years. We have worked in this light and, at the same time, with many problems. And it continued to be this way. There was light, but there were also problems; both belong together.

I was stupid: I tried to put an end to darkness and problems. This futile exercise led me back to Paul. It was he who made me realize: Darkness and light belong together.

There was a further drastic change in 1976, when the name of 'Mission' was taken away and replaced by 'Church' (as Papua was included, we called it ELC-PNG). [16]

The white gown was taken over by us black leaders from you whites. This has opened our eyes to the problems of our young people, and we have discovered the problems of young criminals. But Yara's group has conquered the way of life of the young criminals. [17]

From 1976-84, the church reached the villages of the people. Thus, people no longer used to say: ELC-PNG is the church, but: I am the church.

In 1983, the light was fighting with darkness. The Gospel was there, but many problems were also there. At that time, an expatriate said to me: 'It seems that the many problems will overwhelm the Gospel'. I answered: 'I planted the Gospel in my own ground, and it will grow there. From time to time they can cut off leaves and branches, but the plant will grow.'

When light and darkness were fighting each other, we had little money but a lot of the Gospel. Today we have plenty of money, but little of the Gospel. When we talk about money, we talk for a long time. When we talk about the Gospel we only talk for a short time. Young people are full of enthusiasm when they start to work, but they become tired quickly if they receive no money for their work. This is how I see the present situation.

Where there is the Gospel, we also find bad things like stealing, fornication, etc. They are there together with the Gospel. But they cannot take away the Gospel. The Gospel has a way of doing away with these things. That is like the life of Peter. I liken all Christians in ELC-PNG to Peter, who denied the Lord, but was reinstated by the Lord. There is a number of new groups (sects) around these days, but I am not worried. My church is not worried. My Christians may leave me, but I will bring them back. How come I'm so confident? Because this is a local church.

The biblical passage I always refer to when speaking about those who left us is Luke, chapter 15. We will not bring them back by quarrelling and fights. If I quarrel, I commit a sin. If I work in harmony, there is a possibility of bringing them back.

It is the work of the headmen to bring those back who have left us. Because of this problem, we founded a 'Good-News Department' in our District in 1983. Even more than that, I declared the whole Bishop's office to be a 'Good-News office'.

On young people:

This District has many young people. Therefore, many young people turn to us. Some want help in their problems, others join us in our work, full of zeal.

The young ones are mobile, the old ones are stable. Both must cooperate with their respective gifts.

On stewardship:

The good thing about the Hagen District is that the younger ones are ready to follow their leaders. I never pushed them, but always tried to convince them as a teacher. Some are quite occupied by business activities. But the church's business is people. The church has to work with people. And people, in turn, will support the church. Thus, some business people gave us sums of Kina 2,000 and Kina 1,500 for equipment for a congregational office.

On the church:

The church is like a garden; if we work hard enough in the garden, we will by God's blessing always reap the fruits. I think of the parable in Mark, chapter 4: 'Good fruits grow together with the weeds'. Who is the church? I am the church. If I include myself, then there is a church. That is also like a garden. First, it yields only enough to feed me, but later when it becomes bigger it can also support others. The church brings people together.

On church and mission:

The church is also in motion. If there is only faith in the church, then we are still in darkness. If there is faith and mission, we are a church. Last year, 30 people volunteered to work as evangelists. That is what I waited for. Now I can go back to my home District, because evangelists are sent out by the Hagen District.

On work and workers in the congregation:

If there is too much difference between what a worker says and what he does, it will ruin the congregation. I believe in the congregation. Whenever a congregation has a worker whose deeds correspond to his words, there will be good results of the work. The congregation is God's garden. What we plant, will grow in God's garden. What we destroy, we destroy in God's garden.

The headman is the evangelist of the village. If he does not work well, he destroys the village.

The pastor has the main task of administering the sacraments. But I would like to see more pastors take over confirmation instruction; after all, they have studied theology.

The pastor has to train elders in counselling. The main task of the elders is counselling. To hear confession is the work of elders, together with the pastors. The headmen have to make a plan for the pastor's work. The headman is the 'boss' of the pastor. I keep telling the pastors: The headmen are your bosses. Since the headmen are the evangelists of a village, it is their task to visit families in their houses.

On missionary work of ELC-PNG:
It is no coincidence that the word 'Evangelical' is the first word in the name of our church. Today, the task of counselling members of a congregation is our 'evangelistic' work.

On work in town — social work:
The task in town is not too big for the church. There we have to do our mission work. I cannot always help everyone in his bodily needs, but I can help him to come to Jesus. The church should be more open also to accept people with problems in their training institutions. I keep asking myself: Why don't we accept young criminals in theological training?

Once a young criminal stole one of my hens, so I took another hen and prepared some food. I invited him, and he ate with me. Later, he asked me why I did not report him to the police. I told him that I can sort out such things in a Christian way. Later, he looked after my hens.

One of the young criminals also stole a pig from me. I gave him ten Kina, as I assumed he was in need. Later, he enrolled in confirmation class and kept supporting me and my family.

On personal motivation:
(He passed me a piece of paper with his Christian name and the Christian name of his wife in Jabem, which were given when they were baptized: *Katusele* [I have been cleansed] and *Kesiwagao* [He is my redeemer].)

This is what Jesus has done for us, and this has kept us working in our church. I have been cleansed, so I want to stay in the light. Therefore, I cannot retire. I retire when I die. Jesus who died for me gave me this name. That is the reason why I keep working in my church. I have to work for a long time in this light in order to cover the short period of darkness in the beginning of my life. I further believe I am a sinner. I have never seen Jesus, but I belong to the 'people of the Holy Spirit'. He does not leave me alone, and assures me of the name I received when I was baptized. I thank God for all the work he has allowed me to do.

Interview 3: with Gedisa Tingasa
(First local President of the Jabem District; co-founder, and experienced counsellor in the Social Concerns Office in Lae; now living in his home village)

Gedisa Tingasa, former District President.

On church and mission:
Right after conversion, the early Christians were charged with the responsibility of proclaiming the Gospel, or rather living the Gospel in a heathen environment by settling in the heathen villages. After they arranged their life according to Christian principles, they took responsibility for promoting the spread of the Gospel, which made them active and responsible agents of fundamental change in society. They were not, as in a later stage, sometimes helpless victims of social change, but rather instrumental agents of change. Also, they worked in a way and in an environment where they had reason to feel superior over against their 'missionary fathers' in communicating with their countrymen, even employing traditional ties or roles to their advantage.

My people are like Paul: strong fighters against the Gospel, and after their conversion daring and bold evangelists. As skilful canoeists, they were very mobile, and they used this skill in spreading the Gospel. The canoes of war were now used in the service of the Gospel of peace.

On the situation in towns:
The missionary work of the church is just now beginning. Whereas this church was strong in missionary outreach and work in the rural areas, we have discovered a new mission field, which is even more challenging than the work in the rural

363

areas. We had to start a new mission endeavour. I see my role in town to heal the rifts that have been developing between 'mission' and 'government'. The deportation of missionaries during World War II was, in terms of 'power', a clear defeat for the so-far dominant group ['mission'], whose aims were largely shared or even internalized by us New Guineans.

Seeing that the influence of the government is ever-increasing, I felt challenged, not as an agent of the mission, but as a responsible PNG leader, to play my role in this conflict by building bridges. I clearly understand the church as being charged with the important task of re-evangelising my people in towns. It is true that we heard and accepted the Gospel, but the inner strength vanished in the course of time. This development is a negative verdict on my work as District leader of the church.

The service and the ministry of us Christians, which brought about such remarkable changes, is no longer effective in a changing situation which is brought clearly to light in an urban setting.
Individuals come to our office (whose interior has been eaten away by ants), and they come from old traditional congregations. My main task is to be a shepherd of the individual sheep, caring for individuals, not leading a big group.

On relationship between the Social Concerns Office and congregations:

I see the congregational work and the contribution of special institutions as complementary, on the basis of mutual help. We work with people who are no longer reached by the traditional congregations.

We try to give the congregational leaders training to enable them to cope with these urban problems. We want to work closely with congregations, and to offer help in severe cases where the congregation cannot cope. We also work with the people who are not members of a congregation.

Our work has opened the eyes of the church to its responsibility and tasks in town. Towns are the prisms which reflect changes in society. I see the work in towns as a challenge which is not always fully met by my church.

On the beginning of the work in rural areas:

The main motive for joining the 'mission' in the beginning of mission work was the expectation of a life without fear. The decision to join the mission

was made on the basis of a comparison between living in constant fear of enemies and sorcery, and the expectation of eventually experiencing a state of peacefully living together. So, in this period of time, belonging to the mission meant being included in a community that lived free from the fear of enemies and sorcery.

The reason behind the decision to join the mission was a careful weighing of the 'power' behind the traditional and the Christian systems.

I myself demonstrated the power of the new system [the Gospel] by eating food prepared by a woman who was regarded by the village as a sorceress. While I was eating, the whole village started wailing, because they believe I would soon be dead. The fact that the 'power' of the old system did not kill me led to a mission break-through in this particular village.

The firm grip of the old system was demonstrated by the loud wailing of women and mothers when the first catechumens were about to be baptized. We had a further breakthrough against the old power system when the first women were to join the congregation. In our traditional customary society, women had a very low status. In the beginning, the work of mission was aimed only at the male members of society.

The barriers which had to be overcome are illustrated in the reaction by members of a traditional society when, for example, the wife of a missionary held her husband's hand; it prompted those observing to say: 'What shameless behaviour!'

I was able to baptize the first woman only after my wife joined me and started to work with the women in the village. Thus, even after a period of understanding the congregation as the context for men peacefully living together considerably free of fear from threats from outside or within the community, the women had yet to become part of this new life-style.

A special problem was the question of polygamy, which we had to face when a traditional 'big man' with a number of wives wanted to join the congregation. Sometimes, the rights which women had when legally married to a traditional leader were simply 'sacrificed' for the sake of the conversion of a leader.

I observed the customs of the Maka people, where the first wife of a leader had the right to employ other women to help her, who were also regarded as wives of the leader, but with lesser rights. This led to the unique situation in which the first wife made the decision about the lot of the other 'wives', when the husband joined the congregation.

On ministry of the church:

As, in the course of time, urban settlements developed, two types of pastors emerged: the pastor in the rural area who has to have his own garden, whom I would call a 'pastor with a digging stick or spade', and the pastor in town who is paid by his congregation and spends a lot of time in studying and attending to office work. So I would like to call him a 'pastor with a ballpen or pencil'. We need this type of pastor since, sometimes, the education of our lay leaders is not good or high enough to meet the challenge of working with people with a higher education in our congregations.

On new patterns of ministry:

In our work in the urban situation, we have to work with families. The family is the basic unit in the urban society, so we have to work with the individual family in order to strengthen our church. In former times, we used to work only with the male leaders of clans or villages, who made the decision for a big group to join the mission. Nowadays, help and counselling in the Social Concerns Office as an institution of the church is increasingly sought by individuals. When working with these individuals, we often find that the problems can be traced back to a family problem. So we have to start anew by working with the family, which in the urban setting is not the extended family, but the nuclear family, as in Western society.

We used to have the traditional patterns of older people intensively preparing young people for marriage. The clan also had a stabilizing effect on marriage by being involved in the preparation and maintenance of a stable marriage.

The church workers have to frequently visit couples and families, and we have to have good written material available to support his personal counselling.

On congregational meetings and the role of the District:

The big traditional meeting of the congregation no longer provides an adequate platform to deal with the problems of individual families. We have overlooked individuals and families to such an extent that many children even of prominent church leaders have turned their back on the church. We have not paid enough attention to this situation in which individual families are no longer ready to discuss openly their problems in the large congregational meetings. If we are not focusing on the individual family in our pastoral work, our church is not going to be strong.

On the level of the congregational assembly, we discuss matters of a wider scope, for example, who is going to go to a seminary to be trained as pastor. The congregational meeting is only the 'mouth'; the family represents the 'legs' and the 'hands', which actually move and work. The group gathered in the congregational meeting speaks about the direction and the aims of our church work, but the actual work is done and implemented by the family.

The church district has the task of coordinating the different activities and acting as a platform for sharing models and experiences in congregational work, thereby encouraging other congregations to benefit from successful models of church work tested and proved at the congregational level. We do not need a power structure working from the top to reach the bottom, but rather a model of sharing experiences from congregations on the grass-root level, for the benefit of other congregations belonging to the same church. We need a pattern which works from the bottom to the top, not a hierarchical structure working the other way around.

On the role of national church leadership:

I see the role of the Bishop and, to a lesser degree, the role of the Church Council as being charged, not in the first place with organizational tasks and executive functions, but primarily responsible for making sure that the preaching and teaching of the church is in accordance with the Gospel and the doctrines of the church. The Bishop has to be freed of managerial tasks and of responsibilities with regard to 'business and land matters'. He must be studying the Scriptures and teaching his pastors. Therefore, I would like to see a division between spiritual guidance and administrative tasks, as has been done in some Highlands districts, where they have the office of a District Bishop and a District President. The Bishop has to be 'clean'. He has the task of studying the Scriptures and seeing to it that the Word of God is preached in a good and proper way.

On personal motivation:

My name is Gedisa, which means in the Jabem language: 'He is risen', and a name is like a compass guiding a big ship. I was as a person called by God, and became an instrument of God's work for my people in my country.

Interview 4: with Honeo Gubung

(Teacher, leader, and President of the Sattelberg Circuit, Morobe Province)

Honeo Gubung,
President Sattelberg Circuit.

On changes:

When our fathers were baptized, they experienced a crucial turn from constant fear to peace. In the beginning, missionaries were involved in negotiations to bring about peace. One of the missionaries was a hot-tempered man who initiated a peace settlement prior to a big baptism. The power of the Gospel was reinforced or demonstrated by a big earth-tremor in 1906. Since the missionaries employed local myths, especially creation myths, it was easier for my fathers to accept the Gospel.

When my people turned to the Gospel, they had the expectation that they would also receive a share of the material goods of the Europeans. The local Christians soon took over missionary work. In the beginning, it was done on the initiative of the missionaries; but later we ourselves, also, were convinced that as we have received the good news we also want to pass it on to others. The spreading of the Gospel was organized in such a way that the missionaries and the local leaders kept in touch with their messengers, and encouraged them in their work in remote areas. In the beginning, the light was shining brightly, but later the congregations lost zeal and dedication. This was a result of outside influences and the observation by local Christians that the Gospel did not produce the expected results.

This attitude came to light quite clearly in the Eemasang Movement. [18] At that time, people used to say: 'The missionary deceived us by withholding the key for obtaining material things'. The local Christians regarded us leaders as siding with the white missionaries, and accused us also of refusing to open access to material belongings. I received letters containing this accusation, and I was even attacked by a person with a knife.

At the same time, the missionaries also suspected us of being involved in the 'cargo movement'. This left us leaders in quite a lonely position.

The movement was triggered partly by the young labourers who worked outside, far away from our closed Christian society back home. And back home, people also thought that the new way of life did not meet their material expectations, despite the fact that the mission had introduced coffee and coconuts as a means to earn money. But this, obviously, was not the answer to the questions and desires in the minds of some local Christians.

World War II was regarded partly as a time of punishment by God for not fully accepting his Word, and this led to a revival of church life in hiding-places in the jungle. On the other hand, the wealth of material objects, demonstrated so plentifully by American soldiers, gave rise to new speculations about ways and means to obtain a share in these goods. So, right after the war, suspicions regarding the whites, and aspirations to obtain 'cargo', surfaced again.

On church and business:

From 1960, our country saw the emergence of business activities, which changed traditional concerns. Rather than looking back to ensure the support of a benevolent God, people started to look to the future of their children. They kept asking themselves: 'What are the future prospects for my children if I as an individual am not involved in money-earning business activities?'

So the outside development encouraged individual heads of the nuclear family to perceive the future of their own children no longer in a framework of village community and communal development, but rather in individual efforts in establishing business activities. In this way, they hoped to secure the future of their children.

In this situation, we leaders of the church pointed to the imminent arrival of God's kingdom, which would give all these worries a secondary importance.

The spheres of life drifted apart. Despite considerable efforts by the church to promote commercial economic development, through communal societies (like Namasu) [19], we viewed economic development as something basically introduced and promoted by the Government. This did not lead to a turning away from the church. However, the emphasis of our people was

366

clearly directed toward economic development. People used to say: 'In town, business development is only possible under Europeans, so we prefer to start our own businesses in rural areas'.

Business and church activities are not seen by my people as mutually exclusive. But some Christians still regard *lotu* [church work] and *bisnis* [economic activities] as alternatives.

On aims of church work today:

Our main aim should be to strengthen the faith and spread the Gospel to the people. The times may have changed, but God and Jesus never change.

We put great emphasis on patrols. Basically we, the Sattelberg congregations, have not changed our ways of working. We Sattelbergers want to follow our own proven way of working.

The National Church and the District give us a few impulses, but we base our work on the insights we have gained from many years of experience. The work of the National Church and the District shows only small results.

On Youth and Women's Work:

Traditionally, the parents were responsible for their children. Today, our young people are looking for their own ways. But we want to keep them in the church.

Women's work has produced some results, but we are going to watch further development.

On life and work of the congregations:

The congregation has become tired. Some say: 'We have contributed a lot, and this kind of work is completed'. Some say: 'Because most of the work is done in Pidgin, we Kate-speaking people cannot contribute any more'. The real reason, however, is that they think only of themselves.

One means of strengthening our work is the conducting of courses for headmen [elders]. In former times, we had the teacher/evangelist, who was the backbone of the work in a congregation. Since we no longer have them, the elders must be trained for the work.

We do not receive any help from outside, no stimulation from visitors. The leadership of the church is far away. At best, they write a letter. My congregations do not know the leaders of the District or the National Church.

On personal motivation:

We church workers know that God has entrusted this earth to us to work on it. In our struggle with 'cargo cult' adherents, we have been strengthened by what Paul writes (in his letter to the Galatians in chapters 3 and 5) about faith and things which are not true or are of a devious nature.

Jesus has paid for my sins. He has promised that we will join him in heaven. This promise has prompted me to work for him. Not because of our merits, but by the grace of God through Jesus, we will be going to heaven. I see this promise and, therefore, I do my work, and as an old man I still work with the church, even climbing steep mountains in my work.

Interview 5: with Sanangke Dole
(Bishop of the Mount Hagen District)

Sanangke Dole,
Bishop Hagen District.

On changes:

Things have changed quite rapidly. In the 1960s, all of the circuits had an expatriate missionary. Things simply changed. We were forced to develop a new way of working when we had fewer and fewer missionaries. We were pleasantly surprised when a gang of youngsters became Christian youth leaders, as in Teka. [17] I see more young people, today, who are ready to work for the church.

God has brought about this change. Many people in our country think only of good education, which will lead them to well-paid jobs. But this has changed, too. Quite a number have heard of our new 'work mission areas', [20] and are ready to work there. This is partly also the result of a determined effort to work with young people, since we are in danger of losing them to small groups and sects. In this respect, our work has changed. In earlier times we turned to heathen in order to baptize them. We have seen the results of this work, but we also noticed that today the children of these former heathens are about to become heathen again. This calls for our attention and action. I received many letters from young people who have big problems. We must, therefore, pay more attention to young people. But the young ones are no longer living in the villages. They attend schools, and they roam around in towns. Therefore, we have to follow them and find them in towns and schools. In former times all the people lived in the villages. Nowadays, the youngsters are in town, and they are in danger of being caught by sects.

On the work of pastors and elders:
Pastors mainly work in villages, but their work-load is not distributed evenly. Some have to attend to too many villages. Their training does not equip them for their work. They learn a lot of theory, but not enough about how to apply it to actual situations. They know that they have to preach on Sundays, but it's not clear to them that they should be visiting the homes of individual families together with the elders. If a pastor does not know his congregation, he will not reach them in his sermon. A pastor has to work closely with his elders.

He has to cooperate with them. He himself will be strengthened by this close cooperation. A pastor has to work with and through the elders. He has to train elders. These headmen are in a position to help the pastor when he has problems with his congregation. The elders are like the strong posts (on which a house is built), for they carry the work. The pastor should be the spiritual animator of the elders. The elders are like the heart, which pumps blood into the veins. (This is the situation in the rural areas. The situation in towns may be different, but I have to study this situation first.)

As the people are scattered all over town, we have problems in visiting them. The churches are well attended in town. People really want to hear God's Word. But we have to establish a network of elders in town, too. First we have to discover the strong Christians, offer them courses, and form small cells or centres from where they can work with people in their settlements.

On church:
Individual Christians have no idea what we mean when we talk about 'church'. We know it is the 'community of saints', but this is not common knowledge for most Christians. When somebody belongs to a congregation, he wants worship services and the Lord's Supper. But the fact that the individual Christian is a member of the big community of saints is not widely known.

When people belong to a congregation, then they want to build their own church first. But when they are asked to contribute to the work of the District or the National Church, they hardly respond.

We have to invest a lot of work yet to make it clear to the individual members of a congregation that they are part of a bigger unit, the church.

When they received their baptismal instruction, this idea was not part of what the evangelist taught them. They told the Bible stories, and said: When you learn them well, you will be baptized and you are on the Christian road. But the people were not taught about the church.

On international connections of the church:
When ELC, the Districts, or Circuits hear about overseas churches, they think in the following way: The road of the Gospel came from them. So support for the Gospel work has also to come from them.

Local congregation and National Church:
The local congregation is, in spiritual terms, the church. We will go to heaven without the help of the central office in Lae. As far as financial support is concerned, that is different. Many congregations expect to receive outside help. This is sad, because when we receive something, the blessing remains with those who give. If we give, the blessing remains with us.

Many people say: 'I feel I am the church (in spiritual terms). But when it comes to giving, I feel others are the church'.

On future perspective of work:
First, I want to find out who is ready to work for God, and who is like a car without a battery, and constantly has to be pushed. I want to start working with the active members of the congregation, who in turn by their good example can reach others and set them in motion. This is our way of working in Hagen. If people see something illustrated by a clear example, they will be set in motion by this example.

On personal motivation:
For me, Romans chapter 8 is important: 'Nothing shall separate me from the love of God'.

Many prayers are answered only after years. The same happened to me in the process of understanding many parts of the Bible. Despite the answers of my teacher, many things in the Bible were not clear to me. But now I feel many things in the Bible have become clear to me.

I see God answering my prayers by making so many people ready to work with us.

I have experienced in my life that God knows my problems and needs. Many a time I did not know how I could get soap, kerosene, and other things. But God has sent somebody who helped me. God's big net-bag is full of blessing and grace. And every morning when we get up and start our work, he empties his net-bag on us. The Lord's blessing is not hidden. We realize it in our work, our life, and in our family.

I shall work hard in order to keep us co-workers united, to help many people to join God's kingdom. To listen to and to bear problems of others is for me a sign of God's blessing. If people no longer talk openly to me about their problems, I remain no longer under God's burden, but also no longer under God's blessing.

Interviews 6 and 7: with Bapiangnu Sike
(President of the Kate District, Morobe Province) and **Sam Sorenu** (Teacher and Stewardship Director of the Kate District, Morobe Province)

Bapiangnu Sike,
President Kate District.

On commissioning of workers:
The congregation is no longer the sending body for their workers. They are stationed by the Church Council after they have completed their training. This is a very impersonal procedure. The congregation is deprived of its right to send its messengers, and, therefore, is not continuing the old practice of a public festive service of farewell for them, strengthening them, accompanying them, and keeping in contact with them during their time of service. This new practice of sending workers without close cooperation, not to speak of initiatives, by the home congregation, is mainly practiced with pastors graduating from Martin Luther Seminary. They are viewed by their home

congregation in line with other students who attend tertiary institutions to get trained for a well-paid job. The key to this job is assumed to be the certificate attesting the successful completion of their studies.

On stewardship:
The members of the congregations have money, but they are not motivated to give. There is competition between the need to support a worker and the contributions that are asked for the work of the District and the National Church.

The system of giving and receiving should not be initiated by the District or on the Circuit level, but on the congregational level. If, for example, a congregation receives a new pastor, they do not feel a special obligation to support the seminary that trained him, but rather they are worried at the prospect of having to provide for an additional worker.

Sam Sorenu:
The most pressing need for the church is not institutions, but care for the workers the church already has. If there is not enough food available for the two visitors already in my house, I do not invite new guests.

On elders:
Elders in villages are facing tough competition from other village leaders, such as community government officials, teachers, medical staff, etc. Many people claim to be leaders today. Therefore, leaders of the congregation must be well qualified and ready to compete successfully with other leaders to establish their leadership. This necessitates a good training program for elders, so that they can offer satisfying options or solutions for the villagers, not only in terms of 'religious affairs' but also in other concerns of a village.

Their insights in, and understanding of, the complexity of today's village problems also require them to have a good grasp of the present economic and political development in PNG. The old, proven, and respected part of traditional leadership has to be upgraded in order to maintain or regain their leading role in village affairs.

We cannot take it for granted that church elders are good preachers, not to speak of their ability to cope with the sects and small religious groups which are increasingly turning to the villages. Both functions of a religious leader in a village require a solid grounding in Scripture, and, at least, basic knowledge about fundamental aspects of the teachings and practices of sects.

369

President Bapiangnu Sike:

The elders themselves feel a desperate need for such training, and keep asking the District to make efforts to re-establish this training program. [21] The Mount Hagen District also feels the need for such a program.

ELC-PNG will never be in a position to station pastors in every village. And the villages will not be able to maintain a church worker coming from outside. The many villages of PNG, therefore, need able and well-qualified elders, who are already established in the village and are living their life like the rest of the villagers.

On relationship between institutions and congregations:

By establishing central offices in a District, one only creates the wrong impression that things are taken care of. And the villagers no longer feel responsible for making their own efforts on the grass-roots level. They will only say: 'We now have an institution or an office to take care of this work, so our own efforts are not needed any longer'.

We now have, for example, chaplains in central hospitals. So, people in the villages feel they no longer have to care for and visit their sick people in town.

The villages which used to be the very centre of church work, feel more and more left alone. Their influence is dwindling. Villagers no longer feel important and responsible. Institutions seem to be taking over their contribution. They also no longer feel involved in the decision-making process. The actions of the church and the government are neither understood nor supported by them, because they were not included in the process of discussion leading to decisions.

Sam Sorenu:

What the church and the government are doing to the villagers is like a big box containing a number of things the villagers do not know and do not understand. Nobody is close to the villagers these days.

Bapiangnu Sike:

It is of central importance that the leaders of the church maintain or re-establish personal communication with the villagers. A letter or any other form of 'paper communication' is in PNG rural society no substitute for meaningful personal communication. Visits with congregations also give the leader a chance to maintain his roots in the village. There is a possibility of the village 'forgetting' somebody if he is not seen for a long time. And, on the other hand, the villagers and the members of the church lose the feeling of belonging if they are not visited by their leaders.

Sam Sorenu:

The villagers are utterly confused. Some circuits still draw from the presence of an overseas worker as their 'figure of integration' in a wider context, or from the past experiences of working together with such a person.

On the 'inner situation' of the church, as reflected in stewardship:

Sam Sorenu:

If I look at the church from within, it is like a sow worrying only about how to fill her stomach and pushing aside the hungry piglets. If I look at it from the outside, it is like a featherless bird sitting in his nest waiting to be fed by somebody. I use this illustration to point to an attitude of my church with regard to contributions coming from overseas partner churches and money-earning business ventures, and I regard them as 'food' for the featherless bird in his nest.

To come back to my first illustration about the sow: I wanted to illustrate the selfish behaviour of the congregation, seeing collections only as an attack on the money in their pockets. Even the former bishop's 'work mission appeal' [22] was basically seen as an attempt to pull out money from people's pockets.

The pastors are sometimes careful not to encourage too much giving for the District, the institutions, or the National Church. They are afraid that they may not get enough salary if too much money is given for 'outside purposes'.

Even the elders are often somehow half-heartedly appealing to the congregations, for fear the pastor may be getting too much money.

We fail in educating the congregations by making them aware of how much God has given to them as the central motive for their giving.

Giving by congregational members has decreased. When they still gave garden products and animals, the value of collections was higher. By reducing the giving to money I see two dangers: 1) Amounts of up to one or ten shillings was still good giving in former times, but is not sufficient today. Old 'targets' in giving, which are no longer adequate, are still customarily observed. 2) Cash is still quite scarce in villages, and many items can only be obtained by using cash (like school fees, taxes, and household items). Giving should, therefore, to a much greater extent include crops and animals, which are not as scarce as money is in villages.

Coming back to the illustration of the sow: She is not aware that the food she greedily swallows is given to her by God.

Bapiangnu Sike:

In this connection I would like to refer to the fourth petition in the Lord's Prayer.

On personal motivation:
Sam Sorenu:

God granted me insights which he has not granted in the same way to others. Therefore, I am under obligation to do my work, regardless of what others think and do. We have to help our people. We are not eager to enhance our own reputation, but we are eager to help the people to change, and to understand God's will. Therefore, we continue to work.

Interview 8: with Sila Esori
(Voluntary Women's Worker of the Goroka District, Eastern Highlands Province)

*Sila Esori, Women's Worker
Goroka District.*

On changes and growth in Women's Work:

Women's Work as an organized branch of church work originated in the towns, and gradually spread to the rural areas. On a number of out-stations, however, women's work was started by wives of missionaries with house girls and wives of local church workers. The first local people in charge of this work were pastors and evangelists. The local women only contributed by giving crops as offerings.

I left my village when I married my husband, who belonged to a different tribe. At the time of our marriage, my husband was not yet baptized. So, my first missionary task was to bring my husband closer to my church [Comment of her husband: 'Sila persuaded me to come to church services, so I was baptized'].

When I came to Goroka in 1966, there was no women's work done; we only attended the regular church services. When women's work was started, I attended the gatherings. In one of these meetings, the leader asked me to pray publicly. Although I prayed regularly in my home, I had never prayed in public before. So, I asked the other women to close their eyes while I was praying so that they would not see my face and realize that I was trembling. This 'success' gave me the courage to pray regularly in meetings of our women's group and gradually to take a more active part in the group, like reading biblical texts, and, first with the help of an expatriate women's worker and then on my own, to lead Bible studies. Besides regular meetings and Bible studies, we also had a course to learn knitting, and we were in charge of keeping the church clean and decorating it for services. Later, we also took over Sunday-school work. When I had to lead my first Bible study for a national women's meeting, I 'practised' it first in Sunday-school in my small group.

When the overseas women's worker left, I was alone in charge of a local women's group in North Goroka. It was hard for the other local women to accept a leading role by a local women. The men were happy with our work, as we supported church work with our collections.

We continued to work with local women in charge of the group. But we also invited wives of expatriate church workers to join us. And, together with them, we also started making blankets and hand-bags, and making visits in the hospital to bring food and books to the patients, to listen to them and to pray with them. We also had visits to the gaol, with services for the prisoners, and especially we cared for female inmates.

When the activities of our group grew, and we used the money we collected for our own expanding work, this aroused the jealousy and indignation of the male church leaders. And some of them started to question and discredit our activities. They even tried to split our group and hinder our activities, especially in gaol. This had partly to do with envy caused by our successful work, and partly with our gaining independence in financial matters as well.

We readily accepted and included in our program some initiatives by expatriate women in social and diaconal work. When some of the women from overseas left, we somewhat scaled down our activities but carried on with the work. A big boost for our activities was the hosting of the national women's course in Goroka. In preparation for that event, we also involved the women from the rural areas and prepared Bible studies for the national

371

conference. In this way, we were able to make an input on the national level and share our experience with women's groups from different districts.

We also extended our programs to rural areas. We conducted courses for women's group and women's leaders. This was a good experience for the women in the circuits, as well as for us. In looking back, I would like to say that our roles have changed. The Europeans started the work; in the meantime, we local women reached a clear concept about our role, and the expatriate women only joined us in a supportive manner.

We took an active part in supporting the former bishop's 'work mission appeal', and in helping poorer circuits with clothing, as well as supporting two evangelists in heathen areas. We also care for the mentally handicapped in the Goroka hospital.

On women's work and training institutions:

There is good cooperation. We help them sometimes. Students are good in doing Sunday-school work, but they lack experience and are not too effective in women's work. We do not get many impulses for district women's work from the institutions.

On women's work and congregation:

There are benefits from our work. We keep the district leaders informed about our activities. Usually we get support and cooperation from pastors in our courses in rural areas in our programs. Circuits are open for this new kind of work. Top district leadership is supporting us.

On women's work done by Government:

There is good cooperation. They do the same work as we are doing, or, more accurately, they are using our work as the basis for theirs.

A certain danger lies in the Government's readiness to give subsidies too quickly. This is sometimes the cause of friction. Some groups are founded just to have a basis for a financial request to the Government.

On the main emphasis of women's work:

We work with mothers to achieve positive results for their family and the Christian congregation. We want the women to realize that they are worth something and have a mandate for work in the church. Our church is a 'male-dominated' church. Mission work was mainly concerned with men and leaders of tribes. The church did not pay much attention to women.

On personal motivation:

Nobody has appointed me to do this work, and nobody is paying me for my work. That is one of

372

the reasons I was always able to maintain my 'independence' over against interferences from male church workers, and it kept me faithfully in a work I myself chose to do.

Initially, my husband did not support my work. But he later supported my work, because he realized it is worthwhile to help other families to live together in the same harmonious and peaceful way in which we are living together in our own family. The parable of the three servants in Matthew 25 made me actively start women's work. I did not want to hide God's present, so I started to do this work.

Interview 9: with Pastor Uram Panok
(Circuit President of the Wanuma-Circuit, Madang District, Madang Province)

Uram Panok, President Wanuma Circuit.

On changes:

In the beginning, the people in Wanuma readily accepted the Gospel. The fights ceased. First baptisms took place. School work was started.

When representatives of the Government reached Wanuma, things changed, and the Mission was no longer so well received. People started to plant and sell coffee, and to engage in trade-store businesses. Their attention shifted from church to business. But today people realize that the business returns from coffee and trade stores are quite meagre, and so they are searching for the right road.

When the first missionary built the mission station, the expectations of the local people started to grow. So they helped voluntarily and full of joy, without asking for payment, to build up the station. They received only a small amount of money for their help to buy clothes and salt. The people were quite content, and hoped the situation would remain like that.

When, however, the Government took over the airstrip and paid full wages for work at the airstrip, and when the Agriculture Department started some projects, especially the young people started to say: 'The missionaries only told us a useless story without relevance. They just deceived us. Now we are seeing real positive results.' They started their own trade stores and other business activities, and were no longer active or interested in the church work.

But these activities, which were mainly started by young people, did not bring the results expected, so the older people said to the younger ones: 'Your activities are not successful either. We, the old ones, at least experienced the end of constant fighting and the end of bad and shameful magical practices. This experience meant an important change in our lives.'

When the younger ones embarked on business activities they also made use of magical practices, and in doing so felt encouraged by the constant stressing of 'local customs' by government voices like Prime Minister Michael Somare.

When an expatriate missionary wanted to discuss their magical practices [especially ritual killings: *sanguma*] with the local *sanguma* experts, they did not show up for this discussion, giving the following reason: 'The whites are not ready to reveal their secrets, so we are also not going to reveal our own secrets'.

At baptism, only some of the magical objects were burnt or openly exposed; some were still kept by the people.

When mission work was started in Wanuma, people were ready to change their way of life and accept the Christian way of life. They just kept a few of their magical objects to have a possibility to revive the old practices again, should the need arise to use them again.

On the diminishing of initial joy and trust:

The combination of developmental ideas introduced by Government with old magical practices was the decisive factor. Admittedly, the Mission was also busy in the area of development, but the scope and the financial backing of government programs led people to feel: Now we are experiencing the real thing. The real power is with the Government.

In earlier times (the times of first contact with the Mission), we thought: The Mission offers the road to success, but now we see the Government shows us the real road to success.

So, people were very enthusiastic about government activities, and when turning away

from church activities they also turned away from God's Word.

But this enthusiasm also faded, as the government activities did not produce the expected results.

Today, they have a lot of second thoughts: Maybe we have left a good road. So, many are coming back to the church; they build new churches, and ask for evangelists. But some are still following the old way.

On the work of circuit leadership:

We started to work joyfully, but soon encountered many problems. This was the time when we conducted many courses to strengthen our co-workers. But when back in their place of work, they had a lot of problems. So, we visited the co-workers in their villages. But those patrols or visits were not successful, either, as we did not stay long enough. Now, we stay for one week in a village and conduct courses. This way we are able to strengthen our co-workers.

On future emphasis of work:

More young people must have theological training in the seminaries. And more workers must work closer and more intensively with smaller congregations.

The big church services alone cannot change the life of men.

The real missionary work is to work with individuals in their houses. We have to start by taking his problems seriously. We cannot speak about God's Word too soon. Finally, we must pray together.

The big conversions and baptisms brought about by tribal leaders are not sufficient. I must visit people while they are doing their work in the garden, and then talk about the work they are doing. I cannot immediately talk about God's Word. If we have sufficient workers who live and work close to the people, the church will become strong.

On congregations:

The people are not bad, but they do not know Jesus well enough, yet. So they have problems, and we, consequently, have problems, too.

It is our first aim to revive and strengthen the congregation, and to reactivate what they have learnt when they were baptized.

The church of tomorrow will be a church of the young people who today are still trying to find their way. But I see them stand up and reach this goal. I do not regard the congregation as big-headed. They are just like sheep without a shepherd.

On preaching and the Lord's Supper:

If I am not prepared well and, consequently, my preaching is poor, the congregation becomes tired.

There are some who purposely do not participate in the Lord's Supper. They are afraid their magical power might become weak. This kind of people are very hard to bring back to the congregation. Some want to stay in both camps. They want to be people participating in evil practices and, at the same time, to stay in the light. They are far away from the church, because their thoughts and what they say do not correspond.

On personal motivation:

I have experienced God's blessing in my life, the life of my family, and in my garden. Even in hard times, this blessing has kept me. When I was young, I knew a lot of heathen practices, as I was the son of a chief. But I soon discovered that this is not good. The Holy Spirit called me. I went to an evangelist-training school, and was baptized when I completed this training. I was totally inexperienced when I started my work. But it was not me alone who walked this road. Somebody kept holding my hand. So, I do not want to leave this hand.

When a young man comes to me who is willing to work for the church, then I tell him that my experience with God has been a good one. Be prepared for this experience. It will not be easy. But he has used me, a weak human being, as his tool. He will also use you and strengthen you for his work.

Interview 10: with Bamokenare Ateike

(Teacher, President of the Ulap Circuit, Kate District, Morobe Province)

Bamokenare Ateike, President Ulap Circuit.

374

On changes:

I noticed a marked change in the attitude of the people toward the church in the years 1940 to 1942. Prior to that time, people were very much concerned with church work.

At the start of the missionary work, everyone was full of joy and followed God's Word. The Word of God brought an end to fighting, and initiated a way of living together peacefully in harmony. During that time, we had no 'second thoughts' [about having accepted the Gospel]. Prior to that time, we lived in fear, especially of *sanguma* [ritual killings].

Due to the power of the Holy Spirit, people were converted; a large number were baptized and became evangelists. They thought: 'Since we are baptized now and follow God's path, the Lord will take us and lead us into heaven'. They were motivated by biblical texts such as Revelation chapter 21.

At that time they willingly followed the authority of their Christian leaders, especially the elders, evangelists, and teachers.

When they were baptized, they thought: 'Now our way to heaven is open'. They were very active before baptism, but once they were baptized their zeal ceased. They thought: 'We have reached the goal, so now we don't have to be active any longer'.

In the span of time from conversion to World War II, the main problem for the church work was the attitude of the people who thought by being baptized they already had their 'ticket to heaven'. But this attitude — although it was prevalent in all congregations — was at that time never openly articulated.

During World War II, people had the experience of God helping them in a beneficial manner. We continued to work. We carried the school desks into the jungle to continue school work. All Christians hid in the jungle, and we experienced the power of God during this time.

We also saw soldiers with a lot of equipment and an over-abundance of everything. This observation gave rise to the following ideas: All these things were not produced by the whites, but by our ancestors. The whites got hold of all these products by closing the 'door' on us. Instead of delivering the goods to us, the rightful owners, they kept the goods for themselves.

These ideas came into existence during the 'big fight' [World War II]. We, the church workers, were not idle; we prayed, and God gave us strength to subdue these ideas. Nowadays, it looks as if these thoughts no longer prevail, but we do not know for sure what the thoughts of the people are. Outwardly, it looks as if this kind of thinking has ended in our area.

On role of local church workers in this situation: [23]
The people said to us: 'You are only the labour boys of the whites. Just look at your poor standard of living, and compare it to the high standard of the whites'. But we kept saying to them: 'We know that the goods of the whites are a result of their hard work. God told Adam already: "In the sweat of your face you shall eat bread ..." (Gen. 3:19).'

On missionaries and other whites:
The standard of living of missionaries was regarded by some people as the same as other white people. But some people also saw a difference, as the missionaries stayed overnight with the people in a village and walked our steep mountains.

At that time, we were unaware that the missionaries were so well supported and equipped by their home churches. We only discovered that after we had access to the financial reports which were made available to us after ELCONG was founded.

During the war, we observed how the whites handled all their equipment (machinery, ships, etc.) and their supplies in such a careless manner that we could not help but get the impression that their affluence is unlimited.

These attitudes and observations are still in the people's minds today. But the power of the Holy Spirit is at work, and has changed the ideas of some people.

On church workers:
The main problem, today, is that many church workers think or say: 'If we receive sufficient money from the congregation, then we are in a position to do good work'. If this does not happen, then their work is without zeal. Many of the young workers, I am afraid to say, lack inner commitment to their work.

The congregations do not neglect the church worker completely. They say: 'If you do good work among us, then we are also prepared to support you well'.

I can speak of my own experience. I worked for ten years in Sio, and the congregation hardly helped me at all. I built my house. I worked as a teacher full-time, and conducted services regularly. In contrast to my own experience, today I observe that the new workers are asking for high salaries. But when people, the congregation, are under the impression that the worker is not working hard enough, they see no reason to give him a higher salary.

The new church workers have a different attitude than we old church workers. The consequences are obvious: Both the workers and the congregation lack motivation for good cooperation, and the work collapses.

We are aware of this problem. Therefore, we visit the congregations and their workers frequently to strengthen workers and congregations, and to stop the effects of this development.

We, the old workers, are waiting for our reward in heaven, but the church workers nowadays want their reward here and now. What happens later is at God's discretion.

If the Holy Spirit is at work in them, the younger workers will understand what we older workers try to tell them. The younger ones also know what the aim of church work is. But I see the Holy Spirit and God's power at work to change this situation.

On National Church and congregation:
The local congregation is God's congregation, and is the very root of the church. There is a danger of regarding only the District or ELC-PNG as church, not the local congregation.

On other influences:
The competition between government and church is not so central in our area as in other areas. The effects of business ventures are negative only to a certain extent.

On leaders and elders:
To strengthen the church and her work, it is necessary for leaders on the circuit, district, and national church level to frequently visit congregations and workers.

The local elders have a central position as mediators between congregations and their workers. They have the task of explaining the basic concerns of God's Word distinctly. They are the ones who are close to the people; therefore, courses for elders are of the utmost importance. The young elders themselves want good training.

Interview 11: with Zabut Nail

(Pastor, former Youth Coordinator of the Madang District, Madang Province)

Pastor Zabut Nail, Madang District.

On cooperation between local and overseas church workers:

We always sat together to discuss and plan our work. We local pastors and elders, together with you expatriate workers, always worked as a team. One of the team was not instructing or teaching others; we contributed equally. We worked together on an equal platform. No one was superior.

Things were different when I was a pastor in Wewak. There I no longer had the possibility of a fruitful exchange with an expatriate partner. So I fully turned to my congregation. I made many visits to be in a position to get to know my congregation better and, consequently, to help the members of my congregation in a better way. I showed my face everywhere: in the streets, in the cinema, together with my family at 'social nights', in the local hotel. I did not talk about services or prayers; I just wanted to be close to my congregation. I looked for my sheep wherever I could find them. The telephone became an important instrument of my ministry. This work, which was accompanied by constant prayer, gave me a lot of joy — no matter whether I was working with our people in the army, the police force, or among the refugees.

After that period, I took over as youth coordinator of the Madang District. I found a lot of challenges, and I was introduced to a number of interesting tasks. Some of the District leaders showed reponsibility, while others were not ready to give things over to other co-workers. At that time, I

started to realize that the leadership of the District was constantly quarrelling among themselves. This led to the withdrawal of many able workers to their own villages or own areas of work. The work on District level was just going around in circles. Nobody thought ahead (of the future). Everybody blamed lack of money for this state of affairs. But I kept working for 12 Kina in half a year. We still have a lot of meetings, but we are not encouraging each other any more to look for creative ways of cooperation.

There is an office, there are people who are responsible, but the connections with the individual congregations are no longer functioning. We have gatherings of congregations, we have discussions, we have services, but we are lacking direction. It is of utmost importance to visit each other, to see each other.

We have elders, we have congregations who are ready for cooperation, but they hardly see their leaders.

On headmen and the congregation:

In former times, we used to have six headmen who were recognized as leaders, who were able to keep the people together as a group and work together with the people. When the bell rang, people encouraged each other to go the services, and so they attended their services full of joy. After the service, the elders sat together with the people discussing church work and encouraging their people to join in congregational activities. Each part of the village had Bible studies and prayer meetings.

But today the headmen no longer fulfil their task, no longer inform the congregation, no longer lead the congregation. They are no longer the shepherds who lead their flock in order to keep the flock alive. Some people go to church, some stay in their houses. They no longer rejoice about God's Word. A lot of quarrelling goes on. There are a lot of problems. One reason for this is the poor way of preaching. People cannot eat only bananas. No, they also have to eat taros and many other things.

For many today, their house has become only a place to sleep in. They no longer discuss things with their wives, their families, their congregation. Today we talk about our gardens, about business. But some are still spiritually alive.

On perspectives of church work:

First, we have to analyse the situation. We have nobody to thoroughly analyse the situation. The elders are not of one mind. If they were of one mind, the work would progress.

The leadership is weak. Who will revive the congregation? We have to turn back to the old way of doing theings when we worked cheerfully.

We again need the old charismatic leaders, who were able to inspire the congregation. This is the task of the pastors today. The most important thing is to revive the congregation. Even the Lord's Supper, Baptism, and other congregational activities are of secondary importance; but the pastor has to revive (give new life to) the congregation.

Interview 12: with Yara Muramel
(District Youth Coordinator of the Hagen District, and leader of the Teka youth revival movement)

Yara Muramel,
District Youth Leader Mt Hagen.

On experience with the life of the church (congregation) prior to his conversion:
The life and activities of the congregation did not present anything that attracted me or made me feel like joining these activities. It was simply of no interest to me. They only sang hymns. The sermons I heard did not attract me. I was mildly interested in guitar music. So, after my conversion I thought songs with the guitar have to be part of the church's program. This should make services more attractive. The services must not be boring. They must be filled with life and joy to attract people.

I did not go to church, because nobody made any efforts to be close to us young people and invite us. Nobody was our father or shepherd. Nobody pursued me and was ready to become my father. As we were a big congregation, the pastor was only busy administering the sacraments.

The headmen acted as if they were responsible only for those who were already firm members of the congregation. They did preach, but after they had preached they did not think much about their sermons in their daily life. They even participated in our stolen goods (loot).

The evangelist was busy only with his confirmation class. I accepted what he told us in confirmation instruction, but he did not oppose our gang practices.

On examples of Christian life:
I did not see any attractive example, not even outside my own congregation. I did not discover any attractive example in other churches, either. I found out in this period of my life that the church was concerned only with the leaders of the village. At Christmas, for example, they presented dramas directed at the leaders of the village (with subjects like *Moka* [big pig exchanges]), their own reputation, and their own conversion. But we young people felt that all of that had nothing to do with our life. Something else which drove me out of the services was the custom of having to sit quietly. So we used to fall asleep, and, consequently, told the church workers we might as well sleep in our houses.

On preaching and prayers:
The parables used in preaching were aiming only at the old people (with illustrations like *Moka*). But we were no longer familiar with these old customs, and we were not touched or reached by these parables, which we did not understand.

Their prayers never touched me. They prayed for an awfully long time. But I was not clear about their prayers. So I felt like sleeping. If only they had told us something about the meaning of prayer, it would have been easier for us. But they only said: 'Let's pray'. We had to learn the Lord's Prayer by heart, but we were not clear about the meaning and purpose of prayer.

On attractive services for young people:
Singing and joyful songs make the services attractive for us young people. Songs with guitar and drums will attract young and old ones alike. The music attracts them, so they attended the services.

Lame songs do not awake a congregation. We must employ drama and plays. That is something people will understand. There must be something that attracts the little ones, the young ones, and the grown-ups at the same time. We must choose songs which appeal to all three groups. It should be the same way with the sermons. We have to find out who has the gift of preaching, so people are not bored when listening to a sermon.

For services with young people, we also change the liturgy. Liturgy is only a crutch for those lacking creativity, or for those too lazy to prepare services well. Before praying, we prepare the congregation by saying, for example: Now we speak with God. The same applies to preaching: We must be ready now to listen to the Word of God.

When I attended a 'social night', everything was diligently explained. We knew what was going on, and we could easily follow. It must be like that in church, too. People must be clear about what is happening.

On the church:

The church is like a man. The National Office is like the head with eyes, ears, and mouth. The middle part of the body is the District. That is the biggest part of the body. It digests the food, and thus channels energy to the individual members of the body. The hands are the various departments of a District, like women's work, youth work, etc. The legs are the Circuits. But the place where a human being touches the ground and walks on the ground is the congregation. The congregation carries the whole body. If a human being has no legs, he cannot walk and cannot move.

On the Christian way of life:

The old people have not changed. They still live as they used to live in former times. It is different with the young people. We invite young people to our services when we are together with them in town or in the market. They come to us, and sometimes stay overnight in our village, because they find our services attractive.

When they see that young people no longer steal, rape, and drink, they feel attracted. They also want to try out the road we are following. Some also tried to pull me back to my old way of life. When I remained steadfast, it made them think a lot.

We church workers have to change in such a way that our life and our deeds are not apart (are corresponding).

On the motive of conversion:

Our life on this earth is short, and will soon come to an end. Therefore, I was attracted by the perspective of a life that is eternal. This perspective for eternal life also keeps me from going (sliding) back to something which lasts only for a short period of time. Many young people feel this way today. Young people experience in our services, in our gathering, a prefiguration of life eternal. That is something they want to hang on to.

Endnotes

[1] I did not interview the 'Head Bishop' of the ELC-PNG, the Rt Revd Getake Gam; I wanted to spare him any possible embarrassment as a person in the highest authority in ELC-PNG.

[2] Gedisa is now 75 years of age, Honeo is well over 70, and Mambu is 63 years old.

[3] See Interview 2.

[4] See end of Interview 2.

[5] See Interview 3.

[6] See Interview 4.

[7] See Interview 10.

[8] See Interview 9.

[9] See Interview 12.

[10] See Interview 3.

[11] See Interview 5.

[12] See Interview 2.

[13] See Interview 8.

[14] See also Interviews 6 and 7.

[15] Sir Zurewe Zurenuo became the first local 'Head Bishop' in 1973; Mambu became District President of the Hagen District in 1968, and Bishop of the Hagen District in 1972.

[16] Bishop Zurewe issued the 'Declaration of Autonomy' on July 2, 1976.

[17] Yara Muramel (see Interview 12) was a former gang leader of a gang of young criminals from Teka village near Mt Hagen. After his conversion in prison, he and other gang leaders and members became active church members and church workers. Yara Muramel is at present coordinator of youth work in the Hagen District.

[18] 'This religious movement was initiated by Christian leaders in an attempt to revive and strengthen the flagging faith and life of the people', John G. Strelan, *Search for Salvation* (Adelaide: Lutheran Publishing House, 1977), 21. See also J. Strelan's contribution in this volume, ch 15.

[19] *Native Marketing and Supply Service Ltd* — in short, Namasu — was started in 1959 by LMNG, and had strong roots and many shareholders in the Finschhafen and Sattelberg area (see ch 18).

[20] Each District of ELC-PNG is responsible for remote areas at the fringes of the Districts as special 'work mission areas'. In the same category belong traditionally non-Lutheran areas, where nowadays a number of Lutheran migrants are spiritually taken care of by the 'older' Districts of ELC-PNG.

[21] Elders' training was started again in Heldsbach. After a break of some years, this training, which was originally started by the Revd H. Gerber, was resumed in mid-1985 under the leadership of Pastor Bonene.

[22] This appeal was initiated and promoted with much emphasis by Bishop Zurewe. The money collected was to support the first 'overseas missionary' of ELC-PNG, the Revd Nawon Mellombo, who was the first PNG pastor to work with Aborigines in the Lutheran Church of Australia.

[23] See also Interview 4.

Chapter 12

The Church and its Ministry

by Helmut Horndasch

In spite of the fact that ELC-PNG has had its origin in the work of missionaries from various overseas churches, it has not adopted the form of any of its supporting churches in the development of its ministry. While the supporting churches follow the pattern of one ordained ministry, ELC-PNG has developed its own characteristic form of multiple ministry. Not just one, but a variety of ministries equally share in the responsibility for carrying out the work of the church. In other words, ELC-PNG is not a clerical church centered around the office of the pastor, but, rather, a congregations' church with many members sharing in the bearing of church responsibility. The local congregation as a whole is acting out its church responsibilities.

Up to the present time, participation of non-ordained members in the preaching of the Word and in the governing of the church is quite evident. For half a century, the office of elder was of greater significance for the life of the church than the ordained ministry. In such 'living congregations', as Keysser used to call them, able Christians took turns in leading the daily devotions. Admonition aimed at Christian conduct in the community was exercised mutually. From there it was only a minor step for Sunday services and Christian education, the visiting of the sick, funerals, marriage instruction and weddings, the hearing of confessions and handling cases of church discipline, to be also carried out and/or supervised by the congregation itself.

In such expressions of congregational life lie the very beginnings of the spiritual ministry in ELC-PNG, long before theological seminaries were established, and qualified men were formally trained for and ordained to the Ministry of the church.

Fontius, when speaking about the very first beginnings of Christian witnessing by New Guineans to New Guineans, called them 'pre-forms of the ministry'. His criterion for doing so was the very fact that those early witnesses were carrying the Word of reconciliation (2 Cor. 5:19) to places and people who had not yet heard it. This is never done unless the Holy Spirit prompts people to do so. [1] If this is a legitimate theological interpretation of their Christian witnessing, those people cannot be denied the privilege of participating in the ministry of the

381

Word — even though they had not yet been baptized.

The first witnesses, first bearers of the ministry, as the said writer calls them, certainly did not administer the Sacraments. Rather, they carried out spontaneous preaching — or something even less intentional, as they carried on the Christian practice of singing hymns, praying, and telling Bible stories to fellow-villagers who had never heard them. All this started when the students of the first station schools returned to their villages and continued to have devotions in the evening, as they were used to doing on the mission station. Vetter wrote: 'We were very pleased to hear that our boys from Kwalansam came together every night in their home village and had evening devotions with song and prayer, as is being done on the station'. [2] Other students who went to Bogadjim and other places for plantation work also gathered regularly for evening devotions and Sunday services, inviting others to attend. One of these young men wrote to his missionary: 'O missionary, we have not forgotten God. In the evenings we come together and sing. On Sundays we tell the *Miti* [Good News] and share it with others who come.' [3]

When Senior Flierl in later years reflected on the work of so-called mission helpers, he would include all those from whom he and his fellow pioneer missionaries had received help in their evangelizing efforts, 'young and old people, starting right from the time when we first settled in this country'. [4] The missionaries first had considerable problems with the language. Flierl tells the story of how he made his first attempts to preach the Gospel in villages. His station helpers who accompanied him saw the difficulties the missionary was having expressing himself properly, and lost patience after a while. Already knowing what he was trying to say, they cut in and preached the Gospel themselves. That happened more than once. Although not yet baptized, such young men became the missionaries' helpers also in their efforts to spread the Gospel in the villages.

It is reported that, in those early days, even a tribal chief or some of the older men, though not yet prompted to identify themselves with the new message, sometimes spoke up and lent their authority to the missionary by calling upon the village people to take to heart what they had just heard from the missionary.

Such examples of informal witnessing clearly show the collective way of thinking which is typical of New Guinea. It remained an important factor in later years when a more formalized ministry of public preaching began to develop. The Sattelberg congregation, for example, could not envisage baptizing individuals without the whole tribe having given its consent first. In the Kalasa village of Tunge, it was not only an individual sorcerer who gave up his black magic; when he did so, the whole village population revealed their secret practices, and produced hundreds of magic packages which were used for sorcery. Thereafter the whole group of Tunge villagers went to the neighbouring areas witnessing to their fellow people of the effect which the Gospel had had on their life. [5] This was spontaneous evangelism carried by the group of people who had experienced the liberating power of the *Miti* in their own communal life. The baptism of the Tunge people followed some time later. [6]

What consequences can be drawn from such joint action for the understanding of the nature of the ministry of the church and of the congregation? Conversion was experienced in the beginning primarily not by individuals but by groups. A Christian village or group of clans, therefore, became the basic unit of the growing New Guinea church. The Christian life and the functions of a congregation were shared by all members. An indigenous concept of the priesthood of all believers was the starting-point for the further formal organization of the church's ministry and ministries. It says much for the missionaries that they could envisage Christianity and their own missionary work in terms of groups and social units as well as that of individuals.

As sincere and effectual as such spontaneous communal evangelistic movements and group conversions in the early days of New Guinea mission may have been, there is still another side to it. When it was primarily the group that made the decision to become Christian and to be baptized, the group could easily consider that the *Miti* was also at their disposal. The ministry of the Word, then, tended to be seen as their own affair — even to the extent that it was limited to the tribe and

382

enclosed within its confines. Genuine missionary outreach, however, always tends to transcend existing ethnic and even linguistic limitations. Tribal-group interests must never be allowed to cloud the universal claim of the Gospel to all mankind.

In general it has to be said, however, that the very beginnings of congregational ministry were kept free from tribal misconceptions. Those earliest forms, or pre-forms, of an indigenous ministry established a pattern for both the church's and the congregations' ministry that to some degree is still followed in the ELC-PNG today.

Congregational Ministries

It remains debatable whether the terms 'ministry', 'pre-forms' or 'earliest forms of the ministry' ought to be used for the spontaneous (sometimes even unintentional) witnessing to the new way of the *Miti* of the early helpers and pupils of the pioneer missionaries. A permanent ministry, however, can come into existence only after there is a congregation.

According to W. Freytag,[7] the term 'ministry' may be used in a rather broad way to include all forms of leadership in a congregation, even those forms which have been taken over from traditional community life. When conversions occur in groups and traditional social units, it is but natural that the previous forms of leadership will, perhaps with some changes, be continued in the new Christian community, and provide very good leadership potential. The early New Guinean congregations, especially in the Finschhafen area, show clear evidence of the fact that there was some leadership continuity in structure — and sometimes even in personnel.

The Elder

In the beginning, the missionaries were rather hesitant to entrust local Christians with congregational tasks, although they were encouraged by their home Board to do so. In a lecture on 'The Task of Establishing Congregations in New Guinea', the Neuendettelsau Mission Inspector M. Deinzer said:

> The missionary has to look for helpers in the area of catechetical instruction, visiting the villages, supervising the Christians, as well as for

Elder Mokiong — Sattelberg congregation

conducting Sunday services, and for teaching in schools.[8]

Senior Flierl took this up in a paper read at the annual Missionaries Conference of 1907: 'We need mission helpers of various kinds, to be more precise: of four categories'. He then goes on first to describe the functions of a congregational elder 'who sees more and learns more [in his village] than the white missionary can ever see and hear'. Flierl secondly lists catechists (he even thinks of women catechists!) who could give basic instruction to classes in every village in preparation for baptism, and later possibly also for confirmation. And, most important of all, he thinks of teachers for elementary village schools. From their ranks in future years might come the first ordained pastors.[9] It was a kind of programmatic lecture that Flierl gave on that occasion. Later years evidenced how right he was when he outlined the development of congregational life in the scattered villages under an indigenous leadership and ministry.

Village elders had a wide area of responsibility. They not only had the duty of looking after the religious activities of their

383

village congregation, but also had to concern themselves with the people's daily life. Under the guidance of the Holy Spirit, they laboured toward maintaining an orderly village life in every respect. Generally speaking, there was but little separation between the village community and the Christian congregation. With the multitude of tasks to be carried out, especially in larger villages, it became impossible for one man to meet all obligations. Therefore, in such places two — or even three — elders were required, sharing the tasks equally.

Although the ministry of the elder was regarded as quite an important office, no special qualifications were thought necessary for holding this office. Elders could be ordinary village people, not necessarily literate. Far more important was that they were known as earnest and mature Christians who were guided and instructed by the Holy Spirit himself. For their formal qualifications it was enough that they had received baptismal instruction and had been baptized, that thereafter had regularly attended Sunday services and further Christian instruction, and that they confessed their sins and took part in Holy Communion — that is, that they were full church members in good standing. The missionaries were expected to further train, guide, and supervise them as much as time and energy would allow. For quite some time, there was no clear distinction between the office of the elders and ordinary membership in the congregation; the concern of the elder always was also the concern of the congregation. So, the ministry of an elder was, in some ways, a hidden ministry; the congregation as a whole was not simply left with a passive role to play.

In still another respect the office of the elder was a real congregational ministry. Elders were never paid; they received no Mission funds nor did they receive financial remuneration from their congregations. Their ministry was, and still is, an honorary one.

It was not until the late 1970s that the formal training of elders was given some thought (see later in this chapter). Nevertheless, it must be stated again: In the Lutheran Church in New Guinea, the office of the elder is not only the oldest of all congregational ministries; right from the beginning, holders of the office have also taken part in the teaching and preaching of

the Word. In the light of this, it is rightly to be regarded as the first indigenous form of the Ministry of the Church.

The Teacher-Preacher

During the first 20 years, whenever and wherever a new mission station was founded, a school was started, too. Regular schooling was regarded as an important means for the spreading of the Gospel. This was the regular missionary approach of those times, used by almost all Protestant missions, and by the Roman Catholics as well. Senior Flierl was not exceptional at his mission station at Simbang when he added a large schoolroom to his first house. Because the adult population did not seem very interested in their preaching, missionaries turned to the young:

> When we preach to the adult people, it is like a few drops of rain upon dry ground. These people are not sufficiently prepared to understand our message and to grasp its meaning. A more lasting effect on the more receptive youth is needed, so that our preaching will be met with more understanding. [10]

In their optimism about schooling, Flierl and his fellow pioneer missionaries, however, underestimated the difficulties which stood in the way of such a new venture. The illiterate people of New Guinea had no idea what a school meant, and they mistook schooling as a kind of hobby of the missionaries. After a few days the pupils would stay away; they even wanted to get paid for coming to school!

So, it took some time before schooling proved a good means for spreading the Gospel. In subsequent years, young men were willing to come to the mission station from remoter villages, but they could not go to and fro every day. This led to the setting up of boarding schools, which turned out to be very advantageous to missionaries and pupils alike. Moreover, the missionaries always needed useful helpers on the station, so the pupils had an opportunity to earn some money.

The actual motive for coming to school in these early years was not so much their longing for education, or even for learning about the Word of God, but rather the wish to get some money and to acquire European trade goods, tools, and the like. It took many years before the real value of school instruction was recognized.

In the mid-1890s we hear for the first time of 25 pupils who were willing to stay for 10 months on the mission station (and in school); later, the minimum time for staying became a full year.

In 1906, the Finschhafen Mission had established eight mission stations, and there were small but growing Christian congregations at these places. The majority of the villages, however, remained untouched by the *Miti*. It had become clear by that time that mission stations could no longer be built so close to each other that European missionaries could reach out to every local village. Any further Christianizing of the people would be done only with well-trained indigenous 'mission helpers' who could work as teachers, evangelists, and preachers of the Gospel in the more remote areas.

In that very year, Senior Flierl in a circular letter to all stations encouraged his fellow-missionaries to go ahead in finding and training such helpers, as he used to call them:

> What others, i.e. other missions, have brought about with the help of local mission helpers, we should be able to do, too. That is, we should start with the training of mission helpers, as our Home Board has strongly encouraged us to do.

The training of such helpers was necessary for the expansion and continuation of the work. It was felt that Christianizing the established centres would soon come to an end, and therefore this was the right time to select suitable helpers and to train them.

> We are full of hope that they will be of great help for us in the ministry of the Gospel. God chose what the world looks down upon and despises, and He has trained children and babies to offer perfect praise.[11]

In the years after 1906, in one area after the other around Finschhafen, the population en masse turned to Christianity; and, as a result, the missionaries and the young congregations were faced with an enormous task. Not so much missionary outreach through schooling was needed now, but rather further instruction in the Christian faith. 'Our children must not grow up as ignorant as we did. In their childhood they have to be taught the *Miti*', the older folk said. The more they turned away from traditional religion, the more Christian instruction was asked for — and that demanded an extensive educational system. In the beginning, when no

trained teachers were available, the villagers resorted to self-help. Former pupils at the mission station schools were called to start at least some kind of schooling. It may have been of poor educational quality, yet it was the village people themselves who demanded that their children be given religious instruction.

These humble beginnings of an educational system in the New Guinea Church show the roots of the church/mission school system in baptism. A Christian congregation needs its own system of education in the Christian faith — for the adults, and especially for their baptized children. From these roots it also became clear that the village teacher very often was also the village preacher. It was basically a congregational office, and, therefore, is to be seen as another form of the Ministry of the Word.

When formal teacher-training was established in later years, the graduates of the seminaries at Hopoi, Heldsbach, and Amron were qualified not only for teaching in church/mission schools; at the graduation ceremony, they also received a formal call and commission for preaching the Word of God. This liturgical act was never described as, or considered to be, an ordination to the Ministry of the Word; it was in fact, a commissioning for preaching only, and the administration of the Sacraments was in no way included. Nevertheless, in most vernacular languages as well as in Pidgin, one and the same word 'blessing' was used for this kind of teachers' commissioning and for the ordination of pastors in later years. It may seem an imprecise expression, lacking theological differentiation, yet the New Guinean terminology shows precisely how these men were regarded by their congregations as both teachers in school, and preachers of the Word in church. Rightly, the former term 'mission helper' had been replaced by 'teacher-preacher'.[12]

It was from the ranks of these teacher-preachers that congregations in later years chose their first candidates for pastoral training. Congregations chose men who through their preaching and the exercise of other congregational duties had won the respect of congregations and elders alike. In the years of growing constitutional church autonomy, many local congregations, circuits, and districts chose their leaders and presidents from the elite of the teacher-preachers. Some of them applied for formal ordination later, others did not; regardless of this, they held equal positions in church leadership and in exercising episcopal rights. Even though this situation seems to have come to an end by now, it would be a mistake to look upon it as an extraordinary or even emergency measure. It was but a logical consequence of the early years, when the pioneer missionaries were ready to share the Ministry of the Word with elders and teachers. In this way the New Guinea Church had been blessed with a host of indigenous ministers of the Word long before the first formal ordination of pastors had taken place.

The Evangelist

Though evangelists in the New Testament rank among the first ministries in apostolic times (Eph. 4:11; Acts 21:8), the older churches were rather reluctant to recognize a specific evangelistic ministry. The New Guinea missionaries also hesitated to establish such an office; they rather named them 'mission helpers', who shared with them the evangelistic task. In the Madang area, Totol (= angel, messenger) was a more appropriate term for the evangelistic ministry. New Guinean Christians, both younger and older, evangelizing among their fellow village people, were the very motor of missionary outreach in New Guinea. This kind of spontaneous evangelism came into being, as has been pointed out in the first section of this chapter, even before the first baptisms had taken place. This was the initial, and at the same time most effective, way of communicating the Gospel to the heathen. The first student messengers were not even baptized yet — let alone having any kind of commissioning — yet through them the Miti went to the people faster and further than the expatriate missionaries ever could have done in those years.

But the task of evangelization did not stop there. As soon as the first congregations came into being, the missionaries tried to find Christians who were willing to do evangelistic work in neighbouring areas beyond their own clan. Here considerable obstacles had to be overcome. There was nothing in traditional religion that could serve as a starting-point for

386

communicating a religious message or practice with people other than their own. The missionaries' first attempts to win co-workers for a missionary outreach beyond the borders of clan and tribe were anything but successful. Decker, referring to evangelistic work, complained (1906): 'To make a sacrifice for the Lord is still something unknown to our people'. [13] Pilhofer comments: 'It is not surprising that after many vain attempts the missionaries reduced their evangelistic demands to the Christians to a minimum.' [14] Yet there were at least some hopeful indications that the early New Guinean Christians were not altogether unreceptive to the Great Commission of our Lord (for details of the first evangelistic activities of New Guinean Christians among their tribal trade partners, see ch 2).

The expatriate missionaries did not forget the obligation (also for newly-baptized Christians) to spread the Gospel beyond the confines of the small existing congregations, and tried their best to make at least some of the new converts ready for it; the results, however, remained meagre. One reason for this may be seen in their mission-centred approach. As the term 'mission helper' suggests, they could think of evangelistic work only in terms of assistance given to their own missionary activities. Accordingly, the first men who dared to do some kind of evangelistic work 'abroad' (outside their own tribal confines) lacked the sending and support of their own congregations; they (and their families) regarded themselves as 'helpers of the missionaries' rather than as people sent by their respective congregation.

This pattern was thoroughly changed when Christian Keysser at Sattelberg directed the first four men to their congregation when they were prepared to go as evangelists to the far-away Hube tribes. He suggested that the responsibility of sending them was theirs, and not his (for details, see ch 2). Keysser was ready to instruct these men for work among the Hube people, but the sending body had to be the Sattelberg congregation. Finally, the four men and their families were commissioned for the evangelistic task in a congregational service in September 1908; and they went out into an area which in those days hardly any outsider, New Guinean or European, dared to enter.

With that, the ministry of evangelists was inaugurated in the New Guinean church. The commissioning service clearly showed that it was the young Sattelberg congregation who was sending its evangelists, and not the Mission or the missionary. Accordingly, these evangelists were never paid out of Mission funds; the members of their home congregation took it upon themselves to sustain their workers financially, as well as spiritually through prayer and regular visitation.

During the next decades, this pattern of evangelistic ministry by the indigenous congregation proved the greatest blessing the New Guinean church had ever received. Other congregations, of the Jabem-speaking area as well as the Kate-speaking one — and, after some time, also in the Madang area (Rhenish Mission) — followed suit. It is hard to conceive how the almost-impassable mountain regions in all three coastal areas of the Lutheran Mission could ever have been reached, and congregations founded there, without the service of innumerable evangelists. They took it upon themselves to be commissioned and sent with their families to live in 'foreign' regions beyond their own clan and tribe, to be witnesses for Christ, and to win people for him. If, according to 1 Corinthians 9, witnessing to Christ and founding a congregation is an apostle's work, the New Guinea church has had many apostles of its own: indigenous missionaries and evangelists who have spread the Gospel throughout their own country.

The growing New Guinea church did not spend much effort in reflecting on its various ministries, nor was it thought necessary clearly to distinguish between the offices of teacher and evangelist. Whatever formal training evangelists received in the early years was given at the teachers' seminaries at Hopoi, Heldsbach, and Amron. Teachers in newer areas became the evangelists, as well — just as, in the older areas, teachers were also the preachers to the local congregations. Yet it should be kept on record that there was (and in some areas of the church still is) a specific evangelistic ministry, whether it was formally recognized as such, or was included in a more general term. Historically, the evangelists deserve the credit for having

Evangelists Ngezinu,

Mainao,

Hungto

387

done the front-line work in carrying the *Miti* ever and again beyond tribal and geographical borders, and thereby evangelizing the interior regions of New Guinea.

The Pastor

Historically, the pastor in the New Guinea church has been a latecomer. For years, elders, teacher-preachers, and evangelists carried out most of the functions within the congregations and beyond. Only in exceptional cases were these men given permission to baptize people or, even more rarely, to dispense Holy Communion. The administration of the Sacraments for a very long time was reserved for the ordained missionaries. Whatever the nature of commissioning ceremonies for evangelists and teachers may have been, they were never called or considered to be ordination to the Ministry of the Church. The permission to administer Baptism was given to certain men *ad hoc*, for special occasions only. It seems that the Christians' participation in evangelizing, preaching, and leadership of the congregations was so high a challenge for them that the necessity for another office, that of the ordained ministry, scarcely entered their thinking.

An exception was Janggoeng, the first Jabem teacher at Hopoi. In 1928, he wrote to Senior Flierl asking for further training for himself and for some of his co-workers, with the goal of eventually becoming ordained:

> I want to do the work which the Lord has given us all to do. I know that you missionaries have tested us natives during the years that have passed, and that the great and important office which our Lord Jesus Christ gave his disciples has fallen upon you, and that you are administering it now. I am continually thinking about this most important office; therefore, I would like to express the wish whether you could not also bestow it upon me and on some others whose heart urges them. It would be something very great if you would give that good, which came from the Lord, to me and to my fellow-workers … I must think of the wind which blows across the high mountain peaks. It does not break only the crowns of the trees up there in the heights, but also the trees down in the lowlands. What the Kate evangelists have experienced, we evangelists on the coast would also like to experience. [15]

By 'the wind which blows across the mountains' Janggoeng was referring to the

388

evangelist Haringke of Tobou in the Hube mountains, who had received permission from the Sattelberg congregation to perform the very first baptism at Kuluntufu in 1917. Apparently this had not gone without notice among his New Guinean fellow-workers.

Flierl's direct answer to Janggoeng is not known, but there was certainly no immediate response from the missionaries' side. They, rather, wondered whether the congregations themselves felt the need for such a step. Would they know what kind of service ordained pastors should render for the good of all? Would they be willing to contribute toward the support of a pastor and his family when he was called to devote most of his time to his ministerial tasks? The missionaries realized that they had previously neglected to raise these questions in the minds of the people. Unless the congregations themselves were clear on the concept of the ordained ministry, on whom to choose for further training, and on their own willingness to support those men as pastors, the whole undertaking would fail. On no account would the expatriate missionaries force something upon the New Guinean congregations which they did not fully subscribe to — and if not regarded as their own concern, would not feel responsible for, either.

In 1938, the Director of the Basle Mission, Karl Hartenstein, carried out a survey on ministerial training, asking various missionaries and training institutions about their concept of an indigenous ordained ministry. The returns of the two leading men in seminary training of the Finschhafen Mission reflected the general trend of thinking of those years. The missionaries in no way were rushing into setting up an indigenous ministry. S. Lehner wrote:

> In a sense, every church needs ministers. So far in the larger circuits we have worked with our mission helpers and congregational elders, of whom some have been given the right to baptize, others to marry people. Recent development, however, urges us to confer further ministerial functions upon men who have stood the test in order to relieve the missionary. Therefore, the last Mission Conference has resolved that mission-helpers/teachers who have faithfully worked for years should be called back for a six-months' course of further training. This has been laid before the congregations for discussion. They are asked to return their findings to us. [16]

In a similar way, G. Pilhofer replied:

The congregation needs a ministry. But it does not need the kind of ministry we have in our home churches. It is much better if the young churches take their bearings from the example of apostolic and post-apostolic times. There was no ministry which absorbed all spiritual functions of a congregation. A ministry in that sense leads the congregations to passivity ... With regard to indigenous pastors (shepherds), it is not a question of a particularly high standard of education. They must be above the average intellectual level of their fellowmen. Far more important is that they are of strong character, independent men who know what they want, who can say of themselves: 'I know in whom I believe'. They must be men who have had a personal encounter with Christ. With regard to their formal education, the first requirement is not that of a training in European theology. The theology of our pastors has to be an indigenous theology which can provide the answers to religious questions of their people, which interprets their history, and enables them to give Christian advice on spiritual trends among their people. [17]

When World War II had ended, and missionaries were allowed to return to their former field of work, the issue of an indigenous ordained ministry gained enormous momentum.

God has shown us unmistakably that in future the missionaries will have to play an entirely different role in the development of our local congregations. The development will be directed away from a mission-centred to a church-centred orientation of our whole enterprise. More than in the past, the mission will have to put emphasis on the development of good indigenous leaders, and delegate ministries to them. [18]

The relationship between the various existing congregational offices of elders, teachers, and evangelists now came into focus. The senior American missionary, E. Pietz, voiced such questions, which apparently were a matter of concern among the local leaders of the church:

The elders were quite concerned that the present arrangement of congregational leadership be retained, and that the pastors be only a supplement to make a more capable and mature congregation ... Without the ministry of the elders, the congregation would soon become weak and ineffective. In the larger congregations, the pastor would be on an equal level with the elders. [19]

Unfortunately, we do not have adequate documentary material of the fears and concerns that were raised on the congregational level, and especially by those who so far had taken the lead. Mission President J. Kuder was not ready to treat this lightly:

It is the fear that by establishing the ministry — at least the ministry after the pattern of the home church — we undermine the structure of the New Guinea congregations, as it has developed hitherto. [20]

The strength of the New Guinea community has always been the ability to think and act as a group. There were people with all kinds of abilities and functions, but each one with his function and ability served the group, and not primarily his own 'aggrandizement' (Kuder). From the very beginning of the church, group-decisions of the people were sought, and group activity promoted, by missionaries and evangelists.

The early missionaries found existing in New Guinea a well-developed communal organization on which they were able to craft the new concept of a community of God. They were successful in inculcating into the congregations the idea of group responsibility for the conduct of all congregational activities. The elders were elected as the leaders of this activity. [21]

The question was raised at what stage of development the right to exercise the functions of the ordained ministry should be turned over to a congregation. How soon could the congregational leaders take over and exercise this function of the pastoral ministry? The question along such lines, however, is put the wrong way, as Kuder pointed out in his paper:

Wherever there is a Christian congregation, there also are the rights and authority for the exercise of the functions of the public office of the church, i.e., of the ministry ... Where the Gospel is preached and accepted, and men come into the kingdom of God through faith, there is the church and there must also be the Ministry of the Word. [22]

In a rather prolonged process of almost 20 years, interrupted by the years of World War II, the ordained ministry in the New Guinean Church was finally established. The lengthy discussions on all levels, however, were not wasted time. This process avoided the forcing of a Western concept of the ordained ministry upon congregations who had developed specific forms of their own that were worthy of

Heldsbach Teachers Training School (1931).

being preserved. The multiple ministry which had developed from the beginning had proved itself in a blessed history of evangelizing and of shepherding congregations. Credit must also be given to the expatriate missionaries who were sensitive to what had developed so far, and who refrained from lightly introducing the pattern of their home churches. However, it still remains to be seen whether this multiple ministry will hold its place in the second century of New Guinean church history.

Training for the Ministry

To a modern student of church history who has little acquaintance with the New Guinean situation, it may be confusing that in the Lutheran Church the term Ministry has broader application than in most churches elsewhere. In line with this, ministerial training in this context includes more than pastors' training only.

As has been pointed out above, in the first three decades, at least three specific congregational offices — elder, teacher, and evangelist — all shared in the public preaching of the Word and were the backbone of congregational life. That applied to organization as well as to spiritual leadership on the basic level of the congregation. A review of the training for the ministry, therefore, has to pay attention to teachers', evangelists' and elders' training as well as what commonly is considered pastoral training in theological schools. This will be done here in more or less chronological order.

390

Teachers' Training

Historical events that eventually led to the establishing of teachers' training schools in the various areas have been touched on in previous chapters (ch 2, 3, 4, 7, 8), and need not be repeated here.

Rightly, H. Hage in the next chapter calls it 'more than teachers' training'. For the growing New Guinea Church up to the late 1950s, teachers' training was 'the heart of its evangelization program'. As teacher-preachers, the graduates of the training schools in Heldsbach (since 1914), Hopoi (since 1923), Amron (since 1936), and Rintebe (since 1952), played an important role in congregational life and in the village community. [23] In newer areas, the schools had a definite missionary influence, reaching far beyond the actual Christian congregation. Vicedom once wrote:

> In a heathen area one can observe the great value of schools for mission work ... Schools have roused the interest also of the older people. Whenever they happened to pass by the school building, they would stop and sit down with the children and listen for a while. [24]

The teachers' training schools had a three-fold task: to train young men for teaching in village schools; to train them for service in the village congregations; to train them for actual mission work in new areas. In reality, most of the students tended to volunteer for service in new mission areas, rather than — as one might have expected — to become teachers in the older congregations. [25]

The training schools were self-supporting as far as the students' living was concerned; they built their own houses and planted their own gardens. And in matters of school discipline, the student body did not depend on the missionaries' authority; pastoral care was exercised by themselves in groups. One evening each week was set aside for counselling. The students also had a say in weightier decisions of school life, such as whether somebody had to be dismissed. The system of self-support and self-government was set up mainly with the aim of preparing the prospective congregational leaders for their participation in village life, lest they develop the feeling that teachers were entitled to live above the average standard of people in rural areas.

The students, for their part, were very conscious of the fact that the eyes of their home congregation rested upon them while they were in training. This definitely had a positive effect on school and community life. The students who had been sent by their congregations certainly did not want to disappoint their own people; misbehaving in school would have brought 'shame' upon the congregation at home.

The teachers' training schools set high goals for both academic and moral achievements. For the concept of this kind of teaching-preaching ministry to succeed in the church, it was very advantageous that a group of gifted missionaries be called to do seminary work, and that the first generation of these educators be allowed to stay for a rather long period in it. H. Zahn was responsible for the Jabem Seminary from 1911 to 1932. After him, J. Streicher and then S. Lehner took over until World War II ended all regular school work. The Kate Seminary was headed from the very beginning in 1910 until 1930 by G. Pilhofer, and he was followed by W. Flierl, H. Neumeyer, M. Helbig, and A. Wagner. In the Madang area, the steady development of the training program was unfortunately halted by a change in language policy. The initial Amele training school of A. Wullenkord, and the Graged training school at Urit (Kurum) founded by H. George, were combined at Amron in 1936 with E. Hannemann in charge. After being in operation for only a few years, World War II brought all institutional work to a temporary standstill.

It goes without saying that this type of training for the ministry of teacher-preachers reached its high point in the years preceding World War II. The growth of the church, both in depth and width (in its congregational life and in its missionary outreach) would not have been possible without the product of these schools. As well, in those years church and mission were able to organize the school system and their teachers' training schools according to what they regarded as most necessary for church growth and spiritual development. Since the Australian government educational system was almost non-existent, the church was able to shape its school system according to its own requirements, without interference from secular educational policies. And they certainly made best use of that situation.

That, however, was to change after the War. For one more decade (1946-1955), the pre-war mission school system continued, again producing a host of well-trained teacher-preachers for congregational ministry, as well as for the enormous missionary advance in the Highlands. But from 1955 on, the Lutheran school system came under growing pressure to comply with the administration's educational policy of making New Guinea an English-speaking country, and demanding that all educational work be done in English.

This policy of all-English education eventually undermined the Lutheran school system. It was not the use of the English medium as such; actually, the Mission had already set up its own all-English training school at Bumayong three years prior to the administration's strict orders. It was the new concept of education that caused so much unrest within the church school system. No longer was schooling an activity based on baptism and required for nurture in the Christian faith. Not the church, but the administration, now set goals in education — and, of course, these goals were secular ones. If an open clash between the administration's and the church/mission's policy was to be averted, the church had to forgo its concept of the teacher as one form of its public Ministry of the Word. A teacher in future might also be a preacher; but no longer was the teacher-preacher the ultimate goal of teacher-training, even when carried out in church institutions.

Evangelists' Training

In the years prior to World War II, there was no specific evangelists' training in terms of schools or training programs. However, most men who actually undertook evangelistic work in new areas had gone through some kind of schooling program. In many cases, elementary schooling of four years in the village school was all that they had received; at least, they could read and write.

But there were others who were sent by their congregations to new areas with no schooling at all. Living an exemplary life as Christians; acting as mediators and peacemakers in fights; showing a new kind of life without using sorcery or succumbing to the deadly law of retaliation and revenge: this was the kind of language which was well understood by illiterate people in newer areas. What those evangelists had to preach and teach, they knew by heart: Bible stories, the Lord's Prayer, the articles of the Creed. Even in the 1950s and 1960s we still read in missionaries' reports of

the good services of illiterate evangelists in new Highland areas.

There were, of course, more qualified evangelistic workers, partly working as teacher-preachers, partly working as the very missionary pioneers in areas where an expatriate could hardly survive. These were the ones whom H. Neumeyer had in mind when he wrote that the students in general preferred to work in mission areas (see note 25). So, the term teacher-preacher could also be rendered as teacher-evangelist. According to the concept of 'congregational mission' (see ch 2), the older congregations were ready and willing to let some of their best-educated young men go into evangelistic work. For the older congregations that often meant sacrifice; they themselves were always in need of more teachers.

As has been pointed out, the teachers' seminaries pre-war served as training institutions both for the teaching and the evangelistic ministry of the church. In fact, it was hard to draw a sharp line of distinction between those two functions. When this combined training pattern for the ministry faced a crisis in the mid-1950s, a new and more specific form of

Sattelberg evangelists and teachers.

evangelistic training had to be found. That was when the church/mission's Bible School Program began.

As detailed in chapter 13, the church's alternative to the administration's exclusive all-English school system faced obstacles from many sides. At the elementary level, *Tok Ples* schools in the long run had little chance of acceptance by the people as an equal alternative to public English-language schools. And at the secondary level, the *Tok Ples* school program was encumbered by the vague hopes of ambitious young men who for some reason had fallen out of the all-English system — even though on this level the church's Pidgin schools offer a genuine alternative to the public English-language schools. As valuable as such schools have been in the last two decades for hundreds of young men and women, evangelists' training as a form of ministerial training definitely suffered a setback.

In the late 1950s and the 1960s the newly-established District Bible Schools took over what the English teacher-training institutions could no longer do: prepare young men with four or six years of village schooling for the evangelistic/congregational Ministry of the Word.

It was intended — and for some years this was achieved — to establish a Bible School for evangelistic training in each of the six Districts of ELCONG: Gabmazung (1957) and Mainyanda (1965) for the Jabem/Lae District, Kalasa (1956) for the Kate District, Begesin (1953) and Amron (1958) for the Madang District, Onerunka (1961) for the Goroka District, Kewamugl (1957) for the Chimbu District, and Kentagl (1963) for the Hagen District.

Partly due to the ever-changing program for Bible Schools, partly due to a decreasing demand for evangelists in newer areas, partly simply because of inadequate student enrolments, one school (Kalasa) was closed altogether, and others were changed as to their objectives. At present, only the Amron School serves as a specific training institution for the evangelistic ministry. The rest of the *Tok Ples* Bible Schools do not exclude evangelistic activities, but they can hardly be regarded as specific training institutions for the evangelistic ministry of the church. It could well be that new developments will force ELC-PNG to change its policy and to give evangelists' training a higher priority in its ministerial training program than it had received during the last two decades.

A First Attempt: Formal Elders' Training

It is not quite correct to say that training for the earliest of all congregational offices, that of elder, was not given due thought. From the beginning, it was the missionaries' very concern to find reliable and responsible men to be — as they then saw it — 'their eye and ear' in the village congregations.[26] Soon, however, the functions of the elder changed into a kind of ministry in its own right. 'I asked the people of each district [group of neighbouring villages] to select two out of their midst', Keysser reported in regard to the Sattelberg congregation. 'Those selected stay on the station over Sunday to be led a bit further and deeper. They then shall pass on to their fellow-Christians what they have learnt.'[27] What Keysser reported undoubtedly became general practice: those who were chosen as elders received further instruction in the Christian faith and also in how to exercise their duties and rights in the proper way. Though this was seldom done in a formal or even institutionalized way, the congregational elders were given special attention by their missionaries. In the very meaning of the word, it was in-service-training by and through the missionaries. In later years, this was carried on by the respective circuit authorities, and remained so until very recently.

In the late 1970s, at least one of the Districts gave thought to a more formal training for congregational elders. In 1978, the Kate District started a first elders' course of nine months at their school centre at Heldsbach, with H. Gerber in charge. It was a combined theory-practice course, including 'fieldwork programs' on weekends in neighbouring and home villages. In these programs, the elders were helped and supervised by circuit leaders and, where viable, also by expatriate missionaries.

> Our aim is to enable the leaders [elders] to preach, or to preach better, and how to take care of a congregation ... [For this kind of course] no academic standards are required other than the ability to read and write. We like to start them off, open their eyes, and show them a direction. However, we do feel responsible for their continuing training.[28]

The first course in '78/79 roused so much interest, even enthusiasm, among those who attended and others who had heard of it, that two further well-attended courses were conducted. After an interruption of four years, Bonene, who had been lecturer and principal of the Pastors' Seminary at Logaweng, was secured in 1985 to re-start this promising training program at Heldsbach. Despite the success and promise of this first attempt to set up a more formal elders' training at District level, the idea has so far not been taken up by other Districts. This, however, is not to say that the elders have not been given due attention. Pastors and missionaries are only too well aware that this office is the very basic one for the life of the local congregation. It remains to be seen whether informal in-service-training at the local or circuit level, or a more formal and institutionalized training like the Heldsbach experiment — or both — will become the pattern in future years.

Pastors' Training

Even though the Lutheran Mission at Finschhafen and Madang claimed some 60,000 Christians at the time of the outbreak of World War II, there was still no regular indigenous ordained ministry. It was felt by the missionaries, and perhaps even more so by some congregational leaders, that the time was ripe for the next step in church growth. At the Mission Conference at Malalo in 1939, attended also by representatives from the Jabem and Kate Districts, it was resolved that short training courses leading to ordination should be started without further delay. This resolution was prompted by a feeling of urgency due to political events. Two such courses were started soon after at Malalo and at Heldsbach. But it was already too late; the outbreak of war put an untimely end to these first beginnings.

Jabem Pastors' Training Courses

M. Lechner started the first Pastors' Course for Jabem-speaking congregations at Malalo in 1939. Four older teachers were enrolled: three of them, Mikael, Timote, and Ruben from the Malalo congregation, and Elias from Taemi/Deinzerhill. Lechner could teach the course only for a year before he was interned in Australia in July 1940. The four candidates were ordained

394

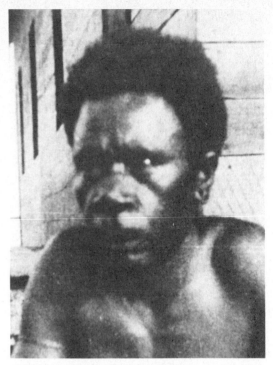

P. Mikael of Malalo congregation.

as pastors by S. Lehner at a District meeting at Malalo in December 1940. [29]

Although Lechner's internment brought his involvement to an abrupt end, Lehner was allowed to stay on in the country until 1943. He instructed another three candidates for the ministry: Taegejam of Bukawa congregation, Naeman of Jabem, and Philemon of Lae congregation.

Instruction was begun at Hopoi. Later, when the station was heavily bombed, they withdrew to a makeshift bush camp at Apo in the hinterland of Bukawa. Taegejam was ordained by Lehner already in February 1942 after a short two months' initial period of instruction; after Lehner's internment, he served the Bukawa congregation for many years. Naeman received initial training from H. Boettger at the Mission printery at Logaweng, and was ordained by Taegejam in March 1942; thereafter, he joined Lehner's course at Hopoi/Apo before taking over his first teacher's pastoral work. For more than 25 years he faithfully served the Jabem congregation at Ngasegalatu.

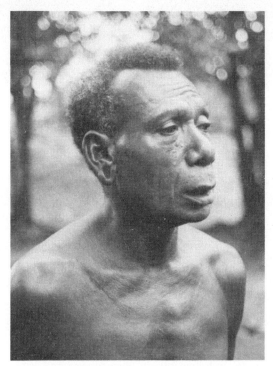

P. Naeman of Ngasegalatu congregation.

P. Taegejam of Bukawa congregation.

Philemon joined this wartime course at Hopoi/Apo at the request of his Ampo congregation. When instruction ceased in September 1943, he returned to Lae just before the actual fighting began in the Huon Gulf area. Philemon was ordained by his two pastor colleagues, Taegejam and Elias, in June 1944, at a time when there were no expatriate missionaries left in New Guinea. It was Philemon whom the first American missionary inquiry team unexpectedly met in September 1945 during a baptismal service held at Labu near Lae (see ch 6).

Though no official files were kept during these years of unrest, it is on record that the above men were the first seven ordained pastors of the Lutheran Church in New Guinea. In hindsight, it may be said that it was a late beginning — in fact, too late a beginning — for pastors' training, with World War II soon putting all New Guinea into crisis. The events of war then delayed formal pastors' training for another full ten years.

After the war, upon the recommendation of the Mission Conference, H. Streicher conducted another Jabem pastor's course at Hopoi in 1951/52, with 17 men graduating in November 1952, and receiving ordination the following month. Streicher was quite self-critical in regard to his work. He had set himself high standards for pastors' training, but 'many things had to be left unfinished'.[30] He felt strongly that the training period of future candidates should be longer, and that their training should be done more thoroughly than had so far been possible.

Kate Pastors' Training Courses

In April 1939, G. Pilhofer started the first pastors' course with older Kate evangelists and teachers at Heldsbach. A total of 15 men had been carefully chosen by their congregations from all circuits of the Kate District. They were: Zurenuo from Sattelberg; Qangengge, Mosangang, Mariong, Manasupe, and Hungto from Hube; Sanangke and Bajape from Wareo; Meki from Heldsbach; Gawamba and Surenoi from Kalasa; Matai from Sio; Akikepe from Ulap; Basawepe from Boana; and Esanangke from Zaka. Unfortunately, the instruction lasted for only six months; in September 1939, Pilhofer was taken away and interned in Australia. That turn of events brought abrupt and precipitous

395

P. Rabisang of Sattelberg congregation.

end to the first Kate pastors' course, and the 15 men returned to their former places of work. Eleven years later, after the missionaries were allowed to return to New Guinea, A. Metzner resumed the training in 1950 with almost the same group of men at Sattelberg. By December, 14 candidates had concluded their training, and subsequently received ordination at the Kate District Conference (1950).

In the meantime, however, another beginning of pastors' training had been made at Boana in 1948. The Kate District had asked G. Bergmann to conduct a pastors' training course at his station. After two years of instruction, the 13 graduates received ordination at Boana in November 1949.[31] These 13 men actually became the first ordained Kate pastors, preceding those who had enrolled in the first course of 1939, but had completed the course and been ordained only in 1950. In '51/52, a second course was conducted by Bergmann at Boana. H. Strauss and L. Goetzelmann each came for three weeks to help with the training.

In order to further redress the shortage of pastors, and to avoid a one-sided training program, another course was conducted by K.

Munsel at Tapen. This course was divided up into three periods of three-to-four months each during 1954, 1955, and 1956; neither the missionary nor the participants could afford to be taken away from their regular work for a longer period of time. However, 15 candidates were presented to the Kate District Conference at Heldsbach in 1956 for ordination.

Yet another pastors' course was held at Boana in 1957/58. When the first course at the new Seminary at Logaweng began in 1957, the number of applicants far exceeded the capacity of the new school. Accordingly, Bergmann was asked to conduct another two-year course at his station for all those who had not been accepted at Logaweng.

So, the number of pastors' courses of the Kate District (and for some Kate-speaking Highlands candidates) totalled six, prior to the work at the combined Logaweng Seminary.

Pastors' Training Courses in the Madang District

In the Madang District, the missionaries tended to follow the way Munsel had conducted his course at Tapen: They called in some of their ablest, proven church workers for several three-month courses. The training in both theoretical and practical subjects continued over a period of five years. The first three-month pastors' course was started by G. Reitz at Begesin in 1950, and was continued there from April to June the following year. For the next two years, the course was transferred to Bongu, with P. Schulz in charge.

The situation at Bongu, however, became very difficult. Especially in the second year it became quite evident that they were not wanted there. At first, the people in the surrounding villages had expected much from the Sunday visits of the pastor candidates. However, as soon as they realized that these men were not providing any material wealth with their coming, the people's interest waned. One Sunday, the visiting candidates were shown the writing on the wall at Janglam village. It read: 'Last year you came and worked energetically among us; but now leave us alone. We wish to remain just as we are.'[32]

Though unwanted, the men persevered with their visiting in the villages near Bongu. The people's reaction was almost the same

396

Pastors Loc, Ud, Liwa and Fulalek (Madang).

everywhere: The pastor candidates got no food, nor were there any other signs of hospitality. Schulz commented in his report: 'One wonders how many other candidates for the ministry are so thoroughly tested.' Both students and teachers continued to work in this climate of insult and scorn, and could well have been expected to become discouraged after months of such harsh treatment. However, the situation evoked a much different response. The students kept asking the question: 'Why are the people so unresponsive?' Finally, they discovered that the people believed in the 'coming of the cargo', because of promises made by a former missionary. At least, that was what they claimed.

P. Mileng, Karkar congregation.

From April to July 1954, that Madang pastors' course was concluded on Karkar with R. Pech in charge, and culminated in the ordination of the first four pastors of the Madang District at the Elders' Conference held at Kaul village. The pastors ordained were: Ud, Baite, Mileng, and Kautil.

A further course was started on Karkar with 20 students in 1955/56, with R. Pech again in charge. It was continued and concluded at Biliau in 1957 by H. Wuest. At the 1957 District Conference at Minderi, 13 graduates were ordained.

Up to the opening of the ELCONG Pastors' Seminary in Logaweng in 1957, a total of 85 pastors had been trained in various District courses, beginning with the courses at Malalo and Heldsbach before the war. All graduates

P. Katiwa, Henganofi congregation (Eastern Highlands).

subsequently received ordination, and were put to work by their respective District.

Senior Flierl Seminary, Logaweng

As far back as 1950, the Lutheran Mission Conference decided 'that we set as our aim the establishment of one Theological Seminary for the Lutheran Mission Field in New Guinea, the students to be graduates of our several Teacher Training Schools'. This resolution was passed after the presentation and thorough discussion of J. Kuder's study paper 'Native Leadership and Clergy'.[33] There was no doubt that the church urgently needed more and better trained pastors for shepherding the flock, and for helping and guiding other congregational workers.

When the Evangelical Lutheran Church of New Guinea (ELCONG) was founded in 1956, the establishment of a joint theological seminary at Logaweng was one of the first decisions made. In remembrance of the Lutheran pioneer missionary in New Guinea, the Seminary was to be called Senior Flierl Seminary. The three supporting churches in America, Germany, and Australia mediated a considerable grant from the Lutheran World Federation for building the new theological institution. The partner churches in America and Australia even sent volunteer short-term workers to do the construction work.

The Seminary actually began its work in 1957, although building was not yet complete. The official opening was held only in 1959. In the first course, some 26 students were enrolled from the three coastal districts. Instruction was given in the three church languages: Kate, Jabem, and Graged. Pidgin and some English were used only as colloquial media for the life on the campus. The first European missionaries teaching at the Seminary were: L. Goetzelmann for the Kate group, H. Streicher for the Jabem group, and P. Freyberg for the Graged group. The three language-groups formed three parallel courses at the seminary.

As soon as the first two-year course was ended, two New Guinean teachers were added to the staff: P. Geyammalo for the Jabem group, and Wabing for the Kate group. The Madang group had its first indigenous teacher, Malek, only in 1968. In subsequent years, as the student enrolment increased, the teaching staff,

Senior Flierl Seminary Logaweng. Chapel and classrooms.

both expatriate and New Guinean, was enlarged accordingly.

The system of choosing students for the seminary differed very little from the way the candidates had been selected by the various congregations for the previous courses at District level. The first courses at Logaweng consisted mainly of teachers and evangelists who were chosen and sent by their congregations to be trained as pastors. Prior to being chosen, they had faithfully worked in village schools, and had also been preaching for years in the church. Streicher gave a striking comment on this sending principle in his first Seminary Report in 1957:

> [The students'] coming was not a matter of their own choice. They have been chosen by their congregations for their task. Nobody would want to give the impression that he would regard himself worthy and capable for the work of a pastor. Otherwise, if they fail, it would be their own fault. It is the congregation that bears the responsibility and therefore picks the men.

Nevertheless, the candidates seemed to be aware of why they were really at the seminary. They appeared to be very willing 'to confirm their call'. [34]

In view of the considerable experience which the students had already gained in preaching, the teachers initially concentrated on Bible studies and homiletics in order 'to find the Papuan way to prepare and preach sermons'. [35] Other subjects, such as Church History, the Lutheran Faith, Ethics, Liturgics, and Church Order, were taught concurrently.

It took some time before the parallel courses at the seminary finally were combined into a joint-course system, and a general curriculum for all three language-groups was developed. [36] From 1965 on, all language sections had courses lasting for three years; from 1975, this was extended to a five-year training program with one intervening year of vicarage. The medium of teaching in the course of time also changed to Pidgin, [37] with the three Church languages being used only for homiletics, and in the church services at the seminary. In later years, the use of vernaculars was reduced even more, being confined to optional courses only.

Most of the students in the earlier courses were married. Provision had to be made for family units to live together at the seminary. This gave the Logaweng community the chance to live as an *ad hoc* Christian congregation, having a normal spiritual life in worship and work, exercising discipline among themselves, and caring for the sick and for the children. Regular times for Communion services were set by the congregational meeting, and Baptism was administered for the new-born as in a normal village congregation. This pattern of normal village life also provided the opportunity for additional education of the women, especially in preparing them for their future task as a pastor's wife. Bible studies were conducted with them all, and younger women were trained for Sunday-school and Christian womens' work. Here the wives of the expatriate missionaries had a welcome field of work of their own.

Logaweng was a very carefully-chosen place for theological training, also in so far as enough church/mission-owned garden land was available to allow each family (or single student) to grow most of his own food. That made the institution partly self-reliant, and reduced the operating costs considerably. In addition, the students were not diverted from

Studying.

the pattern of subsistence farming which is still the way of life for some 80% of the population in New Guinea. Most Lutheran pastors are expected to live and work in such a rural setting. Through Lutheran Economic Service (see ch 18), some assistance was given to the Seminary by seconding two agricultural workers and providing the means for simple mechanical farming.

Highlands Seminary, Ogelbeng

At the 1960 Highlands Conference, the long-felt need of recruiting pastors from the Highlands circuits, and then having them work there, was thoroughly discussed. It was resolved that experienced men of the Highlands congregations, teachers and evangelists, should be trained for pastoral work, in addition to those who were being sent for training at Logaweng. Hermann Strauss of Ogelbeng Circuit was assigned the task of building up such a school, and starting pastoral training. He was able to begin in December 1961 with 15 students, and was assisted by two Kate teachers, Mugarenang and Muratie. The medium of instruction was Kate. From the beginning, the training for the ministry was done in close connection with practical evangelistic work in the circuit.

Initially, the training courses were of two years' duration; however, in 1971, a three-year system of two parallel classes was introduced. Subsequently, a detailed curriculum equivalent approximately to the level of instruction at Senior Flierl Seminary was made obligatory. Credit for developing this curriculum goes to H. Junker.

In 1971, a new venture with the approval of the Highlands circuits was tried. A number of students from St Timothy Seminary at Birip, the school for congregational workers of the (then) Wabag Lutheran Church, were enrolled at Ogelbeng, together with other non-Kate-speaking trainees from the Highlands. These men then formed a Pidgin-speaking class, running parallel to the Kate class. The teaching staff was increased accordingly (H. Bamler from the Goroka District, and J. Klein from Menyamya-Siassi, together with pastors Kongie from the Chimbu District and Karayo from the Madang District). The departure of J. Klein in
400

Ogelbeng seminary buildings. Chapel in foreground, classroom and housing in background.

1974 stalled this experiment until 1982, when students of the (now) Gutnius Lutheran Church joined the courses at the Highlands Seminary.

Beginning in 1986, Ogelbeng Seminary will provide a full five-year program of theological education. In their fourth year, students will do their vicarage in selected congregations. With an average of 25 students per class, around 100 students are expected on campus, most of them married. Since the majority of the students' wives had had very little formal education, programs of adult literacy have been started, and active womens' work is carried out among the women living on the seminary campus, mainly by the wives of the resident expatriate lecturers.

Daily devotions and Sunday services at the seminary are the practical field for students and teachers in homiletics and liturgics. Besides that, much evangelistic work is being done in the surrounding Ogelbeng Circuit, in Mt Hagen town, and among the youth in town and in schools.

It is a tradition at Ogelbeng that students do not receive handouts from the Church (or Mission), provided there is no famine or disaster impoverishing them. The rule is that they attend school in the forenoons, and tend their gardens in the afternoons, thus never interrupting the village routine of subsistence farming which will also be required from them when they later are stationed as pastors in the predominantly-rural areas of the Highlands. [38]

St Timothy Seminary, Birip

The Seminary of the Gutnius Lutheran Church in the Enga Province (see ch 8) was opened in 1960 under the name 'Birip Lutheran School for Church Workers'. First teacher and principal from 1960-65 was Dr Willard Burce. Initially, instruction was given in Enga; later, it had to be changed to Pidgin so that non-Enga students from the more western circuits of the church in Kopiago, Pogera, and Paiala could be included. This change also made possible a student exchange program with the ELCONG Highlands Seminary at Ogelbeng. This exchange has continued since 1982 when eight students were enrolled at Ogelbeng (in addition to 15 students at Martin Luther Seminary at Lae). St Timothy Seminary in 1985 had 46 students enrolled. [39]

Martin Luther Seminary, Lae

For this section of ministerial training, see the special contribution by H. Lutschewitz later in this chapter.

New Challenges for the Ministry

In the first decade after World War II, theological training was clearly aligned with congregational life and evangelistic work in the villages. That was the environment from which the pastor candidates came, and to which they returned after having concluded their training. The contest of faith in the everyday life of the village community with its traditional religious background was well known to the first generation of pastors.

These men also knew that, wherever they were stationed, they had to fit into that life-pattern if they were to do the work expected of them as pastors. The support which a congregation was expected to give to its pastor was very much in line with the way congregations had supported their teachers and evangelists: They were supposed to build him a house, make available sufficient garden land for him and his family, and occasionally also help him with his gardening; at Christmas, they used to pay out a token sum of money as 'cash salary'. Such a system of support incorporated teachers, and now also pastors, fully into life of their villages. At the same time, it was fully adapted to circumstances and conditions of rural New Guinea where subsistence farming is the normal way of living. In current popular terminology, here was a rural kind of 'tent ministry' in which pastor and teacher — like the Apostle Paul, the professional tent-maker — earned his living with his own hands.

This situation changed swiftly in the 1950s and 1960s. The country adopted compulsory education. Its economy shifted to industrial production, trade, and commerce. In the context of South-East Asian development, there was no other choice for New Guinea than to catch up with other developing countries. All this had its immediate effects on the hitherto fairly uniform village system of life. Spiritually, the effect was quite paradoxical: religious practices typical of former times emerged, with a renaissance of traditional rites in stark contrast to other modern progressiveness and all the trends of emancipation. New Guinea began to change to a multi-level social and cultural structure.

With society, the church also had to change — and, in particular, its ministries and ministerial training. This change was expecially felt in the theological seminaries. With the beginning of the third decade of pastoral training, the challenge of so-called modern Papua New Guinea was brought to the fore. The seminaries had to take this into account in the planning of their training programs. One sign was the obligatory adoption of Pidgin as a medium of instruction both at Logaweng and Ogelbeng. This modern Melanesian language in particular is an adequate expression of the occurring blend of traditional and modern western values.

The planning and establishing of an English-language theological seminary also belongs into this context of change. From 1963 to 1965, a very lively and sometimes even hot discussion ensued. The use of the English language as such in theological training was not the real issue; it was, rather, the whole problem of language as a means of communication in theology and preaching. On the one hand, theological training has to confront and grapple with current intellectual trends; on the other, the proclamation of the church has to penetrate the innermost recesses of a man's heart and mind if it is to lead to repentance and faith. How much would theological trianing in the modern academic medium of English aid or impede that very process?

No less a challenge for the ordained ministry of the church is the new social-prestige structure of society which assumes an important role in any swiftly-developing country. Influential and well-paid positions can be found only in government service or in business enterprise. Employment here, however, is made dependent on English education. Is mastering this language, then, the key to influence and to the kind of 'good life' which traditionally was the ultimate goal of every man and woman in New Guinea?

In this context, the ministry of the church can also find itself drawn into the maelstrom of social prestige. On the one hand, it is an evangelistic necessity that the English-speaking leaders of the nation, along with the socially-advanced prestige groups, have preachers and spiritual advisers who educationally are their equals. On the other hand, the ministry of the church is in danger of being evaluated in terms of social status. It makes an observer think when one sees to what degree salary and status questions of pastors have been pushed to the foreground — and not by educationally-advanced pastors only. In years to come, it will be a major task for the church to maintain the servant-character of the ordained ministry over against any kind of social prestige thinking. It will likewise be difficult to preserve the unity of the ministry within the church and a solidarity of the ministry with the congregation. [40]

In its short history of 100 years, ELC-PNG has developed a broad understanding of the ministry of the church, not necessarily limited by educational standards or by the rite of ordination. It has unfolded Luther's concept of the priesthood of all believers to a much higher degree than in most of its overseas partner-churches. So far it has also withstood to a certain degree the trends of having its congregational structures shaped along the lines of the ordained ministry. Teachers, elders, and (to a lesser degree now) evangelists are recognized congregational ministries alongside the office of the ordained pastor. It can rightly be asked whether ELC-PNG will be able to preserve this broader understanding of the ministry in the future. In today's society with its pressures to conform to the Western model in all sections of life, it certainly will not be easy to counteract the modern inclination toward educational elitism. ELC-PNG must not conform with a trend which can conceive only of the academically-trained and graduated pastor as the future leader of congregations and of the church.

New Training Programs

Even within the framework of a manifold ministry, the New Guinean church will have to pay greater attention to the entire training program for pastors in coming years. There is still a considerable shortage of pastors, partly due to the fact that the first generation of ordained men were trained when they were already in their 40s and 50s. Many of them are no longer in active service or have died.

In view of this, the Kerowagi Synod of ELC-PNG in 1980 resolved that special short courses be conducted, again for older church workers who had been faithful in their work. After having successfully completed such a course, these men may be ordained and stationed as pastors in the congregations they have been serving. These courses are not meant to be a permanent set-up for a kind of parallel pastoral training to the existing seminaries; rather, they are seen as a stop-gap measure until such time as the shortage of pastors is overcome.

For giving further training to those already in the ministry, an Office for Continuing Education has been set up. It has been made compulsory for the three seminaries to conduct two in-service-training courses for pastors annually. These courses will be part of the seminaries' regular training program. The seminary faculties will be responsible for conducting such courses in consultation and cooperation with the said office.

Such courses fill a need, and the pastors undoubtedly appreciate them. Each course is scheduled to run for five to six weeks. Almost all active pastors have gone through such a course of in-service-training by now. It has been suggested that in future these courses should even be extended. It is intended, as a rule, that every pastor attend such in-service-training after every five years of service — with Martin Luther Seminary graduates perhaps even after every three years.

402

Lutheran Bible College

The church is in need not only of more pastors, but also of other church workers such as evangelists, religious instruction teachers, parish workers, women's workers, youth leaders, etc. Therefore it was decided in 1981 that a new church college be set up for the training of such church workers. This training college is specifically meant for younger men and women with some high school education who would be willing to do church work, but who are not well enough prepared for any kind of spiritual leadership. The site chosen for the college is Banz, and its proposed name is Lutheran Bible College.

After some lengthy discussions, plans have been refined, and the first draft of the curriculum has been worked out. The two first years will concentrate on basic biblical studies for all students enrolled; after this period, professional training courses for specific church work will be added. The college is scheduled to begin operations in 1986 with a first class in the basic Bible study program.

Looking Back and Looking Ahead

Looking at the Lutheran Church in Papua New Guinea, at its humble beginnings in 1886 and its growth within the first century, one can rightly say that its very existence is a miracle of God. 'God chose what is low and despised in the world' (1 Cor. 1:28). If the expatriate missionary had been the sole bearer of the Gospel, and if his station had been the only centre of activity, mission work would have had only very limited results. By the Holy Spirit's working, not only were the people's hearts and minds after some time opened to the *Miti*; he also moved men and women in overwhelming numbers to take up the manifold ministry of witnessing to that Gospel in their own villages, and way beyond in heathen areas.

It is a characteristic of the Lutheran Church in Papua New Guinea that there is no essential difference between the ordained and non-ordained ministries in the congregation. No doubt, the church is aware of the various kinds of ministry in its midst, and that each one is given its own charisma. Among the Lutheran churches in the world, the New Guinea church is almost unique in the way so many members take an active part in publicly proclaiming the Word of God. Many of these workers — often unduly labelled 'lay-missionaries' — made an extraordinary contribution not only in their specific field of work, but also as preachers and witnesses to Christ, both in words and conduct. In this, the New Guinean church has been teaching its overseas co-workers, and through them has also made a very valuable theological contribution to the understanding of the Ministry of the Church. This approach has been a blessing to the New Guinea church, and may prove a blessing also to other churches — a blessing that can still be unleashed by trusting the Holy Spirit's gift of faith to all believers, and by entrusting many of its baptized membership with the Great Commission which the Lord has given to all his disciples.

Training for the Ministry at Martin Luther Seminary

by Hermann Lutschewitz

In the year that the Lutheran Church commemorates its beginning in Papua New Guinea a hundred years ago, Martin Luther Seminary (MLS) has just entered its third decade of existence. Its academic work started on February 6, 1966 on the premises of Balob Teachers College, and it remained there as a guest institution for five years. MLS was able to celebrate the graduation of its first seven students on its own new campus, only a kilometre from Balob and the ELC-PNG Headquarters, in November 1971.

MLS was obviously a latecomer in the institutional and theological development of the Lutheran Church in PNG. This fact reflects, on the one hand, the understanding of the ministry as being something broader than just a pastor-oriented venture. On the other hand, it shows the difficulties the Lutheran churches had with establishing what is now MLS. Not only had the planning period been complicated by the need to reach agreement among all those involved; the initial years were also painful because of an ongoing debate within ELCONG itself, and among the overseas supporting partners as well. This slow process was a threat to the very existence of the young seminary, and a continuous frustration to staff and students alike. Later on, the performance of MLS — and, even more so, of its graduates — was under constant scrutiny, and criticism was always readily available.

That critical period has come to an end as MLS completes its 20th year of operation. It has won a recognized place within the churches concerned and also within the country. Its early uneasy relationship with the other two seminaries has given way to mutual acceptance and support.

The Beginnings

From the first mention in official minutes of an English-language theological college to the actual start of MLS, four-and-a-half years went by. If the five initial years when MLS was a guest at Balob Teachers College are added, the whole phase of establishing the Seminary took ten years.

Recommendations and resolutions of many different church bodies — local and international — were abundant and often controversial.[41] And yet, in this jungle of opinions and decisions, a constantly-growing will emerged to create a theological training program in which English would be the language of instruction. One might compare that painful and frustrating process to a meandering river — so typical of Papua New Guinea — which, in spite of many diversions and much going around in circles, does finally reach the sea.[42]

At the 15th Field Conference of Lutheran Mission New Guinea in 1961, several resolutions were passed requesting the forming of 'Higher Bible Schools' to pick up students for theological training after the completion of Standard VI.[43] The first of these schools was to be started in Boana/Kate District. A year later, the LMNG Conference recommended to the ELCONG Districts the beginning of an 'English Pastors' Course' as early as January 1963.[44] Dr G.O. Reitz was asked to 'prepare a paper concerning ministerial training in English to be presented to the Districts and circulated amongst L.M. staff'.[45]

Parallel to this process, however, the option of participation in the Pacific Theological College in Suva/Fiji was kept open. No strong commitment was made, for there was obviously a desire to measure one's own potential first.[46]

404

After the first steps toward an English-language theological college were taken, the discussion fanned out immensely: to the Districts of ELCONG, to the existing seminaries, to subsequent LMNG conferences, Executive Council meetings, to the partner churches and mission societies overseas and their Joint Committee on New Guinea.

For and Against English Theological Training

Instead of going through individual statements and resolutions, it might be best to summarize the reasons given for and against theological training in English.

The positive stand was taken because of missionary, educational, and political reasons. If the church is to be adequately represented in its dealings with its own government, well-educated national theologians are needed. On the international scene, the church also needs to speak independently through competent people of its own, rather than through foreign interpreters.[47] It was also felt that the church could not isolate itself from the general educational trend of the country, and therefore would have to use English as a means of theological instruction.

The heart-beat of the promotion of English however, was the missionary concern. Some people thought that English might emerge as a solution to the multi-language dilemma of PNG,[48] and that the church should be ready for this possibility. As well, the church should be in a position to meet already-existing needs for English-trained chaplains, as they were required in places like high schools, the university, the police and defence forces, and at corrective institutions. In addition, the ongoing changes in society would require well-versed pastors who could respond to the questions and challenges of the members of the church, especially of the youth.[49]

The arguments against an English-language seminary program were, on the one hand, drawn from the fear that the church might be alienated from its very roots in PNG, and on the other hand, from the problem of finding the financial support for the future graduates. It was felt that English-trained pastors would no longer be suitable for the congregational ministry of the church, in particular in the rural areas, and that the graduates would finally end up in special callings. It was argued that they would not be able to transmit in their mother tongues and in the local situation what they had learnt in theology. Rather, it was feared, these theologians would shape the New Guinea church gradually into a Western one; they might run into personal difficulties when confronted with historical-critical exegesis as it was developed in Europe. If any English-trained pastors were needed at all, one thought, a very small number would do, as their financial demands would be beyond the means of the ordinary congregation. Concerns were further expressed that a split in the clergy might be created, leading to a *clerus major* of MLS-trained pastors over against a *clerus minor* of pastors trained in other theological schools. [50]

Discussion of the Arguments

The time for arguing pro and con the English training of pastors is now over, due to the course which education in general took in PNG, and also to the very existence of MLS and to the contribution its graduates have made to the whole church. Nevertheless, it is still worthwhile looking at some of the controversial issues of that time.

It was not only the Australian administration of Papua and New Guinea which favoured the English language as the means of formal education; the government of independent Papua New Guinea also has continued to do so, even though it avoided making a definite decision as to the question of a national language. If the Lutheran churches of PNG had passed up the chance to start an English-language seminary, they would have excluded themselves from the educational context in PNG. They, then, would not have been able to provide adequate theological training for many young people coming out of the English school system who felt called into the ministry of the church. The church would also have been hampered in reaching out to that portion of the population which had undergone secondary and tertiary education. The Lutherans might even have been restricted from offering chaplains for government-sponsored institutions.

One very obvious result of the language policy of the government is that the church school system in Pidgin and Kate has shrunk tremendously, or is already almost non-existent at the elementary level. Even the Pidgin seminaries are no longer able to fill their ranks with students from these schools; increasingly they receive their students from English schools, though from a level below high school completion.

Looking at the fundamental changes taking place in PNG, it is without doubt important to have theologians who are able to tap English literary resources which help them to understand and to respond to the challenges of today. Even though most people are still living in rural (sometimes very remote) communities, they have all been affected to some degree by the changes taking place. [51] Life in PNG today is a complex blend of many different traditional and Western forms of behaviour shaping politics, business, education, medicine, agriculture, law, communication, housing, transport, and the whole fabric of tribes, clans, families, of man-woman relationship, of bride prices, marriages, and parenthood. The church is caught up in all this, too, and needs competent shepherds of its flock.

The demand for English worship services is on the increase, also reflecting the new development taking place. Among the twelve Lutheran congregations in Lae, at least six English services are held on Sundays. This is not to be regretted. Why should people use English only as a secular language during their working hours, and not also for worship?

However, what about the unity of the clergy in the Lutheran churches of PNG? It can happily be said that there is so far no theological split, despite the enormous educational variety, not to mention the tribal diversity. The different standards of theological training are not simply the result of the English training of pastors. The Pidgin seminaries have also gradually lengthened their training program to the present five-year course, and their graduates, too, vary considerably in regard to their formal theological education. In addition to that, there are the so-called short-course pastors with much less formal training (see the earlier section of this chapter). To speak of a *clerus minor* and *major* in New Guinea is simplifying and misjudging the reality; rather, we should be grateful that in such a multi-faced ministry and

405

highly-diversified clergy we find an astounding harmony and cooperation.

As far as the distribution of MLS graduates goes, one has to admit that a certain concentration of their stationing has taken place: all pastors in Port Moresby, for example, come from MLS; in towns, MLS graduates often outnumber others. As has been implied above, MLS graduates are called into government institutions and into high school chaplaincies and teaching positions. But there are more and more MLS graduates now serving in a rural ministry. In fact, there is a heightened interest among them in the grass-roots ministry.

Finally, some thoughts ought to be added in regard to the commitment of MLS-trained pastors, for they have been criticized harshly for their dedication and endurance under normal congregational circumstances. Only carefully-prepared statistical material embracing all seminaries of the Lutheran churches and of other denominations over a long enough period of time could really measure how MLS graduates fare. It is my personal impression that they differ little from others in their commitment and faithfulness. It cannot be denied that there have been MLS students who simply wanted to receive further education at MLS in order to get employment elsewhere. However, because of a more specialized training program for government and business jobs, and because of the changing employment market, MLS graduates now have less chance than ever to find work in sectors other than the church, and this has led to greater realism among students. Another stabilizing factor is that more and more mature men have been enrolled at MLS, having left a career behind them for the sake of becoming a pastor.

One further comment: The criticism regarding the endurance of MLS-trained pastors also needs to be addressed. It is surprising, at least from a Western perspective, how many Papua New Guineans give up jobs and simply sit back. Economically that is possible; most people still have refuge in their home villages, where one can till one's own land and build one's own house. PNG is not overpopulated, and a real urban consciousness is only gradually developing. Early retirement is also sought by some people because of the burden of continuous professional stress, which people

were not exposed to in former generations. Since these above-mentioned trends seem to apply to all of society, pastors who give up need to be seen and judged in this context if we are to be fair to them.

A Joint Seminary

MLS was different from the other Lutheran seminaries at Logaweng, Ogelbeng, and Birip (but similar to Balob Teachers College) in that it came into being as a combined effort of the three Lutheran Churches and Missions in New Guinea in the 1960s. In June 1965, the Convention of the (then) Wabag Lutheran Church decided to be part of the English-language seminary, and from 1966 on supported MLS through personnel and finances beyond its actual student proportion. The Australian Lutheran Mission and the Siassi/Menyamya Lutheran congregations also took part in the planning and establishing of MLS right from the beginning.

The first Faculty meeting consisting of Dr G.O. Reitz and J.G. Strelan took place in November 1965. The Seminary started its actual instruction ten weeks later on February 6, 1966 with a Faculty of three (including Mr D. Gerber as lecturer for general studies). With these initial seminary teachers, each one of the three participating Churches/Missions had provided a staff member for MLS.

The Studies Program

The Studies Program in the first two years includes general studies, a theological foundation program, and personal spiritual clarification and growth, including aspects of congregational life. Early attention is also given to preaching and the preparation of sermons, for students in New Guinea are expected to preach while still in training. Specific educational courses equip the student for his many avenues of teaching in schools and in confirmation classes. Along with classroom activities goes practical involvement in all fields of church work, such as home visitation, youth work, hospital calling, conducting Sunday-school, and leading congregations in worship.

In the advanced studies program (third and fourth year), the students undertake a core program in theology, and are given a choice for special areas of interest, such as communication and media work, cross-cultural studies, advanced education, or psychology. A full year is set aside for vicarage, which may take place in a rural congregation or in an urban environment. Most of the vicars come back to their last year in seminary with a sharpened sense of the needs of the people and of their own shortcomings.

At graduation, students receive their Diploma or the Bachelor Degree of Theology. On this occasion they are also given a call by a church leader for their first assignment as a pastor. Ordination normally takes place within the next twelve months.

As Martin Luther Seminary completes its second decade, one can only be thankful for what it has been able to achieve. It has always had students who felt called to become servants of Christ, and it has always had teachers who did their work with love and dedication. It is the hope of students and staff alike that the Triune God may continue to grant his blessing to this seminary in the years ahead, so that it may continue to be a blessing to his church and to the country of Papua New Guinea.

Endnotes

[1] H. Fontius, *Mission — Gemeinde — Kirche* (Erlangen: Evang. Luth. Mission, 1975), 49-59, 'Vorformen von Amt und Gemeinde'.

[2] K. Vetter, Kirchliche Mitteilungen 5/1893.

[3] Quoted by G. Pilhofer, I, 107.

[4] J. Flierl, *Wunder der goettlichen Gnade* (Tanunda: Auricht's, 1931), 13.

[5] G. Pilhofer, *Geschichte der Neuendettelsauer Mission in Neuguinea* (Neuendettelsau: Freimund-Verlag, 1961), vol. I, 179 (hereafter quoted only by volume and page number).

[6] Some more instances of spontaneous evangelistic movements in the early days of Lutheran Mission, both by individuals and by groups of people, could be added. For the Madang area, see H. George, First Half-Yearly Report, 1916; H. Eckershoff, Second Half-Yearly Report, 1917; A. Wullenkord, First Half-Yearly Report, 1921 (Barmen Archives). Also the Bongu story of the *Lan-tamo* could be quoted in this context (see ch 3).

[7] W. Freytag, *Reden und Aufsaetze I* (Munich: Christian Kaiser Verlag, 1960), 260-262.

[8] M. Deinzer, Jahrbuch der Bayerischen Missionskonferenz, 1907, 8.

[9] J. Flierl, *Wunder der goettlichen Gnade*, 80.

[10] *Ibid*, 45. This was written down when he already lived in retirement, yet one can sense something of the frustration of the early years.

[11] J. Flierl, *Denkschrift fuer unsere Heimatleitung*, 1906 (Lae Archives).

[12] For this change, see also Pilhofer, II, 43, footnote 73.

[13] J. Decker, letter dated 16.7.1906 (Neuendettelsau Archives).

[14] G. Pilhofer, I. 183.

[15] Janggoeng, in a letter to J. Flierl, dated October 28, 1928 (Lae Archives).

[16] S. Lehner, Answer to Questionnaire of Dir. Hartenstein, 1938 (Lae Archives).

[17] G. Pilhofer, Answer to Questionnaire of Dir. Hartenstein, (Lae Archives).

[18] S. Lehner, The Development of a Native Clergy, 1946, 16 (Lae Archives).

[19] E. Pietz, The Development of a Native Clergy, 1948, 3 (Lae Archives).

[20] J. Kuder, Native Leadership and Clergy, 1950, 2 (Lae Archives).

[21] *Ibid*, 5.

[22] *Ibid*, 6.

[23] Each of these established District Training Schools had had its forerunners: Heldsbach at Masang (1910) and Zaka (1912); Hopoi at Logaweng (1907/1911); Amron at Amele (1923) and Urit (1924). For the Highlands, a teachers training school was established at Rintebe in 1952, which operated on the same lines as the three coastal schools. For details see ch 13.

[24] G. Vicedom, 'Erfreuliches Erwachen', *Neuendettelsauer Missionsblatt* 1/1935.

[25] See H. Neumeyer, Annual Report, Kate Seminary 1938: 'It is very hopeful to see that until now the thought of becoming a teacher (in the home congregation) is of less importance. The idea of doing mission work still remains the goal we are trying to achieve.'

[26] G. Bamler, in a paper read at the 1906 Mission Conference (Lae Archives).

[27] Chr. Keysser, Annual Report Sattelberg, 1907 (Lae Archives).

[28] H. Gerber, Annual Report, Leadership Training, Heldsbach, 1979 (Lae Archives).

[29] In fact, these four men were the first ordained indigenous pastors of the Lutheran Church in New Guinea. Their ministry, however, was very short-lived. Mikael of Malalo was killed in 1943 in a Japanese bombing raid; Ruben was captured and detained by the Japanese army, and died soon after his release from detainment; Timote worked only for a short time at Mumeng before his early death; Elias was relieved of his duties after a short period of work in his home congregation of Taemi because of old age.

[30] H. Streicher, Jabem Pastors' Course, Hopoi, 1952 (Lae Archives).

[31] Their names were given by one of the participants as follows: from Sattelberg congregation Farenu, Wahawete, Manasunu, Muhujupe; from Kalasa: Bataningnuwe, Batamae, Tuno; three from Hube, of whom he remembered by name only Iwindinga; from Ulap-Sio Hiskia, Ateng; and from Boana Hariepo.

[32] P. Schulz, Pastors' Course, Buged, 1953 (Lae Archives).

[33] Lutheran Mission Conference, resolution 50:56. See also note 20.

[34] H. Streicher, Logaweng Seminary Report — Jabem Section, 1957 (Lae Archives).

[35] Logaweng Seminary Report, 1958 (Lae Archives).

[36] In the beginning years, neither the commencing of the various courses nor the graduating of the students was done at the same time, due to differing resolutions of the respective District Conferences. After the second Graged course was completed in 1962, the Madang District withdrew for three years from the ELCONG Seminary. In 1965, they rejoined with their students in an all-Pidgin class, which then became the model for all classes.

[37] Some courses in the years 1965-67 were given in English.

[38] The section on the Highlands Seminary, Ogelbeng was contributed by the Revd H. Bamler, Kleinhaslach, Germany.

[39] Information provided by Dr Willard Burce, Lae.

[40] A. Koschade, *New Branches on the Vine* (Minneapolis: Augsburg Publishing House, 1967), 152.

[41] A list compiled by G. Reitz in 1984 numbers 162 occasions between 1961 and 1968 when the matter was brought up for discussion.

[42] H. Fontius, *Mission — Gemeinde — Kirche* (Erlangen: Verlag der Ev.-Luth. Mission, 1975), 162-165, accuses those who promoted the English Seminary of shady, illegal, and questionable methods. Unfortunately, space does not allow a detailed debate on the matter here.

[43] Lutheran Mission New Guinea, Conference Minutes, resolutions 61:109-11.

[44] Lutheran Mission Conference Minutes, resolution 62:139.

[45] Lutheran Mission Education Committee, resolution 62:16.

[46] Lutheran Mission New Guinea, Executive Committee, resolutions 61:236; 62:358 and 359.

[47] Lutheran Mission Conference Minutes, resolution 62:139.

[48] Expatriate Meeting at Kate District Conference, 1962.

[49] Theological Education Committee (Madang), resolution 62:8 and 9; Committee on Ministry and Ministerial Training of Lutheran Mission Conference, 1963, Minutes Appendix 52,53; Lutheran Mission Conference 1965, Minutes, 19; Joint Committee for Theological Education, Lae, October 24-26, 1966.

[50] 1965 Lutheran Mission Conference Minutes, 19.

[51] This has been clearly seen and well described by A. Repp in his 'Report in Reference to MLS Lae', *The new New Guinea* (Lae: typescript, 1968), 3-23.

Chapter 13

Languages and Schools

by Hartley B. Hage

Already in 1886, the flying foxes of Finschhafen were well-equipped with ultra-sonic squeakers and echo-sensitive ears and wingtips to find a pathway through thick jungle in the dark, tropical night. By comparison, Senior Flierl was ill-equipped to penetrate the jungle of languages that confronted him. No tape recorders, no word processors, and no computers were available to him and his fellow-missionaries. In their wisdom, they decided to make only a narrow pathway through this jungle by using one or two local languages, which they hoped everyone would learn.

Little could these men know that the centenary of their arrival would be celebrated in a language for which they had the lowest possible esteem. That Pidgin might one day become the church's pathway through the linguistic jungle was quite beyond their wildest dreams. That thousands of people might praise Almighty God in Pidgin, as well as in other indigenous languages, was unthinkable. Equally as amazing for them would have been the thought that a foreign language such as English could become the medium of instruction for children.

Schools were the obvious tools for making the pathway envisaged by the early missionaries. Here, the children would learn the chosen languages which would eventually unite clans and tribes into one family of God. How cruel history can be! The very same tools used for promulgating the church languages were later used by the secular authorities to destroy them.

In spite of geographic obstacles, health problems, staff shortages, policies of governments, and the destruction of war, the Lord Jesus Christ used language and school mightily to bring his people the Gospel and to fulfil his promise: 'I will build my church'.

Choosing Church Languages

Even before the arrival of Europeans, members of neighbouring tribes learnt each others' languages to some extent. Where trade friendships existed, boys were sent to live with other groups to learn the language. The Rai Coast people, for example, sent boys to Madang to learn Graged.

The first missionaries worked in the particular language of their area, and produced

409

Deinzerhill school boys with missionaries Decker (left) and Lehner.

some literature. However, to continue in this way was soon recognized to be quite impracticable. Too many languages would be involved. It would be a waste of precious resources and a hindrance to the evangelization of the people. A language policy had to be decided on. After years of discussion, it was agreed to use Kate and Jabem in the Finschhafen and Lae areas, and Graged in the Madang area. These three finally became the church languages.

It was Mission policy that the local language be used for work among first-generation adults. In schools, however, the church language was to be used from the outset. This policy was reaffirmed as late as 1948. [1] By and large, the system of using church languages was reasonably successful, although the degree of success varied from one district to another.

The great pity was that in the early years not enough missionaries had the vision, humility, and courage to opt for a single vernacular. When it was too late to change, and when the church vernaculars were under attack from the government, this was regretted. In 1954, the Mission President wrote: 'The day the Mission

410

decided to use separate vernaculars as school languages, they also decided that none of them would become the official language of the people'. [2] When the first theological training school was planned for Logaweng, Finschhafen, it was suggested that the Mission had a last chance to make one of the church languages the *lingua franca* of the church. It would be the language used at the seminary. This did not happen.

Even if there were three church languages, it still has to be admitted that they had a unifying influence in the country. When the Territory Administration threatened the virtual destruction of the church language program in schools at the beginning of 1959, President Kuder pointed this out to the Minister of Territories in Canberra, Australia. He stressed the fact that through the church vernaculars a large number of tribes who had been enemies or even total strangers to one another, were joined together into one large community. He cited the example of Kate, which had originally had been spoken by some hundreds of people but was now used by 100,000. [3] Of course, not all spoke Kate fluently. What was true of Kate

Kate village school at Ogelbeng.

was also true of Jabem and Graged to a lesser degree.

The church languages in the coastal areas live on, but they struggle for survival. They were a gift from the Mission to the Lutheran Christians of Papua New Guinea. And finally, the giver had no choice but to leave it to the discretion of the recipient what to do with the gift. Whether Pidgin and English will remain the church languages of the future will depend to a large extent on national and international developments.

A Kate Vision for the Highlands

Tribal animosity posed a problem for the Mission, and it was hoped to overcome it in the Highlands through the introduction of Kate. A start was made before World War II, but it was in 1947 that a clear policy was formulated. It stated 'that we continue the use of Kate as the vernacular for our teaching program in the Central Highlands'.[4]

The reasons given for this important and sometimes controversial policy are enlightening.

1. There are 15 distinct language groups in Lutheran Mission areas.
2. One tribal group in the Highlands would not be willing to accept the language of another.
3. Use of local vernaculars involving much language research would delay the educational program considerably, and make the cost of printing literature in all vernaculars quite prohibitive.
4. Kate literature from the past 50 years is readily available.
5. Kate is structurally similar to the Central Highlands languages.
6. Kate is received without prejudice.
7. Several thousand people already have a working knowledge of Kate, and many thousands of others are learning it.
8. Teachers from the coast must be employed for the next decade.
9. The Mission has Kate-speaking missionaries available, who could use Kate as a medium in the teaching of English.

In addition to these factors, it must be remembered that these years were a critical period of rebuilding after the interruption and destruction of the war. Both missionaries and finance were at a premium.

411

'Later there was no choice but to drop Kate'.

Making a policy was relatively easy, but there were problems with the everyday usage of Kate. A fine New Guinean solution was found in the Kewamugl school in 1950.

> A step taken by our school boys is worthy of mention. Having at first refused to try to speak Kate outside the school, after much admonition, and with the added incentive of the presence of the Asaroka boys, they resolved several months ago to use Kate exclusively, outlawing their own languages on the station. They planted a shrub as a reminder of this promise, and they have pleasantly surprised me by keeping it,

writes school missionary P. Freyberg. [5]

Ten years after the first policy decision, it came up for review. Certain advantages of using local vernaculars, like Medlpa and Kuman, were recognized. But then it was decided, rather curiously,

> that we hold to the principle that Kate should be the school language in elementary education in the Central Highlands, but exceptions be made where the need arises and, in those cases, local group languages or Pidgin English may be used. [6]

It was further recommended that the local language be used in religious instruction for the

first years of schooling, until such time as the children knew sufficient Kate.

Soon after the Mission re-affirmed its policy in 1957, winds of change began to blow. The government made no secret of its determination to introduce its own policy for the Highlands. English was to be used in schools there, and the teaching of Kate was to be ruled out. Only one of the local vernaculars or Pidgin could be used in preparation for the teaching of English. The dilemma for Lutheran schools in the Highlands was acute.

In 1960, a missionary from the Rintebe school outlined the problem.

> It seems that our idea of using the major vernaculars such as Medlpa, Kuman, and Kamano is not going to work. People in fringe areas don't know enough of the language. Literature will have to be produced in all of them. One wonders who will do this. Where will they get the time, and how good a job will be done to ensure good instruction? [7]

It was suggested that Pidgin must be seen as an alternative.

In the village schools seeking government recognition, there was no choice but to drop

412

Church Conference — 'Pidgin was the only possible means of communication'.

Kate. However, in the evangelism-training schools of the Highlands, known as District Bible Schools, a choice of language was possible. But even there, the winds of change were felt. By 1964, the Kentagl District Bible School of the Western Highlands was using Pidgin as the teaching medium, for the first two years as a minimum. Others gradually followed this lead, and Kate began to die rather quickly. A great hope of the church for the Highlands remained unfulfilled. Time had simply run out.

Reluctant Acceptance of Pidgin

Over the years, a number of missionaries had stressed the importance of producing literature in a common language such as Pidgin, for the growth of a united church. After all, the three church languages had a divisive as well as a unifying effect. But it was not until 1956 that the Mission officially recognized Pidgin as a language. Even then, it was done rather carefully so as not to jeopardize the continued use of the church languages. It was

> resolved that we recognize Pidgin as an acceptable language for the promulgation of the Gospel, and wherever it is deemed advisable by

the circuits, in consultation with their Districts concerned, schools be conducted in this language.[8]

Former attitudes had changed.

In Finschhafen, Pidgin was hardly used after the German Administration moved to Madang in 1891. The missionaries had no time for it. 'One's hair would stand on end when one listened to the gibberish.'[9] Pidgin was branded as being incapable of expressing a truly indigenous experience, and as lacking in clarity and terminological precision. If missionaries had been able to agree on the use of only one church vernacular, the practical need for using Pidgin would hardly have arisen within the church.

As it was, whenever people of different language groups were involved in church conferences, Pidgin was the only possible means of communication. This was particularly true in the towns that grew so quickly after World War II. Services there were held in the church languages whenever possible, but many of the workers in the town compounds needing spiritual care and nurture simply did not understand Kate, Jabem, or Graged. Pidgin had

413

to be used. So, the Pidgin *Lotu Buk* took its place beside the other hymn books of the church. The use of Pidgin may have been regarded by some as a necessary evil, but there was no other alternative.

To use English in the compounds was quite out of the question. It was not even considered as a long-term possibility, as evidenced by a 1956 resolution.

> Whereas we do not believe that English will in the foreseeable future become the language of the people of this country and whereas Pidgin may one day be the unifying language of the New Guinean Church, resolved that we prepare for this greater use of Pidgin by periodic instruction in the religious use of Pidgin in our higher schools and that the production of religious and other materials in Pidgin be encouraged. [10]

When the Evangelical Lutheran Church of New Guinea (ELCONG) was organized in 1956, its membership spoke a multitude of languages. So Pidgin became a useful tool for communication. At least, there was less need for multiple translation of proceedings. Pidgin also became one of the languages used for the church's newspaper, and by 1974 it was the only language in use for this purpose.

Another pressure for the greater use of Pidgin came from the growth of government schools after 1945. This growth meant that an increasing percentage of the church's children no longer learnt to speak, read, or write one of the church languages. Pidgin was the best available medium for a spiritual ministry to most of them.

As a result of government policy to recognize only English schools, a complete system of Pidgin schools was set up by the Mission and Church, including a Teachers Training School at Rintebe. But it was done most reluctantly. The 1960 Mission Conference decided that Pidgin schools should only be established where there was no possibility of conducting a school in a church language. Furthermore, and quite significantly, such Pidgin schools should continue only until necessary school materials in local languages could be provided, and teachers trained to use them. That day never came.

More than anything else, the release of the New Testament in Pidgin in February, 1969, gave this language respectability. It has

414

increasingly become the language of the church, and most publications of the church are now produced in Pidgin. Nevertheless, the struggle between Pidgin and English for national recognition is probably far from over.

English — Path to Prosperity

New Guinea was for many decades a colonial country. A natural result was the introduction of the colonizers' language. Until 1914 it was German, and then it was English. The latter has had the greatest repercussions for the education program of the Lutheran Church. Especially during World War II, the American and Australian soldiers made quite an impact in the area of language, elevating English considerably. Several of the 1946 Conference Reports of missionaries refer to the desire of New Guineans for English and for technical training. Rightly or wrongly, these were seen to be the two keys opening the door to the white man's technology and wealth, of which so much had been seen during the war years.

Reading the signs of the times, the 1947 Mission Conference took positive action, and resolved that the Conference 'adopt the policy of making available in English and in all Mission vernaculars, all literature prepared for use in our Mission'. [11] In retrospect, this can only be judged a laudable plan requiring far more human and financial resources than were ever available. Immediately after a devastating war, a spirit of optimism was vital.

The next significant move was the establishment in 1952 of the Mission's all-English school at Bumayong, near Lae. This was a first for the Mission, and at this stage it certainly had no plans to abandon its vernacular education program. The Bumayong school was simply meant to meet an additional need within the church. By 1955, the Administration's Education Advisory Board, which had earlier agreed on the importance of using the vernacular as the medium of instruction in village schools, was coming under pressure from Canberra. The Australian government was beginning to demand the sole use of English for all educational work in New Guinea. It looked as if Lutheran Mission had moved in the right direction.

Not everyone was convinced of the wisdom of these developments. Doubts were expressed

The Pidgin New Testament being officially released, Madang, 1969.

by missionaries on the field. And before the Goroka Valley English School was opened in 1956, reservations were expressed by one of the overseas supporting partners.

> By carrying out the educational program as proposed by the Field, we are taking the first step towards the final end of our own school work ... If we expand the educational program in the suggested way, the congregations will again depend on the Mission in a branch of the work which they used to do independently, guided only by the missionaries. [12]

In the matter of dependency, no one can deny the accuracy of this prophecy. In the last decade, Lutheran schools have become solidly dependent on government and church finance.

A year later, the question of English schooling was still being hotly debated. Dr Kuder expressed the thoughts of many with his question: 'Does anyone believe that our people could find in English an adequate medium to express their faith or to convey to the heart a meaningful Christian message?' [13] The concern on the part of missionaries was genuine. Equally genuine was the desire of the church members to learn English. Not a few of them had linked their hopes for a better future to this language.

In 1952 an all-English School was opened at Bumayong, a forerunner of today's High School.

Whatever effort it might take, whatever sacrifice it might require, this was the mountain they were prepared to climb. For them it was the path to prosperity.

A one-class English village school.

A Selective School System

Structures in education are dynamic. New situations require new approaches. As the Mission work in Papua New Guinea grew and the number of congregations increased, the educational requirements became ever more demanding. Gradually, a system evolved with a broad base of village schools catering for all pupils. It then built up, through a process of selection, to look much like a razor-back mountain, with a small percentage of those village school pupils reaching the higher schools.

The Lutheran school system has, of course, altered during the course of the past 100 years (for details of educational developments in the Siassi-Menyamya and Enga areas, see chs 7,8). But the most common form has been that of a four-stage program. The village school instruction extended over a period of four years, the station or circuit school for two years, the middle or area school for four years, and the Teachers Training School for two more years. In the present English system, pupils may attend the Community School, and Teachers College. Those who qualify may gain

416

entrance to other tertiary institutions, or even to the university.

Whatever the system, the question of wastage arises. With the advent of English teaching, certificated teachers, and short-term overseas teachers, the concept of wastage became a lively issue. Teachers felt that if only a few of their pupils went on to higher schools, their efforts were largely wasted. Their feelings can be appreciated, and their criticism of the selection process starting at the end of the fourth year of village schooling is understandable. The problem has still not been solved. The large number of school leavers after the sixth year of primary school remains one of the country's major educational and social problems.

The concept of wastage belongs to the latter part of the Mission's history. Originally, the fact that perhaps ten out of fifty village-school pupils could continue at a higher school would not have been considered wastage. Rather, the village-school teacher had accomplished what he set out to do, namely, to carry the children through a four-year course. He had a sense of fulfilment. The fact that ten children could go on to the station school was in the nature of a bonus for his efforts as a teacher.

From the outset, it had been the aim of Lutheran Mission to link congregation and school as closely as possible. Consequently, the congregations were involved with the selection process of students from one level to another. And the idea that only the highest academic achiever should be chosen to attend a higher school was not compatible with the concept of a living relationship between congregation and school.

Four main factors played a part in selection of students, and they give an insight into the church's educational philosophy at the time.
1. The character of a student was often the first and most important consideration.
2. A student's personal wishes were ascertained. If he were rather uncertain about continuing, he could often be encouraged or persuaded to consider the hopes that the congregation had for him.
3. Past scholastic record and academic potential were appraised.
4. The selection process included a sincere concern for the principle of representation. If

at all possible, every circuit or congregation should have some students at all higher schools.

It is worthwhile looking more closely at the fourth point, regarding representation. It goes back to the link between school and congregation. The school belonged to everyone, and everyone needed a life-line to it. Furthermore, a congregation felt that if it had no students in the Teachers Training School it might well end up with a shortage of teachers. Since these men were also preachers and evangelists, the congregation regarded representation as a guarantee for its very survival. When the demands of the government in regard to the English language and school registration forced a change in the selection process, there was much questioning. With a good deal of dismay, the congregations saw academic excellence being given pride of place, and the matter of representation becoming a minor consideration. It will have taken them some time to appreciate the national, rather than the congregational, approach to education.

Ever-Changing Bible Schools

The name 'Bible School' once designated a boarding school for the training of evangelists. It was later applied to the non-English or Exempt Schools of the church. Rather than have them closed, the church changed them to Bible Schools. The prospect of an educational vacuum in Christian villages was completely unacceptable. If a congregation could not have a recognized English school, then it was determined to meet its responsibilities in another way. And so the Village Bible Schools continued the church's literacy program. For Lutheran children, the Bible, catechism, and hymn book were to remain a vital part of their Christian heritage.

At the beginning of 1962, missionaries in conference resolved

> that until such time as there are enough qualified teachers, we divide our educational program into a dual system whereby all certificated teachers and selected permit teachers feed their pupils into our English schools, and that the other teachers work towards making their pupils literate in a vernacular and prepare them for a fuller congregational life and service. [14]

In view of the Administration's stated aim of achieving universal primary education in English within 15 years, this dual system was simply meant to be a stop-gap measure.

At the time, there was some uncertainty concerning a definition of the word 'school'. To avoid any possible misunderstanding or legal complications, it was agreed to call these non-schools Religious Literacy Centres. Two years later, the Mission Conference recommended to the church that the name be changed to Village Bible Schools. Two reasons were given. Firstly, the final aim of the Religious Literacy Centres was that children learn to read and to understand God's Word. Secondly, in communication with non-Mission people, the New Guineans would have a name describing the essential character of these schools. And this would minimize the danger of possible misunderstanding.

A complete Pidgin curriculum was to be prepared for the Bible Schools to serve as a model for any other vernacular programs. Tremendous effort was put into the production of programs and lesson guides. Yet, there was always a serious dearth of materials. It all happened too quickly, with thousands of children suddenly requiring books. Especially was this true in the Highlands. Coastal schools could at least make use of old Kate, Jabem, and Graged materials prepared years ago. There were 12 years to be covered, following the old pattern of village, circuit, district, and teachers' training schools.

At first, the dual education system functioned under two separate authorities within the church. The English program had its Mission Education Officer, and the vernacular program its Religious Literacy Officer, together with their respective committees. The first New Guineans to hold the respective offices were Mr Sakey Ronu and Mr Elisha Gware. Liaison between the two offices increased over the years to the point of amalgamation in 1978, with a Lutheran Education Board and Assistant Secretaries for the various departments.

The Village Bible School program had its ups and downs. In some areas it was warmly welcomed, while in others it was merely tolerated. It has to be remembered that it was intended to be only a stop-gap measure. In spite of that, at its peak, some 700 teachers were

Sakey Ronu, first indigenous Education Officer.

teaching thousands of children in schools which were not open doors to lucrative jobs and professions. But within a few years that picture was to change dramatically, with a decline in teachers and students. Before that happened, something different was tried.

From 1968 onwards, a new concept for Bible Schools began to emerge. The Revd E. Jaeschke spear-headed the development from a Bible School to a *Tok Ples* School program (that is, a vernacular school program in distinction to the foreign language school program).

> If built up carefully and methodically, it could become a very valuable service to the developing Church. In addition, there is the possibility it could become an example and a forerunner for the whole school system for all missions, and also for the Administration. [15]

The new program was developed in great detail.

In 1972, a consultation was held in Madang at which the principles, objectives, and aims of the *Tok Ples* School program were set up. Following this, the Synod of the Church formally changed the names of Bible Schools to *Tok Ples* Schools. Not only the name changed; the

418

essential character of the schools also changed. They could more accurately be described as vocational schools. It was intended that they be an alternative to the English schools.

In spite of great efforts to prepare a new curriculum and to improve the professional standing of the teachers, the outgoing tide could not be stemmed. The number of teachers and pupils in the *Tok Ples* program began to decline alarmingly. English schools were becoming more available to the people, and they were not particularly attracted to the *Tok Ples* Schools. By 1984, the last of these schools in the Highlands had closed. The Kate District was still fairly supportive of its Kate schools, and a few non-English schools remained in the Jabem District where there were no English schools. Otherwise, little remains apart from the upper level of the *Tok Ples* program, and that caters for Grade 6 school leavers from the English program.

The percentage of school-age children unable to attend an English Community school is still high. For example, in the Aseki Circuit it is estimated that only 13 per cent of the children attend school. In other areas, that percentage will be much higher, but the challenge for the church remains. If the Bible Schools and *Tok Ples* Schools are no longer welcomed in the villages, then the congregations will have to find some other way to teach their children and make them literate.

Attractions of English Schools

Attendance at an English school brought with it a certain prestige. Those New Guineans able to converse in English formed a kind of elite. English schooling was seen to be the key to jobs, wealth, entrance into European society, and overseas travel.

When the first all-English school of the Mission was opened at Bumayong in 1952, specific aims were drawn up. They are interesting, because they reveal not only the hopes of the Mission but also certain fears. Pride and alienation from the congregations could easily become a by-product of English education.

> 1. Pupils should be discouraged from looking at their training as something higher than the education at other institutions. The only difference lies in the language medium.

2. The pupils are sent and supported by their congregations, and therefore are expected to serve their congregations and their church.
3. The aim is to prepare pupils for leadership, as teachers, candidates for the Theological Seminary, medical training, technical training, clerical positions within the church, and to serve in business enterprises within the church.
4. The hope is that some will hold prominent positions in the church, and form a liaison between the outside world and the church. [16]

After Bumayong opened its doors, one English school after another was established: Goroka Valley (Asaroka) in 1956, Kewamugl in 1957, and Kitip in 1959. After some years, the schools at Bumayong, Asaroka, and Kitip became Junior High Schools, together with the schools at Baitabag and Heldsbach. By 1965, the Mission was prepared to build up these schools into full High Schools. However, before the plan could come to fruition, a process of consolidation was set in motion. The 1966 Synod of the Church decided to close all the Lutheran High Schools except Asaroka (for the Highlands) and Bumayong (for the coastal district). For many indigenous and expatriate folk, this development brought much sadness.

As things have developed in the latter years, the former Junior High Schools are experiencing a rebirth. Kitip has re-opened, and the Madang and Chimbu Districts of the church are working toward the same end. With the help of overseas donor funds, their wishes may well be fulfilled. Something that will be watched with interest is the possible establishment of an independent Church High School with maximum church control.

At the 1962 Mission Conference, a plan far more ambitious than that of High Schools was considered. It was hoped that the foundations of what would later develop into a school of university level would soon be laid. As we now know, Lutheran Mission never made a serious move in that direction, much to the disappointment of some missionaries.

When the Mission realized its plight due to the government's impending decrees regarding the use of English in schools, it decided in 1957 to request short-term teachers. That sounds quite straight-forward, until it is realized that certain principles were involved. For this reason, some missionaries had strong reservations. They saw it as a move toward secularization of

In 1957 short-term teachers from overseas were introduced to boost the English program (School in Tiria).

the education program, and a possible undermining of the Mission's long-standing policy of learning a New Guinean language and having a year or two of orientation. A short term of two years' service would permit neither.

Weighted against this argument was the stark fact that in 1959 a total of 407 Mission candidates sat for their 'A' certificate examination. Two hundred and nine passed, and only about 20 of them were from Lutheran Mission. So, the short-termers came, from overseas churches and from other voluntary agencies. It was not the ideal solution to a problem, but these men and women made a valuable contribution to the education program of the Church.

The backbone of the Lutheran education program, of course, was the village schools. There were some 600 of these one-teacher schools, with more than 30,000 children enrolled, when the language crisis arose. Faced with the alternative of losing their schools or introducing English, the circuits simply converted them into one-teacher English schools. However, it soon became evident that a teacher working alone quickly lost much of his ability in the English language.

419

The backbone of Lutheran education were the 600 village schools (School at Maranenan, Watut).

In 1968, the Missions' Education Officer advised circuits of the aim to build up all schools to three-teacher schools as soon as possible. A year later, no one-teacher schools were to be reported on the Quarterly Returns unless they had the specific sanction of the MEO. No mention on the returns meant no school supplies and no salary. Faced with such an ultimatum, congregations simply had to give in.

Villagers who had proudly maintained their little bush school for decades experienced a sense of bereavement. Those who gained a consolidated community school were delighted. Consolidation has continued, and all the church's registered schools now teach the children for a full six years before there is any selection for admission to a High School.

National independence in 1975 brought with it a natural desire for localization of teaching positions. An interesting comment came from the Lutheran Education Officer in 1978 regarding staffing of Lutheran High Schools: 'We are very pleased to report that 83% of the teachers are from PNG, and we are looking forward to the day we can report 100%
420

of the teachers are Nationals'. [17] By 1984, all Head Masters and Deputy Head Master positions had been localized.

Lutheran children attending government English schools have presented the church with a real challenge. Efforts have been made to give religious instruction to all of these children. To this end, the Church now makes a gift of books and other materials for Christian Education classes to all schools that have Lutheran children enrolled.

A national spirit, along with the English school system, may be expected to raise hopes which can only be partially fulfilled. There are obvious limits to what a nation can afford for education, and there are limits to what a church can contribute as a partner in the national education system. Attractions of an English education offer no protection against the disillusionment of unemployment, with its resultant social disruption. The Utopian path to prosperity hardly makes for contentment in the humble life of village agriculturalists. But for a people adept at climbing mountains, even these obstacles will not appear unconquerable.

Jabem Girls' School, opened at Bula in 1956.

Girls' Schools

The first attempts to open a District Girls School at Finschhafen in 1907 were opposed by the congregations, so the plan was dropped. Another way to improve the education of girls was found. House-boys on Mission stations were replaced by girls, who learnt sewing, mending, washing, cooking, and hygiene. Sometimes they also attended the station school, and had opportunity to join in the daily worship life of the station. Eventually, two station schools for girls were founded. Miss Dora Flierl began a school at Heldsbach in 1912; and the school at Kalasa was opened some years later by Mrs K. Wacke.

After World War II, Mrs A. Welsch opened a school at Amele, enrolling 20 girls from the Amele circuit. Then in 1948, girls from other areas in the Madang District were able to attend the school too. For congregations to send girls to a Mission station other than their own was something new. Mrs Welsch set her students the goal of becoming kindergarten teachers. By 1951, no less than 15 of her graduates were teaching 154 children in 11 villages. Four years later, the school was transferred to Nobonob, and became the Madang District Girls School.

Missionaries put a high priority on girls' schooling, but it was not always easy to convince the New Guineans of such a need. Nevertheless the Kate District Girls School opened at Raong in 1954, and the Jabem Girls School at Bula in 1956. It took until 1963 for the Western Highlands Girls School to be established at Tiria.

The following aims for girls' schools were drawn up in 1958:

1. To ground all students in the essentials of Christian home-making.
2. To prepare selected students for spiritual work among village women.
3. To train Kindergarten and Sunday-school teachers.
4. To prepare selected students for later training as nurses or certified 'A' teachers.

Teachers attempted to achieve these aims as best they could with a limited staff. They were assisted by New Guinean women.

Soon there was an emphasis on raising academic standards. The 1965 Mission Conference asked the District Girls Schools to enrol girls who had completed Standard 6. They were then to receive training in religious instruction, Sunday-school teaching, leadership in Bible study, church language, mothercraft, first aid, cooking, sewing, handcrafts, and garden work — all this, along with a modified general education for a period of two or three years. These were noble but hardly attainable goals. And before they could become properly established, these same schools were either closed or had their curriculum changed once again.

The day of coeducational High Schools was about to dawn. In fact, the Conference that modified the District Girls Schools curriculum, as mentioned above, made another noteworthy decision:

> that all District Junior High Schools make provision for coeducational training for those girls meeting the qualifications, and appointed by the congregations for the purpose of becoming teachers, graduate nurses, social workers, and other possible courses, i.e. domestic science teachers or commercial work. [18]

Following the closure of the District Girls Schools, Domestic Science Bible Schools were opened in a number of locations. In 1984, there were again District Girls Schools at Baitabag, Kentagl, Tarabo, and Sattelberg, operating within the Workman Training Department of the Church.

Much More Than Teachers' Training

Teachers' training may be called the heart of an education program. For the Mission, it was also at the heart of its evangelization program.

Serious discussions about training teachers began surprisingly early in the history of the Mission. Only six years after the first two men were baptized in 1899, both the Jabem and Kate Missionaries' Conferences of 1905 considered the possibility of establishing Teachers Training Schools. Right from the outset, there was general agreement that a living union between congregation and school would be essential. What this meant in practical terms may well surprise the modern student.

At one Seminary or Teachers Training School, the students had an oral examination at the close of each year's study. This was held in the presence of New Guinean and missionary representatives of the congregations. Then, at the graduation service, the teachers were formally handed back to their congregations,

422

who then assigned them to their field of labour. At the same service, a new class was formally received.

Small District Centres

The first tentative steps toward training teachers were taken at Logaweng with Jabem-speaking students. The Revd G. Bamler found five students from Deinzerhill willing to begin studies in 1907, but the course came to an untimely conclusion after several months. In 1909, he trained a group of seven students for the whole year. But it was all a little premature. There were only a few, small Jabem congregations at the time, and they needed further instruction before properly understanding the implications of involvement with a training school. By 1911 this point had been reached, and the Revd H. Zahn was able to carry on the work successfully. In 1914, no less than 21 students were welcomed to Logaweng. Jabem teachers' training continued there until a new school was opened at Hopoi in 1924. A flourishing work ended there when Balob Teachers College opened in Lae in 1965.

In 1910, representatives of all the Kate congregations gathered at Masang (Simbang III), together with many missionaries, to dedicate their first Teachers Training School.

Kate Teachers Training School

The 14 students beginning a three-year course had the Revd G. Pilhofer as their teacher. Interest in this new venture was high, and more than 1,000 New Guineans attended the graduation service of the 13 men who completed their training. In 1913, the school moved to Zaka, but found a new and permanent home at Heldsbach the following year. There was a move in 1964 to close the school as a Teachers Training Centre, but that was only an interlude. In 1967 it again opened as the Training Centre for Kate Bible School teachers. The Synod of the Church in 1984 gave it a new task, to train full-time teachers for religious instruction in non-Lutheran Community Schools.

At Finschhafen the Mission had two separate language areas, with two training schools. In **Madang** there were also two linguistic arrangements with two separate schools. The Revd A. Wullenkord founded the

Heldsbach Teachers Seminary with the Revd G. Pilhofer.

Jabem Teachers Seminary with the Revd H. Zahn.

423

Amele Teachers Seminary with the Revd A. Wullenkord and family.

first Teachers Training School at Amele in 1923, using the Amele language. On Karkar Island a second school was built at Urit (Kurum) in 1924. The Revd H. George began with a class of 24 students, teaching them in the Graged language.

Union of the two Madang district schools came with a decision of the 1932 Field Conference of Lutheran Mission Madang, to use Graged as the church language. (At that time, Finschhafen and Madang were two separate Mission organizations.) Toward the end of 1934, the new school at Amron, some 12 kilometres from Madang, opened its doors. In the latter years, the school has trained evangelists rather than teachers.

Educational developments in the **Highlands** were seriously hampered by World War II. Finally, the 1950 Mission Conference took action to establish a Teachers Training School at Rintebe, not far from Goroka. The Revd A. Frerichs began the work there with Mr R. Tews, and in 1958 a group of 25 teachers graduated. This was the first time in the Highlands that a class of Lutheran students had completed the 12 years of instruction necessary
424

to become teachers. Prior to this time, a number of Highland boys had graduated from the church's other training schools.

Need for Centralization

When the government became quite adamant about its language policy, English teachers' training had to become a reality. In 1957, the Mission selected 32 students from its three Training Centres, and sent them to Amron for an extra year's training, using English exclusively. At the end of the year they sat for the government examination, being the first group of Lutheran Mission teachers to do so. The following year, the other three training schools also began presenting students for the certificate examinations. Meanwhile, the English Training School moved from Amron to Bumayong in 1958, to begin the higher level 'B' course training. It closed at the end of 1962, after which the 'B' course trainees attended the Administration Teachers College at Port Moresby.

If we go back to the early period of the Mission, we come across an interesting proposal. Mission Inspector Steck, who visited

Education Secretary, Martin Helbig, welcomes the guests of honour at the dedication of Balob Teachers College in 1964.

the Field in 1914-15, suggested combining the two existing Teachers Training Schools at one place, namely, Logaweng. He argued that a single school with two teachers could achieve more than two schools with one teacher each. The truth of his observation cannot be denied. Still, it did not eventuate, and in due course the Mission actually had five Teachers Training Schools, each with one or two missionary teachers working with one or more New Guinean teachers. With the demand for higher educational standards, something else had to be done. In 1960, the Mission decided 'that the combined Teachers Training College for the coastal districts be built on the Malahang property' near Lae. [19] The plan at that stage was to retain Rintebe as the college for the Highlands, but this plan was later dropped. Also dropped was the plan to build at Malahang, in favour of Bumayong. Eventually, it was agreed to build the college across the road from the Ampo headquarters of Church and Mission, near Lae.

No sooner were plans afoot for a central college, than voices were raised in warning. Such a large institution, they maintained, would tend to weaken the link between trainees and their home congregations. It would also destroy the sense of responsibility that congregations and district once had toward their District Training Centres. On both counts they were right; the price of progress had been correctly identified. Oddly enough, then, a minority report presented to the 1963 Mission Conference would have made matters even worse. It proposed sending students to the Administration Teachers College instead of building a new Church College. After graduation, they were to be given a course lasting approximately six months to prepare them for teaching in Lutheran schools. The proposal was reasonable, but not generally accepted.

Balob Teachers College was dedicated in 1964, and began with classes in 1965. Mr F. Stolz was the first Principal, and he was assisted by a staff of seven to train 99 students. Twenty years later, the college had 349 students with 25 staff members. Quite significantly, the college has also served the Wabag Lutheran Church, and what was then known as the Australian

Lutheran Mission. From 1969, the Anglican Church also supplied students and some staff. Financial support and representation on the school board is based on the percentage of students attending. Nevertheless, Balob is considered an institution of the Evangelical Lutheran Church — Papua New Guinea (formerly ELCONG). It draws some K20,000 annually from the church budget. The Gutnius Lutheran Church (Wabag) is considered a direct partner, and the Anglicans are associate partners. [20]

Over the years, Lutheran enrolments at Balob Teachers College have averaged approximately 50 per cent of the student body. That fact alone has presented opportunities and challenges in the social and religious life of the college. Those students who fulfil the requirements are granted a certificate of Christian Education in addition to their teaching diploma. The certificate helps a teacher to be posted to a Lutheran school. Balob has now graduated more than 2,000 teachers, and it continues to work under its motto: 'To Serve'.

Bible School Teachers Training

In the same year that Balob was dedicated, Rintebe began with Bible School teachers' training. This was in accordance with the Mission's decision 'that Rintebe begin a program of training for teachers for the new Religious Literacy program', and that 'Rintebe become the ELCONG Teachers Training Centre for the Religious Literacy program'. [21]

Aerial view of Balob Teachers College.

426

Kate teachers were also trained at Rintebe in 1965 and 1966, after which this training returned to Heldsbach.

It had been hoped that all Literacy Centre training (later called Bible School, and still later *Tok Ples* School) could be conducted at Rintebe in the Pidgin language, no matter what the medium of instruction would eventually be in the classroom. This was not to be. Those who entertained such hopes failed to appreciate fully the pedagogical difficulties of such a scheme. Moreover, they had underestimated the significance of the Kate language and the Heldsbach school location for the people of the Kate District. It was, after all, from Heldsbach that so many teacher-preachers went to evangelize the Highlands. Heldsbach was a spiritual centre, and its re-establishment was a boost for the Kate language itself. In view of the Mission's determination to close Heldsbach as a Teachers Training Centre in 1964, it is almost ironic that all non-English teacher's training for years 1-6 was transferred there in 1982, following the closure of Rintebe as a training centre.

A rather short-lived venture of the church was the District Bible School Teachers Training at Kitip in the Hagen District. Its task was to train teachers for the six District Bible Schools, and this was begun in 1971 by the Revd H. Hage. Among the students were several men who had been teaching at the Senior Flierl and Highlands seminaries. After completion of the course, they returned there. In 1979, Rintebe began a training course for years 7-8 of the Bible School program, so taking over the work started at Kitip.

A Sacred Commission

Teachers' training in the Mission and Church has been much more than the title suggests. From the outset, the aims of teachers' training were three-fold:

1. Men were to be trained as teachers.
2. They were to be trained for service in the congregations, for leading in the worship life of the congregation, and for assisting in confirmation and catechumen instruction.
3. They were to be trained for evangelization of the heathen.

These basic aims changed little with the passage of time, and it is understandable that

Former Sattelberg Circuit President Ronu.

the Training Centres were first known as Seminaries. For decades, Lutheran teachers have also been preachers, and as the Church celebrates 100 years of missionary activity in New Guinea, many teachers will still be active in their congregations, even if not to the same extent as formerly.

It is undoubtedly true that there have been instances where school work suffered because of a teacher's involvement in the congregation. From a purely educational standpoint, such a situation could be viewed rather critically, as it was in the 1950s and '60s. But while the school was still seen to be an integral part of the congregation, and not simply a recognized unit of a national education system, what the teacher did for the school and the congregation could be viewed positively as his total contribution and service.

Any consideration of teachers' training must include the subject of the divine call. To graduate from one of the church's Teacher Training Schools was much more than successful completion of a course of instruction. Graduates of past years believed that they were responding to a call of God. As young men, they had been sent by their congregations to the school, and they had felt themselves under a continuing spiritual bond with the congregations. Furthermore, they believed that the office committed to them on the day of graduation was sacred. Consequently, they took the laying on of hands, as the office of teacher was committed to them, most seriously. Missionaries sometimes held fears about this action and possible misunderstandings of it, but it was continued for years. Along with the teachers, congregations held the office in high regard.

All this needs to be remembered and appreciated if the heartache of teachers in the latter years is to be comprehended. Just because they could not successfully teach in English and meet other and new pedagogical demands, they felt harshly criticized and discarded. Such judgments were quite out of harmony with their call into the office of a Christian teacher. Assessment of their work was nothing new. For years, missionaries and other New Guinean teachers had inspected their schools, making critically constructive comments. But it had not been suggested, even by implication, that they were worthless. Because of language requirements, many teachers felt they had no choice but to resign. At the same time, they felt that something sacred was being ruthlessly attacked. In fairness to many of the inspectors, it must be said that they could not have an appreciation of the teacher's call.

Graduation customs reveal much about the way in which teachers perceived their work. Two examples illustrate this well. At Hopoi, in 1956, each student lit the candle he was holding, from the altar candles, and carried it into the congregation. It was a symbolic action the men would remember for years. There was also a meaningful custom at Heldsbach, followed for years. The following description was written in 1954.

> In accordance with old tradition the 71 students, together with their native teachers had a two-day farewell retreat. The place which they elaborately prepared for this occasion in a secluded corner of the jungle near the creek did not lack beauty or solemnity. One of the main features of their program was that everyone present delivered a short farewell message based on a word of

Scripture, or an event of Church history or Mission history, or some folklore. The series of talks were interrupted by singing and prayer, and concluded with a native-style banquet. [22]

Curriculum Foundations

If the graduates were conscious of the sanctity of their office, so were the teachers who trained them. They were particularly aware of this when preparing the various courses. Missionaries had to create their own curriculum, write books, and devise their own teaching methods and programs of work. By trial and error it was found that a set of daily lesson guides, prepared for each day and year, gave the best results. It may not have left much room for teacher initiative or innovation, but for men unused to the discipline of a daily routine the method was good. The training of teachers required much dedication and humility, along with patience. One man who worked in this field for years wrote:

> We are only too well aware of all shortcomings and of how far we still are from turning out better and abler men. But things cannot be forced. We have to be satisfied with gradually aiming at greater things and accomplishments in the course of years and generations. [23]

Now, this approach was fine until New Guinea was thrust on the world stage, and other nations were clamouring for her independence. Almost without warning, the gradual approach to improvement was tossed overboard.

Modern students may well be surprised at the breadth of curriculum found in schools years ago. One example is that of the Amron school.

In the years 1932-42, students had a six-year stay at the school, leading to graduation as teachers. Subjects listed were: Reading, Writing, Arithmetic, Christianity I and II, Graged, Singing, Sports (native games), Hygiene, Geography, English, Physics, Biology, Physiology, Manual Training (carving), Practice Teaching, Church History, Botany, and Zoology. The goal of all the Teachers Training Schools was to give students as thorough and broad an education as time and resources permitted.

There was a philosophy of Christian education, even if it was not spelt out in great detail. The Principal of Amron for many years, Dr E. Hannemann, wrote:

Dr E. Hannemann, Principal of Amron Teachers Seminary for many years.

How could an institution such as our Amron Central school address itself one-sidedly to what is commonly called the spiritual side of man? The Papuan man is a unit, a man indivisible: his body and soul, his present hopes and his future needs, all phases of the life which is and which is to come represent a unit. For that reason our Christian school presents knowledge concerning all branches of science which explain the universe and which show where animistic and magical beliefs are false. [24]

On this basis the curriculum was planned.

Gratefully Remembered

Teachers' training has taken place within a boarding situation, and it is especially here that the New Guinean assistants of past years will be gratefully remembered by missionaries and students alike. At Hopoi they were: Male Nedelabu, Anam David, Tingasa Gedisa, and Ida Jalingnomsing. At Heldsbach: Mitie, Fuapo, and Mufuanu Butik, all of whom served for many years, even decades. At Urit: Mileng, Jas, and Sapush. At Amron: Lapan, Tanggoi, Pah, Gulal, Jabon, and Los. They understood the students much better than the Europeans, and

428

First Mission Printery at Logaweng.

gave invaluable leadership in the community life of the school. Without their sacrificial and dedicated help, a handful of missionaries could not possibly have trained an army of teachers for Lutheran schools.

Many more dedicated teachers ought to be remembered, also those who served their congregations faithfully in often remote places. This, however, cannot be done in a church history as this, as much as they deserved it.

Printing Presses in the Service of Mission and Church

Only two years after the first Kate and Jabem evangelists were sent out, the printery was begun at Logaweng in 1909 by the Revd G. Bamler. In 1914, the Revd H. Boettger took over the work, which was so vital for the language and school programs of the Church and Mission. Before printing was begun at the field, all materials had to be produced overseas, often causing long delays. For the Mission in the Madang area, some printing was done at Urit on Karkar Island. The year 1935 saw the building of a printery at Gonob, adjacent to Amron, with the Revd J. Mager in charge.[25]

Printery at Nagada after World War II.

429

Timong Langwa, who served the Church as a printer for almost 60 years.

When World War II compelled the overseas missionaries to leave their posts, the presses continued working. A few New Guineans, trained in the workshop at Logaweng, continued printing hymnals, in spite of air attacks, until the supplies of paper ran out. Eventually both printeries, at Gonob and Logaweng, were bombed and destroyed. A new printery to serve the whole Mission was built at Nagada after the war. It remains there to this day.

Many developments have taken place since the first printery was established. There has been continuing modernization of equipment resulting in a more efficient operation, with an ever-increasing volume of books and other materials being printed. More and more New Guineans have been employed, assuming ever greater responsibility. By 1971, no less than 35 New Guineans worked at the Nagada printery, including nine apprentices and four tradesmen. In the following year, four of the five main departments were supervised by nationals.

The printeries have served Church and Mission well, providing hymnals, histories, New

430

Testaments, language helps, catechisms, Sunday-school leaflets, Sunday text explanations, church newspapers, and a host of school books, teaching aids, and other materials. One of the most exciting projects undertaken was the printing of the Pidgin New Testament for the Bible Society in an edition of 40,000 in 1969.

In the immediate post-war years, the printery at Nagada made no attempt at being self-supporting. Mission funds supported the Mission personnel working there, and paid the New Guineans too. At the same time, the production of literature was subsidized, often by as much as 40 per cent. Even after the formation of Kristen Pres Inc. in 1969, with Luther Press at Nagada as the production division, more than 50 per cent of production was being subsidized by its own revenue. In spite of this, the new organization, incorporating separate production and sales divisions, was reported to be self-supporting by 1970.

The sale of books had for a long time been handled by the printeries themselves. But in 1966 a **Christian Book Centre** was dedicated in the town of Madang. The first manager, Mr F. Lamparter, planned on opening a network of bookshops throughout the whole Mission. This goal was pursued with vigour, and the growth of sales was spectacular. In the first year of operation, sales figures were $40,000, and by 1969 they exceeded $160,000. After a short four-year association with Lutheran Mission New Guinea, the Christian Book Centre became part of the publishing company known as Kristen Pres Inc. Nevertheless, the service to schools and congregations of the church continued.

A more recent development has been the appointment of a Book Committee by the church. The committee is responsible for finding writers of books and for deciding which books may be printed in the name of the church. It also recommends which books shall be subsidized. Naturally, it works hand in hand with the printery. And with the constant revision of books used by the church, the printery will continue in its servant role for many more generations.

Upgrading, Updating, Uplifting

Innovation and improvization, graduating

and gathering, training and retraining, characterize the history of Lutheran education in PNG. In 1917, the first Kate graduating class was recalled for one year's training. This might be called the beginning of refresher courses. Most annual refresher courses, however, have extended over a week or two. They have involved much expenditure of money and effort on the part of the Mission. Years ago, for instance, teachers were flown to the coast from the Highlands, and mission ships carried hundreds of teachers each year, free of charge. In 1955, no less than 260 teachers attended the Kate Refresher Course at Heldsbach. To that number would have to be added the teachers attending the Jabem and Graged courses.

A feast of topics was available at the courses. One course listed the following: English, Geography of Europe, Arithmetic, Improvement of Handwriting, Teaching Methods, Introduction to Paul's Epistles to the Romans and Corinthians, Daily Scriptural addresses, Treatment of the Cargo Cult from economical, psychological and religious angles, and Question Box. Such a gathering was also the time to introduce any new text-books and programs of work or daily lesson plans.

Refresher courses were times of reunion, the importance of which should not be underestimated. Teachers often lived far away from home and relatives, experiencing a sense of physical and social isolation. So, these courses were times of spiritual renewal, as well as academic refreshment.

Wherever Refresher Courses were held, there was a need to supply food. Mostly, the students at the Training Centres planted extra gardens just for this purpose. In other cases, the local communities became involved. In 1955, some 70 New Guinean teachers and nearly all the Western Highlands missionaries gathered for a course. One of the participants reported:

> Two days before the Refresher Course we stood amazed and dumbfounded as a line of local people (it took over 5 minutes to pass us), Christians and heathen, the luluai, tultuls, elders, women, men and children brought firewood, sweet potatoes, sugar cane, bananas, pineapples, vegetables and stacked and piled it high in the cook house. It was a heart-warming act on the part of the locals to support or endeavour to refresh their teachers. [26]

Things have changed. The present-day teacher may apply for scholarships within PNG or overseas to improve himself. Provinces also hold annual in-service weeks for teachers. All this is provided for the certificated teachers. For the *Tok Ples* School teachers, the church also conducts in-service courses for one or two weeks. No doubt, the modern in-service courses have much in common with the old-fashioned Refresher Courses. It is but one way to improve and help.

Surely unique was the system of school inspections adopted by the Mission for many years. Missionary teachers from the Middle or Area Schools, together with those from the Teachers Training Schools, went on inspection once a year. In addition, New Guinean teachers who had been appointed as so-called Head Teachers by congregations, visited all the schools in their areas twice a year. The latter reported their findings to the Teachers Training School. Inspection results were often discussed at Refresher Courses, too.

Sadly, it was the demand of the education authorities to raise standards and to emphasize the teaching of English that broke down the system of inspection for a number of years. And yet, that was just the time when regular inspections were crucial. There were two reasons for fewer inspections. Firstly, missionaries could not leave the classroom because lessons had to be taught in English. In former times, the New Guinean assistants could take over, since they could work in the vernacular. Secondly, because of the demands to achieve higher standards, teachers felt they had to spend as much time as possible in the classrooms. Inspection trips might take as long as four or five weeks. This they felt they could not afford.

In 1964, the Sattelberg circuit received a full-time missionary teacher as inspector of schools, and that broke new ground in the Mission. Other circuits and districts of the church followed suit. For example, in 1967 the Madang District of the church had a supervisor responsible for 30 recognized schools with 96 teachers. He could visit all schools several times that year, and many were actually visited five or six times. Before long, New Guineans were trained as inspectors, and took over from the expatriates. Once the church teachers joined

431

the National Teaching Service, government inspectors took over, and they make inspections for the purpose of teacher upgrading. But the church still has a role to play. It has District Education Secretaries, who visit schools to help them maintain their Lutheran identity.

It may seen a little strange in modern times, but a means used to upgrade the schools was to lower the enrolment age. Grown men and women have not always been excluded from beginners' classes in village schools. It was felt that those keen enough to learn should be given the opportunity. Many succeeded quite well, while others tended to impede the progress of the class. From 1956, efforts were made to enrol in village schools only children not more than ten years of age. Even that sounds old. Before long, the age of admission declined still further. That brought with it other problems. Young children could not be expected to walk long distances each day, or to go away to boarding schools. The latter problem was overcome by spending six years instead of four in the local school. As for the first problem, where the population is sparse, the villages small and scattered, and the terrain harsh, there is no solution.

Lack of good roads, lack of public transport, and lack of finance have made a regular support system for teachers quite difficult. And yet it is amazing what has been achieved at times. For example, at Omkolai, the teachers came to the station weekly for special English lessons. That entailed a long, hard walk. At Ega, the teachers came every second Tuesday. The lessons they had to use for the next two weeks were discussed, and special English lessons were also given. Twice in the year, the government officer also gave some instruction.

Although he may not have been qualified as an educator, the circuit missionary played a key role in the support of teachers. When he went on trips throughout the circuit to visit the congregations, he also visited the schools and helped the teachers in many ways. At the Mission station, he often spent many hours each week assisting the teacher. Not to be forgotten are the missionary wives, who played a vital role in the upgrading of schools and in boosting the morale of teachers.

432

In the boarding schools especially, the worship life of the school community provided students with a daily renewal of their spiritual life. Particularly helpful were the evening prayer meetings. These times of communion with their Heavenly Father and with each other strengthened many a student in times of discouragement, loneliness, and temptation.

Quite different, but still uplifting in their own way, were the extra-curricular activities at the schools, which were many and varied. Drawing classes to inculcate an appreciation of indigenous Melanesian designs took their place alongside carving, translation work, composition of hymns, and photography. One school set up a bakery, using a 44-gallon drum as an oven, baking six loaves at once. Another school built dams, and started Tilapia farming. Cocoa planting and forestry took the fancy of others. One group of boys wanted to learn carpentry, so the teacher guided them in building a two-storey dormitory. Choir singing and competitions with other schools became a favourite activity. A number of schools formed conch-shell bands, while others settled for brass instruments or recorders. Ever popular were the numerous ball games that European students play throughout the world. Flierl's first students at Simbang could not have imagined how interesting and enjoyable school could actually be.

Sweat of Self-Support

Sweaty and gleaming bodies on the playing fields of New Guinea are a common sight, and the playing fields of schools are no exception. Not quite as pleasant as playing soccer is the task of students to make gardens and support themselves. Cutting down the jungle, burning and clearing, turning the soil, or just making holes in the ground, all produce perspiration in abundance.

It is true that Senior Flierl hired students for the first school because they were simply not interested in sitting at desks. However, they were attracted by tools. So, the school satisfied a desire for material things which they wanted. One cannot blame a group of heathen boys for this, and it is difficult to see what other means the first missionaries could have employed to persuade the boys to come. But this method was not to continue.

Teacher students grow their own food.

When the first Teachers Training Schools were being started, the character of these schools was the subject of serious discussion. Should they be purely training schools as found in European countries, or should the character of a New Guinea village be incorporated into the life of the school? It was decided to follow the latter course. The policy of responsibility through self-support was adopted. So, students built their own dormitories, made their own gardens, and cooked their own food. When the yield from the gardens was good, they could sell some food and purchase personal items like clothing and soap. [27]

The Mission did not want people becoming Christians purely for material gain. And the policy of self-support also meant that congregations felt a direct responsibility for their students and the school. This was all good. However, it did mean that time spent in the gardens could not be spent in the classrooms. The price of this self-support policy was the limitation it put on scholastic progress. As late as 1948, the Mission Conference resolved to uphold the former rule of self-support for the station schools.

It has to be admitted that self-support meant sacrifice. One missionary reported seeing pupils who had carried sweet potatoes for two days, only to discover that a few potatoes did not buy many slates. At one Mission station, a number of classes were ready to start school, but there were no gardens for the children. So the missionary took action.

> When the parents brought their children I addressed them and asked them if they would care for their children as the bush-fowls do? I must give them credit at the end of this year, that not a single time have the children come to me and complained that they were hungry. The parents have brought food for the children each week and have helped them to make their gardens. [28]

Is there a sweatier job than pit-sawing? When the people of the Ulap circuit were encouraged to build permanent schools in place of their bush schools, the policy of self-support was bent just a little. From profits of the bulk-store, 20 sheets of iron were donated to those groups willing to pitsaw timber for a new school. The remainder of the materials they had to purchase themselves. By the sweat of their brows they built their schools.

The 1956 Mission Conference heard pleas for release from self-support. Teachers wanted students in higher schools freed from some of their outside work. The general opinion was that, instead of changing the policy of self-help, the use of oxen or tractors could be considered. These would be supplied by the plantations. Later on, school fees were introduced, and these also released students somewhat from self-support. Parents and congregations paid for release.

Congregations were generally quite happy to support students in the Area Schools and Teachers Training Schools. But when the former system of student selection and teacher allocation changed, so did the attitude of the congregations. Instead of the congregation selecting the students for admission to higher schools, a school inspector did this on the basis of written tests; instead of the congregations being involved in the stationing of teachers, this was done by a higher council of the church.

People were not impressed. Students whom they had supported for years might not even return to their district. The new system created some hard feeling and an accompanying lack of interest in the larger educational institutions of the church and in the students attending them. It may be small comfort for the congregations, but in a small way the church prepared them for what lay ahead. With the introduction of the National Teaching Service, Lutheran teachers, like all others, are stationed by a government committee.

Before the National Teaching Service was introduced in 1970, the old policy of self-support was modified little by little. Government subsidies were accepted and used for school maintenance, as well as for student support. Nowadays, under the National Education System, local people are responsible for constructing and maintaining schools. In education, the local community has to a large degree replaced the congregation.

Perhaps the old Mission policy of self-support has the durability of a New Guinea hardwood. Of particular interest is the action of the Church Council in 1977 approving a recommendation that schools develop self-help projects to become as independent as possible of outside financial help. [29] It may be that school, soil, and sweat will unashamedly continue their partnership.

Power-Play of Subsidies

Lutheran missionaries in PNG came from different national backgrounds, but on the principle of separation of Church and State there was no disagreement. In regard to schools, the desire was to retain as much independence from government control as possible. To complicate matters, though, there were people in other missions in PNG who regarded it as the duty of governments to assist missions in education. For many years they were in the minority, and most saw the loss of autonomy in education as too high a price to pay for any form of aid. At the 1928 Administration-Missions Conference, the Missions voted against receipt of subsidy.

By the end of World War II attitudes had changed considerably, as Lutherans soon discovered. In 1947, Dr J. Kuder reported to his co-workers:

In the past we have not been willing to receive subsidies because of the obligations involved in such acceptance. In this unwillingness to receive

subsidies we stand more or less alone. It was quite evident at the [Administration-Missions] conference held at Port Moresby, that other missions considered such subsidies as their right. Some well-thought out policy is called for. [30]

Given the competition that would soon develop between missions, especially in the Highlands, Lutheran Mission could hardly be expected to stand alone for very long. Lutheran students would simply opt for schools receiving government subsidies.

Irresistible Pressures

Two years after that Port Moresby conference, the Mission was still wrestling with the problem, one that had international overtones. In the matter of subsidies, the United Nations would play a role, as Dr Kuder had realized.

It would be well to realize what the situation is in which New Guinea finds itself. New Guinea is a Trust Territory of the United Nations ... In practically every nation associated with the United Nations free, secular and compulsory education is the rule. In every such nation there are large grants for education on the nation's budget. [31]

He also noted that the UN representatives would not be impressed with the amount the Australian Government spent on education in New Guinea. Criticism would follow.

In view of the attitude of the UN, there would certainly be some pressure put on Lutheran Mission to accept subsidies, since it had one of the largest school systems in New Guinea at the time. Of course, it is also true that the largest percentage of New Guinea's educational costs were not visible at all; they were borne by the congregations. Looking at the situation realistically, a good part of the cost was in the form of work done for the teacher in his gardens in lieu of salary. The self-support system in the boarding schools of the church greatly reduced expenditure of money. Since there was no valuation of such hidden costs, it was possible for UN representatives simply to ignore them to suit their own purposes.

Also to be considered in the subsidy issue was the concern that if Lutheran Mission refused aid it would force the hand of the Administration to set up schools in competition. In some areas, this did actually happen. Like it or not, the policy of refusing subsidies had to be revoked. In 1950, the Mission certainly had the option of rejecting or of accepting subsidies. However, the 1970 National Education Act showed rather clearly that the treasured philosophy of autonomy in education could not have been upheld for long, anyhow.

The historic decision relating to the acceptance of subsidies was made at the 1950 Lutheran Mission Conference: 'Resolved that we accept the Administration's educational subsidy'.[32] It was also decided to give teachers $6 a year from the subsidy. This gradually increased, as the amount of Grant-in-aid money increased.

At first, the Mission had remarkable freedom in determining just how this money was to be spent. In 1953, it made a list of materials that could be purchased for Village Schools. It was restricted to items like text books, writing materials, and teachers' equipment. Most were not given free, but the price was substantially reduced for the pupils. Higher Schools could purchase maps, globes, charts, clocks, and reference books.[33]

It was possible to involve students in the decision-making process. At one Teachers Training Centre, they made three categories for which subsidy money would be used: essentials, emergencies, and desirables. The subsidy money was then apportioned, and a record of expenditure kept by the students. When extra money was required for essential food toward the end of the year, it was taken from the category of desirables, and so ended the students' pocket money. No one complained, because it had all been their decision right from the outset. And valuable lessons were learnt.

By 1955, there was talk of government withdrawal of subsidies, and it was more than rumour. The Administration was planning to withdraw subsidies from non-English schools, and the Mission President correctly predicted the following year that

> The policy is to let us have subsidies and then when we have learned to depend on them threaten to withdraw them unless conformity with the official policy is accepted.[34]

In the face of such difficulties, there was some bravado. One missionary likened the loss of subsidy to Damocles' sword hanging over people's heads, but he felt that trade stores could do just as good a job of subsidizing as the government. Others argued for using plantation profits to augment teachers' salaries. Neither suggestion was found acceptable, although individual circuits and congregations did use trade store profits from time to time to assist their schools.

Gradual Transformation

Once the subsidy door had been opened a little by accepting government Grant-in-aid, it was pushed open still further. The original Mission policy of self-support was slowly transformed into subsidy-support. Of course, it is true to say that the Mission had in effect always been subsidizing the school system by supplying European teachers for the Higher Schools at no cost to the congregations. Still, there were no direct payments to New Guinean teachers or students from Mission funds. This was to change, as requests to alter Mission policy came from many quarters. Teachers and students alike were reeling under the pressure to raise standards.

Calls for direct monetary assistance were countered with words of caution.

> We should consider carefully whether we have any other basis on which to present the claims of the children of New Guinea for an education than that of service. Once service is not any longer the motive, but a monetary consideration becomes so, have we not started on a road which gets slipperier the farther along one travels it? In other words, can a monetary incentive within the means of our New Guinea congregations and Church do more than whet the appetite but never satisfy?[35]

Who will deny that these were words of wisdom? And yet, the spirit of service and a better salary are not mutually exclusive. In any event, the 1957 Mission Conference took the step of recommending to ELCONG that certificated teachers receive the full government subsidy available to them, but that this money be channelled through the circuits.

The idea of channelling subsidy moneys through congregational treasuries was an attempt at suggesting to teachers that they were still servants of the church, in spite of government subsidy. To be quite honest, it was little more than a token gesture. Teachers knew the true source of the new generosity, and rather naturally began to regard the government rather than the congregations as their Papa. Such a feeling blossomed fully once teachers began receiving their pay cheques directly from government sources, and Lutheran teachers were receiving the same salary as government teachers under the National Teaching Service. This is not to suggest a disloyalty on the part of Lutheran teachers, only a new awareness.

Easing the Pain

In the initial stages, a considerable amount of subsidy unhappiness was created by virtue of discrepancies. One teacher in an English school could be receiving a salary of $160 per annum, while his non-certificated colleague, doing comparable work, received only $20 or less for his labours. Worse still was the plight of many Village Bible School teachers, who often received the grand salary of $5. Comparisons may be odious, but they also hurt. Fortunately, the problem no longer exists in the English schools, and in the *Tok Ples* schools the pain has been alleviated.

> For teachers of Hap 7 [year 7] or higher K45 a month from the *Tok Ples* budget is paid from Ampo. The District or school projects are to pay a similar amount. Hap 1-6 teachers receive K40 *Bel Gut Mani* [present] a year from the *Tok Ples* Budget. The local congregation is responsible for regular support of these teachers usually with a salary of K100 a year. [36]

Clearly, the unhappy situation of 1957 is not as unhappy any more in 1984.

Unavailability of government subsidy for non-English schools created a problem that called for an immediate soution if they were to be saved. Overseas funds were available. On the basis of a submission, the Bavarian Lutheran Church, Germany, provided almost $100,000 in aid. This was available in 1965, and helped to pay for the operation of the Rintebe Teachers Training Centre for two years. It also provided a 50 per cent subsidy for school supplies in Village Bible Schools, as well as higher Bible Schools. Morale was considerably improved. Other major grants have been made since then from a number of sources. German funding agencies still support the *Tok Ples* Budget, which subsidizes the salaries of non-English teachers.

Subsidy spells power. The government used that power in persuading the church to change its language policy for schools. It used that power again to convince the church to join

436

Teacher Wahawete refused mission money for his school.

the National Teaching Service at the highest level. To a greater or lesser degree, the availability of subsidy money from overseas was instrumental in changing the Bible Schools of the church to *Tok Ples* Schools. Overseas agencies were not able to give aid to purely religious schools, but could assist vocational schools. What could be more logical than obtaining money for the survival of the non-English schools, and then changing their character in order to qualify for assistance?

In at least one instance, subsidy money was refused. The New Guinean teacher Whawete insisted that not a single cent of mission money be used for permanent buildings at the Kalasa Bible School. He waited until the Kate District had collected $800 for a classroom. Not many others had an inclination to follow his example.

Bold New Concepts

An interesting development was the establishment of a Contingency Reserve Fund by the church in 1977. From the fund, subsidies could be given to the districts of the church to help pay for specialists of one kind or another. For example, the Heldsbach non-English

Teachers Training School employed two experienced certificated teachers, and was able to pay them salaries more or less equivalent to what they were getting before.

At the beginning of this century, Mission policy was responsibility through self-support. But in 1982, responsibility through subsidy was being advocated. The church's Education Secretary, Mr Sakey Ronu, put a case for the 148 Lutheran Community Schools, or Lutheran English Primary Schools.

> I feel that the Church as a whole has a responsibility to give actual support to the individual schools in two main areas: in the Christian Education programme of the schools and in the building programme of the community schools. [37]

The church responded by establishing the Community School Assistance Fund. The Lutheran Education board minutes of March, 1983, reveal that K24,000 had been distributed to 25 schools. The Board is requesting the church to make available K100,000 annually for the fund. In addition to such a direct church grant, the Community School Assistance Fund receives money from the schools themselves.

Each Lutheran Community School is expected to contribute 50 toea per pupil per annum to the fund. Compared with actual needs, the amount raised in this way would be little more than a drop in the bucket. But it is a novel self-support scheme. Quite significantly, it reflects the corporate sense of responsibility and corporate assistance which has been so much a part of indigenous culture. The great unknown is whether the corporate sense of responsibility can be maintained on the national level as readily as it has been maintained on the local village level.

Sounds of War

Warriors' headdresses may be decorated with its feathers, but the sounds of war have little in common with the song of the bird of paradise. Happily, a beautiful bird forms part of the national emblem rather than the weapons of war, although the sounds of war have often silenced the happy sounds of children at school during the past 100 years. Children's education has been interrupted by tribal fighting. Concerned relatives have appeared at the school door, demanding to take students home because of possible revenge. And fear has robbed children of their concentration in class. But it is not tribal warring that has had the most serious long-term effects on the schools of the church.

Wars originating in other countries have left deep scars in Papua New Guinea. World War I (1914-1918) brought hardships for the missionaries, but there was little interruption to schooling. Fortunately, the last ship to arrive before the start of hostilities brought a large consignment of paper for the Mission printery. So schools and congregations could be supplied with essential books even during those years.

World War II (1939-1945) brought disaster for schools. Some missionary teachers were interned, while others had to return to their home countries. What sorrow the military authorities brought students when they removed their beloved school fathers! Yet, it was a blessing in disguise. If they had all been allowed to remain, it is extremely doubtful that the Japanese soldiers would have left many alive. As it was, most were able to return to their schools after the war.

Death and destruction rained from the skies like a tropical downpour. Numerous school buildings were destroyed, or damaged. Yet, in spite of danger, it was not uncommon for teachers to continue working in school. Others were obliged to carry cargo for the army. Many simply had to flee the war zones, together with children and parents.

After the war, a mammoth task of rebuilding lay ahead for educators. One thing was sure: Things would never be quite the same again. New Guineans had been closely involved in the war, and it left its mark on the minds, hearts, and aspirations of the people. One returning missionary observed changes in his students.

> They were more inclined to make decisions independently, without first asking the missionary for permission or advice. Another change is their stronger desire to gain knowledge. Their efforts are more persistent than formerly, especially in secular subjects, such as English language. [38]

Shortages characterized the post-war period. For at least five years, no teachers were graduated. Little wonder that demand was far greater than supply. Figures given for the Kate

437

District in 1951 are truly startling. The number of children attending village schools in that year rose by 1,800 to more than 9,000. To cater for that kind of situation, circuits placed partially trained or untrained men in charge of schools, until no less than 10 per cent of all teachers were in that category. This was a deplorable situation, resulting directly from war.

Modern students do well to ponder the effects of armed conflict. Just after the war, some pupils were writing on sheets of corrugated iron flattened out, because they had neither slates nor paper. Everywhere it was a case of sharing and improvising. On Karkar Island in 1946, some 600 pupils had 200 slates and 60 slate pencils between them. In other schools, a single reader had to be shared by half a dozen pupils. Home-made exercise books were made by sewing together duplicated lined sheets.

In spite of all the shortages, schools functioned. The initiative often came from New Guinean teachers, because there were no missionaries in the area. The striking of empty steel cylinders signalled the start of the school day; the litter of war had become a school bell,

'The striking of an empty steel cylinder signals the start of a new school day.'

438

and issued its daily, grim reminder of the sounds of war. For children and for education, peace is much to be preferred.

Great Expectations of Governments

Surprising as it may seem, it was not until 1913 that the German Administration of New Guinea took any direct interest in the schools of the Mission. Similar lack of interest was shown by the Australian Administration across the border in Papua. There may be various explanations for this. Possibly, education was simply left to the Missions. Perhaps some felt that the population was not really capable of learning. Undoubtedly, others were of the opinion that an educated tribe would be more difficult to control. But once the Administration became interested, it tended to criticize the Mission schools which it had earlier ignored. Maybe it operated on the premise that attack is the best means of defence.

During the German administration, Governor Hahl sent a circular to all Missions in the Protectorate. In this interesting document of December 1913, he demanded that German be taught instead of Pidgin, because that was to be eliminated. To the circular he attached a draft of a school ordinance, which was to come into effect from January 1915. Hahl's ordinance stated that 'The Governor shall exercise general supervision over all schools in the Protectorate of German New Guinea'. [39] That meant that all schools had to notify the government of their existence. War intervened in 1914, however, and Australia took over the administration of the territory, but did not enforce Hahl's ordinance.

If war had not intervened in 1914, Lutheran Mission could have experienced the kind of agony it went through in 1958. Hahl was determined that

> In native schools no living language except German, other than the language of the natives current at the locality where the school is situated, is permitted as the language of instruction. In the place of the native language current at the school locality a language kindred to it may be used with the consent of the Governor. [40]

Cooperation and Control

Papua and the Mandated Territory of New Guinea were formally united under one Australian Administration in 1946, and a

Department of Education was formed. At the time, the government had no schools in Papua, and only six primary schools in New Guinea with 500 students. The fledgling department soon announced its policy.

> The general principle is not to duplicate Government and Mission projects in one area, providing the Missions are able and willing in due course to conduct schools in their own areas on lines prescribed by the Administration and to fit them into its general educational plan. [41]

At the same time, the department planned to exercise control over all secular teaching in all schools, to give guidance, to assist with essential equipment, and to provide for approval or registration of Mission schools and teachers. Without a doubt, Lutheran Mission would soon have felt the effects of that policy, incorporated in the 1952 Education Ordinance. [42]

Hahl's ordinance had been shelved because of war. The 1952 ordinance could not be fully implemented either, because of events in Australia. A new Federal Government had taken office, and demanded a complete reorganization of the Department of Education in PNG. Grossly understaffed as it was, this task made implementation of the whole ordinance impossible. Nevertheless, certain aspects were applied immediately.

The 1952 ordinance made provision for an Education Advisory Board, which included representatives from Missions, appointed by the Administrator. Lutheran Mission was fortunate to have one representative on that Board. Furthermore, the ordinance gave the Director of Education the power to determine the language or languages of instruction to be used for secular education in a school. It also became mandatory for the Mission to apply for registration for all of its schools.

Co-workers in Crisis

Within Lutheran Mission, a school had always been a school, and a teacher had always been a teacher. To be sure, they were not all of the same standard, and that fact was no secret. Still, the brotherhood of Christian teachers remained intact. Once the 1952 Education Ordinance required all schools to be classified, this brotherhood of teachers was endangered. The government's aim was to put all schools into categories as an incentive for up-grading weaker ones. As such, the idea was commendable, but it introduced into the Mission's school system elements of inferiority and shame. This was not conducive to promoting a spirit of fellowship, and something precious had been dealt a severe blow.

The three categories of schools became known as registered, recognized, and exempt schools. Among other requirements, a school could only be registered if it was in the charge of a certificated teacher. Where the teacher had only a permit to teach, it was placed in the lower category of a recognized school. Both types of schools received assistance from the government in the way of school materials. Since Lutheran Mission had no certificated New Guinean teachers until 1958, all Lutheran schools in the charge of a New Guinean teacher were placed in the lower category. There were a handful of missionaries with teachers' training who could be certificated, but the outlook for Lutheran schools was grim. The Mission could only be thankful that events in Australia made full implementation of the ordinance impossible. Any schools not registered or recognized were illegal, and subject to a fine.

Because the Department of Education found that it could not possibly inspect all Mission schools by March 1, 1955, it had to exempt them from the penal clause. Hence the third category, that of exempt schools. However, there was no room for complacency. A circular memorandum issued in 1958 gave warning: 'It is the policy of the Department to encourage and induce the Missions to raise the standards of efficiency of all Exempt schools until they merit Recognition or Registration'. [43] Even at that stage, government inspectors found it impossible to inspect all schools, and many of Lutheran Mission's exempt schools in isolated areas were never visited. It took another ten years before the government came up with the final solution, and exempt schools were officially classified as non-schools and placed right outside the Department's concern and statistical records. It was a neat way of tidying up. But already then missionaries were suggesting that one day these non-schools would again attract the attention of the Department. That has now happened. The 1983 Education Act required the registration of all so-called permitted schools. Once again, the church's vernacular and Pidgin schools have been drawn back into the orbit of the government's attention. What the consequences will be remains to be seen, and what the true purpose of it is remains unknown. If it does nothing else, it will assist the government in clarifying just how far it still has to go in reaching the objective of universal primary education announced by the Administrator on January 30, 1959.

Changing Directions

Great were the expectations of the government of the day, as it issued a press statement entitled 'Plan For Universal Primary Education'. Without question, the plan was visionary, but for Lutheran Mission it was like a bolt of lightning that struck mercilessly. The educational storm clouds had been gathering for some time, but the severity of the government's action left many in shock.

> It is recognised that the objective of universal primary education can be attained only with the goodwill and close cooperation of the Christian Missions ... It must be clearly understood that universal primary education means universal literacy in English ... Payment of grants-in-aid for vernacular schools which do not teach English will cease at the end of 1959 ... Missions using as teaching media vernacular languages which are not the mother tongues of the children attending school, are informed that in 1960 schools where the children are taught in a 'foreign' vernacular will not be exempted but closed. This is in accordance with the provision of the Education Ordinance which empowers the Director of Education to determine the language. [44]

The Director of Education appeared in person at the Mission Conference a matter of days after the press statement to reiterate what the Administrator had written. He added that the plan was to achieve universal primary education in English within 15 years. Twenty-five years later, that goal lies in the dim and distant future.

On the basis of such a categorical statement regarding exempt schools, it could only be concluded that the church's numerous schools in that classification would be compelled to close their doors. But was that God's will also? What the Administrator could not foresee in 1959 was how world events would soon intervene. The report of the United Nation's 1962 delegation to PNG dealt a body

blow to the policy of universal primary education. It wanted an educated elite produced as quickly as possible with a view to granting PNG its independence. [45] At the same time, the UN Trusteeship Council was emphasizing the urgent need to develop university education.

Faced with the pressure of such intense and negative world-wide publicity, the Administration virtually had to change the directions of its educational policy. For Lutheran Mission, this meant a breathing space in which to upgrade many more of its existing schools and have them registered as English schools. It also had time to organize some of its resources for an alternative program of Christian education in Bible Schools. Even if the government had to change directions, it could and did plan for a national system of education.

At the Crossroads

The 1968 synod of the church was aware of the proposal, and wrestled with the problem of what its attitude should be to a National Education System. It expressed agreement with the government's aim to raise the educational standards of schools. However, it wished to retain final authority over its schools and teachers. [46] Of course, wishes are one thing, and possibilities are another. Years before, the church had built up a large English school system with the help of government finance, and there was no way it could possibly carry on without such massive aid. It was clearly a case of join the system or pull out of education.

The Principal of Balob Teachers College at the time saw both advantages and disadvantages of joining the national system.

> The Church will now be represented on the District Education Boards, which will have considerable power in each District. Previously the Church's voice was only heard in an advisory capacity. She will now be represented when the actual decisions are being made. Although not all will agree, I feel that the fact that all teachers will receive equal salaries and can be promoted on an equal basis with Administration teachers, should help to improve the standard of work in the Church schools. Of course there are disadvantages. [47]

He mentioned the possibility of losing a number of Head Teacher positions in the Church's schools, and the loss of freedom for Lutheran high school students in other districts to attend either the Bumayong or Asaroka Lutheran High Schools.

Never before had the Church and Mission been in the position of having to make an educational decision with such far-reaching consequences. The matter was debated sincerely, prayerfully, and vigorously. A study committee with ten members was appointed. Subsequent events are shrouded in mystery, as detailed in a paper presented to the 1971 Mission Conference.

> It seems impossible, but nevertheless it is a fact, that the next action of the Church with regard to the National Teaching Service proposal is found in ELMIS Council (comprised of Church and Mission representatives) minutes of June, 1970, and states simply and bluntly: 'Resolved that all Primary "T" Schools of ELCONG enter the National Teaching Service as Category "A" (full membership)'. With those few words the matter was closed. It was not the subject of any resolution at the 1970 Synod. [48]

Truly puzzling was the fact that absolutely no reference was made to any findings of the duly-appointed study committee. Quite legitimately, the question was asked whether those making the decision had bowed to pressure from overseas.

Only three months before the momentous decision of ELMIS Council, a Consultation was held in Lae between representatives of the Lutheran Church, Lutheran Mission, and representatives of the overseas Supporting Partners. That Consultation made the recommendation that all Lutheran church schools in the English program enter at category "A" level. Perhaps there was no alternative, but the procedure adopted certainly put into question the independence and final authority of the Synod of the Evangelical Lutheran Church of New Guinea.

In 1983, the old Education Act of 1970 was replaced with a new National Education Act. It continues to guarantee the Christian identity of schools, and the right to give religious instruction daily, for a period of 30 minutes. In keeping with the old Act, it also has all teachers and schools firmly in government control. While PNG continues to have a government sympathetic to the Christian Church, there may well be no great cause for concern. Should the opposite be the case one day, it does not take much imagination to realize what havoc could be created in Lutheran schools. It would be the hope of all that Christian schools might continue to flourish in PNG, so that the invitation of the Saviour of the world might be heard by all the nation's boys and girls:

> 'Let the children come to me, do not hinder them; for to such belongs the kingdom of God' (Mark 10:14).

Bibles and Hymnals

Early Christian Literature

by Karl Goerner and Herwig Wagner

Before any effective evangelistic work can be accomplished, God has ordained the sweat of studying languages. Missionaries in Papua New Guinea from deep personal struggles have learnt the truth of that statement.

The very beginning of that struggle came when an employee of the New Guinea Company gave Johann Flierl a small collection of some 50 words in the Jabem language spoken around Finschhafen. From that moment, he and his fellow-missionaries began to work their way into the jungle of New Guinea languages. Then came the hard second step: putting the spoken language into written form. But it was not long before the early missionaries were able to start teaching some boys the art of reading and writing in their mother tongue.

It is impossible to survey in detail the missionaries' efforts in linguistics, and the contribution they have made in developing a New Guinean vernacular literature, which began with handwritten copies of Bible stories and with the translation of liturgical parts of the Christian worship. However, an enormous amount of work has gone into producing a variety of catechetical and educational literature. This was highlighted in 1924 when a translation of the complete New Testament in the Jabem language was published. Other translations were soon to follow. The first complete Bible in a New Guinea vernacular, the Kate language, was ready for print in 1978.

The following table lists only printed translations (and revisions) of the complete

New Testament or the Bible that have been produced by Lutherans. There are many more vernacular translations by members of the Summer Institute of Linguistics (SIL). Parts of the Bible and collections of Bible stories for educational use had been translated and printed much earlier. It would be a worthwhile study of its own to find all translations of Bible parts and Bible story books, often existing in only duplicated or manuscript form, that have been produced during the first 100 years of the Lutheran Church in Papua New Guinea. It goes without saying that all editors/translators have been working with indigenous speakers of the respective language.

Dr Georg Pilhofer.

442

New Testament and Bible Translations

Language	Vernacular Title	Publication	Editor/Translator
Jabem	Binglênsêm Waku	London 1924	H. Zahn
	— rev. edn	Stuttgart 1935	
	— rev. edn	Canberra 1973	
	Bibolo Dabung	Port Moresby 1980	(shortened version of Bible)
Kate	Miti Qâlicne	Stuttgart 1938	G. Pilhofer
	Miti Qâri	London 1965	W. Flierl, K. Munsel, C. Schneuker
	Tiri Papia Qizec	Port Moresby 1978	K. Munsel (complete Bible)
Graged	Temaneknen Faun	London 1960	E. Hannemann
Melpa	Kaentik ik Kontnga	London 1965	H. Strauss
Kuman	Die Bibel in der Kumansprache	Mutdapilly n.d.	W. Bergmann
Adzera	Sising bini	Port Moresby 1976	K. Holzknecht
Lae-Wampar	Fenefon Ngarobingin	Port Moresby 1984	K. Holzknecht
Pidgin	Nupela Testamen	Madang 1969	
	Nupela Testamen na ol Sam	Port Moresby 1978	

Hymnals

A second segment of Christian literature comprises hymnals or song books. Christian songs provide the first authentic indigenous response of early New Guinean Christianity to the proclamation of evangelists and missionaries, and how that message has been understood by the people. In fact, with the indigenous hymns, Christian literature reaches out into the pre-literate field of oral traditions.

Christian songs sprang up spontaneously in almost every local language where the Gospel was proclaimed. They were sung at the village meeting houses and fire places. Often they originated from anonymous sources, sometimes even years before the first people of

Heinrich Zahn.

Male, assistant to Heinrich Zahn in the translation of the Jabem New Testament.

443

Dr Willy Flierl working with Elder Esonuwe (centre) and Circuit President Honeo.

Dr H. Strauss with translation assistant, Pastor Woworicke.

Karl Holzknecht handing over one of the first printed copies of the Azera New Testament.

that region were baptized into the church. These indigenous Christian songs were a response of faith to the Gospel; at the same time, they were an evangelistic means of spreading the Good News in a form that was entirely indigenous.

Printed hymn books contain but a small portion of the songs which have been composed and which are sung in local congregations. Even so, it is a characteristic of the Lutheran Church in Papua New Guinea that translations of European hymns today take up only a small section in the printed hymn books of the various languages. When faith responds creatively to the Word of God as it has been heard and grasped, people will do this in their mother tongue. The New Guinea Church can be proud of these documents of faith in their own languages.

A beginning of indigenous hymnology has also been made in more recent years in Pidgin, the new *lingua franca* of the country. Most of the hymn books listed below also contain liturgies and some parts of Luther's Small Catechism for religious instruction.

Language	Vernacular Title	Publication	Editor
Jabem	Alanem Abumtau	Neuendettelsau 1898	H. Vetter
	Wue Tabung	Logaweng 1909	H. Zahn
	— rev. edn	Logaweng 1911	H. Zahn
	Wê Dabung	Logaweng 1917	H. Zahn
	Lêng Ngagôling	Logaweng 1927	H. Zahn
	— rev. edn	Finschhafen 1932	
	— rev. edn	Madang 1960	W. Stoll

Konrad Munsel and his translation team.

Kate	Gahe â Mitifipapia	Logaweng 1906	Ch. Keysser
	Gaepapia	Logaweng 1913	Ch. Keysser
	— rev. edn	Finschhafen 1933	W. Flierl
	Lutheran Gae Buk	Madang 1960	C. Schneuker
	— rev. edn	Madang 1973	W. Geisselbrecht
Graged	Me Katechismus kitek	Logaweng 1916	
	Kanambug mai		
	Kanam Buk	Madang 1958	
Amele	Duebuk	Finschhafen 1929	A. Wullenkord
	Due Buk	Madang 1946	
	— rev. edn	Madang 1980	I. Amman
Nobonob	Kaiak tituanak nai	Logaweng 1916	F. Schuetz
	Ahietak nai ele		
	Ahietak Buk	Madang 1946	R. Inselmann
	— rev. edn	Madang 1963	I. Amman
Lae-Wampar	Anutu zob fon iri	Logaweng 1920	K. Panzer
	Ngaeng wampar amed		
Adzera	Ampan mara ram sanaban	Madang 1967	K. Holzknecht
	da Katekismus		
Ono-Kalasa	Ekeket-Kisi	Logaweng 1912	K. Wacke
Zia	Papia sasagao erauwa	Logaweng 1914	K. Mailaender
	Anutura ungweng tang	Logaweng 1917	K. Mailaender
Hamtai	Apa-Buk	Neuendettelsau 1984	H. Fink
Kafe	Yagame Mono Avontafera	Madang 1977	H. Bamler
Pidgin	Lotubuk	Madang 1950	E. Hannemann
	— rev. edn	Madang 1963	J. Sievert
	Rejoice and Sing	Adelaide 1979	G. Gerhardy
	Paradais Song	Madang 1979	C. Rohrlach
	Songs bilong Yangpipel	Madang 1978	
	Songs for Today	Madang 1978	
	Yumi singim Song	Madang 1979	A. Reinhardt
	Song bilong ol Pikinini	Madang 1979	

The Pidgin New Testament is officially launched 1969 (Dr Paul Freyberg at left).

Church Papers

A most remarkable feature of Christian literature in Papua New Guinea has been the early publication of vernacular churchpapers.

In the beginning, it was the missionaries who attempted to create a feeling of solidarity among the widely-scattered congregations of their area by publishing a monthly or bi-monthly paper, thereby seeking to overcome the complacency of Christian tribes and villages. Soon, however, local church leaders and teachers began to see the value of a printed medium of communications, and made the churchpapers an instrument of their own. They shared their experiences in the Christian faith with a wider readership. News from the newer (mission) areas was printed and broadcast, devotional articles and biblical meditations with a typical New Guinean touch were published.

This makes the early volumes of the three churchpapers a most valuable resource for the history of the church, as New Guineans themselves have seen it, and also for the first beginnings of an indigenous Melanesian theology expressed in a non-scholarly form.

After World War II, the vernacular churchpapers gradually have been replaced by English and Pidgin parallel editions of a church-wide paper.

Language	Name of Paper	Published	
Jabem	Jaeng Ngajam	1905-1963	with several interruptions
Kate	Ââkesing	1911-1964	
Graged	Krist Medain Totol	1909-1983	irregularly after World War II
English	New Guinea Lutheran	1962-1973	
Pidgin	Niugini Lutheran	1962-	

447

Totol

Kristen nadin

Gragetnen, Panutibunen, Siasnen, Bilianen

Melamalnen, Matugasnen, Krakarnen, Asainen

Jahr 1.	Januar 1909.	N. 1.

Jesus itase lak.

**Maria Jesus Betelem nen inau lak, sain
me lon König Erodes Jeruslem nen ma-
do ime.   Patui-mañau dal makaiu dise.**

Graged churchpaper, first issue, January 1909.

Jaeŋŋajam.

7	July	1927

Biŋ ŋacgejob ŋajamŋa. (Akac nêm Biŋ lênsêm wakuc ma
taôm asam. Joaŋ 10.) Apômtau Jesu kêsam tau gebe ŋacgejob
ŋajam aê, ma eŋ ŋacgejob ŋajam biŋŋanô. Eŋ gêwa ŋacgejob kwa-
lecŋa ŋam sa gêdêŋ aêac, ma aêac talic gêŋ samob naŋ eŋ gêwa
sa kêpi ŋacgejob secwaga, naŋ tau gêgôm ŋagêŋ keso teŋ kêtôm
êsêac atom. Kêam sec ŋamalac to lausiŋ dêdêŋ eŋ ma eŋ kêkôgeŋ,
gêc atom, nê dombageŋ sêcsêja. Eŋ kêkôgeŋ ma gêjam nê lau
kêsi ma kêkêŋ katu gêjô êsêac gebe êsêac sêmoa to ôliŋsamuc
ma eŋ tau êkêŋ tau êjô êsêac. Ŋacgejob ŋajam tonaŋ kêtêc ŋandaŋ
kapôêŋ teŋ atom, kêkêŋ tau samucgeŋ gêdêŋ nê ŋacjo. Ŋam tageŋ
tonaŋ gebe eŋ têtac gêwiŋ nê domba aêac ŋanô to samucgeŋ.
Embe têtac êwiŋ aêac atom, oc êc su me êŋgôm gêŋ kapôêŋ teŋ

Jabem churchpaper, July 1927.
448

11   Nowembe   1933

Printed by Lutheran Mission, Finschhafen. New Guinea.
Editor   H. Neumeier Heldsbach, Printer. G. Horrolt

Honesulec eele dâŋ.

Âgofâc maŋnâŋecte fuŋne ʒiŋuc ta-niŋkeekac: Gienâŋec sâcne baŋgopeneŋ iŋuc muhuc sâkebâbâc juhapene qaqazu Pilhoferzi fisilâ gienâŋec honesulec ehuc muekac: Kecʒi bâsifuckeekic, kecʒi sâcne baekic. I gie baeŋgopeneŋzi biaŋkekac â sâqolekac mi muhapene Pilhofer e gie soŋaŋzi fisilâ honesulec eme mocwâc bâtiŋnelâ baeŋgopeneŋ.

Âgofâc i mâleŋko wiac qazunâleweczi fisilâ gie honesulec eme mocwâc bâtiŋ-neeŋgopeneŋ. Â gielusâko faic juekac.

wec. Eha ʒâhec doc bame lolâ balapie honelâ maŋnezi mocwâc mumuhehec eme lalâ sahac mecne qâqâtâc mecne mâmâc sipilickelâ alictacjâmbâŋ ewec.

O âgofâc, ilec ŋifecne ʒiŋuc fokac: Nâŋâc Jesule kikefuŋ jueŋgopeneŋ, i mi-tisawa mi bajueŋgopeneŋ. Moneŋmafale sasecwac mâmâc fonâlekac Ilec haesâc ʒiŋuc mueŋgopieŋ: No moneŋmafa pitic-ne fuanaleme muzac sondacgieo mitio lazapo. Ilec haeo ŋehuc gienane bape moneŋmafa moc fuanaleme bunane biaŋkeha miti manazepac. Iŋuc muhuc

Kate churchpaper, November 1933.

Endnotes

[1] Lutheran Mission Executive Committee, minutes, res. no. 1948-71.

[2] J. Kuder, Mission Conference Annual Report, 1954.

[3] J. Kuder, 'The Case for Church Languages', Letter to Paul Hasluck, Canberra, dated 22.10.59; found in an unpublished thesis by Meg Duncan, 'The Lutheran Missions In New Guinea: Their Work and Influence on Education, 1886-1972', pp clxxv-cxcvi.

[4] Lutheran Mission Conference, minutes, res. no. 1947-82.

[5] P. Freyberg, Mission Conference Annual Report, Central Highlands School, Kewamugl, 1950.

[6] Lutheran Mission Conference, minutes, 1957; Central Highlands School Language Committee.

[7] K. Theile, Mission Conference Annual Report, Rintebe Education Centre, 1960.

[8] Lutheran Mission Executive Committee, minutes, res. no. 1956-330.

[9] A. Hoffmann, quoted by G.L. Renck, 'New Guinea Pidgin Teaching: Policy of the Lutheran Church', in S.A. Wurm, ed., *Language, Culture, Society, and the Modern World* (Canberra: Australian National University, 1977), fasc. 1, 662.

[10] Lutheran Mission Executive Committee, minutes, res. no. 1956-331.

[11] Lutheran Mission Conference, minutes, res. no. 1947-86.

[12] G. Vicedom, 'Memorandum re Missionary Policy' — comment on policy of Ninth Annual Field Conference, 1955.

[13] J. Kuder, Mission Conference Annual Report, 1957.

[14] Lutheran Mission Conference, minutes, 1962-71.

[15] E. Jaeschke, 'Thoughts on the Bible School Programme in New Guinea', Report to Leipzig Mission Society, 1.7.1968.

[16] Lutheran Mission Conference, minutes, 1953, p 50.

[17] S. Ronu, Report to New Guinea Coordinating Committee, 1978.

[18] Lutheran Mission Conference, minutes, res. no. 1964-173.

[19] Lutheran Mission Conference, minutes, res. no. 1960-52.

[20] G. Mueller, Private correspondence, 8.10.1984.

[21] Lutheran Mission Conference, minutes, res. no. 1964-219.

[22] W. Flierl, Mission Conference Annual Report, 1954.

[23] J. Streicher, Mission Conference Annual Report, 1950.

[24] E. Hannemann, *Norma at Amron* (published by The Mission Auxiliary of the ALC, n.d.), 25.

[25] For list of Mission personnel serving in Printeries and Bookstores, see Appendix.

[26] Mission Conference Annual Report, 1955.

[27] G. Pilhofer, *Die Geschichte der Neuendettelsauer Mission in Neuguinea* (Neuendettelsau: Freimund Verlag, 1963), vol. II,47.

[28] W. Bergmann, Mission Conference Annual Report, 1963.

[29] Report to New Guinea Coordinating Committee, 1977.

[30] J. Kuder, Lutheran Mission Conference, minutes, 1947.

[31] J. Kuder, Mission Conference Annual Report, 1949.

[32] Lutheran Mission Conference, minutes, res. no. 1950-37.

[33] Lutheran Mission Conference, minutes, res. no. 1953-165.

[34] J. Kuder, covering letter to 1956 Conference Minutes.

[35] J. Kuder, Mission Conference Annual Report, 1958.

[36] G. Mueller, private correspondence, 8.10.1984.

[37] S. Ronu, Report to New Guinea Coordinating Committee, 1982.

[38] M. Heist, Mission Conference Annual Report, Jabem Schools, 1947.

[39] M. Duncan, 'The Lutheran Mission in New Guinea', p lxxvi.

[40] *Ibid.*

[41] *Ibid*, 260.

[42] *Ibid*, cxiii.

[43] *Ibid*, clx.

[44] *Ibid*, cxl.

[45] *Ibid*, 364.

[46] ELCONG Synod, minutes, res. nos. 1968-12 and 1968-13.

[47] F. Stolz, Circular, 12.8.1970.

[48] H. Hage, 'The Place of the Bible Schools in the Church's Programme', Lutheran Mission Conference Paper, 1971, 46.

Source Material

Access to Lutheran Mission New Guinea Conference reports, minutes, papers, and covering letters — as cited in the notes — was obtained through the Office of the Board for Overseas Mission and Church Cooperation of the Lutheran Church of Australia in Adelaide.

Other material:
ELC-PNG Tok Pisin Edukesen Semina, 16-20 Nov. 1981.

Inglis Edukesen Woksop, 12-26 Aug, 1982.

Policy Book for ELC-PNG Education Department (Draft).

Chapter 14

Sculptures and Paintings

An Indigenous Expression of the Christian Faith

by Hermann Reiner

There are various ways in which Christian faith may find its indigenous expression: in sermons, hymns, or — as a characteristic feature of New Guinean congregations — in dramatizations. Such forms of expression certainly are evidence of the fact that Christianity has become part and parcel of the culture of a people. The same holds true of painting and sculpture as indigenized forms of the Christian faith.

It is almost impossible in one chapter to give a detailed account of the many and varied expressions of art within the Lutheran Church of Papua New Guinea. Rather, I shall try to show the mainstream of development by a number of examples of sculpture and painting.

In my opinion there are four phases to be made out — though sometimes overlapping in different areas, because the Gospel did not reach all the people at the same time. First, we notice a naive representation of biblical themes. The second stage is marked by an imitation of European models. The third phase then tries to introduce traditional motifs but is still not free from European influence. It is only in the final phase that a homogeneous indigenous style in architecture, sculpture, and painting is achieved. For each of these four stages, typical examples will be given in this chapter.

Paintings in the Kotna Church

Fascinating pieces of art of the first phase are the pictures painted by the Kate evangelist S. Qakomo in the late 1950s for the church at Kotna near Mt Hagen. They show in six scenes the artist's understanding of the Life of Christ according to the Apostles' Creed. At one point, however, he has added a statement in his sequence of paintings: he has included Christ's baptism by John at the Jordan. This is rather significant. It indicates the artist's intention to depict also the life of the followers of Christ: birth, conversion and baptism, suffering, death and resurrection, and life everlasting. Qakomo is no way influenced by the modern or any other style of painting. His pictures are more like pre-historical cave paintings. And yet, what expression and power lie in his testimony! These are Bible stories preached and painted for illiterate people.

451

Let us now look at the pictures and thus familiarize ourselves with the artist's thoughts and reflections.

The Birth of Jesus

The shepherds' field: The angelic messenger seems to hover above the shepherds, who are depicted only as heads. The angel directs them to Bethlehem. They are on their way to the stable to behold the miracle of incarnation. Over and above the scene of Bethlehem hover some queer mute faces. They have no message for the shepherds, and therefore no mouth, either. Are these the heavenly hosts? Or perhaps the spirits of ancestors who just watch without being able to interfere? Whatever they may be, they express the pre-Christian mind and world-view of New Guineans: Every member of society feels himself watched, and knows his life is being controlled by spiritual powers who may have good or evil intentions.

The stable: In the little hut on the left side there is hardly room for Mary and Joseph with the child. The child, of course, is brown. He is painted in the likeness of an ancestral figure who was worshipped in the pre-Christian era. However, this is the message: From now on, this child of Bethlehem is to be adored; the ancestors have lost their power.

And above all this, we see the star which guided the wise men. It looks like a requisite fetched by the angels to grace the stage of salvation.

The Baptism of Jesus

The contrast in style, between the ornamental frame of the pictures, done in a masterly way, and the biblical scene painted, is quite obvious. Ornamental decorations have an old tradition in Melanesia, but not so scene painting.

Jesus himself appears small and humble, compared with the huge figure of John the Baptist. Jesus and John are the only figures within the scene who are complete. Above all is the dove, the symbol of the Holy Spirit. There are two groups of witnesses: on the right side the disciples of Christ, and on the left the disciples of John. The latter represent the Gentiles who have to resign after the coming of Christ.

Baptism is understood as initiation, that is, a new start in life. Here the painter expresses his own experience. Baptismal instruction in New Guinea often coincided with preparation for the work of an evangelist. The celebration of the day of baptism was often at the same time the farewell for the person as an evangelist. Soon after that, they had to leave (as in Qakomo's

Johavezi-Jesu
niti opâ ruacnewec.

case, for the Highlands), and perhaps never see their relatives again.

Jesus before Pilate

Jesus is captured. His enemies are displayed as vicious creatures of darkness who cannot bear the light of the day — like evil spirits out of old ghost-stories. Jesus himself is the only human figure, but with a halo around his head.

In the background are the tools of war: spears, clubs, arrows, and even weapons of modern warfare. On the right side, we see Jesus before the High Priest with a tiara shaped like a crescent, possibly copied from a European illustration. Even features of the trial are visible: Jesus is handcuffed, and stripped of his clothes, his hands covering his nakedness. But he never loses his majesty.

Jesu-rombiŋ.

Kiarao-barambiŋ.

Crucifixion

The day has dawned. Jesus carries his cross. In the background we notice the merciless mob gaping at the spectacle. For all that, Jesus is unperturbed. He wears the crown of thorns. In the foreground is Simon of Cyrene carrying his hoe, which indicates that he comes from his garden; behind him, a soldier who forces him to carry the cross.

On the right side, Jesus is crucified, his blood flowing down to the ground. The women under the cross embrace his body lovingly. They are drawn much bigger than John and another (?) disciple, who appear small and humble at the right side. This may indicate that their faith was weaker than the women's, who stayed faithfully with Jesus until the end.

Resurrection and Ascension

The risen Christ is shown with a flag in his hand. His face is strange and mask-like; the face of the angel to the right is bright. In sharp contrast, the guardians of the grave look dark and gloomy, indicating their state of mind. On the left side, we are given the artist's concept of ascension. Christ ascends into heaven between two angels in a humble position. On both sides of the rising Lord we see the grey phantom of the ancestors and other pagan spirits. This is like saying: 'Be not afraid, for Christ now is given

454

all authority and power in heaven and on earth'. Below are the eleven disciples who have just been blessed and commanded to spread the Gospel until their Lord's second coming.

The Day of Judgment

This is a colourful painting. Christ is shown with a sickle in his hand to gather his harvest, as it is written in Revelation. He is 'clothed in a long robe [which reaches to his feet], and with a golden girdle round his breast; his head and his hair ... white as white wool ... his eyes ... like a flame of fire, his feet ... like burnished bronze, refined as in a furnace' (Rev. 1:13-15). In his hand is the sceptre, an emblem of royal might. On his head he wears a crown, the emblem of the Creator even in pre-Christian times. The crown is ornamented like the front board of a canoe. Angels are trumpeting in every direction, as if to enlarge the light which radiates from his throne, and to drive away all darkness. Suns, moons, and stars are shown to indicate that he comes with the clouds of the sky. The heavenly King is accompanied by 'a cloud of witnesses', the full number of believers.

All in all, this sequence of six paintings in the church at Kotna is an impressive witness of the faith and the depth of belief of the first generation of Christians in Papua New Guinea.

Dawidi of Obasega

For the second period of art development within the New Guinean church, I have chosen the church in Ngasegalatu/Finschhafen. Most of it is the work of Dawidi of Obasega village, who is presently regarded as one of the most outstanding artists of the Lutheran Church in Papua New Guinea.

This is how Dawidi himself related the story of the new Ngasegalatu church:

We started building the church at Ngasegalatu in 1954, and finished it by 1957, when it was dedicated.

Our old house of God was build by the previous generation, and it was dedicated in 1938. Shortly thereafter, the war broke out, and we had to leave everything here behind, and hide in the jungle.

455

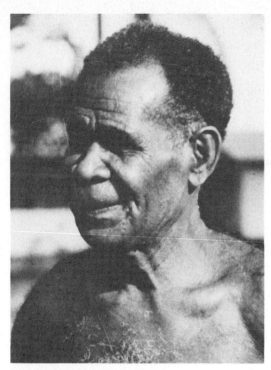

Dawidi from Obasega village.

When the Japanese army came, they used our church as a barrack. They used to cook their meals there. When the American pilots saw the smoke coming up from the building, they riddled the roof with machine guns. After that, the Australian and American troops came and destroyed what was left. They even sawed off some of the posts because they did not like the wood-carvings. So, after we came back to our village when the war was finished, we found our church greatly damaged.

We had many discussions what to do. How could we have our services in a church with such a brittle framework? It might collapse one day and bury all of us. How could we get a new church? That was the question which our elders and pastor discussed for a long time without finding an answer. Where can we find the money to buy construction material? When discussing this matter again on a certain Saturday, I got up and suggested to the meeting: 'Why are we talking and talking? Appoint one man from each village here. They must be strong men. We'll start working and then you will see it yourselves. That is my plan.' The meeting followed my advice, and selected seven strong men. They were to work with me. Before the war, Missionary Herrlinger had given us a large pit-saw. During the war years, I had hidden it in the jungle. I now fetched this and cleaned it.

Then we went together into the forest and started cutting down trees. Each time a tree was felled, we built a platform around it and started pit-sawing it into slabs and boards. Months later, I told the congregational meeting to ask all the people from Mange to Kamlaua to turn up at Obasega and carry boards and beams to the church-site. They came, and we picked up the boards from various sites and brought them to the village. I must add that the pit-sawing took us a long time — much longer than I am able to explain now. The trees were not always readily available.

I was against buying timber from a commercial sawmill. After all, we had our own timber stand. Before continuing, let me explain why I was against buying timber from outside. Many years ago, when a new church was dedicated at Ampo (Lae), Pastor Theile from Australia gave the sermon. Afterwards, he said to us: 'You call this a church? Where I live, such a building would not be called a house of God. It is rather like a car- or a tool-shed. I wish you people of New Guinea would start building your own churches, instead of asking European master builders to build churches for you. You New Guineans have axes, and you have plenty of trees'. When he asked: 'Where did you get the boards for this church?', we said: 'From the Mission sawmill at Butaweng'. Theile went on: 'Does your forest consist of prairie grass? I think you are in a position to build churches yourselves, without the help of white men.'

I have never forgotten these words, and so I told our people: 'We have axes. And we have timber. Let us use it instead of buying timber from a sawmill in Lae.' And so we built our church. When the church was built in the years from 1954 to 1957, I was still a teacher in my home village. Before the war, I was first a student and then a teacher at Hopoi Teachers Seminary, working together with the missionaries Zahn and Streicher. After that, I became teacher here at Ngasegalatu. During the war, I was head teacher for the whole area, and many teachers were entrusted to me. We never stopped the school work, not even during the war. When fleeing into the jungle, we used to build shelters first, but immediately thereafter a school was built.

The Ngasegalatu Church

Dawidi, the master builder of the Ngasegalatu church, and also the one who carved most of the sculptures in that church, made the following comments on this outstanding example of church architecture and art in Finschhafen.

The ornament outside the church above the entrance was carved for our old church, built in 1938. The man who did it thought of Noah. The carving shows two hands stretched out to take the returning dove to the safety of Noah's ark. With this picture he wanted to say: The church of God is like the ark. Whoever enters it is under the protection of God, just as he protected Noah and his family. When the flood receded, Noah sent out a dove and it returned with a leaf from a tree in its beak. For Noah this was a sign that the earth again would be green. Pre-war this carving was inside the church. When the new church was completed, I put it on the outside just above the entrance.

Ancestor Posts and Apostles Posts: The outer posts of the church are carvings of ancestor figures, as was done for the ceremonial houses of our forefathers. In olden times, such ancestor posts were put up at these houses because they were believed to be the homes of the spirits. I did not consider it right to have these figures inside a Christian church. However, they should not be forgotten. Therefore I wanted to display them outside the church to indicate the origin of the people who enter the house of God. These figures were not without meaning. They were symbols of taboos: You shall not steal; you shall not commit adultery; you shall not break the tribal law. Anyone in the vicinity of such posts was not allowed to commit any sin or cause scandal.

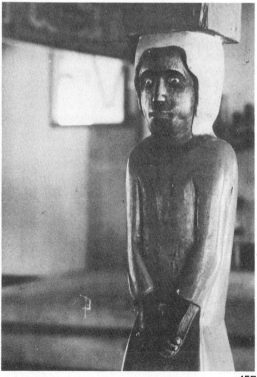

The posts inside the church, which I carved, depict the new life of the reborn Christian. In the letter to the Ephesians, we read: 'He made some as posts in His Church, and He Himself, Jesus, being the main post' (Eph. 2:20, Jabem translation).

Canoe Board Ornaments: On the ceiling, right above the pulpit, there is a piece of old traditional decoration which has its special story. Some time ago I asked some Tami islanders and also some Jabem people to revive some of their old traditions. I told them: 'Has not God given you artistic abilities? Why not use them for our church? You used to embellish your canoes with special designs, as you have them from your forefathers. The Lord has also given such gifts to our generation. Such are gifts which he has granted to us New Guineans.' As a result of this reminder, the people started painting again. One man particularly had a dream in which he saw somebody arriving in a canoe. It was furnished with ornaments of a special design. Immediately after he awoke, he made a sketch in order not to forget it. Afterwards, he did it on a big canoe board. This painting now is in our church. It shows various motifs well known to us in daily life: for

instance, a snake which attacks a common crab. Or a lizard and a scorpion. We notice a sea-horse, a creature which is reputed to be dumb and slow, but which hides between the coral for safety.

Above the pulpit is the Luther rose, which I designed to identify our church. Other denominations also have their marks and symbols. I therefore mounted the Luther rose in a prominent place to show all the visitors that this is a Lutheran church.

The Pulpit: Let us now turn to the pulpit, the place of preaching. We Jabem people are fishermen. Our canoes are made for the purpose of going out to bring in a haul of fish. Another purpose of the canoe is to make trips to other places along the coast. By canoe the Gospel has been carried from here to Malalo and to the Siassi Islands. So I thought I would make the pulpit in the shape of a canoe. There is another thought which prompted me to make a canoe-like pulpit. Jesus himself preached from a boat on the Sea of Galilee. A multitude of people pushed him more and more toward the sea shore, and so he asked Peter to row him out a few yards. If Jesus had been in New Guinea, he certainly would have used a canoe.

The canoe-boards I decorated with the traditional motifs of our forefathers. There is one type of canoe which has an opening in the middle of both sides enabling the waves to lap through, so that a person does not have to bail water all the time. With this I wanted to demonstrate to the younger

generation that our forefathers, too, had quite ingenious minds. In our language this gadget is called a *Selenggeme*. On both sides of it I carved two birds, looking out. They are only a decoration, and have nothing to do with the ark of Noah.

On the front of the canoe I made the place for the preacher. On its four sides are the symbols of the four evangelists. The two images on the right side have the following meaning: The lion represents Mark. He was not a true disciple of Jesus or apostle, who personally experienced Jesus' healings, death, and resurrection. His Gospel is based on the stories of Peter and Paul. He therefore is like a lion. A lion keeps on following his prey until he catches it. No obstacle is too high for him. This is Mark. He followed his 'prey' and related it in his Gospel, although he himself had never seen Jesus.

Matthew has the image of an angel. He followed Jesus and saw his death and resurrection. He heard the very words of Jesus, and marvelled at his healing power. This he reports in his Gospel. Thus, he is like an angel and herald of his Lord. To the left a large bird is shown, an eagle. He flies high up into the blue sky. From a bird's-eye view he sees everything. Nothing remains hidden. This is how I portrayed John. John is the one who not only related what had happened in the past; he

sees also into the future. He is like a large bird which flies up high enough to see the turning of a road which others who stay on the ground cannot see.

The fourth image is for Luke. He was no direct disciple of Jesus, either. He simply recounts what he has heard. He is like a bull or an ox which does not leave out one single leaf of a tree or blade of grass. He devours it all. Luke did not excuse himself by saying: 'I am a doctor. What has the preaching of the Word to do with me?' No, he became an evangelist. On the middle part of the pulpit is a lamb, holding a flag with the emblem of a cross. This is the Lamb of God, our Lord Jesus Christ.

The Chancel: For the altar I made two carvings. The front piece of the altar shows a man holding a lamb in his arm. This is Jesus who says: 'I am the Good Shepherd'. When I painted this, I had never seen a sheep before, and so I had to copy it from pictures.

Jesus has the colour of our skin, but the hair I left long. I did not dare to portray him with our curly hair. Right and left of the altar I carved two angels each with six wings, as in Isaiah's vision: 'With two he covered his face, with two he covered his feet, and with two he flew (Isa. 6:2). The two palm branches on the lower side of the front piece are only adornment without a deeper meaning.

The picture in the upper part shows a man and three women. This is the meaning of it: When Jesus wandered about in Palestine, he had many followers, men and women, who saw his miracles and believed in him; they witnessed the miracle of the wine, his healings, his death and resurrection. However, as soon as Jesus was captured and persecuted, their faith vanished, and they deserted him. Only Peter and John followed him from a distance. At Herod's house, even Peter left him. The only ones who never left him were the women and John. They held out unceasingly and followed him on his way to the cross. How is it that John held out? Where did he get his strength? It was the peace of his Lord and his love which held him. And the women? Peace, faith, and love in their hearts made them also follow Jesus to the cross. And here they are standing under the cross. Why did all the men run away? What happened to Peter? His heart was full of anger. He wanted to fight. Whoever is controlled by fear and anger cannot remain with Jesus. He is pulled away by outside forces. All the young men were afraid, too. Above the chancel, two angels hold a scroll. This was painted and carved for the old church by my uncle. He did it during the war, when we were

hiding in the jungle. At that time we had settled on a mountain called Tarabe. This was done on the advice of the Australian government, so that they could provide us with some additional food. At Tarabe our pastor said: 'We cannot live here like heathens. We want to have a church.' And so a church was built out of bush material. As decoration for this church, my uncle carved and painted this piece which is now in our new church. The meaning of it is: God did not desert us. In his eyes we were not worthless. God remained with us, even in the jungle, and sent his angels to guard us. The words on the scroll say: 'Jesus is good, he saved me!'

The angel who is holding the candles I had carved in 1938 for the old church. Being a teacher and elder at that time, I felt that I should do something for the adornment of the church. I carved the piece without having any model. All three arms, including the candle holder, are made from one single piece of wood. The body is also made from one piece, as are the hands. When I started it, I wanted to make legs as well, but then time run out on me. After all, I had a full-time job as a teacher. As a base for the angel, I then decided to carve four butterflies. Butterflies in their weightlessness, I thought, are earthly images of the angels in heaven.

Another carving, here, shows Moses who lifts up a snake. In the wilderness, the Israelites were afflicted with a plague of poisonous snakes. On God's command, Moses erected the image of a snake. Whoever looked at it was healed. I had the carving designed only as a sketch. Since I was short of time, I gave it to my son Yakotung who carved and finished it. Even our fathers knew that you can heal a sickness with a substance similar to the affliction. This is how the poisonous snakes could be warded off by the elevated snake. The Apostle Paul said likewise: 'God made Christ answerable for our sins so that we would be freed from the bondage of sin'. Jesus also testified: 'As Moses lifted up a serpent in the wilderness, so must the Son of Man be lifted up' (John 3:14).

So far the story of Dawidi from Obasega, a New Guinean teacher, who in his artistic creations expressed his faith and the faith of his fellow-Christians. In this period, as evidenced by the carvings in his home church at Ngasegalatu, he was, in my opinion, influenced somewhat by European art. This was to change in later years; more and more he developed his own style (third phase).

The Chapel of Martin Luther Seminary, Lae

The comments on the altar for this building are again those of Dawidi:

> The builder of the church at Martin Luther Seminary at Lae, Lester Rohrlach, asked me to carve the altar. He even had procured a suitable piece of timber, but otherwise left it entirely to me. The altar should be an elevated table in the centre of the church, equally visible from all sides. In thinking it over, I decided that the legs should be a special feature of the table. They should be like drums as they were used by our forefathers, and still are in use now. The drums had an important function. When war was declared, the drums summoned the warriors. The drums also sounded when peace was celebrated. Then the people would be happy and express their joy by dancing and singing. Thus, the drum is the symbol for strain and for battle, and at the same time for peace celebration and for joy. We carved four drums to be the table legs, and put a richly decorated table slab on them. For wall decorations we used motifs of canoe boards. Their design is actually not Christian, but traditional ornamental art.

The Church at Kwalansam

For the church at Kwalansam I wanted to carve a crucifixion scene which was different from the usual ones. It was not to be the naked Jesus of Golgotha, bowed down to death, but the Son of God as a child — the child Jesus, wearing the vestments of a bishop and the crown of a king, signifying his dignity and sovereign exaltation. Jesus became man, and was born as a child, but not as an ordinary human child. He is the King, the Son of God, to whom all power in heaven and earth is given. Therefore I gave him a crown to wear on his head. At the same time he is the bishop for his disciples and for all those who believe in him. He is also the high priest who acts on our behalf before God. Jesus is a new Moses who leads his people through the wilderness. In the battle with the Amalekites, he stood on the mountain and raised his hands to God; and, as long as he held his hands up, the children of Israel were victorious. Likewise, Jesus' hands of blessing were also held spread out on the hill of Calvary to strengthen us for our life's battle. Above him is a star as an expression of his greatness, and underneath a lamb, for he himself is the Good Shepherd.

Right in the centre is the baptismal font. The carving again shows traditional motifs, two sea-horses between a leaf. Sea-horses, as I said before, are harmless and rather slow. When an enemy is

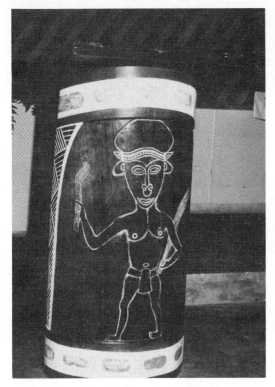

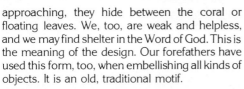

approaching, they hide between the coral or floating leaves. We, too, are weak and helpless, and we may find shelter in the Word of God. This is the meaning of the design. Our forefathers have used this form, too, when embellishing all kinds of objects. It is an old, traditional motif.

Seminary Chapel at Logaweng

For the church at Logaweng I carved the two lecterns. The picture on the left lectern shows a man holding a burning torch. He brings light to the people. Whoever opens the Bible and preaches God's Word is like a man who lights a fire and brings light to the people who sat in darkness. And whoever hears the Word of God exposes himself to the light. He acknowledges his sin and sees his own faults, as he sees the stone or the snake on the road at night by the light of a torch. The picture on the right side shows a man who holds a conch shell horn. Whoever proclaims God's Word is like a man who sends out horn signals. The people come together and listen to the message which he has to give.

I also did the pulpit of the Logaweng church. One picture shows a sower who broadcasts his seed. The other one shows a man who lights a fire and in the left hand he carries a torch to let it burst into flames.

Simbang Memorial Church

The Simbang church is an example of the fourth period. Here Dawidi was able to realize his own concept of an indigenous New Guinean church building: architecture, sculptures, ornaments, all of the same design. The result is impressive.

Again let us follow the comments of the artist himself:

After the decision which was made at the Malalo District Synod to build a Johann Flierl Memorial Church at Simbang, a committee planned the building. Two of the senior missionaries, Baer and Holzknecht, were present, and the elders of our congregations.

I put my concept before them. My idea was to build a church in the style our forefathers built the men's houses. Our forefathers, though living in the time of darkness, had all sorts of skills and traditions.

When the Mission came, they got rid of all their traditions, good and bad. Now I wanted to build a church decorated with the ornaments of our forefathers. Christian symbols I thought to confine to the chancel area. The walls and posts, however, I wanted to do in a traditional design with many symbols of our forefathers. The committee members, after listening attentively, declared themselves to be in agreement.

Soon after, I ordered boards and posts, and selected some men to assist me, and we began carving. During the Malalo District Synod the question was discussed: Can a church be built like a traditional men's house? After discussing it at length, it was decided that it could be done. A men's house is for the entire community. People sit there and discuss matters of daily life or recount stories of the past. In the early days, decisions about war or death-magic were also made at such places. Having had the consent of the people, I asked Lester (Rohrlach, the church architect) to draw up a plan of a men's house and not a church. Men's houses are open sitting places on posts, just with a roof overhead. This was the pattern we wanted to follow when planning the Memorial Church. And this is how it was done.

Now, as for the outer posts, they were carved like posts of the traditional ceremonial houses. In this particular case, they were not to have the symbols of just one particular village, but of the whole region. A variety of symbols is carved on the various posts. One shows a man in his particular war-array. Another wears the emblem of the crocodile on his headband; this means he is as strong as a crocodile. A third one wears only the tail of a fish; that is to say, 'I am not yet an experienced fighter', or 'I am here only to help in the fight'. One man has a snake on his headband; he compares his strength with that of a snake. Another headband has the form of a shark.

To sum it up: All headbands indicate the attributes of the men who wear it. Thus, they revealed to friend and foe alike: I am experienced! I am feared! I kill swiftly like a crocodile! I pierce unexpectedly like a snake! An encounter with me is as deadly as with a shark!

Ceremonial (or spirit) houses of our forefathers also were places of refuge (sanctuaries). Any man who had forfeited his life, but who reached the spirit house, was safe; he had entered the taboo area. No blood was to be shed there. The posts of a ceremonial house mark the taboo area. Pursuers would stop there and say: Oh, he escaped. It is similar with the House of God, where God's Word is to be heard. On that thought I have preached on several occasions: The House of God is the place where people can take refuge. Whenever we have disputes, anger, or fighting, we can flee to the House of God, put aside everything which parts us, and sit next to one another as brothers and sisters who listen to God's Word.

On the ceiling I painted ornaments which our fathers used when decorating their canoes. They

466

did not like plain boards, and so they decorated them with traditional designs. All around the church we have listed on wooden slabs the names of all mission stations and the year they were founded. This is to mark the route the Gospel has taken on its way through Papua New Guinea.

The altar of the church is very simple. The only symbol is a huge cross with the Crucified. Left and right of the crucifix are candleholders shaped like the traditional neck-rests, so to speak, the head-pillows of our forefathers. They had good reasons for using them. Because those neck-rests were rather uncomfortable, they resulted in having only light sleep; otherwise, they might sleep too deeply to hear the coming of their enemies. To stress this point I carved both an owl and a pig on the neck-rest. The pig usually sleeps under the house of its owner and, as soon as enemies approach the house, the pig warns the sleepers by his loud squeal. Similarly, the owl; as soon as a stranger enters the village, it sounds a warning cry to wake the villagers. Hearing the owl's calling, the warrior jumps to his feet, lest the enemy overtake him by surprise.

The candles are to show the light of the Gospel in the midst of a heathen territory. The candleholder rests on the neck-rests of our forefathers to remind the new generation of Christians: Awake, for the Lord is near. Be ready! He will come like a thief in the night.

Chapter 15

New Challenges

Traditional and New Religious Movements

by John G. Strelan

Gospel in Cultural Context

The Lord God, in his wisdom, did not commit to angels the task of proclaiming his Gospel. He placed this work into the hands of flesh-and-blood men and women. These human proclaimers of the Gospel are members of particular cultures; they speak certain languages; they hold to tried and tested world-views; and they operate with sets of perceived and unperceived presuppositions and assumptions. In short, those who proclaim the Gospel are products of their age and culture. They have received the Gospel from others, internalized it, and made it part of themselves and their culture.

As these historically- and culturally-bound evangelizers go about their work, they find that the shape and content and emphases of their proclamation are influenced by their own personal and cultural background and experiences. The apostle Paul is the example *par excellence*. The influences which shaped Paul's message and methods were many and varied. Those more-easily identified are: Palestinian and Hellenistic Judaism; Greek and Roman culture and religion, especially the mystery religions; and, above all, his personal conversion-experience on the road to Damascus.[1] Martin Luther is another example: the influences which shaped his theology, in particular his emphasis on 'justification by faith', have been documented many times over.[2] Although more effort needs to be made to identify the religious and cultural influences which went into the formation of a Flierl or a Keysser, we may say with confidence that these men and their colleagues were all children of their age; the Gospel passed through their own cultural-historical-personal matrix before they shared it with the men and women and children of Papua New Guinea.

If those who proclaim the Gospel are culturally-bound children of their age, what shall we say about those who hear the Gospel? At one point in the history of Western civilization, when evolutionary theory was influential, many intelligent people firmly believed that so-called 'primitive' man had very little culture, and no religion. So, for example, Sir Samuel Barker, an English traveller, reported to the Ethnological Society of London in 1866 that the Dinka and Shilluk of the Upper Nile had no religion, 'nor is

469

the darkness of their minds enlightened by even a ray of superstition'.[3] A century of research and experience has shown that such a view is, of course, quite absurd. Every ethnic and tribal group has its own distinctive, well-developed, and integrated culture, of which religion is often a dominant and pervasive part.

The Gospel, then, is never preached into a religious or cultural vacuum. Those who hear the Gospel already have a culture and religion of their own; and when they hear the Gospel, they proceed to interpret it in the light of their own religious beliefs and cultural values, presuppositions, and world-view. They evaluate the Gospel in terms of its usefulness for meeting present felt needs as well as their hopes and aspirations for the future — both in this life and, perhaps, for a life to come.

In a cross-cultural missionary situation — with proclaimers of the Gospel speaking from their own religious and cultural experience to hearers who have a different set of cultural and religious experiences — distortions and misunderstandings of the Gospel message are bound to arise. Indeed, this is what happened already in the time of the early church. As we piece together the history of the early church, we have to conclude that within 25 years of the 'beginning of the gospel' (Mark 1:1), the apostolic message was being misunderstood, misinterpreted, and misapplied. Although Walter Bauer's pioneering monograph, *Orthodoxy and Heresy in Earliest Christianity*, has come under increasing fire in recent years,[4] it is still recognized as a brilliant demonstration of how 'out of a fluid, amorphous primitive Christianity there gradually emerged a polarized antithesis between secondary developments, known to us as orthodoxy and heresy'.[5]

But one does not need to read Bauer's work in order to see that the apostolic message was quickly distorted and misunderstood. The New Testament itself bears witness to this fact. The letters of Paul, especially Galatians and the Corinthian correspondence, contain polemics against distortions of the Gospel. Likewise, the Johannine corpus clearly testifies to the presence in the church of doctrinal aberrations which later came to full flower in what came to be known as Cerinthianism, Gnosticism, Docetism, and so forth.

470

In short, what happened in the early church, already within the lifetime of Christ's chosen apostles, was that, when the Gospel message was proclaimed, the proclaimers meant one thing and the hearers often heard something different. It was not long before 'other gospels' (Galatians 1:8,9) were abroad in the church, and different streams and movements arose, some of which would later be classed as 'orthodox', and some as 'heretical'.

If the Gospel message proclaimed by the Lord's chosen apostles was so quickly distorted, twisted, and misunderstood, then it should come as no surprise that the same fate befell the preaching of Flierl and Bergmann and Keysser *et al* in Papua New Guinea. The Lutheran missionaries who came to Simbang and Astrolabe Bay at the end of the 19th century were children of their age; they came with their own cultural baggage, their own pre-understanding of the Gospel and its implications for life. It is to their credit that they were conscious of the fact that they were not preaching that message into a religious vacuum. They were aware that the peoples of Papua New Guinea possessed a well-developed belief-system which was fundamental to their cultures. The early Lutheran missionaries established a pattern of study of the religions, myths, rituals, languages, and cultures of the people among whom they worked — a pattern which has continued to the present day.

It is outside the scope of the present chapter to describe in detail the religious beliefs and practices of the peoples to whom the early missionaries brought the Gospel (see ch 1). Lawrence and Meggit, the editors of a symposium on Melanesian religions, characterize the 'seaboard religions' of Melanesia (which includes those encountered by early missionaries) as follows:

> There is strong emphasis on autonomous creative or regulative spirit-beings and also on the dead. In many places, there are totemic beliefs. Distant ancestors tend to be forgotten, while recent ghosts are regarded as the protectors of their living descendants. Ritual for deities and ghosts, although embodying elements of placation, is based on the confidence that, properly approached, they will automatically serve man's interest. Religion, therefore, pervades man's whole intellectual life.[6]

The religious beliefs and practices of the people to whom the first Lutheran missionaries brought the Gospel, are undergirded, validated, and given life and meaning by a number of traditional myths. Myths in Melanesia function as means of explaining and justifying present customs and conditions, as well as providing the dynamic for change. Myths in Melanesia are alive and powerful — and fluid, for they are constantly being reinterpreted to fit changing conditions.

One myth which must be mentioned here, both because of its broad provenance, and also because of its deep influence on the Melanesians' response to the Christian message and Western culture and technology, is the myth of the Two Brothers. This myth occurs with many variations, in many parts of Melanesia: from the north-east coast of Papua New Guinea, to the Sepik, to Vanimo, to Rabaul, to Finschhafen and the Huon Gulf, and elsewhere. [7] The basic story line concerns two brothers, Manup and Kilibob, sons of Anut, the creator-god. Manup was the elder brother, Kilibob the younger. The myth begins with a quarrel between Manup and Kilibob:

> Kilibob invented canoe-building and wood-carving. One day Manup's wife stole one of Kilibob's arrows and forced him to tattoo its incised design on her pudenda. Manup was furious and tried to murder Kilibob. Eventually the two brothers left Karkar. Manup made a canoe and sailed north. But Kilibob made a very large canoe and then created men, pigs, dogs, fowls, food plants, and artefacts, all of which he put on board. He sailed to Madang, where he carved out Dallman Passage and the yam islands by shooting arrows at the mainland. He then sailed down the Rai Coast, again leaving new islands and reefs in his wake. At each coastal village, he put a man ashore, giving him the power of speech, food plants, a bow and arrows, a stone axe and adze, rain, and ritual formulae. East of Saidor, he crossed over to Siassi, where he settled and was visited by Manup, with whom he was reconciled. [8]

In some versions, the roles of the two brothers are reversed, and the cause of the quarrel varies. Furthermore, in some versions, the reconciliation between the two brothers still lies in the future. It was expected that the two brothers would return to Madang, and, after weathering a series of apocalyptic-like events, they would settle their differences, and be reconciled.

This myth of Manup and Kilibob was the seminal and archetypal myth behind many of the religious movements which broke out in many parts of Melanesia from 1850 onward.

To summarize: Early Lutheran missionaries came to Papua New Guinea with their own language, culture, and religious beliefs and practices. They proclaimed the Gospel, the dynamic and motivating force of their missionary endeavours, to a people with a vastly different language, culture, and religious system. In this situation, the potential for distortion and misunderstanding of the message was enormous.

But several other factors need to be considered at this point. First, the method which the early missionaries chose to follow in spreading the Gospel message. The missionaries determined that, as soon as possible, the group which made a decision 'for' the Gospel should be encouraged to send several members from within the group to a neighbouring village, where they would settle, try to live as Christians, and speak the Christian message to any who cared to listen. Elsewhere in this volume an account has been given of the often-heroic work done by these early converts to Christianity. [9] It is not our purpose to discuss the pros and cons of this method. But it should be noted that the majority of folk who left their home village to live and work in an alien village were newly-baptized Christians, with a maximum amount of faith, perhaps, but a somewhat-lesser amount of Christian knowledge and understanding. Often they were illiterate. Often the missionary was able to visit them only once or twice a year. [10] The question must be asked: By the time the Gospel message had been passed on from village A to village B to village C, and so forth, just how garbled and distorted had it become?

Secondly, Johannes Flierl and his co-workers adopted the practice of giving gifts to the people among whom they wished to work. As a means of establishing contacts and making friends with people, this action was appropriate and in keeping with Papua New Guinean custom. But it was also in keeping with another local custom, namely, that one gives, initially, smaller gifts as tokens of a larger, the real, the essential gift, which is to follow. One Papua New Guinean pastor, when asked, in

1959, to comment on this practice, is said to have replied:

> Their action was correct. They used the small gifts only as a bait. But within the bait was the hook of God's Word hidden. The people snapped after the bait and so were seized by the Word of God and pulled close. [11]

True enough. But the question remains: How many 'snapped after the bait' because they saw in the Gospel an alternative, perhaps superior, means of achieving the pragmatic and man-centred ends of their traditional religion?

The purpose of the foregoing discussion has been to highlight the fact that, when Lutheran missionaries came to Papua New Guinea with the Gospel, it was, humanly speaking, inevitable that the proclamation of, and living witness to, the Gospel would result in religious and cultural ferment; it would result in misconceptions and distortions of the Christian message; and it would give rise to rival movements, movements which tried to put a Christian skin on to the framework of traditional religions, new wine into old bottles.

In the pages which follow, we will attempt to trace the history and describe the morphology of several major religious movements which arose in so-called 'Lutheran' areas, that is, on the north-east coast of Papua New Guinea, centred on Madang, and on the Huon Peninsula, centred on Finschhafen. This will be followed by a study of two more-recent movements, one in the Garaina area of the Morobe Province, and one in the Enga Province. While we review these movements, note will be taken of how the church responded, at the grass-roots level, and 'officially'. The chapter concludes with a discussion of the points on which the religious movements challenge the Lutheran church to examine itself, its policies, its practice, its theology, its worship life, and its role in Papua New Guinea society.

Madang Area

When the missionaries from the Rhenish Mission Society began work at Buged, Siar Island, Karkar Island, and other places in and around Madang in the period 1887-1897, they heard the myth of the Two Brothers. Missionary Hoffmann recorded the myth as he heard it from the Buged people in 1895, and he sent it home to be published in the *Berichte der*

472

Rheinischen Missionsgesellschaft (1897). [12] The missionaries also heard stories about visits to Bongu on the Rai Coast of the Russian scientist Nikolai Miklouho-Maclay, in the period between 1871 and 1883. The people identified Miklouho-Maclay, together with other European visitors to the Rai Coast, as pagan deities, and to some extent, as spirits of the dead. [13] Miklouho-Maclay, who impressed the people with his constant courtesy and quiet courage, was especially the object of speculation: Could he be the younger brother, Kilibob, returned to share a new kind of material culture with his people? No one could be sure; at the least, he was a deity, a source of wealth and of superhuman knowledge. And he was a friend. [14]

The people's experience, however, with the settlers and traders and government officials who followed Maclay, was not so pleasant. Many groups lost land as it was 'bought' by representatives of the German New Guinea Company. [15] At first it was thought that these Europeans were hostile deities; but later the people realized that the colonial rulers and exploiters were mortal (and killable).

By 1903, a serious anti-European sentiment had developed in and around Madang. July 26, 1904 was set as the day on which all German government officers, traders, and male missionaries in Madang were to be killed. However, an informer from Bilia divulged the plot, and the revolt failed. The conspirators were rounded up, and preparations were made to return them to their homes where compensation payments were to be arranged. This mild response on the part of the government changed overnight when it was found that labourers from the Finschhafen (Neuendettelsau Mission) area were involved in the planned revolt. Fearing a wide-spread conspiracy, the government took drastic action: nine putative leaders of the revolt were summarily executed; seven were imprisoned in Rabaul. The final retributive act on the part of the government took place in 1912 when, in response to another abortive uprising, most of the people of Siar, Bilia, and Panutibum were exiled, and their lands alienated. [16]

The Madang revolts of 1904 and 1912 were traumatic events for both church and people. On the one hand, the missionaries, who had laboured for 16 years before baptizing the first convert (in 1903), 'petitioned their Barmen headquarters to give up New Guinea as a thankless field of thorns'. [17] The people, on the other hand, had to reinterpret the Manup-Kilibob myth in order to explain the failure of the revolts. The new interpretation said that the Melanesians had acted stupidly (in the mythical past), and so they lost the secret of the good life as a result of their own foolishness. Kilibob's military superiority and his more-effective technology were gifts from the gods. That was why the Europeans had guns, while the Melanesians were obliged to use only bows and arrows. The only hope for the future lay in the early return and reconciliation of the two brothers. [18]

The decade after 1904 was a time for what Hannemann calls 'passive resistance' [19] — minimal cooperation with the government; withholding of labour and the refusal to pay taxes — which came to an end soon after the exile of the Siars in 1912. Then followed several decades of 'accomodation' (Hannemann [20]), during which time full cooperation was offered to the government and the missions. Many baptisms took place in swift succession: 127 at Bongu in 1913; 177 Bel villagers at Graged Island in 1919. In 1921, the first baptism (121 adults) was held at Kabailo on Karkar Island. [21]

Hannemann [22] suggests that when the people embraced Christianity they were deliberately embracing a new culture: the lifestyle imposed on them by the government, and reinforced by the missions, required that they clothe themselves with the new religion which validated and empowered that way of life, that is, Christianity. In other words, as Peter Lawrence observes, 'Christianity was attributed the same relationship to the new material culture as the pagan religion was thought to have to the old'. [23]

The Christianity which was adopted by many people at this time was not that preached by the missionaries, but one adapted by the people themselves to match the materialism and man-centredness of their traditional religions. The main stories and truths of Christianity became, when combined with elements of traditional thinking, the basis for a new myth concerning the origin of 'cargo'. And Christian faith, ethics, and ritual was seen as a means of obtaining 'cargo', that is, the good,

desirable, life in all its aspects: spiritual, social, material, political, and economic. [24]

It appears, then, that in the Madang area in the 1920s, the rush to baptism, the church services and the prayer meetings, the hymn-singing, the ban on dancing and on ceremonies honouring the spirits of the dead, the strict observance of the Christian ethic — all this was, for many people, not a conversion to genuine Christianity, but a participation in what has been called 'the first recognizable cargo cult in the southern Madang District: that is, the first organized ritual specially designed to activate a deity to send Western goods'. [25]

It seems that at least 50% of the population of the Madang district believed that the brand of Christianity which was being preached by many local evangelists and other church workers, was the 'official' version, having the imprimatur of the missionaries. [26] Relationships between the people and the missionaries in the 1920s were amicable enough, but they were, as Lawrence concludes, 'based on complete mutual misunderstanding'. [27] Only in retrospect were missionaries able to grasp fully what had happened, and to see what a challenge this quasi-Christian cargo movement presented to the church to reexamine its proclamation and practices, and to take more careful note of how the people were interpreting and applying the Christian message.

Finschhafen Area

In order to maintain historical continuity in this survey, it is necessary at this point to shift focus from the work in the Madang area, and to look at what happened in the 1920s among the Lutheran congregations which had evolved from the work of missionaries of the Neuendettelsau Mission Society among the Kate-speaking peoples and neighbouring tribes on the Huon Peninsula. [28]

Missionary Christian Keysser held his farewell service at Sattelberg on March 14, 1920. Several years after his departure — and perhaps as a reaction to his departure — the Sattelberg congregation experienced a period of spiritual lethargy, characterized by dereliction of duty on the part of some leaders, a lack of interest in evangelism and worship and church discipline, a decline in moral standards, and uneasy relationships with the missionary. The

Selembe, Sattelberg; station manager, teacher, church leader, and later Paramount Luluai.

Desiang, a leader of the Eemasang movement.

missionary, Leonhard Flierl, was responsible for a geographically-vast circuit, far beyond the strength of one man. Flierl was opposed on many counts by Selembe, an energetic and influential leader who had served the government for some years at Rabaul, and who returned in the early 1920s to Sattelberg, accompanied by his New Ireland wife.

However, in 1927 there began at Sattelberg what appeared to be a Christian revival movement. This movement was known as *Eemasang* (= house-cleaning).[29] It began with the conversion (or reconversion) of Selembe. He received a message from the Holy Spirit, he said, who warned him of the consequences of his evil ways. Quickly Selembe influenced other leaders to follow him along the road of repentance and renewal of life, and soon a regular revival had developed.

Eemasang aimed at renewal of the individual and of the congregation. It worked for repentance, a change of heart, confession of sins, acknowledgment that God is holy, and that no unclean or sinful person can stand alone before him. A typical *Eemasang* meeting began with the singing of hymns, followed by prayer, 474

an inspirational address, and earnest prayers in which the participants' utter unworthiness and sinfulness was stressed. Then all those who wished to change their ways were invited to come forward, make their public confession, and pledge to strive to live a godly life. Their confession and promise was acknowledged and confirmed with a brief prayer by one of the *Eemasang* leaders.[30]

Eemasang was a people's movement; the missionaries took a back seat. It spread rapidly from Sattelberg until it embraced all the Kate people; it also moved into the Hube area. Inevitably, all kinds of accretions crept in. Spiritual pride and arrogance began to rear its head. Some 'renewals' were short-lived. By the end of 1933, *Eemasang* had died out, partly because it had achieved its stated goals, partly because no movement of this nature can sustain itself for more than several years, and partly because some of the leading men in *Eemasang* were found to be involved in what Keysser calls the 'money-making swindle' (*Geldzauberschwindel*). We turn, now, to a consideration of the 'swindle', which was, in fact, a cargo movement.[31]

In 1922, two men of the Wemora tribe, Tutumang and Mutari, returned from Rabaul with their heads full of ideas of how to acquire the wealth and superior technology of the Europeans. Rabaul, it should be borne in mind, was the centre of racial, industrial, and ideological ferment in the 1920s, a ferment which culminated in the Rabaul Strike of 1929. [32] Rabaul was also the town where Selembe, the *Eemasang* leader, had worked for some years prior to his return to Sattelberg.

The cult which was developed by Tutumang and Mutari (who were joined in the leadership by Tikombe), had its ritual centre in money-houses which were erected in the bush. Money was collected from cult adherents, and then 'holed' shillings were matched with whole shillings (that is, male and female) in an attempt to produce more shillings. Alternatively, coins were held with bamboo tongs and boiled over a fire to bring out offspring coins. The words which were associated with these acts are not known to us. Symbols of the cult were the 'money-machines', which consisted of a simple box with a tin can and string, perhaps also with a bell. In 1927, a European trader actually sold the cult leaders a cash register. [33] The money which was stored in these 'money-machines' was extremely volatile: it could turn into stone just as easily as it could turn into money.

The cargo cult began in 1922, and lasted, on and off, until 1938. In 1927, the movement was, for the first time, brought out into the open by Christians. As a consequence, four villages were refused baptisms and the Eucharist. [34] But then the cult went underground, until it reappeared in 1930 in harness with the *Eemasang*. The rituals of *Eemasang* (prayer, singing, confession, promises) were diverted to the cargo movement, and became part of the essential ritual. If money did not multiply as expected, the fault lay with the people's failure to repent, and confess, and so forth.

Eemasang leaders, such as Selembe and Desiang, were prominent participants in the cargo movement. In 1933, a campaign was conducted in an effort to root out the cult. The effort achieved only partial success, for the cult erupted once more in 1936. Finally, in 1937, the cult leaders were publicly exposed by 'missionary Winkler's sharing the common indigenous ability to dream a "true" dream, in which he recognized prominent evangelists as the leaders of the cult in the Hube area; and next morning discovering four magic money-making machines in a secret room'. [35]

What was the church's reaction to this movement? Repentant participants, together with loyal church members, proposed that all baptisms, communions, weddings, and funerals be suspended. In addition, they accepted Pilhofer's stipulations: all cult secrets had to be revealed, and all collected moneys handed over; all cult members had to attend instruction classes; an apology was to be offered to the missionaries; and the ringleaders were to be handed over to the government for punishment. Finally, the Sattelberg-Hube congregations, at the insistence of their former missionary Keysser, sent a letter of 'apology' to the Neuendettelsau authorities, and in a solemn ceremony on July 3, 1938, they planted a tree, erected a plaque, and pledged never again to be involved in the money cult. [36]

What was the actual relationship between *Eemasang.* and the 'money-magic' cult? Certainty is impossible, given the meagre information at our disposal. However, there are indications that the *Eemasang*, for some people at least, was not a 'marvellous movement of sanctification' as Senior Flierl called it, but rather a phase in a cargo movement. These indications are: (1) The cargo movement leaders and the *Eemasang* leader all had spent time in Rabaul. (2) The cargo movement started five years earlier than the *Eemasang*. (3) Selembe was the instigator of *Eemasang*, and also a leading participant in the cargo movement. (4) The three reported interventions by the congregation (in 1927, 1933, and 1937) all came at points which correspond exactly to a common pattern in cargo movements, namely, (a) an initial use of traditional ritual to expedite the arrival of the 'cargo' (= the period 1922-27, at which point congregational action was taken); (b) a turning to Christian beliefs and rituals as an alternative to the traditional rituals (= the *Eemasang* period, 1927-33, at which point there was again congregational intervention); and (c) a synthesis of traditional and Christian ritual and beliefs (= the period 1934-37, at which point the congregation intervened once more). In 1938 the movement was thought to have died; but, as we shall see, it merely slumbered until 1946, when it awoke once more in a slightly modified form.

Upikno Movement (Kalasa)

In 1933, an independent, but related, movement arose in the Kalasa area under the leadership of Upikno, an illiterate Christian from Gitua.[37] Upikno was assisted by the teacher Fenzongnuc, who functioned as his secretary. Upikno heard 'voices' which commanded repentance and prayer and the destruction of material possessions in order to demonstrate true humility and trust. Upikno tried to interest other church workers in his movement, and to keep the movement hidden from the missionary Wacke. When this failed, the 'voices' became anti-white and apocalyptic in tone.

Upikno received another 'voice' message which, as Pech notes, rewrites the 'Two Brothers mythological scenario' thus:

> The Whites were also black at first. Only much later they prepared themselves by repentance and prayer so that I could bless them, so that they became white. At that time I also gave them huge warehouses, so that they could become masters. But the missionaries are guilty because they hid the fact that I wanted you to have the great warehouses too. Their local assistants are hopeless — disregard them! Get rid of their titles. Get rid of all devotions with song, biblical address, and prayers. Get rid of the remaining coconuts on the palms. Only so can the heavenly warehouses descend to earth. Take care not to stir out-of-doors at night. If someone does, it will be his fault if the heavenly store does not descend.
>
> Great cannons will stand at Qambu too, and many warehouses. Then the Brown people will become white, but the Whites will receive another quite distinctive colour.[38]

Upikno's movement infected many Christians in Gitua, Sialum, and Qambu, and also in the region inland from Kalasa. Eventually, in 1935, disillusionment began to set in. The promised goods from heaven had not arrived. The Gitua people confessed their foolishness and their sinfulness in following Upikno. They repented and turned to the Gospel with renewed zeal. However, in 1938, Missionary W. Zischler reported that the Gitua had not really recovered from the effects of Upikno's movement. Zischler speaks of disunity and quarrelling, a lack of interest in school work and

476

in evangelistic outreach.[39] Upikno's movement flared and died, but its influence, especially in the reworking of the myth of the Two Brothers, continued on for many decades.

Letub Movement (Madang)

While the church on the Huon Peninsula was meeting the challenges and changes introduced by *Eemasang* and cargo movements, in the Madang region changes were taking place in the relationship between missionaries and people. The period of 'accomodation', in which a cargo movement based on a 'Christian' myth had flourished, came to an end in the latter half of the 1920s. The cargo activity, which attempted to use Christian stories and ritual, had not borne fruit. The missionaries had not revealed to their converts the secret of the *as bilong kago* and the *rot bilong kago* (the source of the good life and the way to obtain it). Frustration and bitterness set in. The deepening economic depression on the world scene made the settling of the 'cargo' question a matter of great urgency. 'From 1929 onwards', Pech notes, 'the discussions at the Lutherans' local and district church conferences were dominated by this topic, particularly when matters calling for village finance, such as teachers' salaries and improved living conditions in the villages, were under review.'[40]

Feelings and frustrations came out into the open when the Buged people asked Missionary Hanselmann to place the following matter on the agenda for the 1934 conference:

> Why do we not learn the secret of cargo? You people hide the power of the Europeans from us. Our possessions are quite worthless; those of the white men are really worth while. We understand all the work of Europeans, but they obstruct us. We want to progress, but they keep us down as *kanakas*. True, the Mission has taught us Christianity, but it does not help us black people in a practical way. The white men are hiding the cargo secret from us. We are destined to be complete paupers, absolutely destitute.[41]

Nothing was settled at the Buged conference. At the Sagalau conference (1935), the missionaries themselves raised the question of 'cargo' expectations, and pointed to the problems of a general congregational malaise, a renewed interest in traditional dancing, and a distrust of missionaries. Although delegates admitted the problems and resolved to do something about them, 'the older missionaries deemed it advisable to suspend the administration of the sacraments until the individual congregation had shown evidence of a change for the better'. [42] The decision to withhold the Sacraments was reaffirmed after the 1936 conference at Sangpat on the Rai Coast, at which the missionaries were again openly accused of withholding from the people the secret of 'cargo'. [43]

By the end of the 1930s, then, Christianity had been tried and found wanting as a means of present 'salvation', as the people understood it. It is not surprising that, in the late 1930s and the early 1940s, several cargo movements developed which had their roots in the traditional religion, but which included some Christian elements as well. In short, they were syncretistic. [44]

The Letub Cult [45] was based partly on the Letub dance — which had been discontinued and was now revived by its owners, the Mabonup people, who in turn sold it to their neighbours — and partly on a revised, syncretistic version of the Manup-Kilibob myth. The revised version said, in brief, that Jesus-Manup was the deity and culture-hero of the Madang peoples, while Adam and Eve were the culture-heroes of the Europeans. The Jews held Jesus-Manup captive in heaven (in or above Sydney, Australia). The Letub ritual was designed to free Jesus-Manup from his bondage so that he could return to Papua New Guinea with his ships and cargo, and he could supervise the introduction of the new, good life. [46]

The Letub movement spread rapidly, fanned in 1939 by rumours that war had begun in Europe. No one person was recognized as leader of the movement, although Kaut, a young *tultul* from Kauris, who had spent some time working in Rabaul, was sponsored by some people as a likely 'king of Madang'. By 1940 the majority of villages in the environs of Madang were occupied with Letub-related activity:

> church meetings with prayer and confession, prophecies, healings, Letub dances, seances in cemeteries — all of which were justified as worshipping God. The thought underlying all was that when every village had joined the movement

and observed the ceremonies as they understood them, the cargo would come. [47]

The missionary Inselmann and some faithful Christians worked to keep the lines of communication open with the Letubists. In 1941, a conference was held at Barahin, attended only by nationals. No agreement was reached; the Letubists reiterated their conviction that the European missionaries were still withholding from them the secret of 'cargo'. On December 10-13, 1942, with the Japanese occupation of Madang expected at any moment, a baptism of infants and catechumens was held. At this gathering there was also a general renunciation of Letub. [48] But, in many cases, this renunciation was shortlived.

When the Japanese occupied Madang and district on December 18, 1942, they were welcomed by many Letubists as saviours sent by the ancestors. Kaut of Kauris became at this time a leader in persuading Letub followers to cooperate with the Japanese and to revive the Letub. [49] Meanwhile, a rival movement had begun at Milkuk under the leadership of Tagarab, an ex-policeman who had worked in Rabaul, taken part in the Rabaul Strike of 1929, and had been imprisoned for a short time. [50] Tagarab based his teachings on a version of the Manup-Kilibob myth. He said that missionaries had taught the people to pray to a false god so that the people's prayers would be deflected from the true cargo deity. Because of this deception, God-Kilibob had sent the Japanese to drive out the Europeans and to bring the 'cargo'.

Tagarab's ritual involved the singing of hymns, prayers, and sermons — all directed to the true cargo deity. The Ten Commandments were to be strictly observed; fighting was to cease; love magic and adultery was to be abandoned; and the Japanese were to be given full cooperation. Tagarab developed a large following among Lutheran Christians; but eventually it became evident that the Japanese were in the country to exploit — not to 'save' — the people, and disillusionment set in. In the end, Tagarab himself announced that he would henceforth direct his ritual activity toward working for the return of the Allies. Tagarab was executed by the Japanese during their retreat to the Sepik.

Kukuaik Movement (Karkar Island)

To complete the picture in the Madang area, it is necessary to backtrack several years, and visit Karkar Island, the site of a movement known as Kukuaik.[51] The first known Karkar religious revival movement had occurred in 1926 (a year before *Eemasang* in Sattelberg). Although this movement arose as part of the preparation for the imminent return of Christ, and although it had no overt 'cargo' elements, the Takia people, when reflecting on this movement at a later date, regarded it as the start of the activities which culminated in Kukuaik.[52]

During the 1930s, the Karkar islanders made serious efforts to synthesize traditional and Christian beliefs. Dissatisfaction with Europeans — government officers, traders, planters, and missionaries — also developed on Karkar in the 1930s. Kukuaik was seen by its leaders as, in part, a protest movement against European domination and exploitation.[53]

Kukuaik itself began in 1940 when Yas of Kabailo, a leader of the Bagabag congregation, tried to stir up his lethargic people by urging confession of sins, restitution of ills, and a feast of reconciliation. The Karkar circuit conference gave Kukuaik its blessing, and recommended it to all congregations in the circuit. It happened that at this time some unusual natural phenomena were observed: extreme drought, an influenza epidemic, blood-red sunsets, meteors, comets, bright stars, strange mirages, and mysterious lights. These phenomena, together with rumours of approaching war in the Pacific, served to develop a great sense of apocalyptic expectancy, and built a 'euphoric sense of brotherhood never experienced there before — or since'.[54]

But Kukuaik, which affected Christians and non-Christians alike, turned into a cargo movement, with a doctrine similar to that of the cargo movement in the Southern Madang District, 1913-1933.[55] Under the leadership of Kubai of Boroman, graveside prayer-meetings were conducted, people spoke in tongues, and there was mass hysteria. Many new songs were written and sung during this period. 'Kukuaik', McSwain concludes, 'was largely Christian [in form], but the assumptions upon which it was based were pagan'.[56]

Kubai named January 1, 1942 as the day on which the world as it is presently known would end, and on which a new world, favourable to the Karkars, would emerge. But New Year's Day brought, not a new world, but police from Madang (the police party included Tagarab and Yali). The Kukuaik leaders, or reputed leaders, were arrested and imprisoned in Madang. They were released on January 21 when Japanese planes bombed and strafed Madang.

Reflections

The foregoing survey of the challenges which traditional and syncretistic religious thinking and movements presented to the fledgling Lutheran churches in the Madang area and on the Huon Peninsula, shows that the experiences and the responses in both areas were similar. In both areas, the movements arose from within the congregations. In both areas, there were some movements which were based on traditional religious thinking and ritual, some movements which were a mixture of traditional and Christian beliefs and practices, and also examples of movements which began as ostensibly 'Christian' revivals but ended up as cargo movements. In both areas, missionaries were, with a few notable exceptions, the last to recognize the extent of the challenge which the movements presented to the congregations; and in both areas, congregational leaders were themselves infected by the movements, or were slow to take action against them. In both areas, the response of the missionaries and the faithful Christians was, in some cases, an attempt at understanding and dialogue; but more often the decision was made to suspend the Sacraments and other services of the church until such time as those caught up in the movement repented, confessed their folly, and once more sought the services and fellowship of the Christian congregation.

Here is not the place to explore the reasons for the similarity of experiences. Some factors are obvious: the same Gospel was preached by foreigners to people with similar traditional world-views and religious beliefs and practices. Church polity introduced into both areas was much the same. Two factors which are not so obvious, and which need further investigation are, first, the extent of communication between people of the Finschhafen area and people of the Madang area. We know that, traditionally, there were trading links between these two areas. We also know that missionaries and congregational representatives from the Finschhafen area visited congregations in the Madang area. And we have already noted that labourers from the Finschhafen area were implicated in the 1904 revolt in Madang. Secondly, it is noteworthy that at least seven of the leaders of the religious movements which broke out in the 25 years from 1925 in both areas, had all worked in Rabaul, namely: Selembe, Tutumang, Mutari, Mambu, Kaut, Tagarab, and Yali. This suggests that a detailed study of the religious, political, social, and economic scene in Rabaul in the period of 1910-1930 would be relevant for an understanding of the events described in the preceding pages.

Yali Movement (Rai Coast)

The Lutheran church survived World War II in Papua New Guinea, only to have to face immediately another formidable challenge. In the 25 years after the establishment of a provisional civil government in Port Moresby in 1945, countless cargo movements and other religious and socio-economic movements broke out all over Melanesia.[57] Areas served by the Lutheran church received their share of such movements.

The most notable and influential movement of the period was that led by Yali Singina (1912-1975) of Sor village on the Rai Coast. His story has been told by Peter Lawrence in *Road Belong Cargo*, and need not be repeated here.[58] Suffice it to say that Yali, an Allied war hero because of his coast-watching activities, attempted to start a Rai Coast Rehabilitation Scheme during the period 1945-48. However, the scheme was perverted by former followers of the Letub, and it developed into a cargo movement.

At first, Yali repudiated cargo doctrine. But when he saw that the promises concerning the good life which had been made by the Australian government during the war were not going to be kept, he turned against the government and the churches, and gave himself fully to developing his movement as a pagan revival.

[Yali] assumed that there were two separate religions in New Guinea, each constituted in roughly the same way and each powerful in its own sphere. First, there was Christianity, with its two deities (God and Jesus Christ), spirits of the dead, and multiple totems. God and Jesus Christ were responsible for the material and social culture of the Europeans ... This was the Europeans' secret. They would never reveal more than its externals to outsiders and would resist any attempt to purloin it — as, for example, by means of cargo ritual ... Second, there was the native religion, which had its own deities, spirits and totems. These deities were responsible for the New Guinea material and social culture, to which he would now encourage his people to return. Beyond the European modifications written into the new 'Laws' he had drawn up, there was to be no further compromise between the two ways of life.[59]

Although Yali tried to divorce the pagan revival from the cargo movement, he was unable to resist the spirit of the times. By 1949, the pagan revival had become a full-blown cargo movement, with Yali as messiah and king, and Gurek, a native of Hapurpi village, as its chief prophet and ideologue. As a result of charges laid against him by missionaries and government officers, Yali spent five years in gaol (1955-59). This did little to decrease his popularity, and in the 1960s the Yali movement spread rapidly, partly through contagion, and partly through deliberate 'mission' efforts on the part of Yali-ists. Yali repudiated the 'cargo' aspects of his movement in 1973, and he died in 1975, the year Papua New Guinea became an independent sovereign state.

The influence and geographical spread of Yali-ism was enormous in the late 1950s and 1960s. From the Rai Coast it spread to the North Coast, to the Sepik, to the Ramu, to Long Island, down the coast to the Huon Peninsula, to Lae and environs, to Boana, to the Markham Valley, and even into the Eastern Highlands region. J.F. Wagner surveyed mission station reports from the period 1952-1962 and found reports of Yali-influenced movements, or independent cargo movements, or at least 'cargo' talk, from the following places: Bunabun, Begesin, Amele, Buged, Ogelbeng, Mumeng, Tapen, Kaiapit, Asaroka, Tarabo, Sattelberg-Hube, Boana, Kalasa, Biliau, Ega, Raipinka, Malalo, Wanuma, Ulap, Zaka, Kotna, Kabak, Karkar, Omkolai, Tiripini, and Agotu.[60]

Skin Guria Movement (Hube)

It is impossible to report here on all these movements, and to note how local Christians responded to the particular movement in their area. Let one case-study suffice: that of the *skin guria* (body-shaking) movement among the Hube of the Morobe Province.[61] In mid-1946, three men — Anzirong from Ko village, Boteteng from Simbeng, and Ipongi from Zewezang — received a revelation from the ancestors:

> Anutu gave the paradise called Eden to men, which was taken away again because of the transgression of Adam and Eve. But the Whites have found Eden again, by means of the spirits of their ancestors. Our Eden is waiting too, and it will be obtained through proper conduct and certain behaviour — of course, only with the assistance of the ancestors. When Jesus rose from the dead and had ascended into heaven, he opened the door for life on earth [this life], as well as the one for life in heaven [the life to come]. However, the Whites have closed the door for life on earth to us, and they have concealed the truth from us. Therefore one of the dead will rise again after three days, as Christ did, to lead us the way through this door to earthly life.[62]

The 'proper conduct and certain behaviour' spoken of in the revelation, included the following: a strict, military-style regimentation of village life; drilling with imitation rifles; careful personal and communal hygiene; a blameless life; public and private prayers; hymn-singing; and speaking in tongues and 'shaking'. The expectation was that 'cargo' was to come in planes, ships, and trucks. Paired bush houses were erected in various localities: one for the men to have their secret meetings, and one for the 'cargo' which was to come.

The movement spread like wildfire, out of the Burum valley, to Mindik, to Kuat, to Kuluntufu. It came to a head at Kuluntufu where, it is reported, cultists reflected on the words of Christ in Luke 9:24, and determined to sacrifice two of their young men in an effort to obtain the good life.[63] There is also evidence that the movement spread to the Buangs where, under the leadership of Joveing Petrus, it was known as *Tapi-tapi* (= we are climbing up the steps to the good life).[64]

Both the church and the government responded to the *skin guria* movement in the Hube and the Buangs. In the Hube, the leaders
480

of the movement were brought before a meeting of Christians at Ogeramnang. At this meeting, the cult was denounced, and the leaders of the cult were struck with branches of a shrub which was traditionally used for counter-magic. A large stone was inscribed with the details of the meeting, and then erected as a *tambu* at the entrance to the station church. Small replica stones were placed at strategic points in the area.[65]

In the Buangs, a meeting took place at Mapos II village: between Joveing and his followers on the one hand, and Missionary Horrolt and other church leaders on the other. Joveing defended his position and his practices. Horrolt opposed him and, according to reports, was successful in convincing Joveing and his people that they should give up *Tapi-tapi* and should return to the Christian faith. Unfortunately, Joveing's change of heart was short-lived. He continued to oppose and challenge church leaders, and even succeeded in having three of them taken to court. They were found not guilty of all charges, and released. However, they refused to press counter-charges against Joveing. 'Then', Simon Stephen says, 'the cult prophet and all his followers repented and joined again the Christian Church. This was in 1947, and most of them are still serving today.'[66]

A second wave of cargo activity hit the Hube area in 1956, a third in the early 1960s, a fourth in 1968, and a fifth in 1970. All these movements were related to *skin guria*, but they are known as movements of the Tanget Cult, a cult which continues to the present day.[67] The initial impulse for Tanget was supplied by a series of dreams experienced by Kopa Oziong from Nomaneneng village. These dreams gave instructions for the planting of the *tanget* shrub (*cordyline terminalis*), the collection of money, the observance of military discipline, and the practice of personal hygiene. The use of the *tanget* shrub — traditionally thought to have magic powers — was to ensure the arrival of the cargo, and to emphasize indigenous identity and status over against the Europeans.[68]

The doctrine and ritual of Tanget was actively spread by Sariong from Katken village and Akinu from Mindik. But other leaders also arose in specific localities, notably Nubos Etek from Zewezang village. Nubos later became influential in the Pitenamu Society, a direct offspring of Tanget.[69]

What was the response of the church to Tanget activity, indeed, to all the cult activity of the post-war period? Robert Adams summarizes accurately the situation with regard to Tanget:

> Increased conflict between the movement members and the church leaders was also a very significant factor [in the expanded influence of Tanget]. A decline in the position of the church, together with increasing resistance to church injunctions against polygamy, had brought great tension between cult and church authority. Although villagers have not broken with the church and still attend services, large groups have been subject to church discipline for long periods, and widespread tension existed.[70]

Church Reactions

On the wider church level, efforts were made in 1964 to generate greater understanding of cargo cults, and to provide Christians with a strategy and a statement of faith with which to oppose cargo cults. At the Eighteenth Field Conference of Lutheran Mission New Guinea (January 28-February 6, 1964), several missionaries presented lengthy studies on cargo cults.[71] These papers gave information on the cults, their history, beliefs, rituals, hopes, and expectations. The papers are evidence of a genuine effort by missionaries to understand the cargo cults on their own terms, and to develop a pastoral approach to a ministry to cargo cultists.

A Cargo Cult altar.

Later in 1964, at the Fifth General Synod of the Evangelical Lutheran Church of New Guinea, a Statement of Faith over against cargo ideas was debated and adopted. The statement was based on a Kate version emanating from Sattelberg, which had been translated into English by Willy Flierl. But the minutes of the Synod were written in Pidgin; it is this version, therefore, which is the official one, and which is given here in English translation:

A STATEMENT OF FAITH TO CORRECT FALSE IDEAS ABOUT CARGO
I am a member of the church of Jesus Christ and I believe his holy Word. I therefore confess that:

1. God created all the things which are in this world, and they are here to serve my physical needs.
2. God says that I must apply myself diligently to the work he has given me to do, and earn my daily bread with sweat and toil.
3. Therefore I must place my trust in God, I work and I pray, and I thank God for his blessing.
4. There is no way in which a man can obtain manufactured articles, money, or other material goods from cemeteries, mountains, lakes, or holes in the ground.
5. Therefore, I must not pray [to the dead] in cemeteries. I must not speculate about different ways of obtaining cargo. I must not try to induce fits of shaking or quivering. I must not prepare a place in the bush to pray [for cargo]. I must not pursue cargo through dreams and in many other ways. These things are nothing but illusions and deceptions of Satan.
6. If I see people doing these things, or if I hear people talking in this way, I will not believe them. I will reject what they say and do. They are ignorant and misguided people.
7. Sometimes a person says: I have heard the voice of an angel; or he says that a message came to him on the wind and he heard it when he was praying; or he says that in a dream he received a prophetic message or that he communicated with a spirit. This is a trick of Satan himself.
8. Therefore, I will not listen to anyone who tries to promote cargo activity. Instead, I will expose him [or: it] before the congregation and oppose all such foolish ideas. I am a member of the church of God, and now I want to stand fast on the Word of God and fight against the lies of Satan.

May Christ the Lord help me and give me his strength to defeat foolish ideas about how to get cargo.[72]

481

Lo-Bos Movement (Bongu-Buged)

Study papers and statements of faith did not, of course, put an end to cargo movements. The Yali movement continued unabated, as did the Tanget Cult and other movements. We will look now, briefly, at later developments within the Yali movement and the Tanget Cult.

The Yali movement, or *wok bilong Yali* as it is now known, has become institutionalized to some extent in what is called the *lo-bos* movement. *Lo* in the name *lo-bos* refers to traditional rules and customs for social behaviour. Careful keeping of these laws and rules will ensure a state of harmony in the community. If a state of *lo* is achieved, then the 'good time' will arrive. The function and responsibility of the *lo-bos* is to look after village *lo*.[73]

The *lo-bos* movement is especially strong in the Bongu-Buged area of the Southern Madang District. There it outnumbers Christians by about 10 to 1. Christians and *lo–bos* adherents have learnt to co-exist, each one trying to establish a state of *lo* by their own lights.

Each group follows what has become its fixed tradition, determined ultimately by their different answer to the question: Which Brother is the primary and ultimate source of *lo*? And with which group of ancestors is he connected — the New Guinean ancestor-descendants of the brother who stayed, or the ancestor-descendant of the crewmen of the brother who sailed away, and has returned in the new Christian era?[74]

In Madang town, Beig Wen has attempted to take over the leadership of the *wok bilong Yali*.[75] Beig Wen is from Kauris village (the same village as Kaut of Letub fame); he is a former Lutheran church councillor, and a former secretary and confidant of Yali. He prefers the title 'ministo' to 'lo-bos'. He meets regularly with his co-believers in a house on Modilon Road in Madang for reflection and meditation on the sayings and commands of Yali, which are preserved in an exercise book. Yali is venerated as the 'Melanesian Jesus'. His predecessors, such as Mambu and Tagarab, are thought to have filled roles equivalent to that of the Old Testament prophets.

According to Garry Trompf, Beig Wen teaches that there are two plans of salvation, one for the White and one for the Madang people. Trompf construes these two plans diagrammatically thus:[76]

	Good Period	Bad Period	Good Period	
Macro-history of the Whites	Abraham to Moses	Angered prophets	Jesus (revealing the right road)	Expected return of Jesus
Macro-history of the Blacks	Ancestral time, ordered around the male cult	Competition between Christianity and tradition	Yali (revealing the right road)	Expected return of ancestors (including Yali)

It is worth noting that, according to Beig Wen's eschatology, the crucial future event is the *taim bilong tumbuna*, the return of the ancestors. The ancestors will bring, not 'cargo' — Beig Wen rejects the epithet 'cargo cultist' — but a return to the cooperation which existed between the Madang people during the pre-contact period, that is, in the *taim bilong tumbuna*. Beig Wen's view of the future is modelled on the traditional ideals of reciprocity and community in the Madang villages. His

482

vision is non-racist; it embraces all peoples of goodwill and cooperation, whether Black or White. But the vision is centred on the return of the ancestors, including Yali.[77]

In the Beig Wen-led *wok bilong Yali*, Trompf concludes:

We now witness a self-conscious concern to develop a radical Melanesian alternative to the Christian churches, yet one which seeks to earn respectability without aligning itself to a *lotu* ... or with any Christian church or sect.[78]

Pitenamu Society (Hube)

To conclude this survey of tradition-based movements which have challenged the Lutheran church in Papua New Guinea during the first 75 years of the 20th century, we note a later development in the Tanget Cult, namely, the evolution of the Pitenamu Society. [79]

Pitenamu began life in Lae in 1969 as the 'Hube Company', an investment scheme organized by Puling Sapa and Nakes Sauwia Marigi. Both men had been exposed to Tanget activities, but neither claimed any particular cultic knowledge or power.

During 1971-72, the enterprise expanded rapidly in and around Lae, gaining support from a number of different tribal groupings, especially from the Pindiu, Tewae, Nawae, and Mumeng areas (hence the name: Pi-te-na-mu). In 1971, the business became closely allied with the fledgling Pangu Pati, and with the Tanget Cult. Thus, the business enterprise became a movement of a political, socio-economic, and religious nature. It had one foot in traditional religious beliefs and practices, and one foot in Western business practices and principles.

Nake died in 1973, and was replaced by Nubos Etek, a leading figure in the Tanget Cult. Nubos, Adams says, 'brought the Society great ritual authority together with considerable drive and organisational capacity. This gave a more explicit and purposeful approach to the process of wealth generation, both secular and non-secular'. [80]

Under Nubos's leadership, a number of *mani haus* were erected near Lae and Bulolo, and Pitenamu attracted a wide following — also among Lutherans, including some pastors and church workers. Pitenamu became a movement which endeavoured to generate wealth and prosperity by Western business methods, undergirded by the ritual and doctrine of the Tanget Cult. It seems that Pitenamu's association with Tanget created far more hopes and expectations than simply a sharing of material wealth.

Pitenamu met with a great deal of opposition from the church and from the government, especially at the local government level. Adams, however, is of the opinion that at the village level Pitenamu enjoyed wide-ranging support, especially in the Hube area. In the church, at the local level, opinion was divided, often bitterly divided. Sometimes physical action was taken which was hardly seemly for Christians. At the Church District level, the then-President of the Jabem District, Gedisa Tingasa, headed a committee which had been set up to investigate Pitenamu. This comittee was formed in response to complaints brought to the 1973 Lae District *Sam* by Christians from Nawae. After tracing the history, development, and practices of Pitenamu, President Gedisa concluded the committee's report as follows:

> At the *Sam* we heard the name 'Pitenamu Society'. This is a good name. But those who have given the movement this name have done so in order to disguise cargo cult activity ... Cargo cult is what kind of business? We members of the committee have investigated the roots of cargo cult. We find that cargo cult is a deception. Its father is Satan. Cargo cult encourages adultery and fornication. We must rouse ourselves to help the sheep in our care. [81]

Finally, to round out this survey of cargo movements and the church's response, we note that in 1975 a National Lutheran Pastors Conference was held in Lae. At this conference, Pastor Sorum Saulgaria (now President of the Amele Circuit, Madang), presented a paper which dealt, in part, with cargo cults. It touched off a lively discussion. The final paragraphs of Pastor Saulgaria's paper reflected the consensus of those present. He wrote:

> One question is paramount: What shall we pastors and the church do about cargo cults and cargo thinking? We can't hope for a quick end to cargo activity. Get rid of it in one place and it pops up elsewhere ...
> We church workers must not get angry with cargo cultists. If we do, they won't listen to us, and they won't change. But if we deal gently with them, then they might be inclined to listen. The situation doesn't call for the use of a hammer, it requires tact and gentle persuasion.
> We must also be careful lest we cause them to feel 'shame'. All they will do then is accuse the church of ruining their work. So we have to take an indirect approach when we talk with them. This, I believe, is the right way to go about it.
> When a cargo cult erupts, we must not exclude the cultists from the church. Why not? Because when the movement loses momentum, they will be afraid and they will feel they are not welcome in the church. They will be greatly ashamed. So let's not think of excluding them from the church. If we exclude them, we won't get them back. They will

483

remain outside of the church, and turn with greater zeal to cargo activity.[82]

Bilip Grup Movement (Garaina)

There are indications that the *wok bilong Yali* with its *lo-bos* movement, and the Tanget Cult with its Pitenamu Society, will be the last of the great 'classical' cargo movements to challenge the churches in Papua New Guinea. That is not to say that cargoism will disappear; rather, it is to say that in the future the hopes and expectations and objectives of cargo ideology will find a different form of expression.[83]

The religious movements which offered challenges to the churches in the 1970s and 1980s had, in many cases, no overt 'cargo' leanings, even though some of them were clearly grounded in traditional, pre-Christian thinking. These movements may be grouped loosely into two categories: revival or 'Spirit' movements, and independent church movements. These two categories are not mutually exclusive, inasmuch as some of the 'Spirit' movements, as Barr notes, 'have the potential of becoming independent churches or organizations'.[84]

An example, from a Lutheran area, of a 'Spirit' movement which developed into an independent church, is the *Bilip Grup* movement among the 5000 Guhu-Samane-speaking people who live inland along the Waria river valley to the south of the Morobe Province.[85] The Sub-district headquarters of the government, and the Circuit headquarters of the Lutheran church, are at Garaina.

Since the 1920s, the Lutheran church has been the only church working in the area. The Summer Institute of Linguistics (SIL) has been working in the region since 1958. During the period 1971-74, the SIL operated an 'academy' in the Garaina area which offered Bible study, homiletics, music, reading and writing, hygiene, community development, art, agriculture, an elementary course in Morse Code, and so forth. This 'academy' influenced the development of the Bilip Grup movement.

The Garaina area had experienced other religious movements before the Bilip Grup began in 1976. In 1963-65 a cargo movement, led by Budzo, affected some villages in the Au-Wakaia region. More significantly, a future Bilip Grup leader named Togololo had, in the early 484

1970s, 'initiated a series of activities which included intense prayer, the seeking of the Holy Spirit, and *tanget* planting, all of which he apparently kept secret from the authorities and the expatriates'.[86] Togololo had worked in Finschhafen for some years.

The Bilip Grup movement began in 1976 under the leadership of Ubabae of Au village, and his wife Tongipo; these two regard themselves as the originators and over-all leaders and directors, with Mumure of Muniva and Sopera of Au as the main helpers. The movement seems to have begun partly in response to visionary experiences of the leaders, partly as a reaction to disillusionment with the government and with economic conditions generally, and partly as an attempt to offer an alternative to what was seen as deadness and atrophy in the life and worship of the Lutheran church.

By 1980, the Bilip Grup movement had gathered tremendous momentum, involving about two-thirds of the Guhu-Samane population. It was active in 14 inland villages and three coastal villages; and it was finding support among Garaina residents in Lae. The movement was sufficiently developed for an outside observer to identify some characteristic features:[87] There was a strong emphasis on the study and understanding of the contents of the New Testament, and of taking it into the heart in 'true belief'. Men, women, and children memorized great slabs of the New Testament, with special emphasis on passages from the Revelation. One person is reported to have eaten pages of the recently-translated New Testament in an attempt to get at the real basis or source of Christianity.

With the emphasis on study of Revelation, there developed a keen expectation of the return of Christ, which in turn gave rise to an emphasis on confession of sins, conversion, and renewal. Evil ways of life — sorcery, ancestor ritual, adultery, drunkenness, juvenile delinquency, and so forth — had to be abandoned. A strong ban was placed on traditional ceremonial dancing and feasting, as well as modern dancing and alcohol consumption. Certain men and women in the movement were recognized as having the ability to detect sin in another person. These people were called 'disciples'. Those in whom sin was discerned were instructed to make an offering of pigs or chickens as atonement. Confession was usually made to movement leaders, following Lutheran church practice.

Another important dimension of the movement was the special outpouring of the Holy Spirit. This began in Au village in 1980, and spread from there to other villages. Possession by the Spirit was marked by crying, hanging from the roof, singing and dancing, and fainting fits. Some people were able to speak in tongues. Special visions, signs, and miraculous cures were reported. From 1980 onwards, worship services took on a very vigorous and ecstatic style.

The main elements of worship services were the singing of hymns to traditional and modern melodies, always with instrumental accompaniment (guitars), Bible reading and commentary, individual recitation of Bible verses (especially good performances were applauded), and spontaneous prayer by the whole congregation simultaneously. In earlier stages of the movement, all-night prayer vigils were held in the bush, on mountain-sides, or in places previously believed to be inhabited by spirits.

Later, the more dramatic manifestations of Spirit-possession gave way to the gifts of preaching and teaching, discerning sin, and the abilities of 'wireless' people and 'scientists'. 'Wireless' people receive messages about God's will for the community; 'scientists' receive knowledge for their work from the Holy Spirit in prayer and worship. It is expected that these 'scientists' will eventually gain a full measure of scientific knowledge, only a small portion of which they had received at the SIL 'academy' in 1971-74.

Wendy Flannery is of the opinion that in the Bilip Grup movement there are latent popular millennarian and 'cargoist' expectations. The emphasis on the imminent return of Christ engendered hopes for an immediate and radical transformation of the present life. The arrival of the benefits of the 'good time' was thought to be dependent upon prayer, faith, the power of Jesus, and the activities of the dead relatives. In recent years, the 'cargo' kind of beliefs and activities have died down, and people have become involved again in agriculture, community work, and small business enterprises.

What has been, and is, the relationship between the Lutheran church and the Bilip Grup? At first the church tried to involve the group's leaders and members in combined Bible studies and courses organized by the church. Even when the deteriorating relationship between the Bilip Grup and the church developed into open conflict, and even violence, efforts were made to keep dialogue going between the two sides. Finally, the Circuit President and Council imposed a one-year ban on the Sacraments, involving the whole Circuit at village level, and including for a time the Circuit Missionary, Borzel. After a short time, the ban was lifted in the case of those who remained faithful to the Lutheran church. But for Bilip Grup adherents, the ban was still in force at the time of writing (1984).

Lutheran church opposition to the Bilip Grup centred on the fact that the movement was being organized and developed independently of official church sanction and supervision. Concern was also expressed over the growing divergence between the patterns of worship of the Bilip Grup and of the Lutheran church. Church officials were also worried about what was seen as excesses which accompanied the possession by the Spirit, and also about the 'cargo' overtones of some of the beliefs and practices of the Bilip Grup.

In 1982, a delegation of Bilip Grup leaders met with Bishop Getake Gam, and asked his permission to become an independent Lutheran church. Bishop Gam denied that he had the authority to grant such permission. For a year the matter remained unresolved, during which time some people began to express dissatisfaction with the movement, and unease about being deprived of the Sacraments. Some tension also developed among the leaders of the Bilip Grup. However, in April 1983, the Bilip Grup members formed their own independent church. Over 400 people were rebaptized, and joined the new church, known as the Papua New Guinea Renewed Life Church (RLC). Part of the official Lutheran response to this development was to defrock the Lutheran pastor who serves as pastor of the Renewed Life Church. Early in 1985, the church had an estimated 1000 members, with two daughter congregations in

Lae. Local Lutheran leaders in the Garaina area understand well the appeal and attraction which the Renewed Life Church has for the Garaina people. One Lutheran elder is reported to have said:

> It [the Renewed Life Church] is a strong movement, because it has its roots in the thinking and feelings of the people of this land. It is like a tree which is firmly rooted in our soil. We have no fear of those movements which are brought to us by a white person, supported by a couple of Papua New Guinean helpers. These sects come and go. But, that which has taken root in our own soil — that remains. [88]

Spirit Movement (Enga)

From Garaina in the Morobe Province we turn to the Enga Province for an example of a 'Spirit' movement which did not develop into an independent church, but which arose from within the Lutheran church and was finally integrated into the life of the church. The movement in question began in 1979 in Matianda Valley of the Kandep region of Enga Province, among members of the Gutnius Lutheran Church of Papua New Guinea (GLC-PNG). [89] The movement did not evolve around any one person. It spread by contagion, and developed new leadership in each community.

Missionary Gary Teske, who made an in-depth study of the movement in the Kandep area, emphasizes the fact that

> what was spread was an EXPERIENCE, not a set of dogmas or tenets. In other words, it was not like the introduction of a new church with a complete or partial confession of faith and practice. It was almost totally a spread of an emotional/social experience. [90]

Characteristic features of the movement included the following: First, a cathartic conversion experience. The subject experienced shaking and dancing, and babbled in a strange language. He or she fell to the ground, often physically prostrate. People who had received the Spirit previously scrutinized the faces of the possessed ones, and decided whether they had sin or guilt which needed to be purged. If sin and guilt was discerned, then confession was required. This process — shaking, falling to the ground, and confession — would continue, perhaps several times, until at last a look of peace passed over the person's
486

face: a sign that the Spirit was truly present. Teske comments that 'the whole experience seemed to be one of working through that [wrestling and struggling] to some sort of peace and a **feeling** of forgiveness and reconciliation with God'. [91]

Secondly, people spoke in tongues, dreamed dreams, and saw visions. Dreams were often the means by which a 'prophet' (that is, a scrutinizer or discerner of sins) was chosen. The 'prophet' was able, by means of visions, to 'see' the wrongs and sins which people had committed. One prophet claimed the ability to discern whether a sick person would die or be healed.

Thirdly, miraculous healings were experienced:

> One evangelist named Jon had an ailment which left him with bloodshot eyes. Some of the prophets sat with him in his house praying, and divined that someone had worked sorcery on him by putting a stick in the fireplace. The stick was found and removed, and Jon's eyes cleared up immediately. [92]

Fourthly, the focal point of the movement was the local church building. Teske reports one incident in which, as the result of a vision, a group of young people built a small house on top of a mountain where ancestral spirits resided, and which was traditionally the site of important pig sacrifices. [93] However, apart from this one example, and several unattested rumours of people praying in cemeteries, the usual focal point for 'Spirit' activity was the local church building.

How did the GLC-PNG and its pastors react to the 'Spirit' movement? [94] Some (older) pastors adopted a 'hands off' policy; they did not get involved, not even in the frequent Bible studies and the spirited debates on whether the spirit received was good or evil. Other (mainly younger) pastors saw the movement as a good thing for the church. It built up rather than tore down. It actually contributed new workers to the Lutheran church. Tensions there were, but at no time was there a threat of a split.

Tensions arose between those who had 'received the Spirit' and those who had not (at least not in a dramatic way). Tension arose between husbands and wives, as one or the other was caught up in the movement and failed to pull his or her weight at home. School children were sometimes adversely affected by the movement: neglecting their schoolwork and staying away from school. And since the 'Spirit' experience flowered especially among the young and the women, tensions sometimes developed between the generations and between the sexes. There was potential for tension to arise between the 'prophets' of the movement and the pastors and evangelists in the congregations. But, by and large, these people tended to work together in harmony.

By 1983, the movement had lost its momentum, and the intense activity had slackened off. Some congregations had settled into a pattern of worship which included the ministry of the 'prophets'. However, in 1983, a fresh, localized outbreak of the movement was reported. It followed the pattern of earlier outbreaks. Teske reports 'a great deal of cooperation between the evangelists there and the appointed prophet (who also happens to be an evangelist from a neighbouring congregation) in looking after the new people having the experience'. [95]

It is outside the scope of this chapter to report on the many 'Spirit' and revival movements, and the independent churches which have arisen in Papua New Guinea since 1975. However, it is important to keep in mind that, just as cargo cults challenged all the established churches, and not only the Lutheran church, so too the more-recent 'Spirit' and revival movements have occurred in all parts of Melanesia, and not only in 'Lutheran' areas. [96]

Reflections: A Challenge to the Church

To conclude this chapter, we shall endeavour to pinpoint a number of areas in which traditional and new religious movements have offered, and still offer, a challenge to the church to re-examine various facets of its life and work.

1. The religious movements, especially the traditional ones, call upon the Lutheran church to undertake, as Rufus Pech says, 'an evaluation of the relative merits of the Christian message of the coming Saviour in time and at the end of time, and the typical Melanesian primal myth in any of its ethnocentric and tribocentric versions'. [97] There is ample evidence to show that, throughout the history of mission in Melanesia, the Christian message

A challenge to the Church.

has been understood by the receptors as a possible substitute for, or alternative to, traditional myths; it is thought to have the same function, the same power, and the same efficacy as Melanesian primal myths. The church will not really have come to grips with the problem of misunderstanding and misinterpreting the Gospel, and of how the church itself is missing the mark in its preaching, until it undertakes a serious theological evaluation of primal myths in Melanesia, and discovers the fundamental questions which Melanesians are asking by means of these myths.

2. The church is challenged to face squarely the question of what role, if any, ancestors, spirits (malign and benign), and other powers, play in the life of Christian people. Involved here is also the matter of dreams and visions, the work of traditional healers, and also theological questions concerning the person and work of the Holy Spirit and his gifts. The church may quite properly speak of the indigenization of the church: of its theology, its worship, its practice. But the church needs to discover just what forms this indigenizing has taken at the village level. Theodor Ahrens suggests that the church should ask questions like these:

> What sense of christian appreciation and/or christian distinctiveness is displayed as christian communities and individual christians relate to meaningful and crucial sections of their cultural traditions?
> What kind of response to the biblical message, if any, do communities and individuals give, as they relate to the crucial concerns and needs of their societal environment?
> What sense of christian solidarity, and what sense of mission, does a church display in these responses and relationships?
> How, if at all, is the reconciling presence of Christ witnessed to in the liturgy, preaching, singing, praying, meetings and organizational structure of the church?
> What does the church in all these relationships and responses say about Jesus Christ and about herself in terms of discipleship? [98]

The religious movements of the past century have shown that Papua New Guineans have wanted to make Christianity part of the warp and woof of their lives; they have wanted it to have meaning and purpose in their total existence. But they have not been willing to stop

488

being Melanesians in the process. The religious movements also show that many Lutheran Christians see the organized church as irrelevant. Lo-bos meetings, for example, seem to have more relevant items on their agendas, items which touch the daily lives of the people, than do the meetings of the church.

3. It is, perhaps, in the area of worship that the religious movements challenge the church to most urgent and serious self-examination. The use of Christian and quasi-Christian worship forms by followers of traditional religious movements show that many Lutherans see worship as a 'work' which they perform, a 'work' which, if properly carried out, will result in the receipt of the looked-for benefit. Hence the oft-heard question: 'We stap kaikai bilong lotu?' (Where are the results of our worship and religion?). Education is urgently needed on the why of worship.

Many Lutheran Christians seem to be bothered by the fact that traditional Lutheran forms of worship have no evident 'power'. By way of contrast, the cargo rituals and many of the worship services of the revival and 'Spirit' movements, appear to abound with 'power': there is healing, shaking, and speaking in tongues; sins are identified and hidden sins are revealed and punished immediately; sorcery is uncovered; and the future is revealed. The focus is on worship which has practices and forms which produce effects, experiential effects, among the participants. [99] In the light of the traditional importance which is placed on the need to gain access to 'power', [100] it is not surprising that many people, including Lutheran Christians, apply the criterion of what Teske calls 'effective power' to worship services. Teske adds:

> I think the question, 'What is the power in worship and how is it present and how can we know that it is present? needs to be seriously addressed. Also, what is the place of experience in worship? I fear that the cultural adaptations made in the worship of the mainline churches are little more than cosmetic daubs of paint, and in reality it still requires a person with a knowledge of 16th-century theology and church history to appreciate what is going on. [101]

The newer religious movements have exposed the drabness and unattractiveness of much of what passes for worship in the Lutheran church. One of the most common complaints made by Lutherans (and other members of mainline churches) who are attracted to the new religious movements is that the worship of the churches is lifeless, boring, and meaningless. [102] Worship in the mainline churches is not seen as total worship. People are not provided with the opportunity to worship in the fullness of their being. Much of the worship in the churches is intellectualized; it is emotionally and physically restricting and restrictive. [103]

What is it that is so attractive to Melanesians in the worship style of the 'Spirit' and revival movements? Robinson Moses, a Melanesian and a member of the United Church, answers:

> Worship has become more meaningful, exciting, satisfying, fulfilling, and alive. Participants sense the presence of God, Jesus Christ, and the Holy Spirit. Thus worship sessions can last for two hours or more without the people getting bored or tired. The order of service is flexible, and there is plenty of room for creative expression. This is evident when guitars, kundu drums and other instruments are used to accompany singing. Hand clapping and hand raising are spontaneous expressions of joy and praise ... Prayers offered are more intense and soul- or heart-searching ... The singing of hymns is much more alive, and the words sung are fully meant. New tunes are set to familiar hymns, giving them a new vitality. Young people participate fully in the worship life of the Church, and many of them are local preachers. [104]

Certainly, in the matter of worship, the Lutheran church has much to learn from the new religious movements. [105] This is not to say that the Lutheran church should totally reject its rich liturgical heritage and blindly follow the lead of the movements; but it is to say that 'those commissioned to revitalize worship by the development of new forms should note with respect how the New Religious Movements provide for the whole person's total involvement in worship more adequately than do some of the older churches'. [106]

4. Another feature of 'Spirit' and revival movements which is instructive for the Lutheran church is the great interest which is taken in Bible reading, study, and discussion. Ross Weymouth [107] notes four outstanding points concerning the use of the Bible in revivals in Melanesia:

1. There is a growing interest in the Scriptures.

2. The direction which a revival movement takes 'depends to a large extent upon a group's knowledge and understanding of the Bible'.
3. The particular form which a movement takes is normally related to a group's interpretation of the Scriptures, which in turn depends on the heritage it has received from its founding church or missionary.
4. 'The permanence of the movement, even though the excitement may wane, depends upon the continuing study of the whole counsel of God as revealed in the Scriptures.'

This interest in, and dependence upon, the Scriptures on the part of recent religious movements challenges the Lutheran church in two directions: First, it should encourage pastors and other qualified people to offer a Bible-teaching ministry to members of the movement. Experience has shown that usually such an offer is gladly accepted. Secondly, the Lutheran church itself needs to make a concerted effort to develop genuine scriptural literacy among its people. The Scriptures have to be made available to all members of the church, especially the Old and the New Testament in Pidgin and the major vernaculars. Leaders, both men and women, need to be

District Bishop Yanadabing Apo.

489

The women of the church have their meetings.

given the skills to conduct fruitful Bible studies. And a church-wide Bible study program, such as the one developed by the Jabem District under the leadership of Bishop Janadabing Apo, needs to become an on-going feature of the church's life.

5. Finally, brief mention must be made of the role of women in the new religious movements.[108] While some older, traditional movements did have women leaders, the majority of them were male-led and male-oriented. However, in the newer movements it is noticeable that women are full participants, and often they play a leading part. The reasons for this are complex, but certainly it is part of the change which is taking place in the status and role of women in Papua New Guinea society.[109] It is also probably a reaction to women's dissatisfaction with the lethargy in male-dominated churches; and it probably reflects disgust with the drinking, fighting, and economic irresponsibility of their menfolk. There is, in fact, in the Goroka and Chimbu Provinces an active women's business organization which was formed precisely in protest against the ineptitudes and

490

irresponsibilities of men in economic matters.[110]

The point for the Lutheran church to ponder is that the time is fast approaching when the women in the church in Papua New Guinea will follow their sisters in other parts of the world and ask for, demand, the right of greater participation at all levels of the church's activities, including worship. The signs are there in the new religious movements, in society, in politics, and in the economic sphere. Rather than react to a crisis situation, charged with emotion and with political overtones, the church would do well now to address the women's concerns, both from a theological and practical point of view.

In this chapter we have attempted to describe and understand some of the major traditional, new, and on-going religious movements which have arisen within, or alongside of, the Lutheran church in Papua New Guinea during the 100 years of its existence. We have seen how the church responded to these movements, and we have suggested major areas of the church's life and work which need

'Serve the Lord with gladness.'

to be examined in the light of the challenges presented by these movements.

If, sometimes, the church has not been shown in the best light, and if, sometimes, the criticism has been harsh, this has been made necessary by the goal of this chapter: to help the Lutheran church to see itself more clearly; to help the church to understand where it has been, where it is now, and where it is going; and to help the church to grasp with renewed zeal its mandate for ministry to the people of Papua New Guinea on into the 21st century.

Endnotes

[1] See H.J. Schoeps, *Paul: The Theology of the Apostle in the Light of Jewish Religious History* (Philadelphia: Westminster, 1961), 13-50; H. Hamann, 'The Background of St Paul's Gospel', *Australasian Theological Review*, XXVI (4, 1955), 105-118.

[2] For example, Ph. Watson, *Let God be God!* (Philadelphia: Fortress, 1947); G. Ebeling, *Luther: An Introduction to his Thought* (Philadelphia: Fortress, 1970).

[3] Quoted by G. Leinhardt, *Social Anthropology* (London: Oxford University Press, 1964), 146.

[4] For example, I.H. Marshall, 'Orthodoxy and Heresy in Earlier Christianity', *Themelios*, 2,1 (September 1976), 5-14. The second German edition (1964) of Bauer's work was published in English translation by SCM Press (London) in 1972.

[5] J.M. Robinson, 'The Dismantling and Reassembling of the Categories of New Testament Scholarship', in Robinson and Koester, eds., *Trajectories through early Christianity* (Philadelphia: Fortress, 1971), 16.

[6] P. Lawrence and M.J. Meggitt, eds., *Gods, Ghosts and Men in Melanesia* (Melbourne: Melbourne University Press, 1965), 23.

[7] Cf. Rufus Pech, 'Myth Dream and Drama: Shapers of a People's Quest for Salvation', STM Thesis, Columbus, Ohio: Trinity Lutheran Seminary, 1979, 89-141. Pech notes (p 76) that he reviewed 20 recorded variations of the myth.

[8] Peter Lawrence, *Road Belong Cargo: A Study of the Cargo Movement in the Southern Madang District New Guinea* (Melbourne: Melbourne University Press, 1964), 22 (hereafter cited as *Road*).

[9] See chapter 2.

[10] Johann Flierl, *E-emasang, or A Marvellous Movement of Sanctification in our Lutheran Mission-Church, New Guinea* (Tanunda: Board of the N.G. Mission, n.d.), 32: '[The] various mission-assistants have to do the greater part of the teaching and preaching of the divine word. The white missionary can only be at one place at the time . . .' The evangelist school started at Logaweng by Missionary Bamler in 1907 gave the men training in basic Christianity and rudimentary skills, in a 2-year course. Even with this schooling, the Christian knowledge and experience of these men was negligible when compared with the knowledge and experience of the traditional religionists.

[11] Quoted by J.F. Wagner, 'The Outgrowth and Development of the Cargocult', mimeographed, 1964, 63.

[12] Pech, 'Myth dream', 82, offers an English translation of Hoffmann's recording of the myth. With it should be compared the version recited 80 years later by Tanok Galopi of Bongu, and recorded by Theodor Ahrens in T. Ahrens and W.J. Hollenweger, *Volkschristentum und Volksreligion im Pazifik*. Perspektiven der Weltmission, Volume 4 (Frankfurt/Main: Otto Lembeck, n.d.), 75-80.

[13] Lawrence, *Road*, 63. On Maclay, see the biography by E.M. Webster, *The Moon Man: A Biography of Nikolai Miklouho-Maclay* (Melbourne: Melbourne University Press, 1984).

[14] See E.F. Hannemann, 'Village Life and Social Change in Madang Society', n.d. (ca 1943), mimeographed. Hannemann says (pp 24,25) that the people called Maclay *Tibud* (= spirit, demigod).

[15] P.J. Hempenstall, *Pacific Islanders under German Rule* (Canberra: Australian National University Press, 1978), 167-170.

[16] On the Madang Revolts, see Hannemann, 'Village Life', 26-28; Hempenstall *Pacific Islanders*, 180-189; W. Kigasung, 'Early Native Resentment to European Presence in Madang', *Yagl-Ambu*, 4 (4,1977), 248-263.

[17] Hempenstall, *Pacific Islanders*, 183.

[18] Cf Lawrence, *Road*, 70,71.

[19] 'Village Life', 28.

[20] *Ibid*, 37: 'The period between 1914 and the early 20s was a time of quiet submission. The natives made concessions to Euro-Australian rules and regulations at the expense of their own *Kibiaing* (rules or orders)'.

[21] Pech, 'Myth dream', 161.

[22] 'Village Life', 30.

[23] Lawrence, *Road*, 74.

[24] *Ibid*, 75.

[25] *Ibid*, 80.

[26] E.F. Hannemann, 'Le Culte de Cargo en Novelle-Guinée', *Le Monde Non-Chrétien*, VIII (1948), 944.

[27] Lawrence, *Road*, 85.

[28] The history of the beginnings of the work in the Finschhafen area has been told in chapter 2.

[29] Flierl, *E-emasang*, 21-27; Christian Keysser, *A People Reborn* (Pasadena: The William Carey Library, 1980), 236-252 (German original: *Eine Papuagemeinde*. Neuendettelsau: Freimund-Verlag, 1950. Second edition).

[30] Keysser, *A People Reborn*, 248.

[31] *Ibid*, 253-259; Pech, 'Myth dream', 167-169.

[32] See: 'The Rabaul Strike: A European View', and 'Inquiry into the Strike', in B. Jinks, P. Biskup, and H. Nelson, eds., *Readings in New Guinea History* (Sydney: Angus and Robertson, 1973), 244-255.

[33] Pech, 'Myth dream', 167; Keysser, *Reborn*, 255.

[34] Keysser, *Reborn*, 257.

[35] Pech, 'Myth dream', 169, note 1.

[36] Keysser, *Reborn*, 258,259, makes no mention of the fact that in February and March 1938, he had written five letters to the Sattelberg congregation in which, among other things, he demanded that the Sattelbergers apologize, and that they erect a memorial to their 'malice and unprecedented mistrust'. cf. T. Ahrens, 'The Flower Fair Has Thorns as Well: Nativistic Millennialism in Melanesia as a Pastoral and Missiological Issue', *Missiology*, XIII (1,1985), 70.

[37] Pech, 'Myth dream', 169-173; Wagner, 'Outgrowth', 7-13; Karl Wacke, 'Upikno und die durch ihn entstandene Bewegung im Kalasagebiet', 1934, typescript.

[38] Pech, 'Myth dream', 171,172, based on Wacke, 'Upikno', 13. Pech has 'abbreviated and re-arranged [the message] chronologically to suit a Westerner's historical sense' (171).

[39] Wilhelm Zischler, *Annual Report*, 1938, 2 (Neuendettelsau: Archives).

[40] Pech, 'Myth dream', 174.

[41] Lawrence, *Road*, 89, loosely translating the Pidgin text given by Hannemann, 'Le Culte', 945,946.

[42] Rudolf Inselmann, 'Letub, the Cult of the Secrets of Wealth', MA Thesis, Hartford Seminary Foundation: Kennedy School of Missions, 1944, 108.

[43] *Ibid*, 109.

[44] Lawrence, *Road*, 92.

[45] On Letub, see Inselmann, 'Letub', *passim*, and Pech, 'Myth dream', 92-98.

[46] For details of the revised myth, see Lawrence, *Road*, 92-94.

[47] Pech, 'Myth dream', 183,184.

[48] Inselmann, 'Letub', 130.

[49] *Ibid*, 132-134.

[50] On Tagarab, see Lawrence, *Road*, 98-110.

[51] *Kukuaik* means 'watchfulness, alertness'. On the Kukuaik movement, see Frederick Henkelmann, 'Kukuaik', Narer, 1942, typescript; Romola McSwain, *The Past & Future People: Tradition and Change on a New Guinea Island* (Melbourne: Oxford University Press, 1977), *passim*.

[52] McSwain, *Past & Future*, 91.

[53] *Ibid*, 93.

[54] Pech, 'Myth dream', 189 quoting a personal communication from Missionary J. Hafermann.

[55] See earlier in this chapter.

[56] McSwain, *Past & Future*, 68.

[57] For a survey of these movements, see John G. Strelan, *Search for Salvation: Studies in the History and Theology of Cargo Cults* (Adelaide: Lutheran Publishing House, 1977), 36-50.

[58] Lawrence, *Road*, 116-221.

[59] *Ibid*, 177,178.

[60] Wagner, 'Outgrowth', 192-197.

[61] R. Adams, 'The Pitenamu Society', in Wendy Flannery, ed., *Religious Movements in Melanesia Today (1)* (Goroka: The Melanesian Institute, 1983), 134-135; H. Gerber, 'The so-called Cargocult a neo-animistic movement in the Hube', n.d., mimeographed, 5-11.

[62] Gerber, 'Cargocult', 5.

[63] It is not clear whether this plan was carried out. Gerber, 'Cargocult', 10,11 says it was.

[64] Simon Stephen, 'The *skin guria* Movement in the Buang Area', 1979, mimeographed, 2.

[65] Adams, 'Pitenamu', 134.

[66] Stephen, 'Buang', 12. Stephen's paper is based entirely on oral reports from people who still remember the events of 1946-47.

[67] On Tanget Cult, see Adams, 'Pitenamu', 135-140; Gerber, 'Cargocult', 11-23.

[68] The significance of the *tanget* shrub is discussed by Adams, 'Pitenamu', 137,138, and Stephen, 'Buang', 1,2.

[69] See section later in this chapter.

[70] Adams, 'Pitenamu', 136,137.

[71] The papers were: J.F. Wagner, 'The Outgrowth and Development of the Cargo Cult'; H. Wagner and R. Hueter, 'A Field Study of the Bongu-Buged Circuit'; J. Kuder, 'The Cargo Cult and its Relation to the Task of the Church'.

[72] The English translation is taken from Strelan, *Search for Salvation*, 93. The Pidgin original is given in the same book, 106.

[73] On the *lo-bos* movement, see Theodor Ahrens, 'New Buildings on Old Foundations', *Point*, 1 (1974), 29-49; Theodor Ahrens, 'Christian Syncretism', *Catalyst*, 4 (1,1974), 3-40; Theodor Ahrens, 'Kirche, Volkschristentum und Volksreligion in Melanesien', in T. Ahrens and W.J. Hollenweger, *Volkschristentum*, 11-72; Louise Morauta, *Beyond the Village: Local Politics in Madang, Papua New Guinea* (Canberra: Australian National University Press, 1974), 39-49 and *passim*.

[74] Pech, 'Myth dream', 228.

[75] Garry Trompf, 'The Theology of Beig Wen', *Catalyst*, 6 (3,1976), 166-174; Garry Trompf, 'Independent Churches in Melanesia', *Oceania*, LIV (1,1983), 67,68.

[76] Trompf, 'Independent Churches', 67,68.

[77] Trompf, 'Beig Wen', 169.

[78] Trompf, 'Independent Churches', 68.

[79] Adams, 'Pitenamu', 142-164. Unless otherwise indicated, the information given here on Pitenamu is taken from Adams' study.

[80] *Ibid*, 148.

[81] 'Kagokat i kirap long Lae Distrik', n.d. (ca 1974), mimeographed, 5.

[82] Sorum Saulgaria, 'Kain Kain Lotu na Bilip bilong ol Tumbuna', in Peyandi Lepi, ed., *Ripot Bilong Namba Wan Nasenal Luteran Pasto Konprens* (Lae: Evangelism Department of the ELCONG, 1975), 38,39.

[83] See Garry Trompf, 'What has happened to Melanesian Cargo Cults?', in W. Flannery, ed., *Religious Movements in Melanesia Today (3)* (Goroka: The Melanesian Institute, 1984), 29-51.

[84] John Barr and Garry Trompf, 'Independent Churches and Recent Ecstatic Phenomena in Melanesia: A Survey of Materials', *Oceania*, LIV (1,1983), 50. For a survey of revival and 'Spirit' movements, see John Barr, 'A Survey of Ecstatic Phenomena and Holy Spirit Movements in Melanesia', *Oceania*, LIV (2,1983), 109-132. For a survey of independent churches in Melanesia, see Trompf, 'Independent Churches', and the articles in W. Flannery, ed., *Religious Movements in Melanesia Today (2)* (Goroka: The Melanesian Institute, 1983).

[85] For information on the Bilip Grup, I rely entirely on Wendy Flannery, 'Bilip Grup', in Flannery, *Religious Movements (2)*, 155-193. In some sections, extracts have been made from a precis of her work supplied by Sr Flannery.

Since completing this chapter, I have had the opportunity to read a doctoral dissertation by Amy Burce, 'Knowledge and Work: Ideology, Inequality, and Social Process in the Waria Valley, Papua New Guinea' (Stanford University, 1983). Dr Burce was actually doing her fieldwork among the Guhu-Samane people when the movement which became known as the Bilip Grup started. Her report of the movement is given in chapter 10 of her thesis, 'Guhu-Samane Millennarianism' (pp 324-366). The reports by Flannery and by Burce complement and support each other. Burce, however, gives more details on the beginnings of the movement, and also makes the point that for some time there were two competing factions, each one vieing for the support of the Guhu-Samane.

[86] Flannery, 'Bilip Grup', 163,164.

[87] *Ibid*, 164-177.

[88] Quoted by Hannes Gaenssbauer, 'Bericht ueber meine Dienstreise nach Papua-Neuguinea, 3.2. — 15.3. 1985', dupl. Neuendettelsau, 1985, 8.

[89] I rely on Gary Teske, 'The Holi Spirit Movement among the Enga Lutherans', in Flannery, *Religious Movements (2)*, 113-136. See also the report of the movement among Catholic Engas by Tony Krol and Simon Es, 'Enga Catholics and the Holy Spirit Movement', in Flannery, *Religious Movements (2)*, 137-143. For a report on revival movements in the Highlands of Papua New Guinea, see Wendy Flannery, 'All Prophets: Revival Movements in the Catholic and Lutheran Churches in the Highlands', *Catalyst*, 10 (4,1980), 229-257.

[90] Teske, 'Enga Lutherans', 114.

[91] *Ibid*, 115.

[92] *Ibid*, 119.

[93] *Ibid*, 122.

[94] For a report on responses by both Lutheran and Catholic workers to various 'Spirit' and revival movements, see W. Flannery, 'All Prophets', 241,242.

[95] Teske, 'Enga Lutherans', 123.

[96] See the bibliography given in note 84 above.

[97] Pech, 'Myth dream', 229.

[98] Theodor Ahrens, 'Local Church and Theology in Melanesia', *Point* (2,1978), 142,143.

[99] See Gary Teske, 'Worship the Father in Spirit and Truth', in Flannery, *Religious Movements (2)*, 244.

[100] For discussions of the importance of 'power' in Melanesian thinking, see: Theodor Ahrens, 'Concepts of Power in a Melanesian and Biblical Perspective', in J. Knight, ed., *Christ in Melanesia (Point 1977)* (Goroka: The Melanesian Institute, 1977), 61-74; Esau Tuza, 'Spirits and Powers in Melanesia', in N. Habel, ed., *Powers, Plumes and Piglets* (Adelaide: Australian Association for the Study of Religions, 1979), 97-108; T.W. Dye, 'A Theology of Power for Melanesia', Part I, *Catalyst*, 14 (1,1984), 57-75.

[101] Teske, 'Worship', 248.

[102] See the statements recorded by Flannery, 'Bilip Grup', 182,183.

[103] Brian Schwarz, 'African Movements and Melanesian Movements', in Flannery, *Religious Movements (3)*, 22. Schwarz follows Harold Turner here.

[104] Robinson Moses, 'A Theological Assessment of Revival Movements', in Flannery, ed., *Religious Movements (3)*, 188.

[105] See the suggestions made by Alexander Dawia, 'Indigenizing Christian Worship', *Point* (1,1980), 52,53.

[106] Schwarz, 'African Movements', 23.

[107] Ross Weymouth, 'The Bible and Revival Movements', in Flannery, *Religious Movements (3)*, 206,207.

[108] See Wendy Flannery, 'Mediation of the Sacred', in Flannery, *Religious Movements (3)*, 139-141.

[109] See the various articles in *Point* (2,1975).

[110] See Karl Goerner, 'Emanzipationsbewegung im Kargokultgewand?' 1982, typescript, 4: 'Wir Frauen bebauen den Garten, pfluecken den Kaffee und ziehen die Schweine gross, aber unsere Maenner geben dieses hart verdiente Geld leichtfertig aus, indem sie es vertrinken oder beim Kartenspiel verlieren. Nun wollen wir zeigen, dass wir es besser verstehen, sinnvoll mit dem Geld umzugehen.'
For information on this business activity, including the work of the Goroka Women's Investment Corporation, see two studies by Lorraine Sexton: '*Wok Meri*: A Women's Savings and Exchange System in Highland Papua New Guinea', *Oceania*, LII (3,1982), 161-198; and 'Little Women and Big Men in Business: A Gorokan Development Project and Social Stratification', *Oceania*, LIV (2,1983), 133-150.

Chapter 16

Younger People Looking at Their Church

by various authors

The Revd G. Neumeister, for some years Lutheran Chaplain at the University of Papua and New Guinea, requested a number of his students and others to give their opinion on their Church. They have freely expressed their views and conceptions, positively as well as critically. The following pages give a good deal of their thoughts. No attempt has been made to get them into a more systematic order or thematic outline. All these contributions have been reproduced exactly as they were written.

A student of the University of PNG reflects on the time and kind of first contact of his people with Lutheran missionaries in the Garaina area. He assesses the impact of the Christian message on the life of his people.

Christianity and Melanesian Culture

Many accusations have been levelled against the church being an agent for destroying the culture of Melanesian societies. This, in my opinion, is a gross generalization; considering the course of church activities and the things it has achieved it seems to me that the church should be complimented.

First Contact and Achievements

The church, at least for me, deserves credit because the first work of the civilization in the area began with the work of christianization. The first Lutheran missionary to land on the shore of Finschhafen was Senior Flierl, on the twelfth of July 1886. After establishing the station at Finschhafen, the missionaries began their mission to the North, West, and South. It was while on this missionary advance that they encountered Garaina (Garaina lies to the South of Morobe Province).

It was in early 1900s that the first missionary entered the area. During this period, people were still fighting each other, and consequently, there was very little interaction amongst the people. However, the missionaries' penetration eventually united the people and kept them from fighting and killing. In the first instance, the people were not accommodating to the missionaries because they could not communicate adequately. The problem of imparting messages was immense but they communicated using gestures. While they were struggling to communicate with each other, the missionaries managed to inform the people that

497

Entering the University of Papua New Guinea.

Students at a social gathering.

they were their friends and not their enemies. Then the missionaries taught the people the Kate language. It is a language spoken by certain villages around the Finschhafen area. It was in this language that they eventually taught people about the Bible.

Point of Contact

People became suspicious about who the missionaries were and where they had come from. They thought they were their dead ancestors returning to help them, but such misconceptions were suppressed in the course of their involvement with the missionaries. When the missionaries began preaching about the most powerful God and the incarnation of God in human form, people readily accepted the notion. As the notion of spirits and supernatural was already prevalent in their societies, they had no difficulty in believing the message. From their own experience their own fate depended on their relationship with other human beings and the spirits. To avoid confusion, the word 'spirit' here exclusively refers to the spirit of the dead.

The concept of God coming down from heaven to take up human form was not too difficult for them to comprehend. People perceived God as a 'big spirit' most powerful, almighty and eternal. In their traditional ancestoral spirits' worship they had similar practices, so God was understood as a spirit and was perceived in that understanding.

Another student who introduces himself as a spiritual and not a social member of the Lutheran Church, pinpoints achievements and failures of the church against the background of experiences in his home region.

My contribution for most part is based on the experience of oneself and is referenced to the small community (or in fact a large one), the Mape area in the Finschhafen District of the Morobe Province of Papua New Guinea.

Changes toward Better Ways of Life

Just as it was with other Christian churches, God has used the Lutheran Church so effectively in bringing peace into the land in terms of clan hostilities and evil practices. In

Women and girls being instructed.

brief, the church has done so much good as Christianization and laying the foundation of educational opportunities in the area are concerned. Consequently one of the good fruits of the church's establishment is that, once upon a time girls and young women with admirable qualities could not live beyond their teens. They were the main victims of evil practices, especially when they found themselves caught between men, each desiring to marry them as possible wives. Thanks be to God, that the church has made sure that such evil practices are eliminated, and that just within five years of Christianity in the area girls could enjoy life longer than their predecessors. Of course there are countless others that one can think of with respect to social, economic and spiritual aspects.

The Church and Traditions

The bad side of church's involvement of course cannot be denied. Church had in its shortsightedness, viewed all traditional practices and values as evil although some may have been beneficial in various aspects. It is quite regrettable to find that many of the helpful values were consequently abandoned; and there is general consciousness in the minds of the people that practices involving bush herbs and roots for medical purposes or otherwise are evil. No doubt there is a misunderstanding that only the white men's medicines and values of life are the best and ideal, although most of them have the same origin as those of traditional medicine. Of course there is no dispute about the fact that some of the traditional practices were evil, hence their elimination in the society was and is justifiable.

The Lutheran Church and Other Churches

Furthermore the Church or those who played a role in the church may also be blamed for the way in which people have come to view other Christian denominations around them. The Church has brainwashed the simple minds in such a way that people have become so traditional in their thinking about the church and its teachings. There are obvious implications that Lutherans, both in urban and rural areas, have the idea that the Lutheran Church is the only and ideal denomination that upholds the real truth of the Good News, and no other
500

denomination. This could further lead to the danger of passing judgement on non-Lutherans as being non-Christians. For instance, at one occasion a person who was baptised and brought up in a Lutheran Community, later became a member of S.D.A. Church. This, to the Lutheran Church elders particularly, was the worst sin that person could commit; at least that was their implication I could gather. The person concerned was consequently regarded as an outcast and was banned from having anything to do with the Lutheran Church and its community simply, because he had made his choice to become a member of a church other than the Lutheran Church.

As well as that, people in the rural villages are so led to believe that by allowing non-Lutherans to share the Word of God with them will only confuse and threaten their faith, thus often non-Lutherans are not allowed to preach the Good News to the people. There is possible danger also, that with such misunderstandings and attitudes people may be led to commit themselves to the Lutheran Church itself rather than to God as far as the spiritual side of life is concerned. I for one, find it very disturbing to see that people may be or are in fact fighting for a wrong course. I fear that people are having pride of being Lutherans rather than acknowledging the fact that God is for all and works equally in all denominations, and it is not the Church as such, it is the faith in the Word of God and in His Son Jesus Christ, no matter which denomination one belongs to.

A New Approach

Perhaps it is about time the Church had done something to read just the minds of the people, especially in the rural areas of the country so that they exactly know whom they are for, either for the Lutheran Church, or for God through the Lutheran Church. Of course, it is up to the people to receive their good and acceptable values and practices in consultation with the Church and authorised authorities. The church has therefore, an obligation to correct, if one may say so, 'spiritual abnormalities' it may have caused, and perhaps show us the real direction to salvation.

Bofeng Dadae, a student of Economics at the University of PNG, once again emphasizes the benefits of Christianity in the past. At the same time he points out some deficiencies as he sees them in the Church of today.

Childhood

I was brought up in a small village of Davot in the Kabwum area of Morobe Province. I was fortunate enough to be born into a family in which my father was a first-baptized Christian and a first local missionary. As a small boy I used to get interested in listening to the Bible Stories from my elder family members. Surprisingly enough, unlike me, my father had to be trained by his forefathers at the age of seven how to fight with the enemies.

First Contact and Achievements

Congratulations to the white missionaries and the evangelists from the Finschhafen area who brought the good news to my area (1920-30). The pride and bravery of the missionaries (of course with God's help) was the contributing factor to the wiping away of the tribal fightings and the pagan practices that prevailed. The power of the Holy Spirit was moving — people were quickly and easily converted to Christianity.

Obedience was the centre in which all activities were being carried out. Any person found stealing or getting involved in corrupt practices received appropriate treatment. Not from man but from God. For instance, a man who decided to go hunting on Sunday would inevitably run into dangers.

Indeed the Church has played a significant role in the development of people's life both physically and spiritually. The church was very active during the first contact. How about today?

Alarming Features

The comparison between the past and the present situation is somewhat alarming. Lack of cooperation within the community, decreasing numbers of people attending Sunday services and religious activities, increased number of young people marrying outside the church, fornication, adultery, more concentration on business activities are a few examples of how my village is like today. It is frightening, because another Sodom and Gomorrah is descending. What are the main causes of continuous deterioration in people's Christian faith? There

are two major ones: (1) How the Word of God is delivered to the people, and (2) rapidly growing influence by need of possessing material wealth. In the former case, the preachers (pastors, teachers, elders) present very good sermons but is it not enough. People cannot absorb and put into practice what you preach unless you become a good example practically. For instance, is it right for the preacher to use physical confrontation to solve the land dispute? Is it right for him to sleep with young women even though he is married? Does the Bible contain any provisions which warn Christian leaders on how they should live?

On Preachers and Preaching

Obviously, it is quite impossible for one to live a perfect life, but at least the preachers should be the 'salt and light' to the people. I believe, complete dedication to God's service is very significant for the preachers and their family members.

As a genuine Lutheran church member I do not believe in charismatic worships as exercised by the sects, but at least we need some energetic or dynamic preaching by the

Proclaiming the Gospel with fervour and life.

501

ordained pastors who went through theological seminaries. Think of how you attract people's attention and concentration so that God's Word does not fall on deaf ears. Why do many believers go asleep as the sermon is being delivered? Succinctness should be adapted by the preachers. A sermon preached in 15 minutes is better understood than that of 30 or 45 minutes. Let the Holy Spirit speak through you. A boring and unclear sermon is the one that is presented by the preacher out of his own thoughts. It is quite difficult to judge which preacher is spiritually motivated, but if there is liveliness in your preaching then surely that is the work of the Holy Spirit. More criticisms have been made here purposely to inform our leaders to take appropriate actions.

In his view of the Church, John Muingnepe, a graduate of the University of PNG and occasional preacher, tackles the question of Western theology and method of preaching in the context of Melanesia.

Proclamation in Melanesia

The fundamental objective of the existence of the church is to preach the Gospel. Preaching is the goal of exegesis and hermeneutic reflection, but preaching in Melanesia could cause adverse effects if the hermeneutic approach of the church does not embrace our history and culture. The Teutonic manipulation of theology in Melanesia naturally affects the church's hermeneutic approach. (I use the term 'hermeneutic' here, because we don't have a better one.) Therefore the image of church's hermeneutic in Melanesia has the face of the West. The corollary to the foreign approach to proclamation is a misinterpretation of the contemporary context of Melanesia. Because our approach to proclamation is fundamentally foreign, and is not rooted in our Melanesian tradition, therefore it cannot strive to mature in the present, thus is far more incomprehensible to many.

Just as the new hermeneutics of Ebeling, Fuchs and others has sought to recapture the vital message of Luther and the Reformation Fathers for the benefit of their sons, we must improve on this so-called new hermeneutics in a bid to seek the wisdom of our ancestors and their message for us in the present.

502

Preaching in Melanesia must be genuine and appropriate. It must enable an act of understanding spanning the gulf between the biblical message and our existence today. And we cannot do it with the western tradition which has degenerated into corruptible, objectifying language of a technological society that turns man into an object to be controlled and manipulated like other things. The Church in Papua New Guinea exists to preach the Gospel, therefore its theology needs to embrace the real profound needs of the people. Theology must address the social and economic conditions of the people. It must prepare people to live in this world because there are so many people missing out on their share and the church just cannot tell them to lay up their treasure for the life to come without doing something for the share of the poor in this life on earth.

First Converts and Hermeneutic Principles

There was a time when the first Christian converts in our country who were not print-oriented and therefore not literate, preached the gospel with all its own freshness and relevance in the mother tongue. And because there were so few missionaries, the proclamation of these early converts was not done under direct missionary supervision. They spread the gospel while the missionaries were far away. They heard and told the story in the context of their own experience and their own culture.

There are two sound principles advanced by the so-called school of new hermeneutics. Our grand-parents knew and followed these rules without direct supervision and regulation by their missionaries. The first is that one must proclaim the gospel in the language and culture of the people, in the vernacular. For many today this involves resisting the temptation to be 'learned' and 'proper'. To our first convert grandparents this was no problem at all. Innocent of western education they were so trapped within their culture as to have no other choice. Limited by illiteracy they were forced to elaborate on a Bible story with imagination which would make it meaningful to them and their hearers. Rural folk still crowd churches, particularly when there is no seminary graduate, just to hear the gospel spoken in this same relevant and moving way. But there is wonder as to why the so-called contemporary educated

Melanesians are far away from this distinctly Melanesian style.

The second hermeneutic principle is that the gospel must speak to the contemporary man and his needs. Those first converts felt no compulsion to be supervised and regulated. They showed little or no inclination to follow the literalistic interpretations which the foreign church devised to meet the foreign plantation settlers, miners, and so on, and to justify exploitation. On the contrary they looked for answers to their community and their people's needs. They never condoned punitive actions and exploitation in gold mines and plantations, but were committed to changing these conditions by active propagation of the gospel. They never condoned their own lifestyle but were committed to the vital message of Christ in their own way.

No Place for Abstractions

'Hermeneutics', as I would like to use the word, is a code word for putting the gospel on a tell-it-like-it-is basis. If the goal of Teuton hermeneutics is that of detheorising the gospel

and getting to people where they are — making it flexible — the typical Teutonic, particularly German intellectual pattern that prevails in our Seminaries and Bible colleges, simply has not allowed students of hermeneutics to practicalise what it is all about. For instance, students are taught and produced as scholars who then in the actual work are using scholastic approaches and thus are unable to reach the real profound needs of the people. In our state of theological subordination and captivity Melanesians are prone naturally to theorize over much, not realizing that our culture and congregations have little place for abstractions.

Reorientation

When we have departed from our traditional religious practices and are interpreting the Scriptures white-style, we are risking severe loss of interest and audience. Western Christianity which we are so committed to, seems to be losing the battle to reach the crucial needs of the people who have to live in the kind of world we are entering into — a world of economic exploitation, political oppression, social injustice and religious subordination.

University students during a lecture.

A Melanesian hermeneutic style might just help to reverse the trend. May God graciously help us not to completely assimilate our values to those that are driving western man to social and spiritual suicide: acquisitiveness for example, numbness of heart, and machine idolatory. To the extent that these things are kept at bay from our experiences, to that extent Melanesians are qualified to take the lead in the role of leadership in theology in Melanesia.

In his capacity as school inspector of the Church Tok Ples Education, Johan F. van Bruggen meets many young people in the Bible Schools of the Church. They, along with other young people from various villages, have been open enough to tell him about their grievances and concerns as they look at the church. In diary-entry style, the author shares their thoughts with us.

I remember a young man in a village near Mt Hagen saying to me: 'Many members of the Lutheran Church do not really have a strong faith in God; as a result, the Holy Spirit is not able to work strongly in our church.'

On Church Workers

The church service is over. I 'enjoyed' the service. The headman who preached did a fine job. He was well prepared and his message was relevant. 'Why didn't you come to the service? You would have liked it', I asked a young active church member.

'When this man preaches, I do not want to be in church. Sometimes he is drunk and then his mouth is full of filth. I want to listen to the Good News he brings, but I keep thinking of the bad things he says when he is drunk. So it is better for me not to go to church when he preaches.'

A Bible School, 1983. During a visit to this school, one of the students wants to see me.
'Can I get a transfer?'
'Why would you want one?'
— Silence —
'Did you talk with your headteacher?'
'No.'
'Well . . .'
He looks at me: 'I am not happy here. I thought I'd come to a school where I would learn more about God and His Word. I want to know

504

. . . I work with the young people in my village and I have not been able to help them as well I'd like to . . . We have our Bible lessons here, but so much is wrong in our school. If I think of what some of our teachers and students do, then these Bible lessons just do not make much sense . . .'

On Faith and Spiritual Power
November 1984, a village near Wau.

I am here with a group of former Bible school students, now all working in their respective villages. While travelling to the village on Sunday morning, we meet lots of young people as well as grown-ups walking along the road. I am told that they are on their way to various church services in Wau: Baptist, Four-Square, Morobe Gospel Fellowship, and others. We arrive in an almost deserted village. The service starts a little later. A handful of mostly elderly people with a few scattered youth fill the very front part of the church. The rest of this large beautiful building stays empty.

In the afternoon the Pentecostals return. I invite a few to sit with our team. One of them is Jeremiah, and I recognize him immediately as one of the three students that were expelled from the Bible school in 1980. He does not seem to have lost any of his joy and honesty in these four years. He talks freely and openly about his life and work.

'What made you people leave the Lutheran Church? What do you feel is lacking in this church?' are our questions. The answers come readily and we write them down. The first three are as follows:
1. The Lutheran Church lacks the power of the Holy Spirit.
2. Many church workmen lack a strong faith and do not show good examples to their flock in the way they talk and live. And so they are not able to give good food to their sheep.
3. And this again makes the Word of God powerless, that is, it can not change man's behaviour. Repentance is very important in the Kingdom of God, but the Lutheran Church does not show this.

On Reforming the Church
Markham, Sunday morning, November 1984.
The church is full, with young people sitting

right up in the front. There is an atmosphere of expectancy in the air.

Young people from the Hagen District have spent the Reformation week-end with this congregation. The leader of this team has given an hour-long sermon which kept everybody spellbound. His main point: The Lutheran Church came into being because of all the changes that Luther brought about. And we should not be afraid to reform our church again, so that it truly becomes the body of Christ. Through faith alone: Where is this faith? ... Living in Christ: Where is Christ? ... Filled with the Holy Spirit: Where is the Holy Spirit?

The congregation is as if electrified. I could see it on the faces of the people that packed the church. I could hear it in the moving words spoken by the president of the congregation at the end of the service. And the congregation is hungry for more of this spiritual food.

But next Sunday, the disappointment is great: The person whose turn it is to preach has gone off to some other commitment. There is no sermon.

'We did not know, so nobody is prepared' is the explanation given. It is not the first time that this has happened, but this time the congregation does not accept it passively: There is some kind of angry explosion as the people are upset. 'Let's go and join the Seventh Day Adventists!', I overhear a young man say. An ex-Bible school student lashes out at a leader with some hard comments: 'You leaders do not care a bit for the sheep. They are starving, and you give them nothing to eat!'

There is a spontaneous meeting of concerned people after the service. We feel that God, through the 'Hagen Sunday' and this morning's 'disastrous' service, has opened a door. Plans are made for a fellowship evening the following Sunday.

Will the young people come? The signs are promising. Every afternoon some young men come up to the station to practise new songs to be sung during the fellowship meeting.

The next Sunday evening, the church is full! And the fellowship evening is beautiful! And so it has been every Sunday night since. More and more young people are drawn into preparing and participating in the fellowship meetings. There is a hunger for God's Word that is really astonishing.

On the Role of Church Elders
A village in the Hagen District, September 1984.

I have shown the crucifixion and resurrection parts of the film *Jesus of Nazareth*. As usual, the film has made a deep impression on the audience. The reactions are varied. Some sit still, lost in thoughts; others cry; some are noisy (to conceal their true feelings?). One remark is shattering. It is the youth leader who makes it.

'When I watched the schemes and tactics of the Pharisees, I had to think of our headmen. They do the same thing!'

'What do you mean?', I asked, rather shocked. The response is almost bitter.

'They stop Jesus from doing His work in this congregation, just as the Pharisees tried to stop Him from doing His work. They are not standing up for Jesus, they are standing up for themselves. And anybody who in his words and actions really wants to show Jesus to others is suspect, and is being watched very carefully. Some weeks ago, a fight almost broke out between another village and ours. They had killed our pigs already. Some of our headmen wanted us young people to fight. We were told to be prepared and to stay in the village and play cards, a thing we abandoned years ago. It seemed as if all the good work had been destroyed. No more fellowship nights or prayer meetings ... But we youth leaders stood our ground. We felt very strongly that God had not abandoned us. We told the warriors of the other village that we did not have anything to fight with, and that we were not going to make these things again, because we did not want to fight. Three times they came to fight, and three times we stood very close to them and told them that we were not going to. And we told not only our enemies; we also gave this message to our headmen and the young men who felt not quite sure of themselves.

Our Church Members and the Life of Christ
Village Teka near Mt Hagen.

We are gathered in the church for a Communion service. While we wait for the service to start, young people from Teka and Hagen town lead us in joyful singing. One song is just finished when the bell of the Teka Pentecostal church starts to ring. The two

'Some of our headmen wanted us young people to fight.'

church buildings are very close, and the sound is clear for everybody to hear.

The young man that leads the singing asks the congregation: 'Is it true that we have to join the Pentecostal Church in order to meet Jesus and be filled with the Holy Spirit, as the members of that congregation tell us?' It is mostly the young people that answer with a clear No.

'We can meet Jesus in the Lutheran Church, we can experience the power of the Holy Spirit right here and now, but we must be prepared! As long as we Lutheran stay *tubel-Christians* (limping on both legs), as long as we do not allow God to take full control of our lives, we won't be able to meet Him here, and the Holy Spirit will not be able to guide and direct our lives. But if we truly believe, then we will see God's glory right here in the Lutheran Church!'

The congregation sings the song:
Mi tokim yu pinis, sapos yu bilip
bai yu lukim glori bilong God.
(John 11:40)

The joyful singing completely drowns out the bell-ringing of the Petecostal church.

506

Yaungere Gipe, a dedicated and committed leader of the English-speaking youth-group in Lae, calls upon his church to become a church which cares. From his own experience in a town situation, he challenges the church to make every effort to meet the various needs of her people following the example of Christ.

The message of the church is still the greatest the world has ever heard, but it has lost its original sense of urgency and importance. The leadership, since localization, has apparently lacked hindsight and foresight. It has also apparently been indecisive and often complacent. Enemies of the church from inside as well as outside the church are succeeding in turning the church into a materialistic, secularistic, or worldly-oriented organization. The net effect of these factors is that the original visions and commitments of Christ have not been properly adhered to. The original visions and commitments are in some danger of being watered-down, if they aren't already.

Where and how has the church not been able to adhere to the principles of the Lord? If the Lord's aim was to make man free and a

St Paul's Lutheran Church, Lae.

complete moral and spiritual being in relation to God and mankind, then the Lord endeavoured to meet man's basic needs — physiological, spiritual, moral and mental needs. It was in meeting these needs that the Lord has set man free to be whole and complete.

My point is to spell out what I believe are Christians' basic needs in Papua New Guinea, and the role the Lutheran Church has not been playing, or rather should be playing in meeting these needs.

Employment and Housing

Since the first European contacts, men's need for employment and income has clearly taken new forms, namely, the capitalist modern sector was introduced, and it is now becoming part of the everyday life of Papua New Guineans, Christians and non-Christians alike. Simultaneously, the ways and means for the meeting of these needs have changed (and are continuing to change).

As the country is 'progressing', the pool of people desiring wage or salary employment is tending to rise, whilst the supply of available jobs for particular skills are either stagnant or declining. In short, the demand for wage or salary jobs is outstripping the supply of jobs available.

Even though many of these suffering people are members of the Lutheran Church, the attitude and resources of the church are such that the church is not assisting her members in this sector to meet their basic needs.

The church needs to have men and women of foresight and of Christian vision who will see and respond to these needs of the modern Christian. In the Lutheran tradition, giving of tithes and offerings is voluntary and not a strict requirement for the members. Preaching on tithing or offerings is done rarely by Lutherans. But certain passages of the Bible speak loudly about them, for example, Malachi 3:6-12. A consequence of these attitudes of tithing and offerings is that, compared with the givings of some newer churches, the Seventh Day Adventist, Baptists, etc., many Lutheran Church members are quite poor givers of tithes and offerings. As a result the church lacks funds in doing these necessary tasks of meeting man's needs, including employment and income needs.

In the subsistence sector, the Church could furthermore assist her members in building better houses, particularly in areas where present housing structures are health hazards. Assistance could be given in terms of advice in housing structures and techniques. But because the church sees housing as a private need of men, she doesn't assist very much. Also, her resources are quite inadequate.

Nevertheless, she could assist her members in a number of ways. She could, for instance, follow the examples of the Roman Catholic Church and the Salvation Army in constructing and renting-out hostels to her members.

People Need Love and Fellowship

As a basic need God has intended that man gives and receives love and fellowship. Traditionally, this need was met by society, perhaps not perfectly, but there was a social security system which made sure that there were no unloved and no socially isolated individuals. People stood together both in good times and bad; and these needs were met.

507

Better housing conditions in towns are necessary.

In modern time it is quite difficult for a Christian to have his needs of love and fellowship satisfied, especially if he is a newcomer in the town environment. It is difficult because of a number of reasons. People from different clans and tribes live in towns. Also, the philosophy of profit presupposes that there be competition and striving for individual improvement of living conditions — hardly the conditions for the finding of love and fellowship.

Although people do come together in linguistic, clan, or tribal groups by their own will, the church needs to teach people the Christian basis for those gatherings. The church also needs to be actively involved in creating Christian environments in which people can gather together, such as encouraging Christian fellowship groups (adult and youth), encouraging Christian sportsmanship, activity-oriented clubs, such as women's sewing clubs.

Of course, the church is at present creating some Christian environment, but she is not doing this as actively as she should.

Education and Health
The Word of God says implicitly that man

508

should have education (about God and man's environment) and health (in body, soul, and mind) as basic needs of life. Indeed for the Lutheran Church of Papua New Guinea provision of educational and health needs have become important caring activities. And this work should continue because the present general educational strategy of Papua New Guinea is either elite or gain-oriented. The results are not positive. Many thousands of young people are (and will be) 'drop-outs' of the formal educational system and feel neglected and disappointed when they don't get selected for further education or for jobs.

In this situation the church has both formal and informal education programs. In the formal sector, the main rationale is to train a professional or semi-professional work-force to become leaders of the church in the modern environment, e.g. teachers, pastors, evangelists, etc. In the informal sector, the main rationale is to train leaders in the subsistence, basically village environment, and to fulfil aims such as increasing the rate of literacy. Given these rationales, the church has been producing elite people who are upholding a church structure which however does not respond very well to the needs of the majority of the people. These rationales should therefore be re-formulated, a new educational strategy be drawn up, which should be people-oriented.

The main rationale for the church's health services is to 'cure' and bring people with diseases and illnesses back to health, so that these people can be free to be able to serve God and man; and to 'assist' the disabled, as gestures of Christ's love.

The World Health Organization has a slogan of achieving health for all by the year 2000. Their emphasis is on universal primary health care. The church should be emphasizing this as well. In my opinion the basic people's needs are to know basic preventive health care methods, least-cost approach to family health care, and Christian approach to health care.

Other Social Concerns

There are other needs that come about as a result of socio-economic and cultural changes. Some examples which can be placed in this category are: alcoholism, crime, family problems and divorces, 'rascals', victims of social and legal injustices, etc.

Until very recently the church did not see these needs as possible areas of her ministry — she had concentrated her attention in the subsistence sector. In former times, the church did not have trained personnel to deal with the many-faceted problems of the Christians in the modern capitalistic sector; for example, she did

Social concerns.

not have trained counsellors or specialists for urban-oriented ministry.

However, the church is beginning to expand her activities into the modern sector, such as the Social Concerns Office. These are commendable efforts and should be continued and further expanded.

I refer specifically to juvenile delinquents. Many young people who are educational drop-outs are turning toward crime. Institutions and comprehensive re-education and social adjustment programs should be set up, and these youngsters absorbed into them. Such Christian programs are being conducted in many other countries.

The Need for Jesus Christ

Apart from God, man cannot rule the world in peace and justice — history has shown man's dismal failure in these respects. Man is in need of God. Man is in need of Jesus Christ.

Preaching of the Gospel ought to be seen as most important and urgent. The world has major problems, and Christ is returning soon. These thoughts ought to move the church into immediate action.

To do that, the church needs to sit down and define what she means by the phrase 'people need Jesus Christ'. I don't think the Church should be satisfied with just having people baptized as infants and later confirm them. As a basic spiritual need, the Lutheran Christians need to grow in faith and become mature Christians. It is understood that God gives the growth, but the workers must be doing their part to provide nourishment, and to water them regularly.

In both the traditional and modern sectors there are Lutherans who are in need of balanced spiritual nourishment as well as care and love. For example, in certain areas in the Madang and the Morobe Provinces, people have been misled by cargo cult (millennarian) leaders. If these are not a product of lack of balanced spiritual nourishment, love and care, then what are they a product of?

However, the present attitudes and resources of the church are such that these basic needs of the Christians are not being met adequately. The Church's emphasis on 'grace alone' and 'faith alone' tends to make Christians complacent at times. It is understood that Martin

A new generation, ready 'to grow in faith and become mature Christians'.

Luther had preached against human effort as the means of salvation, and that the Church's teachings have been built around Luther's emphasis of that time. However, the church does not equally and properly emphasize obedience and work as the fruit of God's working in people's lives. As a result, I see two effects of Lutheran teachings on Christians' lives. First, often God's grace becomes a soft pillow for lazy Christians. Second, many Christians tend to view human efforts in religious activities as ways of getting some sort of reward from God, Christ, or the church, instead of viewing them as fruit of God's Spirit working in them. Both are sins. And the church must teach clearly that these are sins.

Spiritual Renewal

As a basic spiritual need, God has intended that His people who have fallen into sin and apostasy be renewed and restored into fellowship with Him. This is shown clearly in the Bible.

But there is a real danger that legalistic and complacent Christians will view God's renewal negatively and oppose it to the peril of their

510

souls. At the same time there is a real danger of misrepresenting the real Gospel in the guise of renewal. In fact, in the world today many kinds of Christian renewal groups have emerged, and whilst some genuinely represent the real Gospel, there are others with another, false gospel. The false gospels are whipped up by the devil to confuse the multitudes.

In view of these dangers, the leaders and members of the Lutheran Church need to be wary and cautious. First, they need to understand clearly what the real Gospel is, and secondly, bring about genuine Christian renewal based on the real Gospel.

Concerning resources, the staff and leaders in the church need to be renewed persons who can lead also others to renewal. If they themselves are not renewed persons, it will be difficult to organize and sustain a church-wide renewal.

Mr T. Kim, a post-graduate student of education at the University of PNG by the time he wrote his contribution, compliments the Church (besides other achievements) for what has been accomplished in the field of training of church-workers. Among the number of shortcomings as he sees them, he stresses the lack of publications and communications within the church.

From a Christian point of view, the Lutheran Church of Papua New Guinea has achieved a number of important aspects. They are:

Full Localization

It has been very encouraging to note that we have a good number of national pastors throughout the country. Many of the important issues within the church have been discussed involving the national pastors. This is I think a tremendous achievement by the church in the country today.

An Active Youth Movement

Many of our youth groups established in the provinces and even at village level are organized by the young leaders of this country. Involving Christian ideas with the youth activities is an achievement of the faith that the youth groups have in the Lutheran Church.

Established Church Training Programmes and Health Services

The Lutheran Church of PNG has established some very effective training institutions in our country. The graduates of such institutions have contributed to the national development of this country. Many of the Lutheran Church leaders are at the top of the country of PNG and its government. Lutherans are also keeping very effective health services for its members and for members of other denominations, especially in the rural areas of the country.

Many Dedicated and Committed Church Workers

In comparison with many other churches in PNG, the Lutheran Church is not so active in terms of church activities, but it has got some of the very dedicated and committed people who believe in Jesus Christ. They do their work in some very isolated areas. I have witnessed many who didn't care whether their family has got enough to eat or to wear. Some even in the

towns, if they are not paid regularly, carry on with their work.

Since the establishment of the Lutheran Church of Papua New Guinea, it has played and is playing a very vital role within the development of the human life. However, there are also some negative implications worth mentioning at this point.

1. It lacks an efficient administration of the church activities. The business arm of the church activities is essential, but it lacks good management and expansion. Every human being must work hard to obtain his living, but it has to come from the Christian beliefs. Of course, in order to live on this earth you need to have first the spiritual needs satisfied and the bodily need would come later. Both are essential for the human life. So far a number of very dedicated church workers had difficulties especially in terms of bodily needs, but that didn't withdraw them from their work as pastors or evangelists. Church work cannot be very effective if there is no physical support from the community.

2. There is a lack of cooperation between two Lutheran Churches, Gutnius Lutheran Church and the Evangelical Lutheran Church of Papua New Guinea. Church workers between these two churches are competitive in terms of their work. They feel that they are working much more harder than others, and therefore they do not accept comments or suggestions from other churches. They lack the exchange of ideas and problems between each other.

3. Lacking financial assistance from overseas Lutheran churches. The main overseas churches who have been involved in the Lutheran Church organization are the German, American, and the Australian Lutherans. There is very little support from these countries in terms of financial assistance. In our own church services there is no generating revenue, and so we depend largely on individual collections. Individual collection is good because it is a return of one's thanksgiving to God. Whatever one is benefiting comes from God as a gift, and the collections are to be made before God from the individual persons.

4. It fails in communicating with its members and does not promote its believers.

The Lutheran Church has not sufficiently publicized to its members what important

511

activities are taking place in the country. Lack of information has created dissatisfaction and less active involvement in the church by its members. The members are confused, and many have left the Lutheran Church to join other churches. As human beings, people are easily convinced and tempted to lose their faith because of other attractions. It happens today that members are seeking to join other churches because sometimes they do not know much about themselves and the church they are belonging to. Our church still lacks publications which create a vital communication between individuals and groups.

Finally, I want to say that the expressed views on the positive and on the negative sides of the church today are entirely my own views. The power to change and to realize some of the ideas as to church activities, however, still remains with our Lord God, the Heavenly Father.

Chapter 17

Medical and Diaconal Work

by Christa Gerhardy

Medical Work and Women's Work

After mission work had been carried out in Papua New Guinea for 75 years, Dr T. G. Braun said in 1961:

> It is our ardent desire that also in the future the Lord may continue to bless the medical work as a means of physical helping and healing and that it may be a true witness to Jesus Christ. At the same time, may He help the young church to aspire to a true 'diaconia' which will serve Him only. [1]

Medical work and women's work have had many points of contact over the years. The missionary and his wife were the first ones to treat the sick, to bandage sores and give injections. And it was the missionary's wife who took young New Guinean women into her home, not merely to help with the housework, but also to teach them hygiene and an orderly family life. These women were taught to follow Jesus, to serve Him as wife and mother, and then also to teach what they had learnt to their own people.

It is out of this that the medical work grew with its hospitals, health centres, aid posts, and schools of nursing, as also the work among the women through girls' schools and women's worker-training schools. Subsequently, the nurses were taught to help the women in the villages, to lead Bible studies, and to teach Sunday school. The women's worker-trainees were taught hygiene, prevention of sickness, and how to tend the elderly and sick in the village. This did not mean a duplication of services, for, in both medical work and women's work, a service of love was given by followers of Christ to their fellowmen with the intention of serving the whole person. This did not satisfy only the physical needs, or only the spiritual needs, but served the whole person physically, spiritually, socially, and psychologically.

Irmgard Bergmann (Horndasch) wrote in 1969:

> 'Diaconia' is there already. Hundreds of girls and women are serving the children and the village women, the old and the sick, very faithfully without getting a cent. They are not organized, and they have no written rule, but they are obedient servants of Christ, ready to serve and to give. [2]

What is here said of dedicated service in women's work applied equally among the men and women in the medical service.

513

Early Medical Mission in New Guinea

Today it is hard to understand what conditions were like when medical mission work began in Papua New Guinea. Almost all New Guineans who lived at an altitude of less than 1000 metres suffered from chronic malaria. Forty per cent of all infants died before the age of two years. All were worm-infested, and many had tropical ulcers and yaws. There were also the diseases which had been introduced by Europeans, such as whooping-cough, smallpox, typhus, dysentery, tuberculosis, and scabies, against which the New Guinean had no resistance. The heathen thought of disease and illness as a result of sorcery or as punishment for a broken taboo. Missionaries lived in small widely-separated settlements, and transportation was extremely difficult, and many a missionary or his wife became seriously ill, or even died, without the opportunity to see a doctor or a nurse.

When the German government took control, it stationed doctors in the capitals, first at Madang, and later at Rabaul. But their efforts were concentrated mainly on the white population. New Guineans in general did not yet trust white doctors sufficiently to seek medical help.[3]

Concerning the menace of malaria in those years, Konrad Vetter wrote in a letter of 1891:

> The fever takes all the strength out of us white people, so that only the strength of a child is left in a grown man.[4]

G. Pfalzer also wrote from Finschhafen:

> As a rule every newcomer comes down with fever regularly every fourteen days. I myself was sick with malaria for 23 days out of the 31 in May. After about six months the fever comes only every four weeks. This continued for the next ten years.[5]

Malaria also took its toll in Madang among the Rhenish missionaries; and the beautiful Madang area was to become known as the graveyard of the Rhenish Mission

Remembering Their Names

From the beginning, therefore, every mission station also had a small clinic, and work with the sick began with the first pioneer missionary.

Among the first settlers in Finschhafen was Frieda Goetz, who came from Germany as a housekeeper for her brother, an employee of 514

the New Guinea Company. She became the first nurse on the field when she joined the Mission in 1889, and worked for eight years caring for the sick and convalescing missionaries at Sattelberg.[6]

Dr Wilhelm Frobenius from Bavaria in Germany joined the Mission in 1890, but was stationed in Madang with the Rhenish Mission. He made his headquarters at Siar, and worked there for ten years. Finschhafen at that time had a government doctor, Dr O. Schellong. Missionary Karl Saueracker took lessons from an Australian dentist, and was the only dental technician for some time in what was then called Kaiser Wilhelmsland.

Both mission fields, Madang and Finschhafen, suffered greatly through not having any trained medical personnel for two decades. All missionaries proceeding to the field had to have some medical experience and to be as self-reliant as possible.

Dr Robert Koch, who was in charge of the Research Hospital in Bogadjim in 1900, advised the Lutheran missionaries to take prophylactic quinine and to have their living quarters

Dr Wilhelm Frobenius, first Lutheran medical missionary (1890–1900).

screened. This had a very significant influence on the health of the missionaries.[7]

Rosette Keppler arrived in 1904 from Australia, and served faithfully as a medical helper for 38 years. She went to New Guinea against medical advice (a heart murmur had been diagnosed), yet she was to outlive and give longer service than most of her contemporaries. Besides doing general nursing, she served as the field midwife to the mission wives along the coast. Going from station to station, she delivered the babies at home, and also cared for the families at the same time. In her 38 years of midwifery in New Guinea, she never lost either a mother or a baby. She claimed that much of her success in midwifery was due to having learnt to wait patiently for nature to do its part in deliveries. As a kind and understanding midwife, she had confident and relaxed mothers, a factor which greatly reduced complications.[8]

Sister Mathilde Lindner, a midwife from Germany, arrived in 1908 to work in Finschhafen. She later married the missionary Georg Pfalzer, and left the field in 1914.

Sister Mathilde Wagner, also a trained midwife, came from Germany, and later married Missionary Panzer. They worked together at Gabmazung until 1926.

Missionary Johann Stoessel from Germany had had some medical training prior to his coming to New Guinea in 1911, and was said to have been the first male nurse. At Butaweng, Finschhafen, he set up the Immanuel Hospital, where he continued to work until 1922. Although an ordained missionary, he gave a great deal of his time to medical work. His knowledge and advice were widely sought, and his work held in high regard. He seems to have had the confidence of people from both the Jabem and Kate areas, and performed numerous operations.[9]

Sister Ida Voss, a trained deaconess and nurse, arrived from USA in 1921. She worked at setting up a new hospital at Dari, on Finschhafen Harbour, opposite Madang Island. Later, she worked in various outstation bush hospitals until marrying Victor Koschade in 1924.

After the two mission fields had been without a trained doctor for 23 years, the Iowa Synod in America sent Dr A. B. Estock to Immanuel Hospital in 1923. He was already an experienced missionary from Africa. 'The intention was to send a physician to New Guinea for the benefit of the mission personnel; in the course of time medical work should be extended to the natives.'[10] However, because of his age, Dr Estock had difficulties in adjusting, and left the field in 1926 after three years' service at Dari. The people distrusted him (as well as all the white man's medical abilities), for the fear of losing 'soul matter' was too deeply ingrained.[11]

Sophie Desguisne from USA first came out in 1923 to care for a number of sick mission staff on Karkar Island and Sattelberg. While on furlough, she took a nursing course, and then returned to be Dr Braun's assistant at Finschhafen until she married Stephan Lehner in 1933.

Also from USA was Sister Hattie Engeling, a trained nurse and midwife. After her arrival in 1924, she worked first in Finschhafen, and later at Amele, Madang. She married Dr T. G. Braun, and together they gave many years of service to the people of Papua New Gunea.

In 1928, Sister Gretchen Tamminga, a nurse from Germany, came to the field via USA. She had two male orderlies in training, and it was she who stated in reports that the local people were losing their fear of hospitals as a place where people would only die. However, many still came to the hospital only after their own 'medicines' had failed. She also had good contact with the medical *tultuls* in the villages, and considered that they were doing their best.

Dora Flierl, the daughter of Johann Flierl, born in Simbang in 1890, took a nursing course in Adelaide before beginning her work at the Heldsbach hospital in 1927. Mairupe Ngami was the first full-time medical orderly who worked with Dora, helping her to keep records.[12]

Concerned for the sick mission personnel on the field, the Neuendettlesau Board sent out Sister Helene Moll in 1927. She is noted for the extensive travelling she did from station to station. Returning after World War II, she worked mainly in the laboratory at Buangi hospital at Finschhafen. A further arrival from Germany, in 1929, was Sister Sophie Bezler. Trained in dentistry, she worked at Kalasa, and later in Finschhafen.

Hospital at Heldsbach with Sister Dora Flierl.

Dr T.G. Braun, inaugurator of the Lutheran Medical Service.

The hospitals in those days were only slightly-improved huts, but it was the loving, devoted care that the nurses and doctors gave which helped much in the recovery of their patients.

Dr Theodore G. Braun

The Revd F. Braun showed the concern of his home Board when he wrote from America:

> Medical mission has a higher aim than caring for the sick and curing their ailments; it is more than a mere humanitarian enterprise; it manifests the love of God toward man, and the medical missionary must be a true disciple of Christ, his Master, fit for the ministry of healing and mercy. [13]

Acting from that standpoint, the American Board called a medical missionary, Dr Theodore G. Braun, with a specific assignment. 'He was to serve the whole field; a hospital was to be built and regular mission work to be done among the natives.' [14] Over the years, this was achieved in quite a remarkable way. Dr Braun inaugurated the medical services for the Lutheran Church in New Guinea, and himself spent 42 years helping his beloved people of New Guinea. Before taking up his work in New

Kakoko Hospital, Finschhafen.

Guinea, he went to Tuebingen and Hamburg in Germany to further his knowledge of tropical medicine. En route to Madang, he also conferred with Dr Cilento in Australia, since he had been a government physician in New Guinea.

Dr Braun arrived in Madang on his twenty-sixth birthday, March 29, 1930, a strong-willed, but dedicated young man. However, he had a number of lessons to learn about the new culture he was now entering. He later often enjoyed relating one incident in particular.

Within hours of his arrival at the wharf at Madang, he was called to Amele to attend a child with black-water fever. He was given a decrepit old horse, 'Makis', and four young men as his helpers. At the Wagol river, they motioned to him to dismount in order to cross the wooden grass-roofed bridge. The horse stopped, sensing the gravity of the situation, but not he. How dare it act like a stubborn 'Missouri mule' and not carry him across? No horse was going to dictate to the new young doctor, who was determined to show that he was an experienced horseman, having learned the art of riding in South Dakota.

'The horse went on, the bridge came down, and horse and I were swimming in the water — grass-roof, planks, and other belongings floating around us', a grinning Dr Braun recounted later. Depite the dunking, Dr Braun carried on, arriving at the Amele hospital only to find that the child was recovering sufficiently not to need his help. He had learnt two lessons that day, he said: 1) You listen to New Guineans' advice when travelling with them; 2) bridges in those days were not made for horses, but only for humans. [15]

When Dr Braun was posted to Finschhafen, he found the existing hospital inadequate, and reported this to his home church. Money for a new building was raised by the women of the American Lutheran Church, and two Australian carpenters built Kakoko, the new hospital on a small hill near Finschhafen Harbour, which was dedicated on December 18, 1932. The following year, Hertha Keysser, a daughter of Christian Keysser, who had been born at Sattelberg, returned to New Guinea as a trained nurse. She worked at Kakoko until she married Wilhelm Fugmann in 1935. Thereafter, together with him, she continued to serve the church until retirement in 1972. During Dr Braun's first year, an influenza epidemic swept through the country. In his area alone, Dr Braun recorded 1500 to 1600 deaths.

Dr Braun and the Mission Conference soon came to the conclusion that 'medical work would only be beneficial if the Christian congregations would be part of it. This meant training of indigenous workers and the payment would need to come from the congregations. The aim was that the church itself would take over the work and continue it.' [16]

Sister Hattie Engeling had similar ideas: 'From the first day that she saw shy New Guinean children with their equally shy mothers, she longed for the time when these children

Amele Hospital, Madang.

'... men like Jambungnu from Kalasa'.

would play a vital role in helping their own people fight illness, so prevalent in the Amele area. Her dream was a school of nursing for young men and women.' [17] When Dr Braun and Sister Hattie Engeling were married in 1932, they pursued their common ambition.

However, Dr Braun reported: 'Unfortunately at this time an opinion prevailed that it would not be good to have Germans and Americans work on the same field. (An appropriate resolution was formed by the Home Boards.)' [18] Dr Braun was sent to Madang, and Dr Martha Koller from Germany (1933-1938) took over the hospital at Finschhafen.

Dr Koller, a very lively and active woman doctor, made many trips throughout the mission field — mostly on horseback, since there was no other means of transport at that time. After Dr Koller left, Dr Alfred Stuerzenhofecker (1937-1940), also from Germany, took over the care of Kakoko. He likewise had the responsibility of looking after a mission field extending from Mt Hagen to Morobe, and from Ulap to Mumeng. Both doctors made every effort to train medical assistants. Men like Zozinggao from the Mape area, and Jambungnu from Kalasa, to name only two out of dozens trained, served their congregations for many years.

When Dr Braun went to the Madang mission field, the Lutheran women of America again raised money to build a hospital. This second hospital, erected at Amele, 24 km from Madang, was dedicated in 1935. There Dr and Mrs Braun immediately began to train medical orderlies. In June 1934, Dr Braun was one of the six missionaries who made an exploratory expedition into the Highlands, where he found neither tuberculosis nor malaria. [19]

Sisters Emma Blum and Hilda Hauert from America, together with Frieda Klotzbuecher from Australia, arrived in 1935 to help the growing medical work.

'Bruder' Karl Kirsch, a deacon from Neuendettelsau, trained in nursing and in dentistry, came in 1932 and began work at Kakoko. Concerning these early days, he related the following:

> We were able to begin our work in Papua New Guinea when heathendom was still very strong. But especially in our medical work we could notice on the one hand the inner freedom received from the gospel and on the other hand the great fear of evil and death. The sick did not want to come to hospital. We had to go to the villages to see them and win their confidence. The first years were mainly taken up with gaining people's confidence. Slowly more people came to hospital. But, if someone died, the hospital was empty again the next day, and we started all over again. Soon we took three young men, two Heldsbach schoolboys and one from Malalo, to train. They were shy at first, but soon settled in and progressed very well. After three years of training they were all sent to outstations — Jambungnu to Kalasa, Zozinggao to Sattelberg, and Ngasengom to Malalo. Ngasengom died early, but the other two continued to work faithfully for the church for thirty years. [20]

During those years, several more nurses came to work for the church: Sister Lydia Seidler (USA), 1931 at Ulap; Esther Venz (Australia), 1936 at Madang; Frieda Schoenwald (USA), 1936, Clara Pech (Australia), 1936, Elfriede Stuerzenhofecker (Germany) 1936, Hedwig Ruf (Germany), 1937, all at Finschhafen; and Marie Kroeger (USA), 1940 at Madang. A number of these nurses subsequently married and continued their services, some until retirement.

When Dr Agnes Hoeger from North Dakota, USA arrived at Amele Hospital in September 1935, Dr Braun was freed to do more fieldwork to visit and advise the nurses on outstations and conduct health surveys.

With the Australian Lutheran Mission taking over the mission work on the Siassi Islands in 1936, Missionary Harold Freund and his wife Dora paid special attention to the treatment of yaws for which intravenous injections were now available.

The World War II Period

At the outbreak of the war in 1939, Dr Hoeger took over Kakoko Hospital in Finschhafen; however, following the Japanese attack in 1942, she was evacuated to Australia. She had hoped to return to New Guinea with the United States Army, but instead found herself serving as an army physician in Peru. [22]

Most missionaries were now either evacuated or interned. At Amele, Dr and Mrs Braun, together with Sisters Klotzbuecher and Kroeger, remained. Dr and Mrs Braun had been given the offer to leave before the Japanese landed, but, as Dr Braun said: 'We did not feel like leaving our post. We wanted to keep our word to our New Guinean Christians.' [23] After the Japanese occupation of Madang (1942), Dr Braun detailed his medical orderlies to hide drugs and medicines in caves near the hospital. On New Year's Day 1943, right after the morning service, the Japanese arrived to take the staff prisoners. Together with Catholic

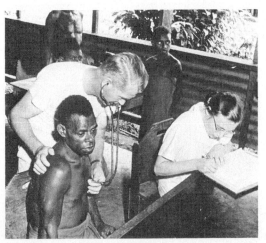

'Bruder' Karl Kirsch, giving injections.

missionaries, they were moved from one prison camp to another. In February 1944, they were taken by boat to Hollandia (now Jayapura/West Irian). As the Allied Forces advanced, the prisoners were finally abandoned and liberated by American troops on April 25, 1944 (for a more detailed account of the months as Japanese prisoners of war and of the deaths which occurred on the boat, see ch 4).

Work Goes On

It may seem that the medical work came to a standstill during the war years; however, this was not so. To be sure, no reports were written, but many a faithful medical orderly, trained by the church, continued his work in his own village.

Siming from Graged Island in Madang was Dr Braun's first medical orderly. He had begun with a contract in 1935 at Sujau in Amele, and later told how he and other orderlies continued their medical work with the medicines they had hidden in caves near Jelso. He and Fulalek from Aijab, who had begun as a medical orderly with Dr Braun in 1936, built a hut deep in the bush to hide the medicines. They continued intravenous injections of Neosalversan against yaws, treated malaria with quinine, and dressed the many sores. One day, they were reported to the Japanese, and had to appear before the court. Siming recalls how they took his wife and family away, and tied him up to kill him. 'The Japanese had their bayonets ready', Siming said. 'I was not worried; they could only kill my

Medical Orderly Fulalek (later pastor).
520

body. But then they did not do it. God helped me, I know.'

Fulalek, too recalls how he was called to appear before the Japanese: 'One stood on either side of the house, with his bayonet. Another was inside the house entrance, a finger on the trigger of his pistol. I knew he intended to kill me. I bowed down before him, head on the ground as was their custom, and as they insisted we also do. But then he did not shoot; the pistol fell out of his hand, he came over to me, hugged me, and we both cried. Then they cooked food, and we ate together. God helped us and saved us.' [24]

From 1943 until 1944 they worked with the Japanese, Siming patrolling in the Nobonob area and along the North Coast as far as Sek, and Fulalek in the Bogadjim and Ramu areas. They treated their own people and the Japanese. After Madang was recaptured by the Australians, they had a hospital in Jabob near the Gum river. Fulalek and Siming rounded up the other medical orderlies who had been trained by Dr Braun, and they all worked with the Australian New Guinea Administrative Unit (ANGAU) until 1946. The following year Fulalek returned to Sujau, Amele. The hospital there had been bombed, but in its place he built up a small bush dispensary and began work. When Fulalek was asked why he wanted to work for Dr Braun and the church, he told how Mrs Braun had asked him as a schoolboy to help her treat sores and later help with Sunday School. 'I wanted to work for the church because I knew that the Gospel had changed me and made me a new man. Medicines and operations can make the body better, but it is the Gospel that makes a new man.' [25]

Regarding the period of the war, Dr Braun said in 1946:

Medical work never ceased in the Madang field ... During the Japanese occupation, medical orderlies carried out their work in the jungle and the villages. Thousands of injections for yaws were given, and skin-grafts done. The greatest joy to us is that they never lost sight of the fact that they were to serve their fellow-men in need (not merely the Ameles or the Grageds). They felt themselves as one group which had no tendency to break up into tribal factions. They even trained others. [26]

New Guineans on the whole were loyal to the Allies, and many helped the soldiers in need;

they carried them over treacherous terrain so they could be evacuated. An Australian soldier, the Revd Richard Piper, wrote a popular tribute to their care in which he called them 'Fuzzy-Wuzzy Angels', and said: 'The look upon their faces made us think that Christ was black.' [27]

Restoration After the War

After the end of the war in 1945, Dr Fricke, Executive Secretary of the American Mission Board, and Missionary John Kuder visited New Guinea to assess the situation on the field. The physical plant of the mission was wrecked; however, as Dr Fricke said: 'The mission is gone, but the church is still here'. They inspected the huge 119th Field Hospital of the American Army situated at Buangi in Finschhafen. It had permanent buildings and everything that was needed except a maternity ward. The Mission negotiated with the Army, and bought the hospital and equipment for the nominal sum of US$10,000, which was collected by the women of the American Missionary Federation. As the hospital was larger than required, part of it was transported by boat up the coast to Madang (approximately 320 km) as a favour by the American Army. From there it was taken by truck to the Gum river and laboriously transported across the mouth of the river by canoes. Trucks then made innumerable trips to transport the equipment and materials to the hospital's new site, Yagaum, 13 km south-west of Madang. Here a new two-hundred-bed hospital was built. Nagede, one of the early medical orderlies of Dr Braun, had negotiated with his people for the ground and donated it. Volunteers from America and Australia did the construction work, setting up the buildings on high ground where there was also a reliable well to supply the staff and patients with sufficient water. The official opening took place on July 22, 1950.

At Finschhafen, missionaries arrived back toward the end of 1945 and early in 1946. Germans, however, were delayed. Work began immediately at Buangi; and, not long

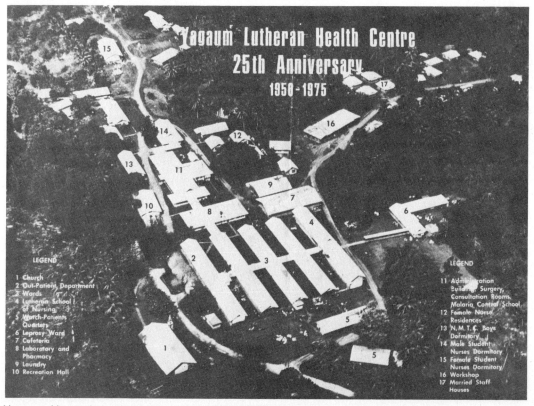

Yagaum Hospital, aerial view.

521

afterwards, Dr and Mrs Braun returned to the field to be stationed there. Dr Braun set out to rebuild and strengthen the church's medical program. In his report to the church in December 1946, he wrote:

Each centre has to be a centre of evangelistic activity and a point from which knowledge of disease prevention radiates. The program cannot stand if we should lose our contact with evangelistic mission work or if the members of our staff are not consecrated to their task and willing to work overtime if necessary.' [28]

Hattie Braun worked in all departments of the hospital and assisted her husband in the theatre. She supervised the nursing care and taught the indigenous staff. One of the first men to be taught was Kito from Sattelberg, who came in March 1946. He continued medical work until his retirement in 1983, having completed the building of the Kito Health Centre at Sattelberg. Kito had already worked for the church during the war with Adolf Wagner. [29] Sisters Ella Walborn and Ruth Heber arrived in July 1946 to work at Buangi.

When Dr Agnes Hoeger returned in October 1946, she was sent to Madang. This area being as yet without a hospital, she travelled throughout Amele, Nobonob, Karkar, and Bongu to concentrate on health promotion and disease prevention. She initiated the Maternal Child Health (MCH) program in New Guinea, thanks to experience she had gained while working in Peru during the war. Dr Hoeger wrote twelve health lectures in Pidgin, recognizing that health education would be a major factor in eradicating belief in sorcery. She also taught the missionary wives to conduct clinics on every mission station. By October 1947, there were thirteen clinics in Nobonob, Amele, Graged Island, Bongu, Biliau, Bunabun, Karkar, and Begesin. [30] Soon pre-natal care was also added.

The earlier-trained medical orderlies, like Siming, Fulalek, and Joseph, helped with the injection program to eradicate yaws, which was now brought under control. They also conducted child health clinics. By mid-1949, Fulalek reported 200 babies attending regularly for clinics, and he gave health talks to their mothers. Siming had built up a bush hospital on Graged Island where he treated yaws and

522

leprosy, and held baby clinics, besides treating common everyday illnesses. [31]

Dr Hoeger wrote in her report in 1948:

Evangelistic work must go hand in hand with medical work. Modern medicines and health education can benefit those New Guineans most who are on a firm Christian footing, and who have overcome most of their superstitions and fears of sorcery.
Our medical mission work rests upon the kind of New Guinean medical assistant whom we train. They must first and foremost have steadfast Christian character or else their work is of little avail. Those who train these people must be qualified professionally and also be spiritual leaders, who can show their trainees and patients what it means to be a Christian. [32]

Yagaum Hospital

Dr Hoeger transferred to Buangi in 1950 when Dr and Mrs Braun came to Madang to begin the work in the new Yagaum Hospital. Sisters Phyllis Schirmer (USA), Myra Lehmann (Australia), Ella Walborn (USA), and a number of New Guinean medical orderlies were there from the outset. Myra Lehmann concentrated her work on Maternal Child Health Clinics. Later, Sisters Gladys Koschade (Australia), Alta Madden (USA), as well as Beatrice Welland (USA), a pharmacist, arrived. Many of the staff members began at Yagaum and from there moved on to Buangi and other centres.

In 1952-53, Yagaum was extended by adding two more wards, several classrooms, and a leprosy annex, bringing the bed capacity to 353.

Dr and Mrs Erwin Heist from USA came in 1953, and worked with Dr Braun for many years. Other nurses who came during this period were Sisters Maria Horn and Else Strauss, as well as laboratory technician Rosemary Schad, all from Germany. Sisters Hilda Matzner (USA) and Melva Schneider (Australia) arrived in 1955, Melva doing the Maternal Child Health fieldwork for several years. Yagaum essentially became a major hospital and training school, and for many years the fieldwork was secondary. In 1956, Yagaum was still the only adequate major hospital in the country. [33] Statistics for 1956 show that there were 3,376 inpatients, 3,666 outpatients, 896 surgical operations, and 42 leprosy inpatients. 223 mission members and 234 non-mission members had been treated.

The Nursing School

Training of medical orderlies began as early as 1935 when the first hospital at Sujau, Amele, was dedicated. Before that time, some of the sisters had trained helpers on the job. Dr and Mrs Braun with the help of nursing sisters from America and Germany now trained young men in the Pidgin language. In 1939-1940, Siming and Fulalek, together with Dr Braun, wrote an Anatomy and Physiology book in the then church language, Graged (today called Bel).

In the early days, it was unheard of for women to be trained; this was reserved only for men. However, because of her influence and her love and devotion for the Amele people, Hattie Braun was able to persuade them to let girls start training as nurses at Yagaum after World War II. [34]

Sister Marie Reitz (USA), who had arrived at Yagaum in 1951, developed the first syllabus for a four-year training of medical orderlies. Some of the pre-war orderlies were also included in the classes and given regular instruction: Fulalek from Amele; Siming, Kaman, and Joseph from Graged Island; Guru from Nobonob; and Sue from the Rai Coast. 'Their assistance and understanding of mission medical work is invaluable in the Madang area', Dr Braun said. [35]

The first group of medical orderlies received their certificates in 1955. Among them were the first two women ever trained, Sunei from Aijab (Fulalek's eldest daughter), and Dabung from Siar. Fulalek himself went on to train as a pastor; he returned in 1957, and was ordained as hospital chaplain. Until 1968 he held two positions: medical orderly and chaplain. Thereafter, until his retirement in 1972, he worked as a pastor only. [36]

Since there were no guidelines from the Health Department in regard to nurse-training, each school had to develop its own program as it saw fit to meet the health needs of the country. Pidgin continued to be used until 1961, when the English language and the syllabus from Port Moresby were introduced. In 1963 the first group of aid-post orderlies took the Health Department examination and received their certificates.

In 1964, the Nursing Council of Papua New Guinea was established. Yagaum was given partial recognition; until 1968, it was possible for

School of Nursing: left, Sr Melodie Olson; right, Sr Christa Lindner and Sr Lesley.

all students after three years' training to sit for an examination from the Papuan Medical College. Successful students studied for a further year and four months at the Papuan Medical College before sitting for their finals. Those who did not go to Port Moresby tried to gain the aid-post orderly certificate at Yagaum.

On July 20, 1966, representatives of Lutheran Mission New Guinea (LMNG), New Guinea Lutheran Mission (NGLM), and the Australian Lutheran Mission (ALM) gathered at Yagaum to establish a recognized school of nursing. Dr E.J. Wright from Port Moresby inspected the school, and recommended that the dormitories for students and teaching facilities be improved, and that there be an increase in teaching staff. [37]

For some years prior to this, the trained European staff at Yagaum had been built up considerably. More nurses with double and triple certificates came to the field; others underwent studies to equip themselves further for teaching positions. Sisters Merla Garrett (Australia) and Christa Lindner (Germany) joined the staff early in 1962. Sister Marie Reitz, who had begun the nurse training program, retired from teaching in 1964 and transferred to Kotna. Sister Lindner took charge of the training school, and most of the trained staff at Yagaum, including Hattie Braun, were involved in the teaching.

In May 1968, representatives of the above-mentioned Lutheran missions, together with their respective churches, inaugurated The Lutheran School of Nursing (LSON) with its own board of directors and articles of association. Sister M. Garrett was appointed principal. The Nursing Council granted its approval in October of that year. From that time on, the Territorial Nurses had their full training at Yagaum, took the Territorial final examinations, and were fully recognized. The first graduation of eleven male and female nurses took place in 1970.

Mr Ken Cramer (Australia), who had previously been in Menyamya, joined LSON in 1969. Miss Melodie Olson (USA) from the Wabag Lutheran Church followed, as did Sister Jane Rittal (USA) in 1974. Sister Rittal had been the matron of the hospital since 1968. Mr Banak Umul, from Karkar, a territorial nurse from

524

Dr J. Kuder hands certificate to Top Nurse of PNG, Wilson Waesa, later Director of Medical Service.

Yagaum and Port Moresby, took over the nursing service from her.

Between 1973 and 1975, Sister Garrett was seconded to the Nursing Council of Papua New Guinea for several periods of three months at a time, to write guides on a variety of subjects for teachers of Enrolled Nurses. [38] During this time, Sister Lindner served as acting principal until 1975, prior to Independence. Wilson Waesa then became principal; that same year, Sister Lindner left the service on her marriage to Missionary Gordon Gerhardy.

Wilson Waesa had graduated from LSON in 1971, with the distinction of being 'Dux of Papua New Guinea'. [39] During 1973-1974 he attended the Papua New Guinea Paramedical College in Port Moresby to take a post-graduate course, and received his Diploma in Nursing Education. He also attended a Management Course at the Administrative College. In 1978, Waesa became principal and tutor at Braun Health Centre Nursing Aide/APO School, Finschhafen. Isaac Samuel, who had also graduated from LSON and later gained a Diploma in Nursing Education, became the principal of LSON.

LSON continued to educate men and women from the coastal and Highlands regions as APOs, nursing aides, enrolled and registered nurses. It made a major contribution in preparing nurses to staff that vast and populous Highlands area in the hectic years leading up to Independence. It was the aim of the School to educate Christian nurses for Papua New Guinea. Daily devotions and weekly Bible studies were an integral part of the program. The students were encouraged to have devotions with the patients in the wards and to conduct Sunday school. The girls were instructed in women's work, and visited the nearby villages weekly to meet with the women. The men took their turn in taking services or part thereof on Sundays.

Due to the scaling down of Yagaum Hospital (all the acute cases were now treated at Madang General Hospital), the staff arranged to have the nurses gain their surgical experience at the latter hospital. At the end of 1975, the School moved campus to the Madang Hospital, where some classrooms and dormitory facilities were made available, and became the LSON, Madang.

In 1976 Sister Garrett served for six months as project officer for the Nursing Council. The book, *Obstetrics and Gynaecology for Nurses*, written by Christa Gerhardy and Merla Garrett, and later enlarged, was published by Kristen Pres Inc., Madang in 1978. It is used in all Schools of Nursing throughout Papua New Guinea. [40]

From 1978 to 1980, Sister Garrett was Church/Government Health Liaison Officer, nominated by the Churches' Medical Council to represent the 25 churches and missions involved in medical work. In her 1978 annual report, Merla wrote: 'It is of great benefit to the churches to have representation at headquarters, so that the churches' point of view can be put to the Department of Health and vice versa'. [41] Sister Garrett left Papua New Guinea in 1980.

Funds were sought and made available to build phase one of the Lutheran School of Nursing across the street from the Madang General Hospital. The dormitory of the male students, the mess, classrooms, library, and administration bloc were dedicated in January 1982. Ken Cramer, who had been with LSON for many years, regarded it as a highlight to see a number of students who had graduated (and received further training) coming back to the School as members of the teaching staff, and others holding responsible positions in either church or government. [42] Ken left the field in 1982.

Today Mr Vincent Michaels, a graduate of the School with a Diploma in Nursing Education, is the principal. Other staff are Arigina Banzumai, Amad Uma, Tony Natile, Dorothy Degnitz, Margaret Voigt, Paula Ingebritson, and E. Cecilia part-time. Sister Voigt (Australia), who first came to New Guinea in 1963, worked at Yagaum, Kotna, and Karkar, and is now a member of the School faculty, says:

> The best part of working at the LSON is to see the students gradually becoming more conscientious and capable nurses, and also to hear from graduates who work in isolated stations, coping with frightening situations and having regular devotions with their patients. It has been good, over the last twelve months with less expatriate staff, to see the national teachers take more responsibility in the running of the School and experience a better team-work at the School. [43]

Yagaum on a Lower Scale of Activities

Yagaum had its peak time in the 1960s with a large number of specialized staff: nurses, laboratory technicians, secretaries, X-ray technicians, anaesthetists, and up to three or four doctors at the one time, as well as many national nurses. But it was Papa and Mama Braun who gave the tone to the place, being like parents to all. They had never had any children of their own, so Pastor Fulalek and his wife gave their son, Teddy, to the Brauns out of gratitude and love for all that the couple had done for them and their fellow New Guineans.

A leprosy hospital was built in 1963 from money given by the Swedish Church. One hundred patients at all stages of leprosy lived there, and were taught handcrafts in order to become more self-reliant. Sisters Ursula Johst (Germany) and Margaret Kloster (Holland), together with Joseph Son from Graged, cared for them. In 1970, Bapie, an APO from Tapen, took over the running of the unit.

Many other doctors have worked at Yagaum for varied periods of time: Doctors Garner, Stime, Trudel, Stinson, Baer, Driedger, Fuglestad, and Scholz, to mention some of them. A few of the many nurses were the following: from Germany — Ruth Schirmer, Grete Pommer, Johanna Florek, Karin Keuler, Karin Mueller, Karin Kubina, Christa Lindner, Maria Rebelein, and Rotraud Streicher; from Australia — Merla Garrett, Eva Landmann,

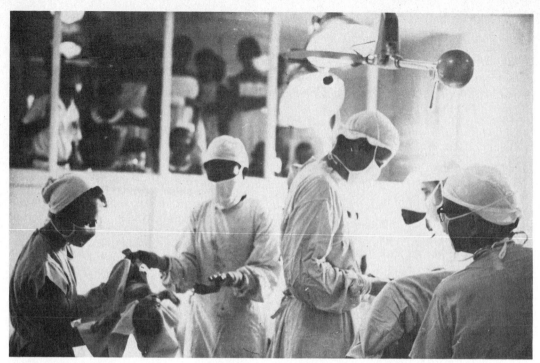

Surgery at Yagaum.

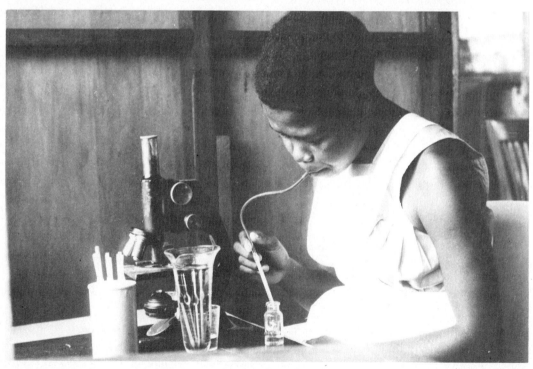

Laboratory technician at work.

Eleanor Zerna; from USA — June Hetrick, Beatrice Scheele, Bonnie Olson; and from Canada — Jackie Ulmer and Dolores Hall.

In August 1972, Dr W. D. Symes, then Director of Health, and Dr H. Helberg from the World Council of Churches, visited Yagaum. The recommendation was made that Yagaum should scale down its services, as an independent country would not be able to support two large hospitals in such close proximity as Yagaum and the Madang General Hospital. The church, in any case, was not in a position to afford the ever-increasing running costs of this hospital.

That same year, Dr and Mrs Braun retired, and were spared from experiencing the changes that had to come about in the hospital which they had so devotedly helped to build up for people they dearly loved. Hattie Braun and Theodore Braun had spent 48 and 42 years of their lives respectively in Papua New Guinea. On the eve of their return to the USA, they said: 'Our main aim has been to bring the gospel and to train the people of New Guinea so that they, in turn, can further the work in their villages.' [44] Dr Braun died on March 10, 1980, and Mrs Braun on January 26, 1984 in Nebraska, USA.

In the ensuing years, the hospital, because of its age, needed more and more repairs. The Church was not able to meet the costs, and the government had its commitments at the Madang General Hospital only 12 km away. A rationalization agreement was worked out with the government hospital: acute medical and

Dr and 'Mama' Braun, who spent over 40 years in Papua New Guinea.

surgical cases would be taken care of in Madang, while TB, leprosy, and long-term patients would be cared for at Yagaum.

In 1976, Yagaum became a health centre without a doctor, and has continued to serve the Amele people in this capacity ever since. Today Frances Yamu is in charge, and his staff comprises: Ubias Samuel in charge of MCH, Natera, Givae, Ayo, Piwok, and Kiom. Albrecht Woelfel (Germany) is also now stationed at Yagaum, as the Project Officer of Lutheran Medical Services. He visits all outstations of the church to advise and to supervise in planning, maintenance, and new projects.

Lutheran Medical Services

Medical service has been given by the church to its people ever since mission work began in New Guinea. For many years Dr Braun was in charge of the program — in effect, as director.

Dr Mary Fritsch (Australia) recalls from her time in 1969 as medical director her joy at seeing firsthand on her inspection visits New Guineans and expatriates running health centres and clinics in all sorts of places, under all sorts of conditions, far away from the comparatively well-established setting of Yagaum or Butaweng, and doing this so nobly and mostly uncomplainingly. [45]

In 1970, at the Eighth Synod of ELCONG at Ogelbeng, the medical work was established as a separate department. [46] In 1971, the Lutheran Medical Services Board, at its February meeting, appointed Dr Nate Stime (USA) as acting director, and Charles Pfarr (USA) as business manager of the department. [47] From 1973 to 1975, Dr Des Scholz (Australia) served as the medical director. Sister M. Garrett (1975-1977) and Mr K. Cramer (1978) were in turn acting directors of Lutheran Medical Services (LMS). Wilson Waesa was appointed acting director in 1979; when this became a full-time position in 1980, Wilson moved to Madang to set up the office of LMS — quite a tremendous task.

From 1976 to 1978 Wilson was also chairman of the Churches' Medical Council, and from 1979 to 1985 he represented the CMC as a member of the Nursing Council for PNG. Today he is deputy chairman of the CMC and on its executive committee. The office of LMS is

527

now sited in Lae, and Ruth Johnston (America) has become Wilson's secretary and adviser. Wilson feels strongly about the course to be taken and says:

> The medical work is mission work! I am not a theologian, but I know that when Christ was in this world He did medical work. Therefore it is wrong to say that the only work of the church is to preach the Gospel. I am happy about all that is happening in our hospitals. Many have developed their own mission program. There is still much to do ... I therefore propose that:
> 1) Hospitals and aid-post staff must work closely with the congregational pastor;
> 2) There should be a pastor appointed to care for each hospital;
> 3) There should be spiritual materials available to help the staff of the hospitals and the chaplains;
> 4) The medical work of the church must be made known in its schools and seminaries;
> 5) All medical workers should receive some Bible School training. [48]

Today LMS consolidates, plans, organizes, and supervises the medical work of ELC-PNG. It also runs *Was long Sipsip* workshops, to produce materials which can be given to the LMS staff and patients to help them in their daily work to care for the sick and to proclaim the Good News. [49]

Buangi Hospital

Dr Agnes Hoeger transferred from Madang to Buangi in 1950, and was for Finschhafen what Dr Braun was for Madang. After coming into the Finschhafen area, she immediately set up MCH services. Sister Clara Rohrlach took over this work when she and her husband David returned after the war. David Rohrlach was the maintenance officer for all buildings and equipment, and was also responsible for the rebuilding of Buangi over the years. When David and Clara Rohrlach retired in 1973, they had given 40 and 37 years of service respectively.

Sister Helene Moll, one of the pre-war nurses who came from Germany in 1927, returned after the war and worked at Buangi, mainly in the laboratory, until her retirement. Sister Kaethe Wirth (Germany) worked first at Buangi, and later at Gaubin. When Bruder Karl Kirsch returned in 1951, he was based at Buangi, placed in charge of all congregational aid-posts and expected to establish new ones.
528

Those set up were at Sattelberg, Keregia, Wareo, Boa, Taemi, Wagezaring, Siraring, and Sariau. Bruder Karl said:

> The work gave me much satisfaction; I felt how necessary it was to give help and advice in each centre and how much these men, who did outstanding work in isolation, appreciated my coming, even though it meant I was away from home more and more. [50]

Sister Emma Ruck (Germany) came to Buangi in 1957, where she worked and taught until 1973. Many more overseas nurses worked at Buangi over the years, among whom were: Elvira Koop (Australia), 1956, Rosemarie Lechner (Germany), 1957, Joan Kotzur (Australia), 1957, Kaethe Schwaner (Germany) 1963, Margarete Bertelsmeier (Australia), to mention only some. Sister Heather Borgelt (Australia) took over the MCH work in 1959, and was later joined by Sister Hazel Knopke (Australia).

Training of national nurses was soon begun in Pidgin. Among Ruawe from Sattelberg started his training at Buangi in 1958. He was later sent to Yagaum to upgrade his training and gain experience in the laboratory. When he graduated at Yagaum in 1962, he returned to Buangi to work in the laboratory. He says:

> When I came to Buangi, there were few who could help me, and I had to find my own way in the work. We had a lot of work in those days with the outbreak of a whooping-cough epidemic, hookworm, anaemia, and TB. Norma Arntson, a laboratory technician from USA, was a great help to me, and we worked well together. [52]

In 1963, Among married Jama, a nurse who had trained at Yagaum and worked at Buangi, and who is now at Butaweng. Thinking both of her medical work and her Sunday-school teaching, she said:

> I am happy that God gives me this work to do. He has cared for me and my family all these years, and now my husband and I can still help the sick and tell them about Jesus. [53]

Fuawe Somanu from Sattelberg began his nursing training at Buangi in 1951, and graduated in 1955. He worked in aid-posts, then at Buangi and later at Butaweng, retiring in 1978. In 1984 when his village, Sosoninko, needed a village aide, he volunteered to help. As he says: 'I am old, but I am still able to help my people, as long as God gives me strength'. [54]

Dr Mary Fritsch arrived on the field in 1958, and spent most of her time in the Finschhafen area. She was present when the rebuilt Buangi hospital was opened in 1959. Money for this project had been raised by the Lutheran women of Australia, a number of whom came to PNG for the dedication service. Dr Mary spent most of her time in the country as the superintendent of Buangi and of the Butaweng Chest Hospital. In 1960, she acted as medical officer at the Finschhafen government health station. Shortage of staff required her to serve as medical officer for both Butaweng and Yagaum hospitals in 1968-1969. Whenever she was absent from Butaweng, the sisters took charge of the hospital.

Relating the many difficulties of those times, Dr Mary recalled

> road washaways, landslides and bridges collapsing (one even collapsed sideways while I was in a combi-van on it, and it was only a crazy iron post piercing the window and impaling itself in the car's roof which prevented the van and us ten folk inside from crashing twenty feet into the creek-bed below!). There were the uncertainties of plane flights, the vulnerability of boats and canoes, the difficulties of patients trying to get themselves to medical help, of others on home-made stretchers, jeeps and coastal ships, etc. [55]

Dr Ursula Jehles (Germany) was in charge of Buangi hospital from 1961 to 1964; thereafter she took care of the medical outstations Wagezaring, Sariau, and Siraring. After her leaving, Drs Meding (Germany), Marubbio (USA), and others worked at Buangi after having received medical orientation at Yagaum. Dr Kahu Sugoho from Bukawa village near Lae was the first-ever qualified national medical practitioner in New Guinea. He joined the staff of Buangi in 1970. After attending the aid-post school at Malahang for two years and receiving a medical assistant certificate, he spent four years at the Fiji School of Medicine, which gave him his Diploma (surgery, medicine, and obstetrics) in 1955. In Noumea, New Caledonia, he acquired a certificate for health education in 1957. Tropical medicine and public health was studied in Fiji again in 1961, and from the East-West Centre in Hawaii he was graduated in 1969 with a certificate in paediatrics. Dr Sugoho was held in high regard by all the staff and patients as a fine doctor who showed Christian compassion for his patients.

Eighteen months after coming to Buangi, Dr Sugoho was replaced by Dr Stime (USA). Dr Sugoho left to join the Public Health Department and was appointed to headquarters. [56] He is now building up his own private practice in Lae.

Sister Barbara Dolling transferred from Awelkon to Buangi and took over the MCH work. She did much to update the training of the nurses as APOs and as child-health and midwifery orderlies, so that they could be recognized by the government. Most of these nurses went to serve on outstations such as Siassi, Menyamya, Zaka, Garaina, Malalo, Aseki, and Wagezaring. Missionary wives who were nurses gave their support to these girls in their work.

Butaweng — Braun Health Centre

In Finschhafen on the southern side of the Mape River was the Butaweng Chest Hospital, built by the government and staffed by the Lutheran Church. It was officially opened in December 1958. Dr Mary Fritsch took charge of it until 1959; Dr Agnes Hoeger then took over and remained until her retirement in 1965, having completed almost thirty years of service in the country.

Dr Fritsch again took over, and recalls the richness and uniqueness of the congregational and communal life at Butaweng. Baptisms, marriages, and deaths all took place. With 400 patients destined to stay for two years' treatment, two New Guinean pastors, three medical orderlies, Ed Tscharke (Australia), Hilda Hauert (USA), and Doug Kohn (Australia), the caretaker, much loving concern showed itself during this time. Dr Fritsch wrote: 'I'll never forget trying to describe to the patients sitting in the chapel after Wednesday devotions and with the moon sailing by outside, that man had just landed on the moon! [57]

It was at this time that a basket-making and craft program was set up for the good and comfort of the patients. Sisters Liesel Kummer (Germany), Christine Schulz (Australia), Elizabeth Ruediger (Australia), and the deacon Dieter Klemp (Germany) worked at Butaweng, with Sister Ruediger taking charge many times during the absence of Dr Mary Fritsch. Dr Mary married Rudolf Gutner in 1970, and left the field at the end of that year.

Braun Health Centre, Butaweng.

During the 1970s, due to a change of treatment and rationalization of health services, the number of patients decreased steadily. Since Buangi needed more and more costly repairs, it was decided to merge Buangi and Butaweng at the latter place at the end of 1973. To accommodate the staff, a number of buildings were transferred across the river to Butaweng which then became a general hospital with two TB wards. The official opening took place on November 2, 1974. The hospital became a health centre under the new classification of the National Health Plan, and was given the name 'Braun Health Centre' in honour of Dr T. G. Braun.

David Wallis (Australia) worked as pharmacist and hospital administrator for a number of years at Butaweng. He had first come as a volunteer pharmacist to Yagaum, where he met Eunice Henslin (USA), a laboratory technician. Both David and Eunice did much for the spiritual life of Butaweng. Since their return to Australia in 1979, Manasseh Katur from Siassi has taken over as hospital administrator. Both he and his wife, Mamba Katur, are now
530

giving Butaweng stability in this time of frequent staff changes.

In 1975, the nursing staff was almost completely localized, with Mr Adin Wagim serving as 'matron', and Sister Irene Suaka as the deputy matron. Staff nurses were Jokobet Jawal, Atu Gedisa, Eta Koarang, Baleb Aikum, and Jenny Akae. All the local staff were trained at LSON, and some had taken post-graduate training. Sister Dolling, who was in charge of MCH work, and the only expatriate sister at the time, writes:

It has been and still is a joy to be working side by side with all the national nursing staff and to see how capably they take responsibility. [58]

The following doctors also served at the Braun Health Centre: Dr H. Steinacker (Germany), Dr and Mrs R. Brown (New Zealand), Dr J. Hershey (USA), Dr N. Nickerson (USA), Dr M. Kaiser (Germany), Dr E. Schumacher (Germany). Dr Hermann Munsel (Germany) is the present officer in charge.

Today Braun Health Centre trains both men and women as aid-post orderlies and nursing aides. With the instruction in English, these students are fully recognized after they have taken their final examinations. Mr Elia McNeil is the principal, and Sister Mamba Katur and Gewe Yamsob are the tutors. The health centre is responsible for all the medical services of the Finschhafen sub-province, which has a population of 52,000 and covers 1,550 square miles of some of the most rugged mountains in Papua New Guinea.

> We are confronted with a real challenge to improve the health of these people. We need dedicated staff with much fortitude and stamina for the strenuous patrolling into the remote mountain areas, where few if any roads exist

says Sister Barbara.[59] There have been two teams of MCH workers headed by Sister Dolling and her counterpart Anike Titus, from Labu near Lae, doing the clinics by foot or by car to bring primary health care to the people. Mindik, Pindiu, Siassi, and Menyamya have MCH nurses stationed to do the patrolling, but they need to be visited and advised by staff from the Health Centre. The government has recognized Sister Barbara's contribution to health care by awarding her the Independence Medal in 1977 and the Queen's Silver Jubilee Medal in 1979.

Village midwife courses have been run by staff from the Health Centre at various locations. Village midwives live in their own villages, and many mothers are able to give birth there with the help of these women.

Braun Health Centre records show a marked decrease in patients admitted over the last years. Sister Katur attributes this fact to the increased concern of the staff in primary health care, where the emphasis lies on prevention of diseases rather than cure.[60]

A village aid program has also been commenced and is being run on a trial basis. Dr Kaiser, Mr Thompson Meteke (APO Supervisor from Siassi), and Sister Baleb Aikum from Karkar until recently were organizing the program.

Gaubin/Karkar Island

Karkar, a volcanic island 50 km north of Madang, created many health problems for the early missionaries, and a number died of malaria. The Japanese occupied the island in 1943, and after the war the health of the population was very poor, many being afflicted with yaws, ulcers, and malaria.

Edwin Tscharke and his wife Tabitha began the medical work there after the war. Edwin had been called as a carpenter to Finschhafen early in 1941. However, through his enlistment in the army, he received training as a medical assistant and worked with ANGAU in various areas. He married in March 1945, was discharged from the army in April 1946, and accepted a call to medical mission work.

Edwin and Tabitha's first assignment was to accompany twelve head of cattle, eight pigs, eight ducks, and fifty chickens on the MV *Montoro* from Australia. This consignment was needed to rebuild the supply of livestock depleted by the war. Arriving in Lae for the first field conference in January 1947, Ed Tscharke was confronted by the resolution of the conference: 'Tscharke to go to Karkar, to build a hospital and set up health services'.[61]

For six months, Ed Tscharke worked with Dr Braun at Buangi, gaining experience especially in minor surgery and intravenous injections. In August 1947, Dr Braun considered it was time for Ed to collect surplus army building material, and to try to get to Karkar to implement the resolution of the first field conference. Ed sketched a building plan and showed it to Dr Braun. Although he seemed to have some misgivings, Dr Braun said: 'You are going to build it and work in it, so go ahead'.[62] And when Dr Braun farewelled the Tscharkes, he gave them this advice:

> Tscharke, do not do patrols to get patients, like the army taught you. Your work must be good so people will want to come to you. If you have few or no patients, then I will say your work is poor. Another point you must remember: Work with the congregations and discuss your problems with them.[63]

On arrival at Karkar, all the building materials were unloaded at Kurum beach. Even though there was no house, Tabitha was prepared to stay and pioneer with Ed. The first patient soon arrived on a pinnace boat with a huge scalp wound. The only place to give any treatment was on the bullet-ridden kitchen table in the home of the plantation manager, Jack Lindner. And it was night-time, and Tabitha had to be sent back to the beach to find the surgical equipment. Nevertheless, by hurricane lamp Ed sutured the wound, and the patient eventually made a good recovery.

Gaubin Hospital, Karkar Island.

Where to build the hospital was a question not lightly answered, as Ed was aware of the New Guineans' emotional and sacred attachment to their ground, and wanted to forestall any later ground disputes. The land chosen and drained was the swampy, severely-bombed beach-front, a non-productive part of the Kurum plantation. As Ed said:

I have always believed in the value of the community and the strength of the congregation and its leaders. If one is prepared to sit down and communicate a problem and seek their help in solving it jointly, they are ready to work with such a person. The building of the hospital was a challenge to be solved along these lines. [64]

Pastor Mileng of Karkar was a great help to the Tscharkes. During the building period, there was increasing need to begin with medical work. After discussions, the Tscharkes began with NAB injections against yaws every Monday. In the first year, some 13,000 injections were given.

Gaubin Hospital was officially opened in June 1948. When Ed asked Dr Braun for staff, he was told: 'Do as I am; train your own', [65] so Ed set out to begin an APO and MCH training school. Nagu from Kaul village was among the first twelve students. He later took pastoral training and was commissioned as assistant pastor in 1963. Most of his time was then spent in chaplaincy, but he also continued with medical work.

At this time, no literature in Pidgin was available for nurses, so Ed wrote a 300-page

Pidgin Medical Handbook in conjunction with Dr Hoeger. In 1958, Ed wrote another book in Pidgin: *Better Health and Hygiene for New Guinea People.*

Among the nursing sisters who worked at Gaubin were: Elvira Koop from Australia, who mainly did MCH work; Kaethe Wirth and Ursula Johst, both from Germany; Joan Kotzur, Melva Schneider, Esther Schulz, Margaret Voigt, and Pam Logan, all from Australia. Sister Logan did much to upgrade the training program. With funds from the donor agency 'Bread for the World', the hospital was rebuilt as a more permanent structure.

The population of Karkar in 1947 was just under 9,000. Today it is approximately 27,000. Gaubin today is a 180-bed health centre, which covers the general health needs of the communities of Karkar and Bagabag islands, as well as the needs of the hired labourers. The services cover inpatient and outpatient care, surgery, obstetrics, X-ray, laboratory, pharmacy, TB and leprosy control, and paraplegic care. Rural MCH work is a very important outreach from Gaubin. The trained staff at the health centre itself today comprises Ed Tscharke and the national nurses Kiboni, Tigua, and Galung.

The school trains APOs and nurse aides to government-required standards, and challenges them to be active in evangelistic work. From early days it has been the practice at Gaubin that after every delivery a prayer of thanks be offered with the mother and relatives,

532

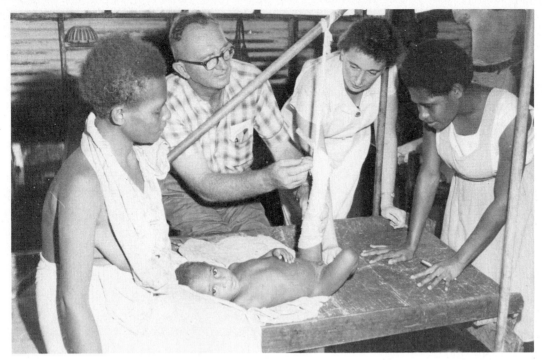

Mr E. Tscharke and Sr E. Schulz attending to a patient.

and that, before surgery, one of the staff prays with the patients.

Sister Dolores Hall (Canada), who first came to New Guinea in 1966 and worked at Yagaum, is now the tutor of the training school. Her assistants are Banloi, Siming, and Gamok.

The faithful and dedicated work done by the Tscharkes has been recognized and acknowledged. In 1974, Ed received the Member of the British Empire award, and in 1978, the Queen's Silver Jubilee Award; as well, he was the recipient of the Paul Harris Fellow Award in 1982 from Rotary International.

Ed and Tabitha, looking back over their 44 years of service in the church, acknowledge the tremendous blessings and abiding presence of our Lord whose promises remain true through dark and bright days, as Jesus said, "I will never leave you nor forsake you".' [66]

Wagezaring/Hube

Today a road is being built from Finschhafen to Pindiu to help the heavily-populated hinterland of the Hube circuit. But in 1956, when the first permanent hospital was built, there was no such road, and it was difficult to bring supplies to Wagezaring from the airstrip at Pindiu. This 50-bed hospital was built by the Hube people themselves, and functioned well with three medical orderlies. However, more help was needed at Wagezaring, and the 1959 Field Conference decided to send Bruder Karl Kirsch who, until then, had worked at Buangi.

No sooner had Karl and Babette Kirsch arrived in Wagezaring in 1959 than a severe influenza epidemic swept through the area. Almost overnight, the whole of Hube was affected. Many were seriously ill, and before long there were over 200 patients in the hospital, as Bruder Karl recalls:

> They were lying everywhere; in, and under, and next to the beds. A few days later, the medical orderlies also became ill. Now my wife and I were the only ones to take care of the sick. For two weeks we worked day and night, never getting undressed and rarely off our feet ... No one died in the hospital, but many died in the villages ... This epidemic was like a baptism of fire for us and the people, and from the beginning it bound us closely to the people. [67]

With money from Queensland Sunday schools and 'Bread for the World', a 100-bed hospital was completed in 1965. As Bruder Karl was trained in dentistry, he was able to take care of the teeth of the patients as well.

Bruder Karl trained his own staff, whom he described as being all conscientious and dedicated men. Sotine Rias from Ungsesu village trained under Dr Braun at Buangi, and went to Wagezaring in 1952 as the first medical worker. There he built the first hospital, and later worked with Bruder Karl. He retired in 1984 after 35 years with Lutheran Medical Services. At his farewell he said:

> The good health service in Pindiu has changed the health of the Hube people, helped them to get education and develop their land. Now this work is in the hands of the younger men and this work must go ahead. [68]

Bruder Karl retired in 1970 after 37 years of service, and was replaced by Fred Nusch and his wife, who also was a nurse. Later, Wamao Rendung, a graduate of LSON, took over the health centre. Today, Omin Gunua, a health extension officer seconded to Wagezaring by the government, and registered nurses Teine, Kugeva, and Minuigal work at the health centre.

Bruder Karl recently wrote about his work:

> The Lord has done great things for us; in that we rejoice. At our departure one of the Hube headmen said to us as we shook hands with him, 'You have become part of us; you are real Hube people; only your skin stayed white, but your home is in Hube and we would have liked to bury you here with us'. [69]

This was a great tribute paid to a couple who spent their life in helping the people of Papua New Guinea.

Etep — Ulap

Etep is a hospital established 13 km up into the mountains from Wasu. Sister Erna Matthias (USA) was stationed there soon after she arrived in New Guinea in 1947. At that time it was to be a hospital for leprosy patients.

The Ulap hospital was another 7 km further inland. Sister Ella Walborn (USA), who arrived in 1946 and worked first with Dr Braun at Buangi and Yagaum, began work at Ulap in the early 1950s. She worked there for 19 years, caring for many orphans, as well as doing her routine work. In 1969, the hospital became an aid-post, and all general patients from then on attended Etep.

534

Sr Maria Horn, Etep.

The bush-material buildings at Etep were gradually replaced by permanent buildings. National staff trained at Buangi and Yagaum were a great asset in the work, for they could speak the local languages, and the Ulap people were reluctant to use Pidgin. Fotaneo from Ulap, after attending Bible School and then receiving his training as a medical orderly at Buangi, has worked there conscientiously since 1953.

Denzunde Akikepe from Ulap, the daughter of the well-known Ulap church leader Pastor Akikepe, did her four-year general nursing course at Yagaum, and began work at Etep in 1960. In order to gain government recognition, Denzunde did further studies at Buangi before returning to Etep.

Sister Maria Horn (Germany) came to Etep in 1965, thereby releasing Sister Matthias for service at Awande hospital, Okapa. Sister Horn had arrived on the field in 1953, and had previously worked at Yagaum and Awande. Etep is now a health centre, caring for leprosy and general patients. The fact that Sister Horn has done a great deal in the rehabilitation of the leprosy patients accounts for the happy and contented atmosphere among the patients.

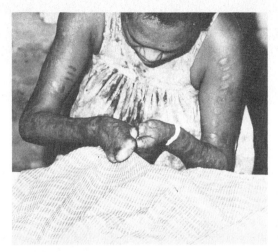
A leprosy patient.

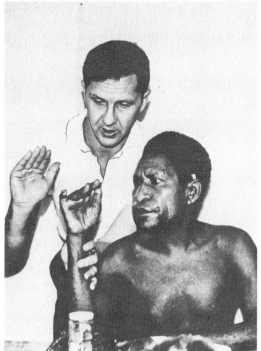
Mr Charles Pfarr, founder of Kotna Hospital.

Staffing changes are frequent now among the national workers, due to further education, marriage, and family wishes. This makes it difficult for the work at the health centre to run smoothly, and many extra hours of work have to be put in by the older faithful workers. During 1983, ten students from LSON and a number of nurse aides were assigned to Etep to gain practical experience. 'It was a great joy to have them', writes Sister Maria, 'and they have been a great help to us too.' [70]

That same year, 29 new leprosy patients were found on patrol. TB is still increasing, though home visits are being carried out regularly. The health centre had 850 inpatients and 23,250 outpatients for the year. In eleven MCH clinics, 3,567 children were seen and 335 in schools. A total of 107 days were spent on patrols, and seven aid-posts supervised. The staff all help with the daily devotions in the wards and with Sunday school.

Ogelbeng - Kotna

Ogelbeng, the mission station near Mt Hagen, was the first place in the Western Highlands where a general and leprosy hospital was gradually built up. Mr Charles (Chuck) Pfarr (USA), who had come to New Guinea in February 1947 as a construction worker, received some medical training under Dr Braun in Finschhafen in 1948. Later that year, he began medical work in a one-room building at Ogelbeng. Working faithfully with him was the medical orderly Zozinggao, who later started a secondary hospital at Siraring in his home Mape area (Finschhafen). In the last four months of 1948, they treated 25,000 patients. Gradually the hospital was enlarged over a period of years to twelve leprosy wards, a dispensary, and a church. Since there was no medical staff available, Chuck trained his own.

In 1950, he treated over 47,400 outpatients and had 600 inpatients; in addition to that, he trained 20 men and 11 women. That year, 110 leprosy patients were also registered. Chuck was the first trained medical worker in the Hagen area in those days; Togoba, the leprosy hospital, was the only other place with trained staff. His departure on leave in 1951, as well as other reasons, led to the closure of the hospital. Mrs Elfriede Strauss and Dr Elisabeth Jaeschke were thereafter permitted to do dispensary work only, as the government had opened a hospital in nearby Mt Hagen.

During his leave in USA, Chuck took a nursing course. On his return to New Guinea in 1952, he was placed at Kotna, north-east of Mt Hagen, and began to build up medical work there. He found most of his former medical aides working for the government, where they were highly praised. [71] Chuck Pfarr and his wife Julia took care of the medical patients as well as of all the infants and orphans of leprosy patients. As the 112-bed hospital needed a qualified medical officer, Dr Elisabeth Jaeschke was stationed at Kotna with her husband the Revd Ernst Jaeschke in 1968. Dr Jaeschke took over the medical work, and Chuck continued his administrative, supervisory, training, and building tasks.

When he went on leave, Sister Ursula Johst, from Germany, replaced him in 1960. Chuck Pfarr was later transferred to Yagaum, where he first worked as X-ray technician and later as hospital administrator. In 1963, Sister Margaret Voigt (Australia) transferred to Kotna, to be followed in 1967 by Sister Ursula Schwermer (Germany) who had worked in Buangi since 1954. Eventually Kotna conducted three-year courses for hospital orderlies, both men and women.

Dr Ingrid Lutschewitz also worked at Kotna for a short time before she was stationed with her husband, the Revd Hermann Lutschewitz, at Tiripini. There she continued to do medical work and advised government medical workers in the area. In her later years at Lae, Dr Lutschewitz acted as chief adviser to all mission staff, faithfully counselling many expatriates as well as many New Guineans.

Zero Kalong, a territorial nurse, joined the staff at Kotna in 1967. The work-load also increased, for the child health services covered a population of 17,760 in 57 villages, with 3,403 children under five years enrolled. [72] Sister Karin Keuler, who had first come in 1962 to Yagaum and Buangi, was now assigned to help. Today the staff consists of Sister Sinika Multanen (from Finland via Australia), and trained nurses Kumai, Alois, and Jack. During 1983, there were 1,495 inpatients and 18,448 outpatients. In the MCH work, figures show 11,446 under five years seen and examined, as well as 620 schoolchildren. 63 aid-posts are being supervised from this health centre. The health centre staff conducts morning and evening devotions as well as Sunday services. 'Our outreach with the Good News on free weekends to the villages in the Dei Council area has been a great blessing to us too. Our Lord has blessed this work so wonderfully', Sister Multanen writes. [73]

536

Sigimaru

The church established medical work at Sigimaru near the government patrol post and airstrip of Karimui in the Eastern Highlands in 1965. Werner Metze, a nurse from Germany, was the first trained worker in the area. There was evidence that a large percentage of the population had leprosy; however, these patients, were taken care of by government and research workers from Australia. The hospital, later called a health centre, was generally staffed by a single registered nurse at any one time: Sister Johanna Florek (1968-71), Sister Karin Kubina (from 1971 onwards), as well as several trained APOs. When Sister Kubina left, the health centre was localized. Sister Florek established MCH clinics, and had 1,250 children under five years enrolled. All clinics and patrols had to be done on foot.

Since 1972, Sigimaru has a permanent building for obstetrics and emergency cases. The general wards are made of bush materials with a fireplace in the centre. Registered nurses Munog T., Munog H., and Kautil, with APOs Baisor, Dara, and Yalubut staff the health centre today.

Awande

Awande Hospital was built in 1961 in the Kuru region of the Eastern Highlands, near Okapa. It was established to accommodate patients with the illness called *kuru*, and to become a research centre.

Kuru was first noted in 1952-53 by the anthropologists R. M. and C. H. Berndt among the Fore, Yate, and Usarufa people. [74] The word *kuru-kuru* in the Fore language means 'trembling from fear or cold'. *Kuru* is an acute degenerative disorder of the central nervous system, with a uniform pattern from onset to death. All cases were fatal within four to twelve months, and no cause was then known. In some villages, over 3% of the population succumbed to *kuru* every year. The victims were mainly women, although in childhood both sexes were affected equally.

The disease was first brought to the attention of Dr Vincent Zigas, District Medical Officer at Goroka at that time. Close observation of the disease began. Blood specimens and brain tissue were sent to Melbourne, but no infectious agent could be isolated. Early in

1957, Dr D. C. Gajdusek of the National Institute of Health, Bethesda, Maryland, USA, joined Dr Zigas. The Kuru Research Centre was begun at Okapa, and the disease came under intensive study. The people themselves, however, had no doubt in their minds as to what was the cause of the disease; for them it could only be sorcery.

Due to many young women dying, the children left behind often became malnourished and had to be specially cared for. Sister Eva Hasselbusch (Germany) came to the Okapa government hospital in 1959 to take care of the *kuru* patients and many orphans. She wrote: 'Thanks to God for allowing Okapa to be run by the Lutheran Mission. Twelve years ago Christianity was not known here.' [75]

Awande was built and dedicated in November 1962. Sister Maria Horn (Germany) was the first trained sister who worked with the doctors studying the disease. At the beginning, many *kuru* patients came; however, when no cure for the disease was found and all hospitalized patients died, they preferred to stay in their villages and to die surrounded by their relatives.

As studies of the disease continued, it was found that *kuru* was caused by a slow latent and temperate virus infection, probably being transmitted through cannibalism, as children and women mainly consumed the brains of the dead. When cannibalism was prohibited, the disease declined markedly.

Kuru in earlier years was called 'Laughing Death' because patients had an unusually happy expression on their faces, even when dying. The Nobel Prize was awarded to Dr D. C. Gajdusek in 1976 for his research into *kuru*. [76]

Another great service the hospital gave was its care for the many orphaned infants, who might well have followed their mothers into the grave. Weaning in that area usually took place only at the age of 18-24 months. Many children were brought to the hospital in an advanced state of malnutrition. In 1966 there were seventy orphans at Awande. It was the loving care and patience of the sisters, nurses, and aides which helped the children to grow strong again. The staff taught the older brothers and sisters (who came along with them as 'watch patients') to feed them with sweet potato and with peanut-milk balls. These children stayed three to four years, and then returned to their villages. [77]

By 1968 the hospital ceased to function as a *kuru* hospital and was closed. Sister Erna Matthias, who had changed places with Sister Maria Horn, concentrated her efforts on village visits to the few *kuru* patients that still existed and did MCH work. Together with two national nurses from Yagaum and Buangi, she cared for a population of 19,000. Of these, 1,201 were enrolled in the MCH clinics. The team spent five days a week on clinics, and enlisted all the APOs in the area to help with the work.

Awelkon-Lablab/Siassi Islands

Medical work on Rooke Island started before the war with the arrival of the first missionaries. It was picked up again after the war in 1946 when the missionaries returned. Sister Lorna Hamdorf (Australia) and Sister Jean Nagel (wife of the Revd Keith Nagel from Australia) were the first two nursing sisters. After gaining some experience and orientation en route at Buangi with Dr Braun and Dr Hoeger, they were part of the first missionary group that returned to the Awelkon station, 10 km inland from Gizarum. The mission house had not been destroyed during the war, so they had shelter.

Medical work was begun immediately by treating the many tropical ulcers. This was done mainly with foments and sulphonomide powder dressings, for very little penicillin was available at that time. A small clinic was erected after a few months, but not many people made use of the facilities. The nurses made patrols on foot to the villages to treat the sick.

Two more Australian sisters (after orientation at Buangi first) came to the Mission in January 1948: Rita Heinrich and Irma Mischke. Sister Heinrich recently recalled those first days at Buangi:

I remember how depressed we were at first to see the long wards full of patients, and not knowing how to converse with them, let alone care for them. We remember, though, how friendly and happy they were. [78]

After learning simple pathology procedures and gaining other practical experience, they set out by boat from Finschhafen to Rooke Island, 100 km across the open sea, and then the final 10 km inland on horseback.

A permanent dispensary was being built, and there were some bush huts for patients — if they stayed for treatment. Most patients had to be found and treated in the villages. Hardly any women came for deliveries, but there was no knowledge of orphans either. Right from the start, two young local men always helped the sisters, and were being trained on the job. Yaws was widely spread. At first intravenous injections of Neosalversan were given, and later penicillin was used. MCH clinics were also commenced in villages around the station.

There was no airstrip or government post on the island, and the six-weekly visit of the MV *Umboi* to the mainland (at first) was the only opportunity to send serious cases to the doctors in Finschhafen. Rita recalls how they had to do an amputation on a man who had his hand blown to bits with explosives while fishing.

> There was nothing else we could do. I had seen an amputation done, so I told Irma Mischke what to do, while I gave the anaesthetic. The patient made a good recovery. [79]

Rita Heinrich married Art Fenske in 1950. They went to live on Graged Island, where Rita continued her medical work from a little room in her laundry. Quite a few babies were born there, too. After 18 years on Graged Island, the Fenskes moved to Madang town, where Rita continued her medical work. Today she has a little dispensary on the verandah of her house, and every morning she takes care of the sick.

Other sisters from Australia who came to Awelkon — mostly after orientation in Finschhafen — were Sisters Lois Blaess, Irene Dreckow, Ruth Wedding, and Sheila Gaulke. TB and malaria were the major problems after yaws had been eradicated with penicillin. By 1956 the hospital had permanent buildings.

Later, a second hospital was established at Lablab on the other side of the island, with Sister Ruth Wedding the first sister in charge. When she went on leave, Sister Dreckow relieved her, and had to cope with three major epidemics at once: whooping-cough, measles, and chickenpox. The whole community, including the medical orderlies, was affected. More than 100 patients were at the hospital for weeks. This was the last whooping-cough epidemic on Rooke Island, as Triple Antigen immunizations were now covering the island. [80]

Sisters Edna Huf and Barbara Dolling, both triple-certificated nurses, arrived from Australia in August 1957. Medical orderlies were trained on the job, many of them school-leavers after 538

four years of schooling. They were taught to do dressings, give injections, and recognize simple diseases, as well as taking care of the hospital, grounds, gardens, and equipment. Some went with Missionary Harold Freund to Menyamya when that field opened. In 1975, the Health Department allowed some of these men to sit for the APO certificate in order to become recognized. Nikonal Ambalis was in charge of Awelkon, and Soten Ampar in charge of Lablab, both registered APOs.

Sister Edna Huf spent eight years at Awelkon. She recalls her time on the island as a time when she realized the constancy of God's loving presence:

> The days of miracles are not over. There was a very sick child for whom we could do nothing more, then suddenly there was rapid recovery! Or the mother haemorrhaging to death through complications in labour; we did all we could physically do. How thankful we were when she survived the flight to Lae and the subsequent caesarean operation. There were many more cases — premature babies, gastro-enteritis, meningitis, tetanus — in which, as we saw the patient recover, we could not but give thanks and praise to God Almighty. [81]

On one occasion, Soten Ampar went on patrol by canoe when the mission boat *Karapo* had been out of order for some time. What should have been a few hours' work turned out to be a long and dangerous adventure. He was stranded on an island for five days before he was finally able to begin to paddle his way homeward. However, the canoe was then caught in heavy seas, and broke up. Soten and the others in the canoe were saved only by the grace of God who protected them in the heavy surf.

Sister Barbara Dolling, who spent over 12 years at Awelkon, tells of many emergencies in which, as she said, 'the Lord took over'. One such occasion was when

> Kiva Nathaniel, a two-year-old boy, ran into his father's axe. A large gaping abdominal wound was the result, intestines gaping through the severed peritoneum. I had permission to send the boy on to Lae. The plane came, but the winds became too strong for take-off; it was too risky. On conferring again with the doctor in Lae, I was told to go ahead and suture the abdomen under local anaesthetic. The operation took three hours, mother and father holding the boy. A miraculous healing took place without infection. [82]

Jasaking Namang, a medical orderly trained at Yagaum, was very competent in making a diagnosis and giving treatments. He was excellent in suturing, reducing fractures, and applying plaster casts. In 1970, when Sister Dolling transferred to Buangi, Jasaking took charge of the station; later, when Awelkon was taken over by the government, he took charge of Lablab.

Lablab has remained a health centre of the church, and has been staffed by nationals for many years. Today a health extension officer, Matthew, seconded by the government, is in charge; he has two registered nurses, Jokobet Jawal and Karant, working with him as well as some APOs.

Kapo-Kwaplalim/Menyamya

Kapo and Kwaplalim are two health stations in the Menyamya area, a mountainous area west of Wau and Bulolo.

Menyamya itself had a national APO working on the station in 1960 when the mission's first trained medical worker, Ken Cramer, arrived from Australia (after spending three months on Rooke Island for orientation). A two-roomed bush-material clinic was built for Ken and his APO co-worker, Jateng, at Kwaikuma station. After three years, this medical centre was transferred over the mountain ridge to the more populous area of Kapo. As there were no roads, every nail and

sheet of iron had to be carried on the backs of the local people for the three-hour walk from Menyanya to Kapo, in order to build the 18-bed health centre.

In 1963, a second medical worker arrived from Siassi: Sister Dulcie Seiffert, who later became Mrs Ray Ramm.

At Kapo, Ken Cramer began training young local men as medical orderlies. When they became competent in their work, Jateng returned to Siassi. Some of these men are still working today either for the church or the government.[83] James Miti is one of them. He writes:

> When I started school in 1955 and learnt to read and write, it was then that I heard about Jesus. I bought myself a Basic English Bible and read it continually. I read the stories about Jesus — how He was the Doctor who helped and healed many men and women. Jesus says, 'If a man believes in Me and shows love to his fellowmen with works of love, he will receive eternal life'. I believed these words of Jesus and decided to start medical work. I was first at Kwaikuma and later at Kapo.[84]

After five years he became the head medical orderly, and was able to attend to all the cases that came in.

James tells of a little one-week-old boy, Peter Kasu, who became very sick, and was near to death. James and Ken Cramer attended to him every hour, both day and night, in the hope of saving his life. Gradually he improved and became well again. James writes:

Kwaplalim Hospital.

Restoring life to the child was not something I did by my own strength or skill. No! I worked with my thoughts always fixed upon Jesus, the Master and Doctor. I prayed to Him, He heard my prayer and helped me in this work to restore Peter Kasu. The words of Jesus in Luke 6:36 where Jesus says, 'Be full of pity, even as your Father is full of pity', are my guide. They are the words I try to obey. [85]

James later took charge of the Menyamya aid-post.

Ken Cramer remembers well the early years, when the patients were brought to the health centre only after their own medicine had failed. Of course, this was very often too late, and events seemed to suggest that the white man's medicine was not much good, either. But hygiene in those days was almost non-existent as far as the patient was concerned.

There were other problems, too. Patients would leave the clinic after dressings had been applied, and would remove the bandages to reinforce their netbags! The staff also had to wrestle with the apathy of the people; for those who did come for treatment, one dose of medicine was expected to be sufficient to cure almost all ills. And there were the numerous superstitions and cases of sorcery. But understanding gradually improved, and many joys were experienced.

The Menyamya people had traditional midwives, and only the midwife was permitted to cut the cord at delivery. Ken Cramer had his hand smacked once, when he attempted to cut the cord! [86]

In 1966, a permanent 18-bed hospital was opened at Kapo. It had been financed by the sale of used postage stamps through 'Stamps for Missions', a fund-raising project of the youth of the church in Australia.

Sister Dulcie Seiffert had commenced MCH clinics, and started giving Triple Antigen injections, but this was difficult to get under way among people who did not understand the reasons. Sister D. Wegener (Australia) began MCH work at Kwaplalim in 1964. Reports indicated that she was serving 3,355 people, and had 310 children enrolled. Tetanus also was a major problem at that time; the three cases treated in one month all made good recovery.

Health Patrol in the Menyamya mountains.

Sister Beryl Heinrich (Australia) came to work at Kwaplalim in 1965. At that time, the MCH enrolment was 730, and there was great need to combat malnutrition. 'Befriending these people, patiently seeking to help them, and witnessing to them at every opportunity is a precious and satisfying calling', said Sister Beryl. [87]

Sister Joan Dutschke relieved Ken Cramer at Kapo in 1967. Sister Dutschke had been serving on Rooke Island, and brought with her five well-trained medical orderlies: James and Jesse (who had been in medical work for many years), and Caleb, Dan, and Reuben. All these men were able to take the responsibility of the hospital when the sister was absent. They were also a tremendous help when it came to interpreting.

In the recent past, Sisters Karin Mueller and Christa Wegenast, both from Germany, spent much of their time patrolling in the area. Sister Denise Dockery (New Zealand) came as a volunteer to work with the Lutheran Medical Services in Menyamya. Later, she was joined by Sister Linda Manning (England), also a volunteer. With malnutrition a major problem in the area for many years, Mrs Thompson, a nutritionist, was appointed to work together with the Department of Primary Industries and Lutheran Medical Services. She initiated centres where local girls are now trained in nutrition. They work with the mothers, helping them to cook, feed their children, and grow gardens. The value of this experiment lies in the fact that these girls are able to converse with and understand the local people better than anyone from outside.

Today, Kwaplalim is a sub-health centre. Linda Manning, with three trained nurse aides from Braun Health Centre and Gaubin, work there. They care for the community school which is next door, and every Wednesday the nurses give health talks to the school children. Kapo is now an aid-post with two trained APOs, and with Amos in charge. Menyamya church centre is the base for the MCH team, led by Sister Dockery and nurses Michaels and Gagum. Their main work consists in patrolling, holding clinics, and supervising the aid-posts. When the nurses are on the station, they are on call for obstetrics at the Menyamya government health centre. This health centre is run by a Health Extension officer, and there is good cooperation between the church and government. Each centre has a large nutrition unit for combating malnutrition.

In the course of the history of the medical program of the church, three aims have emerged. First, there has been a deep concern to bring primary health care to the people of Papua New Guinea by teaching them to help themselves. Secondly — and very prominently — there has been a succession of a great number of overseas and national medical workers carrying out a dedicated healing ministry. The third aim has been to educate men and women to bring primary health care to every community, as well as actual care for the sick. Young national leaders of Lutheran Medical Services continue to emphasize today what many faithful workers in the earlier years have taught: that medical work is God-given, and that only those who have Christ's love in their hearts can find true joy in this service.

Work with the Women in Papua New Guinea

Women in Papua New Guinea traditionally have had a subordinate standing in their society. The woman was primarily the worker and sexual partner of her husband. She carried the heavy netbags (*bilums*) with fruits from the garden, collected the firewood, cooked food, and cleaned the house and surroundings. She bore children and brought them up. She made mats, netbags, and grass skirts. The man protected and owned the woman. With bow and arrows he led the way; she followed, carrying heavy loads, including children. The bride-price compensated the family of the girl for a lost worker, but also helped to ensure that the husband would care for his wife; otherwise, she may have returned to her clan. The woman in this society faced life completely subordinate to her husband and the power of the clan; she had no individual freedom or independence.

However, with the coming of the missionaries and the Word of God, the social

Carrying heavy loads, including children.

Mrs M. Wacke and her girls.

standing of the woman is changing. As a woman from Sio said:

> We women in New Guinea were the lowest and most despised beings. But through baptism we are equal; we are freed. Now we, as well as men, are God's creation, His beloved children. [88]

Men and women have heard the Word of God, and have been received into the Christian congregation. Here, when the Christian concept of marriage and family life is followed, the role of the woman changes dramatically.

It was the missionary's wife who first saw the need of her sister in Christ in New Guinea. In her she saw one also of 'a chosen race, a royal priesthood, a holy nation, God's own people'. It was for her, too, to 'declare the wonderful deeds of him who called [her] out of darkness into his marvellous light' (1 Peter 2:9).

Early Beginnings

The first moves to introduce girls to household duties and to teach them at mission stations were made at Sattelberg and

Heldsbach. Mrs E. Keysser was the first missionary's wife to employ girls, and she was soon followed by others. In Heldsbach, the daughters of Senior Flierl started a small girls' school. Later, Mrs M. Wacke at Kalasa mission station did some outstanding work among the women and girls. At times she had up to 30 girls at the station to teach them Bible lessons as well as reading and writing, and household duties.

Dinekpain in the Mandang District

Mrs Adele Welsch can be regarded as the founder of organized women's work in the Lutheran Church in this country. She arrived on the field in 1922. In Amele and Begesin, like most of the missionaries' wives, she taught young women in her house to become Christian wives and mothers, and helped them to fulfil their duties 'to declare the wonderful works of our Lord'. In the 1930s she cared for and taught the wives of the first evangelists to the Highlands, when they were not able to accompany their husbands immediately to their place of work. These women were taught Bible study, singing, sewing, nutrition, and domestic science.

With the onset of World War II, Mrs Welsch was evacuated to Australia in 1941; however, she was able to return in 1946 as the first missionary woman allowed back to the field. Tragically, she had lost her husband, Jacob Welsch, and Nagi, their adopted son, during the war. But she returned to make her home again with the Amele people. Qaildec and Ud, two faithful New Guineans, built their houses on either side of the station so that there would be men to protect her. [89] And, with the sanction of the congregation, she started a girls' school.

One day she had a visit from a young woman who has since come to be called 'the first Bible Woman in the New Guinea Lutheran Church'. [90] This was Ahigol of Aijab village in the Amele Circuit, who had been a student of 'Mama Welsch' in Amele and Begesin before the war. She said:

> Mama, you have lost Nagi and your husband in the war. I too lost my husband and child. Now we both will work for our Lord together. [91]

Ahigol, also known as Ahin, is now in her seventies and still works for the Lord, teaching Religious Instruction at the Behil Community School near her home. Reflecting on her many years working with the women, she commented in conversation:

> I ask myself, 'Why is the Word of God no longer sweet for the women today?' They think only of business and making money. Have we not taught them well enough? [92]

Being without children, Ahigol today is a lonely woman. There is no one to help her in her old age (children are the 'old age pension' of Papua New Guinea).

Mojou from Gonoa also was a faithful worker with Mama Welsch, following her to Nobonob and later to Madang town. The women they trained were sent back to their villages to start kindergarten work and teach Sunday school. Mojou said:

> I did not get married, I wanted to be free to spread the Word of God. I went to Nobonob and Karkar, and looked after the nurses at Yagaum. God helped me in my work. He strengthened me when I became ill with asthma. The work has borne fruit. In earlier times women lived in fear; they were under Satan. But the Word of God made them free. His Spirit made the woman to be a Christian woman. [93]

Mojou lives today with her people in Gonoa, almost blind and still suffering from asthma.

Mama Welsch retired in 1957 at the age of 67, but was called back to New Guinea only one year later. The church recognized her extraordinary abilities, and now appointed her to begin and lead the women's work as such. It had become obvious that women had more and more responsibilities in the village, as many men went to the towns to work. It was Mama

Mrs A. Welsch.

Ahigol (left) and Mojou.

543

Welsch who was able to build bridges in a church where many people from different parts of the world and different parts of New Guinea lived and worked together. In her busy life she was often heard to say: 'Odio (Good-bye), don't stop me. The Lord has given grace to my journey. I must hurry to Amele, to tell them about Jesus.' [94] She died in Germany on January 21, 1980, after having spent 41 years in Papua New Guinea.

This was the beginning of women's work in the Madang District, known there as *Dinekpain*. Gail Wilson (USA) and Deaconess Merna Thamm (Australia) followed in Mama Welsch's footsteps, and many New Guinean sisters went through the Baitabag girls' school to become teachers and workers. Today Mariesa Galah is the Madang District women's worker. At the girls' school at Baitabag today, young women are trained to be women's workers. Taunas from Amele has been the head-teacher at the girls' school for the last six years.

Gejamsao in the Jabem District

'Women's work in the Jabem District began with the first missionaries', says Gabby Gedisa,[95] leader of *Gejamsao* work in her district. All the missionaries took girls into their homes, and taught them hygiene, nutrition, sewing, singing, and Bible studies. Subsequently, they went back to their villages and started small groups of *Gejamsao*, which means 'help for women'.

In 1956, an English school for girls was opened at Bula. Here Mrs Bayer and her daughter, Hedwig (from Germany), were the first teachers; later, June Prange (USA) and Sister Waltraud Keller (Germany) continued the work. The girls in the school were taught Bible study and how to teach Sunday school. After completion of their schooling, these girls went home to their villages, worked with the women, and held Sunday school for the children on Sunday afternoons.

Elsie Walther (Germany), who was in charge of the guest house at Lae, began women's work in the Jabem District. After first working with her house girls, she branched out into Butibam and other surrounding villages. It was she who also began women's work at Sio. She was followed by Violet Stang (USA).

At all times, the overseas workers had national co-workers with them. Gengosoo Geyadabing from Wedilu-Hopoi worked for many years in the Gejamsao office in Lae. In 1954, it was not yet common for girls to go to school. Gengosoo's parents and village people opposed her desire for education, but, with the help of the missionary, the congregation and elders agreed for her to go to Nobonob (Madang). After four years' training, she returned to her village to work with the children. Gengosoo said: 'The people have scant respect for a woman, and I received poor support ... It didn't worry me much. My heart and soul were wrapped up in just doing my work.' [96]

In 1964, she became the first New Guinean woman to be appointed to work in the Gejamsao office in Lae. When the elders and people of the place where she was working at the time heard of her appointment, they were angry and scoffed at her: 'She's been working in the village (instead of marrying) and so has no children. She just wants to go to town so that she can bear a child there.' Recalling this, Gengosoo said:

> Other similar slander and accusations were said against me, and I had not a soul who stood by me or supported me. I said nothing and went to work with Elsie Walther until October 1964 when she left to get married in Australia. I was left alone in the work until 1965 when Sister Violet Stang arrived. [97]

Gengosoo and Sister Violet travelled through the ten circuits of the Lae District, gathering women, expounding the Scriptures to them, and stimulating them to take an active part in the congregations to 'declare the wonderful works of God'. In Gengosoo's words:

> I am devoted to this work now and have no desire to leave it. I feel strongly that God has called me for this work as the words in John 15:16 say, 'I have chosen you for Myself. And I put you to work so that you may go and bear fruit, fruit that will last.' [98]

Gabby Gedisa from Laukano village, Malalo, came to the Gejamsao office after a year of teacher-training at Rintebe in 1972. Among her circuits there are four in which there is a particular language-barrier: Kaintiba, Aseki, Menyamya, and Wantoat. There the message is not getting through because the women do not speak Pidgin, and the young girls are not happy to meet with the women. But she says:

544

Now that we have begun to develop the *Was long Sipsip* program for the women, I hope that the work will run better. We also need follow-up visits of our women's workers who were trained in the four girls' schools of the church. We need more printed material in Pidgin which our women can use at the grass-roots level. [99]

In 1980, Gabby attended a course in Fiji. Since then, she has realized the need to cooperate more with other organizations such as the Welfare Office, YWCA, CWA, and Morobe Women's Association. She is now the vice-president of the Morobe Women's Association and also the leader of the Jabem Gejamsao. Through these positions, she considers she is able to explain to the women in the village the program of the government, and to bring the work of the church into the government's program. She adds:

I thank God for giving me strength to do this work; I know that I have not always worked well, but I do know that it is God who leads and guides me. [100]

The church saw the necessity for women's work. However, at the same time, it was cautious that this program should not develop into something apart from the church, but always remain integrated in the life of the church.

A Program Develops in the Kate District

In the Kate District, the first girls' school was opened at Raong in 1961, with 56 students. Irmgard Bergmann (Germany) was the first teacher, and Basanu Habu the matron. In the same year, the second teacher, Traude Hofmann (Australia), arrived. Irmgard Bergmann wrote of those times:

One cannot say that the woman has no rights in everyday life. A man who had married a woman from another clan brought his daughter to me at Raong. He looked lovingly at her, and to me he said strongly, 'Be sure nothing happens to this girl! I trust you. I give her into your hands. She belongs to my wife, but I have paid much money to the relatives of my wife. Now she is mine!' Note that she was his own daughter. [101]

Apart from the routine subjects at the school, much time was spent teaching the girls sewing and embroidery, and how to teach Sunday school. In March 1962, the Women's World Day of Prayer was observed for the first time in the Kate District.

Basanu Habu (centre) talking to women.

545

Toward the end of 1962, Dorothea Wagner (Germany) began Bible study for the women at Sattelberg, where her husband was the missionary. She gathered the women from 12 villages belonging to the Wemo congregation, and every Saturday afternoon about 200 attended. After the Wagners left for Logaweng, the Wemo women continued with their weekly Bible studies, and Basanu Habu helped them greatly. In 1965, for the first time at a Kate District conference, the women had their own meeting, and Dorothea Wagner gave the Bible study. It was at this time that the Sattelberg women declared the beginning of women's work, and asked for Irmgard Bergmann to be called specifically for this task.

A statement of the Kate District on women's work in 1964 relates, among other things:

> We shall not see the women's work and the women's meetings in the congregation as something new or foreign. It was the Word of God that brought and still brings a new honour and social standing for the woman. Therefore women's work shall not become a separate function of the congregation. The Christian life is not only meant for men but also for women. We need Christian mothers who will bring up their children in a Christian way, that is, if we want better Christian families. Therefore women's work and the women's meetings shall be part of the congregational life. The leaders of the congregation, the pastors and elders, must therefore take an active part in these meetings. They shall choose a suitable Christian woman to be the leader of the women's work and of their meetings in specific areas. The main fruit of these women's meetings shall be practical love for the neighbour and works of mercy. This shall be directed mainly towards the elderly and sick in the villages, who are often neglected. They shall be visited, helped and advised. The main function of the woman lies in the bringing up of her children. The mothers are the best and first teachers of their children. [102]

Irmgard Bergmann returned from Germany in February 1966 to begin the women's work of the Kate District. She had no co-workers or guidelines, and made Sattelberg her headquarters. The Saturday afternoon Bible study meeting still continued, and a sewing lesson was added. Much time was spent travelling through the circuits. Circuit President Honeo and his wife went to Dedua in the

Sattelberg circuit with Irmgard to introduce women's work. The same was done in the other circuits over the next months.

In April 1966, the first seven girls were trained in a three-month course at Sattelberg. More buildings were needed for a school to be established there, but the work went ahead. The next year, 18 girls were trained in a four-month course.

There were varied reactions on the part of the men in the Kate District toward women's work. District President Mufuanu and Circuit President Honeo were positive and helpful, but people in the villages were often sceptical, and even opposed the idea. Two young ex-students from Sattelberg, Heninipe and Mumure (and later, Mukjak), came to be co-workers with Irmgard. Every year there were trips and courses to train more workers. In response to an invitation in 1969, Mrs Bergmann and Mrs Honeo visited Hagen, Chimbu, and Goroka districts to introduce women's work. A trip to Tiripini followed in 1970, where there was to be the first baptism, and the idea was to encourage the practice of monogamy. 'Never again!' writes Irmgard, without further comment. [103]

Heninipe and Mumure often took over the work on the station. Heninipe visited Germany in 1974, and was married that same year soon after her return. Heninipe writes:

> Now that I am married, I still work with the women. I have come to realize more the difficulties women have in doing this work, but I have also come to see the fruits of the work of the Holy Spirit, the change the Word of God has brought about in women. I thank God for this. [104]

It was only in 1974 that the women's work of the Kate District first had its own budget. Buildings were financed through gifts both from overseas and from the offerings of all the Kate vilages. The latter each gave £1.0.0 to finance a house for the girls.

In 1975, Irmgard Bergmann married the missionary Helmut Horndasch. The Women's Worker training school was taken over by Fare from Boana (who had already done five years of teaching), and Dapeo of Kabwum (who had just finished teacher-training at Heldsbach).

Ten years earlier, Dapeo Qafirigu's parents had wanted her to take the Sunday school course which was offered in 1965, but she refused. As she herself later said: 'I was not

Irmgard Horndasch and Dapeo.

interested. All I wanted to do was plant my garden, feed the pigs, and find a boy-friend.' [105] A mere two years later, she was ready to take that course. When she told her parents, her mother laughed and said: 'How come you are wanting to do this work now? For two years you turned your back on it!' However, when they realized that she was serious, they promptly agreed and encouraged her.

When Dapeo returned from the course and tried to gather the children together for Sunday school, she met with opposition. The people were not clear about her intentions or her work. One man closed the church doors; the village schoolteacher closed his classrooms to her; as a result, she had nowhere to meet with the children. However, she eventually found a small house which served as her Sunday-school room. She says: 'God cannot be found only in the church. I know He was with us in the little bush-house.' [106]

When a call came in 1969 for young girls to go to Sattelberg to train as women's workers, Dapeo was chosen to go. Her parents told her: 'We put you in God's hands. You must follow

Him. If you die or harm befalls you, we will still be happy.' [107]

After five years at the school, Dapeo was sent to Germany to receive two years' further training at Hesselberg. Upon her return, the work of the Sattelberg school and the District women's work were separated. Today, Hofagao from Garaina, Epe from Kabwum, and Depo from the Highlands are the teachers, and Dapeo is the leader of the District work. She travels most of the year, visiting the nine circuits and the women's workers at the grass-roots level. She holds courses and speaks about the work with the women whenever she gets a chance. Dapeo writes about her work:

I believe that God calls His workers into the work. The garden is very big, and much work needs to be done. The life of the church is not at the national level, but at the grassroots, in each house, each family. Many are hungry for the Word of God. They are Christians, but they need to be fed with the Word of God. Much needs to be done to strengthen the faith of all — men, women, and children — so they come to know the Triune God. [108]

547

Women's Work in the Goroka District

The District of the Eastern Highlands, Goroka, has its Women's Worker training school at Tarabo. This school was begun in 1963 by Maria Gedisa from Hopoi in the Jabem District. Maria was one of the first graduates of the Bula girls' school, and one of the first New Guinean teachers at Bula, teaching there for five years before undertaking her teacher-training at Rintebe. After her graduation, she was asked to start Tarabo Girls School. She said: 'Yes, I'll do it. This is my work!' [109] She began with 72 girls, taking one class in the morning, and another in the afternoon. Since 1981, Waizo Addy from Kalasa teaches at the school. Elaine Schutz, wife of the Tarabo missionary Rodney Schutz (Australia), helps to carry the load.

Women's work in the town of Goroka started in 1970, with Lissy Schuster from Germany and Sila Esori as the first workers. When Lissy left in 1974, Sila continued the work. Although she has had only three years' schooling at Kewamugl, she gathers the women for Bible study and prayer in each of the compounds. The women make and gather presents for the evangelists and pastors at Christmas. They visit mothers with a new baby and bring food. Hanna Ahrens also has helped Sila with the work in the hospital and the prison.

In 1981, Gisela Hamann from Germany and her co-worker Wahayu Salaki were appointed to the women's work in this District. Wahayu comes from the Finintugu Circuit, and was trained at Onerunka Bible School for four years. After working for one year in her circuit, she spent a year with Basanu Habu at Kundiawa to learn more about the work.

Wahayu says about her work:

There are many problems in our work, and I often feel like running away, but God is always near. He strengthens me and I am happy to do His work. There is still a great need to work with the women and children in our District. [110]

Gisela Hamann comments on the work:

Wahayu and I would not have been able to do the work without Mama Sila's help. She has a lot of experience, and it was a great blessing that she joined us in this work. [111]

The ten circuits of the District have been visited over the last years, and one-week courses have been held for the women. These courses have been well attended, and the women are eager

548

and cheerful listeners. A literacy course has also been started for women, many of whom are illiterate. Their children all go to school, but they themselves have never had the chance. The pastors and evangelists in the Goroka District were very reserved at first in regard to women's work, but this has changed lately. Elders and pastors are interested in the work, and now even offer help with Bible studies and other lessons. In some circuits, the men are attending the meetings, too. It seems they have come to realize how very important the work with the women is for the church, the home, and the family.

Hagen District Women's Work

The women's work in the Hagen District is slowly developing. Many problems have caused the closure of the Women's Worker training school at Tiria, but it is hoped that soon this school will function again. Women like Deaconess Leona Zadow from Australia and the missionaries' wives Bernice Imbrock (USA), Renate Menzel, and Hedwig Hertle (both from Germany), helped the work.

Noman Wapi, who finished her training at Baitabag in 1981, is now the leader of the work for the Hagen and Southern Highlands districts with their 17 circuits. Noman experiences many difficulties, mainly relating to the vast distances she has to travel, and the fact that there are still tribal fights in the area. 'But the women are eager to receive the Word of God, and are always happy to see me', [112] she says.

Chimbu District

The beginnings of women's work in the Chimbu District go back to 1964 when Linda Hahn (USA) and later Margaret Jericho (Australia) began work there. The latter concentrated mainly on Religious Instruction lessons for schools. [113]

Basanu Habu came to the Chimbu in 1972 and began work in the District's eleven circuits in 1973. She has had an interesting career. Basanu's home was at Sattelberg. In the early 1950s, she worked as a house-girl for the Metzner family, where she learnt many things which benefited her later when she trained as a nurse at Yagaum. She became matron for the girls at Raong, and later house-mother for the nurses at Yagaum Hospital. At Banz she

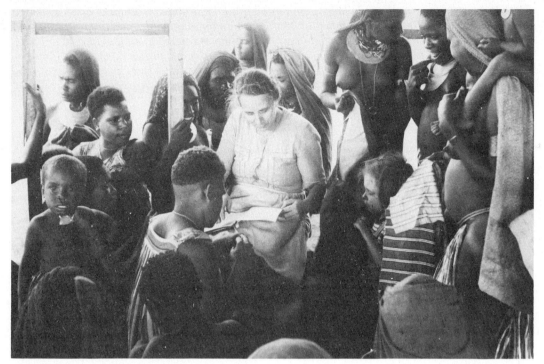

Mrs H. Hertle at a Womens' Meeting.

attended a leadership training course. The first of her several visits to Germany was the first visit by a woman from Papua New Guinea to that country. At that time she trained at Hesselberg.[114] She now resides in Kundiawa, from where she directs the women's work in the Chimbu District.

One-week courses are held in all circuits, with up to 200 women attending some of them. Basanu teaches the women Christian family life, Bible studies, Sunday school, stewardship, literacy, and other ways to help the work of the church. Dagang, the wife of the late District President Baniepe, is now Basanu's co-worker. She attends all the courses and helps with them.

A great deal of opposition is faced in the work. Discussing her work, Basanu reported:

> Many of the women do not understand the work. All they think of is how to get a good name and make money through business, thinking that their offerings will bring the cargo. Men too are doubtful about the purpose of women's work. If it brings no cargo, they consider that there is no point in doing the work. This applies mainly to the townspeople. My circuit work makes me happy.

To those who oppose her, she answers:

> God has appointed me to do this work. I shall die in it. You cannot close my mouth, for I shall continue with the work. A woman who wants to do this work must be united with Jesus Christ. The talk of people cannot harm one. All that you have and all you are, you must give to the work of God.[115]

Siassi

Prior to 1958, the only students at the Gelem school on Rooke Island, Siassi, were married men. It was Joan Eckermann (Australia), wife of missionary Con Eckermann, the headmaster, who recognized that the wives of these men would have to receive some training if they were to be good help-mates for their husbands later. First of all, these girls were taught hygiene, and learnt to use soap and water daily. It was not long before they had their first sewing lesson. In 1958, when married men no longer were accepted at the school, and the school became co-educational, Joan Eckermann started a class with five young schoolgirls, teaching them Bible stories, cooking, sewing, and child-care. Each year the number of students increased, and sewing

549

classes became a routine subject every afternoon. By 1963, there were 90 girls at the school, at first very shy, but quickly gaining confidence through their training.[116]

Deaconess Vida Mibus from Australia was called to Siassi as a women's worker. However, as there was a shortage of teachers at Gelem, she was appointed to become a full-time teacher instead. Vida and many of her co-workers left a deep influence on the women of Siassi. Hundreds of girls who passed through the station schools were changed to a greater or lesser degree by the education they received, and they in turn have influenced others at home.[117]

Apart from the schools, there were also the many missionary wives who trained girls in their homes, or who worked with the wives of the station workers. At one stage, the government welfare officer was invited to introduce the idea of women's clubs to the islands. At first this was successful, but enthusiasm later waned.

Since 1973, a number of young girls from Siassi have been trained as women's workers at Baitabag, and have returned to their homes to continue to work with the women in the villages.

In 1982, Dora Steven was appointed to be the leader of women's work on Siassi. Dora herself had been a schoolgirl at Gelem High School, and then did teacher-training at Balob Teachers College. Now married, she runs courses for the women in different areas and at the District centre.

> We teach the women Bible study, cooking, sewing, nutrition and health. Many women attend and are happy to learn more. One of the main problems we face on Siassi is that there is need to go out to villages and small islands, but there is no transport.[118]

Menyamya

Deaconess Merna Thamm was called in 1955 to work among the women and girls in the Menyamya field.[119] Three years later, when restrictions in the outlying areas were lifted, she left Menyamya station in 1958 to start a school for girls at Kwaikuma. There were 28 girls in the first class, many of them already having been marked for a future husband though only nine or ten years old. In July 1963, a girls' school was begun on Concordia station. Three of the original 28 girls at Kwaikuma were among the

Merna Thamm started working at Menyamya in 1955. Today she teaches at Martin Luther Seminary.

18 girls in the new school. Besides the usual school subjects, the girls learnt sewing, hygiene, cooking, and gardening methods, as well as other things which could better equip them for the role of Christian wife and mother. As mothers, they would be able to teach their children a God-pleasing way of life from infancy on in their homes. Today, local women's workers who have been trained at Baitabag are working with the women in the villages throughout the Menyamya area.

The Seminaries

Work with the women is also being given attention today at the three theological seminaries: Martin Luther Seminary at Lae, the Highlands Seminary at Ogelbeng, and Senior Flierl Seminary at Logaweng/Finschhafen. The wives of the students are being taught a regular course, either by the wives of the lecturers at the seminaries or by a women's worker. The aim is to equip these women, some of whom are illiterate, to be a greater help to their husbands in the ministry, and to be able to teach both their own children and other women in the villages.

The women's work of the Evangelical Lutheran Church of Papua New Guinea is formally organized on congregational, circuit, district, and national levels. Women's work falls under the ELC-PNG Evangelism Department, and in the past has been the responsibility of the director of the department.

In 1981, the position of full-time women's coordinator was created to take over women's work on the national level. Currently, the district and circuit levels of the church have full-time women's leaders, whereas congregational and parish levels rely on volunteers.

Samarida Yamu from Bukawa is the first women's co-ordinator. She was born in 1960 in Tigidu. After her four years of high school, she was able to study theology at Martin Luther Seminary in Lae. Sama considers that

> the women's work of ELC-PNG is decentralized and slowly progressing. It is a new task for our church, and we are still struggling to come up with a clear organization in which our women can see for themselves the purposes and challenges of women's work. [120]

The national women's committee meets twice a year to plan the work in the districts. Every two years, there is a week-long national course for the women of ELC-PNG. Support for such courses comes directly from the women, and not from the national office. In these courses, the women study the Word of God, learn more about their role as Christian women, and take up the responsibilities of an altar guild.

Sama in 1984 made the pertinent comment:

> What the women of ELC-PNG lack is leadership training. In June 1985 there will be the very first leadership course for the District leaders and for teachers of the Seminary women's courses, girls' schools, and women's worker training schools. LWF has been asked to subsidize this course. [121]

In the development of the women's program of the church, there is much evidence of courageous witness and dedication, quietly and unobtrusively carried out. The power and blessing of God can be clearly seen in the work that has been done. But very much still needs to be accomplished to give spiritual help to Christian wives, mothers, and other women, young and old, in these rapidly-changing and difficult times.

Endnotes

[1] Theodore Braun, in *75 Jahre Neuguinea-Mission 1886-1961*, H. Neumeyer, ed. (Neuendettelsau: Missionsanstalt, 1961), 24.

[2] Irmgard Bergmann, *Women's Work in a Changing Rural Society* (unpublished, 1969), 15.

[3] Theodore Braun/Christa Lindner, 'Der Dienst am kranken Menschen', in Wolfram von Krause, ed., *Junges Neuguinea* (Neuendettelsau: Freimund Verlag, n.d.), 193.

[4] Quoted by Georg Pilhofer, *Die Geschichte der neuendettelsauer Mission in Neuguinea* (Neuendettelsau: Friemund Verlag, 1961-63), I, 82.

[5] *Ibid.*

[6] Ellen Kettle, *That They Might Live* (Sydney: F.P. Leonard, 1979), 6. For short biographical references to Lutheran Mission personnel (until 1960), see E.A. Jericho, *Seedtime and Harvest in New Guinea* (Adelaide: UELCA New Guinea Mission Board, 1961) 79-157.

[7] *Junges Neuguinea*, 193.

[8] E. Kettle, *That They Might Live*, 28.

[9] W. Flierl, *Miti Fua Ngeing Ewec* (Madang: Lutheran Mission Press, 1962), 191.

[10] F. Braun and C.V. Sheatsley, *On Both Sides of the Equator* (Columbus, Ohio: The Lutheran Book Concern, 1937), 115.

[11] *Ibid.*

[12] E. Kettle, *That They Might Live*, 48.

[13] F. Braun and C.S. Sheatsley, *On Both Sides of the Equator*, 128.

[14] *Ibid*, 129.

[15] Dr Th. Braun, Personal Conversation, 1968.

[16] Th. Braun, Personal Conversation, 1968.

[16] Th. Braun, in *Junges Neuguinea*, 194.

[17] Margaret Cramer, 'People Call them "Mama" and "Papa"', *Post-Courier* (July 21, 1969), 8.

[18] *Junges Neuguinea*, 194.

[19] Albert C. Frerichs, *Anutu Conquers in New Guinea* (Columbus, Ohio: The Wartburg Press, 1957), 60.

[20] Karl Kirsch, Personal Correspondence, 1984.

[21] E. Kettle, *That They Might Live*, 50.

[22] Dr Agnes M. Hoeger, Personal Correspondence, 1984.

[23] Margaret Cramer, 'Japanese Took Them into Captivity', *Post-Courier* (July 22, 1969), 4.

[24] Siming-Fulalek Interview, 7.9.1981.

[25] *Ibid.*

[26] LMNG Medical Report, 1946.

[27] Quoted by A. Frerichs, *Anutu Conquers in New Guinea*, 77.

[28] LMNG Medical Report, 1946.

[29] Kito, Personal Correspondence, 1984.

[30] Dr A. Hoeger, Personal Interview, 1983.

[31] E. Kettle, *That They Might Live*, 217.

[32] LMNG Medical Report, 1948.

[33] E. Kettle, *That They Might Live*, 217.

[34] Christa Lindner, *Lutherische Schwesternschule, Yagaum, Neuguinea* (unpublished, 1971), 1.

[35] LMNG Report, 1947.

[36] Siming-Fulalek Interview, 7.9.81.

[37] Ch. Lindner, *Lutherische Schwesternschule,* 2.

[38] Merla Garrett, Personal Correspondence, 1985.

[39] Wilson Waesa, Personal Correspondence, 1984.

[40] M. Garrett, Personal Correspondence, 1985.

[41] ELC-PNG Annual Report, 1978.

[42] Ken Cramer, Personal Correspondence, 1984.

[43] Margaret Voigt, Personal Correspondence, 1984.

[44] *Highland News* (August 1972), 22.

[45] Dr Mary Guntner, Personal Correspondence, 1984.

[46] Report on 8th Synod, Ogelbeng, 1970, res. 10.

[47] Lutheran Medical Services Board Minutes, February 15-16, 1971, res. 2:71 and 3:71.

[48] *Concordia, 67* (Neuendettelsau, September 1982), 25.

[49] W. Waesa, Personal Correspondence, 1984.

[50] Karl Kirsch, Personal Correspondence, 1984.

[51] E. Kettle, *That They Might Live,* 217.

[52] Among Ruawe, Personal Correspondence, 1984.

[53] Jama Ruawe, Personal Correspondence, 1984.

[54] Fuawe Somanu, Personal Interview, 1984.

[55] Dr M. Guntner, Personal Correspondence, 1984.

[56] Dr Kahu Sugoho, Personal Correspondence, 1970.

[57] Dr M. Guntner, Personal Correspondence, 1984.

[58] Barbara Dolling, Personal Correspondence, 1984.

[59] *Ibid.*

[60] Mamba Katur, Personal Correspondence, 1984.

[61] Edwin Tscharke, Personal Correspondence, 1984.

[62] Edwin Tscharke, *A Quarter Century of Healing* (Madang: Kristen Pres, 1973), 10.

[63] *Ibid.*

[64] E. Tscharke, Personal Correspondence, 1984.

[65] E. Tscharke, *A Quarter Century of Healing,* 20.

[66] E. Tscharke, Personal Correspondence, 1984.

[67] K. Kirsch, Personal Correspondence, 1984.

[68] *New Guinea Lutheran, 23* (September 1984), 15.

[69] K. Kirsch, Personal Correspondence, 1984.

[70] ELC-PNG Missionary Report, Maria Horn, 1983.

[71] LMNG Reports, C. Pfarr, 1948-1953.

[72] E. Kettle, *That They Might Live,* 237.

[73] ELC-PNG Missionary Reports, Sinika Multanen, 1983.

[74] R.M. Berndt, 'A Devastating Disease Syndrome', *Sociologus* 8, (1968), 114-128.

[75] LMNG Annual Report 1960, Eva Hasselbusch.

[76] E. Kettle, *That They Might Live,* 260.

[77] Chr. Lindner, *Laughing Death on the Last Unknown* (unpublished, 1966).

[78] Rita Fenske, Personal Correspondence, 1984.

[79] *Ibid.*

[80] E. Kettle, *That They Might Live,* 222.

[81] *The Challenge, 4* (1966), 43.

[82] Barbara Dolling, Personal Correspondence, 1984.

[83] Ken Cramer, Personal Correspondence, 1984.

[84] *The Challenge, 4 (1966), 14.*

[85] *Ibid,* 16.

[86] K. Cramer, Personal Correspondence, 1984.

[87] *The Challenge, 5* (1967), 43.

[88] Hans Wagner, in *Junges Neuguinea,* 103.

[89] Hilde Schoettler, Personal Correspondence, 1984.

[90] *The Challenge, 6* (1968), 32.

[91] H. Schoettler, Personal Correspondence, 1984.

[92] Ahigol, Personal Interview, May 1984.

[93] Mojou, Personal Interview, May 1984.

[94] *Concordia, 65* (Neuendettelsau, June 1980), 76.

[95] Gabby Gedisa, Personal Correspondence, 1984.

[96] *The Challenge, 9* (1971), 39.

[97] *Ibid.*

[98] *Ibid.*

[99] G. Gedisa, Personal Correspondence, 1984.

[100] *Ibid.*

[101] *Junges Neuguinea,* 105.

[102] *Ibid,* 104.

[103] I. Horndasch, Personal Correspondence, 1984.

[104] Heninipe Kuria, Personal Correspondence, 1984.

[105] Dapeo Qafiriju, Personal Correspondence, 1984.

[106] *Ibid.*

[107] *Ibid.*

[108] *Ibid.*

[109] *The Challenge, 8* (1970), 25.

[110] Wahaju Salaki, Personal Correspondence, 1984.

[111] Gisela Hamann, Personal Correspondence, 1984.

[112] Noman Wapi, Personal Correspondence, 1984.

[113] Basanu Habu, Personal Interview, January 1985.

[114] *Concordia, 65* (Neuendettelsau, June 1980), 55-56.

[115] Basanu Habu, Personal Interview, January 1985.

[116] *The Challenge, 2* (1964), 42.

[117] *The Challenge, 6 (1968), 28.*

[118] Dora Steven, Personal Correspondence, 1984.

[119] *The Challenge, 2* (1964), 10.

[120] Samarida Yamu, Personal Correspondence, 1984.

[121] *Ibid.*

Unprinted source material
Interviews and Tape Recordings:
Ahin Ahigol, 1984; Habu Basanu, 1985; Theodore Braun, 1968; Agnes M. Hoeger, 1983; Saulgeria Mojau, 1984; Fulalek, 7.9.1981; Siming, 7.9.1981.

Personal Correspondence:
Ken Cramer, 1984; Barbara Dolling, 1984; Rita Fenske, 1984; Somanu Fuawe, 1984; Merla Garrett, 1985; Gabby Gedisa, 1984; Mary Guntner, 1984; Dolores Hall, 1984; Gisela Hamann, 1984; Agnes Hoeger, 1983; Irmgard Horndasch, 1984; Mamba Katur, 1985; Karl Kirsch, 1984; Heninepe Kuria, 1984; Wapi Noman, 1984; Dapeoc Qafirigu, 1984; Among Ruawe, 1984; Jama Ruawe, 1984; Hilde Schoettler, 1984; Dora Steven, 1984; Kahu Sugoho, 1970; Edwin Tscharke, 1984; Margaret Voigt, 1984; Wilson Waesa, 1984; Salaki Wahayu, 1984; Sama Yamu, 1985.

Chapter 18:

The Socio-Economic Concern of the Church

by Wilhelm Fugmann

New Guinea 100 years ago was an unknown country to the missionary fathers who arrived on its shores. There were no roads, no cars, no ships, and no shops. In order to survive, they had to build their own houses and grow their own food. The most basic requirements for the survival had to be imported. With the help of their New Guinean friends, they built roads and houses, churches and schools. Later on, they brought ships and cars and aeroplanes to enable the *Miti* (Word of God) to travel beyond the horizon. The story of the church's socio-economic concern is also the story of many missionaries from overseas who were not ordained to the Ministry of the Word.

Now the time has come when national church leaders are at the helm. It is the time when overseas missionaries have to give a true account of stewardship. May this account be acceptable in the eyes of God and also in the eyes of our New Guinean brothers and sisters. We built the scaffold to enable the church to grow. The time has now come when the scaffold must be removed, so that the church may grow in 'breadth and length and height and depth' (Eph. 3:18).

The Supply Service

The first missionaries were anything but private evangelists going to an unknown country to preach the Gospel. They were commissioned by their home churches, and provided with the means to carry out their task. They were expected to be good stewards in the use of such means, and to give regular accounts.

Finschhafen 1886-1914

For the first three months after landing in New Guinea, Johann Flierl had no particular worries about looking after his bodily needs. The German Governor von Schleinitz invited him to have meals at the government canteen. In October, after Karl Tremel had arrived, the two missionaries decided to open up a mission station at Simbang. Now they had to fend for themselves. The first financial account[1] which Flierl sent to his home board covered the time from July 12, 1886, to March 30, 1887, and amounted to £202.14.0. In 1889, Georg Pfalzer arrived in New Guinea. Besides his missionary work, he was given the job of business manager/treasurer. He carried this dual role through until his retirement.[2]

During the first five years, the missionaries could obtain their supplies from the German New Guinea Company, which had its headquarters at Finschhafen. According to a directive from Berlin, the New Guinea Company was 'to supply the missionaries as far as possible and let them have groceries and other supplies at reduced prices'.[3] The New Guinea Company at that time was also responsible for the administration of the new colony. Thus, it had to have a large European staff. When, in 1891, an epidemic broke out and killed 13 out of 40 staff, the rest decided to give up that 'unhealthy place' and to move to Madang. In vain they tried to convince the missionaries to follow them. Flierl and his compatriots decided to stay and take the risk of being on their own and far away from any source of supply.

With the exodus of the New Guinea Company, the missionaries had to arrange for a common purchasing agency. The nearest supply base was at Madang, approximately 240 kilometres away. Thus, in 1892 Georg Pfalzer wrote to his home board: 'In future we have to do our purchasing on a communal basis'.[4]

Besides satisfying their own needs, the missionaries obtained the much-wanted steel goods for their New Guinean neighbours. Trading itself became a valuable means of communication, and it may well be said that the constantly improving relationship between missionaries and New Guineans was due in no small degree to the exchange of goods. The Mission supplied the tools, and the New Guineans the vegetables and potatoes. All mission stations had small boarding schools, and the white men not only taught the schoolboys reading and writing, but also handed them seeds and plants of new products such as corn, pineapple, and pawpaw.

The mission supply house at that time was at Simbang. Every two months, a coastal ship would call at Langemak Bay to unload supplies and mail. In 1901, a change took place. The New Guinea Company decided to start a coconut plantation at Finschhafen. Now Finschhafen, which for the last ten years had been a forgotten place, came to life again. Since the shipping company would not call at two

Georg Pfalzer in front of his house at Pola (1892).

556

places, and decided in favour of Finschhafen, the missionaries at Simbang were left high and dry. The mission reacted quickly by acquiring a piece of land at Finschhafen to build a mission station combined with a supply house. The new station was known as Pola. From then on, Pfalzer was the missionary and business manager at Finschhafen. In 1904, he was also appointed Imperial Postmaster. The work at Pola grew to such an extent that Pfalzer was unable to look after his spiritual work as well as the supply and finance of the mission. An additional missionary, Georg Stuerzenhofecker, had to be called. By 1908, the Lutherans had established 14 mission stations, in addition to a sawmill, a printery, a health station, and two plantations. In Mr Friedrich Laur a store manager was found who was able to take over the receiving and distribution of goods. The mission had become a big undertaking, and trade stores were part and parcel of the general service.

The New Guineans made full use of the opportunities to sell their vegetables, sweet potatoes, tobacco, and copra to the mission, and in turn buy salt, kerosene, and steel goods. Mission trade stores have often been criticized by outsiders, but they have not known what they were talking about. As late as 1939, there was no trading facility between Lae and Madang, except one store owned by a Chinese trader. The people had to rely on mission trade stores. It may well be said that this service was part of the Lutheran understanding of serving the whole man. The groundwork had been laid for a development which later was followed up by Namasu and/or the Cooperatives.

The final goal of the first generation of missionaries was to become economically independent of overseas contributions. On December 16, 1907, Johann Flierl wrote to his home board:

> Most probably, of all the German missions working overseas, ours is the one which costs the least. On the stations we keep dairy cattle, poultry, and we even raise pigs. My ideal would be a mission-church which works without contributions from outside. [5]

Developments at Madang

The Rhenish Mission had started mission work at Madang by sending Wilhelm Thomas and Friedrich Eich to New Guinea in 1887.

In terms of supply and communication, the missionaries around Madang had a somewhat easier start. The New Guinea Company had established itself at Bogadjim and later Madang. Madang was a port of call for overseas ships. There were stores at Madang, and consequently there was no need for a common purchasing agency. Another feature was that the missionaries received a full salary, and each one had to fend for himself. Finschhafen had the communal system, which meant that everything for living was provided, except personal items, and the mission staff received 1,000 Marks pocket-money per year. At Madang, the missionaries had to buy groceries and kitchen utensils, and if they wanted poultry and cattle, they paid out of their own pocket. In Finschhafen, everything was common property. The missionaries at Madang were more free and independent. The Finschhafen staff, however, grew together to be a more closed community. The Madang system was the more expensive as far as overall expenditure was concerned. In a report by the Director of the Rhenish Mission, dated 27/8/1909, we read:

> The proximity of the European settlement (at Madang) makes itself felt even in another way. The expenses in relation to the very narrow strip of country which we have occupied around Madang are very high. [6]

It could be said that the Rhenish Mission at that time was not an economic unit as was Finschhafen, but a group of largely independent mission stations. Thus, the role of the man in charge of the finance at Madang was not nearly as important as at Finschhafen. In Madang, Wilhelm Blum had taken care of the books for many years, besides doing his spiritual work.

Developments Since the First World War (1914-1939)

Georg Pfalzer had served the mission for 25 years. His last job was arranging and supervising the building of a motor schooner at Rabaul. Together with Captain Jericho, he brought the new ship, which was called *Bavaria*, to Finschhafen. Meanwhile, the Mission had been in the process of building a large 130x36 feet supply house. This had become an urgent necessity, since large and varied stocks, ranging from an anchor to safety pins, had to be kept.

Supply House, Finschhafen (1914).

The trading section played an important role, and goods were imported from Australia, Germany, and the East. The Mission was not unprepared for Pfalzer's retirement. Already since 1911, Missionary Johann Ruppert had served as a second man at Pola. Since he had been a banker prior to his theological training, he was able to fill the vacant position very well.

When in August 1914 World War I broke out, the Mission Supply House was well stocked with goods of every description. This proved to be a great advantage, because Finschhafen was immediately cut off from the outside world. Johann Flierl wrote in a letter dated February 20, 1915: 'Our coastal vessel was last here in July last year. For seven months we have now been cut off. We are, at the moment, 50 adults and 30 children stationed at over 18 different places.'[7] After such a long time, the shortage was being felt, and the Mission introduced a rationing system. Contract labourers had to be paid off. There was a shortage of diesel fuel for the *Bavaria*, and also a shortage of medicine. The little group of missionaries far away from their homeland was hard pressed. The natural thing was to look to their Lutheran friends in

558

Australia. After all, Flierl's wife was an Australian pastor's daughter, and there were Australians serving in the Mission. From the very beginning, the Australian Lutherans were partners in the common work. Many of their pastors had studied at Neuendettelsau. Among them was F. Otto Theile, pastor at Bethany near Brisbane. He had always been regarded as a great friend of the New Guinea mission. To him Johann Flierl wrote, asking for help. Meanwhile, Theile, on his own, had already organized a relief consignment for New Guinea.

Another church which had always shown great interest in the work in New Guinea was the Iowa Synod in the United States. Many pastors of that church hailed form Germany, and had studied at Neuendettelsau. Some years prior to the war, Johann Flierl had made a trip to the United States to interest the Lutherans in the New Guinea work. Now this paid off. Already before the war, the American Lutherans had collected approximately 50,000 Marks per year, and sent it regularly to Neuendettelsau. Now, instead of sending it there, they transferred the money to Pastor Theile. These moneys, together with the Australian contributions, helped to send at least the most important supplies to the hard-stricken area. The Rhenish missionaries at Madang were not left out, although they were not directly connected with the Lutheran bodies in Australia, Germany, and the United States. They were, however, friends and co-workers in the great task of bringing the Gospel to the people in New Guinea. The Director of the Rhenish Mission, Pastor Kriele, wrote about this much later: 'It will never be forgotten what the Australian and American Lutherans did for the Rhenish Mission'. [8] Johann Flierl, the senior missionary at Finschhafen, wrote in a similar way: 'Through the love and support of our friends and brethren in the United States and Australia the Lord sustained us right through the terrible war years'. [9]

In spite of all the shortages, privation, and anxieties, the war years passed without a serious incident. Then peace came. What about the future? The contributions and value of the relief consignment which had been sent to New Guinea amounted to £35,000. This had been just enough to keep the Mission going. However, now the storehouses, larders, and cash boxes were depleted. Houses and physical plants had deteriorated because of shortage of funds. The missionaries' salaries had not been paid for more than four years. What would happen to the orphaned missions? It was touch and go.

The Lutherans could have lost their Mission Field for political and/or financial reasons. The political side was quite obvious. The Australian Government, which was the new master of the colony, did not want German missionaries. They wanted to hand over the Lutheran work to a different denomination.

It was at that time that the world-wide connections of Neuendettelsau began to bear fruit. The Australian and American Lutherans rallied and acted. The President of the Iowa Synod in the United States, Dr F. Richter, went to Australia, and through his good offices Australian Lutherans joined hands, thus opening the way for a common takeover of the Lutheran work in New Guinea. On May 12, 1921, a directive by the Australian Government entrusted the Lutheran work in New Guinea to the newly-formed United Evangelical Lutheran Church in Australia, which was to run this work

jointly with the Iowa Synod. A Board of control, comprised of Australian nationals, was formed. Its duty was to control fully all property of the former Neuendettelsau and Rhenish Mission Societies. These societies had ceased to exist, as far as the Australian Government was concerned. The Lutheran Mission New Guinea had been born. The Director of this new Lutheran Mission was Pastor F.O. Theile, whose office was situated in Brisbane. In him the Lord had provided the Mission with an outstanding personality, who until his death in 1945 served the Mission well and faithfully. Theile made many trips to New Guinea, and represented the Mission to the Government. He was the financial coordinator between the various churches and the treasury in New Guinea. A man of outstanding organizational talents, he knew his mission inside out. He had the gift of bringing together the three nationalities to work for the common goal.

Now that the new parties had taken over the work in New Guinea, the immediate financial worries for the Mission were over. The outstanding debts were paid, and the missionaries received their allowances. Many of them were ill and worn out, and overdue for furlough. Some of them took the opportunity for a vacation in Australia. New staff arrived from the United States, as well as from Australia.

Within the business section, the next 20 years were marked by many staff changes. In 1921, the first American couple who arrived at Madang were Mr and Mrs F. Knautz. Mr Knautz first worked together with the treasurer of the former Rhenish Mission, the Revd W. Blum. In 1925, when Blum left New Guinea, Mr Knautz took over the responsibility for the financial affairs of the district. After 1921, when the amalgamation of the two mission fields had taken place, it became obvious that it was wise to adopt the Finschhafen communal system also at Madang. This meant that a new mission supply house had to be found. This was started by Mr Knautz at Ragetta, and later transferred to Madang. In Finschhafen, Mr R. Laur, who had served the Mission for 17 years, had to leave because of ill-health. His successor was Mr Paul Deutscher, an Australian from Victoria. By 1928, Johann Ruppert had served the mission as a treasurer for more than 14 years. He was a very sick and worn-out man, who had carried the

Supply House, Madang (1921).

burden of finance at a most difficult time. He died soon after his return to Germany.

The next few years brought many changes. The German societies claimed a more active part in the work, which led to a number of conferences. For a while, the Rhenish Mission Society took over its former mission field at Madang. However, this arrangement lasted only three years. Since the Rhenish Mission had too many commitments in other parts of the world, it could not do justice to the Madang District and so it withdrew in 1932. After these somewhat painful changes, the Lutheran Mission Finschhafen was taken over by Neuendettelsau, and the Lutheran Mission Madang by the American Lutheran Church. Both organizations accepted Director F.O. Theile as coordinator and uniting link. Already in 1929, Neuendettelsau had sent out Mr Emil Daub, a trained accountant, to bring order to the books at Finschhafen. With Neuendettelsau now fully responsible for the work, it was felt that someone who had some knowledge of the home situation should be sent to assist at Finschhafen. The then acting-treasurer at Neuendettelsau, Mr Wilhelm Fugmann, was
560

sent out in 1933.

Both Fugmann and Daub worked well together, Daub being the business manager and Fugmann his assistant. This happy collaboration had to be interrupted in 1935, when Fugmann was transferred to Lae/Malahang to open up a branch of the Finschhafen supply house. This had become necessary because of the newly-begun mission work in the Highlands, and the acquisition of an aeroplane. After six months' ground-work, Fugmann was called back to Finschhafen to take over the managership of the Supply Centre. Daub had been called to be the secretary to the Superintendent, with special responsibility for land matters.

Fugmann's place at Lae/Malahang was taken over by Mr O. Wallent, who after a short time decided to train as mission pilot. In his place, Martin Boerner took over the branch. The second man in Finschhafen was Mr E. Guth, who had arrived from Germany in 1938.

Let us now turn back once more to the situation when Neuendettelsau took over the responsibility for staffing and financing the Lutheran Mission Finschhafen. In contrast to the Rhenish Mission, Neuendettelsau had only one mission field, that is, the New Guinea field. Under normal circumstances, both in terms of finance and personnel, the Bavarians could easily have done justice to the work. However, the depression in Germany in 1932 and soon after that the rise of the Nazi Government created extraordinary circumstances. Stringent currency regulations were introduced, and no money could leave Germany. The Lutheran Mission had grown to 26 outlets, including mission stations, a hospital, a printery, a health station, a building department, a supply house, an aviation as well as a shipping department, and, last but not least, the plantations. Already in 1932, the conference of missionaries decided to ask for a 10 per cent salary cut to alleviate the financial position. This meant that a married couple would receive an annual salary of £54. In 1935, the missionaries decided to take another 10 percent salary deduction in order to finance the purchase of a much-needed smaller coastal vessel, the M.V. *Velka*. [10]

In 1933, the Lutheran Missions had been asked by the Administrator of the country to open up mission stations among the hundreds of thousands of people living in the Central Highlands. How could any mission refuse such a call? Financially, this meant a further strain. In September 1933, the Mission was informed that in view of the scarcity of foreign exchange, the German Government had disallowed the sending of trade goods from Germany for the benefit of German missionaries. This was another blow. The Mission required cash for buying diesel oil, rice for the labour line, and many other things necessary for the running of such a large enterprise. During the first few years, the Mission managed somehow, mainly because of good copra prices. The situation deteriorated in later years. While in 1932 the copra prices were as high as £22 per ton, it went down to £7 in 1938. This meant a loss of income of between £5,000 to £7,000 per year. There was no other way but to cut down expenses wherever possible. In 1938, the Mission had to introduce a 20 per cent cut in all the station budgets. Private orders, for which the field treasury normally would pay and deduct from the salaries, were disallowed. In the conference/executive minutes of that time we find the sentence: 'Either we receive at least

DM 70,000 in cash or else part of the work, probably the highland, has to be abandoned'. [11] Soon after that, World War II broke out, and then all financial and organizational worries disappeared like a little cloud. Instead, fear and trepidation of a far greater dimension befell the missionaries. For the next five or six years most of them lived in the internment camp. The beloved work had to be left behind.

After World War II

After a war which had brought devastation and ruin to the physical plant of the Mission, there was no time to meditate on whether or not the Mission should retain its own supply system. If you wanted to get things done, you had to do them yourself. European and Chinese-owned shops were mushrooming all over the country, but none of them would have been efficiently able to assist the Mission in its great task of reconstruction. As a supply centre Finschhafen was not viable, Lae had become the centre of communication and trade, and at Madang there had been a mission supply centre. So, supply houses were opened in both centres, their main task being to obtain building materials and general supplies as quickly as possible and send them out to the stations. The first storeman at Madang was Mr Alwin Zimmermann, a South Australian, who served the mission as a 'Jack-of-all-trades'. He was assisted by Mr B. Jaeschke, who, prior to the outbreak of World War II, had been plantation manager at Nagada plantation near Madang. In Lae, a young Canadian, Mr D. Daechsel, had arrived in July 1947. For a while he was responsible for the supply base there, but soon he took over Madang. The supply system was no longer connected with the treasury; business manager and treasurer were separate positions. The business manager was a pre-war man, Mr Ross Boettcher, and the treasury went to Mrs Ann Wenz, who had some previous accounting experience. In 1950, Fugmann returned and was stationed at Lae. He became the supply house manager at Lae, and also took over some of the duties of the business manager.

The big question still remained: Should or could the Mission afford two supply centres? Madang had a better harbour and was nearer to the Highland, which was served from that centre. The mission conference in 1953

561

decided against Lae. Fugmann was asked to carry through the amalgamation of the Lae and Madang supply centres. All supplies for Lutheran Mission were from now on imported via the port of Madang, and distributed from Madang harbour and airport.

The speed with which the physical plant of the Mission was built up after the war is shown by the fact that, in 1953, 87 mission stations, plantations, schools, hospitals, and private households had to be supplied. In 1952, sales by the two supply houses amounted to £150,000, and later it went up as high as £500,000. At the height of Lutheran mission activities in Papua New Guinea, there were over 500 Europeans working for the Lutheran Mission. This included the wives, who certainly did a fair share of the work. The supply house had to stock 4000-5000 different items, or else provide them locally. The Lutheran Mission Supply House also served as a buying agent for more than 20 different Missions working in Papua New Guinea. At times, there were between 15 and 20 Europeans working in the supply house. It would be impossible to mention all the people and their comings and goings. Besides Daechsel and Fugmann, who carried a fair share of work and responsibility in the supply department, two Australians have to be mentioned: Mr Ron Johnstone from Brisbane and Mr Harold Ziegeler from South Australia. Both men worked for over 20 years within Mission Supply and communication. Both had arrived in New Guinea in 1952, and helped to bear the brunt of the first years after amalgamation. Two more personnel changes should be mentioned briefly: Fugmann went on furlough in 1955, and after his return did not join the Mission Supply System but started Namasu. Daechsel was manager until 1965, when he was relieved of his duties and became business manager. He was succeeded by quite a number of different managers.

Meanwhile, the situation had considerably changed toward the end of the 1960s. The communal system which the early missionaries had introduced had proved to be a great blessing. But 80 years had passed, and the system now showed its shortcomings. Such a system is invaluable in a smaller community, where the people know each other well. It is a different story, however, within a large

562

community, with hundreds of people coming from different nationalities and different social backgrounds. The outward circumstances had also changed considerably. Whereas the missionary fathers were almost dependent on the Mission Supply House, the new generation had plenty of opportunities to purchase their supplies at some of the many businesses which had opened up from Lae to Mount Hagen, and from Madang to Wau. So, in 1969/70 the communal system was abandoned in favour of a full salary. This had some decisive consequences for the Mission Supply House. People around Mount Hagen and some other places preferred to go shopping at the nearest town, and see what they were getting for their money. The usefulness of the Supply House declined, and in 1970 the conference of missionaries decided to sell out. The trading section for the New Guineans had been taken over previously by Namasu. On October 1, 1972, the Lutheran Supply House Madang was sold.

For 80 years the Missions Supply System had served a very useful purpose. It saved the missionaries from wasting their time in providing for the things which they needed to do the work. It had served the New Guineans at a time when no other source of supply was open to them. The Mission, on its way to becoming the church, had taken another step forward.

(For a list of Mission personnel who served in the Supply Department, see the appendix.)

Transportation

Papua New Guinea a hundred years ago was one of the least-developed countries in the world. The difficulties with which the first missionaries were confronted seemed to be insurmountable. They found an almost inpenetrable country of mountains and valleys covered with rain forest. How could they ever reach the various tribes living in the 'lost corners' of 'a land that time forgot'? While shipping and aviation certainly played an important role in opening up the country, we cannot overlook what happened with regard to road transport.

Bush Tracks

The very first missionaries who came to New Guinea could not do much about improving the bush tracks. The people were not interested in communicating with outsiders. They were fearful of enemies from every side. In the mountain areas, people built their villages on ridges which were hard to reach and easy to defend.

The first mountain area in which this changed on account of the acceptance of the Gospel was around Sattelberg and Wareo. Christian Keysser and Leonhard Wagner encouraged the people to give up their isolated hamlets, and live together in larger villages which could be connected with better bush paths, even suitable for travel by horse. In one of his books, Christian Keysser describes how the German government officer Berghausen was offered a horse for his travels through the Sattelberg hinterland. Berghausen doubted very much, on account of previous experiences in other parts of New Guinea, whether horse travel would be possible. When he came back from his trip he was full of praise for what he had seen, and said: 'I received an excellent impression. These people are by far the most advanced in New Guinea'. [12]

The new-won freedom from fear had encouraged these young Christians to build 'roads on which the *miti* could travel', as they expressed it. As time went on, similar developments could be noticed in other areas. As the Gospel took possession of the minds of the people, their old fears and hatreds disappeared, and they no longer felt imprisoned in their tribal area. Now they began to move about.

It may be said that the building of better roads went hand in hand with the spreading of the Gospel in the Morobe and Madang district. Everywhere, the missionaries encouraged the building of roads, or at least paths suitable for travelling by horse. Along the coast, local canoes could be used. But when the work spread inland, it meant building suitable lines of communication. With the introduction of steel implements, such as axes, knives, and shovels, work went ahead at great speed. As the influence of Christianity grew, the desire of the people to connect up with the pulsating life of the outside world grew at the same time. The

Traditional Transport (Markham Valley).

563

Traditional Bridge.

driving force behind the new movement everywhere was the evangelists. When Australian patrol officers later on began to travel in the mountain areas, they found the going much easier than normally would have been the case. [13] Indeed, these men made an outstanding contribution to the opening of their country.

Roads

Johann Flierl can well be called the first missionary of the mountains. It was perhaps not so much his own idea, but divine guidance, which brought this about. The Flierl family had lived at Simbang for over five years (1886-1891), when constant illness in the family almost forced them to leave the country. The only alternative was to find a healthier place, free of malaria, perhaps on top of a mountain. After a first exploration, which brought the Missionaries Flierl and Pfalzer to a mountain called Sattelberg, it was decided to build a mission station there. Later, perhaps, it could also be used as a health station for missionaries to get away from the hot coastal climate for a while. In November 1892, Flierl and his family moved to Sattelberg.

564

The first thing to do was to improve the bush track. Flierl and Pfalzer had taken two days to reach the top of the mountain. Very soon, sick mission-members and their families used the new station to recuperate. At that time, they had to be carried over the bush tracks by hammocks. Later, Flierl supervised the improvement of the track so that a two-wheeled ox-cart could be used. The ox-cart was pulled by four oxen, and carried 800 pounds of supplies. Later again, even an ambulance ox-cart was added to the equipment. Afterwards, Mr E. Paul Helbig, an Australian, supervised the building of another road up Sattelberg mountain, which then became the road for trucks and jeeps. Today, one travels from Heldsbach to Sattelberg in 30 minutes.

In the Madang area, the longest road for many years was the one built from Madang to Amele by V. Koschade, assisted by Dr Theodore Braun. It was 16 miles long, and it made possible the transport of patients and supplies by truck. Later on, a three-mile road was constructed from Nagada plantation to Amron Teachers Training School.

Mule Train, Markham Valley.

The role which horses had in the transportation system must not be overlooked. Some missionaries had to cover areas of between 2,000 and 3,000 square miles in order to visit the last village within their circuit. This could not have been done without the use of horses. The early Finschhafen missionaries received five horses as a gift from mission friends in Australia. However, the horses were not well suited for mountain work. The Mission then imported ponies from Makassar Celebes, which were then crossed with the Australian horses. These cross-breds proved to be eminently suitable for mountain work. Horses were used after World War II on many mountain stations. According to a report from 1931, the Mission at that time had 76 horses and six mules at Finschhafen, and approximately 50 horses in the Madang area.

When the work in the Markham Valley started, the larger type of horses proved to be excellent carriers for men and material. The missionaries could travel much faster over long stretches of country. There were no roads whatsoever in the Markham Valley. At the beginning, the Gabmazung station — near Nadzab — was supplied by the canoes of the Labo people, who had to row their canoes upstream and took two days to reach the destination. Later on, the Mission employed horses and mules to carry the supplies as far as Ongga. A report by Mr Otto Sperr notes that in future the stations Gabmazung, Kaiapit, and Kambaidam were to be supplied by mule-train.[14] Sperr says he had made 15 trips from Lae to Ongga. During that time, he had carried approximately five tons of cargo. When Sperr died as a result of an accident, Martin Boerner took over his work. He was assisted by a mixed-race man, Robi Kraus. Boerner carried this work through until 1934. In one of his reports, Boerner mentions that the freight rate from Lae to Kaiapit was nine pence per pound, which was far too high. He continues: 'As there are no roads in the Markham valley the ideal mode of transportation undoubtedly would be by aeroplane'.[15] Boerner had a team of 12 horses and mules, and carried thousands of pounds along the valley to keep the Mission stations going. The last trip was made in January 1935. After that, the mission aeroplane took over.

565

First motor car at Finschhafen.

Modern road to the Highlands.

Motor Vehicles

The first government-built road on the mainland of New Guinea was a dirt road linking up the goldfields at Wau and Bulolo with the coast. At Finschhafen and Madang, the Lutheran Mission had a short stretch of road, and in each location one motor vehicle. That was all.

The great change came about after World War II. During the war, the army constructed roads all over the country, particularly along the coast. Thousands of jeeps and trucks were imported from the United States to move men and material. What was left over after the war, could be purchased at a very reasonable price. Thus, the Mission entered the age of motorization. Nearly all the coast missionaries had jeeps. The highlanders were not as fortunate, since roads to the Highlands and within it were not yet built. The Australian Administration, however, in its endeavour to open up the country, induced the people of New Guinea on the coast, as well as in the Highlands, to work certain days of the week to build or repair roads. With the introduction of the Local Government Councils, road construction became obligatory for these bodies. Later on, to build the highways, road machinery was imported and overseas contractors were hired to do the job properly. The Mission would not and could not stand aside in this great work. Many side roads connecting up with the main highways were built by the Mission. In certain places where the building of a road did not receive first priority by the Administration, the Mission stepped in and constructed roads and bridges. For instance, a road was built by Mr Behrendorff from Nagada plantation to Nobonob on top of the Hanselmann Mountain. A road was constructed by D. Kohn from Timbulim plantation to the Johann Flierl Seminary at Logaweng. Quite a network of roads was built in the Sialum-Kalasa area by H.J. Wiederhold. He also built two bridges there. Very soon after the war, Mr R. Sherer, an American, built a bridge over the Gum River near Madang, and one over the Mape River at Finschhafen.

The building of roads was soon followed by the purchase of more motor vehicles by the Mission. Mr Louis Winter, the director of building and technical service of the Mission, wrote in 1959 that in 1950 there was one motor vehicle in the Highlands; in 1955, three; and in 1959, eighteen. In the coastal districts, every missionary with access to a road already had his jeep. In his report, Winter goes on to say that with the opening up of the Highland road it would be necessary to station a mechanic at Goroka, and equip him with the necessary tools for doing repair work on motor cars and electrical plants in use at the mission stations. The Mission, as far back as 1950, had erected a large workshop in Lae, which was run by Mr A. Zimmermann. In 1955, Madang got its workshop, in 1959, Finschhafen, and in 1960, Goroka. In 1966, a workshop was started in Mount Hagen to serve the technical needs in the Western Highlands. According to the statistics of 1967, the Lutheran Mission had 135 motor vehicles, 35 tractors, and 15 motor bikes. Nearly all the mission stations had power plants. All mission plantations, as well as school stations with large garden areas, had tractors to help in the production of food. Consequently, with all this technical equipment, there was plenty of work for the five workshops of the Mission.

Up to the end of the 1960s, all vehicles were mission-owned. In the long run, however, this proved to be unsatisfactory, and so it was decided to change the whole system. A special vehicle fund was established, from which the missionaries could draw, to finance the purchase of their own motor cars. Such loans could be repaid by charging for the number of kilometres run on behalf of the work.

The mission workshops served not only Mission members, but also congregations, private groups of motor vehicle owners, and individuals who wanted to avail themselves of the service offered. Thus, these workshops were fully utilized.

Technical Services

As shown in the previous section, the Mission had no choice but to build up the nucleus of a technical service organization. The workshops not only served the automotive section to keep the cars running, but also had to repair and maintain the power plants. After World War II, all mission stations were furnished with home generating plants, to bring electricity to the schools, hospitals, and living quarters for the people living in isolated places. It was, however, beyond the ability of the average ordained man to make repairs. Early in 1970, the men of the Church and Mission planned to hand over all work which so far had been done in the name of Lutheran Mission to the Evangelical Lutheran Church of Papua New Guinea. For the time being the work was carried on, but in 1975, when Lutheran Mission New Guinea ceased to exist as a legal entity, ELCONG took over the various services, such as building, repair shops for radio, the automotive section. All these aspects of technical service were combined into a new independent organization, which called itself Lutheran Technical Service.

It had its own legal status and its own set of books. All work done for the church or individuals had to be charged on a break-even basis. While, at the beginning, all the workshops, the radio shop, and a new organization called Ampo Builders were included in Lutheran Technical Service, it soon became evident that there were not enough clients to keep the workshops going. The situation had changed considerably. Motor vehicles were no longer mission-owned, which meant that the individuals could choose the nearest workshop. Some missionaries preferred to use the commercial garages. There were also less overseas staff as potential customers, which made it very hard for the workshops to break even. The first one to be given up was the radio repair shop. This was followed by the garages at Lae, Madang, Mount Hagen, and Finschhafen. The equipment was sold to local groups, who continued for a while and then gave up. The only ones which are still operating under the name of Lutheran Technical Service is the Goroka workshop and Ampo Builders.

The growth of Lutheran work in Papua New Guinea could never have been so rapid without the services of devoted laymen, who made it possible for the ordained missionaries to concentrate on their main task of preaching and teaching. (For a list of Mission personnel in Technical Services, see the appendix.)

Shipping

Finschhafen, 1886-1942

Right from the very beginning of missionary activities in New Guinea, the question of communication with the outside world and between the mission stations loomed large in the minds of the missionary fathers. There were no roads, except for a few bush paths used by the New Guineans. The greatest part of the country was covered by dense jungle. Thus, travel by sea offered itself as the only means of communication. During the first 20 years, the missionaries travelled by open canoe. The coastal people, particularly the Tami Islanders, were seasoned sailors, and would make trips as far as Lae to the south-west or Siassi Islands to the north-east.

In 1906, a request was made to the Home Board at Neuendettelsau to grant the necessary money for the purchase of a small sailing vessel. Pfalzer, who was then business manager of the Mission, wrote: 'For twenty years we have put up with open canoes; it is about time we got a proper seacraft'. [16] In 1907, a vessel was built in Hong Kong. Captain Ruwolt, a native of Bremen, Germany, was hired to skipper the ship. In memory of the landing of Lutherans on New Guinea soil, it was called *Simbang*.

However, a sailing ship proved to be unsuitable; it could sail with the wind, but not against it. Sometimes it had to wait two months for suitable sea conditions. It was never able properly to serve the eight mission stations along the coast from the Siassi Islands to Morobe in the south. Without a proper and safe seagoing vessel, personnel and supplies of a fast-growing Mission could never be transported to their destination. This soon became evident when in 1913 Missionary G. Pilhofer, together with 25 students, travelled from Finschhafen to Morobe in three small open canoes, a distance of 324 kilometers. That the party safely reached their destination is a miracle. In the same year, Missionary Decker, who had returned from a furlough in Europe, wanted to reach his station, Deinzerhill, before Christmas. He waited for seven days to make the short trip to his station. One night, when he thought the sea was calm, he attempted the trip. The boat struck a reef, turned over, and sank. Mrs Decker and their two young sons were drowned.

In the meantime, the Mission had ordered a motor vessel which was to be built by a Japanese firm in Rabaul. The new vessel was 24 metres long and six metres wide. It was two-masted, so it could sail with favourable winds,

Traditional sea transport.

Sailing boat 'Simbang'.

Ted Radke, Captain.

and it had a 52 hp motor. Launched on May 4, 1913, the new ship was named *Bavaria* after the German state where Sunday-school children had gathered the needed 50,000 Marks. [17] The *Bavaria* could carry 50 tons. Captain Samuel Jericho, an Australian, was in command. Unfortunately, he was killed in an accident caused by heart failure in 1916. By that time, the world was at war, and no new captain could be obtained from abroad. Thus, the Mission engaged non-mission members available in New Guinea. This was not very satisfactory, and one left after another. From 1917 to 1920, Wilhelm Schulz, an Australian lay-missionary, helped out. He was replaced by Captain Engel, a contract captain. He proved to be a good choice. In 1922 Theodore Radke, an Australian lay-missionary, became captain of the *Bavaria* until 1932. He was assisted by Hermann Miers, who arrived in 1925. During the intervening periods, E.P. Helbig also assisted.

The *Bavaria* proved to be a great help, since from 1914 to 1924 no overseas ship called at Finschhafen. The *Bavaria* had to transport copra from Finschhafen to Madang, and return with supplies. At the end of 1931,

M.V. 'Bavaria'.

Radke went to Australia on furlough. When he returned, he was employed by Lutheran Mission Madang. The new captain, Hermann Miers, who was assisted by L. Behrendorff and D. Rohrlach as mechanics, died two years later from a lung infection, and was replaced by D. Rohrlach as captain, with L. Schirmer as the new mechanic.

The ship was rebuilt twice, once in 1932 under Miers, and again in 1937/38 under D. Rohrlach. Often it had been on reefs. Twice it had lost its screw. Three times the main anchor was lost. The sailing facilities sometimes proved to be a great asset in getting the ship safely back to port. When war came, the *Bavaria* was used to evacuate many people in the face of the Japanese advance. Then it was sunk on official orders, to prevent its falling into the enemy's hands.

The history of the *Bavaria* is closely connected with the Lutheran advance in the Morobe District. The good old *Bavaria* carried more than 150,000 missionaries, evangelists, teachers, and village people during its lifetime. Many times the ship was in great danger, but the Lord held his saving hand over 'his messenger *Bavaria*'.

In 1925, the Sunday-school children of the Iowa Synod in the United States purchased a motor launch which was called *Iowa*. For a while, this sea craft served mainly along the gulf stations between Lae and Finschhafen. Later, it was transferred to Madang, and the Finschhafen mission purchased another motor launch which was paid for by the missionaries by having 10 per cent of their salaries deducted. This was called VELKA (*Vereinigte Evangelisch-Lutherische Kirche in Australien*), in memory of the contribution made by the Australian Lutherans to work in New Guinea.

Madang, 1887-1942

Shortly after the arrival of the Rhenish missionaries at Madang, the need was felt to purchase a small sailing boat. While the transport of personnel could be done on canoes from Siar and Graged, the movement of a larger number of people or supplies had to be done by open boats. Workers from the Mioko Island from the Bismarck Archipelago manned the oars, and sometimes were assisted by a small sail when the wind was favourable. Sea travel on open boats was dangerous. Missionary Kunze, on a trip from Siar to Karkar Island, a distance of 60 miles, drifted back and forth in the open sea for four days and three nights. Kunze called the trip 'a ride with death'. Finally the boat was grounded at Bagabag Island, where strangers took the unconscious man, covered with boils from the sea water, into their homes until he recovered his strength. Missionary Barkemeyer made a notable two-day trip from Bogadjim to Karkar in July 1895 through heavy volcanic dust to tell the missionaries that they were to be evacuated because of the volcanic eruption on the island. Barkemeyer delivered his message, but died a few days later from an accidental gun wound. Meanwhile, the Mission home board had sent out a sailor, August Pilkuhn, who died after having been in New Guinea for only nine months.

In 1907, the Rhenish missionaries applied to their home board for a motor vessel. This enabled the Westphalian Sunday-school children to finance an attractive project. Thus, the mission was able to buy a motor vessel which was named *Westphalia*. They engaged a captain-mechanic, August Glitz. After a test run, the ship was sent on an eight-hour trip to the Rai Coast. There it struck a reef and was lost. This was indeed a bitter disappointment to the missionaries in the Madang area, to the home board in Barmen, and, last but not least, to the children in Westphalia who had raised the money.

However, none of the parties gave up. The missionaries ordered a new ship, and the children of the Rhenish church collected sufficient money to buy another one. This time it was called *Rheno-Westphalia*. In 1910, it arrived in New Guinea. Its overall length was 51 feet, and its width 11 feet. Captain Glitz sailed the *Rheno-Westphalia* till 1913, when he was replaced by the mechanic, Mr Loesel. When Loesel died in 1916, the ship was run, in succession, by W. Schulz, T. Radke, and H. Alt.

After Radke had returned from furlough in Australia in 1930, he was transferred to Madang. Meanwhile, the *Rheno-Westphalia* had become too small for the growing work in the Madang district. The missionaries felt that a newer and bigger boat was necessary. This proved to be an ideal project for the Sunday-school children of the newly-formed American Lutheran Church,

M.V. 'Rheno Westphalia'.

and they raised the funds to buy a new ship. Radke went to Hong Kong and supervised the building of the hull, which then was towed to Madang, where the new engine was installed and the superstructure built. This new boat was named *Totol*. It had an overall length of 80 feet, and was regarded as an excellent ship. Unfortunately, it had a short life. When the war came to New Guinea, the *Totol* was used to evacuate people from New Britain to the mainland. As the Japanese forces came nearer, the ship was hidden in an mangrove swamp in Nagada harbour, where it was discovered and later bombed and sunk.

Shipping from 1946 to 1972

After World War II, the two Missions, Lutheran Mission Finschhafen and Lutheran Mission Madang, were united into one body: Lutheran Mission New Guinea. This meant that from now on all shipping would be directed from one place. The obvious choice for a home port of Lutheran ships was Madang, with its excellent harbour.

At the end of World War II, the transport situation by sea was hopeless. Many of the small ships which had provided a service before the war were destroyed. The first ship which Lutheran Mission acquired after World War II was a small vessel which had been used by Guinea Airways between Lae and Salamaua, prior to the outbreak of the war. It was refitted by Mr D. Rohrlach, the pre-war captain of the M.V. *Bavaria*, and renamed *Maneba*. For almost two years he skippered it, until he was assigned a different job. The *Maneba* proved to be an excellent ship, which served the Mission for almost 30 years.

Otherwise, the ships left over after the war were usually not very suitable. For instance, the Mission purchased a rescue boat from the army. It was of plywood construction, built for the express purpose of rescuing pilots drowned at sea. This ship made some trips, but sank after hitting a reef on the Rai coast. A second ship, called *Totol II*, proved unsuitable because of design faults. After several months, it was sold for use in river transport. Again the Mission was left without a boat, except for a small pinnace called *Victor*, which did excellent service, particularly around Madang and Finschhafen, but could not be employed on long trips.

M.V. 'Simbang'.

Then the vessel *Warambu*, a 70 foot cutter, was purchased to fill the gap until a new Mission ship could be built. It served the Mission well, and was sold after the new ship had arrived in New Guinea. The new ship, with the historic name *Simbang*, was built in Brisbane. It was 80 feet long, and had a capacity of 114 passengers and 80 tons of cargo. The cost to the Mission of £36,000 was raised partly by Sunday-school children in the United States. It was put into service at Madang on June 14, 1953, under the command of Captain B. Jaeschke. Later on, Arthur Fenske served as captain for many years. During the 1950s and 1960s it was the only ship on the north coast of New Guinea which ran according to a regular schedule. Its main ports of call were Madang, Biliau, Yarra, Wasu, Sialum, Finschhafen, Lae, and Morobe southward, and Kurum, Bunabun, and Bogia northward. With the *Simbang, Maneba* and *Warambu*, approximately 200,000 men, women, and children were carried during the 1950s and 1960s. Thousands of tons of supplies and produce were transported to and from the main ports. The growth of the Mission during that time would have been unthinkable without the services of the *Simbang*. Thousands of evangelists, teachers, and missionaries were carried from their homes to their places of work, and vice versa. The men manning these ships deserve to be commended: captains, engineers, and crews. In a regular year they spent 250 days away from home.

In 1971, the Mission decided to order a new ship to replace the *Simbang*, which had been in service for nearly 20 years. This new ship, which was to be called *Totol*, arrived in September 1972. Meanwhile, the shipping department grew, and the Mission had a number of short-term contract captains. In 1970, Captain H. Iversen, a foreign-going master, joined the Mission. He was particularly interested in initiating a training program for indigenous seamen, such as captains, engineers, and coxwains. The formal training of the deck officers was done by Michael Roussau, also a foreign-going master.

Lutheran Shipping

Until September 1972, Lutheran Shipping was a service department of the Lutheran

573

Mission, and fully integrated in its accounting system. Any profits derived from shipping would go to the Mission treasury, and any expenses would be paid by the Mission.

In view of the impending cessation of Lutheran Mission as a legal body and the transfer of all properties and assets to the church, steps had to be taken to facilitate the takeover by the church. A consultation, which acted as a planning body, was held between the representatives of the national church and the overseas churches which had been supporting the mission work. This took place at Lae in February-March 1970. The vital question with which the participants were confronted was: Should the future church be burdened with an organization which developed as the need grew, but with a structure strictly modelled on European concepts, or should the future structure be far simpler? It was felt that some of the service departments had to be retained because public facilities were not sufficiently available. They should, however, be established as independent commercial enterprise owned, but not run, by the church.

Accordingly, in 1972, Lutheran Shipping established itself as an independent shipping company owned by the church and run by a Board of Directors. Ever since that time, Lutheran Shipping has stood on its own feet and has grown by leaps and bounds. In 1974, it purchased the assets and goodwill of L. & S. Traders for $200,000, including the M.V. *Junel* and *Deanel*. With this purchase, the only serious competitor on the New Guinea coast had gone out of business. No other action has contributed more to the image that Lutheran Shipping is no longer a service department of the church, but a commercial enterprise. During the first four years all profits were retained to build up its fleet of coastal vessels and to repay some loans which had been granted to the company. Since 1976, annual payments to the church have been made on interest of the capital as well as 80 per cent of the net profit, while 20 per cent is retained for the renewal of the fleet. Members of the Lutheran Church on official trips, as well as all school children, travel at half fare, and all cargo shipped on behalf of the Church receives a 50 per cent reduction on the freight rates.

574

The company at the moment owns and operates eight coastal vessels. [18] Lutheran Shipping trains its own seafaring personnel, in close cooperation with the Government Nautical School at Madang. Twenty engineers, 15 small ships captains, and 14 coxwains have received certification.

The company also operates its own Marine Engineering Shop, where company-owned vessels, as well as indigenously-owned ships, are repaired and refitted. Four small motor vessels have been built on behalf of New Guinea villagers. In its fibreglass section, the company has made 25 lifeboats, as well as liferafts. Another section within the company's workshop manufactures steel trusses for churches and schools, as well as steel frame forms, truck canopies, and water tanks.

Lutheran Shipping is a flourishing and well-run company, which is making a great contribution to the development of Papua New Guinea. However, it must be mentioned that there is great opposition to the policy of Lutheran Shipping to carry beer on its ships. The increase of alcoholism throughout the country has had disastrous consequences for the community, and many people feel that a Christian church should not be involved in facilitating the consumption of alcoholic beverages. Sooner or later, the church will have to make a decision on a moral issue of great concern to many Christians.

(For a list of Mission personnel in the Shipping Department, see the appendix.)

Mission Aviation

New Guinea is a rugged country, with cloud-covered mountains, lonely beaches, and deep valleys. It is a country hard to traverse. Up to the late 1920s, the interior was a blank spot on the maps of the world. In 1928, two Australian patrol officers crossed the island from the Sepik to the Fly River. With them, word reached the outside world that the Central Highlands of New Guinea was thickly populated. Ivan Champion and Charles Karius saw some of the Western Highlands, and at about the same time the pioneer missionary Leonhard Flierl stood on the hills east of Bena Bena and had a first glimpse of the fertile Goroka valley. When one speaks of the opening of the Central Highlands, one thinks of names such as the Leahy brothers, Jim Taylor, and, last but not least, Wilhelm Bergmann. Jim Taylor, the young government patrol officer, wrote enthusiastically to his superior officer at Salamaua:

> We are on the threshold of a new era in New Guinea. If this density of population around Kainantu is maintained across to the Sepik river, there must be 200,000 people.

Later investigations revealed that there were more, perhaps half a million.

So far, the Australian Administration had only a few officers to look after law and order. In the past, the missions had done it better and more peacefully. How could the Government open up the Central Highlands without the assistance of the missions? Both the Catholics and the Lutherans were invited to participate in the great task. How could they ever extend their work with the meagre means at their disposal? So far their peaceful invasion of new and unknown territory had been done step by step, from one tribe to the next. How could they now suddenly make the great leap of 500 km from Lae to Mount Hagen?

Leaving aside their problem for the moment, we turn to look at another development which had taken place at about the same time. Near Mount Kainti and in the adjoining Bulolo valley, gold had been discovered — plenty of gold. White men from all over New Guinea and Australia rushed to the scene. Even government officers gave up their positions in search of gold. These miners needed supplies, tools, and machinery. Thousands of New Guineans were hired to carry these across a 5,000 feet range from Salamaua to Wau. At that time there were no roads, and the supply position became desperate. Obviously the time was ripe to leave the muddy and leach-infested mountain paths, and to use wings. Aviation was introduced in support of the search of gold. Would this also be the answer to the problems of christianizing the mass of people in the Highlands? Could aviation be used in support of the search for souls? Shortly before he retired, the grand old man of the New Guinea Mission, Johann Flierl, wrote to his home board: 'One day we will have to fly like

First Mission aeroplane, 'Papua'. Captain F. Loose (left) and Director Dr Eppelein.

homing pigeons to their cote. The men in search of gold are now trying it out for us'. [19]

Beyond the horizon, hundreds of thousands were waiting, and a friendly government was extending an urgent call for help. How could the Mission refuse this? Indeed, the missionary fathers 'did not confer with flesh and blood', but acted immediately. A research party was sent to the Highlands, and an application was made to the home board to look for a suitable aeroplane. It is one of the great miracles of modern mission history that within 12 months the plane was available and ready for its first flight. This could never have been available and achieved within such a short time without the drive of the Director of Mission at Neuendettelsau, Dr F. Eppelein. He inspired the people of his church to provide the necessary funds. This was not an easy task in 1934, when the Nazis were in power; Hitler was never a friend of Christian missions.

This was a great time for the Lutheran Mission. New Guinean congregations and their leaders were electrified by the development. The Revd Pilhofer wrote to the home board:

> Our poor mountain congregations have already collected 500 shillings for the new plane, yea the evangelists in the Gazub-Hazung area — the door to the highland — decided to go without their annual pay in favour of the new aeroplane. [20]

Meanwhile, the German home board had approached Junkers Aeroplane Factory at Dessau in search of a suitable machine; the Junkers planes had been flying in New Guinea for a number of years. The choice fell on a Junkers F 13 passenger plane with a payload of 1,200 lbs and powered by a 270 hp engine. On the recommendation of Junkers-Dessau, the German Home Board obtained the services of Mr F. Loose, a World War I ace pilot. Pilot and aeroplane arrived in New Guinea in February 1935. Two days later, on February 21, the first flight was made to Kaiapit. Captain Loose was accompanied on that flight by the Revd W. Bergmann. In a little ceremony at Finschhafen the plane was named *Papua*.

Loose proved to be *the* pilot. During his time, approximately 12 aerodromes were constructed by the Mission. He soon became famous for his first landings under most difficult conditions. Fritz Loose had no aerial map, except a sketch made by Missionary Stephen Lehner roughly indicating the mountain ranges,

rivers, and possible landing strips. There was no air traffic control nor, for that matter, radio communication. The pilots had to fly over unknown country almost 400 miles to the furthest point so far known to Europeans in New Guinea.

Lae at that time was a small township, known as *the* air centre of New Guinea. From there, the big Junkers aeroplanes flew to the goldfields at Bulolo and Wau. Lae was also earmarked as the future base for mission aviation. Mr W. Fugmann was delegated to build up the new base. For the first six months, supplies were stored in a makeshift store near Lae aerodrome, and flown from there to the Highlands. After waiting in vain for several months for a building permit, the Mission decided to build its own air base at Malahang plantation. Mr M. Boerner was asked to build the airstrip, the pilot's residence, and the workshops. The Malahang aerodrome was 800 metres long.

In 1936, the first full year of flight operations, the plane made 130 flights and carried, besides a great number of passengers, 62 tons of freight. In 1937 it increased to 190 flights and 80 tons. From November 1937 to October 1938, 199 flights were made. The plane was 450 hours in the air during that time. A flying hour cost the mission £2. Loose wrote in one of his reports that in three years he flew 300,000 kilometres. He carried 280 tons of cargo and 2,400 passengers during that time.

In February 1938, F. Loose left New Guinea, and was followed by Werner Garms. Garms served the Mission until September 1939. After the outbreak of the war, Garms, together with his flight engineer Paul Rabe, secretly took the plane to neutral West New Guinea, which at that time was under Dutch rule. There, at Merauke, on the south coast, it was left to rust away.

The Lutheran Mission was, as far as is known, the first mission in the world to use aviation as a tool in spreading the Gospel. The *Papua* had made history.

After World War II

The war was over, but some of the war-time pilots stayed on and worked for airlines or private operators. Missionaries returned to take up the work which they had left. The churches

First 'Cessna' aeroplane after World War II with prospective 'customers'.

were destroyed, but the church lived. Pastors and evangelists went back to the Highlands. Stations had to be built up again. There was still no road from the coast to the Highlands, and yet supplies had to be shifted. This could only be done by aeroplanes. For five years, Lutheran missionaries, pastors, and evangelist-teachers had to rely on commercial planes.

In the United States, a group of war-time pilots, who had become practising Christians, banded together for the specific purpose of serving missions throughout the world, missions which had to rely on aviation. They called themselves the Missionary Aviation Fellowship. In Australia, a group of war-time flyers joined them, and started the Australian Missionary Aviation Fellowship (AMAF). Its secretary, a South Australian farm-boy, who had served in the Australian forces, accepted an assignment in New Guinea. Mr E. Hartwig thus became the first Lutheran Mission pilot after World War II. He was joined by B. Hutchins, an American, who for the time being acted as mechanic. Lutheran Mission purchased an 'Auster Autocar', a four-seater plane. Operations began in May 1951, but lasted only

until August. On the way from Goroka to Madang the plane crashed, and Hartwig was killed. This was indeed a great shock. Yet, business had to go on. The work in the Highlands simply could no longer rely on commercial flying, which was irregular and costly. Perhaps Lutheran Mission should hand over its flying service to experts. This was done, and the Missionary Aviation Fellowship, which had its headquarters in California, was asked to handle all aviation matters. Soon after, a new Cessna 170, the first of its kind in New Guinea, arrived from the United States. The Mission was also very happy to be able to obtain the services of Mr Charles Mellies, an experienced pilot and also a very able organizer. Together with Mr B. Hutchins, he organized a new program. During the last four months of 1952, they shifted more than 40 tons of supplies and carried 260 persons to their destination.

The two pilots soon realized that in the long run they would never be able to cope with the ever-expanding mission activities in the Highlands, and so they suggested that the main routes from Madang to Banz and Goroka be covered by chartering DC 3 planes, with a

577

Ray Jaensch †. He lost his life while on active service.

carrying capacity of from 6 to 8 tons. A Cessna plane was stationed at Banz to shuttle the supplies from Banz to the various outstations. From then on, every week or fortnight, a fully-loaded DC 3 would fly to Banz and return with a load of sweet potatoes and vegetables for the Yagaum hospital. By 1954, the Lutheran Mission had three Cessna planes, one stationed at Banz and two at Madang.

In 1953, Mr R. Jaensch, a Lutheran pilot from South Australia, arrived in New Guinea. Meanwhile, the MAF activities were sought after by many other missions, and so it was decided that MAF would concentrate on other denominations, while the Lutherans would take over the management of their own fleet. During the following years, Lutheran aviation expanded considerably. In 1953, it accumulated 1,000 flying hours, in 1955 it had risen to 1,200, in 1957 to 1,400, and in 1960 to 1,600. By 1963, the use of DC 3 planes decreased; a new highland road had been completed between Lae and Goroka. The Mission reacted by opening a supply branch at Goroka. All goods were now shifted by road, and flown from Goroka to the outstations.

578

Right in the middle of his work in building up the Lutheran Aviation Service, chief pilot R. Jaensch was killed in a tragic accident. When taking off from Dauta airstrip, an engine defect developed and the plane crashed. Jaensch was severely injured, and died on the flight to the hospital.

As the mission grew in size, the aviation department followed suit. In 1965-66, Lutheran Mission had four aeroplanes stationed at Madang, Lae, and Goroka. In 1967, the planes were 2,477 hours in the air, and transported 7,000 passengers, as well as supplies, to 68 different airstrips. During the following years, there were always between four and five planes in operation.

Toward the end of the 1960s, the aviation department, like any other department within the mission, had to face the question of what would happen if the autonomy of the church were to become a reality. Could the indigenous church be bothered with such a complicated business as aviation?

As an outcome of the Lae consultation between the national church leaders and representatives from overseas churches, the aviation department was advised to form an independent company, owned by the church, but run by a Board. In 1971, this transition from a 'child' of the Mission to an independent service organization took place. The new organization called itself Luta Air. With its own Board of directors, and standing on its own feet, the new airline had to be more stringent in its management. For instance, routes were now plotted, and flights were made only if a payable load of passengers or cargo was available. The growing-process had still not come to a standstill. In 1973, the company planes had been flying 3,500 hours, with six pilots, one flight engineer, and five other staff members. Luta Air gave preferential rates to all cooperating churches and missions, with 50 per cent reduction on the ordinary freight rates. In 1975-76, shortly before its liquidation, the company had a capital of 235,000 Kina.

Meanwhile, the old question was asked again: Would the church even through the Board which had been introduced always be able to run a growing airline? It would, for the time being, always be dependent on overseas personnel. Would it not be better to leave aviation to specialists? Perhaps the Australian Missionary Aviation Fellowship would be a suitable successor. The friendly and close cooperation between the Lutherans and the AMAF had been going on since the time of E. Hartwig. Many pilots flying for Luta Air had been provided by AMAF. Negotiations were started, and in 1977 it was agreed that Luta Air terminate its services. The whole enterprise was sold to AMAF,[21] with the stipulation that preferential rates be granted for all Lutheran Church personnel and air cargo. The proceeds of the sales were handed to the church for long term investment.

Lutheran Aviation had made an outstanding contribution to the churches and also to the development of Papua New Guinea. More than 40 airstrips have been built by the Lutheran people in New Guinea.[22]

During its 30 years of service, including the years before World War II, Lutheran Aviation had an excellent record. Approximately 30,000 passengers were carried over rugged country, and only three passengers lost their lives during that time. Four pilots lost their lives while serving the Church and Mission in Papua New Guinea. We remember their names: Edward Hartwig, Ray Jaensch, Ross Dunhill, and Gavin Hoskin. (For a list of Mission pilots, see the appendix.)

Building Activities

Saw-Milling

Saw-milling was probably introduced by missionaries. They were the first who had to resort to the resources of the land. Governments or white settlers had more money, and could afford to build their houses with imported timber. During the first twenty years, Lutheran missionaries had no sawmill or carpenters available. So, they had to build their own houses out of bush material and soft-wood timber. Later on, pit-sawing was introduced in order to get more permanent buildings. As stations and schools grew in number, it soon became evident that mechanical means of getting sawn timber were needed.

The first missionary who harnessed water power to drive a small sawmill was Georg

First sawmill at Finschhafen/Butaweng.

Bamler. He, together with J. Hertle, erected a sawmill at the Buta Creek near Logaweng. All parts were made of wood, and this proved to be a mistake, for the construction could not stand the stress. The mill broke down after having sawn a few hundred superfeet of timber. Besides, they also found that the creek did not carry sufficient water all year round to drive the wheel. In searching for a better place, the missionaries found an ideal location near the Butaweng river. Proper sawmill equipment was ordered from Germany. This cost the mission 50,000 Marks. Two expert carpenters, Messrs Wirth and Hertle, set the mill up. In September 1913, Johann Flierl reported to his home board: 'I can give you the good news that the new saw mill is now in operation'.[23] This sawmill remained in operation almost up to the beginning of World War II.

The Mission employed two Europeans to utilize the plant fully. Gottried Schulz, an Australian, was responsible for the milling, while Johann Schmutterer, a German, had to do the logging with an ox team. For seven years these two men worked together, and provided timber for building mission stations and the big supply

Johann Hertle with his crew.

house at Finschhafen. Unfortunately, Schulz had to leave in 1920 on account of illness. Schmutterer carried on until 1931, when he left for Germany. After him, Linus Eiermann, a German, continued the work almost to the beginning of World War II. The mill had been in operation for over 25 years. Then the machines were worn out, and the timber stands depleted.

The Mission looked for a new timber stand, and found it near Malahang plantation. Mr Len Behrendorff, an Australian wheelwright, set up a new plant, and by May 1939 the mill was working smoothly. The intention was also to produce timber for sale, and thus help to finance the cost of erecting the new plant. However, in September, when World War II broke out, saw-milling, like all other activities, soon came to an end.

Carpentry

Undoubtedly, the early missionaries had to be handymen. They had to build their own stations and do some farming, besides being preachers and teachers. The first person with some architectural training was Mr Hans Meier. He came to Finschhafen in 1904, and proved to be a great help with building and making surveys for the Mission. He left New Guinea in 1911.

With the arrival of Johann Hertle, a cabinet-maker as well as a fitter and turner by profession, the whole building program of the Mission took a new turn. In over 30 years, he built and rebuilt more than 20 mission stations, 580

churches, and class-rooms. Besides, he taught more than 100 New Guineans the art of carpentry and cabinet-making. [24] Together with his New Guinean carpenters, Hertle supplied the mission stations with furniture, and the classrooms with forms. He repaired wharves, and even helped to repair the Mission aeroplane.

Shortly after the outbreak of the war with Japan, Hertle, with some other missionaries, had to walk across the Owen Stanley ranges from Wau to Port Moresby. In Australia he was interned, and he died in December 1942 at the age of 62, at Tatura Internment Camp.

Johann Hertle had his own building style. He preferred houses with wide verandahs and big airy rooms. He was a strict but very sensible boss to his trainees. The Hertle-trained carpenters were sought after all over the country. In his reports he specifically mentions three outstanding New Guinean carpenters: Elieser from Katika, Yanadabing from Eec, and Komeng from Sattelberg.

The building activities after World War I could hardly keep pace with the extension of missionary activities in the Morobe district. Thus, in December 1924, an Australian carpenter, Christian Claussen, joined the Mission. Claussen was a particularly good teacher of carpentry, and usually had between 15 and 20 trainees. Besides carpentry, Claussen had special courses for pit-sawing. A number of outstanding buildings were erected during his term in New Guinea. Unfortunately, Claussen

Komeng.

Christian Clausen.

died of malaria in 1932. Another man who made a great contribution to the training of craftsmen was Paul Helbig, who first at Salankaua plantation and later at Sattelberg always supervised a small gang of carpenters.

From 1886 to 1939, the Lutheran Mission Finschhafen had built up 30 stations, some of which had eight to ten buildings of different sizes. At Madang, saw-milling and carpentry had taken a different turn altogether. The amount of building there was much less than at Finschhafen. Mission stations were situated close to Madang, and imported timber from Java and Australia could be transported to the building sites with greater ease than at Finschhafen. Most of the stations built prior to World War I were erected by the ordained missionaries themselves. The first carpenter to arrive at Madang (in 1905) was Heinrich Schamann. Prior to taking over Nagada plantation, he built Nobonob. Later on, timber was obtained mainly by making use of the pit-saw.

The situation changed after 1921, when the mission was amalgamated with the Neuendettelsau group at Finschhafen. More

personnel arrived from the United States and Australia, and the work itself expanded considerably. Carpenters and lay missionaries who helped to build up the physical plant of Lutheran Mission Madang were W. Siemers, A. Mild, A. Bertelsmeier, and T. Radke. The old Rhenish Mission stations which were built before the field was taken over by Lutheran Mission Madang were: Amele, Nobonob, Kurum, Keku, Maulon, and Nazadamon. Between the two wars, the following stations were added: Supply House Madang (1925), Biliau (1932), Bunabun (1933), Narer (1933), Kerowagi (1934-35), Begesin (1935), Amron 1936), and Amele Hospital (1937). [25]

Rebuilding Lutheran Mission after World War II

During the war, nearly all the churches, mission stations, schools, and hospitals were destroyed by bombs. The returning missionaries were faced with a situation which was aptly summed up in the statement of the American Pastor Dr Fricke: 'The churches are destroyed but the church lives'. How could so few men rebuild so much? Nearly 40 mission stations had been destroyed. Assistance came

581

from the United States. The Mission Board recruited a group of young men to build up the physical plant which had been lost. They called themselves 'Mission Builders'. The first group arrived in 1946. They erected the most basic buildings, some of steel construction, to house the administrative and the supply section, as well as important schools and the Yagaum hospital. Neither the men nor the material were yet available to build up the mission stations. Most missionaries — and there were only a few who had returned — helped themselves, and often lived in makeshift houses. It is an amazing story which would be well worth telling in full. However, since the rebuilding and the building of 130 mission stations, schools, hospitals, and plantations would almost fill a volume by itself, the writer must desist.

By 1972, the building boom was over. Many institutions had made additions to the first group of buildings. In fact, at some of the places building never stopped. Quite a number of stations and institutions were built up gradually; thus no specific year when they were built can be given. During these 25 years, over 200 well-constructed churches were built.

All this work could never have been carried out without the devoted participation of hundreds, perhaps thousands, of New Guinea craftsmen. In fact, the main work was not done by expatriate mission workers but by nationals. It is most unfortunate that their names cannot be recorded, because of the many changes which occurred. Their names may, perhaps, be forgotten, but their work still exists as a visible expression of partnership in building up the Lutheran Church.

During the last decade, practically all building activities for the church have been carried out by teams of national builders. There is only one expatriate building expert who heads the church service organization which calls itself 'Ampo Builders'. This organization is available for either taking on building contracts or furnishing plans and specifications for New Guinean teams.

With hundreds of buildings going up, how was the Mission going to find the timber? Coastal stations were comparatively well off, since timber could be obtained from commercial sawmills at Bulolo and Lae. The

582

Len Behrendorff with his carpenters.

Highlanders were not so fortunate. There was as yet no road connection, and most of the highland houses had to be built with pit-saw timber, which sometimes took years.

The initiative to start a new sawmill was taken by the Revd F. Scherle, who at that time was stationed at Malalo. There were rich timber stands between Salamaua and Morobe, which belonged to the members of his congregation. Why not develop them commercially as a cooperative enterprise? Lutheran Mission advanced the money to purchase the equipment, and also made available its pre-war saw-miller, Mr Linus Eiermann. Work began in 1955 at Sawet. After about two years of trial and error, the mill reached a capacity of 1,000 logs per year. Over the years, there were many changes in managership. By 1963, the timber resources around Sawet were almost depleted, and the plant was moved to Laukano. By 1966, the new plant had been installed. During the following years, between 400,000 and 700,000 super feet of timber were supplied to the various mission projects. By 1969, the building boom slowed down, and so the work was discontinued.

In the Madang district, a small plant was built by Mr R. Sherer as early as 1952-53. The logging was done by Mr L. Behrendorff, who at that time was in charge of building up the Nobonob Girls School. Later, the work was carried on by Mr W. Johnstone. Another source of supply was a mobile 'Dolmar' saw-milling plant, operated by Mr W. Schulz. Quite a lot of timber for building projects in the Madang district was obtained from Sawet and Laukano.

The building up of the physical plant of Lutheran Mission had taken just about 25 years. Millions of dollars and thousands of man-hours have been invested to set up the basic buildings within which the Evangelical Lutheran Church of Papua New Guinea could carry on the work started by the Mission.

None of this could be done without the whole-hearted support of New Guineans and their expatriate collegues. No outside contracting firm could ever have done so much at such reasonable costs. These men have made an outstanding contribution to building up the church. Indeed, they became real church builders.

(For a list of Mission personnel in Building Activities, see the appendix.)

Radio Communication

Prior to 1935, Lutheran Mission Finschhafen had no telephone or radio link-up with the outside world. Mail and supplies arrived by ships, which called at Finschhafen approximately every four weeks. Urgent messages were sent by carrier overland to Lae, or received from there the same way.

With the arrival of a mission aeroplane in 1935, a direct link between Finschhafen and Lae became a necessity. Application to operate a private transmitting and receiving set was granted. Now, the daily flight plans could be broadcast. This gave the missionaries concerned the necessary warning of when to expect the plane. Any other information of general interest could also be transmitted to Lae or Finschhafen. By turning on their private radio sets, all mission personnel could listen to the daily transmissions. In 1939, when war broke out, the Australian Administration confiscated the sets.

After World War II, Lutheran Mission supported the establishment of Christian Radio Missionary Fellowship, an organization whose aim was to interconnect all mission stations in Papua New Guinea. In 1949, an American lay missionary, Carl Spehr, arrived to set up the Mission's own radio network. This became necessary to broadcast flights and ships' movements. It also provided a service for medical emergencies; aeroplanes or ships could be diverted from their normal routes in cases of emergency. The mother radio station and workshop, which had been set up at Baitabag near Madang at that time, had 13 mission stations hooked up for communication with each other. In 1956, when the main station was shifted to Madang, there were already 23 mission stations participating. Meanwhile, the electronic workshop had to take care of repair and maintenance, and also of all ships and aeroplane radio sets.[26] In 1962, Hans Selke, who then was in charge, reported that 19 new generating plants and wirings of mission stations were made. He highly praised the work of his two New Guinea assistants, Daing and Gapenu.

In 1964, Carl Spehr returned to his homeland, and Mr George Groat, another American, took over the electronic division. In his 1967 report, he stated that in the meantime a network of 73 Lutheran stations had been established. The total number of participants in the Christian radio hook-up system was 300. All denominations took part.

At the beginning of the 1970s, the building of new stations was completed, and consequently the work slackened off in every direction. Commercial radio workshops had been springing up in all major settlements. Electrical contractors could be called in to repair lighting plants and electronic devices. For the Mission, it was no longer a paying proposition to keep up its electrical and electronic service. Thus, in 1974 the workshop was closed down. The supervision of the radio network, as well as the maintenance of transceivers, was entrusted to the Christian Radio Missionary Fellowship at Rugli near Mount Hagen.

(The names of Mission personnel in this section are included in the appendix.)

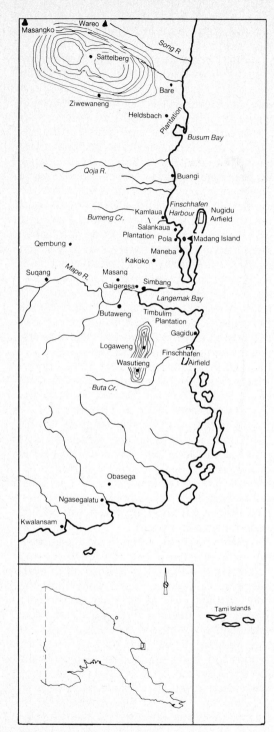

Finschhafen proper.

Plantations

The Finschhafen Plantations, 1904-1939

Finschhafen today consists of a scattered group of settlements and villages situated near the sea and extending from the Ginggala Islands in the south to Scarlet Beach in the north. People living in Gagidu, Timbulim, Butaweng, Logaweng, Maneba, Salankaua, Kamlaua and Heldsbach regard themselves as living in Finschhafen. Finschhafen proper, however, is the actual area around the harbour basin, which is called Maneba and Salankaua. The inner harbour of Finschhafen is able to take small coastal vessels, while the big overseas steamers anchor near Nugidu point.

The Finschhafen plantations consisted of Heldsbach, Salankaua, and Timbulim. Here the basis was laid for the assistance of missionary activities.

Heldsbach

The idea of starting a coconut plantation near the Busum creek was perhaps a secondary thought to Johann Flierl. While in charge of Sattelberg mission station, he realized that Finschhafen was too far away to serve as a base from which goods from the coast could be transported to Sattelberg. Would not Busum be an ideal place for a coastal base, from which supplies could be carted by ox carts to Sattelberg? A school could be opened to take the overflow of pupils from Sattelberg. Cattle could be raised, and additional food grown for the Sattelberg schoolboys. Perhaps a plantation could be started to provide young New Guineans with work near their home. Johann Flierl was a practical man. He immediately wrote a letter to the German Colonial Administration, asking for land around the Busum creek. Within a few weeks he received a reply, saying that 500 hectares could be granted, providing the Mission started to develop a coconut plantation within five years.

Land not actually in use at that time was regarded as Crown land. Even if he wanted to, Flierl could not deal with the New Guineans directly. He was not even allowed to pay any compensation in cash. He therefore paid the people in kind, carefully noting the names of the 44 villagers who had some claim on the land.

Not much time was lost after that. Johann Flierl took it on himself to start the new coastal base at Busum. In memory of Missionary Held, who had died earlier, he called the new place Heldsbach. At Sattelberg he handed over his work to Christian Keysser, and in January 1904 he moved to Heldsbach, leaving his family at Sattelberg. Within three years, with the help of Karl Wacke, who had just arrived from Germany, and with a group of pupils, he cleared the bush, planted field fruits, built roads, dormitories, and classrooms, and finally his own house. Every morning, the schoolboys received lessons in reading and writing. In fact, what had been built was a new mission station. In 1907, Mrs Flierl and the children moved to Heldsbach. Meanwhile Leonhard Flierl, a nephew of the 'Senior', had arrived to help with the school and the outside work.

The actual work of planting coconut trees began in earnest in 1908. Flierl, with the help of his sons Wilhelm and Johannes, as well as his nephew Leonhard, planted 10,000 palm trees between 1908 and 1913 — and this besides the missionary work and the daily lessons for the plantation workers.

Meanwhile, the Flierl sons were gone, and Johann and Leonhard Flierl could not possibly spend more time on the plantation. It needed a full-time manager. Kaspar Doebler, a Bavarian farmer's son, who arrived on December 10, 1913, proved to be the right choice to make this plantation a paying proposition and at the same time a coastal base for the mountain stations, Sattelberg and Wareo. During the 25 years he was responsible for Heldsbach, he trained numerous young New Guineans; he was like a strict but loving father to them. Heldsbach became a vital base for mission work, both spiritually and economically, among the New Guinea people. Though handicapped during World War I because of shortage of funds, Doebler continued with the building up of land available, by planting 16,000 palms. In 1928, he wrote in his report: 'Now the plantation is fully bearing. Generally speaking, more copra cannot be expected and little maintenance is now required.' Copra production at Heldsbach was raised from 10 tons in 1914 to an average of 200 tons per year. The plantation became a money-spinner, and helped the Mission to keep afloat financially during the most difficult period

Kaspar Doebler.

from 1933 to 1939. Besides the fund-raising, New Guineans were trained in regular work, copra was produced, horses and cattle were raised, and products such as coffee and tobacco, as well as vegetables, were purchased. Indeed, the economic involvement of the Mission had become a blessing to the church and to the people of New Guinea. Heldsbach stood for good stewardship.

Salankaua

At the turn of the century, the German New Guinea Company was the great landlord at Finschhafen. It owned almost 800 hectares along the waterfront. Two hundred and sixty hectares were planted with palms. In 1906, it became evident that, because of commitments in other parts of the country, the New Guinea Company was not very interested in their property at Finschhafen. The Lutheran Mission at that time had only one hectare of land, and urgently required more land. After all, Finschhafen was the central place from which ten mission stations had to be supplied. When it became known that perhaps the Company would sell its property, Senior Flierl and his

585

Cattle were imported.

deputy Pfalzer wrote to their home board, proposing the purchase of Salankaua plantation. They reasoned that if the New Guinea Company should sell its property to an opponent of the Mission, it could make things very difficult for the Mission. In their letter to Neuendettelsau, the missionary fathers also stressed the point that many young men around Finschhafen were looking for work elsewhere. Why not provide working opportunities near their homes? Last but not least, a coconut plantation could prove to be a source of income for the Mission and the church. It was not an easy decision for the German home board to make, to undertake such a step. In order to find the necessary finance, they started a special drive. After some negotiations, the property was purchased for 150,000 Marks. [27] Included in the purchase were 766 hectares of land, of which 260 hectares had been planted up with palms, the rest being virgin forest and beach area. Also included were two residences, labour quarters, a copra shed, and also some cattle. The area included the places today known as Salankaua, Maneba, and Timbulim.

On February 18, 1908, Paul Helbig, an

Australian farmer, took over the property, including a labour force of 42 men. There was much sickness among these men. Coming from mountain areas, they were not used to the coast and its malaria. Helbig also found that some of the men had to get used to regular working hours. Very soon it became evident that big patches of the land under cultivation were too poor for continued attention. Plantation labourers also had to load and unload overseas vessels calling at Finschhafen. The cargo which was handled increased so much that in 1912 Helbig had to build a wharf. Since this job was beyond one man, he received help from Johann Hertle, a German carpenter, and from Gottfried Schulz, an Australian farmer.

This plantation, which was situated at the centre of Lutheran activities, was burdened with many and varied tasks. So it became necessary to employ another worker, Samuel Jericho, an Australian farmer. He assisted in the plantation from 1905 to 1912. In 1911, Helbig and his team started to cut the bush on the other side of the Mape river. Soon another plantation (today known as Timbulim) began to take shape. By 1920, the two plantations had 31,000 palms in

The Revd Paul Helbig.

Adolph Obst.

production. However, it soon became apparent that the ground at Salankaua and Timbulim was much poorer than at Heldsbach. Salankaua, even at its best, and with almost twice as many palms as Heldsbach, never produced much more copra than Heldsbach.

In 1922, Helbig's health was such that he had to be replaced. During the next nine years the plantation had five different managers. It was only in 1931 that a certain continuity of management was achieved. Adolf Obst, an Australian farmer's son, who took over the plantation, was a remarkably good organizer. During his nine-years' term as manager, Salankaua produced the maximum revenue for the Mission. And the Mission needed it urgently, since funds from Germany did not suffice to finance the ever-growing extension of Lutheran work, particularly in the Central Highlands. Obst was an all-round man. At times he even had to run the mission ship *Bavaria*. In 1941, with the entry of the Japanese into the war, all the work at Salankaua came to a standstill. Soon the Japanese forces occupied Finschhafen, and Adolf Obst died in action while working for the Allied Command as a 'coast watcher'.

Timbulim

While manager at Salankaua, Helbig managed to plant 7,000 palms on the south side of the Mape river. In 1928, when the number of palms had reached the 10,000 mark, the plantation had to be made independent. The first manager was John Lindner, who served between 1928 and 1932, and he planted a further 6,000 palms. After Lindner went on furlough, Eiermann, a German saw-miller, was asked to look after the plantation while he was still in charge of Butaweng sawmill. He did a remarkably good job, considering that he could only spend a fraction of his time at the plantation. Timbulim was never a success. A strange disease befell the coconut trees, the cause of which has never been found.

After World War II

The three Finschhafen plantations, Heldsbach, Salankaua, and Timbulim, lie within ten miles of one another. Yet formerly they had to be run as separate units. There were no vehicle roads before the war, but only horse tracks interrupted by numerous small creeks.

587

For the Mission, it was much cheaper to transport copra and general cargo by sea.

During World War II, Finschhafen had become the third largest military port in the world, after London and New York. At times there were one million Allied soldiers stationed at Finschhafen. It was one big war city, with a six-lane highway between the Mape and the Buming rivers. Dozens of side roads crisscrossed the plantation and connected numerous warehouses, recreation centres, churches, and picture theatres. Military equipment of all description and in huge quantities were ready for the 'trip' to Japan.

When the war was over and the first batch of missionaries came back, instead of finding the old sleepy mission settlement they found a ghost city, with much of the physical plant of the Mission destroyed. Since no coconuts were gathered during the war, thickets of young palms were growing under the trees. Along the roadside they could see old rusty Sherman tanks, building material, and corrugated iron. The first lay missionary who came back to Finschhafen in November 1945 was Mr David Rohrlach, the pre-war captain of the *Bavaria*.

Soon after Rohrlach came Mr Emil Wagner, the New Guinea-born son of a German missionary. He took over the three plantations, and built them up again. He found himself in a discouraging situation. Salankaua, once a plantation of 27,000 palms, was reduced to a mere 5,000. Heldsbach had suffered less. Of 16,000 palms, 10,000 were left. Timbulim had suffered most. Within the plantation, secondary bush had grown up, and the palms had to be freed from vines. Wagner had to make the best of it to clean the plantations and collect the coconuts. To make it worthwhile, he also collected scrap iron, tyres, motor spirit, and corrugated iron sheets, to help in the rebuilding program. At the end of 1948, he reported that he had made 100 tons of copra during the year. Before the war, the three plantations had an output of 400 tons. Yet the present labour costs were even higher. Many bridges, flimsily built by the army, had to be renewed.

The many cattle, which formerly grazed in the plantations, were gone. However, the faithful foreman Zure of Heldsbach had wisely driven some cattle back into the mountains when the Japanese forces occupied the area. Of these,

The aftermath of the war at Finschhafen.
588

seven head were brought back, and some more were purchased from near Lae to build up the herd again.

During the war, thousands of New Guineans, while serving in the army as carriers and cooks, had come into contact with foreigners. No longer did they regard the Europeans as supermen, but as very human beings, with frustrations and failings. This helped the New Guineans to gain more self-respect. While in the past they had sometimes been too easily satisfied, they now became more ambitious to take things into their own hands. Thus, the time was ripe for closer cooperation in the spiritual as well as in the economic field. The ideal opportunity to practise partnership offered itself in the plantation work. A share-farming system was devised, whereby certain Christian congregations formed themselves into a cooperative with the purpose of taking over some parts of mission plantations. This was the beginning of a very successful cooperation between the Lutheran Mission and the New Guineans, which lasted almost 30 years. Heldsbach plantation was split between cooperatives from Heldsbach villages, Wareo, and Dedua. Salankaua was taken over by a group of cooperatives from the coastal villages and Sattelberg. In Timbulim, a group of people from the Hube mountains built a copra kiln, and started plantation work.

In 1955, Wagner reported that the initial difficulties had now been overcome. The

Zure of Qoia (Finschhafen).

plantations had been cleaned up and freed from undergrowth and war material. The cooperatives were satisfied with the arrangement. It gave them some extra money and, what is more, they felt part and parcel of the common work.

Apart from the cooperatives, the Mission had a labour force of its own to look after the cattle and to undertake the replanting of palm trees. They planted 5,000 palm trees and 5,000 cocoa trees. The cattle herd grew to 90 head. In addition, the plantation had 20 horses, 150 pigs, and 90 goats. Most of the outside work was handed over to the very capable foreman, Zure. In 1959, the copra production reached 136 tons. This was also the year when a new bridge was built over the Mape river. This major construction work was carried out by Mr Russell Sherer from Lutheran Mission Madang. Meanwhile, Mr Wagner had left New Guinea for good, and Mr Don Ruthenberg, a Queenslander, had taken over at Finschhafen. In 1963, the Salankaua part of the plantations were taken over by Horin, a very capable New Guinean. It can be said that both European and New Guinean managers never stopped planting new trees. Some of the increase in copra production is due to this fact. In spite of quite promising results, it must be said that the Finschhafen plantations will always remain a marginal proposition. In order to survive, they need a good manager and reasonable prices for copra and cocoa.

Malahang Plantation

Like the Finschhafen plantations, Malahang was not started primarily as a business enterprise. The Lutherans intended to establish a coastal base for the Jabem-speaking population. Such a base could also become a stepping-stone for further mission work into the interior. After all, the proximity of the wide Markham Valley as a door to the Highlands made it advisable to secure land in that corner of the country. Should any profits accrue later, they could be used for furthering the mission work. First and foremost, however, work had to be provided for young New Guineans in the Gulf and Markham areas. In Dr Hahl, the German Governor, the Mission had a well-meaning friend. He admired the work which was being done around Finschhafen. When contacted about the acquisition of land, he offered 500 hectares of land bordering the Busu river. After discussing matters at the mission conference and obtaining the approval of the home board, Flierl purchased the land. [28]

The building up of the new plantation was entrusted to the Revd Georg Stuerzenhofecker, a Jabem-speaking missionary. On September 12, 1916, he started with the clearing of the bush, employing a group of 35 New Guineans. In the course of the following six years, Stuerzenhofecker cleared 250 hectares and planted 22,000 palms. In 1922, the Mission employed an American farmer, Mr Andrew Freese, and Stuerzenhofecker could be released for spiritual work. Freese stayed for six years, and during that time he planted another 10,000 palms.

Then the time came when the trees which had been planted first should have been ready to carry nuts. However, there was not much fruit to be gathered. Although the palms grew quite well during the first few years, their bearing capacity was surprisingly low. The investors had overlooked the fact that they had started a coconut plantation in an area which once was an old river bed. It was alluvial soil, with a very high acid content. Even at its best, the plantation did not yield more than 150 tons of copra. The cost of keeping such a large plantation clear was tremendous. Malahang was a failure, as far as copra producing was concerned. After Freese left, right up to the outbreak of World War II, four different men tried their very best to make Malahang a success, but without much result.

Meanwhile, events had taken a new turn. In 1934, the work in the Highlands had been started. The Mission had purchased an aeroplane, and Malahang became the base station for the sending of supplies to the highland. An aerodrome and workshop was built. Now the Mission had an ideal setup for further extension. Alas, this all came to an abrupt end when World War II began, in 1939.

During the war, the flat country between Malahang and Nadzab was regarded as *the* strategic point for both the Allies and the Japanese. It is the door to New Guinea. Consequently, all the villages and settlements in that area suffered most. When Linus Eiermann, the last pre-war manager, took over Malahang again after the war, he found devastation, ruins,

bomb holes, dilapidated barracks, big cement slabs, rusty scrap iron, disused vehicles, European and New Guinean squatters, and roads criss-crossing in all directions. Out of 30,000 palms, there were 9,000 left. What could be done with such a place? The obvious thing was to clean the plantation, cut the undergrowth to find the coconuts, and to start from scratch.

Thirty tons of copra were produced in 1947-48. Cattle were imported from Queensland, and fences were built. In 1949, the mission households could be supplied with milk. In 1951, William Meuser, an agriculturist from the United States, made a survey of the plantation's economic viability, and suggested a change from copra production to dairy farming. Subsequently, the Mission obtained the service of Mr George Knopke, a cattleman from Queensland, and started to follow Mr Meuser's advice. Cattle were imported from Australia, and a slaughter-house was built to enable the sale of fresh beef. By 1955, the herd had increased considerably, and 6,000 gallons of fresh milk were produced during the year. In 1961, the production had reached 32,000 gallons, and milk was commercially marketed under the name 'Tropical Dairies'. During a short interval, the sale of milk was discontinued because of public attacks by competitors. Later, these same people were unable to satisfy the increasing public demand for fresh milk, and the plantation entered the market again. By 1963, the plantation had increased its cattle herd to 700 head, and was now worth £110,000. During the following years, Brahman cattle were imported with a view to gradually changing from dairy to beef production. Right up to 1968, the plantation increased its cattle herd, and became one of the outstanding cattle-breeding stations in Papua New Guinea. In 1970, a small portion of the plantation was set aside as a building site for the newest pastors' training institution of the Church, Martin Luther Seminary.

Nagada Plantation

The Rhenish Mission started its work in the Madang area. Whereas Finschhafen was far away from a European settlement, Madang had both a business community and a government district centre. Unlike the people at Finschhafen, New Guineans living around Madang had ample opportunities to find work. The Neuendettelsau Mission had to acquire Salankaua plantation in order to have a base for providing the various mission stations with supplies. Nagada could never have been a base station, since it was too far away from Madang. What then motivated the Rhenish Mission to start work at Nagada? The Revd Blum, the missionary in charge of the business and administrative section, wrote in a letter to his home board:

> We must never forget that it is our main task to preach the gospel of Jesus Christ. This, however, cannot be done without the financial means. It appears that our Lord is providing us with such means in an unusual way. The means are available, all we have to do is to use them. I would go so far as to say that the work at Nagada is to at least 50 per cent mission work. [29]

This is a clear indication of what was in the minds of the Mission when it started plantation work. Furthermore, Nagada was not only to become a mission plantation, but also a school station.

In 1906, the Rhenish Mission purchased from the German Colonial Administration 303 hectares of land north of Madang, known as Nagada. The man who started the work was Gerhard Mange. After his early death, he was followed in 1908 by Emil Wilms. In 1909, Wilms reported that by the end of 1909 55 hectares had been cleared and planted with coconut trees. Unfortunately, Wilms could not stand the climate, and had to return to Germany. After him came Heinrich Schamann, a carpenter by trade, who had come earlier to help in building the mission stations. Soon more land was cleared, and the cattle which so far had been grazing at Nobonob could now be transferred to the plantation. In 1913, Schamann reported the acquisition of an additional 500 hectares of land, of which 120 hectares had been planted up with coconut trees. In 1914, Heinrich Schamann, after a very successful start at Nagada and 10 years' continuous service, was due for long-service leave in Germany. He was replaced by Jacob Welsch, an ordained man. Heinrich Schamann wrote in his report to the home board:

> After Eckershoff was transferred to Kurum I had to take over teaching. It is not an easy job. The children of Ruo village always seem to forget their lessons more quickly than they learned them. [30]

Welsch looked after the plantation, as well as teaching and doing language work. In his report to the home board after the end of the war, he wrote: 'Right after the beginning of the war we had to return some of the workers to their villages because of lack of funds. We only kept 20 men for the most necessary work.' [31] In 1918, Welsch had to take over some other work and was replaced by Missionary Graeb. [32] Meanwhile, the Rhenish Mission was no longer able to exercise the rights of an owner. All German mission property had been entrusted to the newly-formed Lutheran Mission New Guinea, which was under the jurisdiction of the United Evangelical Lutheran Church in Australia and the Iowa Synod in the United States. Adolf Obst was now responsible to the Director of the Mission in Brisbane. Conditions in Nagada had become very favourable, and Obst could reap where others had sown. This does not in any way belittle the efforts of this capable man. In 1929, for instance, he reported that the plantation had a crop of 220 tons of copra. There was also a large herd of cattle which supplied the mission households with milk and butter and beef. In 1930, 250 hectares of land had been planted up with 25,000 palms.

In 1930, the Rhenish Mission took back for a short time its old mission field in New Guinea. Adolf Obst, as a result of the new arrangement, handed over the plantation to Ernst Dahlhaeuser, who had been sent out from Barmen. Obst went to Finschhafen to take over the Salankaua plantation. This second period of Rhenish Mission activities in New Guinea lasted only over two years. Owing to heavy commitments in other parts of the world, they felt they could not make available men and means in sufficient numbers to do justice to the work in New Guinea. Lutheran Mission Madang now became the mission field of the American Lutheran Church.

In 1933, Nagada plantation, after many changes in management, was taken over by Mr Berthold Jaeschke, a young South Australian. His labour line consisted of approximately 80 men from Nobonob, Amele, and Begesin. A large stockyard was built for approximately 300 head of cattle. For the production of approximately 350 tons of copra per year, a new copra kiln was erected. [33] In a special report, Jaeschke mentioned the services and friendship he had received at Nagada from a number of men, New Guineans as well as Europeans. Jack Lindner, his hard-working countryman, together with his gang, split fence posts and made fences as well as copra sheds. Heinrich Schamann built a new copra kiln, and Ray Barber was mostly engaged in pit-sawing for the various building projects in the Madang district. Batet, a leading Christian from Nobonob, was the spiritual leader of the Nagada community at that time. He was a true brother to all. He and his family led an exemplary Christian life. He also conducted the Sunday services, and held many funerals during those years. Jaeschke served at Nagada up to 1941, when he went on long-service leave. The plantation was taken over by August Bertelsmeier, who had been working as a mission carpenter. Bertelsmeier remained at Nagada until he was taken prisoner by the Japanese in 1942.

The Nagada plantation did not suffer as much war damage as the Finschhafen or Malahang plantations, both of which were directly occupied by the armed forces. This caused more devastation than the direct bombing. Nagada, on the other hand, suffered by neglect. When August Bertelsmeier arrived back in New Guinea to take over Nagada, his main task was to cut down the undergrowth and high grass before he could start looking for coconuts.

Meanwhile, a new development had also taken place in Madang. New Guineans, owing to their wartime experiences, were conscious of how much they yet lacked. They wanted to take part in the development of their land. What better chance for a Christian congregation than a nearby mission plantation! The congregation at Amele, under their very capable leader Ud, wanted to become a partner at Nagada. They formed themselves into a cooperative, and took over part of the Nagada plantation on a share-farming basis. Both sides were satisfied with the arrangement. Later on, the Nobonob people did likewise, but it did not work so well, according to Bertelsmeier's reports. In 1951, Louis Winter, an American farmer, took over the work. Meanwhile, the war-time scars had been removed, and the plantation had been well looked after. Winter reported that during the year 210 tons of copra had been shipped. Compared with Finschhafen or Malahang, this

was a record harvest so soon after the war. A taking of £10,424 was split between the two partners. Both sides were highly satisfied. All through the following 20 years, the production could be kept at that level of 200 to 230 tons per year, with the exception of 1962, when a bumper harvest of 300 tons was recorded.

Over the next 20 years, all the managers paid particular attention to making full use of the tremendous grazing capacity of the plantation. The cattle herd grew from 52 head in 1952 to 400 head by 1970, and the milk and meat production accordingly. One of the managers enlarged the poultry section, and eggs were produced at an increasing rate, reaching 11,000 dozen per year in 1969. Indeed, Nagada plantation played an important part in financing the Mission's activities in Papua New Guinea.

Kurum Plantation

After an early tragic and unsuccessful attempt to start mission work on Karkar Island, the Rhenish Mission tried again in 1911 by sending the Revd Eckershoff, who was joined in 1912 by the Revd George. They settled at Kurum because of its suitable harbour facilities. Unknown to them, they had picked a piece of most fertile land. The Mission purchased 200 hectares of land for a mission station and a coconut plantation. It appeared that Kurum was to follow the pattern of Nagada. As at Nagada, the first group of plantation labourers received lessons in religion as well as in reading and writing. For a short time prior to his going on long-service leave, Heinrich Schamann also went to Kurum. After Schamann had gone and the war had broken out, there was no replacement for him in sight. Thus, the Karkar missionaries Eckershoff and George had to look after the plantation right up to 1922, when Mr C. Holtkamp, who had been at Nagada, took over the plantation and trade store at Kurum. Under his management, a considerable part of the plantation was built up. He had to leave New Guinea because of ill-health. In 1930, he was followed by Heinrich Schamann, who, after an absence of 15 years, had again come back to New Guinea to continue work at Kurum. Schamann continued to plant more coconut trees. Another 95 hectares of land were purchased, making a total of about 300 hectares. When World War II broke out, Heinrich

Heinrich Schamann.

Schamann was interned, and Mr Hans Thogerson, an American, was put in charge of Kurum. Soon the Japanese invasion put an end to all peaceful work.

The first plantation manager who took over Kurum after the end of the war was the veteran plantation man, Jack Lindner, who had served the Mission in many ways during his 25 years of service, beginning in 1922. The first thing he had to do was to build a sea wall to protect the plantation from the inroads which the sea had been making. During the first year, he shipped 50 tons of copra. Later, Lindner was helped by Hermann Radke, who took over after Lindner left for Malahang. By 1949, the plantation had picked up considerably, and they harvested 165 tons of copra during the year. The local people were not very much inclined to do plantation work, and so highlanders had to be hired. By 1951, the number of trees bearing had increased to 9,000. In addition, 12,000 cocoa trees had been planted. For the next 20 years, there was a continuous upward trend noticeable, as can be seen from the plantation reports. The amount of copra shipped from Kurum rose from 185 tons in 1951 to 342 tons

in 1971. The cocoa production rose from 14 tons in 1951 to 65 tons in 1971. The cocoa plantation is now fully planted. In 1971, there were 27,000 coconut palms and 57,000 cocoa trees. Kurum had quite a number of managers, who, together with their New Guinean helpers, made Kurum a financial success.

Gizarum Plantation

In 1934, the attention of the officials of the Evangelical Lutheran Church in Australia was drawn to the fact that there was an open door for mission work in New Guinea. It may well be called divine guidance that the first group of emissaries of the church who went to New Guinea came into contact with the Lutherans at Finschhafen. Because of heavy commitments in the Highlands, Finschhafen Lutheran Mission found it difficult to continue work on their Siassi mission field. They therefore suggested that the Australian Lutherans take over the work at Siassi. Negotiations took place, and as a consequence the mission station Awelkon on Rooke Island was ceded to the Evangelical Lutheran Church of Australia.

Two years later, the only plantation on the island which was in the hands of two European planters and traders was offered for sale. This was an excellent opportunity for the Australian Lutheran Mission to establish a broader basis for its work. The plantation consisted of 530 acres, of which 212 had been planted up, and had the only good harbour in the whole group of islands. This property was purchased for £10,000. In order to raise the purchase money, the New Guinea Mission Society was founded. Both the purchase money and the working capital were raised by the Australian church people.

There were other reasons why the Australian Lutheran Mission was keen to take possession of the property. Since Rooke was an island and thus very confined, the missionaries naturally did not want the plantation to fall into the hands of a person inimical to the work of Christian mission, or of a competing denomination. Furthermore, the plantation provided working opportunities for the islanders.

Years later, the New Guinea Mission Society in Australia was dissolved, and the plantation managed by the church through its agent, the Australian Lutheran Mission. Although, during the first years prior to the war, the financial situation gave rise to difficulties, this changed after the war. Then, for many years, the plantation was a source of income for the church, as well as a 'helpmate' to the church in providing shipping and technical services. It also provided working opportunities for the students of the Gelem High School. In spite of the initial difficulties prior to the war, the work had gone ahead tremendously. All available land was planted with coconuts, cocoa, and kapok. The sawmill provided timber for the various housing projects. In 1937, the Mission acquired two vessels. The M.V. *Umboi* enabled the islanders to keep in contact with the outside world, ship their produce, and get their supplies. The stage was set for further development, when World War II broke out and put an end to most activities, at least for the time being. Like many other small coastal vessels, the *Umboi* became a war casualty. As has been pointed out already, after the war the Mission reaped the harvest which had been sown before the war. With a new hope, and full of confidence, the missionary work was taken up again. A new *Umboi* was purchased, which kept up a regular service with the mainland. The sawmill was started again to provide timber for building and repair jobs. During all these years, the Australian Lutheran Mission enjoyed the services of devoted men in the economic field: G. Noack, V. Neumann, L. Noller, E. Thamm, T. Pile, M. Braunack, and others. Much of the success of the plantation is due to their devotion to duty.

After the amalgamation of the two Lutheran churches in Australia, Siassi remained a separate unit for a time, and Gizarum plantation was managed by the Siassi Church Council. Later, the management was taken over by Kambang Holdings, the service organization of the Lutheran Church. Meanwhile, the second *Umboi* was transferred to Lutheran Shipping and put on the Finschhafen run. Since the Siassi people were not part of the bigger Lutheran organization, it was no longer necessary to keep up its own shipping service. Lutheran shipping provided a fortnightly service.

Following the trend of the time, the Evangelical Lutheran Church of Papua New Guinea felt that wherever New Guineans are interested in taking over former mission

plantations, they should be encouraged to do so. Consequently, the Gizarum plantation was sold in 1981 to a New Guinean private investor. The Gizarum plantation had served the Church and Mission for over 40 years, and had provided the means for spiritual work by employing men who were ready and able to serve in God's kingdom. [34]

A New Development

By 1969, it became obvious that in the near future the Lutheran Mission would be handing over its work to an autonomous church. The question arose: Can the national church be burdened in the future with all sorts of activities such as running an airline or a string of workshops, a supply house, or a row of plantations? While nobody doubted that all assets should be kept for the benefit of the church, it was generally felt that the church itself should be set free for its proper mandate.

With regard to plantations, a commission was appointed which, together with two Australian businessmen, Messrs O. Heinrich and J. Singe, studied the plantation set-up. It recommended that the management of plantations should be handed over to Lutheran Economic Service (LES). Thus, in October 1969, an office was opened at Lae with Mr D. Ruthenberg as general manager of LES and Mr N. Bradtke as accountant. From then on, the plantations were run as a separate entity. They now had to fend for themselves. Any losses sustained were no longer carried by the general mission treasury. Any services rendered to the Mission or Church had to be charged. This changed the whole relationship between plantations and the mission stations.

Meanwhile, the situation had also changed in other respects. Many mission stations had become vacant. The supply of milk, meat, and eggs was not required to the same extent, and consequently the upkeep of dairies and poultry farms was a less viable proposition. Fluctuating prices for copra and cocoa, and rapidly increasing labour costs, caused many plantations to become a marginal proposition financially. More and more plantations became a burden instead of an asset to the church. On the other hand, there were ever-increasing and sometimes quite violent claims by former landowners for the return of the land, plus improvement.

In 1976, Kambang Holdings was formed. (See also below, at the end of this chapter.) All income-earning sections of the church were grouped together under the newly-formed company, which was 100 per cent owned by the Evangelical Lutheran Church Property Trust. From now on, it was not the church, but Kambang Holdings whose responsibility it was to dispose of, or otherwise make use of, the income-earning branches of the former Lutheran Mission, as well as of the Gizarum Plantation belonging to the former Australian Lutheran Mission.

On the recommendation of an international team of experts,[35] all business enterprises of the church were to be disposed of in favour of passive investment. However, quite apart from this, the economic situation of the plantations put even more pressure on Kambang Holdings to sell out these holdings as soon as possible. So, concerted efforts have been made to sell these properties.

Gizarum: This plantation was sold in 1981 to an investor who acted on behalf of a local group of people.

Kabak: This small plantation, which was purchased in 1958 by the Lutheran Mission, was usually managed by the missionary in charge of the Kabak circuit. In 1982, it was sold to a group of local people.

Malahang: In 1981, Kambang Holdings decided to sell the plantation to the local people. The land was sub-divided, to keep a portion for future church needs. Since the people were interested in purchasing the land only, the cattle herd was sold off. However, up to the time of writing it has not been possible to finalize the sale, because the purchasers have been unable to organize themselves and agree on the future use of the land.

Finschhafen: In the case of the Finschhafen plantations, Kambang Holdings has been forced to deal with the former landowners. These people have two problems: They have no money, and there is no agreement among themselves as to how they will handle the land once it is sold to them. Kambang Holdings is willing to let them have the land at a minimal cost, but the government insists that a fair price, determined by government valuation, be paid

for the properties. In 1985, the Department of Lands in Port Moresby reported that, on instruction by the Prime Minister, the land in Finschhafen should be acquired by the government.

Nagada: Here again, strong pressure is being exerted by the local people to purchase the land. However, they have the same problem: no money and no unity. Providing unity is reached, Kambang Holdings is prepared to lease the property under Kambang management until such time as the necessary deposit has been earned to acquire a bank loan.

Kurum: Kurum is still quite a profitable plantation, and it is only because of its profits that Kambang Holdings can keep its other plantations going. Meanwhile, an agreement has been reached between the church and the people in Karkar whereby the church guarantees that in the event of sale the property will be sold only to the former landowners, and that the church will give some sort of timetable as to when this may happen.

Just before and since changes brought about by the creation of Kambang Holdings, the management of plantations gradually changed from expatriate management to management by New Guineans. Only Kurum plantation retains the service of an expatriate manager. For many years, New Guineans have played an important role in the management of plantations.

We remember the services of Erinumeng, Tieo, Sawa, and Yateng on Nagada Plantation; of Zure, Aias, and Mitine at Heldsbach Plantation; of Horing at Salankaua; and of Naialor, Yateng, and Mupang at Timbulim Plantation.

(For a list of Mission personnel in Agricultural and Development Work, see the appendix.)

Namasu

The Roots of Namasu[36]

The challenges for Christian missions working in a developing country have always been manifold. Not only are missionaries supposed to spread the Gospel, to teach

595

Namasu headquarters.

children, and to tend the sick, but they are also faced with constant questions of social ills, and of how to raise the general economic standard of the people. When the first missionaries arrived in New Guinea, they found a society in no way ready to listen to the Gospel or to change their way of life. Thus, the groundwork had to be laid for a change of attitude toward life in general. The preaching of the Gospel had to go hand in hand with a general raising of the low standard of living. Here we find the roots of the economic assistance programs which played such a prominent part in the work of the early missionaries. They imported cattle, horses, better strains of pigs, potatoes, new types of vegetables, corn, citrus fruits, and, last but not least, coffee. Yet, at first the people were not at all interested in new-fangled ideas, new crops, or a new concept of work. Thus, missionaries were saddled with bartering and trading from the very beginning. Gradually, it became an accepted thing that a mission station not only had a church, but also a small store, since there was no other trading agency which could have taken care of the needs of the people. The missionary fathers could not very well satisfy their

consciences by saying that their duty was simply to preach the Gospel, and otherwise leave the people to their own devices. They were not dreamers. They built stations, schools, churches, horse-tracks; they started gardens, and put the young students to work where they could acquire a certain practical knowledge. [37] Many of the small coconut plantations along the coast are a direct result of that early pioneering work.

At the beginning of World War II, the Lutheran Mission had 24 mission stations, every one with a trade store providing an essential service to the surrounding population. It was a very modest effort. The amount of goodwill created, however, was infinitely more important. After World War II, the situation changed dramatically. The people had experienced an awe-inspiring invasion. They had been driven from their villages by carpets of bombs. Foreign soldiers equipped with the most modern tools and with a never-ending stream of supplies were taking possession of their country. 'How in all the world can human beings be so rich and so ruthless?' they asked. These experiences changed the outlook of the people.

After the war, the American army dumped millions of dollars' worth of material into the sea. How can you explain such actions to a people unfamiliar with the techniques and economics of war? It is not at all surprising that as a result of these experiences dormant cargo cults swept across New Guinea like a bushfire. 'The Europeans are going to exploit us. They take our country. They have a secret formula of success. Let us get busy making up for lost time.' Old army trucks were pulled out of the bush. Trade stores were opened, involving business which so far seemed to have been reserved for Chinese and for missionaries. The people were not ready to listen. It took years until the storm blew over; but it had left its marks. Old values started to become obsolete, and an ancient community system was being replaced by a modern money economy, bewildering and at the same time fascinating to a race which had hardly passed the threshold of stone age. Money was becoming the criterion of power, wealth, and social standing. Coffee, cocoa, gold, clubs, scout movements, migration schemes, education in every form, betting shops, cooperative societies, dozens of different Christian denominations, and many so far unknown things were literally being forced upon the people. [38] Indeed, a new era had taken hold of New Guinea.

Such was the situation in the 1950s. Immediately after the war, the Mission had decided to discontinue trading. However, circumstances were stronger than ideals. Soon the missionaries on isolated stations found themselves in a situation where they were besieged by thousands of people clamouring for goods. Very reluctantly, they again started to render a service which nobody else at that time was in a position to provide. The kind of help they could give was by no means sufficient. New Guineans who had started to produce coffee and copra, expected marketing and transportation assistance. [39] How could the Mission perform its main task of looking after the spiritual welfare of the people, carry through a large educational and medical program, and at the same time conduct a smoothly-running marketing and supply service? Thus, as far back as 1951, the idea of segregating the industrial and business activities of the Mission, and of handing it over to another organization, was

discussed. Lack of staff prevented the Mission from putting such thoughts into effect. The situation became more pressing every day, and something had to be done. True, there was the mission supply house, but it was geared to supply mission stations with everything from an anchor to a hairpin. There was a so-called trade goods department, but it played a minor role in the mission's supply system. Perhaps one day a supply house serving the indigenous people could be established.

The Birth of Namasu

In 1957, after returning from a furlough in Germany, I was asked by the Mission to supervise the first congregation-owned bulk store at Finschhafen/Sattelberg. At the same time, I was to make a survey of the economic situation in the villages, and possibly come up with certain proposals to materialize the dream of a New Guinean-owned marketing and supply organization. The store at Finschhafen could well be called a forerunner of Namasu. Already as far back as 1949, the Sattelberg Missionary Adam Metzner had handed over the mission trade store to the congregation. It was his idea to use this store as a training ground for New Guineans, as well as a source of income for the congregation to carry out certain projects. Metzner's idea had been followed by other congregations. In most instances, it was only the store at the mission station which had been — in a most informal way — handed over to the congregation. However, at Finschhafen, Metzner, with the assistance of Emil Wagner, had established a bulkstore, which served approximately 30 village outlets.

During a survey trip which brought me to hundreds of villages and gave opportunities for discussion with village leaders, missionaries, and government officers, it became obvious that, particularly in the Morobe District, something should be done without delay. Indeed, if anything worthwhile was to be achieved, the Lutheran Mission had to set up a central buying point and marketing agency capable of looking after the many small buying points and trade stores. Such an organization would possibly have to have its own transportation system to relieve mission ships and aeroplanes.

While supervising the Finschhafen enterprise, I was offered a small coastal vessel, the *Wing Wah*. The proposal to purchase this vessel was put to the elders of the Sattelberg and Malalo congregations. They decided to combine forces and to buy the ship. It was renamed *Mula*, and for many years served both congregations, as well as Namasu later. This was the first case of two congregations working together in the economic field. Others were to follow. The response of the Malalo and Sattelberg people encouraged us to try to build up an all New Guinean-owned company. The basis for such a company would have to be to work with the people and not simply for them.

With these thoughts in mind, a group of missionaries[40] approached the Lutheran Mission Field Conference in 1958 to sponsor the formation of a new company. The decision was not an easy one, for quite a number of missionaries were of the opinion that the church should not get its hands dirty by being involved in business. The new company was to be called NATIVE MARKETING AND SUPPLY SERVICE LTD — in short, NAMASU.[41]

After much discussion, Lutheran Mission Conference 1958 decided to sponsor the formation of Namasu. The company was then registered by the Registrar of Companies in Port Moresby on March 26, 1959, with a nominal capital of £100,000 divided into shares of £1 each.

Now the 'child' was born. It may be worthwhile to sum up the situation which led to the formation of the new company. Namasu was not started according to a pre-conceived and well-laid-out plan. This was its strength and at the same time its weakness. It was started because there was an urgent need to do something in the economic sector, in an area which had been neglected. Lutheran missionaries had found from the very beginning that the inherent religious background of religion and life was a valuable heritage of the people, which should be preserved. Perhaps the founding of Namasu can best be described as a reaction to an existing situation of acute underdevelopment. Could we not perhaps guide the Christian people of this land to apply the Gospel to all aspects of their daily life?

The Growing Up

It is a fascinating and sometimes very complex story which now unfolds. Shortly after the mission conference in February 1959, a valuable property was offered to Namasu at Voco Point, Lae. It consisted of a residence close to the waterside, with cargo shed and a dilapidated wharf. Included in the offer was an old motor vessel, the M.V. *Morna*, which the company did not want. Later, this proved to be the money-spinner for the first year. On April 10, the property was taken over. The first meeting of the new company took place on April 12, and the office-bearers were elected.[42]

During the following share-promotion work, which took me to many parts of the Morobe District, I had the advantage of having been known to many people as the business manager of Lutheran Mission. Within the first year, Namasu had over a thousand share applications. The response and the willingness to participate in the enterprise was almost frightening. Unaware of the many pitfalls, the people's expectations were higher than ours. Constantly they had been cautioned; but what can one do against preconceived ideas? They were also told in no uncertain terms that Namasu was not a savings bank, from which you can withdraw your money at any time. They would become part-owners of a 'hen' which perhaps may be laying some eggs, but you cannot kill the hen if you want eggs. In every speech they were told: 'For every pound you invest you may perhaps get one shilling "profit" at the end of the year'. Looking back today, it can be clearly seen that some of these exaggerated expectations were a kind of cargo cult.

A promotion trip to Australia became necessary, because according to the laws of Papua New Guinea the share capital of any company had to be 60 per cent in the hands of British people or organizations. The New Guineans, however, were not British citizens, and thus could own only 40 per cent. This law was later revoked.

The other outstanding events of the first year of operation were the opening of a shop in the town of Lae, offering religious literature and, as a sideline, carvings from Tami Island.

The most significant undertaking, however, was the starting of a commercial

598

A busy day at Namasu headquarters.

The Namasu fleet at Voco Point.

599

school to educate New Guinean staff members. It was the first school of that type in the Territory of New Guinea. The young men educated there proved to be the most reliable staff members which Namasu ever had;[43] I know of no instance in which any of these men became involved in an embezzlement case.

Toward the end of 1959, Namasu started supplying congregational stores in the Morobe district from Ulap to Zaka. The first 60 tons of coffee had come in for processing, and the airstrip at Pindiu was finished.

Meanwhile, during 1960, the European personnel of the company also had to be increased. The most outstanding acquisition was Mr Arthur Goward, a young Australian accounts clerk who stayed with Namasu for ten years and in 1968 became its general manager.

In February 1960, the company replaced the old *Morna* with a North Sea trawler (80 feet long), which was renamed *Salankaua*. Later on, a small additional coast vessel, the M.V. *Sio*, was purchased. Now the company had three ships: the *Salankaua* as a general carrier and money-spinner, and the two small coastal boats to serve customers along the long drawn-out sea route from Zaka to Saidor. This involvement in shipping, right from the very beginning, was an indication of the company's concern for the people in the outlying areas. The Lutheran Mission at that time had only the *Simbang* serving on that route — a ship far too big to call at the various small ports. For the people, a small ship calling regularly meant a door to the outside world, with patients, evangelists, school children, copra, and merchandise being loaded and unloaded. 1961 was marked by the acquisition of a store at Mumeng, to serve the people in the Mumeng and Buang area.

In 1961, the missionaries of Chimbu and Mount Hagen, W. Bergmann and Strauss, asked Namasu to handle their coffee export. In Lae, a garment factory was opened, employing between six and eight women. Under the direction of Mrs Fugmann, the factory supplied the company with thousands of garments of all descriptions for more than ten years.

During 1962, the first consignments of coffee came by road from the Highlands to Lae. On the north coast, a string of Namasu-constructed copra kilns were erected. The copra purchases increased over 100 per cent,

Opening a new branch (at centre, Stahl Mileng and W. Fugmann).

owing to a regular shipping service. In Wantoat, a new Namasu store was opened.

1963 was marked by the opening of the new coffee factory at Lae and the start of the Highlands work. The ELCONG Highlands Conference had asked Namasu to extend its activities into the Highlands. Both at Banz and Kainantu, land had been acquired. At Banz, a new bulk store was built, the very first in the Highlands.

The increased coastal work made it necessary for the company to acquire another vessel, *Kauri*. The small ships sometimes were away from ten to 14 days, calling at dozens of little places under difficult conditions, picking up produce and selling trade goods. It was never a paying proposition, but a service to the communities. Namasu could afford it only because of the profits made by the *Salankaua* on its commercially-viable runs. Meanwhile, by 1967, Namasu had opened branches at Kainantu, Chimbu, Banz, and Mount Hagen. These branches had been staffed by a group of enthusiastic and well-meaning but inexperienced young Europeans.

In 1968, Namasu had reached sales figures of $2.7 million. It had 7,000 shareholders, and 28 European and over 300 New Guinean employees. [44] In Lae, Namasu had a new administrative building and bulk store. Sufficient land had been acquired for future expansion. Early in 1968, I, the Managing Director, went on furlough, and the Board of Directors appointed a team to carry the burden of management: Mr Arthur Goward, General Manager; Mr Neil Bradtke, Accountant; Mr Norman Goward, Merchandise Manager; and Mr Barry Hicks, Branches Inspector.

However, the year 1968 proved to be a turning-point in the company's history. It was heralded by the explosion of the good ship *Salankaua* in the port of Cape Killerton in October 1968. Unfortunately, the ship had been entrusted to a man who had just received his master's ticket. It blew up while discharging fuel. Fortunately, no human lives were lost. While the ship itself was covered by insurance, the company lost approximately $30,000 earning capacity per year, which would have been sufficient to subsidize the maintenance and running costs for the small ships. For Namasu,

Buying copra at Ronzi, North Coast.

this meant the beginning of the end as far as shipping was concerned.

The Crisis

In trying to give an unbiased account, I shall use as a guideline a research paper submitted by Mr G. Messner to the Board of Directors of Namasu in 1970. Mr Messner, an economist, studied the company's activities, covering the most critical period between 1968 and 1970. In his report, he says the main reasons for the recession were: too rapid growth, lack of qualified staff, and lack of capital.

Some of the figures used in Mr Messner's report will be given in presenting this depressing chapter of the company's development. In most cases, the figures speak for themselves. In some cases, however, personal observations have to be added in order to give a comprehensive picture.

Too rapid growth. In 1968, Namasu had about 20 wholesale outlets, mostly in the Morobe district. The bigger branches were in the Highlands. The three most important branches were at Kainantu, Chimbu, and Mount Hagen. Taking 1967 as the last normal year and 1969 as the absolute 'bottom' in Namasu's history, we find the following figures, covering the three branches.

	1967	1969	
Sales:	$490,000	977,000	(Increase 100%)
Expenses:	$ 36,000	102,000	(Increase 200%)
Profit/Loss:	$ 38,000	-49,000	(Loss 230%)

Taking 1967 as an average year, the branches showed a 7 per cent net profit. If we transfer this to 1969, the three branches would have had to make a net profit of $76,000. Instead, they made a loss of $49,000. This meant a reduced income within two years of $125,000. If we add the loss of income by the *Salankaua*, we find that Namasu was $150,000 poorer in 1969, compared with 1967. In 1968, the company could afford, from its 1967 reserves, to pay a dividend of five per cent. In 1969, this was not possible.

Most reluctantly, I have to relate some of my observations when I came back from furlough in February 1969. Owing to the hasty growth of the Highlands branches, the

602

accounts department at headquarters was far behind. The balance sheet as per June 30, 1968, had not been finalized yet. This meant that the management was in the dark as to the financial position. Yet the Lae merchandise department continued supplying these branches. Meanwhile, the losses in the Highlands branches were accumulating.

The following facts and figures are quoted from notes which were made during a Highlands trip in March-April 1969.

Kainantu: The sales had increased from $158,000 in 1967 to $341,000 in 1969. In his ambition to push the sales, the manager sent truckloads of goods twice a week to Okapa without proper stock-transfer notes. On the way back, the truck driver would bring the cash takings, again uncounted. Nobody knew what stock was at Kainantu, Raipinka, Henganofi, or Okapa. The only book which was kept was the cash book. The expense bill had gone up tremendously. The manager in charge had built up almost a small township on the grounds of Raipinka mission station, without headquarters being aware of it. Thousands of dollars of stock losses were not accounted for.

Chimbu: The sales in Chimbu had gone from $100,000 in 1967 to $300,000 in 1969. The expenses, however, were four times higher than in 1967. In order to boost his sales, the manager had given out goods on a commission basis to 19 different village storekeepers. The arrangement was to pay for the goods as they were sold. The goods were delivered, but the money did not come back at the same rate. The result was a devastating loss by the Chimbu branch.

Mount Hagen: Here we found the same picture. Everything was done to push the sales. Thousands of dollars' worth of cigarettes were sold every month to European traders on a credit basis, while Namasu had to pay cash. The branch was disorganized, the stock unclean. The manager was busy organizing a New Guinean-owned transport company. He built a warehouse on Namasu ground with money received from these people, which caused us no end of trouble. According to the sparse figures available, between $40,000 and $50,000 were not accounted for. The net loss for 1969 was $23,000, whereas there should have been a profit of at least $20,000.

Indeed, it was an ugly picture with which the management of Namasu was confronted in March and April 1969. Within a few weeks, the branch managers were relieved of their duties. However, the harm had been done both to the finance and to the reputation of Namasu. The company's very foundation had been shaken by these erratic happenings. How could this all happen without headquarters even being fully aware of it? Obviously, the lines of communication had been severed. Wasn't there a branches inspector? Wasn't it his duty to visit the branches, and to report his findings? Hadn't management realized that the cash flow was out of balance?

The development in the Highlands had been like an avalanche, which headquarters apparently had been unable to stop. The branch managers' prudence had been outmatched by their ambition to get the highest possible sales figures. The extent of the damage after it had come to light had a demoralizing effect. One leading man, when giving notice some months later, said: 'I have outgrown my usefulness to the company'.

In March 1968, Mr A. Goward had taken over the management of Namasu. Now, in August 1969, he gave notice that he would terminate his contract by the end of the year. Indeed, this was another great loss to the company. This is a true record of what had happened. It does, however, not exonerate the Managing Director or the Board in any way. Both parties have to carry a fair share of what happened in the Highlands, and which led to the disaster of 1969. The development of Namasu up to 1967-68 had not been without problems, yet anything the company touched turned out to be successful. Somehow, we thought we would pull through. In looking back, it must be said that the Highlands work was too big a fish for the company at a crucial period of development. By exposing our co-workers to a situation which they obviously were unable to handle, we had failed them and thereby endangered the company's future. Some Board members later tried to find excuses by saying they were not too well informed. They were, of course, informed. An important step like beginning work in the Highlands or appointing a General Manager, had to have the approval of the Board.

Lack of qualified staff. Mr Messner, in his 1970 report, mentions the lack of qualified staff. Indeed, Namasu's weakest point in its 25 years of existence has always been the lack of qualified staff. Large Australian business houses, banks, or insurance companies were in a much better position. They could transfer ambitious young staff members to New Guinea. For them, a transfer meant an advancement in their career. In the case of Namasu it was different. Namasu had to go to the open market. Young men finding themselves in good positions in Australia would not give up their jobs lightly. The usual rate of successful applicants from recruiting trips to Australia was three or four out of 60 applications. Namasu had a number of very fine men from Australia and Germany, but there were also people who were more a burden than a help. Yet, Namasu needed men with commercial training. In his 1971 report, the Registrar of Cooperatives, when explaining the very high losses of the Chimbu Coffee Society, wrote: 'Inadequate supervision introduces a large element of risk ... the answer is only to be found by employing more qualified staff to safeguard against failure.' Qualified and trustworthy staff, however, were very hard to come by.

The lesson which the management had learnt from the Highlands disaster was that qualified staff is the one and only consideration for expansion. Consequently, no new developments were started after 1969, apart from the aviation program. In spite of a restrictive policy, the Highlands disaster and its aftermath were the beginning of a long series of setbacks. This was not only due to the financial situation. In fact, there was a slight recovery. The main Highlands branches were now in the hands of responsible men, who did all in their power to make up for the losses. For instance, after the disastrous 1969 result, Mount Hagen and Chimbu broke even in 1970, and made profits in 1971. The causes for the continuous misfortunes were of a different nature. These shall be dealt with one by one.

Namasu never was an illegitimate child of Lutheran Mission. It had been conceived with the approval of many New Guineans and a majority of missionaries. There were, however, some antagonists among the mission staff, and also people who had no set opinion and could be swayed by circumstances. As long as Namasu was successful, everything was quiet on the surface. However, no sooner were a string of setbacks visible, than opponents became most vocal in their criticism.

Land. During the founding years, a large piece of unused ground near the mission headquarter at Ampo was left to Namasu to build staff residences. Since the Mission had no use for the land, and since it was quite interested in having the land developed, it let Namasu have it. Unfortunately, the legal side was never attended to. There were other, mostly small pieces of land, which the big landowner Lutheran Mission gave to Namasu for use.

Nobody was too much concerned. However, when the Namasu manager at Raipinka built almost a village on mission ground, the whole land question quite rightly became a bone of contention. Some people said: 'Is Namasu going to encroach further and further to take over mission land?' Objectively speaking, the critics were right. The land questions should never have been left in abeyance. There was, however, another side to it. In Lae, the Mission had never made use of the bush country along the Busu Road. When Namasu used it, the land was considerably improved. Similarly at Raipinka. There were hundred of acres of mission ground which at that time were hardly used, while Namasu had about four or five acres in use. The hard fact remains, however, that enroachments had taken place, and Namasu had to pay for it dearly at a later stage.

Trade competition. During 1967, a change in management of the Lutheran Supply House at Madang became necessary. The new manager, with no mission background whatsoever, immediately regarded Namasu as a trade competitor, and thus the unusual situation arose where the two 'children' of Lutheran Mission — at least in the eyes of the New Guineans — were fighting against each other. The Supply House manager wrote circulars in which he pointed out that the Mission could become independent of overseas contribution by actively trading with the New Guineans. In his circular to missionaries he stated: 'With the Supply House you have a hen which one day could lay golden eggs'. The New

604

Guinea people, on the other hand, were confused by such happenings.

In the Highlands, particularly in the Chimbu district with its tremendous potential, the company was fully accepted by the people. It had, however, the misfortune that the first two managers were anything but successful against the well-established and mighty government-sponsored coffee society. Some of the missionaries were not very happy with the performances of Namasu. They expected more. Their plans for the future were housing for pastors, better salaries, a pension scheme, and possibly all this to be paid from trade profits. Since Namasu did not come up to their expectations, they started their own trading organization under the name of Kuman Holdings. Indeed, a most unpleasant situation arose, which enhanced neither the reputation of some Chimbu missionaries, nor of Namasu.

Exorbitant expectations. Never at any time during the share drive did Namasu make any promises beyond the five per cent dividend. However, the people threw our cautious remarks to the wind. For them, anything which Europeans organized heralded success. By investing a few dollars, they expected Namasu to be a welfare society, to sell goods under the normal price, to pay a 100 per cent dividend, and to act as a savings bank from which you could withdraw your investment at a moment's notice. In one area, Namasu was expected to pay the council tax and the school fee. The question we had to ask ourselves was: Had Namasu become nothing else but a great cargo movement? When in 1969 no dividends could be paid, Namasu's reputation had reached an all-time low.

Worsening staff situation. Namasu was judged by its staff. The expansion had been so rapid that, in spite of screening, not all branch managers were willing to accept the close tie between Namasu and the church. If a man was not a practising Christian and perhaps a hard business man, it very often lowered the reputation of Namasu. This was a constant embarrassment to the management and Board. The accounts section in Lae, after its arrear in 1968, never caught up. We had to replace one accountant after the other. Even people chosen and recommended by a highly reputable accountancy firm in Australia had to be relieved of their duties. The malady in the accounts section led in turn to insufficient control. Although Namasu was blessed with many fine New Guinean staff members, there were cases of embezzlement and thieving and two proven cases of fraud by Europeans.

Shipping. Ever since the loss of the *Salankaua* by fire, the shipping department had been running at a financial loss. The smaller vessels, which were run as a service to under-developed areas, had to be subsidized. In order to make the shipping department more viable, Namasu purchased a ship in Germany, the M.V. *Holfast.* On the surface the ship looked sound, but when it was overhauled in Hamburg the costs went sky-high. This error of judgment brought the company into a very difficult position, and caused a feeling of irritation between management and Board. Management was accused by the Board of not having handled this matter more carefully. Indeed, management failed to keep in touch with the marine workshop in Hamburg before it was too late.

Great Changes

In spite of the 1969 disaster and the subsequent accounts situation — four accounts within two years — which made the control very difficult, management felt that the company would soon again be out of the difficulties, and this in spite of a very serious case of embezzlement by an office manager. However, when the relationship between board and management, particularly the co-directors from Lutheran Mission, became more and more strained, my health was very much affected, and in November 1971 I tendered my resignation. I had grown tired of fighting against the odds. After my retirement, Mr G. Messner, the Mission Comptroller, was appointed to take over temporarily. This change had certainly not brought about an improved relationship between management and Board.

The Mission members within the Board were not sure about their own business acumen. Had they always done their duty in advising and checking the management? Subsequently, most of these men retired and made room for experienced outsiders: Lae business people. Perhaps they could streamline the company and have it run according to hard-and-fast business rules. Meanwhile, Mr Messner had not been idle. He worked out and introduced a new and strictly centralized accounting system.

In July 1972, the new Board had found a general manager in Mr Ramsay, a former army colonel. The new accounting system was to be implemented under him. All branches' accounts were to be kept at headquarters, and managers were to be informed about the results of their trading at the end of the financial period. This caused great unrest among them. Some of the Highlands branches, which previously had made great losses, had meanwhile been staffed by good men, while the quality of accountants at headquarters had not improved very much. In order to carry through the new system, the Board hired more and more Europeans, and finally the head office at Lae was overstaffed. This in turn was resented by the New Guinean staff members. The overhead expenses were far in excess of former years, while the efficiency of headquarters had not increased by the same degree.

When in February 1973 the general share-holders' meeting dealing with the financial result of June 1972 took place, a number of Highlands shareholders revolted. They had come to find out why their company had again not made any profits and consequently no dividends could be paid. The Highlands branches were now working profitably, but the profits were 'eaten up' by the inflated headquarters staff. An additional cause of suspicion was the presence of a number of white business men, who were now the directors of the company. 'Perhaps they were going to exploit Namasu?' At any rate, for the New Guineans this all looked like a threat to the independence of Namasu. During the meeting, the Highlanders submitted a motion asking for a new set of financial reports to be audited by a different firm of auditors, and specifying the profits and losses of each branch. Furthermore, the profit and loss statement should show what amounts of wages were paid each to expatriate and indigenous staff members. The new balance sheet was to be submitted within six weeks to an extraordinary shareholders' meeting. Also submitted was a motion of no confidence in the three European directors. The two mission directors were asked to stay in office. When the series of motions was rejected, the Highlanders walked out of the meeting. The incident had shown that the New Guineans were not just fighting for dividends, but that they feared a takeover of their company by Europeans.

As a consequence of this stormy meeting, Board and management were restructured. The European directors, except the two mission members, withdrew, and were replaced by New Guineans. The new Board now consisted of nine New Guineans and two European missionaries. Its first action was to relieve Mr Ramsay of his duty and elect Mr G. Messner to be the new managing director. The interim solution of a 'manager' and 'outside' directors had cost the company a great deal of money. One of the remaining mission directors, relating the incident, quite rightly said: 'Our attempt to move Namasu away from the church had only succeeded in driving it deeper into the church than ever before'.

Ayo Foundation

In his 1970 report, Mr Messner, who in 1973 became the new Managing Director of Namasu, had already pointed out that Namasu was grossly undercapitalized. This, together with the exorbitant growth, had brought the company into a precarious position. The 'interim period', with its generous expenses account, had not relieved but rather strained the liquidity of the company. The bankers as well as trade creditors became alarmed, and the company now was on the brink of insolvency. The question had to be considered whether or not Namasu should go into liquidation.

With its valuable properties, no shareholder would have lost his money. However, after careful consideration, it was decided for the sake of thousands of shareholders who had put their trust in Lutheran Mission and its 'child' Namasu, to make another attempt to continue. Applications were forwarded to overseas donor agencies, in which the circumstances were explained. Since grants could not very well be given directly to Namasu, the suggestion was made to hand the money to a foundation, which in turn would invest the money in Namasu. The outcome was the formation of Ayo Foundation.

After the legal side was duly taken care of, Ayo Foundation received a grant of $710,000

under the following conditions: Ayo Foundation was to be the sole holder of all shares in Namasu Holding. Namasu Holding was to be the main shareholder and parent company of all Namasu-related companies. The founding members of Ayo Foundation were to consist of two members each of the Evangelical Lutheran Church of Papua New Guinea, the Lutheran Economic Service, and Namasu. Other development-oriented organizations could become members. The Evangelical Lutheran Church was gradually to sell its share parcel in Namasu to make room for prospective shareholders. Part of the grant directed to Namasu via Ayo Foundation was to be repaid within 20 years. The purpose of the Foundation was to support development-related projects in Papua New Guinea out of dividends or repayments of loan. The formation of Ayo Foundation was explained to the shareholders' meeting on September 21, 1973, and unanimously carried.

The New Concept

Namasu had originally been founded to be a 'child' of the Morobe District. Tribal distinction and suspicions had been overcome, or the Sattelberg and Malalo congregations would not have become partners in shipping. With the start in the Highlands, the company had burdened itself with a problem of which management was blissfully ignorant at that time. There had always been slight suspicion on the part of the Highlanders toward the coastals. In fact, the Highlands work of Namasu had been started partly because of the strong plea by the Highlanders to treat them as equals to the coastals. However, for the time being the Highlands work had kept the company so busy that it never gave any thought to possible later conflicts. This dormant mistrust finally came out into the open at the shareholders' meeting in February 1973.

The February meeting had also shown that the centralized accounting system introduced in 1972 had not helped the branch managers and the local people to identify themselves more closely with the company's fortune.

Meanwhile, Messner had worked out a new chart of how Namasu should be reorganized. This was submitted to an extraordinary meeting which took place at Lae on September 21, 1973. Accordingly, Namasu was to be split up into six new companies, which were to take over the respective business within their districts. They were: Namasu Goroka, Chimbu, Kainantu, Morobe, Madang, and Mount Hagen. The underlying thought was to prevent the mother company from being drawn in, in case one of the 'daughters' became insolvent.

Now the stage was set for a new start. Namasu had the shareholders' consent for the restructuring. With the financial grant from overseas donor agencies, it also had the necessary capital to implement Messner's plans. One important element, however, which could spell failure or success, was not as yet in sight: competent and dedicated staff. One of the fundamental ideas of the planners was to spread the available capital as widely as possible, in order not to have all the eggs in one basket. This policy was followed during the ensuing years.

Having abundant capital at its disposal, the planners of Namasu Holdings went far beyond the original aims of the founders, which were to assist New Guineans in rural areas to make use of economic opportunities, and to provide shipping and trade facilities for backward areas. These aims were now changed. According to an interview given to the Port Moresby *Post Courier,* by its manager, Namasu wanted to be 'pacemakers for Papua New Guinea'. [45] The scheme had been introduced in the interest not only of the company's shareholders, but also of the Papua New Guinea community as a whole.

During the following five years, the management implemented its plans for a wide diversification of capital, by floating quite a number of subsidiary companies or becoming partner in already-existing businesses.

A NEW NAMASU
Organizational Chart

Namasu Holdings Pty Ltd

I. Namasu Branches
(converted into subsidiary companies)

1) Namasu Morobe Pty Ltd
2) Namasu Madang Pty Ltd
3) Namasu Goroka Pty Ltd

4) Namasu Chimbu Pty Ltd
5) Namasu Kainantu Pty Ltd
6) Namasu Mount Hagen Pty Ltd

II. Namasu Subsidiary Companies and Investments

7) *PNG Import and Export Pty Ltd*
Namasu in partnership with a Japanese fish cannery

8) *Namasu Coffee Pty Ltd*
In partnership with a German coffee importer

9) *Namkundu Wholesale Pty Ltd*
100 per cent owned subsidiary

10) *Formo Ltd Hong Kong*
100 per cent owned subsidiary

11) *Namasu Australia Pty Ltd*
100 per cent owned subsidiary

12) *Melanesian Soap Pty Ltd*
Namasu minor shareholder

13) *Co-Air Pty Ltd*
Namasu minor shareholder

14) *Pagini Brambles Ltd*
Namasu minor shareholder

15) *Namasu Wharf Pty Ltd*
A subsidiary of Namasu Transport Ltd

16) *Bouara Poultry Pty Ltd*
100 per cent owned subsidiary

17) *A.R. Oslington Pty Ltd*
100 per cent owned subsidiary

18) *Aroweld Pty Ltd*
100 per cent owned subsidiary

19) *Carnell Carriers Pty Ltd*
100 per cent owned subsidiary

20) *Morobe Airways Pty Ltd*
Minor shareholder

21) *Namasu Angoram Pty Ltd*
100 per cent owned subsidiary

22) *Namasu Transport Pty Ltd*
100 per cent owned subsidiary

This is indeed an impressive list of subsidiaries and investments, but at the same time an intricate system was established, requiring a staff of experienced, efficient, and devoted employees.

While it would be impossible for me to deal at length with the performances of a network of 22 companies established between 1973 and 1985, I believe that some of the main developments should be recorded. There is a wealth of reports, letters, statements, as well as personal investigations, from which this has been compiled.[46]

I *Namasu branches*

In 1973, when the Namasu branches became subsidiary companies, they were partly owned by Namasu Holdings and partly by New Guinean shareholders. Here is a short history of performances during that period.

Namasu Morobe showed excellent results up to 1975, when Messrs Kroner and Matu were in charge. After 1975, when they had left, the losses went up to 300,000 Kina. In 1984, the company ceased trading altogether, after the last two shops in Lae had been closed down.

Namasu Madang expanded in 1974 by acquiring a Chinese-owned store with a flourishing trade. After an expatriate manager was hired, the expenses increased but the selling hours were cut down. This, together with an overstocking of useless merchandise, brought the Madang branch to the brink of disaster. Trading ceased, and the shop was leased to an Australian business firm.

Namasu Goroka ceased trading in 1974. Insufficient supervision caused heavy losses.

Namasu Chimbu: After heavy losses sustained by two former managers up to 1969, the performances picked up during 1970 to 1973, owing to the excellent performance of an

608

expatriate manager. When he left, the trading results went down, and it did not take very long before Kuman Holding, the other Lutheran 'child' at Kundiawa, could take over. Namasu Chimbu is now in liquidation.

Namasu Kainantu: This branch has been kept afloat, after having had many ups and downs.

Namasu Mount Hagen: After a cycle of misfortune, the company picked up and showed extremely good results. In 1980-81, it got out of control. While having a turnover of seven million Kina, it showed a profit of only 1/3 per cent of the turnover. The manager had to be relieved of his duty. Under a new manager, it has picked up again and is the only well-functioning Namasu branch in Papua New Guinea.

Why such disappointing results? the reader may ask. The answer is that this is nothing extraordinary, but fits into the general trend which lately can be observed in connection with the cooperative movement, government departments, and many a village business run on a communal basis. Only the strictest supervision by highly efficient experts will safeguard against failure. Indeed, the story of Namasu branches over the last 15 years was no longer a story of lack of capital, but of lack of qualified and reliable staff. There were quite a number of good men of many nationalities working for Namasu, but even a small minority can cause heavy losses if competent supervision is lacking.

II *Namasu Subsidiary Companies and Investments*

PNG Import and Export Pty Ltd: This company was floated in conjunction with a Japanese fish cannery. As a result, Namasu became one of the largest importers of fish in Papua New Guinea, with a turnover of millions

Work inside the coffee factory.

of dollars. Yet it never made excessive profits. In looking back, the present financial comptroller of Namasu Holding says that the company was more or less an invoicing address in Papua New Guinea for the Japanese fish cannery. Meanwhile, it has ceased trading, and the partnership has been dissolved.

Namasu Coffee Pty Ltd: This has been the most successful enterprise within the Namasu group of companies. It had a large European coffee importer as its minor shareholder, which also supplied the manager. The partnership has since been dissolved.

Namkundu Wholesale Pty Ltd: This company has been established to take over some of the work of the merchandise department of the 'old' Namasu. After an unsuccessful start with an indigenous manager, which brought shockingly high losses, the management was handed over to a Chinese businessman who himself had a flourishing business. The agreement was that 'everything had to be obtained from the manager's business'. Again, this venture proved unsuccessful.

Formo Ltd Hong Kong: This company was supposed to act as a purchasing agent for Namasu in Hong Kong. It never became active, and is now in the process of being wound up.

Namasu Australia Pty Ltd was set up to make use of the 'Australian Government Export Incentive Scheme'. In spite of this, the company was not very successful and sustained heavy losses. It is now being wound up.

Melanesian Soap Pty Ltd: Shares have in the meantime been sold.

Co-Air Pty Ltd: Shares have been disposed of.

Pagini Brambles (see Namasu Transport Pty Ltd): An excellent investment.

Namasu Wharf Pty Ltd: This is a subsidiary company of Namasu Transport Pty Ltd. An excellent investment.

Bouara Poultry Pty Ltd: This company traded only a very short time, and incurred heavy losses on account of bad planning. It is now in the process of being wound up.

A.R. Oslington Pty Ltd: Inactive. It is in the process of being wound up.

Aroweld Pty Ltd: A subsidiary of A.R. Oslington.

Carnell Carriers Pty Ltd Popondetta: 100 per cent subsidiary. This is the latest acquisition to the Namasu group of companies. Namasu Wharf Pty Ltd owned 33 per cent of the shares. Meanwhile, the remainder of the share parcel has been acquired in the name of Namasu Morobe Pty Ltd, the idea being that profits from wharf operations at Popondetta will assist in repaying the huge losses of Namasu Morobe.

Morobe Airways Pty Ltd: The Namasu aeroplane, a 'Norman Islander', was sold to Morobe Airways Pty Ltd. In turn, Namasu received a 25 per cent equity in that firm. Later the shares were sold.

Namasu Angoram Pty Ltd: In 1976, a going concern was purchased in Angoram. The early performance was good. Later, because of staff difficulties, heavy losses were sustained. Meanwhile, the property has been sold and the company ceased trading.

Namasu Transport Pty Ltd: This company is an investment company only. It is the owner of all shares in Namasu Wharf Pty Ltd, as well as Pagini Brambles. It is the most successful subsidiary company of Namasu Holdings, owing to the excellent income derived from

Namasu wharves at Lae and the high dividends paid by Pagini Brambles.

Taking a look at the Namasu subsidiary companies and share investments, we find that out of 16 enterprises 11 ceased to be trading or never traded within the given period and are now in the process of being dissolved for various reasons. The most successful divisions of the Namasu group of companies have been the ones dealing with coffee and the Namasu wharf. Namasu coffee has always been an outstanding branch of the company's activities since its inception in 1959. The Namasu wharf, if properly run, cannot but make profits, owing to its strategic position in Lae. Some investments made after 1973 have been extremely successful, such as the partnership with Pagini Brambles, the taking over of the wharf formerly belonging to the Anglicans, and, last but not least, the share parcel in Carnell Carriers Pty Ltd.

Examining the performances during the last 15 years (see Appendix A), we find that after the poor results in 1969-70 the company was picking up in 1971. Then the situation deteriorated, and it became even worse after the sudden change in management. This was followed by a period of instability. It was only in 1977 that the financial result was bettered, owing to an excellent 'coffee year'. Namasu Coffee Pty Ltd made a huge profit. When Messner left in 1978, Namasu experienced an all-time low as far as management was concerned. One general manager stayed for not even one year. His replacement stayed over two years, but had to be relieved of his duties because of incompetence. The question may be rightly asked: How could any Board of Directors employ such men in the first instance? Consequently, the years 1978-80 showed disappointing results compared with the sales figures. To a great degree, this was also due to heavy losses sustained by Namasu Morobe and the setback at Mount Hagen. Last but not least, considerable losses sustained by the subsidiaries helped to eat up profits made in other sections. The subsidiary companies had been superficially planned and badly managed. The good results of 1981-83 are due to the fact that meanwhile Namasu Holdings stopped dilly-dallying in trading in nearly all the places except Mount Hagen. Today, the company derives its income by leasing the wharf to Lutheran Shipping and others, as well as from rents received from Namasu Coffee Pty Ltd and its property at Madang. In addition to this, the investments in Pagini Brambles and Carnell Carriers have proved to be highly profitable.

When we look back and appraise the operations from 1973 to 1985, it is certainly not an overstatement to say that Namasu had a very good start again, with an additional capital influx of $700,000. The subsequent losses were not due to lack of capital, but were solely the result of staff difficulties. The planning had been done without taking into consideration the most vital requirement in any endeavour: the human element.

In summing up the situation, I wish to make the following points:

1) The history of Namasu during the last 15 years proves that it is not the finance available but the human endeavour which either makes or breaks an organization.

2) The assets of Namasu according to an official valuation amount to 3.5 million Kina. The influx of capital in 1973 — even if not always used wisely — saved the company from having to go into liquidation and thus squandering valuable assets.

3) Now the time has come to safeguard these assets, and to discontinue active trading. By turning such assets into passive investments, the shareholders of Namasu — Ayo Foundation — will be able to make a sizeable contribution to the religious, social, and economic development of church and state in Papua New Guinea.

4) The church has no reason whatever to be ashamed of having formed Namasu. There was a time when this company was necessary, and it played an important role in the development of many backward areas. Now the time has come for the church to withdraw and to dedicate its strength to the one and only commission which justifies its existence.

(See also the appendix.)

Winding Up Namasu

Steps have now been taken to enable the church to wind up Namasu Holdings Ltd and to transfer its assets to the church, with a view of discontinuing active trading in favour of passive

Namasu truck on the way to the Highlands.

investments. The following resolutions have been passed by the members of Ayo Foundation Ltd, in order to transfer all Company assets to the Evangelical Lutheran Church of New Guinea Property Trust:

Having considered the objects of the Company, and having considered the purpose for which the ELCONG and the ELCONG Property Trust were established, and

having considered that amongst the objects for which the Church and the Property Trust were established are objects which are similar to the principal objects for which the Company was established, and

having concluded that the objects would be better served by having the management and control of the Company's assets vested in the Trustees of the Church Property constituted according to the ELCONG Property Trust Act, Chapter 1007, the members resolved that

the resolutions of the Directors of the Company, dated July 9, 1985, and set out hereunder be and are hereby ratified.

Resolutions of the Directors:

a) that the shares of Namasu Holdings Ltd held by the Company be transferred to the Evangelical Lutheran Church Property Trust for a consideration of 1 Kina; and

b) the Company assign all its right title and interest in a loan from the Company Namasu Holdings Ltd to the Evangelical Lutheran Church of New Guinea Property Trust for a consideration of 1 Kina.

The above resolutions were unanimously passed by the Annual General Meeting of Ayo Foundations Ltd on August 21, 1985. With this resolution, the road has been cleared for the dissolution of Namasu Holdings Ltd and for the transfer of all its properties to the Evangelical Lutheran Church of New Guinea Property Trust.

Editorial Note

No one but the founder of Namasu himself was in the position to give an accurate account of how this venture in economic enterprise in New Guinea was started. In all fairness to the author, and to the men who have helped him in setting up Namasu, it should be noted how new the concept of this new type of business had been in New Guinea.

A basic principle from the outset was to have local people participating in it with men and means. When Namasu shares were to be offered for sale, however, it was discovered that an old law requiring 60 per cent British capital in any company in the (then) Australian Territory was still in force. That law had first to be changed before any substantial New Guinean participation could be secured. Selling shares to local people, however, involved many very small parcels of three or five shares. This resulted in a lot of pressure being put on the company by people who had only a small holding in it; only later was it realized that the number of shares held or the amount of capital invested meant nothing to the people. Since it was 'their' company — and rightly, they claimed — everybody should have an equal voice in the shareholders' meetings, no matter how many shares they had.

Many other unexpected reactions were also discovered by the Western business mind as new ground was broken in New Guinea. In the 1970s, many people forming companies in New Guinea came to the church seeking information and advice based on Namasu's experiences that would enable them to avoid the traps and pitfalls which Namasu had discovered in this field. The aspect of the positive effects of Namasu is mostly overlooked today when viewing its operations. How much this trail-blazing contributed to the world of business in Papua New Guinea is hard to evaluate; it is, however, considerable.

The first ten years of successful operation of Namasu was a real contribution to the country, for it did fulfil the needs it was set up to cover, namely, a fair deal for the local community in selling their primary produce, and the availability of trade goods at a fair price. Today, keen competition in both fields ensures local people of a fair deal, but, in those initial years, Namasu provided the only means for some reasonable access to the market.

The author must be given due credit for having been game to launch out into the vast unknown of Western-style business enterprise in developing New Guinea. This the founder of Namasu could not contribute himself when giving his account of the beginnings of this business enterprise of the Lutheran Church. It would be regrettable if the

612

readers of this section felt that the Namasu venture ended in complete failure. Far from it! There is also a very positive side, and the editor wishes this to be drawn to the attention of the readers as well.

Lutheran Economic Service

Lutheran Economic Service, a non-profit company limited by guarantee, is an offspring of Namasu. When Namasu was started in 1959, it received a subsidy of DM 200,000 from the German donor agency Bread for the World. This money was to be used specifically for developmental work within Papua New Guinea. Meanwhile, Namasu had been registered as an ordinary trading company, owned by shareholders and with the object of making profits. Thus, its particular status prevented the Company for legal as well as taxation purposes from accepting outright gifts. Consequently, the money was never taken up into the accounts of Namasu, but put into a special bank account under the name Lutheran Economic Development Fund. Out of this fund various projects were financed. As time went on, more and more project requests had to be satisfied, which made it necessary to separate the aid program section from the mother company. On the suggestion of the managing director of Namasu, a non-profit limited company was founded, which was called Lutheran Economic Service. With this step, a way had been opened to receive special grants from overseas for socio-economic purposes, without interfering with either the church treasury or Namasu. The board of the new company consisted of seven members, two each representing the church, the Mission, and Namasu. As a seventh member, the bishop of ELCONG, the Revd Dr John Kuder was elected chairman. Mr W. Fugmann was elected as the secretary. From now on, Lutheran Economic Service acted as a clearing house for moneys received from overseas. All requests for economic, social, or educational projects were directed to overseas agencies via LES.

During the subsequent years, many projects were initiated by Lutheran Economic

Service and financed by Overseas Donor Agencies. While the bulk of finance came from the United States, at the beginning of the 1960s church overseas agencies such as the German Organization Bread for the World or Lutherhyaelpen in Sweden made available funds for underdeveloped countries. These funds were not so much meant to build up church institutions, but rather to help people in such countries to get on their own feet socially and economically. In New Guinea, the Mission and the church always tried to care for the whole man, and thus all mission institutions were geared to that aim. It was therefore only natural that Lutheran Economic Service, in presenting the cases, stressed this particular quality. Right up to 1968, the main purpose of Lutheran Economic Service was the applying, receiving, and channelling of overseas funds to earmarked projects.

In 1968, a survey of mission plantations had become necessary. In anticipation of an early autonomy of the church, it was felt that the mission plantations should be kept strictly separated and put on a commercial basis. Some of their profits should be retained for further expansion and development. The survey was carried out under the chairmanship of Mr O. Heinrich, a prominent Lutheran businessman from Australia. As a result, all mission plantations were entrusted to Lutheran Economic Service as managing agent. With this additional mandate and the growth of general activities, it became necessary to relieve the Namasu manager of this additional work and to open up a separate office. Mr D. Ruthenberg, the plantation manager from Finschhafen, was appointed general manager. From now on, Lutheran Economic Service had a four-pronged program:

1) Receiving and channelling overseas funds to earmarked projects.
b) Management of mission plantations.
c) Management of Asak Cattle Station, Gabmazung Rice Project, and Alkena Agricultural Extension.
d) Involvement in agricultural training at Banz.

Since that time, many changes have occurred. The mission plantations, being now a property of the church, are held by the ELC-PNG Property Trust Fund and managed by Kambang Holdings. The Asak Cattle Station has been handed back to the New Guineans. Today's field of operation of LES consists of:

a) Taking care of rural training, mainly through *Yangpela Didiman,* but also other programs of non-formal rural education.
b) Applying for and channelling overseas funds for socio-economic projects.
c) Administering of special funds for relief work.

Lutheran Economic Service, being a plain service organization, does not produce any income, but rather acts as a mediator between overseas donor agencies and church-initiated projects.

Apart from a great number of smaller projects (see under Appendix B) which were initiated and financed via Lutheran Economic Service, there are some larger ones which deserve special comments.

Gabmazung Rice and Produce Project

Prior to World War II, Lutheran Mission had a mission station near Nadzab, in the Markham Valley, which was called Gabmazung. After the Second World War this station was not continued, since most of the people had become Christians.

When in 1965 the Balob Teachers College was founded, the Mission had to look for a suitable piece of ground to produce food for the student body. Gabmazung offered itself as an ideal place to open a school farm. The Mission asked one of its most experienced farmers, Mr Martin Boerner, to develop the Gabmazung farm project. After six months, the first crop of sweet potatoes and vegetables was ready for consumption. By the end of 1966, the Teachers College and Commercial School at Lae were supplied with 25 tons of food. A wide variety of vegetables was introduced, such as sweet potatoes, corn, sorghum, peanuts, chinese taro, soya beans, cucumbers, tomatoes, and other vegetables. In 1967, the supply went up to 120 tons of vegetables and 125 tons of peanuts. The greatest achievement, however, came in 1968-69, when rice was imported from the Philippines. The first five acres of land were flooded, and the first batch of wet rice ever grown by private enterprise was planted. With an excellent result of four tons per acre, it was proved that wet rice could be grown in New Guinea. Many difficulties had to be overcome

613

until New Guinea rice could be marketed. The consumers were used to white rice grown in Australia, and at first would not accept home-grown brown rice. Later on, this changed, and rice could be marketed, particularly in the Highlands.

In 1970, when Mr Boerner retired from active service, Mr Braunack, an Australian farmer, took over the work in Gabmazung. [47] During his term of service, up to 50 acres of land were used for trial plots, and seed rice was supplied to government agencies. New varieties were planted, and a lot of work went into research. In 1973, Mr Braunack was transferred to take over another job, and two Filipino rice farmers were employed to carry on the work. Later, the Gabmazung farm project was handed over to *Yangpela Didiman* to be used as a training centre within their rural training program. Its earlier function to produce food for the Teachers College is still being kept up.

Agricultural Extension Alkena

In 1961, the mountainous country around Alkena Mission Station was severely hit by frost. The staple diet of the Highlands people is sweet potatoes, and they take between eight and nine months until they can be harvested. The famine-stricken area had to be supplied with rice, which was flown in from Madang. To assist the population to find a more varied type of diet, Lutheran Economic Service was asked to help. Subsequently, in 1963, Mr H. Henker, an agriculturalist from Germany, was stationed at Alkena to do research work and to find different types of tubers and vegetables which could be grown at the extreme altitude of 7,500 feet. Henker had to start from scratch by laying out seed beds and building a road connecting the station to the main road system. After one year, he was replaced by Mr G. Oelschlegel, who stayed for a period of six years. During his time, buckwheat, oats, different types of vegetables, ducks, goats, and fish ponds were introduced. Oelschlegel worked mainly through the evangelists. By visiting them and assisting them to get better gardens, his ideas were disseminated among the mountain population. The people could see for themselves that it pays to use more modern methods, and also to plant a greater variety of produce. When Oelschlegel left in 1970, he wrote in his final report:
614

We have just planted 10 acres of sweet potatoes. Everywhere the evangelists have well-tended gardens. Plenty of potatoes are now grown here and offered for sale at Mount Hagen. It is amazing how much these people have learned in such a short time.

After Oelschlegel had left, Lutheran Economic Service employed indigenous agriculturalists at Alkena. Most of them were graduates from the Agricultural School at Banz. Today, the agricultural station at Alkena is used by *Yangpela Didiman* as a training centre.

Agricultural Extension Eastern Highlands

An extension program similar to Alkena was started in the Eastern Highlands by Mr G. Rometsch. Various school farms were assisted or started at Onerunka, Raipinka, Tarabo, and Rintebe. Their main objective was to feed the student bodies at the various church schools. Quite a lot of unused land was planted up with coffee, soya beans, and different kinds of vegetables and sweet potatoes. Rometsch also constructed a road between Ponampa Mission Station and the town of Kainantu. The work of LES proved to be a great boost to the agricultural development in the Eastern Highlands.

Asak Cattle Station

During the 1960s, Namasu's work along the north coast between Finschhafen and Madang had grown by leaps and bounds. A regular shipping service picked up copra, coffee, and vegetables, and supplied the village trade stores with tools, textiles, and a variety of other goods. The people generally had become wealthier.

The one exception was the Kalasa area, about midway between Finschhafen and Ulap. The wide and undulating grassland which lies between the coast and the mission station was regarded as poor country for growing cash crops. Yet, it appeared to be suitable for cattle raising, as there was plenty of grass, and creeks providing water supplies. Perhaps a cattle project should be started there. With this in mind, LES requested two cattlemen (Knopke and Ruthenberg) to inspect the site. On their recommendation, a plan was prepared and submitted to the German donor organization Bread for the World. Meanwhile, Mr W.

Inspecting site of Asak Cattle Station (from left: Wilhelm Fugmann, Hans-Jakob Wiederhold, and Mufuanu Butik).

Fugmann, while on furlough in Germany, obtained the services of an experienced man, Mr H.J. Wiederhold. With both the man and the means at hand, the project was started toward the end of 1964. During the first 12 months, the infrastructure was thoroughly prepared. In Sialum, a wharf had to be built to land the cattle. A road was built from Sialum harbour to Kalasa and on to Asak over steep coral country. Deep gullies had to be bridged, and fences built. Two hundred head of cattle were either imported or purchased locally.

The project was not started in order to make money, but rather to enable the surrounding villages to start a cattle industry. Up to that time, New Guineans were not used to raising cattle, and so it was decided to go slowly in selling cattle to villages. The village elders were asked to send suitable young men to be trained. During the training period, the trainees were supplied with food and shelter but did not receive any wages. Later, when they returned to their villages, they were given a male and female beast each, and sufficient fencing material to keep the cattle fenced and to change the pasture. Only villages which supplied trainees were eligible to purchase cattle. This precaution was necessary to prevent people from indiscriminately buying cattle and letting them run loose.

During his term of service from 1964 to 1975, Mr Wiederhold built approximately 50 miles of road and many small bridges, among them the 120 feet steel concrete bridge across the Tewai river. New strains of grass were introduced and handed out to the people to improve the pastures.

When Mr Wiederhold left Papua New Guinea, about 35 villages had been supplied with 600 head of cattle. Several hundred had been sold for slaughtering, and approximately 800 head were left at the cattle station. Indeed, Mr Wiederhold had done an outstanding job in building up an infrastructure and starting a cattle industry in an otherwise grossly neglected area of Papua New Guinea. After Mr Wiederhold left, Asak was handed back to the original landowners, and is now managed by a Cattlemen's Association, and used as a breeding station to supply approximately 50 villages with cattle.

Reinhard Tietze inspecting cattle at Banz.

Pig raising at Banz.

Agricultural School, Banz

The first informal training of young New Guineans in agriculture and animal husbandry was done by Lutheran missionaries and plantation managers prior to World War I. There was hardly a mission station without cattle, pigs, poultry, and extensive gardens. After World War II, the Lutheran Mission called an agriculturist from the United States, Mr William Meuser, to study the feasibility of agricultural training in Papua New Guinea. After all, the church had its roots on the land. Meuser arrived in 1951, and was stationed at Malahang plantation, from where he started to make numerous field trips to find out more about indigenous gardening and to see which place would be best suited for starting an agricultural school. The final choice fell on Banz, in the Wagi Valley. In 1955, the Meusers moved to Banz to begin the work there. While the missionaries foresaw that agricultural training would be one of the most important aspects in developing the country, the New Guinea people at that time were not over-enthusiastic about it. There was no famine and no overpopulation. Why should they get entangled with new-fangled ideas?

With the help of Lutheran Mission and a grant from the German donor agency Bread for the World, the new school was built during 1956. In June 1957, the first class of 16 students was enrolled. William Meuser, with a comprehensive knowledge of agriculture and the zeal to make the best of it, expected students to have at least a grasp of the English language.

616

He experienced his first disappointment, for their English was not of a very high standard. Some of the students had failed in their high school exams, and were simply looking for a job. Often the congregations, as well as the students, were not sufficiently motivated. Nobody except the Europeans seemed to be greated interested in agricultural training. For the congregations, Banz seemed to be a Western innovation.

In retrospect, it seems that the curriculum of the school at that time was somewhat too demanding for the students. According to a report of 1960 the students had to take 20 theoretical subjects, and by the end of 1961 they would have to pass their exam in 36 subjects. The students were expected to read text books in English in order to study for themselves. In a later report Meuser writes:

> Now we release 23 students to return to their villages. What will happen to them? Will they be enabled to start community projects or will they be smiled at when they try to practise what they have learned?

In 1968, a group of new students, before starting at Banz, were asked about their motivation to enrol in an agricultural school. Some of them said they were simply trying to get away from home, while others confessed they were looking for another avenue of learning, since they had not passed their high school exams. A third group said they had heard that the students at Banz would be taught tractor driving, and perhaps later on they could get a job as a tractor driver.

Banz Agricultural School became one of the best of its kind in Papua New Guinea, and was equal to, if not better than, the government agricultural colleges. Banz would have been a credit to any country district in the United States or Australia. It turned out excellent men, who found good positions in the agricultural and civil service, with the army and with private planters. However, they were not turned out to serve their own communities. The people living in the villages were not yet ready to accept their services. A Morobe student once said that his people had told him: 'Go back to the white man and find a job there. They have taught you agriculture as they do it.'

Yangpela Didiman

Indeed, if the Lutheran Mission or LES wanted to remain in the field of agricultural training, they had to change their whole concept. The Church and Mission could not afford to educate jobseekers, but had to concentrate on preparing people for service in the rural communities. In 1969, Reinhard Tietze, a German agriculturist, arrived in Banz to serve there as a teacher. During the first few years of his service, he realized that something had to be changed. First of all, the old scholars of Banz should be called back occasionally to be motivated and encouraged in their work. Their old school should keep in contact with them. Perhaps they could become project leaders in their villages. If they could get the people to start community projects such as fish ponds, trial gardens, or poultry farms, life in the villages could become more attractive both for the young people and the older ones. The idea was put before the people, mainly in the Wagi Valley and the Western Highlands. They seemed to be greatly interested and ready for the new projects. The difficulty now was to find sufficient project leaders to satisfy the demand from the villages. It was then and there that it was decided to 'enlist' young men for a short-term course in agriculture, and then to send them out as project leaders.

Within a short time, this new movement, which was called Yangpela Didiman (Young Farmers), was most popular around Banz and its hinterland. Over 100 villages were involved.

An agriculture-cooperative was started, called Kenem Kenem. Within a short time, it had 4,000 members who had paid their entrance fees. The purpose was to obtain seeds, insecticides, tools, day-old chickens, and general farm supplies. Yangpela Didiman had become a people's movement, to be known and admired far beyond the borders of Papua New Guinea. But this movement had grown too fast, and when in 1974 Tietze went on furlough, the movement broke down. The numerous young project leaders were not sufficiently well-prepared to do their jobs. Quite a number of them had collected money which never reached the treasury of the cooperative. There were cases of embezzlement and lack of interest in the work. The cooperative broke down completely. When Tietze came back from furlough, the cooperative was dissolved and all the project leaders except four were sacked. It was a painful but very healthy experience for Yangpela Didiman.

A new start had to be made with the remaining faithful project leaders. Yangpela Didiman now concentrated on assisting and advising project leaders serving at Lutheran Church schools like Heldsbach and Amron, and looking after the work at Alkena and Menyamya. However, the big question was: What would become of Banz? Should the Mission and Church continue to turn out a few experts who were too well educated to go back to their villages? Would it not be better to change the whole system of agricultural training and simplify the curriculum, so as to be able to take people from the villages, train them for a shorter period, and return them to the places from which they had come?

In 1975, Tietze, with a group of young project leaders, made a trip to Indonesia to study agricultural training. There they discovered the system of 'village motivators': people who come from the village and are trained for the villages to return to the village from which they had come. This was the solution also for Papua New Guinea.

Soon after their return, the first group of future village motivators were enrolled at Banz. The criterion for accepting such people was not their formal schooling, but their standing in the community. There were pastors, teachers, evangelists, medical orderlies, councillors, and

617

'Undergoing a 12 month basic training in animal husbandry.'

Working with water buffalo at Banz.

618

ordinary villagers who were called to Banz, if possible with their wives, to undergo a 12-months' basic training in agriculture, animal husbandry, soil conservation, wood-working, village mechanics, and leadership training.

When the trainee arrives, he is allotted half a hectare of land on which he is supposed to grow sufficient food for himself and his family. He may also grow some cash crops to enable him to pay for personal expenses. The morning hours are usually left for classroom and community work, whereas in the afternoon the student is expected to work in his own garden. The 12 months' intensive training aims at preparing the participants to better serve their community after returning home. Their spiritual and mental faculties are sharpened for their future role as a leader in the village. They are not expected to foster community projects, but rather to build up their own farm as an illustration for others. Actions speak louder than words.

The courses are augmented by a 'Motivator Follow-up Program', which is to be seen as part of the training. This is to assist village motivators for at least three years. All motivators are expected to attend at least one in-service training course a year.

Meanwhile, the work of *Yangpela Didiman* has grown beyond the borders of Banz. Training centres have been built up at Alkena, Amron. Gamazung, and Heldsbach, and a village-based mobile training centre was started in Kapo-Menyamya District, Teptep-Finisterre, and other areas. [48]

Agricultural extension work in Papua New Guinea had to go a long way to find out how best to serve the rural communities. In that way, the Agricultural Centre at Banz played an important role. The work there, as well as nation-wide, would have been unthinkable without the devoted service of men like Nataniel Poya, Kamandong Kanai, Maing Kuning, and many expatriate teachers. During 1983, *Yangpela Didiman* Headquarters was moved from Banz to Lae. Lae was chosen because it is also the headquarters of the church, as well as of Lutheran Economic Service.

The time has now come when Lutheran Economic Service is no longer required as a separate company. Its activities can be taken over by a service department within the church. It has served its purpose, and it has served it well.

Summing up this particular section, it may well be said that both Lutheran Mission and the Lutheran Church, during the last 100 years, have made an outstanding contribution to the rural economy of the country.

(A list of Mission personnel who have served in LES is included in the appendix.)

Kambang Holdings Ltd

Kambang Holdings Ltd is the business arm of Lutheran work in Papua New Guinea. During its almost 100 years of existence, Lutheran Mission New Guinea built up a small business empire with the specific aim to serve the church, the Mission, and the people of Papua New Guinea. It consisted of supply houses, plantations, a shipping line, an aviation department, as well as technical services.

These business branches of Lutheran activity may have had their rightful place during the long process of establishing an indigenous church. However, once the building is finished, the scaffold should be removed. This was the opinion of the church leaders as well as of their overseas partner churches.

After some years of discussion and planning, it was decided to form a company with the specific purpose of taking over the business part of Lutheran mission work in Papua New Guinea. Consequently, Kambang Holdings was founded in 1976 as a Registered Company Limited by Guarantee, and 100 per cent owned by the Evangelical Lutheran Trust members. This meant that a person can only be a member of Kambang Holdings if he or she is a member of the Evangelical Lutheran Church of New Guinea Property Trust. The company began its operations in 1976 with four divisions:

Division of Lutheran Shipping
Division of Aviation
Division of Technical Services
Division of Plantations.

Each division has its own management and accounting, but is under the jurisdiction of the mother company.

Since then, the Division of Aviation has been discontinued, and all assets disposed of in favour of the church. Within the Division of Plantations, two properties — Gizarum and Kabak — have been sold, while Malahang plantation was phased out as a plantation in 1981. With regard to the remaining five plantations, their activities are described under the corresponding sections. The Divisions of Shipping and of Technical Services are still actively engaged for their respective purposes.

With the winding up of Ayo Foundation Ltd and the transfer of its assets to the Evangelical Lutheran Church Property Trust, the responsibility for the realization of all church-related business will fall to Kambang Holdings Ltd.

In summing up the financial situation of the Evangelical Lutheran Church of Papua New Guinea at the turn of the first century of Lutheran work in New Guinea, the following points should be made:

1. The Church is in a financially sound position.
2. This is due to the fact that many former enterprises have been sold and the proceeds turned into passive investments in favour of the Church.
3. The process of withdrawing from active business and turning the proceeds thereof into passive investments will have to be actively continued for the sake of the spiritual aims and mandate of the Church.

Endnotes

[1] Neuendettelsau Archives (File, J. Flierl).

[2] Georg Pilhofer, *Geschichte der Neuendettelsauer Mission in Neuguinea*, Vol. II (Neuendettelsau: Freimund Verlag, 1963), 23, 91.

[3] Neuendettelsau Archives (File, G. Pfalzer).

[4] *Ibid.*

[5] Neuendettelsau Archives (File, J. Flierl).

[6] Letter E. Kriele to Deputation, 27/8/1909 (Barmen Archives).

[7] Neuendettelsau Archives (File, J. Flierl).

[8] E. Kriele, *Das Kreuz unter den Palmen* (Barmen: Verlag des Missionshauses, 1927), 185.

[9] Johann Flierl, *Gottes Wort in den Urwaeldern von Neuguinea* (Neuendettelsau: Verlag des Missionshauses, 1929), 95.

[10] G. Pilhofer, II, 94.

[11] Lutheran Mission Finschhafen, Executive Minutes, 1938.

[12] Ch. Keysser, *Eine Papuagemeinde* (Neuendettelsau: Freimund Verlag, 2nd ed., 1950), 248.

[13] Assistant District Officer A. Nurton in a letter to Lutheran Mission Madang: 'During my stay in your district I have met hundreds of teacher-evangelists. Every one of them has shown the utmost cooperation toward the work of the government. These men are highly intelligent, a quality which sometimes is lacking in many Europeans', quoted by Johann Flierl, *Wunder der goettlichen Gnade* (Tanunda: Auricht's Printing Office, 1931).

[14] Neuendettelsau Archives (File, 51/61-64).

[15] Neuendettelsau Archives (File, Transportation).

[16] Neuendettelsau Archives (File, G. Pfalzer).

[17] Without the help of Bavarian Sunday-school children the money could not have been raised.

[18] Personal correspondence from A. Fenske, 8/3/1984.

M.V. *Sungu* built in 1975, replaced *Maneba*. M.V. *Simbang* built in 1977, replaced *Umboi II*. M.V. *Umboi* built in 1978, replaced the old *Simbang*. M.V. *Malalo* built in 1979, replaced *Junel*. M.V. *Mabaya* built in 1980, replaced *Nambutu*. M.V. *Totol* built in 1981, replaced the old *Totol*. M.V. *Nagada* built in 1982, replaced *Deanel*. M.V. *Maneba* built in 1984. With these vessels, the north coast of New Guinea is covered from Samarai via Lae, Finschhafen, and Madang, as far as Vanimo near the Indonesian border, as well as Port Moresby, Rabaul, Kieta, and Manus and Siassi Islands.

[19] Letter J. Flierl to Director Ruf, 24/5/1927 (Neuendettelsau Archives).

[20] G. Pilhofer to home board, 11/10/1934 (Neuendettelsau Archives).

[21] ELC-PNG Church Council Meeting, 7/11/1977.

[22] Airstrips were built at: Agotu, Alkena, Amele, Asaroka, Aseki, Begesin, Biliau, Boana, Dona, Ega, Finintugu, Gabmazung, Heldsbach, Hopoi, Kaiapit, Karkar, Karimui, Keglsugl, Kerowagl, Kalasa, Kogl, Kaintiba, Lablab, Menyamya, Mindik, Mumeng, Malahang, Madang, Hengune, Monono, Nomane, Oglbeng, Omkolai, Pindiu, Rintebe, Ranara, Sialum, Tapen, Tarabo, Teptep, Wabi, Wantoat, Wanuma, Wasu, and Wonenare.
Today most of these airstrips are maintained by the Provincial Government or by local authorities.

[23] Neuendettelsau Archives (File, J. Flierl).

[24] Among the bigger projects which were built under J. Hertle's supervision are: Supply House at Finschhafen, Printery at Logaweng, Health Station at Sattelberg, Teachers Seminaries at Hopoi and Logaweng.

[25] See also F. Braun and C.V. Sheatsley, *On Both Sides of the Equator* (Columbus: The Lutheran Book Concern, 1937).

[26] For instance, 50 transmitters had to be set up and repaired. The work grew to such an extent that an electrical division had to be added. In 1960, this division maintained more than 50 installations.

[27] The purchase was entered in the Land Register at the Imperial District Court at Madang on 15/2/1908.

[28] Neuendettelsau Archives (Letters, J. Flierl, 30/4/1914).

[29] Barmen Archives (Blum to Deputation, March 1914).

[30] Barmen Archives (Schamann, Letter to the home board, 1911).

[31] Barmen Archives (Welsch, Letter to the home board, 1918).

[32] Barmen Archives (Report, Graeb, 1921).

[33] Personal correspondence from B. Jaeschke, 1/8/1984.

[34] Personal correspondence from A.P.H. Freund, 30/7/1984, and documents obtained from G. Noller, 26/4/1984.

[35] *Report and Recommendations* of the International Evaluation Team to the Evangelical Lutheran Church of Papua New Guinea, ed. by Jonathan Preus (mimeographed), Lae, 1977.

[36] It is with great hesitation that I deal with a chapter of church involvement in which I myself was very much engaged. However, since the editors have asked me to include the story of Namasu, I shall make every effort to relate fairly what to me will always not only be a story of success but also of failure and great shortcomings. Having been actively engaged in the economic development for the people of New Guinea for almost half a century, and having had a time of grace and reflection for over twelve years now, I do hope to be able to give an unbiased picture of what has happened. (See also the appendix.)

[37] At the Teachers Seminary at Heldsbach, G. Pilhofer had not only taught his students the elementary skills of teaching children, but also introduced them to the planting of coffee. Every teacher graduate took home some coffee seedlings. In this way, the planting of coffee was spread over a large area. In 1938, the first consignment of coffee grown by New Guineans was exported to Australia by Lutheran Mission.

[38] The old Pastor Zurenuo once exclaimed: 'The old heathenish ways we managed to overcome, but this is beyond us!'

[39] When the representative of the German donor agency Bread for the World, Dr B. Ohse, asked the Director of Native Affairs in 1959 what he thought would be the most important service required by the people, he answered: 'Marketing!'

[40] F. Fugmann, H. Wagner, W. Jacobsen, F. Scherle, and others.

[41] 'Namasu' in the Bukawa language means the inner kernel of a coconut.

[42] The first office-bearers were: Rufus Pech, Carl Radke, Fred Scherle, Wilhelm Fugmann, Alwin Zimmermann, Zurewe Zurenuo, Lot (from Sio), Samasam Isaiah, Samuel Kamdring, and Gideon Apeng. R. Pech was elected chairman, and W. Fugmann managing director. The first secretary was E.B. Davies, and the auditor Carl Schulz, a prominent Lutheran from Australia.

[43] Qohotao from Dedua, Firie from Wareo, Zinguwe from Pindiu, Bumang from Qembung, Jambunke from Wareo, Horgkenare from Boana, Manasing from Kalasa, Rauke from Komba, Kewariong from Hube, Jateng from Malalo, Sangas from Hube, Maire from Raipinka, Kukut from Tapen, Gelinde from Kalasa, and Sanangkepe from Zaka.

[44] During the first nine years the following dividends were paid: 1960: 6%; 1961: 6%; 1962: 7.5%; 1963: 7.5%; 1964: 10%; 1965: 10%; 1966: 10%; 1967: 10%; 1968: 5%.

[45] Interview, given to *Post Courier* by the Namasu Manager, 25/9/1973.

[46] Financial Statements, Namasu Group of Companies, 1959-1984. Report for Directors' Meeting, 28/11/1969. Report, Registrar of Companies, Port Moresby, for 1969. G. Messner, Survey and Projection, 1971-1973. Report, International Team, 1975. W. Fugmann, Neuguinea Situationsbericht, 1972. Letter, ELC-PNG Finance Director to LWF, 1983. Progress Report, Namasu to LWF, 26/5/1983. Report, Chairman of Directors, Namasu, to LWF, 16/3/1984.

[47] Report, Braunack, Gabmazung, 1972/73 (Lae Archives).

[48] *Yangpela Didiman* Report, 1984. The following numbers of village motivators were trained between 1977 and 1984: Alkena, 83; Gabmazung, 45; Banz, 195; Heldsbach, 115; Amron, 107; Kapo, 20; Total: 565. Out of these, 458 (87%) were at work.

Source Material

Lutheran Mission New Guinea, Conference Minutes, 1950-1974.

'Social and Economic Changes in Papua and New Guinea, and their Implications on Christian Missions' (Conference Paper, Lutheran Mission New Guinea). W. Fugmann, 1958.

Wilhelm Fugmann, *Junge Kirche zwischen Steinzeit und Neuzeit*, (Neuendettelsau: Freimund Verlag, 1959).

Namasu, Annual Reports, 1958-1970.

Lutheran Economic Service, Articles of Association, 1966.

'Mission Involvement in Business Training' (Paper submitted to the Third Waigani Seminar by W. Fugmann, 1967).

'Business Activities of Lutheran Mission, Recommendations and Observations', by O. Heinrich and F. Singe, 1967.

I.J. Fairbairn, *'Namasu.* New Guinea's Largest Indigenous Owned Company'. New Guinea Research Bulletin No. 28. (Canberra: Australian National University, 1969).

'Wok Bisnis long ELCONG.' W. Fugmann, 1970.

G. Messner, 'Namasu. Survey and Projection.' 1971.

W. Fugmann, 'Namasu. Its Success and Its Problems.' 1971.

Annual Report, Registrar of Cooperative Societies, 1971.

W. Fugmann, 'Neu Guinea Situationsbericht.' 1973.

'Report and Recommendations of the International Evaluation Team to the Evangelical Lutheran Church of Papua New Guinea, ed. by Jonathan Preus (mimeographed), Lae, 1977.

'The Evangelical Lutheran Church of Papua New Guinea: Report on a Fact Finding Survey', ed. by Theodor Ahrens (Goroka: The Melanesian Institute, 1977).

Kambang Holdings, Articles of Association and Memorandum, 1977.

Namasu Group of Companies
Trading Statistics 1960-1983

Year	Turnover	Profit	Loss
1960	89,000	7,400	
1961	N/A		1,200
1962	206,000	14,500	
1963	242,000	24,000	
1964	734,000	30,000	
1965	1,200,000	80,800	
1966	1,700,000	70,600	
1967	2,100,000	104,800	
1968	2,000,000	3,700	
1969	2,670,000		34,000
1970	2,738,000		32,500
1971	3,330,000		14,400
1972	4,400,000		102,000
1973	4,271,600		34,100
1974	6,517,300		23,751
1975	7,187,000		122,296
1976	11,063,000		97,217
1977	23,530,000	453,000	
1978	14,000,000	22,714	
1979	13,000,000	179	
1980	14,500,000	35,476	
1981	13,500,000	213,000	
1982	18,620,000	242,000	
1983	19,517,000	314,000	

Projects

submitted to Overseas Donor Agencies and controlled by
Lutheran Economic Service

Balob Teachers College, Lae	completely financed
Commercial School, Lae	completely financed
Heldsbach Teachers Training	dormitories, hydro-electric plant, farm machinery
Rintebe Teachers Training	farm machinery
Asaroka High School	dormitories, mess hall, water reticulation system
Kitip High School	water reticulation system
Kentagl Tok Ples School	water reticulation system
Highlands Seminary, Ogelbeng	farm machinery
Senior Flierl Seminary, Logaweng	school farm and machinery
Gaubin Hospital	rebuilding
Asuar Leprosy Colony	completely financed
Yagaum Hospital	kitchen building and mess hall
Butaweng Hospital	rebuilding as a general hospital
Social Concerns Office, Lae	financial assistance
Melanesian Institute, Goroka	financial assistance
Road- and Bridge-building	Sialum-Asak Road
	Kalasa-Dedua Road
	Tewai River bridge (Kalasa)
	Tauri River bridge (Kaintiba)
	Kaudl River bridge (Alkena)
Airstrips	Mindik
	Ponampa
	Tapen
	Sialum
	Qaqa
	Damananang
	Kako
Dolmar Saws	Karkar Island
	Mindik
	Eastern Highland
Sheep	Boana
	Tarabo
Vegetable Projects	Boana
	Menyamya
	Buang
Copra Kilns	three kilns on the Rai Coast

Epilogue

An important aspect of Lutheranism in Papua New Guinea from the very beginning has been the cooperation of various Lutheran churches and Mission bodies with the local Papua New Guinean Christians. The most recent expression of this cooperation has been the compilation of this history.

The history of the Evangelical Lutheran Church in Papua New Guinea is, above all, a manifestation of the boundless grace of God. Despite all the problems and difficulties, physical and spiritual, including the ravages and privations of two world wars, God has blessed his Church. Its growth and expansion has been one of God's miracles of modern missionary history.

The contributions and sacrifices of missionaries and members of the Lutheran Churches from Europe, America, and Australia over the past one hundred years have undoubtedly been considerable. But without the dedication and commitment to the Gospel of countless villagers, church workers, elders, evangelists, and pastors, who have responded so wholeheartedly to the power of God's Word in their lives, the mission would not be what it has become: an autonomous Church.

As the Evangelical Lutheran Church of Papua New Guinea now moves forward into the second century, it is confronted with new challenges and opportunities to proclaim the Gospel in a rapidly changing and secularizing society in a nation which achieved its independence only ten years ago and is seeking to establish its status in the international scene.

As overseas Churches, we have throughout the past 100 years been richly blessed by our involvement with our Papua New Guinean brothers and sisters in spreading the Gospel. Now, in this second century, we look forward to a continuing partnership in the Gospel and stand ready to express this as God opens doors for cooperation and mutual support.

Dr Johannes Hanselmann,
Landesbischof
Evangelical Lutheran Church in Bavaria

Dr Leslie B. Grope,
President
Lutheran Church of Australia

David W. Preus
President
American Lutheran Church

Dr Donald W. Sjoberg
President
Evangelical Lutheran Church in Canada

Prof. D. Peter Krusche
Bischof
Northelbian Evangelical Lutheran Church
626

APPENDIX

A Register of expatriate workers who have served Lutheran Churches in Papua New Guinea

(Workers who died on the mission-field are marked with †)

A. Of the Neuendettelsau Mission and (since 1972) of the Mission Dept of the Lutheran Church of Bavaria

MWB = Neuendettelsau Mission and Mission Dept of the Luth. Ch. Bavaria; ELCA = Evangelical Luth. Ch. of Australia; UELCA = United Ev. Ch. in Aust.; LCA = Luth. Ch. of Aust.; ALC = American Luth. Ch.; LM = Leipzig Mission; NMZ = North Elbian Mission Centre.

Flierl, Revd Johann, D.D.	1886-1930	Founder of LM
& Louise	1888-1930	work in PNG
Tremel, Revd Karl	1886-1894	Evangelism
& Christine	1889-1894	
Bamler, Revd Georg	1887-1928†	Evangelism
& Frieda	1904-1928	
Pfalzer, Revd Georg	1889-1914	Evangelism/
& Mathilde		Administration
Goetz, Frieda Sr	1889-1897	Medical
Vetter, Revd Konrad	1889-1906†	Evangelism
& Maria	1894-1895†	
& Justine	1899-1906	
Hoh, Revd Adam	1892-1914	Evangelism
& Else	1898-1914	
Ruppert, Revd Andreas	1894-1894†	Evangelism
Decker, Revd Johann	1895-1944	Evangelism
& Emilie		
Zwanzger, Revd Andreas	1896-1913	Evangelism
& Margarete	1902-1913	
Held, Revd Friedrich	1897-1901†	Evangelism
Hansche, Revd Ernst Richard	1899-1907	Evangelism
& Clara	1899-1902†	

Keysser, Revd Dr Christian & Emilie	1899-1920	Evangelism/ Literature
Heumann, Emilie (Mrs Keysser)	1902-1920	Education
Zahn, Revd Heinrich	1902-1932	Evangelism/
& Emma	1907-1928	Literature
Lehner, Revd Stephan	1902-1943	Evangelism/Supt.
& Clementine	1902-1931†	
& Sophie		
Wagner, Revd Leonhard	1902-1934	Evangelism
& Lukretia	1908-1934	
Schnabel, Revd Ernst	1902-1930	Evangelism
& Johanna	1908-1928	
Wacke, Revd Karl	1903-1939	Evangelism
& Magdalene	1910-1959	Matron Finsch Hospital
Schlenk, Emilie (Mrs Decker)	1903-1913†	Education
Meier, Hans	1904-1911	Builder
Stuerzenhofecker, Revd Georg	1904-1939	Evangelism
& Marie	1907-1927†	
& Margarete	1930-1939	

Name	Dates	Work
Mailaender, Revd Karl	1904-1929	Evangelism
& Hedwig	1913-1929	
Pilhofer, Revd Dr Georg	1905-1939	Evangelism/
& Elise	1911-1939	Literature
Boettger, Revd Herrmann	1902-1942	Evangelism/Print.
& Elisabeth	1909-1914†	
& Emma	1926-1942	
Raum, Revd Hans	1906-1915	Evangelism
& Marie	1913-1920	
Stolz, Revd Michael	1907-1931	Evangelism
& Maria	1923-1931	
Flierl, Revd Leonhard	1907-1929	Evangelism
& Ottilie	1923-1929	
Goehl, Gottfried	1907-1907	Builder
Ruwolt, Georg	1907-1913	Shipping
Ruppert, Revd Johann	1907-1928	Evangelism/
& Frieda	1911-1928	Admin.
Panzer, Revd Karl	1907-1923	Evangelism
& Mathilde	1912-1926	Medical
Saueracker, Revd Karl	1907-1931	Evangelism/
		Medical
& Agnes	1924-1931	Education
Hertle, Johann	1907-1939	Builder
& Kunigunde	1911-1914†	
& Laura	1926-1939	
Laur, Friedrich	1907-1928	Administration
& Agnes	1926-1928	
Spaeth, Lorenz	1907-1909	Agriculture
Lindner, Mathilde	1908-1914	Medical
(Mrs Pfalzer)		
Oertel, Revd Friedrich	1909-1938	Evangelism
& Christina	1913-1938	
Schmutterer,		
Revd Gottfried	1909-1935	Evangelism
& Magdalena	1913-1935	
Markert, Elisabeth	1911-1921	Medical
Krodel, Wilhelm	1911-1913	Education
Schmutterer, Johann	1911-1931	Builder
& Babette	1922-1931	
Flierl, Sr Dora	1911-1930	Medical/
		Womens work
Stoessel, Revd Johann	1911-1922	Evangelism/
& Charlotte	1911-1922	Medical
Bayer, Revd Friedrich	1911-1930	Evangelism
& Sybilla	1922-1930	Education
	1956-1958	
Wirth, Konrad	1912-1913	Builder
Doebler, Kaspar	1913-1939	Agriculture
& Margarete	1922-1939	
Schneider, Revd Georg	1914-1924	Evangelism
Flierl, Revd Wilhelm, D.D.	1914-1915	Sem./Supt.
	1927-1962	
& Maria	1927-1962	
Schmidt, Babette	1914-1920	Domestic Work
(Mrs Schuster)		
Moll, Sr Helene	1927-1961	Medical
Flierl, Revd Johannes	1927-1966	Evangelism
& Johanna	1927-1966	
Lechner, Revd Matthias	1928-1950	Evangelism
& Kaethe	1929-1950	
Streicher, Revd Hans	1928-1953	Evangelism/
	1957-1961	Literature
& Elise	1929-1953	
	1957-1961	
Bergmann, Revd Wilhelm	1928-1968	Evangelism/
& Luise	1928-1968	Literature
Herrlinger, Revd Jakob	1928-1939	Evangelism
& Rosa	1930-1939	
Bezler, Sr Sophie	1929-1942	Medical
Schroeder, Martha	1929-1932	Education
(Mrs Sperr)		
Eiermann, Linus	1929-1959	Agriculture
& Anna	1937-1959	
Sperr, Otto	1929-1932†	Agriculture
Kracker, Hans	1929-1932†	Agriculture
Neumeyer, Revd Hans	1929-1939	Evangelism
& Tabea	1931-1939	
Vicedom, Revd Dr	1929-1939	Evangelism
Georg, D.D.		
& Gertrud	1931-1939	
Bergman, Revd Gustav	1929-1969	Evangelism
	(1969-1981)	
& Anna	1931-1969	
	(1969-1981)	
Daub, Emil	1930-1939	Administration
& Anna	1933-1939	
Fluegel, Sr Frieda	1930-1962	Medical
(Mrs Horrolt)		
Linsenmeier, Revd Georg	1931-1940	Evangelism
& Margarete	1933-1940	
Methsieder, Revd Lorenz	1931-1939	Evangelism/
& Bertha	1933-1939	Admin.
Boerner, Deacon Martin	1931-1945	Agriculture
	1954-1972	
& Ilse	1936-1945	
	1954-1959	
Keysser, Jutta	1931-1937	Domestic Work
(Mrs F. Bergmann)		
Kirsch, Deacon Karl	1932-1971	Medical
& Babette	1934-1971	
Metzner, Revd Adam	1933-1955	Evangelism
& Traude	1934-1955	
Koller, Dr Martha	1933-1938	Medical
Horrolt, Revd Georg	1933-1962	Evangelism
& Frieda		
Winkler, Revd Martin	1933-1939	Evangelism
& Gunda	1937-1938†	

628

Name	Dates	Work
Bergmann, Revd Friedrich¹ & Jutta	1933-1936	Evangelism
Fugmann, Wilhelm & Hertha	1933-1972	Administration
Keysser, Sr Hertha (Mrs Fugmann)	1933-1972	Medical
Maurer, Revd Hans & Leni	1933-1964 / 1938-1964	Evangelism
Hofmann, Revd Georg & Clara	1933-1952 / 1936-1951	Evangelism
Schnabel, Ruth (Mrs Munsel)	1933-1975 / 1983-1985	Education
Reiner, Revd Hans & Rosa	1934-1940† / 1936-1940	Evangelism
Stuerzenhofecker, Hubert & Babia	1934-1939 / 1937-1939	Agriculture
Zischler, Revd Wilhelm & Else	1934-1942 / 1938-1942	Evangelism
Zimmemann, Revd Martin & Imma	1934-1939 / 1937-1939	Evangelism
Strauss, Revd Dr Herrmann & Elfriede	1934-1971	Evangelism/ Literature
Goetzelmann, Revd Leonhard & Lina	1935-1961 / 1937-1961	Evangelism
Holzknecht, Revd Karl & Helene	1935-1979 (-1983) / 1938-1979 (-1983)	Evangelism/ Literature
Munsel, Revd Konrad & Ruth	1935-1975 / 1983-1985	Evangelism/ Literature/ Seminary
Wagner, Revd Hans & Elisabeth	1936-1966 / 1939-1966	Evangelism
Baer, Revd Michael & Martha	1936-1974 / 1938-1974	Evangelism/Sem.
Stuerzenhofecker, Sr Elfriede (Mrs Strauss)	1936-1971	Medical
Kothe, Else	1937-1939	Domestic Work
Stuerzenhofecker, Dr Alfred & Irene	1937-1940 / 1937-1940	Medical
Hertle, Revd Wilhelm & Hedwig	1937-1977	Evangelism
Ruf, Hedwig (Mrs Hertle)	1937-1977	Medical
Strauss, Wilhelmine	1937-1942	Domestic Work
Wagner, Revd Adolf & Mathilde	1938-1943† / 1939-1941	Evangelism
Guth, Ernst	1938-1939	Administration
Habenstein, Theodor	1938-1939	Builder
Schuster, Revd Wilhelm & Friedlinde	1952-1966 / 1953-1966	Evangelism/ Bible School
Wagner, Revd Friedrich & Lydia	1952-1971 / 1953-1971	Evangelism/ Literature
Wuest, Revd Herrmann & Edit	1952-1958 / 1953-1958	Evangelism
Flierl, Revd Helmut & Liselotte	1953-1971 / 1954-1971	Evangelism/ Bible School
Horn, Sr Maria	1953-	Medical
Strauss, Sr Else	1953-1957	Medical
Bamler, Revd Heinrich & Myra	1953-1974	Evangelism/Sem.
Bayer, Hedwig	1953-1959	Education
Dollinger, Revd Hans & Lore	1954-1970 / 1955-1970	Evangelism/ Bible School
Jacobsen, Revd Werner & Elisabeth	1954-1972 / 1954-1972	Evangelism
Wolfrum, Revd Helmut	1954-1955	Evangelism
Wirth, Sr Kaethe	1954-1959	Medical
Schad, Sr Rosemarie	1954-1958	Medical
Schwermer, Sr Ursula	1954-1970	Medical
Schuster, Elisabeth	1955-1973	Matron KLS/ Womens work
Stief, Revd Johann & Anneliese	1956-1970 / 1957-1970	Evangelism
Walter, Else	1956-1964	Domestic work Womens work
Johst, Sr Ursula	1956-1971	Medical
Eidam, Revd Walter & Margarete	1956-1970	Evangelism/ Bible School
Junker, Revd Herbert & Annemarie	1956-1969 / 1957-1969	Evangelism/Sem.
Pommer, Sr Grete	1957-1962	Medical
Ruck, Sr Emma	1957-1973	Medical
Schuster, Revd Adolf & Barbara	1957-1971 / 1959-1971	Evangelism/ Education
Keller, Sr Waltraud	1957-1961	Education
Horndasch, Revd Helmut & Christel & Irmgard	1957- / 1958-1974†	Evangelism/Sem.
Lechner, Sr Rosemarie (Mrs Hager)	1957-1974	Medical
Diepen, Rolf & Wilhelmine	1957-1963 / 1957-1963	Medical
Bergmann, Revd Heinrich & Irmgard (Mrs Horndasch)	1957-1958† / 1958-	Evangelism / Women's work
Lechner, Matthias & Emma	1958-1973 / 1960-1973	Print.
Hager, Revd Bertold & Rosemarie	1958-1974	Evangelism
Herrlinger, Revd Guenter & Heidrun	1959-1964 / 1959-1964	Evangelism

Name	Years	Role
Kirchhof, Revd Ernst	1959-1969	Evangelism
& Elisabeth	1960-1969	
Fischer, Hanna (Mrs Geisselbrecht)	1959-1974	Medical
Schirmer, Sr Ruth (Mrs Geisler)	1959-1980	Medical
Weber, Revd Eckart	1959-1976	Evangelism
& Brigitte	1960-1976	
Boy, Joachim	1960-1963	Medical
& Ursula	1960-1963	
Huber, Willi	1961-1962	Administration
Jehles, Dr Ursula	1961-1965	Medical
Geisselbrecht, Revd Werner & Hanna	1961-1974	Evangelism/Sem.
Wagner, Revd Dr Herwig	1961-1972	Evangelism/Sem.
& Dorothea	1961-1972	
Steinbauer, Revd Dr Friedrich	1961-1971	Evangelism
& Annemarie	1961-1971	
Keuler, Sr Karin	1961-1970	Medical
Stege, Reinhard	1961-1967	Print.
& Kaethe-Lotte	1962-1967	
Polz, Sr Elfriede (Mrs Metze)	1962-1968	Medical
Kummer, Sr Liesl (Mrs Doerfer)	1962-1979 1986-	Medical
Jacobsen, Revd Wolfgang	1962-1967	Evangelism
& Rosemarie	1962-1967	
Lindner, Sr Christa (Mrs Gerhardy)	1962-	Medical
Heumueller, Revd Erich	1962-1973	Evangelism
& Christa	1962-1973	
Doerfer, Revd Dieter	1962-1979 1986-	Agriculture/Evangelism
& Liesl		
Dahinten, Revd Walter	1962-1974	Evangelism
& Hildegard	1962-1974	
Herrmann, Luise	1962-1966	Matron KLS
Erdenkaeufer, Manfred	1963-1969	Administration
& Leonore	1963-1969	
Metze, Werner	1963-1968	Medical
& Elfriede		
Henker, Hans	1963-1970	Agriculture
& Tina		
Spiller, Hartmut	1963-1967	Education
Seiler, Revd Gottfried	1963-1974	Evangelism/Sem.
& Martha	1963-1974	
Sander, Revd Gerd	1963-1973	Evangelism/Bible School
& Gerdi	1963-1973	
Fink, Revd Hans	1963-1979	Evangelism/Bible School
& Hannelore	1964-1979	
Schwaner, Sr Kaethe	1963-1967	Medical
Berger, Wolfgang	1963-1971	Admin./Youth work
Florek, Sr Johanna	1963-1972	Medical
Rebelein, Sr Maria	1963-1974	Medical
Klein, Revd Anton	1964-1977	Evangelism/Bible School
& Margaret	1964-1977	
Kuenzel, Revd Manfred	1964-1974	Evangelism
& Christine	1964-1974	
Scholz, Monika	1964-1968	Education
van Bruggen, Johan	1964-	Bible School
Soer, Berend	1964-1984	Education
Trillitzsch, Hans-Dagmar	1965-1970	Education
& Marja-Liisa	1965-1970	
Flurer, Hannelore	1965-1969	Education
Lehner, Revd Juergen	1965-1977	Evangelism/Bible School
& Christl	1965-1977	
Meding, Dr Werner	1965-1970	Medical
& Charlotte	1965-1970	
Geisler, Revd Dieter	1965-1980	Evangelism
& Ruth		
Menzel, Revd Dieter	1966-1975	Evangelism
& Renate	1966-1975	
Walz, Revd Klaus	1966-1979	Evangelism
& Heimtraud	1966-1979	
Gaenssbauer, Revd Hans	1966-1975	Evangelism
& Henriette	1966-1975	
Frank, Revd Heinz-Joachim	1966-1975	Evangelism
& Gesine	1966-1974	
Kubina, Sr Karin	1966-1974	Medical
Mueller, Sr Karin	1966-1969	Medical
Rosenstein, Sr Tina (Mrs Henker)	1966-1970	Medical
Tolks, Uwe	1966-1967	Ship.
& Renate	1966-1967	
Mirus, Elisabeth	1966-1971	Matron KLS
Gerber, Revd Horst	1967-1981	Evangelism
& Helene	1967-1981	
Lippmann, Revd Karl	1967-1973 +1980-	Evangelism/Sem.
& Gisela	1967-1973 +1980-	
Laux, Sr Waltraud	1967-1975	Medical
Messner, Gerhard	1968-1973	Administration
& Baerbel	1968-1973	
Fugmann, Revd Gernot	1968-1974 +1983-	Evangelism/MI
& Christa	1968-1974 +1983-	
Meisel, Revd Christoph	1968-1978	Evangelism
& Hilde	1968-1978	
Rometsch, Gotthold	1968-1973 +1978-	Agriculture
& Leena	1968-1973 +1978-	

Name	Dates	Field
Klemp, Deacon Dieter	1968-1981	Medical
Schoenweiss, Revd Wilfried	1968-1973	Evangelism
& Gisela	1968-1973	
Keitel, Revd Manfred	1968-1977	Evangelism
& Rita	1968-1977	
Rottke, Susanne	1968-1971 / 1979-1982	Education
Reiner, Revd Dr Hermann	1969-1976	Evangelism/Sem.
& Elli	1969-1976	
Dommerholt, Johanna	1969-	Education
Nusch, Deacon Friedrich	1969-1975	Medical
& Anneliese	1969-1975	
Lauterbach, Revd Werner	1969-1979	Evangelism/ Bible School
& Christa	1969-1979	
Kroner, Deacon Rudolf	1969-1975 / 1981-1982	Administration
& Brita		
Mickerts, Brita (Mrs Kroner)	1969-1975 / 1981-1982	Education
Bergmann, Revd Dr Ulrich	1969-	Evangelism
& Edelgard	1969-	
Tietze, Reinhard	1969-1979 / 1982-	Agriculture
& Karin	1969-1979 / 1982-	
Baessler, Revd Wolfgang	1970-1975	Evangelism
& Hedwig	1970-1975	
Schrader, Revd Klaus	1970-1983	Evangelism
& Selma	1970-1983	
Wendt, Wolfgang	1970-1973 / 1977-1980	Education
& Beate	1970-1973 / 1977-1980	
Trantow, Revd Juergen	1970-	Evangelism/ Social Conc.
& Ingrid	1970-	
Zimmermann, Revd Manfred	1971-1974 / 1982-	Evangelism/ Bible School
& Gabriele	1971-1974 / 1982-	
Borzel, Revd Rudolf	1971-1981	Evangelism
& Martha	1971-1981	
Tilgner, Sr Hannelore	1971-1975	Medical
Reins, Revd Guenter	1971-1975 / 1982-1985	Evangelism/Sem.
& Monika	1971-1975 / 1982-1985	
Strauss, Werner	1971-	Evangelism/ Youth work
& Liesel	1971-	
Steinacker, Dr Helmut	1972-1976	Medical
& Erika	1972-1976	
Melzner, Dr Joerg	1972-1973	Medical
& Marie Louise	1972-1973	
Wegelehner, Sr Christa	1972-1975	Medical
Hempfling, Rose	1973-1975	Education
Sinner, Margarethe	1973-1975†	Education
Weber, Dr Friedrich-Wilhelm	1973-1976	Education
& Ursula	1973-1976	
Hennings, Revd Wolf	1974-1979	Evangelism
& Cornelia	1974-1979	
Richter, Wilhelm	1974-1978	Education
& Ingrid	1974-1978	
Hagemann, Christine	1974-1978	Education
Weiss, Deacon Lothar	1974-1978	Education
Hebenstreit, Herbert	1975-1976	Agriculture
Waltz, Hermann	1975-1976	Administration
& Marianne	1975-1976	
Walther, Revd Wilhelm	1975-	Evangelism
Rossdeutscher, Heidrun	1975-1976 / 1982-	Education/ Bible School
Fischer, Revd Friedrich	1976-1981	Evangelism
& Gisela	1976-1981	
Henke, Dr Bruno	1976-1979	Administration
& Elisabeth	1976-1979	
Spernau, Volker	1976-1981	Education
& Marianne	1976-1981	
Jerusalem, Manfred	1976-1979	Education
& Hildegard	1976-1979	
Finkernagel, Emil	1977-1978	Administration
Riess, Gerhard	1977-1980	Education
& Heike	1977-1980	
Neumeister, Revd Gerhard	1977-1985	Evangelism
& Dorothea	1977-1985	
Rode, Revd Hubertus	1977-	Evangelism
Arneth, Gudrun	1978-1981	Education
Arnold, Revd Bernd	1978-1983	Evangelism
& Ruth	1978-1983	
Goerner, Revd Karl	1978-1984	Evangelism/Sem.
& Inge	1978-1984	
Wagner, Elisabeth	1978-1981	Matron KLS
Wild, Hans-Guenther	1981-1983	Education
& Luise	1981-1983	
Husel, Manfred	1981-1984	Print.
& Eva	1981-1984	
Krauss, Reinhard	1981-1983	Agriculture
& Brigitte	1981-1982†	
Boehner, Wolfgang	1981-	Youth work
Woelfel, Albrecht	1981-	Medical
& Ilse	1981-	
Pilhofer, Georg	1981-1984	Administration
& Jennifer		
Weberruss, Revd Martin	1982-	Evangelism
& Regine	1982-	

Name	Years	Field
Fugmann, Revd Ekkehard	1982-	Evangelism/Sem.
& Gudrun	1982-	
Wilhelm, Isolde	1983-1985	Matron KLS
Munsel, Dr Hermann	1983-	Medical
& Johanna	1983-	
May, Dr John	1983-	Mel. Inst.
& Margarete	1983-	
Kaul, Hans-Joachim	1983-	Develop. work
& Roswitha	1983-	
Nowitzky, Herbert	1983-1986	Education
Arend, Werner	1983-1986	Education
& Karla	1983-1986	
Knop, Gert	1984-	Agriculture
& Gabriele	1984-	
Hauenstein, Revd Philipp	1984-	Evangelism
& Elfriede	1984-	
Averbeck, Johann	1984-	Agriculture
& Dorothea	1984-	
Lang, Guenter	1984-	Agriculture
& Ursula	1984-	
Mueller-Wolff, Juergen	1984-	Administration
& Renate	1984-	
Milz, Margarete	1985-	Education
Gruber, Sr Gertrud	1985-	Womens work
Ruckriegel, Sr Annelore	1985-	Womens work
Borkenhagen, Norbert	1985-	Education
& Susanne	1985-	
Brinckmeier, Revd Christoph	1985-	Evangelism
& Annemarie	1985-	
Krueger, Revd Dr Wolfgang	1986-	Evangelism
& Ingeborg	1986-	

B. Of the Rhenish Mission, Barmen

Name	Years	Field
Thomas, Revd Wilhelm	1887-1887	Evangelism
Eich, Revd Friedrich	1887-1891	Evangelism
& Margarete	1887-1889†	
Scheidt, Revd Wilhelm	1887-1891	Evangelism
Bergmann, Revd Gustav	1887-1904†	Evangelism
& Karoline		
Kunze, Revd Georg	1888-1899	Evangelism
& Bernhardine	1891-1892†	
& Johanna	1897-1899	
Wackernagel, Revd Hermann	1888-1888†	Evangelism
Klaus, Revd Friedrich	1890-1890†	Evangelism
Boesch, Revd Friedrich	1889-1891†	Evangelism
& Lina	1891-1891†	
Arff, Revd Peter	1889-1893†	Evangelism
& Elly	1891-1895	
Frobenius, Dr Wilhelm	1890-1900	Medical
& Martha	1897-1900	
Dassel, Revd Adolf	1892-1895	Evangelism
& Bertha	1894-1895	
Pilkuhn, August	1892-1892†	Shipping
Hoffmann, Revd Albert	1892-1904	Evangelism
& Henriette	1894-1904	
Barkemeyer, Revd Johannes	1893-1895†	Evangelism
Helmich, Revd Heinrich	1894-1913	Evangelism
& Ida	1897-1913	
Hanke, Revd August	1895-1918	Evangelism
& Laura	1897-1900†	
& Johanna	1902-1918	
Holzapfel, Revd Ludwig	1896-1898	Evangelism
Nebe, Revd Wilhelm	1901-1901†	Evangelism
Koolen, Revd Martinus	1901-1902	Evangelism
Ostermann, Revd Heinrich	1902-1904†	Evangelism
& Auguste	1903-1904	

Name	Years	Category
Blum, Revd Wilhelm	1902-1925	Evangelism
& Marie	1904-1925	
Diehl, Revd Wilhelm	1902-1913	Evangelism
& Luise	1904-1905†	
& Johanna	1907-1913	
Weber, Revd Ernst	1903-1908	Evangelism
& Maria	1907-1908	
Schamann, Heinrich	1905-1939	Plantation
& Lina	1911-1939	
Schuetz, Revd Friedrich	1905-1939	Evangelism
& Elisabeth	1907-1939	
Becker, Revd Karl	1906-1911	Evangelism
& Laura	1908-1911	
Mange, Gerhard	1907-1908†	Plantation
Wilms, Emil	1907-1910	
Eckershoff, Revd Heinrich	1907-1928	Evangelism
& Elisabeth	1909-1928	
Eiffert, Revd Georg	1907-1925	Evangelism
	1930-1935	
& Emma	1913-1925	
	1930-1935	
Glitz, Gustav	1908-1911	Shipping
George, Revd Heinrich	1910-1930	Evangelism
& Elfriede	1912-1930	
Graeb, Revd Ernst	1911-1923	Evangelism
& Minna	1913-1923	
Loesel, Leonhard	1913-1916†	Shipping
Welsch, Revd Jakob	1913-1944†	Evangelism
& Adele	1922-1963	
Wullenkord, Revd Adolf	1913-1930	Evangelism/ Education
& Anna	1922-1930	
Alt, Hermann	1930-1939	Shipping
& Elise	1931-1939	
Dahlhaeuser, Deacon Ernst	1930-1939	Agriculture
& Katharina	1930-1939	
Doege, Revd Walter	1930-1939	Evangelism
& Marianne		
Krueger, Revd Erich	1930-1933	Evangelism
Schoettler, Revd Friedrich	1930-1970	Evangelism
& Hilde	1931-1970	
Stahl, Revd Walter	1930-1939	Evangelism
& Hilde	1931-1939	
Lindner, Revd Gerhard	1931-1933	Evangelism
Hermann, Richard	1931-1932	Plantation
& Luise	1931-1932	
Loos, Bruno	1931-1933	Building
Hofius, Revd Kurt	1952-1963	Evangelism
& Erna	1952-1963	

C. Of the Lutheran Church of Australia and its predecessor Churches

Name	Years	Church	Category
Flierl, Revd Johannes, & Louise (nee Auricht)	1886-1930	UELCA	Evangelism
Keppler, Gottlieb & Elizabeth	1902-1914	UELCA	Agriculture
Keppler, Rose	1904-1942	UELCA	Medical
Helbig, Revd Paul & Ernstine	1906-1951	UELCA	Builder/Evangelism
Jericho, Samuel	1908-1916	UELCA	Shipping
Schultz, Gottfried	1908-1920	UELCA	Agriculture
Wacke, Magdalene	1910-1959	UELCA	Medical
Schulz, Wilhelm	1913-1934	UELCA	Shipping
Schultz, J.F. Wilhelm	1919-1921	UELCA	Administration
Holtkamp, Charles	1921-1928	UELCA	Agriculture

Koschade, Victor & Ida	1921-1936 1953-1954	UELCA	Handyman
Rechner, Agnes (Mrs Karl Saueracker)	1921-1931	UELCA	Education
Lindner, John	1922-1966	UELCA	Agriculture, Technical Service
Obst, Adolf & Anna	1922-1942	UELCA	Agriculture
Radke, Theodore & Emma	1922-1944	UELCA	Shipping
Claussen, Christian & Elizabeth	1924-1932	UELCA	Builder
Deutscher, Paul	1925-1942	UELCA	Supply
Miers, Hermann	1925-1933	UELCA	Shipping
Schloss, Sr Anna (Mrs A. Obst)	1927-1942	UELCA	Medical
Lohe, Wolfgang & Elsie	1928-1942	UELCA	Supply, Agriculture
Uhe, Maria	1928-1941	UELCA	Domestic
Helbig, Clara (Mrs George Hofmann)	1929-1951	UELCA	Domestic
Behrendorff, Leonard & Theodora	1930-1971	UELCA	Builder
Schoettler, Revd Friedrich & Hilde	1930-1970	Rhenish	Evangelism
Giess, Annie (Mrs Wilbur Wenz)	1931-1975	UELCA & ALC	Administration
Helbig, Revd Martin & Frieda	1933-1968	UELCA	Education, Evangelism
Jaeschke, Berthold & Roma	1933-1956 1962-1966	UELCA	Shipping
Rohrlach, David & Clara	1933-1973	UELCA	Shipping, Builder
Lewald, Charles	1934-1935	UELCA	Handyman
Schirmer, Leslie	1934-1941	UELCA	Shipping
Klotzbuecher, Sr Frieda	1935-1944	UELCA	Medical
Wallent, Oswald	1935-1937 1940-1942	UELCA	Supply Aviation
Freund, Revd Harold & Dorothea	1936-1965 1968-1976	ELCA LCA	Evangelism, Literature
Neumann, Victor & Doris	1936-1951	ELCA	Shipping, Agriculture
Noack, Revd Fred & Clair	1936-1940	ELCA	Evangelism
Noack, Gerhard & Grace	1936-1939 1951-1952 1954-1956	ELCA (Wabag)	Builder, Agriculture
Pech, Sr Clara (Mrs David Rohrlach)	1936-1973	UELCA	Medical
Venz, Sr Esther (Mrs R. Boettcher)	1936-1975	UELCA	Medical
Bertelsmeier, August & Sophie	1937-1957	UELCA	Builder, Agriculture
Wagner, Emil & Linda	1937-1957	UELCA	Agriculture
Barber, Raymond	1938-1953	UELCA	Agriculture
Koch, Erich & Blanche	1938-1940	ELCA	Agriculture
Simpfendorfer, Frieda (Mrs Martin Helbig)	1938-1981	UELCA	Administration
Rohde, Theodora (Mrs Leonard Behrendorff)	1939-1971	UELCA	Domestic
Zacher, Arthur	1939-1942	ELCA	Agriculture
Radke, George	1940-1942	UELCA	Technical Service
Tscharke, Edwin & Tabitha	1941-	UELCA	Medical
Brumm, Cyril & Rita	1946-1949	UELCA	Medical
Hamdorf, Sr Lorna (Mrs Louis Heppner)	1946-1970	ELCA	Medical
Kleinig, Armin	1946-1953	ELCA	Agriculture

Nagel, Revd Keith & Jean	1946-1964	ELCA	Evangelism
	1973-1975	LCA	
Eckermann, Revd Conrad & Joan	1947-1975	ELCA	Education, Seminary
Geue, Leslie	1947-1949	ELCA	Technical Service
Heppner, Louis & Lorna	1947-1970	ELCA	Builder
Kohn, Douglas & Elvera	1947-1978	UELCA	Builder
Koop, Gerhard	1947-1948	ELCA	Builder
Lehmann, Sr Myra (Mrs Hermann Radke)	1947-1975	UELCA	Medical
Radke, Hermann & Myra	1947-1975	UELCA	Builder
Sawade, Mervyn	1947-1955	ELCA	Builder, Agriculture
Zimmermann, Alwin & Clara	1947-1971	UELCA	Technical Service
Heinrich, Sr Rita (Mrs Arthur Fenske)	1948-	ELCA	Medical
Kleinig, Revd Ian & Enid	1948-1966	ELCA	Evangelism
Mischke, Sr Irma (Mrs L. Noller)	1948-1953	ELCA	Medical
Koschade, Sr Gladys (Mrs Robert Knie)	1949-1957	UELCA	Medical
Sawade, Victor	1949-1951	ELCA	Agriculture
Victor-Gordon, Mervyn & Torquay	1949-1950	ELCA	Shipping
Whitehead, Vida (Mrs B. Hartwig)	1949-1953	UELCA	Education
Altus, Owen & Joan	1950-1960	ELCA	Education
Fiegert, Revd Ronald	1950-	UELCA	Evangelism, Bible Schools
Hartwig, Bernard & Vida	1950-1953	UELCA	Evangelism
Koschade, Revd Alfred & Beatrice	1950-1956	UELCA	Evangelism
Noller, Lionel & Irma	1950-1955	ELCA	Shipping
Pech, Revd Rufus & Margaret	1950-	UELCA	President LMNG, Seminary
Blaess, Sr Lois	1951-1952	ELCA	Medical
Hartwig, Edwin & Margaret	1951-1951	UELCA	Aviation
Lutze, Revd Theodor	1951-1959	ELCA	Evangelism
Miller, Herbert	1951-1957	ELCA	Agriculture
Radke, Ruth	1951-1974	UELCA	Domestic
	1984-	LCA	
Schulz, Emma	1951-1956	UELCA	Matron
Dreckow, Sr Irene (Mrs Lionel Worrall)	1952-1972	ELCA	Medical
Jeffers, Don	1952-1969	ELCA (Wabag)	Builder
Johnston, Ron & Elizabeth	1952-1975	UELCA	Supply, Aviation
Knie, Robert & Gladys	1952-1957	UELCA	Builder
Noller, Revd Geoffrey & Elinor	1952-1961	ELCA	Evangelism
Renner, Immanuel & Rosalie	1952-1977	UELCA	Education
Rohrlach, Kevin	1952-1953	UELCA	Builder
Uebergang, Rufus & Iris	1952-1956	ELCA	Shipping
Wedding, Sr Ruth (Mrs E. Thamm)	1952-1966	ELCA	Medical
Ziegeler, Harold & Jacqueline	1952-1981	UELCA	Supply, Administration
Fiegert, Audrey	1953-1955	UELCA	Education
Gaulke, Sr Shiela	1953-1957	ELCA	Medical
Jaensch, Ray & Elizabeth	1953-1964	UELCA	Aviation
Jaensch, Elizabeth (Mrs Stan Read)	1964-1975	UELCA	Administration
Knopke, George & Pauline	1953-1968	UELCA	Agriculture
Schmutterer, Gottfried & Christa	1953-1970	UELCA	Builder
Vogt, Louis & Lorna	1953-1967	UELCA	Shipping, Technical Service

Hoopmann, Dr Eric	1951-1952	ELCA	Medical
Mueller, Lotte	1954-1956	ELCA (Wabag)	Supply
Jordan, Revd Morris & Elva	1954-1964	ELCA	Evangelism
Tscharke, Revd Leonard & Claire	1954-1971	UELCA	Evangelism, Education
Beck, Edwin & Evelyn	1955-1957 1959-1963	ELCA UELCA	Technical
Fuhlbohm, Revd Oscar & Eunice	1955-1975	UELCA	Evangelism, Education
Hage, Revd Hartley & Myrtle	1955-1964 1968-1972	UELCA LCA	Evangelism, Education
Noske, Ronald	1955-1960	ELCA	Handyman
Schneider, Sr Melva	1955-1970	UELCA	Medical
Schoettler, Margarete (Mrs W. Eidam)	1954-1970	UELCA and ND	Education
Stoll, Revd Wilhelm & Daphne	1955-1968	UELCA	Education
Stolz, Rosalind	1955-1956	UELCA	Supply
Thamm, Merna	1955-1964 1967-	ELCA LCA	Women's Work Education
Heinrich, Wesley & Gwenneth	1956-1963 1968-1976	ELCA LCA	Technical Service
Jericho, Myra (Mrs Gilbert Kirchhoff)	1956-1971	UELCA	Domestic
Koop, Sr Elvira (Mrs Douglas Kohn)	1956-1977	UELCA	Medical
Schulz, Ruth (Mrs J. Hafermann)	1956-1970	UELCA and ALC	Education
Worrall, Lionel & Irene	1956-1972	UELCA	Education
Bergmann, Hilda	1957-1957	UELCA	Education
Dolling, Sr Barbara	1957-	ELCA	Education
Huf, Sr Edna	1957-1967	ELCA	Medical
Janetzki, Clem & Thelma	1957-1975	ELCA (Wabag)	Builder
Joppich, Arnold & Loris	1957-1967	UELCA	Shipping
Kotzur, Sr Joan	1957-1962	UELCA	Medical
Mibus, Vida	1957-1978	ELCA	Education
Noller, Joan	1957-1960	ELCA (Wabag)	Administration
Ruthenberg, Donald & Voilet	1957	UELCA	Agriculture, Administration
Schneider, Victor	1957-1960	UELCA	Agriculture
Weier, Revd Russell & Selma	1957-1978	ELCA	Evangelism
Wilson, Raymond & Mavis	1957-1958 1961-1961	UELCA	Agriculture
Carlsen, Victor & Lenore	1958-1962	ELCA	Shipping
Carter, Eric & Heimtraud	1958-1961 1965-1968	UELCA	Builder Handyman
Fritsch, Dr Mary (Mrs R. Guntner)	1958-1960 1966-1970	UELCA	Medical
Grieger, Revd Melvyn & Vivienne	1958-1962	ELCA	Evangelism
Heintze, Merle	1958-1960	UELCA	Domestic
Joppich, Oscar & Irene	1958-1959	UELCA	Education
Rohrlach, Revd Colin & Eleanore	1958-1983	UELCA	Education, Seminary
Seiffert, Sr Dulcie (Mrs Ray Ramm)	1958-1971	ELCA	Medical
Thompson, Sr Dell	1958-1959	UELCA	Medical
Adler, Lorna	1959-1961	UELCA	Administration
Auricht, Otto & Ivy	1959-1968	UELCA	Handyman, Guest House

Borgelt, Sr Heather	1959-1964	UELCA	Medical
Collyer, Paul	1959-1964	ELCA (Wabag)	Administration
Fels, Norman & Yvonne	1959-1964	UELCA	Builder
Freund, Roland and Josephine	1959-1970	ELCA (Wabag)	Agriculture
Hasselbusch, Sr Eva	1959-1961	UELCA	Medical
Jericho, Dawn	1959-1961	ELCA	School Matron
	1965-1966	(Wabag)	
	1974-1977	LCA	Guest House
Jericho, Rita	1959-1966	UELCA	Domestic
Kotzur, Colin & Coralie	1959-1975	UELCA	Technical Service
Kuhne, Donald & Jennette	1959-1964	UELCA	Technical Service
Lewis, John (Bill) & Patricia	1959-1973	ELCA	Builder
Obst, Patricia	1959-1963	UELCA	Supply
Rohde, Samuel	1959-1962	UELCA	Namasu
Schulz, William	1959-1966	UELCA	Builder
	1975-1983		
Simpfendorfer, Vida	1959-1960	UELCA	Administration
Spike, Revd Lloyd & Margaret	1959-1969	UELCA	Builder
	1974-1976	LCA	Evangelism
Tanzer, Grace	1959-1960	UELCA	Domestic
Tanzer, Margaret	1959-1960	UELCA	KLS Matron
Von Pein, Theodore	1959-1964	UELCA	Supply
Albanus, Rosalie (Mrs Immanuel Renner)	1960-1977	UELCA	Education
Cramer, Kenneth & Margaret	1960-1982	ELCA	Medical
Gallasch, Maryn (Mrs John Schultz)	1960-1970	UELCA	Administration
Golding, Shirley	1960-1962	ELCA (Wabag)	Administration
Hofmann, Heimtraud (Mrs Eric Carter)	1960-1968	UELCA	Education
Hueppauff, David	1960-1964	UELCA	Technical Service
Jaensch, Ruth	1960-1961	UELCA	Education
Kirsch, Revd Karl-Heinz & Heidi	1960-1970	UELCA	Evangelism, Education
Klein, Revd Rhyall (Jim) & Noreen	1960-1977	ELCA	Evangelism
Loffler, Horace & Sylvia	1960-1964	UELCA	Agriculture
Maas, Jim & Iris	1960-1963	UELCA	Namasu
Pohlner, David & Patricia	1960-1963	UELCA	Shipping, Namasu
Prenzler, Doris	1960-1961	UELCA	Education
Ramm, Ray & Dulcie	1960-1971	ELCA	Supply, Technical Service
Stephan Alfred	1960-1962	UELCA	Namasu
Watts, Sr Barbara	1960-1960	UELCA	Medical
Weier, Don & Gaye	1960-1969	ELCA (Wabag)	Builder
Eschner, Ruth	1961-1962	UELCA	Education
Fletcher, Bernice	1961-1964	ELCA	Education
Kirsch, Marianne	1961-1962	UELCA	Education
Klein, Neville	1961-1961	ELCA	Education
Knopke, Sr Hazel	1961-1970	UELCA	Medical
Kohlhagen, Mavis	1961-1963	UELCA	Domestic
Kuchel, Sr Rosemary	1961-1961	UELCA	Medical
Menzel, Sr Lois	1961-1965	ELCA	Medical
Muckert, Iris (Mrs Jim Maas)	1961-1963	UELCA	Domestic

Riley, Trevor & Gertrude	1961-1967	UELCA	Technical Service
Schultz, John & Maryn	1961-1970	UELCA	Supply, Agriculture
Selke, Hans & Marilyn	1961-1963	UELCA	Technical Service
Zerna, Sr Elinore	1961-1963	UELCA	Medical
Bartminas, Zelma	1962-1964	ELCA (Wabag)	Administration
Batson, Gaye (Mrs Don Weier)	1962-1969	ELCA (Wabag)	School Matron
Bliesner, Leslie & Denise	1962-1968	ELCA	Education
Bradtke, Neil & Colleen	1962-1971	UELCA	Namasu, Administration
Drogemuller, Marlene	1962-1963	UELCA	Education
Garrett, Sr Merla	1962-1980	UELCA	Medical
Guse, Shirley	1962-1963	UELCA	Education
Haapakoski, Vilma	1962-1964	UELCA	Administration
Kirsch, Gerhard & Virginia	1962-1966	UELCA	Education
Kleinschmidt, Jennifer	1962-1962	UELCA	Education
Kotzur, Sr Grace	1962-1963	UELCA	Domestic
Leske, Merl	1962-1963 1965-1967	UELCA	Domestic
McDonald, Charles & Anne	1962-1964	ELCA (Wabag)	Builder
Murden, John & Lola	1962-1964	ELCA (Wabag)	Builder
Noack, Theodore	1962-1964	ELCA (Wabag)	Technical Service
Ottens, Erica	1962-1963	UELCA	Education
Otto, Douglas & Kaye	1962-1973	UELCA	Education
Schulz, Sr Esther	1962-1967	UELCA	Medical
Starick, Colleen (Mrs Neil Bradtke)	1962-1971	UELCA	Education
Strelan, Revd John & Bronwyn	1962-1985	ELCA	Evangelism, Seminary
Von Saldern, David & Margaret	1962-1967	UELCA	Namasu
Weier, Althea	1962-1965	ELCA (Wabag)	Administration
Winderlich, Trevor & Elizabeth	1962-1966	ELCA	Education
Bell, Elaine	1963-1964	UELCA	Education
Cooper, Chris & Marlene	1963-1970	ELCA (Wabag)	Education
Cramer, Noel & Joan	1963-1972	ELCA	Supply
Cramer, Joan	1963-1975	ELCA	Administration
Davis, Sr Margaret	1963-1966	ELCA (Wabag)	Medical
Friebel, Frederick & Margrit	1963-1960	ELCA	Technical Service
Haby, Janice	1963-1967	ELCA (Wabag)	Administration
Harth, Janice	1963-1965	UELCA	Domestic
Israel, Margaret (Mrs Lloyd Spike)	1963-1969 1974-1976	UELCA LCA	Administration
Jacob, Helen	1963-1967	UELCA	Education
Jarrott, Lesley	1963-1964	UELCA	Education
Leske, Roy & Erica	1963-1964	UELCA	Technical Service
MacKenzie, Wendy (Mrs W. Voigt)	1963-1969	ELCA	Education
Mickan, Rex	1963-1964	UELCA	Education
Mirtschin, Lawrence & Janet	1963-1970	ELCA (Wabag)	Technical Service
Obst, Joyleen (Mrs Danny Chan)	1963-1965	UELCA	Administration
Pfitzner, Grace	1963-1966	UELCA	Education
Ruediger, Sr Elizabeth	1963-1970	UELCA	Medical

Schirmer, Glenda	1963-1964	UELCA	Education
	1967-1968		
Schroeter, Rita	1963-1964	UELCA	Education
	1966-1966		
Silins, Enid	1963-1965	UELCA	KLS Matron
Spann, Wendy (Mrs E. Hartung)	1963-1972	UELCA	Education
Stephan, Claire	1963-1965	UELCA	Administration
Venz, Douglas	1963-1966	ELCA (Wabag)	Medical
Voigt, Sr Margaret	1963-1969	UELCA	Medical
	1975-	LCA	
Wieck, Ronda	1963-1964	UELCA	Education
Wilksch, Erica	1963-1968	UELCA	Education
Wurst, Norman & Joy	1963-1968	UELCA	Caretaker
	1971-1972	LCA	Namasu
Ahrens, Evelyn	1964-1967	UELCA	Education
Altus, Desmond & Clair	1964-1967	ELCA (Wabag)	Supply
Bailey, Brieley & Althea	1964-1968	ELCA (Wabag)	Supply
Beattie, Gaye	1964-1965	ELCA (Wabag)	Administration
Blyth, John & Norma	1964-1966	ELCA	Handyman
Burgess, Bronwyn (Mrs John Strelan)	1964-1985	UELCA	Education
Campbell, Gwendoline	1964-1965	UELCA	Domestic
Dutschke, Bradley & Jill	1964-1968	ELCA	Education
Feist, Dennis & Betty	1964-1981	ELCA (Wabag)	Administration
Freiberg, Gaydan & Eunice	1964-1966	ELCA (Wabag)	Builder
Hanckel, Celia	1964-1966	ELCA (Wabag)	Administration
Jahnke, Ronald & Rita	1964-1970	UELCA	Technical Service
Jenke, Maurice & Dawn	1964-1968	UELCA	Supply
Klante, Dorothea	1964-1966	UELCA	Domestic
Little, Graham & Valma	1964-1967	UELCA	Technical Service
McMaster, Evadne	1964-1967	UELCA	Education
Oestmann, Rudolf & Ruth	1964-1965	UELCA	Caretaker, Education
Ottens, Kevin	1964-1966	UELCA	Education
Ruediger, Melva	1964-1969	UELCA	Domestic
Russell, Deane & Nell	1964-1970	ELCA (Wabag)	Builder
Sabel, David	1964-1966	UELCA	Supply
Schwartz, Wilhelm	1964-1968	UELCA	Supply
Schwartzkopff, Margaret	1964-1965	UELCA	Education
	1968-1970	LCA	
Stiller, Theodor & Ulrike	1964-1970	UELCA	Agriculture
Venz, Noel & Olive	1964-1969	UELCA	Builder
Voigt, William & Wendy	1964-1969	ELCA	Education
Wegener, Sr Denise (Mrs Leslie Bliesner)	1964-1968	UELCA	Medical
Weier, Henry & Alice	1964-1966	ELCA (Wabag)	Builder
Wilksch, Harold & Meta	1964-1968	ELCA	Builder
Atze, Brenton & Phyllis	1965-1966	UELCA	Handyman
	1968-1970	LCA	
Behrendorff, Rosalind	1965-1971	UELCA	Administration
Bensch, Norman & Janet	1965-1969	UELCA	Supply
Boyd, Christine	1965-1969	UELCA	Administration

Fidden, John	1965-1967	UELCA	Administration
Franklin, Terrance & Patricia	1965-1967	ELCA (Wabag)	Technical Service
Friebel, Claire	1965-1968	ELCA (Wabag)	Administration
Gallasch, Anthony	1965-1970	UELCA	Technical Service
Gerken, Rosemarie	1965-1974	UELCA	Education
Hartwig, Revd John & Meryl	1965-1967†	ELCA	Evangelism
Hausler, Ray & Eunice	1965-1971	ELCA (Wabag)	Education
Hayter, Colin & Ruth	1965-1972	ELCA	Education
Heinrich, Sr Beryl	1965-1967	ELCA	Medical
Heyne, Dean & Elizabeth	1965-1969	ELCA	Education
Koch, Shirley	1965-1967	ELCA (Wabag)	Administration
Kuhne, Denise	1965-1969	UELCA	Education
Landman, Sr Eva	1965-1967	UELCA	Medical
Lutz, Heather	1965-1967	ELCA (Wabag)	Administration
Muster, Sr Helen	1965-1967	ELCA	Medical
Petschel, Shirley	1965-1968	UELCA	Education
Pohlner, Bernard	1965-1967	UELCA	Education
Poole, Cynthia	1965-1969	UELCA	Education
Rehbein, Noreen	1965-1966	UELCA	Education
Riedel, Revd Erich & Betty	1965-1973	UELCA	Army Chaplain
Ruediger, Denis	1965-1966	UELCA	Supply
Schulte, Kathleen	1965-1968	UELCA	Education
Schultz, Roland & Helen	1965-1966	UELCA	Education
Schurmann, Rosalie	1965-1971	ELCA	Education
Simpfendorfer, Dora	1965-1966	UELCA	Education
Simpfendorfer, Herbert	1965-1968	UELCA	Education
Stolz, Frederick & Lois	1965-1979	UELCA	Education
Winderlich, Revd Robert & Rosemary	1965-1975	ELCA	Evangelism
Zschech, Cheryl	1965-1969	ELCA (Wabag)	Administration
Braunack, Maxwell & Anne	1966-	UELCA	Agriculture
Clarke, Dennis & Yvonne	1966-1968	ELCA	Technical Service
Clarke, Helen	1966-1968	ELCA	Administration
Day, William & Laura	1966-1975	ELCA (Wabag)	Technical Service
Dutschke, Sr Joan	1966-1969	ELCA	Medical
Eckermann, Margaret	1966-1968	ELCA	Education
Freiberg, Sr Edith	1966-1970	ELCA (Wabag)	Medical
Geffert, Paul	1966-1972	UELCA	Agriculture
Gerhardy, Revd Gordon & Christa	1966-	UELCA	Education, Seminary
Geue, Heather	1966-1967 1969-1971	UELCA LCA (Wabag)	Administration
Gloede, Sr Sabine	1966-1968	UELCA	KLS Matron
Grosser, Bruce & Rosemary	1966-1973	UELCA	Supply
Hahn, Adeline	1966-1968	UELCA	Education
Harris, Kaye	1966-1968	UELCA	Administration
Heitmann, Judith	1966-1966	UELCA	Administration
Heppner, John & Gloria	1966-1968 1970-1972	UELCA LCA	Supply
Hueppauff, Christine	1966-1969	UELCA	Administration

Kleinig, Dr Daniel & Mona	1966-1969	ELCA (Wabag)	Medical
Koch, Marion	1966-1966	UELCA	Education
Kuehne, Ronald & Margaret	1966-1982	UELCA	Agriculture
Kumnick, David	1966-1969	ELCA (Wabag)	Education
Kupke, Coralie (Mrs Colin Kotzur)	1966-1975	UELCA	Administration
Larsen, Cecilie	1966-1967	UELCA	Education
Leskie, Raymond & Ruby	1966-1968	UELCA	Technical Service
Loechel, Evon	1966-1967	ELCA	Education
Logan, Revd Cecil & Audrey	1966-	ELCA	Evangelism
Materne, Kenneth & Rhonda	1966-1967	UELCA	Technical Service
Mirtschin, Marlene	1966-1968	ELCA (Wabag)	Supply
Morrison, Brian & Ruby	1966-1970	UELCA	Caretaker
Paech, Dawn	1966-1968	UELCA	Domestic
Pfeiffer, Ian & Kaye	1966-1977	ELCA	Builder
Priebbenow, Revd Arthur & Cynthia	1966-1978	ELCA	Evangelism, Seminary
Schache, Roy & Judy	1966-1979	ELCA (Wabag)	Builder
Schilling, Dorothy	1966-1969	UELCA	Education
Schilling, Graeme & Petryn	1966-1970	ELCA	Builder
Schmidt, Margrit (Mrs Frederick Friebel)	1966-1969	UELCA	Supply
Shillabeer, Rhonda	1966-1968	UELCA	Administration
Starick, Trevor & Linda	1966-1970	ELCA (Wabag)	Technical Service
Stephan, Olive (Mrs Noel Venz)	1966-1969	UELCA	Namasu
Walkenhorst, Erica	1966-1980	ELCA	Administration
Zerner, Dorothy	1966-1969	UELCA	Education
Zwar, Lynnette	1966-1968	UELCA	Supply
Auricht, Norman & Lola	1967-1970	LCA	Education
Bahr, Colleen	1967-1968	LCA	Education
Breddin, Paul & Phyllis	1967-1977	LCA	Education
Hammer, Richard & June	1967-1969	LCA	Education
Hanson, Kenneth & Margaret	1967-1968	LCA	Builder
Helbig, Doris	1967-1968	LCA	Education
Hoffrichter, Faye	1967-1969	LCA	Administration
Jensen, Ruth (Mrs Colin Hayter)	1967-1972	LCA	Education
John, Trevor & Ronda	1967-1969	LCA	Supply
Kotzur, Wilma	1967-1968	LCA	Administration
Kunze, Rolf & Aaltje	1967-1968	LCA	Education
Lange, Gloria (Mrs John Heppner)	1967-1972	LCA	Administration
Latz, Keith & Heather	1967-1969	LCA	Aviation
Lotz, Ruth	1967-1968	LCA	KLS Matron
Mattner, Patricia	1967-1969	LCA (Wabag)	Administration
Mickan, Helen	1967-1968	LCA	Education
Noske, David & Jennifer	1967-1975	LCA	Technical Service
Ritter, Betty	1967-1973	LCA	Administration
Rohrlach, Lester & Elaine	1967-	LCA	Builder
Rossack, Sr Cynthia	1967-1969	LCA	Medical
Samuel, Ronda (Mrs Trevor John)	1967-1969	LCA	Administration
Schultz, Patricia	1967-1972	LCA	Administration

Simpfendorfer, Martin & Adele	1967-1969 1974-1975	LCA	Technical Service
Steinmuller, Paul	1967-1970	LCA	Education
Stoddart, Barry & Kathleen	1967-1973	LCA	Supply
Thomas, David & Faith	1967-1971	LCA (Wabag)	Evangelism
Wolski, Shirley	1967-1969	LCA	Domestic
Zilm, Mary	1967-1972	LCA	Education
Bartel, Sr Dorothy	1968-1976	LCA	Medical
Eckermann, Petryn	1968-1970	LCA	Education
Grosser, Valerie	1968-1970 1970-1972	LCA (Wabag) (KPI)	Administration
Hampel, Lesley & Joylene	1968-1969	LCA	Carpenter
Hoff, Naomi	1968-1969 1970-1979	LCA (Wabag) LCA	Education
Jaeschke, Monica	1968-1972	LCA	Supply
Jantke, Revd Thomas & Lynette	1968-1983	LCA	Evangelism
Jenke, Helen	1968-1970	LCA (Wabag)	Administration
Jorgenson, Elaine	1968-1970	LCA	Administration
Keys, Jillian	1968-1970	LCA	Administration
Keys, Valmai	1968-1968	LCA	Administration
Koehne, Revd Peter & Norma	1968-1976 1980-1985	LCA	Education Seminary
Kruger, David & Elizabeth	1968-1973	LCA	Agriculture
Kuchel, Dorothy	1968-1969	LCA	Education
Kuhl, Delmae (Mrs Ray Materne)	1968-1972	LCA	Administration
Lehmann, David & Hazel	1968-1970	LCA	Supply
Mickan, Douglas & Nancy	1968-1978	LCA (Wabag)	Technical Service
Nietschke, Colin & Margaret	1968-1969	LCA	Supply
Nuske, Ernest & Ruby	1968-1974	LCA	Technical Service
Rosenblatt, Theodore	1968-1970 1972-1973	LCA (Wabag)	Education
Russ, Alan	1968-1974	LCA	Education
Schrapel, Vernon	1968-1969	LCA	Supply
Weckert, Peter	1968-1976	LCA	Education
Wiencke, Christine	1968-1969	LCA	Education
Wundke, Dennis & Karen	1968-1969	LCA	Caretaker, Education
Zobel, Joyce	1968-1970 1971-1973	LCA (Wabag)	Administration
Zwar, Alan & Mary Jo	1968-1970 1975-1976	LCA	Technical Service
Baer, Dr Theodore & Lynette	1969-1970	LCA	Medical
Briggs, Walter	1969-1971	LCA	Supply
Cirulis, Anita	1969-1969	LCA	Education
Dieckmann, Rhonda (Mrs Philip Holzknecht)	1969-1971	LCA	Administration
Dornbusch, Lorraine	1969-1972	LCA	Administration
Geue, Clarrie	1969-1969	LCA	Supply
Grosser, Wilma	1969-1971	LCA	Administration
Hartwig, Max	1969-1971	LCA	Caretaker

Havelberg, Bethne	1969-1971	LCA	Administration
Heinrich, Brian	1969-1971	LCA	Supply
Heyer, Konstantine & Karma	1969-1971	LCA	Education
Hoepner, Keith & Pamela	1969-1973	LCA	Supply
Lange, Sr Roslyn	1969-1972	LCA	Medical
Langford, Andrew & Dawn	1969-1970	LCA	Education
Logan, Sr Pamela	1969-1975	LCA	Medical
MacKenzie, Christine (Mrs Gregory Lockwood)	1969-	LCA	Education
McPhee, Betty	1969-1971	LCA	KLS Matron
Mays, John & Noelene	1969-1971	LCA	Builder
Mibus, Graham & Lynne	1969-1971 1972-1973	LCA	Technical Service Shipping
Mirtschin, Sr Lena	1969-1978	LCA	Medical
Noller, Kaye (Mrs Ian Pfeiffer)	1969-1977	LCA	Education
Oster, Robert	1969-1970	LCA (Wabag)	Education
Peglar, Christine (Mrs Geoffrey Quast)	1969-1974	LCA (Wabag)	Administration
Petering, Carl & Judith	1969-1970	LCA	Education
Petrulis, Klaus & Helen	1969-1971	LCA	Medical
Pfitzner, Kaye	1969-1971	LCA	Administration
Pietsch, Noreen (Mrs Ian Roennfeldt)	1969-1973	LCA	Administration
Quast, Revd Wilton & Deborah	1969-1984	LCA	Evangelism
Roennfeldt, Ian & Noreen	1969-1973	LCA	Aviation
Roll, Colin & Rhonda	1969-1973	LCA	Technical Service
Schiller, Glenda	1969-1971	LCA	Domestic
Schloithe, John & Robyn	1969-1972	LCA	Shipping, Technical Service
Scholz, Gordon & Joyce	1969-1971	LCA	Builder
Schulte, Audrey	1969-1971	LCA	Administration
Schultz, Sr Christine	1969-1971	LCA	Medical
Schutz, Beryl	1969-1970	LCA	KLS Matron
Schwarz, Revd Brian & Janet	1969-1986	LCA	Evangelism
Steiniger, Christa	1969-1970	LCA	Education
Tischler, Sr Bernice	1969-1971 1976-1977	LCA	Medical
Waltrowicz, John & Wendy	1969-1972	LCA	Education
Welke, Revd Peter & Edna	1969-1974	LCA	Evangelism
Young, Peter & Gwenneth	1969-1971	LCA	Caretaker
Bertelsmeier, Sr Margaret (Mrs Volker Steinmann)	1970-1977	LCA	Medical
Day, Colin	1970-1972	LCA	Technical Service
Dornbusch, Rhonda (Mrs Colin Roll)	1970-1973	LCA	Education
Fiegert, Sr Judith	1970-1972	LCA	Medical
Gallasch, Maureen	1970-1971	LCA	Education
Hansen, Malcolm & Valmai	1970-1971	LCA	Technical Service
Highland, Evelyn	1970-1971	LCA	Education
Jewson, Peter	1970-1971	LCA	Supply
Linke, Ruth	1970-1971	LCA	Education
Pech, Marilyn	1970-1975	LCA (Wabag)	Administration

Pietsch, Alethea	1970-1971	LCA	Domestic
Quast, Geoffrey & Christine	1970-1974 1975-1977	LCA (Wabag)	Technical Service
Quast, Patricia (Mrs Roland Weier)	1970-1978	LCA (Wabag)	Medical
Rohde, Trevor	1970-1971	LCA	Agriculture
Rosenzweig, Brian & Vida	1970-1975	LCA	Agriculture
Schermer, Margit	1970-1972	LCA	Domestic
Schmocker, Rose	1970-1972	LCA (Wabag)	Administration
Spence, Noreen	1970-1974	LCA	Women's Work
Stiller, Ruth	1970-1973	LCA	Administration
Strelan, Revd Richard & Joy	1970-1975	LCA	Evangelism
Thomson, Barrie & Valma	1970-1972	LCA	Technical Service
Wilkinson, Joylene	1970-1970	LCA	Administration
Winderlich, Helen	1970-1972	LCA	Education
Wrightson, Jeremy	1970-1971	LCA	Shipping
Wundke, Barry & Elizabeth	1970-1974	LCA	Printing
Zadow, Leona	1970-1979	LCA	Women's Work
Zadow, Terrance & Jane	1970-1973	LCA	Aviation
Cramer, Cheryl	1971-1973	LCA	Administration
Geer, Trevor & Irene	1971-1973	LCA	Technical Service
Graham, Herbert & Noelene	1971-1972	LCA	Handyman
Jericho, Margaret	1971-1972	LCA	Women's Work
Kammermann, Harry & Mary	1971-1973	LCA	Builder
Kupke, Margaret	1971-1974	LCA	Administration
Leske, Desmond & Gwenyth	1971-1972	LCA	Namasu
Lockwood, Revd Gregory & Christine	1971-	LCA	Seminary
McLiesch, Ian & Helen	1971-1973	LCA	Aviation
Matuschka, Bruno & Vilma	1971-1972	LCA	Education
Nitschke, Ron & Lorna	1971-1972	LCA (Wabag)	Agriculture
Peach, Sr Lynda	1971-1973	LCA	Medical
Radke, Doreen	1971-1973	LCA	Domestic
Scholz, Delphine	1971-1972	LCA	Administration
Scholz, Dr Desmond & Roma	1971-1975	LCA	Medical
Thiele, Mervyn & Roslyn	1971-1975	LCA	Caretaker
Von Boehm, Hans & Ruth	1971-1976	LCA	Namasu
Wallis, David & Eunice	1971-1978	LCA	Medical
Bartsch, Revd Malcolm & Anne	1972-1979	LCA	Education
Cramer, Sr Helen (Mrs Graham Koch)	1972-1978	LCA	Medical
Geue, Beverley	1972-1972	LCA	KLS Matron
Lovelock, Edward & Verlie	1972-1974	LCA	Technical Service
Mibus, Neville & Jacqueline	1972-1976 1982-1986	LCA	Shipping
Mickan, Dennis & Roslyn	1972-1980 1982-1985	LCA	Agriculture
Pfeiffer, Lois	1972-1974	LCA	Administration
Schilling, Loris	1972-1974 1976-1978 1981-1983	LCA	Domestic
Simpfendorfer, Edgar & Margaret	1972-1973	LCA	Education

Trimper, Sr Annette	1972-1975	LCA (Wabag)	Medical
Trimper, Sr Carol	1972-1973	LCA (Wabag)	Medical
Zweck, Revd Dean & Dorothy	1972-	LCA	Evangelism, Seminary
Arnold, Denis & Gillian	1973-1975	LCA	Education
Burr, Denis & Mary	1973-1975	LCA	Education
Hausler, Margaret	1973-1975	LCA	KLS Matron
Heinrich, Glenice	1973-1976	LCA	Women's Work
Hoskin, Gavin & Audrey	1973-1974	LCA	Aviation
Huppatz, Ian & Kerri	1973-1980	LCA	Education
Kathage, Wayne	1973-1974	LCA	Education
Kempe, Russell	1973-1975	LCA	Technical Service
Konetschnik, Dr Fredrick & Dr Beris	1973-1973	LCA	Medical
Krieg, Neville	1973-1975	LCA	Aviation
Lambert, Patricia	1973-1977	LCA	Aviation
Lynam, Rosslyn	1973-1974	LCA (Wabag)	Education
Multanen, Sr Sinikka	1973-	LCA	Medical
Vairogs, Sr Laima	1973-1975	LCA (Wabag)	Medical
Dunhill, Helen	1974-1975	LCA	KLS Matron
Dunhill, Ross	1974-1974	LCA	Aviation
Hartwich, Lynette	1974-1980	LCA	KLS Matron
Koch, Graham & Helen	1974-1978	LCA	Aviation
Moll, Ivan & Margaret	1974-1976	LCA	Education
Reschke, Harold	1974-1975	LCA	Education
Shrowder, David & Elizabeth	1974-1975	LCA (Wabag)	Technical Service
Zweck, John & Margaret	1974-1975	LCA	Education
Clode, John & Joyce	1975-1976	LCA	Technical Service
Haeusler, Robin & Cheryle	1975-1977	LCA	Agriculture
Holzknecht, Philip & Rhonda	1975-1977	LCA	Education
Huff, Wendy	1975-1977	LCA	Administration
Roberts, Janet (Mrs P. Martin)	1975-1977	LCA (Wabag)	Administration
Schultz, Alan & Maureen	1975-1977 1982-1983	LCA	Education
Strelan, Revd James & Ruth	1975-1983	LCA	Evangelism
Thamm, Geoffrey	1975-1978	LCA	Technical Service
Weier, Vivian & Juelle	1975-1979	LCA (Wabag)	Supply
Zadow, Bronte	1975-1976	LCA	Aviation
Durow, David & Frances	1976-1979	LCA	Education
Hetzel, David & Rosemarie	1976-1978 1981-	LCA	Education Administration
Behrend, Monica	1977-1979	LCA	Education
Dunn, Graham & Denise	1977-1979 1984-	LCA	Shipping, Technical Service
Gerhardy, Ruth	1977-1978	LCA	Education
Holzknecht, Erich & Sonia	1977-1978 1984-	LCA	Education
Ludwig, Revd Heinz & Lorene	1977-1977	LCA	Evangelism
Moll, Robert & Noela	1977-1978	LCA	Education
Neumann, Kevin	1977-1978	LCA	Aviation

Altmann, Gary & Jenine	1978-1980	LCA (Wabag)	Technical Service
Georg, David	1978-1980	LCA	Agriculture
Seidel, Raymond & Lois	1978-1980	LCA	Education
Borgas, Sr Marie	1979-1980	LCA	Medical
Heinrich, Revd Michael & Jill	1979-1983	LCA	Evangelism
Keller, Revd John & Jennifer	1979-1982	LCA	Evangelism
Maczkowiack, Robert & Anne	1979-1985	LCA	Agriculture
Stoll, Anne-Marie	1979-1980	LCA	Domestic
Cole, Graham	1980-	LCA	Education
Kloeden, Allen & Susan	1980-1981	LCA	Education
Koch, Sr Dianne	1980-1982	LCA	Medical
Kummerow, Esther	1980-1981	LCA	Education
Leschke, Graham & Karen	1980-1981	LCA (Wabag)	Technical Service
Nuske, Ralph & Narelle	1980-1982	LCA (Wabag)	Technical Service
Radke, John & Judith	1980-1982	LCA	Agriculture
Schilling, Raymond & Joanne	1980-1984	LCA	Caretaker
Bailey, Barry & Faye	1981-1984	LCA	Builder
Bothe, Jennifer (Mrs Georg Pilhofer)	1981-1984	LCA and ND	Education
Noll, Karen	1981-1982	LCA	KLS Matron
Noller, Brian & Heather	1981-1981	LCA	Education
Olive, Allan & Faye	1981-1983	LCA	Supply
Oppitz, Andrew	1981-1982	LCA	Education
Rudolph, Peter	1981-1985	LCA	Shipping
Whellum, Julie	1981-1982 1984-1984	LCA	Education
Burgess, Robin & Cheryl	1982-1983	LCA	Education
Kuchel, Revd Geoffrey & Chris	1982-	LCA	Evangelism, Seminary
Launer, Gavin & Raelene	1982-1984	LCA	Caretaker
Lipsys, David & Janet	1982-1983	LCA	Administration, Guest House
Modra, Kevin & Margaret	1982-1983	LCA	Education
Mueller, John	1982-1983	LCA	Technical Service
Pentti, Sr Marita	1982-1984	LCA	Medical
Pfeiffer, Rodney & Patricia	1982-1982	LCA	Education
Kennett, Helen	1983-1984	LCA	KLS Matron
Narnst, Revd William & Christine	1983-	LCA	Evangelism, Seminary
Schutz, Revd Rodney & Elaine	1983-	LCA	Evangelism
Graetz, Lois	1984-1985	LCA	Education
Haar, Revd Richard & Julie	1984-	LCA	Evangelism
Prenzler, Revd John & Dorothea	1984-	LCA	Evangelism
Schiller, Revd Gregory	1984-1984 1986-	LCA	Vicar Evangelism
Dickfos, Stanley & Evadne	1985-	LCA	Administration
Habermann, Kym & Catherine	1985-	LCA	Shipping
Nuske, Kym & Ligita	1985-	LCA	Printing
Pokela, Eric & Lynne	1985-	LCA	Caretaker, Education
Jordan, Revd David & Alison	1986-	LCA	Evangelism
Lewis, Patricia	1986-	LCA	KLS Domestic
Schubert, Daryl	1986-	LCA	Vicar

FINLAND

Immonen, Yuoko & Elvi	1967-1971	Finland LCA	Technical Service
Pusa, Revd Keijo & Mirja	1982-1983	Finland LCA	Evangelism
Huhtinen, Revd Pauli & Marja-Terttu	1985-	Finland LCA	Evangelism

D. Of the American Lutheran Church

Knautz, Friedrich & Emma	1921-1928	Mech./ Administration
Voss, Sr Ida (Mrs Victor Koschade) (& UELCA)	1921-1938	Medical
Voss, Luthilda (Mrs Emil Hanneman)	1921-1924†	Education
Deguisne, Sophie (Mrs S. Lehner) (&ND)(-1965)	1922-1956	Education
Pietz, Revd F. Edward, DD & Adina	1922-1950 1960-1967	Evangelism/Supt.
Siemers, William	1922-1944	Builder
Bertram, Carl	1923-1935	Admin.
Estock, Dr A.B.	1923-1926	Medical
Friese, Andrew	1923-1928	Agriculture
Hannemann, Revd Emil, DD & Luthilda & Emilie	1923-1956	Evangelism/ Sem./Lit
Engeling, Emma (Mrs Theodore Radke) (& UELCA)	1924-1964	Education
Engeling, Sr Hattie, (Mrs Theodore Braun)	1924-1971	Medical
Kalkwarf, Tennie	1924-1926	Education
Reck, Louise	1924-1929	Education
Fliehler, Revd Paul & Lydia	1926-1943†	Evangelism/Supt.
Hanselmann, Revd Roland & Marie	1926-1936	Evangelism
Hueter, Revd George, DD & Anna	1926-1932	Evangelism
Henkelmann, Revd Frederick	1927-1943†	Evangelism
Mager, Revd John & Alice	1927-1950	Evangelism/ Educa./Sem./Lit.
Pfeiffer, William	1927-1933	Agriculture
Braun, Dr Theodore G. & Hattie	1930-1971	Medical
Foege, Revd Heinrich & Frieda	1930-1937	Evangelism
Seidler, Sr Lydia (Mrs Paul Fliehler)	1930-1941	Medical
Schwarz, Hans & Charlotte	1931-1938	Administration
Gruber, Emilie (Mrs Emil Hanneman)	1933-1956	Education
Hannemann, Revd Herbert & Olinda	1934-1968	Evangelism/Lit.
Kuder, Revd John, DD & Louise	1934-1973	Evang./Supt./ Bishop
Blum, Sr Emma (Mrs Herbert Enser)	1935-1946	Medical
Hoeger, Dr Agnes	1935-1967	Medical
Spier, Revd Daniel & Sr Frieda	1935-1937	Evangelism
Taeuber, Erma	1935-1938	Education
Thorgersen, Hans	1935-1940	Technical Service
Inselmann, Revd Rudolf & Edna	1936-1946	Evangelism

Name	Years	Service
Kuehn, Alvin & Marie	1936-1944†	Administration
Schoenwald, Frieda (Mrs Daniel Spier) (Mrs Andrew Mild)	1936-1958	Medical
Boettcher, Ress H. & Esther	1937-1975 / 1936-1975	Administration / Medical Sr
Dott, Revd Harry	1937-1943†	Evangelism
Frerichs, Revd Albert, DD & Sylvia	1937-1976	Evangelism/Administration
Enser, Revd Herbert & Emma	1938-1946	Education/Evangelism
Mild, Revd Andrew & Frieda	1938-1958	Agriculture/Evangelism
Freyberg, Revd Paul, DD & Dorothy	1939-1980 / 1946-1980	Evangelism/Sem./Literature
Hafermann, Revd John & Helen & Ruth	1939-1970	Evangelism/Education
Krebs, Walter	1939-1944†	Printery
Ackermann, Revd Martin	1940-1942	Evangelism
Ander, Revd Hans	1940-1944†	Evangelism
Kroeger, Marie (Mrs Alvin Kuehn)	1940-1944†	Education
Wenz, Wilbur & Annie	1940-1942†	Administration
Banfield, Zoe	1946-1948	Medical
Brandt, Revd Roland & Amee	1946-1972 / 1977-1981	Evangelism/Admin.
Fenske, Arthur & Rita	1946-	Builder/Ship/Admin. Education
Heber, Sr Ruth (Mrs Henry Voss)	1946-1959	Medical
Heist, Revd Martin & Florence	1946-1969	Evangelism/Education/Administration
Kammueller, Jean (Mrs Gerhard Reitz)	1946-1956 / 1962-	Administration
Pfarr, Charles & Julia	1946-1973	Medical
Philippi, Revd Leon & Theophila	1946-1949 / 1954-1972	Builder / Evangelism
Reitz, Revd Gerhard, DD & Jean	1946-1956 / 1962-	Evangelism/Sem./Admin.
Sanders, Helen (Mrs John Hafermann)	1946-1956†	Medical
Scherle, Revd Fred & Edna	1946-1967 / 1972-1981	Evangelism/Social Concerns
Schneuker, Revd Carl & Irene	1946-1961	Evangelism/Education
Schroer, Sherwood & Ruth	1946-1948	Evangelism
Sherer, Russell & Ruth	1946-1963	Technical Service
Walborn, Sr Ella	1946-1970	Medical
Walck, Revd Alfred & Marion	1946-1973	Evangelism/Education/Literature
Wegenast, Clarence & Esther	1946-1949 / 1951-1967 / 1952-1967	Builder/Education
Winter, Louis & Theora	1946-1969 / 1947-1969	Builder/Tech Serv.
Daechsel, Douglas & Doris	1947-1970	Administration
Diemer, Sr Doris (Mrs Douglas Daechsel)	1947-1970	Medical
Goldhardt, Revd Ralph & Julia	1947-1973	Evangelism
Hartung, Edward C. & Esther	1947-1970	Printer
Matthias, Sr Erna	1947-1967	Medical
Muhlenhard, Evelyn	1947-1984	Administration
Schulz, Revd Paul A. & Carrie	1947-1969	Evangelism/Education/Administration
Wolber, Revd Herbert & Daisy May	1947-1953	Evangelism
Diemer, Revd Max & Darlene & Dorothy	1948-1951 / 1958-1985 / 1948-1951† / 1959-1985	Evangelism/Literature
Mansur, Revd Hermann F. & Dorothy	1948-1969	Evangelism
Schirmer, Phyllis	1948-1954	Administration
Miller, Eloise	1949-1954	Education
Spehr, Carl & Marian	1949-1965	Tech. Serv.
Weiland, Beatrice (Mrs Alfred Koschade)	1949-1957	Medical
Madden, Sr Alta	1950-1961	Medical
Meuser, William & Gloria	1950-1970	Agriculture
Tews, Ralph & Ruth	1950-1956	Education
Malcuit, Bruce & Ganelle	1951-1966	Agriculture
Reitz, Marie Sr	1951-1970	Medical
Hueter, Revd Robert & Ruth	1952-1981	Evangelism/Admin.
Sievert, Revd John & Frieda	1952-1972	Evangelism/Literature

Name	Dates	Role
Theile, Revd Kenneth & Juanita	1952-1974	Evangelism/ Educa./Sem.
Heist, Erwin G., MD & Emilie	1953-1967	Medical
Johnson, Thomas & Elizabeth	1953-1968	Aviation
Brown, Revd Harold, Dr Ed & Jane	1954-1972	Evangelism/ Education/ Administration
Huber, Pearlyn	1954-1964	Education
Kulow, David & Laura	1954-1956 1961-1966	Builder Medical
Reitz, Revd Marcus & Pearlyn	1954-1964	Evangelism/ Education
Senff, Alfred, MD & Deborah	1954-1955	Medical
Clark, Revd Merrill & Katherine	1955-1969	Evangelism/ Education
Diers, Revd John & Evelyn	1955-1960	Evangelism/ Education
Graf, Pauline (Mrs George Knopke)	1955-	Education
Kuder, Paul & Edna	1955-1974	Education
Kurtz, Revd Wilmer & Lorraine	1955-1969+	Evangelism
Matzner, Sr Hilda	1955-1963	Medical
Willeke, Wanda	1955-1960	Administration
Amman, Revd Ivan & Lois	1956-1970	Evangelism/Sem.
Arten, Oliver & Shirley	1956-1963	Agriculture
Imbrock, Revd Norman & Bernice	1956-	Evangelism/Sem.
Reents, Revd Jack, D Min & Shirley	1956-1958 1962-1978	Builder Evangelism/ Admin
Schroeder, Revd William & Karen	1956-1958 1962-1980	Builder Evangelism/ Admin
Bergstraesser, Myra (Mrs Heinrich Bamler)	1957-1974	Education
Conlon, Ray & Arlene	1957-1964	Administration
Davis, Revd Benjamin & Loretta	1957-1967	Evangelism
Hetrick, Sr June	1957-1963	Medical
Hueter, Irene	1957-1985	Education
Prange, June	1957-1960 1962-1973 1981-1984	Education
Roepke, Revd Arthur	1957-	Evangelism/Lit./ Educa.
Doermann, Paul, MD & W. Ernestine	1958-1959	Medical
Falk, Revd Dennis & Yvonne	1958-1963	Evangelism
Florer, Carl & Sylvia	1958-1965	Agriculture
Kirchhoff, Gilbert	1958-1972	Maintenance/ Education
& Myra	1956-1958	Main — Miss Child. Schl.
Sansness, Arnold & Ardyna	1958-1966	Agriculture
Schardt, Revd Ronald D. Min. & Else	1958-	Builder Evang./Educa./ Admin
Stang, Violet	1958-	Education/ Evangelism
Walters, David & Sarah	1958-1964	Administration
Ager, Revd Theodore & Dorothy May	1959-1973	Education
Groat, George & Marigold	1959-1975	Admin/ Tech. Serv.
Kempfer, Charlotte	1959-1959	Education
Pavey, L.J. & Margie	1959-1959	Maintenance
Schulz, Revd Alfred & Esther	1959-1973	Evangelism
Schurr, Carolyn	1959-1961 1964-1973 1981-1984	Education
Fry, Allan & Lorraine	1960-1974	Tech. Serv.
Hueter, Revd Richard & Evelyn	1960-1980	Evangelism
Lange, David & Lucille	1960-	Agriculture
Logeman, Sr Fern	1960-1964	Medical
Mesplay, Revd Kenneth & Roselyn	1960-1973	Evangelism
Brandt, Virgil & Eunice	1961-1962	Education
Carlstedt, Rhoda	1961-	Education
Erickson, Revd Alvin & Ina	1961-1974	Evangelism/ Sem.
Fricke, Revd Vincent & Barbara	1961-1967	Evangelism
Hilpert, Revd Theodore & Sharyn	1961-1962	Evangelism/ Sem.
Jamieson, Revd Robert & Marjorie	1961-1977	Evangelism/ Literature
Johnson, Milton & Cecil	1961-1963 1965-1966	Education

Name	Years	Field
Jordal, Revd Paul & Jenine	1961-1963 1965-1975	Education
Lose, W. S. & Mary	1961-1967	Tech. Serv/ Builder
Ryan, Sheldon	1961-1964	Tech. Serv.
Scheele, Sr Beatrice	1961-1972	Medical
Tuff, Revd David & Florence	1961-1974	Evangelism
Bagley, Revd Robert & Naomi	1962-1968	Evangelism
Engebretson, Phyllis	1962-1979	Education
Garner, W. Richard, MD & Charlotte	1962-1965	Medical
Haas, Revd Wayne & Irene	1962-1969	Evangelism
Hartung, Edward & Wendy	1962-1966	Printing
Hintz, Merna	1962-1970	Education/Admin
Kuhens, Galen & Mary	1962-1968	Education
Meland, Norris & Lorraine	1962-1972	Agriculture
Mueller, Gretchen	1962-1965 1967-	Education
Ramin, Robert & Inez	1962-1973	Administration
Sauer, Revd Robert	1962-1975	Evangelism
Schroeder, Marliss	1962-	Education
Woolbert, Marilyn	1962-1964	Education
Arntson, Norma	1963-1977	Medical
Estergreen, Mary	1963-1974	Education
Flatham, Revd Albert & Virginia	1963-1985	Evangelism/ Education
Marubbio, A. Thomas, MD & M. Lavonne	1963-1971	Medical
Norden, Revd Norman & Wanda	1963-1979	Evangelism
Olson, Sr Bonnie	1963-1969	Medical
Ware, Revd John & Ruth Ann	1963-1965	Evangelism
Weiss, Revd Joseph & Glennys	1963-1970	Evangelism
Wilson, Gail	1963-1967	Education
Gunderson, Paul & Harriet	1964-1968	Education
Krause, Elizabeth	1964-1969	Administration
Larson, Ralph & Elizabeth	1964-1966	Education
Senff, Revd Paul & Marie	1964-	Evangelism/ Education
DeMitchell, Sr Geraldine	1965-1968	Medical
Scherer, David & Judith	1965-1969	Aviation
Edwards, Revd Byron & Ellen	1966-1972	Evangelism
Jacobs, Gordon, MD	1966-1970	Medical
Read, Stanley & Elizabeth	1966-1976	Aviation
Scherer, Revd David & Glenyce	1966-1972	Evangelism
Foster, Sr Shirley	1967-1971	Medical
Ingebritson, Revd Joel & Paula	1968-1983 1984-	Sem./Education
NeSmith, Joanne	1968-1973	Administration
Rittal, Sr Jane	1968-1976	Medical
Vogeley, Revd Raymond, DD & Gertrude	1968-1970	Education
Iverson, Helge & Miriam	1969-1980	Shipping
Ledin, Stanley & Florence	1969-1976	Administration
Schutte, Howard & Patricia	1969-1974	Aviation
Solberg, Revd Robert & Judith	1969-1980	Evangelism
Stime, Nathan, MD & Linda	1969-1977	Medical
Stinson, H. Keith, MD & Sally	1969-1972	Medical
Brandt, Thomas & Ena	1970-	Education
Nordvall, Revd Robert & Karen	1971-1982	Evangelism
Ruehle, Mary Jo (Mrs George Zwar)	1971-1974	Education
Blumanthal, Revd Gary	1972-1983	Evangelism
Brown, Robert & Jane	1972-1976	Education
Ashmead, Robert & Lynne	1973-1975	Education
Boyd, Marjorie	1973-1975	Education
Minneman, Jean	1973-	Education
Gilbertson, Revd Gaylen & Stella	1974-1978	Communications
Orest, Thomas & M. Louise	1974-1975	Administration
Winter, Esther	1974-	Education
Zeilinger, Revd Neal & Rhonda	1974-1979	Evangelism
Prasek, Revd Ronald & Virginia	1975-1976	Evangelism

650

Docktor, LeRoy & Ramona	1976-1979	Administration
Heuchert, Evelyn	1976-1978	Education
Neuman, Revd Fred & Kay	1976-1979	Evangelism
Paulson, Revd David & Diane	1976-	Evangelism
Frerichs, Jonathan & Marian	1977-1980	Communications
Hacker, James & Kathy	1977-1984	Administration
Nerison, Rex & Mae	1977-1982	Administration
Spieker, Revd Erich	1977-1978 1985	Shipping Evangelism
Hershey, John, MD & Vickie	1978-1981 1985-	Medical
Perks, J. Carey & Peggy	1978-1984	Administration
Pleiss, Margaret	1978-1980	Education
Riedel, Revd Robert & Ruth	1978-	Evangelism/ Sem.
Grosch, Kenneth & Rosalie	1981-	Communications/ Admin.
Midthun, Revd Eric & Susan	1981-	Evangelism
Niemi, Revd Stanley & Kristin	1981-	Evangelism
Thompson, Gary & Laurel	1981-	Education
VanderZiel, Albert & Ann	1981-1983	Education
Brandt, Samuel	1982-	Administration
Bunai, Elizabeth	1982-1984	Education
Jordahl, Revd Roger, PhD & Clara	1984-	Sem.
Maurer, Revd Dennis, PhD & Carolyn	1984-	Sem.
Monsen, Wayne & Karen	1984-	Education/ Agriculture
Aukee, Waino, D Edu & Sylvia	1985-	Education
Cottingham, Carol	1985-	Education
Meyer, Revd Gregory & Kristen	1985-	Evangelism

E. Of the Lutheran Church — Missouri Synod

Burce, Revd Willard & Elinor	1948-	Evangelism
Hintze, Revd Otto & Jeannelle	1948-1965	Evangelism
Heppner, Louis & Loma	1949-1971	Builder
Kleinig, Revd Ian & Enid	1949-1965	Evangelism
Stotik, Revd Karl & Esther	1950-1978	Evangelism
Wessel, Loren & Beulah	1950-1952	Domestic Work
Jeffers, Donald	1952-1969	Builder
Spruth, Revd Erwin & Lorraine	1952-1978	Evangelism
Dicke, Edward & Phyllis	1953-1975	Administration
Fricke, Wanda	1953-1958	Medical
Hinlicky, George & Miriam	1953-1964	Education
Heinicke, Revd Victor & Norma	1954-1972	Education
Strackbein, Revd Lee & Ruth	1954-1961	Evangelism
Arndt, Revd Gerald & Frieda	1955-1971	Evangelism
Biberdorf, Walter & Audrey	1955-1980	Builder/ Evangelism
Hall, Donald	1955-1956	Builder
Harms, August	1955-1962	Builder
Hoopman, Dr Eric	1955-1956	Medical
Kahre, James & Dorothy	1955-1963	Builder

Name	Years	Department
Lenschow, Norma	1955-1956	Medical
Marquardt, Robert	1955-1957	Builder
Rivers, Clarence	1955-1957	Builder
Schultze, Clarence	1955-1957	Builder
Wagner, Revd William & Ruth	1955-1969	Evangelism
Bauer, Kenneth & Vivian	1957-1963	Education
Busse, Dale & Lucile	1957-	Education
Denman, Marianne	1957-1965	Medical
Fehrmann, Revd Walter & Hildegarde	1957-1964	Evangelism
Gerber, Don & Marjorie	1957-1970	Education
Klomhaus, Dr Alfred & Adeline	1957-1960	Medical
Larson, Revd James & Marie	1957-1974	Evangelism
Noller, Joan	1957-1960	Administration
Wiebe, Reta	1957-1963	Medical
Barbour, Robert	1958-1960	Builder/ Administration
Neubacher, Joseph & Patricia	1958-1963	Education
Schmidt, Walter	1958-1960	Builder
Freund, Roland & Josephine	1959-1971	Agricultural
Redeker, Eunice (Mrs. Ray Hausler)	1959-1973	Education
Simonson, Anita	1959-1966	Medical
Bleeke, Ralph & Margaret	1960-1975	Education
Casson, Edith	1960-1961	Medical
Conner, Dr Clarence & Margaret	1960-1965	Medical
Golding, Shirley	1960-1962	Administration
Kopitske, Revd Harley & Donna	1960-1974	Evangelism
Schaus, David & Dorothy	1960-1965	Education
Schaus, David & Dorothy	1967-1970	Education
Weier, Donald & Valerie	1960-1970	Builder
Cooke, Gary & Svea	1961-1967	Education
Lorenz, David & Joan	1961-1975	Education
Padgett, Revd Stanley & Norma	1961-1962	Evangelism
Schulz, Mildred	1961-1970	Medical
Wenger, Revd Dwight & Rosalie	1961-1966	Evangelism
Yarroll, Donald & Christine	1961-1973	Education
Adler, Richard & Loretta	1962-1982	Education
Brandon, Richard & Elizabeth	1962-1967	Administration
Brandon, Revd Richard & Elizabeth	1977-1980	Evangelism
Budke, Revd Clarence & Ruth	1962-1971	Evangelism
Cooper, Christopher & Marlene	1962-1971	Education
Dahlgren, Henry & Esther	1962-1965	Medical
Frautschi, John & Anna	1962-1967	Medical
Herzog, Revd James & Elizabeth	1962-1967	Evangelism
Hilgendorf, Richard & Joanne	1962-1982	Education
Janetzki, Clem & Thelma	1962-1975	Builder
Kunert, Daniel & Nancy	1962-1981	Education
Lehmann, Arlo & Euleen	1962-1967	Education
Rothenbush, Revd Donald & Muriel	1962-1971	Evangelism
Scheimann, Revd Max & Judith	1962-1973	Evangelism
Schilling, Juanita	1962-1964	Medical
Steffens, Stephen & Elisabeth	1962-1976	Education
Wagner, Revd Merlyn & Janet	1962-1970	Evangelism
Weier, Althea	1962-1965	Administration
Ewald, Elwyn & Phyllis	1963-1968 1970-1973	Education
Finney, Arthur & June	1963-1967	Builder
Hartwig, Lorenz & Sandra	1963-1968	Education
Holst, Revd Robert & Lynne	1963-1968	Evangelism
Houser, Revd David & Mona	1963-1973	Evangelism
Lehman, Terry & Sharon	1963-1974	Education
Loncar, Revd Ronald & Jane	1963 (1 mth)	Evangelism
Marubbio, Dr A. Thos. & Mayvis	1963-1966	Medical
McCormick, Judith	1963-1966	Medical
Priebe, Janet (Mrs Lawrence Mirtschin)	1963-1971	Medical
Rivers, Ronnie & Marlene	1963-1974	Education
Wolff, Garry & Charla	1963-1976	Education
Banke, Eliz. (Mrs Stephen Steffens)	1964-1967	Medical
Barton, James & Carol	1964-1970	Administration
Feist, Dennis & Betty	1964-1982	Administration
Geach, Revd John & Darlene	1964-1969	Evangelism

652

Name	Years	Category
Gessner, Gwendolyn	1964-1972	Medical
Handorf, Lala	1964-1965	Medical
Heidorn, Mark	1964-1974	Education
Ingeman, Frances	1964-1965	Education
Kath, Revd Harvey & Norita	1964-1971	Evangelism
Leland, Nancy (Mrs Douglas Mickan)	1964-1977	Medical
Loth, Judy (Mrs Roy Schache)	1964-1979	Medical
McArthur, Dr James & Mary	1964-1969	Medical
Meyer, Revd Robert & Judith	1964-1975	Evangelism
Reitz, Priscilla (Mrs Mark Heidorn)	1964-1974	Medical
Rhodes, Sandra	1964-1984	Medical
Schmeling, Gerald & Karen	1964-1976	Education
Bloos, Edmund & Luverne	1965-1982	Evangelism
Eckert, Revd Leroy & Lois	1965-	Evangelism
Faber, Judith	1965-1972	Evangelism
Hausler, Ray & Eunice	1965-1973	Builder
Hein, Orville & Glorian	1965-1970	Printer
Kroenke, Robert & Lois	1965-1971	Builder
McMillen, Stanley & Margot	1965-1971	Education
Mirtschin, Lawrence & Janet	1965-1971	Builder
Reinking, Dr Richard & Martha	1965-1970	Medical
Seiler, Revd Brian & Ruth	1965-1967	Evangelism
Vollrath, Paul & Karen	1965-1974	Education
Westermann, Revd T & Florence	1965-1968	Education
Day, Wilfred & Laura	1966-1975	Technical
Degnitz, Dorothy	1966-	Medical
Freiberg, Edith	1966-1970	Medical
Green, Merlyn & Ardys	1966-1978	Domestic
Greenthaner, Edward & Arlene	1966-1975	Evangelism
Hett, Revd Roger & Rosalie	1966-1975	Evangelism
Kleinig, Dr Daniel & Mona	1966-1969	Medical
Lillie, James & Nola	1966 (4 mths)	Education
Rehfuss, Linda	1966-1968	Medical
Reko, Revd H. Karl & Ruth	1966-1972	Evangelism
Sackschewsky, Revd Marvin & Christa	1966-1971	Evangelism
Schaan, Revd Herbert & Alberta	1966-1980	Evangelism
Schrader, Susan (Mrs Dennis Malone)	1966-1975	Medical
Smith, Revd Ernest & Katherine	1966-1976	Evangelism
Venz, Raymond	1966-1969	Medical
Zabransky, Sylvia	1966-1973	Education
Arndt, Revd Warren & Elise	1967-1972	Evangelism
Ettinger, Nancy	1967-1971	Medical
Groenewold, Revd Douglas & Sonia	1967-1973	Evangelism
Gruenhagen, David & Magdalene	1967-1973	Education
Levenhagen, Linda	1967-1972	Medical
Lorenz, Barbara	1967-1969	Education
Lutz, Revd Bernhard & Roberta	1967-1975	Evangelism
Malone, Dennis & Susan	1967-1975	Education
Mohr, Robert & Jeanne	1967-1973	Medical
Pucci, Connie	1967-1973	Education
Reitz, Mary	1967-1969	Education
Russell, Malcolm & Petronella	1967-1971	Builder
Weinhold, Dr Delmer & Judith	1967-1982	Medical
Brennan, Dr Paul & Dorothy	1968-1977	Literature
Ebel, Alfred & Nancy	1968-1978	Education
Herman, Myron & Mavis	1968-1980	Agricultural
Ingebritson, Revd Joel & Paula	1968-1978 1980-1983	Evangelism
Kuhlman, David & Sharryn	1968-1982	Education
Parker, Gary & Darlene	1968-1977	Education
Borchard, Revd Terry & Kathryn	1969-	Evangelism
Dobelstein, Paula (Mrs Joel Ingebritson)	1969-1983	Medical
Groh, Dr Lawrence & Delphine	1969-1970	Medical
Koeneke, LeAnn	1969-1971	Administration
Luedtke, Todd & Janet	1969-1984	Education
Olson, Melodie	1969-1975	Medical
Trinklein, Daniel & Edith	1969-1972	Education
Woodburn, William & Joan	1969-1973	Administration
Zertuche, Karen	1969-1973	Medical
Reinecke, Ruth	1970-1971	Medical
Drumm, Carolyn	1971-1973	Medical

Name	Years	Field
Kohn, Patricia	1971-1975	Education
Dierker, Rebecca	1973-1974	Medical
Muench, Revd Paul & Andrea	1972-1979	Evangelism
Haseley, Revd Stephen & Carol	1973-1980	Evangelism
Herndon, Steven & Barbara	1973-1974	Education
Huse, Gregory	1973-1978	Education
Kunert, Mark & Linda	1973 (2 mths)	Education
Meyer, Revd Lealand & Joan	1973-1981	Evangelism
Pust, Dr Ronald & Kren	1973-1979	Medical
Rall, Revd Ronald & Mary Ann	1973-1981	Evangelism
Rapp, Revd Victor & Margaret	1973-1977	Evangelism
Schmidt, Terry & Ann	1973-1974	Education
Smith, Jeffrey & Esther	1973-1974	Medical
Eggert, Christine	1974 (2 mths)	Education
Mickan, Douglas & Nancy	1974-1977	Builder
Schache, Roy & Judy	1974-1979	Builder
Tumlison, Dr John & Christina	1974-1976	Medical
Peters, Revd Edward & Kathleen	1976-1980 1985-	Evangelism
Bracewell, Earl & Phyllis	1979-	Agricultural
Reedstrom, Kermit & Joyce	1979-1982	Administration
Bock, Revd Gordon & Ruth	1981-1985	Administration
Martin, Dr P.S.S., & Janet	1981-1984	Medical
Smith Dr Dean & Marion	1981-1984	Medical
Benscoter, Revd Randall & Carlene	1982-	Evangelism
Gettner, Donald & Maureen	1982-	Agricultural
Robert, Solomon & Thamary	1982-	Education
Sielaff, David & Cynthia	1982-1984	Education
Hornig, John & Joan	1983-	Administration
Jentz, Revd Paul	1983-	Evangelism
Gause, Revd Mark	1984-	Evangelism
Inglehart, Revd Stephen & Jana	1984-	Evangelism
Matro, Revd Lawrence & Tina	1984-	Evangelism
Otten, Revd David & Danele	1984-	Evangelism
Pennington, James & Karen	1984-	Administration
Rausch, Henry & Susan	1984-	Education
Rittmann, Dr John & Lorraine	1984 (2 mths)	Medical
Schroeder, Revd Mark & Barbara	1984-	Evangelism
Bjornstad, Carsten & Karen	1985-	Education
Eggert, Revd John & Jeanette	1985-	Evangelism
Geerdes, Jody	1985-	Education
Nickerson, Dr Neil & Alice	1985-	Medical

F. Of the Leipzig Mission

Name	Years	Field
Jaeschke, Revd Ernst	1955-1962 1973-1977	Evangelism/ Sem.
& Dr Elisabeth	1955-1962 1973-1977	Medical
Klemm, Revd Hans-Dieter & Hanna	1955- 1956	Evangelism/ Sem.
Hoehne, Revd Friedrich & Heidi (Mrs Kirsch) & UELCA	1955-1958 1956-1970	Evangelism
Weber, Revd Eckard & Ursula	1957-1964 1960-1964	Evangelism
Renck, Revd Guether & Gertrud	1957-1976 1957-1976	Evangelism/ Bible School

Name	Years	Work
Fontius, Revd Dr Hanfried	1959-1972	Evangelism/Sem.
& Gisela	1959-1972	
Walter, Revd Helmut	1959-1971	Evangelism/Sem.
& Ingrid	1959-1971	
Michold, Revd Christoph	1961-1974	Evangelism
& Christine	1961-1974	
Tuerschmann, Revd Wolfgang	1965-1971	Evangelism
& Renate	1965-1971	
Grabowski, Sr Lieselotte	1967-1971	Medical
Ahrens, Revd Dr Theodor & NMZ	1971-1978	Evangelism/MI
& Revd Hanna	1971-1978	
Gericke, Revd Hartmut & NMZ	1966-1980	Evangelism/Sem.
& Margarete	1966-1980	

Name	Years	Work
Jaeschke, Dorothea (Mrs Prenzler) & LCA	1972-1974 1984-	Education
Kaule, Hadwig Julie (Mrs Rauschning)	1970-1980	Education
Rauschning, Revd Rainer & MWB & Hadwig Julie	1970-1980	Evangelism
Lutschewitz, Revd Hermann & MWB & Dr Ingrid	1972-1985 1972-1985	Evangelism/Sem.
Schmidt, Revd Bernd	1971-1973	Evangelism
Knapp, Walter & Waltraud	1971-1974 1971-1974	Education

G. Of the North Elbian Mission Centre

Name	Years	Work
Hamann, Gisela	1975-1978 1981-1984	Education Women's work
Boigs, Manfred & Lotte	1975-1978	Education
Fruehbrodt, Gisela	1977-1980	Education
Dziobek, Fritz & Lilli	1978-1982	Administration
Ehlers, Revd Eyke & Ingrid	1978-1983 1981-1983	Evangelism
Roebbelen, Ulrich & Margret	1978-	Religious Education
Lies, Revd Rudolf & Cynthia	1979-1984	Evangelism
Breckwoldt-Cuhls, Anke	1980-1985	Education
Cuhls, Claus	1980-1985	Education
Eilts, Harm & Helga	1981-	Administration

Name	Years	Work
Feistkorn, Frauke	1981-1985	Handic. child. work
Jordan, Deacon Ulrich & Astrid	1981-1982	Evangelism
Schmidt, Revd Gerhard & Elisabeth	1982-	Evangelism
Zacharias, Dr Wolfram & Dr Anita	1982-	Medical
Deckelmann, Thomas	1983-	Administration
Bernard, Revd Dieter	1984-	Evangelism
Hinrichs, Dieter	1985-	Education
Wittkopf, Sabine (Mrs Hinrichs)	1985-	Education
Riecke, Revd Kurt & Marianne	1985-	Evangelism
Waack, Revd Dietrich & Revd Regina	1985- 1985-	Stud. work Religious Education

Doering, Sr Adella	1964-1968	Medical	Doering, Revd Felix	1935-1968	Evang./Congr.
Leuze, Dorothy	1964-	Educ./	& Hedwig	1937-1968	
		Teacher Training	Hauert, Sr Hilda	1935-1937	Medical
Pinno, Erhard	1964-1966	Education		1958-1966	
& Lorene	1971-1977		Voss, Henry	1946-1972	Builder/Maint.
Scheske, Ray	1964-1970	Education	& Ruth	1946-1972	
& Marilyn	1964-1970		Kurtz, Revd Wilmer	1955-1969	Evang./Congr.
Hall, Sr Dolores	1966-	Medical	& Lorraine	1957-1969	
Landstrom, Connie	1966-1974	Education	Blacklock, Ray	1962-1981	Educ./
Moore, Revd Douglas	1981-1984	Univ. Chaplain	& Norma	1964-1981	Assist. to Bishop
& Karen	1981-1984		Hopkins, Lionel	1962-1968	Education
Haab, Ernest	1983-	Agriculture	& Elva	1965-1968	

Authors

Fugmann, Wilhelm. Served in New Guinea 1933-1972, first as Business Manager of Lutheran Mission, then as Managing Director of Namasu. Now retired. Address: Fichtenstr. 9, 8806 Neuendettelsau, West Germany.

Gaenssbauer, Revd Hannes, Area Secretary for Melanesia of the Department of World Mission, Ev. Luth. Church in Bavaria. Served in New Guinea 1966-1975 as Circuit missionary (Biliau, Begesin), and as Bible School teacher (Amron). Address: Postbox 68, 8806 Neuendettelsau, West Germany.

Gerhardy, Christa (nee Lindner), FCNA. Served in New Guinea as nursing tutor at Yagaum Hospital, and as part-time health teacher at Balob Teachers College, Lae (1962-1977). Since 1978, resides at Senior Flierl Seminary, Logaweng. Address: Box 119, Finschhafen, PNG.

Gerhardy, Revd Gordon J., STM, BA, Dip Ed, Vice-Principal of Senior Flierl Seminary, Logaweng. Serving in New Guinea since 1966, first at Balob Teachers College, Lae, and since 1978 at Senior Flierl Seminary, Logaweng. Address: Box 119, Finschhafen, PNG.

Goerner, Revd Karl, Pastor in the Department of World Mission, Ev. Luth. Church in Bavaria. Served in New Guinea 1978-1983 as Circuit missionary at Nomane and Lecturer at Senior Flierl Seminary, Logaweng. Address: Meisenweg 2, 8806 Neuendettelsau, West Germany.

Hage, Revd Hartley B., Parish Pastor in South Australia. Served in New Guinea as educational missionary 1955-1972 (Heldsbach, Amron, Bumayong, Sattelberg, Rintebe, Goroka, Kitip). Address: 12 Langdon Terrace, Barmera, SA. 5345. Australia.

Horndasch, Revd Helmut F., Director of the Department of Ministerial Training of ELC-PNG. Served in New Guinea from 1957 as congregational and educational missionary at Zaka/Garaina, Rintebe, Heldsbach, and Logaweng. Since 1981, Departmental Head at ELC-PNG Church Office. Address: Box 80, Lae, PNG.

Kuder, Revd John F., DD, Bishop emeritus. Served in New Guinea 1934-1973. President of LMNG (1945-1969) and first Bishop of ELCONG (1956-1973). Address: 352 Garden Road, Columbus, Ohio. 43214. USA.

Loeliger, Carl E., PhD, MA, Senior Lecturer in Religious Studies (1972-1982) and in History (1984) at the University of Papua New Guinea, Port Moresby. Address: PO Box 7, Lubeck, Vic. 3381. Australia.

Lutschewitz, Revd Hermann W.A. Parish Pastor in Germany. Served in New Guinea 1972-1985 as Circuit missionary (Tiripini) and as Lecturer at the Highlands Seminary, Ogelbeng and at Martin Luther Seminary, Lae. Address: Schallershofer Strasse 24, 8520 Erlangen, West Germany.

May, John D., STL, DTh, PhD, Ecumenical Research Officer, Melanesian Council of Churches, at the Melanesian Institute, Goroka since 1983. Address: Box 571, Goroka, EHP, PNG.

Mrossko, Kurt D., Lecturer at the Institute for the Study of World Mission, Department of World Mission of the Ev. Luth. Church in Bavaria. Served in New Guinea 1973-1976 as educationist at Onerunka and Rintebe. Address: Sonnenstrasse 74, 8806 Neuendettelsau, West Germany.

Neumeister, Revd Gerhard, Pastor in the Dept of World Mission, Ev. Luth. Church in Bavaria. Served in New Guinea 1977-1985 as Circuit missionary at Kaiapit and as Lutheran Chaplain at the University of Papua New Guinea, Port Moresby. Address: Haagerstrasse 10, 8806 Neuendettelsau, West Germany.

Noller, Revd Geoffrey D., Parish Pastor in Australia. Served in New Guinea as congregational missionary at Awelkon, Rooke Island, 1952-1960. Address: 4 Cust Street, Rainbow, Vic. 3424. Australia.

Schwarz, Revd Brian H., Assistant Director, Melanesian Institute, Goroka. Serving in New Guinea since 1969, first as congregational missionary at Goroka and Port Moresby, and since 1982 as a research worker at the Melanesian Institute. Address: Box 571, Goroka, EHP, PNG.

Spruth, Revd Erwin L., BA, ThM, DMiss. Parish Pastor in California. Served in New Guinea 1953-1981 as pioneer missionary in the Enga area (Papayuku and Irelya Circuits) and in administrative positions of GLC. Address: 10341 Limetree Lane, Spring Valley, CA. 92077. USA.

Strelan, Revd John G., DTh. Lecturer at Luther Seminary, Adelaide. Served in New Guinea 1962-1984, first as Circuit missionary at Menyamya, and Faculty member of Martin Luther Seminary, Lae since 1966. Address: 36 Austral Terrace, Malvern, SA. 5061. Australia.

Reiner, Revd Hermann, DTh, Dekan. Served in New Guinea 1969-1976 at Mumeng Circuit, Mainyanda Bible School, and Senior Flierl Seminary, Logaweng. Address: Kirchenplatz 2, 8811 Leutershausen. West Germany.

Reitz, Revd Gerhard O., DD. Chief Archivist of ELC-PNG. Serving in New Guinea since 1946 (Circuit missionary at Karkar, Begesin, Amele. District missionary Madang. Principal and Lecturer at Martin Luther Seminary, Lae. LWF Liaison Officer to Indonesia and Lecturer in Theology at Nommensen University, Pematang Siantar 1956-1961). Address: Box 80, Lae, PNG.

Wagner, Revd Herwig, DTh, STM. Professor of Missiology at Augustana Theological Seminary, Neuendettelsau. Served in New Guinea 1961-1971 as congregational missionary (Sattelberg) and Lecturer and Principal of Senior Flierl Seminary, Logaweng. Address: Finkenstrasse 5, 8806 Neuendettelsau, West Germany.

Selected
Bibliography

Ahrens, Theodor. *Unterwegs nach der verlorenen Heimat. Studien zur Identitaetsproblematik in Melanesien.* Erlangen: Verlag der Ev.-Luth. Mission, 1986.

Ahrens, Theodor, and Walter J. Hollenweger. *Volkschristentum und Volksreligion im Pazifik. Wiederentdeckung des Mythos fuer den christlichen Glauben.* Frankfurt: Otto Lembeck, n.d.

Bergmann, Wilhelm. *Die Kumanuku. Die Kultur der Chimbu Staemme.* 4 vols. Mutdapilly: mimeographed, 1970.

Bergmann, Wilhelm. *Vierzig Jahre in Neuguinea.* 10 vols. Mutdapilly: mimeographed, n.d.

Berndt, Ronald M., and Peter Lawrence. *Politics in New Guinea: Traditional and in the Context of Change. Some Anthropological Data.* Nedlands: University of Western Australia Press, 1971.

Blackwood, Beatrice. *The Kukukukus of the Upper Watut.* Oxford: Pitt Rivers Museum, 1978.

Braun, F., and C.V. Sheatsley. *On Both Sides of the Equator.* Columbus, Ohio: The Lutheran Book Concern, 1937.

Brennan, Paul, ed. *Exploring Enga Culture: Studies in Missionary Anthropology.* Wapenamanda: Kristen Pres, 1970.

Brennan, Paul. *Let Sleeping Snakes Lie: Central Enga Traditional Belief and Ritual.* Adelaide: Australian Society for the Study of Religion, 1977.

Brown, Paula. *Highland Peoples of New Guinea.* Cambridge: Cambridge University Press, 1978.

Buerkle, Horst, ed. *Theologische Beitraege aus Papua Neuguinea.* Erlangen: Verlag der Ev.-Luth. Mission, 1978.

Cochrane, Glynn. *Big Men and Cargo Cults.* Oxford: Clarendon Press, 1970.

Dexter, David. *The New Guinea Offensives. Australia in the War of 1939-1945. Series 1, Vol. VI.* Canberra: Australian War Memorial, 1961.

Feldt, Eric. *The Coast Watchers.* Sydney: Pacific Books, 1946.

Fischer, Hans, ed. *Wampar. Berichte ueber die alte Kultur eines Stammes in Papua New Guinea.* Bremen: Uebersee-Museum, 1978.

Finsch, Otto. *Samoafahrten. Reisen in Kaiser-Wilhelms-Land und in Englisch-Neu-Guinea, 1884 und 1885. 2 vols.* Leipzig: Ferd. Hirth und Sohn, 1888; new edition 1977.

Flannery, Wendy, ed. *Religious Movements in Melanesia Today.* 3 vols. Point Series 2-4. Goroka: The Melanesian Institute, 1983/84.

Flierl, Johann. *Fuehrungen Gottes. Ein Rueckblick auf meinen Lebensgang und auf meine 20-jaehrige Taetigkeit in der Mission.*Neuendettelsau: Verlag des Missionshauses, 1899.

Flierl, Johann. *Forty Years in New Guinea. Memoirs.* tr. M. Wiedraenders. Chicago: Wartburg Publishing House, 1927.

Flierl, Johann. *Gottes Wort in den Urwaeldern von Neuguinea.* Neuendettelsau: Verlag des Missionshauses, 1929.

Flierl, Johann. *Wunder der goettlichen Gnade. Geschichte der Gehilfenarbeit in der Lutherischen Mission bei Finschhafen auf Neuguinea.* Tanunda: Auricht's Printing Office, 1931.

Flierl, Johann. *Christ in New Guinea.* Tanunda: Auricht's Printing Office, 1932.

Flierl, Leonhard. *Eemasang. Die Erneuerungsbewegung in der Gemeinde Sattelberg.* Guetersloh: Bertelsmann, 1931.

Flierl, Willy. *Miti Fua Ngeing Ewec* (History of the Lutheran Mission New Guinea and the Indigenous Lutheran Church). Madang: Lutheran Mission Press, 1962.

Frerichs, Albert F. *Anutu Conquers in New Guinea.* Columbus, Ohio: The Wartburg Press, 1957.

Freund, Dorothea M. *I Will Uphold You. The Memoirs of Dorothea M. Freund.* Adelaide: A.P.H. Freund, 1985.

Fontius, Hanfried. *Mission-Gemeinde-Kirche in Neuguinea, Bayern und bei Karl Steck.* Erlangen: Verlag der Ev.-Luth. Mission, 1975.

Forman, Charles W. *The Island Churches of the South Pacific. Emergence in the Twentieth Century.* Maryknoll, NY: Orbis Books, 1982.

Fricke, Theodore P. *We Found Them Waiting.* Columbus, Ohio: Wartburg Press, 1947.

Fugmann, Wilhelm. *Junge Kirche zwischen Steinzeit und Neuzeit.* Neuendettelsau: Freimund Verlag, 1959.

Fugmann, Wilhelm, ed. *Und ob ich schon wanderte im finstern Tal. Vom Leben und Sterben zweier Zeugen Jesu Christi.* Neuendettelsau: Freimund Verlag, 1982.

Gash, N.G., J.F. Hookey, R.J. Lacey, J.L. Whittaker, eds. *Documents and Readings in New Guinea History, Prehistory to 1889.* Melbourne: Jacaranda Press, 1975.

Garrett, John. *To Live Among the Stars. Christian Origins in Oceania.* Geneva/Suva: World Council of Churches, 1982.

Geyammalo, Apo. *Recollections and Experiences of a New Guinea Evangelist.* tr. F.E. Pietz. Dubuque, Ia.

Griffin, James, ed. *Papua New Guinea Portraits. The Expatriate Experience.* Canberra: Australian National University Press, 1978.

Griffin, James, Hank Nelson, Steward Firth. *Papua New Guinea. A Political History.* Richmond, Vic.: Heinemann Educational, 1979.

Habel, Norman C., ed. *Powers, Plumes and Piglets. Phenomena of Melanesian Religion.* Adelaide: Australian Association for the Study of Religion, 1979.

Hahl, Albert. *Governor in New Guinea.* ed. and tr. by P.G. Sack and D. Clark. Canberra: Australian National University Press, 1980.

Hempenstall, Peter J. *Pacific Islanders under German Rule. A Study on the Meaning of Colonial Resistance.* Canberra: Australian National University Press, 1948.

Hilliard, David L. *God's Gentlemen. A History of the Melanesian Mission 1849-1942.* Santa Lucia: University of Queensland Press, 1978.

Holzknecht, Karl. *Die Erforschung und Geschichte des Markhamtales in Papua Neuguinea.* Wiesbaden: B. Heymann Verlag, 1975.

Idriess, Ion.L. *Gold-Dust and Ashes. The Romantic Story of the New Guinea Goldfields.* Sydney: Angus and Robertson, 1933.

Inselmann, Rudolf. *Letub, The Cult of the Secrets of Wealth.* MA Thesis. Hartford Seminary Foundation: Kennedy School of Missions, 1944.

Italiaander, Rolf, ed. *Heisses Land Niugini: Beitraege zu den Wandlungen in Papua Neuguinea.* Erlangen: Verlag der Ev.-Luth. Mission, 1974.

Jaspers, Reiner. *Die missionarische Erschliessung Ozeaniens. Ein quellengeschichtlicher und missions-geographischer Versuch zur kirchlichen Gebietsaufteilung bis 1855.* Munster: Aschendorff, 1972.

Jericho, E.A. *Seedtime and Harvest in New Guinea.* Adelaide: UELCA New Guinea Mission Board, 1961.

Jinks, B., P. Biskup, and H. Nelson, eds. *Readings in New Guinea History.* Sydney: Angus and Robertson, 1973.

Kettle, Ellen. *That They Might Live.* Sydney: F.P. Leonard, 1979.

Keysser, Christian. *Anutu im Papualande.* Neuendettelsau: Freimund Verlag, 2nd edn 1958.

Keysser, Christian. *Buerger zweier Welten.* Wilhelm Fugmann ed. Neuhausen-Stuttgart: Haenssler-Verlag, 1985.
660

Keysser, Christian. *Das bin bloss ich. Lebenserinnerungen, aus dem Nachlass herausgegeben von Wilhelm Fugmann.* Neuendettelsau: Freimund Verlag, 1966.

Keysser, Christian. *A People Reborn.* tr. A. Allin and J. Kuder. Pasadena: William Carey Library, 1980.

Kigasung, Wesley W. *Change and Development in a Local Church. A History of the Bukawa Church since 1906.* MA Thesis. University of Papua New Guinea, 1978.

Kiki, Albert Maori. *Kiki. Ten Thousand Years in a Life-time: A New Guinea Autobiography.* Melbourne: F.W. Cheshire, 1968.

Knight, James, ed. *Christ in Melanesia. Exploring Theological Issues.* (Point 1977). Goroka: The Melanesian Institute, 1979.

Koschade, Alfred. *New Branches on the Vine. From Mission Field to Church in New Guinea.* Minneapolis: Augsburg Publishing House, 1967.

von Krause, Wolfram, ed. *Junges Neuguinea. Ein Informationsbuch.* Neuendettelsau: Freimund Verlag, 1970.

Kriele, Eduard. *Das Kreuz unter den Palmen. Die Rheinische Mission in Neu-Guinea.* Barmen: Verlag des Missionshauses, 1927.

Kunze, Georg. *Im Dienst des Kreuzes auf ungebahnten Pfaden.* Barmen: Verlag des Missionshauses, 3rd edn 1925.

Lacey, Roderic J. *Oral Tradition as History: An Exploration of Oral Sources Among the Enga of the New Guinea Highlands.* PhD Thesis. University of Wisconsin, 1975.

Laracy, Hugh. *Marists and Melanesians: A History of Catholic Missions in the Solomon Islands.* Canberra: Australian National University Press, 1976.

Lawrence, Peter. *Road Belong Cargo. A Study of the Cargo Movements in the Southern Madang District New Guinea.* Melbourne: Melbourne University Press, 1964.

Lawrence, Peter, and M.J. Megitt, eds. *Gods, Ghosts and Men in Melanesia. Some Religions of Australian New Guinea and the New Hebrides.* Melbourne: Melbourne University Press, 1965.

Lehner, Stephan. *Siehe, ich mache alles neu!* Neuendettelsau: Freimund Verlag, 1937.

McCarthy, J.K. *Patrol into Yesterday.* Melbourne: F.W. Cheshire, 1963. Sydney: Angus and Robertson, 1964.

McSwain, Romola. *The Past & Future People: Tradition and Change on a New Guinea Island.* Melbourne: Melbourne University Press, 1977.

Mantovani, Ennio, ed. *An Introduction to Melanesian Religions.* Point Series No. 6. Goroka: The Melanesian Institute, 1984.

Mennis, M. *Hagen Saga.* Port Moresby: Institute of Papua New Guinea Studies, 1982.

Mikloucho-Maclay, Nikolai. *New Guinea Diaries 1871-1883.* tr. C.L. Sentinella. Madang: Kristen Pres, 1975.

Morauta, Louise, *Beyond the Village: Local Politics in Madang, Papua New Guinea.* Canberra: Australian National University Press, 1974.

Narakobi, Bernhard. *The Melanesian Way: Total Cosmic Vision of Life.* Port Moresby: Institute of Papua New Guinea Studies, 1980.

Nelson, Hank. *Black, White and Gold. Goldmining in Papua New Guinea 1878-1930.* Canberra: Australian National University Press, 1976.

Pech, Rufus. *Myth Dream and Drama: Shapers of a People's Quest for Salvation.* STM Thesis. Columbus, Ohio: Trinity Lutheran Seminary, 1979.

Pilhofer, Georg. *Die Geschichte der Neuendettelsauer Mission in Neuguinea.* 3 vols. Neuendettelsau: Freimund Verlag, 1961-63.

Radford, Robin. *Highlanders and Foreigners in the Upper Ramu: The Kainantu Area 1919-1942.* MA Thesis. Port Moresby: University of Papua New Guinea, 1979.

Rappaport, Roy A. *Pigs for the Ancestors. Ritual in the Ecology of a New Guinea People.* New Haven: Yale University Press, 1968.

Rowley, Charles D. *The Australians in German New Guinea 1914-1921.* Melbourne: Melbourne University Press, 1958.

Rowley, Charles. *The New Guinea Villager. A Retrospect from 1964.* Melbourne: F.W. Cheshire, 1972.

Ryan, Peter, ed. *Encyclopedia of Papua and New Guinea.* 3 vols. Melbourne: Melbourne University Press, 1972.

Schmidt, O.H. *Globe-Trotting for the Gospel.* New York: Vantage Press, 1962.

Schwarz, Brian, ed. *An Introduction to Ministry in Melanesia.* Point Series No. 7. Goroka: The Melanesian Institute, 1986.

Somare, Michael. *Sana: An Autobiography.* Port Moresby: Niugini Press, 1975.

Souter, Gavin. *New Guinea: The Last Unknown.* Sydney: Angus and Robertson, 1963.

Spruth Erwin L. *And the Word of God Spread: A Brief History of the Gutnius Lutheran Church — Papua New Guinea.* Doctor of Missiology Thesis. Pasadena: School of World Mission, Fuller Theological Seminary, 1981.

Strauss, Hermann, and H. Tischner. *Die Mi-Kultur der Hagenberg-Staemme im oestlichen Zentral-Neuguinea.* Hamburg: Commissions Verlag Cram, de Gruyter & Co, 1962.

Steinbauer, Friedrich. *Melanesische Cargo-Kulte.* Munich: Delp'sche Verlagsbuchhandlung, 1971.

Steinbauer, Friedrich. *So war's in Tarabo.* Neuendettelsau: Freimund Verlag, 1969.

Strelan, John G. *Search for Salvation. Studies in the History and Theology of Cargo Cults.* Adelaide: Lutheran Publishing House, 1977.

Threlfall, Neville. *One Hundred Years in the Islands. The Methodist United Church in the New Guinea Islands Region, 1875-1975.* Rabaul: Trinity Press, 1975.

Trompf, Garry W., Carl E. Loeliger, eds. *Religion in Melanesia.* 3 vols. Port Moresby: University of Papua New Guinea, 1980.

Tscharke, Edwin. *A Quarter-Century of Healing.* Madang: Kristen Pres, 1973.

Vicedom, Georg. *Church and People in New Guinea.* World Christian Books. London: Lutterworth Press, 1961.

Vicedom, Georg, and H. Tischner. *Die Mbowamb — Die Kultur der Hagenberg-Staemme.* 3 vols. Hamburg: Friedrichsen, de Gruyter & Co, 1943/48.

Vicedom, Georg. *Ein neuentdecktes Papuavolk.* Neuendettelsau: Freimund Verlag, 2nd edn 1940.

Webster, Elise M. *The Moon Man: A Biography of Nikolai Miklouho-Maclay.* Melbourne: Melbourne University Press, 1984.

Wetherell, David. *Reluctant Mission. The Anglican Church in Papua New Guinea 1891-1942.* Santa Lucia: University of Queensland Press, 1977.

Whiteman, Darrell L., ed. *An Introduction to Melanesian Cultures. A Handbook for Church Workers.* Point Series No. 5. Goroka: The Melanesian Institute, 1984.

Whiteman, Darrell L. *Melanesians and Missionaries. An Ethno-historical Study of Social and Religious Change in the South-west Pacific.* Pasadena: The William Carey Library, 1983.

Wigmor, Lionel. *The Japanese Thrust. Australia in the War of 1939-1945.* Series 1, vol. IV. Canberra: Australian War Memorial 1957.

Williams, Ronald G. *The United Church in Papua, New Guinea and the Solomon Islands. The Story of Development of an Indigenous Church.* Rabaul: Trinity Press, 1972.

Wiltgen, Ralph M. *The Foundation of the Roman Catholic Church in Oceania, 1825-1850.* Canberra: Australian National University Press, 1979.

Index

PERSONS

666

PLACES

Agotu (1961)	G	Kabak (1958)	M	Narer (1933)	M
Alkena (1956)	H	Kabwum (1967)	K	Nobonob (1906)	M
Amapyaka (1953)	GLC	Kainantu (1970)	G	Nomane (1958)	Ch
Amele (1916)	M	Kaintiba (1963)	L	Ogelbeng (1934)	H
Ampo (1911)	L	Kaiapit (1918)	L	Omkolai (1948)	Ch
Amron (1936)	M	Kalasa (1919)	K	Onerunka (1934)	G
Asaroka (1937)	G	Kapo (1963)	S/M	Paiela (1962)	GLC
Aseki (1958)	L	Karepa (1961)	Ch	Papayuku (1954)	GLC
Awande (1959)	G	Kentagl (1963)	H	Pausa (1958)	GLC
Awelkon (1931)	S/M	Kerowagi (1934)	Ch	Pawari (1958)	GLC
Baitabag (1947)	M	Kewamugl (1950)	Ch	Ponampa (1961)	G
Banz (1950)	H	Kitip (1959)	Ch	Pt. Moresby (1961)	PM
Begesin (1934)	M	Kogl (1958)	Ch	Rabaul (1967)	Is
Bena Bena (1963)	G	Kokas (1961)	GLC	Raiakama (1956)	GLC
Biliau (1937)	M	Kopiago (1964)	GLC	Raipinka (1935)	G
Birip (1960)	GLC	Kotna (1955)	H	Ranara (1964)	M
Boana (1932)	K	Kumbasakama (1955)	GLC	Raong (1958)	K
Bongu (1895)	M	Kundis (1958)	GLC	Rintebe (1952)	G
Bougainville (1972)	Is	Kurum (1911)	M	Rongo (1958)	G
Buangi (1945)	L/K	Kwaikuma (1955)	S/M	Sattelberg (1892)	K
Bula (1956)	L	Kwaplalim (1957)	S/M	Sirunki (1951)	GLC
Bumayong (1950)	L	Lablab (1951)	S/M	Sumburu (1958)	Ch
Bunabun (1931)	M	Lae (1911)	L	Tapen (1951)	K
Butaweng (1911)	L/K	Laialam (1962)	GLC	Tarabo (1950)	G
Concordia (1963)	S/M	Logaweng (1906)	L	Tinyipaka (1964)	GLC
Deinzerhill (1899)	L	Lyalyame (1967)	GLC	Tiria (1958)	H
Ega (1934)	Ch	Madang (1889)	M	Tiripini (1961)	SH
Etep (1950)	K	Mainyanda (1965)	L	Ulap (1928)	K
Finintugu (1964)	G	Malahang (1915)	L	Wabi (1958)	SH
Finschhafen (1886)	L/K	Malalo (1907)	L	Wagezaring (1959)	K
Gabmazung (1911)	L	Mambisanda (1953)	GLC	Wakumare (1962)	GLC
Gaubin (1947)	M	Maramuni (1961)	GLC	Walapimi (1963)	GLC
Gatop (1951)	K	Marawaka (1967)	G	Wantoat (1960)	L
Garaina (1961)	K	Menyamya (1951)	S/M	Wanuma (1955)	M
Gelem (1948)	S/M	Mindik (1965)	K	Watumanda (1966)	GLC
Gizarum (1938)	S/M	Monono (1949)	Ch	Wau (1951)	L
Goroka (1963)	G	Mt. Hagen (1964)	H	Wonenare (1964)	G
Gurakor (1931)	L	Mukuramanda (1961)	GLC	Yabari (1961)	GLC
Heldsbach (1904)	K	Mumeng (1931)	L	Yagaum (1950)	M
Hopoi (1923)	L	Mungarep (1966)	GLC	Yaibos (1949)	GLC
Irelya (1949)	GLC	Muritaka (1967)	GLC	Yaramanda (1948)	GLC
Jalibu (1955)	SH	Nagada (1906)	M	Yuyane (1962)	GLC
				Zaka (1911)	K

Abbreviations used for Church District/Church

Ch	=	Chimbu District	L	=	Lae District
G	=	Goroka District	M	=	Madang District
GLC	=	Gutnius Lutheran Church	S/M	=	Siassi/Menyamya Congregations
H	=	Hagen District	SH	=	Southern Highlands District
Is	=	Islands District	PM	=	Port Moresby District
K	=	Kate District